FIFTH EDITION

The Paralegal Professional

Thomas F. Goldman, JD
Professor Emeritus
Bucks County Community College

Henry R. Cheeseman, JD, LLM
Professor Emeritus
Marshall School of Business
University of Southern California

PEARSON

Boston Columbus Indianapolis New York San Francisco Amsterdam
Cape Town Dubai London Madrid Milan Munich Paris Montréal Toronto Delhi
Mexico City São Paulo Sydney Hong Kong Seoul Singapore Taipei Tokyo

Editorial Director: Andrew Gilfillin
Executive Editor: Gary Bauer
Editorial Assistant: Lynda Cramer
Director of Marketing: David Gesell
Senior Marketing Manager: Thomas Hayward
Senior Marketing Assistant: Les Roberts
Product Marketing Manager: Kaylee Carlson
Program Manager Team Lead: Laura Weaver
Program Manager: Tara Horton
Project Management Team Lead: Bryan Pirrmann
Project Manager: Susan Hannahs
Operations Supervisor: Mary Fisher
Operations Specialist: Deidra Smith
Senior Art Director: Diane Six
Manager, Product Strategy: Sara Eilert
Product Strategy Manager: Anne Rynearson
Team Lead, Media Development & Production: Rachel Collett
Media Project Manager: Maura Barclay
Cover Designer: Melissa Welch, Studio Montage
Cover Image: DHuss/Getty Images
Full-Service Project Manager: Chrystie Hopkins, Lumina Datamatics, Inc.
Composition: Lumina Datamatics, Inc.
Printer/Binder: LSC Communications
Cover Printer: LSC Communications
Text Font: 10.5/12.5, Janson Text LT Pro

Library of Congress Cataloging-in-Publication is on file with the Library of Congress.

19 2022

ISBN 13: 978-0-13-413086-6
ISBN 10: 0-13-413086-3

BRIEF CONTENTS

PART I THE PARALEGAL PROFESSION 1

CHAPTER 1 The Paralegal Profession 2
CHAPTER 2 Ethics and Professional Responsibility 42
CHAPTER 3 The Paralegal Workplace 86
CHAPTER 4 Technology and the Paralegal 134

PART II INTRODUCTION TO LAW 173

CHAPTER 5 American Legal Heritage and Constitutional Law 174
CHAPTER 6 The Court System and Alternative Dispute Resolution 204
CHAPTER 7 Civil Litigation 240
CHAPTER 8 Criminal Law and Procedure 300
CHAPTER 9 Administrative Law 334

PART III PARALEGAL SKILLS 373

CHAPTER 10 Interviewing and Investigation Skills 374
CHAPTER 11 Legal Writing and Critical Legal Thinking 418
CHAPTER 12 Legal Research 454
APPENDIX A How to Brief a Case 500
APPENDIX B National Federation of Paralegal Associations, Inc. 512
APPENDIX C Model Standards and Guidelines for Utilization of Legal Assistants—Paralegals 522
APPENDIX D Federal Court Name Abbreviations 533
APPENDIX E Effective Learning: How to Study 537
APPENDIX F The Constitution of the United States of America 542
APPENDIX G Internet Resources 557
APPENDIX H Glossary of Spanish Equivalents for Important Legal Terms 560

Glossary 567
Case Index 586
Subject Index 589

CONTENTS

From the Authors *xii*

About the Authors *xiv*

Acknowledgments *xxiii*

PART I THE PARALEGAL PROFESSION *1*

CHAPTER 1

The Paralegal Profession *2*

Learning Objectives *3*
Paralegals at Work *3*
Introduction to the Paralegal Profession *4*
What Is a Paralegal? *4*
What Do Paralegals Do? *5*
Professional Skills *7*
- *Resourcefulness 8*
- *Commitment 9*
- *Analytical Skills 9*
- *Interpersonal Skills 9*
- *Communication Skills 10*

Opportunities for Paralegals *11*
The Future *12*
Paralegal Education in the United States *13*
Career Planning *13*
- *Advice from the Field 13*
- *Types of Educational Programs 14*
- *Making a Personal Assessment and Setting Goals 16*
- *Selecting a Specialty 16*
- *Assessing Your Background 17*

Qualifications to Be a Paralegal *18*
- *Paralegal Certification 18*
- *Minimum Education 18*

Regulating the Practice of Law *21*
- *Regulating the Paralegal Profession 21*
- *State Licensing 22*
- *Federal Practice 30*

Getting Started *31*
Legal Terminology *33*
Summary of key concepts *33*
Working the Web *35*
Critical Thinking & Writing Questions *36*
Video Case Studies *36*
Ethics Analysis & Discussion Questions *37*
Developing Your Collaboration Skills *37*
Paralegal Portfolio Exercise *37*
Legal Analysis & Writing Cases *38*
Working with the Language of the Court Case *38*
Virtual Law Office Experience Assignments *41*

CHAPTER 2

Ethics and Professional Responsibility *42*

Learning Objectives *43*
Paralegals at Work *43*
Introduction to Ethics *44*
Regulation of the Practice of Law *45*
- *The Paralegal and Licensing 46*
- *Penalties for the Unauthorized Practice of Law 47*

Ethical Duties and Obligations *48*
- *Ethical Guidelines and Rules 49*
- *ABA Model Guidelines for the Utilization of Paralegal Services 50*
- *Ethics Codes of Paralegal Associations 50*
- *National Federation of Paralegal Associations 50*
- *National Association of Legal Assistants 50*

Supervision *51*
Competence *53*
Confidentiality and Privilege *54*
- *Confidentiality 54*
- *Confidentiality in a Technology Age 54*
- *Dropbox Privacy Policy 55*
- *Privilege 55*
- *Claim of Privilege 56*
- *Extension of Attorney–Client Privilege to Others 56*
- *The Self-Defense Exception 57*
- *Work Product Doctrine 58*
- *Exceptions and Limitations to the Work Product Doctrine 59*
- *Inadvertent Disclosure of Confidential Information 61*
- *Judicial Views 61*
- *ABA Ethics Opinion 61*
- *Conflict of Interest 63*
- *Fairness to Opposing Party and Counsel 65*

Avoiding UPL *67*
- *Avoiding UPL: Holding Oneself Out 69*
- *Avoiding UPL: Giving Advice 69*
- *Avoiding UPL: Filling Out Forms 70*
- *Avoiding UPL: Representing Clients 70*
- *Avoiding UPL: Guidelines 71*

Legal Terminology *72*
Summary of key concepts *72*

Working the Web 75
Critical Thinking & Writing Questions 75
Video Case Studies 76
Ethics Analysis & Discussion Questions 77
Developing Your Collaboration Skills 77
Paralegal Portfolio Exercise 77
Legal Analysis & Writing Cases 78
Working with the Language of the Court Case 78
Virtual Law Office Experience Assignments 85

CHAPTER 3

The Paralegal Workplace 86

Learning Objectives 87
Paralegals at Work 87
Introduction to the Paralegal Workplace 88
Arrangements and Organization of Law Offices and Firms 88
Solo Practice 88
Small Offices 89
Partnerships 89
Large Offices 89
General Practice 90
Specialty Practice 91
Legal Nurse Consultants and Nurse Paralegals 92
Real Estate 92
Complex Litigation 93
Environmental Law 93
Intellectual Property 93
Elder Law 93
Paralegal Managers 93
Pro Bono Paralegals 93
Government Employment 94
Legal Departments of Corporations 94
Self-Employment 94
Networking 95
Paralegal Tasks and Functions 95
Client Interviews 95
Investigations 96
Legal Writing 97
Legal Research 97
What Paralegals in Legal Specialties Do 97
Administrative Procedures in Law Offices and Firms 102
Conflict Checking 102
Time Keeping and Billing 104
Accounting in the Law Office 106
Family Law 106
Commercial Litigation 106
Litigation 106
Maintaining Law Firm Financial Information 106
Accounting for Client Retainers and Costs 110
Costs Advanced 111
Civil Practice: Fee and Cost Billing 111
Timely Disbursements 111
Trust Accounts 111
IOLTA Accounts 112
Interest-Bearing Escrow Accounts 112
Court Accounting 113
Preparing Your Résumé 113
Résumé Formats 116
Cover Letters 118
References 118
Creating an Electronic Résumé 118
Electronic Résumé Submission 119
Interviewing for a Job 121
The Interview 121
Legal Terminology 122
Summary of key concepts 123
Working the Web 125
Critical Thinking & Writing Questions 125
Video Case Studies 126
Ethics Analysis & Discussion Questions 126
Developing Your Collaboration Skills 127
Paralegal Portfolio Exercise 127
Legal Analysis & Writing Cases 127
Working with the Language of the Court Case 128
Virtual Law Office Experience Assignments 133

CHAPTER 4

Technology and the Paralegal 134

Learning Objectives 135
Paralegals at Work 135
Introduction to Technology and the Paralegal 136
The Need for Computer Skills 136
How Much Do You Have to Know? 138
Technology in the Law Office 139
Technology Usage in the Law 139
Working with In-House Technology Support Staff 139
Issues in Working with Outside Technology Consultants 140
Outsourcing 140
The Impact of the Federal Rules of Civil Procedure 141
Contemporary Practice 142
Computer Hardware 142
Networks 143
Network Rights and Privileges 144
Network Administrator 144
Backing Up Data 144
Wide Area Networks 145
The Internet 145
Online Computer Resources 147
Internet Browsers 147
Search Engines 148
Addresses and Locations 149
Legal Research 150
Formats of Available Information 151
File Attachments 151
Receiving and Downloading Files and Attachments 151
Sending Files 152
Electronic Filing 153
Types of Image Formats 153
Computer and Network Security 153
Firewalls 153
Encryption Technology 153

Encryption 154
Computer Viruses 154
Operating Systems 154
Applications Software 155
Word Processing 155
Spreadsheet Programs 157
Database Programs 158
Presentation Graphics Programs 158
Office Software Suites 159
Specialty Application Programs 159
Training for Hardware and Software Support 159
Electronic Courtroom and Paperless Office 160
The Electronic Courtroom 160
The Paperless Office 160
Future Trends in Law Office Technology 162
Videoconferencing 163
VoIP 163
Voice Recognition 164
Miniaturization and Portability 164
Wireless Technology 164
Remote Access 165
Remote Collaboration 165
Wireless Networks 166
Wireless Devices 166
Cloud Computing 166
Key Terms 167
Chapter Summary 168
Review Questions and Exercises 169
Internet and Technology Exercises 170
Chapter Opening Scenario Case Study 170
Continuing Cases and Exercises 170
Building Your Professional Portfolio 171

PART II
INTRODUCTION TO LAW 173

CHAPTER 5

American Legal Heritage and Constitutional Law 174

Learning Objectives 175
Paralegals at Work 175
Introduction for the Paralegal 176
What Is Law? 176
Fairness of the Law 177
Flexibility of the Law 177
Schools of Jurisprudential Thought 177
History of American Law 179
English Common Law 179
Adoption of the English Common Law in America 179
Civil Law System 180
Sources of Law in the United States 180
Constitutions 181
Treaties 181
Codified Law 181
Administrative Law 181
Executive Orders 182
Judicial Decisions 182
Priority of Law in the United States 182
The Doctrine of Stare Decisis 182
Constitution of the United States of America 183
Federalism and Delegated Powers 184
Doctrine of Separation of Powers 184
Checks and Balances 184
Supremacy Clause 184
Commerce Clause 185
Native Americans 185
Foreign Commerce 186
Interstate Commerce 186
State Police Power 186
Dormant Commerce Clause 186
Bill of Rights and Other Amendments 187
Freedom of Speech 187
Fully Protected Speech 188
Limited Protected Speech 188
Unprotected Speech 188
Definition of Obscene Speech 189
Free Speech in Cyberspace 189
Freedom of Religion 190
Due Process Clause 191
Substantive Due Process 191
Procedural Due Process 192
Equal Protection Clause 192
Legal Terminology 194
Summary of key concepts 194
Working the Web 197
Critical Thinking & Writing Questions 198
Video Case Studies 198
Ethics Analysis & Discussion Questions 199
Developing Your Collaboration Skills 199
Paralegal Portfolio Exercise 199
Legal Analysis & Writing Cases 200
Working with the Language of the Court Case 200
Virtual Law Office Experience Assignments 202

CHAPTER 6

The Court System and Alternative Dispute Resolution 204

Learning Objectives 205
Paralegals at Work 205
Introduction for the Paralegal 206
State Court Systems 206
Limited Jurisdiction Trial Court 207
General Jurisdiction Trial Court 207
Intermediate Appellate Court 208
Highest State Court 208
Federal Court System 210
Special Federal Courts 210
U.S. District Courts 210
U.S. Courts of Appeals 211
Supreme Court of the United States 212
Petition for Certiorari 214
Vote of the U.S. Supreme Court 214

The Process of Choosing a U.S. Supreme Court Justice 218
Jurisdiction of Federal and State Courts *221*
Subject Matter Jurisdiction of Federal Courts 221
Subject Matter Jurisdiction of State Courts 221
Diversity of Citizenship 221
Exclusive and Concurrent Jurisdiction 222
Personal Jurisdiction and Other Issues *222*
Standing to Sue 222
In Personam Jurisdiction 222
In Rem Jurisdiction 222
Quasi in Rem Jurisdiction 223
Long-Arm Statutes 223
Venue 223
Jurisdiction in Cyberspace 223
Forum Selection and Choice-of-Law Clauses 224
E-Courts *224*
Alternative Dispute Resolution (ADR) *224*
Negotiation *224*
Arbitration *225*
Federal Arbitration Act 227
ADR Providers 227
ADR Procedure 227
Decision and Award 227
Other Forms of ADR *228*
Mediation 228
Conciliation 229
Minitrial 229
Fact-Finding 229
Judicial Referee 230
Online ADR *231*
Legal Terminology *232*
Summary of key concepts *232*
Working the Web *235*
Critical Thinking & Writing Questions *235*
Video Case Studies *236*
Ethics Analysis & Discussion Questions *236*
Developing Your Collaboration Skills *237*
Paralegal Portfolio Exercise *237*
Legal Analysis & Writing Cases *237*
Working with the Language of the Court Case *238*
Virtual Law Office Experience Assignments *239*

CHAPTER 7

Civil Litigation *240*

Learning Objectives *241*
Paralegals at Work *241*
Introduction to Civil Litigation *242*
Civil Litigation Paralegal Skills *244*
Managing Client Relationships 244
Tasks of the Civil Litigation Paralegal 245
Interviewing Clients and Witnesses 245
Investigating Facts 245
Conducting Discovery 245
Obtaining Documents and Records 246
Reviewing Records 246
Drafting Pleadings and Other Documents 246
Assisting at Trial 246
Corporate Paralegals in Litigation 246
Litigation Support Manager 247
Pleadings *247*
Time Limits and Pleading Deadlines 247
Complaint 249
Fact and Notice Pleading 250
Filing Fee 261
Electronic Filing 261
Service of the Complaint 262
Responsive Pleadings 264
Answer 264
Cross-Complaint and Reply 265
Intervention and Consolidation 265
Discovery *265*
Litigation Hold 269
The Duty to Preserve Evidence 269
Case Evaluation 269
Preparing for Trial 270
Facilitating Settlement 270
Preserving Oral Testimony 271
Federal Rules of Civil Procedure—Rule 26(a) Disclosure Requirements 271
Information Subject to Mandatory Disclosure 275
Experts and Witnesses 276
Depositions 276
Interrogatories 276
Production of Documents 278
Physical and Mental Examination 279
Requests for Admission 279
E-Discovery *279*
Pretrial Motions *280*
Motion to Dismiss 280
Motion for Judgment on the Pleadings 281
Motion for Summary Judgment 281
Settlement Conference *281*
Trial *281*
Jury Selection 282
Opening Statements 285
Plaintiff's Case 285
Defendant's Case 285
Rebuttal and Rejoinder 286
Closing Arguments 286
Jury Instructions 286
Jury Deliberation and Verdict 286
Entry of Judgment 286
Appeal *286*
Briefs and Oral Argument 287
Actions by the Appellate Courts 288
Legal Terminology *289*
Summary of key concepts *290*
Working the Web *293*

Critical Thinking & Writing Questions 293
Video Case Studies 294
Ethics Analysis & Discussion Questions 294
Developing Your Collaboration Skills 294
Paralegal & Portfolio Exercise 295
Legal Analysis & Writing Cases 295
Working with the Language of the Court Case 297
Virtual Law Office Experience Modules 299

CHAPTER 8

Criminal Law and Procedure 300

Learning Objectives 301
Paralegals at Work 301
Introduction for the Paralegal 302
Parties and Attorneys of a Criminal Action 303
Criminal Procedure 304
Criminal Complaint 304
Arrest 304
Bail 304
Indictment or Information 306
Arraignment 310
Plea Bargaining 310
Criminal Trial 310
Pretrial Discovery 310
Determination of Guilt 311
Crimes 311
Penal Codes and Regulatory Statutes 311
Classification of Crimes 311
Intent Crimes 312
Non-Intent Crimes 312
Criminal Acts as a Basis for Tort Actions 312
Common Crimes 313
Crimes Against the Person 313
Murder 313
Robbery 313
Burglary 313
Larceny 314
Theft 314
Arson 315
Forgery 315
Extortion 315
White-Collar Crimes 315
Embezzlement 315
Criminal Fraud 316
Bribery 316
Criminal Conspiracy 317
Constitutional Safeguards 317
Fourth Amendment Protection Against Unreasonable Searches and Seizures 318
Search Warrants 318
Warrantless Searches 318
Search of Business Premises 318
Exclusionary Rule 318
Fifth Amendment Privilege Against Self-Incrimination 321
Miranda Rights 321
Immunity from Prosecution 322
Attorney–Client Privilege 322
Other Privileges 322
Fifth Amendment Protection Against Double Jeopardy 323
Sixth Amendment Right to a Public Trial 323
Eighth Amendment Protection Against Cruel and Unusual Punishment 324
Legal Terminology 325
Summary of key concepts 326
Working the Web 329
Critical Thinking & Writing questions 329
Video Case Studies 330
Ethics Analysis & discussion questions 330
Developing Your Collaboration Skills 330
Paralegal Portfolio Exercise 331
Legal Analysis & Writing Cases 331
Working with the Language of the Court Case 332
Virtual Law Office Experience Modules 333

CHAPTER 9

Administrative Law 334

Learning Objectives 334
Paralegals at Work 334
Introduction for the Paralegal 336
Administrative Law 337
General Government Regulation 337
Specific Government Regulation 338
Administrative Agencies 339
Cabinet-Level Federal Departments 339
Department of Homeland Security 339
Independent Federal Administrative Agencies 340
State and Local Administrative Agencies 341
Administrative Procedure 342
Administrative Procedure Act 343
Administrative Law Judges 343
Powers of Administrative Agencies 343
Rule Making 344
Code of Federal Regulations 344
Licensing Power 348
Judicial Authority 348
Executive Power 353
Administrative Searches 353
Judicial Review of Administrative Agency Actions 354
Federal Administrative Agencies 354
Equal Employment Opportunity Commission (EEOC) 354
Environmental Protection Agency (EPA) 355
Food and Drug Administration (FDA) 356
Securities and Exchange Commission (SEC) 356
Occupational Safety and Health Administration (OSHA) 357
National Labor Relations Board (NLRB) 357
Consumer Product Safety Commission (CPSC) 358
Federal Trade Commission (FTC) 359
Consumer Financial Protection Bureau (CFPB) 359

Individual Rights and Disclosure of Administrative Agency Actions 360
Freedom of Information Act 360
Government in the Sunshine Act 361
Equal Access to Justice Act 363
Privacy Act 363
Legal Terminology 364
Summary of key concepts 365
Working the Web 367
Critical Thinking & Writing Questions 367
Video Case Studies 367
Ethics Analysis & Discussion Questions 368
Developing Your Collaboration Skills 368
Paralegal Portfolio Exercise 368
Legal Analysis & Writing Cases 369
Working with the Language of the Court Case 369
Virtual Law Office Experience Modules 371

PART III
PARALEGAL SKILLS 373

CHAPTER 10
Interviewing and Investigation Skills 374

Learning Objectives 375
Paralegals at Work 375
Introduction to Interviewing and Investigations 376
Interviews 376
Screening Interview 377
First Meeting 377
Implied Attorney–Client Relationship 377
Statute of Limitations 379
Letters of Engagement and Termination of Engagement 381
Non-Engagement 381
Preparing for the Interview 381
Investigation Checklists 381
Physical Surroundings 383
Dress and Appearance 387
Communication Skills in a Multicultural Society 387*
Cultural Sensitivity 388
Conducting the Interview 389
Listening Skills 390
Leading Questions 391
Open-Ended Questions 391
Discovery Limitations 392
Moral Versus Ethical Considerations 392
Privileged Communication 393
Expert Witnesses 393
Investigating Claims 395
A Defense Perspective 396
Obtaining Official Reports 396
Fact Analysis 397
Locations 397
Tangible Evidence 397
Following a Timeline 401
Freedom of Information Act (FOIA) 401
Locating Witnesses 403
Directories 403
The Web 403
Interviews, Investigations, and Trials 404
Case and Practice Management Software 405
Software 405
Legal Terminology 407
Summary of key concepts 408
Working the Web 410
Critical Thinking & Writing Questions 410
Video Case Studies 411
Ethics Analysis & Discussion Questions 411
Developing Your Collaboration Skills 411
Paralegal Portfolio Exercise 412
Legal Analysis & Writing Cases 412
Working with the Language of the Court Case 413
Case Summary 413
Virtual Law Office Experience Modules 417

CHAPTER 11
Legal Writing and Critical Legal Thinking 418

Learning Objectives 419
Paralegals at Work 419
Introduction to Legal Writing and Critical Legal Thinking 420
Critical Legal Thinking 420
Legal Writing 422
Writing Styles 423
Duty of Candor 423
Preparing Office Memoranda 424
Analysis 431
Editing and Rewriting 431
Preparing Court Briefs 432
Citations 432
Traditional Print Sources 433
***Bluebook* 434**
***ALWD Citation Format* 435**
***Universal Citation Format* 435**
***Other Citation Formats* 435**
Table of Authorities 441
Cite Checking 442
Bluebook and ALWD Compared 443
Legal Terminology 446
Summary of key concepts 446
Working the Web 448
Critical Thinking & Writing Questions 448
Video Case Studies 449
Ethics Analysis & Discussion Questions 449
Developing Your Collaboration Skills 450
Paralegal Portfolio Exercise 450
Legal Analysis & Writing Cases 450
Working with the Language of the Court Case 451
Virtual Law Office Experience Modules 453

CHAPTER 12

Legal Research *454*

Learning Objectives *455*
Paralegals at Work *455*
Introduction to Research for the Paralegal *456*
Legal Research *457*
Creating a Research Plan *457*
What Is the Issue or Legal Question? 458
What Is the Appropriate Search Terminology? 459
What Type of Research Material Is Available? 459
What Jurisdictions Are Involved? 460
What Is the Controlling Law? 461
What Types of Resources Should Be Used? 461
Where Is the Needed Research Material Located? 461
Executing the Research Plan 462
Finding the Law *462*
Primary Sources and Authority 463
Secondary Sources 470
Finding Tools 473
Personal Research Strategy *473*
A Final Word on Executing the Legal Research Plan *475*
Using Printed Legal Reference Works *475*
Updates 477
Constructing a Computer Search Query *477*
Creating a List of Research Terms 481
Computer Research Providers 481
Search Method and Query 482
Creating the Query 482
Using Connectors 482
Search Engines 485
Updating Legal Research *485*
Shepard's 486
GlobalCite™ 487
KeyCite™ 487
V. Cite™ 487
Parallel Citations *488*
Legal Terminology *490*
Summary of key concepts *491*
Working the Web *493*
Critical Thinking & Writing Questions *493*
Video Case Studies *494*
Ethics Analysis & Discussion Questions *494*
Developing Your Collaboration Skills *495*
Paralegal Portfolio Exercise *495*
Legal Analysis & Writing Cases *495*
Working with the Language of the Court Case *496*
Virtual Law Office Experience Modules *497*

APPENDIX A

How to Brief a Case *500*

APPENDIX B

National Federation of Paralegal Associations, Inc. *512*

APPENDIX C

Model Standards and Guidelines for Utilization of Legal Assistants—Paralegals *522*

APPENDIX D

Federal Court Name Abbreviations *533*

APPENDIX E

Effective Learning: How to Study *537*

APPENDIX F

The Constitution of the United States of America *542*

APPENDIX G

Internet Resources *557*

APPENDIX H

Glossary of Spanish Equivalents for Important Legal Terms *560*

Glossary *567*

Case Index *586*

Subject Index *589*

VIDEO CASE STUDY INDEX

PART I THE PARALEGAL PROFESSION

When Friends Ask for Legal Advice 36
Résumé Writing Do's and Don'ts 36
Independent Paralegal 36
Disclosure of Status 76
Confidentiality Issue: Family Exception? 76
Confidentiality Issue: Public Information 77
Preparing for a Job Interview: Résumé Advice 126
Preparing for a Job Interview: Interviewing Advice 126
Interviewing: The Good, the Bad, and the Ugly 126

PART II INTRODUCTION TO LAW

Difference Between a Criminal and a Civil Trial 198
A School Principal Reacts: Student Rights versus the School's Duty 198
Confidentiality Issue: Attorney–Client Privilege 198
Meet the Courthouse Team 236
Jury Selection: Potential Juror Challenged for Cause 236
Settlement Conference with Judge 236
Preparing for Trial: Preparing a Fact Witness 294
Trial: Direct and Cross-Examination of a Witness 294
Attorney–Client Privilege: Confidentiality Issue 330
Administrative Agency Hearing: The Role of the Paralegal 367

PART III PARALEGAL SKILLS

UPL Issue: Working with a Witness 411
Zealous Representation Issue: When You Are Asked to Lie 411
Zealous Representation Issue: Candor to the Court 449
Zealous Representation Issue: Signing Documents 449
Legal Research: Are Books Obsolete? 494
Fees and Billing Issue: Using Time Effectively 494

FROM THE AUTHORS

Welcome to the fifth edition of *The Paralegal Professional*. In the time that has passed since the publication of the first edition, the paralegal profession has undergone a dramatic growth in its importance in the delivery of legal services. Today, the paralegal is viewed as an important member of the legal services delivery team and has the well-deserved status of a professional in the field of law. To be a member of the paralegal profession today requires developing not only conceptual knowledge, but also professional and analytical skills and a firm understanding of the ethical issues and obligations of the paralegal profession in an increasingly challenging work environment. Our goal in the fifth edition is to provide paralegal students and professionals with the foundation on which to grow and excel in this field today and in the future.

In preparing this edition, we interviewed and consulted with members of the legal profession with whom paralegals work, including hiring attorneys and human resource directors; current users of the previous editions of the text; full and adjunct instructors in paralegal studies; and numerous students across the country. Our goals are presenting a text that will enable each student to achieve his or her potential and providing a source of information for use in the workplace. The feedback of everyone we interviewed resulted in several important changes and additions to the text that help bring paralegal practice alive and illuminate the roles and tasks paralegals are asked to assume in today's legal working environment.

The fifth edition is divided into four sections that provide a logical grouping of topics and flexibility as to coverage of the most commonly practiced, substantive areas of law.

Part I: The Paralegal Profession focuses on introducing students to the paralegal profession, career opportunities, the paralegal workplace, ethics, regulation, and the use of technology on the job.
Part II: Introduction to Law provides an overview of law and the American legal system and in succession introduces students to the three areas of procedure: civil, criminal, and administrative. This treatment helps students understand, early in the course, the differences among these three legal arenas.
Part III: Paralegal Skills focuses on introducing students to interviewing, investigation, traditional and online legal research, and writing and critical thinking in the legal field.
Part IV: Legal Subjects provides an overview of the most common individual legal areas of practice. New sections in each of these chapters inform students of employment opportunities related to the field of practice.

An Essentials version of this text is also available that contains just the first three parts of this comprehensive version. It is titled ***The Paralegal Professional***: The Essentials 5th edition.

We are particularly excited about the additional Video Case Studies and exercises created as part of the **Virtual Law Office Experience** in the new **MyLegalStudiesLab** program. These Video Case Studies provide the student with a workplace context for assignments and make it easy to bring the world of the practicing paralegal into the classroom. Videos cover topics such as résumé writing and interviewing for a job, working in a law firm, the courtroom players and their roles, and paralegals performing various procedures and duties. Many of the segments present scenarios dealing with common ethical situations that paralegals will encounter on the job, making it easy to integrate ethics education throughout the course. Portfolio assignments requiring written documents are provided to allow students to demonstrate their mastery of the chapter learning objectives.

Our book has been carefully and thoroughly designed to meet the requirements set forth by the American Bar Association (ABA) and the American Association for Paralegal Education (AAFPE) regarding coverage of paralegal topics, ethical issues, professional skill development, and the other educational requirements of an introductory paralegal education course.

Thomas Goldman
Henry Cheeseman

DEDICATIONS

Dedicated to Sylvia and Henry, the next generation, they are our future and the promise of a brighter future.

Thomas F. Goldman

"There are two things in life for which we are never truly prepared: twins."
(Josh Billings, 1818–1885)

This book is dedicated to Ziva and Xavier, our new twins.

Henry R. Cheeseman

ABOUT THE AUTHORS

Thomas F. Goldman, JD, is Professor Emeritus of Bucks County Community College, where he was a professor of Law and Management and Director of the Center for Legal Studies and the Paralegal Studies Program. He was a member of the Paralegal Studies Advisory Board and mentor at Thomas Edison State College, where he developed an Advanced Litigation Support and Technology Certificate Program in the School of Professional Studies, and implemented the online paralegal studies program for the *New York Times* knowledge network.

He is an author of textbooks in paralegal studies and technology, including *Technology in the Law Office, Accounting and Taxation for Paralegals, Civil Litigation: Process and Procedures, Litigation Practice: E-Discovery and Technology, Abacus Law: A Hands-On Tutorial* and *Guide, Real Estate Fundamentals,* and *SmartDraw Tutorial and Guide.*

An accounting and economics graduate of Boston University and a graduate of Temple University School of Law, Professor Goldman has an active international law, technology law, and litigation practice. He has worked extensively with paralegals and received the award of the Legal Support Staff Guild. He was elected the Legal Secretaries Association Boss of the Year for his contribution to cooperative education of encouraging the use of paralegals and legal assistants in law offices. He also received the Bucks County Community College Alumni Association Professional Achievement Award. He has been an educational consultant on technology to educational institutions and major corporations and is a frequent speaker and lecturer on educational, legal, and technology issues.

Henry R. Cheeseman is Professor Emeritus of the Marshall School of Business of the University of Southern California (USC), Los Angeles, California, where he was a professor of business law and Director of the Legal Studies in Business Program. Professor Cheeseman taught business law, legal environment, corporate law, securities regulation, cyberlaw, and ethics courses in both the Master of Business Administration (MBA) and undergraduate programs of the Marshall School of Business of the University of Southern California. He received the Golden Apple Teaching Award on many occasions by being voted by the students as the best professor at the Marshall School of Business. He has also served at the Center for Excellence in teaching at the university.

Professor Cheeseman has earned six degrees, including a bachelor's degree in finance from Marquette University, both a master's in business administration (MBA) and a master's in business taxation (MBT) from the University of Southern California, a juris doctor (JD) degree from the University of California at Los Angeles (UCLA) School of Law, a master's degree with an emphasis on law and economics from the University of Chicago, and a master's in law (LLM) degree in financial institutions law from Boston University.

Professor Cheeseman is an award-winning author of several business law textbooks published by Pearson Education, including the definitive and highly regarded *Business Law*. Other business law and legal environment textbooks authored by Professor Cheeseman and published by Pearson Education include *Contemporary Business Law, Legal Environment of Business*, and *Introduction to Law*. In addition to being a coauthor with Professor Thomas Goldman of the fifth editions of *The Paralegal Professional* and *The Paralegal Professional The Essentials*, he is also coauthor of *Contract Law for Paralegals* and *Business Organizations for Paralegals*, all published by Pearson Education.

BUILD A SOLID FOUNDATION FOR YOUR PARALEGAL CAREER!

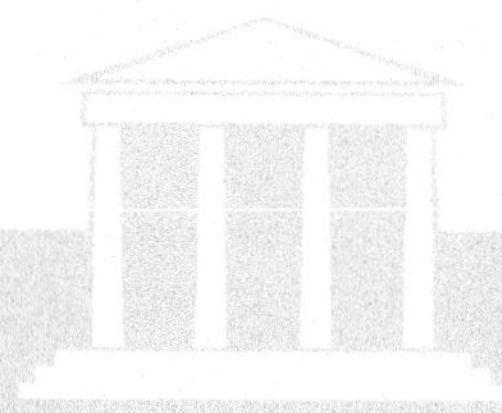

Written by an award-winning team, *The Paralegal Professional* 5e builds the foundation in substantive and procedural legal knowledge and real-world skills that you will need throughout your course of study. The book emphasizes the following:

DEVELOP CRITICAL THINKING AND PROCEDURAL SKILLS!

End-of-chapter material in this edition focuses on developing critical thinking and hands-on skills including the following exercises and assignments:

- Web research exercises
- Critical thinking and writing questions
- Video Case Studies
- Ethics analysis and discussion questions
- Collaborative skill-building exercises
- Legal analysis and writing cases
- Paralegal portfolio building exercises
- Cases for briefing
- Working with the Language of the Court
- Virtual Law Office Experience Assignments

LEARN ABOUT TECHNOLOGY APPLICATIONS IN THE LAW OFFICE

To be effective on the job, you will need to become comfortable using computers and common legal office software. A revised and updated Chapter 4, Technology and the Paralegal, introduces you to the types of application programs and their uses commonly found in law offices today.

UNDERSTAND HOW TO HANDLE ETHICAL SITUATIONS IN THE WORKPLACE

The Paralegal Professional 5e text and package are designed to build a strong foundational understanding of ethical principles for paralegals in the introductory course. Resources include Chapter 2, Ethics and Professional Responsibility; new Ethical Perspective boxes integrated throughout the textbook; and an expanded set of ethics-related video segments from the Paralegal Professional Classroom Video Series Segments.

NEW FOR THE FIFTH EDITION

- *The Paralegal Professional* text has been re-edited to ensure consistency in coverage, use of terminology, and improved readability.
- Three new "Developing Your Collaborative Skills" cases have been added that are designed to be read and used for student group discussions, either in class or as assignments outside of class.
- Six new "Legal Analysis Writing Cases" are included as end-of-chapter assignments. These cases are designed to allow students to analyze cases and reach reasoned decisions based on applying relevant law to the facts of the case.
- There are three new "Working with the Language of the Court Cases." These cases, which are entirely in the original language of the courts, are designed for individual student writing assignments using the IRAC method.
- Information on current and future opportunities in the paralegal profession, including existing and proposed state certification requirements, has been updated in Chapter 1, The Paralegal Profession.
- Changes in the practice of e-filing and the ethical issues resulting from these changes and new cases have been added to the chapter and end of chapter Working with the Language of the Law assignments. This is discussed in Chapter 2, Ethics and Professional Responsibility.
- Chapter 3, The Paralegal Workplace was substantially rewritten to improve the flow of topics and the forms have been updated.
- Chapter 4, Technology and the Paralegal has been rewritten to include new material and coverage of contemporary use of technology in the law office and by the paralegal.
- The U.S. Supreme Court's *Obergefell v. Hodges* decision regarding same-sex marriage is presented in Chapter 5 in the language of the Supreme Court. This case may be used for in class discussion or as an individual writing assignment.
- The role of the paralegal in the litigation process has been revised in Chapter 7 Civil Litigation to include a new case within the chapter and for end of chapter *Working with the Language of the Law* assignments and description of that of the civil litigation paralegal, corporate paralegal, and litigation support paralegal reflect contemporary practice.
- Chapter 10 Interviewing and Investigation skills has been expanded to include two new cases in the chapter end of chapter Working with the Language of the Law assignments
- Chapter 11, Legal Writing and Critical Legal Thinking chart comparing *ALWD* 5th Edition and *Bluebook* 19 is updated.
- Changes in electronic legal research engines and search options are covered in Chapter 12, Legal Research.
- Case law and applications have been updated in all of the substantive law chapters.

KEY FEATURES OF THE TEXTBOOK

PARALEGALS AT WORK CHAPTER OPENER

These opening scenarios offer a hypothetical fact situation that a professional paralegal might encounter on the job. They are designed to stimulate a student's interest in the material to be covered in the chapter.

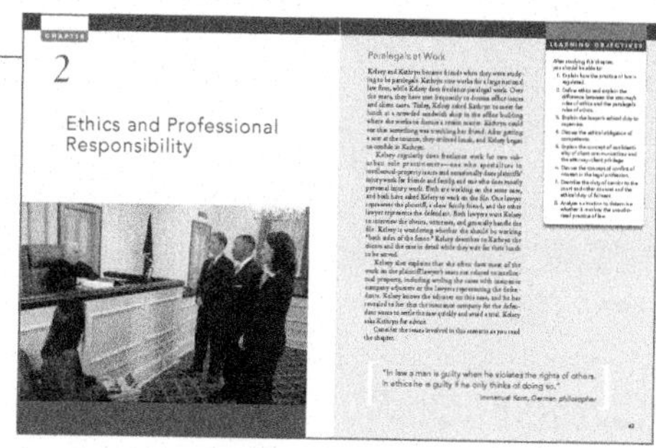

ETHICAL PERSPECTIVE BOXES

These boxes concern hypothetical fact situations and ethical dilemmas that paralegals might face in their professional careers.

ETHICAL PERSPECTIVE

Arkansas Rules of Professional Conduct

RULE 1.7. CONFLICT OF INTEREST: CURRENT CLIENTS

(a) Except as provided in paragraph (b), a lawyer shall not represent a client if the representation involves a concurrent conflict of interest. A concurrent conflict of interest exists if:

(1) the representation of one client will be directly adverse to another client; or

(2) there is a significant risk that the representation of one or more clients will be materially limited by the lawyer's responsibilities to another client, a former client or a third person or by a personal interest of the lawyer.

(b) Notwithstanding the existence of a concurrent conflict of interest under

SIDEBAR BOXES

These boxes provide additional information and commentary on chapter topics.

WISCONSIN RULES OF PROFESSIONAL CONDUCT FOR ATTORNEYS

Contrast and compare the Wisconsin Rules of Professional Conduct for Attorneys, at http://www?.legis.wisconsin.gov/rsb/scr/5200.pdf, with the

SIDEBAR

PARALEGALS IN PRACTICE BOXES

In the fifth edition, we include profiles of paralegals practicing in a variety of practices. Their commentary provides students with insight into the world of practicing paralegals.

Paralegals *in* Practice

PARALEGAL PROFILE

Vicki Voisin

Vicki Voisin, an Advanced Certified Paralegal, is nationally recognized as an author and speaker on ethical issues related to the paralegal profession. She is the creator and presenter of EthicsBasics, a program designed to raise awareness of ethical concerns by legal professionals and corporate employees. She also publishes an e-magazine titled Strategies for Paralegals Seeking Excellence (www.paralegalmentor.com). Vicki is a past president of the National Association of Legal Assistants (NALA) and currently serves on NALA's Advanced Certification Board. She has over 20 years of paralegal experience and is currently employed by Running, Wise & Ford in Charlevoix, Michigan.

issues, the ability to communicate clearly with clients, excellent organizational skills, and attentiveness to detail and accuracy.

I also believe that technology plays an important role in the legal profession. Although technology allows attorneys and paralegals to work faster, it does not necessarily guarantee that all of the work results are accurate. Paralegals should be aware of the potential ethical hazards that technology can introduce, especially in the areas of confidentiality and conflicts of interest. For example, unless done properly, redaction (editing) on electronically filed documents can be uncovered, resulting in the disclosure of confidential and/or privileged information to third parties.

All paralegals should be aware of their ethical obligations and those of an attorney. My advice is to familiarize yourself with the American Bar Association's Model Rules of Professional Conduct, as well as its Guidelines for the Utilization of Paralegal Services. Then become acquainted with the related Model Rules and Guidelines for your particular state, if available. Also, join professional associations to keep abreast of

ADVICE FROM THE FIELD ARTICLES

These articles feature professional advice straight from the experts on interviewing skills, developing your portfolio, professional development, handling clients, and more.

Advice from the Field

TECHNOLOGY IS A TOOL, NOT A CASE STRATEGY IN THE COURTROOM

Michael E. Cobo

The latest legal technology products such as animations and courtroom presentation systems can be very alluring to lawyers. After learning about these products, you may be anxious to use them. But you should keep in mind that technology products are only tools to implement a solution and are not solutions in themselves. The key issue is: What is your case strategy and what do you need to present?

do other exhibits that need to be larger and hold more visual or textual information. Strategically, some exhibits need to be used in conjunction with others or need to be in the view of the jury more often than not.

ASSESS YOURSELF

Before you spend a dime to develop the visual strategy, create a presentation or invest in any technology,

IN THE WORDS OF THE COURT BOXES

Excerpts from key court cases are presented to familiarize students with important legal decisions.

IN THE WORDS OF THE COURT . . .

TRAMMELL V. UNITED STATES, 445 U.S. 40 (1980)
BURGER C. J.

The privileges between priest and penitent, attorney and client, and physician and patient limit protection to private communication. These privileges are rooted in the imperative need for confidence and trust. The priest–penitent privilege recognizes

VIRTUAL LAW OFFICE EXPERIENCE FOR *THE PARALEGAL PROFESSIONAL 5E*

COURSECONNECT ONLINE COURSE WITH THE VIRTUAL LAW OFFICE EXPERIENCE FOR TECHNOLOGY IN THE LAW OFFICE

CourseConnect offers complete online courses that run on common school LMS platforms such as Blackboard, Angel, Canvas, D2L, Sakai, and others. Courses contain interactive lessons covering core topics with assignments and discussion board suggestions using a methodology designed to increase student retention and success in any classroom environment.

Courses and topics are crafted by experts from each discipline and contain a variety of interactive multimedia elements, all levels of cognitive assessments, assignments, discussion questions, MP3 downloadable lectures and detailed instructor resource guides. CourseConnect with the Virtual Law Office Experience is your total online and blended learning solution designed to provide students with the tools they need to confirm their mastery of legal concepts and applications, and then apply their knowledge and skills in a workplace context.

For the instructor CourseConnect courses are accompanied by a complete set of instructor materials, including sample syllabi, lesson plans, and assignments with time-on-task estimates for all activities to assist with acreditation applications.

VIRTUAL LAW OFFICE EXPERIENCE IN COURSECONNECT

Housed within the Media Index in the course are the complete Virtual Law Office Experience modules. Students watch realistic video scenarios, work with case files and documents, and use the technology tools found in the law office to do the work a paralegal will be asked to do in practice. Throughout the course, students build a portfolio of work that demonstrates that they have the training and experience employers are looking for.

- Students engage in a workplace experience as a law office intern.

- Students can see technology being used in the law office and develop an understanding of how best to deploy technology in practice.

- Students build a comprehensive portfolio of workplace products to show potential employers.

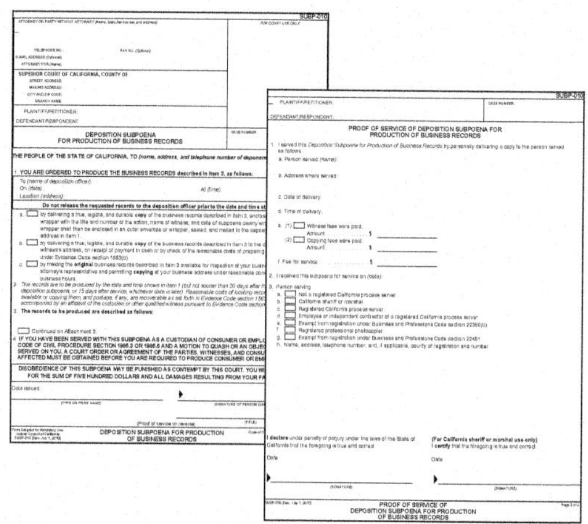

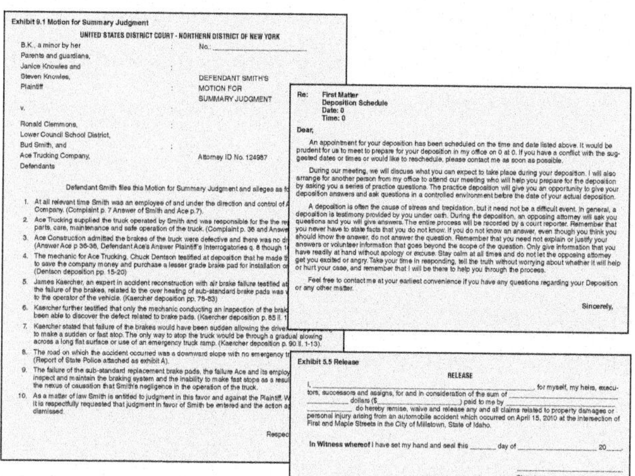

Within the Virtual Law Office Experience, students can access a wealth of resources to complete assignments, including:

- *Ask the Law Librarian Instructional Videos* answer students' research and writing questions.

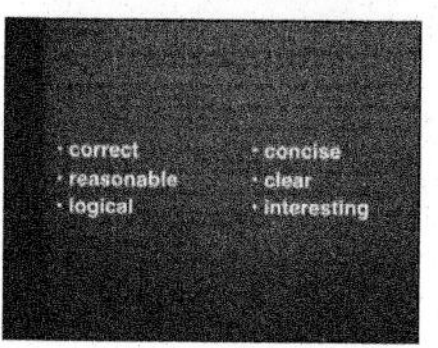

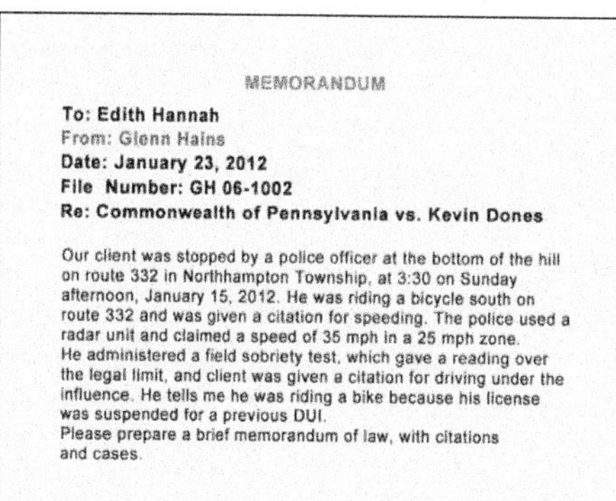

MEMORANDUM

To: Edith Hannah
From: Glenn Hains
Date: January 23, 2012
File Number: GH 06-1002
Re: Commonwealth of Pennsylvania vs. Kevin Dones

Our client was stopped by a police officer at the bottom of the hill on route 332 in Northhampton Township, at 3:30 on Sunday afternoon, January 15, 2012. He was riding a bicycle south on route 332 and was given a citation for speeding. The police used a radar unit and claimed a speed of 35 mph in a 25 mph zone. He administered a field sobriety test, which gave a reading over the legal limit, and client was given a citation for driving under the influence. He tells me he was riding a bike because his license was suspended for a previous DUI. Please prepare a brief memorandum of law, with citations and cases.

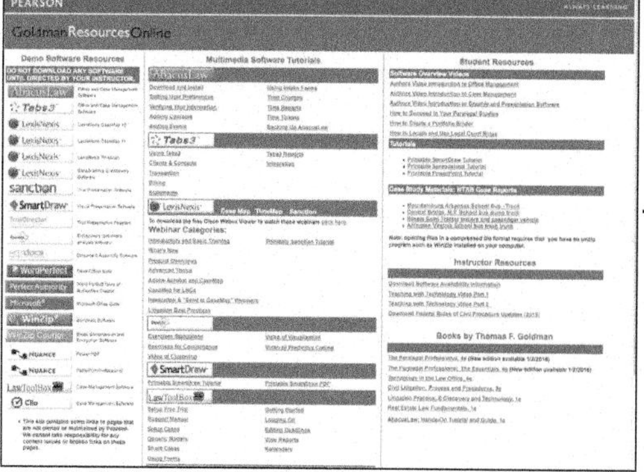

- *Ask Technical Support links* to the Technology Resources Website for technology and legal software support.

AbacusLaw Tutorials,
LexisNexis CaseMap Tutorials,
SmartDraw Tutorials
Sanction Tutorials,
Microsoft Office Tutorials

- *Forms* File contains hundreds of examples of commonly used legal documents for the major legal specialties.

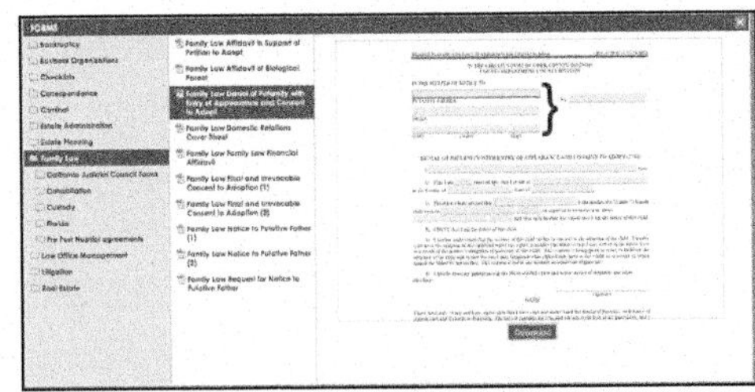

- *Case Materials* contain all of the case information and documents needed to complete assignments.

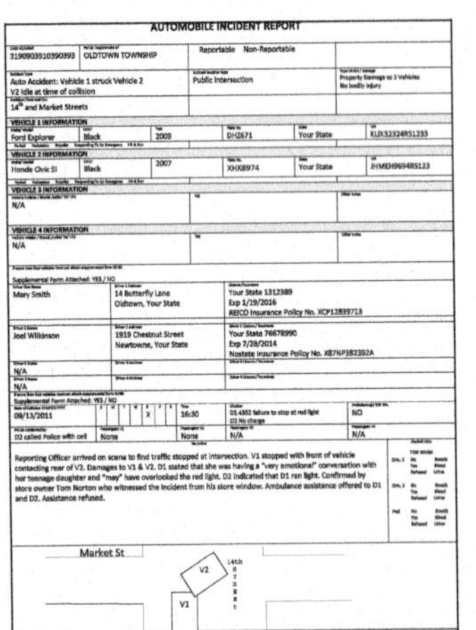

AUTOMOBILE INCIDENT REPORT

OLDTOWN TOWNSHIP

Reportable Non-Reportable

Auto Accident: Vehicle 1 struck Vehicle 2

V2 idle at time of collision

Public Intersection

14th and Market Streets

VEHICLE 1 INFORMATION

Ford Explorer | Black | 2000

VEHICLE 2 INFORMATION

Honda Civic SI | Black | 2007

VEHICLE 3 INFORMATION

N/A

VEHICLE 4 INFORMATION

N/A

Mary Smith | 14 Butterfly Lane, Oldtown, Your State

Joel Wilkinson | 1919 Chestnut Street, Newtowne, Your State

09/13/2011

Market St

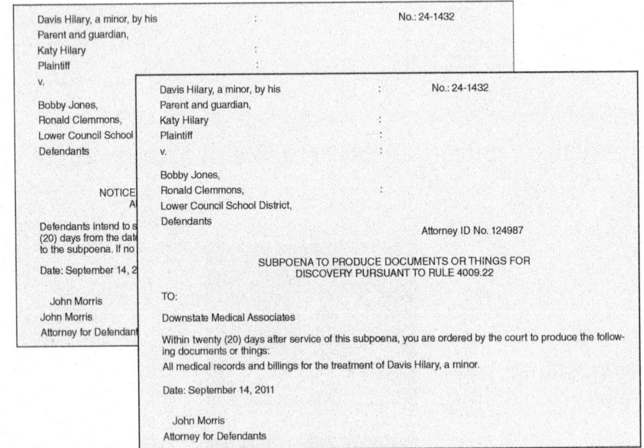

Davis Hilary, a minor, by his
Parent and guardian,
Katy Hilary
Plaintiff
v.
Bobby Jones,
Ronald Clemmons,
Lower Council School District,
Defendants

No.: 24-1432

Attorney ID No. 124987

SUBPOENA TO PRODUCE DOCUMENTS OR THINGS FOR DISCOVERY PURSUANT TO RULE 4009.22

TO:

Downstate Medical Associates

Within twenty (20) days after service of this subpoena, you are ordered by the court to produce the following documents or things:

All medical records and billings for the treatment of Davis Hilary, a minor.

Date: September 14, 2011

John Morris
Attorney for Defendants

Contact your local representative to preview this and other paralegal courses.

TWO CHOICES IN COURSECONNECT COURSES

Introduction to Paralegal Studies (covers the first three parts of the textbook)
Introduction to Paralegal Studies and the Law (covers all four parts of the textbook)

For more information regarding which course and platform application are right for your school, please contact your representative or call 800-635-1579.

INTEGRATE ETHICS INSTRUCTION INTO THE INTRODUCTORY COURSE!

Many paralegal programs struggle with the question of how to integrate dedicated ethics instruction into a paralegal curriculum already packed with coursework. *The Paralegal Professional* 5e text and package are designed to build a strong foundational understanding of ethical principles for paralegals in the introductory course. Resources include:

Chapter 2: Ethics and Professional Responsibility

The fundamental ethics issues and principles are presented in Chapter 2.

Ethical Perspective Boxes Integrated Throughout the Textbook

These boxes present hypothetical fact situations and ethical dilemmas that highlight situations paralegals might face in their professional careers.

Paralegal Practice and Ethics-Related Video Case Study Segments

These videos are located at the book website at www.pearsonhighered.com/careersresources. Many of the segments present situations involving paralegal ethics and illustrate common UPL, Confidentiality, Conflict of Interest, Billing, and Zealous Representation issues.

Need More Coverage of Ethics in a Handy Supplemental Guide?

ETHICS FOR THE PARALEGAL PROFESSIONAL
by Deborah Orlik

If more depth in dealing with ethical issues is desired, this handy guide can be packaged with the textbook at low cost. (ISBN: 0-13-310929-1)

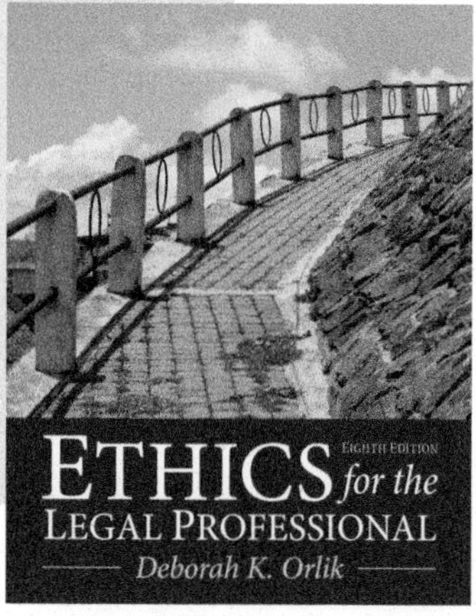

INSTRUCTOR'S MANUAL WITH TOOLKIT FOR NEW INSTRUCTORS

To access supplementary materials online, instructors need to request an instructor access code. Go to **www.pearsonhighered.com/irc**, where you can register for an instructor access code. Within 48 hours after registering, you will receive a confirming email, including an instructor access code. Once you have received your code, go to the site and log on for full instructions on downloading the materials you wish to use.

Instructor's Manual with Test Bank. Includes content outlines for classroom discussion, teaching suggestions, and answers to selected end-of-chapter questions from the text. This also contains a Word document version of the test bank.

- Teaching Suggestions
- Students: How the textbook and Instructor's Manual will help you
- Preparing for Class
- Your First Day of Class
- Model Course Syllabi and Outline
    - One-Semester Course
    - Two-Quarter Course
- Use of Computer Technology
- Content Comparison: Miller, *Paralegal Today* 6e

- Each chapter includes:
    - Teacher to Teacher Notes
    - Pre-Chapter Warm-up
    - Learning Objectives
    - Paralegals at Work
    - Chapter Outline

- Answers to: (includes the questions and the answers)
    - Working the Web
    - Critical Thinking and Writing Questions
    - Ethical Analysis and Discussion Questions
    - Developing Your Collaboration Skills
    - Video Case Studies
    - Paralegal Portfolio Exercises

TESTGEN TEST GENERATOR

TestGen. This computerized test generation system gives you maximum flexibility in creating and administering tests on paper, electronically, or online. It provides state-of-the-art features for viewing and editing test bank questions, dragging a selected question into a test you are creating, and printing sleek, formatted tests in a variety of layouts. Select test items from test banks included with TestGen for quick test creation, or write your own questions from scratch. TestGen's random generator provides the option to display different text or calculated number values each time questions are used.

POWERPOINT LECTURE PRESENTATION PACKAGE

PowerPoint Presentations. Our presentations offer clear, straightforward outlines and notes to use for class lectures or study materials. Photos, illustrations, charts, and tables from the book are included in the presentations when applicable.

ALTERNATE VERSIONS

eBooks This text is also available in multiple eBook formats. These are an exciting new choice for students looking to save money. As an alternative to purchasing the printed textbook, students can purchase an electronic version of the same content. With an eTextbook, students can search the text, make notes online, print out reading assignments that incorporate lecture notes, and bookmark important passages for later review. For more information, visit your favorite online eBook reseller or visit www.mypearsonstore.com.

ACKNOWLEDGMENTS

A round of applause to those whose insights contributed to the learning aspects of the fifth edition. Special thanks to:

Michael Fitch, for his guidance and encouragement early in the development of the project.

Kathryn Myers, for her generosity and kindness in allowing the use of material on portfolios and for the guidance she unknowingly gave by her example of enthusiasm, dedication, and hard work in support of paralegal education.

Lilian Harris, for her constant encouragement and help in developing materials on family law and the needs of tireless paralegal program directors and faculty to teach students the real-world approach.

Richard Opie, for sharing his ideas and materials.

Joy Smucker, for her encouragement in developing soft skills materials.

Deborah Orlik, for her help in really understanding the ethics of the paralegal profession.

Bill Mulkeen, for his encouragement and insights into the educational needs of students.

Don Swanson, an independent paralegal, for his expertise in the role of the paralegal in e-discovery and his total dedication to helping paralegal students by volunteering endless hours to help paralegal educators and authors and sharing real-life experiences and paralegal educational needs.

Members of the AAFPE board, including Pamela Bailey, Marissa Campbell, Christine Lissitzyn, Bob LeClair, Ed Husted, and Carolyn Smoot, for sharing ideas and materials and offering guidance in developing materials for this book that meet the needs of the paralegal student and faculty.

The inspiring panelists and speakers at the AAFPE annual and regional meetings over the past 14 years, for providing insights, guidance, suggestions, and encouragement.

The officers and members of the local and national professional associations, including NALA, NFPA, NALS, and ALA, for allowing the use of materials, but mostly for suggesting topics and real-life issues to be covered.

Paralegal Edie Hannah of Tom Goldman's law office, for her tireless reviews, detail checking, encouragement and support, countless hours on the phone getting materials, and networking with other paralegal professionals to obtain comments and input to make this textbook relevant to working paralegals as well as to students preparing for the profession.

The students in Tom Goldman's classes, for testing the text and online materials in a class setting and graciously providing suggestions and feedback.

Vivi Wang, Tiffany Lee, and Ashley Anderson, Professor Henry Cheeseman's research assistants at the Marshall School of Business at the University of Southern California, for their excellent assistance in conducting legal and paralegal research for this book.

Much gratitude to the reviewers of the fifth edition:

Fifth Edition Reviewer List:

Carina Aguirre, Everest College
Carol Brady, Milwaukee Area Technical College
Glenda Hanson, Renton Technical College
Jane Jacobs, Community College of Philadelphia
Sharee Laidlaw, Salt Lake Community College
Catherine McKee, Mt. San Antonio College
Willie McNeil, Westwood College
Beth Pless, Northeast Wisconsin Technical College
Howard Sokol, Athens Technical College

AND TO REVIEWERS OF THE PAST EDITIONS

Hakim Ben Adjoua, Columbus State Community College
Laura Alfano, Virginia College
Mercedes P. Alonso-Knapp, Florida International University
Sue Armstrong, Central Washington University
Laura Barnard, Lakeland Community College
Laura C. Barnard, Lakeland Community College
Karen Betancourt, University of Texas at Brownsville and Texas Southmost College
Carol Brady, Milwaukee Area Technical College
Linda Cabral Marrero, Mercy College
Chelsea Campbell, Lehman College CUNY
Anderson Castro, Florida International University
Mark A. Ciccarelli, Kent State University, OH
Belinda Clifton, IIA College
Kelly Collinsworth, Morehead State University
Karen Cook, Anne Arundel Community College
Subrina Cooper, University of Southern Mississippi

Jennifer Cote, Madonna University
Brian Craig, Minnesota School of Business—Richfield
Ernest Davila, San Jacinto College North, Texas
Steven A. Dayton, Fullerton College
Stephanie Delaney, Highline Community College
Robert Donley, Central Pennsylvania College
Tara L. Duncan, Everest College, Phoenix, AZ
Jameka Ellison, Florida Metro University—Lakeland
Linda Gassaway, McLennan Community College
Katherine Greenwood, Loyola University
Louise B. Gussin, University of Maryland University College
Laura J. Hansen-Brown, Kaplan University, Florida
P. Darrel Harrison, Miramar College, San Diego, CA
Warren Hodges, Forsyth Technical Community College
Linda Hornsby, Florida International University
Dario Hunter, Mohave Community College
Dee Janssen Lammers, Pima Community College, Tucson, AZ
Jennifer Jenkins, South College—Knoxville
Joy Kastanias, Florida Atlantic University
Alan Katz, Cape Fear Community College
Pierre A. Kleff, Jr., The University of Texas at Brownsville
Nance Kriscenski, Manchester Community College
Diana Lamphiere, Davenport College of Business
Sondi Lee, Camden County College
Carol Linker, University of Toledo
Elaine Lerner, Kaplan College—Online
Victoria H. Lopez, Southwestern College, California
Margaret Lovig, Coastline Community College, California
Ted Major, Shelton State Community College
Robert McDonald, Franciscan University
Alan Mege, LeHigh Valley College
Hillary Michaud, Stevenson University
Sharla Miller-Fowler, Amarillo College
Leslie Miron, Mercy College
R. Eileen Mitchell, University of New Orleans
Anne Murphy Brown, JD, Ursuline College
Dianna Murphy, Morehead State University
Kathryn L. Myers, Saint Mary-of-the-Woods College
Lisa Newman, Brown Mackie College—Atlanta
Anne Oestreicher, Northeast Wisconsin Technical College
Mary People, Arapahoe Community College, Colorado
Deborah Periman, University of Alaska—Anchorage
Anthony Piazza, Dan N. Myers University
Beth Pless, Northeast Wisconsin Technical College
Christy Powers, St. Petersburg Junior College
Judi Quinby, Kennesaw State University
Pat Roberson, New Mexico Junior College
Robin Rossenfeld, Community College of Aurora, Colorado
Wesley K. Sasano, Everest College—Rancho Cucamonga, California
Anne Schacherl, Madison Area Technical College
Labron Shuman, Delaware County Community College
Kathy Smith, Community College of Philadelphia
Deborah Vinecour, SUNY Rockland Community College
John Whitehead, Kilgore College
Alex A. Yarborough, Virginia College at Birmingham

Thomas F. Goldman
Henry R. Cheeseman

PART

I

The Paralegal Profession

Since the late 1960s, the paralegal profession has grown significantly in importance in the delivery of legal services. It has evolved into a profession that demands strong personal skills, a firm foundation in ethics, increasingly higher levels of legal knowledge, and competence in the use of technology. Career opportunities and career choices for the paralegal have never been better. Potential employers are as diverse as the duties paralegals are asked to perform. Today's paralegals need specialized skills in many areas. Formal programs of study and continuing education programs have developed to help individuals obtain and maintain the necessary skills. As with other professions, ethical rules and regulations have evolved to help paralegals avoid conflicts and possible malpractice. These topics will be discussed in Part I.

Chapter 1
The Paralegal Profession

Chapter 2
Ethics and Professional Responsibility

Chapter 3
The Paralegal Workplace

Chapter 4
Technology and the Paralegal

CHAPTER

1

The Paralegal Profession

LEARNING OBJECTIVES

After studying this chapter, you should be able to:

1. Describe the role of the paralegal in the delivery of legal services.
2. Explain the importance of personal skills in career success.
3. Discuss the job opportunities for the paralegal.
4. Describe the educational paths to the paralegal profession.
5. Describe the different approaches to the certification and regulation of the paralegal profession.

Paralegals at Work

On the Friday before Thanksgiving, Ariel sits in the bleachers watching her high school alma mater, Lincoln High, take on Lower Merion High. Ariel's brother, Ethan, is a senior on the football team, and this is his last high school football game.

Ariel graduated from Lincoln in 2012 and went on to get her bachelor's degree with a major in English and a minor in Languages. She spots Mr. Marshall, her high school guidance counselor, and goes over to greet him.

After briefly catching up, Ariel asks Mr. Marshall about the career advice he's given to her brother. Ethan is thinking about a legal career but isn't interested in criminal justice or law enforcement. He's also not sure about the time and dedication it takes to get through law school. Mr. Marshall tells her that he gave Ethan information on local paralegal programs.

Ariel has been working as an editorial assistant for a small publisher of online books. Although she always has plenty of work to do, she's not challenged in her job. She wants to use the technology, language, and writing skills she's developed, as well as have more autonomy and control over her work. Ariel asks Mr. Marshall whether a paralegal career makes sense for her.

Consider these issues as you read the chapter.

> "The great can protect themselves, but the poor and humble require the arm and shield of the law."
>
> *Andrew Jackson*

INTRODUCTION TO THE PARALEGAL PROFESSION

Prior to the late 1960s, many of the functions of today's paralegals were performed by legal staff members with titles such as "legal secretary" and "lay assistant." Much of the work was also performed by law clerks—recent law school graduates who had not yet passed the bar exam. Now, members of the legal community are accustomed to working with paralegals as members of the legal team. As the educational level of paralegals increases, so will the responsibility given to them. In many areas of law, the cost of legal services has increased, and the use of paralegals in many cases permits the delivery of quality legal services at a reduced cost to the client.

Career opportunities for the paralegal have never been better. Paralegals are employed in every area of legal services. They interview clients, conduct factual investigations, do legal research, prepare legal documents, assist at the counsel table in trials, and even represent clients in some administrative hearings. As the use of computer technology has become more commonplace in law offices and courts, paralegals with the necessary skills and training are being used in litigation support and handling electronic discovery issues. They are employed in governments, corporations, and law firms of all sizes.

LEARNING OBJECTIVE 1
Describe the role of the paralegal in the delivery of legal services.

What Is a Paralegal?

A great deal of confusion has arisen as to what the professional in this field should be called or what the professionals should call themselves. The terms **paralegal** and **legal assistant** have been used most frequently in the United States. They are used interchangeably by the **American Bar Association (ABA)**, the **National Federation of Paralegal Associations (NFPA)**, and the **National Association of Legal Assistants (NALA)**. The confusion stems in part from the shift away from the titles of "secretary" or "administrative assistant" or, in some organizations, "law office assistant."

Paralegal (legal assistant) A person qualified by education, training, or work experience who is employed or retained by a lawyer, law office, corporation, governmental agency, or other entity and who performs specifically delegated substantive legal work for which a lawyer is responsible; the equivalent term is legal assistant.

American Bar Association (ABA) The largest professional legal organization in the United States.

National Federation of Paralegal Associations (NFPA) A professional organization of state and local paralegal associations, founded in 1974.

National Association of Legal Assistants (NALA) A professional organization for legal assistants that provides continuing education and professional certification for paralegals, incorporated in 1975.

The exact definition of *legal assistant* has been the subject of discussions by national organizations including the ABA, NFPA, and NALA, as well as many state legislatures, supreme courts, and bar associations. The trend is toward the use of the term *paralegal* and away from the term *legal assistant*. In recognition of this trend, the American Bar Association changed the name of its Standing Committee on Legal Assistants to the Standing Committee on Paralegals.

In 1968, the American Bar Association (ABA) formed the Standing Committee on Legal Assistants (later changed to the Standing Committee on Paralegals). The purpose of this committee was originally to investigate the use of lay assistants in the law office. The ABA gave this committee jurisdiction over standards for the education and training of legal assistants. The committee monitors trends in the field and recommends to the House of Delegates (the policymaking body of the ABA) training programs that meet its standards for quality education.

The American Bar Association's 1997 definition of a paralegal or legal assistant, which has also been adopted by the National Association of Legal Assistants (NALA), is:

> A legal assistant or paralegal is a person qualified by education, training, or work experience who is employed or retained by a lawyer, law office, corporation, governmental agency or other entity and who performs specifically delegated substantive legal work for which a lawyer is responsible.
>
> The comment to the definition by the National Association of Legal Assistants (NALA) further clarifies the definition:
>
> This definition emphasizes the knowledge and expertise of paralegals in substantive and procedural law obtained through education and work experience. It further defines the legal assistant or paralegal as a professional working under the supervision of an attorney as distinguished from a non-lawyer who delivers services directly to the public without any intervention or review of work product by an attorney. Such unsupervised services, unless authorized by court or agency rules, constitute the unauthorized practice of law.

Source: http://www.nala.org/model.aspx#definition

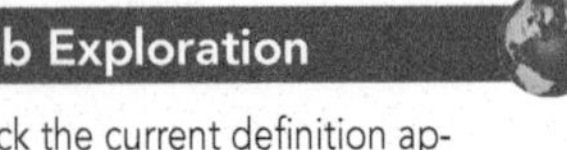

Web Exploration

Check the current definition approved by the American Bar Association at www.abanet.org.

Paralegals *in* Practice

PARALEGAL PROFILE

Vicki L. Karayan

During her 12-year paralegal career, Vicki L. Karayan has worked for both law firms and business corporations. She is currently employed at WellPoint, Inc., in Camarillo, California, the nation's second-largest company in the healthcare industry. As an Advanced Certified Paralegal, her present position of Business Change Advisor focuses on compliance reporting and legal research for the company's consumer marketing department.

I became inspired to pursue a paralegal career after going through a difficult, personal legal battle. After graduating with an associate's degree in Applied Science with a Legal Studies emphasis, I worked in a general practice firm. Later, I worked for a bankruptcy law firm where I eventually became the trainer/staff manager of seven offices. A family move led to a new job in a nationwide bankruptcy firm where I learned to track federal and state regulatory requirements.

In order to work closer to home, I took an Administrative Assistant position in the Medicaid Marketing department for a corporate healthcare company. What started as an entry-level job grew into a whole new position, as I offered better ways to tackle the company's market compliance reporting and legal research, and also helped improve office efficiency and staff training. Three promotions later, I believe I owe much of my career success to actively looking for opportunities to apply knowledge and skills learned from previous jobs and experiences, and from learning how to network with people, building strong working relationships based on ethical practices.

My advice is: try not to limit yourself to traditional paralegal job descriptions. Some of the best opportunities are found by looking "outside the box" and obtaining as many business and technology skills as possible. Finally, find what you love to do, and then network by making new business connections through individuals you already know and others you meet. These contacts can help your work go more smoothly and provide invaluable information in the future.

What Do Paralegals Do?

The primary function of paralegals is to assist attorneys in every aspect of the delivery of legal services, including preparing for hearings, trials, meetings, and real estate closings. In many cases, paralegals do the preparatory work, assisting in the creation of documents and forms, coordinating procedures and other activities, and in many offices maintaining the financial records of the firm.

People tend to think of paralegals as only working in private law offices directly under the supervision of attorneys. Actually, employers of paralegals are just as diverse as the duties paralegals are asked to perform. Many paralegals are employed by state, federal, and local governments, including their regulatory bodies. The paralegal's activities might include analyzing legal material for internal use, collecting and analyzing data, as well as preparing information and explanatory material for use by the general public.

More and more paralegals are coming to the paralegal profession from other professions. For example, they may come from nursing, bringing with them specialized knowledge that they can combine with the legal skills learned in a paralegal program. Their knowledge of medicine, combined with their legal knowledge, gives them a unique ability to analyze specialized material. For example, they are frequently hired to analyze medical materials for trial attorneys, both plaintiff and defense, or are employed as case analysts and claims representatives for health insurance companies. Those with other specialties can take a similar path. For example, those with engineering and other science degrees can find jobs in specialized areas of the law, such as patents and intellectual property. A paralegal with a criminal justice or a forensic science background, for example, may be uniquely qualified to work with criminal defense attorneys and prosecutors.

Web Exploration

Review the Model Standards and Guidelines of the National Association of Legal Assistants at http://www.nala.org/model.aspx.

Prior to the recognition of paralegals as a separate profession, individuals typically acquired specialized knowledge of a narrow legal field through on-the-job training. Someone working with a lawyer—usually a secretary—learned the daily routine

Advice from the Field

PEOPLE SKILLS CRITICAL TO PROFESSIONAL SUCCESS

Kathleen Call, Executive Director, Robert Half Legal

Kathleen Call is Executive Director of Robert Half Legal, a leading staffing service specializing in the placement of legal professionals, ranging from project attorneys and paralegals to administrators, legal secretaries, and other support staff. Robert Half Legal, which works with law firms and corporate legal departments, has offices throughout the United States and Canada.

When you think of which skills will be most important to your career advancement over the next five years, chances are "proficiency with technology" ranks high on your list. Knowledge of key software applications has become a critical success factor in the legal profession. However, to be considered for the best job opportunities in the future, you'll not only need technical competency, but also solid interpersonal skills and problem-solving abilities.

Audio- and video-conferencing, email, corporate intranets and, of course, the Internet have increased exponentially the amount—and speed—of day-to-day professional communication. The expanded use of technology will make it more important for legal professionals to be able to communicate effectively and articulately.

Another significant development driving the need for strong soft skills is the trend toward a more collaborative workplace. In a team-based office environment, diplomacy, flexibility, persuasiveness and management skills are critical. In a survey we commissioned among executives at the nation's 1,000 largest companies, 79 percent of respondents said self-managed employee work teams will increase productivity for U.S. companies. These productivity gains will only be realized, however, if team members can work together effectively. As a result, firms are placing a premium on excellent interpersonal skills.

WHAT ARE PEOPLE SKILLS?

Since soft skills are intangible and therefore hard to quantify, how do you determine whether you have what it takes to succeed? Our firm has identified a composite of key interpersonal traits represented by the acronym "PEOPLE":

Problem-solving abilities (organization, judgment, logic, creativity, conflict resolution)

Ethics (diplomacy, courtesy, honesty, professionalism)

Open-mindedness (flexibility, open to new business ideas, positive outlook)

Persuasiveness (excellent communication and listening skills)

Leadership (accountability, management and motivational skills)

Educational interests (continuous thirst for knowledge and skills development)

A deficiency in these skills can seriously limit your career prospects, whether you're applying for a new job as a legal assistant or seeking to move upward as an attorney within your current firm. Just as workers who failed to enhance their technical skills were left behind by the digital revolution, those who dismiss the significance of PEOPLE skills can find themselves stagnating in dead-end jobs.

ASSESS YOUR STRENGTHS AND WEAKNESSES

While it's relatively easy to measure the development of your proficiency with technology, it's much more challenging to gauge your progress in enhancing your PEOPLE skills. Again, this is primarily because these qualities are more subjective in nature. Since there are no classes on "flexibility" or "positive outlook" at the typical college or university, how do you acquire and upgrade your interpersonal abilities?

The following steps will help you take an accurate inventory of your strengths and weaknesses:

Honestly evaluate your aptitude in each of the PEOPLE skills. Which seem to come naturally? Is there room for improvement in any area?

Ask trusted friends, family members and coworkers for their opinions. How would they rate your PEOPLE skills?

COMMIT TO LEARNING

It takes time and experience to fully develop interpersonal skills, so don't expect to see improvement overnight. Here are some effective strategies to help you continue your progress:

Develop a list of the characteristics you'd most like to develop in yourself. Then brainstorm specific activities that will boost your abilities in your selected areas. For example, if you'd like to refine your leadership skills, volunteer to work on cases that provide the opportunity to supervise others or manage a project from start to finish.

Observe those who demonstrate strong PEOPLE skills in the areas you'd like to improve. How do they apply their abilities in various situations? How are their responses different than what yours would be?

Select a mentor. The best candidate is someone in the legal field whom you admire. Ask your prospective mentor if he or she would advise you, particularly in those PEOPLE skills that you've determined require enhancement. Since it's difficult to see yourself objectively, a mentor's ongoing support and feedback can be invaluable.

Enhance your listening skills. Concentrate on paying close attention to what others are saying. In general, avoid interrupting but ask for clarification when necessary. To prevent misunderstandings, paraphrase information in your own words when you are given complex instructions.

Become a better writer. Read books on effective writing so that you can develop a more concise style, or consider taking a journalism or business writing course. Proofread everything you write, especially email. Because electronic messages are prepared and sent quickly, they can be inadvertently filled with typographical and grammatical errors. In addition, it's important to employ PEOPLE skills in your writing, explaining yourself diplomatically and courteously.

Refine your verbal communication. Know what you want to say before you speak, and use a tone and style appropriate to the audience. When leaving a voice-mail message, organize your thoughts in advance to avoid being vague or rambling. If you're presenting a report to an attorney or client, rehearse a few times so your delivery will be smooth and your message clear.

Become a volunteer. You can acquire stronger leadership and organizational skills through volunteer work. Whether it's becoming involved in a trade association or helping your favorite charity, the skills you develop can be used on the job in a variety of situations.

Seek growth opportunities outside the workplace. Hobbies and leisure-time activities are an enjoyable way to enrich your PEOPLE skills. By coaching your child's soccer team, for example, you'll develop motivational and managerial skills, and become better at dealing with diverse personalities. If you'd like to enhance your creativity, consider taking an art or music class.

tasks and became knowledgeable about that lawyer's specific area of law. Many of these individuals became important sources of information, such as what documents are required for a real estate closing, the steps in preparing and filing estate and trust accountings, or the procedures in preparing and filing pleadings. These were the first paralegals. Today, many of the skills and procedures formerly acquired on the job are taught at institutions specializing in the education of paralegals or legal assistants. These programs may offer a certificate, a two-year associate's degree, a four-year bachelor's degree, or a master's degree.

Professional Skills

LEARNING OBJECTIVE 2
Explain the importance of personal skills in career success.

The skills needed by a paralegal are varied and often depend on the nature of the legal specialty in which one works. Common to all paralegals are certain skills (also known as "soft skills") such as communication, initiative, resourcefulness, problem solving, perseverance, teamwork, leadership, and self-motivation.

Everyone has goals in life. An experienced runner may strive to finish a marathon, or a skilled writer may have a vision of writing a great novel. Achieving a specific goal requires a certain set of skills. If the goal is to be a successful paralegal, certain basic skills are needed. You may already have some of the necessary basic skills, such as

- the ability to read English (unless someone is reading this book to you);
- the ability to communicate at some level in writing or speaking; and
- initiative (you demonstrated this by signing up for this course or picking up this book to learn about the paralegal profession).

In addition, you may have other basic skills, such as

- facility with computers and the Internet;
- the ability to speak a second or third language; and
- a background in medicine, engineering, business, or some other academic or occupational area.

Some other skills are less obvious, such as resourcefulness, perseverance, analytical skills, and interpersonal skills, including cultural sensitivity. These will be explored in greater depth as they are applied to the paralegal profession. We cannot all run a marathon or write a novel, but we can all acquire most of the basic skills by making an effort to improve ourselves and attain the knowledge base to achieve most, if not all, of our goals.

Through hard work and commitment, many people achieve much more than they believed they were capable of. If one is willing to work hard enough, most personal and professional goals can be attained. A good starting point in achieving goals is to understand one's strengths and weaknesses, capitalize on the strengths, and work on overcoming the weaknesses. Exhibit 1.1 shows the top required skills and level of importance for paralegals and legal assistants listed by the American Job Center partner O*Net online.

Resourcefulness

Resourcefulness is the ability to meet and handle situations by finding solutions to problems. It is one of the most valuable skills anyone can have—and one that is not easily taught. A resourceful person in the office is sometimes referred to as the "can-do" person. This is the person who usually finds a creative way to accomplish something everyone else has given up on. Creativity is used to solve the problem by "thinking outside the box" and not limiting the solution to tried-and-true methods. When everyone else says "I can't find this witness," the resourceful person tries a new approach and finds the witness. When others use only an Internet search engine, the resourceful person uses social media websites to locate the witness.

In the legal workplace, the person who gets noticed is the one who finds a way to get the job done in time for the hearing, meeting, or arbitration. He or she is willing to use unconventional means to get the job finished when the power goes out or the computer crashes just before a deadline. Lawyers need resourceful people and reward them to keep them on the team.

Exhibit 1.1 Skills for paralegals and legal assistants

Skills Save Table (XLS/CSV)

Importance	Skill
75	**Reading Comprehension** — Understanding written sentences and paragraphs in work related documents.
69	**Active Listening** — Giving full attention to what other people are saying, taking time to understand the points being made, asking questions as appropriate, and not interrupting at inappropriate times.
66	**Speaking** — Talking to others to convey information effectively.
66	**Writing** — Communicating effectively in writing as appropriate for the needs of the audience.
56	**Critical Thinking** — Using logic and reasoning to identify the strengths and weaknesses of alternative solutions, conclusions or approaches to problems.
53	**Time Management** — Managing one's own time and the time of others.
50	**Active Learning** — Understanding the implications of new information for both current and future problem-solving and decision-making.
50	**Coordination** — Adjusting actions in relation to others' actions.
50	**Judgment and Decision Making** — Considering the relative costs and benefits of potential actions to choose the most appropriate one.
50	**Monitoring** — Monitoring/Assessing performance of yourself, other individuals, or organizations to make improvements or take corrective action.
50	**Service Orientation** — Actively looking for ways to help people.

back to top

Source: National Center for O*NET Development. 23-2011.00. *O*NET OnLine*. Retrieved December 8, 2014, from http://www.onetonline.org/link/summary/23-2011.00

Commitment

Commitment means finishing what one starts. In the old story of the tortoise (turtle) and the hare (rabbit), the tortoise wins the race by being "slow and steady." He wins because of his commitment—putting everything into the race and not stopping until the job is done. Many people start jobs and don't finish them. Others start what seems to be an insurmountable task and—to everyone's amazement—finish, and finish well. Taking on an assignment in a law office requires commitment. Team members are expected to finish the task, whether it is researching a case, writing a brief, filing a pleading, or organizing a file.

As a professional, you are expected to finish tasks within the assigned time frame. There is no excuse for not completing certain tasks, such as filing a complaint with the court before the **statute of limitations** expires or getting the brief to the court by the court-imposed deadline. Even a simple thing like getting to work on time requires commitment.

Not everyone has the commitment necessary to be an effective professional. You have to decide whether you are willing to make the commitment. Others will be depending on you, and if you do not want to commit, admit it to yourself and to the others who are depending on you, and then choose some other activity or profession. Choosing a profession, whether it is the legal profession, the paralegal profession, the medical profession, or the accounting profession, requires a commitment to serve others. As a paralegal professional, you are making a commitment to your clients that you will provide the best professional advice, skill, and effort, and they will depend on your professionalism.

Analytical Skills

Analytical skills involve using a step-by-step process to solve a problem. For example, analytical skills may be used to find a missing witness by analyzing the person's background. The analysis may reveal that the person is part of a group, such as a professional society, that publishes a membership directory. Or analytical skills may be used to find out what made a bottle explode, injuring a client. Determining the actual cause requires a step-by-step analysis of the potential reasons and then narrowing down the possible causes.

One of the basic skills that both law students and paralegal students are taught is legal analysis, or the ability to identify the key facts and legal issues of a case and compare and contrast them to the law and to other cases. This is a skill that develops with time. As you study the law and learn about specific crimes, torts, and other areas of law, you will learn the individual elements of each. You will then be able to determine whether these elements exist in actual cases. For example, in contract law, you will learn what conduct is a valid acceptance of a contract offer, and in tort law, what constitutes reasonable conduct under the circumstances.

SIDEBAR

CREATING AN IMPRESSION

To create a positive impression, try to:

- have a positive attitude
- be diplomatic
- be flexible
- establish a good rapport with others
- be a team player
- be resourceful
- be adaptable
- be thorough

Interpersonal Skills

The ability to communicate and work with others is vital to success as a paralegal, as well as to success in other endeavors. To categorize people, coworkers, colleagues, and employers might be unfair, but we all do it. We think—and sometimes say—things like "He's a pleasure to work with" or "She has clients eating out of her hand." Conversely, we might say things like "She's the most negative person I know" or "He's only out for himself." These comments reflect the other person's interpersonal skills (or the lack of), the ability to communicate and work with others.

How we relate to others can make the job easier or harder. This includes not just other members of the legal team but also clients, witnesses, and opposing parties. Obviously, everyone on the team must have a certain level of trust and confidence in the others on the team. People who have a good working relationship accomplish more and enjoy doing it. By contrast, conflict and tension make the job harder and can cause people to take shortcuts or avoid contact, which can result in poor performance and potential malpractice.

Not everyone has the personality to deal with every type of situation and every type of personality. For example, some may have trouble dealing with difficult clients. But everyone on the legal team has to develop the skills to work with other people or recognize when they may have to have someone else handle certain aspects of a case or a certain client. The skill is in recognizing these situations and making the appropriate adjustments. Some might call this "sensitivity"—to other people's needs, desires, wants, likes, and dislikes.

Cultural differences are discussed later, but in the American culture, for example, people tend to be sensitive to odors—breath, body, environmental. We do not want to offend. Our use of language is another area of sensitivity. We try to avoid using words that we believe will offend the other person in a specific circumstance, such as telling off-color jokes in a religious setting in front of a person of the cloth. Some refer to interpersonal skills as "sensitivity" to other people's needs, desires, wants, likes, and dislikes. The starting point in working with attorneys, paralegals, and support staff, clients, and opposing counsel, court personnel, and others is to be sensitive to these issues. What offends you probably offends others. Being sensitive to how others react to your words, conduct, and actions can provide good clues as to what is acceptable and what is not.

In the past, interpersonal skills were used primarily in face-to-face contact, telephone conversations, and written communications. Today these skills are also necessary in other forms of communication, such as emails and other electronic communications. For example, using the "happy face" and "frowning face" icons [":-)" and ":-("] in an email could be interpreted as overfamiliarity. THE USE OF ALL CAPITAL LETTERS might be interpreted as shouting or anger. Poor spelling and bad grammar in emails are likely to be seen as sloppiness or carelessness. In the past, letters were dictated, typed, proofread, and then signed. Today we often dash off an email without much thought—and sometimes the email reflects just that. How we respond by email affects how our clients view our capabilities and skill.

Communication Skills

Good communication means expressing ideas effectively. The practice of law requires effective communication, both oral and written. The lawyer and paralegal who work together must be able to communicate assignments and information with clarity—and frequently with brevity. Over time, communication will improve as each person comes to understand how the other communicates.

Communication is made more complex by subtleties, nuances, and expressions that may require interpretation or explanation. For example, an attorney who is accustomed to using traditional book methods of research may ask a new paralegal (who has a deep understanding of computer research methods and little traditional book experience) to "check the pocket parts." This means checking for the latest updates or changes to a statute or case law. A paralegal who is accustomed to doing computer research may not understand what this expression means. Or asking a paralegal to "Shepardize" a case may have no meaning to someone who has learned only the Westlaw system, in which the method for checking other cases is called "KeyCiting," or the Loislaw system, which refers to this checking as "GlobalCiting."

Communication can be a major problem in a fast-paced office where information moves very quickly. In the middle of a court hearing, the litigation attorney may send a text message from court to the support paralegal at the office to ask for information about an unexpected case the other side has brought up. Nowadays, we rarely have the time to develop a common written and oral language base for communication among attorneys, paralegals, clients, opposing attorneys, and court personnel. And yet letters, pleadings, contracts, and other written documents must be clear and

SIDEBAR

COMMUNICATION SKILLS

Do I:

- read with comprehension?
- listen effectively and accurately and interpret nonverbal communication?
- write in clear, concise, and grammatically correct English?
- speak in clear, concise, and grammatically correct English?
- use language to persuade?
- tailor the nature of the communication to maximize understanding in the intended audience, including people with different levels of education and different cultural backgrounds?

Source: American Association for Paralegal Education

accurate. In many situations, an idea, request, or demand must be carefully communicated in only one document.

Oral communication must also be clear and precise, and first impressions matter. If a first discussion in person or by telephone is filled with slang or poor grammar, it may create a poor impression of the firm's professionalism, ability, and legal skill. It can influence a client's decision to retain the firm, the inclination of a judge to grant a request, or a court clerk's willingness to give you the help you need.

Opportunities for Paralegals

LEARNING OBJECTIVE 3

Discuss the job opportunities for the paralegal.

The U.S. Bureau of Labor Statistics, in its 2012–2022 projection, indicated a continued demand for legal services from government, individuals, and businesses alike. It further stated that paralegals and legal assistants are expected to account for 46,200 new jobs as legal establishments attempt to reduce costs by assigning these workers more tasks that were once performed by lawyers. This means additional growth of the occupation as well as the need for individuals to replace existing employees. The Labor Department estimates might be increased further by the de facto requirement found in court opinions that more paralegals be used to perform services instead of attorneys, who bill at higher rates.

Web Exploration

Check the latest paralegal statistics in the *Occupational Outlook Handbook* from the Department of Labor, Bureau of Labor Statistics at **http://www.bls.gov/oco/home.htm.**

Projections Data from the National Employment Matrix

				Change, 2012–2022	
Occupational title	**SOC Code**	**Employment, 2012**	**Projected employment, 2022**	**Number**	**Percent**
Paralegals and legal assistants	23–2011	277,000	323,300	46,200	17

Source: *Occupational Outlook Handbook*, 2014–15 Edition, U.S. Department of Labor, Bureau of Labor Statistics, Employment Projections program.

Paralegals held about 277,000 jobs in 2012, according to the Bureau of Labor Statistics, U.S. Department of Labor, *Occupational Outlook Handbook*, 2014–2015 Edition. In 2012, full-time wage-and-salary paralegals and legal assistants had median annual earnings, including bonuses, of $46,990. The top 10 percent earned more than $75,410, and the bottom 10 percent earned less than $29,420. The median annual wages for paralegals and legal assistants in the top five industries as of May 2012 were:

Legal Services	$44,950
Federal Government	$62,400
Local Government	$47,000
State Government	$42,050
Finance and Insurance	$54,670

Source: *Occupational Outlook Handbook*, 2014–2015 Edition, U.S. Department of Labor, Bureau of Labor Statistics.

By comparison, the median annual wage for all occupations in the U.S. economy was $34,750.

Compensation for paralegals varies according to working environment and geographic location. As with most jobs and professions, salaries tend to be higher in large metropolitan areas and lower in small and rural areas. Large firms tend to pay more, and small firms tend to pay less. At times, these variations in compensation can be justified by the costs of working in certain locations, such as higher tax rates and the cost of commuting.

Web Exploration

View current Bureau of Labor Statistics data at **http://www.bls.gov/oes/home.htm.**

The Future

The future of the paralegal profession may be determined by clients who are unwilling or unable to pay what they see as inflated fees for lawyers. The future could also be dictated, to some extent, by the courts. When fee petitions are submitted to courts for approval, important billing issues arise that affect paralegals. This is one of the areas in which the definition of "paralegal" has come into play. For example, certain secretarial or clerical tasks are considered overhead (part of the cost of running the office) and should be performed at no additional cost to the client. However, in some cases, these tasks are charged to the client as paralegal fees. Courts allow charges for paralegal fees but not for secretarial fees. In other cases, higher attorney rates are charged for performing tasks that could have been delegated to a paralegal. Courts have reduced claims for legal fees where using a paralegal for these tasks would have resulted in lower charges.

National Association of Legal Secretaries (NALS) Since 1999, an association for legal professionals. It was originally formed in 1949 as an association for legal secretaries.

For instance, summarizing depositions traditionally has been a task delegated to paralegals. Assume that the paralegal takes two hours to complete the task and the paralegal's time is billed to the client at \$75 per hour. (Don't get excited—that doesn't necessarily have any bearing on what you may be paid.) The client would be charged \$150. For a lawyer to do the same work, if billed out at \$175 per hour, the client would be charged \$350. Unless there is a good reason for the lawyer to do the work, the decision to delegate the work to a lawyer is unfair to the client. A number of court decisions are beginning to focus on the fairness and propriety of attorneys billing for certain services. As other federal and state courts weigh in on this line of decisions, law firms may have to hire more paralegals.

NATIONAL ASSOCIATION OF LEGAL ASSISTANTS MODEL STANDARDS AND GUIDELINES FOR UTILIZATION OF LEGAL ASSISTANTS-PARALEGALS

Preamble

Proper utilization of the services of legal assistants contributes to the delivery of cost effective, high-quality legal services. Legal assistants and the legal profession should be assured that measures exist for identifying legal assistants and their role in assisting attorneys in the delivery of legal services. Therefore, the National Association of Legal Assistants, Inc., hereby adopts these Standards and Guidelines as an educational document for the benefit of legal assistants and the legal profession. . . .

III Standards

A legal assistant should meet certain minimum qualifications. The following standards may be used to determine an individual's qualifications as a legal assistant:

(1) Successful completion of the Certified Legal Assistant (CLA)/Certified Paralegal (CP) certifying examination of the National Association of Legal Assistants, Inc.;

(2) Graduation from an ABA approved program of study for legal assistants;

(3) Graduation from a course of study for legal assistants which is institutionally accredited but not ABA approved, and which requires not less than the equivalent of 60 semester hours of classroom study;

(4) Graduation from a course of study for legal assistants, other than those set forth in (2) and (3) above, plus not less than six months of in-house training as a legal assistant;

(5) A baccalaureate degree in any field, plus not less than six months in-house training as a legal assistant;

(6) A minimum of three years of law-related experience under the supervision of an attorney, including at least six months of in-house training as a legal assistant; or

(7) Two years of in-house training as a legal assistant.

For purposes of these Standards, "in-house training as a legal assistant" means attorney education of the employee concerning legal assistant duties and these Guidelines. In addition to review and analysis of assignments, the legal assistant should receive a reasonable amount of instruction directly related to the duties and obligations of the legal assistant.

Paralegal Education in the United States

LEARNING OBJECTIVE 4
Describe the educational paths for entry into the paralegal profession.

The best-trained, most highly skilled individual is the one most likely to land a job. Given the choice, a prospective employer is more likely to hire an applicant with an associate's degree, a bachelor's degree, or a master's degree in paralegal studies rather than an applicant with only a high school diploma and a paralegal certificate.

An estimated 1,000 paralegal education programs are available in the United States. These programs offer on-site or online instruction or a hybrid format combining online and on-site instruction. Some of these programs have obtained ABA approval, and many are members of the **American Association for Paralegal Education (AAfPE)**, which requires substantial compliance with ABA guidelines as a condition of membership.

American Association for Paralegal Education (AAfPE) A national organization of paralegal educators and institutions offering paralegal education programs.

Career Planning

Career planning should include planning for education and perfecting professional skills. A sound educational plan is built on a foundation of general education courses that will be useful in any occupation and meet basic core requirements for an associate's or bachelor's degree. Occupation-related courses, such as paralegal specialty courses, should be selected with an eye toward transferability and suitability at a higher education level.

This is not to say that all courses must be transferable from one school to another or from an associate's-degree program to a bachelor's- or master's-degree program. Something can be learned from every course you take, even if it is only the realization that you do not wish to pursue a particular area of study. Think of the people you know who have pursued a career only to discover later that they are not interested in that line of work. One of your early educational goals should be to explore areas of actual or potential interest. Many students find a new career path after taking a required class they thought they would not like.

It is also clearer today than ever that successful paralegals must have a solid foundation in computer skills. As a paralegal advances in the profession, he or she must maintain and build upon these skills as computers and software become more sophisticated.

Web Exploration

Check the available resources for paralegal students at the different national paralegal organizations:

National Federation of Paralegal Associations
http://www.paralegals.org

National Association of Legal Assistants
http://www.nala.org

Association of Legal Administrators
http://www.alanet.org

International Paralegal Management Association
http://www.paralegalmanagement.org/ipma/

NALS, the association for legal professionals
http://www.nals.org

Advice from the Field

According to the Department of Labor, employment of paralegals and legal assistants is expected to grow by 17 percent from 2012 to 2022, faster than the average for all occupations. This occupation attracts many applicants, and competition for jobs will be strong. Experienced, formally trained paralegals with strong computer and database management skills should have the best job prospects.

Source: U.S. Department of Labor, *Occupational Outlook Handbook*, 2014–2015 Edition, Paralegals and Legal Assistants.

Web Exploration

See the complete *Occupational Outlook Handbook* of the Bureau of Labor Statistics at http://www.bls.gov/ooh/legal/paralegals-and-legal-assistants.htm.

CHECKLIST My Career Roadmap

- ☐ How can I capitalize on my strengths?
- ☐ My strengths are:
- ☐ Skills I need to strengthen:
- ☐ How can I overcome my weaknesses?
- ☐ My weaknesses are :
- ☐ Skills I need to acquire:
- ☐ Courses I should take:
- ☐ Extracurricular activities for the résumé:
- ☐ Interim work experience I should seek:
- ☐ Volunteer activities:
- ☐ Short-term career goals:
- ☐ Long-term career goals:

The ABA Standing Committee Guidelines require that instruction be at the post-secondary level and contain at least 60 semester hours, including general educational and legal specialty courses, offered by an accredited institution. Of these 60 hours, at least 18 must normally be general education courses and at least 18 must be legal specialty courses.

For purposes of the Guidelines, a "legal specialty course" (1) covers substantive law or legal procedures or process, (2) has been developed for paralegals, (3) emphasizes practical paralegal skills, and (4) meets the instructional requirements of G-301.

> *Source:* http://www.americanbar.org/content/dam/aba/administrative/paralegals/ls_prlgs_2013_paralegal_guidelines.authcheckdam.pdf

Compliance with the ABA and the AAfPE guidelines is voluntary. As stated by the ABA,

> Seeking approval from the American Bar Association is a voluntary process initiated by the institution offering the program. Therefore, the lack of approval does not necessarily mean a paralegal program is not of good quality and reputable.
>
> *Source:* http://www.americanbar.org/groups/paralegals/resources/career_information.html

A majority of paralegal programs have chosen not to undergo the process for approval by the ABA. Many programs may offer a majority of courses in online or hybrid format that do not meet ABA guidelines, which limits the number of such courses that may be offered as part of the program of study.

Types of Educational Programs

The ultimate goals of the paralegal's education are to obtain a good job and to perform at a professional level. The demands on paralegals today require more advanced skills and abilities than in the past. Whereas basic typing, office, and business communications skills might have been acceptable for a starting position in a law firm 20 years ago, greater skills are demanded of those looking for a paralegal position today.

More employers today are also asking for transcripts showing the courses taken and the minimum number of hours of study as spelled out in the ABA guidelines, even for graduates of non-ABA-accredited institutions. However, the reality is that many attorneys do not know what educational requirements are needed to obtain a paralegal degree or certificate. And in many cases, they do not know the elements of the ABA, NFPA, or NALA definitions of "paralegal" or "legal assistant."

Paralegal educational programs generally fall into two categories: those offering a certificate and those offering a degree—either an **associate degree** or a **bachelor degree**. These programs may be offered by a two-year community or junior college or a four-year college or university. A number of business and private **proprietary schools** also offer paralegal programs.

Associate degree A college degree in science (AS), arts (AA), or applied arts (AAS), generally requiring two years of full-time study.

Bachelor degree A college degree generally requiring four years of full-time study.

Proprietary school A private, as opposed to public, institution, generally for profit, offering training and education.

RELEVANT PARALEGAL SKILLS

Skill Development

- Critical thinking skills
- Organizational skills
- General communication skills
- Interpersonal skills
- Legal research skills
- Legal writing skills
- Computer skills
- Interviewing and investigation skills

Acquisition of Knowledge

- Organization and operation of the legal system
- Organization and operation of law offices
- The paralegal profession and ethical obligations
- Contracts
- Torts
- Business organizations
- Litigation procedures

A student's prior educational and professional background will determine, in many cases, which of the programs to select. Those who already have a bachelor's or other higher academic degree may need only the legal specialty courses. Those who come from a specialty background, such as nursing or another science-related field, may want to broaden their education by taking courses of a general nature in addition to the legal specialty courses.

Certificate Programs

Most educational institutions with paralegal or legal assistant programs offer a **certificate** that recognizes completion of a program of study that requires less than what is required to receive a degree. Some certificates award college credits; others do not. For students who already possess a baccalaureate degree, obtaining additional college credits probably isn't an issue. However, for students without an undergraduate degree, programs that do not offer college credit still can be valuable but should be considered carefully. At the very least, the actual time spent in the classroom should be equivalent to the minimums of college credit courses.

Certificate A recognition of the completion of a program of study that requires less than that needed for a degree.

Those planning to transfer should consider whether their credits may be carried over to another institution. Even if they have no immediate intent to continue in school, it would be wise to plan ahead and not lose the hours and credits they have earned in the event they later decide to go on to obtain a degree.

Students should also consider what is acceptable in the community in which they intend to work. Many professional paralegal organizations are reporting that a bachelor's degree is becoming necessary to obtain many paralegal positions. The U.S. Attorney's Office, for example, is requiring at least a four-year degree for a paralegal position.

Associate Degree Programs

Many community colleges and junior colleges offer an associate degree in science (AS), arts (AA), or applied arts (AAS) in paralegal or legal assistant studies. For many students these programs offer a community-based transition into higher education. For others it is a way of getting back into higher education while working at a full-time job or another occupation. Associate degree programs also tend to be a cost-effective educational environment for trying different areas of study before finding an area of concentration.

Web Exploration

The IPMA Position Paper is available at www.paralegalmanagement.org/management-resources/resources-for-paralegal-managers/ipma-position-papers.

Support services are often available for returning students or students who need additional help. Many of these schools offer English courses for those for whom English is a second language. Assistance is also provided for those who need a refresher course or help with study skills after years away from school.

Baccalaureate Programs

Some of the earliest paralegal programs were built on a model in which a bachelor degree was the prerequisite for entering a paralegal program of study. A number of programs now offer a bachelor degree in paralegal studies. One national organization, the International Paralegal Management Association (IPMA), has recommended the bachelor degree as the minimum qualification to enter the profession:

> A baccalaureate degree should be the minimum requirement for employment as a paralegal. Paralegals have assumed many responsibilities previously handled by lawyers. These responsibilities include complex legal issues; clear writing, researching, and critical thinking skills; and a strong academic background. The IPMA believes this accepted professional standard of academic achievement lends greater credibility and respect to increasing paralegal participation in the legal profession.
>
> ***Source:*** International Paralegal Management Association (IPMA), http://www.paralegalmanagement.org/images/stories/documents/education-position-paper.pdf

The increase in professional recognition of paralegals has resulted in their gaining more responsibility, as well as greater expectations regarding their skills and education. As the standing of the paralegal on the legal team rises, so will the demand for those with a broad-based education to serve in those positions. Four-year programs of study are attempting to meet that demand by merging traditional four-year core requirements with legal specialty courses.

The paralegal serving in a family law practice provides a good example of this demand. In the highly charged emotional environment of custody and divorce cases, knowledge of family and child psychology is essential. For those in an intellectual property practice, an understanding of science and engineering is a basic requirement. The four-year time frame allows more flexibility to explore and build skills and knowledge, as well as to meet the increasing demand for broader education.

Graduate Programs

A few colleges and universities now offer graduate degrees in legal studies. Others offer advanced degrees in related areas such as legal administration.

Specialty Certificates

Specialty certificates, such as the legal nurse consultant certificate, offer an excellent entry point into a paralegal career. Specialty certificates combined with degrees in other fields of study, such as nursing, journalism, and computer science, are like a capstone program preparing a person for entry into a new career. One of the greatest demands has been for those with a background in nursing combined with a paralegal education. A growing number of colleges are offering a certificate in legal nurse consulting.

Making a Personal Assessment and Setting Goals

If you are reading this book, you probably have made at least a tentative goal to enter the paralegal profession. The job you ultimately choose should be more than a way to earn an income and should also be work that gives you satisfaction and fulfillment. The paralegal field offers a variety of specialties. An early goal should be to take courses that will help you identify the specialty you would enjoy most. Perhaps you are already experienced in a field that will lead to a specialty, such as nursing, engineering, or law enforcement.

One of the first steps is to assess your own skills and personal qualities. What are your abilities? What are your personality traits? Do you like working under deadlines? Do you enjoy working with certain groups of people, such as the elderly or those with disabilities? As you will find out, the paralegal profession offers opportunities in many types of working environments. Understanding your interests, skills, and preferred working conditions will help you select the best path toward achieving your professional goals.

Selecting a Specialty

It is never too early to set career goals. After you start your first job, you will learn more about the various areas of practice that are available to you. Your ultimate specialty might stem from your educational background, such as journalism or medicine, or from an area of special interest, such as environmental issues. It may also result simply from a preference to work with certain types of clients, such as the elderly people or with disabilities.

CHECKLIST Career Planning

- ☐ My current paralegal job-related skills are:
- ☐ My special interests are:
- ☐ My passions are:
- ☐ My personality traits are:
- ☐ My geographical work and living desires are:
- ☐ My willingness to accept responsibility is:
- ☐ My level of self-motivation is:

A career may take many twists and turns, and it is never too late to make a career adjustment or choose a new path. Many successful individuals begin a career later in life, and schools are full of nontraditional students seeking a career change. For example, there are many former nurses in the paralegal profession who, after working in the medical field for many years, made a change to the paralegal field.

Your decision should be based on a self-evaluation of your likes and dislikes, interests, passions, and any physical or geographic limitations. If you hate to fly, you probably will not want a job that requires travel. If you are not comfortable with strangers, you probably will not want a job as a paralegal investigator for a litigation firm. If you like books and research, you may be interested in working as a firm's librarian or researcher.

Assessing Your Background

As the law has become more specialized, so has the demand for paralegals with more than just paralegal skills. Law firms specializing in medical malpractice frequently look for paralegals who also have a medical background, such as nursing. Firms with large, complex cases often look for someone with computer database skills to manage the files. Paralegals with journalism experience are sought out for their interviewing and writing skills.

Your personal background can be an asset when added to your paralegal certificate or degree. As you begin your professional training, take stock of your entire educational background, special skills, and talents, as well as personal areas of interest. A self-assessment early in your studies helps you recognize your strengths and acknowledge weaknesses that you need to work on.

Assessing Your Skills

You may well have a number of personal skills that will benefit you in the future as a paralegal. You might have great interpersonal skills, communicate well orally and in writing, and be a highly motivated person—all qualities of a good paralegal.

Individuals with language skills are particularly in demand in international law, as well as in working with clients who lack English-language skills. The paralegal who understands a second language or the cultural nuances among clients can be invaluable.

Assessing Your Interests

What are your personal interests? Do you enjoy the outdoors in your free time? If so, working on environmental issues may give you satisfaction. Do you find yourself drawn to volunteering or working in your free time with shut-ins and elderly people?

Selecting Your Electives

Becoming aware of your interests and background knowledge enables you to select the elective courses that can qualify you for work in a specialty field. Taking electives is a good way to explore an area in which you think you might be interested without committing to more than one semester or a few credits of study. Many students find new interests and a potential career direction after taking courses in areas they had not considered previously.

For example, you may find high-technology industries to be exciting and wonder how a paralegal might fit into this growth area. One of the fastest-growing fields is that of intellectual property law. In the age of computers and the Internet, with its global technology marketplace, protection of intellectual property has become a critical concern for individuals and companies alike. Taking a three-credit course in intellectual property may introduce the paralegal student to a new area of interest in a potential growth area of the paralegal profession. This is also true for other emerging areas, such as environmental law and legal nurse consulting.

LEARNING OBJECTIVE 4
Describe the different approaches to the certification and regulation of the paralegal profession.

Qualifications to Be a Paralegal

What are the qualifications that allow someone to call him- or herself a "paralegal" or a "legal assistant" and to be billed as a paralegal? This question is not easy to answer. Just as the practice of law falls to the individual states for regulation, so does regulation of the paralegal profession. Regulations for paralegals lack uniformity in both the state statutes and court rules. Few states have laws such as the California statute shown in Exhibit 1.3. Perhaps the most consistent and universal requirements are those established by the ABA's Standing Committee on Paralegals and the American Association for Paralegal Education (AAfPE), a national association of paralegal educators. These requirements have become the de facto standard for the minimum qualifications necessary for a person to call him- or herself a paralegal or legal assistant.

Paralegal Advance Competency Exam (PACE) The National Federation of Paralegal Associations' certification exam. Candidates must have two years of experience and a bachelor's degree and have completed a paralegal course at an accredited school.

Web Exploration

Detailed information on PACE can be obtained at www.paralegals.org/displaycommon.cfm?an=1&subarticlenbr=888.

Certified Legal Assistant (CLA) A designation by the National Association of Legal Assistants for those who take and pass NALA's two-day comprehensive examination.

ALS (Accredited Legal Secretary) The basic certification for legal professionals from NALS.

PLS (Professional Legal Secretary) The advanced certification for legal professionals from NALS.

International Paralegal Management Association (IPMA) A North American association for legal assistant managers.

PP (Professional Paralegal) Certification from NALS for those performing paralegal duties.

Web Exploration

General information about paralegal certification, including requirements, exam subjects, and testing schedule, can be found at http://www.paralegals.org/includes/get_asset.asp?asset=3168.

Paralegal Certification

Each of the major professional paralegal membership organizations has established a testing program for those who seek a professional designation based on proof of a level of knowledge and skill.

The National Federation of Paralegal Associations (NFPA) administers the **Paralegal Advance Competency Exam (PACE)** to test the competency level of experienced paralegals.

Those who successfully pass the exam may use the designation "PACE-Registered Paralegal" or "RP." Continued use of the designation requires 12 additional hours of continuing legal or specialty education every two years, with at least one hour of legal ethics.

Since 1976, the National Association of Legal Assistants (NALA) has conferred the **Certified Legal Assistant (CLA)** designation upon those who pass its two-day comprehensive examination. In 2004, NALA registered the certification mark "CP" with the U.S. Patent and Trademark Office for those who prefer the term "Certified Paralegal."

To maintain the CLA designation, 50 hours of continuing legal assistant education must be completed every five years. For those who have achieved the initial designation, NALA also offers specialist credentials for those practicing in a specific area of law, such as bankruptcy, intellectual property, civil litigation, probate, and estate planning. Successful completion of these examinations permits the additional designation Certified Legal Assistant–Specialty (CLAS).

NALS offers members and nonmembers the opportunity to sit for three unique certifications dedicated to the legal services profession—ALS, PLS, and PP.

1. **ALS**—the basic certification for legal professionals
2. **PLS**—the advanced certification for legal professionals
3. **PP**—professionals performing paralegal duties

A comparison of the various exams—NALS, NALA, and NFPA—is presented in Exhibit 1.2.

Minimum Education

The **International Paralegal Management Association (IPMA)** is an organization for paralegal management professionals. In its position paper on paralegal education, the IPMA states:

> [N]early 80% of IPMA member organizations require the bachelor's degree when hiring, and many require specific paralegal education and/or give credit for professional certifications.

Legal assistants have assumed many responsibilities formerly handled by lawyers. Working with complex legal issues requires that a legal assistant possess clear writing, researching, and critical thinking abilities.

Exhibit 1.2 Legal certification comparison chart

Comparison of National Level Paralegal Certification Exams©

PLEASE NOTE: The content of the chart below is verified only as to the information about the NFPA® Paralegal Advanced Competency Exam (PACE®) exam and NFPA's new Paralegal CORE Competency Exam (PCCE™). The information regarding the NALA and NALS exams is unverified, and provided for informational and comparison purposes only. The NALS and NALA information below was obtained from publically available sources about those exams. Please contact NALA and NALS for exact details regarding the CLA/CP or PP exams.

Association	NFPA® **Paralegal CORE Competency Exam (PCCE™)**	NFPA® **Paralegal Advanced Competency Exam (PACE®)**	NALA **Certified Paralegal/Certified Legal Assistant Exam (CP/CLA)**	NALS **Professional Paralegal Exam (PP)**
Credential	CORE Registered Paralegal (CRP™)	PACE Registered Paralegal® (RP®)	Certified Paralegal (CP); Certified Legal Assistant (CLA)	Professional Paralegal (PP)
Established	2011	1996	1976	2004
Exam Eligibility (Education and/or Experience)	A bachelor's degree in any subject, a paralegal certificate, no experience or continuing legal education (CLE); OR A bachelor's degree in paralegal studies, no experience or CLE; OR A bachelor's degree in any subject, no paralegal certificate, 6 months of experience and 1 hour of ethics taken in the year preceding the exam application date; OR An associate's degree in paralegal studies, no experience or CLE; OR An associate's degree in any subject, a paralegal certificate, no experience or CLE; OR An associate's degree in any subject, no paralegal certificate, 1 year of experience and 6 hours of CLE, including 1 hour of ethics taken in the year preceding the exam application date; OR Active duty, retired, or former military personnel qualified in a military operation specialty as a paralegal and 1.0 hour of ethics CLE within the year preceding the exam application; OR Candidates who are within two months of graduating and registered for the PCC exam by a director of a paralegal studies program participating in the PCCE Assurance of Learning (AoL) Program at the Partner level; OR A paralegal certificate from a program that meets or exceeds the requirements set forth in NFPA's Short Term Paralegal Program Position Statement, 1 year of experience and 6 hours of CLE, including 1 hour of ethics taken in the year preceding the exam application date;	Associate's degree in paralegal studies obtained from an institutionally accredited and/or ABA approved paralegal program and six (6) years of substantive paralegal experience; OR Bachelor's degree in any course of study obtained from an institutionally accredited school and three (3) years of substantive paralegal experience; OR Bachelor's degree and completion of a paralegal program within an institutionally accredited school (which may be embodied in the bachelor's degree) and a minimum of two (2) years substantive paralegal experience; OR Four (4) years of substantive paralegal experience on or before December 31, 2000.	Graduation from paralegal program approved by ABA or associate degree program or post-baccalaureate certificate program in paralegal studies; or bachelor's degree program in paralegal studies, or paralegal program of 60+ hours, with at least 15 semester hours in substantive legal courses; OR Bachelor's degree in any field plus one year's experience as a paralegal (15 semester hours of substantive legal courses is equivalent to one year's experience as a paralegal); OR High School diploma or equivalent plus seven years' experience as a paralegal under the supervision of an attorney, plus a minimum of 20 hours of CLE within the two year period prior to sitting for the exam.	Five years of experience performing paralegal/legal assistant duties. OR Be a graduate from an ABA approved Paralegal Program. OR Hold a Bachelor degree in paralegal studies. OR Be a graduate from an accredited paralegal program which consists of a minimum of 60 semester hours of which a minimum of 15 hours is substantive law. OR Hold a Bachelor degree in an unrelated field and have one year of experience performing paralegal/legal assistant duties.

(continued)

Exhibit 1.2 Legal certification comparison chart *(continued)*

	OR A high school diploma or GED, 5 years of experience and 12 hours of CLE, including 1 hour of ethics taken in the 2 years preceding the exam application date.			
Exam Fees	$215—Nonrefundable	Member: $25 Application Fee; $225 Exam Fee Non Member: $25 Application Fee; $250 Exam Fee	$250 Member Fee; $275 nonmember Fee; plus testing fees per specific section; *Fees vary by testing center:* One - 1.5-hour session @ each $40 Two - 2-hour sessions @ $40 each Two - 2.5-hour sessions @ $47 each	Member: $225; Nonmember: $275
Testing Dates and Locations	Every day except Sundays and Holidays at Prometric Testing Centers across the United States and Guam, etc. Candidates must take the exam within 90 days of approval of application.	Every day except Sundays and Holidays at Prometric Testing Centers across the United States and Guam, etc. Candidates must take the exam within 90 days of approval of application.	January, May, and September at ACT Testing Centers in most major cities.	First Saturday of March and last Saturday in September in most major metropolitan areas.
Retest	$215; 6-monthwaiting period to apply to retest.	$225 Member Fee; Nonmember $250 Fee. 6 month waiting period to apply to retest.	$60 fee per section for Member & nonmember plus applicable testing center fees for the length of session required for the specific section. *Fees vary by testing center.*	$60/part Member Fee; $70/part nonmember Fee. No waiting period to retest.
Testing Time	Two and one-half (2.5) hours	Four (4) hours	Two years to successfully complete 5 major sections and 4 practice area sections. The time begins on the date any section of the exam is first taken.	One Day
Composition of Exam	**Domain 01: Paralegal Practice** ➢ Paralegal Profession ➢ Ethics and Professional Practice ➢ U.S. Legal System ➢ Legal Research ➢ Legal Writing and Critical Analysis ➢ Communication ➢ Law Office Management and Legal Technology ➢ Civil Litigation **Domain 02: Substantive Areas of Law** ➢ Business Organizations ➢ Contracts ➢ Criminal ➢ Estates, Wills and Trusts ➢ Family ➢ Real Estate ➢ Torts For detailed information please see Appendix A of the PCCE Candidate Handbook available on the NFPA website.	**Domain I** – Administration of Client Legal Matters: conflict checks; develop, organize and maintain client files; develop and maintain calendar/tickler systems; develop and maintain databases; coordinate client services. **Domain II** – Development of Client Legal Matters: client interviews; analyze information; collaborate with counsel; prepare, file, and serve legal documents and exhibits; prepare clients and witnesses for legal proceedings. **Domain III** – Factual/Legal Research: obtain factual and legal information; investigate and compile facts; inspect, evaluate, and analyze evidence; ascertain and analyze legal authority. **Domain IV** – Factual/Legal Writing: communicate with	Federal law and procedure, major subject areas include communications, ethics, legal research, human relations and interviewing techniques, judgment and analytical ability, and legal terminology. Sections of Substantive law include *four mini-examinations* in the areas of American legal system, civil litigation, business organizations, and contracts.[1]	Part 1 – Written Communications: Grammar and word usage, spelling, punctuation, number usage, capitalization, composition and expression Part 2 – Legal Knowledge and Skills: Legal research, citations, legal terminology, the court system and ADR, and the legal skills of interviewing clients and witnesses, planning and conducting investigations, and docketing Part 3 – Ethics and Judgment: Ethical situations involving contact with clients, the public, coworkers, and subordinates; other ethical considerations for the legal profession; decision-making and analytical ability; and ability to recognize priorities Part 4 – All areas of substantive law, including administrative; business organizations and

[1] Information obtained from NALA Website.

(continued)

Exhibit 1.2 Legal certification comparison chart *(continued)*

		client/counsel; draft legal analytical documents. **Domain V** - Office Administration: personnel management; acquire technology; coordinate and utilize vendor services; create and maintain library and legal resources, develop and maintain billing system.		contracts; civil procedure and litigation; criminal; family; real property; torts; wills, trusts, and estates; admiralty and maritime; antitrust; bankruptcy; environmental; federal civil rights and employment discrimination; immigration; intellectual property; labor; oil and gas; pension and profit sharing; taxation; water; workers' compensation[2]
Review Manual	$75 plus tax and Shipping	$82.20 plus tax and shipping	Member $160 plus tax and shipping Nonmember $170plus tax and shipping Mock Exam Member $45 plus tax and shipping Nonmember $55plus tax and shipping	
Certification Renewal - CLE	Every two years from anniversary date of exam: 8 hours of CLE, including 1.0 hour of ethics.	Every two years from anniversary date of exam: 12 hours of CLE, including 1.0 hour of ethics.	Every five years – 50 hours of CLE, including 5 hours of legal ethics.	Every five years – 75 hours of CLE, including 5 hours of legal ethics.
Renewal Fees	Member Fee $35 Nonmember Fee $50 Late Fee $50 in addition to renewal fee.	Member Fee $50 Nonmember Fee $75 Late Fee $50 in addition to renewal fee.	$125	$75
Number Certified	169 (3/14)	575 (3/14)	17,711 (11/13)	>600 (10/15)

[2] Information obtained from NALS website.

Regulating the Practice of Law

To protect the public, certain professions, such as the law, require state licensure as a method of regulating who can practice. Once they are licensed, lawyers must follow the rules found in their state's code of ethics. The ethical code of most states substantially follows the Model Rules of Professional Conduct created by the American Bar Association. A serious violation of these rules can result in the loss of one's license to practice law.

Paralegals, with a few exceptions, have no state license requirement to enter the profession and no uniform code of ethics. State regulations and ethics opinions concerning paralegals are neither uniform nor mandatory. Various paralegal organizations have established their own sets of ethical rules, and violations of these rules can result in a loss of membership in the organization. However, one of the worst ethical pitfalls for a paralegal is the risk of unauthorized practice of law, which can subject a paralegal to prosecution under a state's criminal code. This issue will be discussed in more detail in Chapter 2.

Regulating the Paralegal Profession

Regulation and licensing of the paralegal profession have been some of the hottest topics in the legal and paralegal communities. Each state, through its legislature and court system, regulates and licenses the practice of law. With the development of the paralegal profession has come a new set of concerns and controversies surrounding what constitutes the **unauthorized practice of law (UPL)**, such as who should be permitted to render legal services and under what conditions.

Unauthorized Practice of Law (UPL) Giving legal advice, where legal rights may be affected, by anyone not licensed to practice law.

Exhibit 1.3 California regulation of paralegals

While other state legislatures and courts wrestle with minimum standards, California addressed the requirements in a 2000 amendment to the Business and Professional Code that requires a paralegal to possess at least one of the following:

(1) A certificate of completion of a paralegal program approved by the American Bar Association.
(2) A certificate of completion of a paralegal program at an institution that requires a minimum of 24 semester, or equivalent, units in law-related courses, accredited by a national or regional accreditation organization or approved by the Bureau for Private Postsecondary and Vocational Education.
(3) A baccalaureate or advanced degree and a minimum of one year of law-related experience under an attorney who is an active member of the State Bar of California.
(4) A high school diploma or general equivalency diploma and a minimum of three years' law-related experience under the supervision of a California attorney, with this training being completed before December 31, 2003.

Other states might look to the California statute in deciding the question of who is qualified by education, training, or work experience.

There is a continuing debate between bar organizations and paralegal professional organizations over regulation of the paralegal profession. Generally, the bar organizations, such as the American Bar Association, do not see the need for expending the additional time, effort, and cost for certification of paralegals. Their position is broadly based on the argument that the public is protected by the attorney's obligation to supervise the paralegal and the attorney's responsibility to the public. For the most part, the paralegal profession has sought some level of regulation, certification, or licensure. Somewhere in the middle are increasing numbers of employers of paralegals who want some level of assurance that those they hire are qualified to serve as paralegals. As the responsibilities undertaken by paralegals have increased, so have the educational requirements. Within the legal profession has come a concern as to whether those who hold themselves out as paralegals are truly qualified. Members of the paralegal profession see this as no different from the organized bar monitoring the activities of those holding themselves out as lawyers.

State Licensing

Some states have attempted to set up licensing systems or define who may use the title "paralegal." A case in point is the proposal rejected in 1999 by the New Jersey Supreme Court to license paralegals, which had been developed after five years of study by that court's committee on paralegal education and regulation. If it had been approved, this proposal would have made New Jersey the first state to license paralegals. The approaches of two other states are as follows:

- California leads the nation in setting stringent educational requirements that may become a model for other states. In 2000, California amended its Business and Professional Code to require minimum educational standards for paralegals. See Exhibit 1.3.
- After a number of efforts, a Hawaii State Bar Association task force on paralegal certification developed a voluntary certification proposal for consideration by the Hawaii Supreme Court. This proposal was a compromise that recognized the opposition from some segments of the bar.

To some observers it is obvious that the organized bar is fearful of the incursion of the paralegal profession into the practice of law. For some attorneys, the issue is the possible loss of business. Others are concerned that the quality of legal services will be degraded by those who hold themselves out as members of the legal profession.

Exhibit 1.4 Florida Registered Paralegal

A Florida Registered Paralegal is a paralegal who has met the education, training, certification and work experience required for registration as set forth in Chapter 20 of the Rules Regulating The Florida Bar. A paralegal is a person with education, training, or work experience, who works under the direction and supervision of a member of The Florida Bar and who performs specifically delegated substantive legal work for which a member of The Florida Bar is responsible.

Source: www.floridabar.org

Exhibit 1.5 Ohio State Bar Association Certified Paralegal

The Ohio State Bar Association offers a voluntary credentialing program for paralegals. Individuals meeting the OSBA definition of "paralegal," meeting the eligibility requirements, and passing a written examination will be designated as an "OSBA Certified Paralegal." This credential, along with a logo provided for the purpose, may be used by the paralegal to the extent permitted by the Supreme Court of Ohio's Rules for the Government of the Bar and Rules of Professional Conduct.

OSBA Paralegal Certification provides a valuable credential for paralegals in Ohio through the use of objective standards which measure the training, knowledge, experience, and skill of paralegals. It requires a commitment to excellence and will assist lawyers and law firms in identifying highly qualified paralegal professionals.

Source: http://www.ohiobar.org/pub/?articleid=785

Florida and Ohio are among the states that have addressed the issue of certification of paralegals (see Exhibits 1.4 and 1.5).

For the paralegal, it is a question of status as well as expanding job opportunities. With the establishment of minimum standards comes a certain status that members of a profession are entitled to enjoy. For those who have worked hard to develop their paralegal skills through education and experience, these standards eliminate unqualified individuals from the pool of job applicants. The stated goals of lawyer and paralegal groups are not that far apart: both groups are interested in the delivery of quality legal services at affordable prices and in creating a reasonable standard of living for practitioners.

The traditional role of the attorney in advising and representing clients is limited to those who are admitted to practice as lawyers under the applicable state law. Some exemptions do exist under state law that allow nonlawyers to perform certain services, such as document preparation, which, subject to certain limitations, is permitted under California law. Other states have taken an approach that would allow some to engage in a limited practice, such as those under the Washington State Rule 28, shown in Exhibit 1.6, and the legislative proposal from New York shown in Exhibit 1.7.

In 2003, a study prepared by the Washington State Supreme Court found that a segment of the population did not have adequate access to trained, qualified legal practitioners. The result was the approval of Rule 28: Limited Practice Rules for Legal Technicians.

As stated in the Purpose clause of the rule:

> . . . This rule is intended to permit trained Limited License Legal Technicians to provide limited legal assistance under carefully regulated circumstances in ways that expand the affordability of quality legal assistance which protects the public interest.

Under the rule,

"Limited License Legal Technician" means a person qualified by education, training and work experience who is authorized to engage in the limited practice of

Exhibit 1.6 Washington State Rule 28: Limited Practice Rules of Legal Technicians

ADMISSION AND PRACTICE RULES

RULE 28 LIMITED PRACTICE RULE FOR LIMITED LICENSE LEGAL TECHNICIANS

A. **Purpose.** The Civil Legal Needs Study (2003), commissioned by the Supreme Court, clearly established that the legal needs of the consuming public are not currently being met. The public is entitled to be assured that legal services are rendered only by qualified trained legal practitioners. Only the legal profession is authorized to provide such services. The purpose of this rule is to authorize certain persons to render limited legal assistance or advice in approved practice areas of law. This rule shall prescribe the conditions of and limitations upon the provision of such services in order to protect the public and ensure that only trained and qualified legal practitioners may provide the same. This rule is intended to permit trained Limited License Legal Technicians to provide limited legal assistance under carefully regulated circumstances in ways that expand the affordability of quality legal assistance which protects the public interest.

B. **Definitions.** For purposes of this rule, the following definitions will apply:
   (1) "APR" means the Supreme Court's Admission and Practice Rules.
   (2) "Board" when used alone means the Limited License Legal Technician Board.
   (3) "Lawyer" means a person licensed and eligible to practice law in any United States jurisdiction.
   (4) "Limited License Legal Technician" means a person qualified by education, training and work experience who is authorized to engage in the limited practice of law in approved practice areas of law as specified by this rule and related regulations. The legal technician does not represent the client in court proceedings or negotiations, but provides limited legal assistance as set forth in this rule to a pro se client.
   (5) "Paralegal/legal assistant" means a person qualified by education, training, or work experience; who is employed or retained by a lawyer, law office, corporation, governmental agency, or other entity; and who performs specifically delegated substantive law-related work for which a lawyer is responsible.
   (6) "Reviewed and approved by a Washington lawyer" means that a Washington lawyer has personally supervised the legal work and documented that supervision by the Washington lawyer's signature and bar number.
   (7) "Substantive law-related work" means work that requires knowledge of legal concepts and is customarily, but not necessarily, performed by a lawyer.
   (8) "Supervised" means a lawyer personally directs, approves, and has responsibility for work performed by the Limited License Legal Technician.
   (9) "Washington lawyer" means a person licensed and eligible to practice law in Washington and who is an active or emeritus member of the Washington State Bar Association.
   (10) Words of authority:
      (a) "May" means "has discretion to," "has a right to," or "is permitted to."
      (b) "Must" or "shall" means "is required to."
      (c) "Should" means "recommended but not required."

C. **Limited License Legal Technician Board**
   (1) *Establishment.* There is hereby established a Limited License Legal Technician Board. The Board shall consist of 13 members appointed by the Supreme Court of the State of Washington, nine of whom shall be active Washington lawyers, and four of whom shall be nonlawyer Washington residents. At least one member shall be a legal educator. The members shall initially be appointed to staggered terms of one to three years. Thereafter, appointments shall be for three year terms. No member may serve more than two consecutive full three year terms.
   (2) *Board Responsibilities.* The Board shall be responsible for the following:
      (a) Recommending practice areas of law for LLLTs, subject to approval by the Supreme Court;
      (b) Processing applications and fees, and screening applicants;
      (c) Administering the examinations required under this rule which shall, at a minimum, cover the rules of professional conduct applicable to Limited License Legal Technicians, rules relating to the attorney-client privilege, procedural rules, and substantive law issues related to one or more approved practice areas;
      (d) Determining LLLT Continuing Legal Education (LLLT CLE) requirements and approval of LLLT CLE programs;
      (e) Approving education and experience requirements for licensure in approved practice areas;
      (f) Establishing and overseeing committees and tenure of members;
      (g) Establishing and collecting examination fees, LLLT CLE fees, annual license fees, and other fees in such amounts approved by the Supreme Court as are necessary to carry out the duties and responsibilities of the Board; and
      (h) Such other activities and functions as are expressly provided for in this rule.

(continued)

Exhibit 1.6 Washington State Rule 28: Limited Practice Rules of Legal Technicians *(continued)*

(3) *Rules and Regulations.* The Board shall propose rules and regulations for adoption by the Supreme Court that:
   (a) Establish procedures for grievances and disciplinary proceedings;
   (b) Establish trust account requirements and procedures;
   (c) Establish rules of professional and ethical conduct; and
   (d) Implement the other provisions of this rule.

D. Requirements for Applicants. An applicant for licensure as a Limited License Legal Technician shall:
(1) *Age.* Be at least 18 years of age.
(2) *Moral Character and Fitness to Practice.* Be of good moral character and demonstrate fitness to practice as a Limited License Legal Technician.
(3) *Education.* Have the following education, unless waived by the Board through regulation:
   (a) An associate level degree or higher;
   (b) 45 credit hours of core curriculum instruction in paralegal studies as approved by the Board with instruction to occur at an ABA approved law school or ABA approved paralegal education program; and
   (c) In each practice area in which an applicant seeks licensure, instruction in the approved practice area, which must be based on a curriculum developed by or in conjunction with an ABA approved law school. For each approved practice area, the Board shall determine the key concepts or topics to be covered in the curriculum and the number of credit hours of instruction required for admission in that practice area.
   (d) For the purposes of satisfying APR 28(D)(3), one credit hour shall be equivalent to 450 minutes of instruction.
(4) *Application.* Execute under oath and file with the Board his/her application, in such form as the Board requires. An applicant's failure to furnish information requested by the Board or pertinent to the pending application may be grounds for denial of the application.
(5) *Examination Fee.* Pay, upon the filing of the application, the examination fee and any other required application fees as established by the Board and approved by the Supreme Court.

E. Licensing Requirements. In order to be licensed as a Limited License Legal Technician, all applicants must:
(1) *Examination.* Take and pass the examinations required under these rules;
(2) *Experience.* Acquire 3,000 hours of substantive law-related work experience supervised by a licensed lawyer. The experience must be acquired no more than three years prior to licensure and no more than three years after passing the examination;
(3) *Annual License Fee.* Pay the annual license fee;
(4) *Financial Responsibility.* Show proof of ability to respond in damages resulting from his or her acts or omissions in the performance of services permitted by this rule. The proof of financial responsibility shall be in such form and in such amount as the Board may by regulation prescribe; and
(5) Meet all other licensing requirements set forth in the rules and regulations proposed by the Board and adopted by the Supreme Court.

F. Scope of Practice Authorized by Limited Practice Rule. The Limited License Legal Technician shall ascertain whether the issue is within the defined practice area for which the LLLT is licensed. If it is not, the LLLT shall not provide the services required on this issue and shall inform the client that the client should seek the services of a lawyer. If the issue is within the defined practice area, the LLLT may undertake the following:
(1) Obtain relevant facts, and explain the relevancy of such information to the client;
(2) Inform the client of applicable procedures, including deadlines, documents which must be filed, and the anticipated course of the legal proceeding;
(3) Inform the client of applicable procedures for proper service of process and filing of legal documents;
(4) Provide the client with self-help materials prepared by a Washington lawyer or approved by the Board, which contain information about relevant legal requirements, case law basis for the client's claim, and venue and jurisdiction requirements;
(5) Review documents or exhibits that the client has received from the opposing side, and explain them to the client;
(6) Select, complete, file, and effect service of forms that have been approved by the State of Washington, either through a governmental agency or by the Administrative Office of the Courts or the content of which is specified by statute; federal forms; forms prepared by a Washington lawyer; or forms approved by the Board; and advise the client of the significance of the selected forms to the client's case;
(7) Perform legal research and draft legal letters and pleadings documents beyond what is permitted in the previous paragraph, if the work is reviewed and approved by a Washington lawyer;

(continued)

Exhibit 1.6 Washington State Rule 28: Limited Practice Rules of Legal Technicians *(continued)*

(8) Advise a client as to other documents that may be necessary to the client's case, and explain how such additional documents or pleadings may affect the client's case;

(9) Assist the client in obtaining necessary documents, such as birth, death, or marriage certificates.

G. Conditions Under Which a Limited License Legal Technician May Provide Services

(1) A Limited License Legal Technician must have a principal place of business having a physical street address for the acceptance of service of process in the State of Washington;

(2) A Limited License Legal Technician must personally perform the authorized services for the client and may not delegate these to a nonlicensed person. Nothing in this prohibition shall prevent a person who is not a licensed LLLT from performing translation services;

(3) Prior to the performance of the services for a fee, the Limited License Legal Technician shall enter into a written contract with the client, signed by both the client and the Limited License Legal Technician, that includes the following provisions:

(a) An explanation of the services to be performed, including a conspicuous statement that the Limited License Legal Technician may not appear or represent the client in court, formal administrative adjudicative proceedings, or other formal dispute resolution process or negotiate the client's legal rights or responsibilities, unless permitted under GR 24(b);

(b) Identification of all fees and costs to be charged to the client for the services to be performed;

(c) A statement that upon the client's request, the LLLT shall provide to the client any documents submitted by the client to the Limited License Legal Technician;

(d) A statement that the Limited License Legal Technician is not a lawyer and may only perform limited legal services. This statement shall be on the first page of the contract in minimum twelve-point bold type print;

(e) A statement describing the Limited License Legal Technician's duty to protect the confidentiality of information provided by the client and the Limited License Legal Technician's work product associated with the services sought or provided by the Limited License Legal Technician;

(f) A statement that the client has the right to rescind the contract at any time and receive a full refund of unearned fees. This statement shall be conspicuously set forth in the contract; and

(g) Any other conditions required by the rules and regulations of the Board.

(4) A Limited License Legal Technician may not provide services that exceed the scope of practice authorized by this rule, and shall inform the client, in such instance, that the client should seek the services of a lawyer.

(5) A document prepared by an LLLT shall include the LLLT's name, signature, and license number beneath the signature of the client.

H. Prohibited Acts. In the course of dealing with clients or prospective clients, a Limited License Legal Technician shall not:

(1) Make any statement that the Limited License Legal Technician can or will obtain special favors from or has special influence with any court or governmental agency;

(2) Retain any fees or costs for services not performed;

(3) Refuse to return documents supplied by, prepared by, or paid for by the client, upon the request of the client. These documents must be returned upon request even if there is a fee dispute between the Limited License Legal Technician and the client;

(4) Represent or advertise, in connection with the provision of services, other legal titles or credentials that could cause a client to believe that the Limited License Legal Technician possesses professional legal skills beyond those authorized by the license held by the Limited License Legal Technician;

(5) Represent a client in court proceedings, formal administrative adjudicative proceedings, or other formal dispute resolution process, unless permitted by GR 24(b);

(6) Negotiate the client's legal rights or responsibilities, or communicate with another person the client's position or convey to the client the position of another party; unless permitted by GR 24(b).

(7) Provide services to a client in connection with a legal matter in another state, unless permitted by the laws of that state to perform such services for the client.

(8) Represent or otherwise provide legal or law-related services to a client, except as permitted by law, this rule or associated rules and regulations;

(9) Otherwise violate the Limited License Legal Technicians' Rules of Professional Conduct.

(continued)

Exhibit 1.6 Washington State Rule 28: Limited Practice Rules of Legal Technicians *(continued)*

I. Continuing Licensing Requirements

(1) *Continuing Education Requirements.* Each Limited License Legal Technician annually must complete the Board-approved number of credit hours in courses or activities approved by the Board; provided that the Limited License Legal Technician shall not be required to comply with this subsection during the calendar year in which he or she is initially licensed.

(2) *Financial Responsibility.* Each Limited License Legal Technician shall annually provide proof of financial responsibility in such form and in such amount as the Board may by regulation prescribe.

(3) *Annual Fee.* Each Limited License Legal Technician shall pay the annual license fee established by the Board and approved by the Supreme Court.

J. Existing Law Unchanged. This rule shall in no way modify existing law prohibiting nonlawyers from practicing law or giving legal advice other than as authorized under this rule or associated rules and regulations.

K. Professional Responsibility and Limited License Legal Technician-Client Relationship

(1) Limited License Legal Technicians acting within the scope of authority set forth in this rule shall be held to the standard of care of a Washington lawyer.

(2) Limited License Legal Technicians shall be held to the ethical standards of the Limited License Legal Technicians' Rules of Professional Conduct, which shall create an LLLT IOLTA program for the proper handling of funds coming into the possession of the Limited License Legal Technician.

(3) The Washington law of attorney-client privilege and law of a lawyer's fiduciary responsibility to the client shall apply to the Limited License Legal Technician-client relationship to the same extent as it would apply to an attorney-client relationship.

---

law in approved practice areas of law as specified by this rule and related regulations. The legal technician does not represent the client in court proceedings or negotiations, but provides limited legal assistance as set forth in this rule to a pro se client. To be eligible to be licensed, the applicant in addition to being at least 18 and of good moral character must have

Education. Have the following education, unless waived by the Board through regulation:

(a) An associate level degree or higher;

(b) 45 credit hours of core curriculum instruction in paralegal studies as approved by the Board with instruction to occur at an ABA approved law school or ABA approved paralegal education program; and

(c) In each practice area in which an applicant seeks licensure, instruction in the approved practice area, which must be based on a curriculum developed by or in conjunction with an ABA approved law school. For each approved practice area, the Board shall determine the key concepts or topics to be covered in the curriculum and the number of credit hours of instruction required for admission in that practice area. . . .

E. Licensing Requirements. In order to be licensed as a Limited License Legal Technician, all applicants must:

I. *Examination.* Take and pass the examinations required under these rules;

II. *Experience.* Acquire 3,000 hours of substantive law-related work experience supervised by a licensed lawyer. The experience must be acquired no more than three years prior to licensure and no more than three years after passing the examination;

Exhibit 1.7 New York proposed legislation

A08532 Summary:

BILL NO A08532

SAME AS No same as

SPONSOR Rivera N

COSPNSR

MLTSPNSR

Add Art 167 SS8800 - 8802, Ed L

Requires licensure for the paralegal profession.

A08532 Actions:

BILL NO A08532

07/13/2011 referred to higher education
01/04/2012 referred to higher education

A08532 Votes:

There are no votes for this bill in this legislative session.

A08532 Memo:

BILL NUMBER:A8532

TITLE OF BILL:
An act
to amend the education law, in relation to requiring licensure for the paralegal profession

PURPOSE OR GENERAL IDEA OF THE BILL:
Requiring licensure for the paralegal profession.

SUMMARY OF SPECIFIC PROVISIONS:
Section 1: The education law is amended by adding a new article 167 to read as follows; the board of regents upon the recommendation of the commissioner shall establish a program to require the licensure of paralegals practicing in this state. The program shall define the scope of paralegal practice, establish license application fees and license renewal fees and create an independent board to adopt rules and regulations.

JUSTIFICATION:
Every year more and more attorneys are allowing their paralegals to work extensively on important and complex cases: Cases that impact

(continued)

Exhibit 1.7 New York proposed legislation *(continued)*

the life of their clients and other people involved. Some of these paralegals tend to commit errors that could lead to nightmares for the clients. This legislation would require paralegal to have the qualification necessary in order to provide improved and more professional services to clients of attorneys.

PRIOR LEGISLATIVE HISTORY:
None.

FISCAL IMPLICATIONS FOR STATE AND LOCAL GOVERNMENT:
None.

EFFECTIVE DATE:
This act shall take effect on July 1, 2011.

A08532 Text:

S T A T E O F N E W Y O R K

8532

2011-2012 Regular Sessions

I N A S S E M B L Y

July 13, 2011

Introduced by M. of A. N. RIVERA -- read once and referrec Committee on Higher Education

AN ACT to amend the education law, in relation to requiring li for the paralegal profession

THE PEOPLE OF THE STATE OF NEW YORK, REPRESENTED IN SENATE ANC BLY, DO ENACT AS FOLLOWS:

Section 1. The education law is amended by adding a new article read as follows:

ARTICLE 167

PARALEGAL

SECTION 8800. INTRODUCTION.
8801. PARALEGAL PROGRAM.
8802. USE OF THE TITLE "PARALEGAL".

S 8800. INTRODUCTION. THIS ARTICLE APPLIES TO THE PARALEGAL SION. THE GENERAL PROVISIONS FOR ALL PROFESSIONS CONTAINED IN ONE HUNDRED THIRTY OF THIS TITLE APPLY TO THIS ARTICLE.

S 8801. PARALEGAL PROGRAM. 1. THE BOARD OF REGENTS UPON THE RE DATION OF THE COMMISSIONER SHALL ESTABLISH A PROGRAM TO REQU LICENSURE OF ALL PARALEGALS PRACTICING IN THIS STATE.

2. THE PROGRAM SHALL: (A) DEFINE THE SCOPE OF PARALEGAL PF PROVIDE MANDATORY MINIMUM STANDARDS AND PROCEDURES FOR INITIAI

(continued)

Exhibit 1.7 New York proposed legislation (*continued*)

FICATIONS; AND PROVIDE REQUIREMENTS FOR CONTINUING EDUCATION, CERTIFICATION, AND PROFESSIONAL CONDUCT;

(B) ESTABLISH LICENSE APPLICATION FEES AND LICENSE RENEWAL FEES, WHICH SHALL NOT EXCEED ONE HUNDRED DOLLARS EACH. THE REVENUES GENERATED FROM SUCH FEES SHALL BE USED SOLELY TO ADMINISTER THE PROGRAM AND SHALL BE SET AT A LEVEL THAT DOES NOT EXCEED THE AMOUNT NECESSARY TO ENSURE THE CONTINUED OPERATION OF THE PROGRAM; AND

(C) CREATE AN INDEPENDENT BOARD TO ADOPT RULES AND REGULATIONS, ESTABLISH PROCEDURES, AND ASSIST THE BOARD IN ADMINISTERING THIS SECTION.

S 8802. USE OF THE TITLE "PARALEGAL". ONLY A PERSON LICENSED UNDER THIS ARTICLE SHALL USE THE TITLE "PARALEGAL".

S 2. This act shall take effect on July 1, 2011.

EXPLANATION--Matter in ITALICS (underscored) is new; matter in brackets [ ] is old law to be omitted.

LBD10945

Exhibit 1.8 North Carolina State Bar Paralegal Certification Program

Plan for Certification of Paralegals

The State Bar's interest in the paralegal profession promotes proper utilization of paralegals and assures that legal services are professionally and ethically offered to the public. The Plan for Certification of Paralegals approved by the NC State Bar and adopted by the NC Supreme Court in 2004 will assist in the development of paralegal standards, raise the profile of the paralegal profession, and standardize the expectations of the public and other legal professionals.

The State Bar has worked diligently with attorneys and paralegals across our state to establish a voluntary North Carolina certification program with requirements that are properly defined and that will ensure the credential has value. Through education and experience, the North Carolina certification plan will assist lawyers and administrators in distinguishing paralegals that meet or exceed the skills required for certification. As multi-skilled professionals, paralegals have a diverse knowledge base and must practice effective interpersonal communication skills to maintain collaborative relationships within the legal team. Paralegals, like attorneys, will continue to be held accountable to the highest of ethical and professional standards.

Source: http://www.nccertifiedparalegal.org/

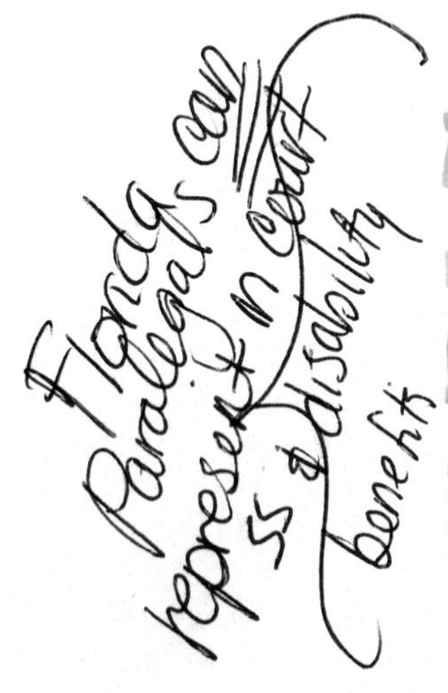

Florida
Paralegals can
represent in court
SS disability
benefit

Federal Practice

Under federal regulations, nonlawyers may represent parties before the Social Security Administration, the Patent Office, and other agencies. However, a conflict may arise between the federal law and state laws that limits this activity. For example, Florida sought unsuccessfully to enjoin a practitioner authorized to practice before the Patent Office, alleging UPL [*Sperry v. Florida*, 373 U.S. 379 (1963)].

Under federal regulations, a paralegal can, without supervision, represent individuals before the Social Security Administration, including appearing before administrative law judges on behalf of clients. Paralegals may appear as representatives of claimants for disability claims; claims regarding Medicare Parts A, B, and C; and cases of overpayment and underpayment of benefits.

As a representative of a claimant before the Social Security Administration, a paralegal may obtain information, submit evidence, and make statements and arguments. The difference between the paralegal and the attorney is only in the matter of direct versus indirect payment for services. The Social Security Administration pays the attorney directly, whereas the paralegal must bill the client for services rendered. Within the Social Security Administration, paralegals are employed as decision writers and case technicians.

Web Exploration

The Kathryn Myers student portfolio article and other information for students can be found on the American Association for Paralegal Education website at www.aafpe.org.

Getting Started

As you start your legal studies and paralegal career, consider the suggestions and advice in the following *Advice from the Field* by a leading paralegal educator.

Advice *from the* Field

THE STUDENT PORTFOLIO

Kathryn Myers, Coordinator, Paralegal Studies, Saint Mary-of-the-Woods College, Paralegal Studies Program

A portfolio is a purposeful collection of student work that is accumulated over time. The material reveals the extent of student learning, achievement, and development. The "portfolio system" is intended to specify knowledge and competence in areas considered necessary to successfully work as a paralegal/legal assistant while leaving the selection of means of documentation of competency to the individual student. Documentation of knowledge and skill acquisition can take a variety of forms, including, but not limited to,

- letters of support
- diaries
- videotapes and audiotapes of work
- pleadings
- memoranda
- course projects
- registration receipts from continuing education and other conferences attended
- proof of membership in professional organizations
- subscriptions to legal publications

Typically, much of the material can be compiled from projects and activities required within courses.

PROCEDURE

The portfolio [should] contain documentation of knowledge and skill acquisition based on the Core Competencies established by the American Association for Paralegal Education. Those core competencies are divided into two areas—skill development and acquisition of knowledge. Within those areas are competencies based on:

Skill Development

- critical thinking skills
- organizational skills
- general communication skills
- interpersonal skills
- legal research skills
- legal writing skills
- computer skills
- interviewing and investigation skills

Acquisition of Knowledge

- organization and operation of the legal system
- organization and operation of law offices
- the paralegal profession and ethical obligations
- contracts
- torts
- business organizations
- litigation procedures

It is understood that [these] areas may overlap somewhat and that [they] do not cover all competencies associated with the program, student growth, or professional success. However, students who perfect these competencies and who perform from this educational base have a foundation for success.

It is suggested that the student purchase a secure container to collect and organize the material, [such as] a hanging file folder or file box. This portfolio may be maintained on computer disk; however, you will not have any graded materials if this is the only method of collection you use.

Students should keep a log of all materials completed. When completing each assignment, [they should] enter the document in the log, with a column to check for inclusion in the campus portfolio and another to check for inclusion in the professional portfolio. Some documents may, of course, overlap in their application.

Students are responsible for the contents of their portfolios. The student should periodically review the

(continued)

contents of the portfolio and add or remove materials based on decisions as to the extent to which the contents adequately represent knowledge and skill acquisition in each of the areas outlined below. This portfolio is not intended to be a compilation of senior level work; rather, it is useful to provide work of varying levels of efficiency to show, among other things, growth and improvement.

CONTENT

To be a successful paralegal/legal assistant, the student must possess a common core of legal knowledge as well as acquire vital critical thinking, organizational, communication, and interpersonal skills. Courses in a student's program should provide the student with the means to develop the competencies, which have been divided into the following sections:

Area 1 Understanding the Profession and Its Ethical Obligations

Area 2 Research

Area 3 Legal Writing

Area 4 Basic Skills

Area 5 Acquisition of Legal Knowledge

Area 6 Professional Commitment Beyond Coursework

Area 7 Evaluation of Professional Growth/Evaluation of Program

Appendix

GUIDELINES FOR SELECTING ENTRIES

When selecting entries, students should bear in mind that each piece is part of a much larger whole and that, together, the artifacts and rationale make a powerful statement about individual professional development. Asking the following questions may help with decision making.

1. What do I want my portfolio to show about me as a paralegal? What are my attributes as a paralegal?
2. What do I want my portfolio to demonstrate about me as a learner? How and what have I learned?
3. What directions for my future growth and development does my self-evaluation suggest? How can I show them in my portfolio?
4. What points have been made by others about me as a paralegal and learner? How can I show them in my portfolio?
5. What effect does my professionalism have upon my peers? How can I show this in my portfolio?
6. What overall impression do I want my portfolio to give a reviewer about me as a learner and as a paralegal?

When decision making about what to include becomes a challenge, it may be helpful to look at each artifact and ask yourself, "What would including this item add that has not already been said or shown?" Remember that portfolios create representative records of your professional development; they are not intended to be comprehensive.

VALUES AND ATTITUDES

Values and attitudes determine the choices we make in our lives. They cross the boundaries of subject-matter areas. Thus, in this final section of your portfolio, you are asked to look at your own values and attitudes and then write a one- to three-page paper in which you reflect upon your own values. Identify one or more values that are important to you. Explain how they influence your choices as a person, parent, future paralegal, voter, and/or citizen of the global community. Include specific examples.

The following questions may help you choose a topic for your essay: What does it mean to be honest? fair? tolerant? open to new ideas and experiences? respect evidence? Which is more important—decreasing the production of greenhouse gases or preserving jobs?

The right to choose how many children we want or controlling world population growth? Freedom to produce pornographic art or the right of children to be sheltered from such experiences? Spending more time with your children or getting a second job so you can buy things you want?

There are no easy answers to these questions. Have fun thinking about your own values. Remember to include specific examples from your own life!

TRANSCRIPTS

Include copies of unofficial transcripts from all colleges and universities that you have attended.

Degree evaluation

Graduation evaluation

Awards or recognitions

Include a copy of your degree evaluation, if you received one.

Include a copy of your graduation evaluation.

Include copies of awards or recognitions you have received.

PROFESSIONAL PORTFOLIO

Modify this inclusive portfolio into a professional portfolio. This professional portfolio will be representative, not comprehensive. Each artifact chosen for inclusion should represent at least one significant aspect of you and/or your accomplishments that can be translated into employability. Use these guidelines to prepare your professional portfolio:

1. Prepare your portfolio as a showcase of your best work—your highest achievements. This will involve selecting from artifacts in your portfolio and adding new ones.
2. Do not send your portfolio when you apply for a job. Rather, include in your cover letter a statement concerning your portfolio. For example: "Throughout my paralegal studies program at ________ College, I developed a professional portfolio that clearly and concisely exhibits my attributes as a paralegal. I would be pleased to share this portfolio with you during an interview."
3. If granted an interview, take your portfolio with you. Be prepared to present the highlights. Practice presenting it effectively. In some instances, you might be asked to present it at the beginning of the interview, and in other instances, you might use it as a source of evidence or enhancement of a point you make in the interview. Interviewing practices vary widely from employer to employer. Portfolios are most likely to be reviewed in situations where the employer is familiar with the abilities of a paralegal.
4. If the interviewer(s) is particularly interested and would like to examine your portfolio more closely, offer to leave it if at all possible. You should make explicit arrangements for collecting it and, of course, follow through as planned. It could be that your portfolio will create the impression that tips the scales in your favor.
5. Remember—it is likely that some people in a position to hire are not familiar with professional portfolios as you know them. Take time to concisely explain that developing your portfolio has been a process of reflection and evaluation that has helped you to know yourself as a paralegal and to establish a foundation for career-long professional development. To some extent, presenting your portfolio will inform the interviewer about both you and the portfolio concept and process.
6. Keep your portfolio up to date. As you continue to gain experience and to grow professionally, alter it to reflect your development. It is not only your first job application that may be enhanced by a well-prepared and presented portfolio but developing your portfolio is an excellent foundation for meeting any expectation of continuing legal education.

CONCLUSION

It is my hope and intention that by your creating this portfolio, you have an opportunity to reflect upon your education and to emphasize to yourself and others that you are capable and qualified to perform as a paralegal. It is time to believe in you. Good luck!

Reproduced with permission of Kathryn Myers.

Concept Review *and* Reinforcement

LEGAL TERMINOLOGY

ALS (Accredited Legal Secretary) 18
American Association for Paralegal Education (AAfPE) 13
American Bar Association (ABA) 4
Associate degree 14
Bachelor degree 14
Certificate 15
Certified Legal Assistant (CLA) 18
International Paralegal Management Association (IPMA) 18
Legal assistant 4
National Association of Legal Assistants (NALA) 4
National Association of Legal Secretaries (NALS) 12
National Federation of Paralegal Associations (NFPA) 4
Paralegal 4
Paralegal Advance Competency Exam (PACE) 18
PLS (Professional Legal Secretary) 18
PP (Professional Paralegal) 18
Proprietary school 14
Unauthorized Practice of Law (UPL) 21

SUMMARY OF KEY CONCEPTS

What Is a Paralegal?

Definition	A paralegal, or legal assistant, is "a person qualified by education, training, or work experience who is employed or retained by a lawyer, law office, corporation, governmental agency or other entity who performs specifically delegated substantive legal work for which a lawyer is responsible" (American Bar Association, 1997).

What Do Paralegals Do?

Function of Paralegals	The primary function of paralegals is to assist attorneys in preparing for hearings, trials, meetings, and closings.

Professional Skills

Definition	Some professional skills are called "soft skills." These include communication skills, initiative, resourcefulness, problem solving, commitment, teamwork, leadership, and self-motivation.
Resourcefulness	The ability to meet and handle a situation and find solutions to problems.
Commitment	The ability to complete what one starts out to do.
Analytical Skills	Analytical skills involve following a step-by-step process to solve a problem.
Interpersonal Skills	The ability to work with people.
Communication Skills	Good communication means expressing ideas effectively—both orally and in writing.

Career Planning

Career Planning	Career planning includes educational planning and a plan for perfecting professional skills.
Paralegal Education in the United States	An estimated 1,000 paralegal education programs are available in the United States. These programs are offered in on-site, online, and hybrid formats combining online and on-site instruction. Some of these programs have ABA accreditation.
Qualifications of a Paralegal	Qualification guidelines have been established by the American Bar Association's Standing Committee on Paralegals and the American Association for Paralegal Education.
Types of Educational Programs	1. Certificate programs 2. Associate degree programs 3. Baccalaureate programs 4. Graduate programs 5. Specialty certificates
Paralegal Certification	PACE (Paralegal Advance Competency Exam) of the National Federation of Paralegal Associations
	CLA (Certified Legal Assistant) title given by the National Association of Legal Assistants
	ALS (the basic certification for legal professionals of NALS)
	PLS (the advanced certification for legal professionals of NALS)
	PP (Professional Paralegal certification of NALS)
Making a Personal Assessment and Setting Goals	1. What are your other job skills? 2. What are your personality traits? 3. Do you like working under deadlines? 4. Do you like working with certain groups of people? 5. What are your personal interests? 6. Recognize your strengths. 7. Acknowledge weaknesses.

Selecting a Specialty	Your decision should be based on a self-evaluation of your likes and dislikes, interests, passions, and any physical or geographic limitations.
Assessing Your Background	Doing a self-assessment early in your studies offers you an opportunity to recognize your strengths and develop them and to acknowledge weaknesses that you need to address.
Regulating the Practice of Law	
Reasons for Regulating the Practice of Law	The practice of law is regulated by state government and court rule to protect the public from incompetent and unscrupulous practitioners.
Regulating the Paralegal Profession	The traditional role of the attorney in advising and representing clients is limited to those who are admitted to practice as lawyers under applicable state law. Some exemptions do exist that allow nonlawyers to perform certain services under state law.
State Licensing	To address the issue of the unauthorized practice of law, some states have enacted legislation requiring a license to perform certain paralegal functions.
Federal Practice	Under federal regulations, nonlawyers may represent parties before the Social Security Administration, the Patent Office, and other agencies.
Opportunities for Paralegals	
Compensation Issues for the Paralegal	In 2010, the median annual salary for full-time paralegals was $46,680. Income level will vary by specialty, size of firm, and geographical area. The U.S. Department of Labor projects that this profession will continue to grow at 18% per year through the year 2020.
The Future	
Career Planning	As courts require the use of paralegals to reduce legal costs, law firms may have to hire more paralegals and delegate more work to them.

WORKING THE WEB

1. Review the latest information on standards for paralegals of the ABA Standing Committee on Paralegals website at www.americanbar.org/groups/paralegals.
2. Review the latest "blawg" postings on Paralegals at www.abajournal.com/blawgs/topic/paralegals/.
3. The Bureau of Labor Statistics' publication *Occupational Outlook Handbook* is updated regularly. Download a copy of the current version on Paralegals and Legal Assistants and compare the salary ranges with those in this text. Have they changed? www.bls.gov/oco/ocos114.
4. One of the significant issues for paralegals over the past years has been whether paralegals are classified as exempt with respect to overtime under the U.S. Department of Labor regulations. Download a copy of the current presentation on executive, administrative, and professional exemption at www.dol.gov/whd/flsa/index.
5. Print out a copy of the mission statement or homepage of each of the major national paralegal associations:
   a. International Paralegal Management Association: www.paralegalmanagement.org
   b. NALS, the association for legal professionals: www.nals.org
   c. National Federation of Paralegal Associations: www.paralegals.org
   d. National Association of Legal Assistants: www.nala.org
   e. Association of Legal Administrators: www.alanet.org
6. Compare your skills with the list of knowledge or competencies required of principal legal administrators at www.alanet.org/about/knowledgelist.

CRITICAL THINKING & WRITING QUESTIONS

1. How does the American Bar Association define the term "paralegal"?
2. What are the minimum qualifications that a paralegal should meet?
3. What is the role of the paralegal in the legal system?
4. Why should those planning to become paralegals or legal assistants get a well-grounded education and develop the necessary skills before seeking employment?
5. How can one satisfy the court that one is qualified as a paralegal and not merely as a legal secretary?
6. What is the advantage to the paralegal in obtaining the PACE or CLA designations?
7. What educational plan makes the most sense for you? Why?
8. How can a candidate for a paralegal position demonstrate that he or she has the qualifications for employment as a paralegal?
9. Why would an employer, such as the U.S. Attorney's Office, require a four-year degree for those seeking a paralegal position?
10. Complete the Career Planning checklist and assess your personal skills and professional goals. Based on your answers, how well prepared are you for a career as a paralegal? What skills need development?
11. How does assessing your interests and skills help in choosing a career path?
12. What skills are required to be a paralegal and why are they important?
13. Complete the Strengths and Weaknesses checklist on page 13 of this chapter.
14. Why are good English writing and speaking skills important for the paralegal?
15. Complete the My Career Roadmap checklist of this chapter.
16. How can you use the Strengths and Weaknesses checklist in preparing your personal career roadmap?
17. What advantages might a person have in entering the paralegal profession later in life?
18. What actions have you observed in other people that demonstrated their resourcefulness? What qualities have others recognized in you that would be considered "resourceful"?
19. How can you demonstrate the characteristic of "commitment"?
20. Start to network by setting up a meeting with a working paralegal and preparing a list of questions to ask at that meeting.

Building Paralegal Skills

VIDEO CASE STUDIES

When Friends Ask for Legal Advice

Dante, a paralegal, is approached by a friend for legal advice about his apartment lease. His landlord is refusing to allow him to have a dog in his apartment.

After viewing the video case study at the book website at www.pearsonhighered.com/careersresources, answer the following:

1. Would a paralegal working in a real estate office be able to give advice as an incidental activity?
2. Is advising the person that you are a paralegal enough to avoid UPL in this situation?
3. What is the law in your state on UPL? How would it address this situation?

Résumé Writing Dos and Don'ts

Two human resource directors in a law office review some of the résumés they have received and discuss the errors people often make in submitting job applications.

After viewing the video case study at the book website at www.pearsonhighered.com/careersresources, answer the following:

1. Why are a good résumé and cover letter so important in getting a paralegal position?
2. What are some of the skills human resource directors look for in new hires?
3. Make a list of skills you need to acquire and courses you should take in pursuing your paralegal studies.

Independent Paralegal

Don Swanson, President of Five Star Legal, an independent paralegal service, discusses the pros and cons of being an independent paralegal.

After viewing the video case study at the book website at www.pearsonhighered.com/careersresources, answer the following:

1. What are the advantages and disadvantages of working as an independent paralegal?
2. Are there any regulatory issues in your jurisdiction around working as an independent paralegal?

ETHICS ANALYSIS & DISCUSSION QUESTIONS

1. Does your state, whether by statute, regulation, code, guideline, or court rule, define "Paralegal" or "Legal Assistant"? If it does, what is that definition and where is it defined? If not, should it formally define the term? Explain why or why not.
2. Does your state have a statute or court rule on the regulation of paralegal or legal assistant practice? What are the requirements to practice as a paralegal or legal assistant? Does the law define the practice in some other terminology?
3. Does your state have minimum educational requirements for paralegals? Should there be a set of minimum qualifications? Explain why or why not.
4. Does having a set of minimum educational requirements eliminate the need for a set of ethical guidelines? Explain.

DEVELOPING YOUR COLLABORATION SKILLS

Working on your own or with a group of other students, review the scenario at the beginning of the chapter, and discuss the employment options and educational issues involved.

1. Discuss why Ethan and Ariel should or should not consider a paralegal career. What are the advantages or disadvantages? What strengths or skills can Ethan and Ariel bring to this career?
2. Working individually or in a group, complete the following:
   a. Summarize, in writing, your career advice to Ethan and Ariel.
   b. Share your advice with other students or groups. Does your group have any additional advice or recommendations?
   c. Take on the role of Ethan or Ariel. Might they have any other questions for Mr. Marshall about the paralegal profession? Make a list of additional questions. Where might Ethan and Ariel get additional information about the paralegal profession?
3. Select a spokesperson who can summarize and present your group's recommendations to the class.

PARALEGAL PORTFOLIO EXERCISE

Create a folder on your computer or on a removable storage device with the items listed as tabs below. Or, using a three-ring binder, start a portfolio of your work and accomplishments in this course. Include any work you are doing in other courses that best represents your growing "skill set." Prepare binder tabs with the following headings, and insert them in your binder:

A. Understanding the Profession and Its Ethical Obligations
B. Research
C. Legal Writing
D. Basic Skills
E. Acquisition of Legal Knowledge
F. Professional Commitment Beyond Coursework
G. Evaluation of Professional Growth/Evaluation of Program
H. Appendix

The portfolio may ultimately be used to show prospective employers samples of your work. For job interviews, it may be more convenient to have a hard copy of the best portfolio items.

LEGAL ANALYSIS & WRITING CASES

Doe v. Condon 341 S.C. 22, 532 S.E.2d 879 (2000)

The Unauthorized Practice of Law and the Paralegal

A paralegal asked the court if he could conduct unsupervised "wills and trusts" seminars for the public, "emphasizing" living trusts during the course of his presentation and answering estate-planning questions from the audience. He proposed a fee-splitting arrangement with his attorney–employer.

The South Carolina Supreme Court ruled: The activities of a paralegal do not constitute the practice of law as long as they are limited to work of a preparatory nature, such as legal research, investigation, or the composition of legal documents, which enables licensed attorney–employer to carry a given matter to a conclusion through his own examination, approval, or additional effort. . . .

. . . The paralegal plays a supporting role to the supervising attorney. Here the roles are reversed. The attorney would support the paralegal. Petitioner would play the lead role, with no meaningful attorney supervision and the attorney's presence and involvement only surfaces on the back end. Meaningful attorney supervision must be present throughout the process. The line between what is and what is not permissible conduct by a non-attorney is sometimes unclear as a potential trap for the unsuspecting client. . . It is well settled the paralegal may not give legal advice, consult, offer legal explanations, or make legal recommendations.

Questions

1. Why is the practice of law limited to licensed attorneys?
2. What tasks may a paralegal perform?
3. What tasks may a paralegal not perform?
4. Why does the answering of legal questions about the need for a will or a trust constitute the unauthorized practice of law (UPL)?
5. Why is a fee-splitting arrangement between a lawyer and a paralegal prohibited?

Note: If in South Carolina, include the parallel citation: 341 S.C. 22. The Lexis citation for this case is 2000 S.C. LEXIS 125.

Sperry v. Florida 373 U.S. 379 (1963)

Petitioner, not a lawyer and not admitted to practice in Florida as a lawyer, was nevertheless authorized to practice before the U.S. Patent Office pursuant to federal statute (35 U.S.C. § 31). The Florida Bar sued to prevent him from representing patent applicants, preparing and prosecuting the patent claims, and advising applicants in the State of Florida.

The Supreme Court, in holding that the Petitioner was permitted to perform tasks incident to prosecuting of patent claims, said,

> by virtue of the Supremacy Clause, Florida may not deny to those failing to meet its own qualifications the right to perform the functions within the scope of the federal authority.

The Court further stated,

> since patent practitioners are authorized to practice before the Patent Office, the State maintains control over the practice of law within its borders except to the limited extent for the accomplishment of the federal objective.

Questions

1. Does this decision allow anyone to practice before any federal agency without being licensed?
2. What are the prerequisites for nonlawyers to act on behalf of others before federal agencies?
3. What steps would a paralegal have to take to prosecute patent claims?

WORKING WITH THE LANGUAGE OF THE COURT CASE

Missouri v. Jenkins

491 U.S. 274 (1989)
Supreme Court of the United States

Read the following case excerpts. Information on preparing a briefing is provided in Appendix A: How to Brief a Case. In your brief, prepare a written answer to each of the following questions.

1. What is the difference between "market rates" for paralegals and the cost to the attorney for paralegal services?
2. Does billing for paralegal services at market rates unfairly benefit the law firm?

3. According to this court, how is a reasonable attorney's fee calculated?
4. How does the public benefit from allowing paralegals to be billed at market rates?
5. Does this court believe that a reasonable attorney's fee should include paralegal fees?

Brennan, J., delivered the opinion of the Court.

This is the attorney's fee aftermath of major school desegregation litigation in Kansas City, Missouri. We [are hearing this case to decide] should the fee award compensate the work of paralegals and law clerks by applying the market rate for their work?

I

This litigation began in 1977 as a suit by the Kansas City Missouri School District (KCMSD), the school board, and the children of two school board members, against the State of Missouri and other defendants. The plaintiffs alleged that the State, surrounding school districts, and various federal agencies had caused and perpetuated a system of racial segregation in the schools of the Kansas City metropolitan area. . . . After lengthy proceedings, including a trial that lasted 7½ months during 1983 and 1984, the District Court found the State of Missouri and KCMSD liable. . . . It ordered various intradistrict remedies, to be paid for by the State and KCMSD, including $260 million in capital improvements and a magnet-school plan costing over $200 million.

The plaintiff class has been represented, since 1979, by Kansas City lawyer Arthur Benson and, since 1982, by the NAACP Legal Defense and Educational Fund, Inc. (LDF). Benson and the LDF requested attorney's fees under the Civil Rights Attorney's Fees Awards Act of 1976, 42 U.S.C. § 1988. Benson and his associates had devoted 10,875 attorney hours to the litigation, as well as 8,108 hours of paralegal and law clerk time. For the LDF, the corresponding figures were 10,854 hours for attorneys and 15,517 hours for paralegals and law clerks. Their fee applications deleted from these totals 3,628 attorney hours and 7,046 paralegal hours allocable to unsuccessful claims against the suburban school districts. With additions for postjudgment monitoring and for preparation of the fee application, the District Court awarded Benson a total of approximately $1.7 million and the LDF $2.3 million. . .

Both Benson and the LDF employed numerous paralegals, law clerks (generally law students working part-time), and recent law graduates in this litigation. The court awarded fees for their work based on Kansas City market rates for those categories. As in the case of the attorneys, it used current rather than historic market rates in order to compensate for the delay in payment. It therefore awarded fees based on hourly rates of $35 for law clerks, $40 for paralegals, and $50 for recent law graduates. [. . .]

III

Missouri's second contention is that the District Court erred in compensating the work of law clerks and paralegals (hereinafter collectively "paralegals") at the market rates for their services, rather than at their cost to the attorney. While Missouri agrees that compensation for the cost of these personnel should be included in the fee award, it suggests that an hourly rate of $15—which it argued below corresponded to their salaries, benefits, and overhead—would be appropriate, rather than the market rates of $35 to $50. According to Missouri, § 1988 does not authorize billing paralegals' hours at market rates, and doing so produces a "windfall" for the attorney.

We begin with the statutory language, which provides simply for "a reasonable attorney's fee as part of the costs." Clearly, a "reasonable attorney's fee" cannot have been meant to compensate only work performed personally by members of the bar. Rather, the term must refer to a reasonable fee for the work product of an attorney.

Thus, the fee must take into account the work not only of attorneys but also of secretaries, messengers, librarians, janitors, and others whose labor contributes to the work product for which an attorney bills her client; and it also must take account of other expenses and profit. The parties have suggested no reason why the work of paralegals should not be similarly compensated, nor can we think of any. We thus take as our starting point the self-evident proposition that the "reasonable attorney's fee" provided for by statute should compensate the work of paralegals, as well as that of attorneys.

(continued)

The more difficult question is how the work of paralegals is to be valuated in calculating the overall attorney's fee.

The statute specifies a "reasonable" fee for the attorney's work product. In determining how other elements of the attorney's fee are to be calculated, we have consistently looked to the marketplace as our guide to what is "reasonable." In *Blum v. Stenson*, 465 U.S. 886 (1984), for example, we rejected an argument that attorney's fees for nonprofit legal service organizations should be based on cost. We said: "The statute and legislative history establish that 'reasonable fees' under § 1988 are to be calculated according to the prevailing market rates in the relevant community . . ." A reasonable attorney's fee under § 1988 is one calculated on the basis of rates and practices prevailing in the relevant market, i.e., "in line with those [rates] prevailing in the community for similar services by lawyers of reasonably comparable skill, experience, and reputation," and one that grants the successful civil rights plaintiff a "fully compensatory fee," comparable to what "is traditional with attorneys compensated by a fee-paying client."

If an attorney's fee awarded under § 1988 is to yield the same level of compensation that would be available from the market, the "increasingly widespread custom of separately billing for the services of paralegals and law students who serve as clerks," all else being equal, the hourly fee charged by an attorney whose rates include paralegal work in her hourly fee, or who bills separately for the work of paralegals at cost, will be higher than the hourly fee charged by an attorney competing in the same market who bills separately for the work of paralegals at "market rates." In other words, the prevailing "market rate" for attorney time is not independent of the manner in which paralegal time is accounted for. Thus, if the prevailing practice in a given community were to bill paralegal time separately at market rates, fees awarded the attorney at market rates for attorney time would not be fully compensatory if the court refused to compensate hours billed by paralegals or did so only at "cost." Similarly, the fee awarded would be too high if the court accepted separate billing for paralegal hours in a market where that was not the custom.

We reject the argument that compensation for paralegals at rates above "cost" would yield a "windfall" for the prevailing attorney. Neither petitioners nor anyone else, to our knowledge, has ever suggested that the hourly rate applied to the work of an associate attorney in a law firm creates a windfall for the firm's partners or is otherwise improper under § 1988, merely because it exceeds the cost of the attorney's services. If the fees are consistent with market rates and practices, the "windfall" argument has no more force with regard to paralegals than it does for associates. And it would hardly accord with Congress' intent to provide a "fully compensatory fee" if the prevailing plaintiff's attorney in a civil rights lawsuit were not permitted to bill separately for paralegals, while the defense attorney in the same litigation was able to take advantage of the prevailing practice and obtain market rates for such work. Yet that is precisely the result sought in this case by the State of Missouri, which appears to have paid its own outside counsel for the work of paralegals at the hourly rate of $35.

Nothing in § 1988 requires that the work of paralegals invariably be billed separately. If it is the practice in the relevant market not to do so, or to bill the work of paralegals only at cost, that is all that § 1988 requires. Where, however, the prevailing practice is to bill paralegal work at market rates, treating civil rights lawyers' fee requests in the same way is not only permitted by § 1988, but also makes economic sense. By encouraging the use of lower cost paralegals rather than attorneys wherever possible, permitting market-rate billing of paralegal hours "encourages cost-effective delivery of legal services and, by reducing the spiraling cost of civil rights litigation, furthers the policies underlying civil rights statutes."

Such separate billing appears to be the practice in most communities today. In the present case, Missouri concedes that "the local market typically bills separately for paralegal services," and the District Court found that the requested hourly rates of $35 for law clerks, $40 for paralegals, and $50 for recent law graduates were the prevailing rates for such services in the Kansas City area. Under these circumstances, the court's decision to award separate compensation at these rates was fully in accord with § 1988.

IV

The courts correctly granted a fee enhancement to compensate for delay in payment and approved compensation of paralegals and law clerks at market rates. The judgment of the Court of Appeals is therefore Affirmed.

VIRTUAL LAW OFFICE EXPERIENCE MODULES

If your instructor has instructed you to complete assignments in the Virtual Law Office program, complete the Virtual Law Office assignments as assigned by your instructor. These assignments are designed to develop your workplace skills. Completing the assignments for this chapter will result in producing the following documents for inclusion in your portfolio:

VLOE 1.1	Skills and Tasks Self-Assessment Form
VLOE 1.2	Personal calendar for the next four months

CHAPTER

2

Ethics and Professional Responsibility

Paralegals at Work

Kelsey and Kathryn became friends when they were studying to be paralegals. Kathryn now works for a large national law firm, while Kelsey does freelance paralegal work. Over the years, they have met frequently to discuss office issues and client cases. Today, Kelsey asked Kathryn to meet for lunch at a crowded sandwich shop in the office building where she works to discuss a recent matter. Kathryn could see that something was troubling her friend. After getting a seat at the counter, they ordered lunch, and Kelsey began to confide in Kathryn.

Kelsey regularly does freelance work for two suburban sole practitioners—one who specializes in intellectual-property issues and occasionally does plaintiffs' injury work for friends and family, and one who does mostly personal injury work. Both are working on the same case, and both have asked Kelsey to work on the file. One lawyer represents the plaintiff, a close family friend, and the other lawyer represents the defendant. Both lawyers want Kelsey to interview the clients, witnesses, and generally handle the file. Kelsey is wondering whether she should be working "both sides of the fence." Kelsey describes to Kathryn the clients and the case in detail while they wait for their lunch to be served.

Kelsey also explains that she often does most of the work on the plaintiff lawyer's cases not related to intellectual property, including settling the cases with insurance company adjusters or the lawyers representing the defendants. Kelsey knows the adjuster on this case, and he has revealed to her that the insurance company for the defendant wants to settle the case quickly and avoid a trial. Kelsey asks Kathryn for advice.

Consider the issues involved in this scenario as you read the chapter.

LEARNING OBJECTIVES

After studying this chapter, you should be able to:

1. Explain how the practice of law is regulated.
2. Define ethics and explain the difference between the attorney's rules of ethics and the paralegal's rules of ethics.
3. Explain the lawyer's ethical duty to supervise.
4. Discuss the ethical obligation of competence.
5. Explain the concept of confidentiality of client communications and the attorney–client privilege.
6. Discuss the concept of conflict of interest in the legal profession.
7. Describe the duty of candor to the court and other counsel and the ethical duty of fairness.
8. Analyze a situation to determine whether it involves the unauthorized practice of law.

> "In law a man is guilty when he violates the rights of others. In ethics he is guilty if he only thinks of doing so."
>
> Immanuel Kant, *German philosopher*

INTRODUCTION TO ETHICS

Every profession has a set of rules that members of that profession are expected to follow. These rules typically set forth the minimum in ethical behavior—the very least each professional should do. In the field of law, these rules are referred to as "the rules of ethics" or "the rules of professional responsibility."

Each state regulates the right to practice law, and therefore each state has adopted its own rules of **ethics**. The supreme court or legislature of each state has created a committee or board that is authorized to enforce these rules of professional responsibility. States typically have a bar association to receive and investigate complaints against lawyers. Most states have adopted some form of the American Bar Association's **Model Rules of Professional Conduct**. This provides a high degree of consistency in the **ethical guidelines** for the legal profession across the country.

Ethics Minimally acceptable standards of conduct in a profession.

ABA Model Rules of Professional Conduct A recommended set of ethics and professional conduct guidelines for lawyers, prepared by the American Bar Association and originally released in 1983.

Ethical guidelines Rules of minimally acceptable professional conduct.

Exhibit 2.1 NALA Code of Ethics and Professional Responsibility website

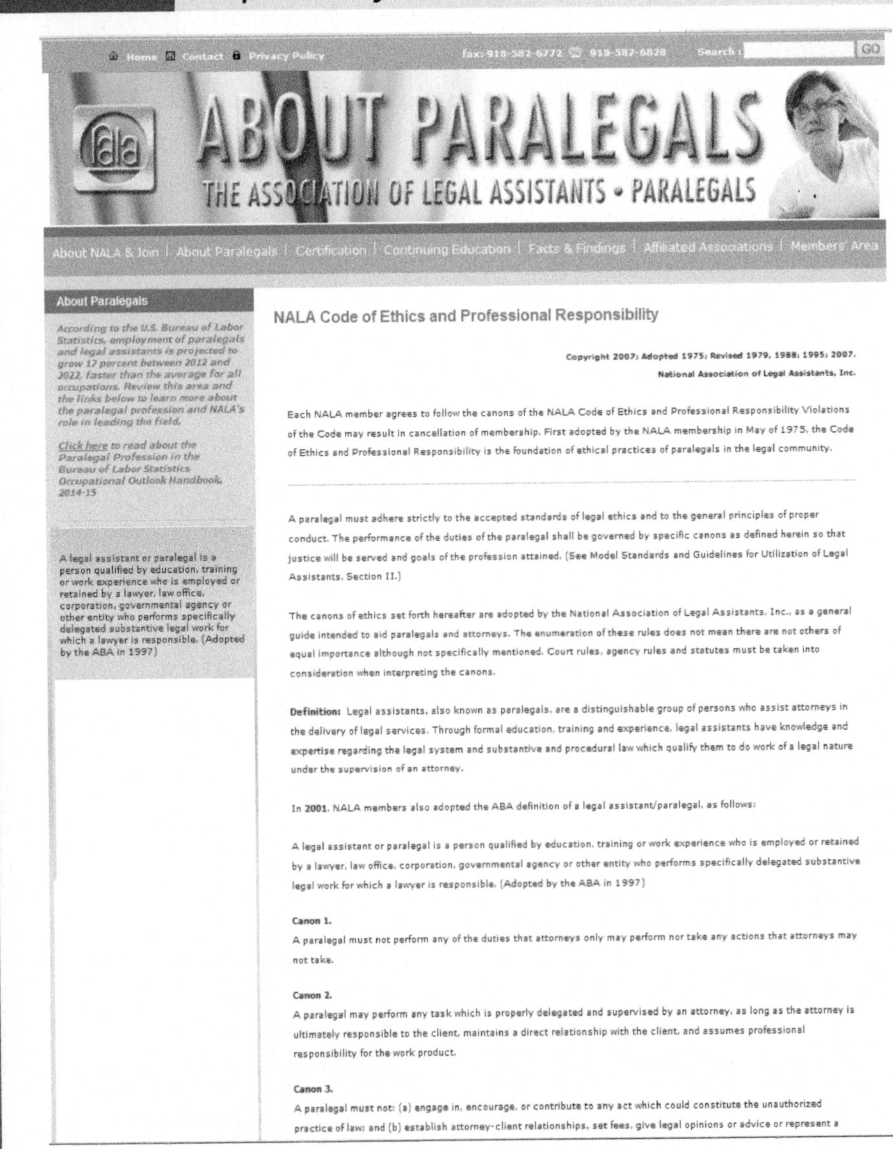

NALA Code of Ethics and Professional Responsibility

Copyright 2007; Adopted 1975; Revised 1979, 1988; 1995; 2007.
National Association of Legal Assistants, Inc.

Each NALA member agrees to follow the canons of the NALA Code of Ethics and Professional Responsibility Violations of the Code may result in cancellation of membership. First adopted by the NALA membership in May of 1975, the Code of Ethics and Professional Responsibility is the foundation of ethical practices of paralegals in the legal community.

A paralegal must adhere strictly to the accepted standards of legal ethics and to the general principles of proper conduct. The performance of the duties of the paralegal shall be governed by specific canons as defined herein so that justice will be served and goals of the profession attained. (See Model Standards and Guidelines for Utilization of Legal Assistants, Section II.)

The canons of ethics set forth hereafter are adopted by the National Association of Legal Assistants, Inc., as a general guide intended to aid paralegals and attorneys. The enumeration of these rules does not mean there are not others of equal importance although not specifically mentioned. Court rules, agency rules and statutes must be taken into consideration when interpreting the canons.

Definition: Legal assistants, also known as paralegals, are a distinguishable group of persons who assist attorneys in the delivery of legal services. Through formal education, training and experience, legal assistants have knowledge and expertise regarding the legal system and substantive and procedural law which qualify them to do work of a legal nature under the supervision of an attorney.

In **2001**, NALA members also adopted the ABA definition of a legal assistant/paralegal, as follows:

A legal assistant or paralegal is a person qualified by education, training or work experience who is employed or retained by a lawyer, law office, corporation, governmental agency or other entity who performs specifically delegated substantive legal work for which a lawyer is responsible. (Adopted by the ABA in 1997)

Canon 1.
A paralegal must not perform any of the duties that attorneys only may perform nor take any actions that attorneys may not take.

Canon 2.
A paralegal may perform any task which is properly delegated and supervised by an attorney, as long as the attorney is ultimately responsible to the client, maintains a direct relationship with the client, and assumes professional responsibility for the work product.

Canon 3.
A paralegal must not: (a) engage in, encourage, or contribute to any act which could constitute the unauthorized practice of law; and (b) establish attorney-client relationships, set fees, give legal opinions or advice or represent a

Web Exploration

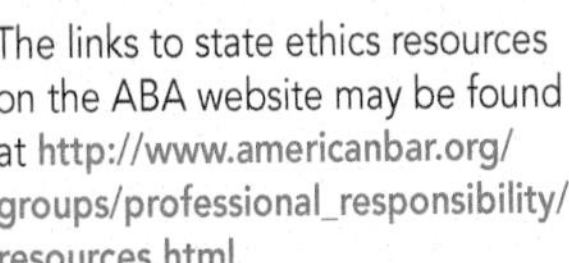

The links to state ethics resources on the ABA website may be found at http://www.americanbar.org/groups/professional_responsibility/resources.html.

Web Exploration

The American Bar Association's Center for Professional Responsibility website has links to other national, state, and international ethics resources. One of the resources available online is its report on the status of individual state review of Professional Conduct Rules. The full report may be viewed at http://www.americanbar.org/groups/professional_responsibility/resources/professionalism/professionalism_codes.html.

National paralegal associations, such as the National Association of Legal Assistants (NALA) and the National Federation of Paralegal Associations (NFPA), also have ethics guidelines. These organizations require members to conduct themselves in accordance with these guidelines as a condition of continued membership in the organization.

Exhibit 2.2 A portion of the NFPA Ethics Documents website

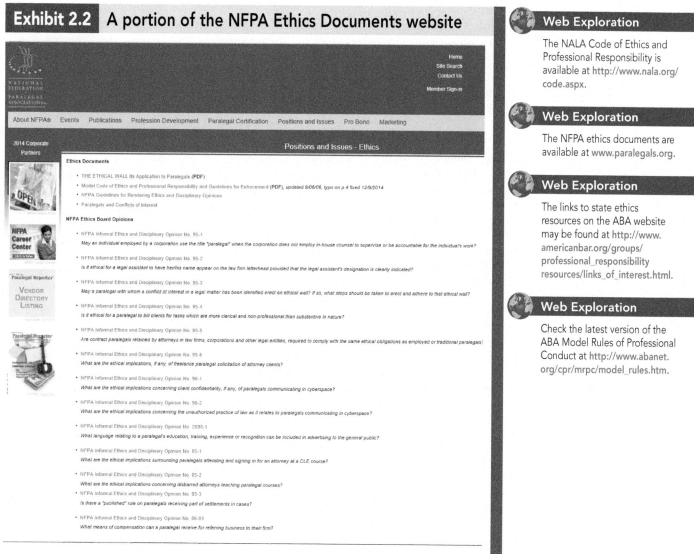

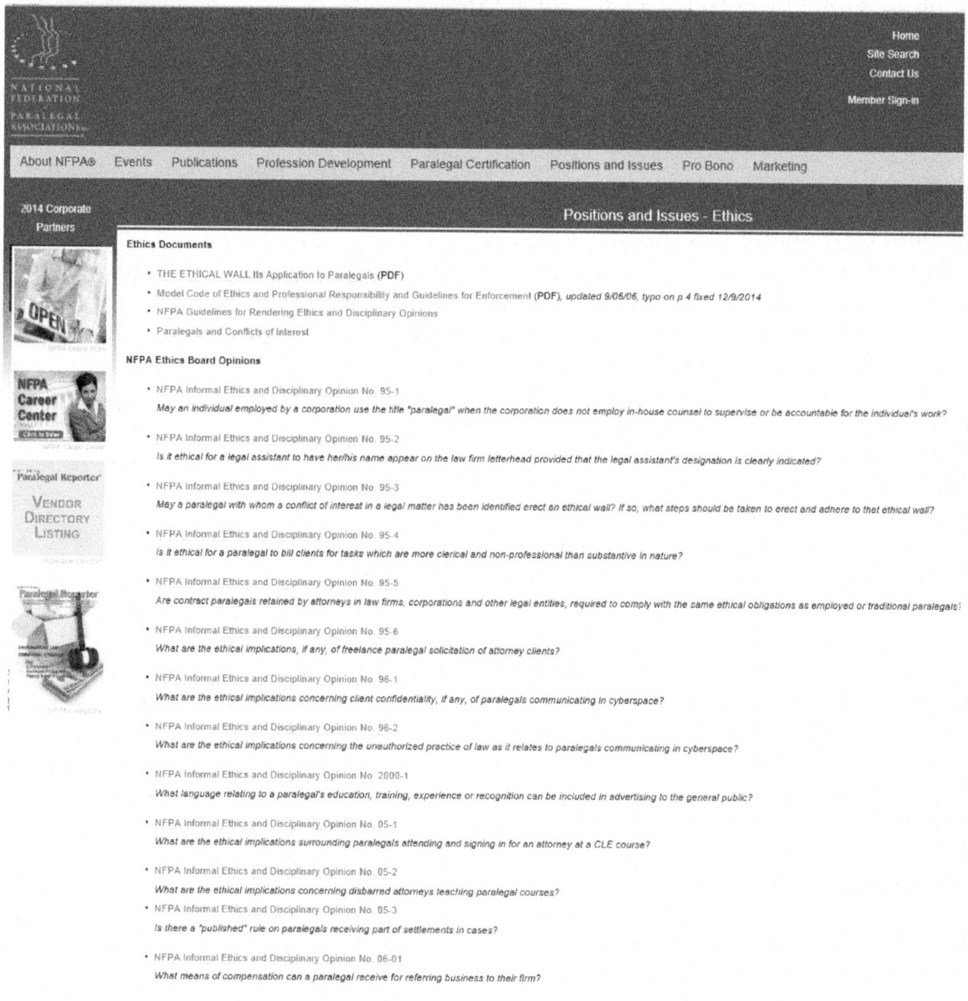

NATIONAL FEDERATION PARALEGAL ASSOCIATIONS

Home
Site Search
Contact Us
Member Sign-in

About NFPA® | Events | Publications | Profession Development | Paralegal Certification | Positions and Issues | Pro Bono | Marketing

2014 Corporate Partners

NFPA Career Center

Paralegal Reporter Vendor Directory Listing

Positions and Issues - Ethics

Ethics Documents

- THE ETHICAL WALL Its Application to Paralegals **(PDF)**
- Model Code of Ethics and Professional Responsibility and Guidelines for Enforcement **(PDF)**, *updated 9/06/06, typo on p 4 fixed 12/9/2014*
- NFPA Guidelines for Rendering Ethics and Disciplinary Opinions
- Paralegals and Conflicts of Interest

NFPA Ethics Board Opinions

- NFPA Informal Ethics and Disciplinary Opinion No. 95-1
  May an individual employed by a corporation use the title "paralegal" when the corporation does not employ in-house counsel to supervise or be accountable for the individual's work?
- NFPA Informal Ethics and Disciplinary Opinion No. 95-2
  Is it ethical for a legal assistant to have her/his name appear on the law firm letterhead provided that the legal assistant's designation is clearly indicated?
- NFPA Informal Ethics and Disciplinary Opinion No. 95-3
  May a paralegal with whom a conflict of interest in a legal matter has been identified erect an ethical wall? If so, what steps should be taken to erect and adhere to that ethical wall?
- NFPA Informal Ethics and Disciplinary Opinion No. 95-4
  Is it ethical for a paralegal to bill clients for tasks which are more clerical and non-professional than substantive in nature?
- NFPA Informal Ethics and Disciplinary Opinion No. 95-5
  Are contract paralegals retained by attorneys in law firms, corporations and other legal entities, required to comply with the same ethical obligations as employed or traditional paralegals?
- NFPA Informal Ethics and Disciplinary Opinion No. 95-6
  What are the ethical implications, if any, of freelance paralegal solicitation of attorney clients?
- NFPA Informal Ethics and Disciplinary Opinion No. 96-1
  What are the ethical implications concerning client confidentiality, if any, of paralegals communicating in cyberspace?
- NFPA Informal Ethics and Disciplinary Opinion No. 96-2
  What are the ethical implications concerning the unauthorized practice of law as it relates to paralegals communicating in cyberspace?
- NFPA Informal Ethics and Disciplinary Opinion No. 2000-1
  What language relating to a paralegal's education, training, experience or recognition can be included in advertising to the general public?
- NFPA Informal Ethics and Disciplinary Opinion No. 05-1
  What are the ethical implications surrounding paralegals attending and signing in for an attorney at a CLE course?
- NFPA Informal Ethics and Disciplinary Opinion No. 05-2
  What are the ethical implications concerning disbarred attorneys teaching paralegal courses?
- NFPA Informal Ethics and Disciplinary Opinion No. 05-3
  Is there a "published" rule on paralegals receiving part of settlements in cases?
- NFPA Informal Ethics and Disciplinary Opinion No. 06-01
  What means of compensation can a paralegal receive for referring business to their firm?

Web Exploration

The NALA Code of Ethics and Professional Responsibility is available at http://www.nala.org/code.aspx.

Web Exploration

The NFPA ethics documents are available at www.paralegals.org.

Web Exploration

The links to state ethics resources on the ABA website may be found at http://www.americanbar.org/groups/professional_responsibility resources/links_of_interest.html.

Web Exploration

Check the latest version of the ABA Model Rules of Professional Conduct at http://www.abanet.org/cpr/mrpc/model_rules.htm.

Regulation of the Practice of Law

LEARNING OBJECTIVE 1
Explain how the practice of law is regulated.

Just as the practice of medicine and other professions is regulated, the practice of law is regulated in an attempt to protect the public from incompetent and unscrupulous practitioners. The purpose of regulating and monitoring those who practice law can be found in the Preamble to the Illinois Supreme Court Rules of Professional Conduct:

> The practice of law is a public trust. Lawyers are the trustees of the system by which citizens resolve disputes among themselves, punish and deter crime, and determine their relative rights and responsibilities toward each other and their government. Lawyers therefore are responsible for the character, competence and integrity of the persons whom they assist in joining their profession; for assuring access to that system through the availability of competent legal counsel; for maintaining public confidence in the system of justice by acting competently and with loyalty to the best interests of their clients; by working to improve that system to meet the challenges of a rapidly changing society; and by defending the integrity of the judicial system against those who would corrupt, abuse or defraud it.

For certain occupations and professions, such as law, a license is required in order to offer services to the public. In some professions, obtaining a license may be as simple as completing a form and providing proof that the requirements for education and experience have been satisfied. But for the profession of law, a qualifying examination is required after proving that the necessary legal education has been obtained.

The examination is generally referred to as the "bar exam." The word *bar* is derived from an old custom in courtrooms of using a physical railing to separate the public, who observe court proceedings from a rear seating area, from the front area of the court where the judge, jury, witness stand, and counsel tables are located. Only attorneys are permitted to "pass the bar" and enter this front area.

The bar examination tests the applicant's basic legal knowledge and attempts to ensure a minimum standard of competency. Passing the exam is the first step in getting "admitted to practice." Candidates are admitted upon the recommendation of the state or local bar examiners and an introduction and motion by an existing member of the bar of that court. Admission is completed by a ceremony where attorneys are sworn in by the court to which they are admitted to practice.

Admission to practice before one court does not automatically authorize practice before other courts. Each state has its own rules and standards. Generally, admission to the highest court of the state confers admission to all of the lower courts of that state. The right to practice before the various federal courts requires a separate application and admission to practice. Admission to federal court is generally granted upon motion of an existing member of the court bar upon submission of proof of good character and proof of admission to practice before the highest court of the state.

In some states, prior admission in one state for a required period of time is sufficient for admission to another state without taking the exam. However, today's rules have generally eliminated these alternative methods of admission to the practice of law. Even seasoned attorneys seeking admission to states such as Arizona, California, and Florida must retake the examination for that state in order to be admitted.

The rules that must be followed in the practice of law are found in each state's code of professional responsibility or canon of ethics. Most states have adopted the American Bar Association's Model Rules of Professional Conduct, with some variation. The rules of conduct are enforced by state disciplinary committees, and sanctions may be imposed against offending attorneys. Complaints about breaches of ethical behavior are referred to a committee for investigation, or a committee may act upon the recommendation of a court. Minor infractions may subject the lawyer to reprimand or censure. Serious cases may result in temporary or permanent loss of the license to practice law, called *disbarment*.

Unauthorized Practice of Law (UPL) Giving legal advice, if legal rights may be affected, by anyone not licensed to practice law.

The **Unauthorized Practice of Law (UPL)** is a statutory criminal violation, and complaints of UPL are generally referred to the state's attorney for prosecution. It should be noted that some other ethical breaches may also be violations of a criminal statute. For example, attorneys who breach a client's trust by taking money out of the client's fund are guilty of violating both an ethical rule and the criminal law against theft.

The Paralegal and Licensing

There are, with a few exceptions, no state licensing requirements for working as a paralegal. Some states, such as California, Maine, and North Carolina, have enacted legislation establishing licensure of paralegals to perform some of the functions often performed by lawyers. Generally, these rules are an attempt to regulate unsupervised freelance or independent paralegals who provide document preparation services. At best, these laws carve out a small part of law practice that may be performed by nonlawyers without their being charged with the unlawful practice of law. But no jurisdiction allows anyone other than a licensed attorney to give legal advice or opinions.

Even the selection of the correct form is considered a lawyer's function, as specified in the California Business Code.

There is a fine line between lawful activity and the unlawful practice of law. Recommending or selecting a form could impact a person's legal rights and may subject the unlicensed person to a charge of UPL. The issue for the paralegal is knowing when explaining information or helping someone fill in a blank form is UPL.

Although each state is free to define the practice of law differently, the statutes have certain elements in common. A typical definition of the "practice of law" is that of Rule 31of the Rules of the Supreme Court of Arizona:

> A. "Practice of law" means providing legal advice or services to or for another by:
>
> (1) preparing any document in any medium intended to affect or secure legal rights for a specific person or entity;
> (2) preparing or expressing legal opinions;
> (3) representing another in a judicial, quasi-judicial, or administrative proceeding, or other formal dispute resolution process such as arbitration and mediation;
> (4) preparing any document through any medium for filing in any court, administrative agency or tribunal for a specific person or entity; or
> (5) negotiating legal rights or responsibilities for a specific person or entity....

Penalties for the Unauthorized Practice of Law

Some states have specifically addressed the issue of the unauthorized practice of law by paralegals and legal assistants. For example, Pennsylvania has enacted a statute that makes it a misdemeanor for "any person, including, but not limited to, a paralegal or legal assistant who within this Commonwealth, shall practice law . . ." 42 Pa. C.S.A. § 2524.

In Florida it is also UPL for anyone claiming to be a paralegal or legal assistant who does not meet the state definition of the title as specified in the Florida Bar regulations:

> Florida Bar Regulation Rule 10-2.1 Generally
>
> ■ Whenever used in these rules the following words or terms shall have the meaning herein set forth unless the use thereof shall clearly indicate a different meaning:
> (a) **Unlicensed Practice of Law.** – The unlicensed practice of law shall mean the practice of law, as prohibited by statute, court rule, and case law of the state of Florida.
> (b) **Paralegal or Legal Assistant.** – A paralegal or legal assistant is a person qualified by education, training, or work experience, who works under the supervision of a member of The Florida Bar and who performs specifically delegated substantive legal work for which a member of The Florida Bar is responsible. A nonlawyer or a group of nonlawyers may not offer legal services directly to the public by employing a lawyer to provide the lawyer supervision required under this rule. **It shall constitute the unlicensed practice of law for a person who does not meet the definition of paralegal or legal assistant to use the title paralegal, legal assistant, or other similar term in offering to provide or in providing services directly to the public** [emphasis added].
>
> Fla. Bar Reg. R. 10-2.1

The drafters of these statutes were concerned that the title of paralegal or legal assistant would be misinterpreted as meaning that a person has been admitted to practice law. However, an unresolved question in Pennsylvania and other states is what specific conduct constitutes the "practice of law." Because that interpretation will vary from state to state, paralegals must be aware of how courts have defined the unauthorized practice of law in each jurisdiction they work in.

In those states that have enacted legislation to regulate paralegal activity, some guidance is offered by definitions within the statutes. For example, California defines activities permitted by an "Unlawful Detainer Assistant" or a "Legal Document Assistant":

Chapter 5.5. Legal Document Assistants and Unlawful Detainer Assistants

Article 1. General Provisions

6400(a) "Unlawful detainer assistant" means any individual who for compensation renders assistance or advice in the prosecution or defense of an unlawful detainer claim or action, including any bankruptcy petition that may affect the unlawful detainer claim or action.

(b) "Unlawful detainer claim" means a proceeding, filing, or action affecting rights or liabilities of any person that arises under Chapter 4 (commencing with Section 1159) of Title 3 of Part 3 of the Code of Civil Procedure and that contemplates an adjudication by a court.

(c) "Legal document assistant" means:

(1) Any person who is not exempted under Section 6401 and who provides, or assists in providing, or offers to provide, or offers to assist in providing, for compensation, any self-help service to a member of the public who is representing himself or herself in a legal matter, or who holds himself or herself out as someone who offers that service or has that authority. This paragraph does not apply to any individual whose assistance consists merely of secretarial or receptionist services.

LEARNING OBJECTIVE 2

Define ethics and explain the difference between the attorney's rules of ethics and the paralegal's rules of ethics.

Ethical Duties and Obligations

Ethics are the minimally acceptable standards of behavior in a profession. Ethical conduct is expected and required of every member of the legal team, including attorneys, paralegals, litigation support staff, information technologists, and outside consultants. All members of the legal team, including nonlawyer members, must understand their ethical obligations and how the ethics rules are to be followed and enforced.

Ethical guidelines are enforced by the court in the jurisdiction where the attorney is practicing or where a case is being tried. These rules are as much a part of the administration of justice as the rules of civil or criminal procedure and the rules of evidence. The supervising attorney of every legal team must follow the ethics rules and ensure that the members of the legal team follow the same rules. As law firms utilize more outside consultants and experts, they must carefully consider who has the responsibility to instruct the nonlawyer members of the team and who is responsible for ensuring their compliance. While it is ultimately the responsibility of the lawyer to supervise these nonlawyers, in many cases this obligation falls to the paralegal or litigation manager.

Among the ethical obligations of the attorney, and the legal team acting as agent of the attorney, are:

- Competency (Model Rules of Professional Conduct, Rule 1.1),
- Confidentiality [Model Rules of Professional Conduct, Rule 1.6(A)],
- Conflicts of Interest (Model Rules of Professional Conduct, Rule 1.7),
- Candor (Model Rules of Professional Conduct, Rule 3.3),
- Fairness to Opposing Party and Counsel (Model Rules of Professional Conduct, Rule 3.4), and
- Duty to Supervise (Model Rules of Professional Conduct, Rules 5.1 and 5.3).

Related to the ethical duty of confidentiality are the rule of attorney–client privilege and the **work product** doctrine under **Federal Rules of Evidence** Rule 501. These rules of evidence bar the legal team from having to testify and protect from disclosure work that the legal team has prepared for trial.

Federal Rules of Evidence The rules governing the admissibility of evidence in federal court.

Ethical Guidelines and Rules

Lawyers generally need to follow only one set of ethics rules. These rules are enacted by the state legislature and are adopted by the supreme court of the state in which lawyers practice.

Most states have adopted the Model Rules of Professional Conduct (MRPC), prepared by the ABA and originally released in 1983. Each state reviews the MRPC and adopts either the entire set or portions of it, as it thinks appropriate for its jurisdiction.

Unlike the MRPC for lawyers, no single source of ethical rules exists for the legal assistant. Legal assistants must follow state statutes and conduct themselves in conformity with the rules of professional conduct and ethics opinions applicable to attorneys. The two major legal assistant organizations, the National Federation of Paralegal Associations (NFPA) and the National Association of Legal Assistants (NALA), provide ethical codes for their members.

Although legal assistants are not governed directly by the ethical rules for attorneys, there is an intertwined relationship among the lawyer, the client, and the paralegal. Under the MRPC, the lawyer ultimately is responsible for the actions of the paralegal. What the paralegal does or does not do can have a real impact on the lawyer's duties and obligations to the client.

Paralegals *in* Practice

PARALEGAL PROFILE

Vicki Voisin

Vicki Voisin, an Advanced Certified Paralegal, is nationally recognized as an author and speaker on ethical issues related to the paralegal profession. She is the creator and presenter of EthicsBasics, a program designed to raise awareness of ethical concerns by legal professionals and corporate employees. She also publishes an e-magazine titled Strategies for Paralegals Seeking Excellence *(www.paralegalmentor.com). Vicki is a past president of the National Association of Legal Assistants (NALA) and currently serves on NALA's Advanced Certification Board. She has over 20 years of paralegal experience and is currently employed by Running, Wise & Ford in Charlevoix, Michigan.*

The most important paralegal skills needed in the law office where I work are familiarity with court rules and ethical issues, the ability to communicate clearly with clients, excellent organizational skills, and attentiveness to detail and accuracy.

I also believe that technology plays an important role in the legal profession. Although technology allows attorneys and paralegals to work faster, it does not necessarily guarantee that all of the work results are accurate. Paralegals should be aware of the potential ethical hazards that technology can introduce, especially in the areas of confidentiality and conflicts of interest. For example, unless done properly, redaction (editing) on electronically filed documents can be uncovered, resulting in the disclosure of confidential and/or privileged information to third parties.

All paralegals should be aware of their ethical obligations and those of an attorney. My advice is to familiarize yourself with the American Bar Association's Model Rules of Professional Conduct, as well as its Guidelines for the Utilization of Paralegal Services. Then become acquainted with the related Model Rules and Guidelines for your particular state, if available. Also, join professional associations to keep abreast of trends, and attend continuing education programs as often as possible.

Model Guidelines for the Utilization of Legal Assistant Services A set of guidelines by the ABA policymaking body, the House of Delegates, intended to govern the conduct of lawyers when they are utilizing paralegals or legal assistants.

ABA Model Guidelines for the Utilization of Paralegal Services

In 1991, the ABA's policymaking body, the House of Delegates, initially adopted a set of guidelines intended to govern the conduct of lawyers when utilizing paralegals or legal assistants. These guidelines were updated in 2002 to reflect the legal and policy developments that had taken place since 1991.

Attorneys are bound by the ethical code adopted by the state in which they practice. As a general rule, whatever the ethical rules forbid the attorney from doing, they also forbid the paralegal from doing. Paralegals, therefore, can look to their state's adopted set of rules, or code of professional responsibility, for guidance in deciding what is appropriate or inappropriate from an ethical perspective.

By the rule of agency, the paralegal, as an agent of the supervising attorney, also becomes an agent of the client. The attorney is an agent of the client, and the paralegal is a subagent. As a subagent, the same duties that are owed to the law firm are also owed to the client.

A question that arises in firms engaged in corporate and securities practice is whether the paralegal can purchase securities (stock) in a client corporation. Some firms have written policies prohibiting members of the firm, including paralegals, from purchasing the securities of client corporations. A more complex issue is that of the propriety of using information obtained from the client to purchase or sell the client's securities. The use of inside information to trade stocks is generally a violation of federal securities laws. If a purchase or sale was made based upon material inside information, or information not generally available to the public, the trade may be illegal.

For the attorney, guidance is available under Model Rule 1.7 and the comments to the rule, which provide that an attorney must refuse employment when personal interests, including financial interests, might sway professional judgment. To the extent that this rule applies to the attorney, good judgment would dictate that it applies to the paralegal as well.

Web Exploration

The National Associations' Ethics Codes and ethical guidelines can be reviewed at:

National Federation of Paralegal Associations
http://www.paralegals.org/displaycommon.cfm?an=1&subarticlenbr=330

National Association of Legal Assistants
http://www.nala.org

NALS, the Association for Legal Professionals
http://www.nals.org

Association of Legal Administrators
www.alanet.org

Ethics Codes of Paralegal Associations

The paralegal profession has no unified code of ethics. State regulations and ethics opinions applicable to paralegals are not uniform. However, national organizations such as the National Association of Legal Assistants and the National Federation of Paralegal Associations each provide a uniform code of ethical conduct for their members.

National Federation of Paralegal Associations

The National Federation of Paralegal Associations, Inc. (NFPA) is a professional organization composed of paralegal associations and individual paralegals throughout the United States and Canada. Members of NFPA reflect the diversity of the paralegal profession and vary widely in background, experience, and education. NFPA promotes the growth, development, and recognition of the paralegal profession as an integral partner in the delivery of legal services.

In April 1997, the NFPA adopted its Model Disciplinary Rules to enforce the NFPA Model Code. However, unlike the sanctions for violations by an attorney of the state-adopted rules of ethics, such as loss of the right to practice (disbarment), no such sanctions exist for a breach of association rules by a paralegal, except loss of membership.

National Association of Legal Assistants

The National Association of Legal Assistants (NALA), formed in 1975, is a leading professional association for legal assistants. NALA provides continuing professional education, development, and certification, and is best known in the profession for its Certified Legal Assistant (CLA) examination. The ABA Standing Committee on Paralegals has recognized the CLA designation as a mark of high professional achievement.

Supervision

Under Rules 5.1 and 5.3 of the Model Rules of Professional Conduct, the **supervising attorney** has an ethical obligation to supervise all who work on a case, including their ethical conduct. Each person supervised by the attorney is the **agent** of the attorney. Under agency law, the agent and the **principal**—the attorney—have a **fiduciary relationship** to each other. The agent must obey the reasonable instructions of the principal, and the principal is presumed to know everything the agent learns in the ordinary course of working for the attorney on the case. The attorney is ultimately responsible for the ethical conduct of the agent.

Under Rule 5.1, partners and lawyers with managerial authority in the firm must ensure that other lawyers' conduct conforms to the ethical code. Under Rule 5.3(b), supervising attorneys with direct authority over nonlawyers have an ethical obligation to ensure that the conduct of those persons is compatible with the obligations of the lawyer. Under Rule 5.3(b), what happens in the handling and processing of a case by the legal team is ultimately the responsibility of the supervising attorney, including any ethical breaches.

The attorney is the one to whom the client looks for professional advice and/or resolution of a case. The attorney will suffer any sanctions that result from a failure by members of the legal team to follow and enforce the ethical rules. These sanctions can come from two sources: the court hearing the underlying action and the attorney disciplinary agency. The court typically punishes this type of misbehavior with monetary sanctions to compensate the other side for the time and effort they expended or will expend because of the abuse. The attorney disciplinary agency's punishment can

LEARNING OBJECTIVE 3
Explain the lawyer's ethical duty to supervise.

Supervising attorney The member of the legal team to whom all others on the team report and who has ultimate responsibility for the actions of the legal team.

Agent A party who acts on behalf of another.

Principal A party who employs another person to act on his or her behalf.

Fiduciary relationship A relationship under which one party has a duty to act in the interest and benefit of another while acting within the scope of the relationship.

ARTICLE VIII. ILLINOIS RULES OF PROFESSIONAL CONDUCT OF 2010

RULE 5.1: RESPONSIBILITIES OF PARTNERS, MANAGERS, AND SUPERVISORY LAWYERS

(a) A partner in a law firm, and a lawyer who individually or together with other lawyers possesses comparable managerial authority in a law firm, shall make reasonable efforts to ensure that the firm has in effect measures giving reasonable assurance that all lawyers in the firm conform to the Rules of Professional Conduct.

(b) A lawyer having direct supervisory authority over another lawyer shall make reasonable efforts to ensure that the other lawyer conforms to the Rules of Professional Conduct.

(c) A lawyer shall be responsible for another lawyer's violation of the Rules of Professional Conduct if:

(1) the lawyer orders or, with knowledge of the specific conduct, ratifies the conduct involved; or

(2) the lawyer is a partner or has comparable managerial authority in the law firm in which the other lawyer practices, or has direct supervisory authority over the other lawyer, and knows of the conduct at a time when its consequences can be avoided or mitigated but fails to take reasonable remedial action.

include, in extreme cases, disbarment or suspension from practice before the court for a period of time, or, in less extreme cases, public or private censure. In addition, under some circumstances, "unfair" litigation tactics may result in a suit for malpractice by the client against the attorney and the law firm.

The paralegal may have a duty to determine that there is a properly existing supervising attorney to avoid potential liability, as spelled out in the words of the court in the *Tegman* case below, and more fully reported in the end-of-chapter material.

IN THE WORDS OF THE COURT ...

***TEGMAN V. ACCIDENT & MED. INVEST.*, 107 WN. APP. 868, 875-876, 30 P.3D 8, 13-14, 2001 WASH. APP. LEXIS 1890, 9-11 (WASH. CT. APP. 2001)**

. . . Mullen contends that her status as a paralegal precludes a finding that she was engaged in the practice of law. She argues that a paralegal is, by definition, someone who works under the supervision of an attorney, and that it is necessarily the attorney, not the paralegal, who is practicing law and owes a duty to the clients. Her argument assumes that she had a supervising attorney. The trial court's determination that Mullen was negligent was dependent on the court's finding that Mullen knew, or should have known, that she did not have a supervising attorney over a period of several months while she was at AMI. Had Mullen been properly supervised by an attorney at all times during her employment with AMI, plaintiffs presumably would have no case against her. Rather, her supervising attorney would be responsible for any alleged wrongdoing on her part.

Web Exploration

A list of commissions and committees may be seen at http://www .americanbar.org/groups.html.

RULES GOVERNING THE MISSOURI BAR AND THE JUDICIARY RULES OF PROFESSIONAL CONDUCT

RULE 4-5.3: RESPONSIBILITIES REGARDING NONLAWYER ASSISTANTS

With respect to a nonlawyer employed or retained by or associated with a lawyer:

a. a partner, and a lawyer who individually or together with other lawyers possesses comparable managerial authority in a law firm, shall make reasonable efforts to ensure that the firm has in effect measures giving reasonable assurance that the person's conduct is compatible with the professional obligations of the lawyer;
b. a lawyer having direct supervisory authority over the nonlawyer shall make reasonable efforts to ensure that the person's conduct is compatible with the professional obligations of the lawyer; and
c. a lawyer shall be responsible for conduct of such a person that would be a violation of the Rules of Professional Conduct if engaged in by a lawyer if:
   (1) the lawyer orders or, with the knowledge of the specific conduct, ratifies the conduct involved; or
   (2) the lawyer is a partner, or has comparable managerial authority in the law firm in which the person is employed, or has direct supervisory authority over the person and knows of the conduct at a time when its consequences can be avoided or mitigated but fails to take reasonable remedial action.

Source: http://www.courts.mo.gov/courts/ClerkHandbooksP2RulesOnly.nsf/?c0c6ffa99df4993f86256ba50057dcb8/f264eb01f0599e3186256ca6005211e3?OpenDocument

Competence

LEARNING OBJECTIVE 4
Discuss the ethical obligation of competence.

ABA Model Rule of Professional Conduct 1.1 requires that lawyers provide competent representation to a client. **Competent** representation requires the legal knowledge, skill, thoroughness, and preparation that are reasonably necessary for the representation. The standards require, at a minimum, an understanding of the **rules of court.** These rules continue to grow in number and complexity, especially those regarding electronic discovery. New rules require greater levels of knowledge in order to competently represent clients. Further, lawyers must be able to communicate with clients in the language of technology about methods of creation and sources of electronic documents and the methods for retrieving them and processing them for submission to opposing counsel and the court about highly technical issues involved in the case. This may require an attorney to retain outside consultants or to associate with attorneys who are familiar with the issues. As explained in the Formal Opinion of the Association of the Bar of the City of New York in the Ethical Perspective below, the use of interpreters of the language of technology is similar to the use of foreign language interpreters.

Competence/competent The minimum level of knowledge and skill required of a professional.

Rules of court A court's rules for the processing and presentation of cases.

ETHICAL PERSPECTIVE

The Association of the Bar of the City of New York Formal Opinion 1995-12 Committee on Professional and Judicial Ethics July 6, 1995, Action: Formal Opinion

... DR 6-101(A)(2) mandates that "[a] lawyer shall not . . . [h]andle a legal matter without preparation adequate in the circumstances." Adequate preparation requires, not only that a lawyer conduct necessary legal research, but also that he or she gather information material to the claims or defenses of the client. See *Mason v. Balcom*, 531 F.2d 717, 724 (5th Cir. 1976). The lawyer's inability, because of a language barrier, to understand fully what the client is telling him or her may unnecessarily impede the lawyer's ability to gather the information from the client needed to familiarize the lawyer with the circumstances of the case. This makes communication via the interpreter vital since it may be the only practical way that a free-flowing dialogue can be maintained with the client, and the only means by which the lawyer can actually and substantially assist the client.

The duty to represent a client competently, embodied in DR 6-101(A)(1), requires a lawyer confronted with a legal matter calling for legal skills or knowledge outside the lawyer's experience or ability, to associate with lawyers with skills or knowledge necessary to handle the legal matter. When a lawyer is confronted with a legal matter requiring non-legal skills or knowledge outside the lawyer's experience or ability and these skills or knowledge are necessary for the proper preparation of the legal matter, DR 6-101(A)(2) appears to require that the lawyer associate with professionals in other disciplines who possess the requisite skills or knowledge needed by the lawyer to prepare the legal matter. The interpreter appears to be the type of professional envisioned by EC 6-3's observation that "[p]roper preparation and representation may require the association by the lawyer of professionals in other disciplines." When the need for an interpreter is apparent or it is reasonable to conclude that an interpreter is required for effective communication, failure to take steps with the client to secure an interpreter may be a breach of the duty to represent the client competently....

WISCONSIN RULES OF PROFESSIONAL CONDUCT FOR ATTORNEYS

SIDEBAR

Contrast and compare the Wisconsin Rules of Professional Conduct for Attorneys, at http://www?.legis.wisconsin.gov/rsb/scr/5200.pdf, with the American Bar Association Model Rules of Professional Responsibility, at http://www.abanet.org/cpr/mrpc/mrpc_toc.html, and the ethical rules in your jurisdiction.

WISCONSIN RULES OF PROFESSIONAL CONDUCT FOR ATTORNEYS

SCR 20:1.1 Competence

A lawyer shall provide competent representation to a client. Competent representation requires the legal knowledge, skill, thoroughness and preparation reasonably necessary for the representation.

LEARNING OBJECTIVE 5

Explain the concept of confidentiality of client communications and the attorney–client privilege.

Privilege A rule of evidence that protects certain forms of communication from disclosure at trial. The attorney–client privilege provides that communication between the attorney and client in obtaining legal advice may not be required to be revealed in court.

Confidentiality A duty imposed on the attorney to keep communications from clients secret. The rule enables clients to obtain legal advice by allowing the client to freely and openly give the attorney all the relevant facts.

Confidentiality and Privilege

All members of the legal team must understand their obligations with regard to the duty of confidentiality and attorney–client privilege. The differences in these related concepts can be confusing. There are two sets of rules: ethical rules and rules of evidence. Confidentiality is an ethical obligation. **Privilege** is a rule of evidence.

Confidentiality

The ethical obligation to keep client information confidential is founded on the belief that clients should be able to tell their attorneys everything about their case so the attorney can give proper legal advice. **Confidentiality** is an ethical obligation. Rule 1.6 of the ABA's Model Rules requires that lawyers "not reveal information relating to representation of a client" until the client gives informed consent to the disclosure after being advised of the consequences of disclosure, except for disclosures that are "impliedly authorized." Everything the lawyer or the members of the legal team learn about the case from every possible source is to be kept confidential. For example, if the client's case is written up in the local newspaper, the story may report details of the case. Even though these details are made public, the members of the legal team are not free to discuss them. The details are still to be kept confidential. They may not be discussed with someone who has read the newspaper and who is not on the team.

Confidentiality in a Technology Age

The rules of confidentiality were created when clients and their attorneys generally met in face-to-face meetings or through written, paper-based documents. Maintaining confidentiality was potentially easier: close the conference room door and make sure no one could hear the conversation, or secure the paper documents in a locked file cabinet. In contemporary practice, the communications may be in any number of electronic forms, including email, video chat, text message, or Web-based input forms. Maintaining electronic communications and electronically created and saved documents creates new issues that must be considered to avoid a breach of confidentiality. Limiting access to electronic messages to only those with a need to know is a starting point. Limiting access frequently requires the use of password-protected computers to access messages and documents. It also requires planning where the confidential electronic documents are stored. In-house storage may require additional safeguards and password protections and, at the very least, a thought-out protocol for who has access and where and under what security conditions documents are stored. Storage at remote cloud- or Internet-based storage services, such as Microsoft OneDrive (formerly SkyDrive) or DropBox, requires a close look at the terms and conditions of service of the cloud-based storage service. Among the questions to consider are their treatment of law enforcement subpoenas, access to data by internal or external personnel, and the treatment of the data if payment is delayed or they go out of business, are acquired, or merge. For example:

Dropbox Privacy Policy

Last Modified: April 10, 2013

... ***Compliance with Laws and Law Enforcement Requests; Protection of Dropbox's Rights.*** We may disclose to parties outside Dropbox files stored in your Dropbox and information about you that we collect when we have a good faith belief that disclosure is reasonably necessary to (a) comply with a law, regulation or compulsory legal request; (b) protect the safety of any person from death or serious bodily injury; (c) prevent fraud or abuse of Dropbox or its users; or (d) to protect Dropbox's property rights. If we provide your Dropbox files to a law enforcement agency as set forth above, we will remove Dropbox's encryption from the files before providing them to law enforcement. However, Dropbox will not be able to decrypt any files that you encrypted prior to storing them on Dropbox....

https://www.dropbox.com/privacy

Security is always an issue with computers and Web-connected systems. The newspapers are full of stories of unauthorized access to computer systems. For the law firm, the duty of confidentiality may require extra effort to protect the data of clients as part of the duty of confidentiality. In some cases this may be satisfied by encrypting the electronic files so as to require a sophisticated system to access them.

Breach of confidentiality may also happen when confidential information is accessed on portable computer devices, such as smartphones, tablets, and portable computers. Most obvious in risk is the opening of confidential documents in public places, such as in coffee shops, on airplanes, on trains, and in waiting rooms, where others may be able to read the screen. Less obvious is the use of Internet connections in the same places that are part of a wireless network that is not secure or that others may use to access the portable device.

PRACTICE TIP

All portable devices should require the use of passwords to open, access, and use the device and have installed software that allows the remote erasing of contents to prevent unauthorized access in the event of the loss of the device.

Privilege

All communication between the client and the lawyer for the purpose of obtaining legal advice is protected by **attorney–client privilege.** This rule of evidence protects the client by preventing the attorney from being required to reveal information communicated by the client. Note that the information is also confidential, but privilege is different from the duty of confidentiality. The privilege only applies when the lawyer is questioned under oath. At that point, the attorney must invoke the privilege, saying, "I refuse to answer because that is confidential information covered by the attorney–client privilege." This could happen any time the attorney is under oath. Some examples are responses to interrogatories or requests for production of documents, testimony in court, in a deposition, or before a grand jury. Only the client can waive the privilege and allow the attorney to reveal protected information. The privilege may not be waived by the attorney. It is the client's right to preserve the privilege except in limited circumstances, such as when the information is about a crime of violence that the client is about to commit.

Attorney–client privilege
A rule of evidence permitting an attorney to refuse to testify as to confidential client information.

Web Exploration

Review the most current version of Rule 1.6 on Confidentiality in your jurisdiction with the American Bar Association Model Rules of Professional Conduct at the American Bar Association website at www.abanet.org/cpr/mrcp/rule1.6.html.

The attorney–client privilege is founded on the assumption that encouraging clients to make the fullest disclosure to their attorneys enables the latter to act more effectively. We have recognized that an attorney's effectiveness depends upon his ability to rely on the assistance of various aides, be they secretaries, file clerks, telephone operators, messengers, clerks not yet admitted to the bar, and aides of other sorts. The privilege must include all the persons who act as the attorney's agents.

Von Bulow v. Von Bulow, 811 F. 2d 136 (2d Cir. 1987)

For the privilege to apply, the client must keep the information secret. If the client reveals the same information to someone other than the attorney or legal staff, the privilege is lost. The concept of privilege also extends to persons while acting within certain roles, such as:

1. Spouse
2. Clergy–penitent
3. Doctor–patient
4. Psychotherapist–patient
5. Participants in settlement negotiations

In the *Von Bulow* case, the court confirmed that the principle of privileged communications extends not just to the attorney but also to legal support staff who work on the team.

Normally, the disclosure of the privileged information to a third party will act as a waiver of the privilege. One exception is the common interest exception, as explained in the *O'Boyle* case, where multiple parties individually represented by separate counsel are aligned against the same opponent.

Claim of Privilege

Claim of privilege Preventing the disclosure of confidential communications as evidence based on a recognized privilege.

The attorney–client privilege is not automatically invoked. The person claiming the privilege (usually the client) has the burden to establish its existence, called a **claim of privilege**.

> To sustain a claim of privilege, the party invoking it must demonstrate that the information at issue was a communication between client and counsel or his employee, that it was intended to be and was in fact kept confidential, and that it was made in order to assist in obtaining or providing legal advice or services to the client.
>
> *SR Int'l Bus. Ins. Co. v. World Trade Ctr. Prop.*, No. 01 Civ 9291 (S.D.N.Y. July 3, 2002), quoting *Browne of New York City, Inc. v. Ambase Corp.* 150 F.R.D. 465 (S.D.N.Y. 1993)

IN THE WORDS OF THE COURT ...

O'BOYLE V. BOROUGH OF LONGPORT,
218 N.J. 168, 176, 94 A.3D 299, 303, 2014 N.J. LEXIS 787, 1 (N.J. 2014)

CASE SUMMARY

OVERVIEW

HOLDINGS: [1]-The New Jersey Supreme Court expressly adopted the common interest rule that the common interest exception to waiver of confidential attorney-client communications or work product due to disclosure to third parties applied to communications between attorneys for different parties if the disclosure was made due to actual or anticipated litigation for the purpose of furthering a common interest and was made in a manner to preserve the confidentiality of the disclosed material and to prevent disclosure to adverse parties; [2]-The Court, in applying that rule, held that the private attorney's protected attorney work product remained privileged despite its disclosure to the third-party municipal attorney because the materials were shared in a manner calculated to preserve their confidentiality, in anticipation of litigation, and in furtherance of a common purpose.

Extension of Attorney–Client Privilege to Others

It is now accepted that the efficient administration of justice requires lawyers to engage others, such as legal assistants, accountants, and other experts. This would not be possible if the privilege did not extend to these agents of the attorney, including, most recently, public relations firms. The U.S. District Court for the Southern District of New York summarized the law, stating:

> the privilege in appropriate circumstances extends to otherwise privileged communications that involve persons assisting the lawyer in the rendition of legal services. This principle has been applied universally to cover office personnel, such as secretaries and law clerks, who assist lawyers in performing their tasks. But it has been applied more broadly as well. For example, in *United States v. Kovel*, the Second Circuit held that a client's communication with an accountant employed by his attorney were privileged where made for the purpose of enabling the attorney to understand the client situation in order to provide legal advice.
>
> *IN RE Grand Jury Subpoenas dated March 24, 2003 directed to (A) Grand Jury Witness Firm and (B) Grand Jury Witness*, M11-188 (USDC, S.D.N.Y.) (June 2, 2003)

IN THE WORDS OF THE COURT . . .

***TRAMMELL V. UNITED STATES*, 445 U.S. 40 (1980)**
BURGER C. J.

The privileges between priest and penitent, attorney and client, and physician and patient limit protection to private communication. These privileges are rooted in the imperative need for confidence and trust. The priest–penitent privilege recognizes the human need to disclose to a spiritual counselor, in total and absolute confidence, what are believed to be flawed acts or thoughts and to receive priestly consolation and guidance in return. The lawyer–client privilege rests on the need for the advocate and counselor to know all that relates to the client's reasons for seeking representation if the professional mission is to be carried out. Similarly, the physician must know all that a patient can articulate in order to identify and to treat disease; barriers to full disclosure would impair diagnosis and treatment.

IMPLIED ATTORNEY–CLIENT RELATIONSHIP

An implied attorney–client relationship may result when a prospective client divulges confidential information during a consultation with an attorney for the purpose of retaining the attorney, even if actual employment does not result.

Pro-Hand Sers. Trust v., Monthei, 49 P.3d 56, 59 (Mont. 2002).

In the modern practice of law, the attorney must rely on others, such as paralegals, legal secretaries, investigators, and law clerks, to assist in the vigorous representation of the client. These agents must also be covered by the attorney–client privilege; to do otherwise would obligate the attorney to guard every document, exhibit, and pretrial memorandum from the eyes of everyone on the legal team and perform every task personally, including interviews of clients and witnesses, the typing of reports and memoranda, fact and legal research, and the preparation of trial exhibits and documents. This is clearly not desirable or cost effective for the client or the administration of justice.

The Self-Defense Exception

The rules concerning the duty of confidentiality and attorney–client privilege are not absolute. Lawyers who are accused of wrongdoing (either intentional or negligent) by their clients must be able to defend themselves. This defense may require the use of confidential privileged information. Therefore, lawyers will not be bound by the rules of confidentiality and privilege in this situation because of an inherent right to **due process.** This is frequently referred to as the "**self-defense exception.**"

Due process An established course of judicial proceedings or other activity designed to ensure the legal rights of an individual.

Self-defense exception The right to reveal a client confidence when necessary to defend oneself against a claim of wrongful conduct.

One of the most significant cases involving the self-defense exception is *Qualcomm, Inc. v. Broadcom Corp.* In this case, substantial sanctions were assessed against the client. In response, the client made accusations of wrongdoing by outside counsel as part of its attempt to exonerate itself.

THE PENNSYLVANIA RULES OF PROFESSIONAL CONDUCT RULE 1.6(C)(4) PROVIDES

(c) A lawyer may reveal such information to the extent that the lawyer reasonably believes necessary:

... (4) to establish a claim or defense on behalf of the lawyer in a controversy between the lawyer and the client, to establish a defense to a criminal charge or civil claim or disciplinary proceeding against the lawyer based upon conduct in which the client was involved, or to respond to allegations in any proceeding concerning the lawyer's representation of the client.

IN THE WORDS OF THE COURT ...

UNITED STATES DISTRICT COURT SOUTHERN DISTRICT OF CALIFORNIA
CASE NO. 05CV1958-RMB (BLM)

Qualcomm, Inc, Plaintiff

v.

Broadcom Corp, Defendant

ORDER REMANDING PART OF ORDER OF MAGISTRATE COURT RE MOTIONS FOR SANCTIONS DATED 1/07/08

... Qualcomm filed four declarations of employees, in spite of the fact it had maintained its position of invoking attorney–client privilege. All four declarations were exonerative of Qualcomm and critical of the services and advice of their retained counsel. None were filed under seal.

This introduction of accusatory adversity between Qualcomm and its retained counsel regarding the issue of assessing responsibility for the failure of discovery changes the factual basis which supported the court's earlier order denying the self-defense exception to Qualcomm's attorney–client privilege. *Meyerhofer v. Empire Fire & Marine Ins. Co.*, 497 F.2d 1190, 1194-95 (2d Cir. 1974); *Hearn v. Rhay*, 68 F.R.D. 574, 581 (E.D. Wash. 1975); *First Fed. Sav. & Loan Ass'n v. Oppenheim, Appel, Dixon & Co.*, 110 F.R.D. 557, 560-68 (S.D.N.Y. 1986); A.B.A. Model Rules of Prof. Conduct 1.6(b)(5) & comment 10.

Accordingly, the court's order denying the self-defense exception to the attorney–client privilege is vacated. The attorneys have a due process right to defend themselves under the totality of circumstances presented in this sanctions hearing where their alleged conduct regarding discovery is in conflict with that alleged by Qualcomm concerning performance of discovery responsibilities. See, e.g., *Miranda v. So. Pac. Transp. Co.*, 710 F.2d 516, 522-23 (9th Cir. 1983)....

The full opinion of the court may be viewed at www.ediscoverylaw.com/Brewster.pdf.

Work product doctrine
A qualified immunity from discovery for "work product of the lawyer" except on a substantial showing of "necessity or justification" of certain written statements and memoranda prepared by counsel in representation of a client, generally in preparation for trial.

Work Product Doctrine

The **work product doctrine** provides a limited protection for material prepared by the attorney, or those working for the attorney, in anticipation of litigation or for trial. The work product doctrine is different from both the attorney–client privilege and the duty of confidentiality. The attorney–client privilege and the duty of confidentiality relate to any information provided by the client regardless of whether it involves potential litigation. The work product doctrine applies only to work created in anticipation of litigation, or for trial.

Exceptions and Limitations to the Work Product Doctrine

The work product doctrine does not cover documents prepared in the normal operation of the client's business, such as sales reports, data analysis, or summaries of business operations:

> The work product doctrine does not extend to documents in an attorney's possession that were prepared by a third party in the ordinary course of business and that would have been created in essentially similar form irrespective of any litigation anticipated by counsel.
>
> *In Re Grand Jury Subpoenas,* 318 F.3d 379 (2nd Cir. 2002)

In other words, the client cannot obtain protection for internal business documents by giving them to the attorney. Giving them to the attorney does not make them work product; they are not protected from discovery by the other side simply because they are in the possession of the attorney.

IN THE WORDS OF THE COURT ...

Work Product Doctrine

***ELECTRONIC DATA SYSTEMS CORPORATION V. STEINGRABER,* 4:02 CV 225 USDC, E.D. TEXAS, 2003.**

The work product doctrine is narrower than the attorney–client privilege in that it only protects materials prepared "in anticipation of litigation [Fed. R. Civ. P. 26(b)(3)], whereas the attorney–client privilege protects confidential legal communications between an attorney and client regardless of whether they involve possible litigation."

IN THE WORDS OF THE COURT ...

Work Product Doctrine

***HICKMAN V. TAYLOR,* 329 U.S. 496 (1947)**

The U.S. Supreme Court recognized the work product doctrine and its importance, saying:

Proper preparation of a client's case demands that he assemble information, sift what he considers to be the relevant from the irrelevant facts, prepare his legal theories and plan his strategy without undue and needless interference. That is the historical and the necessary way in which lawyers act within the framework of our system of jurisprudence to promote justice and to protect their clients' interests.

This work is reflected, of course, in interviews, statements, memoranda, correspondence, briefs, mental impressions, personal beliefs, and countless other tangible and intangible ways—aptly though roughly termed by the Circuit Court of Appeals in this case as the "work product of the lawyer." Were such materials open to opposing counsel on mere demand, much of what is now put down in writing would remain unwritten.

An attorney's thoughts, heretofore inviolate, would not be his own. Inefficiency, unfairness and sharp practices would inevitably develop in the giving of legal advice and in the preparation of cases for trial. The effect on the legal profession would be demoralizing. And the interests of the clients and the cause of justice would be poorly served....

... [W]here relevant and non-privileged facts remain hidden in an attorney's file and where production of those facts is essential to the preparation of one's case, discovery may be properly had.

***Hickman v. Taylor* and the Federal Rules of Civil Procedure.** The revision to the federal rules on discovery modifies some of the protection under the work product rule in federal courts and in those state courts that use the federal rules as guidance. Rule 26 provides an exception to the work product rule allowing access to some material prepared in anticipation of litigation, as explained in Federal Rules of Civil Procedure 26(B)3:

> 3) Trial Preparation: Materials.
> (A) Documents and Tangible Things. Ordinarily, a party may not discover documents and tangible things that are prepared in anticipation of litigation or for trial by or for another party or its representative (including the other party's attorney, consultant, surety, indemnitor, insurer, or agent). But, subject to Rule 26(b)(4), those materials may be discovered if:
> (i) they are otherwise discoverable under Rule 26(b)(1); and
> (ii) the party shows that it has substantial need for the materials to prepare its case and cannot, without undue hardship, obtain their substantial equivalent by other means.
> (B) Protection Against Disclosure. If the court orders discovery of those materials, it must protect against disclosure of the mental impressions, conclusions, opinions, or legal theories of a party's attorney or other representative concerning the litigation.

IN THE WORDS OF THE COURT ...

HAWKINS V. DISTRICT COURT OF FOURTH JUDICIAL DIST., 638 P.2D 1372, 1376-1377, 1982 COLO. LEXIS 527, 7-11 (COLO. 1982)

Against a backdrop of varied judicial interpretations, the United States Supreme Court in 1970 promulgated Fed. R. Civ. P. 26(b) as part of a major revision calculated to integrate into one rule the standards regulating the scope of pretrial discovery. *Advisory Committee Notes, supra* at 490. C.R.C.P. 26 parallels Fed. R. Civ. P. 26 and became effective April 1, 1970, shortly after the United States Supreme Court approved the federal counterpart. Rule 26(b)(3) provides in pertinent part:

"[A] party may obtain discovery of documents and tangible things otherwise discoverable under subsection (b)(1) of this Rule and prepared in anticipation of litigation or for trial by or for another party or by or for that other party's representative (including his attorney, consultant, surety, indemnitor, insurer, or agent) only upon a showing that the party seeking discovery has substantial need of the materials in the preparation of his case and that he is unable without undue hardship to obtain the substantial equivalent of the materials by other means. In ordering discovery of such materials when the required showing has been made, the court shall protect against disclosure of the mental impressions, conclusions, opinions, or legal theories of an attorney or other representative of a party concerning the litigation."

Rule 26(b)(3) broadens the scope of discovery to include matters formerly protected by some courts under the work product doctrine. Materials prepared "in anticipation of litigation or for trial" enjoy a qualified immunity from discovery in that they are discoverable only upon a showing by the party seeking discovery of a substantial need for such materials in the preparation of his case and an inability without undue hardship to obtain their substantial equivalent by other means. C.R.C.P. 26(b)(3), like Fed. R. Civ. P. 26(b)(3), draws no distinction between trial preparation materials [1377] compiled by an attorney and those prepared by some other agent of a party. However, as the rule makes clear, the court in ordering the discovery of trial preparation materials must protect the "mental impressions, conclusions, opinions, or legal theories" of the attorney or other representative of the party. Documents and other tangible things not prepared "in anticipation of litigation or for trial" are discoverable so long as they appear "reasonably calculated to lead to the discovery of admissible evidence." C.R.C.P. 26(b)(1).

Rule 26(b)(3) is not intended to protect from general discovery materials prepared in the ordinary course of business. *Advisory Committee Notes, supra,* at 501. Courts generally have held that reports made and statements taken by an insurance adjuster for an insurance company in the normal course of investigating a claim are prepared in the regular course of the company's business and, therefore, not in anticipation of litigation or for trial. The rationale for such an approach was cogently expressed in *Thomas Organ Co. v. Jadranska Slobodna Plovidba,* 54 F.R.D. 367, 373 (D.C.N.D. Ill. 1972).

Inadvertent Disclosure of Confidential Information

In the practice of law, confidential or privileged information is sometimes disclosed inadvertently. An email may be sent to the wrong address, the wrong number may be speed dialed on a fax machine, or a letter may be sent in the incorrect envelope. The admissibility of the inadvertently disclosed documents will depend on the individual jurisdiction, and courts follow no single policy.

Judicial Views

There are three judicial views on handling the inadvertent disclosure of confidential and privileged information: (1) automatic waiver; (2) no waiver; and (3) balancing test.

1. **Automatic waiver**—These cases hold that once confidentiality is breached, the privilege is automatically waived. There is nothing that will redeem the privilege, and therefore the documents may be used by the party that received them by accident.
2. **No waiver**—Under this theory, the privilege is only destroyed when a client makes a knowing, voluntary waiver of the privilege. Therefore, the attorney's inadvertent disclosure does not constitute a waiver.
3. **Balancing test**—Courts using the balancing test look to several factors: (1) the nature of the methods taken to protect the information, (2) efforts made to correct the error, (3) the extent of the disclosure, and (4) fairness. Remedies under this test may include unlimited use of the disclosed materials, the court-ordered return of documents, or disqualification of attorneys who have reviewed inadvertently disclosed documents.

Web Exploration

The complete version of the Formal Opinion can be found at: http://www.nycbar.org/ethics/ethics-opinions-local/1995-opinions/1134-formal-opinion-1995-12.

ABA Ethics Opinion

The ABA's long-standing view on inadvertent disclosure was contained in its opinion 92-368, which advocated for confidentiality of privileged materials to protect the client, and imposed a burden upon receiving attorneys to not review privileged material and to return it following instructions given to them by the disclosing attorney. The ABA has issued a formal opinion modifying 92-368, which states:

> A lawyer who receives a document from opposing parties or their lawyers and knows or reasonably should know that the document was inadvertently sent should promptly notify the sender in order to permit the sender to take protective measures. To the extent that Formal Opinion 92-368 opined otherwise, it is hereby withdrawn.

However, the ABA has not given direction as to what should happen to the attorney who reads the inadvertently disclosed document and whether the information can be used by the other side. Each jurisdiction may have a different rule. The California courts have addressed these questions in *Rico v. Mitsubishi Motors Corp.*

IN THE WORDS OF THE COURT . . .

RICO V. MITSUBISHI MOTORS CORP.,
42 CAL.4TH 807 (2007), 171 P.3D 1092, 68 CAL.RPTR. 3D 758

Here we consider what action is required of an attorney who receives privileged documents through inadvertence and whether the remedy of disqualification is appropriate. We conclude that, under the authority of *State Comp. Ins. Fund v. WPS, Inc.* (1999) 70 Cal. App. 4th 644 (State Fund), an attorney in these circumstances may not read a document any more closely than is necessary to ascertain that it is privileged. Once it becomes apparent that the content is privileged, counsel must immediately notify opposing counsel and try to resolve the situation. . . .

Moreover, we agree with the Court of Appeal that, "when a writing is protected under the absolute attorney work product privilege, courts do not invade upon the attorney's thought processes by evaluating the content of the writing. Once [it is apparent] that the writing contains an attorney's impressions, conclusions, opinions, legal research or theories, the reading stops and the contents of the document for all practical purposes are off limits. In the same way, once the court determines that the writing is absolutely privileged, the inquiry ends. Courts do not make exceptions based on the content of the writing." Thus, "regardless of its potential impeachment value, Yukevich's personal notes should never have been subject to opposing counsel's scrutiny and use."

ETHICAL PERSPECTIVE

Arizona Ethics Rules

ER 1.6. CONFIDENTIALITY OF INFORMATION

(a) A lawyer shall not reveal information relating to the representation of a client unless the client gives informed consent, the disclosure is impliedly authorized in order to carry out the representation or the disclosure is permitted or required by paragraphs (b), (c) or (d), or ER 3.3(a)(3).

(b) A lawyer shall reveal such information to the extent the lawyer reasonably believes necessary to prevent the client from committing a criminal act that the lawyer believes is likely to result in death or substantial bodily harm.

(c) A lawyer may reveal the intention of the lawyer's client to commit a crime and the information necessary to prevent the crime.

(d) A lawyer may reveal such information relating to the representation of a client to the extent the lawyer reasonably believes necessary:

- **(1)** to prevent the client from committing a crime or fraud that is reasonably certain to result in substantial injury to the financial interests or property of another and in furtherance of which the client has used or is using the lawyer's services;
- **(2)** to mitigate or rectify substantial injury to the financial interests or property of another that is reasonably certain to result or has resulted from the client's commission of a crime or fraud in furtherance of which the client has used the lawyer's services;
- **(3)** to secure legal advice about the lawyer's compliance with these Rules;
- **(4)** to establish a claim or defense on behalf of the lawyer in a controversy between the lawyer and the client, to establish a defense to a criminal charge or civil claim against the lawyer based upon conduct in which the client was involved, or to respond to allegations in any proceeding concerning the lawyer's representation of the client; or
- **(5)** to comply with other law or a final order of a court or tribunal of competent jurisdiction directing the lawyer to disclose such information.

Conflict of Interest

LEARNING OBJECTIVE 6

Discuss the concept of conflict of interest in the legal profession.

The basis of the **conflict of interest** rule is the belief that a person cannot be loyal to two clients whose interests are adverse to one another. Lawyers cannot represent two clients with actual or potentially conflicting interests, such as a husband and wife in a domestic relations case. An attorney also may not represent a client when the attorney has a financial interest in the subject matter of the case, such as when the attorney is a partner in a real estate transaction. Nonlawyer members of the legal team must also avoid conflicts of interest. For example, both sides of a case may not use the same paralegal. However, in many cases, the lines are not as clear.

Conflict of interest A situation where the interest of one client is directly adverse to the interest of another client.

Rule 1.7 of the Model Rules of Professional Conduct addresses conflicts of interest. A lawyer should not represent another client if "representation of one client will be directly adverse to another client" unless both clients give their informed consent to the dual representation, and the consent is confirmed in writing. The lawyer's personal interests or those of third parties who are not clients, such as family members, may also create a risk of a conflict that must be avoided.

Clearly, a lawyer should not accept an engagement if the lawyer's personal interests or desires will, or with reasonable probability will, adversely affect the advice to be given or services to be rendered to the prospective client. The client is entitled to independent advice from members of the legal team, meaning that the advice is not influenced by any concern for personal gain on the part of the lawyer. The information that creates a conflict of interest is not limited solely to that of the attorney representing a client. It also includes the information held by another member of the legal team, including the legal assistant.

Conflict of interest and in-house counsel. A question of conflict of interest arises when the attorney is employed by a corporation and performs services for the clients or customers of the employer corporation. As stated in the *Mid-America* case below, "the in-house counsel is employed by Mid-America, not the client, and has a direct conflict of interest." The question for the paralegal then is: If the purported supervising attorney has a conflict of interest and cannot represent the individual client, are they a supervising attorney or is the paralegal unsupervised and therefore performing legal work? A claim of supervision as a defense to UPL may

ETHICAL PERSPECTIVE

Arkansas Rules of Professional Conduct

RULE 1.7. CONFLICT OF INTEREST: CURRENT CLIENTS

(a) Except as provided in paragraph (b), a lawyer shall not represent a client if the representation involves a concurrent conflict of interest. A concurrent conflict of interest exists if:
- **(1)** the representation of one client will be directly adverse to another client; or
- **(2)** there is a significant risk that the representation of one or more clients will be materially limited by the lawyer's responsibilities to another client, a former client or a third person or by a personal interest of the lawyer.

(b) Notwithstanding the existence of a concurrent conflict of interest under paragraph (a), a lawyer may represent a client if:
- **(1)** the lawyer reasonably believes that the lawyer will be able to provide competent and diligent representation to each affected client;
- **(2)** the representation is not prohibited by law;
- **(3)** the representation does not involve the assertion of a claim by one client against another client represented by the lawyer in the same litigation or other proceeding before a tribunal; and
- **(4)** each affected client gives informed consent, confirmed in writing.

not be sufficient when the alleged supervising attorney has a conflict of interest. As previously discussed in the *Tegman* case, a paralegal is negligent if they know or should know there is a lack of supervision.

IN THE WORDS OF THE COURT ...

IN RE MID-AMERICA LIVING TRUST ASSOCS., 927 S.W.2D 855, 1996 MO. LEXIS 56 (MO. 1996)

Mid-America paralegals contact the client and verify the information in the workbook. The paralegals, based on input from in-house counsel, the review attorney, or personal experience, decide which form of trust would be the most appropriate and draft the initial documents from blank prototypes. The prototypes include forms for single and married persons in community and noncommunity property states. The marital trust prototype includes joint marital trust documents and separate trust documents. There are documents for estates having tax consequences and forms for pour-over wills, durable and general powers of attorney, health care declarations, and health care powers of attorney.

The trust documents, workbook, and attorney check are then mailed to the review attorney. The review attorney sometimes communicates directly with the client, but not always. The paralegal makes changes if directed to by the attorney. The documents are then mailed to the trust associate, who delivers the documents for execution by the client. Mid-America also provides assistance in retitling assets and preparing quitclaim deeds. . . .

Referral attorneys, as well as in-house attorneys, have also been found to suffer from a conflict of interest. Obviously, an attorney's interests are divided by simultaneously working for a trust marketing company and attempting to represent the company's clients. *The Florida Bar*, 613 So. 2d at 428; *Volk*, 805 P.2d at 1117 ("The respondent considered the corporation to be her client, not the individual purchasers of the trusts."); *Macy*, 789 P.2d at 189; Matter of Pearce, 246 Mont. 313, 806 P.2d 21, 22 (Mont. 1990). However, attorneys who regularly receive referrals from trust marketing companies, without being directly employed by them, also have been found to suffer from a conflict of interest. An attorney's advice may be tainted by his desire to continue receiving referrals. See Rule 4-1.7(b); Rule 4-5.4(c); *Cassidy*, 884 P.2d at 310-12. . . .

Mid-America Gathered Information From Individuals for Use in Determining What Type of Trust Was Appropriate for Those Individuals and Preparing Trust Documents.

Merely gathering information for use in a legal document does not necessarily constitute the unauthorized practice of law. See *Martin*, 642 N.E.2d at 79; *The Florida Bar*, 613 So. 2d at 428. However, that is not all that the trust associates did here. The trust associates were required to help the clients fill out a workbook, a detailed questionnaire in which the client listed all their assets and made various legal choices. For instance, the client decided whether the durable power of attorney would be springing or immediate, which assets they wanted included in the trust, and who they wished to designate as trustee, executor, or guardian. The trust associates were provided a training manual that defined legal terms, delineated the duties of appointed persons, and emphasized important choices the client must make throughout the workbook. The trust associates were not merely collecting information to fill in standardized forms as otherwise might have been approved by *Hulse* and *In re First Escrow*. Instead, they also were giving legal advice to the clients about choices to be made and the legal effects of those choices....

... B. Attorney Supervision and Review

Respondents also argue that paralegals draft all documents under the direct supervision of Mid-America's in-house attorney and that a review attorney selected by the client makes certain that the documents are appropriate for the client. Apparently, respondents believe this review is sufficient to "cure" any unauthorized practice of law. In reality, any mitigating effect the attorneys might have comes too little and too late in the marketing scheme....

...(ii) Review Attorney

Likewise, the review attorney cannot "cure" Mid-America's unauthorized practice of law for three reasons. First, and most obviously, the review attorney enters the picture too late. Mid-America's non-lawyer trust associate has already given legal advice to the client regarding the client's legal affairs, recommended and sold a trust instrument, and received valuable consideration. Mid-America has also drafted a custom document tailored to the client's particular needs, prior to the participation of the review attorney....

... Second, participation by review attorneys in Mid-America's trust marketing businesses violates the rules of conduct for the legal profession and, therefore, cannot cure the unauthorized practice of law. See Rule 4-5.4(c); Rule 4-5.5(b). Recent opinions from Colorado, Iowa, and Ohio have confirmed that attorneys reviewing or drafting legal documents recommended or drafted by non-attorneys are aiding in the unauthorized practice of law or working with a conflict of interest.

CANDOR AND FAIRNESS IN LITIGATION

LEARNING OBJECTIVE 7

Describe the duty of candor to the court and other counsel and the ethical duty of fairness.

Litigation is the practice of advocacy, which involves advocating a legal position to the court or persuading a trier of facts to accept a set of facts. Although an attorney must be an aggressive advocate for the client, it is also the duty of the attorney to avoid any conduct that undermines the integrity of the process. The duty to the client to persuasively present the case is qualified by the ethical obligation of **candor**, meaning that the lawyer must not mislead the court or opposing counsel with false statements of law or of facts that the lawyer knows to be false. Without mutual respect, honesty, and fairness, the system cannot function properly.

The duty of candor may simply mean that the attorney presents the current case and statutory law, even when the most current version is not favorable to the position taken. This duty requires making a complete search for *all* the law, statutory enactments, and case law, and not just the law that favors the client's position. In an age of digital information, huge numbers of electronic cases may need to be searched, and it is easy to overlook a few, or not run the search as thoroughly as possible. Not making the proper inquiry of the client's staff, or not thoroughly searching all of the law, may lead to sanctions, and potentially worse—disbarment.

Candor A duty of honesty to the court.

Fairness to Opposing Party and Counsel

Fairness in the practice of law has probably been an issue for as long as there has been an adversarial justice system. A number of bar associations have established professionalism centers such as that of the American Bar Association Center for Professional Responsibility (http://www.americanbar.org/groups/professional_responsibility.html). Attorneys are advocates for their clients and occasionally forget that the purpose of the legal system is justice for all. The ethical rule of fairness to opposing counsel and parties is an attempt to ensure justice is done even if one's client loses the case. Each side is expected to use its best knowledge and skills to present its position fairly and provide evidence for the **trier of fact** to determine where the truth lies. Destroying, falsifying, or tampering with evidence destroys the fabric of the system, and society loses confidence in it. The most familiar example occurs in criminal cases where the prosecutor does not turn over, as required, **exculpatory evidence** that might show that the defendant is innocent.

Trier of fact The trier of fact decides what facts are to be accepted and used in making the decision. It is usually a jury, but may be a judge who hears a case without a jury and decides the facts and applies the law.

Exculpatory evidence Evidence that tends to prove the innocence of the accused or prove the facts of the defendant's case.

ETHICAL PERSPECTIVE

Proposed Michigan Standards for Imposing Lawyer Sanctions [Without Commentary] (Submitted in June 2002 by the Attorney Discipline Board)

Preface

These Michigan Standards for Imposing Lawyer Sanctions were adopted by the State of Michigan Attorney Discipline Board (ADB or Board) on [date] under the authority granted by the Michigan Supreme Court in its order dated [date], and are intended for use by the Attorney Discipline Board and its hearing panels in imposing discipline following a finding or acknowledgment of professional misconduct. Pursuant to the Court's order, these standards may be amended by the Board from time to time. The Court may at any time modify these standards or direct the Board to modify them.

(6.0) Violations of Duties Owed to the Legal System

(6.1) False Statements, Fraud, and Misrepresentation to a Tribunal. The following sanctions are generally appropriate in cases involving conduct that is prejudicial to the administration of justice or that involves dishonesty, fraud, deceit, or misrepresentation to a tribunal:

(6.11) Disbarment is generally appropriate when a lawyer, with the intent to deceive the tribunal, makes a false statement, submits a false document, or improperly withholds material information, and causes serious or potentially serious injury.

(6.12) Suspension is generally appropriate when a lawyer knows that false statements or documents are being submitted to the tribunal or that material information is improperly being withheld, and takes no remedial action, and causes injury or potential injury.

(6.13) Reprimand is generally appropriate when a lawyer is negligent either in determining whether statements or documents submitted to a tribunal are false or in taking remedial action when material information is being withheld and causes injury or potential injury.

RHODE ISLAND RULES OF PROFESSIONAL CONDUCT

RULE 3.3 CANDOR TOWARD THE TRIBUNAL

(a) A lawyer shall not knowingly:
   (1) make a false statement of fact or law to a tribunal or fail to correct a false statement of material fact or law previously made to the tribunal by the lawyer;
   (2) fail to disclose to the tribunal legal authority in the controlling jurisdiction known to the lawyer to be directly adverse to the position of the client and not disclosed by opposing counsel; or
   (3) offer evidence that the lawyer knows to be false. If a lawyer, the lawyer's client, or a witness called by the lawyer, has offered material evidence and the lawyer comes to know of its falsity, the lawyer shall take reasonable remedial measures, including, if necessary, disclosure to the tribunal. A lawyer may refuse to offer evidence, other than the testimony of a defendant in a criminal matter, that the lawyer reasonably believes is false.

(b) A lawyer who represents a client in an adjudicative proceeding and who knows that a person intends to engage, is engaging or has engaged in criminal or fraudulent conduct related to the proceeding shall take reasonable remedial measures, including, if necessary, disclosure to the tribunal.

(c) The duties stated in paragraphs (a) and (b) continue to the conclusion of the proceeding, and apply even if compliance requires disclosure of information otherwise protected by Rule 1.6.

(d) In an ex parte proceeding, a lawyer shall inform the tribunal of all material facts known to the lawyer that will enable the tribunal to make an informed decision, whether or not the facts are adverse.

OREGON RULES OF PROFESSIONAL CONDUCT (12/01/06)

RULE 3.4 FAIRNESS TO OPPOSING PARTY AND COUNSEL

A lawyer shall not:

(a) knowingly and unlawfully obstruct another party's access to evidence or unlawfully alter, destroy or conceal a document or other material having potential evidentiary value. A lawyer shall not counsel or assist another person to do any such act;

(b) falsify evidence; counsel or assist a witness to testify falsely; offer an inducement to a witness that is prohibited by law; or pay, offer to pay, or acquiesce in payment of compensation to a witness contingent upon the content of the witness's testimony or the outcome of the case; except that a lawyer may advance, guarantee or acquiesce in the payment of:
   (1) expenses reasonably incurred by a witness in attending or testifying;
   (2) reasonable compensation to a witness for the witness's loss of time in attending or testifying; or
   (3) a reasonable fee for the professional services of an expert witness.

(c) knowingly disobey an obligation under the rules of a tribunal, except for an open refusal based on an assertion that no valid obligation exists;

(d) in pretrial procedure, knowingly make a frivolous discovery request or fail to make reasonably diligent effort to comply with a legally proper discovery request by an opposing party;

(e) in trial, allude to any matter that the lawyer does not reasonably believe is relevant or that will not be supported by admissible evidence, assert personal knowledge of facts in issue except when testifying as a witness, or state a personal opinion as to the justness of a cause, the credibility of a witness, the culpability of a civil litigant or the guilt or innocence of an accused;

(f) advise or cause a person to secrete himself or herself or to leave the jurisdiction of a tribunal for purposes of making the person unavailable as a witness therein; or

(g) threaten to present criminal charges to obtain an advantage in a civil matter unless the lawyer reasonably believes the charge to be true and if the purpose of the lawyer is to compel or induce the person threatened to take reasonable action to make good the wrong which is the subject of the charge.

Adopted 01/01/05
Source: http://www.osbar.org/_docs/rulesregs/orpc.pdf

Web Resources

The Pennsylvania Bar Association Professionalism website may be viewed at: http://www.pabar.org/public/committees/proflism/about/welcome.asp.

Avoiding UPL

LEARNING OBJECTIVE 8
Analyze a situation to determine whether it involves the unauthorized practice of law.

Every paralegal must carefully consider the question of how to avoid UPL. Although there is much uncertainty about what constitutes UPL, some general guidelines are provided.

ETHICAL PERSPECTIVE

Colorado Supreme Court

RULE 3.4. FAIRNESS TO OPPOSING PARTY AND COUNSEL

Annotations

Comment

(1) The procedure of the adversary system contemplates that the evidence in a case is to be marshaled competitively by the contending parties. Fair competition in the adversary system is secured by prohibitions against destruction or concealment of evidence, improperly influencing witnesses, obstructive tactics in discovery procedure, and the like.

(2) Documents and other items of evidence are often essential to establish a claim or defense. Subject to evidentiary privileges, the right of an opposing party, including the government, to obtain evidence through discovery or subpoena is an important procedural right. The exercise of that right can be frustrated if relevant material is altered, concealed or destroyed. Applicable law in many jurisdictions makes it an offense to destroy material for [the] purpose of impairing its availability in a pending proceeding or one whose commencement can be foreseen. Falsifying evidence is also generally a criminal offense. Paragraph (a) applies to evidentiary material generally, including computerized information.

Source: http://www.coloradosupremecourt.com/Regulation/Rules/appendix20/statdspp88f6.html

IN THE WORDS OF THE COURT ...

UNITED STATES DISTRICT COURT SOUTHERN DISTRICT OF CALIFORNIA
CASE NO. 05CV1958-B (BLM)

Qualcomm Inc.

v.

Broadcom Corp.,

ORDER GRANTING IN PART AND DENYING IN PART DEFENDANT'S MOTION FOR SANCTIONS AND SANCTIONING QUALCOMM, INCORPORATED AND INDIVIDUAL LAWYERS

b. Referral to the California State Bar

As set forth above, the Sanctioned Attorneys assisted Qualcomm in committing this incredible discovery violation by intentionally hiding or recklessly ignoring relevant documents, ignoring or rejecting numerous warning signs that Qualcomm's document search was inadequate, and blindly accepting Qualcomm's unsupported assurances that its document search was adequate. The Sanctioned Attorneys then used the lack of evidence to repeatedly and forcefully make false statements and arguments to the court and jury. As such, the Sanctioned Attorneys violated their discovery obligations and also may have violated their ethical duties. See e.g., The State Bar of California, Rules of Professional Conduct, Rule 5-200 (a lawyer shall not seek to mislead the judge or jury by a false statement of fact or law), Rule 5-220 (a lawyer shall not suppress evidence that the lawyer or the lawyer's client has a legal obligation to reveal or to produce).

Web Exploration

Contrast and compare Rule 1.6(c)(4) of the Pennsylvania Rules at http://www. padisciplinaryboard.org/documents/RulesOfProfessionalConduct.pdf with the American Bar Association Model Rules of Professional Responsibility at http://www.abanet.org/cpr/mrpc/mrpc_toc.html and the ethical rule in your jurisdiction.

ETHICAL PERSPECTIVE

Review the most current version and comments to Rule 1.6 on Confidentiality of Information of the American Bar Association Model Rules of Professional Conduct at the American Bar Association website: http://www.abanet.org/cpr/mrpc/rule_1_6.html.

Avoiding UPL: Holding Oneself Out

A common thread in the law of UPL is the prohibition against "holding oneself out" as a lawyer when not admitted to practice law. Florida defines UPL as follows:

> Any person not licensed or otherwise authorized to practice law in this state who practices law in this state or holds himself or herself out to the public as qualified to practice law in this state, or who willfully pretends to be, or willfully takes or uses any name, title, addition, or description implying that he or she is qualified, or recognized by law as qualified, to practice law in this state, commits a felony of the third degree ...
>
> Chapter 2004-287, Senate Bill 1776.

For paralegals, one of the most basic rules in avoiding UPL is to inform the parties with whom they are dealing that they are not lawyers. Paralegals must not hold themselves out as being anything other than a paralegal, and parties who have contact with the paralegal must know the limited role a paralegal has on the legal team.

Making sure clients understand the role of the paralegal can be a challenge. For some clients, the paralegal is their main contact with the law firm and is the one through whom all documents and information are communicated. Some may believe that because a paralegal is a person with advanced training and knowledge, he or she can perform some of the functions normally performed by lawyers, such as giving legal advice and opinions.

Some clients may come from backgrounds where the distinctions between lawyers and other staff members are not clear. For example, some may come from countries with legal systems where legal professionals play different roles or where different terms are used for those who perform legal-type functions, such as notaries. For persons for whom English is a second language, problems in translation may contribute to the misunderstanding.

Paralegals must immediately make it clear that they are paralegals and not lawyers. In a first meeting with anyone, whether that person is a client, witness, opposing attorney, or a courthouse staff member, the wisest course of action is to advise him or her of one's position as a paralegal. A short statement such as "I am the paralegal for attorney [name of attorney]" may be sufficient to put the other party on notice. Business cards and letterheads, where permitted, should clearly state the title of paralegal. Correspondence should always include the title of paralegal as part of the signature block. In its Business Code, California has attempted to protect the public by requiring the following statement to be made to prospective clients:

> (4) The statement: "I am not an attorney" and, if the person offering legal document assistant or unlawful detainer assistant services is a partnership or a corporation, or uses a fictitious business name, "(name) is not a law firm. I/we cannot represent you in court, advise you about your legal rights or the law, or select legal forms for you."

This provision tries to avoid the problem of a paralegal misleading the public into thinking he or she is a lawyer when limited services are provided, such as document preparation.

Never allow the other party to think you are anything other than what you are—a professional who is a paralegal. For those who are not familiar with the role of the paralegal, you may have to clarify what the paralegal can and cannot do in your jurisdiction.

Avoiding UPL: Giving Advice

Every state prohibits anyone other than a licensed attorney from expressing legal opinions. A paralegal cannot give legal opinions or advice. This rule sounds simple, but actually following it can be complicated. Paralegals must carefully monitor their communications to avoid giving legal advice or rendering a legal opinion. Certain clients and those seeking "a little free advice" may not respect the limitations on the paralegal's role in the legal system.

Certain statements addressed to a paralegal should send up a red flag. A request from a client to prepare a power of attorney or some other document "without bothering the lawyer" should give the paralegal pause. Even in a social setting, legal advice may be casually requested, and the statement "I am not an attorney" or "I cannot represent you in court, advise you about your legal rights or the law, or select legal forms for you" may need to be repeated.

If legal rights may be affected, it is probably legal advice. However, this is not always easy to determine. Consider the seemingly innocent question, "How should I sign my name?" If a person is signing a document in a representative capacity as the officer of a corporation or on behalf of another person under a power of attorney, she must indicate that capacity when signing. Telling the client to simply sign her name without also telling her to indicate her representative capacity might be considered giving legal advice because the client's legal rights could be affected if he or she does not indicate representative capacity.

Avoiding UPL: Filling Out Forms

Filling out forms for clients can also be a source of trouble. In some jurisdictions, paralegals are permitted to assist clients in preparing certain documents. Other courts, however, view this assistance as rendering legal advice. As one Tennessee court has stated,

> As a general matter, other courts have held that the sale of self-help legal kits or printed legal forms does not constitute the unauthorized practice of law as long as the seller provides the buyer no advice regarding which forms to use or how the forms should be filled out.
>
> *Fifteenth Judicial District Unified Bar Association v. Glasgow*, No. M1996-00020-COA-R3-CV, 1999 Tenn. App. LEXIS 815 (Tenn. Ct. of App., Dec. 10, 1999)

A Florida court considering this issue held that UPL consists of

> a nonlawyer who has direct contact with individuals in the nature of consultation, explanation, recommendations, advice, and assistance in the provision, selection, and completion of legal forms engages in the unlicensed practice of law . . . [W]hile a nonlawyer may sell certain legal forms and type up instruments completed by clients, a nonlawyer "must not engage in personal legal assistance in conjunction with her business activities, including the correction of errors and omissions. . . .
>
> *The Florida Bar v. We The People Forms and Service Center of Sarasota, Inc.*, 883 So.2d 1280 (Fla. 2004)

Avoiding UPL: Representing Clients

Nonlawyers are sometimes permitted to represent another person before a judicial or quasi-judicial board, such as an administrative agency. However, it is often difficult to know under what circumstances this is acceptable. Some jurisdictions and administrative agencies do permit those who are not licensed or admitted to practice to appear in court or before administrative law judges or referees on behalf of clients. Under limited circumstances, law students may represent clients under the guidance and supervision of an attorney, depending on the jurisdiction, the nature of the action, and the level of the court.

Acting as a legal representative has traditionally been the role of lawyers. But even lawyers are not always permitted to represent certain parties. A lawyer admitted to practice in one state may not necessarily be permitted to represent the same client in another state. Lawyers admitted to practice in one jurisdiction, however, may ask the court of another jurisdiction for permission to appear and try a specific case. This is a courtesy usually granted for a single case, and the trial attorney is usually required to retain a local attorney to act as co-counsel and advise as to local rules and procedures.

Generally, only duly admitted lawyers in the jurisdiction may represent parties. But this rule has been modified to allow law students in some states to represent parties in certain situations, under appropriate supervision. In some states, a nonlawyer employee may represent a business in some proceedings before administrative agencies or before the minor judiciary, such as small claims courts. There is no uniformity among the rules concerning when nonlawyers may represent parties or before which agencies or courts. Any appearance before a court must be approached carefully. Even something very minor, such as the presentation of a request for continuance of a case, may be considered the practice of law by some courts.

The rules for appearing before federal and state administrative agencies also lack uniformity. Some federal agencies specifically permit nonlawyers to appear. The Social Security Administration allows representation by nonlawyers to nearly the same extent as lawyers. The U.S. Patent Office also permits nonlawyer practice. Some state agencies, by specific legislation or administrative rule, also permit representation by nonlawyers.

Avoiding UPL: Guidelines

The Model Standards and Guidelines for the Utilization of Legal Assistants written by the National Association of Legal Assistants (NALA) provide guidelines for avoiding UPL:

Guideline 1 Legal Assistants Should:

1. Disclose their status as legal assistants at the outset of any professional relationship with a client, other attorneys, a court or administrative agency or personnel thereof, or members of the general public.

Guideline 2 Legal Assistants Should Not:

1. Establish attorney–client relationships; set legal fees; give legal opinions or advice; or represent a client before a court, unless authorized to do so by said court; nor
2. Engage in, encourage, or contribute to any act that could constitute the unauthorized practice of law.

Guideline 3 Legal Assistants May Perform Services for an Attorney in the Representation of a Client, Provided:

1. The services performed by the legal assistant do not require the exercise of independent professional legal judgment;
2. The attorney maintains a direct relationship with the client and maintains control of all client matters;
3. The attorney supervises the legal assistant;
4. The attorney remains professionally responsible for all work on behalf of the client, including any actions taken or not taken by the legal assistant in connection therewith; and
5. The services performed supplement, merge with, and become the attorney's work product.

Concept Review *and* Reinforcement

LEGAL TERMINOLOGY

ABA Model Rules of Professional Conduct 44
Agent 51
Attorney–client privilege 55
Candor 65
Claim of privilege 56
Competence/competent 53
Confidentiality 54
Conflict of interest 63
Due process 57
Ethical guidelines 44
Ethics 44
Exculpatory evidence 65
Federal Rules of Evidence 49
Fiduciary relationship 51
Model Guidelines for the Utilization of Legal Assistant Services 50
Principal 51
Privilege 54
Rules of court 53
Self-defense exception 57
Supervising attorney 51
Trier of fact 65
Unauthorized Practice of Law (UPL) 46
Work product doctrine 58

SUMMARY OF KEY CONCEPTS

Regulation of the Practice of Law

Purpose of Regulation	The practice of law is regulated by state government and court rule in an attempt to protect the public from incompetent and unscrupulous practitioners.
The Paralegal and Licensing	With a few exceptions, there are no state licensing requirements for one to work as a paralegal—unlike the procedures that lawyers must follow to practice law.
Unauthorized Practice of Law	Giving legal advice, if legal rights may be affected, by anyone not licensed to practice law.
Penalties for the Unauthorized Practice of Law	Some states specifically address the issue of unauthorized practice, making it a criminal offense.

Ethical Duties and Obligations

Expected Behavior	Ethical behavior is expected and required of every member of the legal team: attorney, paralegal, litigation support, information technologist, and outside consultant.
	Ethical obligations of lawyers are enforced by the court in the jurisdiction where the attorney is practicing or where the case is being tried.

Ethical Guidelines and Rules

	Every profession develops a set of guidelines for those in the profession to follow. These may be codes of conduct or ethical guidelines. These codes typically set forth the minimum in ethical behavior—the very least each professional should do.
BA Model Guidelines for e Utilization of Paralegal rvices	A set of guidelines intended to govern the conduct of lawyers when utilizing paralegals or legal assistants.

Uniformity of Paralegal Ethics	No single source of ethical rules is set out for the paralegal. At present, unlike a violation by an attorney of the state-adopted rules that can result in loss of the right to practice (disbarment), no such sanction exists for a paralegal's breach of association rules, except loss of membership.
Ethics Codes of Paralegal Associations	1. National Federation of Paralegal Associations, Inc. 2. National Association of Legal Assistants

Supervision

Duty to Supervise	The obligation to ensure ethical conduct is that of the supervising attorney under the ethical obligation to supervise all who work on the case for the attorney.
Competence	Competent representation requires the legal knowledge, skill, thoroughness, and preparation reasonably necessary for the representation.

The Duty of Confidentiality, Attorney–Client Privilege, and the Work Product Doctrine

Attorney–Client Privilege	1. This privilege is a rule of evidence that applies in cases where the Rules of Evidence apply: a court of law, a deposition, or other places where a witness is under oath, such as interrogatories, responses to requests for documents, or grand jury hearings. 2. The "privilege" belongs to the client, not to the attorney. 3. The person claiming the privilege, usually the client, has the burden to establish the existence of the privilege.
Confidentiality	This is a duty imposed on the attorney and each member of the legal team working under the supervision of the attorney to enable clients to obtain legal advice by allowing the client to freely and openly give the members of the legal team all the relevant facts without fear of disclosure of these facts, except in limited situations, such as to prevent commission of a crime or to defend against a client's suit.
Confidentiality in a Technology Age	Maintaining electronic communications and electronically created and saved documents creates new issues that must be considered to avoid a breach of confidentiality. Limiting access to electronic messages to only those with a need to know is a starting point.
Claim of Privilege	The person claiming the privilege, usually the client, has the burden to establish the existence of the privilege.
Extension of Attorney–Client Privilege to Others	The efficient administration of justice requires the privilege to extend to agents of the attorney.
Self-Defense Exception	Lawyers accused of wrongdoing by their clients must be able to defend themselves, including the use of confidential privileged information because of an inherent right to due process.
Work Product Doctrine	1. The work product doctrine provides a limited protection for material prepared by the attorney or those working for the attorney in anticipation of litigation or for trial. 2. The work product doctrine is different from both the attorney–client privilege and the duty of confidentiality. The attorney–client privilege and the duty of confidentiality relate to information provided by the client regardless of whether the information involves potential litigation.

Exceptions and Limitations to the Work Product Doctrine	The work product doctrine does not cover documents prepared in the normal operation of the client's business, such as sales reports, data analyses, or summaries of business operations.
Exception to the Third-Party Document Exception	Courts have made an exception when a lawyer is trying to find out the other party's strategy by asking about documents already in his/her possession.
Inadvertent Disclosure of Confidential Information	The treatment will depend on the individual jurisdiction. The courts follow no single policy.
Judicial Views	The three judicial views on handling the inadvertent disclosure under the attorney–client privilege are: 1. automatic waiver 2. no waiver 3. balancing test
Conflict of Interest	The basis of the conflict of interest rule is the belief that a person cannot be loyal to two clients whose interests are adverse to one another.
Candor and Fairness in Litigation	
	It is the duty of the advocate to avoid any conduct that undermines the integrity of the process. The duty to the client to persuasively present the case is a duty qualified by the ethical obligation (candor) to not mislead the court or opposing counsel with false statements of law or of facts that the lawyer knows to be false.
Fairness to Opposing Party and Counsel	The ethical rule of fairness to opposing counsel and parties is an attempt to ensure justice is done even if one's client loses the case.
Avoiding UPL	
Avoiding UPL: Holding Oneself Out	Parties with whom the paralegal has contact must know the limited role the paralegal plays on the legal team.
Avoiding UPL: Giving Advice	A paralegal cannot give a legal opinion or legal advice. If legal rights may be affected, it is probably legal advice.
Avoiding UPL: Filling Out Forms	A nonlawyer who explains, recommends, advises, or assists in the selection, completion, and corrections of errors and omissions of legal forms may be guilty of UPL.
Avoiding UPL: Representing Clients	1. Some jurisdictions and administrative agencies do permit those who are not licensed or admitted to practice to appear in court or before administrative law judges or referees on behalf of clients. 2. There is no uniformity among the rules outlining when nonlawyers may represent parties or what specific agencies or courts nonlawyers can appear before. Any appearance before a court must be approved carefully. 3. Even a minor activity, such as a request for continuance of a case, may be considered by some courts to be the practice of law. 4. Some federal agencies specifically permit nonlawyers to appear, such as the Social Security Administration and the U.S. Patent Office.
Avoiding UPL: Guidelines	**Guideline 1** Legal assistants should disclose their status as legal assistants at the outset of any professional relationship with a client, other attorneys, a court or administrative agency or personnel thereof, or members of the general public.

Guideline 2
Legal assistants should not:

1. establish attorney–client relationships, set legal fees, give legal opinions or advice, or represent a client before a court, unless authorized to do so by said court; nor
2. engage in, encourage, or contribute to any act that could constitute the unauthorized practice of law.

Guideline 3
Legal assistants may perform services for an attorney in the representation of a client, provided that:

1. the services performed by the legal assistant do not require the exercise of independent professional legal judgment;
2. the attorney maintains a direct relationship with the client and maintains control of all client matters;
3. the attorney supervises the legal assistant;
4. the attorney remains professionally responsible for all work on behalf of the client, including any actions taken or not taken by the legal assistant in connection therewith.

WORKING THE WEB

1. Download the latest ethics opinions and guidelines from the NALA website at www.NALA.org.
2. Download any ethics updates from the NFPA website at www.paralegal.org.
3. Download a personal reference copy of the Model Rules of Professional Conduct from the ABA Center for Professional Responsibility at www.americanbar.org/cpr.
4. Use a Web browser or search engine to find the URL (Web address) for your state or local bar association website that provides guidance or opinions on legal ethics.
5. Use the Internet to locate the most current version of the ethical rules as used in your jurisdiction. Save the Internet address for future reference.
6. Use the Internet to find ethics opinions or sources of information on ethics in your jurisdiction.

CRITICAL THINKING & WRITING QUESTIONS

1. What is the general theory or rationale for regulating the practice of law? How is this applied?
2. Why is "just giving advice" potentially the unauthorized practice of law?
3. How would regulation of the paralegal profession assure the public of quality legal services?
4. When may nonlawyers represent clients?
5. How can the paralegal avoid UPL?
6. How do unauthorized-practice-of-law statutes protect the public?
7. Why should the paralegal be familiar with the ABA Model Rules of Professional Conduct?
8. How do the ABA Model Guidelines for the Utilization of Legal Assistant Services define the role of the paralegal in the law office?
9. Does a paralegal's violation of the ethics rules of the national paralegal associations have the same impact as attorneys violating the ethical rules on the right to practice?
10. Would a paralegal dating a client have a conflict of interest? How could such a relationship create compromising influences and loyalties?
11. What are the reasons for protecting privileged communications?
12. Under what circumstances might a paralegal have a conflict of interest when taking a new job at a different law firm?
13. What are the potential dangers in paralegals moonlighting?
14. What is a conflict of interest under the Model Rules of Professional Conduct?

15. Does a client have an attorney–client privilege regarding information given to a paralegal during the preparation of a case? Explain.
16. What duty does a paralegal owe to the supervising attorney?
17. How is a paralegal an agent of the client?
18. In a possible conflict of interest, with whom does the ultimate decision rest?
19. Under what circumstance must a lawyer or a paralegal refuse employment?
20. What is required to invoke the attorney–client privilege?
21. What information is covered under the work product doctrine?
22. What is the duty of the trier of fact?
23. What is exculpatory evidence?
24. What is the purpose of ethics?
25. What is the purpose of the confidentiality rule in the legal setting?
26. What is the difference between the duty of confidentiality and the attorney–client privilege?
27. Can the confidentiality between attorney and client be lost? Explain.
28. Can the attorney–client privilege be lost? Explain.
29. What are the judicial approaches to the inadvertent disclosure of confidential information?
30. What ethical guidelines, if any, does your state follow?
31. What is the ethical obligation of a paralegal to the firm's client?
32. What is the ethical obligation of the paralegal to the court?
33. What is the ethical obligation of a litigation support staff member to the client? To the court? Of a litigation support person from an outside firm or consultant? Explain.
34. In addition to the attorney–client relationship, are there other relationships where there is a privilege? Why would it apply to others not in an attorney–client relationship?
35. How is a claim of privilege made?
36. Why is the attorney–client privilege extended to others working for the attorney?
37. What is the purpose of the self-defense exception to the confidentiality rule?
38. Why is conflict of interest an issue for the legal team?
39. What is required to invoke the attorney–client privilege? Explain sufficiently for a non-legal team member to be able to understand.
40. What information is protected by the work product doctrine?
41. Do the ethical rules of "fairness" prevent lawyers from aggressively advocating their client's position?
42. Why would a partner in a law firm be required to supervise the other lawyers in the firm?
43. How can members of the legal team demonstrate that they have been adequately supervised?

Building Paralegal Skills

VIDEO CASE STUDIES

Disclosure of Status

A client is meeting with his new attorney and the attorney's paralegal. He expresses some concerns about the confidentiality of information given to the paralegal.

After viewing the video case study at the book website at www.pearsonhighered.com/careersresources, answer the following:

1. Does the paralegal have a duty to reveal his or her status as a paralegal? Does the supervising attorney have the duty?
2. Is the paralegal bound by the same rules of confidentiality as the lawyer?
3. Is the paralegal covered under the attorney–client privilege?

Confidentiality Issue: Family Exception?

Paralegal Judy meets with her mother in a public coffee shop and tells her mother details of the case she is working on that has her "stressed out."

After viewing the video case study at the book website at www.pearsonhighered.com/careersresources, answer the following:

1. Does being "stressed out" change the rules of confidentiality?

2. Is there a privilege that permits discussing the facts of a case with a family member?
3. Can the facts be discussed if names are left out?

Confidentiality Issue: Public Information

A law firm has a case that has received coverage in the local newspaper. Two of the paralegals from the same law firm are having coffee in a public coffee shop. One of the paralegals, who is not assigned to the case, reads an article about the client and asks her friend, who is working on the case, about the accuracy of the article.

After viewing the video case study at the book website at www.pearsonhighered.com/careersresources, answer the following:

1. How does public disclosure of information about a client or a case change the paralegal's responsibility to maintain confidentiality?
2. Are there any ethical issues in discussing cases in a public area?
3. Is the paralegal who is not working on the case under any duty of confidentiality?

ETHICS ANALYSIS & DISCUSSION QUESTIONS

1. Are paralegals held to the same standard as attorneys when there is no supervising attorney?
2. What is the paralegal's duty to the client when the paralegal's employer breaches its duty to the client?
3. Who is responsible for the quality of the legal work performed for a client—the attorney or the paralegal?
4. Assume you have graduated from a paralegal program at a local college. While you are looking for a job where your talents can be properly utilized, a friend asks you to help him fill out a set of bankruptcy forms using a computer program he purchased at the local office supply megawarehouse. The program is designed to pick out the exemptions after the requested information has been plugged in. See *In Re Kaitangian*, Calif. 218 BR 102 (1998). Is this the unauthorized practice of law?

Paralegal Ethics in Practice

5. Assume you are offered the opportunity to work with a local law firm providing living trust services to the public. Your responsibility would be to make presentations to community groups on the advantages of living trusts. After each session, any interested person would be able to meet with you, and you would fill out the forms, collect the fee, and send the completed form and half the fee collected to the law firm for review and transmittal to the client. You would retain half the amount collected as your fee. See *Cincinnati Bar Assn. v. Kathman*, 92 Ohio St. 3d 92, 748 N.E.2d 1091 (2001). What ethical issues are involved? Explain.

DEVELOPING YOUR COLLABORATION SKILLS

Working on your own or with a group of other students assigned by your instructor, review the scenario at the beginning of the chapter.

1. In a group or individually, identify all the potential ethical issues involved in this scenario.
2. Imagine that a local lawyer who knows both Kathryn and Kelsey is sitting next to them and overhears their conversation. The lawyer then sends a letter to the local Ethics Board. Have one group represent the Ethics Board, one group represent Kathryn's employer, and another group represent Kelsey's employers.
   a. How should the Ethics Board respond?
   b. How should the lawyers Kelsey works for respond?
3. Summarize the advice the group would give to Kathryn and Kelsey and to the law firms that employ them.

PARALEGAL PORTFOLIO EXERCISE

Prepare a memorandum of law for submission to a potential employer, outlining the existing regulations in your state for paralegals and the application of any unauthorized practice of law statutes. Include complete citations to any cases, statutes, or regulations and the Internet addresses of any state or local ethics sites for lawyers and/or paralegals.

LEGAL ANALYSIS & WRITING CASES

In re Aretakis, 791 N.Y.S.2d 687 (App. Div. 2005)

An attorney made certain statements public that were taken from a complaint filed against him with the state committee on disciplinary standards, in violation of the rules on confidentiality of proceeding on complaints against attorneys.

The court stated:

> The Court of Appeals has observed that Judiciary Law § 90 and its counterparts reflect a policy of keeping disciplinary proceedings involving licensed professionals confidential until they are finally determined. The policy serves the purpose of safeguarding information that a potential complainant may regard as private or confidential and thereby removes a possible disincentive to the filing of complaints of professional misconduct. The State's policy also evinces a sensitivity to the possibility of irreparable harm to a professional's reputation resulting from unfounded accusations—a possibility which is enhanced by the more relaxed nature of the [proceedings]. Indeed, professional reputation "once lost, is not easily restored."

Questions

1. Can the reputation of a professional be tarnished by disclosure of unsubstantiated claims of ethical breaches?
2. Once tarnished, can a professional's integrity be reestablished?
3. Is the greater good served by allowing all disciplinary complaints to be made public?

WORKING WITH THE LANGUAGE OF THE COURT CASE

Tegman v. Accident and Medical Investigations

107 Wash App. 868, 30 P.3d 1092, 68 Cal.Rptr. 758 (Wash. Ct. App. 2001) Court of Appeals of Washington, Division One

Read the following case excerpted from the Court of Appeals opinion. Review and brief the case. In your brief, answer the following questions:

1. How does this court define "the practice of law"?
2. What is the standard or duty of care that this court imposes on a paralegal who does not have a supervising attorney?
3. What action does this court suggest that a paralegal take when it becomes clear that there is no supervising attorney?
4. Why should a paralegal contact the supervising attorney immediately upon being given a case to handle?
5. Based on this case, should a paralegal advise the client that he or she is a paralegal? If so, when? Why?

Becker, Mary K., A.C.J.

Between 1989 and 1991, plaintiffs Maria Tegman, Linda Leszynski, and Daina Calixto were each injured in separate and unrelated automobile accidents. After their accidents, each plaintiff retained G. Richard McClellan and Accident & Medical Investigations, Inc. (AMI) for legal counsel and assistance in handling their personal injury claims. Each plaintiff signed a contingency fee agreement with AMI, believing that McClellan was an attorney and AMI a law firm. McClellan has never been an attorney in any jurisdiction. McClellan and AMI employed Camille Jescavage, [a] licensed attorney.

Jescavage learned that McClellan entered into contingency fee agreements with AMI's clients and that McClellan was not an attorney. [Attorneys for AMI] settled a number of cases for AMI, and learned that McClellan processed settlements of AMI cases through his own bank account.

In July 1991, McClellan hired Deloris Mullen as a paralegal. Mullen considered Jescavage to be her supervising attorney, though Jescavage provided little supervision. Jescavage resigned from AMI in the first week of September 1991. McClellan told Mullen that her new supervising attorney would be James Bailey. Mullen did not immediately contact Bailey to confirm that he was her supervising attorney. [He] later told Mullen he was not.

While at AMI, Mullen worked on approximately 50–60 cases, including those of [the] plaintiffs. Mullen was aware of some of McClellan's questionable practices and knew that there were substantial improprieties involved with his operation. Mullen stopped working at AMI on December 6, 1991, when the situation became personally intolerable to her and she obtained direct knowledge that she was without a supervising attorney.

When she left, she did not advise any of the plaintiffs about the problems at AMI. After Mullen left, McClellan settled each plaintiff's case for various amounts without their knowledge or consent, and deposited the funds in his general account by forging their names on the settlement checks.

The "practice of law" clearly does not just mean appearing in court. In a larger sense, it includes "legal advice and counsel, and the preparation of legal instruments and contracts by which legal rights are secured." Mullen contends that her status as a paralegal precludes a finding that she was engaged in the practice of law. She argues that a paralegal is, by definition, someone who works under the supervision of an attorney, and that it is necessarily the attorney, not the paralegal, who is practicing law and owes a duty to the clients. Her argument assumes that she had a supervising attorney.

The trial court's determination that Mullen was negligent was dependent on the court's finding that Mullen knew, or should have known, that she did not have a supervising attorney over a period of several months while she was at AMI. The label "paralegal" is not in itself a shield from liability. A factual evaluation is necessary to distinguish a paralegal who is working under an attorney's supervision from one who is actually practicing law. A finding that a paralegal is practicing law will not be supported merely by evidence of infrequent contact with the supervising attorney.

As long as the paralegal does in fact have a supervising attorney who is responsible for the case, any deficiency in the quality of the supervision or in the quality of the paralegal's work goes to the attorney's negligence, not the paralegal's.

In this case, Mullen testified that she believed James Bailey was her supervising attorney after Jescavage left. The court found Mullen was not justified in that belief. Mullen testified that she had started to distrust McClellan before he informed her that Bailey would be her supervising attorney. Mullen also testified that she did not contact Bailey to confirm that he was supervising her. Bailey testified at a deposition that he did not share Mullen's clients and she did not consult him regarding any of her ongoing cases. He also said that one of the only conversations he remembers having with Mullen with respect to AMI is one where he told her that he was not her supervising attorney after she raised the issue with him. This testimony amply supports the trial court's finding that Mullen was unjustified in her belief that Bailey was her supervising attorney.

[Mullen] continued to send out demand and representation letters after Jescavage left AMI. Letters written by Mullen before Jescavage's departure identify Mullen as a paralegal after her signature, whereas letters she wrote after Jescavage's departure lacked such identification. Even after Mullen discovered, in late November 1991, that Bailey was not her supervising attorney, she wrote letters identifying "this office" as representing the plaintiffs, neglecting to mention that she was a paralegal and that no attorney was responsible for the case. This evidence substantially supports the finding that Mullen engaged in the practice of law.

Accordingly, we conclude the trial court did not err in following *Bowers* and holding Mullen to the duty of an attorney. The duty of care owed by an attorney is that degree of care, skill, diligence, and knowledge commonly possessed and exercised by a reasonable, careful, and prudent lawyer in the practice of law in Washington.

The court found that the standard of care owed by an attorney, and therefore also by Mullen, required her to notify the plaintiffs of: (1) the serious problems concerning the accessibility of their files to persons who had no right to see them, (2) the fact that client settlements were not processed through an attorney's trust account but, rather, McClellan's own account, (3) the fact that McClellan and AMI, as nonlawyers, had no right to enter into contingent fee agreements with clients and receive contingent fees, (4) the fact that McClellan was, in fact, engaged in the unlawful

(continued)

practice of law, and that, generally, (5) the clients of McClellan and AMI were at substantial risk of financial harm as a result of their association with AMI. Mullen breached her duty to her clients in all of these particulars.

We conclude the finding is supported by substantial evidence. Accordingly, the trial court did not err in concluding that Mullen was negligent.

Although Mullen was a paralegal, she is held to an attorney's standard of care because she worked on the plaintiffs' cases during a period of several months when she had no supervising attorney. The fact that she did not render legal advice directly does not excuse her; in fact, her failure to advise the plaintiffs of the improper arrangements at AMI is the very omission that breached her duty. Under these circumstances it is not unjust to hold her accountable as a legal cause of the plaintiffs' injuries. As all the elements of negligence have been established, we affirm the judgment against Mullen.

Affirmed.

WE CONCUR: AGID, J., COLEMAN, J.

This case also was scheduled to be published in the Washington Appellate Reports, and if cited in the courts of Washington, would require that citation as well. This case has a Lexis number of 2001 Wash. App. LEXIS 1890.

RUBIN V. ENNS

23 S.W.3d 382 (Texs. App.-Amarillo 2000)
Texas Court of Appeals, Seventh District

1. Does the court's "rebuttable presumption" test work? Would any other test work better?
2. Using the court's "rebuttable presumption" test, would there be some temptation on the part of the second law firm to obtain confidential information that the paralegal learned at the first law firm?
3. Do the ethics standards of the American Bar Association and paralegal associations adequately address the ethical conflicts that paralegals face? Discuss.

FACTS

Inda Crawford was employed as a legal assistant by the law firm of Hicks, Thomas & Lilienstern (HTL) for a number of years prior to May 1999. During her employment with the HTL law firm, HTL represented Michael Rubin and other real estate agents in a lawsuit against Westgate Petroleum and other defendants. Crawford worked on this case as a legal assistant for HTL and billed 170 hours of work on the case.

In May 1999, Crawford left her employment at HTL and went to work for the law firm Templeton, Smithee, Hayes, Fields, Young & Heinrich (Templeton). Templeton represented Westgate Petroleum and the other defendants in the previously mentioned lawsuit. Rubin and the other real estate agents in this case filed a writ of mandamus with trial court judge the Honorable Ron Enns to have the Templeton firm disqualified as counsel for Westgate et al. because Crawford had now switched firms.

Rubin argued that because Crawford had previously worked on the case for the HTL firm, the opposing counsel she now worked for should be disqualified from representing the opposing side in the lawsuit. The trial court judge denied the petitioners' writ of mandamus. The petitioners appealed.

ISSUE

Should the writ of mandamus be approved disqualifying a law firm that represents one side of a lawsuit because a legal assistant who worked for the law firm that represented the other side of the lawsuit has now switched firms and works for the law firm sought to be disqualified?

BOYD, CHIEF JUSTICE

In *Phoenix Founders, Inc. v. Marshall*, 887 S.W.2d 831, 835 (Tex. 1994), the court had occasion to discuss at some length circumstances such as the one before us in which a paralegal has changed employment from a law firm on one side of a case to a law firm on the other side of the case. In doing so, it recognized the countervailing interests involved and noted with approval the ABA suggestion that any restrictions on the nonlawyer's employment should be held to the minimum standard necessary to protect confidentiality of client information. In the course of its discussion, the court held that a paralegal or legal assistant who changes employment and who has worked on a case is subject to a conclusive presumption that confidences and secrets were imparted. While the presumption that a legal assistant obtained confidential information is not rebuttable, the presumption that the information was shared with a new employer is rebuttable.

Such distinction was created to ensure that a nonlawyer's mobility would not be unduly restricted. However, the court emphasized that the only way the rebuttable presumption could be overcome would be (1) to instruct the legal assistant not to work on any matter on which the paralegal worked during the prior employment, or regarding which the paralegal had information relating to the former employer's representation; and (2) "to take other reasonable steps to ensure that the paralegal does not work in connection with the matters on which the paralegal worked during the prior employment, absent client consent."

The trial court also had before it copies of a May 17, 1999, memo from Joe Hayes, managing partner of the Templeton firm, addressed to all the lawyers and staff of the Templeton firm. In the memo, Hayes designated two cases (one of which underlies this proceeding) as those about which Crawford might possess confidential information. In the memo, the recipients were instructed that Texas Disciplinary Rules 1.05(b)(1) and 5.03(a) prohibited them, as Crawford's supervising employers, "from revealing any confidential information she might have regarding the cases." The memo also advised that to satisfy the requirements of the Disciplinary Rules, as well as those set forth by the Supreme Court in the *In Re American Home Products Corporation* case, the firm was implementing the following six policies and procedures, effective immediately:

1. Inda shall not perform any work or take any action in connection with the Westgate case or the Seger case [the second, unrelated, case].
2. Inda shall not discuss the Westgate case or the Seger case, or disclose any information she has concerning these cases, with anyone.
3. No lawyer or staff member shall discuss the Westgate case or the Seger case with Inda, or in her presence.
4. All computer information relating to the Westgate case and the Seger case shall be removed from the firm's computer system. No future information concerning either the Westgate case or the Seger case shall be stored in any electronic medium but, rather, kept solely in hard copy form with the files in the respective case.
5. The files in the Westgate case and the Seger case shall be kept in locked files under my supervision. No one shall have access to those files other than me, and those to whom I have given specific authority to access these files. Inda shall not have access to these files or the area where the files are to be maintained. At the close of each business day, all documents relating to these cases shall be placed in their respective files, which shall be returned to their storage places, which shall then be locked.
6. Inda shall not be given access to any of the files pertaining to the Westgate case or the Seger case, or their contents. None of the documents pertaining to either of these cases shall be disclosed to Inda, discussed with her, or discussed in her presence.

Our review of the record before the trial court convinces us that we cannot say he abused his discretion in arriving at his decision to deny the motion to disqualify the Templeton law firm. Accordingly, realtors' petition seeking mandamus relief must be, and is, denied.

DECISION AND REMEDY

The Court of Appeals affirmed the trial court's denial of the writ of mandamus, thus permitting Crawford to work for the second law firm, which had imposed sufficient safeguards to ensure that confidential information obtained at the first law firm was not disclosed to the second law firm.

The court also may find that the lower court has made an error that can be corrected, by sending the case back to the lower court, and remand the case to the lower court, to take additional action or conduct further proceedings. For example, the lower court may be directed to hold further proceedings in which a jury hears testimony related to the issue of damages and makes an award of monetary damages.

An appellate court will reverse a lower court decision if it finds an error of law [in] the record. An error of law occurs if the jury was improperly instructed by the trial court judge, prejudicial evidence was admitted at trial when it should have been excluded, prejudicial evidence was obtained through an unconstitutional search and seizure, and the like. An appellate court will not reverse a finding of fact unless such finding is unsupported by the evidence or is contradicted by the evidence.

(continued)

JANSON V. LEGALZOOM.COM, INC.

802 F. Supp. 2d 1053; 2011 U.S. Dist. LEXIS 84939; 87 A.L.R.6th 757

United States District Court for the Western District of Missouri, Central Division

1. What service may LegalZoom provide that does not violate the unauthorized practice of law (UPL) statute?
2. What role does technology have in determining the UPL?
3. What specific conduct did the court determine was the UPL?

I. Background

A. Relevant Uncontroverted Facts

. . . LegalZoom maintains a website—www.legalzoom.com—which offers online legal document forms and services.

First, LegalZoom's website offers blank legal forms that customers may download, print, and fill in themselves. . . .

In addition to such blank forms, LegalZoom's website also offers an internet portal, which is the subject of this dispute. With respect to the services offered through the internet portal, . . .

Among the legal documents available through LegalZoom's internet portal are business formation documents, estate planning documents, pet protection agreements, and copyright, trademark, and patent applications. After making an initial selection, the customer enters answers to questions via a "branching intake mechanism" (or decision tree), referred to on the website as an "online questionnaire." Customers type in answers to the questions contained in the online questionnaire. In some cases, customers select an alternative from a list of choices or checkboxes provided by LegalZoom. The branching mechanism skips questions for sections of the questionnaire that are inapplicable based on the customer's prior answers. For example, the questionnaire for a last will and testament asks if the customer has children; if the customer's answer is "no," questions about the customer's children are skipped and the customer is taken to a different next question than if the customer's answer had been "yes."

The online questionnaire process is fully automated. No LegalZoom employee offers or gives personal guidance on answering the questions, although information relevant to the customer's choice sometimes appears on the screen. For example, when completing the questionnaire to purchase a last will and testament, a question appears: "Would you like to protect your personal representative from liability?" After the question, there appears on the screen: "How did most people answer this question?" followed by "yes."

When the customer has completed the online questionnaire, LegalZoom's software creates a completed data file containing the customer's responses. A LegalZoom employee then reviews that data file for completeness, spelling and grammatical errors, and consistency of names, addresses, and other factual information. If the employee spots a factual error or inconsistency, the customer is contacted and may choose to correct or clarify the answer.

After the review of the data file, LegalZoom's software automatically enters the information provided by the customer via the online questionnaire into the LegalZoom template that corresponds with the type of document sought by the customer. LegalZoom's templates include standardized language created by attorneys (licensed outside the state of Missouri) to apply to common consumer and business situations. The software also removes sections of the template that are inapplicable based on the customer's answers to the [*1056] questionnaire. For instance, if a customer has answered that she has no children in responding to the online questionnaire for a last will, no provisions for bequests to children are included in the final document. All information [**6] entered by a customer (other than payment and shipping) is used by the software to fill in LegalZoom's template. In other words, the software does not edit or select from the information entered by the customer.

After the customer's data has been input into the template, a LegalZoom employee reviews the final document for quality in formatting—e.g., correcting word processing "widows," "orphans," page breaks, and the like. The employee then prints and ships the final, unsigned document to the customer. In rare cases, upon request, the document is emailed to the customer. . . .

As Plaintiffs have stated, the overarching issue in this case is whether Defendant LegalZoom has violated Missouri law by engaging in the unauthorized practice of law. . . .

Mo. Rev. Stat. § 484.020. Section 484.010 provides:

1. The "practice of the law" is hereby defined to be and is the appearance as an advocate in a representative capacity or the drawing of papers, pleadings or documents or the performance of any act in such capacity in connection with proceedings pending or prospective before any court of record, commissioner, referee or any body, board, committee or commission constituted by law or having authority to settle controversies.
2. The "law business" is hereby defined to be and is the advising or counseling for a valuable consideration of any person, firm, association, or corporation as to any secular law or the drawing or the procuring of or assisting in the drawing for a valuable consideration of any paper, document or instrument affecting or relating to secular rights or the doing of any act for a valuable consideration in a representative capacity, obtaining or tending to obtain or securing or tending to secure for any person, firm, association or corporation any property or property rights whatsoever....

C. The Missouri Supreme Court's Interpretation of the Unauthorized Practice of Law

The Missouri Supreme Court has repeatedly emphasized that the "judicial branch of government has the power to regulate the practice of law." *In re Thompson*, 574 S.W.2d 365, 366 (Mo. 1978)....

When applying Missouri's unauthorized practice of law statute, the Missouri Supreme Court has written:

This [statutory] definition of "law business" . . . is adequate for the issue before us, [but] it should also be noted that it is impossible to lay down an exhaustive definition of "the practice of law." . . . In any event, the General Assembly may only assist the judiciary by providing penalties for the unauthorized practice of law, the ultimate definition of which is always within the province of this Court....

Thus, to apply Missouri's unauthorized practice of law statute, this Court must decide whether LegalZoom's conduct fits within the Missouri Supreme Court's definition of the unauthorized practice of law.

1. Hulse and Thompson

Two foundational cases are cited throughout the Missouri Supreme Court's jurisprudence on the unauthorized practice of law.... *Hulse v. Criger*, 363 Mo. 26, 247 S.W.2d 855 (Mo. 1952) (en banc), which generally involve businesses providing a legal document preparation service for their customers.

Meanwhile, Defendant LegalZoom argues that its website providing access to online document assembly software is the functional equivalent of the "do-it-yourself" divorce kit approved for sale by the Missouri Supreme Court in *Thompson*, 574 S.W.2d at 366.

In 1952, the Missouri Supreme Court decided *Hulse*, explaining that its regulation of the unauthorized practice of law "is not to protect the Bar from competition but to protect the public from being advised or represented in legal matters by incompetent or unreliable persons." *Hulse*....

Thompson relied most heavily on the Florida Supreme Court's reasoning in *Florida Bar v. Brumbaugh*, 355 So.2d 1186 (Fla. 1978). Thompson quoted Brumbaugh's holding as follows:

We hold that Ms. Brumbaugh, and others in similar situations, may sell printed material purporting to explain legal practice and procedure to the public in general and she may sell sample legal forms.... In addition, Ms. Brumbaugh may advertise her business activities of providing secretarial and notary services and selling legal forms and general printed information. However, Marilyn Brumbaugh must not, in conjunction with her business, engage in advising clients as to the various remedies available to them, or otherwise assist them in preparing those forms necessary for a dissolution proceeding.

Although Marilyn Brumbaugh never held herself out as an attorney, it is clear that her clients placed some reliance upon her to properly prepare the necessary legal forms for their dissolution proceedings. To this extent we believe that Ms. Brumbaugh overstepped proper bounds and engaged in the unauthorized practice of law.... While Marilyn Brumbaugh may legally sell forms ... and type up instruments which have been completed by clients, she must not engage in personal legal assistance in conjunction with her business activities, including the correction of errors and omissions.

... While *Thompson* did not involve notary services of any kind, it reached a similar conclusion as *Brumbaugh* with respect to the sale of legal self-help

(continued)

goods: "[T]he advertisement and sale by the respondents of the divorce kits does not constitute the unauthorized practice of law so long as the respondents and other[s] similarly situated refrain from giving personal advice as to legal remedies or the consequences flowing therefrom." *Thompson*.... Thus, it became the law in Missouri, as it is in other jurisdictions, that the practice of law does not include the sale of "do-it-yourself" kits, which include blank legal forms and general instructions. . . .

...3. Application of Missouri Law to LegalZoom's Conduct

In its Motion for Summary Judgment, ... the Court must decide whether a reasonable juror could conclude that LegalZoom did engage in the unauthorized practice of law, as it has been defined by the Missouri Supreme Court....

... It is uncontroverted that Defendant LegalZoom's website performs two distinct functions. First, the website offers blank legal forms that customers may download, print, and fill in themselves.... Such a "do-it-yourself" kit puts the legal forms into the hands of the customers, facilitating the right to pro se representation.

It is the second function of LegalZoom's website that goes beyond mere general instruction. LegalZoom's internet portal is not like the "do-it-yourself" divorce kit in *Thompson*. Rather, LegalZoom's internet portal service is based on the opposite notion: we'll do it for you. Although the named Plaintiffs never believed that they were receiving legal advice while using the LegalZoom website, LegalZoom's advertisements shed some light on the manner in which LegalZoom takes legal problems out of its customers' hands. While stating that it is not a "law firm" (yet "provide[s] self-help services"), LegalZoom reassures consumers that "we'll prepare your legal documents," and that "LegalZoom takes over" once customers "answer a few simple online questions."

None of the Missouri Supreme Court cases cited by the parties are directly on point, due to the novelty of the technology at issue here. However, the weight of the authority that does exist indicates that businesses may not charge fees for a legal document preparation service, although they may sell goods—including blank forms and general instructions—to facilitate the consumer's own preparation of legal documents. The "do-it-yourself" divorce kit in *Thompson*, upon which Defendant relies so heavily, was not a service but purely a product. Thompson did not even address the question of document preparation in *Thompson* because the issue was not before it—the purchaser of the kit prepared the document, not the company that sold the kit.

Thompson relied heavily on *Brumbaugh*, where the Florida Supreme Court allowed not only the sale of self-help legal goods, but also allowed for parallel notary services. Nonetheless, *Brumbaugh* held that the notary could only "type up instruments which have been completed by clients," and could not "assist them in preparing those forms" or otherwise "engage in personal legal assistance in conjunction with her business activities, including the correction of errors and omissions." *Brumbaugh*....

Here, LegalZoom's internet portal offers consumers not a piece of self-help merchandise, but a legal document service which goes well beyond the role of a notary or public stenographer. The kit in *Thompson* offered page upon page of detailed instructions but left it to the purchaser to select the provisions applicable to their situation. The purchaser understood that it was their responsibility to get it right. In contrast, LegalZoom says: "Just answer a few simple online questions and LegalZoom takes over. You get a quality legal document filed for you by real helpful people." ... Thus, LegalZoom's internet portal sells more than merely a good (i.e., a kit for self-help) but also a service (i.e., preparing that legal document). Because those that provide that service are not authorized to practice law in Missouri, there is a clear risk of the public being served in legal matters by "incompetent or unreliable persons." *Hulse*, ... "Our purpose must be to make sure that legal services required by the public, and [e] ssential to the administration of justice, will be rendered by those who have been found by investigation to be properly prepared to do so ... " Id.

That Defendant's legal document service is delivered through the internet is not the problem. The internet is merely a medium, and LegalZoom's sale of blank forms over the internet does not constitute the unauthorized practice of law. Nor would LegalZoom be engaging in the unauthorized practice of law if it sold general instructions to accompany those blank forms over the internet (as may already be the case).

LegalZoom's legal document preparation service goes beyond self-help because of the role played by its human employees, not because of the internet medium. LegalZoom employees intervene at numerous stages of the so-called "self-help services." ... First, after the customer has completed the online questionnaire, a LegalZoom employee reviews the data file for completeness, spelling and grammatical errors, and consistency of names, addresses, and other factual information. If the employee spots a factual error or inconsistency, the customer is contacted and may choose to correct or clarify the answer. Later in the process, after the reviewed information is inserted into LegalZoom's template, a LegalZoom employee reviews the final document for quality in formatting—e.g., correcting word processing "widows," "orphans," page breaks, and the like. Next, an employee prints and ships the final, unsigned document to the customer. Finally, customer service is available to LegalZoom customers by email and telephone. . . .

LegalZoom does maintain that the documents "do not affect any rights at all before the customers themselves sign, execute, and (in some cases) file them." ...

Defendant's argument on this narrow point does not withstand scrutiny. The statute prohibits, inter alia, "assisting in the drawing for a valuable consideration of any paper, document or instrument affecting or relating to secular rights. . ." Mo. Rev. Stat. § 484.010.2. In other words, there is no requirement that secular rights be affected the moment the document is produced. If that were the case, then the non-lawyers in Eisel, Carpenter, and Hulse could have simply left the room before the legal documents were signed to avoid Missouri's regulation of the practice of law. Moreover, the paper, document, or instrument can either affect or relate to secular rights. . . . Mo. Rev. Stat. § 484.010.2.

Because Defendant fails to rebut Plaintiffs' claim that the papers, documents, or instruments at issue here "affect[ ] or relat[e] to secular rights," id.—which is quite clear, based on the undisputed facts—the Motion for Partial Summary Judgment is granted.

VIRTUAL LAW OFFICE EXPERIENCE MODULES

If your instructor has instructed you to complete assignments in the Virtual Law Office program, complete the Virtual Law Office assignments as assigned by your instructor. These assignments are designed to develop your workplace skills. Completing the assignments for this chapter will result in producing the following documents for inclusion in your portfolio:

VLOE 2.1	Office memo on the ethical obligation of confidentiality and the rules of attorney–client privilege
VLOE 2.2	Checklist of guidelines to avoiding UPL, including how a paralegal or secretary should answer questions from clients and potential clients

CHAPTER

3

The Paralegal Workplace

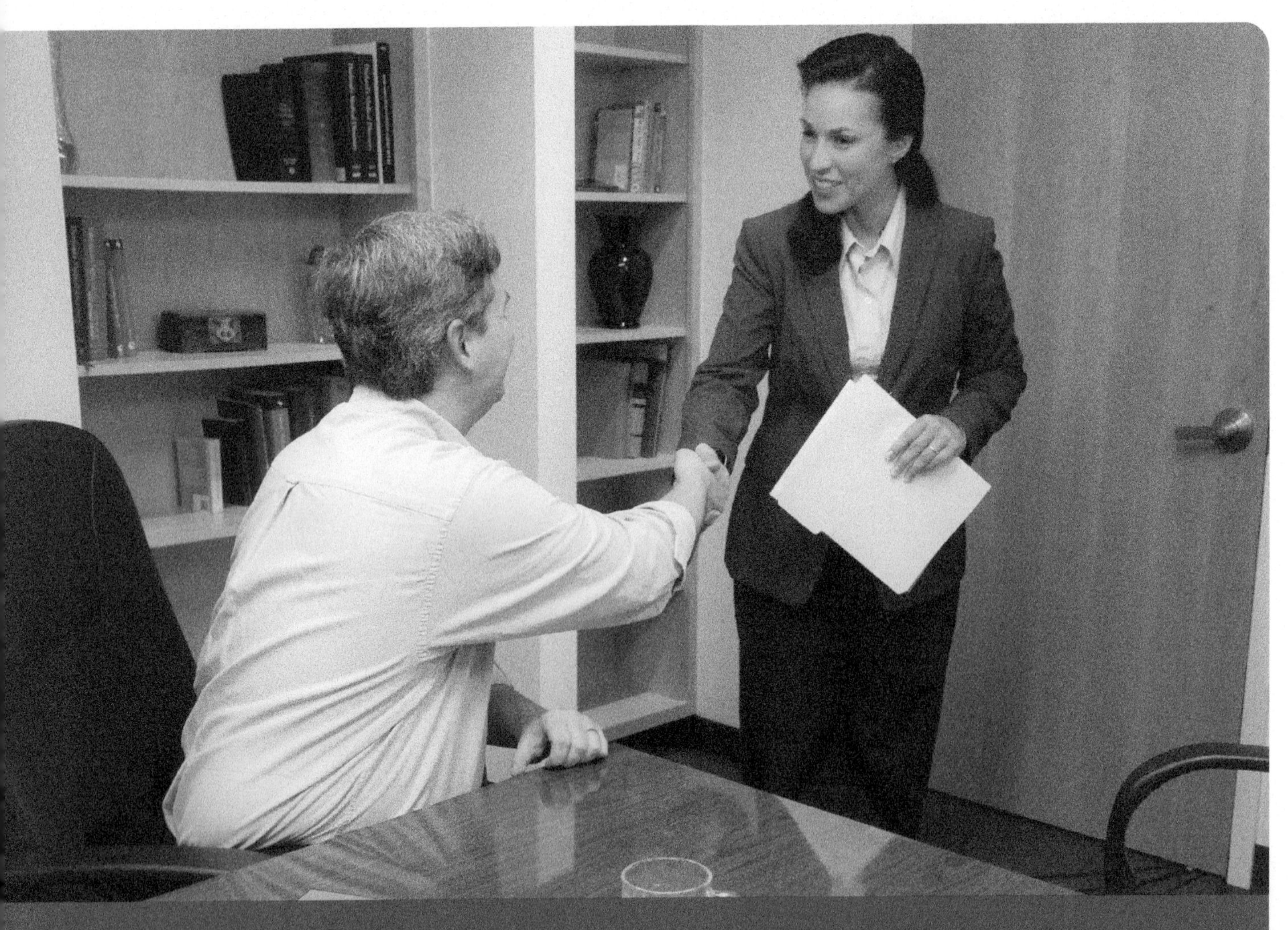

LEARNING OBJECTIVES

After studying this chapter, you should be able to:

1. Describe the different types of practice arrangements of lawyers and law firms.
2. Describe the tasks and functions performed by paralegals.
3. Describe the administrative procedures found in most law offices.
4. Prepare a traditional résumé and an electronic résumé.
5. Plan for a successful job interview.

Paralegals at Work

Law Offices
Goldenberg, Bradley, and Luria

INTEROFFICE MEMO

TO: Natasha Weiser
FROM: Cary Moritz, Office Manager
SUBJECT: Mentoring for New Hires

All of us at Goldenberg, Bradley, and Luria welcome you to our firm. We know you had other job opportunities but believe you will be professionally satisfied and challenged by working here.

The paralegal profession has changed dramatically since I first started in this field, and the one thing we can count on is more change. Please know that you can call on me at any time for advice and guidance. No question is too big or too small.

After all these years, I have seen a number of major changes in the profession. When I started out, we were hired based on keyboarding skills and basically operated as secretaries. Today, more and more lawyers treat us as a part of the legal team and demand of us as much, if not more, than they do new law graduates.

In your new job as a paralegal for Goldenberg, Bradley, and Luria, you frequently will represent our firm as the client's first point of contact and be responsible for conducting initial interviews with clients. As you prepare your interview strategies, please use me as a sounding board. It is important to build rapport so clients will feel comfortable sharing sensitive and personal information with someone who is, at first, a complete stranger. As time goes on, clients often become most comfortable with the paralegal assigned to their case.

As a paralegal, you will be expected to follow a case and do much of the administrative work, such as keeping track of the time and costs associated with each case. Bookkeeping and accounting skills can be a real plus! When I first started, I did only litigation work. When the lawyers in my firm found out that I had been a bookkeeper and had taken accounting classes, I was asked not only to work in

> "A lawyer's time and advice are his stock in trade."
>
> *Abraham Lincoln*

the estates area but also was given responsibility for some of the in-office accounting. This is something to think about as you develop your professional skill set. Getting a bachelor's degree eventually led to my job as an office manager. Additional education is always a plus!

Please know that you can count on me to help you succeed in the present and also to plan and prepare for future endeavors here at Goldenberg, Bradley, and Luria.

Consider the issues involved in this scenario as you read the chapter.

INTRODUCTION TO THE PARALEGAL WORKPLACE

As the paralegal profession has evolved, so too have the duties and roles of the paralegal within the legal system and elsewhere. The earliest legal assistants were probably legal secretaries who developed specialized skills while working for an attorney in one of the legal specialties. As the need for specialized skills became more obvious, legal assistant programs and paralegal programs were created to teach the requisite skills.

In the classic sense, a paralegal performs those tasks and activities that assist the supervising attorney in representing clients. In the broader view, the paralegal performs many of the same functions that attorneys perform, under the supervision of an attorney but limited by laws and regulations on the unauthorized practice of law (UPL). The paralegal's actual tasks and functions vary according to the type of practice, size of the firm or organization, and skill of the individual paralegal.

Arrangements and Organization of Law Offices and Firms

LEARNING OBJECTIVE 1
Describe the different types of practice arrangements of lawyers and law firms.

The classic image of the law firm was of the sole practitioner working alone in a small office in a small town. The more modern view portrayed in movies and on TV is that of a large national or global law firm. In between are small partnerships and other types of organizations in which paralegals work—corporations, insurance companies, government agencies, and consulting firms composed of accountants, lawyers, and management consultants.

Solo Practice

Solo practice One lawyer practicing alone without the assistance of other attorneys.

A **solo practice** is one lawyer practicing alone without the assistance of other attorneys. Solo practitioners still exist, not only in small towns but in large metropolitan areas as well. The solo practitioner may be the type of employer who depends most on the skills of the paralegal in running the office, working with clients, and assisting at trial. A solo practice offers perhaps the greatest challenge and opportunity for the paralegal who wishes to be involved in every aspect of a law practice. Tasks that otherwise might be assigned to an associate will fall to the paralegal to perform.

In a litigation practice or a practice in which the attorney is frequently out of the office to attend meetings, the paralegal becomes the main point of contact and the coordinator between clients and the attorney. In solo practices, jobs that might be done in larger firms by an accounting staff, such as preparation of payroll and maintenance of client escrow accounts, frequently are done by the paralegal. Many solo practitioners consider their paralegal to be a key resource in the practice of law.

Small Offices

Small offices may consist of individual practitioners sharing space, or partnerships. For the small practitioner, the cost of maintaining an adequate law library, conference room, office space, and office equipment can be significant. Therefore, small firms frequently share these common services while separating client practices. The lawyers may work in similar fields, such as criminal law or family law, or they may have practices that are very different, such as estate law and insurance defense work. Depending upon the arrangement, the practitioners might refer clients to one another, but each attorney is personally responsible for the client and the client relationship.

Small offices Small-office arrangements ranging from individual practitioners sharing space to partnerships.

Depending upon the arrangement, personnel such as a receptionist, secretary, or paralegal might be shared. In these situations the paralegal must be certain which of the attorneys is the supervising attorney with regard to each client. The paralegal who is working for more than one attorney in a sharing arrangement might be privy to confidential information that may not be shared with the other attorneys in the office unless they are working on the same case. In some respects, this can be thought of as an "ethical wall" environment. At the very least, the paralegal and the attorneys must clearly understand the ethical issues involved.

Partnerships

A **partnership** may consist of two or more persons who have joined together to share ownership of a business and any profit or loss from that business. Each of the partners has responsibility for the other partner and the practice. Partnerships in small-office arrangements may be "true" partnerships, sharing all aspects of the practice, or they may be partnerships in name only. In the latter case, the paralegal must consider the same ethical issues as in other office-sharing arrangements.

Partnership Two or more persons or corporations that have joined together to share ownership and profit or loss.

Within a partnership, a paralegal may work for more than one of the partners, and in effect, the partners share the paralegal's services. This can be difficult for the paralegal when two or more of the partners demand something at the same time, with the same sense of urgency. The fact that each of the partners will consider him- or herself to be "the boss" can create a delicate situation for the paralegal.

A common solution in many offices is for one of the partners to be the primary supervising attorney for the paralegal, through whom the other partners funnel work requests. From an ethical point of view, this delineates which attorney is the supervising attorney for the clients and files the paralegal concentrates on and at the same time clarifies the lawyers' responsibilities under the rules of professional conduct.

Large Offices

Many of the **large law offices** that exist today grew from smaller, more traditional law offices. These firms expanded over the years, adding partners and associates along the way. At one time, these larger law firms were regional, confined to major cities such as New York, Chicago, Philadelphia, and Los Angeles. As the national economy grew and corporate clients expanded around the country, many firms established offices in other large cities, giving them a presence in different regions. The growth of the global economy has taken large firms one step further, with some establishing offices in foreign countries. As a result, the large law firms have taken on the characteristics of large corporations, with some firms merging to add to their specialty areas of the law and expand the availability of legal services.

Large law offices Large law offices are an outgrowth of traditional law offices that have expanded over the years, adding partners and associates along the way.

For the paralegal, the large office can be an exciting and dynamic area of practice. The paralegal might work with clients who have diverse backgrounds or are located in other regions or countries; some cases may require paralegals to travel on their own or with other members of the legal team. For clients, one of the values of a large law firm is the availability of a number of legal specialties within one legal services provider. For the paralegal, this offers the opportunity to work in different legal fields.

Working in a large law firm also has some disadvantages. There may be fewer opportunities to form personal relationships with clients and other members of the

ETHICAL PERSPECTIVE

Lawyers Who Share Offices

It is "impermissible for unaffiliated attorneys to have unrestricted access to each other's electronic files (including email and word-processing documents) and other client records. If separate computer systems are not utilized, each attorney's confidential client information should be protected in a way that guards against unauthorized access and preserves client confidences and secrets."

Source: District of Columbia Ethics Opinion 303.

legal team. In some firms, just as in any large organization, "playing politics" also becomes an issue. A paralegal's status, as well as some of the perks and benefits of the job, may depend on the status of the individual's supervising attorney. At the same time, the opportunities for advancement in a large firm might outweigh the disadvantages.

Unlike the small office, in which the paralegal might serve as bookkeeper, office manager, receptionist, and second chair in litigation, a large firm typically hires support staff for each of these functions. Bookkeeping or accounting departments usually handle payroll, check requests, and other financial issues. In the larger firms, even the job of making copies takes place in a duplicating department, and the firm might have a mailroom for handling incoming and outgoing mail.

The large law firm also has specialized components to provide different types of services. Law firms in the United States frequently have litigation specialists who spend their time in actual litigation of cases, while other attorneys within the same firm rarely, if ever, go to court. The role of the latter is to work with clients and, when the need arises, prepare materials for the litigation department. In some ways this is similar to the structure of the English legal system, in which one type of lawyer, called a "solicitor," deals directly with clients, and a different type of lawyer, called a "barrister," litigates the cases.

Just as the law has become more complex, lawyers also have come to specialize in narrow areas of practice such as environmental law, intellectual property law, health-care law, insurance law, tort law, and family law. This means that paralegals in large law firms also become specialists within their supervising attorney's primary field. Large firms encourage clients to use the firm for all of their legal needs, so a lawyer in the firm frequently refers clients to other specialists within the firm while remaining the primary contact with those clients. Some firms have lawyers whose expertise is in getting new clients. These lawyers, often former politicians and government officials, frequently are referred to as the "rainmakers." They use their network of contacts to obtain clients and then refer the clients to the specialists within the firm.

Compensation for attorneys within large firms is generally based on how much new business the attorney has brought in, as well as how many billable hours the supervising attorneys and their paralegals have been able to bill. In this kind of environment, the paralegal who is able to maintain strong relationships with clients is an invaluable asset to the firm.

General Practice

General law practice A practice that handles all types of cases.

A **general law practice** is one that handles all types of cases. This is the type of practice many people think of as the small-town lawyer—the generalist to whom everyone in town goes for advice. The reality is that generalists practice in cities as well as in small towns throughout the country. Their practices are as diverse as the law itself, handling everything from adoptions to zoning appeals. As general practitioners, they serve a function in law similar to that of the general family practice doctor in medicine.

Lawyers in this type of practice often work in several areas of law within the same day—attending a hearing in small-claims court in the morning, preparing a will before lunch, having a lunch meeting with an opposing attorney to discuss settlement of an accident case, helping someone who is forming a corporation, and in the evening, appearing at a municipal government meeting to seek a zoning approval. For many, the general practice is the most exciting type of practice, with a continually changing clientele offering all sorts of legal challenges. The paralegal in this environment has the opportunity to work with many different types of clients on many different types of legal matters. The challenge in this type of practice is to stay current in each of the areas the attorney practices.

Specialty Practice

A **specialty practice** is involved in one area of law. Lawyers with specialty backgrounds, such as engineering, might choose to work in patent or intellectual property law. Those coming into the legal profession with accounting backgrounds might specialize in tax matters. Others have special interests and passions, such as working with senior citizens in an elder law practice or protecting the interests of children as child advocates or practicing criminal law.

Specialty practice A specialty practice is involved in practice in one area of law.

Because of the increasing complexity of the law, legal specialists frequently receive referrals from attorneys in general practice or in other specialties. The paralegal working for a specialist often acquires such a high level of knowledge in a specific area that it may rival that of many general practitioners. One of the dangers for the paralegal with this extent of specialty knowledge is that other attorneys could ask the paralegal for answers to questions in that specialty where the answers border on, or actually result in, the unauthorized practice of law.

Paralegals *in* Practice

PARALEGAL PROFILE

Ann W. Price

Ann W. Price, RP, has been a paralegal for over 25 years, working in different-sized law firms in diverse practice areas. Ann is currently employed as a Litigation Paralegal Specialist in the U.S. Department of Justice's Environment and Natural Resources Division in Washington, D.C. She is a PACE™ Registered Paralegal, which means she has passed the Paralegal Advance Competency Exam, a certification test developed by the National Federation of Paralegal Associations (NFPA).

In my first few paralegal positions, I was either the only paralegal in the office or one of two paralegals supporting several attorneys. Because these were small law firms, I was given a large degree of responsibility right from the start. I routinely prepared client correspondence, assisted with discovery (gathering and managing evidence), interviewed clients, and attended trials.

Next, I worked in larger law firms, specializing in food and drug law and environmental law. As a food and drug law paralegal, I researched congressional reports, the *Federal Register*, and other news and legal databases to summarize findings that might be of interest to the firm's clients. As an environmental law paralegal, I worked on all phases of discovery, trial preparation, and arbitration proceedings in Superfund cases that mostly involved municipal landfill cleanups.

My next two jobs were both related to paralegal management for large law firms with hundreds of attorneys. In one of these positions, I was an active paralegal in addition to my management duties. Eventually, I became a paralegal manager where my duties were entirely managerial. I currently work for the U.S. Department of Justice's Environment and Natural Resources Division, where I provide litigation support to approximately 60 attorneys.

There are pros and cons in every type of legal work setting. Paralegals in large law firms are usually paid a larger salary, but the work they perform is often far less substantive than the work performed by paralegals in smaller firms. Large firms often give the most substantive work to the associate attorneys, particularly those right out of law school. In smaller firms, every person is expected to be able to meet any need the case requires. Also, in larger firms, there is often pressure to meet a specified number of client billable hours; many smaller law firms do not even set a minimum.

In my various jobs, the basic skills used and the work performed did not change significantly from practice area to practice area. However, the terminology and legal resources varied considerably. Continuing legal education opportunities are more prevalent in larger law firms than smaller ones. In smaller firms, education is generally limited to on-the-job training. Most law firms in the metro D.C. area, particularly the large ones, require a four-year degree, and many want a paralegal certificate as well. Individuals with two-year degrees are more likely to find employment at smaller firms, at least for their first paralegal job.

Because specialty law practices are often dependent on referrals from other firms, there is a natural tendency for paralegals in these specialties to accommodate referring attorneys by trying to answer questions of a legal nature. To avoid a potential claim of unauthorized practice of law, the paralegal must diplomatically avoid giving legal advice, even to an attorney from another firm.

A primary job function for the paralegal in a specialty practice is maintaining relationships with other law firms and their paralegals and secretaries. The paralegal obtains referrals for the supervising attorney and the firm as a result of relationships developed in professional associations with paralegals at other firms. For example, another paralegal may recommend his or her friend who works for a lawyer specializing in the area sought.

In many areas of specialty, the paralegal becomes a vital team member. Paralegals with skills in specific substantive areas perform services that allow the attorney to concentrate on other matters. In addition, the paralegal may handle office management tasks and other functions such as coordinating between members of the professional team and the client.

Legal Nurse Consultants and Nurse Paralegals

Nurse paralegals or legal nurse consultants Nurses who have gained medical work experience and combine it with paralegal skills.

Nurse paralegals or legal nurse consultants are nurses who combine prior medical work experience with paralegal skills. Becoming a legal nurse consultant or a nurse paralegal is an ideal career opportunity for nurses with clinical nursing experience who want to work in the legal environment. Entry to most nurse paralegal education programs requires a current license as a registered nurse and 2,000 to 6,000 hours (usually one to three years) of clinical nursing experience. Some programs are open to those with an associate's degree in nursing, but usually a bachelor's degree in nursing is desired.

Nurse paralegals draw upon their knowledge of medical terminology, medical procedures, and nursing practice to decipher medical records for the legal community. The most obvious advantage is their ability to analyze medical records from both medical and legal standpoints. Their experience also enables them to conduct more effective interviews with clients, fact witnesses, and expert witnesses in cases of medical malpractice or personal injury. Graduates of these programs often work as independent nurse consultants for law firms and insurance companies. Others find in-house positions with insurance companies and law firms specializing in medical malpractice and personal injury.

Although the ABA considers the nurse paralegal and legal nurse consultant to be part of the paralegal profession, the American Association of Legal Nurse Consultants (AALNC) views this role as a subspecialty of nursing. In March 1998, the Standing Committee on Legal Assistants (now named the Standing Committee on Paralegals) of the American Bar Association decided that "legal nurses and legal nurse consultants fall squarely within the ABA definition of 'paralegal/legal assistant.'" By contrast, the AALNC has defined the legal nurse consultant as a specialty practitioner of nursing whose education should be developed and presented as specialty nursing curricula by nurse educators in partnership with legal educators. The ethical code and regulations that must be followed may depend on which professional organization legal nurse consultants are associated with.

Web Exploration

Further information on legal nurse consulting can be obtained at www.aalnc.org.

Real Estate

Paralegals with real estate sales or title insurance backgrounds can perform many of the tasks associated with a real estate practice, such as communicating between buyers and sellers, coordinating the documentation for settlements, and preparing documents for recording purposes. Completing a course of study for becoming a licensed salesperson or a real estate broker provides a paralegal with knowledge in the practices and procedures of real estate transactions. In addition, familiarity with real estate terminology facilitates effective communication with attorneys and clients.

Complex Litigation

Complex litigation takes many forms, from class-action lawsuits to complex product-liability cases. Paralegals working in complex litigation typically oversee the requests for document production and maintain indexes, usually on computer databases, of the paperwork generated from the litigation. In large cases, the paralegal might supervise a staff of other paralegals or law students in summarizing discovery documents. At trial, these paralegals frequently coordinate the production of exhibits.

Complex litigation Cases involving many parties, as in a class action, or a case involving multiple or complex legal issues.

Environmental Law

Environmental law covers everything from the cleanup of toxic waste dumps to protection of wildlife and the environment. A challenge for the environmental paralegal is in locating and obtaining public records and other documents necessary to establish environmental claims. Some of this documentation may predate computer records, such as those documenting toxic waste dumps created during World War II and the early 1950s.

Environmental law An area of the law dealing with the protection of the environment.

Intellectual Property

The **intellectual property** paralegal assists with the formalities of protecting intellectual property, including patents, trade secrets, copyrights, and trademarks. The two main areas in this field are (a) prosecution, which involves establishing the priority of the claims that will result in the granting of the patent or copyright, and (b) litigation, which protects those rights against claims by others, such as in patent infringement cases.

Intellectual property Protection of intellectual property interests, such as patents, trademarks, and copyrights.

Elder Law

With the aging of the population has come an increased need to protect the rights of the elderly and help them obtain all the benefits to which they are entitled. This includes simple tasks such as helping individuals apply for Social Security, Medicare, or Medicaid benefits. It also entails working with the elderly to create estate plan documents, powers of attorney, and healthcare directives. The paralegal or legal assistant is increasingly becoming an advocate for the elderly, in many cases working in a pro bono capacity or through social service agencies. **Elder law** has also come to include the additional services of helping the elderly work through the maze of health insurance and government benefits.

Elder law Advocacy for the elderly.

Paralegal Managers

As paralegal staffs have grown, so has the need for someone to manage these personnel. Higher turnover rates and increased specialization have increased the need for someone to hire, supervise, train, and evaluate paralegals. The largest firms appoint a managing partner to handle these management and human resources tasks. But in many smaller firms, these duties fall to the individual with the title of **paralegal manager**. In many firms this person not only manages the paralegals but also serves as a liaison between the paralegals and the attorneys. An attorney usually does not have the time to handle the nonlegal tasks required of a manager, so a paralegal manager fulfills this role. The paralegal manager acts as a leader, mentor, employee advocate, supervisor, trainer, evaluator, problem solver, and resource manager for those he or she manages. This new specialty is well recognized and is supported by its own organization, the International Paralegal Management Association.

Paralegal manager Someone who hires, supervises, trains, and evaluates paralegals.

Web Exploration

Check the latest IPMA News at the IPMA website, www.theipma.org

Pro Bono Paralegals

Pro bono means working without compensation on behalf of individuals and organizations that otherwise could not afford legal assistance. Much of this work is performed by legal aid offices and community legal service programs. As members of professional associations, paralegals participate in pro bono activities at varying levels and time commitments. For example, the Massachusetts Paralegal Association supports a

Pro bono Working without compensation on behalf of individuals and organizations that otherwise could not afford legal assistance.

number of pro bono projects. In one of these, the Family Law Project, paralegals partner with attorneys to help handle domestic violence cases without compensation. Pro bono work is seen as part of an ethical obligation of the legal profession.

Government Employment

Government employment Working for federal, state, and local government agencies and authorities.

Federal, state, and local governments are large employers of paralegals, and they are expected to be utilized even further in **government employment** at every level in the future. Many of these positions are found in administrative agencies such as the Social Security Administration, where paralegals work as decision writers, case schedulers, and case specialists. Just as the private law firm has discovered the value of the paralegal on the legal team, so have government law offices such as the U.S. Attorney's Office and the Office of the Solicitor General. These offices are involved with both criminal prosecutions and civil litigation where the government is a party. Many other agencies that conduct administrative hearings utilize paralegals at all levels.

Legal Departments of Corporations

Many people think of a corporate legal department as a relaxed but conservative environment, where there is little activity other than drafting minutes of meetings and filing corporate records with federal and state governments. In reality, these departments can be very busy, dynamic environments to work in.

In the global economy, many corporations are engaged in international trade. There is a large body of law that relates to compliance with trade regulations, and international trade creates a host of unique issues related to the laws of the countries with which the domestic corporation may be doing business. For example, the transfer and sale of certain high-tech equipment must have prior government approval. Sales involving shipments to other countries require letters of credit and currency conversions. The paralegal is in the middle of these transactions, juggling the requirements from both the legal and sales or marketing perspectives. Paralegals with foreign language skills find themselves in even greater demand in handling communication issues. Those with cultural ties to the countries with which the corporation is doing business may be very useful in avoiding mistakes resulting from miscommunications or cultural misunderstandings.

DuPont, one of the largest corporations in the United States, provides a great example in the utilization of paralegals. In an effort to reduce costs, DuPont created a legal model that many companies have adopted.

Self-employment Working independently either as a freelance paralegal for different lawyers or, when authorized by state or federal law, performing services for the public.

Self-Employment

Paralegals also have some opportunities to work independently, although state regulations may limit some of the opportunities for paralegal **self-employment**.

THE LEGAL MODEL ADAPTS TO CHANGE

Since 1992, the DuPont Legal Model has continued to adapt and change to meet the challenges in today's corporate law. That's because the Legal Model remains a dynamic process that undergoes almost continuous re-engineering and refinement in order for us to remain competitive.

For this reason, the Legal Model encourages our legal network of Primary Law Firms (PLFs) and Service Providers to adopt a culture of efficiency and cost control, to evaluate work processes and create more effective ways of delivering legal services.

A web-based knowledge management system for our PLFs and Service Providers

New alternative fee arrangements

New performance metrics

Six Sigma initiatives

Source: http://www.dupontlegalmodel.com/initiatives/

Where authorized by federal law, the paralegal may actively represent clients without the supervision of an attorney, such as before the U.S. Patent Office or Social Security Administration. Many paralegals work as freelancers for different attorneys, usually on a case-by-case basis. In addition to the normal ethical obligations regarding confidentiality and conflict of interest, the freelance paralegal must observe the ethical guidelines on advertising in the local jurisdiction and avoid the appearance of being available to render legal advice.

Networking

Networking is important for every paralegal, regardless of the size or type of working environment. It is essential to establish contacts with others to share questions and information. Many paralegals develop a referral list of other paralegals they can call to get a quick answer to a new problem. Most paralegals are not too proud to call their contacts for help in meeting deadlines or getting necessary forms—whether those contacts are across the street, across the state, or across the country. During interviews, hiring attorneys sometimes ask about the paralegal's networking activity.

For the paralegal, networking may also be the key to obtaining a job. Success in finding employment often depends not only on what you know but also whom you know. Knowing the right person, or someone who can refer you to the right person, can lead to new opportunities.

Networking The establishment of contact with others with whom questions and information are shared.

Paralegal Tasks and Functions

LEARNING OBJECTIVE **2**
Describe the tasks and functions performed by paralegals.

The actual tasks and functions the paralegal performs vary according to the type of practice, the size of the firm or organization, and the skill of the individual paralegal. Some of the more general tasks include:

- conducting interviews
- maintaining written and verbal contacts with clients and counsel
- setting up, organizing, and maintaining client files
- preparing pleadings and documents
- reviewing, analyzing, summarizing, and indexing documents and transcripts
- assisting in preparing witnesses and clients for trial
- maintaining calendar and "tickler" (reminder) systems
- conducting research, both factual and legal
- performing office administrative functions including maintaining time and billing records

Client Interviews

Paralegals are often the first line of contact with clients. Although paralegals may not ethically or legally give legal advice or set legal fees, they frequently conduct the initial interview with the client. This might involve taking the initial client information and preparing a client data sheet (see Exhibit 3.1) or conducting a more in-depth interview to determine the facts of the matter for the attorney's review. Frequently, the paralegal continues to function as the contact point between the client and the supervising attorney or law firm. In this role, paralegals must establish rapport with clients and earn their confidence.

The paralegal must always be keenly aware of ethical limitations in dealing with clients. This is especially true when the client develops a high level of confidence in dealing with the paralegal. When clients have confidence in a paralegal, they might have a tendency to ask the paralegal for advice and recommendations instead of "bothering" the attorney. Providing such advice or recommendations may be in violation of laws against the unauthorized practice of law.

SIDEBAR

DOCUMENT SPECIALIST OR PARALEGAL?

Under the definition enacted by the Maine legislature, anyone calling himself or herself a paralegal or legal assistant must work under the supervision of an attorney. Independent paralegals no longer can use the title "paralegal" or "legal assistant." This has resulted in some of them changing the name of their freelance business to "document specialist" (*Bangor Daily News*, August 16, 1999).

The California legislature has enacted a law prohibiting self-help legal document service providers from receiving compensation unless the legal document assistant is registered in the county where the service is provided and provides a bond of $25,000.

Exhibit 3.1 Client data sheet

CLIENT DATA SHEET

	ACTION TAKEN/REQUIRED
1. Client Name:	
2. Client/Matter Number:	
3. Client Address:	
4. Phone: Work:	
Home:	
Fax:	
5. Email Address:	
6. Social Security No.:	
7. Date of Birth:	
8. Marital Status:	
9. Client Contact:	
10. Matter:	
(a) Adverse Party:	
(b) Date of Incident:	
(c) Statute of Limitations Period:	
(d) Statute of Limitations Date:	
11. Opposing Counsel:	
12. Opposing Counsel Address:	
13. Opposing Counsel Phone:	

For example, to the client, the question, "Should I make my son my power of attorney?" seems simple. However, the answer to this question is actually complex and involves many legal consequences, so it must be referred to the supervising attorney. Another example of the unauthorized practice of law might be helping the client complete blank legal forms, such as bankruptcy forms or will forms purchased at a retail store.

Investigations

The paralegal may be asked to act as the direct representative of the supervising attorney in conducting an investigation of a pending case. A paralegal trained in a specific area of law understands the facts that must be developed for a case in that area, as well as the available sources for that information. A paralegal who has had the opportunity to observe an attorney presenting evidence at trial will have a good sense of what makes good demonstrative evidence, such as models and photographs. For example, an understanding of how photographs will be used at trial and what questions will be asked about the photographs in direct examination and cross-examination will enable the paralegal to be certain that the photographs have been taken from the correct angles, with the correct landmarks or measurements included.

Interviews conducted by the paralegal in preparation for trial could qualify for protection under the attorney–client privilege, just as they do when conducted by attorneys. The paralegal must be aware of how interview material may be used and potentially obtained by opposing parties and act to protect clients' privileged communication.

Legal Writing

Paralegals frequently are called upon to maintain written communications with clients, opposing attorneys, and the court. These may be in the form of correspondence, memoranda of law, or briefs for the court. Many paralegals become extremely adept at drafting complaints and supporting briefs and memoranda. Although the content is ultimately the responsibility of the supervising attorney, a paralegal with good writing skills is an invaluable asset. Well-written and well-reasoned documentation prepared by the paralegal can be easily reviewed, signed, and transmitted by the attorney, saving valuable time.

Legal Research

In the modern law office, legal research is conducted with both books and the Internet. Legal research today requires the ability to use online legal services such as LexisNexis, Westlaw, VersusLaw, and Loislaw, as well as government websites. The ability to conduct research of case law, statutes, and regulatory rules and procedures gives the paralegal a major advantage and can lead to job opportunities and advancement in many firms.

What Paralegals in Legal Specialties Do

In addition to the various general tasks that most paralegals or legal assistants perform, those working in specialty areas may also perform more specialized tasks that require special knowledge, education, or skill beyond the basic skills and knowledge required of all paralegals. The following are some of the tasks that paralegals in specialty practice perform.

General business practice:

- Draft lease agreements
- Draft partnership agreements
- Draft noncompetition agreements
- Prepare real estate sales agreements and attend real estate closings
- Draft contracts for business arrangements and new ventures
- Draft employee agreements

Debtor and creditor rights:

- Draft correspondence complying with state and federal regulations concerning debt collection
- Prepare documentation to support garnishment proceedings
- Arrange for execution of judgments, including publication of notice of sales and levies on personal property
- Transfer judgments to other jurisdictions
- Prepare, file, and terminate Uniform Commercial Code financing statements
- Assist clients in filing bankruptcy petitions, including the preparation of schedules and proofs of claim
- Prepare Chapter 11 debtor's financial statements
- Attend Chapter 13 confirmation hearings

Corporate practice:

- Determine availability of and reserve corporate and fictitious names
- Prepare and file fictitious name registrations
- Prepare articles of incorporation, minutes, and bylaws for the corporation
- Prepare, issue, and transfer stock certificates
- Prepare shareholder agreements
- Prepare applications and file for employer identification numbers and tax registration numbers
- Prepare and file annual reports
- Prepare and file articles of dissolution
- Prepare and file securities registrations and required filings with state regulatory agencies and the Securities and Exchange Commission

Environmental law:

- Track information with regard to Superfund sites
- Determine applicability of brownfields laws to client property
- Research history of properties to determine environmental activity
- Obtain appropriate information about sites from state and federal environmental agencies
- Obtain documentation and assist in the preparation of environmental audits

Family law:

- Collect information from clients with regard to current or prior marital status
- Interview clients and collect information with regard to child support (see Exhibit 3.2)
- Draft prenuptial agreements
- Draft divorce complaints and responsive pleadings
- Prepare motions for support
- Prepare motions for custody and visitation
- Prepare property settlement agreements
- Prepare protection-from-abuse petitions
- Prepare petitions for termination of parental rights
- Prepare adoption petitions

Immigration law:

- Prepare applications and petitions for filing with the U.S. Citizenship and Immigration Services (USCIS; formerly Immigration and Naturalization Service) (see Exhibit 3.3)
- Coordinate translation of foreign documents
- Prepare immigration and nonimmigration visa applications
- Coordinate activities with clients in foreign jurisdictions seeking entry into the United States
- Assist clients in obtaining work visas for working in foreign countries
- Assist clients in the preparation of documentation to prove claim of marital status for submission to USCIS

Intellectual property:

- Conduct patent and trademark searches
- Prepare applications for patents, trademarks, or copyrights (see Exhibit 3.4)
- Assist in the preparation of documentation for proceedings regarding opposition, interference, infringement, and similar issues

Exhibit 3.2 Child support data form

______________________ v. ______________________ No. ______________________

THIS FORM MUST BE FILLED OUT

(If you are self-employed or if you are salaried by a business of which you are owner in whole or in part, you must also fill out the Supplemental Income Statement which appears on the last page of this Income and Expense Statement.)

INCOME AND EXPENSE STATEMENT OF

____

I verify that the statements made in this Income and Expense Statement are true and correct. I understand that false statements herein are made subject to the penalties of 18 Pa.C.S. §4904 relating to unsworn falsification to authorities.

Date: ______________ Plaintiff or Defendant: ______________________

INCOME

Employer: ______________________

Address: ______________________

Type of Work: ______________________

Payroll Number: ______________________

Pay Period (weekly, biweekly, etc.): ______________________

Gross Pay per Pay Period: $ ______________________

Itemized Payroll Deductions:		
	Federal Withholding	$ ________
	Social Security	________
	Local Wage Tax	________
	State Income Tax	________
	Retirement	________
	Savings Bonds	________
	Credit Union	________
	Life Insurance	________
	Health Insurance	________
	Other (specify)	________
	________	________
	Net Pay per Pay Period	$ ________

OTHER INCOME: (Fill in Appropriate Column)

	Weekly	*Monthly*	*Yearly*
Interest	$ ________	$ ________	$ ________
Dividends	________	________	________
Pension	________	________	________
Annuity	________	________	________
Social Security	________	________	________
Rents	________	________	________
Royalties	________	________	________
Expense Account	________	________	________
Gifts	________	________	________
Unemployment Comp.	________	________	________
Workmen's Comp.	________	________	________
________	________	________	________
Total	________	________	________
TOTAL INCOME			$ ________

- Coordinate activities and filings with foreign patent, trademark, and copyright attorneys and agents
- Work with engineers in preparation of applications and defense of patents and trade secrets
- Draft licensing agreements for intellectual property

Exhibit 3.3 Sample Citizenship and Immigration Services form

Application For Naturalization

Department of Homeland Security
U.S. Citizenship and Immigration Services

USCIS
Form N-400
OMB No. 1615-0052
Expires 09/30/2015

For USCIS Use Only	Date Stamp	Receipt	Action Block
Remarks			

Type or print all your answers in black ink. Type or print "N/A" if an item is not applicable or the answer is "none" unless otherwise indicated. Failure to answer all of the questions may delay USCIS processing your Form N-400. **NOTE: You must complete Parts 1. - 14.**

Part 1. Information About Your Eligibility *(Check only one box or your Form N-400 may be delayed)*

Enter Your 9 Digit A-Number:
► A-

You are at least 18 years old **and**

1. ☐ Have been a Permanent Resident of the United States for at least 5 years.
2. ☐ Have been a Permanent Resident of the United States for at least 3 years. In addition, you have been married to and living with the same U.S. citizen spouse for the last 3 years, **and** your spouse has been a U.S. citizen for the last 3 years at the time of filing your Form N-400.
3. ☐ Are a Permanent Resident of the United States, and you are the spouse of a U.S. citizen, **and** your U.S. citizen spouse is regularly engaged in specified employment abroad. *(Section 319(b) of the Immigration and Nationality Act)*
4. ☐ Are applying on the basis of qualifying military service.
5. ☐ Other (explain):

Part 2. Information About You *(Person applying for naturalization)*

1. **Your Current Legal Name** *(do not provide a nickname)*

   Family Name *(Last Name)* | Given Name *(First Name)* | Middle Name *(if applicable)*

2. **Your Name Exactly As It Appears on Your Permanent Resident Card** *(if applicable)*

   Family Name *(Last Name)* | Given Name *(First Name)* | Middle Name *(if applicable)*

3. **Other Name(s) You Have Used Since Birth** *(include nicknames, aliases, and maiden name if applicable)*

   Family Name *(Last Name)* | Given Name *(First Name)* | Middle Name *(if applicable)*

Human resources law:

- Draft documents for tax-sheltered employee benefit plans
- Draft deferred compensation plans
- Prepare and file for Internal Revenue Service determination letters for plans
- Prepare and file annual reports such as 5500 series Internal Revenue Service forms
- Calculate employer and employee contribution levels and limitations
- Draft, review, and distribute summary plan descriptions

Litigation:

- Investigate factual allegations of cases
- Assist in locating witnesses and physical evidence
- Draft summonses, complaints, answers, and other responsive pleadings
- Organize and maintain litigation files
- Assist in the preparation of trial notebooks
- Gather, review, summarize, and index documents for trial
- Locate and arrange for interviews with expert witnesses

Exhibit 3.4 Copyright form

Copyright Office fees are subject to change. For current fees, check the Copyright Office website at www.copyright.gov, write the Copyright Office, or call (202) 707-3000.

Privacy Act Notice: Sections 408-410 of title 17 of the *United States Code* authorize the Copyright Office to collect the personally identifying information requested on this form in order to process the application for copyright registration. By providing this information you are agreeing to routine uses of the information that include publication to give legal notice of your copyright claim as required by 17 U.S.C. §705. It will appear in the Office's online catalog. If you do not provide the information requested, registration may be refused or delayed, and you may not be entitled to certain relief, remedies, and benefits under the copyright law.

Form TX
For a Nondramatic Literary Work
UNITED STATES COPYRIGHT OFFICE

REGISTRATION NUMBER

TX TXU

EFFECTIVE DATE OF REGISTRATION

Month Day Year

DO NOT WRITE ABOVE THIS LINE. IF YOU NEED MORE SPACE, USE A SEPARATE CONTINUATION SHEET.

1

TITLE OF THIS WORK ▼

PREVIOUS OR ALTERNATIVE TITLES ▼

PUBLICATION AS A CONTRIBUTION If this work was published as a contribution to a periodical, serial, or collection, give information about the collective work in which the contribution appeared. Title of Collective Work ▼

If published in a periodical or serial give: Volume ▼ Number ▼ Issue Date ▼ On Pages ▼

2

a NAME OF AUTHOR ▼ DATES OF BIRTH AND DEATH Year Born ▼ Year Died ▼

Was this contribution to the work a "work made for hire"? ❑ Yes ❑ No

AUTHOR'S NATIONALITY OR DOMICILE Name of Country OR { Citizen of ______ Domiciled in ______

WAS THIS AUTHOR'S CONTRIBUTION TO THE WORK Anonymous? ❑ Yes ❑ No Pseudonymous? ❑ Yes ❑ No If the answer to either of these questions is "Yes," see detailed instructions.

NATURE OF AUTHORSHIP Briefly describe nature of material created by this author in which copyright is claimed. ▼

b NAME OF AUTHOR ▼ DATES OF BIRTH AND DEATH Year Born ▼ Year Died ▼

Was this contribution to the work a "work made for hire"? ❑ Yes ❑ No

AUTHOR'S NATIONALITY OR DOMICILE Name of Country OR { Citizen of ______ Domiciled in ______

WAS THIS AUTHOR'S CONTRIBUTION TO THE WORK Anonymous? ❑ Yes ❑ No Pseudonymous? ❑ Yes ❑ No If the answer to either of these questions is "Yes," see detailed instructions.

NATURE OF AUTHORSHIP Briefly describe nature of material created by this author in which copyright is claimed. ▼

c NAME OF AUTHOR ▼ DATES OF BIRTH AND DEATH Year Born ▼ Year Died ▼

Was this contribution to the work a "work made for hire"? ❑ Yes ❑ No

AUTHOR'S NATIONALITY OR DOMICILE Name of Country OR { Citizen of ______ Domiciled in ______

WAS THIS AUTHOR'S CONTRIBUTION TO THE WORK Anonymous? ❑ Yes ❑ No Pseudonymous? ❑ Yes ❑ No If the answer to either of these questions is "Yes," see detailed instructions.

NATURE OF AUTHORSHIP Briefly describe nature of material created by this author in which copyright is claimed. ▼

NOTE
Under the law, the "author" of a "work made for hire" is generally the employer, not the employee (see instructions). For any part of this work that was "made for hire" check "Yes" in the space provided, give the employer (or other person for whom the work was prepared) as "Author" of that part, and leave the space for dates of birth and death blank.

3

a YEAR IN WHICH CREATION OF THIS WORK WAS COMPLETED This information must be given in all cases. ______ Year

b DATE AND NATION OF FIRST PUBLICATION OF THIS PARTICULAR WORK Complete this information ONLY if this work has been published. Month ______ Day ______ Year ______ ______ Nation

4

COPYRIGHT CLAIMANT(S) Name and address must be given even if the claimant is the same as the author given in space 2. ▼

See instructions before completing this space.

TRANSFER If the claimant(s) named here in space 4 is (are) different from the author(s) named in space 2, give a brief statement of how the claimant(s) obtained ownership of the copyright. ▼

DO NOT WRITE HERE OFFICE USE ONLY
APPLICATION RECEIVED
ONE DEPOSIT RECEIVED
TWO DEPOSITS RECEIVED
FUNDS RECEIVED

MORE ON BACK ▸ • Complete all applicable spaces (numbers 5-9) on the reverse side of this page. • See detailed instructions. • Sign the form at line 8.

DO NOT WRITE HERE
Page 1 of ______ pages

- Prepare written interrogatories
- Assist in preparing for and conducting depositions including videotape depositions
- Prepare or obtain subpoenas (see sample in Exhibit 3.5) and arrange for service
- Coordinate, assist, and arrange for trial exhibits
- Obtain jury pool information and assist in the selection of jury members
- Attend trial and assist in the handling of witnesses, exhibits, and evidence
- Prepare contemporaneous summaries of witness statements during trial

Exhibit 3.5 Subpoena

AO 88 (Rev. 02/14) Subpoena to Appear and Testify at a Hearing or Trial in a Civil Action

UNITED STATES DISTRICT COURT

for the

____________________)
Plaintiff)
v.) Civil Action No.
____________________)
Defendant)

SUBPOENA TO APPEAR AND TESTIFY AT A HEARING OR TRIAL IN A CIVIL ACTION

To:

____
(Name of person to whom this subpoena is directed)

YOU ARE COMMANDED to appear in the United States district court at the time, date, and place set forth below to testify at a hearing or trial in this civil action. When you arrive, you must remain at the court until the judge or a court officer allows you to leave.

Place:	Courtroom No.:
	Date and Time:

You must also bring with you the following documents, electronically stored information, or objects *(leave blank if not applicable)*:

The following provisions of Fed. R. Civ. P. 45 are attached – Rule 45(c), relating to the place of compliance; Rule 45(d), relating to your protection as a person subject to a subpoena; and Rule 45(e) and (g), relating to your duty to respond to this subpoena and the potential consequences of not doing so.

Date: __________

CLERK OF COURT

OR

____________________ ____________________
Signature of Clerk or Deputy Clerk *Attorney's signature*

The name, address, e-mail address, and telephone number of the attorney representing *(name of party)* __________
____________________, who issues or requests this subpoena, are:

Notice to the person who issues or requests this subpoena

If this subpoena commands the production of documents, electronically stored information, or tangible things before trial, a notice and a copy of the subpoena must be served on each party in this case before it is served on the person to whom it is directed. Fed. R. Civ. P. 45(a)(4).

LEARNING OBJECTIVE 3

Describe the administrative procedures found in most law offices.

Conflict checking Verifying that the attorneys in the firm do not have a personal conflict and have not previously represented and are not currently representing any party with an adverse interest or conflict with the potential client.

Administrative Procedures in Law Offices and Firms

Certain administrative procedures, such as conflict checking and time keeping, are common to most, if not all, law offices. Depending on the size of the law firm and the nature of the practice, a paralegal also may be called upon to perform certain financial activities, such as preparing invoices, maintaining client escrow accounts, maintaining trust accounts, preparing payroll records, preparing court-required accounting, and completing real estate settlement forms.

Conflict Checking

Conflict checking is necessary to verify that current and prior parties or matters handled by the firm will not result in a conflict of interest when accepting a new client or matter. Checking for conflicts of interest is essential to complying with ethical rules against representing competing interests. Some firms still rely on manual systems of paper lists and index cards containing the names of clients, opposing parties, and opposing attorneys in every case handled by the firm. But now, many offices use computer database software for conflict checking, and the names of clients, opposing parties, counsel, and law firms can be quickly searched electronically. However, determining conflicts is difficult where there has been only indirect representation.

Attorneys and paralegals who change firms may have to undergo a preliminary conflict check before they can accept or start employment. A conflict arises when the former firm and the new firm are or were on opposite sides of a case. It may be a conflict for someone who has had access to information about a case to switch to the firm representing the opposing party. Before starting employment, confidential disclosure for the limited purpose of conflict checking could prevent a serious ethical violation. In some cases, the conflict of interest may result from a financial interest such as stock ownership or investments. Making full disclosure of these potential conflict situations to the supervising attorney or to the appropriate conflict checker with the firm is important.

In many cases, the conflict can be resolved by isolating the individual from information about the case—sometimes called building an "ethical wall." An ethical wall, also known as a Chinese wall, is an attempt to shield a paralegal or lawyer from access to information about a case when there is the possibility of a conflict of interest. Most courts permit the establishment of an ethical wall to protect the parties from a conflict of interest or breach of confidentiality. As commented by a Connecticut trial court in an unpublished opinion:

> . . . The court does not subscribe to the argument that, as a matter of law, screening would be ineffective when a nonlawyer switches employment to "the other side." The ABA opinions indicate that a law firm can set up appropriate screening and administrative procedures to prevent nonlawyers from working on the other side of those common cases and disclosing confidential information. . .

Devine v. Beinfield, No. CV930121721 S, 1997 Conn Super Lexis 1966 (Ct. Sup. Jul. 1, 1997)

The Nevada Supreme Court specifically addresses the issue of conflict of interest as it relates to paralegals in the *Leibowitz* case.

IN THE WORDS OF THE COURT . . .

LEIBOWITZ V. EIGHTH JUDICIAL DISTRICT COURT, 119 NEV. 523, 78 P.3D 515 (2003)

The Nevada Supreme Court overturned a 1994 ethics opinion, *Ciaffone v. District Court*, 113 Nev. 1165 945 P.2d 950 (1997), that prohibited paralegals from working for a firm that represents any client that had an adversarial relationship to any client of the former employer law firm. The court summarized the rationale for the ethical wall and provided an instructive guide.

> As pointed out by the amici's brief, the majority of professional legal ethics commentators, ethics tribunals, and courts have concluded that nonlawyer screening is a permissible method to protect confidences held by nonlawyer employees who change employment. Nevada is in a minority of jurisdictions that do not allow screening for nonlawyers moving from private firm to private firm.
>
> Imputed disqualification is considered a harsh remedy that "should be invoked if, and only if, the [c]ourt is satisfied that real harm is likely to result from failing to invoke it."
>
> This stringent standard is based on a client's right to counsel of the client's choosing and the likelihood of prejudice and economic harm to the client when severance of the attorney–client relationship is ordered. It is for this reason that the ABA

(continued)

opined in 1988 that screening is permitted for nonlawyer employees, while conversely concluding, through the Model Rules of Professional Conduct, that screening is not permitted for lawyers. The ABA explained that "additional considerations" exist justifying application of screening to nonlawyer employees (*i.e.*, mobility in employment opportunities which function to serve both legal clients and the legal profession) versus the Model Rule's proscription against screening where lawyers move from private firm to private firm. In essence, a lawyer may always practice his or her profession regardless of an affiliation to a law firm. Paralegals, legal secretaries, and other employees of attorneys do not have that option.

We are persuaded that *Ciaffone* misapprehended the state of the law regarding nonlawyer imputed disqualification. We therefore overrule *Ciaffone* to the extent it prohibits screening of nonlawyer employees.

When a law firm hires a nonlawyer employee, the firm has an affirmative duty to determine whether the employee previously had access to adversarial client files. If the hiring law firm determines that the employee had such access, the hiring law firm has an absolute duty to screen the nonlawyer employee from the adversarial cases irrespective of the nonlawyer employee's actual knowledge of privileged or confidential information.

Although we decline to mandate an exhaustive list of screening requirements, the following provides an instructive minimum:

(1) *"The newly hired nonlawyer [employee] must be cautioned not to disclose any information relating to the representation of a client of the former employer."*
(2) *"The nonlawyer [employee] must be instructed not to work on any matter on which [he or] she worked during the prior employment, or regarding which [he or] she has information relating to the former employer's representation."*
(3) *"The new firm should take . . . reasonable steps to ensure that the nonlawyer [employee] does not work in connection with matters on which [he or] she worked during the prior employment, absent client consent [i.e., unconditional waiver] after consultation."*

In addition, the hiring law firm must inform the adversarial party, or their counsel, regarding the hiring of the nonlawyer employee and the screening mechanisms utilized. The adversarial party may then: (1) make a conditional waiver (*i.e.*, agree to the screening mechanisms); (2) make an unconditional waiver (eliminate the screening mechanisms); or (3) file a motion to disqualify counsel.

However, even if the new employer uses a screening process, disqualification will always be required—absent unconditional waiver by the affected client—under the following circumstances:

(1) *"[W]hen information relating to the representation of an adverse client has in fact been disclosed [to the new employer]"; or, in the absence of disclosure to the new employer,*
(2) *"[W]hen screening would be ineffective or the nonlawyer [employee] necessarily would be required to work on the other side of a matter that is the same as or substantially related to a matter on which the nonlawyer [employee] has previously worked."*

Once a district court determines that a nonlawyer employee acquired confidential information about a former client, the district court should grant a motion for disqualification unless the district court determines that the screening is sufficient to safeguard the former client from disclosure of the confidential information. The district court is faced with the delicate task of balancing competing interests, including: (1) "the individual right to be represented by counsel of one's choice," (2) "each party's right to be free from the risk of even inadvertent disclosure of confidential information," (3) "the public's interest in the scrupulous administration of justice," and (4) "the prejudices that will inure to the parties as a result of the [district court's] decision."

Time Keeping and Billing

Keeping track of billable time is critical in ensuring that the law firm will be compensated properly for its advice and efforts on behalf of clients. Time records are the basis for most law firm billings, and without accurate time records, billings cannot be made. Responsibility for tracking time extends beyond just the attorneys and includes paralegals, and in some cases, secretaries and clerks.

Billing is one of the most important functions in a law firm. Without billing, there is no revenue to pay expenses and salaries. Yet despite its being so essential, in many offices, billing is not treated with enough care.

The propriety of fees is addressed in Rule 1.5 of the Model Rules of Professional Conduct and is addressed by the ethical rules in most jurisdictions. The Utah Rules of Professional Conduct provide as follows.

Rule 1.5 Fees

(a) A lawyer shall not make an agreement for, charge or collect an unreasonable fee or an unreasonable amount for expenses. The factors to be considered in determining the reasonableness of a fee include the following:
  (a)(1) the time and labor required, the novelty and difficulty of the questions involved and the skill requisite to perform the legal service properly;
  (a)(2) the likelihood, if apparent to the client, that the acceptance of the particular employment will preclude other employment by the lawyer;
  (a)(3) the fee customarily charged in the locality for similar legal services;
  (a)(4) the amount involved and the results obtained;
  (a)(5) the time limitations imposed by the client or by the circumstances;
  (a)(6) the nature and length of the professional relationship with the client;
  (a)(7) the experience, reputation and ability of the lawyer or lawyers performing the services; and
  (a)(8) whether the fee is fixed or contingent.

(b) The scope of the representation and the basis or rate of the fee and expenses for which the client will be responsible shall be communicated to the client, preferably in writing, before or within a reasonable time after commencing the representation, except when the lawyer will charge a regularly represented client on the same basis or rate. Any changes in the basis or rate of the fee or expenses shall also be communicated to the client.

(c) A fee may be contingent on the outcome of the matter for which the service is rendered, except in a matter in which a contingent fee is prohibited by paragraph (d) or other law. A contingent fee agreement shall be in a writing signed by the client and shall state the method by which the fee is to be determined, including the percentage or percentages that shall accrue to the lawyer in the event of settlement, trial or appeal; litigation and other expenses to be deducted from the recovery; and whether such expenses are to be deducted before or after the contingent fee is calculated. The agreement must clearly notify the client of any expenses for which the client will be liable whether or not the client is the prevailing party. Upon conclusion of a contingent fee matter, the lawyer shall provide the client with a written statement stating the outcome of the matter and, if there is a recovery, showing the remittance to the client and the method of its determination.

(d) A lawyer shall not enter into an arrangement for, charge or collect:
  (d)(1) any fee in a domestic relations matter, the payment or amount of which is contingent upon the securing of a divorce or upon the amount of alimony or support, or property settlement in lieu thereof; or
  (d)(2) a contingent fee for representing a defendant in a criminal case.

(e) A division of a fee between lawyers who are not in the same firm may be made only if:
  (e)(1) the division is in proportion to the services performed by each lawyer or each lawyer assumes joint responsibility for the representation;
  (e)(2) the client agrees to the arrangement, including the share each lawyer will receive, and the agreement is confirmed in writing; and
  (e)(3) the total fee is reasonable.

Web Exploration

View the comments to the Utah rules at http://www.utcourts.gov/resources/rules/ucja/ch13/1_5.htm.

The billing of clients is not limited to the time of lawyers but may also include that of paralegals. As the 11th Circuit Court of Appeals has stated:

> We have held that paralegal time is recoverable as part of a prevailing party's award for attorney's fees and expenses, [but] only to the extent that the paralegal performs work traditionally done by an attorney. Quoting from *Allen v. United States Steel Corp.*, 665 F.2d 689, 697 (5th Cir. 1982): "To hold otherwise would be counterproductive because excluding reimbursement for such work might encourage attorneys to handle entire cases themselves, thereby achieving the same results at a higher overall cost."
>
> *Jean v. Nelson*, 863 F. 2d 759 (11th Cir. 1988)

Client expense records, by contrast, are usually well maintained because a check is usually written, which provides a documented record for billing purposes. But for billable time, a record must be kept by the attorney, paralegal, or other legal team member. This information frequently is recorded manually on pieces of paper called time slips or time records. Client bills are prepared manually from these records.

More offices are now using time and billing software, such as AbacusLaw. Most of these programs allow for random entry of individual time record information, which is then automatically sorted by client and project or case. These programs also allow for the entry of fees and costs expended and application of retainers, which may be included in the final billing report.

Accounting in the Law Office

In the law office working environment, your ability to understand basic financial issues makes you a more valuable member of the law office team. Unlike retail, wholesale, or manufacturing businesses that trade in goods or commodities, a law firm is a business that, as Abraham Lincoln once said, deals in "time and advice."

A major function of the legal support staff is to keep track of the time the lawyers and support staff spend on a case and then bill the client for the time expended. Financial records must be kept accurately for matters related to specific clients or for internal office activities that are part of the overall cost of running the office. If accurate records are not kept, the law office may fail or close.

When funds belong to clients, errors in internal documentation, court documents, and tax returns may result in malpractice claims. At worst, errors may result in a loss or misappropriation of client funds, which can lead to sanctions, disbarment, or criminal prosecution.

In addition to understanding the internal accounting needs of a law firm, it is useful to understand the accounting and financial affairs of clients. Understanding accounting and financial reports and documents is essential in many areas of law today.

Family Law

Domestic relations cases may involve concerns related to property settlement, support, and alimony. In prenuptial agreements today, there is an increasing demand for full financial disclosure. A basic understanding of the nature and the sources of a family's financial information will enable the paralegal to prepare the necessary documents. As an example, Exhibit 3.6 shows selected pages from the New Jersey Family Part Case Information form.

Commercial Litigation

Commercial litigation typically involves actions resulting from claims of breach of contract or disputes over interpretations of provisions of a contract. This field is often very complex because of the financial implications of contract breaches and remedies. The tasks of finding, analyzing, and presenting financial information increasingly fall on litigation paralegals.

Litigation

Even in the simplest of litigation matters, a measure of damages has to be computed. Calculations of wages lost, projection of future losses, and the current or present value of a case may have to be computed or reviewed for accuracy.

Maintaining Law Firm Financial Information

Law firms, like any other business, have numerous financial obligations. Utility bills and employees must be paid on a regular basis, and accurate records must be maintained to determine which costs are chargeable to individual clients. Firms must also keep records of client funds in separate escrow accounts.

Records of the various receipts and disbursements are used to prepare the firm's tax documents. These may include filings of quarterly and annual employee withholding, income tax returns, and reports for independent contractors such as freelance paralegals, court reporters, and investigators.

Exhibit 3.6 New Jersey family case information

Part D - Monthly Expenses (computed at 4.3 wks/mo.)

Joint Marital or Civil Union Life Style should reflect standard of living established during marriage or civil union. Current expenses should reflect the current life style. Do not repeat those income deductions listed in Part C - 3.

	Joint Life Style Family, including _____ children	Current Life Style Yours and _____ children
SCHEDULE A: SHELTER		
If Tenant:		
Rent	$	$
Heat (if not furnished)	$	$
Electric & Gas (if not furnished)	$	$
Renter's Insurance	$	$
Parking (at Apartment)	$	$
Other charges (Itemize)	$	$
If Homeowner:		
Mortgage	$	$
Real Estate Taxes (if not included w/mortgage payment)	$	$
Homeowners Ins. (if not included w/mortgage payment)	$	$
Other Mortgages or Home Equity Loans	$	$
Heat (unless Electric or Gas)	$	$
Electric & Gas	$	$
Water & Sewer	$	$
Garbage Removal	$	$
Snow Removal	$	$
Lawn Care	$	$
Maintenance/Repairs	$	$
Condo, Co-op or Association Fees	$	$
Other Charges (Itemize)	$	$
Tenant or Homeowner:		
Telephone	$	$
Mobile/Cellular Telephone	$	$
Service Contracts on Equipment	$	$
Cable TV	$	$
Plumber/Electrician	$	$
Equipment & Furnishings	$	$
Internet Charges	$	$
Home Security System	$	$
Other (itemize)	$	$
TOTAL	$	$
SCHEDULE B: TRANSPORTATION		
Auto Payment	$	$
Auto Insurance (number of vehicles: ____)	$	$
Registration, License	$	$
Maintenance	$	$
Fuel and Oil	$	$
Commuting Expenses	$	$
Other Charges (Itemize)	$	$
TOTAL	$	$

(continued)

Exhibit 3.6 New Jersey family case information *(continued)*

Description	Title to Property (P, D, J)[1]	Date of purchase/acquisition. If claim that asset is exempt, state reason and value of what is claimed to be exempt.	Value $ Put * after exempt	Date of Evaluation Mo./Day/Yr.
1. Real Property				
2. Bank Accounts, DC's (identify institution and type of account(s))				
3. Vehicles				
4. Tangible Personal Property				
5. Stocks, Bonds and Securities (identify institution and type of account(s))				
6. Pension, Profit Sharing, Retirement Plan(s), 401(k)s, etc. (identify each institution or employer)				
7. IRAs				
8. Businesses, Partnerships, Professional Practices				
9. Life Insurance (cash surrender value)				
10. Loans Receivable				
11. Other (specify)				

TOTAL GROSS ASSETS: $__________

TOTAL SUBJECT TO EQUITABLE DISTRIBUTION: $__________

TOTAL NOT SUBJECT TO EQUITABLE DISTRIBUTION: $__________

[1] P = Plaintiff; D = Defendant; J = Joint

Revised to be effective September 1, 2013, CN: 10482 (Court Rules Appendix V)

page 8 of 10

Regular use of a consistent system will simplify the completion of financial reports. By using a standard system of accounting, lawyers, bookkeepers, paralegals, and secretarial personnel can easily communicate information about charges and revenues that can be used by anyone who needs the information, including outside accountants and auditors.

Reconstructing or organizing a client's financial information is a common task in many law offices. In many cases, clients deliver piles of financial documents and expect the law office personnel to sort, classify, and organize these seemingly unrelated pieces of paper for use in income tax returns, estate tax returns, settlements, and other instances where financial information is needed. Knowing how to attack the piles of paper can save time, stress, and frustration.

Safekeeping of client property and segregation of client funds from those of the law firm are important ethical obligations imposed under Rule 1.15 of the Model Rules of Professional Conduct and the ethical rules of most jurisdictions. For example, the rule in South Dakota provides in part:

Rule 1.15 Safekeeping Property

(a) A lawyer shall hold property of clients or third persons that is in a lawyer's possession in connection with a representation separate from the lawyer's own property. Funds shall be kept in a separate account maintained in the state where the lawyer's office is situated, or elsewhere with the consent of the client or third person. Other property shall be identified as such and appropriately safeguarded. Complete records of such account funds and other property shall be kept by the lawyer and shall be preserved for a period of five years after termination of the representation. A lawyer may deposit the lawyer's own funds in a client trust account for the sole purpose of paying bank service charges on that account, but only in an amount necessary for that purpose. A lawyer shall deposit into a client trust account legal fees and expenses that have been paid in advance, to be withdrawn by the lawyer only as fees are earned or expenses incurred.

(b) Upon receiving funds or other property in which a client or third person has an interest, a lawyer shall promptly notify the client or third person. Except as stated in this Rule or otherwise permitted by law or by agreement with the client, a lawyer shall promptly deliver to the client or third person any funds or other property that the client or third person is entitled to receive and, upon request by the client or third person, shall promptly render a full accounting regarding such property.

(c) When in the course of representation a lawyer is in possession of property in which two or more persons (one of whom may be the lawyer) claim interests, the property shall be kept separate by the lawyer until the dispute is resolved. The lawyer shall promptly distribute all portions of the property as to which the interests are not in dispute.

(d) Preserving Identity of Funds and Property of Client.

  (1) All funds of clients paid to a lawyer or law firm, including advances for costs and expenses, shall be deposited in one or more identifiable bank accounts maintained in the state in which the law office is situated and no funds belonging to the lawyer or law firm shall be deposited therein except as follows:

    (i) Funds reasonably sufficient to pay bank charges may be deposited therein.

    (ii) Funds belonging in part to a client and in part presently or potentially to the lawyer or law firm must be deposited therein, but the portion belonging to the lawyer or law firm may be withdrawn when due unless the right of the lawyer or law firm to receive it is disputed by the client, in which event the disputed portion shall not be withdrawn until the dispute is finally resolved.

  (2) A lawyer shall:

    (i) Promptly notify a client of the receipt of his funds, securities, or other properties.

    (ii) Identify and label securities and properties of a client promptly upon receipt and place them in a safe deposit box or other place of safekeeping as soon as practicable.

    (iii) Maintain complete records of all funds, securities, and other properties of a client coming into the possession of the lawyer and render appropriate accountings to his client regarding them.

    (iv) Promptly pay or deliver to the client as requested by a client the funds, securities, or other properties in the possession of the lawyer which the client is entitled to receive. . .

The complete rule may be viewed at http://www.sdbar.org/Rules/Rules/PC_Rules.htm.

Accounting for Client Retainers and Costs

Retainer A payment at the beginning of the handling of a new matter for a client. This amount may be used to offset the fees for services rendered or costs advanced on behalf of the client.

Law firms frequently request a **retainer**—a payment from a client at the beginning of a new matter. This amount may be used to offset the fees for services rendered or costs advanced on behalf of the client. Unless there is some other legally permissible arrangement, these funds do not belong to the law firm until they have been earned by rendering a service, or actual costs have been incurred. Unused amounts may have to be returned to the client and those expended accounted for to the client. Social Security Administration Model Fee Agreement Language is shown in Exhibit 3.7.

Under the rules of professional conduct in many states, a written fee agreement is required in contingency fee cases, whereas in other types of cases it is preferred but not required.

A new approach to providing legal services is sometimes called "unbundled" legal services, or "discrete task representation." This refers to a broad range of discrete tasks that an attorney might undertake, such as advice, negotiation, document review, document preparation, and limited representation.

A lawyer may also request a nonrefundable retainer. This is a common practice when the client does not want the law firm to be able to represent the opposing party in a pending legal action and is seen most commonly in family law or divorce actions. Legal ethics prohibit taking on a client when there is a conflict of interest. In cases of nonrefundable retainers, a statement of application of the funds should be made as a matter of financial accounting practice.

Exhibit 3.7 Social Security Administration Model Fee Agreement Language

Fee For Services

My representative and I understand that, for a fee to be payable, the Social Security Administration (SSA) must approve any fee my representative charges or collects from me for services my representative provides in proceedings before SSA in connection with my claim(s) for benefits.

We agree that, if SSA favorably decides the claim(s), I will pay my representative a fee equal to the lesser of [**Insert** a number less than or equal to 25 percent] percent of the past-due benefits resulting from my claim(s) or [**Insert** a number less than or equal to the applicable specified dollar limit established pursuant to section 206(a)(2)(A) of the Social Security Act (e.g., $5,300, $6,000)].

Review of the Fee

We understand that one or both of us may request review of the fee amount, in writing, within 15 days after SSA has notified us of any amount my representative can charge.

- My representative may ask SSA to increase the fee, and [Insert he or she] has informed me that [Insert he or she] will do so if [Insert the conditions under which the representative might seek a fee higher than the fee otherwise agreed upon].
- I may ask SSA to reduce the fee.
- An affected auxiliary Social Security beneficiary, if any, may ask SSA to reduce the fee too.
- Also, if SSA approved the fee agreement, the person(s) who decided my claim(s) may ask for a reduction of the fee under the agreement if, in his or her opinion, my representative did not represent my interests adequately or the fee is clearly excessive for the services provided.

If someone requests review, SSA generally would send the other(s) a copy and offer an opportunity to comment on the request and provide more information to the person reviewing the request. SSA then would finally decide the amount of the fee and notify us in writing whether the fee increased, decreased, or did not change.

We both have received signed copies of this agreement.

Source: http://www.ssa.gov/representation/model_fee_agreement_language.htm#&sb=2

Costs Advanced

Law firms typically pay directly to the court any fees for filing documents for the client. In some cases, the costs of stenographers, expert witnesses, duplication of records, travel, phone, and copying will also be advanced. The firm must keep proper accounting for these items to be able to bill a client properly or charge the amounts expended against prepaid costs or retainers. Good practice is to include in the initial client fee letter the nature and amount of costs that will be charged for these various items.

Civil Practice: Fee and Cost Billing

In a civil litigation practice, fees may be calculated on an hourly rate, as a contingent fee, or as a combination of the two. The time records for each member of the firm must be obtained, either from the hard copies of time records or the computer printout of hours spent working on the case. The actual time may be reported to the client chronologically, with all activity by each person who worked on the file integrated with all the others, or it may be listed separately for each individual.

One of the difficulties in billing is calculating the correct amount for each person at his or her respective hourly rate. Senior partners, junior partners, associates, and paralegals may bill at different rates. It is thus good practice to calculate the total for each billable person separately and then collectively. The totals of the individuals, of course, must equal the grand total. A comparison should be made to check mathematical accuracy.

At one time, firms prepared client bills manually from paper copies of time records or other office documents. Now, many firms prepare the client billing using a computer program. Most of these programs allow input of the individual time records in a random order, which can then be sorted automatically by client and project. In addition to time billing, these programs allow the entry of costs expended for inclusion in the final billing.

Timely Disbursements

As part of the settlement of a case for a client, the opposing side may pay the amount of the cash settlement to the lawyer. These funds must be retained in a separate escrow account until they are disbursed to the client and may not be commingled with the lawyer's own funds. Records of the receipt and disbursement of these funds must be maintained properly to avoid charges of misuse of client funds.

A lawyer is not required to make disbursements until the draft or check has cleared. A check or draft is deemed cleared when the funds are available for disbursement. However, lawyers may not retain the amount for an unreasonable time. The client is entitled to earn the potential interest on the amount to be disbursed. The lawyer is not entitled to keep the amount and earn interest for his or her own account.

Trust Accounts

A **trust account** or fiduciary account contains the client's funds and should never be commingled with those of the firm or the individual attorney. A clear record of all trust transactions must be maintained. In many cases, such as trusts, estates, or cases involving children, detailed reports must be filed with the court following the court-imposed rules (as shown in Exhibit 3.8). When a checking account has been established, the check register is a primary source for creating any necessary reports. With some larger accounts, checking accounts may not have been set up. Many trust and estate accounts are invested in money market funds, stocks, bonds, and mutual funds.

Trust account A separate account where the funds of the client must be held.

Exhibit 3.8 Selected provisions of the rules of practice and procedure in the probate courts of the state of New Hampshire

RULE 108. FIDUCIARY ACCOUNTING STANDARDS

The following standards shall be applicable to all interim and final accountings of Administrators, trustees, guardians and conservators, required or permitted to be filed with the Court.

A. Accounts shall be stated in a manner that is understandable by Persons who are not familiar with practices and terminology peculiar to the administration of estates, trusts, guardianships and conservatorships. . . .
B. A Fiduciary account shall begin with a concise summary of its purpose and content. The account shall begin with a brief statement identifying the Fiduciary, the subject matter, the relationship of Parties interested in the account to the account, and, if applicable, appropriate notice of any limitations on or requirements for action by Parties interested in the account. . . .
C. A Fiduciary account shall contain sufficient information to put parties interested in the account on notice as to all significant transactions affecting administration during the accounting period. . . .

Keeping a clear record is made more difficult by the potential for periodic increases and decreases in value that are not actually realized—referred to as "paper gains and losses." These exist on paper but have not been realized by the actual sale or transfer of the assets. Any investments by the attorney of assets held in trust must be authorized by the client or by state law. Separate records should be maintained showing the activity in each of the trust accounts, including all deposits, interest, disbursements, and bank charges.

IOLTA Accounts

IOLTA account Where the amount is too small to earn interest, court rules require the funds be deposited into a special interest-bearing account, and the interest is generally paid to support legal aid projects (Interest on Lawyers Trust Account).

When the amount of a client's funds is too small to earn interest, many states, by court rule, impose an obligation to deposit these funds into a special interest-bearing account called an **IOLTA account** (Interest on Lawyers Trust Account). Interest generated from these small accounts is paid to a court-designated agency, usually a local legal aid agency, to fund their activities. Because the cost of setting up small individual accounts is greater than the interest earned, or the amount deposited is so small that no interest would accrue to the client, everyone wins by having these funds generate some income for the public good. Reconciliation of this account is simpler because no accounting has to be made for interest accruing to the client.

Interest-Bearing Escrow Accounts

Lawyers frequently are asked to act as escrow agents or to retain client funds for future disbursements. In some cases, the amounts may be significant. As a fiduciary, the lawyer must treat these funds in the same manner as would any prudent investor. If the amount is sufficient to earn interest, the amount earned belongs to the client, not to the attorney, and must be accounted for to the client.

If client funds are earning interest, attorneys are expected to open separate accounts for each client. In opening these accounts, the client's Social Security number or other employer identification number should be used. If the law firm maintains the account under its own tax identification number, it will have to report interest annually to the client and to federal and state governments.

A significant body of law has emerged to avoid money laundering. In a law firm this may require reporting when significant amounts of cash are received. The problem is balancing the money-laundering rules and the attorney–client privilege. When amounts in excess of $10,000 are received in cash from a client, current legislation and regulations must be consulted.

Opening an account with a financial institution requires a federal tax identification number. This identification number may be that of the client, the trust, the estate, or another legal entity. In some cases, the financial institution may require copies of any documentation that created the client entity, such as the trust documents, death certificate, or decedent's will. The financial institution needs this documentation to comply with existing regulations on federal withholding, money-laundering, or large-deposit-reporting obligations.

Court Accounting

In addition to the preparation and filing of federal and state estate tax returns, the fiduciary often has to file an accounting with the local court that administers or supervises trust and estate matters. These **court accounting** reports are designed to show that the fiduciary has administered the estate or trust properly.

Court accounting An accounting with the local court that administers or supervises trust and estate matters. These reports are designed to show that the fiduciary has properly administered the estate or trust.

In many jurisdictions, reports are also required in civil cases involving minors. Tort settlements that are negotiated between the insurance company or defendant and the minor's parent or guardian are subject to the approval of the court. This usually requires submitting a brief accounting of the expenses, including counsel fees, the proposed disbursements to compensate for out-of-pocket expenses, and the proposed investments of the proceeds until the minor reaches a certain age. In cases involving minors, all of the parties are considered fiduciaries who must act in the best interest of the minor.

Local practice and court rules will dictate the form and methods of fiduciary accounting, called the "uniform system of accounts." The basic objective of the uniform system of accounts is to present the financial information in a consistent manner that is understandable to the court and all interested parties. The parties are entitled to full disclosure, clarity, and, when appropriate, supplemental information. Exhibit 3.9 is a sample of a model executor's account template using the uniform system of accounts. The uniform system of accounts has been accepted by some jurisdictions without formal court rule, but in others has been included in the local court rules.

Preparing Your Résumé

LEARNING OBJECTIVE 4
Prepare a traditional résumé and an electronic résumé.

Getting a job requires presenting your credentials in a persuasive manner. A well-prepared résumé is usually the first impression you will make on a prospective employer.

A **résumé** is a short description of a person's education, a summary of work experience, and other supporting information that potential employers use in evaluating a person's qualifications for a position in a firm or other organization. Exhibits 3.10 and 3.11 provide examples. You should prepare a résumé as you see yourself today, and then look at your résumé from the perspective of a future employer. What areas do you need to strengthen to demonstrate your ability to perform the type of job you would like to have?

Résumé A short description of a person's education, a summary of work experience, and other related and supporting information that potential employers use in evaluating a person's qualifications for a position in a firm or an organization.

You should look at your résumé as a continuing work in progress. Constantly update your résumé to include any new job responsibilities, part-time employment skills and qualifications, and special achievements. Add meaningful items to your résumé such as courses, skills, and outside interests that will set you apart from other applicants and land you that first paralegal job after you complete your training.

Exhibit 3.9 Model executor's account template sample—Pennsylvania Orphans' Court

ORPHANS' COURT RULES

MODEL EXECUTOR'S ACCOUNT

First and Final Account

FIRST AND FINAL ACCOUNT OF

William C. Doe, Executor

For

ESTATE OF John Doe, Deceased

Date of Death:	November 14, 1978
Date of Executor's Appointment:	November 24, 1978
Accounting for the Period:	November 24, 1978 to November 30, 1979

Purpose of Account: William C. Doe, Executor, offers this account to acquaint interested parties with the transactions that have occurred during his administration.

The account also indicates the proposed distribution of the estate.[1]
It is important that the account be carefully examined. Requests for additional information or questions or objections can be discussed with:

[Name of Executor, Counsel or other appropriate person]
[address and telephone number]

[*Note:* See discussion under Fiduciary Accounting Principle II with respect to presentation of collateral material needed by beneficiaries.]

Note

In Pennsylvania the date of first advertisement of the grant of letters should be shown after the date of the personal representative's appointment.

[1] Optional—for use if applicable.

Summary of Account

	Page	*Current Value*	*Fiduciary Acquisition Value*
Proposed Distribution to Beneficiaries[1]	645	$102,974.56	$ 90,813.96
Principal			
Receipts	636		$160,488.76
			2,662.00
Net Gain (or Loss) on Sales or Other Disposition	638		$163,150.76
Less Disbursements:			
Debts of Decedent	639	$ 485.82	
Funeral Expenses	639	1,375.00	
Administration Expenses	639	194.25	
Federal and State Taxes	639	5,962.09	
Fees and Commissions	639	11,689.64	19,706.80
Balance before Distributions			$143,443.96

(continued)

Exhibit 3.9 Model executor's account template sample—Pennsylvania Orphans' Court *(continued)*

FIDUCIARY ACCOUNTING STANDARDS

Distributions to Beneficiaries	641	52,630.00
Principal Balance on Hand	641	$ 90,813.96
For Information:		
Investments Made	642	
Changes in Investment Holdings	642	
Income		
Receipts	643	$ 2,513.40
Less Disbursements	643	178.67
Balance Before Distributions		$ 2,334.73
Distributions to Beneficiaries	644	2,334.73
Income Balance on Hand		-0-
Combined Balance on Hand		$ 90,813.96

[1]Optional—for use if applicable.

Receipts of Principal

Assets Listed in Inventory (Valued as of Date of Death)			*Fiduciary Acquisition Value*
Cash:			
First National Bank—checking account		$ 516.93	
Prudent Saving Fund Society—savings account		2,518.16	
Cash in possession of decedent		42.54	$ 3,077.63
Tangible Personal Property:			
Jewelry—			
1 pearl necklace			515.00
Furniture—			
1 antique highboy		$ 2,000.00	
1 antique side table		60.00	
1 antique chair		55.00	2,115.00
Stocks:			
200 shs.	Home Telephone & Telegraph Co., common	$ 25,000.00	
50 shs.	Best Oil Co., common	5,000.00	
1,000 shs.	Central Trust Co., capital	50,850.00	
151 shs.	Electric Data Corp., common	1,887.50	
50 shs.	Fabulous Mutual Fund	1,833.33	
200 shs.	XYZ Corporation, common	6,000.00	90,570.83
Realty:			
Residence—	86 Norwood Road West Hartford, CT		$ 50,000.00
	Total Inventory		$146,278.46
Receipts Subsequent to Inventory (Valued When Received)			
2/22/79	Proceeds of Sale—Best Oil Co., rights to subscribe received 2/15/79	$ 50.00[1]	
3/12/79	Fabulous Mutual Fund, capital gains dividend received in cash	32.50	
5/11/79	Refund of overpayment of 1978 U.S. individual income tax	127.80	
9/25/79	From Richard Roe, Ancillary Administrator, net proceeds on sale of oil and gas leases in Jefferson Parish, Louisiana	10,000.00	$ 10,210.30

[1]Proceeds of sale of rights may be treated as an additional receipt, as illustrated here, or may be applied in reduction of carrying value as illustrated on page 646 of the Model Trustee's Account. Either method, consistently applied, is acceptable.

Exhibit 3.10 Sample functional résumé

SARA MARKS

2222 Market Way
Brooklyn, NY 11223
(212) 555-8634 (Home)
(212) 555-9234 (Office)

EDUCATION
Reading College, Brooklyn, NY, 2008
Associate of Science degree, GPA 4.0
Paralegal Major—ABA-approved program
Dean's List, Vice President of the Honor Society

EMPLOYMENT HISTORY
Paralegal field work, Brooklyn, NY, 2006 to 2008
Advisor, Small Claims Court and the Brooklyn Department of Consumer Affairs
- Assisted claimants with small claims forms
- Counseled individuals on consumer affairs issues

Registration and admissions clerk, Brooklyn, NY, 2004 to 2006
Reading College
- Registered incoming and returning students
- In charge of organizing the filing system, creating more efficiency in the office

Cosmetologist and Barber, Brooklyn, NY, 2000 to 2004
- Self-employed
- Handled all phases of business, including purchasing, bookkeeping, and payroll

SPECIAL SKILLS
- WordPerfect, Microsoft Office Suite
- Excellent ability to communicate with general public

PROFESSIONAL AFFILIATIONS
Manhattan Paralegal Association

Excellent references available upon request

After you have gathered all of the necessary information and put it into a proper résumé form, then review it. Does the résumé reflect the information you want to communicate to a prospective employer? Try to look at it with an open, objective mind. Employers are looking for individuals who demonstrate a good work ethic, a willingness to accept responsibility and take direction, and the skills necessary for the job for which they are applying.

Set your roadmap for the job you wish to obtain. What additional education, training, or skills are required? This should determine your future course of study. Work-study programs and cooperative education are good ways to demonstrate on-the-job training. Depending upon your goals, resources, and time frame, a specialized certificate such as a paralegal certificate, a degree in paralegal studies, or a bachelor's degree in paralegal studies will certainly demonstrate your level of interest and ability to achieve the minimum level of education for the job.

Résumé Formats

Many formats may be used in preparing a résumé. These are sometimes referred to as functional, chronological, reverse chronological, combination, technical, and

Exhibit 3.11 Sample chronological résumé

MICHAEL C. SMITH

2345 Oregon Street, #A
Portland, OR 98765
(363) 282-7890

EDUCATION
Paralegal Certificate, General Litigation, 2008
University of Portland (ABA approved)
Curriculum included:

Family Law	Paralegal Practices and Procedures
Criminal Law	Legal Research and Writing
Civil Litigation	Estates, Trusts, and Wills

Bachelor of Science Degree
Transportation and Distribution Management
Golden Gate University, San Francisco, CA

EXPERIENCE
Paralegal Practice
- Drafted memos to clients
- Prepared notice of summons
- Conducted research for misdemeanor appeal cases
- Prepared points and authorities for motions
- Observed bankruptcy and family law court proceedings
- Completed necessary documents for probate
- Wrote legal memoranda

Administration and Management
- Participated in new division startup
- Dispatched and routed for the transportation of 80 to 120 special education students daily
- Supervised between 20 and 25 drivers
- Designed and implemented daily operation logs
- Liaison between drivers and school officials or parents
- Evaluated various conditions when assigning routes and equipment

EMPLOYMENT HISTORY

Susan Hildebrand, Attorney, Portland, OR Paralegal Intern	2008
Laidlaw Transit, Inc., San Francisco, CA Dispatch Manager	2002 to 2008
Hayward Unified School District Teaching Assistant	2001 to 2002
San Mateo Union High School District Office Clerk	2000 to 2001

electronic formats. There are no hard-and-fast rules for choosing a résumé format, except perhaps putting your name and contact information at the top. Always remember that the main purpose of the résumé is to get a job interview and, you hope, employment.

The **chronological résumé format** presents education and job history in a time sequence, with the most recent experience listed first. An alternative format is the reverse chronological résumé format, with the latest job listed last. Some suggest that the chronological résumé is the form used most commonly in the legal field. The **functional résumé format** usually gives a summary of the individual's qualifications and current experience and education without emphasizing dates of employment.

Chronological résumé format Presents education and job history in chronological order, with the most recent experience listed first.

Functional résumé format Gives a summary of the individual's qualifications with current experience and education without any emphasis on dates of employment.

The combination résumé format combines the chronological and functional résumé formats.

If responding to an ad in the paper, tailor your résumé to the job description or to the job listing of the individual employer. You may have to develop résumés in more than one format if the job openings require different skill sets. For example, the résumé sent to an employer looking for someone with specific computer skills should show these skills first. A job description looking for depth of experience probably should use the chronological approach.

Common elements of most résumés include:

- Heading, with your name and contact information.
- Career objective, concise and to the point, geared to the job description of the position you seek.
- Education, generally at the beginning of the résumé if you are a recent graduate, including specific academic honors and awards if applicable to the job.
- Experience, including paid and unpaid activities, showing the employer the skills you have to offer.
- Activities, listed briefly, unless directly related to the job description, including professional organizations and educational and volunteer activities.

Cover Letters

Cover letter A brief letter sent with a document identifying the intended recipient and the purpose of the attachment.

Always include a **cover letter** with your résumé. This applies to email applications as well. The cover letter creates the first impression and demonstrates your ability to communicate in writing. Take the time to be sure it properly reflects who you are and what skills you have. The cover letter should be brief, as your qualifications will be covered in the accompanying résumé.

The cover letter should describe the job you are seeking, summarize your qualifications, request an interview, and express a desire for the job. If possible, address the cover letter directly to the person who is responsible for the hiring decision. Be sure to spell the person's name correctly and include the correct job title.

Just as you may need different résumés for different jobs, you should personalize each letter for the specific job application.

References

References may be requested in advertisements. Even if they are not, you may wish to add them to your résumé. Select your references carefully—they are frequently called or contacted for comment as part of the hiring process. Those you select must be contacted, and their permission obtained, before you use their names as references. Faculty members and former employers are frequently asked to be used as references. In some schools and workplaces, there are policies that limit the information that may be given about employment dates or attendance. An employer following up on one of these references may make a negative inference from the limited information given.

Keep in touch with those who do agree to give a reference and who will say good things about you to a potential employer. Keep them informed on your latest work and other extracurricular activities such as charity or pro bono work so that they may speak knowledgeably about you if contacted.

Creating an Electronic Résumé

A growing number of employers are using computers to search the Internet for job applicants and to sort electronically through the résumés they receive.

Human resources managers search through résumés received online or through Internet sites by entering a few words or phrases that describe the required skills and qualifications for the position they are trying to fill. Only the résumés in the computer system that match these electronic sorting terms and phrases are considered for the job. To have your résumé considered, you will need an electronic résumé in addition to the conventional printed résumé.

Computer programs that are used to search résumés generally look for certain descriptive words, similar to the key words used to conduct legal research. For example, to highlight your initiative, words such as "initiated," "started," "created," or "introduced" should be used. For leadership skills, use words such as "directed," "guided," or "organized." To attract interest in your problem-solving skills, use words such as "evaluated," "reorganized," "simplified," "solved," or "eliminated." Be sure to use these types of key words in your electronic résumé where appropriate to make your résumé stand out from the others. A good starting point is to gather all the information highlighted in the résumé checklist.

Electronic Résumé Submission

Increasingly, potential employers and employment agencies require applicants to submit résumés and writing samples electronically, usually as an attachment to an email. If you plan to send your résumé as an attachment to an email, be sure it will look presentable on the receiver's screen and can be printed out if desired.

You cannot be certain that the recipient has the same version of the word processing program you used to create the documents. In some cases the recipient will not have a compatible document viewer and may not be able to open or read your documents. One solution is to convert the documents to PDFs. Most word processing programs allow documents to be saved in the PDF or PDF/A format, which preserves the visual image of the document. There is almost universal access to software for reading PDFs, and a number of companies, such as Nuance and Adobe, provide free PDF readers. After you create your résumé, save a copy in the PDF format for electronic distribution. If you have writing samples that you may need to submit, save those in PDF format as well.

The first line of your résumé should contain only your full name. Type your street address, phone and fax numbers, and email address on separate lines below your name.

CHECKLIST Résumé

Personal information

- ☐ Name
- ☐ Address

Education

- ☐ High school
  - ☐ Year of graduation
- ☐ College
  - ☐ Year of graduation
  - ☐ Degree
  - ☐ Grade point average or class rank

Work experience

- ☐ Current or last employer
  - ☐ Position(s) held
- ☐ Prior employer
  - ☐ Position held and dates

Specific skills

- ☐ Office skills
- ☐ Computer skills
- ☐ Language skills
- ☐ Other job-related skills

Other

- ☐ Organizational memberships
- ☐ Licenses/certifications

Because many human resource managers search by key words, you should include a key word section near the top of your résumé. List nouns that describe your job-related skills and abilities. If you have work experience with specific job titles such as "paralegal," list these key words as well. Also include language proficiency or other specialty qualifications such as "nurse paralegal" or "fluent in Spanish."

After you have created your résumé, save it again as a PDF file. Email the résumé to yourself or to a friend to confirm that it transmits correctly and has the desired appearance.

Think of getting a job as a process that starts with the résumé, continues through the interview, and ends with the follow-up to the interview as shown in the checklist for interview strategies.

CHECKLIST Interview Strategies

Getting Ready

- ☐ Write résumé.
- ☐ Make contacts.
- ☐ Network.
- ☐ Make appointments from mass mailings, telephone solicitations, and network contacts.

Before the Interview

- ☐ Know your résumé.
- ☐ Be familiar with a typical application form.
- ☐ Know something about the company or firm. Check the Martindale-Hubbell or Standard and Poor's directories.
- ☐ Have a list of good questions to ask the interviewer and know when to ask them.
- ☐ Rehearse your answers to possible interview questions, then rehearse again.
- ☐ Plan a "thumbnail" sketch of yourself.
- ☐ Know the location of the interview site and where to park, or become familiar with the public transportation schedule.
- ☐ Be at least 10 minutes early.
- ☐ Go alone.
- ☐ Bring copies of your résumé, list of references, and writing samples in a briefcase or portfolio.
- ☐ Check local salary ranges for the position.
- ☐ Be prepared to answer questions regarding your salary expectations.
- ☐ Try to anticipate problem areas, such as inexperience or gaps in your work history.
- ☐ Be prepared to handle difficult questions, and know how to overcome objections.

The Introduction

- ☐ Dress the part.
- ☐ Do not smoke, eat, chew gum, or drink coffee prior to or during the interview.
- ☐ Maintain good eye contact and good posture.
- ☐ Shake hands firmly.
- ☐ Establish rapport and be cordial without being overly familiar.
- ☐ Be positive—convert negatives to positives.
- ☐ Keep in mind that first impressions are lasting impressions.

The Interview

- ☐ Provide all important information about yourself.
- ☐ Sell yourself—no one else will.
- ☐ Use correct grammar.
- ☐ Do not be afraid to say, "I don't know."
- ☐ Ask questions of the interviewer.
- ☐ Do not answer questions about age, religion, marital status, or children unless you wish to. Try to address the perceived concern.
- ☐ Find out about the next interview or contact.
- ☐ Find out when a decision will be made.
- ☐ Shake hands at the end of the interview.

After the Interview

- ☐ Immediately document the interview in your placement file.
- ☐ Send personalized thank-you letters to each person who interviewed you.
- ☐ Call to follow up.

Source: Andrea Wagner, *How to Land Your First Paralegal Job* (Upper Saddle River, NJ: Prentice Hall, 2001), pp. 163–164.

Interviewing for a Job

LEARNING OBJECTIVE 5
Plan for a successful job interview.

Most students today work at part-time or full-time jobs while pursuing their education. These might be summer jobs, holiday fill-in positions, or full-time jobs. The interviews for these positions provide opportunities to perfect your interviewing skills. Interviewing for a job can be highly stressful, but careful preparation can reduce the stress and help you put your best foot forward so you can get the job you are seeking.

After the interview, you should review what happened and the results of the interview in order to improve your interviewing skills. Even if you obtain the job, you'll want to learn what you did correctly that helped you to get the job, as well as what you could have done better, to prepare for future interviews.

The Interview

An interview for a job need not be intimidating. With a little preparation and research, you can appear confident and make a good impression. Preparation starts with carefully reading the job description and the requested qualifications. Be sure that you can answer questions related to these qualifications, such as your experience in the particular area of law or special training in the use of legal specialty software. Research the firm by looking at its website, or by finding articles about the firm or its lawyers online. Prepare a list of questions that demonstrate your interest in the firm and the particular job, as shown in the checklist of interview questions. After you leave the interview, analyze your performance in the interview by reviewing the post-interview checklist. Then prepare and send a thank-you note to the person with whom you interviewed to make a positive, lasting impression.

Advice from the Field

THE PARALEGAL'S PORTFOLIO

Kathryn Myers, Coordinator, Paralegal Studies, Saint Mary-of-the-Woods College, Paralegal Studies Program

INTERVIEW

Q: How did the practice of assembling a portfolio come about?

A: This portfolio is actually based on the old concept of the "artist's portfolio." Anyone who is involved in a "hands-on" profession has utilized this concept for years.

Q: Instead of pictures, what do you mean when you speak of a portfolio for paralegal students?

A: A portfolio for paralegal students consists of two parts. One part is for my use in the program. The students have growth papers for each class, plus a series of other papers. I look at the collection of work to determine whether the paralegal program is doing what it says it will and whether it needs to be changed. I have modified a number of classes based on the material in this portfolio.

The other part is a professional portfolio. The students pull material from the above portfolio and create their own professional portfolio to take on interviews. This contains a copy or copies of their résumé, transcripts, selected writing samples, projects, or any other document they believe would be useful at the interview. Employers have been very impressed with this presentation.

Q: Do potential employers ever balk at seeing something that bulky? If so, how would you suggest handling it?

A: This has not been a problem for my students. As indicated earlier, we "create" two portfolios—one program-related and the other for professional purposes. I think this eliminates any problems at the interview.

Q: What is the most important thing about a portfolio?

A: The most important thing in the professional portfolio appears to be that the employer has another tool to assess the quality of the potential employee. Grades do not mean that much anymore. An "A" at [our college] may well come

(continued)

from a more demanding curriculum than an "A" at another institution. There is no basis for comparison unless the employer knows the grading scales/demands of the different programs. However, having a portfolio of material allows the employer to see what an interviewee can do.

Q: With that in mind, what should a paralegal student keep in mind when putting together the portfolio?

A: How a student puts a portfolio together says a lot about the student. I encourage students to incorporate both good and "not so good" work. That shows the employer that the interviewee can learn and can improve. Students collect material as they go through the program rather than waiting until the end.

Students should highlight their growth, their abilities, and their determination. They need to provide documentation that can show abilities that counter any poor grades that might appear on the transcript. This shows potential employers that test-taking is not necessarily the be-all, end-all to grades.

Most of all, the students need to let themselves shine through within the portfolio materials. Each student is unique, and each has different talents to highlight. That is the value of the portfolio.

Kathryn Myers is Coordinator, Paralegal Studies, Saint Mary-of-the-Woods College, Paralegal Studies Program. Used by permission.

CHECKLIST Questions to Ask at the Interview

- ☐ How does the firm evaluate paralegals?
- ☐ What is the growth potential for a paralegal in the firm?
- ☐ Why did the prior paralegal leave?
- ☐ How is work assigned?
- ☐ What support services are available to paralegals?
- ☐ What consideration is given for membership in paralegal associations?
- ☐ Does the firm provide any assistance for continuing education for paralegals?

CHECKLIST Analyzing How I Handled the Interview

- ☐ I arrived early for the interview.
- ☐ I greeted the interviewer warmly, with a smile and a firm handshake.
- ☐ I maintained good posture.
- ☐ I did not smoke or chew gum during the interview.
- ☐ I spoke clearly, using good grammar.
- ☐ I demonstrated enthusiasm and interest.
- ☐ I was able to answer questions asked of me.
- ☐ I sent a thank-you note within 24 hours after the interview.

Concept Review *and* Reinforcement

LEGAL TERMINOLOGY

Chronological résumé format 117
Complex litigation 93
Conflict checking 102
Court accounting 113
Cover letter 118
Elder law 93
Environmental law 93
Functional résumé format 117
General law practice 90
Government employment 94
Intellectual property 93
IOLTA account 112
Large law offices 89
Networking 95
Nurse paralegals or legal nurse consultants 92
Paralegal manager 93
Partnership 89
Pro bono 93
Résumé 113
Retainer 110
Self-employment 94
Small offices 89
Solo practice 88
Specialty practice 91
Trust account 111

SUMMARY OF KEY CONCEPTS

Arrangements and Organization of Law Offices and Firms

Solo Practice	In a solo practice, one lawyer practices alone without the assistance of other attorneys.
Small Offices	Small offices range from individual practitioners sharing space to partnerships.
Partnerships	Partnerships consist of two or more persons or corporations that have joined together to share ownership of a business and profit or loss from that business.
Large Offices	Large offices are an outgrowth of traditional law offices that have expanded over the years, adding partners and associates along the way.
General Practice	Generalists handle all types of cases.

Specialty Practice

Legal Nurse Consultants and Nurse Paralegals	Nurses who have gained medical work experience and combine it with paralegal skills.
Real Estate	Paralegals in this field can benefit from experience in real estate sales or from title insurance agencies.
Complex Litigation	Complex litigation requires document production and maintaining indexes, usually on computer databases, of the paperwork generated from litigation.
Environmental Law	Environmental law covers everything from toxic waste dumps to protection of wildlife.
Intellectual Property	Intellectual property is concerned with the formalities of protecting intellectual property interests, including patent rights, trade secrets, and copyrights and trademarks.
Elder Law	Elder law is concerned with protecting the rights of the elderly and obtaining all the benefits to which they are entitled.
Paralegal Managers	Paralegal managers hire, supervise, train, and evaluate paralegals.
Pro Bono Paralegals	Pro bono paralegals work without compensation on behalf of individuals and organizations that otherwise could not afford legal assistance.
Government Employment	Paralegals are found in administrative agencies and federal offices involved with both criminal prosecutions and civil litigation.
Legal Departments of Corporations	Paralegals handle documents, technology, and investigations, juggling legal, sales, and marketing perspectives.
Self-Employment	State regulation may limit the opportunities or restrict paralegal self-employment. Where authorized by federal law, the paralegal may actively represent clients without the supervision of an attorney.
Networking	Networking involves establishing contact with others to exchange questions and information.

Paralegal Tasks and Functions

1. Conducting interviews
2. Maintaining written and verbal contacts with clients and counsel
3. Setting up, organizing, and maintaining client files
4. Preparing pleadings and documents
5. Reviewing, analyzing, summarizing, and indexing documents and transcripts
6. Assisting in preparing witnesses and clients for trial
7. Maintaining calendar and tickler systems
8. Conducting research, both factual and legal
9. Performing office administrative functions including maintaining time and billing records

Administrative Procedures in Law Offices and Firms

Conflict Checking	The purpose of conflict checking is to verify that current and prior representations of parties and matters handled will not present a conflict of interest for the firm in accepting a new client or legal matter.
Time Keeping and Billing	In any law firm, it is essential to carefully keep track of expenses and billable time.

Accounting in the Law Office

Maintaining Law Firm Financial Information	A paralegal needs to understand the internal accounting needs of the firm and to understand and prepare client financial information.
Accounting for Client Retainers and Costs	A retainer is a payment at the beginning of the handling of a new matter for a client. This amount may be used to offset the fees for services rendered or costs advanced on behalf of the client.
Civil Practice: Fee and Cost Billing	Fees may be calculated on an hourly rate, as a contingent fee, or as a combination of the two.
Timely Disbursements	Lawyers cannot retain settlement funds for an unreasonable time.
Trust Accounts	Trust accounts are used for holding the client's funds separately.
IOLTA Accounts	Where the amount is too small to earn interest, court rules require that the funds be deposited into a special interest-bearing account, the interest generally being paid to support legal aid projects (Interest on Lawyers Trust Account).
Interest-Bearing Escrow Accounts	If the amount held for a client is sufficient to earn substantial interest, it should be deposited into an interest-bearing account for the benefit of the client.
Court Accounting	A court accounting is an accounting with the local court that administers or supervises trust and estate matters. These reports are designed to show that the fiduciary has properly administered the estate or trust.

Preparing Your Résumé

Résumé Formats	A résumé is a brief description of a person's education, a summary of work experience, and other related and supporting information that potential employers use in evaluating a person's qualifications for a position in a firm or an organization.
Chronological Résumé Format	Presents education and job history in chronological order, with the most recent experience listed first.
Functional Résumé Format	Gives a summary of the individual's qualifications with current experience and education without emphasizing dates of employment.

Cover Letters	The cover letter creates the first impression and is a sample of your writing skills.
Creating an Electronic Résumé	A growing number of employers use computers to search the Internet for job applicants, sorting résumés electronically.
Converting a Traditional Résumé into an Electronic Résumé	Traditional word processing documents may not be readable in electronic form and need to be converted to a readable format.
Interviewing for a Job	
The Interview	Careful interview preparation can help to eliminate some of the stress and help you put your best foot forward.

WORKING THE WEB

1. Check and download from the websites of the various paralegal professional associations information on paralegal occupational opportunities:
   a. National Association of Legal Assistants at www.nala.org
   b. National Federation of Paralegal Associations at www.paralegals.org
   c. International Paralegal Management Association at www.paralegalmanagement.org
   d. American Association of Legal Nurse Consultants at www.aalnc.org
   e. The American Association of Nurse Attorneys at www.taana.org
2. What paralegal opportunities are posted at www.monster.com?
3. What online resources are available to help in creating résumés?
4. What online career resources are available at:
   a. Career Resource Library at www.labor.state.ny.us
   b. America's Job Bank at www.careeronestop.org/jobsearch/findjobs/state-job-banks
   c. Wall Street Journal at www.careers.wsj.com
   d. CareerWEB at www.employmentguide.com
5. What law firms in your area have a website that offers employment opportunities? Use the Martindale-Hubbell Legal Directory to find the law firms.

CRITICAL THINKING & WRITING QUESTIONS

1. What are the different forms of practice arrangements that lawyers use?
2. What are the advantages and disadvantages of working for a lawyer in solo practice?
3. What are the advantages and disadvantages of working in a small multi-lawyer office or partnership?
4. What are the advantages and disadvantages of working in large law offices or firms?
5. Would working in a specialty practice be less stressful than working in a general practice?
6. What are the advantages and disadvantages of working in a corporate legal department?
7. Why would a law firm want to hire a nurse paralegal?
8. What additional costs might a paralegal incur in working in a large-city practice in contrast to a small-town office?
9. Why would a paralegal who specializes in one legal field be at greater risk for the unauthorized practice of law?
10. Other than revealing potential employment opportunities, what advantages does networking have for a paralegal?
11. Are interviews conducted by paralegals considered privileged?
12. Why is doing a conflict check important?
13. Is it necessary to do a conflict check before starting employment at a new law firm? Why?
14. When is an ethical wall required?
15. What steps should be taken to ensure that a proper ethical screen is in place?
16. Why is accurate time keeping important to the paralegal and the law firm?
17. What is a retainer?
18. What is an IOLTA account, and what is the reason behind maintaining one?
19. What is the purpose of filing a court accounting?
20. What is the objective of a uniform system of accounts?

21. Prepare the résumé you would like to have five years from now. How would this résumé help you in selecting courses, extracurricular activities, and interim employment?
22. Prepare your current résumé in print form. What format did you use? Why?
23. Convert your print résumé to an electronic résumé. Email a copy to your instructor if requested.
24. How does assessing your interests and skills help in preparing your personal résumé?

Building Paralegal Skills

VIDEO CASE STUDIES

Preparing for a Job Interview: Résumé Advice

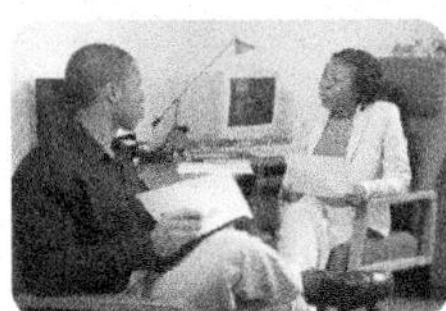

Paralegal student Reed meets with a college counselor for advice about preparing his résumé and obtains some suggestions for enhancing his résumé and preparing a cover letter.

After viewing the video case study at the book website at www.pearsonhighered.com/careersresources, answer the following:

1. Prepare an outline of your résumé with the appropriate sections, and save it as a template for future use.
2. Complete the résumé using the template by adding your current qualifications and experience.
3. Prepare and print out a copy of the résumé using the paper you would use for submitting a résumé to a potential employer.
4. Prepare the résumé for electronic submission with an email. Prepare and send the email to yourself as if you were the potential employer.

Preparing for a Job Interview: Interviewing Advice

Paralegal student Reed meets with his college counselor to obtain advice about interviewing for a job. His counselor helps him with some of the questions he may be asked that trouble him.

After viewing the video case study at the book website at www.pearsonhighered.com/careersresources, answer the following:

1. Pair up with another student and role-play with one of you acting as the human resource director and the other the applicant.
2. Make a list of questions you would ask as the interviewer.
3. Make a list of questions you would ask as the applicant.
4. Conduct the interview in front of the class or another person who can offer comments and critiques of the interview.
5. Prepare a follow-up note to the interviewer.
6. What are questions that cannot be asked? If they are asked, how will you respond to them?

Interviewing: The Good, the Bad, and the Ugly

Three paralegals are applying for a job at a prestigious law firm. Each presents him- or herself in a different manner and with a distinctive style.

After viewing the video case study at the book website at www.pearsonhighered.com/careersresources, answer the following:

1. Make a list of suggestions for each of the three applicants on what they should have done or can do in their next interview to make the most positive impression.
2. What interviewing rules did each applicant follow? What rules did they violate?
3. How important is the way you dress for an interview? Explain.

ETHICS ANALYSIS & DISCUSSION QUESTIONS

1. In changing jobs from one firm to another, how does the paralegal avoid a conflict of interest?
2. What ethical and UPL problems do freelance paralegals face that those working in a single firm do not?

3. What ethical issues might arise in determining the paralegal's supervising attorney when the paralegal is working in a small firm of three attorneys?
4. Say you are working as a paralegal in a small law office shared by three attorneys, each of whom is a solo practitioner. To save money, they share a law library and a fax machine, and they use a common computer network with separate workstations but with a common file server to save files because it has an automatic backup system. You work for each of the lawyers as the need arises, answering phones and generally performing paralegal services. See District of Columbia Ethics Opinion 303. What issues of confidentiality should be considered? As the office paralegal, are there any conflict of interest problems?

Paralegal Ethics in Practice

5. You hold a bachelor's degree in paralegal studies from a prestigious college. You want to work as an independent paralegal. May you advertise in the local newspaper and put a sign on the door of your office that uses the term "paralegal," according to your state law?

DEVELOPING YOUR COLLABORATION SKILLS

Working on your own or with a group of other students, review the scenario at the beginning of the chapter, discussing the changes and opportunities in the paralegal profession.

1. Divide the class into groups of three. One person will play the role of Cary Moritz and another the role of Natasha Weiser. The third person will act as recorder and presenter.
2. Role-play Natasha's first day on the job. She receives the memo from Cary and goes to her office to offer her thanks.
   a. What additional questions could Natasha ask Cary?
   b. What additional advice could Cary offer?
3. The recorder keeps detailed notes of the conversation.
4. Once the role-play is completed, the group summarizes the expectations that Natasha and Cary would have of the other in their working relationship.
5. Repeat the activity, with students exchanging roles.

PARALEGAL PORTFOLIO EXERCISE

Develop your résumé, using the functional format to prepare the résumé you would like to have when you finish your education as a paralegal. List the skills you expect to develop or learn before you apply for your desired paralegal position.

LEGAL ANALYSIS & WRITING CASES

Jean v. Nelson, 863 F.2d 759 (11th Cir. 1988)

Reimbursement for Paralegal Time under Federal Statute

The district court awarded, and the 11th Circuit Court of Appeals upheld, reimbursement for time spent by paralegals and law clerks where the work normally was done by an attorney. The hourly rate awarded was $40, the rate at which the law firm whose paralegals and clerks were involved bills its clients.

The government challenges the rate awarded and contends that paralegal time is compensational only at the actual cost to the plaintiff's counsel. In the context of a Title VII case, [the court] held that paralegal time is recoverable as "part of a prevailing party's award for attorney's fees and expenses, [but] only to the extent that the paralegal performs work traditionally done by an attorney. To hold otherwise would be counterproductive because excluding reimbursement for such work might encourage attorneys to handle entire cases themselves, thereby achieving the same results at a higher overall cost."

Questions

1. Does this rationale encourage lawyers to use paralegals?
2. Does this decision facilitate the availability of lower-cost quality legal services?
3. Should an attorney be allowed to charge more than out-of-pocket costs for paralegal services?

In Re Busy Beaver Bldg. Centers, Inc., 19 F.3d 833 (3rd Cir. 1994)

Paralegal Fees Based on Skill Level

In deciding the propriety of awarding paralegal fees in bankruptcy cases, the court held:

As is true with recently graduated attorneys, entry-level paralegals perform the more mundane tasks in the paralegal work spectrum, some of which may resemble those tasks generally deemed "clerical" in nature. Yet, even with these tasks, paralegals may have to bring their training or experience to bear, thereby relieving attorneys of the burden of extensive supervision and ensuring the proper completion of tasks involving the exercise, or potential exercise, of some paraprofessional judgment. Of course, the appropriate rate the attorney will command for paralegal services will ordinarily parallel the paralegal's credentials and the degree of experience, knowledge, and skill the task at hand calls for . . . [P]urely clerical or secretarial tasks should not be billed at a paralegal rate, regardless of who performs them.

The short of it is that the market-driven approach of the [bankruptcy act] § 330 permits compensation for relatively low-level paralegal services if and only if analogous non-bankruptcy clients agree to pay for the same, and then only at that rate. [T]hose services not requiring the exercise of professional legal judgment . . . must be included in "overhead."

We cannot agree that in all cases the general ability of a legal secretary to perform some particular task determines whether a paralegal or a legal secretary is the appropriate, most efficient, employee to perform it at any given instant. At times, temporal constraints may foreclose the delegation option. At other times, a paralegal—or, for that matter, an attorney—can more productively complete a clerical task, such as photocopying documents, than can a legal secretary.

Questions

1. How can the attorney prove the skill level of paralegals when seeking compensation for paralegal services?
2. Will this kind of reasoning by the court force attorneys to hire more skilled paralegals?
3. Would the existence of a certificate or degree in paralegal studies be useful in proving that the person who worked on a case was a paralegal?

WORKING WITH THE LANGUAGE OF THE COURT CASE

Phoenix Founders Inc. v. Marshall, 887 S.W.2d 831 (1994)

Supreme Court of Texas

Read the following case, excerpted from the state supreme court's opinion. Review and brief the case. In your brief, answer the following questions.

1. What is the danger in hiring a paralegal who has worked at a competing law firm when handling a case on appeal?
2. What is the supervising attorney's responsibility in hiring a paralegal who has worked at another law firm?
3. What steps must be taken when hiring a paralegal who worked at another law firm that represents an opposing party?
4. What instructions should the paralegal who worked at another firm be given when hired?
5. Under what general circumstances will a law firm be disqualified after hiring a paralegal?

Spector, Justice, delivered the opinion of the Court, in which Hillips, Chief Justice, and Gonzalez, Hightower, Hecht, Doggett, Cornyn, and Gammage, Justices join.

In this original proceeding, we consider whether a law firm must be disqualified from ongoing litigation because it rehired a legal assistant who had worked for opposing counsel for three weeks. We hold that disqualification is not required if the rehiring firm is able to establish that it has effectively screened the paralegal from any contact with the underlying suit. Because this standard had not been adopted in Texas prior to the trial court's disqualification order, we deny mandamus relief without prejudice to allow the trial court to reconsider its ruling in light of today's opinion.

The present dispute arises from a suit brought by Phoenix Founders, Inc. and others ("Phoenix") to collect a federal-court judgment against Ronald and Jane Beneke and others. The law firm of Thompson & Knight represented Phoenix in the original federal-court suit, which began in 1990 and ended in 1991, and has also represented them in the collection suit since its commencement in 1992. The Benekes have been represented in the latter suit by the firm of David & Goodman.

In July of 1993, Denise Hargrove, a legal assistant at Thompson & Knight, left her position at that firm to begin working for David & Goodman as a paralegal. While at David & Goodman, Hargrove billed six-tenths of an hour on the collection suit for locating a pleading. She also discussed the case generally with Mark Goodman, the Benekes' lead counsel. After three weeks at David & Goodman, Hargrove returned to Thompson & Knight to resume work as a paralegal. At the time of the rehiring, Thompson & Knight made no effort to question Hargrove in regard to potential conflicts of interest resulting from her employment at David & Goodman.

Three weeks after Hargrove had returned, counsel for the Benekes wrote to Thompson & Knight asserting that its renewed employment of Hargrove created a conflict of interest. The letter demanded that the firm withdraw from its representation of Phoenix. Hargrove resigned from Thompson & Knight the next week, after having been given the option of either resigning with severance pay or being terminated. The firm itself, however, refused to withdraw from the case. The Benekes then filed a motion to disqualify.

This Court has not previously addressed the standards governing a disqualification motion based on the hiring of a nonlawyer employee. With respect to lawyers, however, this Court has adopted a standard requiring disqualification whenever counsel undertakes representation of an interest that is adverse to that of a former client, as long as the matters embraced in the pending suit are "substantially related" to the factual matters involved in the previous suit. This strict rule is based on a conclusive presumption that confidences and secrets were imparted to the attorney during the prior representation [Coker, 765 S.W.2d at 400].

We agree that a paralegal who has actually worked on a case must be subject to the presumption set out in Coker; that is, a conclusive presumption that confidences and secrets were imparted during the course of the paralegal's work on the case. We disagree, however, with the argument that paralegals should be conclusively presumed to share confidential information with members of their firms. The Disciplinary Rules require a lawyer having direct supervisory authority over a nonlawyer to make reasonable efforts to ensure that the nonlawyer's conduct is compatible with the professional obligations of the lawyer.

The Texas Committee on Professional Ethics has considered the application of these rules in the context of a "right hand" legal secretary or legal assistant leaving one small firm and joining another that represents an adverse party. The Committee concluded that the Rules do not require disqualification of the new law firm, provided that the supervising lawyer at that firm complies with the Rules so as to ensure that the nonlawyer's conduct is compatible with the professional obligations of a lawyer. This view is consistent with the weight of authority in other jurisdictions.

The American Bar Association's Committee on Professional Ethics, after surveying case law and ethics opinions from a number of jurisdictions, concluded that the new firm need not be disqualified, as long as the firm and the paralegal strictly adhere to the screening process set forth in the opinion, and as long as the paralegal does not reveal any information relating to the former employer's clients to any person in the employing firm. A number of courts have since relied on the ABA's opinion to allow continued representation under similar conditions.

Underlying these decisions is a concern regarding the mobility of paralegals and other nonlawyers. A potential employer might well be reluctant to hire a particular nonlawyer if doing so would automatically disqualify the entire firm from ongoing litigation. This problem would be especially acute in the context of massive firms and extensive, complex litigation. Recognizing this danger, the ABA concluded "any restrictions on the nonlawyer's employment should be held to the minimum necessary to protect confidentiality of client information" [ABA Op. 1526].

We share the concerns expressed by the ABA, and agree that client confidences may be adequately safeguarded if a firm hiring a paralegal from another firm takes appropriate steps in compliance with the Disciplinary Rules. Specifically, the newly hired paralegal should be cautioned not to disclose any information relating to the representation of a client of the former employer. The paralegal should also be instructed not to work on any matter on which the paralegal worked during the prior employment, or regarding which the paralegal has information relating to the former employer's representation. Additionally, the firm should take other reasonable steps to ensure that the paralegal does not work in connection with matters on which the paralegal worked during the prior employment, absent client consent after consultation. Each of these precautions would tend to reduce the danger that the paralegal might share confidential information with members of the new firm. Thus, while a court must ordinarily presume that some sharing will take place, the challenged firm may rebut this presumption by showing that sufficient precautions have been taken to guard against any disclosure of confidences.

Absent consent of the former employer's client, disqualification will always be required under some circumstances, such as (1) when information relating to the representation of an adverse client has in fact been

(continued)

disclosed, or (2) when screening would be ineffective or the nonlawyer necessarily would be required to work on the other side of a matter that is the same as or substantially related to a matter on which the nonlawyer has previously worked. Ordinarily, however, disqualification is not required as long as "the practical effect of formal screening has been achieved."

In reconsidering the disqualification motion, the trial court should examine the circumstances of Hargrove's employment at Thompson & Knight to determine whether the practical effect of formal screening has been achieved. The factors bearing on such a determination will generally include the substantiality of the relationship between the former and current matters; the time elapsing between the matters; the size of the firm; the number of individuals presumed to have confidential information; the nature of their involvement in the former matter; and the timing and features of any measures taken to reduce the danger of disclosure. The fact that the present case involves representation of adverse parties in the same proceeding, rather than two separate proceedings, increases the danger that some improper disclosure may have occurred. Evidence regarding the other factors, however, may tend to rebut the presumption of shared confidences.

The ultimate question in weighing these factors is whether Thompson & Knight has taken measures sufficient to reduce the potential for misuse of confidences to an acceptable level. Because we have modified the controlling legal standard, the writ of mandamus is denied without prejudice to allow the trial court to reconsider the disqualification motion in light of today's opinion. The stay order previously issued by this Court remains in effect only so long as necessary to allow the trial court to act.

RAMIREZ V. PLOUGH, INC., 12 CAL. RPTR. 2D 423 (CT. APP. 1992)*, COURT OF APPEALS OF CALIFORNIA

Read and, if assigned, brief this case. Prepare a written answer to each of the following questions. Note the words of the California Supreme Court on appeal.

1. How does this case illustrate the clients' cultural differences?
2. Are the views of the parent in this case the same as your own? Would you have conducted yourself in the same way as the parent?
3. What ethical obligation does the paralegal have to be sure the client who does not speak the same language understands the advice given? Does it matter if it is medical directions, as in this case, or legal advice?
4. Does a law firm have a higher duty to a non-English-speaking client than a drug company, such as the defendant in this case, does in selling a product?
5. Does the law firm have a duty to explain cultural differences in the American legal system and its procedures to non-English-speaking, non-native-born clients?

Thaxter, Judge

Jorge Ramirez, a minor, by his guardian ad litem Rosa Rivera, appeals from a summary judgment in favor of Plough, Inc. Appellant sued Plough alleging negligence, product liability, and fraud. The action sought damages for injuries sustained in March of 1986 when Jorge, who was then four months old, contracted Reye's Syndrome after ingesting St. Joseph Aspirin for Children (SJAC). Plough marketed and distributed SJAC.

Reye's Syndrome is a serious disease of unknown cause characterized by severe vomiting, lethargy, or irritability, which may progress to delirium or coma.

In December 1985, the Food and Drug Administration (FDA) requested that aspirin manufacturers voluntarily place a label on aspirin products warning consumers of the possible association between aspirin and Reye's Syndrome. Plough voluntarily complied and began including a warning and insert in SJAC packaging. On June 5, 1986, the Reye's Syndrome warning became mandatory.

In March 1986, SJAC labeling bore the following warning: "Warning: Reye's Syndrome is a rare but serious disease which can follow flu or chicken pox in children and teenagers. While the cause of Reye's Syndrome is unknown, some reports claim aspirin may increase the risk of developing this disease. Consult a doctor before use in children or teenagers with flu or chicken pox." In addition, the SJAC package insert included the following statement: "The symptoms of Reye's Syndrome can include persistent vomiting, sleepiness and lethargy, violent headaches, unusual behavior, including disorientation, combativeness,

* *If citing in a California court, add "15 Cal. App. 4th 1110" after the case name and before the citation from the California Reporter, set off by commas. Ramirez v. Plough, Inc., 15 Cal. App. 4th 1110, 12 Cal. Rptr. 2d 423 (1992)*

and delirium. If any of these symptoms occur, especially following chicken pox or flu, call your doctor immediately, even if your child has not taken any medication. Reye's Syndrome is serious, so early detection and treatment are vital."

Rosa Rivera purchased SJAC on March 12, 1986, and administered it to appellant, who was suffering from what appeared to be a cold or upper respiratory infection. She gave appellant the aspirin without reading the directions or warnings appearing on the SJAC packaging. The packaging was in English and Ms. Rivera can speak and understand only Spanish. She did not seek to have the directions or warnings translated from English to Spanish, even though members of her household spoke English.

The trial court granted Plough's motion for summary judgment on the grounds that "there is no duty to warn in a foreign language and there is no causal relationship between plaintiff's injury and defendant's activities."

It is undisputed that SJAC was marketed and intended for the treatment of minor aches and pains associated with colds, flu, and minor viral illnesses. The SJAC box promised "fast, effective relief of fever and minor aches and pains of colds." . . . In March 1986, federal regulations requiring a Reye's Syndrome warning had been promulgated and were final, although not yet effective. . . . The scientific community had already confirmed and documented the relationship between Reye's Syndrome and the use of aspirin after a viral illness. There is no doubt Plough had a duty to warn of the Reye's Syndrome risk.

The question thus is whether the warning given only in English was adequate under the circumstances. Respondent argues that, as a matter of law, it has no duty to place foreign-language warnings on products manufactured to be sold in the United States and that holding manufacturers liable for failing to do so would violate public policy.

While the constitutional, statutory, regulatory, and judicial authorities relied on by respondent may reflect a public policy recognizing the status of English as an official language, nothing compels the conclusion that a manufacturer of a dangerous or defective product is immunized from liability when an English-only warning does not adequately inform non-English-literate persons likely to use the product.

Plough's evidence showed that over 148 foreign languages are spoken in the United States and over 23 million Americans speak a language other than English in their homes. That evidence plainly does not prove that Plough used reasonable care in giving an English-only warning. Plough, then, resorts to arguing that the burden on manufacturers and society of requiring additional warnings is so "staggering" that the courts should preclude liability as a matter of law. We are not persuaded.

Certainly the burden and costs of giving foreign-language warnings is one factor for consideration in determining whether a manufacturer acted reasonably in using only English. The importance of that factor may vary from case to case depending upon other circumstances, such as the nature of the product, marketing efforts directed to segments of the population unlikely to be English-literate, and the actual and relative size of the consumer market which could reasonably be expected to speak or read only a certain foreign language. Plough presented no evidence from which we can gauge the extent of the burden under the facts of this case.

Ramirez submitted evidence that Plough knew Hispanics were an important part of the market for SJAC and that Hispanics often maintain their first language rather than learn English. SJAC was advertised in the Spanish media, both radio and television. That evidence raises material questions of fact concerning the foreseeability of purchase by a Hispanic not literate in English and the reasonableness of not giving a Spanish-language warning. If Plough has evidence conclusively showing that it would have been unreasonable to give its label warning in Spanish because of the burden, it did not present that evidence below.

. . . [I]f we accepted Plough's arguments in this case, in effect we would be holding that failure to warn in a foreign language is not negligence, regardless of the circumstances. Such a sweeping grant of immunity should come from the legislative branch of government, not the judicial. In deciding that Plough did not establish its right to judgment as a matter of law, we do not hold that manufacturers are required to warn in languages other than English simply because it may be foreseeable that non-English-literate persons are likely to use their products. Our decision merely recognizes that under some circumstances the standard of due care may require such warning.

Because the evidence shows triable issues of material fact and because Plough did not establish its immunity from liability as a matter of law, its motion for summary judgment should have been denied.

(continued)

RAMIREZ V. PLOUGH, INC., 6 CAL.4TH 539, 863 P.2D 167, 25 CAL. RPTR.2D 97 (1993)

California Supreme Court on Appeal—Opinion
Kennard, J.

IV

. . . We recognize that if a Spanish language warning had accompanied defendant's product, and if plaintiff's mother had read and heeded the warning, the tragic blighting of a young and innocent life that occurred in this case might not have occurred. Yet, as one court has aptly commented, "The extent to which special consideration should be given to persons who have difficulty with the English language is a matter of public policy for consideration by the appropriate legislative bodies and not by the Courts." (*Carmona v. Sheffield* (N.D.Cal. 1971) 325 F. Supp. 1341, 1342, affd. *per curiam* (9th Cir. 1973) 475 F.2d 738.) (**4b**) We hold only that, given the inherent limitations of the judicial process, manufacturers of nonprescription drugs have no presently existing legal duty, within the tort law system, to include foreign-language warnings with their packaging materials. . . .

Mosk, J.

I concur. I write separately to emphasize the majority's caveat that "We do not . . . foreclose the possibility of tort liability premised upon the *content* of foreign-language advertising. For example, we do not decide whether a manufacturer would be liable to a consumer who detrimentally relied upon foreign-language advertising that was materially misleading as to product risks and who was unable to read English language package warnings that accurately described the risks. No such issue is presented here . . ."

. . . Evidence of the content, timing, duration, and scope of distribution of foreign-language advertising bears substantially on the question whether a non-English-literate consumer has been materially misled about product risks, and a trial court must consider that evidence if properly presented.

The majority do not define "materially misleading as to product risks," leaving that issue for another day—a day likely to arrive soon, given the high probability that foreign-language media will continue to expand in California.

MARTINEZ V. TRIAD CONTROLS, INC., 593 F. SUPP. 2D 741, 763-765, 2009 U.S. DIST. LEXIS 626, 50-54, 22 OSHC (BNA) 1758 (E.D. PA. 2009)

Read the following case, excerpted from the district court's opinion. Answer the following questions.

1. When is there a duty to warn in a language other than English?
2. Is this case consistent with the Ramirez case above?

I. BACKGROUND

This case arises out of a July 30, 2003 accident at Laneko Manufacturing ("Laneko") in Royersford, Pennsylvania that resulted in the amputation of several fingers on the right hand of Plaintiff Fernando Martinez. On that day, Plaintiff and a co-worker, Joshua Thumm ("Thumm"), were [3] operating a CMC Bliss 300 ton mechanical power press (the "press") to form metal parts for the automobile industry. The press was equipped with two sets of die, which allowed two different metal parts to be formed at the same time. The press was operated using controls called "palm buttons." Palm buttons are point of operation safety devices that require a worker to have both hands on the buttons (rather than in the press) before the press's ram will descend. Each set of palm buttons is designed to protect both hands of one worker. The press at issue was designed to accept two sets of palm buttons, thereby ensuring that both members of the two-man team had their hands clear of the press. However, at the time of the accident, a "dummy plug" was being used in place of one of the sets of palm buttons, so that the press could operate with only one set of buttons.

C. FAILURE TO WARN

Ingersoll-Rand argues that the portion of Plaintiff's strict liability claim that is based on its alleged failure to warn should be dismissed because Plaintiff has failed to meet his burden of proof. "In failure to warn cases . . . recovery is sought on the theory that the product is 'unreasonably dangerous' when 'unaccompanied by a warning with respect to nonobvious dangers inherent in the use of the product.'" Fisher, 296 F. Supp. 2d at 566. . . . "To proceed on a failure to warn theory, a plaintiff must establish that (1) a warning was either absent or inadequate, and (2) the user would have avoided the risk had he been advised of it by the seller." *Blake v.*

Greyhound Lines, Inc., 448 F. Supp. 2d 635, 642 (E.D. Pa. 2006) (citation omitted). To show that a warning was inadequate, a plaintiff must show that the deficiency in warning made the product unreasonably dangerous. . . . To establish causation, "the plaintiff must establish that it was the total lack or insufficiency of a warning that was both a cause-in-fact and the proximate cause of the injuries." *Pavlik v. Lane Ltd./ Tobacco Exps. Int'l*, 135 F.3d 876, 881 (3d Cir. 1998) (citations omitted). "While the question of causation in Pennsylvania is normally for the jury, 'if the relevant facts are not in dispute and the remoteness of the causal connection between the defendant's negligence and the plaintiff's injury clearly appears, the question becomes one of law.'" Id. . . .

Plaintiff's expert Dr. Ryan identifies two alleged failures by Ingersoll-Rand: (1) the warning labels on the press were not of adequate durability to remain legible for the effective life of the press; and (2) Ingersoll-Rand failed to warn adequately of the point of operation hazard inherent in power presses. Plaintiff does not understand English. Thus any failure to properly affix the existing warnings, which were in English, or provide additional warnings in English would have been futile and as such was not a cause in fact of Plaintiff's injury.

Dr. Ryan, however, suggests that Ingersoll-Rand should have provided the above-discussed warnings in Spanish. . . . Different courts in different contexts have come to different conclusions regarding the adequacy of English-only warnings for non-English-speaking plaintiffs. For instance, in *Ramirez v. Plough, Inc.*, 6 Cal. 4th 539, 25 Cal. Rptr. 2d 97, 863 P.2d 167, 174-78 (Cal. 1993), the California Supreme Court held that manufacturers of nonprescription drugs, which were subject to FDA regulations, were under no duty pursuant to tort law to provide warnings in languages other than English. The California Supreme Court asserted that decisions about non-English warnings in this context were especially appropriate for legislative bodies rather than courts. . . . In contrast, in *Stanley Indus., Inc. v. W.M. Barr & Co.*, 784 F. Supp. 1570, 1574-76 (S.D. Fl. 1992), the district court held that it was a question for the jury whether the defendant had failed to provide adequate warnings in Spanish where the defendant targeted the large Hispanic population in Miami through Hispanic-oriented media in selling the device in question.

In the instant case, the Court does not find it necessary to consider the apparent blanket barrier to liability adopted by the California Supreme Court in *Ramirez*, as the instant case can be decided on narrower grounds. In contrast to Stanley Industries, there is no evidence that Ingersoll-Rand intended to target Spanish-speaking populations or reasonably expected that its press would be sold to or used by Spanish speakers. Indeed, the press was manufactured and sold in Ontario, Canada, in 1978. See generally Profile of Hispanic community in Canada, attached to Ingersoll-Rand Mot. as Ex. R (illustrating the small Hispanic population in Canada). After considering relevant cases, Professor Keith Sealing suggests liability should exist for failing to provide Spanish-language warnings where (1) the product is sold or used in a geographic area of dense Hispanic population; (2) the product has been marketed [765] toward Hispanics, such as on Spanish-language cable television; or (3) the product is used in an industry with a large percentage of Hispanic workers, such as the migrant farm industry. . . . If the Court allowed liability here, it would suggest the need for too many warnings in too many languages when it would not be foreseeable that such warnings would be useful. Accordingly, Ingersoll-Rand's Motion will be granted as to Plaintiff's claim for liability for failure to warn.

VIRTUAL LAW OFFICE EXPERIENCE MODULES

If your instructor has instructed you to complete assignments in the Virtual Law Office program, complete the Virtual Law Office assignments as assigned by your instructor. These assignments are designed to develop your workplace skills. Completing the assignments for this chapter will result in producing the following documents for inclusion in your portfolio:

VLOE 3.1	Personal résumés and a cover letter in paper and electronic format
VLOE 3.3	1. Critique of each applicant, including suggestions for improvement for the next time they interview. 2. A thank-you letter for each interview.

CHAPTER

4

Technology and the Paralegal

LEARNING OBJECTIVES

After studying this chapter, you should be able to:

1. Explain why computer skills and the need to understand the language of technology are essential in law offices and court systems.
2. Explain the use of the technology in the law office.
3. Discuss the impact of the Federal Rules of Civil Procedure on electronic documents and the use of technology in the law.
4. Explain the functions of the components of a computer system in a law office.
5. Explain the features and functions of a computer network in a law office.
6. Describe the types of software used in a law office and the functions they perform.
7. Describe the features of the electronic courtroom and the paperless office.
8. Discuss the future trends in law office technology.

Paralegals at Work

Attorneys Edith Hannah and Alice Hart have decided to combine their practices to form the Hannah & Hart Law Office. Ms. Hannah has had a thriving practice for 35 years, but Ms. Hart has been in practice for only 5 years. The Hannah law firm is located across the street from the county courthouse and the Hart office a block from the federal courthouse and government complex in a neighboring city 20 miles away. Both attorneys rely heavily on their paralegal staff to run their businesses. Elma Quinn has worked for Ms. Hannah for 25 years, and Cary Moritz has been with Ms. Hart for only 3 years.

When Elma first visited the Hart office, she was surprised to see how small Ms. Hart's library was compared to Ms. Hannah's library. She also noticed that the Hart office had fewer filing cabinets and boxes and no accounting and client ledger books.

Elma sat down next to Cary's workstation and asked, "Where do you store all of your files? We have at least a dozen heavy fireproof file cabinets and a rented warehouse room full of boxes of closed files. I've heard of the paperless office, but you must have records somewhere. And how do you do legal research without a decent law library?" Cary explained that they are able to access almost everything they need for research online and use their Internet subscriptions to find all of the latest cases, statutes, and regulations. He further explained that all the client files and records are kept on the computer system.

Elma expressed her real concern to Cary: "I come from the 'old school.' We use paper files and ledger books. How much will I have to learn if they decide to use your computer system?" She was also concerned about interactions between the offices. "It takes an hour to travel between the offices. I don't want to be the one to drive back and forth to exchange documents. I also know the attorneys spend most

> "Laws too gentle are seldom obeyed; too severe, seldom executed."
>
> Benjamin Franklin, *Poor Richard's Almanack* (1756)

of their time in court. I just don't see how they will be able to find the time to work together."

When these firms combine their offices, do you think they will have any problems combining files, clients, and office procedures? Consider the issues involved in this scenario as you read this chapter.

INTRODUCTION TO TECHNOLOGY AND THE PARALEGAL

The use of technology in the law office, the court system, and the courtroom has changed the way many traditional procedures are performed. Paper files have given way to electronic documents that reside on computer servers and cloud-based Internet repositories instead of in boxes and file cabinets. The computer and the Internet are increasingly used not just for traditional document preparation, but also for maintaining client databases, keeping office and client accounting records, researching, filing documents with the court, presenting cases at trial, and attracting new clients through firm websites. Communications between colleagues and clients have changed from traditional paper documents to electronic methods including email, texting, postings on social media sites, and audio and video conferencing calls using the Internet.

Computer technology is used in the following ways in the law office:

word processing—preparing documents
electronic spreadsheets—performing financial calculations and financial presentations
time and billing programs—recording billable time accurately and invoicing clients
accounting programs—managing firm financial records, payroll, and client escrow accounts
calendaring—tracking deadlines, appointments, and hearing dates
graphic presentation software—preparing persuasive presentations
trial presentation software—organizing trial presentations
Internet search engines—searching for accurate and current legal information and factual information to support a case
databases—maintaining records and documents
document scanning—converting documents to electronic format
document search features—locating relevant material in documents and exhibits
email and document delivery—communicating electronically
e-discovery—finding and reviewing discoverable electronic data
online collaboration—using the Internet to work collaboratively
online electronic document repositories—storing and accessing documents remotely

Web Exploration

Compare the results of the latest survey information with the data listed to the right. The full survey may be viewed at the International Practice Management Association website at http://www.theipma.org/.

The Need for Computer Skills

LEARNING OBJECTIVE 1

Explain why computer skills and the need to understand the language of technology are essential in law offices and court systems.

Computer devices are being used with greater frequency to communicate and share information in **digital format** between remote offices, courthouses, government agencies, and clients. In the past, paper had to be physically copied and sent, frequently by a costly messenger service or express mail service. Now, electronic files are increasingly shared as **attachments** to emails. Large files can be exchanged almost instantaneously anywhere in the world, without any **hard copy**. Electronic files do not have the same issues with physical safety as paper documents. However, electronic files do have their own issues with security and **confidentiality**.

The legal team is increasingly using the Internet for more than just pure legal research. Most government information can be obtained through the Internet. Finding businesses and individuals is now handled most efficiently through Web search engines such as Google, Bing, and Yahoo! More legal firms are developing and using websites for their own businesses, as shown in Exhibit 4.1.

The increase in the use of electronic filing and documents in litigation and the number of federal and state rules and case law on electronic discovery are increasing the demand for skills and knowledge in the use of technology. Increasingly, the legal team must work with technology professionals in order to use computers and electronic data effectively. Thus everyone on the legal team must now have a working familiarity with computers and the types of computer programs used in the law office.

At one time, the equipment in the average law office consisted of a typewriter, an adding machine, and a basic duplicating machine. Paper was king, with every document being typed, edited, retyped—and frequently retyped again. In each instance, a paper copy was produced and delivered to the supervising attorney for review and additional changes. It was then returned for retyping and eventually sent to the client, to the opposing counsel, or filed with the court. File cabinets abounded in the law office, and numerous boxes of paper files were stored in back rooms, warehouses, and other storage locations. But now, the trend is toward eliminating paper in the law office through the use of computer technology and software. In most law offices

Digital format A computerized format utilizing a series of 0s and 1s.

Attachments A popular method of transmitting text files and graphic images by attaching the file to an email.

Hard copy A paper copy of a document.

confidentiality In the legal field, any information with regard to a client, learned from whatever sources, that is to be kept in confidence by the legal team.

Exhibit 4.1 Typical law firm website

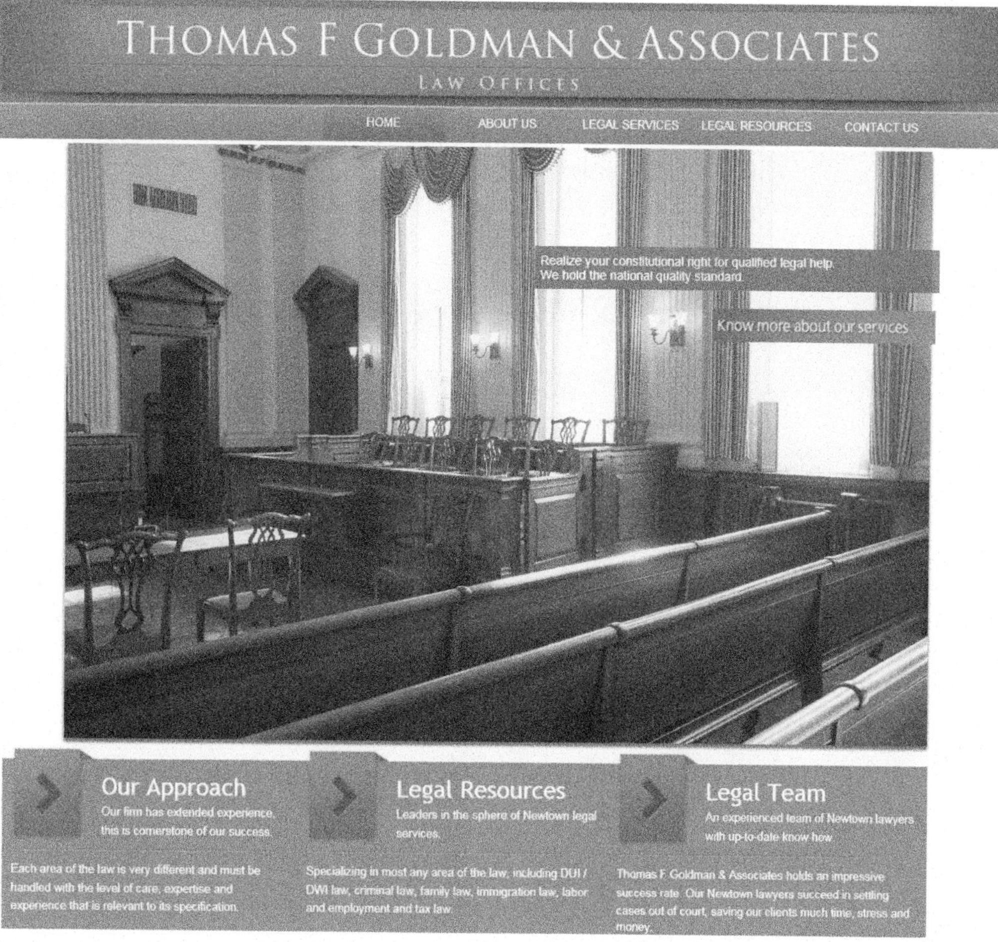

today, there are no typewriters; instead, computers are used to prepare documents using word processing software. The typical duplicating machine is now a multifunction device that can scan, print, copy, and fax documents.

Members of the legal team frequently work from locations other than the firm's main office, such as a home office, satellite office, or another firm. In some cases, they may be working in a different part of the country or world. Face-to-face meetings are being replaced with audio and video conferencing. But no matter where each team member works, he or she may need access to the case data or electronic files. One solution is to have all of the files stored electronically in a cloud-based **electronic repository**, a data storage server on a secure, protected file server that authorized users may access over the Internet.

Electronic repository An off-site computer used to store records that may be accessed over secure Internet connections.

Members of the team may also use the Internet to work together using **online collaboration** software. This software allows several persons to see the same document simultaneously and, in some cases, to make on-screen notes and comments. A number of companies provide services and software that converts case documents to electronic format and stores the documents on a secure server. Exhibit 4.2 shows a typical remote litigation network.

Online collaboration Using the Internet to conduct meetings and share documents.

In some cases, each group thinks it is communicating to the other, but in reality, the words used by one group may have a different meaning to the other group. For example, the word *protocol* has multiple definitions. To the legal team, *protocol* is defined as "a summary of a document or treaty; or, a treaty amending another treaty, or the rules of diplomatic etiquette" (*Black's Law Dictionary*—West Group). To the technology specialist, *protocol* is defined as "a set of formal rules describing how to transmit data, especially across a network" [Free On-Line Dictionary of Computing (http://foldoc.org)]. Another example is the word *cell*. To the criminal lawyer, a cell is a place where clients are held in jail. To the computer support staff, it is a space on a spreadsheet where a piece of data is displayed. Lawyers, paralegals, other members of the legal team, and the members of the technology support team must learn each other's language, because understanding such differences in terminology is essential to working together effectively and meeting the needs of clients.

Lexicon of Technology
The field of law has developed its own lexicon of terms that enables those in the legal community to communicate effectively and with precision. The technology world also has developed its own nomenclature. An understanding of the language of technology is thus a prerequisite to understanding the technology found in the law office, the courthouse, and the client's business. The legal team and the technology support team must learn each other's language in order for one team to communicate its needs and solutions to the other.

How Much Do You Have to Know?

What is important is knowing enough to know what you do not know and to be able to find the information or someone who does know. It is thus necessary for members of

Exhibit 4.2 Secure remote access for the legal profession

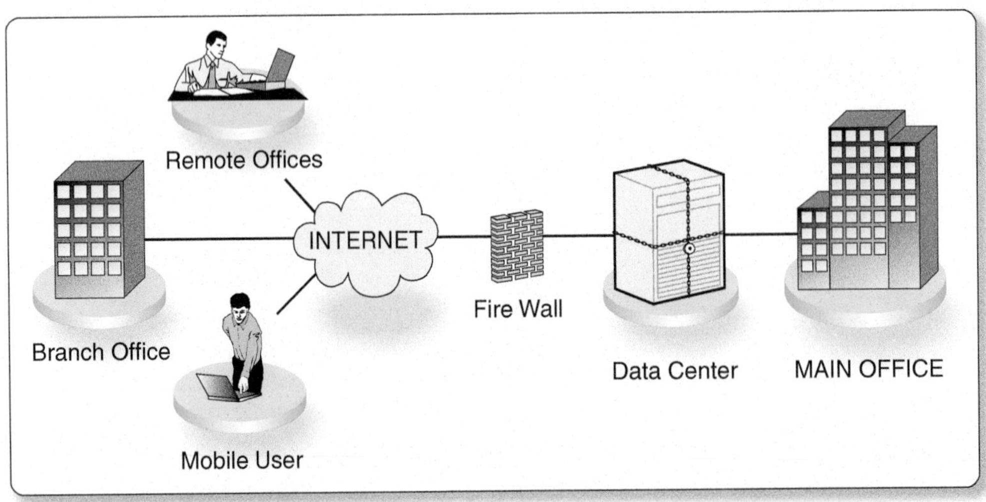

the legal team to understand basic computer concepts and be able to communicate with those who are the experts. Having a basic understanding of what different computer programs are used for in the legal environment is a good starting point. For instance, find out what word processing, spreadsheet, or database programs are used in the daily support of the legal team. Learn and understand the differences in the software and computer tools used by the litigation specialist and those used by the in-house legal support team. Most important is the ability to communicate with both the legal side and the technology side of a firm. Learn the language of the IT specialists—what some refer to as "geek talk." Keep current by reading the professional journals, legal newspapers, and online blogs for new tools and services being offered to make the job of legal and litigation teams more efficient. Attend local, regional, and national technology shows for the legal industry to see the products and services available. Ask questions, and learn enough to make suggestions for updating and changing the tools of your profession.

Technology in the Law Office

Technology Usage in the Law

LEARNING OBJECTIVE 2
Explain the use of the technology in the law office.

The role of technology in the law has evolved in a few years from a minor role, such as the stand-alone word processor, to a ubiquitous element in the management of law offices of all sizes. Computers are now being used for everything from word processing to accounting functions, such as computerized timekeeping, payroll, or tax return preparation. In some offices, telephone systems even use a computerized attendant to answer the phone without human intervention. The use of technology in litigation was once limited to large law firms working on big cases for wealthy clients who could afford to pay for the technology. Today, however, even the smallest law firm and litigator must use technology. Some courts and government agencies require computerized filing. Records previously available in paper form, such as medical records in litigation cases, are now provided electronically. The result is that offices of all sizes now need to have computer or technology support.

Larger law offices, corporate legal departments, and government offices usually have a technical support staff, frequently called the **IT**, or information technology, department. The IT staff handles questions and issues concerning the use and implementation of technology in general and computers and software in particular. Smaller offices may have a person who is unofficially responsible for the same type of support. This person is usually the most tech-savvy member of the staff—a lawyer, a paralegal, a secretary, a "friend" of the office, or a relative of a staff member—and is sometimes referred to affectionately as the office "geek."

IT Information technology, or the technology support staff within organizations.

Working with In-House Technology Support Staff

In the past, technology support was limited to supporting on-site computer systems and software. The advances in portable computers and wireless technologies, however, have expanded the demands placed on IT departments to include supporting the legal team outside the office. Members of the legal team who are working from remote locations on their wireless laptops, smartphones, and electronic tablets or other devices may need to be able to access files on office file servers or on remote electronic repositories. In addition, services must be provided for technology beyond computers and software. Litigation teams may require support for video recording depositions at out-of-office or out-of-town locations, and trials may require the use of sophisticated presentation equipment.

The IT department may not have the resources in people, hardware, or software to support every demand. If the IT staff is frequently called in at the last moment, they may not have the time to gear up to support the immediate needs of the legal team. But when the support staff has time to prepare, they can usually find a way to support many

Remote access Accessing a file server or computer from a remote location using the Internet.

potential applications, whether they are **remote access** issues or graphic-intense litigation needs. Of course, IT staff can offer the best support to the legal team when they are involved early in the process and when it is clear what the legal team needs to accomplish. For instance, if the use of a computer simulation is being considered for presenting a case at trial, calling in the IT staff in the early stages of the litigation may save time and money. In that situation, for example, the IT staff may need time to consider such issues as whether the courthouse has the necessary equipment to show the simulation, whether specialty equipment must be obtained or used, or whether the graphics can be delivered in a format compatible with the law firm's trial presentation software.

Issues in Working with Outside Technology Consultants

There are many types of independent technology consultants who can provide services with computer, software, and multimedia technology. Selecting the correct consultant is a matter of understanding what is needed. Consultants may be needed to fix a computer or peripherals such as a printer or monitor. Many outside companies are retained for a period of time on a maintenance contract to provide coverage as needed and at a fixed rate. Others are hired as needed for support or maintenance at an hourly rate.

Media consultants are also frequently called on to assist in a variety of situations. Some are called upon to prepare graphic presentations ranging from individual exhibits to multimedia simulations. Others are called upon simply to operate equipment or assist in trial presentations.

To obtain the best service from the consultant, the legal team must speak the same language as the consultant when defining the scope of service and the desired results. Hiring a consultant who uses a system that is incompatible with the legal team's system can be a costly mistake or even a disaster—one sometimes not discovered until the actual day of trial. For example, if the legal team is using PC-based hardware and software and the consultant is using Mac OS (the operating system used by Apple computers), the consultant might produce the final product in a version that works only on an Apple computer. Although such a gross oversight might seem unlikely, it has been known to happen.

The ownership of the consultant's work product must also be addressed. Is it "work for hire" that will be owned by the law firm or client, or is it a creative work that is owned by the consultant and may be used in any way he or she wishes?

Outsourcing

Outsourcing Use of persons or services outside of the immediate office staff.

Outsourcing has become a buzzword for shipping work out of the office or out of the country to save money. Some of the services that can be performed in-house are better outsourced. For years, many law firms have outsourced the payroll function instead of preparing payroll checks and tax returns in-house. The confidentiality of information about salaries may dictate that an outside firm handle the payroll process so that only a few people in the office have access to critical payroll information. In a similar vein, accounting functions may be outsourced to an outside bookkeeping or accounting firm.

IT support may also be outsourced. For example, using an outside computer consultant to provide support for hardware and software is a form of outsourcing. Such support may simply involve a help desk that is located in a foreign location answering questions.

Information technologist A member of the legal team who has legal and technology skills and primarily supports electronic discovery activities.

Electronic data is created and stored in many formats using many different software applications. While there are some commonly used protocols, formats, and methods for data creation and storage, the lawyers and paralegals on the legal team cannot be expected to have the same specialized technical knowledge as an **information technologist** has. The handling of electronic records requires the input of these information technology specialists. Even the IT specialist may need to engage the assistance of additional specialists in rarely used methods, software, or hardware. In some cases, such as those involving erased data or damaged storage media, a forensic expert may need to be called in.

IT specialists understand current information systems; the methods of producing, reproducing, and accessing electronic documents; and the problems that may be encountered in handling documents. IT specialists must therefore be part of the legal team.

The Impact of the Federal Rules of Civil Procedure

LEARNING OBJECTIVE 3
Discuss the impact of the Federal Rules of Civil Procedure on electronic documents and the use of technology in the law.

The revisions to the Federal Rules of Civil Procedure and many state court rules of civil procedure and related cases on electronic discovery have had a major impact on the role of technology in the practice of law and the advice given to clients. Members of the legal team who had given only passing notice to the inroads of computers and electronic documents can no longer ignore the impact of this technology. The new federal rules organize and formalize what had once been a patchwork of court rules and case law on electronic discovery.

The new rules specifically address the issue of the increased use of electronic documentation in all aspects of business and personal life. Whereas people once used a pen or a typewriter to write a letter, today the communication method of choice is more likely an email or text message. The federal courts have, through the rules of civil procedure, acknowledged the role of electronically stored information and the impact it has on litigation. Many state and local courts have implemented their own rules, which are often fashioned after the federal rules.

The legal team must always consider the impact of technology on documents connected with current litigation and on electronic communications internally and with clients. They must also consider the impact of technology on documents and related electronic communications that could be connected with potential litigation. One important consideration is document retention, including email documents. The ability to retain documents is limited mainly by available storage space. The more space available, the greater the number of documents that can be stored, and the longer they can be retained. With electronic files, the ability to retain documents is virtually limitless. It is therefore necessary for the legal team to carefully consider the rules and procedures for retaining and storing potentially sensitive documents.

Technology has had a significant impact not only on the ability to retain documents but also on the ability to find and access those documents. For a litigator, stored documents can be a source of a potential "**smoking gun**"—a document on which the case hinges and that may be introduced into evidence. For example, a document may admit a course of conduct, such as removing a safety feature for the sake of saving money. In some classic product liability or antitrust cases, tractor-trailer loads of documents have been produced, and a document may be "hiding" in a maze of possibly thousands of pieces of paper, waiting for other parties to find it. For example, in a well-known product liability case, a manufacturer was alleged to have sold a dangerous product despite knowing that it was defective. The smoking gun was an internal company report stating that the potential monetary damages from lawsuits would be less costly than changing the design. But the plaintiff team's serendipitous discovery of this document was like finding a needle in a haystack.

Smoking gun A document hidden among old files that would conclusively impeach or destroy the credibility of a witness or be evidence that conclusively determines an issue.

With technology and a big enough budget, all of the paper documents in a case can be scanned electronically, a format that allows an electronic search for the smoking gun. The search can be made easier if the documents are delivered by the opponent in a searchable electronic format pursuant to a proper discovery request. Clients from major corporations to small neighborhood mom-and-pop stores are eliminating paper in favor of electronic records. Letters are being replaced with email, checks with electronic payments and orders placed online.

Contemporary smoking-gun documents may include emails, text messages, or similar electronic communications that are generated and stored in an organization's or client's data server. An example might be emails confirming a pattern of discrimination against specific employees based on age, sex, or other protected classes.

The potentially massive delivery of documents in electronic form also raises concerns that these electronic documents may contain privileged or confidential information. These documents may need to be delivered to the opposing side in compliance with an electronic discovery request without the opportunity to check each document for privileged or confidential material.

Contemporary Practice

In recent years, courts, clients, and law firms have taken a closer look at how the use of technology can reduce costs and increase efficiencies. For courts with reduced staff, increased demands, limited funding, and budget cuts, the use of technology has become essential to be able to handle more cases in less time. Clients, facing their own financial constraints, look to their law firms to offer services more efficiently and at lower costs. For law firms, revenue reductions have directly impacted the size of staff, requiring the remaining staff to do more. Effective use of technology has become one of the main solutions, allowing greater productivity, reducing the need for expensive travel for face-to-face meetings, and cutting costs for document creation and storage.

The legal team, whether a sole practitioner with a legal secretary or a mega-member international law firm with in-house technical support, can no longer ignore the role of technology in the practice of law. Everyone on the legal team must understand the use and the role of various technologies in counseling, representing clients, and managing the law firm.

LEARNING OBJECTIVE 4
Explain the functions of the components of a computer system in a law office.

Computer Hardware

Computer hardware is the tangible or physical parts of a computer system. Every **computer system** includes at least one input device, a central processor, and at least one output device. A system may be as small and portable as a digital watch, smartphone, or tablet computer or as large as a **mainframe** computer requiring a large room to house it.

Older models of computers, some of which are still found in law offices, are large, ugly metal boxes connected to large, bulky, and heavy video monitors, sometimes taking up half of a desktop. Newer models are smaller and less obtrusive. In some offices, the computer system consists of a portable laptop computer, weighing as little as two to three pounds, with a docking station to connect it to a flat-screen monitor, an external keyboard and mouse, an Internet connection, and the office network.

Computers have not only become smaller; they have also increased in speed and functionality. On older models, opening more than one document would use most of the computer system's resources, slowing it down or even "freezing" or stopping the processing of data. Newer models will run well even while multiple documents are open or multiple applications are running at the same time, such as Word documents, Excel spreadsheets, calendaring programs, and timekeeping applications. Exhibit 4.3 shows a monitor displaying four programs that are running at the same time.

The ability to perform multiple functions simultaneously is in part a result of the increase in processing speed of newer **central processing units (CPUs)**, and the availability of inexpensive dynamic or volatile computer memory, called **random access memory (RAM)**. A CPU is the computer "chip" that interprets computer instructions and processes data, and RAM is the temporary computer memory that stores work in progress.

Hardware of all sizes requires software instructions to run and perform desired functions. Software is basically the instructions that tell the system how to perform each function. **Operating system** software provides the basic instructions for starting up the computer and processing the basic input and output activities. The processing of data requires additional applications software, such as that used for word processing and financial data processing.

Computer hardware A term encompassing all of the tangible or physical items of a computer system, including computers, monitors, printers, fax machines, duplicators, and similar items that usually have either an electrical connection or use batteries as a power source.

Computer system A combination of an input device, a processor, and an output device.

Mainframe A large computer system used primarily for bulk processing of data and financial information.

Central Processing Unit (CPU) The computer chip and memory module that perform the basic computer functions.

Random access memory (RAM) Temporary computer memory that stores work in process.

Exhibit 4.3 Four-page display in Microsoft Office Suite

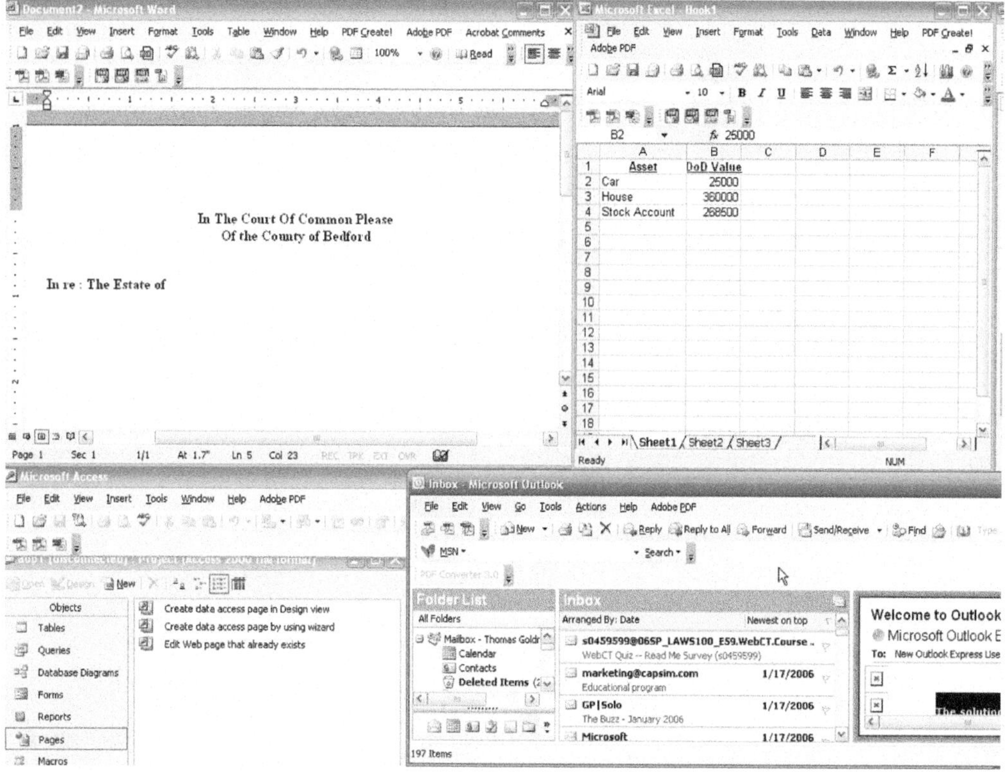

Source: Reprinted with permission from Microsoft Corporation.

Just as an automobile depends on fuel to operate, so the computer is dependent on a power source. All computer components must have a power source, such as an electrical outlet or battery, to operate the CPU, RAM, and output devices, such as the computer monitor and printer. After the power is turned off, computers cannot remember data or information that was on the screen unless it was saved to a permanent memory device. Power is also required to write the information on devices such as hard disk drives, USB memory devices, removable memory (SD) cards, CDs, or DVDs. These permanent memory devices do not require power to retain data—they only write or read the data to or from a computer.

Operating system A basic set of instructions to the computer on how to handle basic functions, such as how to process input from "input devices" like the keyboard and mouse, the order in which to process information, and what to show on the computer monitor.

Uninterruptible power supply (UPS) battery backup systems are frequently used to guard against loss of work in process when there is a temporary power loss or outage. A UPS is a battery system that can supply power to a computer or computer peripheral for a short period of time. The length of time the computer will continue to work after loss of its permanent power supply depends on the size of the battery in the UPS; it may be as short as a few minutes or as long as an hour or more. The UPS is only designed to allow time to save the current work-in-process files and shut down the computer normally in the event of a major power outage.

Uninterruptable Power Supply (UPS) A battery system that can supply power to a computer or computer peripheral for a short period of time.

Networks

LEARNING OBJECTIVE 5
Explain the features and functions of a computer network in a law office.

In the contemporary law office, a **workstation** generally consists of a single personal computer, a monitor, and a printer. A **computer network** is a group of workstations connected together. A network may consist of as few as two workstations. In large law firms, a network may link hundreds of workstations and other devices such as shared printers and fax machines, all connected through a network file server. Exhibit 4.4 is a typical computer network in a law office.

Exhibit 4.4 Typical network system

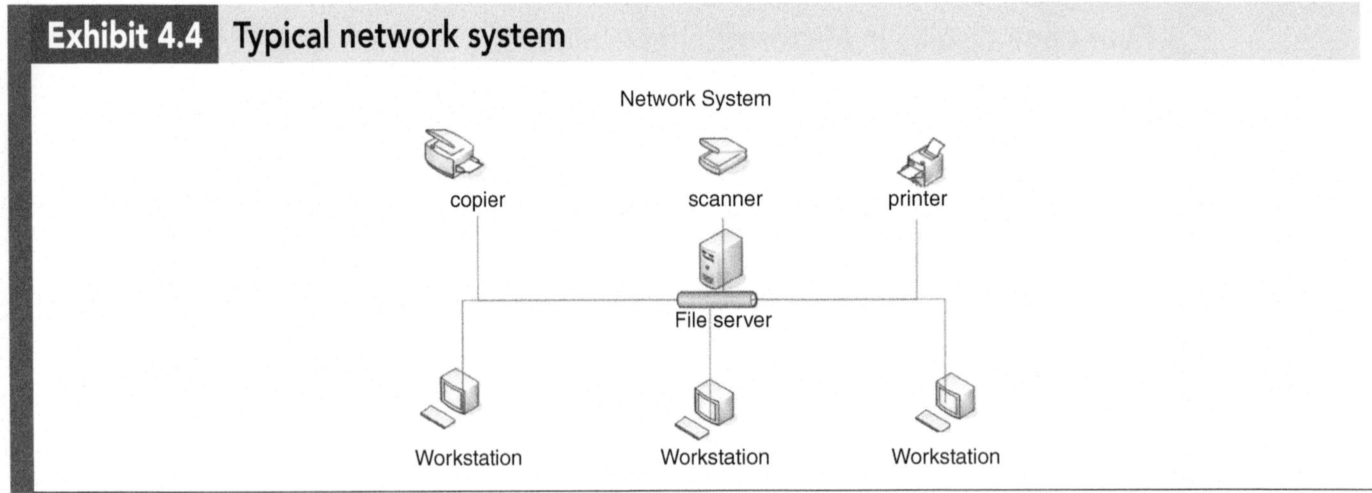

Workstation A computer connected to a network that is used for access consisting of a monitor, an input device, and a computer.

Computer network A set of workstations connected together.

Network file server A separate computer in a network that acts as the "traffic cop" of the system, controlling the flow of data.

Network rights and privileges Rights or privileges that determine who has access to the server, the data stored on the server, and the flow of information between connections.

A **network file server** is a separate computer that acts as the "traffic cop" for the system, controlling the flow of information between workstations, the file server, and other peripheral devices. It also handles requests to use the resources of the system or to access data stored there. The server requires network operating software that tells it how to communicate with the connected workstations and peripheral devices. These computers and devices are referred to as "connections."

Network Rights and Privileges

Network software has security protocols that limit access to the file server, peripheral devices such as printers, or other workstations. These rights to access the server and the other devices are sometimes called "**network rights and privileges.**" The rights or privileges determine who has access to the server, the data stored on the server, and the flow of information between connections.

Network Administrator

Network administrator The network administrator usually is the person with the highest level of access to the network file server.

Law offices that use network servers generally use them as the central repository for all electronic files. Although an individual workstation can store documents or data, it is usually stored centrally as well. Maintaining files in a central location offers a level of protection by limiting access to those who have the proper authorization, most often requiring a password for access. The person with the highest level of access to the network server is called the **network administrator**.

Limiting access to files on a file server is one method to ensure confidentiality in a large office. File access can be limited by assigning passwords to files and granting password access only to those with a need to view and work on those specific files. Because each file or folder can be password-protected separately, ethical walls can be established by restricting access to only those who are working on a case.

Backing Up Data

Backup of data Making a copy of critical files and programs in case of a loss of the original files.

The regular **backup of data** is an essential function to prevent loss of critical files and office data in the event of a disaster such as a flood, fire, earthquake, or tornado. When files are stored only on a workstation, they are backed up only if the workstation user remembers to do so. With everything on one central file server, backups can be automated to make copies of everyone's files regularly.

It is a good policy to back up the file server daily and store the duplicate copy in a safe location away from the server location, such as a fireproof safe or a bank safe deposit box. It can be disastrous to have to reconstruct files, court-filed documents, and other essential information after a devastating storm, flood, or fire destroys a law firm's records.

Advice from the Field

TECHNOLOGY IS A TOOL, NOT A CASE STRATEGY IN THE COURTROOM

Michael E. Cobo

The latest legal technology products such as animations and courtroom presentation systems can be very alluring to lawyers. After learning about these products, you may be anxious to use them. But you should keep in mind that technology products are only tools to implement a solution and are not solutions in themselves. The key issue is: What is your case strategy and what do you need to present?

An expensive, ill-planned use of technology may result in losses at trial. These losses, or even an uncomfortable implementation of a technology product, may ultimately cause some to feel the experiment was unsuccessful and abandon future use of courtroom technology.

On the other hand, such potentially devastating results can be avoided by carefully planning a case strategy with the same care as you would plan a general trial strategy. The pitfalls will be avoided and you will present a more effective case to the trier of fact.

The trial team must remember that it is the message, not the medium, that wins at trial. Take this opportunity to vary the presentation media and develop some exhibit boards or utilize an overhead. Certain exhibits are displayed best as foamcore boards. Timelines or chronologies generally lend themselves to a board, as do other exhibits that need to be larger and hold more visual or textual information. Strategically, some exhibits need to be used in conjunction with others or need to be in the view of the jury more often than not.

ASSESS YOURSELF

Before you spend a dime to develop the visual strategy, create a presentation or invest in any technology, make a critical self-assessment. Will you be comfortable with the strategy and the technological tools that will be developed for the trial? The most effective visual communication strategy will never be effective if it is never implemented or is delivered without conviction because you are not comfortable using the tools.

The effective use of technology involves (1) creating an inventory of the visual requirements, (2) selecting the proper technologies, medium and tools, and (3) being prepared to properly use the products to implement your case strategy.

Wide Area Networks

Time can be saved by sharing information electronically instead of by personal delivery or courier, even within a city, building, or floor. Many firms—even some as small as two people—maintain multiple office sites, such as a downtown and a suburban location or a main office and a satellite office across from the courthouse. Each of these offices may have a separate computer network.

With high-speed communication lines, these separate networks may be connected to form a **wide area network** or "network of networks." Access to a workstation on one of the networks allows access to the other networks in the system and the peripherals attached to the network, such as network printers. This allows a person in one office to print documents on a printer in another office. Files may be shared among all the members of the legal team regardless of the office where they are physically located.

Wide area network A network of networks. Each network is treated as if it were a connection on the network.

The Internet

The **Internet** may be thought of as simply a very large group of computers linked together, with the ability to search all the connections for information. An office in which all of the computers are networked together is much like a small version of the Internet. Each person's computer is connected to other people's computers, generally with a main computer where the shared data files and the software reside. The network operating system controls the connections and how the requests from each computer are handled and directed. This main control computer usually is referred to as the file server (see Exhibit 4.5).

Internet A group of computers worldwide, linked together, with the added ability to search all the connections for information.

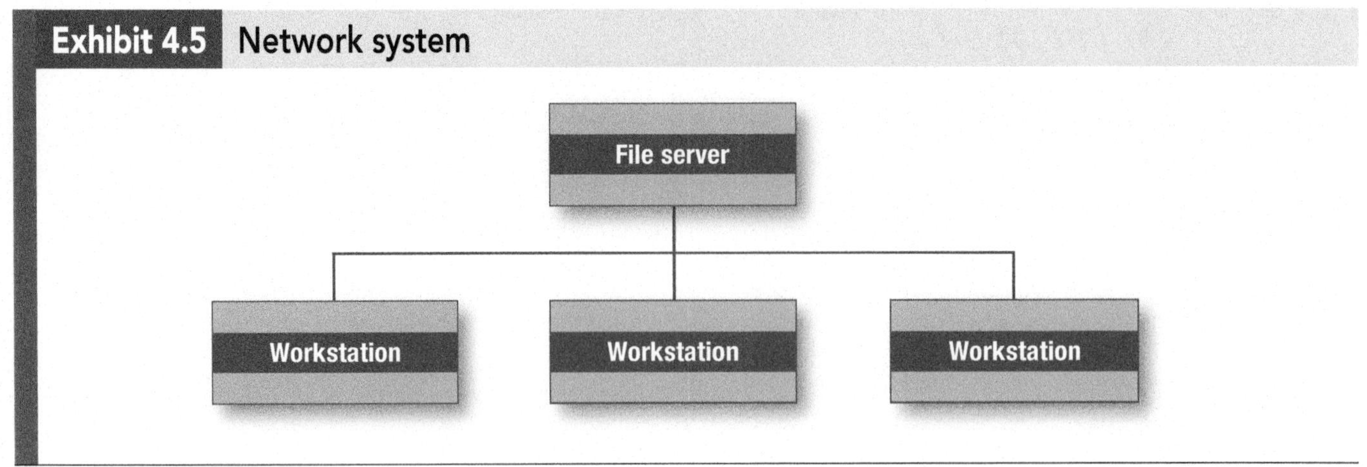

Exhibit 4.5 Network system

Local area network (LAN) A network of computers at one location.

Internet service provider (ISP) The company providing the connection between the user and the Internet.

Modem A device that translates electronic signals to allow computers to communicate with each other.

The **local area network (LAN)** search tool is usually a program such as Microsoft Windows Explorer (not to be confused with the Internet browser Internet Explorer) that locates files on the local computer or the other computers that have shared access. Exhibit 4.6 shows the Explorer screen, and Exhibit 4.7 shows the Search companion.

Internet service providers (ISPs) provide local or toll-free access numbers that most people use to connect to their service. A **modem** is used to translate the electronic signals for transmission so the computers can "talk" to each other. The modem converts (modulates) the information from the keyboard and computer into a form that can be transferred electronically over telephone lines, cable connections, and radio waves.

At the receiving end of the signal is another modem that reconverts (demodulates) the signal into a form usable by the computer. Speeds of transmission vary widely, depending on the modem and the ISP service. A multipage document will take longer to transmit or receive than a single-page document. As with most services, the higher the speed, the higher the cost. The cost of a high-speed connection will depend upon the volume of data regularly sent or received.

Perhaps less obvious is the size of the files in a graphic format. Most government forms are available in a graphic form rather than a text form. A single one-page

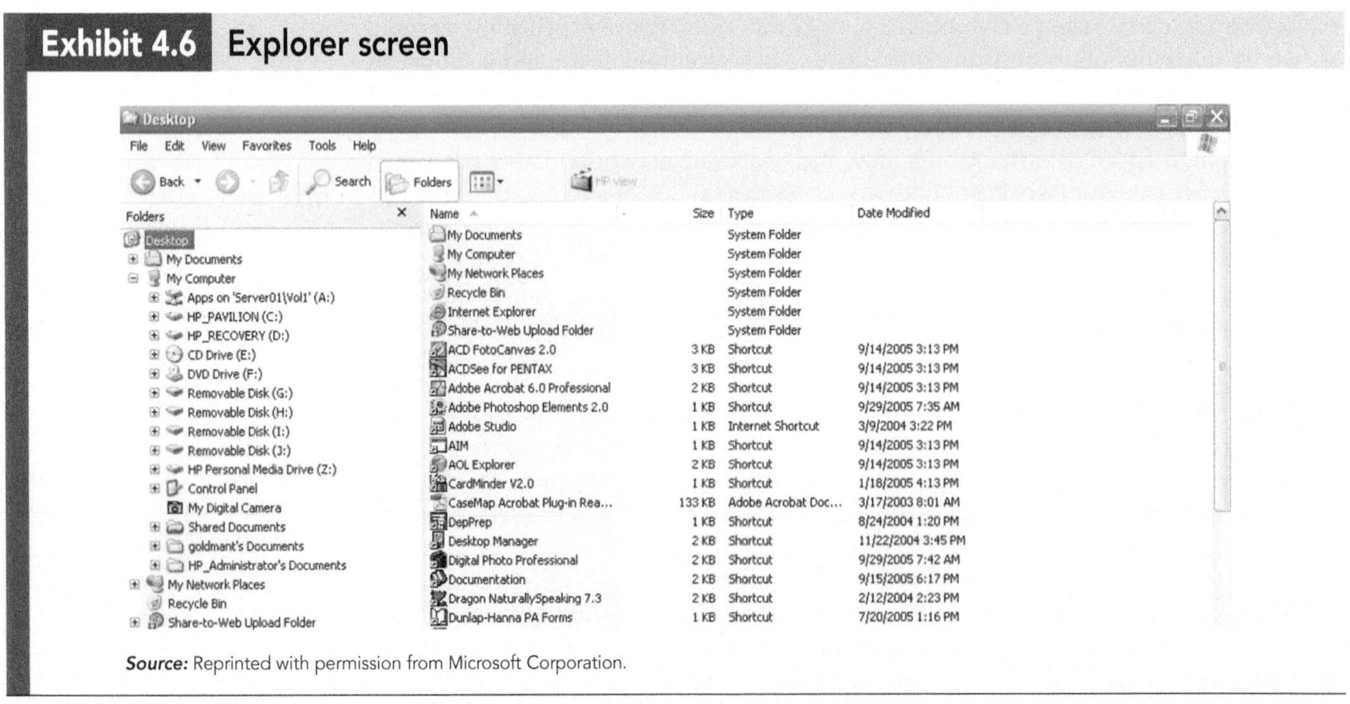

Exhibit 4.6 Explorer screen

Source: Reprinted with permission from Microsoft Corporation.

Exhibit 4.7 Search companion

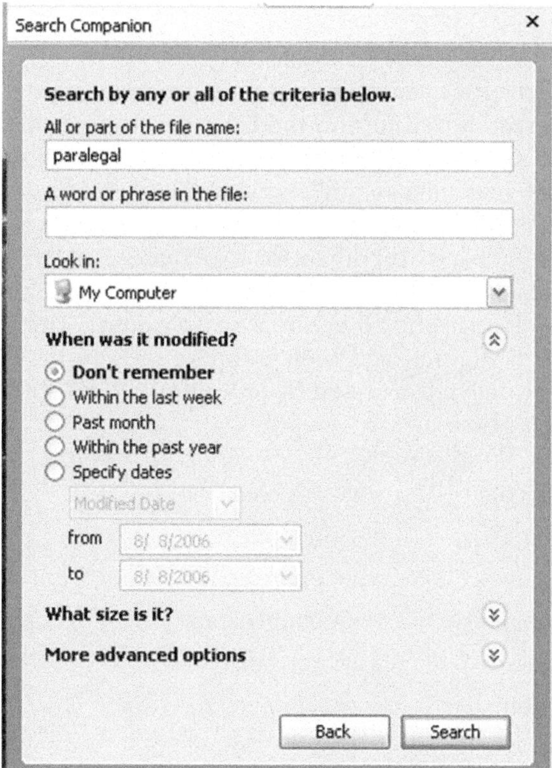

Source: Reprinted with permission from Microsoft Corporation.

form in graphic format may be the equivalent of a 10-page text document. If such forms or other graphic documents are transmitted frequently, it might be advisable to upgrade to a high-speed line.

Online Computer Resources

The number of Internet resources increases daily. But finding information is easy when you know the specific source and the precise information being sought. If the exact source is known, the user may enter the computer address of the specific page or document and obtain the result almost instantly. However, in many cases the user will have to locate information about a specific item without first knowing where to find it.

Internet Browsers

Internet browser A program that allows a person to use a computer to access the Internet.

An **Internet browser** is a program that allows a person to access the Internet. Unless the computer has a direct connection to a computer database, a browser is needed. A few of the most popular Web browsers are Microsoft Edge, Microsoft Internet Explorer, Google, and Firefox. These browsers typically are used with Internet service providers that do not themselves provide any content but rather act as an intermediary between the user and the World Wide Web. Some services, such as MSN, provide content such as news and weather and specialty sections for sharing information, along with Internet connections and email.

Internet browsers such as Google, Firefox, Microsoft Edge, and Internet Explorer provide search features that allow a search of available Web resources. These searches require only inputting into the search engine a word or phrase to obtain a listing of potentially relevant information. Specialized search engines, such as Google and Yahoo!, use highly developed algorithms to search for relevant information and return a listing in order of relevancy and with amazing accuracy.

All of the browsers basically provide two main screens—one to display email (see Exhibit 4.8) and another to display content and Internet search results (see Exhibit 4.9.)

Search Engines

Internet search engine An Internet search engine is a program designed to take a word or set of words and locate websites on the Internet.

An **Internet search engine** is a program designed to take a word, or set of words, and search websites on the Internet. Among the available Internet search engines, each searches in a different fashion. The same search request may generate totally different results on different search engines.

The number of search engines is expanding constantly. Some search engines are more suitable than others for legal searches. Many search engines are designed for use by children and families, so they may not return the results needed.

Uniform Resource Locator (URL) The address of a site on the Internet.

It is useful to create a search query, run it through a number of different search engines, and then compare the results. Each of the search engines shown below may be accessed by entering its **URL (uniform resource locator)** in your web browser:

Ask.com	www.ask.com
Dogpile	www.dogpile.com
Excite	www.excite.com
Google	www.google.com
Zoo	www.zoo.com
Yahoo!	www.yahoo.com

Exhibit 4.8 Email display

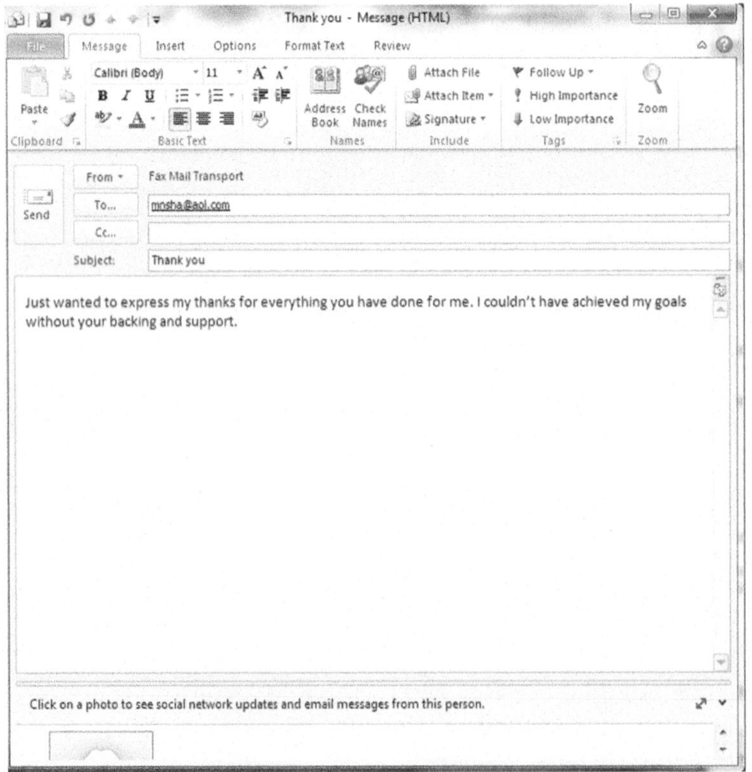

Used by permission of Microsoft.

Exhibit 4.9 Internet browser

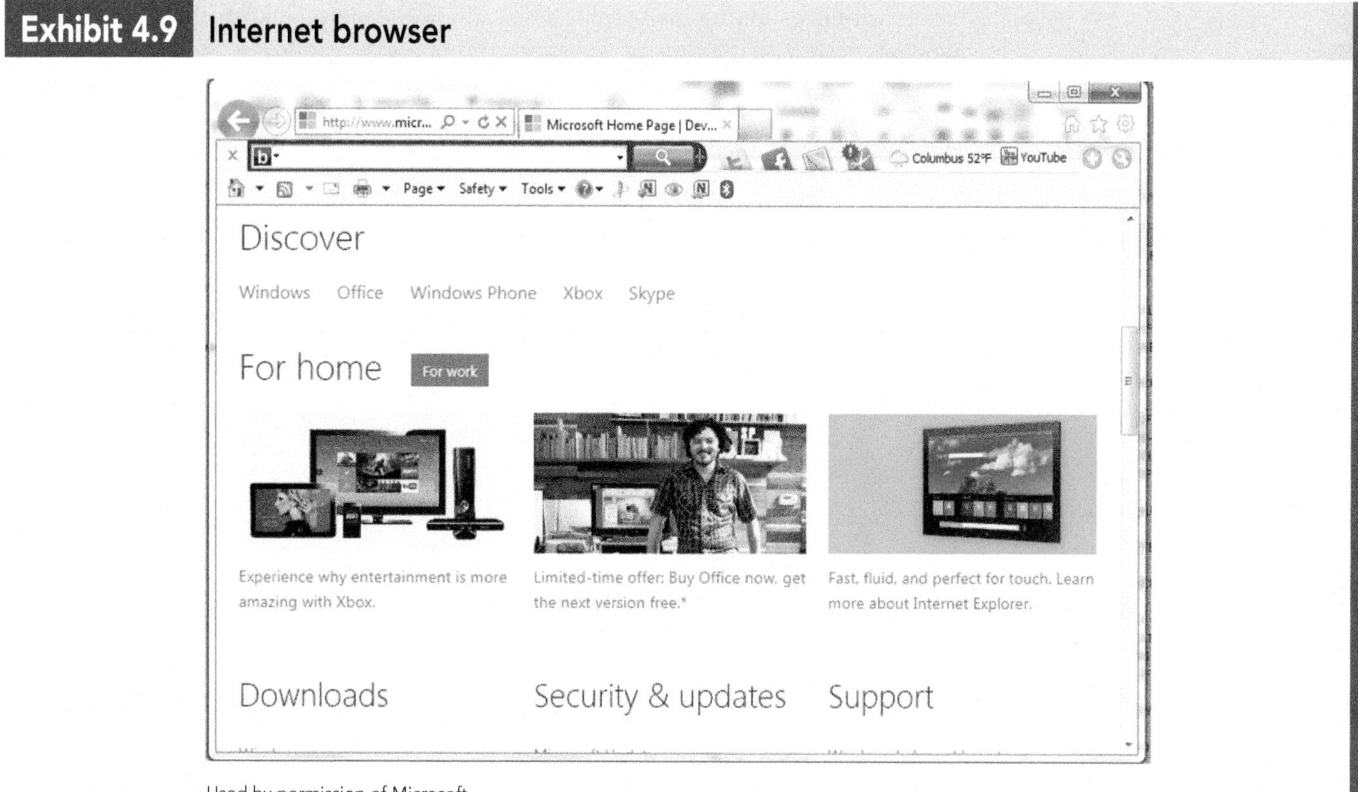

Used by permission of Microsoft.

Upon executing the search, some of the information will be shown immediately on the screen and will not require any more searching. The data—such as a phone number, address, or other limited information—may be copied manually or printed out to capture the displayed page. Other information may be in the form of large text or graphic files. These may be many pages long or in the form of graphic image files, such as PDFs. For example, the tax forms available from the Internal Revenue Service are presented in PDF format.

It should be remembered that the addresses of websites tend to change frequently. It is a good idea to keep a list of frequently used websites handy and update it regularly.

Web Exploration

Obtain copies of tax forms from the Internal Revenue Service at www.irs.gov.

Addresses and Locations

It is usually easier to find something when the user already has some information about its location. We find people by looking for their home or business address or their telephone number. The modern equivalent of a telephone number is the **computer address and location**. Web pages also have addresses, known as uniform resource locators, or URLs.

The URL is made up of three parts:

Protocol://Computer/Path

The **protocol** is usually "http" (hypertext transfer protocol). The "Computer" above is the name assigned to the computer on the Internet, such as www.bucks.edu. The "Path" is the directory or subdirectory on the computer where the information can be found.

The URL may be thought of as a file cabinet in which the protocol is the name of the file cabinet, the computer is the drawer in the file cabinet, and the path is the file folder in the drawer. However, not all URLs have a path as part of the address.

Computer address and location The modern equivalent of a person's telephone number is the email address. Pages on the Internet also have addresses known as the uniform resource locator (URL), made up of three parts: protocol, computer, and path.

Protocol In a URL, the required format of the web address.

Part of the naming protocol is a domain nomenclature, with three-letter extensions that designate the type of website. Common extensions are:

.org	organizations
.edu	educational institutions
.com	commercial operations
.gov	government agencies
.biz	business
.mil	military

In addition, there are two-letter extensions assigned to countries, such as

.jp	Japan
.fr	France
.uk	United Kingdom

These designations refer to the country where the computer is located.

Many people save information about websites for future use, either as a copy, on cards, or in a database. The website profile checklist below provides suggested headings for such lists.

In determining the authenticity of information found on the Internet, knowing whether the computer is a commercial site (.com or .biz) or a government site (.gov) is sometimes useful. Some websites may appear to be official government websites containing official information but actually are private sites. For example, the official URL for the Internal Revenue Service is www.irs.gov. This is not to be confused with the unofficial private website www.irs.com. To obtain the official Internal Revenue Service forms and information, you must use the official site, www.irs.gov.

Potentially one of the biggest time savers for the paralegal is the ready availability of legal forms, files, and other information on the Internet. Public information that at one time would have required a trip to the courthouse or other government office is now instantly available without leaving the law office. This information may come from public or private sources. Government information typically is available without cost or at minimal cost. Private information may be free to all or provided at a cost per use, per page, or per time period (such as a month).

Legal Research

In the law office, one of the most important uses of the Internet is to do research, both factual and legal. Using powerful search engines, such as Google, Yahoo!, and Ask.com, can help the paralegal locate almost any information that is available on the Internet. More legal research is being conducted on the Internet as law offices reduce the size of paper-based law libraries in favor of online resources. A number of companies provide access for a fee to case law, statutory material, and other secondary legal sources. Among the most widely used of these are Westlaw, LexisNexis, Loislaw, and VersusLaw. Although some websites offer information without charge, most do not have the depth of information that the paid sites offer. The Cornell University Law School site is among the most popular of the free sites.

Web Exploration

Check the free resources of the Cornell Law School website at http://www.law.cornell.edu/.

CHECKLIST Website Profile

- ☐ Address (URL):
- ☐ Name of organization or site:
- ☐ Key subject:
- ☐ Secondary subject:
- ☐ Cost:
- ☐ Comments:

Formats of Available Information

Most of the items that are displayed can be printed using a printer attached to a computer. At the top of most Web browsers is a printer icon or a Print command within the FILE menu at the top of the page. Clicking on the icon or word PRINT in the FILE pull-down menu will initiate the print process. Patience may be necessary, as the computer may have to take some time to access the original source of the information. Clicking several times will not speed up the process and may actually result in several copies of the same information being printed.

File Attachments

A popular method for transmitting text files and graphic images is by **attachment** of the file to an email. This is much easier than it sounds. Today, almost everyone has an email address, whether at home, at work, or both. To send or receive emails requires the use of an Internet service provider and a browser, such as Internet Explorer, or an email program. In a typical email, text is entered on the keyboard and transmitted to the email account of a recipient, who reads it online. Virtually any file can be attached and sent with an email. The receiver need only click the mouse on the attachment, which may appear as an icon at the bottom of the email. In most cases, the file will open using the same program with which it was created, such as Microsoft Word, Corel WordPerfect, or Adobe Acrobat. Occasionally, a file may be in a format that the receiver does not have the software to open. This is particularly true with regard to graphic images, pictures, and drawings.

File attachment The attachment is a popular method for transmitting text files, and occasionally graphic images, by attaching the file to an email.

Receiving and Downloading Files and Attachments

The method for downloading files and attachments is the same. Users should first determine the directory (folder) into which they will be downloading these files. In Windows, this usually is a folder called My Download Files or My Files. If there is no existing folder, Windows Explorer can be used to create a file with a name assigned to it. Windows Explorer may be found in the Start directory under Programs.

Most of the files attached to an email will be word processing files created and saved as either Word or WordPerfect documents. The user may want to save these files directly into the Word or WordPerfect directory. Attachments may also be opened immediately instead of saving for later use. Alternative file formats may be offered, such as Word, WordPerfect, or PDF, so it is important to be sure you have the appropriate program on your computer that can open and view the file.

Normally, text files and graphic images are static files; by themselves, they do not perform any function but must be used with another program such as a word processor or graphic image viewer. It has become common, however, to send attachments that have within them mini-programs called "macros" that perform functions when activated, such as calculating sums in spreadsheets. Others are self-contained programs containing animations, such as screensavers.

Some program files have an extension of either ".exe" or ".com." Files with these extensions may run automatically after downloading. Therefore, greater caution must be taken in downloading files with these or other unknown file extensions, which may contain macros (mini-programs) with formulas that run automatically and

CHECKLIST To Retrieve and Download a Form

- ☐ Select a file format.
- ☐ Select the file(s) you wish to receive. To select multiple items, hold down the Control button while selecting.
- ☐ Click the Review Selected Files button. A Results page will be displayed with links to the file(s) you requested.
- ☐ Select the file title to retrieve.

may contain computer viruses, as discussed below. Remember that it is not enough to depend on the sender being a reliable source, as even the most reliable source can have a security breach that allows a virus to be attached to a file, or the source may be forwarding files from other, less reliable sources without checking the files before sending them to you.

Sending Files

Some Internet service providers (ISPs) limit the amount of information that may be sent at one time, depending on the speed of the connection and how busy the system is at different times of the day. This may limit the number of pages that may be sent at one time. With increased transmission speed, or bandwidth, comes the ability to transmit much larger files and more pages at the same time.

Increasingly, large-size graphics files and images such as photographs are sent attached to emails. The amount of time required to send a file depends on the size of the file and the bandwidth it is traveling across. Bandwidth may be thought of as a pipeline through which only a limited amount of product can be transmitted at any one time. The larger files require more bandwidth to avoid slowing down the system. To more equitably share the limited bandwidth available, ISPs and network operators limit the number of files or the size of files that one user may transmit, either permanently or temporarily during peak usage times. In some offices, the same limitations may be imposed to overcome the bandwidth limitation. Files may be transmitted in a compressed format, frequently referred to as zip files. Large files are run through a program that compresses them before being sent. The recipient of the compressed file then must uncompress the file before being able to read it.

A number of programs are available to compress and decompress files. Some of these are operated manually through several steps, and other programs perform the task automatically. For occasional use, the manual method is acceptable, but with the increasing number of compressed files, it may be more efficient to purchase one of the automatic programs. Trial versions of some of these decompression programs may be downloaded from the Internet without charge from software companies that will then encourage the user to buy the full version after the trial period expires.

ETHICAL PERSPECTIVE

Arizona Law Firm Domain Names Opinion No. 2001-05 (March 2001) Summary

A law firm domain name does not have to be identical to the firm's actual name, but it must comply with the Rules of Professional Conduct, including refraining from being false or misleading. And it may not imply any special competence or unique affiliation unless this is factually true. A for-profit law firm domain name should not use the domain suffix ".org" nor should it use a domain name that implies that the law firm is affiliated with a given nonprofit organization or governmental entity. [ERs 7.1, 7.4, 7.5]

ETHICAL PERSPECTIVE

Ohio Rule on Commercial Law-Related Websites

Ohio lawyers may not participate in a commercial law-related website that provides them with clients if the arrangement entails prohibited payment for referrals or if the business is engaged in the unauthorized practice of law. (Ohio Supreme Court Board of Commissioners on Grievances and Discipline opinion 2001–2)

Electronic Filing

A number of courts have established procedures for filing pleadings electronically. Each court is free to set up its own rules and procedures, which must be consulted before one attempts to use their service. The Internal Revenue Service and some states have combined in a joint effort to allow electronic filing of both the federal and state individual income tax returns in one step. The local or state tax authority retrieves the information from the Internal Revenue Service. A feature of this service, known as IRS e-file, is the return receipt when the federal and state governments receive the form.

Types of Image Formats

With increasing frequency, the Internet is being used to obtain needed forms, such as government agency forms, tax forms, or court forms. Even the best-equipped office will require one form or another that is not in the office files. It may be an unusual federal tax form or a form from another state. Most federal government forms use the PDF format, and many state agencies use it as well.

Computer and Network Security

As law offices, courts, and clients become more dependent upon the use of computers and the Internet, security has become a critical issue. Within a computer network, a virus or malicious program introduced into one workstation can adversely impact every workstation on the network and the network file server itself. Any workstation is a potential access point for programs that could corrupt the files stored on the system. In rare cases, employees have introduced annoying or potentially harmful programs as a way to get even with an employer. Part of the solution to these types of issues is to limit access to the network, such as by restricting the ability to access the file server from workstations, limiting the ability to make changes to operating systems, or limiting activity to saving documents.

The use of the Internet from workstations has also introduced the potential for unauthorized parties to gain access to the computer network—referred to as "**hacking**." In some instances, the person wants to gain access to information in files stored on the network. In other cases, the intent is to undermine the integrity of the system by modifying files and programs or introducing computer viruses that can delete files, programs, or operating systems.

Hacking Unauthorized access to a computer or computer network.

Firewalls

A **firewall** is a program designed to limit access to a computer or a network. Depending upon the complexity of the program, it may totally restrict access or limit access to certain kinds of programs or sources. For example, many parents use a form of a firewall designed to limit their children's access to certain kinds of programs and websites that are deemed to be unacceptable.

Firewalls Programs designed to limit access to authorized users and applications.

A firewall can be a two-edged sword for the paralegal: it prevents unauthorized access to the network, but it may also prevent the paralegal from accessing the firm's files from an off-site location, such as a courthouse, a client's office, or opposing counsel's offices. It is important to check a connection to be sure it will allow data to be accessed from a remote location before it is needed for a trial, deposition, or presentation. With enough time, almost any issue may be resolved with the local system administrator.

Encryption Technology

Encryption technology basically permits a computer user to put a lock on information to protect it from being accessed by others. Encryption technology is like a lock on a house.

Encryption Encryption is technology that allows computer users to put a "lock" around information to prevent access by others.

ETHICAL PERSPECTIVE

Interception of Electronic Communications

Interception or monitoring of email communications for purposes other than assuring quality of service or maintenance is illegal under the Electronic Communications Privacy Act of 1986, as amended in 1994. [18 U.S.C. B2511(2)(a)(i)]

Without the lock in place, unwanted persons can easily enter the house and steal its contents; with the lock in place, it is more difficult to enter and take the house's contents. Encryption software lets computer users scramble information so that only those who have the encryption code can enter the database and use the information.

Encryption

Confidential or privileged information sent over the Internet is frequently encrypted by the sender and unencrypted by the receiver because of the concern that it will be intercepted when transmitted over the Internet. Encryption programs use algorithms (mathematical formulas) to scramble documents. Without the proper password or encryption key, unauthorized persons are not able to read the files and determine their content.

The levels of protection offered by the different encryption programs are much like different types of combination locks. The least security is provided by a two-number combination lock frequently found on inexpensive luggage. As the numbers required for opening the lock increase to three, four, or more numbers, the security also increases. It is not hard to see how the two-digit combination lock can be quickly opened, while the four-digit lock requires more time and effort. For an amateur computer hacker with simple encryption-breaking software, a basic encryption program might be thought of as equivalent to a two- or three-number combination lock. The higher-level program, with tougher algorithms designed to thwart a professional code-breaker, would be like a lock with four or more digits. As computers become faster, more sophisticated methods will be required.

Computer Viruses

Unfortunately, some people take sadistic pleasure in developing and disseminating programs that attack and destroy computer programs, internal operating systems, and occasionally entire hard drives. These programs are known as **computer viruses.** Viruses range from those that create only a minor inconvenience to those that can destroy data and cause shutdowns.

Computer viruses Viruses are programs that attack and destroy computer programs, internal computer operating systems, and occasionally the hard drives of computers.

Some simple precautions can prevent disaster. Virus-protection programs, such as those sold by Norton, McAfee, and others, are as important to have on a computer as the computer operating system itself. This should be the first program loaded onto a new computer.

Antivirus programs scan the computer to identify the presence of viruses, and the better programs eliminate the virus entirely. Every disk should be scanned with an antivirus program before being used. Files that are downloaded from other computers or over the Internet should also be checked. As good as these programs are, they quickly go out of date as new viruses are unleashed. Therefore, these virus-checking programs should be updated regularly.

LEARNING OBJECTIVE 6

Describe the types of software used in a law office and the functions they perform.

Operating Systems

The two most popular computer systems are the PC ("personal computer") and the Apple. The original designs of these two systems were built around different central processor chips manufactured by different companies—Intel in the case of the PC, and Motorola for Apple. Each computer system requires its own unique operating system.

Although both computer systems have their advocates, the PC has had a dominant position in the legal and business communities, where computers are mainly used for writing text and performing mathematical computations. The Apple system achieved a dominant position in the graphic and artistic communities. The legal community has been increasingly switching to or adopting the Apple product line from iPhone to iPad to Mac laptop computers.

In 2006, Apple started to utilize the same CPU manufacturer as the PC manufacturers, allowing the new Apple computers to use **software** for both systems on its computers. Microsoft Windows™ is the most commonly used computer operating system for the personal computer. The latest version, Windows 10, is designed to take advantage of increased computer operating speeds and better graphics. However, different versions of the Windows operating system may be found in the workplace.

Software Programs containing sets of instructions that tell the computer and the other computer-based electronic devices what to do and how to do it.

Among the newer operating systems gaining followers is the Linux operating system. It is offered as an alternative to Microsoft operating systems and is provided without a license or royalty fee, but with the agreement that any improvements will be made available without a fee to anyone using the system.

Applications Software

Applications software programs perform specific tasks, such as preparing documents, sorting information, performing computations, and creating and presenting graphic displays. These are the programs used in the management of the law office and the management of client cases.

Applications software Programs that perform specific tasks such as word processing.

Word Processing

Written communication and document preparation are at the heart of every law office. This writing may include letters to clients, other counsel, or the court, as well as contracts and pleadings. Achieving clarity and accuracy in writing frequently means writing, rewriting, and correcting the same document, sometimes multiple times by different members of the legal team. Computerized word processing makes it possible for other team members to easily make or suggest changes to a document before it reaches its final form. Word processing files are sent electronically to the appropriate members of the legal team for review. Changes or revisions are frequently made to the electronic copy by each reviewer. If several people are working on a document, the changes made by each person may be monitored using built-in features such as MS Word's "**Track Changes**" tool. This feature shows the original text, the deleted text, and the new text by a series of strikethrough lines over the deleted text. It also shows margin notes within the document. Exhibit 4.10 shows an original Word file, the changes inserted, old text with a strikethrough line, and the final version with the changes still showing in the margin of the document. When the final document is completed, it may be sent by email, fax (directly from the computer without printing), and in many jurisdictions, filed electronically with the court.

Track Changes As found in MS Word, a feature that shows the original text, the deleted text, and the new text, as well as a strikethrough line for deleted text, the underlining or highlighting of new text, as well as margin notes in the document.

Today, the most commonly used program in the law office is the word processor. Although many different word processing programs are available, most members of the legal community use either WordPerfect™ or Microsoft Word™. These programs have built-in software tools that check spelling and grammar and allow customized formatting with a variety of type sizes and font styles in the same document—functions that were not possible with a typewriter. Some offices use other programs, each with its own file format.

Most word processing programs allow the opening and saving of files in the file formats of other word processing programs. When a file is saved, a **file extension**

File extension A period followed by three characters, added to the end of the file name, to identify the program or format in which the file has been saved.

Exhibit 4.10 Microsoft Word Track Changes

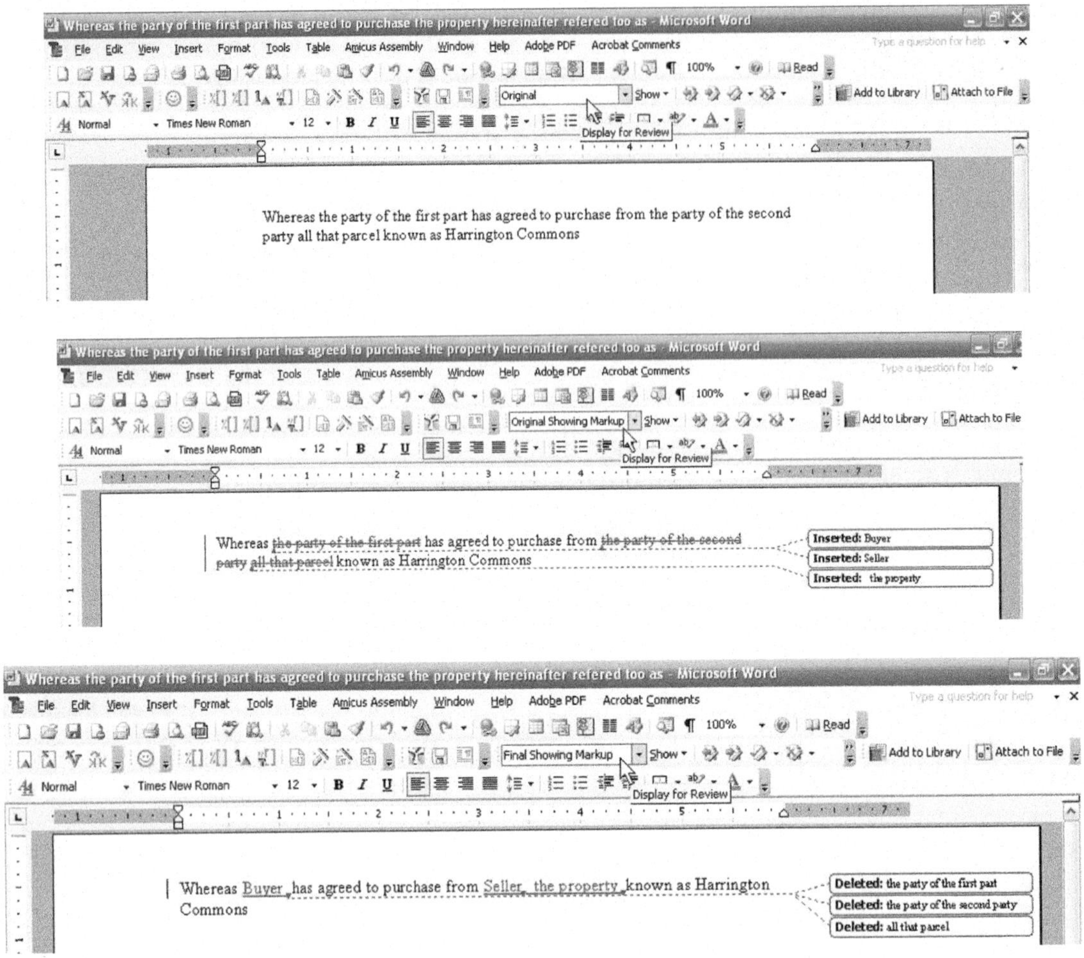

Whereas the party of the first part has agreed to purchase the property hereinafter refered too as - Microsoft Word
Original
Display for Review
Whereas the party of the first part has agreed to purchase from the party of the second party all that parcel known as Harrington Commons
Original Showing Markup
Whereas the party of the first part has agreed to purchase from the party of the second party all that parcel known as Harrington Commons
Inserted: Buyer
Inserted: Seller
Inserted: the property
Final Showing Markup
Whereas Buyer has agreed to purchase from Seller, the property known as Harrington Commons
Deleted: the party of the first part
Deleted: the party of the second party
Deleted: all that parcel

Source: Reprinted with permission from Microsoft Corporation.

(a period followed by a series of characters) is added to the end of the file name identifying the program or format in which the file has been saved. For example:

File type:	Extension:
Microsoft Word 97–2003	filename.doc
Microsoft Word 2007–2016	filename.docx
WordPerfect	filename.wpd
Microsoft Works	filename.wps
Web documents	filename.htm
Rich text file word processing format	filename.rtf
Text file word processing format	filename.txt

WordPerfect has many other features that increase productivity. Newer versions have a feature that simulates the Microsoft Word workspace. Files are saved with the document properties, such as type font and type size, and document formatting details. The saved files also include instructions to the computer on how to display the document, security features, and hidden information, such as the Track Changes information. WordPerfect also has built-in viewers that allow it to open and read almost every word processing document format used over the past 30 years and permitting them to be saved in different formats.

ETHICAL PERSPECTIVE

Document Comparison Software

The history of changes and other information about a document is called *metadata*. When using Track Changes or similar comparison features, be sure to remove the metadata before sending it to the opposing counsel, the client, or the court.

The history of the changes made to a document may offer the reader insight into the strategy of the case. For example, the final price the client is willing to pay may have appeared in the original draft and not the offer letter that was sent to the opposing party. Word Help offers instructions on how to remove this information. WordPerfect has the option "Save without Metadata," making it easy to quickly remove private or sensitive data from within office documents.

Spreadsheet Programs

Many areas of legal practice require the calculation and presentation of financial information. For example, in a family law practice, family and personal balance sheets and income and expense reports are routinely prepared for support and equitable distribution hearings. Estate lawyers must submit an "accounting" to the court for approval, showing details of how the fiduciary handled the financial affairs of the estate or trust. Litigation firms must at some point prepare documentation showing the receipts and disbursements for cases, for court approval.

As shown in Exhibit 4.11, a calculation involved in the handling of an estate may be as simple as multiplying the number of shares owned by a decedent by the value on the date of death ("D of D"), and then calculating the profit or loss when the stock was sold. Without a **spreadsheet program**, all of the calculations would have to be done manually, using a multicolumn form known as a "spreadsheet or accountant's working papers." The information would then have to be typed in a report for submission to the court, the beneficiaries, or the taxing authorities.

Spreadsheet programs
Programs that permit the calculation and presentation of financial information in a grid format of rows and columns.

Using a computerized spreadsheet, such as Microsoft Excel or Corel Quattro Pro, the numbers are entered in cells, as shown in Exhibit 4.11. A formula is assigned to the cell in which the result is to be displayed. For example, a formula might direct the application to "multiply column C by column D," and then display the result in column E. The computerized spreadsheet may be laid out in the format acceptable to the court, and then printed without reentering the data, or copied into word processing documents using simple "Cut" and "Paste" operations.

The use of computer spreadsheets reduces the errors that would result from manual calculations or retyping information. However, care must be taken to make sure that the formula is accurate and performs the desired calculation.

PRACTICE TIP

Even expert spreadsheet users will enter a set of sample numbers to test the formulas they have entered.

Exhibit 4.11 Excel spreadsheet

Excel File Edit View Insert Format Tools Data Window Help

	A	B	C	D	E	F	G	H
1	Date	Description	# of shares	D of D value	Total Value	Sales Price	Gain/(Loss)	
2	3/14/07	Product Guild Limted	100	$58.23	$5,823.00	$6,250.00	$427.00	
3								
4								
5								
6								
7								
8								
9								
10								
11								
12								

Row → Cell ↑ Column ↓

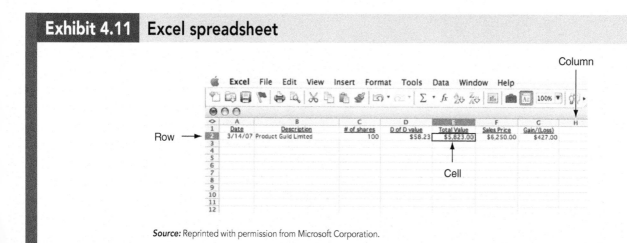

Source: Reprinted with permission from Microsoft Corporation.

Many offices use spreadsheet templates much like forms are used in word processing. For example, a real estate settlement spreadsheet with formulas and headings may be saved without any data. Because the formulas do not change and the form has proven accurate, it may be used as a template for other clients' real estate settlements.

Database Programs

Database program An electronic repository of information of all types that can be sorted and presented in a meaningful manner.

A **database program** is a repository of information that can be sorted and presented in a meaningful manner. Before electronic databases became available, law offices used a manual card system to keep track of the names of clients and opposing parties. These cards would be searched to determine any possible conflicts of interest in representing new clients. For a small office, this system may work. But for a larger office with many attorneys, using a card system for entering and searching large amounts of information is not realistic.

Computerized database software, such as Microsoft Access and Corel DB, will allow timely, accurate access to information by every authorized member of the legal team. For example, information may be stored in a database that includes the names, contact information, and personal data, such as birthdates, of every client, opposing party, witness, or opposing counsel that any member of the firm has ever had contact with. With a few keystrokes, a list can be prepared for checking for conflicts of interest, or a computer search can be performed for any matter in which a particular name appears.

An electronic database may also be used in maintaining client relations. Many firms use client information to send birthday and anniversary greetings or to provide updates on specific changes in the law for which the client has consulted the firm previously.

Presentation Graphics Programs

It has been said that a picture is worth a thousand words. Presentation graphics software, such as WordPerfect Presentation (see Exhibit 4.12) and Microsoft PowerPoint, are often used by attorneys to create high-quality slide shows and drawings. These graphic presentations can include text, data charts, and images.

Exhibit 4.12 WordPerfect Presentation

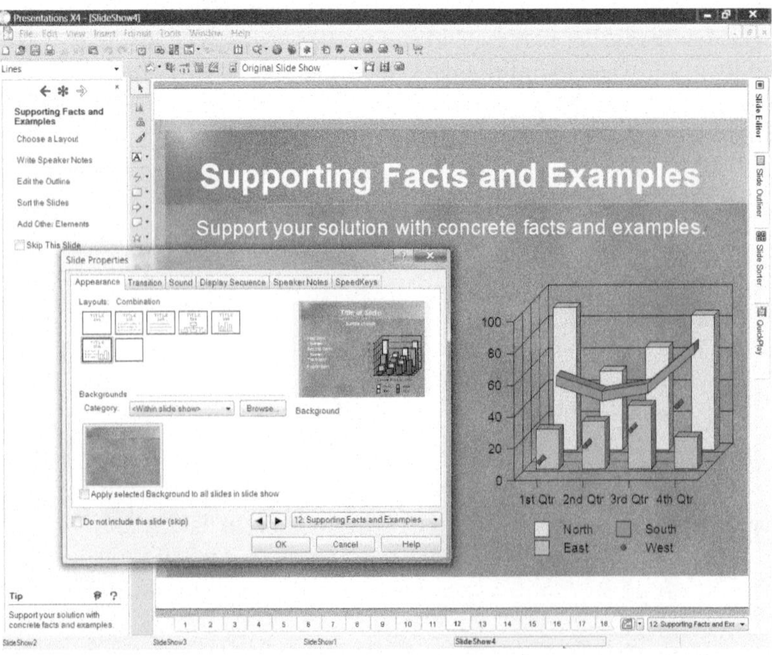

Source: WordPerfect screen shot reprinted with permission of Corel.

One of the advantages of these programs is their flexibility. They can be used to prepare and display the presentation using a computer, with or without a projector, and to print out paper copies for distribution. Presentation programs typically provide stock templates of graphics, artwork, and layout as a sample that the user can easily modify. More advanced users can add sound clips, still photos, video clips, and custom graphics from other programs.

Office Software Suites

Office software suites are sets of commonly used office programs. They manage data, manipulate financial or numeric information, or display images and graphics presentations. Some of the tools in the two most common program suites, Microsoft Office and Corel WordPerfect, are shown below.

Office software suites Software consisting of commonly used office programs that manage data, manipulate financial or numeric information, or display images and presentations.

	Microsoft Office	Corel WordPerfect Office
Word processor	Word	WordPerfect
Spreadsheet	Excel	Quattro Pro
Database	Access	Paradox
Presentation graphics	PowerPoint	Presentation
Graphics	Visio	Presentation Graphics

Software suites are usually delivered on one CD, or downloadable from the Internet enabling all the programs to be loaded at one time, which simplifies matters and saves installation time. With common features and appearance, it is easier to switch between programs and copy information between the programs. For example, part of a spreadsheet may be copied into a word processing document.

Specialty Application Programs

Specialty application programs combine many of the basic functions found in software suites, word processing, database, spreadsheet, and graphic presentation programs, and are tailored for law office case and litigation management. They simplify the management of a law office with the use of customized input screens and preset report generators.

Most legal specialty software falls into the following categories:

- Office management
- Case management
- Litigation support
- Transcript management
- Trial presentation

Specialty application programs Programs that combine many of the basic functions found in software suites, such as word processing, database management, spreadsheets, and graphic presentations, to perform law office, case, and litigation management.

Training for Hardware and Software Support

To be efficient, each user of the office computer system must be trained in the features and procedures of that system. Each office tends to have its own method of filing electronic documents, whether on individual personal computers or workstations, on the office network file server, or on an outside data repository. In an ideal world, a reference guide—where everything is documented, easy to read, and completely understandable—would be available to each employee. But in the real world, people may need instruction on everything from the basics, such as where the on–off switch is located, to more sophisticated tasks, such as how to connect with a remote office file server or Internet-based data repository and download a file.

Someone must do the training. Again, in an ideal world, an IT person would do the training in-house. In the real world, however, few offices have this resource.

Often, some of the basics are taught by the more-experienced people in the office. But in most law practices, one or more outside sources are used. The person or company that sold or installed the hardware or software may also offer training. Manufacturers may offer online help or telephone support. In some cases, classes may be offered at local educational institutions, either for credit or as noncredit offerings. Many bar associations and paralegal organizations offer courses, including some for continuing education credit. Many specialty software vendors also offer training from a basic to an advanced level.

LEARNING OBJECTIVE 7

Describe the features of the electronic courtroom and the paperless office.

Electronic Courtroom and Paperless Office

Computer technology is changing the way law offices and court systems operate. The ease of creating documents such as letters, contracts, and emails has resulted in an explosion in the quantity of documents. At the same time, cases are going to trial faster because of the demand for "quicker justice," allowing less time to prepare and present a case in court. The result has been a rapid growth in the use of electronic documentation and computerized case management.

The Electronic Courtroom

Increasingly, judges are embracing the use of electronics and computer-based systems in the courts. The initial reluctance to adopt new technology is giving way to acceptance of tools that enhance the speedy administration of justice.

One of the earliest uses of technology in the courtroom was the playing of videotaped depositions of expert witnesses on TV monitors in court. Getting experts to testify in person is difficult when the trial schedule is uncertain. Many professionals, such as noted surgeons and medical forensics experts, have active, lucrative practices and demand compensation for time lost while waiting to testify. This compensation can range into the thousands of dollars per hour, and the average litigant can rarely afford this cost. A videotape or electronic recording of a deposition can be used during trial as a cost-effective method of presenting expert witnesses, or witnesses who for reasons of health or distance would not otherwise be available to testify personally.

Courtrooms are now being outfitted with computers and audiovisual presentation systems, as judicial budgets allow. Exhibit 4.13 shows the U.S. Tax Court's electronic courtroom in Virginia. Computerized courtrooms are often seen in televised trials, with computer monitors at the counsel tables, the judge's bench, the jury box, and for each of the court support personnel.

Litigation support software is used at trial to display documentary evidence, graphic presentations, and simulations of accident cases. As a witness identifies documents during testimony, relevant portions of the documents can be displayed for everyone to see at the same time, without having to pass paper copies to everyone. Lawyers can rapidly search depositions and documents on their laptop computers to find pertinent material for examination or cross-examination of the witness.

The electronic courtroom is also used in many jurisdictions for preliminary matters in criminal cases in which the judge is at a central location and the defendants are located at various lock-up facilities. Video cameras and monitors are used so that the parties can see each other during the proceeding.

The Paperless Office

Paperless office The paperless office is one in which most documents are created and stored electronically.

To some, the ideal office has no paper documents, or "hard copies." An office where all documents are created and stored electronically is sometimes referred to as the "**paperless office**," or "electronic office." Although it is difficult to imagine for those who have grown up in the world of paper documents, the paperless office is rapidly becoming reality.

Exhibit 4.13 U.S. Tax Court's electronic courtroom

In the traditional office, documents that are created electronically with word processing software or received by fax or email are then printed for distribution and review. In the paperless office, documents created with word processor programs are sent electronically to the attorney for review. Paper documents are converted into electronic files using scanners and related software. One of the advantages of the paperless office is portability. This requires inexpensive portable computer memory, a computer to store and transport the documents, and small, lightweight computers to display them.

With the help of modern scanning technology, secure methods for transmitting documents, protocols for the use of electronic documents, and rules of court permitting electronic submissions, the paperless law office is now becoming the norm.

Portable Document Format (PDF)

One of the basic requirements of a system of electronic documentation is the ability to save documents in a format that cannot be easily changed. Anyone who has received a word processing document knows that it may be changed, saved, and presented as an original. The graphic image format (gif) and portable document format (PDF) are formats that the recipient cannot easily change.

Anyone can view PDF documents by downloading a free PDF reader from Nuance or Adobe. However, creating documents in PDF format requires specialty software such as Adobe Acrobat or Nuance PDF Creator or the built-in ability in the program such as newer word processing programs. As this format has become more widely accepted, attorneys have become more willing to scan and store documents in PDF format, eliminating the need to return the original paper copies to the client.

The PDF/A format is a variation of the PDF format, which is now required by the federal courts for electronic filing and by many state courts and government agencies. Created by the Library of Congress, this open universal standard for electronic documents contains archival features allowing use into the future without additional software.

Web Exploration

Acrobat tutorials "Introduction to PDFs," "Acrobat 101," and "Acrobat 201" may be found at www.casesoft.com/student.asp.

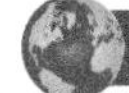
Web Exploration

Samples of PDF files can be downloaded from the Internal Revenue Service at www.irs.gov.

Scanning

The hardware originally used for scanning (converting paper documents to electronic form) was costly and frequently unreliable. Today, scanning has become a common feature in office printers and copy machines. Modern scanners provide double-sided (front and back) scanning of documents with a high degree of accuracy and at a relatively low cost. Double-sided scanning is found today in multifunctional devices featuring printing, scanning, copying, and faxing, at prices under $100. These devices, when coupled with application software, allow virtually anyone to create electronic documents.

Scanning and storing of paper documents has become easier with the development of software such as PaperPort by Nuance. This software provides easy-to-use, high-speed scanning and document capture. As a document management application, it allows for organizing, finding, and sharing of both paper and digital documents.

LEARNING OBJECTIVE 8
Discuss the future trends in law office technology.

OCR

Sometimes documents have to be converted from a graphic image to a format that allows for editing in a word processor or other suite of applications. The software used for this conversion has come to be referred to as optical character recognition (OCR). Products such as OmniPage, by Nuance, permit any scanned page, PDF file, or other image or document file to be converted quickly and accurately into one of a number of different editable formats, including Microsoft Word or Corel WordPerfect.

Future Trends in Law Office Technology

Law offices are under constant pressure to be more productive. Increased costs have led law office managers to look for new ways to use technology to increase productivity. Further, clients and the courts are unwilling to approve fees and costs when more cost-effective methods are available. In addition, the demand for speedy justice in the courts has resulted in less time to prepare and present cases. Thus the legal team must work faster and become more productive. Advances in computer technology are providing solutions to help deal with these constraints.

Looking ahead to what's on the technological horizon is imperative to the smooth and profitable functioning of the law office. Anticipating and incorporating new technology in turn requires IT knowledge and savvy, whether it is provided by in-house staff or external technology consultants. A chief information officer or chief technology officer at a corporate firm must anticipate change and plan for it in concrete and innovative ways. Those responsible for IT at smaller firms must also be well informed of technology trends. They must assess when a new tool should be added to their technology repertoire—and when it should be avoided.

The legal team is an increasingly mobile workforce. Working outside of the office is a fact of life for trial attorneys and their support staff. The litigation team may spend much of their time in courthouses, or taking depositions at other offices. These activities may take place across the street, across the country, or around the globe. Increasingly, the support staff must also work outside the traditional law office. In some cases, this work is outsourced to other firms or companies in remote locations. In addition, some lawyers, paralegals, and litigation support staff work from home. With advances in technology, it is possible for these team members to connect with the main office and access all the needed files and electronic resources through a computer at home. These workers are sometimes referred to as **teleworkers**.

Teleworkers People who work from remote locations, typically home.

Technology is developing much faster than we could have expected even a few years ago. As Raymond Kurzweil writes in his essay "The Law of Accelerating Returns" (2001),

> An analysis of the history of technology shows that technological change is exponential, contrary to the common-sense "intuitive linear" view. So we won't experience

> 100 years of progress in the 21st century—it will be more like 20,000 years of progress (at today's rate). The "returns," such as chip speed and cost-effectiveness, also increase exponentially. There's even exponential growth in the rate of exponential growth.

The following section describes a sample of the emerging technology, some of which is currently available and in use at some law firms and some of which is still under development. The list is not exhaustive but gives an idea of what businesses might expect to see in the near and distant future.

Videoconferencing

Videoconferencing is the use of the Internet, telephone lines, or special satellite systems to transmit and receive video and audio signals in real time. This technology allows parties in several locations to see and hear each other during a conference, as shown in Exhibit 4.14.

Videoconferencing Conferencing from multiple locations using high-speed Internet connections to transmit sound and images.

Many law firms and their clients currently use videoconferencing on a regular basis as a method of "face-to-face" communication when parties are at remote sites, such as depositions, hearings, or conferences. Modern technology has reduced the cost and increased the ease of use to the point that some people conduct regular telephone calls as video calls using their smartphones or tablet computers with built-in cameras and free Internet software applications like Skype and Apple FaceTime. For minimal additional cost, Skype calls may include multiple parties. The use of this service has become so ubiquitous that the term for video calling another person is referred to as "Skyping."

Videoconferencing is also used in many courts at various stages of court proceedings, most often at the early stages of a criminal case. This technology is now being recognized by some court rules. For example, Section 885.52(3) of the Wisconsin Supreme Court Rules defines videoconferencing as "interactive technology that sends video, voice, and data signals over a transmission circuit so that two or more individuals or groups can communicate with each other simultaneously using video monitors." The Wisconsin rules further establish the requirements under which videoconferencing can be used in court proceedings, permitting the use of this technology in all aspects of criminal and civil litigation. Rules such as these are designed to make emerging Web-based technologies available to litigants, as long as certain requirements are met. Videoconferencing and other technologies can be expected to become important tools in litigation practice.

VoIP

Voice over Internet Protocol (**VoIP**) is a method for transmitting voice communication over the Internet rather than through traditional telephone company services; Skype, mentioned above, is such a VoIP service. A smartphone, tablet computer, or any

VoIP Voice over Internet Protocol is an Internet replacement for traditional telephone connections.

Exhibit 4.14 Legal team collaboration using video conferencing

computer with a microphone and headset or speaker is used to complete a call to another computer or telephone over the Internet. The communication operates through software installed on a computer, and may include both voice and images. At first, VoIP was limited by the inability to connect calls to or from a conventional telephone. But services such as Yahoo Messenger and Skype now provide options that permit calling conventional phones at a very nominal rate, sometimes as low as one cent per minute.

At one time, conducting a videoconference required going to a special location and paying a substantial fee. Now, the relatively low cost and ease of use of VoIP make teleconferencing, including videoconferencing, a reality for those who previously could not afford such services. Anyone with a computerized device with a microphone, speakers, and video camera can set up a videoconference from almost anywhere an Internet connection is available.

Voice Recognition

Voice recognition Computer programs for converting speech into text or commands without the use of other in/out devices such as keyboards.

Voice recognition software has been around for a number of years as an alternative to typing. This software converts spoken words into text on the screen. Many will remember trying out earlier versions of speech recognition programs and finding them to be lacking in accuracy. But improved technology has brought this software to a level of accuracy approaching, and in some cases exceeding, the accuracy of typing. Speech-enabled devices include smartphones, pad devices, and GPS devices. With programs such as Dragon Naturally Speaking (Legal Version), it is now possible to dictate working drafts of legal documents directly into almost any other program, including word processors, spreadsheets, and databases, without touching a computer keyboard. The document may then be sent to another member of the legal team electronically. This software has become so advanced that portable dictation devices can be used outside of the office and later connected to the office computer to transcribe documents without the intervention of a typist. And the benefits to the legal team in productivity and efficiency are significant. Transcribing speech at up to 160 words a minute, voice recognition software far outpaces the average typist's speed.

The underlying technology found in voice recognition software is now being used in automated response systems that replace live operators and receptionists at some firms. It is also used in products that help those who cannot use a keyboard because of physical disabilities such as carpal tunnel syndrome. Smartphones such as the Apple iPhone, and Android-based phones such as the Samsung phone, use voice recognition software to replace keystrokes.

Miniaturization and Portability

The trend in computers and computer devices, including smartphones and tablets, has been toward light weight, portability, and extended battery life. Some laptops now weigh less than three pounds and are more powerful than some older desktop systems. They may include all of the capabilities of desktop systems, including built-in Web cameras for videoconferencing. Similarly, virtually all cell phones are smartphones, and both tablets and smartphones today are capable of taking and displaying photos and video, preparing documents, sending emails, and accessing the Internet—functions that formerly required large, hard-wired computer devices.

Wireless Technology

Only a few years ago, wires or cables were necessary to access networks or to set up network connections. Today, networks may be set up among workstations, servers, and peripherals using wireless technology. Remote access is also possible with the use of a wireless Internet connection using laptops and cell phones with built-in Internet access.

Many offices today are equipped with wireless telephones and wireless Internet networks. In addition, the worldwide availability of inexpensive high-speed Internet connections, or "hotspots," has expanded the use of wireless technologies. Wireless Internet is available on airplanes, an idea inconceivable a few years ago, allowing productivity even during long airplane flights. Wireless devices allow constant communication and enable work to be performed virtually anywhere, such as at home, at the courthouse, in an airport lounge, at a coffee shop, on airplanes, and even on cruise ships. Staff members may connect to their office's wireless network through the Internet or cellular network using wireless hardware built into the smartphone or other computerized device.

Remote Access

Remote access allows members of the legal team working on cases out of the office to connect with the office file server or other Internet data repository to retrieve documents, work on them, and send them to other members of the legal team or clients anywhere in the world. If a hard copy is needed, documents may be printed on any printer accessible over the Internet, including printers in remote office locations, public access points in airports, clients' offices, and courthouses. Exhibit 4.15 is an example of a typical remote access configuration that provides security for the data and limits access to authorized users.

Remote Collaboration

Remote collaboration involves members of the legal team and clients at multiple locations working together as if they were in the same physical location. Software conferencing programs allow team members to share files while communicating and seeing each other on the same screen with the use of small cameras on the desktop or built into their laptop computers. The same remote access technology also allows the taking of witness statements from remote locations while the parties see each other or view exhibits on the computer screen.

Remote collaboration Working on a common document utilizing remote access by two or more parties.

With high-speed Internet connections, true real-time videoconferencing has become a reality. In the past, slower connections restricted how much information could be transmitted and increased the time needed to send a document. Slower speeds also prevented the availability of full-motion, full-screen video. High-speed Internet connections now allow users to transmit both sound and images simultaneously. With the introduction of fiber-optic and cable Internet services, videoconferencing from multiple locations is now available at many offices.

Exhibit 4.15 Secure remote access for the law office

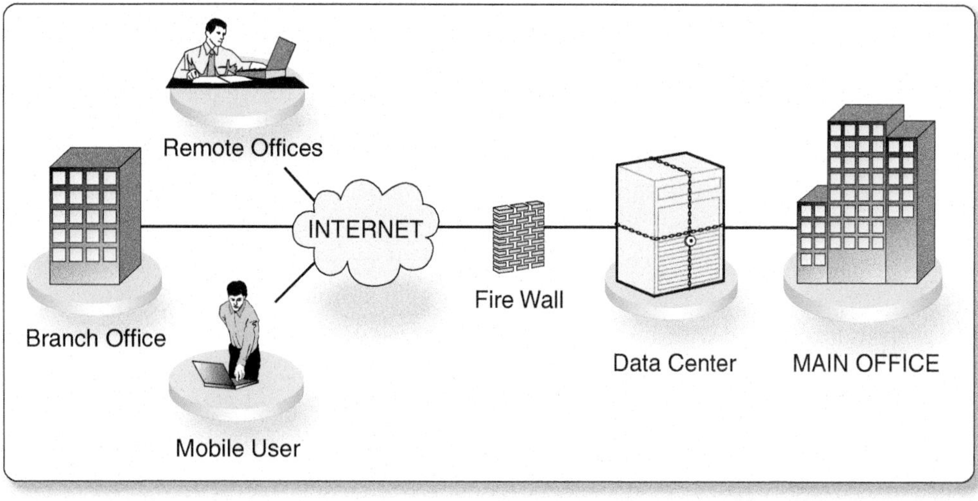

Wireless Networks

Wireless computer networks A wireless network uses wireless technology in place of wires for connecting to the network.

Wireless networks are like cell phone networks in that both use radio waves to transmit signals to a receiver. Cell phone systems use cell towers located at strategic points all over the world that receive the signals from cellular devices. Similarly, wireless networks use wireless access points, which are essentially receivers of radio signals that convert the signals so that they can be transmitted to a computer or to the Internet.

Unlike cell phone towers, these access points have a more limited range of only a few hundred feet. Many of these access points, or "hotspots," are provided in coffee shops, airport lounges, hotels, libraries, bookstores, and other locations. Businesses often offer wireless access without charge, or at a nominal fee, to encourage customers to patronize them.

Hotspot A wireless access point, generally in a public area.

With the growth of wireless **hotspots**, lawyers and paralegals may be connected anywhere in the world and may send documents electronically back and forth with the same ease as sending them within the same building. And with cellular connections provided through internal or plug-in accessories, computers can access the Internet over areas where the Internet was not previously accessible.

Wireless Devices

Most smartphones, tablets, laptops, and similar computerized devices have hardware and software that enables them to be wirelessly connected to the Internet without the need of a hotspot. Subscriptions to data services are provided by most major cellular providers such as AT&T, Verizon, and Sprint. These services can provide Internet access virtually anywhere there is cellular coverage. The popularity of these wireless services has resulted in many newer-generation laptops having the feature built in, thus eliminating the need for external cards.

Thin client A computer system where programs and files are maintained on a centralized server.

Web Resource

The State Bar of Texas Practice Management Program blog, The Practice Manager, offers valuable information on a variety of practice-related topics at http://lpm-newsletter.blogspot.com/.

Cloud Computing

"Cloud computing," or "**thin client**," as it has been called, has emerged in which all files are maintained on a centralized or cloud server, such as Microsoft OneDrive (formerly called SkyDrive) or DropBox. The thin client model offers some additional level of control and prevents the loss of information that would occur if someone's computer were lost or damaged. Another example of cloud computing is Software as a Service (SaaS), such as Office 365 from Microsoft. The service charges a monthly fee for use of its software when needed.

CHECKLIST✓

Use the following checklist as a tool to assess how your firm uses technology and to discover areas you might want to address in the future.

- ☐ Which functions are automated now? Which additional functions do you wish to automate?
- ☐ Are existing pieces of equipment mutually compatible?
- ☐ Does everyone in the office use the same software?
- ☐ Are word processing procedures standardized?
- ☐ Is the billing system interfaced with the accounting system?
- ☐ Are checks drawn on law firm accounts computer-generated or manually prepared?
- ☐ Are you using software to keep track of client expenses, such as copies, faxes, long-distance calls, and postage?
- ☐ Are telephone messages delivered accurately and in a timely manner?
- ☐ Does the office get flooded with paper interoffice memoranda?
- ☐ Is the payroll prepared in-house? Is it handled manually or with software?
- ☐ Do the attorneys often carry boxes of documents to the courthouse?
- ☐ Do the paralegals spend hours preparing manual document index systems?
- ☐ How does the firm check for conflicts of interest?
- ☐ What type of calendaring system do you use for docket control and scheduling?

Source: Gisela Bradley, Law Practice Management Program, State Bar of Texas.

Note Taking *and* Collaboration

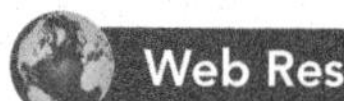

Web Resources

Contrast and compare West Virginia Rules of Professional Conduct Rule 1.1 with the analogous rule in the American Bar Association Model Rules of Professional Conduct. Then compare these to the ethical rule in your jurisdiction.

Electronic note taking is rapidly replacing paper format note taking. It is common to see people in meetings, conferences, courtrooms, and libraries taking notes using laptops, tablets, and smartphones. In some cases the notes are even created using voice recognition software. The advantages include legibility as opposed to what can sometimes be referred to as unreadable hieroglyphic handwriting. Electronic files are easier to store and organize within the computer or are saved on servers or cloud-based storage sites.

One of the more popular programs for taking notes is Microsoft Office OneNote. Created and stored electronically, these notes can be sorted and searched by words and phrases to find needed information previously stored. OneNote may be used as a collaboration tool using the Share feature of OneNote, as shown in Exhibit 4.16.

Exhibit 4.16 Microsoft OneNote

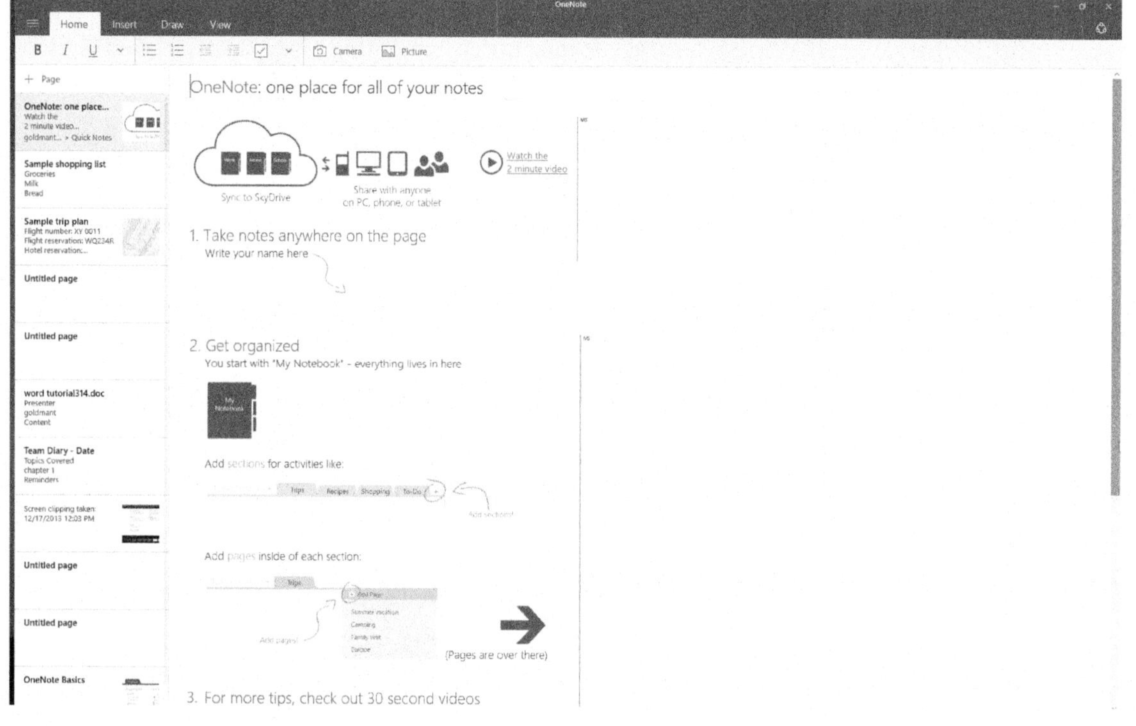

Concept Review *and* Reinforcement

KEY TERMS

attachments 136
confidentiality 137
digital format 136
electronic repository 138
hard copy 136
hotspot 166
information technologist 140
IT 139
online collaboration 138
outsourcing 140
remote access 140
remote collaboration 165
smoking gun 141
teleworkers 162
thin client 166
videoconferencing 163
voice recognition 164
VoIP 163
wireless computer network 166

CHAPTER SUMMARY

Introduction to Technology in the Law Office	Computer technology is used in many ways in the law office: electronic spreadsheets time and billing programs accounting programs calendaring graphic presentation software trial presentation software Internet search engines document scanning document search features e-mail and document delivery online collaboration online document repositories
Impact of the Federal Rules of Civil Procedure	New federal rules that became effective in December 2006 specifically addressed the issue of the increased use of electronically stored documentation. New federal court rules on electronic discovery and electronically stored documents and emerging case law on electronic discovery are creating increased demand for skills and knowledge in the use of technology in civil litigation.
Technology Support in the Law Office	In larger law offices, corporate legal departments, and government offices, there is usually a technical support staff.
Technology Usage in the Law	The role of technology in the law has evolved in a very small number of years from a minor function to a ubiquitous element in the management of law offices of all sizes.
Working with In-House Technology Support Staff	Litigation teams may require support for videotaping depositions at out-of-office or out-of-town locations. Trials may require the use of sophisticated presentation equipment. All members of the legal team may need access to the home office files on the office file servers from remote locations on their wireless laptops.
Issues in Working with Outside Technology Consultants	Outside companies may be retained to service hardware or provide support to software used in the office. They may be retained on a maintenance contract basis to provide coverage as needed for a period of time or for a fixed rate. Others may be hired as needed at an hourly rate.
Outsourcing	Work may be shipped out of the office to an outside contractor to save money. Some service providers are located overseas.
Information Technologists as Members of the Legal Team	Information technologists are members of the legal team who combine legal skills and technology skills.
Training for Hardware and Software Support	To be efficient, each user of the office computer system must be trained in the features and procedures of that system.
How Much Do I Really Need to Know?	What is important is knowing enough to know what you do not know and to be able to find someone who does know.
Understanding the Language of Technology	An understanding of the language of technology is a prerequisite to understanding the technology found in the law office, the courthouse, and the client's business.
Future Trends in Law Office Technology	The legal team is under pressure to be more productive. Advances in computer technology are providing ways for the team to achieve this greater productivity.
Videoconferencing	Videoconferencing employs technology that transmits sound and video simultaneously, in real time. It allows remote conferences, hearings, and depositions among parties located at separate sites.

VoIP	Voice over Internet Protocol is a computer substitute for the use of traditional telephone connections.
Voice Recognition	Voice recognition software allows spoken words to be converted directly into text. Speech-enabled devices include cell phones, personal digital assistants (PDAs), and other handheld devices.
Miniaturization and Portability	The trend in computers and related devices has been toward miniaturization and portability.
Wireless Technology	Wires and cables are no longer necessary to access networks or to set up network connections. Today, they may be set up using wireless technology in a wireless network.
Remote Access	Team members working on cases outside of the office can connect with the office file server to access documents.
Remote Collaboration	The legal team can work collaboratively from multiple locations as if in the same physical location through software conferencing programs. This technology allows the sharing of files while team members communicate with and see each other on the same screen using small cameras on the desktop or built into laptop computers.
Wireless Computer Networks	Wireless computers use radio signals to transmit information to wireless access points. These wireless networks can be used to connect to the Internet.
Wireless Laptop Connections	Laptops may access the Internet using built-in or plug-in devices and a subscription service that provides access anywhere there is a cellular connection. In cloud computing, programs and files are maintained on a centralized server. Each user has access through a terminal called a thin client.

REVIEW QUESTIONS AND EXERCISES

1. Prepare a detailed list of the ways technology is used in the law office and courts.
2. How can members of the legal team use computers to share information?
3. How can the Internet be used to attract new business for the law office?
4. How has the use of technology changed the skills needed to work in a law office?
5. How can the computer help members of a legal team work together when they are not in the same physical location?
6. Explain, with examples, how the Internet is used today by law offices and the courts.
7. Why does the legal team need to have a working familiarity with computers and the different types of computer software programs? Give examples.
8. How have the new Federal Rules of Civil Procedure impacted the legal profession?
9. What is the role of the information technology department in a law office?
10. How can "hotspots" be used by the legal team?
11. Why is it necessary for members of the legal team to be able to communicate with those in a support or user position about technology as it relates to the legal community? Give examples.
12. Why is the quantity of documents increasing in litigation?
13. How has technology changed the roles of the members of the legal team?
14. Why would a law firm use an outside technology support firm?
15. What are the underlying reasons for the difficulty some legal team members may have in communicating with the IT staff?
16. Do members of the legal team need to know everything about the computers and software they use?
17. How can a member of the legal team learn about the technology used in a law office? Give specific examples.
18. How will videoconferencing change the way law is practiced in the future?
19. Is it realistic for members of a legal team to do work from home?

Building Your Professional Skills

INTERNET AND TECHNOLOGY EXERCISES

1. Use an Internet search engine to find an article on the use of outsourcing in the legal community.
2. Locate at least three Internet resources on technology used in law practices. Save the Internet addresses for future use.
3. Using information available on the Internet, prepare a job description for each of the different members of a legal team. Include descriptions of the skills that are necessary to manage a law practice in the age of technology.
4. Prepare a memo to the legal team on how the IT department can aid the team and the issues in working together.

CHAPTER OPENING SCENARIO CASE STUDY

Use the opening scenario for this chapter to answer the following questions. A new attorney is having a discussion with an experienced paralegal who has agreed to help him open an office.

1. What are the office and legal functions for which technology can be used in a start-up law office? What technologies would best serve those functions?
2. What technologies would be most helpful in a litigation practice where the attorney is frequently in court? How would those technologies help a trial attorney be more efficient and productive?
3. What issues are involved in using an outside software, hardware, or Internet consultant in setting up a law office?
4. Prepare a checklist of *minimum* software and hardware requirements for a start-up office. Prepare a second checklist of *recommended* technology needs. Be specific. Print out and save a copy for future reference.
5. What, if any, additional minimum or recommended items should be added to the list in question 4 for a trial attorney establishing a new law practice?
6. Use the Internet to find the prices for the equipment and software on the checklists in questions 4 and 5. Prepare a budget for acquiring hardware and software for the new law office.

CONTINUING CASES AND EXERCISES

1. Prepare a list of calendar entries for the course, including times and locations for class, library sessions, tests, assignment deadlines, and other class-related calendar items. Using an electronic calendar program, create a calendar as if it were a docket control system. Set up warnings or alarms in the system to alert you when certain dates are approaching.
2. Owen Mason, Esq., is a young, technology-aware attorney just starting out in a new legal practice. He thought the Internet would be a good source of potential business. However, as a clerk in the federal court, he did not have the opportunity to look at many law office websites. He asks for your help in designing his Web page.
   a. Using the Internet search tools available to you, locate the websites of law firms in your area, as well as around the country. Make a list of the best and the worst features of these websites.
   b. Prepare your recommendations for Mr. Mason, including details and, if possible, screen printouts. Make a list of the Web addresses of each of the sites that you feel demonstrate the good, the bad, and the ugly.

BUILDING YOUR PROFESSIONAL PORTFOLIO

1. Keep a log of the time you spend in this course. Use the following format:

Date	Start	Stop	Elapsed	Code	Description
8-19-2015	8:00	9:00	1.00	AC	Attend class on ethics

Record the actual time spent (you can round to 1/10 of an hour) using these suggested codes. The descriptions in parentheses are analogous activities that would be billed in a real law practice.
AC—class attendance (conference with supervising attorney)
T—travel to and from class (travel)
RRM—time reading and researching material (research)
PA—time preparing assignments (drafting documents)
TP—time spent preparing for tests (preparation)
T—time taking tests (trial)
M—other miscellaneous items (miscellaneous)

2. Internet resources
   a. Start a list of resources available on the Internet as you progress through the text and complete assignments. To get started, the Internet resources from this chapter have been inserted. Remember that Web addresses change often, so update your list regularly.
   b. Locate at least three Internet resources on technology used in law practices. Save the Internet addresses for future use.

Subject	Source	Topic	URL	Date of entry
Ethics	ABA	Model rules of professional conduct	http://www.americanbar.org/groups/professional_responsibility.html	
State ethics opinions		Your state ethical rule opinions		
Dictionary	FOLDOC	Computing	http://foldoc.org	
Federal Court Rules—Civil	Legal Information Institute	FRCP	www.law.cornell.edu/rules/frcp	
Federal Court Rules—Criminal		FRCRMP	www.law.cornell.edu/Rules/FRCRMP	
State and Local Court Rules—Civil				
State and Local Court Rules—Criminal				

PART

II

Introduction to Law

The aspiring paralegal professional must become familiar with the American legal heritage and how the law developed in this country over the centuries. This includes learning the historical and current sources of federal and state law. In addition, a professional paralegal should have knowledge of the Constitution of the United States of America and how it structures the federal government, delegates power to the federal government, reserves powers to the states, and protects us from unwelcome government intrusion into our lives. A paralegal professional must have knowledge of the American court system and the process of judicial and nonjudicial dispute resolution. A working knowledge of the civil litigation process, criminal litigation and procedure, and administrative law is also a necessary part of a paralegal professional's education. Part II, "Introduction to Law," provides the paralegal professional student with this knowledge.

Chapter 5
American Legal Heritage and Constitutional Law

Chapter 6
The Court System and Alternative Dispute Resolution

Chapter 7
Civil Litigation

Chapter 8
Criminal Law and Procedure

Chapter 9
Administrative Law

CHAPTER

5

American Legal Heritage and Constitutional Law

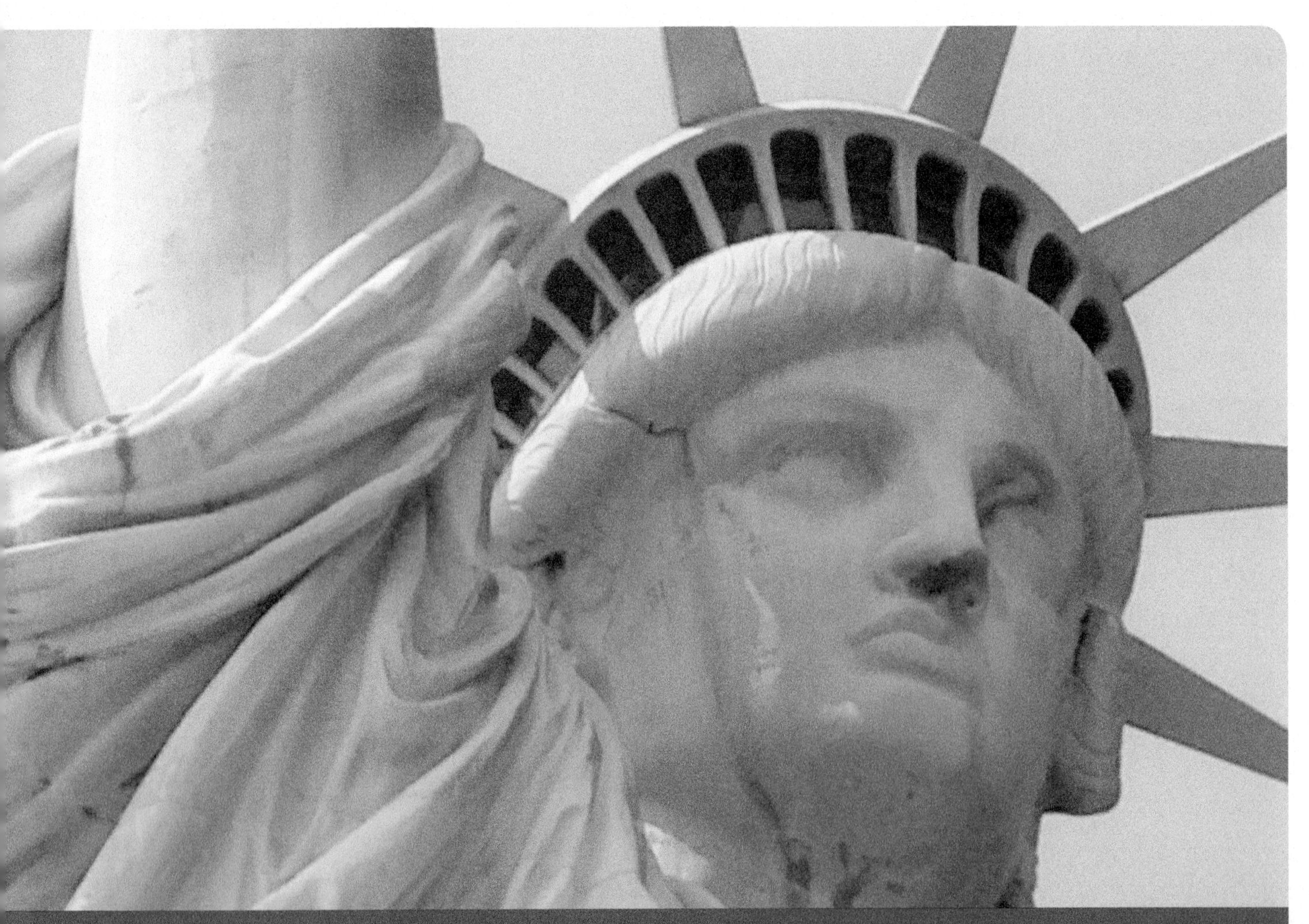

Paralegals at Work

You are a paralegal at a large law firm that specializes in handling issues in constitutional law. You work for Vivian Kang, a senior partner of the firm. One day Ms. Kang calls you into her office and tells you that a new client, Mr. Hayward Storm, has retained the law firm. Ms. Kang asks you to sit in with her during an interview with Mr. Storm.

Mr. Storm tells the following story: For more than twenty years he has been on radio and television, primarily as a disc jockey and talk show host. Mr. Storm most recently hosted television shows where he behaved outlandishly, using vulgar language, having guests appear on the show nude, telling disgusting jokes, and doing other things that offended many people. Mr. Storm also hosted a radio show in which he used profanity and offensive language. The Federal Communications Commission (FCC), a federal government agency, is responsible for regulating radio and television. The FCC has fined Mr. Storm and his employer for engaging in such conduct over the television and radio airwaves.

In addition, Mr. Storm explains that he will be leaving regular radio and television and has been hired to be a disc jockey for satellite radio broadcasts. He is making this change because satellite radio currently is not regulated by the FCC. Mr. Storm plans to continue his usual offensive programming on satellite radio and says he will increase his extreme language and conduct because of satellite radio's lack of FCC regulation. However, he is concerned that Congress will enact a federal statute granting the FCC the power to regulate satellite radio.

Consider the issues involved in this scenario as you read this chapter.

LEARNING OBJECTIVES

After studying this chapter, you should be able to:

1. Recognize the professional opportunities for paralegals in the area of constitutional law.
2. Define *law* and describe the functions of law.
3. Explain the fairness and flexibility of the law.
4. List and describe the sources of law in the United States.
5. Explain the doctrine of separation of powers and describe the checks and balances built into the U.S. Constitution.
6. Describe the Supremacy Clause of the U.S. Constitution and the preemption doctrine.
7. Describe the Commerce Clause of the U.S. Constitution.
8. Describe freedom of speech and other protections guaranteed by the Bill of Rights.
9. Describe the Equal Protection Clause and the tests used to determine whether it has been violated.
10. Explain a paralegal's duty to avoid conflicts of interest.

> "We the People of the United States, in Order to form a more perfect Union, establish Justice, insure domestic Tranquility, provide for the common defense, promote the general Welfare, and secure the Blessings of Liberty to ourselves and our Posterity, do ordain and establish this Constitution for the United States of America."
>
> *Preamble to the Constitution of the United States of America*

INTRODUCTION FOR THE PARALEGAL

A paralegal must have a foundation in the basic sources of the law of the United States. Our society makes and enforces laws that govern the conduct of the individuals, businesses, and other organizations that function within it. In the words of Judge Learned Hand, "Without law we cannot live; only with it can we insure the future which by right is ours. The best of men's hopes are enmeshed in its success" (*The Spirit of Liberty*, 1960).

Human beings do not ever make laws; it is the accidents and catastrophes of all kinds happening in every conceivable way that make law for us.

Plato, *Laws IV*, 709

Although U.S. law is based primarily on English common law, other legal systems, such as Spanish and French civil law, have also influenced it. The other main sources of law in this country are the U.S. Constitution, state constitutions, federal and state statutes, ordinances, administrative agency rules and regulations, executive orders, and judicial decisions by federal and state courts.

Paralegals should be well-rounded professionals who have an understanding of this country's founding, its constitutional protections, and the current debates concerning the application of constitutional language in these modern times. To that end, this chapter provides an overview of the nature and definition of law, the history and sources of law, and the U.S. Constitution.

LEARNING OBJECTIVE 1
Recognize the professional opportunities for paralegals in the area of constitutional law.

The feature at the bottom of the page discusses the career opportunities for paralegal professionals in the area of constitutional law.

What Is Law?

LEARNING OBJECTIVE 2
Define *law* and describe the functions of law.

The word *law* is used in many different contexts, and its definition is very broad. *Black's Law Dictionary*, fifth edition, defines *law* as follows:

> Law, in its generic sense, is a body of rules of action or conduct prescribed by controlling authority, and having binding legal force. That which must be obeyed and followed by citizens subject to sanctions or legal consequences is a law.

Law That which must be obeyed and followed by citizens subject to sanctions or legal consequences. A body of rules of action or conduct prescribed by controlling authority, and having binding legal force.

Law consists of rules that regulate the conduct of individuals, businesses, and other organizations within society. Laws are intended to protect persons and their property from unwanted interference from others and forbid persons from engaging in certain undesirable activities.

CAREER OPPORTUNITIES FOR PARALEGALS IN CONSTITUTIONAL LAW

The Constitution of the United States of America is one of the most important documents ever drafted. The U.S. Constitution created a new country, one that was not ruled by kings, queens, monarchs, or dictators. The country was one of the world's first democracies—a crucial development in the history of the world.

The Constitution is considered a "living document" that has continually been applied by the United States Supreme Court and other courts to an ever-changing society. As a result, the interpretation of the Constitution has constantly evolved since its ratification more than two centuries ago.

Some members of the paralegal profession will work in practice areas that frequently involve issues in constitutional law. This is an exciting field to participate in. Paralegals who work in this area will be called upon to conduct legal research relating to constitutional provisions and amendments, find relevant cases that interpret constitutional language, and assist lawyers who present cases to the courts regarding constitutional issues. Some members of the paralegal profession will be fortunate to work on cases that will be heard and decided by the U.S. Supreme Court.

All paralegals should be familiar with several major provisions and protections of the U.S. Constitution and its amendments:

- The Supremacy Clause
- The Commerce Clause
- Freedom of speech
- Freedom of religion
- The Due Process Clause
- The Equal Protection Clause

In addition to the above provisions, paralegals should understand how the Constitution structures the federal government with its built-in checks and balances, how it grants powers to the government, and how it establishes protections against certain intrusions by the government into our lives. The Constitution of the United States of America is set forth in its entirety in Appendix F to this book.

Fairness of the Law

LEARNING OBJECTIVE 3
Explain the fairness and flexibility of the law.

On the whole, the American legal system is one of the most comprehensive, fair, and democratic systems of law ever developed. Nevertheless, that system often produces errors and unjust results. These include mistakes and abuses of discretion by judges and juries, unequal applications of the law, and procedural mishaps, which sometimes allow guilty parties to go unpunished.

In *Standefer v. United States*, 447 U.S.10, 100 S.Ct.1999, 1980 U.S. Lexis 127 (U.S., 1980), the U.S. Supreme Court *affirmed* (let stand) the criminal conviction of a Gulf Oil Corporation executive for aiding and abetting the bribery of an Internal Revenue Service agent. The agent had been acquitted in a separate trial. In writing the opinion of the Court, Chief Justice Warren Burger stated, "This case does no more than manifest the simple, if discomforting, reality that different juries may reach different results under any criminal statute. That is one of the consequences we accept under our jury system."

Flexibility of the Law

Paralegals new to the profession may be surprised to find that American law is quite flexible. The law is generally responsive to cultural, technological, economic, and social changes.

> Example Laws that are no longer viable—such as those that restricted the property rights of women—are often repealed.

This flexibility in the law leads to some uncertainty in predicting the results of lawsuits. However, laws cannot be written in advance to anticipate every dispute that could arise in the future. Therefore, general principles are developed to be applied by courts and juries to individual disputes. The following quote from Judge Jerome Frank addresses the value of the adaptability of law (*Law and the Modern Mind*, 1930):

> The law always has been, is now, and will ever continue to be, largely vague and variable. And how could this be otherwise? The law deals with human relations in their most complicated aspects. The whole confused, shifting helter-skelter of life parades before it—more confused than ever, in our kaleidoscopic age.

The nation's armour of defence against the passions of men is the Constitution. Take that away, and the nation goes down into the field of its conflicts like a warrior without armour.

Henry Ward Beecher
Proverbs from Plymouth Pulpit, 1887

The continuing potential for unexpected problems in our society requires a legal system capable of fluidity and pliancy. Our society needs a court system that, with the able assistance of lawyers, can constantly adapt the law to the realities of ever-changing social, industrial, and political conditions. Although changes to the law should not be considered lightly, rules must be somewhat impermanent and flexible.

The legal system may appear to be flawed in its uncertainty, but the ability of the law to be flexible and adaptable is of immense social value.

Sometimes it takes years for the law to reflect the norms of society. Other times, society is led by the law. The major functions served by law are listed and described in Exhibit 5.1.

Schools of Jurisprudential Thought

The philosophy or science of the law is referred to as **jurisprudence**. Scholars of jurisprudence attempt to explain the nature of law and how legal systems and institutions develop. These philosophers can be grouped into the following major categories:

Jurisprudence The philosophy or science of law.

- The **natural law school** postulates that the law is based on what is "correct." Natural law philosophers emphasize a *moral* theory of law—that is, law should be based on morality and ethics. People "discover" natural law through reasoning and by choosing between good and evil. Documents such as the U.S. Constitution, the Magna Carta, and the United Nations Charter reflect this theory.

Exhibit 5.1 Functions of the law

1. Keeping the peace (such as by punishing certain activities or making them crimes)
2. Shaping moral standards (for example, by enacting laws that discourage drug and alcohol abuse)
3. Promoting social justice (for example, by enacting statutes that prohibit discrimination in employment)
4. Maintaining the status quo (such as bypassing laws that prevent the forceful overthrow of the government)
5. Facilitating orderly change (such as bypassing statutes only after considerable study, debate, and public input)
6. Facilitating planning (for example, by designing laws to allow businesses to plan their activities, allocate their productive resources, and assess the risks they take)
7. Providing a basis for compromise (as in systems where more than 90 percent of all lawsuits are settled without the need for a trial)
8. Maximizing individual freedom (for example, the rights of freedom of speech, religion, and association granted by the First Amendment to the U.S. Constitution)

The law is not a series of calculating machines where definitions and answers come tumbling out when the right levers are pushed.

William O. Douglas
The Dissent, A Safeguard of Democracy, 1948

- The **historical school** believes that the law is an aggregate of social traditions and customs that have developed over the centuries. The law is an evolutionary process, and the law gradually reflects changes in the norms of society. Thus, historical legal scholars look to past legal decisions, or precedent, to solve contemporary problems.
- The **analytical school** maintains that the law is shaped by logic. Analytical philosophers believe that results are reached by applying principles of logic to the specific facts of the case. The emphasis is on the logic of the result rather than on how the result is reached.
- The **sociological school** asserts that the law is a means of achieving and advancing certain sociological goals. Followers of this philosophy, known as *realists*, believe that the purpose of law is to shape social behavior. Sociological philosophers are unlikely to adhere to past law as precedent.
- The philosophers of the **command school** believe that the law is a set of rules developed, communicated, and enforced by the ruling class, and that the law does not truly reflect society's morality, history, logic, or sociology. This school maintains that the law changes when the ruling class changes.
- The **critical legal studies school** proposes that legal rules are unnecessary and are used as an obstacle by the powerful to maintain the status quo. Critical legal theorists (sometimes referred to as "Crits") argue that legal disputes should be solved by applying arbitrary rules based on broad notions of what is "fair" in each circumstance. Under this theory, subjective decision making by judges would be permitted.
- The **law and economics school** proposes that promoting market and economic efficiency should be the central goal of legal decision making. This school is called the "Chicago School" of jurisprudence because it had its roots at the University of Chicago. This school proposes, for example, that free-market principles, cost–benefit analysis, and supply-and-demand theories should be used to determine the passage of legislation and the outcome of lawsuits.

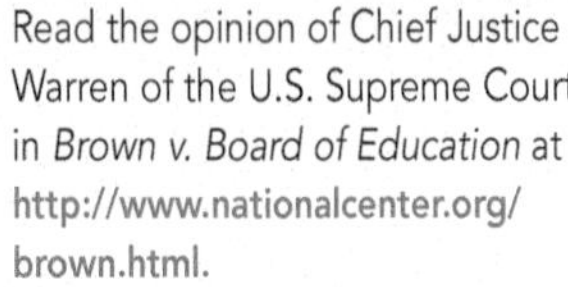

Read the opinion of Chief Justice Warren of the U.S. Supreme Court in *Brown v. Board of Education* at **http://www.nationalcenter.org/brown.html.**

History of American Law

Every person in the United States should have a basic knowledge of this country's legal history. Paralegals in particular need to know the history of the law in the United States and how the law developed to become what it is today.

When the American colonies were first settled, the English system of common law was generally adopted as the system of jurisprudence. English common law became the source of much of the law of the American colonies and eventually of the United States of America. This was the foundation from which American judges developed a common law in the United States.

English Common Law

English **common law** was law developed by judges who issued written opinions when deciding cases. The principles announced in these cases became precedent for later judges deciding similar cases. The English common law can be divided into cases decided by the following courts:

Common law Law developed by judges who issue their opinions when deciding cases. The principles announced in these cases become precedent for judges to later decide similar cases.

- **Law courts.** After 1066, William the Conqueror and his successors to the throne of England replaced various local laws with one uniform system of law. The king or queen appointed loyal followers as judges in each area of the kingdom. These judges were charged with administering the law in a uniform manner in what were called **law courts.** Law at this time tended to emphasize form (legal procedure) over the substance (merits) of the case. The only relief available in law courts was a monetary award for damages.
- **Chancery (equity) courts.** Because of the sometimes unfair results and the limited relief available in the law courts, a second set of courts—the **Court of Chancery (or equity court)**—was established, under the authority of the Lord Chancellor. Those who believed that the decision of a law court was unfair or that the law court could not grant an appropriate remedy could seek relief in this court. The Chancery Court inquired into the merits of the case and was less concerned with legal procedure. The Chancellor's remedies were called *equitable remedies* because they were shaped to fit each situation. Equitable orders and remedies of the Court of Chancery took precedence over the legal decisions and remedies of the law courts.
- **Merchant courts.** As trade developed in the Middle Ages, the merchants who traveled around Europe developed certain rules to solve their commercial disputes. These rules, known as the "law of merchants" or the *law merchant*, were based upon common trade practices and usage. Eventually, a separate set of courts, called the **merchant courts**, was established to administer these rules. In the early 1900s, the merchant court was absorbed into the regular law court system of England.

Two things most people should never see made: sausages and laws.

An old saying

Adoption of the English Common Law in America

All the states of the United States of America (except Louisiana) base their legal systems primarily on the English common law. The law, equity, and merchant courts have been merged so that most U.S. courts permit aggrieved parties to seek both law and equitable orders and remedies.

The importance of common law to the American legal system is described in the following excerpt from Justice William Douglas's opinion in the 1841 case of *Penny v. Little*, 4 Ill. 301, 1841 Ill. Lexis 98 (Ill., 1841):

> The common law is a beautiful system, containing the wisdom and experiences of ages. Like the people it ruled and protected, it was simple and crude in its infancy, and became enlarged, improved, and polished as the nation advanced in civilization,

virtue, and intelligence. Adapting itself to the conditions and circumstances of the people and relying upon them for its administration, it necessarily improved as the condition of the people was elevated. The inhabitants of this country always claimed the common law as their birthright, and at an early period established it as the basis of their jurisprudence.

Civil Law System

Another important legal system that has developed in the Western world is the Romano-Germanic **civil law system**. This legal system, commonly called the *civil law*, dates to 450 B.C., when Rome adopted a code of laws for its citizens. A compilation of this Roman law, called the *Corpus Juris Civilis* (the Body of Civil Law), was completed in A.D. 534. Later, two national codes—the French Civil Code of 1804 (the Napoleonic Code) and the German Civil Code of 1896—became models for countries that adopted civil codes.

In contrast to Anglo-American common law, in which laws are created by both judges and legislatures, the Civil Code and the statutes that expand and interpret it are the sole sources of the law in most civil law countries. Thus, cases are adjudicated by simply applying the code provisions or statutes to a specific set of facts. In some civil law countries, court decisions do not have the force of law.

Some states in America—particularly states that have a French or Spanish heritage, such as Louisiana and the southwestern states—have incorporated civil law into their legal systems.

LEARNING OBJECTIVE 4
List and describe the sources of law in the United States.

Sources of Law in the United States

In the more than 230 years since the founding of this country, U.S. lawmakers have developed a substantial body of law. The laws of the United States are extremely complex.

Paralegals often are called upon to conduct legal research to find relevant laws and judicial decisions that affect the cases or projects to which they are assigned. It is therefore important for them to know the sources of these laws. The sources of modern law in the United States are discussed in the following sections.

U.S. Congress, Washington, D.C. The U.S. Congress, which is a bicameral system made up of the U.S. Senate and the U.S. House of Representatives, creates federal law by enacting statutes. Each state has two senators and is allocated a certain number of representatives, based on population.

Constitutions

The **Constitution of the United States of America** is the supreme law of the land. This means that any law—federal, state, or local—that conflicts with the U.S. Constitution is unconstitutional and, therefore, unenforceable.

Constitution of the United States of America The supreme law of the United States. The Constitution of the United States of America establishes the structure of the federal government, delegates powers to the federal government, and guarantees certain fundamental rights.

The principles enumerated in the Constitution are extremely broad, because the founding fathers intended them to be applied to evolving social, technological, and economic conditions. The U.S. Constitution is often referred to as a "living document" because it is so adaptable.

States also have their own constitutions, often patterned after the U.S. Constitution, though many are more detailed. Provisions of state constitutions are valid unless they conflict with the U.S. Constitution or any federal law.

Treaties

The U.S. Constitution provides that the president, with the advice and consent of the U.S. Senate, may enter into **treaties** with foreign governments. Treaties become part of the supreme law of the land. With increasing international economic relations among nations, treaties will become an even more important source of law affecting business in the future.

Treaty A compact made between two or more nations.

Codified Law

Statutes are written laws enacted by legislatures. The U.S. Congress is empowered by the Commerce Clause and other provisions of the U.S. Constitution to enact **federal statutes** to regulate foreign and interstate commerce.

Statute Written law enacted by the legislative branch of the federal and state governments that establishes certain courses of conduct.

Examples Federal statutes include laws that cover antitrust, securities, bankruptcy, labor, equal employment opportunity, environmental protection, and consumer protection.

State legislatures enact **state statutes**.

Examples State statutes include state corporation laws, partnership laws, workers' compensation laws, and the Uniform Commercial Code.

The statutes enacted by the legislative branches of federal and state governments are organized by topic in code books. Law that has been recorded and organized in this way is referred to as **codified law**. Paralegals are often called upon to conduct research to find codified law that may apply to cases they are assigned to.

State legislatures often delegate lawmaking authority to local government bodies, such as cities and municipalities, counties, school districts, and water districts. These governmental units are empowered to adopt laws called **ordinances**.

Ordinance Law enacted by local government bodies, such as cities and municipalities, counties, school districts, and water districts.

Examples Traffic laws, local building codes, and zoning laws are types of ordinances. Ordinances are also codified.

Administrative Law

The legislative and executive branches of federal and state governments are empowered to establish **administrative agencies** to enforce and interpret statutes enacted by Congress and state legislatures. Many of these agencies regulate business.

Examples Congress has created numerous agencies such as the Securities and Exchange Commission (SEC) and the Federal Trade Commission (FTC).

The U.S. Congress or state legislatures usually empower these agencies to adopt administrative rules and regulations to interpret the statutes that the agencies are authorized to enforce. These rules and regulations have the force of law. Administrative agencies usually also have the power to hear and decide disputes. Their decisions are called *orders*. Because of their power, administrative agencies often are informally called the "fourth branch" of government.

Executive Orders

Executive order An order issued by a member of the executive branch of the government.

The executive branch of the federal government is headed by the president of the United States. In each state, the governor is the head of the executive branch. The executive branch is empowered to issue **executive orders**. This power is expressly delegated by the legislative branch and is implied from the U.S. Constitution and state constitutions.

Example On October 8, 2001, President George W. Bush, by executive order, established within the Executive Office of the President an Office of Homeland Security to be headed by the Assistant to the President for Homeland Security.

Judicial Decisions

Judicial decision A ruling about an individual lawsuit issued by federal and state courts.

When deciding individual lawsuits, federal and state courts issue **judicial decisions**. In these written opinions, the judge or justice usually explains the legal reasoning used to decide each case. An opinion often includes interpretations of statutes, ordinances, administrative regulations, and legal principles applied to the case. Many court decisions are reported in books available in law libraries.

Priority of Law in the United States

The U.S. Constitution and treaties take precedence over all other laws. Federal statutes take precedence over federal regulations, and federal law takes precedence over any conflicting state or local law. State constitutions rank as the highest state law, and state statutes take precedence over state regulations. State law takes precedence over local laws.

The Doctrine of *Stare Decisis*

Based on the common law tradition, past court decisions become precedents for deciding future cases. Lower courts must follow the precedents established by higher courts. That is why all federal and state courts in the United States must follow the precedents established by U.S. Supreme Court decisions.

The courts of one jurisdiction are not bound by the precedents established by the courts of another jurisdiction, although they may look to each other for guidance. Thus, state courts of one state are not required to follow the legal precedents established by the courts of another state.

Stare decisis Latin phrase meaning "to stand by the decision." Adherence to precedent.

Adherence to precedents is called ***stare decisis*** ("to stand by the decision"). The doctrine of *stare decisis* promotes uniformity of law within a jurisdiction, makes the court system more efficient, and makes the law more predictable for individuals and businesses. A court may change or reverse its legal reasoning later if a new case is presented to it and a change is warranted.

The doctrine of *stare decisis* is discussed in the following excerpt from Justice Musmanno's decision in *Flagiello v. Pennsylvania*, 417 Pa. 486, 208 A.2d 193 (Pa., 1965):

> Without *stare decisis*, there would be no stability in our system of jurisprudence. *Stare decisis* channels the law. It erects lighthouses and flies the signals of safety. The ships of jurisprudence must follow that well-defined channel which, over the years, has been proved to be secure and worthy.

Constitution of the United States of America

LEARNING OBJECTIVE 5

Explain the doctrine of separation of powers and describe the checks and balances built into the U.S. Constitution.

Prior to the American Revolution, each of the thirteen original colonies was a separate sovereignty under the rule of England. In September 1774, representatives of the colonies formed the Continental Congress. In 1776, the colonies declared their independence from England, and the American Revolution ensued.

The Constitutional Convention was convened in Philadelphia in May 1787 with the primary purpose of strengthening the federal government. After substantial debate, the delegates agreed to a new U.S. Constitution, which was reported to Congress in September 1787. State ratification of the Constitution was completed in 1788. Since that time, many amendments, including the Bill of Rights, have been added to the Constitution.

The U.S. Constitution serves several major functions:

1. It creates the three branches of the federal government (executive, legislative, and judicial) and allocates powers to these branches.
2. It grants the federal government certain authority to enact laws and enforce those laws.
3. It protects individual rights by limiting the government's ability to restrict those rights.

The Constitution of the United States is not a mere lawyers' document: it is a vehicle of life, and its spirit is always the spirit of the age.

Woodrow Wilson
Constitutional Government in the United States, 1927

The Constitution itself permits amendments to address social and economic changes.

The first page of the Constitution of the United States of America is shown in Exhibit 5.2.

Exhibit 5.2 The Constitution of the United States

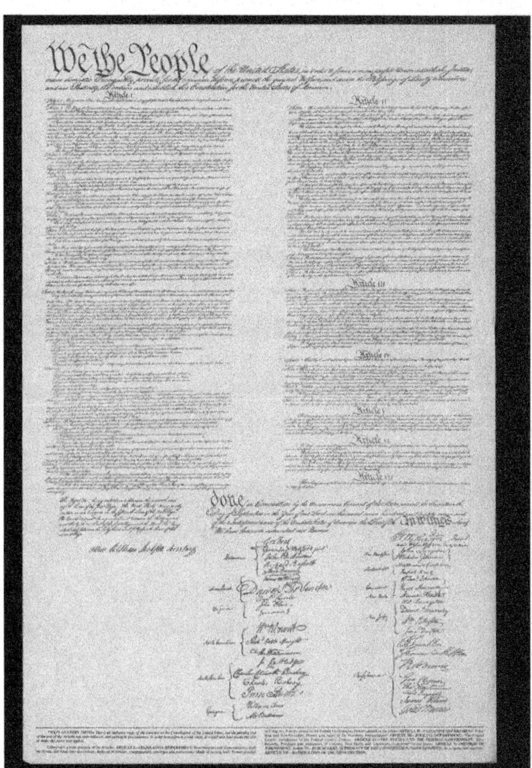

Federalism and Delegated Powers

Federalism The U.S. form of government, in which the federal government and the 50 state governments share powers.

The U.S. form of government is referred to as **federalism**, which means that the federal government and the 50 state governments share powers. When the states ratified the Constitution, they delegated certain powers to the federal government. These **delegated powers**, also called **enumerated powers**, authorize the federal government to deal with certain national and international affairs. State governments have powers that are not specifically delegated to the federal government by the Constitution and are empowered to deal with local affairs.

Doctrine of Separation of Powers

Legislative branch The part of the U.S. government that makes federal laws. It is known as Congress and consists of the Senate and the House of Representatives.

Executive branch The part of the U.S. government that enforces the federal law; it is headed by the president.

Judicial branch The part of the U.S. government that interprets the law. It consists of the Supreme Court and other federal courts.

The first three articles of the Constitution divide the federal government into three branches:

1. **Article I** of the Constitution establishes the **legislative branch**. This branch is bicameral, consisting of the Senate and the House of Representatives, and is collectively referred to as *Congress*. Each state is allocated two senators. The number of representatives to the House of Representatives is determined by the population of each state. The current number of representatives is determined by the 2010 census.
2. **Article II** of the Constitution establishes the **executive branch** by providing for the election of the president and vice president. The president is not elected by popular vote, but instead by the Electoral College, whose representatives are appointed by state delegations.
3. **Article III** establishes the **judicial branch** by creating the Supreme Court and authorizing the creation of other federal courts by Congress.

Checks and Balances

Checks and balances A system built into the U.S. Constitution to prevent any one of the three branches of the government from becoming too powerful.

Certain **checks and balances** are built into the Constitution to ensure that no one branch of the federal government becomes too powerful. Some of the checks and balances in our system of government are as follows:

1. The judicial branch has authority to examine the acts of the other two branches of government and determine whether these acts are constitutional.
2. The executive branch can enter into treaties with foreign governments only with the advice and consent of the Senate.
3. The legislative branch is authorized to create federal courts and determine their jurisdiction and to enact statutes that change judicially made law.
4. The president has veto power over bills passed by Congress. A vetoed bill goes back to Congress, where a vote of two-thirds of the members in each chamber is required to override the president's veto.
5. The president nominates persons to be U.S. Supreme Court justices, and many other federal judges, but the U.S. Senate must confirm the candidate before he or she becomes a judge.
6. The House of Representatives has the power to impeach the president for certain activities, such as treason, bribery, and other crimes. The Senate has the power to try the impeachment case, which requires a two-thirds vote of the Senate to impeach the president.

Web Exploration

Visit the website http://www.senate.gov/. Click on the word "Senators." Who are the two senators who represent your state in the U.S. Senate? Go to each senator's website and email the senator, expressing your view on a legal issue in which you are interested.

Web Exploration

Visit the website http://www.house.gov/. Who is the person who represents your home district? Go to that representative's website and read about his or her position on a current legal issue. What is the issue, and what is your representative's view on it?

LEARNING OBJECTIVE 6

Describe the Supremacy Clause of the U.S. Constitution and the preemption doctrine.

Supremacy Clause

The **Supremacy Clause** establishes that the federal Constitution, treaties, federal laws, and federal regulations are the supreme law of the land (U.S. Const. Art. VI, § 2). State and local laws that conflict with valid federal law are unconstitutional.

The concept that federal law takes precedence over state or local law is called the **preemption doctrine**.

Supremacy Clause A clause of the U.S. Constitution that establishes that the federal Constitution, treaties, federal laws, and federal regulations are the supreme law of the land.

Congress may expressly provide that a specific federal statute exclusively regulates a specific area or activity. No state or local law regulating the area or activity is valid if there is such a statute. More often, though, federal statutes do not expressly provide for exclusive jurisdiction. In these instances, state and local governments have concurrent jurisdiction to regulate the area or activity. But any state or local law that "directly and substantially" conflicts with valid federal law is preempted under the Supremacy Clause.

Example The United States government entered into treaties with other countries that established the size and length of oil tanker ships. Thus, oil tankers can transport oil between different countries using the same oil tankers. The state of Washington enacted a law that permitted only smaller oil tankers to enter its Puget Sound watercourse, which connects to waters of the Pacific Ocean. Oil tanker companies sued the state of Washington, arguing that the state law was unconstitutional. The U.S. Supreme Court held that the state law conflicted with federal law and was therefore preempted by the Supremacy Clause. *Ray v. Atlantic Richfield Co.*, 435 U.S. 151, 98 S.Ct. 988, 1978 U.S. Lexis 18 (U.S., 1978).

Commerce Clause

LEARNING OBJECTIVE 7

Describe the Commerce Clause of the U.S. Constitution.

The **Commerce Clause** of the U.S. Constitution grants Congress the power "to regulate commerce with foreign nations, and among the several states, and with Indian tribes" (U.S. Const. Art. I, § 8, cl. 3). Because this clause authorizes the federal government to regulate commerce, it has a greater impact on business than any other provision in the Constitution. Among other things, this clause is intended to foster the development of a national market and free trade among the states.

The U.S. Constitution grants the federal government the power to regulate three types of commerce. These are:

1. Commerce with Indian tribes
2. Commerce with foreign nations
3. Interstate commerce

Commerce Clause A clause of the U.S. Constitution that grants Congress the power "to regulate commerce with foreign nations, and among the several states, and with Indian tribes."

Native Americans

Before Europeans arrived in the "New World," the land had been occupied for thousands of years by those we now refer to as Native Americans. When the United States was first founded over two centuries ago, it consisted of the original thirteen colonies, all located in the east, and primarily on the Atlantic Ocean. At that time, the U.S. Constitution delegated to the federal government the authority to regulate commerce "with the Indian tribes" (U.S. Const. Art. I, § 8, cl. 3). This included tribes in the original thirteen states as well as in the territory that was to eventually become the rest of the United States of America.

Web Exploration

Visit the website of the National Museum of the American Indian at www.nmai.si.edu.

Example The federal government enacted the Indian Gaming Regulatory Act,[1] wherein the federal government authorized Native American tribes to operate gaming facilities. This act sets the terms of casino gambling and other gaming activities on tribal land. Today, casinos operated by Native Americans can be found in many states. Profits from the casinos have become an important source of income for members of certain tribes.

[1] 25 U.S.C. §§ 2701–2721.

Foreign Commerce

Foreign commerce Commerce with foreign nations. The Commerce Clause grants the federal government the authority to regulate foreign commerce.

The Commerce Clause gives the federal government the exclusive power to regulate commerce with foreign nations. Direct or indirect regulation of **foreign commerce** by state or local governments violates the Commerce Clause and is therefore unconstitutional.

Example Suppose the state of Michigan imposes a 20 percent sales tax on foreign automobiles sold in Michigan but only a 6 percent tax on domestic automobiles. This act would violate the Commerce Clause because Michigan would be regulating foreign commerce differently than state commerce. If Michigan placed a 20 percent sales tax on all automobiles sold in Michigan, this would not violate the Commerce Clause. Under its foreign Commerce Clause power, the federal government could enact a federal law that places a 20 percent tax on foreign automobiles sold in the United States.

Interstate Commerce

Interstate commerce Commerce that moves between states or that affects commerce between states.

The Commerce Clause gives the federal government the authority to regulate **interstate commerce**. Originally, the courts interpreted this clause to mean that the federal government could regulate only the commerce that moved *in* interstate commerce between states. The modern interpretation, however, allows the federal government to regulate activities that *affect* interstate commerce.

Under the "effects on interstate commerce" test, the regulated activity does not itself have to be in interstate commerce. Thus, any **intrastate commerce** (commerce within a state) that has an effect on interstate commerce is subject to federal regulation. Theoretically, this test subjects a substantial amount of business activity in the United States to federal regulation.

Example In the famous case of *Wickard, Secretary of Agriculture v. Filburn*, 317 U.S. 111, 63 S.Ct. 82, 1942 U.S. Lexis 1046 (U.S., 1942), a federal statute limited the amount of wheat a farmer could plant and harvest for home consumption. Filburn, a farmer, violated the law. The U.S. Supreme Court upheld the statute on the grounds that it prevented nationwide surpluses and shortages of wheat. The Court reasoned that wheat grown for home consumption would affect the supply of wheat available in interstate commerce.

State Police Power

Police power Power that permits states and local governments to enact laws to protect or promote the public health, safety, morals, and general welfare.

The states did not delegate all power to regulate business to the federal government. They retained the power to regulate much intrastate and interstate business activity that occurs within their borders. This is commonly referred to as the states' **police power**.

Police power permits states (and, by delegation, local governments) to enact laws to protect or promote the public health, safety, morals, and general welfare. This includes the authority to enact laws that regulate the conduct of business.

Examples State environmental laws, corporation and partnership laws, property laws, and local zoning ordinances and building codes are enacted under state police power.

Dormant Commerce Clause

If the federal government has chosen not to regulate an area of interstate commerce that it would otherwise have the power to regulate under its Commerce Clause powers, this area of commerce is subject to what is referred to as the **Dormant Commerce Clause**. A state, under its police power, can enact laws to regulate that area of commerce. However, if a state enacts laws to regulate commerce that the federal government has the power to regulate but has chosen not to regulate, the Dormant Commerce Clause prohibits the state's regulation from **unduly burdening interstate commerce**.

Unduly burdening interstate commerce To unlawfully restrict or limit commerce among states. Laws may be enacted by a state to protect or promote the public health, safety, morals, and general welfare, as long as those laws do not unduly burden interstate commerce.

Example Under its interstate commerce powers, the federal government could, if it wanted to, regulate corporations. However, the federal government has chosen not to. Thus, states regulate corporations. Assume that one state's corporation code permits only corporations from that state but from no other state to conduct business in that state. That state's law would unduly burden interstate commerce and would be unconstitutional.

Bill of Rights and Other Amendments

LEARNING OBJECTIVE 8

Describe freedom of speech and other protections guaranteed by the Bill of Rights.

In 1791, the states approved the ten amendments commonly referred to as the **Bill of Rights**, and they became part of the U.S. Constitution (see Exhibit 5.3). The Bill of Rights guarantees certain fundamental rights to natural persons and protects these rights from intrusive government action. Most of these rights, or "freedoms," also have been found applicable to so-called artificial persons, such as corporations.

Bill of Rights The first ten amendments to the Constitution. They were added to the U.S. Constitution in 1791.

The First Amendment to the Constitution guarantees the rights of free speech, assembly, and religion. In addition to the Bill of Rights, seventeen amendments have been added to the Constitution. Two important clauses from these amendments are the Due Process Clause and the Equal Protection Clause. These amendments are continually litigated and are frequent subjects of U.S. Supreme Court opinions.

I disapprove of what you say, but I will defend to the death your right to say it.

Voltaire

Freedom of Speech

One of the most important freedoms guaranteed by the Bill of Rights is the **freedom of speech**. Many other constitutional freedoms would be meaningless without it. It should

Freedom of speech The right to engage in oral, written, and symbolic speech protected by the First Amendment.

Exhibit 5.3 Bill of Rights

be noted, however, that the First Amendment's Freedom of Speech Clause protects speech only, not conduct. The U.S. Supreme Court places speech into three categories: (1) fully protected speech, (2) speech with limited protection, and (3) unprotected speech.

Fully Protected Speech

Fully protected speech Speech that cannot be prohibited or regulated by the government.

Fully protected speech is speech that the government cannot prohibit or regulate. Political speech is an example of such speech.

Example The government could not enact a law that forbids citizens from criticizing the current president.

The First Amendment protects oral, written, and symbolic speech.

Example If a person burns the American flag in protest of a government policy, this is symbolic speech that is protected by the First Amendment.

Limited Protected Speech

Limited protected speech Speech that the government may not prohibit but that is subject to time, place, and manner restrictions.

The Supreme Court has held that certain types of speech are only **limited protected speech** under the First Amendment. Although the government cannot forbid this type of speech, it can subject it to restrictions of time, place, and manner. The following types of speech are accorded limited protection:

- **Offensive speech** is speech that offends many members of society. The Supreme Court has held that offensive speech may be restricted by the government under time, place, and manner restrictions. Note, however, that "offensive" speech is not the same as "obscene" speech.

  Example The Federal Communications Commission (FCC) can regulate the use of offensive language on television by limiting such language to times when children would be unlikely to be watching, such as late at night.

- **Commercial speech** is speech such as advertising and business solicitation. The Supreme Court has held that commercial speech is subject to proper time, place, and manner restrictions.

  Example A city could prohibit billboards along its highways for safety and aesthetic reasons as long as other forms of advertising (such as print media) are available to the commercial advertiser.

Unprotected Speech

Unprotected speech Speech that is not protected by the First Amendment and may be forbidden by the government.

There are certain types of speech that the U.S. Supreme Court has held have no protection under the Freedom of Speech Clause. These types of speech may be entirely prohibited by the government. The Supreme Court has held that the following types of speech are **unprotected speech** under the First Amendment and may be totally forbidden by the government:

- dangerous speech (including such speech as yelling "fire" in a crowded theater when there is no fire);
- fighting words that are likely to provoke a hostile or violent response from an average person;
- speech that incites the violent or revolutionary overthrow of the government (however, the mere abstract teaching of the morality and consequences of such action is protected);
- defamatory language;
- child pornography; and
- obscene speech.

Definition of Obscene Speech

The definition of **obscene speech** is quite subjective. As Justice Stewart stated, "I know it when I see it." *Facobellis v. Ohio*, 378 U.S. 184, 84 S.Ct. 1676, 1964 U.S. Lexis 822 (U.S., 1964). In *Miller v. California*, the Supreme Court determined that speech is obscene under these circumstances:

1. the average person, applying contemporary community standards, would find that the work, taken as a whole, appeals to the prurient interest;
2. the work depicts or describes, in a patently offensive way, sexual conduct specifically defined by the applicable state law; and
3. the work, taken as a whole, lacks serious literary, artistic, political, or scientific value. 413 U.S. 15, 93 S.Ct. 2607,1973 U.S. Lexis 149 (U.S., 1973).

States are free to define what constitutes obscene speech. Movie theaters, magazine publishers, Web operators, and other media producers are often subject to challenges that the materials they display or sell are obscene and therefore are not protected by the First Amendment.

Free Speech in Cyberspace

In our digital age, constitutional provisions drafted centuries ago must often be applied to new technologies. Once or twice in a century, a new medium comes along that presents redundancy problems in applying freedom-of-speech rights. Recently this has been true of the Internet.

The U.S. Congress enacted the Communications Decency Act to regulate the Internet. This statute made it a felony to knowingly make "indecent" or "patently offensive" materials available on computer systems, including the Internet, to persons under 18 years of age. Penalties such as fines, prison terms, and loss of licenses were imposed for those convicted of violating the Act.

The American Constitution is, so far as I can see, the most wonderful work ever struck off at a given time by the brain and purpose of man.

W. E. Gladstone
Kin Beyond Sea, 1878

Immediately, cyberspace providers and users filed lawsuits challenging the provisions of the Act as violating their free speech rights under the First Amendment. Proponents of the Act countered that these provisions were necessary to protect children from indecent materials.

The U.S. Supreme Court decided to hear this issue and came down on the plaintiffs' side, overturning certain provisions of the Communications Decency Act. The Court found that the terms "indecent" and "patently offensive" were too vague to define and criminally enforce. The Court reasoned that limiting content on the Internet to what is suitable for a child would result in an unconstitutional limitation of adult speech. It further pointed out that parents can regulate their children's access to the Internet and can install blocking and filtering software programs to protect their children from seeing adult materials.

The Supreme Court declared emphatically that the Internet must be given the highest possible level of First Amendment free speech protection. The Supreme Court stated,

> As the most participatory form of mass speech yet developed, the Internet deserves the highest protection from government intrusion.

The Court also reasoned that because the Internet is a global medium, there would be no way to prevent indecent material from flowing over the Internet from abroad.[2]

---

[2] *Reno v. American Civil Liberties Union*, 521 U.S. 844, 117 S.Ct. 2329, 1997 U.S. Lexis 4037 (Supreme Court of the United States, 1997).

Protest, Los Angeles, California. The Freedom of Speech Clause of the First Amendment to the U.S. Constitution protects the right to engage in political speech. Freedom of speech is one of Americans' most highly prized rights.

Freedom of Religion

The U.S. Constitution requires federal, state, and local governments to be neutral toward religion. The First Amendment actually contains two separate clauses regarding religion:

Establishment Clause A clause in the First Amendment that prohibits the government from either establishing a state religion or promoting one religion over others.

1. The **Establishment Clause** prohibits the government from either establishing a state religion or promoting one religion over another.

   Example An Alabama statute authorized a one-minute period of silence in school for "meditation or voluntary prayer." The U.S. Supreme Court held that the statute endorsed religion, and therefore was invalid.[3]

   Example Copies of the Ten Commandments were prominently displayed in large gold frames and hung alone in two county courthouses in Kentucky so that visitors could see them. The U.S. Supreme Court held that this violated the Establishment Clause.[4]

Free Exercise Clause A clause in the First Amendment that prohibits the government from interfering with the free exercise of religion in the United States.

2. The **Free Exercise Clause** prohibits the government from interfering with the free exercise of religion in the United States. Generally, this clause prevents the government from enacting laws that prevent individuals from practicing their chosen religion.

   Example The federal, state, or local governments could not enact a law that prohibits all religions or that prohibits churches, synagogues, mosques, or temples. The government could not prohibit religious practitioners from celebrating their major holidays and high holy days.

---

[3] *Wallace v. Jaffree*, 472 U.S. 38, 105 S.Ct. 2479, 1985 U.S. Lexis 91 (Supreme Court of the United States, 1985).

[4] *McCreary County, Kentucky v. American Civil Liberties Union of KY*, 545 U.S. 844, 125 S.Ct. 2722, 2005 U.S. Lexis 5211 (Supreme Court of the United States, 2005).

Of course, this right to be free from government intervention in the practice of religion is not absolute.

Example Human sacrifices are unlawful and are not protected by the First Amendment.

In the following feature, a paralegal professional shares her experience of working on a constitutional law case.

Due Process Clause

The **Due Process Clause** provides that no person shall be deprived of "life, liberty, or property" without due process of law. This means that although the government is not prohibited from taking a person's life, liberty, or property, it must follow a certain process to do so. The Due Process Clause is contained in both the Fifth and the Fourteenth Amendments. In the Fifth Amendment, the Due Process Clause applies to federal government action. In the Fourteenth Amendment, the Due Process Clause applies to state and local government action. There are two categories of due process: *substantive* and *procedural*.

Due Process Clause A clause that provides that no person shall be deprived of "life, liberty, or property" without due process of law.

Substantive Due Process

Substantive due process requires that government statutes, ordinances, regulations, and other laws be clear on their face and not overly broad in scope. The test of

Paralegals *in* Practice

PARALEGAL PROFILE

Charlotte A. Sheraden-Baker

Charlotte A. Sheraden-Baker started her career as a legal secretary after graduating from high school. After taking time out to raise a family, she resumed work as a legal secretary while attending night school to obtain her paralegal degree. In 2000, she graduated as Paralegal of the Year with an Associate of Applied Science degree, the oldest person in her class. After convincing her firm they needed another paralegal, Charlotte was promoted and continued evening classes to obtain her Bachelor of Arts degree. She currently works for the law firm of Warner, Smith & Harris in Fort Smith, Arkansas, where she has been employed for the last 14 years.

I work for a general practice that has 13 partners and 3 associates. I recently assisted in a constitutional law case that was appealed to the Arkansas Supreme Court over a First Amendment issue. Our client was a party to a lawsuit between two groups of a local temple. Both thought they were entitled to make governing rules for the temple and maintain its original assets and location. Since the matter could not be resolved between the opposing parties, the state court judge was asked to rule, and he determined that an election should be held, whereby the temple members would decide.

In the process, my firm's attorneys contended that the judge overstepped his duties by overriding the already-established governing documents of the temple and assigning a different definition as to who was a member of the congregation and entitled to vote. It was argued that the judge had prohibited the free exercise of religion, as guaranteed by the First Amendment of both the federal and state constitutions. Our case was lost on appeal because it was determined the judge did not intrude into anyone's religious rights. Nonetheless, the case was a great learning experience in my legal career.

At the state court level, some of my pretrial duties included preparing, gathering, and duplicating exhibits; copying and keeping up to date on important documents; making lists of witnesses and exhibits; and more. At trial, my primary job was to ensure that the judge, court clerk, and court reporter had all the necessary documents; monitor exhibits offered, admitted, or rejected; organize witnesses and keep track of their appearances and testimony; and take notes on testimony to help with the attorney's upcoming examinations.

My duties at the state Supreme Court level were slightly different. For any case that is appealed, each party prepares a brief and responds to the other party's brief within a short time. Then the case is set for oral argument before the state Supreme Court. Preparation of appellate briefs is complicated and precise, as the Supreme Courts require specific style, format, and content. I was asked to monitor filing deadlines, obtain the local trial transcripts and submit them to the Supreme Court, prepare an extensive summary of the pertinent trial testimony for the appeal brief, and verify or "Shepardize" all cases cited in the brief itself.

whether substantive due process is met is whether a "reasonable person" could understand the law well enough to be able to comply with it. Laws that do not meet this test are declared *void for vagueness.*

Example A city ordinance that makes it illegal for persons to wear "clothes of the opposite sex" would be held unconstitutional as void for vagueness because a reasonable person would not be able to clearly determine whether his or her clothing violates the law.

Procedural Due Process

Procedural due process A category of due process that requires that the government give a person proper notice and a hearing of the legal action before that person is deprived of his or her life, liberty, or property.

Procedural due process requires that the government give a person proper notice and a hearing of the legal action before that person is deprived of his or her life, liberty, or property. The government action must be fair.

Example If the federal or state government brings a criminal action against a defendant for an alleged crime, the government must notify the person of its intent (by charging the defendant with a crime) and provide the defendant with a proper hearing (a trial).

Web Exploration

How does Louisiana law differ from that of the other 49 states? Go to https://en.wikipedia.org/wiki/Law_of_Louisiana

Example If the government wants to exercise its power of eminent domain and demolish a person's home to build a highway, the government must (1) give the homeowner sufficient notice of its intention, and (2) provide a hearing. Under the **Just Compensation Clause** of the Fifth Amendment, the government must pay the owner just compensation for taking the property.

LEARNING OBJECTIVE 9

Describe the Equal Protection Clause and the tests used to determine whether it has been violated.

Equal Protection Clause

Equal Protection Clause A clause that provides that state, local, and federal governments cannot deny to any person the "equal protection of the laws."

The **Equal Protection Clause** of the Fourteenth Amendment, as interpreted by the U.S. Supreme Court, provides that state, local, and federal governments cannot deny to any person the "equal protection of the laws." The clause is designed to prohibit invidious government discrimination, and prohibits governments from enacting laws that classify and treat similarly situated persons differently. Both natural persons and businesses are protected.

The Equal Protection Clause has not been interpreted literally by the U.S. Supreme Court. The Court has held that some government laws that treat people or businesses differently are constitutional. It has established three different standards for determining whether such government action is lawful:

Strict scrutiny test A test that is applied to classifications based on a *suspect class* (such as race, national origin, citizenship) or that involves *fundamental rights* (such as voting).

1. ***Strict scrutiny test.*** Any government activity or regulation that classifies persons based on a "suspect class" (such as race, national origin, and citizenship) or involves a "fundamental right" (such as voting) is reviewed using a strict scrutiny test. Under this standard, most government classifications of persons based on race are found to be unconstitutional.

   Example A government rule that permitted persons of one race, but not of others, to receive government benefits such as Medicaid would violate this test. But affirmative action programs that give racial minorities a "plus factor" when considered for public university admission is lawful, as long as it does not constitute a quota system.

Intermediate scrutiny test A test that is applied to classifications based on a *protected class* (such as gender or age).

2. ***Intermediate scrutiny test.*** The lawfulness of government classifications based on *protected classes* other than race (such as gender and age) is examined using an intermediate scrutiny test. Under this standard, the courts determine whether the government classification is "reasonably related" to a legitimate government purpose.

Example A rule prohibiting persons over a certain age from military combat would be lawful, but a rule prohibiting persons over a certain age from acting as government engineers would not be. With regard to a person's gender, the U.S. Supreme Court has held that the federal government can require males, but not females, to register with the military for a possible draft.

3. ***Rational basis test.*** The lawfulness of all government classifications that do not involve suspect or protected classes is examined using a rational basis test. Under this test, the courts will uphold government regulation as long as there is a justifiable reason for the law. This standard permits much of the government regulation of business.

   Example Providing government subsidies to farmers but not to those in other occupations is permissible.

Rational basis test A test that is applied to classifications not involving a suspect or protected class.

The ethical duty and social responsibility of a paralegal professional to avoid conflicts of interest is discussed in the following feature.

LEARNING OBJECTIVE 10
Explain a paralegal's duty to avoid conflicts of interest.

ETHICAL PERSPECTIVE

Paralegal's Duty to Avoid Conflicts of Interest

Ms. Jennifer Adams is hired as a paralegal at a law firm with expertise in real estate development law. She recently left a paralegal position at another law firm to take this new position.

At the new firm, Ms. Adams is assigned to work for Mr. Humberto Cruz, a senior partner. He is an expert in complex real estate transactions, representing clients in the purchase, development, and leasing of large shopping malls. One client Mr. Cruz represents is Modern Properties L.P., a limited partnership that constructs and operates retail shopping malls across the country.

One day Mr. Cruz asks Ms. Adams to attend a meeting with him and the president of Modern Properties L.P. At the meeting, the president discloses a dispute that the partnership has with a tenant, Third National Bank, concerning its lease at a mall constructed and operated by Modern Properties L.P. The president explains that Third National Bank has filed a lawsuit against Modern Properties L.P. The president further explains that the partnership wants Mr. Cruz to represent the partnership in this lawsuit.

Ms. Adams realizes that her prior law firm represented Third National Bank in many lawsuits, and that she had worked on several of those cases. During the course of this work, she became privy to confidential information about Third National Bank, including its financial condition, operations, and legal strategy. Does Ms. Adams have a conflict of interest? If so, what should she do?

PARALEGAL'S ETHICAL DECISION

Model and state paralegal codes of ethics and professional responsibility provide that a paralegal is under a duty to avoid conflicts of interest. Thus, a paralegal cannot conduct work on any matter where there would be a conflict of interest with a present or past employer or with a client.

Thus, Ms. Adams must immediately disclose the fact that she previously worked on cases involving Third National Bank at the prior law firm where she was employed and that because of that employment she possesses confidential information about Third National Bank. Because of this conflict of interest, Ms. Adams must excuse herself from working on the *Third National Bank v. Modern Properties L.P.* case.

Concept Review *and* Reinforcement

LEGAL TERMINOLOGY

Administrative agencies 181
Analytical school of jurisprudence 178
Bill of Rights 187
Checks and balances 184
Civil law system 180
Codified law 181
Command school of jurisprudence 178
Commerce Clause 185
Commercial speech 188
Common law 179
Constitution of the United States of America 181
Court of Chancery (or equity court) 179
Critical legal studies school of jurisprudence 178
Delegated powers 184
Dormant Commerce Clause 186
Due Process Clause 191
Enumerated powers 184
Equal Protection Clause 192
Establishment Clause 190
Executive branch 184
Federal statutes 181
Federalism 184
Free Exercise Clause 190
Freedom of speech 187
Fully protected speech 188
Historical school of jurisprudence 178
Intermediate scrutiny test 192
Interstate commerce 186
Intrastate commerce 186
Judicial branch 184
Judicial decision 182
Jurisprudence 177
Just Compensation Clause 192
Law 176
Law and economics school 178
Law courts 179
Legislative branch 184
Limited protected speech 188
Merchant courts 179
Natural law school of jurisprudence 177
Obscene speech 189
Offensive speech 188
Ordinances 181
Police power 186
Preemption doctrine 185
Procedural due process 192
Rational basis test 193
Separation of powers 000
Sociological school of jurisprudence 178
Stare decisis 182
State statutes 181
Statutes 181
Strict scrutiny test 192
Substantive due process 191
Supremacy Clause 185
Treaty 181
Unduly burdening interstate commerce 187
Unprotected speech 188

SUMMARY OF KEY CONCEPTS

What Is Law?

Definition of *Law*	Law consists of a body of rules of action or conduct prescribed by a controlling authority and having binding legal force.
Functions of Law	The main functions of the law are to: • keep the peace; • shape moral standards; • promote social justice; • maintain the status quo; • facilitate orderly change; • facilitate planning; • provide a basis for compromise; and • maximize individual freedom.
Fairness	Although the American legal system is one of the fairest and most democratic systems of law, abuses and mistakes in the application of the law still occur.

Flexibility	The law must be flexible to meet social, technological, and economic changes.

Schools of Jurisprudential Thought

Natural Law	This school postulates that law is based on what is "correct"; it emphasizes a moral theory of law—that is, law should be based on morality and ethics.
Historical	These scholars believe that law is an aggregate of social traditions and customs.
Analytical	Students of this school maintain that law is shaped by logic.
Sociological	These thinkers assert that the law is a means of achieving and advancing certain sociological goals.
Command	Philosophers of this school believe that the law is a set of rules developed, communicated, and enforced by the ruling class.
Critical Legal Studies	This school maintains that legal rules are unnecessary and that legal disputes should be solved based on a general concept of fairness.
Law and Economics	Scholars of this school believe that promoting market efficiency should be the central concern of legal decision making.

History of American Law

English Common Law	English common law (or judge-made law) forms the basis of the legal systems of most states in this country. Louisiana bases its law on the French civil code.

Sources of Law in the United States

Constitutions	The U.S. Constitution establishes the federal government and enumerates its powers. Powers not given to the federal government are reserved to the states. State constitutions establish state governments and enumerate their powers.
Treaties	The president, with the advice and consent of the Senate, may enter into treaties with foreign countries.
Codified Law	• Statutes are enacted by Congress and state legislatures. • Ordinances and statutes are passed by municipalities and local government bodies to establish courses of conduct that must be followed by covered parties.
Administrative Agencies	Administrative agencies are created by the legislative and executive branches of government. They may adopt rules and regulations that govern conduct.
Executive Orders	Executive orders are issued by the president and state governors.
Judicial Decisions	Courts decide controversies by issuing decisions that state the holding of each case and the rationale the court used to reach that decision.

Doctrine of Stare Decisis

Definition	*Stare decisis* means "to stand by the decision." This doctrine requires adherence to precedent.

Constitution of the United States of America

Scope	The Constitution consists of seven articles and 27 amendments. It establishes the three branches of the federal government, enumerates their powers, and provides important guarantees of individual freedom. The Constitution was ratified by the states in 1788.

Basic Constitutional Concepts	*Federalism:* The Constitution created the federal government, which shares power with the state governments. *Delegated powers:* When the states ratified the Constitution, they delegated certain powers, called *enumerated powers*, to the federal government. *Reserved powers:* Those powers not granted to the federal government by the Constitution are reserved to the states. *Separation of powers:* Each branch of the federal government has separate powers: • the legislative branch has the power to make the law; • the executive branch has the power to enforce the law; and • the judicial branch has the power to interpret the law. *Checks and balances:* Certain checks and balances are built into the Constitution to ensure that no one branch of the federal government becomes too powerful.

Supremacy Clause

The Supremacy Clause stipulates that the U.S. Constitution, treaties, and federal law (including both statutes and regulations) are the supreme law of the land. State or local laws that conflict with federal law are unconstitutional. This is called the *preemption doctrine.*

Commerce Clause

- The Commerce Clause authorizes the federal government to regulate commerce with foreign nations, among the states, and with Native American tribes.
- The federal government has broad power to regulate any activity (including intrastate commerce) that affects interstate commerce.
- Police powers are powers reserved to the states to regulate commerce.

Bill of Rights and Other Amendments

- The Bill of Rights consists of the first ten amendments to the Constitution. They establish basic individual rights. The Bill of Rights was ratified in 1791.
- In addition to the ten amendments of the Bill of Rights, there are seventeen other amendments to the U.S. Constitution.

Freedom of Speech

The Freedom of Speech Clause of the First Amendment guarantees that the government shall not infringe on a person's right to speak. It protects oral, written, and symbolic speech. This right is not absolute—that is, some speech is not protected and other speech is granted only limited protection. The U.S. Supreme Court has placed speech in the following three categories:

1. *Fully protected speech:* Speech that cannot be prohibited or regulated by the government
2. *Limited protected speech:* Types of speech that are granted only limited protection under the Freedom of Speech Clause—that is, they are subject to governmental *time, place, and manner restrictions:*
   - offensive speech
   - commercial speech
3. *Unprotected speech:* Speech that is not protected by the Freedom of Speech Clause:
   - dangerous speech
   - fighting words
   - speech that advocates the violent overthrow of the government
   - defamatory language
   - child pornography
   - obscene speech

Freedom of Religion

There are two religion clauses in the First Amendment. They are:

1. *Establishment Clause:* Prohibits the government from establishing a state religion or promoting religion.
2. *Free Exercise Clause:* Prohibits the government from interfering with the free exercise of religion. This right is not absolute; for example, human sacrifices are forbidden.

Due Process Clause

The Due Process Clause provides that no person shall be deprived of "life, liberty, or property" without due process. There are two categories of due process:

1. *Substantive due process:* Requires that laws be clear on their face and not overly broad in scope. Laws that do not meet this test are *void for vagueness.*
2. *Procedural due process:* Requires that the government give a person proper *notice* and *hearing* before that person is deprived of his or her life, liberty, or property. An owner must be paid *just compensation* if the government takes his or her property.

Equal Protection Clause

The Equal Protection Clause prohibits the government from enacting laws that classify and treat "similarly situated" persons differently. This standard is not absolute and the government can treat persons differently in certain situations. The U.S. Supreme Court has applied the following tests to determine if the Equal Protection Clause has been violated:

1. *Strict scrutiny test:* This test applies to *suspect classes* (such as race, national origin, and citizenship) or involves a fundamental right (such as voting).
2. *Intermediate scrutiny test:* This test applies to other *protected classes* (such as sex or age).
3. *Rational basis test:* This test applies to government classifications that do not involve a suspect class, a fundamental right, or a protected class.

WORKING THE WEB

1. Go to the website http://www.usconstitution.net/const.html. Scroll down to "Amendment 7." When was this amendment ratified? What does this amendment provide? Explain.
2. Visit the website http://www.archives.gov/exhibits/charters/charters.html. A page titled "The Charters of Freedom—A New World Is at Hand" will appear on your computer screen. Do the following exercises:
   a. On the page shown, click on the third icon from the left. Read the article titled "The Spirit of the Revolution—The Declaration of Independence." What did the Declaration of Independence do? Explain.
   b. On the page shown, click on the sixth icon from the left. Read the article "The Constitutional Convention—Creation of the Constitution." How many states were required to ratify the Constitution?
   c. At the top of the page shown, click on the second-to-last icon from the right. Read the article "Expansion of Rights and Liberties—The Right of Suffrage." What amendment to the U.S. Constitution gave women the right to vote? What year was this amendment ratified?
3. Go to http://www.nps.gov/stli/learn/historyculture/index.htm to read a history of the Statue of Liberty. Visit the World Heritage website describing the Statue of Liberty at http://whc.unesco.org/en/list/307.

CRITICAL THINKING & WRITING QUESTIONS

1. Define the term "law." Is this an easy concept to define? Why?
2. Should the language of the U.S. Constitution be applied according to its original meaning, or should it be applied in a more expansive sense? Explain.
3. What is the power of the legislative branch of government? What is a statute?
4. Do you think the U.S. Supreme Court makes law when it interprets the U.S. Constitution? Explain.
5. What is the doctrine of *stare decisis*? Why is this doctrine important?
6. What does the doctrine of separation of powers provide? Can you give any examples where the separation of the powers of the three branches of government is blurred?
7. What is the purpose of the doctrine of checks and balances? Can you give any examples where one branch of the government limits the power of another branch of the government?
8. What does the Supremacy Clause provide? What would be the consequences if the Supremacy Clause did not exist? Explain.
9. What does the Commerce Clause of the U.S. Constitution do? Explain.
10. The First Amendment to the U.S. Constitution contains the Freedom of Speech Clause. Explain the differences between fully protected speech, partially protected speech, and unprotected speech.
11. The U.S. Constitution guarantees freedom of religion. Explain the difference between the Establishment Clause and the Free Exercise Clause. Can you give a possible example of a legitimate government restriction of a religious practice?
12. What does the Equal Protection Clause provide? Explain the differences between the strict scrutiny test, intermediate scrutiny test, and rational basis test.

Building Paralegal Skills

VIDEO CASE STUDIES

Difference Between a Criminal and a Civil Trial

An interview with Judge Kenney, a trial court judge, who discusses the difference between a civil and a criminal trial.

After viewing the video case study at the book website at www.pearsonhighered.com/careersresources, answer the following:

1. What are the differences in the burdens of proof in a criminal and a civil matter?
2. What protections does the U.S. Constitution afford those accused of criminal acts?

A School Principal Reacts: Student Rights versus the School's Duty

In an altercation on a school bus, it is claimed that the student involved had a contraband knife on his person. As a result, the principal has ordered that the student be searched for the knife.

After viewing the video case study at the book website at www.pearsonhighered.com/careersresources, answer the following:

1. Does a student have a constitutional right of privacy?
2. Does the school have a right to search a student?
3. Are the school district and those working for it immune from suit for the actions taken?

Confidentiality Issue: Attorney–Client Privilege

Paralegal Alicia Jackson meets with a client to review answers to documents that must be sent to opposing counsel. While reviewing the answers, the client tells her about a potentially fraudulent claim.

After viewing the video case study in MyLegalStudiesLab, answer the following:

1. Does the attorney–client privilege apply to information given to a paralegal?
2. To whom does the privilege belong?
3. How is the attorney–client privilege different from the duty of confidentiality?

ETHICS ANALYSIS & DISCUSSION QUESTIONS

1. Are there any ethical issues in expressing one's personal feelings while working on a case? What if you have strong feelings against the client's position?
2. Does the American system of law depend on members of the legal team to put aside their personal beliefs and work diligently on unpopular cases or issues? How does this ensure equal justice and allow for change in the system?
3. You are working in a law firm for an attorney who has had a series of strokes that have caused a permanent reading disability and memory impairment. Do you have any ethical obligation to the attorney's clients? Do you have any ethical obligation to the firm and to the attorney? See Philadelphia Ethics Opinion 2002–12 (2000). See also Texas Ethics Opinion 522 (1997).

DEVELOPING YOUR COLLABORATION SKILLS

With a group of students, review the facts of the following case. Then as a group, discuss the following questions.

1. What does the Supremacy Clause provide?
2. Did the product label warn of the possible side effects and injuries suffered by the plaintiff?
3. What did the New Hampshire state law require for labeling the product? How was this different from federal requirements?
4. What was the defendant pharmaceutical company's defense against liability to the plaintiff?
5. Who wins and why?

Mutual Pharmaceutical Company, Inc. v. Bartlett

In 1978, the Food and Drug Administration (FDA), a federal government agency, approved a nonsteroidal anti-inflammatory pain reliever called sulindac under the brand name Clinoril. At the time, the FDA approved the labeling of the prescription drug, which contained warnings of specific side effects of the drug. When the Clinoril patent expired, the law permitted other pharmaceutical companies to sell generic versions of sulindac under their own brand names. Federal law requires that genetic sellers of drugs use the exact labeling as required on the original drug, without alteration.

Mutual Pharmaceutical Company, Inc. (Mutual) manufactured and sold a generic brand of sulindac. Karen L. Bartlett was prescribed sulindac for shoulder pain and the pharmacist dispensed Mutual's generic brand of sulindac to her. Bartlett soon developed an acute case of toxic epidermal necrolysis. The results were horrific. Sixty percent of the surface of her body deteriorated and burned off. She spent months in a medically induced coma, underwent 12 eye surgeries, and was tube-fed for a year. She is now severely disfigured, has a number of physical disabilities, and is nearly blind. The original patented drug's label, and therefore Mutual's generic brand label, did not refer to the possible side effect toxic epidermal necrolysis.

The state of New Hampshire law required stricter warnings on prescription drugs than federal laws. Bartlett sued Mutual for product liability under New Hampshire law. The jury of the U.S. district court found Mutual liable and awarded Bartlett more than $21 million in damages, and the U.S. court of appeals affirmed the award. Mutual appealed to the U.S. Supreme Court, asserting that the federal labeling law pre-empted New Hampshire law under the Supremacy Clause.

Source: Mutual Pharmaceutical Company, Inc. v. Bartlett, 133 S.Ct. 2466, 2013 U.S. Lexis 4702 (Supreme Court of the United States, 2013)

PARALEGAL PORTFOLIO EXERCISE

Research and find an article that discusses a Federal Communications Commission (FCC) clash with a radio, cable, or television station regarding the subject matter that it may broadcast. Write a memorandum, no longer than two pages, that discusses this dispute and the outcome of the case.

LEGAL ANALYSIS & WRITING CASES

McCreary County, Kentucky v. American Civil Liberties Union of Kentucky

McCreary County and Pulaski County (the counties), Kentucky, placed in their courthouses a large, gold-framed copy of the Ten Commandments. In both courthouses, the Ten Commandments were prominently displayed so that visitors could see them. The Ten Commandments hung alone, not with other paintings and such. The American Civil Liberties Union of Kentucky (ACLU) sued the counties in U.S. district court, alleging that the placement of the Ten Commandments in the courthouses violated the Establishment Clause of the U.S. Constitution. The U.S. district court granted a preliminary injunction ordering the removal of the Ten Commandments from both courthouses. The counties added copies of the Magna Carta, the Declaration of Independence, the Bill of Rights, and other nonreligious items to the display of the Ten Commandments. The U.S. district court reissued the injunction against this display, and the U.S. court of appeals affirmed. The counties appealed to the U.S. Supreme Court.

Question

1. Does the display of the Ten Commandments in the counties' courthouses violate the Establishment Clause?

Source: McCreary County, Kentucky v. American Civil Liberties Union of Kentucky, 545 U.S. 844, 125 S.Ct. 2722, 2005 U.S. Lexis 5211 (Supreme Court of the United States, 2005)

Reno, Attorney General of the United States v. Condon, Attorney General of South Carolina

State departments of motor vehicles (DMVs) register automobiles and issue driver's licenses. State DMVs require automobile owners and drivers to provide personal information—including a person's name, address, telephone number, vehicle description, Social Security number, medical information, and a photograph—as a condition for registering an automobile or obtaining a driver's license. Many states' DMVs sold this personal information to individuals, advertisers, and businesses. These sales generated significant revenues for the states.

After receiving thousands of complaints from individuals whose personal information had been sold, the U.S. Congress enacted the Driver's Privacy Protection Act of 1994 (DPPA). This federal statute prohibits a state from selling the personal information of a person unless the state obtains that person's affirmative consent to do so. South Carolina sued the United States, alleging that the federal government violated the Commerce Clause by adopting the DPPA.

Question

1. Was the Driver's Privacy Protection Act properly enacted by the federal government pursuant to its Commerce Clause power?

Source: Reno, Attorney General of the United States v. Condon, Attorney General of South Carolina, 528 U.S. 141, 120 S.Ct. 666, 2000 U.S. Lexis 503 (Supreme Court of the United States, 2000)

WORKING WITH THE LANGUAGE OF THE COURT CASE

Obergefell v. Hodges

135 S.Ct. 2584, 2015 U.S. Lexis 4250 (2015)
Supreme Court of the United States

Read the following excerpt from the U.S. Supreme Court's opinion. Review and brief the case. In your brief, answer the following questions.

1. What does the Due Process Clause of the Fourteenth Amendment provide?
2. What does the Equal Protection Clause of the Fourteenth Amendment provide?
3. What were the issues that the U.S. Supreme Court was asked to decide?
4. What decision did the U.S. Supreme Court reach? What reasoning did the Supreme Court use in reaching its decision?

Kennedy, Justice (joined by Ginsburg, Breyer, Sotomayor, and Kagan)

The Constitution promises liberty to all within its reach, a liberty that includes certain specific rights that allow persons, within a lawful realm, to define and express their identity. The petitioners in these cases seek to find that liberty by marrying someone of the same sex and having their marriages deemed lawful on the same terms and conditions as marriages between persons of the opposite sex.

These cases come from Michigan, Kentucky, Ohio, and Tennessee, States that define marriage as a union between one man and one woman. The petitioners are 14 same-sex couples. The respondents are state officials responsible for enforcing the laws in question.

Petitioners filed these suits in United States District Courts in their home States. Each District Court ruled in their favor. The respondents appealed the decisions against them to the United States Court of Appeals for the Sixth Circuit. It consolidated the cases and reversed the judgments of the District Courts.

The petitioners sought certiorari. This Court granted review, limited to two questions. The first, presented by the cases from Michigan and Kentucky, is whether the Fourteenth Amendment requires a State to license a marriage between two people of the same sex. The second, presented by the cases from Ohio, Tennessee, and, again, Kentucky, is whether the Fourteenth Amendment requires a State to recognize a same-sex marriage licensed and performed in a State which does grant that right.

With the exception of the opinion here under review and one other, the Courts of Appeals have held that excluding same-sex couples from marriage violates the Constitution. After years of litigation, legislation, referenda, and the discussions that attended these public acts, the States are now divided on the issue of same-sex marriage.

Under the Due Process Clause of the Fourteenth Amendment, no State shall "deprive any person of life, liberty, or property, without due process of law." The fundamental liberties protected by this Clause include most of the rights enumerated in the Bill of Rights. In addition these liberties extend to certain personal choices central to individual dignity and autonomy, including intimate choices that define personal identity and beliefs. Over time and in other contexts, the Court has reiterated that the right to marry is fundamental under the Due Process Clause. This analysis compels the conclusion that same-sex couples may exercise the right to marry.

The nature of marriage is that, through its enduring bond, two persons together can find other freedoms, such as expression, intimacy, and spirituality. This is true for all persons, whatever their sexual orientation. There is dignity in the bond between two men or two women who seek to marry and in their autonomy to make such profound choices. The right to marry thus dignifies couples who wish to define themselves by their commitment to each other. Same-sex couples have the same right as opposite-sex couples to enjoy intimate association.

As all parties agree, many same-sex couples provide loving and nurturing homes to their children, whether biological or adopted. And hundreds of thousands of children are presently being raised by such couples.

This Court's cases and the Nation's traditions make clear that marriage is a keystone of our social order. Marriage remains a building block of our national community. There is no difference between same and opposite-sex couples with respect to this principle.

The right of same-sex couples to marry that is part of the liberty promised by the Fourteenth Amendment is derived, too, from that Amendment's guarantee of the equal protection of the laws. Indeed, in interpreting the Equal Protection Clause, the Court has recognized that new insights and societal understandings can reveal unjustified inequality within our most fundamental institutions that once passed unnoticed and unchallenged.

It is now clear that the challenged laws burden the liberty of same-sex couples, and it must be further acknowledged that they abridge central precepts of equality. Here the marriage laws enforced by the respondents are in essence unequal: same-sex couples are denied all the benefits afforded to opposite-sex couples and are barred from exercising a fundamental right. Especially against a long history of disapproval of their relationships, this denial to same-sex couples of the right to marry works a grave and continuing harm. And the Equal Protection Clause, like the Due Process Clause, prohibits this unjustified infringement of the fundamental right to marry.

These considerations lead to the conclusion that the right to marry is a fundamental right inherent in the liberty of the person, and under the Due Process and Equal Protection Clauses of the Fourteenth Amendment couples of the same-sex may not be deprived of that right and that liberty. The Court now holds that same-sex couples may exercise the fundamental right to marry. No longer may this liberty be denied to them. The State laws challenged by Petitioners in these cases are now held invalid to the extent they exclude same-sex couples from civil marriage on the same terms and conditions as opposite-sex couples.

The Court, in this decision, holds same-sex couples may exercise the fundamental right to marry in all States. It follows that the Court also must hold — and it now does hold — that there is no lawful basis for a State to refuse to recognize a lawful same-sex marriage performed in another State on the ground of its same-sex character.

Petitioners ask for equal dignity in the eyes of the law. The Constitution grants them that right.

The judgment of the Court of Appeals for the Sixth Circuit is reversed.

It is so ordered.

VIRTUAL LAW OFFICE EXPERIENCE MODULES

If your instructor has instructed you to complete assignments in the Virtual Law Office program, complete the Virtual Law Office assignments as assigned by your instructor. These assignments are designed to develop your workplace skills. Completing the assignments for this chapter will result in producing the following documents for inclusion in your portfolio:

VLOE 5.1 Memo on the school's right to censor student newspaper and electronic deliveries

CHAPTER

6

The Court System and Alternative Dispute Resolution

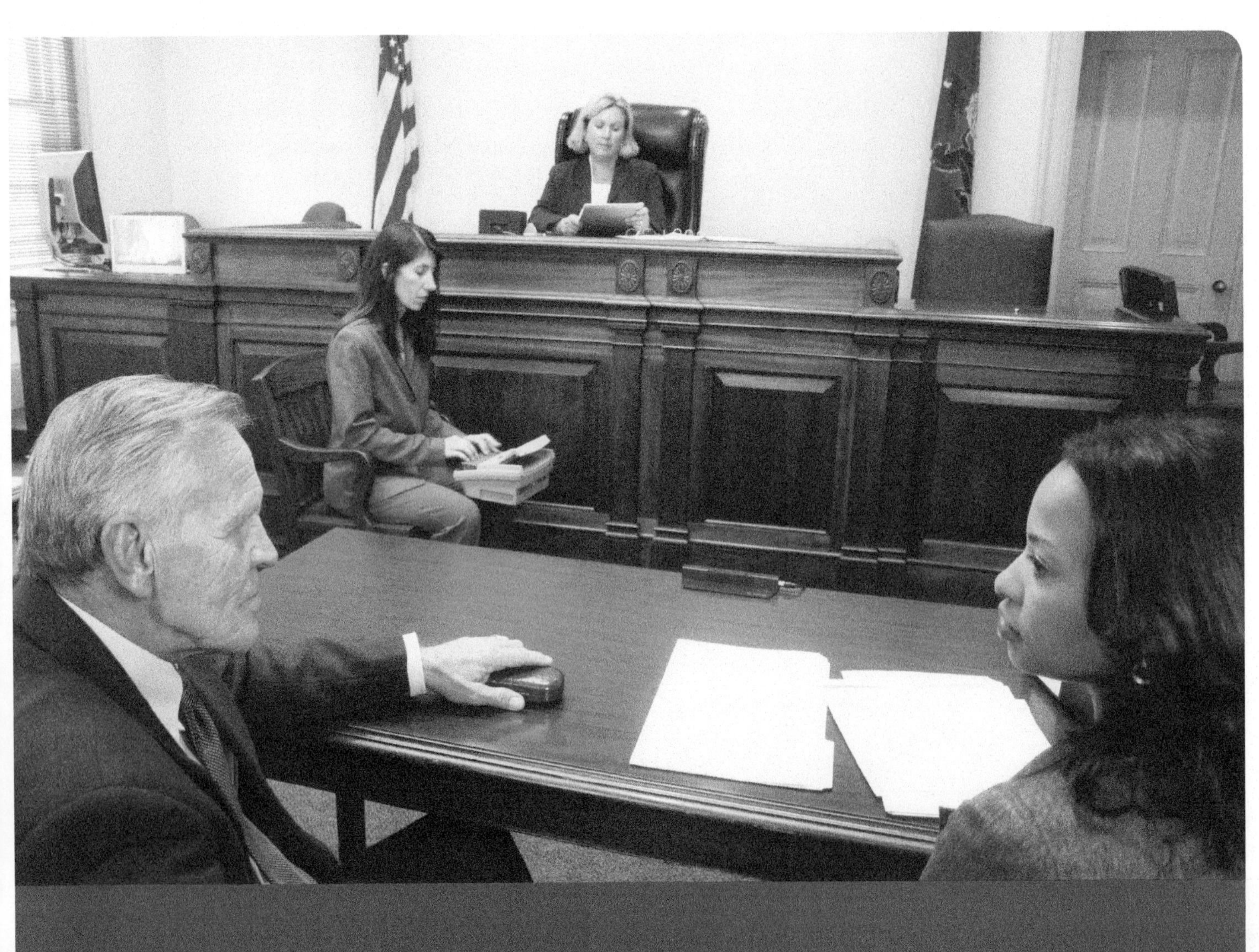

Paralegals at Work

You have applied for a position as a paralegal at a law firm that specializes in litigation. Most of the law firm's practice is in the area of torts, particularly representing plaintiffs in negligence cases. The firm has scheduled an interview with you. On the day you arrive for the interview, you are called into the office of Ms. Harriet Green, a senior partner in the firm. Ms. Green wants to assess your knowledge of judicial and nonjudicial dispute resolution. Ms. Green informs you that she will tell you the facts of a case and will ask you several questions about the case.

Ms. Green explains that Ms. Heather Andersen has retained the law firm to represent her as plaintiff in an accident case. Ms. Green explains that Ms. Andersen was driving her automobile on the main road of your city when Mr. Joseph Burton, driving another automobile, ran a red light and hit Ms. Andersen's vehicle, causing her severe physical injuries, as well as pain and suffering. The law firm plans to file a lawsuit for negligence against Mr. Burton. Ms. Andersen is a resident of your state. Mr. Burton is a resident of another state who was visiting your state when the accident occurred.

Ms. Green asks you the following questions: What is a complaint? In what court or courts can our law firm file the complaint on behalf of Ms. Andersen? If we lose the case at trial, to what court can Ms. Andersen appeal the trial court's decision? After the case is filed in the court, is there any way of resolving the case in favor of Ms. Andersen before the case goes to trial?

Consider these issues as you read the chapter.

LEARNING OBJECTIVES

After studying this chapter, you should be able to:

1. Recognize the professional opportunities for paralegals in litigation.
2. Describe the state court systems.
3. Describe the federal court system.
4. Describe the U.S. Supreme Court and how cases reach the Court.
5. Explain subject matter jurisdiction of federal and state courts.
6. Describe *in personam* jurisdiction of courts.
7. Recognize the professional opportunities for paralegals in alternative dispute resolution.
8. Explain the use of arbitration.
9. Explain the use of mediation and other forms of alternative dispute resolution.
10. Explain a paralegal's duty to provide pro bono services to the public.

> "I was never ruined but twice; once when I lost a lawsuit, and once when I won one."
>
> *Voltaire*

LEARNING OBJECTIVE 1
Recognize the professional opportunities for paralegals in litigation.

INTRODUCTION FOR THE PARALEGAL

The court systems and the procedures to bring and defend lawsuits are complex. To be a valuable member of the legal team, a paralegal should be knowledgeable about court systems, how a lawsuit proceeds to trial, and how it is decided in court.

Some parties to a dispute will choose to settle a case without a trial, or have the case reviewed or decided by a private party rather than by the courts. Thus, a paralegal should also be knowledgeable in the procedures for having disputes resolved outside of the court system.

The glorious uncertainty of law.

Thomas Wilbraham
A toast at a dinner of judges and counsel at Serjeants' Inn Hall

The two major court systems in the United States are (1) the federal court system and (2) the court systems of the 50 states and the District of Columbia. Each of these systems has **jurisdiction** to hear different types of lawsuits. The process of bringing, maintaining, and defending a lawsuit is called **litigation**. Litigation is a difficult, time-consuming, and costly process that must comply with complex procedural rules. Although not required, most parties employ a lawyer to represent them when they are involved in a lawsuit.

Litigation The process of bringing, maintaining, and defending a lawsuit.

Several forms of nonjudicial dispute resolution have been developed in response to the expense and difficulty of bringing a lawsuit. These methods, collectively called alternative dispute resolution (ADR), are being used more and more often to resolve disputes.

Paralegals are especially valuable in providing support to lawyers who are engaged in litigation and alternative dispute resolution. Paralegals interview clients, prepare documents to be submitted to courts, conduct legal research, and assist lawyers during the proceedings.

This chapter focuses on the various court systems, the jurisdiction of courts to hear and decide cases, the litigation process, and alternative dispute resolution. The following feature discusses the career opportunities for paralegal professionals in courts and litigation.

LEARNING OBJECTIVE 2
Describe the state court systems.

State Court Systems

Paralegal professionals should be familiar with the **state court system** in which they will be assisting attorneys. Each state and the District of Columbia have a separate court system. Most state court systems include:

- Limited jurisdiction trial courts
- General jurisdiction trial courts
- Intermediate appellate courts
- A supreme court (or highest state court)

CAREER OPPORTUNITIES FOR PARALEGALS IN COURTS AND LITIGATION

Many paralegals are fortunate to have the opportunity to work in a special environment—the court system. Paralegals are often hired by state and federal courts to assist judges in the preparation of cases for trial. They may also assist a judge or justice by conducting research, briefing arguments, preparing documents, and fulfilling other duties.

In addition to working for the courts directly, many more paralegals are employed by attorneys who represent clients who are involved in litigation. These paralegals may work for either plaintiffs' or defendants' attorneys in civil lawsuits involving breach of contract, negligence, product liability, business litigation, and other civil matters. These lawsuits may be in either state or federal courts.

Paralegals are also hired to work for prosecutors and defense attorneys in the area of criminal law. These paralegals assist the attorneys to prepare for and assist during trial. Criminal cases are brought in either state or federal courts, depending on whether the crimes alleged are under state or federal statutes.

A paralegal who works for the courts or litigation attorneys must have a detailed knowledge of the court systems that serve the jurisdiction that he or she works in. However, even paralegals who work in positions that are not directly involved in litigation should have knowledge of the country's court systems.

Limited Jurisdiction Trial Court

State **limited jurisdiction trial courts**, which sometimes are referred to as *inferior trial courts*, hear matters of a specialized or limited nature.

Limited jurisdiction trial court A court that hears matters of a specialized or limited nature.

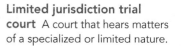

Examples Limited jurisdiction trial courts include traffic courts, juvenile courts, justice-of-the-peace courts, probate courts, family law courts, courts that hear misdemeanor criminal law cases, and those that hear civil cases involving lawsuits of less than a certain dollar amount. Because these courts are trial courts, evidence is introduced and testimony is given. Most limited jurisdiction courts keep a record of their proceedings. Their decisions usually can be appealed to a general jurisdiction court or an appellate court.

Web Exploration

Use www.google.com to find out if your state has a small claims court. If so, what is the dollar limit for cases to qualify for the small claims court?

Many states also have **small claims courts** to hear civil cases involving small dollar amounts (such as $5,000 or less). Generally, the parties must appear individually and cannot have a lawyer to represent them. The decisions of small claims courts are often appealable to general jurisdiction trial courts or appellate courts.

General Jurisdiction Trial Court

Every state has a **general jurisdiction trial court**. These courts often are called **courts of record** because the testimony and evidence at trial are recorded and stored for future use. These courts hear cases that are not within the jurisdiction of limited jurisdiction trial courts, such as felonies, civil cases above a certain dollar amount, and other categories. Some states divide their general jurisdiction courts into two divisions: criminal cases and civil cases.

General jurisdiction trial court (court of record) A court that hears cases of a general nature that are not within the jurisdiction of limited jurisdiction trial courts.

General jurisdiction trial courts hear evidence and testimony. The decisions these courts hand down are appealable to an intermediate appellate court or the state supreme court, depending on the circumstances.

Courthouse, St. Louis, Missouri. State courts hear and decide the majority of cases in the United States.

Intermediate Appellate Court

Intermediate appellate court An intermediate court that hears appeals from trial courts.

In many states, **intermediate appellate courts** (also called *appellate courts* or *courts of appeal*) hear appeals from trial courts. These courts review the trial court record to determine any errors at trial that would require reversal or modification of the trial court's decision. Thus, the appellate court reviews either pertinent parts of the trial record or the entire record from the lower court. No new evidence or testimony is permitted. The parties usually file legal briefs with the appellate court that state the law and the facts that support their positions. Appellate courts usually grant the parties a short oral hearing.

Appellate court decisions are appealable to the state's highest court. In less populated states that do not have an intermediate appellate court, trial court decisions can be appealed directly to the state's highest court.

Highest state court The top court in a state court system. It hears appeals from intermediate state courts and certain trial courts.

Web Exploration

Go to Exhibit 6.2. Find the website for your state or district or territory and go to this website. What is the name of the highest court? In what city is the highest court located?

Highest State Court

Each state has a **highest state court** in its court system. Most states call this highest court the *supreme court*. The function of a state supreme court is to hear appeals from intermediate state courts and certain trial courts. The highest court hears no new evidence or testimony. The parties usually submit parts of the lower court record or the entire lower court record for review. The parties also submit legal briefs to the court and typically are granted a brief oral hearing. Decisions of state supreme courts are final unless a question of law is involved that is appealable to the U.S. Supreme Court.

Exhibit 6.1 shows a typical state court system. Exhibit 6.2 lists the websites for the court systems of the 50 states and the jurisdictions in the United States.

Exhibit 6.1 A typical state court system

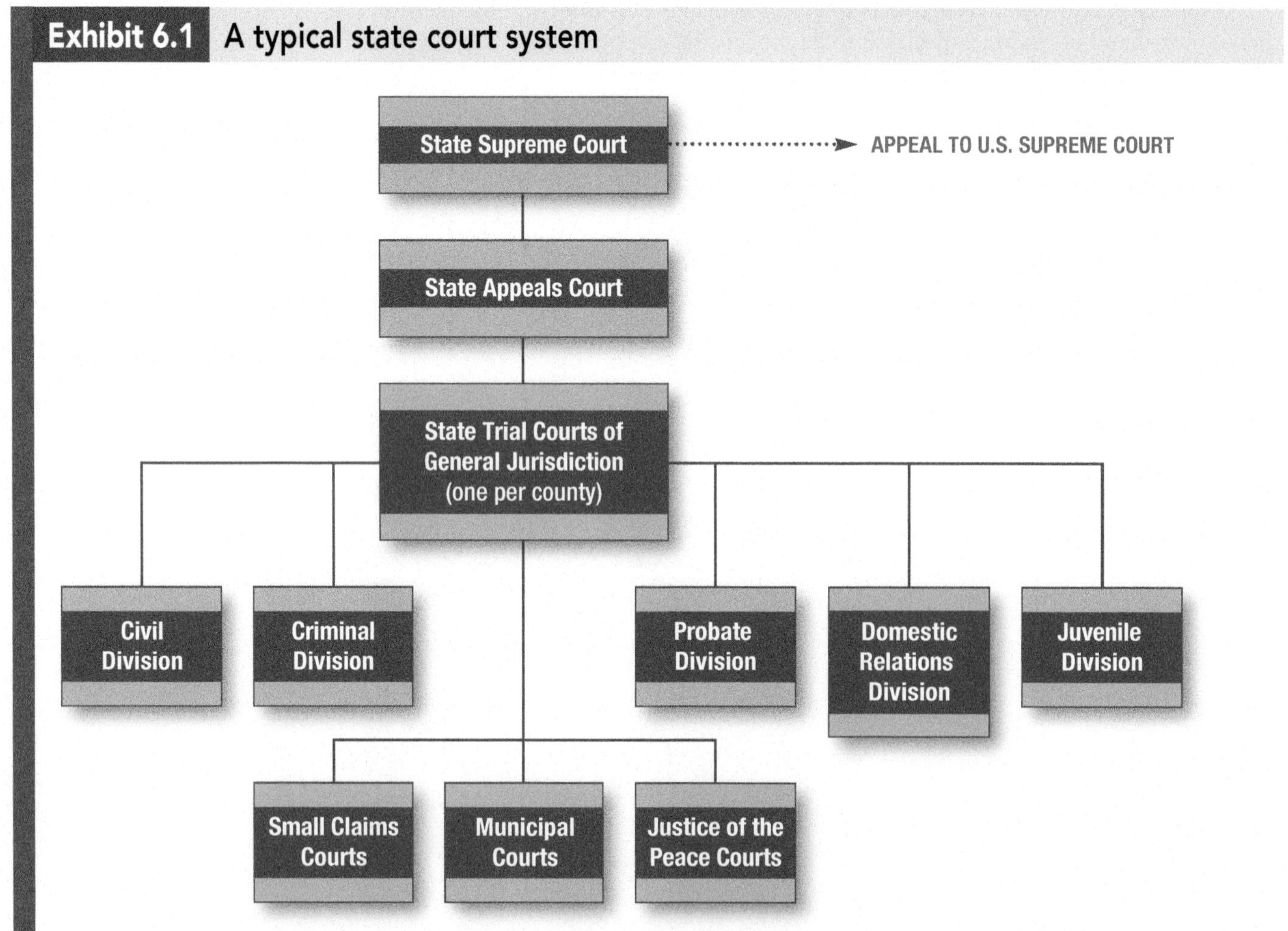

Exhibit 6.2 Websites for state court systems and jurisdictions

State	Website
Alabama	www.judicial.state.al.us
Alaska	www.state.ak.us/courts
Arizona	www.azcourts.gov
Arkansas	www.courts.state.ar.us
California	www.courts.ca.gov
Colorado	www.courts.state.co.us
Connecticut	www.jud.state.ct.us
Delaware	www.courts.state.de.us
District of Columbia	www.dccourts.gov
Florida	www.flcourts.org
Georgia	www.georgiacourts.org
Guam	www.guamsupremecourt.com
Hawaii	www.courts.state.hi.us
Idaho	www.isc.idaho.gov
Illinois	www.state.il.us/court
Indiana	www.in.gov/judiciary
Iowa	www.judicial.state.ia.us
Kansas	www.kscourts.org
Kentucky	www.courts.ky.gov
Louisiana	www.lasc.org
Maine	www.courts.state.me.us
Maryland	www.courts.state.md.us
Massachusetts	www.mass.gov/courts
Michigan	www.courts.michigan.gov
Minnesota	www.mncourts.gov
Mississippi	www.mssc.state.ms.us
Missouri	www.courts.mo.gov
Montana	www.montanacourts.org
Nebraska	court.nol.org
Nevada	www.nvsupremecourt.us
New Hampshire	www.courts.state.nh.us
New Jersey	www.judiciary.state.nj.us
New Mexico	www.nmcourts.com
New York	www.courts.state.ny.us
North Carolina	www.nccourts.org
North Dakota	www.ndcourts.com
Ohio	www.sconet.state.oh.us
Oklahoma	www.oscn.net/oscn/schome
Oregon	www.courts.oregon.gov

(continued)

Exhibit 6.2 Websites for state court systems and jurisdictions *(continued)*

State	Website
Pennsylvania	www.pacourts.us
Puerto Rico	www.ramajudicial.pr
Rhode Island	www.courts.ri.gov
South Carolina	www.judicial.state.sc.us
South Dakota	www.ujs.sd.gov
Tennessee	www.tsc.state.tn.us
Texas	www.courts.state.tx.us
Utah	www.utcourts.gov
Vermont	www.vermontjudiciary.org
Virginia	www.courts.state.va.us
Virgin Islands	www.visuperiorcourt.org
Washington	www.courts.wa.gov
West Virginia	www.courtswv.gov
Wisconsin	www.wicourts.gov
Wyoming	www.courts.state.wy.us

LEARNING OBJECTIVE 3
Describe the federal court system.

Federal Court System

Paralegal professionals are sometimes involved in assisting attorneys who practice before one of the many federal courts. Article III of the U.S. Constitution provides that the federal government's judicial power is vested in the Supreme Court. The Constitution also authorizes Congress to establish "inferior" federal courts in the **federal court system**. Pursuant to this power, Congress has established special federal courts, the U.S. district courts, and the U.S. courts of appeal. Federal judges are appointed for life by the president with the advice and consent of the Senate (except bankruptcy court judges, who are appointed for 14-year terms, and U.S. Magistrate Judges, who are appointed for 8-year terms).

Special Federal Courts

Special federal courts Federal courts that hear matters of specialized or limited jurisdiction.

The **special federal courts** established by Congress have limited jurisdiction. They include:

- **U.S. Tax Court:** Hears cases involving federal tax laws
- **U.S. Court of Federal Claims:** Hears cases brought against the United States
- **U.S. Court of International Trade:** Hears cases involving tariffs and international commercial disputes
- **U.S. Bankruptcy Court:** Hears cases involving federal bankruptcy laws

U.S. District Courts

U.S. district courts The federal court system's trial courts of general jurisdiction.

The **U.S. district courts** are the federal court system's trial courts of general jurisdiction. The District of Columbia and each state has at least one federal district court;

U.S. District Court, Las Vegas, Nevada This is the Lloyd D. George United States District Court for the District of Nevada, which is located in Las Vegas, Nevada. This is a federal trial court. This court, along with the other U.S. district courts located throughout the country, hears and decides lawsuits concerning matters over which it has jurisdiction. State, Washington, D.C., and U.S. territory courts hear and decide matters over which they have jurisdiction. The process of bringing and defending lawsuits, preparing for court, and the trial itself is complicated, time-consuming, and expensive.

the more populated states have more than one. The geographical area that each court serves is referred to as a *district*. At present, there are 94 federal district courts. These courts are empowered to impanel juries, receive evidence, hear testimony, and decide cases. Most federal cases originate in federal district courts.

Web Exploration

Go to http://www.uscourts.gov/courtlinks/. Click on "District Court." Click on your state. What is the location of the U.S. district court closest to you?

U.S. Courts of Appeals

The **U.S. courts of appeals** are the federal court system's intermediate appellate courts. The federal court system has 13 circuits. "**Circuit**" refers to the geographical area served by a court. Eleven are designated by a number, such as the "First Circuit," "Second Circuit," and so on. The twelfth circuit is located in Washington, D.C., and is called the District of Columbia Circuit.

U.S. courts of appeals The federal court system's intermediate appellate courts.

As appellate courts, these circuit courts hear appeals from the district courts located in their circuit, as well as from certain special courts and federal administrative agencies. The courts review the record of the lower court or administrative agency proceedings to determine whether any error would warrant reversal or modification of the lower court decision. No new evidence or testimony is heard. The parties file legal briefs with the court and are given a short oral hearing. Appeals usually are heard by a three-judge panel. After the panel renders a decision, a petitioner can request a review *en banc* by the full court.

Web Exploration

Go to http://www.uscourts.gov/courtlinks/. Click on "Court of Appeals." Click on your state. What is the location of the U.S. court of appeals closest to you?

A thirteenth circuit court of appeals was created by Congress in 1982, called the **Court of Appeals for the Federal Circuit**. Located in Washington, D.C., this court has special appellate jurisdiction to review the decisions of the Court of Federal Claims, the Patent and Trademark Office, and the Court of International Trade. This court of appeals was created to provide uniformity in the application of federal law in certain areas, particularly patent law.

The map in Exhibit 6.3 shows the 13 federal circuit courts of appeals. Exhibit 6.4 lists the websites of the 13 U.S. courts of appeals.

Exhibit 6.3 Map of the federal circuit courts

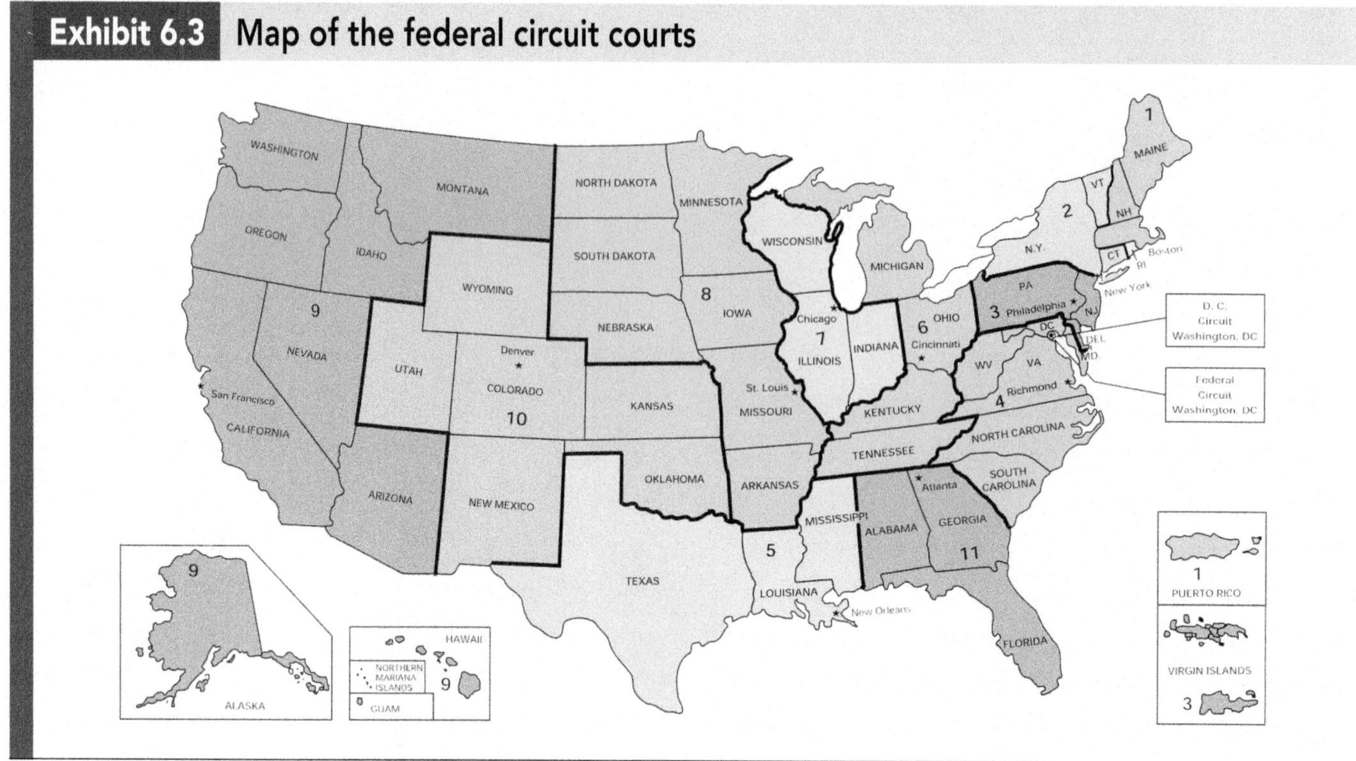

Exhibit 6.4 Websites for federal courts of appeal

United States Court of Appeals	Main Office	Website
First Circuit	Boston, Massachusetts	www.ca1.uscourts.gov
Second Circuit	New York, New York	www.ca2.uscourts.gov
Third Circuit	Philadelphia, Pennsylvania	www.ca3.uscourts.gov
Fourth Circuit	Richmond, Virginia	www.ca4.uscourts.gov
Fifth Circuit	Houston, Texas	www.ca5.uscourts.gov
Sixth Circuit	Cincinnati, Ohio	www.ca6.uscourts.gov
Seventh Circuit	Chicago, Illinois	www.ca7.uscourts.gov
Eighth Circuit	St. Paul, Minnesota	www.ca8.uscourts.gov
Ninth Circuit	San Francisco, California	www.ca9.uscourts.gov
Tenth Circuit	Denver, Colorado	www.ca10.uscourts.gov
Eleventh Circuit	Atlanta, Georgia	www.ca11.uscourts.gov
District of Columbia	Washington, D.C.	www.dcd.uscourts.gov
Court of Appeals for the Federal Circuit	Washington, D.C.	www.cafc.uscourts.gov

Supreme Court of the United States The highest court in the United States, located in Washington, D.C. The Supreme Court was created by Article III of the U.S. Constitution.

LEARNING OBJECTIVE 4

Describe the U.S. Supreme Court and how cases reach the Court.

Supreme Court of the United States

The highest court in the land is the **Supreme Court of the United States,** located in Washington, D.C. Paralegals should be familiar with the role of the Supreme Court, its jurisdiction, the types of cases it hears, and how it decides cases. This Court is composed of nine justices who are nominated by the president and confirmed by the Senate. The president appoints one justice as **chief justice**, who is

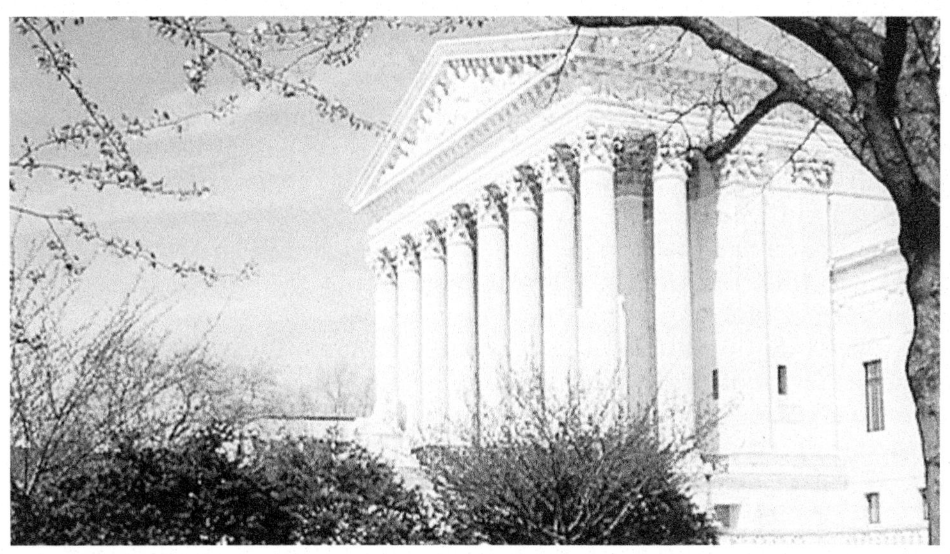

Supreme Court of the United States, Washington, D.C. The highest court in the land is the Supreme Court of the United States, located in Washington, D.C. The U.S. Supreme Court decides the most important constitutional law cases and other important issues it deems ripe for review and decision. The Supreme Court's unanimous and majority decisions are precedent for all the other courts in the country.

responsible for the administration of the Supreme Court. The other eight justices are **associate justices.**

The **U.S. Supreme Court** is an appellate court that hears appeals from federal circuit courts of appeals and, under certain circumstances, from federal district courts, special federal courts, and the highest state courts. The Supreme Court hears no evidence or testimony. As with other appellate courts, the lower court record is reviewed to determine whether an error has been committed that warrants a reversal or modification of the lower court's decision. Legal briefs are filed, and the parties are granted a brief oral hearing. The Supreme Court's decision is final and cannot be appealed.

Exhibit 6.5 illustrates the federal court system.

Exhibit 6.5 Federal court system

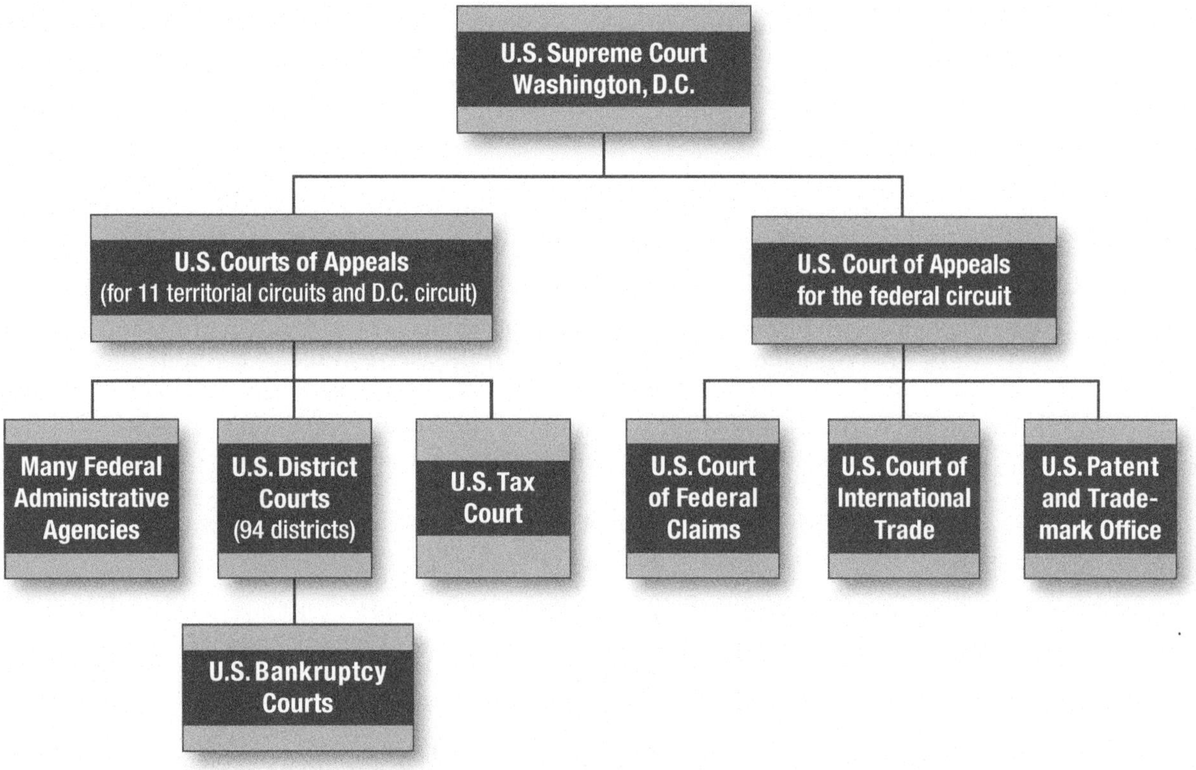

- U.S. Supreme Court Washington, D.C.
  - U.S. Courts of Appeals (for 11 territorial circuits and D.C. circuit)
    - Many Federal Administrative Agencies
    - U.S. District Courts (94 districts)
      - U.S. Bankruptcy Courts
    - U.S. Tax Court
  - U.S. Court of Appeals for the federal circuit
    - U.S. Court of Federal Claims
    - U.S. Court of International Trade
    - U.S. Patent and Trademark Office

Petition for *Certiorari*

Petition for *certiorari* A petition asking the Supreme Court to hear one's case.

Writ of *certiorari* An official notice that the Supreme Court will review one's case.

A party wishing to bring a case before the Supreme Court must file a **petition for *certiorari*** asking the Court to hear the case. If the Court decides to review a case, it will issue a **writ of *certiorari***. Because the Court issues only about 100 opinions each year, writs are usually granted only in cases involving very important issues.

The justices meet once a week to discuss which cases merit review. The votes of four justices are necessary to grant an appeal and schedule an oral argument before the Court (the "rule of four"). Written opinions by the justices are usually issued many months later.

The U.S. Constitution gives Congress the authority to establish rules for the appellate review of cases by the Supreme Court, except in the rare case where mandatory review is required. However, Congress has given the Supreme Court discretion to decide what cases it will hear.

Exhibit 6.6 shows a petition for *certiorari* to the U.S. Supreme Court.

Vote of the U.S. Supreme Court

Each justice of the Supreme Court, including the chief justice, has an equal vote. The Supreme Court can issue the following types of decisions:

- **Unanimous decision**. If all of the justices voting agree as to the outcome and reasoning used to decide the case, it is a unanimous opinion. Unanimous decisions are precedent for later cases.

  Example If all nine justices hear a case, and all nine agree to the outcome (the petitioner wins) and the reason why (such as that the Equal Protection Clause of the U.S. Constitution had been violated), this is a unanimous decision.

- **Majority decision**. If a majority of the justices agree to the outcome and reasoning used to decide the case, it is a majority opinion. Majority decisions are precedent for later cases.

  Example If all nine justices hear a case, and five of them agree as to the outcome (the petitioner wins) and all five of those justices also agree to the same reasoning (the Equal Protection Clause of the U.S. Constitution has been violated), it is a majority opinion.

- **Plurality decision**. If a majority of the justices agree to the outcome of the case, but not to the reasoning for reaching the outcome, it is a plurality opinion. A plurality decision resolves the case as to those parties, but it is not precedent for later cases.

  Example If all nine justices hear a case, and five of them agree as to the outcome, but not all of these five agree as to the reasoning, this is a plurality decision. For example, the petitioner wins, but three base their vote on a violation of the Equal Protection Clause and two base their vote on a violation of the Freedom of Speech Clause of the U.S. Constitution. Five justices have agreed to the same outcome, but those five have not agreed for the same reason. The petitioner wins his or her case, but the decision is not precedent for later cases.

- **Tie decision**. Sometimes the Supreme Court sits without all nine justices present because of illness or conflict of interest or because a justice has not been confirmed to fill a vacant seat on the court. In the case of a tie vote, the lower court decision is affirmed. These decisions are not precedent for later cases.

  Example A petitioner won her case at the court of appeals. At the U.S. Supreme Court, only eight justices hear the case. Four justices vote for the

Web Exploration

Go to the website of the U.S. Supreme Court at www.supremecourtus.gov. Who are the nine justices of the U.S. Supreme Court? Who is the chief justice? What president appointed each justice, and what political party did each of those presidents belong to?

Exhibit 6.6 Petition for *certiorari* for the case *Fisher v. The University of Texas*

No. 11-

IN THE

Supreme Court of the United States

ABIGAIL NOEL FISHER,

Petitioner,

v.

UNIVERSITY OF TEXAS AT AUSTIN et al.,

Respondents.

ON PETITION FOR A WRIT OF CERTIORARI TO THE UNITED STATES COURT OF APPEALS FOR THE FIFTH CIRCUIT

PETITION FOR A WRIT OF CERTIORARI

BERT W. REIN
Counsel of Record
WILLIAM S. CONSOVOY
THOMAS R. MCCARTHY
CLAIRE J. EVANS
WILEY REIN LLP
1776 K Street, N.W.
Washington, DC 20006
(202) 719-7000
brein@wileyrein.com

Attorneys for Petitioner

September 15, 2011

238053

COUNSEL PRESS
(800) 274-3321 • (800) 359-6859

(continued)

Exhibit 6.6 Petition for *certiorari* for the case *Fisher v. The University of Texas* (continued)

i

QUESTION PRESENTED

Whether this Court's decisions interpreting the Equal Protection Clause of the Fourteenth Amendment, including *Grutter v. Bollinger*, 539 U.S. 306 (2003), permit the University of Texas at Austin's use of race in undergraduate admissions decisions.

ii

PARTIES TO THE PROCEEDING AND RULE 29.6 STATEMENT

Petitioner in this case is Abigail Noel Fisher.

Respondents are the University of Texas at Austin; David B. Pryor, Executive Vice Chancellor for Academic Affairs in His Official Capacity; Barry D. Burgdorf, Vice Chancellor and General Counsel in His Official Capacity; William Powers, Jr., President of the University of Texas at Austin in His Official Capacity; Board of Regents of the University of Texas System; R. Steven Hicks, as Member of the Board of Regents in His Official Capacity; William Eugene Powell, as Member of the Board of Regents in His Official Capacity; James R. Huffines, as Member of the Board of Regents in His Official Capacity; Janiece Longoria, as Member of the Board of Regents in Her Official Capacity; Colleen McHugh, as Chair of the Board of Regents in Her Official Capacity; Robert L. Stillwell, as Member of the Board of Regents in His Official Capacity; James D. Dannenbaum, as Member of the Board of Regents in His Official Capacity; Paul Foster, as Member of the Board of Regents in His Official Capacity; Printice L. Gary, as Member of the Board of Regents in His Official Capacity; Kedra Ishop, Vice Provost and Director of Undergraduate Admissions in Her Official Capacity; Francisco G. Cigarroa, M.D., Interim Chancellor of the University of Texas System in His Official Capacity.

Plaintiff-Appellant below Rachel Multer Michalewicz is being served as a respondent herein.

(continued)

Exhibit 6.6 Petition for *certiorari* for the case *Fisher v. The University of Texas* (continued)

iii

TABLE OF CONTENTS

	Page
QUESTION PRESENTED	i
PARTIES TO THE PROCEEDING AND RULE 29.6 STATEMENT	ii
TABLE OF CONTENTS	iii
TABLE OF APPENDICES	v
TABLE OF CITED AUTHORITIES	vi
PETITION FOR A WRIT OF CERTIORARI....	1
OPINIONS BELOW.........................	1
JURISDICTION............................	1
CONSTITUTIONAL PROVISION INVOLVED..	1
INTRODUCTION............................	2
STATEMENT OF THE CASE	5
A. History Of UT's Admissions Program.....	5
B. Proceedings Below	11

(continued)

Exhibit 6.6 Petition for *certiorari* for the case *Fisher v. The University of Texas* (continued)

iv

Table of Contents

	Page
REASONS FOR GRANTING THE PETITION. .	19
I. The Constitutional Issues In This Case Are Critically Important	19
II. Review Is Required Because The Fifth Circuit's Analysis Conflicts With This Court's Equal Protection Decisions	23
A. The Court Should Correct The Fifth Circuit's Unwarranted Deference To UT	23
B. This Court Should Correct The Fifth Circuit's Abandonment Of Strict Scrutiny.	29
III. The Court Should Grant Review To Clarify Or Reconsider *Grutter* To The Extent It Can Be Read To Justify UT's Use Of Race In Admissions	35
CONCLUSION	36

petitioner, and four justices vote for the respondent. This is a tie vote. The petitioner remains the winner because she won at the court of appeals. The decision of the Supreme Court sets no precedent for later cases.

A justice who agrees with the outcome of a case but not the reason proffered by other justices can issue a **concurring opinion**, setting forth his or her reasons for deciding the case. A justice who does not agree with a decision can file a **dissenting opinion** that sets forth the reasons for his or her dissent.

Exhibit 6.7 illustrates an opinion by the U.S. Supreme Court.

The Process of Choosing a U.S. Supreme Court Justice

In an effort to strike a balance of power between the executive and legislative branches of government, Article II, Section 2 of the U.S. Constitution gives the president the power to appoint Supreme Court justices "with the advice and consent of the Senate." This means that the majority of the 100 senators must approve the president's nominee in order for that nominee to become a justice of the U.S. Supreme Court.

Exhibit 6.7 Opinion of the U.S. Supreme Court: *Brown v. Board of Education*

SUPREME COURT OF THE UNITED STATES

Nos. 1, 2, 4 AND 10.—OCTOBER TERM, 1953.

1	Oliver Brown, et al., Appellants, *v.* Board of Education of Topeka, Shawnee County, Kansas, et al.	On Appeal From the United States District Court for the District of Kansas.
2	Harry Briggs, Jr., et al., Appellants, *v.* R. W. Elliott, et al.	On Appeal From the United States District Court for the Eastern District of South Carolina.
4	Dorothy E. Davis, et al., Appellants, *v.* County School Board of Prince Edward County, Virginia, et al.	On Appeal From the United States District Court for the Eastern District of Virginia.
10	Francis B. Gebhart, et al., Petitioners, *v.* Ethel Louise Belton, et al.	On Writ of Certiorari to the Supreme Court of Delaware.

[May 17, 1954.]

MR. CHIEF JUSTICE WARREN delivered the opinion of the Court.

These cases come to us from the States of Kansas, South Carolina, Virginia, and Delaware. They are premised on different facts and different local conditions,

(continued)

Exhibit 6.7 Opinion of the U.S. Supreme Court: *Brown v. Board of Education* (continued)

Supreme Court of the United States

No. 1 ---- *, October Term, 19* 54

Oliver Brown, Mrs. Richard Lawton, Mrs. Sadie Emmanuel et al., Appellants,

vs.

Board of Education of Topeka, Shawnee County, Kansas, et al.

Appeal from *the United States District Court for the* -------------------- *District of* Kansas.

This cause *came on to be heard on the transcript of the record from the United States District Court for the* ------------ *District of* Kansas, ------------ *and was argued by counsel.*

On consideration whereof, *It is ordered and adjudged by this Court that the judgment of the said* District ---------------- *Court in this cause be, and the same is hereby,* reversed with costs; and that this cause be, and the same is hereby, remanded to the said District Court to take such proceedings and enter such orders and decrees consistent with the opinions of this Court as are necessary and proper to admit to public schools on a racially nondiscriminatory basis with all deliberate speed the parties to this case.

Per Mr. Chief Justice Warren,

May 31, 1955.

A president who is elected to one or two four-year terms in office may have the opportunity to nominate justices to the U.S. Supreme Court who, if confirmed, may serve many years after the president leaves office. President Barack Obama was inaugurated in January 2009, and within months after taking office, had the opportunity to nominate a justice for the Supreme Court when a justice retired. President Obama nominated Sonia Sotomayor for the seat. Sotomayor was confirmed to the Supreme Court by a majority vote of the U.S. Senate, becoming the first Hispanic person to be a justice of the U.S. Supreme Court and the third female appointed to the Court. In 2010, President Obama had a second opportunity to nominate a justice when another justice retired from the Court. The president nominated Elena Kagan, formerly the U.S. solicitor general. Kagan was confirmed by a majority vote of the U.S. Senate.

Jurisdiction of Federal and State Courts

LEARNING OBJECTIVE 5

Explain subject matter jurisdiction of federal and state courts.

A federal or state court must have **subject matter jurisdiction** to hear a case. Article III, Section 2 of the U.S. Constitution sets forth the jurisdiction of federal courts. These courts have *limited jurisdiction* to hear cases involving federal questions and cases involving diversity of citizenship. State courts also have jurisdiction to hear various types of cases that cannot be handled by federal courts. The jurisdiction of federal and state courts to hear cases is discussed in the following paragraphs.

Subject matter jurisdiction Jurisdiction over the subject matter of a lawsuit.

Subject Matter Jurisdiction of Federal Courts

Federal courts have jurisdiction to hear cases based on the subject matter of the case. They have jurisdiction to hear cases involving "federal questions." **Federal question** cases are cases arising under the U.S. Constitution, treaties, and federal statutes and regulations. There is no dollar amount limit on federal question cases that can be brought in federal court.

Federal question A case arising under the U.S. Constitution, treaties, or federal statutes and regulations.

Example A lawsuit involving federal securities law concerns a federal question (involving a federal statute) and will be heard by a U.S. district court.

Subject Matter Jurisdiction of State Courts

State courts have jurisdiction to hear cases involving subject matters that federal courts do not have jurisdiction to hear. These usually involve state laws.

Examples State courts may have jurisdiction to hear cases involving the subjects of real estate law, corporation law, partnership law, limited liability company law, contract law, sales and lease contracts, and negotiable instruments.

Diversity of Citizenship

A case involving a state court subject matter may be brought in federal court if there is **diversity of citizenship**. Diversity of citizenship occurs if the lawsuit involves (a) citizens of different states, (b) a citizen of a state and a citizen or subject of a foreign country, and (c) a citizen of a state and a foreign country as plaintiff. A corporation is considered a citizen of the state in which it is incorporated and in which it has its principal place of business. The reason for giving federal courts diversity jurisdiction was to avoid the bias against nonresidents that might occur in state courts. The federal court must apply the appropriate state's law in deciding the case. The dollar amount of the controversy must exceed $75,000 to be brought under diversity jurisdiction. If this requirement is not met, the action must be brought in the appropriate state court.

Diversity of citizenship A case between (1) citizens of different states, (2) a citizen of a state and a citizen or subject of a foreign country, and (3) a citizen of a state and a foreign country where a foreign country is the plaintiff.

Example Henry, a resident of the state of Idaho, is driving his automobile in the state of Idaho when he negligently hits Mary, a pedestrian. Mary is a resident of the state of New York. There is no federal question involved in this case; it is an automobile accident that involves state negligence law. However, there is diversity of citizenship: Henry is from Idaho, while Mary is from New York. Usually the case must be brought in the state in which the automobile accident occurred because this is where most of the witnesses and evidence will be from. But in this case, Mary may bring her lawsuit in federal court in Idaho. If she does so, the case will remain in federal court. If Mary brings the case in Idaho state court, it will remain in the Idaho state court if Henry agrees; however, Henry can move the case to federal court.

Exclusive and Concurrent Jurisdiction

Federal courts have **exclusive jurisdiction** to hear cases involving federal crimes, antitrust, bankruptcy, patent and copyright cases, suits against the United States, and most admiralty cases. State courts cannot hear these cases.

State and federal courts have **concurrent jurisdiction** to hear cases involving diversity of citizenship and federal questions over which federal courts do not have exclusive jurisdiction (such as cases involving federal securities laws). If a plaintiff brings a case involving concurrent jurisdiction in state court, the defendant can remove the case to federal court. If a case does not qualify to be brought in federal court, it must be brought in the appropriate state court.

LEARNING OBJECTIVE 6
Describe *in personam* jurisdiction of courts.

Personal Jurisdiction and Other Issues

A court does not have the authority to hear all cases within its subject matter jurisdiction. To bring a lawsuit in a court, the plaintiff must have *standing to sue*. In addition, the court must have *jurisdiction* to hear the case, and the case must be brought in the proper *venue*. These topics are discussed in the following paragraphs.

Standing to Sue

To bring a lawsuit, a plaintiff must have **standing to sue**. This means the plaintiff must have some stake in the outcome of the lawsuit.

Example Linda's friend Jon is injured in an accident caused by Emily. Jon refuses to sue. Linda cannot sue Emily on Jon's behalf because she does not have an interest in the result of the case.

In Personam Jurisdiction

***In personam* (personal) jurisdiction** Jurisdiction over the parties to a lawsuit.

Service of process A summons being served on a defendant to obtain personal jurisdiction over him or her.

Jurisdiction over a person is called ***in personam* jurisdiction**, or **personal jurisdiction**. A *plaintiff*, by filing a lawsuit with a court, gives the court *in personam* jurisdiction over him or her. The court must also have *in personam* jurisdiction over the *defendant*, which is usually obtained by having a summons served to that person within the territorial boundaries of the state. Serving a summons is referred to as **service of process** and is usually accomplished by personally hand-delivering the summons and complaint to the defendant.

If personal service is not possible, alternative forms of notice, such as mailing the summons or publishing a notice in a newspaper, may be permitted. A corporation is subject to personal jurisdiction in the state in which it is incorporated, has its principal office, and is doing business.

A party who disputes the jurisdiction of a court can make a *special appearance* in that court to argue against imposition of jurisdiction. Service of process is not permitted during such an appearance.

In Rem Jurisdiction

***In rem* jurisdiction** Jurisdiction to hear a case because of jurisdiction over the property at issue in the lawsuit.

A court may have jurisdiction to hear and decide a case because it has jurisdiction over the property at issue in the lawsuit. This is called ***in rem* jurisdiction** ("jurisdiction over the thing").

Example A state court would have jurisdiction to hear a dispute over the ownership of a piece of real estate located within the state. This is so even if one or more of the disputing parties lives in another state or states.

Quasi in Rem Jurisdiction

Sometimes a plaintiff who obtains a judgment against a defendant in one state will try to collect the judgment by attaching property of the defendant that is located in another state. This is permitted under ***quasi in rem* jurisdiction**, or **attachment jurisdiction.**

***Quasi in rem* (attachment) jurisdiction** Jurisdiction allowing a plaintiff who obtains a judgment in one state to try to collect the judgment by attaching property of a defendant located in another state.

> Example If a plaintiff wins a monetary judgment against a defendant in a Florida state court, but the defendant's only property is located in Idaho, the Idaho state court has *quasi in rem* jurisdiction to order the attachment of the defendant's property in Idaho to satisfy the Florida court judgment.

Long-Arm Statutes

In most states, a state court can obtain jurisdiction over persons and businesses located in another state or country through the state's **long-arm statute**. These statutes extend a state's jurisdiction to nonresidents who were not served a summons within the state. The nonresident must have had some *minimum contact* with the state, as held in the leading case of *International Shoe Co. v. Washington*, 326 U.S. 310, 66 S.Ct. 154, 1945 U.S. Lexis 1447 (U.S., 1945). In addition, maintenance of the suit in a particular jurisdiction must uphold the traditional notions of fair play and substantial justice.

Long-arm statute A statute that extends a state's jurisdiction to nonresidents who were not served a summons within the state.

The exercise of long-arm jurisdiction is generally permitted over nonresidents who have (1) committed torts within the state (as where a plaintiff is alleged to have caused an automobile accident in the state), (2) entered into a contract either in the state or that affects the state (and the party allegedly breached the contract), or (3) transacted other business in the state that allegedly caused injury to another person.

Venue

Venue requires lawsuits to be heard by the court with jurisdiction nearest the location in which the incident occurred or where the parties reside.

Venue A requirement that lawsuits be heard by the court with jurisdiction that is nearest the location in which the incident occurred or where the parties reside.

> Example Harry, a Georgia resident, commits a felony in Los Angeles County, California. The California Superior Court, located in Los Angeles, is the proper venue because the crime was committed in Los Angeles County and the witnesses are probably from that area.

Occasionally, pretrial publicity may bias jurors located in an otherwise proper venue. In these cases, a **change of venue** may be requested so that a more impartial jury can be found. However, courts generally frown upon *forum shopping*, in which a party looks for a favorable court without a valid reason for changing venue.

Jurisdiction in Cyberspace

Obtaining personal jurisdiction over a defendant in another state has always been difficult for courts. Today, with the Internet allowing persons and businesses to reach millions of people in other states electronically, particularly through websites, new issues have arisen as to whether courts have jurisdiction in cyberspace. For example, if a person in one state uses the website of an Internet seller located in another state, can the user sue the Internet seller in his or her state under that state's long-arm statute?

A seminal case that addresses jurisdiction in cyberspace is *Zippo Manufacturing Company v. Zippo Dot Com, Inc.*[10] In addressing jurisdiction of Internet users, the court created a "sliding scale" in order to measure the nature and quality of the commercial activity effectuated in a forum state through a website. The court stated:

> At one end of the spectrum are situations where a defendant clearly does business over the Internet. If the defendant enters into contracts with residents of a foreign jurisdiction that involve the knowing and repeated transmission of computer files over the Internet, personal jurisdiction is proper. At the opposite end are situations where

[10] 952 F.Supp. 1119, 1997 U.S. Dist. Lexis 1701 (W.D. Pa. 1997).

> a defendant has simply posted information on an Internet Web site which is accessible to users in foreign jurisdictions. A passive Web site that does little more than make information available to those who are interested in it is not grounds for the exercise of personal jurisdiction. The middle ground is occupied by interactive Web sites where a user can exchange information with the host computer. In these cases, the exercise of jurisdiction is determined by examining the level of interactivity and commercial nature of the exchange of information that occurs on the Web site.

Applying this standard is often difficult and depends on the circumstances of the case.

Forum Selection and Choice-of-Law Clauses

In a contract, parties sometimes agree as to what courts will have jurisdiction to hear a legal dispute. Such clauses are called **forum selection clauses**.

Forum selection clause A contract provision that designates a certain court to hear disputes concerning nonperformance of a contract.

Choice-of-law clause A contract provision that designates a certain state's or country's law to be applied to disputes concerning nonperformance of a contract.

In addition to agreeing to a forum, the parties also often agree as to what state's or country's law will apply in resolving a dispute. These clauses are called **choice-of-law clauses.**

E-Courts

In a conventional court system, litigation can be a cumbersome process. The clients, lawyers, and judges involved in the case are usually buried in documents. These documents include pleadings, interrogatories, motions, research, depositions, evidence, briefs, memorandums, and numerous other documents. By the time a case is over, reams of paper are stored in dozens, if not hundreds, of boxes. In addition, court appearances for even very small matters must be made in person, and are usually time-consuming.

> Example Lawyers often wait hours for a 10-minute scheduling conference or other conference with a judge. The time it takes to drive to and from court also has to be taken into account, which in some areas may amount to hours.

The Internet has radically changed how lawyers and courts operate. It has enabled many communications between lawyers and courts to be conducted electronically. Today, the Internet and other technologies have enabled the use of **electronic courts**, or **e-courts**, also referred to as **virtual courthouses**. Technology also allows for the **electronic filing**, or **e-filing**, of pleadings, briefs, and other documents related to a lawsuit. In addition, technology allows for the scanning of evidence and documents into a computer for storage and retrieval and for emailing correspondence and documents to the court, opposing counsel, and clients. Scheduling and other conferences with the judge or opposing counsel are held via telephone conferences and email.

e-court A court that either mandates or permits the electronic filing of pleadings, briefs, and other documents related to a lawsuit. Also called a *virtual courthouse.*

Many courts have instituted electronic document filing and tracking. In some courts, e-filing of pleadings and other documents is now mandatory. Companies such as Microsoft and LexisNexis have developed systems to manage e-filings of court documents.

LEARNING OBJECTIVE 7
Recognize the professional opportunities for paralegals in alternative dispute resolution.

Alternative Dispute Resolution (ADR)

The use of the court system to resolve major disputes can take years and cost thousands, if not millions, of dollars in legal fees and expenses. In commercial litigation, the normal business operations of the parties are often disrupted. To avoid or lessen these problems, businesses are increasingly turning to methods of **alternative dispute resolution (ADR)** to resolve disputes. The most common form of ADR is *arbitration*. Other forms of ADR are *negotiation*, *mediation*, *conciliation*, *minitrial*, *fact-finding*, and using a *judicial referee*.

Alternative dispute resolution (ADR) Methods of resolving disputes other than litigation.

The following feature discusses the career opportunities for paralegal professionals in alternative dispute resolution.

Negotiation

Negotiation A procedure in which the parties to a dispute engage in negotiations to try to reach a voluntary settlement of their dispute.

The simplest form of alternative dispute resolution is engaging in negotiation between the parties to try to settle a dispute. **Negotiation** is a procedure whereby the parties

CAREER OPPORTUNITIES FOR PARALEGALS IN ALTERNATIVE DISPUTE RESOLUTION

The growth in the use of alternative dispute resolution to resolve disputes has been phenomenal. Alternative dispute resolution is just that—an alternative to using the litigation process and court systems to resolve disputes.

The most common form of alternative dispute resolution is arbitration. The United States Supreme Court has upheld the use of arbitration in many types of disputes. Arbitration is used particularly in contract disputes, because many contracts contain arbitration clauses; that is, the parties to the contract have agreed not to use the court systems to resolve their disputes. Instead, they have expressly agreed that an arbitrator, and not a jury, will decide the matter. Most major companies have placed arbitration agreements in their contracts.

Examples Arbitration clauses appear in contracts to purchase goods, lease automobiles, employ services, and other types of contracts. Also, arbitration clauses are included in many employment contracts. Thus, if an employee has a dispute with his or her employer, the dispute goes to arbitration for resolution because the employee has given up his or her right to use the court system by agreeing to the arbitration clause.

Mediation also has become an indispensable method of helping to resolve disputes. In mediation, the mediator does not act as a decision maker, but instead acts as a facilitator to try to help the disputing parties reach a settlement. Mediation is often used in family law matters, particularly in settling divorce cases.

Paralegals who work on business-related matters, contract disputes, and family law matters should have a thorough understanding of alternative dispute resolution. These paralegals are often called upon to help attorneys prepare for arbitration, mediation, and other forms of alternative dispute resolution. The following sections address the major forms of alternative dispute resolution.

to a dispute engage in discussions to try to reach a voluntary settlement of their dispute. Negotiation may take place before a lawsuit is filed, after a lawsuit is filed, or before other forms of alternative dispute resolution are pursued.

In a negotiation, the parties are often represented by attorneys. During the proceedings, the parties usually make offers and counteroffers to one another. The parties or their attorneys also may provide information to the other side that would assist the other side in reaching an amicable settlement.

Many courts require that the parties to a lawsuit engage in settlement discussions prior to trial. The judge must be assured that a settlement of the case is not possible before he or she permits the case to go to trial. Judges often convince the parties to engage in further negotiations if they determine that the parties are not too far apart in their positions.

If a settlement of the dispute is reached through negotiation, a settlement agreement is drafted that contains the terms of the agreement. A **settlement agreement** is voluntarily entered into by the parties and resolves the dispute. Each side must sign the settlement agreement for it to become effective. The settlement agreement usually is submitted to the court, and the case is dismissed based on execution of the agreement.

Settlement agreement An agreement voluntarily entered into by the parties to a dispute and that settles the dispute.

Arbitration

LEARNING OBJECTIVE 8
Explain the use of arbitration.

Paralegals working in many areas of the law—litigation, contract law, business law, and such—will encounter arbitration clauses in some of the cases they are working on. In **arbitration**, the parties choose an impartial third party to hear and decide the dispute, called the **arbitrator**. Arbitrators usually are selected from members of the American Arbitration Association (AAA) or another arbitration association.

Arbitration A form of ADR in which the parties choose an impartial third party to hear and decide the dispute.

Labor union agreements, franchise agreements, leases, and other commercial contracts often contain **arbitration clauses** that require disputes arising out of the contract to be submitted to arbitration. If there is no arbitration clause, the parties can enter into a **submission agreement**, whereby they agree to submit a dispute to arbitration after the dispute arises.

Arbitration clause A clause in a contract that requires disputes arising out of the contract to be submitted to arbitration.

Arbitration often has many benefits over litigation. It is less expensive, is completed faster, and is decided by a person who is knowledgeable in the area of law that is in dispute. However, some consumers and employees who are subject to arbitration agreements argue that arbitration unfairly favors businesses and employers.

In the past, some courts were reluctant to permit arbitration of a dispute or found that arbitration agreements were illegal. However, in a series of cases, the U.S. Supreme Court upheld the validity of many types of arbitration clauses or agreements.

Exhibit 6.8 is a form for a demand for arbitration.

Exhibit 6.8 Demand for arbitration

American Arbitration Association
Dispute Resolution Services Worldwide

_______________ ARBITRATION RULES
(ENTER THE NAME OF THE APPLICABLE RULES)

Demand for Arbitration

MEDIATION: If you would like the AAA to contact the other parties and attempt to arrange mediation, please check this box. ☐
There is no additional administrative fee for this service.

Name of Respondent			Name of Representative (if known)		
Address:			Name of Firm (if applicable):		
			Representative's Address		
City	State	Zip Code	City	State	Zip Code
Phone No.		Fax No.	Phone No.		Fax No.
Email Address:			Email Address:		

The named claimant, a party to an arbitration agreement dated _______________, which provides for arbitration under the _______________ Arbitration Rules of the American Arbitration Association, hereby demands arbitration.

THE NATURE OF THE DISPUTE

Dollar Amount of Claim $	Other Relief Sought: ☐ Attorneys Fees ☐ Interest ☐ Arbitration Costs ☐ Punitive/ Exemplary ☐ Other _______

AMOUNT OF FILING FEE ENCLOSED WITH THIS DEMAND (please refer to the fee schedule in the rules for the appropriate fee) $

PLEASE DESCRIBE APPROPRIATE QUALIFICATIONS FOR ARBITRATOR(S) TO BE APPOINTED TO HEAR THIS DISPUTE:

Hearing locale_______________ (check one) ☐ Requested by Claimant ☐ Locale provision included in the contract

Estimated time needed for hearings overall: _______hours or _______days	Type of Business: Claimant _______________ Respondent_______________

Is this a dispute between a business and a consumer? ☐Yes ☐ No
Does this dispute arise out of an employment relationship? ☐Yes ☐ No

If this dispute arises out of an employment relationship, what was/is the employee's annual wage range? Note: This question is required by California law. ☐Less than $100,000 ☐ $100,000 - $250,000 ☐ Over $250,000

You are hereby notified that copies of our arbitration agreement and this demand are being filed with the American Arbitration Association's Case Management Center, located in (check one) ☐ Atlanta, GA ☐ Dallas, TX ☐ East Providence, RI ☐ Fresno, CA ☐ International Centre, NY, with a request that it commence administration of the arbitration. Under the rules, you may file an answering statement within the timeframe specified in the rules, after notice from the AAA.

Signature (may be signed by a representative) Date:			Name of Representative		
Name of Claimant			Name of Firm (if applicable)		
Address (to be used in connection with this case):			Representative's Address:		
City	State	Zip Code	City	State	Zip Code
Phone No.		Fax No.	Phone No.		Fax No.
Email Address:			Email Address:		

To begin proceedings, please send two copies of this Demand and the Arbitration Agreement, along with the filing fee as provided for in the Rules, to the AAA. Send the original Demand to the Respondent.

Please visit our website at www.adr.org if you would like to file this case online. AAA Customer Service can be reached at 800-778-7879

Source: Reprinted with permission of American Arbitration Association.

Federal Arbitration Act

The **Federal Arbitration Act (FAA)** was originally enacted by Congress in 1925 to reverse the long-standing judicial hostility to arbitration agreements in English common law and American courts (9 U.S.C. Sections 1 et seq.). The Act provides that arbitration agreements involving commerce are valid, irrevocable, and enforceable contracts, unless some grounds exist at law or equity to revoke them (such as fraud or duress). The FAA permits one party to obtain a court order to compel arbitration if the other party has failed, neglected, or refused to comply with an arbitration agreement.

Federal Arbitration Act (FAA) A federal statute that provides for the enforcement of most commercial arbitration agreements.

About half of the states have adopted the **Uniform Arbitration Act**, which promotes the arbitration of disputes at the state level. Many federal and state courts have instituted programs to refer legal disputes to arbitration or another form of alternative dispute resolution.

ADR Providers

ADR services are usually provided by private organizations or individuals who are qualified to hear and decide certain disputes. For example, the **American Arbitration Association (AAA)** is the largest private provider of ADR services. The AAA employs persons who are qualified in special areas of the law to provide mediation and arbitration services in those areas. These persons are called **neutrals**.

For example, if parties have a contract dispute involving an employment, construction, or Internet contract, or other commercial contract or business dispute, the AAA has a special group of neutrals that can hear and decide these cases. Other mediation and arbitration associations are located throughout the United States and internationally.

ADR Procedure

An arbitration agreement often describes the specific procedures that must be followed for a case to proceed through arbitration. If one party seeks to enforce an arbitration clause, that party must give notice to the other party. The parties then select an arbitration association or arbitrator as provided in the agreement. The parties usually agree on the date, time, and place of the arbitration. This can be at the arbitrator's office, a law office, or any other agreed-upon location.

At the arbitration, the parties may call witnesses to give testimony, and introduce other evidence to support their case or refute the other side's case. Rules similar to those followed by federal courts are usually adhered to at the arbitration. Often, each party pays a filing fee and other fees for the arbitration. Sometimes the agreement provides that one party will pay all of the costs of the arbitration. Arbitrators are paid by the hour or day, or another agreed-upon method of compensation.

Decision and Award

After the hearing is complete, the arbitrator reaches a decision and issues an **award**. The parties often agree in advance to be bound by the arbitrator's decision. This is called **binding arbitration**. In this situation, the decision and award of the arbitrator cannot be appealed to the courts. In **non-binding arbitration**, the decision and award of the arbitrator can be appealed to the courts. However, courts usually give great deference to an arbitrator's decision and award.

If a decision and award have been rendered by an arbitrator, but a party refuses to abide by the arbitrator's decision, the other party may file an action in court to have the arbitrator's decision enforced.

Example A contract dispute between Northwest Corporation and Southeast Corporation goes to binding arbitration. The arbitrator issues a decision that awards Southeast Corporation $5 million against Northwest Corporation.

Paralegals *in* Practice

PARALEGAL PROFILE
Kathleen A. Stradley

Kathleen A. Stradley is a Certified Arbitrator and Certified Mediator with 26 years of paralegal experience. She also is an Advanced Certified Paralegal and Civil Litigation Specialist. Since 1998, Kathleen has worked as an independent contractor of litigation support and consulting services in North Dakota and Minnesota. She assists trial attorneys and corporations with case management and trial preparation. She also serves as a private arbitrator and mediator in legal disputes.

Becoming involved in alternative dispute resolution (ADR) has been an interesting process. Before starting my own business, I worked for several law firms and a corporation in Ohio and North Dakota. During that time, I was aware that ADR could save a lot of time and money. However, I did not know much about putting ADR into practice. So, I enrolled in an intense course that allowed me to obtain my mediator certification after 40 hours of training.

A short time later, I trained for a new binding arbitration program for the North Dakota Workers' Compensation Bureau. This program provided employees and employers with the option of binding arbitration rather than a formal administrative hearing or judicial solution. Instead, a hearing was held in front of three arbitrators, one from each of three societal areas: labor, industry, and the public. For about a year, I served as a public sector arbitrator and chairperson for the panel. After the panel was reduced to one person, I continued to serve as an arbitrator for Workers' Compensation hearings.

Later, I served as an arbitrator and mediator through the American Arbitration Association (AAA) for family, commercial, personal injury, employment/workplace, and construction industry claims. In 1997, after a terrible flood destroyed my hometown of Grand Forks, North Dakota, I mediated in many disaster-related commercial and construction disputes, as well as family law cases. In more recent years, I spoke with a number of disaster victims who experienced an ADR process. Most of them agreed that ADR was a valuable course of action that helped them rebuild their homes and lives.

Due to mandatory arbitration provisions in most contracts, and the trend of court ordered dispute resolution proceedings, I think there will be fewer trials in the future. Instead, I believe more and more lawsuits will be resolved with alternative methods. Cases using ADR proceedings typically involve fewer documents. However, these documents need to be prepared much earlier, and in greater detail, than cases that are tried in court with a jury. In mediation, each party submits their statement of the case and its value to the mediator in advance of the mediation. In arbitration, the evidence is submitted to the arbitrator in advance of the arbitration. ADR proceedings usually occur after discovery is completed and well in advance of the scheduled trial.

Source: Stradley, Kathleen A., "ADR: Changing Ground." *Facts & Findings, the Journal for Legal Assistants* 30(4) (January 2005): 16–17. Career Chronicle Edition 2004, NALA.

If Northwest Corporation fails to pay the award, Southeast Corporation can file an action in court to have the award enforced by the court.

In the feature above, a paralegal professional discusses her experience in alternative dispute resolution.

LEARNING OBJECTIVE 9
Explain the use of mediation and other forms of alternative dispute resolution.

Other Forms of ADR

In addition to arbitration and negotiation, other forms of ADR are available, such as *mediation*, *conciliation*, *minitrial*, *fact-finding*, and using a *judicial referee*. These forms of ADR are discussed in the following paragraphs.

Mediation

Mediation A form of negotiation in which a neutral third party assists the disputing parties in reaching a settlement of their dispute.

Mediator A neutral third party who assists the disputing parties in reaching a settlement of their dispute. The mediator cannot make a decision or an award.

Mediation is a form of negotiation in which a neutral third party assists the disputing parties in reaching a settlement of their dispute. The neutral third party is called a **mediator**. The mediator usually is a person who is an expert in the area of the dispute, or a lawyer or retired judge. The mediator is selected by the parties by agreement. Unlike an arbitrator, however, a mediator does not make a decision or an award.

A mediator's role is to assist the parties in reaching a settlement, usually as an intermediary between the parties. In many cases the mediator will meet with the parties at an agreed-upon location. The mediator will then meet with both parties, usually separately, to discuss each side of the case.

After discussing the facts of the case with each side, the mediator will encourage settlement of the dispute and will transmit settlement offers from one side to the other. In doing so, the mediator points out the strengths and weaknesses of each party's case and gives his or her opinion to each side as to why they should decrease or increase their settlement offers.

Then the mediator gives his or her opinion to the parties as to what he or she believes to be a reasonable settlement of the case, and usually proposes settlement of the dispute. The parties are free to accept or reject the proposal. If the parties agree to a settlement, a settlement agreement is drafted, and execution of the settlement agreement ends the dispute. The parties, of course, must then perform their duties under the settlement agreement.

Example Parties to a divorce action often use mediation to try to help resolve the issues involved in the divorce, such as division of property, payment of alimony and child support, custody of children, and visitation rights.

Exhibit 6.9 is a form for a request for mediation.

Conciliation

Conciliation is often used when the parties refuse to face each other in an adversarial setting. A person called a **conciliator** helps the parties reach a resolution of their dispute. The conciliator schedules meetings and appointments during which information can be transferred between the parties. A conciliator usually carries offers and counteroffers for a settlement back and forth between the disputing parties. A conciliator cannot make a decision or an award.

Although the role of a conciliator is not to propose a settlement of the case, many often do. In many cases, conciliators are neutral third parties, although in some circumstances the parties may select an interested third party to act as the conciliator. If a settlement is reached through conciliation, a settlement agreement is drafted and executed by the parties.

Conciliation A form of dispute resolution in which a conciliator transmits offers and counteroffers between the disputing parties in helping to reach a settlement of their dispute.

Conciliator A third party in a conciliation proceeding who assists the disputing parties in reaching a settlement of their dispute. The conciliator cannot make a decision or an award.

Minitrial

A **minitrial** is a voluntary private proceeding in which the lawyers for each side present a shortened version of their case. Representatives of each side attend the minitrial and have the authority to settle the dispute. In many cases, the parties also hire a neutral third party, often someone who is an expert in the field concerning the disputed matter, who presides over the minitrial. After hearing the case, the neutral third party renders an opinion as to how a court would most likely decide the case.

During a minitrial, the parties get to see the strengths and weaknesses of their own position and those of the opposing side. Once the strengths and weaknesses of both sides are exposed, the parties usually are more realistic regarding the merits of their positions, and the parties often settle the case. The parties also often settle based on the opinion rendered by the neutral third party. If the parties settle their dispute after a minitrial, they enter into a settlement agreement.

Minitrials serve a useful purpose in that they act as a substitute for the real trial, but are much shorter, less complex, and less expensive to prepare for. Resolving a dispute through a minitrial is often preferable to an expensive and more risky trial in court.

Minitrial A voluntary private proceeding in which the lawyers for each side present a shortened version of their case to representatives of the other side, and usually to a neutral third party, in an attempt to reach a settlement of the dispute.

How many a dispute could have been deflated into a single paragraph if the disputants had dared to define their terms.

Aristotle

Fact-Finding

In fact-finding, the parties to a dispute will employ a neutral third party to investigate the dispute. The fact-finder is authorized to gather real evidence, prepare demonstrative evidence, and prepare reports of his or her findings.

A fact-finder is not authorized to make a decision or award. In some cases, a fact-finder will recommend settlement of the case. The fact-finder presents the evidence

Exhibit 6.9 Request for mediation

American Arbitration Association
Dispute Resolution Services Worldwide

REQUEST FOR MEDIATION

Name of Responding Party			Name of Representative (if known)		
Address:			Name of Firm (if applicable)		
			Representative's Address:		
City	State	Zip Code	City	State	Zip Code
Phone No.		Fax No.	Phone No.		Fax No.
Email Address:			Email Address:		

The undersigned party to an agreement contained in a written contract dated ________________, providing for mediation under the ________________________________ Mediation Procedures of the American Arbitration Association, hereby requests mediation

THE NATURE OF THE DISPUTE

CLAIM OR RELIEF SOUGHT (amount, if any):

AMOUNT OF FILING FEE ENCLOSED WITH THIS REQUEST: $

Mediation locale____________________ (check one) ☐ Requested by Filing Party ☐ Locale provision included in the contract

Type of Business: Filing Party ______________________ Responding Party_________________________

You are hereby notified that copies of our mediation agreement and this request are being filed with the American Arbitration Association's Case Management Center, located in (check one) ☐ Atlanta, GA ☐ Dallas, TX ☐ East Providence, RI ☐ Fresno, CA ☐ International Centre, NY, with a request that it commence administration of this mediation.

Signature (may be signed by a representative) Date:			Name of Representative		
Name of Filling Party			Name of Firm (if applicable)		
Address (to be used in connection with this case):			Representative's Address:		
City	State	Zip Code	City	State	Zip Code
Phone No.		Fax No.	Phone No.		Fax No.
Email Address:			Email Address:		

To begin proceedings, please send two copies of this Request and the Mediation Agreement, along with the filing fee as provided for in the Rules, to the AAA. Send the original Request to the responding party.

Please visit our website at www.adr.org if you would like to file this case online. AAA Customer Service can be reached at 800-778-7879

Source: Reprinted with permission of American Arbitration Association.

and findings to the parties, who may then use such information in negotiating a settlement if they wish.

Judicial Referee

If the parties agree, the court may appoint a **judicial referee** to conduct a private trial and render a judgment. Referees, who are often retired judges, have most of the powers of a trial judge, and their decisions stand as a judgment of the court. The parties usually reserve the right to appeal.

Online ADR

Several services now offer **online arbitration**. A party may register the dispute with the service and then notify the other party by email of the registration. Most online arbitration requires the registering party to submit an amount that the party is willing to accept or pay to the other party in the online arbitration. The other party is afforded the opportunity to accept the offer. If that party accepts the offer, a settlement has been reached. The other party, however, may return a **counteroffer**. The process continues until a settlement is reached or one or both of the parties remove themselves from the online ADR process.

Online dispute resolution The use of online alternative dispute resolution services to resolve a dispute.

Online arbitration The arbitration of a dispute using online arbitration services.

Several websites also offer **online mediation** services. In an online mediation, the parties sit before their computers and sign onto the site. Two chat rooms are assigned to each party. One chat room is used for private conversations with the online mediator, and the other chat room is for conversations with both parties and the mediator.

Online mediation The mediation of a dispute using online mediation services.

Online arbitration and mediation services charge fees for their services, but the fees are usually reasonable. In an online arbitration or mediation, a settlement can be reached rather quickly without paying lawyers' fees and court costs. The parties are also acting through a more detached process rather than meeting face-to-face or negotiating over the telephone, either of which could result in verbal arguments.

The ethical duty and social responsibility of a paralegal professional to provide pro bono services to the public is discussed in the following feature.

LEARNING OBJECTIVE 10
Explain a paralegal's duty to provide pro bono services to the public.

ETHICAL PERSPECTIVE

A Paralegal's Duty to Provide Pro Bono Services to the Public

Mr. Alvarez is a paralegal who works directly with Ms. Dawson, a partner at their law firm. In addition to her practice with the law firm, Ms. Dawson volunteers to work one evening per week at a domestic abuse center that serves women and children.

At the center, Ms. Dawson interviews domestic abuse victims and pursues whatever legal actions can be taken to assist the victims and their families. This often includes obtaining restraining orders, government assistance, and spousal and child support. All of Ms. Dawson's services at the domestic abuse center are provided pro bono. The term *pro bono* is short for the Latin phrase *pro bono publico*, which means "for the public good." Pro bono work is provided free of charge.

One day, Ms. Dawson asks Mr. Alvarez whether he would be interested in volunteering to help her one night each month at the domestic abuse shelter. Ms. Dawson explains that she could use his assistance as a paralegal to help conduct interviews, prepare documents, and obtain government and other assistance for the domestic abuse victims and their families. Mr. Alvarez would be under the supervision of Ms. Dawson while working at the center. Does a paralegal owe an ethical duty to provide pro bono services to the public?

Model and state paralegal codes of ethics do state that a paralegal has an ethical duty to provide pro bono services. Thus, a paralegal should strive to provide pro bono services under the supervision of an attorney or as authorized by a court. It is best if these services are provided to assist the poor, persons with limited education, and charitable programs, or to protect civil rights.

PARALEGAL'S ETHICAL DECISION

Because a paralegal owes an ethical duty to provide pro bono services to the public, Mr. Alvarez should agree to assist Ms. Dawson at the domestic abuse shelter one evening each month in order to fulfill his duty to the public. This would be an excellent way for Mr. Alvarez to satisfy his ethical duty as a paralegal professional.

Concept Review *and* Reinforcement

LEGAL TERMINOLOGY

Alternative dispute resolution (ADR) 224
American Arbitration Association (AAA) 227
Arbitration 225
Arbitration clauses 225
Arbitrator 225
Associate justices 213
Attachment jurisdiction 223
Award 227
Binding arbitration 227
Change of venue 223
Chief justice 212
Choice-of-law clause 224
Circuit 211
Conciliation 229
Conciliator 229
Concurrent jurisdiction 222
Concurring opinion 218
Counteroffer 231
Court of Appeals for the Federal Circuit 211
Courts of record 207
Dissenting opinion 218
Diversity of citizenship 221
E-courts 224
Exclusive jurisdiction 222
Federal Arbitration Act (FAA) 227
Federal court system 210
Federal question 221
Forum selection clause 224
General jurisdiction trial court 207
Highest state court 208
In personam jurisdiction 222
In rem jurisdiction 222
Intermediate appellate courts 208
Judicial referee 230
Jurisdiction 206
Limited jurisdiction trial courts 207
Litigation 206
Long-arm statute 223
Majority decision 214
Mediation 228
Mediator 228
Minitrial 229
Negotiation 224
Neutrals 227
Non-binding arbitration 227
Online arbitration 231
Online mediation 231
Personal jurisdiction 222
Petition for *certiorari* 214
Plurality decision 214
Quasi in rem jurisdiction 223
Service of process 222
Settlement agreement 225
Small claims courts 207
Special federal courts 210
Standing to sue 222
State court system 206
Subject matter jurisdiction 221
Submission agreement 225
Supreme Court of the United States 212
Tie decision 214
Unanimous decision 214
Uniform Arbitration Act 227
U.S. Bankruptcy Court 210
U.S. courts of appeals 211
U.S. Court of Federal Claims 210
U.S. Court of International Trade 210
U.S. district courts 210
U.S. Supreme Court 213
U.S. Tax Court 210
Venue 223
Virtual courthouses 224
Writ of *certiorari* 214

SUMMARY OF KEY CONCEPTS

State Court Systems

Limited Jurisdiction Trial Court	This state court hears matters of a specialized or limited nature (such as misdemeanor criminal matters, traffic tickets, or civil matters under a certain dollar amount). Many states have created small claims courts that hear civil cases involving small dollar amounts (under $5,000, for example) in which parties cannot be represented by lawyers.
General Jurisdiction Trial Court	This state court hears cases of a general nature that are not within the jurisdiction of limited jurisdiction trial courts.
Intermediate Appellate Court	This state court hears appeals from state trial courts. The appellate court reviews the trial court record in making its decision. No new evidence is introduced at this level.
Highest State Court	Each state has a highest court in its court system. This court hears appeals from appellate courts and, where appropriate, trial courts. It reviews the record in making its decision, and no new evidence is introduced. Most states call this court the *supreme court*.

Federal Court System

Special Federal Courts	Specialized federal courts have specialized or limited jurisdiction. They include: *U.S. Tax Court:* hears cases involving federal tax laws *U.S. Court of Federal Claims:* hears cases brought against the United States *U.S. Court of International Trade:* hears cases involving tariffs and international commercial disputes *U.S. Bankruptcy Court:* hears cases involving bankruptcy law
U.S. District Courts	U.S. district courts are federal trial courts of general jurisdiction that hear cases that are not within the jurisdiction of specialized courts. Each state has at least one U.S. district court; more heavily populated states have several district courts. The area served by one of these courts is called a *district*.
U.S. Courts of Appeals	U.S. courts of appeals are intermediate federal appellate courts that hear appeals from district courts located in their circuit and, in certain instances, from special federal courts and federal administrative agencies. There are 12 geographical circuits in the United States. Eleven serve areas composed of several states, and one covers only Washington, D.C. A thirteenth circuit court—the *Court of Appeals for the Federal Circuit*—is located in Washington, D.C., and reviews patent, trademark, and international trade cases.

Supreme Court of the United States

U.S. Supreme Court	The Supreme Court is the highest court of the federal court system. It hears appeals from the circuit courts and, in some instances, from special courts and U.S. district courts. The Court, located in Washington, D.C., is composed of nine justices, one of whom is named chief justice.
Decisions by the U.S. Supreme Court	*Petition for* certiorari *and writ of* certiorari: To have a case heard by the U.S. Supreme Court, a petitioner must file a petition for *certiorari* with the Court. If the Court decides to hear the case, it will issue a writ of *certiorari*.
Voting by the U.S. Supreme Court	*Unanimous decision:* All of the justices agree as to the outcome and reasoning used to decide the case. The decision becomes precedent. *Majority decision:* A majority of justices agree as to the outcome and reasoning used to decide the case. The decision becomes precedent. *Plurality decision:* A majority of the justices agree to the outcome but not to the reasoning. The decision is not precedent. *Tie decision:* If there is a tie vote, the lower court's decision stands. The decision is not precedent. *Concurring opinion:* A justice who agrees as to the outcome of the case but not the reasoning used by other justices may write a concurring opinion setting forth his or her own reasoning. *Dissenting opinion:* A justice who disagrees with the outcome of a case may write a dissenting opinion setting forth his or her own reasoning.

Jurisdiction of Federal and State Courts

Subject Matter Jurisdiction	The court must have jurisdiction over the subject matter of the lawsuit. Each court has limited jurisdiction to hear only certain types of cases.

Limited Jurisdiction of Federal Courts	Federal courts have jurisdiction to hear the following types of cases: *Federal question:* cases arising under the U.S. Constitution, treaties, and federal statutes and regulations. There is no dollar amount limit. *Diversity of citizenship:* cases between (a) citizens of different states, (b) a citizen of a state and a citizen or subject of a foreign country; and (c) a citizen of a state and a foreign country where the foreign country is the plaintiff. The controversy must exceed $75,000 for the federal court to hear the case.
Jurisdiction of State Courts	State courts have jurisdiction to hear cases that federal courts do not have jurisdiction to hear.
Exclusive Jurisdiction	Federal courts have exclusive jurisdiction to hear cases involving federal crimes, antitrust, and bankruptcy; patent and copyright cases; suits against the United States; and most admiralty cases. State courts may not hear these matters.
Concurrent Jurisdiction	State courts hear some cases that may be heard by federal courts. State courts have concurrent jurisdiction to hear cases involving diversity of citizenship cases and federal question cases over which the federal courts do not have exclusive jurisdiction. The defendant may have the case removed to federal court.

Personal Jurisdiction and Other Issues

Standing to Sue	To bring a lawsuit, the plaintiff must have some stake in the outcome of the lawsuit.
In Personam Jurisdiction (or Personal Jurisdiction)	The court must have jurisdiction over the parties to a lawsuit. The plaintiff submits to the jurisdiction of the court by filing the lawsuit there. Personal jurisdiction is obtained over the defendant by *service of process.*
In Rem Jurisdiction	A court may have jurisdiction to hear and decide a case because it has jurisdiction over the property at issue in the lawsuit (such as real estate property located in the state).
Quasi in Rem Jurisdiction (or Attachment Jurisdiction)	A plaintiff who obtains a judgment against a defendant in one state may utilize the court system of another state to attach property of the defendant located in that other state.
Long-Arm Statutes	These statutes permit a state to obtain personal jurisdiction over an out-of-state defendant as long as the defendant had the requisite minimum contacts with the state. The out-of-state defendant may be served process outside the state in which the lawsuit has been brought.
Venue	A case must be heard by the court that has jurisdiction nearest to where the incident at issue occurred or where the parties reside. A *change of venue* will be granted if prejudice would occur because of pretrial publicity or some other legitimate reason.
Forum Selection Clause	This clause in a contract designates the court that will hear any dispute that arises out of the contract.
Choice-of-Law Clause	This clause in a contract designates which state's or country's law will apply in resolving a dispute.

Alternative Dispute Resolution (ADR)

ADR	ADR consists of *nonjudicial* means of solving legal disputes. ADR usually requires less time and money than litigation.
Negotiation	Negotiation is a procedure whereby the parties engage in discussions to try to reach a voluntary settlement of their dispute.

Arbitration	In arbitration, an impartial third party, called the *arbitrator*, hears and decides the dispute. The arbitrator makes an award that is appealable to a court if the parties have not given up this right. Arbitration is designated by the parties pursuant to: *Arbitration clause:* Agreement contained in a contract stipulating that any dispute arising out of the contract will be arbitrated. *Submission agreement:* Agreement to submit a dispute to arbitration after the dispute arises.
Federal Arbitration Act (FAA)	The FAA is a federal statute establishing that arbitration agreements involving commerce are valid, irrevocable, and enforceable contracts, unless some grounds exist at law or equity to revoke them (such as fraud or duress).
Other Forms of ADR	
Mediation	In mediation, a neutral third party, called a *mediator*, assists the parties in trying to reach a settlement. The mediator does not make an award.
Conciliation	In conciliation, an interested third party, called a *conciliator*, assists the parties in trying to reach a settlement of their dispute. The conciliator does not make an award.
Minitrial	A minitrial is a short proceeding in which the lawyers present their cases to representatives of each party, who have the authority to settle the dispute.
Fact-Finding	In fact-finding, the parties hire a neutral third person, called a *fact-finder*, to investigate the dispute and report his or her findings to the adversaries.
Judicial Referee	With the consent of the parties, the court can appoint a judicial referee (usually a retired judge or lawyer) to conduct a private trial and render a judgment. The judgment stands as the judgment of the court and may be appealed to the appropriate appellate court.
Online ADR	Online ADR is a form of alternative dispute resolution in which the parties use an online provider of ADR services. This could be online arbitration, online mediation, or other forms of online ADR.

WORKING THE WEB

1. Go to www.nala.org/supreme.aspx and read the information under the title "The US Supreme Court and Paralegals."
2. Go to www.fisc.uscourts.gov. Click on "About the Court" and read the description of the court.
3. Visit the website http://www.law.cornell.edu/supct/index.html. Find the most recent decision of the U.S. Supreme Court. Read the case heading and the summary of the case. Who were the parties? What issue was presented to the Supreme Court? What was the decision of the Supreme Court?
4. Go to www.adr.org. Go to "Areas of Expertise" and click on "Olympics and Sport Doping Disputes" and read the description of the arbitration of these disputes.
5. Find the homepage for the courts in your state. What are the names of the courts in your state? Draw a diagram of the courts in your state. Include limited jurisdiction courts, general jurisdiction trial courts, appellate courts, and the highest state court.

CRITICAL THINKING & WRITING QUESTIONS

1. Describe the difference between state limited jurisdiction courts and general jurisdiction courts.
2. What are the functions of the state intermediate courts and the highest state courts?
3. List the special federal courts, and describe the types of cases that each of these courts can hear.
4. What is the function of U.S. district courts? How many are there?
5. What is the function of U.S. courts of appeals? How many U.S. courts of appeals are there? How does the Court of Appeals for the Federal Circuit differ from the other U.S. courts of appeals?

6. What is the function of the U.S. Supreme Court? How many justices does the Supreme Court have? How does the chief justice differ from the associate justices?
7. Explain the difference between a federal court's jurisdiction to hear a case based on (1) federal question jurisdiction and (2) diversity of citizenship jurisdiction.
8. What is a long-arm statute? What is the purpose of a long-arm statute?
9. What is venue? When can a change of venue be granted?
10. What is the difference between judicial dispute resolution and nonjudicial alternative dispute resolution? Why would one be preferred over the other, and who would have a preference?
11. Define arbitration. Describe how the process of arbitration works. What is an award?

Building Paralegal Skills

VIDEO CASE STUDIES

Meet the Courthouse Team

An interview with Judge Kenney, a trial judge, who introduces members of the courthouse and the roles they serve as members of the courtroom team.

After viewing the video case study at the book website at www.pearsonhighered.com/careersresources, answer the following:

1. What type of relationship should the paralegal develop with the courthouse team?
2. In addition to the courtroom team, what other members of the courthouse should the paralegal know about?

Jury Selection: Potential Juror Challenged for Cause

Trial counsel for a case, which is going to be tried before a jury, are interviewing the individual potential jurors to select an appropriate jury member.

After viewing the video case study at the book website at www.pearsonhighered.com/careersresources, answer the following:

1. What is the role of the jury in the justice system?
2. Why are the attorneys allowed to request that certain individuals not be allowed to serve on a jury?
3. Is everyone guaranteed a right to a jury trial in the American system of justice?

Settlement Conference with Judge

Opposing counsel meet with Judge Lee prior to the start of the trial. The trial judge is presenting the strengths and weaknesses of each side in an attempt to get the parties to settle the case.

After viewing the video case study at the book website at www.pearsonhighered.com/careersresources, answer the following:

1. How is a settlement conference with a judge before trial like an alternative method of dispute resolution?
2. Is the judge in the settlement conference being unfair to one side or the other?
3. Why is the judge trying to settle the case before trial?

ETHICS ANALYSIS & DISCUSSION QUESTIONS

1. May a paralegal represent a client in court?
2. Are a paralegal's time records or calendar subject to the attorney–client privilege?
3. You have been appointed as a trustee of a client's children's educational trust. You need to petition the court for a release of the funds for noneducational purposes—paying the taxes on the trust income. May you appear alone as the trustee and represent the trust in the court proceedings? Would a nonlawyer or nonparalegal be permitted to appear?

See *Ziegler v. Nickel*, 64 Cal. App. 4th 545, 75 Cal. Rptr. 2d 312, 1998 Cal. App. Lexis 500 (Cal. App., 1998).

DEVELOPING YOUR COLLABORATION SKILLS

With a group of students, review the facts of the following case. Then, as a group, discuss the following questions.

1. What is a forum-selection clause?
2. Why do companies include forum-selection clauses in their contracts?
3. Is the forum-selection clause in the Facebook agreement enforceable?
4. If there were no forum-selection clause, could the case have been brought in New York?
5. If you have a Facebook account, have you read the Terms and Service Agreement?

Fteja v. Facebook, Inc.

Facebook, Inc. is a Delaware corporation with its principal place of business in Palo Alto, California. Facebook operates the world's largest social networking website. During the Facebook sign-up process an applicant is asked to fill out several fields containing personal and contact information. The user is asked to click a button that reads "Sign Up." The user is asked to enter more information and then a page displays a second "Sign Up" button where the following sentence appears: "By clicking Sign Up, you are indicating that you have read and agree to the Terms of Service." A hyperlink is available that may be clicked to find Facebook's Terms of Service agreement. The agreement contains a forum-selection clause that stipulates that any disputes between Facebook and the user will be brought exclusively in a state or federal court located in Santa Clara County, California.

Mustafa Fteja, a resident of Staten Island, New York, was an active user of facebook.com. In order to have obtained a Facebook account, Fteja would have followed Facebook's signup procedure. Fteja alleges that defendant Facebook disabled his Facebook account without justification and for discriminatory reasons because he is a Muslim. Fteja alleges that Facebook has caused him harm in all his personal relationships and ability to communicate and thus caused emotional distress and assaulted his good reputation among his friends and family. Fteja filed an action in New York Supreme Court in New York County against Facebook, Inc. Because of diversity of citizenship of the parties—Fteja is a resident of New York and Facebook is a corporation incorporated in Delaware with principal offices in California—Facebook moved the case to the U.S. district court for the southern district of New York. Facebook made a motion to transfer this action to the U.S. district court for the northern district of California pursuant to the forum-selection clause.

Source: Fteja v. Facebook, Inc., 841 F.Supp.2d 829, 2012 U.S. Dist. Lexis 12991 (United States District Court for the Southern District of New York, 2012)

PARALEGAL PORTFOLIO EXERCISE

Based on the facts of the case described in the opening scenario, prepare and complete the following documents from the facts of the scenario.

1. A complaint to file the case on behalf of the plaintiff against the defendant in the appropriate trial court of your state.
2. The defendant's answer to the complaint.

LEGAL ANALYSIS & WRITING CASES

Richtone Design Group v. Live Siri Art

Richtone Design Group LLC (Richtone) is a New York LLC that owns the copyright to the Pilates Teacher Training Manual and licenses fitness instructors to teach "pilates" exercise programs. Live Siri Art, Inc. is a California corporation owned by Siri Galliano. Richtone learned that Live Siri Art and Galliano were selling the pilates manual over a website for profit without permission. They sold several copies of the manual to New York residents, making only about $1,000 in sales in New York from 2000 to 2012. Defendants have no office, property, or bank accounts in New York. Richtone brought a copyright infringement lawsuit against Live Siri Art and Galliano in U.S. district court in New York, alleging that the defendants were subject to personal jurisdiction in New York based on New York's long-arm statute. The defendants Live Siri Art and Galliano defended, alleging that they were not subject to suit in New York because they were residents of California, that they did not have the requisite minimum contacts with New York to be subject to suit in that state, and that to make them defend the lawsuit in New York violated their due process rights. The defendants made a motion to dismiss the New York lawsuit based on lack of personal jurisdiction.

Question

1. Are the defendants subject to lawsuit in New York?

Source: Richtone Design Group v. Live Siri Art, 2013 U.S. Dist. Lexis 157781 (United States District Court for the Southern District of New York, 2013)

Bertram v. Norden, et al.

Four friends, John Bertram, Matt Norden, Scott Olson, and Tony Harvey, all residents of Ohio, traveled to the Upper Peninsula of Michigan to go snowmobiling. On their first day of snowmobiling, after going about 135 miles, the lead snowmobiler, Olson, came to a stop sign on the snowmobile trail where it intersected a private driveway. As Olson approached the sign, he gave the customary hand signal and stopped his snowmobile. Harvey, second in line, was going too fast to stop, so Olson pulled his snowmobile to the right side of the private driveway. Harvey, to avoid hitting Olson, pulled his snowmobile to the left and went over a 5- or 6-foot snow embankment. Bertram, third in line, going about 30 miles per hour, slammed on his brake, turned 45 degrees, and slammed into Olson's snowmobile. Bertram was thrown from his snowmobile. Norden, fourth in line, could not stop, and his snowmobile hit Bertram's leg. Bertram's tibia and fibula were both fractured and protruded through his skin. Bertram underwent surgery to repair the broken bones.

Bertram filed a lawsuit against Olson, Harvey, and Norden in a trial court in Ohio, claiming that each of his friends was liable to him for their negligent snowmobile operation. A Michigan statute specifically stated that snowmobilers assumed the risks associated with snowmobiling. Ohio law did not contain an assumption of the risk rule regarding snowmobiling. The three defendants made a motion for summary judgment.

Question

1. Does Michigan or Ohio law apply to this case?

Source: Bertram v. Norden, et al., 823 N.E.2d 478, 2004 Ohio App. Lexis 550 (Court of Appeals of Ohio, 2004)

WORKING WITH THE LANGUAGE OF THE COURT CASE

Duell v. Kawasaki Motors Corporation, U.S.A. and East Coast Cycles, Inc.

962 F.Supp.2d 723, 2013 U.S. Dist. Lexis 108429 (2013)
United States District Court for the District of New Jersey

Read the following excerpt from the opinion of the U.S. district court and brief the case. In your brief, answer the following questions.

1. Describe personal jurisdiction.
2. What does a state's long-arm statute permit?
3. What test does *International Shoe Company v. Washington* require to be met to find personal jurisdiction over an out-of-state defendant?
4. What facts did the court cite that would establish New Jersey's personal jurisdiction over the out-of-state defendant in this case?

Simandle, Chief District Judge

Defendant East Coast Cycles operates a regional motorcycle store, Powersports East, at 620 Pulaski Highway in Bear, Delaware, which sells multiple brands of motorcycles and power equipment. Defendant is an authorized dealer of Kawasaki motorcycles. East Coast does not have, and has never had, any employees, sales representatives, other agents based in New Jersey, nor does it have a place of business in New Jersey.

On November 18, 2010, Plaintiffs Douglas and Heather Duell, New Jersey residents, purchased a new Kawasaki motorcycle from East Coast as a Christmas present for their minor son, who is identified in this litigation by his initials "D.D." D.D. first operated the motorcycle on December 25, 2010, at which time an accident occurred, injuring D.D.

On November 26, 2012, Plaintiffs commenced this action against Defendants East Coast Cycles and Kawasaki Motors Corporation, U.S.A., alleging that East Coast negligently assembled the motorcycle's throttle mechanism, causing D.D. to crash the bike and sustain serious and permanent injuries.

East Coast filed a motion to dismiss for lack of personal jurisdiction. The Duells oppose the motion and have mustered evidence through certifications and documents supporting the exercise of personal jurisdiction in New Jersey over East Coast. If a defendant maintains "continuous and substantial" forum contacts, general jurisdiction can be exercised.

New Jersey's long arm statute confers jurisdiction to the extent allowed by the U.S. Constitution. The

Due Process Clause of the Fifth Amendment requires a plaintiff to show that a defendant has "certain minimum contacts with the forum such that the maintenance of the suit does not offend traditional notions of fair play and substantial justice." *International Shoe Company v. Washington*, 326 U.S. 310, 66 S.Ct. 154, 1945 U.S. Lexis 1447 (U.S., 1945).

East Coast generates between $6.5 million and $7 million in revenue every year. The vast majority of East Coast's revenue is derived from sales of motorcycles in its Delaware store. From 2002–2012, East Coast sold 1,903 vehicles to residents of New Jersey, out of a total 15,943 vehicles. In other words, New Jersey residents accounted for 12 percent of all motorcycle sales at Powersports East during that decade.

The Duells, New Jersey residents, assert they have purchased four motorized vehicles from East Coast since 2003, of which the present motorcycle, purchased in 2010 was the fourth. East Coast knew that all sales to Plaintiffs would be used at their home in Quinton Township, Salem County, New Jersey. East Coast warranted and serviced the Duells' vehicles and always offered to pick up the vehicles from the Duells' residence in New Jersey for servicing.

East Coast admits that it conducts regular business over the Internet directly with residents in New Jersey. East Coast also maintains a Facebook page, YouTube page, and Twitter account to share information with consumers and to promote events they sponsor. East Coast's YouTube account contained a video promoting a "Tax Free Delaware" to entice customers from neighboring jurisdictions that charge sales tax, including New Jersey, to purchase vehicles in Delaware. Indeed, Plaintiff Douglas Duell stated that avoiding paying New Jersey sales tax by making this major purchase in Delaware was a motivating factor in dealings with East Coast. East Coast's Facebook page also advertised an annual motorcycle ride along the New Jersey shore that originated in New Jersey.

The courts have applied general jurisdiction to companies that advertise and regularly solicit sales within the relevant forum. When looking at the totality of East Coast's contacts with New Jersey, this Court determines general jurisdiction to be appropriate. Even though East Coast does not have any physical presence in New Jersey, that fact is not necessary to establish general jurisdiction. The numerous continuous and purposeful contacts East Coast maintains with New Jersey allow the Court to exercise general personal jurisdiction.

East Coast has maintained contacts with New Jersey for at least 10 years showing that they are continuous in addition to being substantial. These contacts are sufficient to show that East Coast could reasonably expect to be brought to court in New Jersey without offending the Due Process Clause of the constitution. Exercising general personal jurisdiction over East Coast in no way offends the traditional notions of fair play and substantial justice.

For the reasons explained above, the Court's exercise of personal jurisdiction over Defendant East Coast Cycles is proper. The motion to dismiss will be denied.

VIRTUAL LAW OFFICE EXPERIENCE MODULES

If your instructor has instructed you to complete assignments in the Virtual Law Office program, complete the Virtual Law Office assignments as assigned by your instructor. These assignments are designed to develop your workplace skills. Completing the assignments for this chapter will result in producing the following documents for inclusion in your portfolio:

VLOE 6.1 List of documents and information for arbitration

VLOE 6.2
1. Outline of the elements of the actionable civil wrongs of assault and battery
2. Description of any conduct by the plaintiff that supports these causes of action
3. List of people to consider calling as witnesses, and questions to ask them in arbitration

VLOE 6.4
1. Summary of the arbitration for the case file
2. Copy of local rules for appealing from an arbitration hearing
3. Procedural checklist with any forms for appealing from an arbitration in your jurisdiction

CHAPTER

7

Civil Litigation

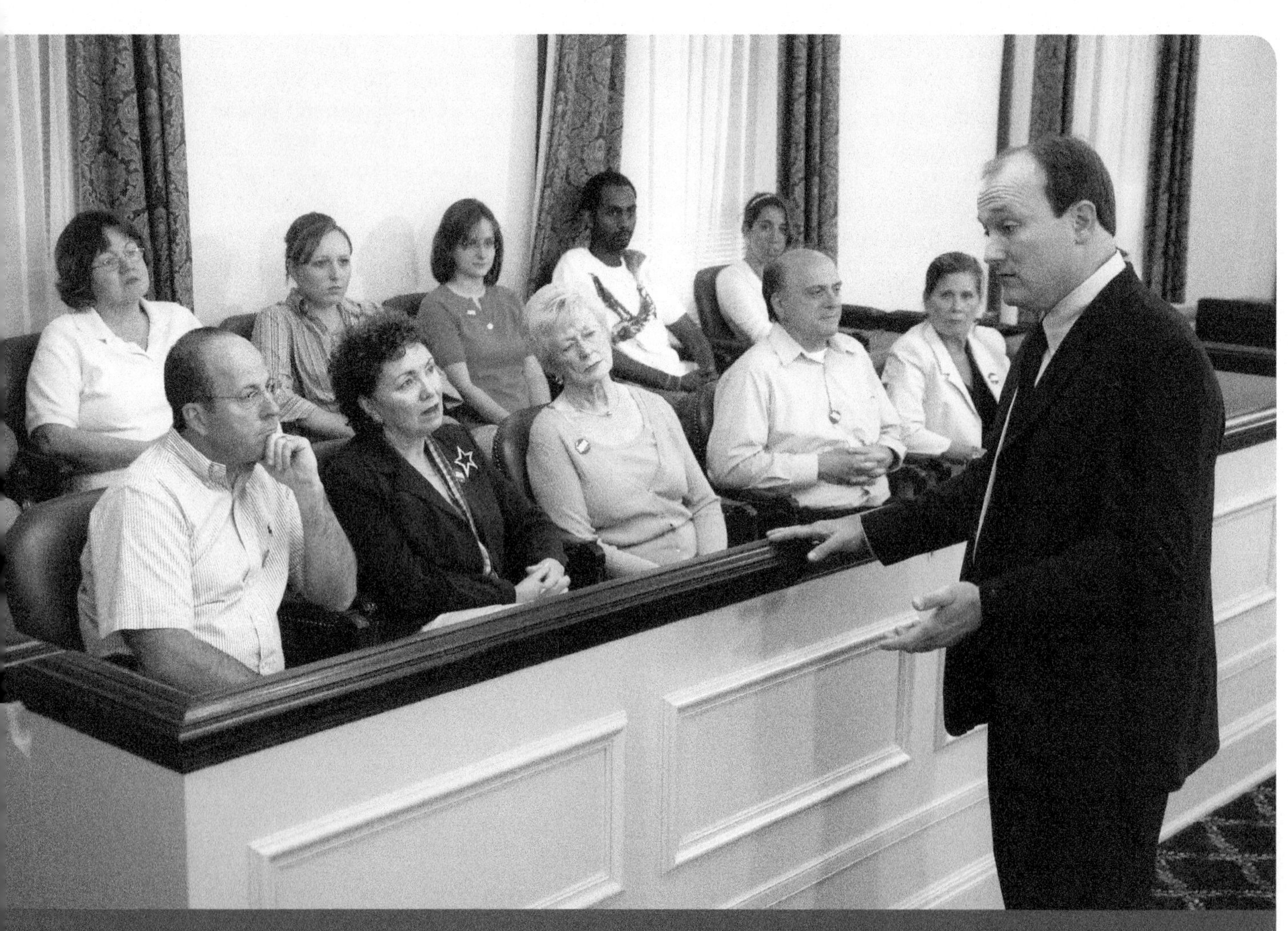

LEARNING OBJECTIVES

After studying this chapter, you should be able to:

1. Explain the role of the paralegal in the litigation process.
2. Describe the types of civil litigation pleadings and their purposes.
3. Explain the purpose of discovery in the litigation process.
4. Explain the use of pretrial motions and settlement conferences.
5. Describe the steps in a trial.
6. Describe how a case is appealed and what decisions can be rendered by an appellate court.

Paralegals at Work

Rowan, a middle school student, and his sister Isis, a high school student, were passengers on the last school bus of the day. They were on their way home after Rowan's basketball practice and his sister's choir practice. The bus had made its regular stops and was on a public highway when it was struck by a large commercial truck. Rowan's injuries were severe enough to prevent him from playing basketball for the rest of the season on his school team and on a local club team that was in the championship game. Isis had been practicing and eagerly looking forward to traveling with the school choir on an invitational European tour, but she would miss this trip as a result of her injuries.

Their parents have retained your law firm, on a contingent fee basis, to pursue a claim for their children's injuries and their out-of-pocket expenses. A review of the medical bills shows expenses in excess of $75,000 for each child. The accident was investigated by the National Transportation Safety Board, which issued a report indicating the probable cause of the accident was the failure of the brakes on the truck. In his initial police statement, the truck driver indicated that he had had no problems with the vehicle before the accident and that he relied upon the mechanics in the maintenance facility to maintain the vehicle, especially the brakes. The trucking company has denied any liability. No initial reports or documentation were provided by the trucking company to the police because all of the truck and maintenance records are kept in electronic format at the company's corporate headquarters in another state.

Consider the issues involved in this scenario as you read the chapter.

> "Discourage litigation. Persuade your neighbors to compromise whenever you can. Point out to them how the nominal winner is often a real loser—in fees, and expenses, and waste of time. As a peacemaker, the lawyer has a superior opportunity of being a good man. There will still be business enough."
>
> Abraham Lincoln, *Notes on the Practice of Law* (1850)

INTRODUCTION TO CIVIL LITIGATION

Civil litigation involves legal disputes between parties seeking a remedy for a civil wrong or to enforce a contract. It differs from criminal litigation, where the government enforces a law or brings a prosecution for the breach of a law. The parties to civil litigation may be individuals, businesses, or, in some cases, government agencies. Although the fundamental process is the same for most jurisdictions, the procedures may vary.

Generally, the filing of a legal dispute with a court happens after the parties have determined that they cannot resolve their differences amicably through negotiation or the use of alternative dispute resolution methods. One of the first steps in the civil litigation process is to determine in which courts the case could be filed. In the United States, subject to jurisdictional requirements, cases can be filed in federal or state court. Within the state or federal court system, there may be multiple courts having the power to hear the same cause of action. The choice of a specific court may be based on geographical convenience or trial strategy.

Many lawyers specialize in civil litigation, in which a plaintiff sues a defendant to recover money damages or seek some other remedy for the alleged harm the defendant caused the plaintiff. It may be based on an automobile accident, an alleged breach of contract, a claim of patent infringement, or any of a myriad of other civil wrongs.

In a civil case, either party can appeal the trial court's decision once a final judgment is entered. In a criminal case, only the defendant can appeal. The appeal is made to the appropriate appellate court.

Litigation The process of bringing, maintaining, and defending a lawsuit.

Paralegals often work for lawyers who specialize in civil litigation seeking monetary damages or other remedies. The litigation process, or **litigation**, consists of bringing, maintaining, and defending a lawsuit.

Civil litigation is an area in which a paralegal's analytical, research, writing, and other abilities are truly put to the test. Paralegals who work in the litigation field must have a thorough knowledge of the litigation process, the rules of evidence, and court procedure, as well as the technology used in discovery, electronic filing, and trial presentation.

A paralegal's first introduction to a new lawsuit often begins with the scheduling of the initial conference with a client, when the law firm is first retained to represent the client as either a plaintiff or a defendant. Many times, the paralegal's first work assignment is to sit in on the initial conference between the attorney and the client and take notes. These notes are used in setting up the client or case matter file.

The paralegal usually is the one to start the new client or case file for the lawsuit. This may involve setting up the client file in the office electronic billing system and creating a case file for the specific litigation matter. Some clients have many case matters. For example, an insurance company represented by a law firm may assign many different cases to the firm, each having a separate case matter file, but there is usually only one client file for the insurance company.

Setting up a new client and case matter may include preparing client fee agreement letters for the supervising attorney's review and obtaining available evidence, documents, and other items relevant to the case. Each attorney has his or her own system for preparing a case for trial (or settlement), and the paralegal may have his or her own way of preparing the file as well. In paperless offices, this usually involves entering the information electronically into a case management system.

The paralegal is often assigned to help draft the pleadings for the case. In addition, the paralegal may contact the client for information, interview the client, draft requests for production of documents and other evidence, and assist in the preparation of depositions to be taken or attended by the supervising attorney.

At this stage, the paralegal is involved in the case as much as his or her supervising attorney. Because of their knowledge of a case, paralegals can be indispensable in the preparation for lawyer–client meetings, discovery, depositions, and settlement conferences.

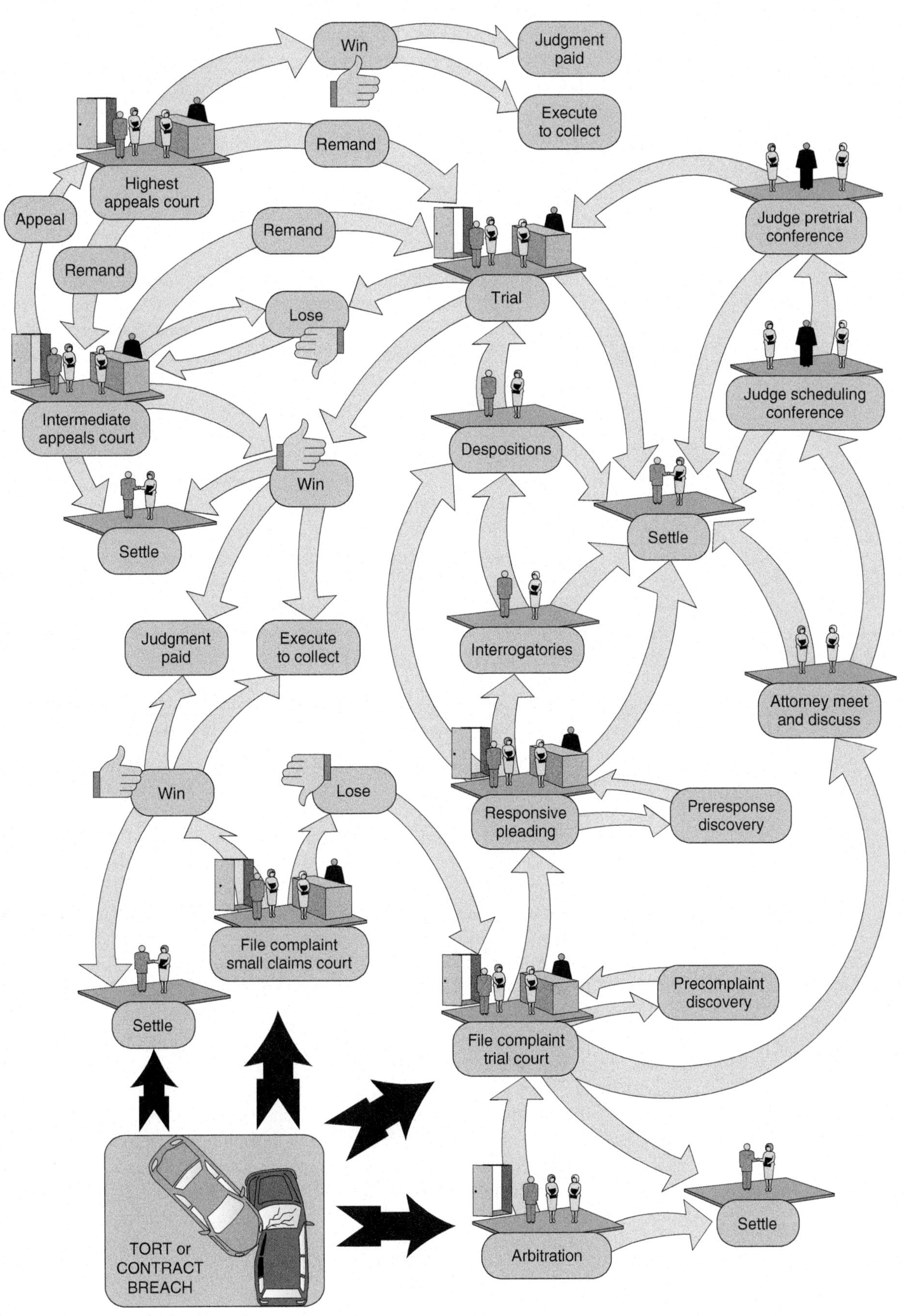

Civil Litigation Process

PRACTICE TIP

Continuing education courses offer the lawyer and the paralegal an opportunity to learn about new areas of law or update their knowledge of specialty areas. Many courses offer discounts for paralegals and special rates for lawyer–paralegal teams who attend together.

If the case is to go to trial, the paralegal is usually called upon to help conduct the legal research that will be used in the brief of the case to be submitted to the court. The paralegal's responsibility is to help organize the case and to use all available technology to prepare the case for trial. During the trial, the paralegal becomes indispensable in assisting the attorney to present the case on behalf of the client.

Civil Litigation Paralegal Skills

LEARNING OBJECTIVE 1

Explain the role of the paralegal in the litigation process.

Civil litigation is a process that requires the assembly of information and evidence, analysis of facts and law, preparation of material for trial presentation and post-trial appeals, and execution of judgments. Typically, these tasks are completed through a team effort. The lawyers, paralegals, litigation support staff, investigators, information technologists, and other support staff handling a case are frequently referred to collectively as the **legal team**. Law firms have structures that define everyone's function in the litigation process. In some law firms, that structure is formalized in a written office manual with detailed job descriptions. Other law firms are less structured, with more flexibility and loosely defined roles that frequently overlap. The members of the legal team in all working environments are ultimately accountable to the clients who hire and depend on them for competent legal representation. Each member of the team shares the total responsibility, performing other assigned functions and helping others on the team when the need arises. Successful legal teams allow for flexibility that will result in success in the litigation process. Some of the functions are defined by the permissible role the person can play in the courtroom. For example, only lawyers admitted to practice before a particular court may appear on behalf of clients. Paralegals and litigation support staff typically may sit at counsel table to assist the attorney, but some local rules may restrict even that activity, relegating the role to an associate attorney.

Litigation is often a fast-paced process with sudden deadlines and demands imposed by changing trial schedules, availability of witnesses, and changing trial strategy. Civil litigation can be exciting and stimulating; it can also test the stamina of the legal team. Everyone must be willing to pitch in to meet deadlines and be fully prepared to appear in court. There may be late nights spent researching and preparing for every move or strategy the other side may make.

Obviously, the paralegal must have a basic knowledge of the law and of how the courts function. Depending on the area of practice, additional knowledge may be required in legal specialties such as intellectual property, medical malpractice, and estate law. Knowledge of unique rules in specialized courts, such as those for bankruptcy, tax, or probate, might also be necessary.

That does not mean that paralegals must know everything. But they do need to know how to research new areas of the law, locate court rules, and find other sources of information efficiently and effectively.

The skills needed by a paralegal are varied, and they depend in some cases on the nature of the legal specialty in which one works. All paralegals need certain basic skills and attributes, such as resourcefulness and dedication, as well as analytical, interpersonal, and communication skills. This is especially true for the civil litigation paralegal. Litigation attorneys come to depend on their civil litigation paralegals in the same way a surgeon depends on a nurse in the operating room. While the lawyer is thinking through the strategy and preparing mentally, the paralegal is making sure everything comes together. The paralegal manages the scheduling of clients and witnesses, prepares exhibits and audiovisual equipment, and completes last-minute research.

Managing Client Relationships

Clients involved in civil litigation may be individuals, small or medium-sized businesses, or large corporate clients. The typical client contact with individuals and smaller businesses is directly with the individuals concerned. Working with corporate clients may be indirect—the client contact is the inside corporate counsel for the corporation. Inside corporate counsel generally selects the outside law firms and monitors the handling of civil litigation. Maintaining positive client relationships is a critical area of the practice of law. Clients want to be kept informed and have their inquiries answered promptly. In the inside counsel–outside law firm relationship, communication may occur via electronic sharing of information. With every client, minimizing the cost of litigation is important. It may be more important with inside counsel because of the need to budget the expenditures for senior management and justify the costs of every piece of litigation.

It is important that the legal team, and particularly the paralegal (who may be the person having the most direct and frequent contact with the client), understand the client's views and values. Corporate or business clients frequently refer to these views and values as the corporate culture. In some cases, clients are more concerned with the principles involved in the litigation than they are with the costs. In others, cost-consciousness dictates a very lean budget for litigation and a desire to do a cost-benefit analysis of the litigation decisions. In all cases, the paralegal becomes the eyes of the attorney and must keep counsel informed of the cost incurred—in effect, monitoring the litigation budget. Because it is often the paralegal on the legal team who hires the outside vendors or sees the time records, the paralegal is often in the best position to monitor the budget.

Tasks of the Civil Litigation Paralegal

The civil litigation paralegal may be called on to perform many tasks—interviewing clients and witnesses, investigating facts, organizing and managing case files, conducting factual and legal research, drafting pleadings and memos of law, scheduling and assisting in depositions, and even operating the trial presentation software in court. In addition to these tasks related to client representation, the paralegal should expect to be responsible for certain administrative tasks such as checking for conflicts of interest and maintaining time records for billing purposes.

Interviewing Clients and Witnesses

The litigation paralegal is often the point of contact between the law firm and others, including clients, witnesses, opposing counsel, and the court. Paralegals with strong interpersonal and communication skills will be well suited to interview clients and witnesses and maintain personal contact during the case. During this important phase of civil litigation, the paralegal must encourage open communication to obtain information easily.

Investigating Facts

Another key component of the process of civil litigation is investigating the facts that have been described by the client. If at all possible, the legal team will attempt to verify through independent means the story the client has shared. It is human nature for people to relay events in such a way as to present themselves in the best possible light. It is not lying; it's perception and human nature. The resourceful civil litigation paralegal will know what records and information can be easily obtained and how to do so. Investigation of facts includes obtaining and reviewing records.

Conducting Discovery

Paralegals play an important role in the discovery process. Discovery is a step in the litigation process in which the parties share information relevant to their dispute. Successful discovery requires a familiarity with the rules of court and, increasingly, the rules relating to the discovery of electronically stored information (ESI) and files. The methods used to locate, preserve, and produce the electronically stored documents require a new set of skills and knowledge of specialty terminology.

Obtaining Documents and Records

In many litigation cases, paralegals will be asked to obtain copies of documents. Those documents relate in some way to the case on which the paralegal is working, and they will enable the legal team to better evaluate the strengths and weaknesses of the client's case. However, in this time of identity theft, privacy laws, and regulations, record keepers are understandably reluctant to freely provide copies of documents. The resourceful paralegal will know the procedures required to obtain these records. In fact, many paralegals have their own reference manual of information listing the procedures, agencies, Web addresses, contact people, fees (if any), and forms necessary to obtain documents. Electronically stored document recovery may also require technical knowledge of accessing and opening documents stored in various electronic formats (such as PDF format) or those that have been compressed to save space and must be uncompressed using a specialty software program to unzip the files.

Reviewing Records

Analytical skills developed by paralegals are essential to reviewing records. When the paralegal reviews records, he or she should look for consistencies and inconsistencies with the client's story and that of other witnesses, noting these in the report to the supervising attorney. Medical records are particularly troubling for paralegals because they may contain many unfamiliar medical terms and symbols. Access to a good medical dictionary or website will help the paralegal to understand the nature of injuries and the cause of those injuries. Increased litigation involving technology, such as faulty computer modules in cars causing sudden acceleration, requires an understanding of the technical terminology or access to references like the medical dictionary in a personal injury case.

Paralegals need to be inquisitive and creative when reviewing records. Understanding terminology is not the sole object of a records review. Knowing what information is significant to the legal team (and potentially admissible as evidence) and finding facts in the records that support or contradict the client's case are examples of the art of being a paralegal.

Drafting Pleadings and Other Documents

Paralegals with good written communication skills can expect to be asked to draft pleadings and documents. The paralegal must be sure that the supervising attorney is actually supervising this task and ultimately signing the pleadings that are filed. Any document that affects a person's legal rights must be approved and signed by a person licensed to practice law in the particular jurisdiction or court, such as that required under federal Rule 11. A paralegal may assist by preparing drafts of these documents, but the supervising attorney must review, revise, correct, and sign them. To do otherwise may subject the paralegal to unauthorized practice of law charges.

Assisting at Trial

At trial, paralegals provide a wide variety of services to the attorney, such as ascertaining which electronic equipment is available in the courtroom (and which must be supplied by the legal team), ensuring that witnesses arrive at the appointed time, presenting exhibits, and keeping notes of what occurs daily during the trial.

Corporate Paralegals in Litigation

Most large corporations, and many smaller companies, have in-house counsel. In some companies, in-house counsel directs the activities of a large staff of attorneys, paralegals, and other legal support staff. Depending on the nature of the business and the needs of the corporation, in-house counsel staff may litigate cases or refer them to outside counsel and supervise the activities of the outside legal team where claims arise or rights need to be enforced. In-house paralegals may have a supervisory role in the litigation process, making sure deadlines are met, reviewing documents prepared by outside counsel, and monitoring the budget for the litigation. When outside counsel is retained, the paralegals' primary role is the maintenance of the relationship among outside counsel, in-house counsel, and corporate officers and employees whose testimony may be required. When in-house counsel litigates cases, paralegals perform the same functions as those working in private legal practices.

Litigation Support Manager

One of the emerging opportunities for experienced paralegals is as managers of litigation support—coordinating and facilitating the technology needs of the legal team. Contemporary litigation requires the use of technology for obtaining, organizing, and presenting evidence. All paralegals will have some level of responsibility with regard to technology. In large law firms the litigation support manager may serve to coordinate the technology for the entire firm. The lawyers on the team frequently delegate technology concerns to the litigation support manager so that the lawyers can concentrate on strategy, analysis, and preparation for trial. The paralegal must work with the technology support personnel and in-house or outside consultants. Paralegals must explain the needs of the legal side while understanding the possibilities and limitations of the technical side. In this role, they must frequently educate the non-legally trained IT staff on the ethical obligations of the legal profession.

Pleadings

LEARNING OBJECTIVE 2
Describe the types of civil litigation pleadings and their purposes.

Pleadings are the documents that are filed with a court to commence or respond to a lawsuit. In the initial pre-filing phase, it is important to be familiar with the applicable rules of the court in which the action is to be filed and tried. The form of the pleadings and the procedure for filing and serving the pleadings are dictated by the rules of the court in which the action is filed. The rules vary between federal and state courts. Within the same court system, there may also be local practice rules that amend or supplement the standard rules.

Pleadings The paperwork that is filed with the court to initiate or respond to a lawsuit.

The initial pleading filed by the plaintiff is designed to give the party being sued notice of the filing of the lawsuit. The initial responsive pleading answers the claims made by the plaintiff or adds other parties that the responding party believes are responsible for the plaintiff's losses. The initial pleadings also define the case. The complaint establishes the alleged wrong and the claims for relief. The answer filed by the defendant establishes the defenses to the plaintiff's claims.

Time Limits and Pleading Deadlines

The first time limit that must be determined in every potential civil action is when the time limit will expire for filing a particular cause of action. With the exception of the crime of murder, every wrong, whether civil or criminal, has a time frame within which a party must bring suit or lose his right to sue. This time period is referred to as the **statute of limitations**. In some civil cases, this period may be short as thirty or sixty days. For example, under some states' laws designed to protect their primary tourist businesses, such as the ski resort industry, the time for giving notice to a ski resort operator of a potential claim for injuries on the ski slopes is very short. More typical statutes of limitations require commencement of a cause of action for personal injuries within two or three years of the injury.

Statute of limitations A law that establishes the period during which a plaintiff must bring a lawsuit against a defendant.

Advice from the Field

GETTING CASE ANALYSIS OFF TO A FAST START

by DecisionQuest

From your first conversation with a prospective client, you're learning about the dispute that led the individual or corporation to seek counsel. There are many benefits to taking a systematic approach to analyzing this knowledge. Not least of these is the favorable impression you'll make on those who retain you.

The following article presents a method for organizing and evaluating the facts about any case. And it illustrates how the early results of this dispute analysis process can be used to great effect in an initial case analysis session with your client.

When you take this approach to case analysis, you'll gain a thorough understanding of the dispute and clarify your thinking about it. And, as you sort out what you do know about the case, you'll find it easy to identify what you don't know and need to find out.

The process focuses on creating four analysis reports: a Cast of Characters, a Chronology, an Issue List, and a Question List. These reports provide a framework for organizing and evaluating critical case knowledge. If multiple people are involved in the analysis process, the reports provide a way to divide responsibility and share results. Moreover, once you standardize the analysis work product, it's easy to compare the findings in one matter to the analysis results from other similar disputes.

You should create your case analysis reports using database software, not a word-processor. Database software makes the knowledge you're organizing far easier to explore and evaluate. For example, using database software, it's easy to filter your Chronology so it displays only facts that have been evaluated as being particularly troublesome.

CAST OF CHARACTERS

Create a Cast of Characters that lists the individuals and organizations you know are involved in the dispute. This report should also catalog key documents and other important pieces of physical evidence. Capture each player's name and a description of the role the person, organization, or document plays in the case.

Also include a column in which you can indicate your evaluation of cast members. Even if you don't evaluate every player, it's essential to note the people and documents that are particularly worrisome, as well as the basis for your concerns. If you follow my recommendation that you build your dispute analysis reports using database software, you will find it easy to filter the entire cast list down to the problem players you've identified.

CHRONOLOGY

A chronology of key facts is a critical tool for analyzing any dispute. As you create the chronology, important factual disputes and areas of strength and weakness become obvious.

Begin by listing the fact and the date on which it occurred. As you enter each fact, be sure to make the important details about the fact explicit. For example, rather than simply stating "Gayle phoned David," write "Gayle phoned David, and asked him to shred the Fritz Memo." Remember that your chronology should be a memory replacement, not a memory jogger.

Since you're analyzing the case within weeks of being retained, there will be many facts for which you have only partial date information. For example, you may know that Gayle called David about the Fritz Memo sometime in June of 1993, but be unsure as to the day within June. When you run into this problem, a simple solution is to substitute a question mark for the portion of the date that's undetermined, e.g., 6/?/93.

In addition to capturing the fact and the date, be sure to list a source or sources for each fact. Now, in the early days of a case, it's likely that the sources of many of the facts you are entering in your chronology are not of a type that will pass muster come trial. However, by capturing a source such as "David Smith Interview Notes," you know to whom or what you will need to turn to develop a court-acceptable source.

The mission in early dispute analysis is to take a broad look at the potential evidence. Therefore, your chronology should be more than a list of undisputed facts. Be sure to include disputed facts and even prospective facts (i.e., facts that you suspect may turn up as the case proceeds toward trial). You'll want to distinguish the facts that are undisputed from those that are disputed or merely prospective. Include in your chronology a column that you use for this purpose.

Finally, include a column that you use to separate the critical facts from others of lesser importance. A simple solution is to have a column titled "Key" that you set up as a checkbox (checked means the fact is key, unchecked means it's not). If you're using database software, filtering the chronology down to the key items should take you about 2 seconds.

ISSUE LIST

Build a list of case issues including both legal claims and critical factual disputes. If the case has yet to be filed, list the claims and counter-claims or cross-claims you anticipate.

Rather than listing just the top-level issues, consider breaking each claim down to its component parts. For example, rather than listing Fraud, list Fraud: Intent, Fraud: Reliance, and so on as separate dimensions.

In addition to listing a name for each issue, create a more detailed description of it. The description might include a brief summary of each party's position on the issue and, if it's a legal issue, the potential language of the judge's instruction.

As your case proceeds to trial, your Issue List will increase in importance. You'll use the Issue List to return to the Cast of Characters and Chronology and establish relationships between each fact, each witness, each document, and the issue or issues to which it relates. Once you've made these links, it will be easy to focus on the evidence that's being developed regarding each issue and to make decisions about case strategy based on this analysis.

QUESTION LIST

When you start case analysis early, your knowledge of the dispute is sure to be incomplete. But as you map out what is known about the case, what is unknown and must be determined becomes clear.

Each time you come up with a question about the case that you can't readily answer, get it into your Question List. You'll want your report to include a column for the question and another column where you can capture notes regarding the answer. Also include a column for evaluating the criticality of each question. Use a simple A (extremely critical), B, C, and D scale to make your assessment. Other columns to consider for your Question List are "Assigned To" and "Due Date."

The analysis reports you've begun are "living" ones. As you head toward trial, keep working on your Cast of Characters, your Chronology, your Issue List, and your Question List. These analysis reports will do far more than help you think about your case. They'll serve a myriad of concrete purposes. They'll help you keep your client up-to-date, plan for discovery, prepare to take and defend depositions, create motions for summary judgment, and make your case at settlement conferences and at trial.

In medical malpractice claims, the limitations period doesn't begin to run out until the plaintiff becomes aware or should have become aware of the injury. For example, in a claim for medical malpractice arising from a foreign object, such as a surgical sponge, being left in the person during an operation, a patient may not be aware for several years of the medical malpractice committed by the surgeon, until the cause of persistent pain is finally diagnosed. It would not be fair for the time limit to start when the injury was caused—the date of the original surgery. Fundamental fairness requires that the time frame begin when the patient learns of the cause of the injury.

In other types of cases, the time limit may also not begin until a point in the future. Societal concepts of justice allow **minors** (children) who suffered an injury during their minority to bring a cause of action after they reach the **age of majority**, usually eighteen years of age. In these cases, the statute of limitations starts on the birthday on which the individual reaches the age of majority in the applicable jurisdiction.

In contract cases, statutes of limitations vary depending upon the particular cause of action pursued. For example, a contract dispute may involve a violation of the Uniform Commercial Code (UCC), which imposes a four-year statute of limitations. However, the same dispute, if framed as a breach of contract under the common law, may be subject to a six-year statute of limitations. It may also involve some other cause of action with a different limitations period under state law. Bringing the cause of action under the appropriate statute may give new life to a case for which the UCC limitation has expired.

Plaintiff The party who files a complaint.

Complaint

The **plaintiff** (the party who is suing) must file a **complaint**, in some jurisdictions called a plaintiff's original petition or summons, with the proper court. The content and form of the complaint will vary depending on each court's procedural rules.

Complaint The document the plaintiff files with the court and serves on the defendant to initiate a lawsuit.

A complaint must name the parties to the lawsuit, allege the ultimate facts and law violated, state the remedy requested, and recite a "prayer for relief" to be awarded by the court. The complaint can be as long as necessary, depending on the complexity of the case.

Many courts follow the federal practice of "**notice pleading**," requiring only that causes of action be stated in general terms sufficient to give the defendant notice of the allegations. Other state courts follow the traditional form, "**fact pleading**," requiring a more detailed allegation or description of the basis for the action.

Fact and Notice Pleading

In the federal courts and in some state courts, the complaint need only provide general allegations of the wrongful conduct, called notice pleading. The U.S. Supreme Court described the history and reasoning for the notice pleading requirement in the case of *Bell Atlantic Corp. v. Twombly* (No. 05-1126), 425 F. 3d 99:

> . . . Rule 8(a)(2) of the Federal Rules requires that a complaint contain "a short and plain statement of the claim showing that the pleader is entitled to relief." The rule did not come about by happenstance and its language is not inadvertent. The English experience with Byzantine special pleading rules . . . made obvious the appeal of a pleading standard that was easy for the common litigant to understand and sufficed to put the defendant on notice as to the nature of the claim against him and the relief sought. Stateside, . . . the highly influential New York Code of 1848, which required "[a] statement of the facts constituting the cause of action, in ordinary and concise language, without repetition, and in such a manner as to enable a person of common understanding to know what is intended." . . . Substantially similar language appeared in the Federal Equity Rules adopted in 1912. See Fed. Equity Rule 25 (requiring "a short and simple statement of the ultimate facts upon which the plaintiff asks relief, omitting any mere statement of evidence").
>
> A difficulty arose, however, in that the Field Code and its progeny required a plaintiff to plead "facts" rather than "conclusions," a distinction that proved far easier to say than to apply. As commentators have noted,
>
> "it is virtually impossible logically to distinguish among 'ultimate facts,' 'evidence,' and 'conclusions.' Essentially any allegation in a pleading must be an assertion that certain occurrences took place. The pleading spectrum, passing from evidence through ultimate facts to conclusions, is largely a continuum varying only in the degree of particularity with which the occurrences are described."
>
> . . . ("[T]here is no logical distinction between statements which are grouped by the courts under the phrases 'statements of fact' and 'conclusions of law'"). Rule 8 was directly responsive to this difficulty. Its drafters intentionally avoided any reference to "facts" or "evidence" or "conclusions." . . . ("The substitution of 'claim showing that the pleader is entitled to relief' for the code formulation of the 'facts' constituting a 'cause of action' was intended to avoid the distinctions drawn under the codes among 'evidentiary facts,' 'ultimate facts,' and 'conclusions' . . .").
>
> Under the relaxed pleading standards of the Federal Rules, the idea was not to keep litigants out of court but rather to keep them in. The merits of a claim would be sorted out during a flexible pretrial process and, as appropriate, through the crucible of trial . . . ("The liberal notice pleading of Rule 8(a) is the starting point of a simplified pleading system, which was adopted to focus litigation on the merits of a claim"). Charles E. Clark, the "principal draftsman" of the Federal Rules, put it thus:
>
> "Experience has shown . . . that we cannot expect the proof of the case to be made through the pleadings, and that such proof is really not their function. We can expect a general statement distinguishing the case from all others, so that the manner and form of trial and remedy expected are clear, and so that a permanent judgment will result."

Web Exploration

Go to http://www.almd.uscourts.gov/forms/generic_complaint_format.pdf to view a sample format of a complaint filed in the U.S. district court.

The sample complaint in Exhibit 7.1 is an example of a notice pleading in federal court. Other states require fact pleading, in which the plaintiff must plead specific facts that constitute the wrongful conduct. Exhibit 7.2 is a sample state trial court fact pleading complaint filed in New York. Exhibit 7.3 is a bilingual notice to plead to a complaint.

Exhibit 7.1 Notice complaint filed in federal court

UNITED STATES DISTRICT COURT - NORTHERN DISTRICT OF NEW YORK

B.K., a minor by her	:	No.: ______________________
Parents and guardians,		
Janice Knowles and	:	
Steven Knowles,		COMPLAINT
Plaintiff	:	CIVIL ACTION - NEGLIGENCE
v. :		
Ronald Clemmons,	:	Jury Trial Demanded
Lower Council School District,		
Bud Smith, and	:	
Ace Trucking Company,		Attorney ID No. 124987
Defendants :		

Plaintiff in the above captioned action alleges as follows:

JURISDICTION

1. Plaintiff and defendants are residents of different states and the amount in controversy exceeds $75,000.00, exclusive of interest and costs as specified in 28 U.S.C. §1332.

PARTIES

2. Plaintiff is B.K. a minor whose interests are represented by her parents and natural guardians, Janice and Steven Knowles, adult individuals, husband and wife, residing at 1243 Asbury Avenue, Bennington, Vermont (hereinafter Plaintiff).
3. Defendant, Ronald Clemmons is an adult individual residing at 24 Logan Street, Albany, New York (hereinafter Defendant Clemmons).
4. Defendant Lower Council School District is a governmental unit duly authorized and existing under the laws of the State of New York with its principal place of business being 701 Wilkes Road, Albany, New York (hereinafter Defendant School).
5. Defendant Bud Smith is an adult individual residing at 332 S. Hearn Lane, Pittsfield, Massachusetts (hereinafter Defendant Smith).
6. Defendant Ace Trucking Company is a corporation duly organized and existing under the laws of the State of New York with its principal place of business being 2501 Industrial Highway, Center Bridge, New York (hereinafter Defendant Ace).
7. At all relevant times, Defendant Clemmons, a 69 year old, duly licensed school bus driver, was employed by and under the direction, supervision and control of Defendant School.
8. At all relevant time Defendant Smith, a 46 year old, duly licensed truck driver, was employed by and under the direction, supervision and control of Defendant Ace.
9. On October 21, 2010, after finishing his regular route, Defendant Clemmons drove to Albany City School No. 18 and loaded 44 children, ages 5 to 9 years old, and 8 adults for a scheduled field trip.
10. Plaintiff, who was 7 old on the date in question, was a passenger on the bus, seated on Row 10 Seat F. A true and correct copy of the bus seating chart is attached hereto, made a part hereof and labeled as Exhibit "A".
11. At approximately 10:30 a.m., the bus was traveling north on SR-30A between 15 and 25 mph as it approached the intersection with SR-7. The north- and southbound traffic on SR-30A was controlled by an advance warning sign that indicated a stop ahead, a stop sign, flashing red intersection control beacons, pavement markings that included the word "STOP", and a stop bar.

(continued)

Exhibit 7.1 Notice complaint filed in federal court *(continued)*

12. Defendant Clemmons, who was looking for SR-7, saw the posted stop sign, slowed, but did not stop the bus, which then entered the intersection.
13. Upon entering the intersection, the bus was struck on the right side behind the real axel by a dump truck operated by Defendant Smith.
14. Defendant Smith was driving the dump truck with utility trailer, owned and operated by Defendant Ace. Defendant Smith was traveling about 45 mph westbound on SR-7. East- and westbound traffic on SR-7 at the intersection with SR-30A was controlled by flashing yellow intersection control beacons.

Count I - Plaintiff v. Defendant Clemmons

15. Plaintiff incorporates by reference the allegations contained in paragraphs 1 through 14 as though fully set forth at length herein.
16. Defendant Clemmons was negligent when he failed to stop the school bus at a stop sign.
17. As a result, Plaintiff was injured when the impact of the dump truck with the school bus she was thrown about the interior of the school bus striking her head and shoulders on the side and roof of the bus resulting in a fractured skull and fractured vertebra at C3 and 4, contusions and abrasions suffering damages, as follows:
    a. surgical treatment and repair of a fractured skull;
    b. placement of a halo brace upon her head and shoulders for stabilization and healing of vertebra fractures as C3 and 4;
    c. physical therapy to rehabilitate and restore the normal use of her head and neck;
    d. medical expenses related to the treatment and rehabilitation for the injuries sustained;
    e. time lost from school while hospitalized and unable to attend school;
    f. arranging and paying for private tutors to come to her home for missed school instruction;
    g. inability to participate in soccer, Daisy Scouts and other of life's pleasures, and;
    h. such other damages as will be proved at trial of this matter

Wherefore plaintiff requests this Honorable court enter judgment in her favor and against the Defendants in an amount exceeding $75,000 plus interest, costs, attorneys fees and such other relief as deemed equitable.

Count II - Plaintiff v. Defendant School

18. Plaintiff incorporates by reference the allegations contained in paragraphs 1 through 14 as though fully set forth at length herein.
19. Defendant School failed to properly supervise, control and direct its employee Defendant Clemmons
20. As a result of Defendant School negligence in employing and supervising Defendant Clemmons the collision of October 21, 2010 occurred causing plaintiff to suffer, as follows:
    a. surgical treatment and repair of a fractured skull;
    b. placement of a halo brace upon her head and shoulders for stabilization and healing of vertebra fractures as C3 and 4;
    c. physical therapy to rehabilitate and restore the normal use of her head and neck;
    d. medical expenses related to the treatment and rehabilitation for the injuries sustained;
    e. time lost from school while hospitalized and unable to attend school;
    f. arranging and paying for private tutors to come to her home for missed school instruction;
    g. inability to participate in soccer, Daisy Scouts and other of life's pleasures, and;
    h. such other damages as will be established at the trial of this matter.

Wherefore plaintiff requests this Honorable court enter judgment in her favor and against the Defendants in an amount exceeding $75,000 plus interest, costs, attorneys fees and such other relief as deemed equitable.

(continued)

Exhibit 7.1 Notice complaint filed in federal court *(continued)*

Count IV - Plaintiff v. Defendant Smith

21. Plaintiff incorporates by reference the allegations contained in paragraphs 1 through 14 as though fully set forth at length herein.
22. Defendant Smith was negligent in the operation and control of a dump truck driving too fast for conditions while approaching an intersection with flashing yellow lights.
23. As a result, Plaintiff was injured upon the impact of the dump truck with the school bus she was thrown about the interior of the school bus striking her head and shoulders on the side and roof of the bus resulting in a fractured skull and vertebra at C3 and 4 and suffered damages as follows:
    a. surgical treatment and repair of a fractured skull;
    b. placement of a halo brace upon her head and shoulders for stabilization and healing of vertebra fractures as C3 and 4;
    c. physical therapy to rehabilitate and restore the normal use of her head and neck;
    d. medical expenses related to the treatment and rehabilitation for the injuries sustained;
    e. time lost from school while hospitalized and unable to attend school;
    f. arranging and paying for private tutors to come to her home for missed school instruction
    g. inability to participate in soccer, Daisy Scouts and other of life's pleasures, and;
    h. such other damages as will be established in the trial of this matter.

Wherefore plaintiff requests this Honorable court enter judgment in her favor and against the Defendants in an amount exceeding $75,000 plus interest, costs, attorneys fees and such other relief as deemed equitable.

Count V - Plaintiff v. Defendant Ace

24. Plaintiff incorporates by reference the allegations contained in paragraphs 1 through 14 as though fully set forth at length herein.
25. Defendant Ace was negligent in failing to inspect and correct mechanical deficiencies to the brake system, the air hose linking the truck and the trailer, permitting use of a dump truck to pull a trailer, allowing its driver to operate a vehicle not designed to pull a trailer, and failed to properly supervise and train employee Smith concerning the rules of the road.
26. As a result of Defendant Ace's negligence the dump truck struck the school bus in which Plaintiff was a passenger, injuring her when upon impact she was thrown about the interior of the school bus striking her head and shoulders on the side and roof of the bus resulting in a fractured skull and vertebra at C3 and 4 and suffered the following damages:
    a. surgical treatment and repair of a fractured skull;
    b. placement of a halo brace upon her head and shoulders for stabilization and healing of vertebra fractures as C3 and 4;
    c. physical therapy to rehabilitate and restore the normal use of her head and neck;
    d. medical expenses related to the treatment and rehabilitation for the injuries sustained;
    e. time lost from school while hospitalized and unable to attend school;
    f. arranging and paying for private tutors to come to her home for missed school instruction;
    g. inability to participate in soccer, Daisy Scouts and other of life's pleasures, and;
    h. such other damages as will be established at the trial of this matter.

(continued)

Exhibit 7.1 Notice complaint filed in federal court *(continued)*

Wherefore plaintiff requests this Honorable court enter judgment in her favor and against the Defendants in an amount exceeding $75,000 plus interest, costs, attorneys fees and such other relief as deemed equitable

Respectfully submitted,
Mason, Marshall and Benjamin
ATTORNEYS FOR PLAINTIFF

____
Ethan Benjamin, Esquire
Attorney ID #
Mason, Marshall and Benjamin
Address
Albany, New York
Phone
Fax
Email

VERIFICATION

I, JANICE KNOWLES, verify that I am authorized to make this verification. I verify that the Complaint is true and correct to the best of my knowledge, information and belief. I understand that false statements herein are made subject to the penalties of perjury relating to unsworn falsification to authorities.

Date: ____________________ ____________________
JANICE KNOWLES

I, STEVEN KNOWLES, verify that I am authorized to make this verification. I verify that the Complaint is true and correct to the best of my knowledge, information and belief. I understand that false statements herein are made subject to the penalties of perjury relating to unsworn falsification to authorities.

Date: ____________________ ____________________
STEVEN KNOWLES

Exhibit 7.2 Sample state trial court fact pleading complaint

IN THE SUPREME COURT OF NEW YORK FOR ALBANY COUNTY

B.K., a minor by her	:	No.: ______________________
Parents and guardians,		
Janice Knowles and	:	
Steven Knowles,		
Plaintiff	:	Civil Action - Negligence
v.	:	
Ronald Clemmons	:	Jury Trial Demanded
Lower Council School District,		
Bud Smith, and	:	
Ace Trucking Company,		Attorney ID No. 124987
Defendants	:	

COMPLAINT

NOW comes the plaintiff, by her attorneys, Mason, Marshall and Benjamin and brings this complaint alleging as follows:

1. Plaintiff is B.K. a minor whose interests are represented by her parents and natural guardians, Janice and Steven Knowles, adult individuals, husband and wife, residing at 1243 Asbury Avenue, Albany, New York (hereinafter Plaintiff).
2. Defendant, Ronald Clemmons is an adult individual residing at 24 Logan Street, Albany, New York (hereinafter Defendant Clemmons).
3. Defendant Lower Council School District is a governmental unit duly authorized and existing under the laws of the State of New York with its principal place of business being 701 Wilkes Road, Albany, New York (hereinafter Defendant School).
4. Defendant Bud Smith is an adult individual residing at 332 S. Hearn Lane, Albany, New York (hereinafter Defendant Smith).
5. Defendant Ace Trucking Company is a corporation duly organized and existing under the laws of the State of New York with its principal place of business being 2501 Industrial Highway, Center Bridge, New York (hereinafter Defendant Ace).
6. At all relevant times, Defendant Clemmons, a 69 year old, duly licensed school bus driver, was employed by and under the direction, supervision and control of Defendant School.
7. At all relevant time Defendant Smith, a 46 year old, duly licensed truck driver, was employed by and under the direction, supervision and control of Defendant Ace.
8. On October 21, 2010 at approximately 7:20 a.m. Defendant Clemmons began transporting students to school on his regular morning route driving a 2005 full size school bus owned and operated by Defendant School.
9. On October 21, 2010 at approximately 8:50 a.m., after finishing his regular route, Defendant Clemmons drove to Albany City School No. 18 and loaded 44 children, ages 5 to 9 years old, and 8 adults serving as chaperons for a scheduled field trip to the Pumpkin Patch in Central Bridge, New York, about 40 miles from the school.
10. Plaintiff, born on June 12, 2003, being 7 years of age on the date in question, was one of the passengers, seated on Row 10 Seat F of the bus. A true and correct copy of the bus seating chart is attached hereto, made a part hereof and labeled as Exhibit "A".
11. Although familiar with the Central Bridge area, Defendant Clemmons had never been to the Pumpkin Patch.

(continued)

Exhibit 7.2 Sample state trial court fact pleading complaint *(continued)*

12. Defendant School did not provide its driver, Defendant Clemmons with directions or a map to the site.
13. Defendant Clemmons asked a chaperone for directions which were obtained from a secretary in the school office.
14. Each school bus passenger seat was equipped with three color-coded lap belts, one color coded belt for each passenger in a seat. Each child was seated and restrained with a lap belt before the trip began for purposes of safety and supervision.
15. Departing the school about 9:20 a.m., Defendant Clemmons took the New York State Thruway west to exit 25A onto Interstate-88 (I-88) and then traveled west on I-88 toward exit 23, the intended exit.
16. Defendant Clemmons was confused about the directions to the Pumpkin Patch and exited at exit 24, the wrong exit. Clemmons stopped the bus on the exit 24 ramp, turned the bus around, returned to I-88, and continued traveling to exit 23, the correct exit.
17. At the end of the exit ramp for exit 23, Defendant Clemmons turned right onto State Route 30A (SR-30A) and started looking for State Route 7 (SR-7).
18. At approximately 10:30 a.m., the bus was traveling north on SR-30A between 15 and 25 mph as it approached the intersection with SR-7. The north- and southbound traffic on SR-30A were controlled by an advance warning sign that indicated a stop ahead, a stop sign, flashing red intersection control beacons, pavement markings that included the word "STOP", and a stop bar.
19. At the same time, Defendant Smith was driving a dump truck towing a utility trailer owned and operated by Defendant Ace. Defendant Smith was traveling about 45 mph westbound on SR-7. East- and westbound traffic on SR-7 at the intersection with SR-30A was controlled by flashing yellow intersection control beacons.
20. As the school bus approached the intersection, several children on board saw the sign for the Pumpkin Patch that was beyond the intersection and yelled.
21. Defendant Clemmons, who was looking for SR-7, saw the posted stop sign, slowed, but did not stop the bus, which then entered the intersection where the dump truck struck it on the right side behind the rear axle.

Count I - Plaintiff v. Defendant Clemmons

22. Plaintiff incorporates by reference the allegations contained in paragraphs 1 through 21 as though fully set forth at length herein.
23. Defendant Clemmons was negligent when he failed to stop the school bus at a stop sign breaching his duty to operate a vehicle in accordance with the rules of the road in effect in the state of New York for purposes of safety and traffic control.
24. Defendant Clemmons breached the duty of care owed to the passengers of the bus when he violated the rules of the road failing to stop at the traffic control device.
25. As a direct result of Defendant Clemmons' negligence in the operation of the school bus, Plaintiff was injured when upon impact of the dump truck with the school bus she was thrown about the interior of the school bus striking her head and shoulders on the side and roof of the bus resulting in a fractured skull and fractured vertebra at C3 and 4, contusions and abrasions.
26. As a result of the injuries sustained by Plaintiff she has suffered damages as follows:
    a. surgical treatment and repair of a fractured skull;
    b. placement of a halo brace upon her head and shoulders for stabilization and healing of vertebra fractures as C3 and 4;
    c. physical therapy to rehabilitate and restore the normal use of her head and neck;
    d. medical expenses related to the treatment and rehabilitation for the injuries sustained;

(continued)

Exhibit 7.2 Sample state trial court fact pleading complaint *(continued)*

e. time lost from school while hospitalized and unable to attend school;
f. arranging and paying for private tutors to come to her home for missed school instruction;
g. inability to participate in soccer, Daisy Scouts and other of life's pleasures, and;
h. such other damages as will be proved at trial of this matter

Wherefore plaintiff requests this Honorable court enter judgment in her favor and against the Defendants in an amount exceeding $25,000 plus interest, costs, attorneys fees and such other relief as deemed equitable.

Count II - Plaintiff v. Defendant School

27. Plaintiff incorporates by reference the allegations contained in paragraphs 1 through 21 as though fully set forth at length herein.

28. Defendant School failed to properly supervise, control and direct its employee Defendant Clemmons as follows
    a. failure to obtain proper medical certification of a bus driver known to have a heart condition, hypertension, and Type I Diabetes in violation New York Department of Motor Vehicles Article 19-A;
    b. failure to provide map and directions for driver's destination;
    c. failure to establish a policy to limit the eligibility of senior drivers known to be easily confused, distracted and unable to focus on multiple stimuli, and;
    d. such other negligence as may be discovered in preparation of the trial of this matter.

29. As a result of Defendant School negligence in employing and supervising Defendant Clemmons the collision of October 21, 2010 occurred causing plaintiff to suffer, as follows:
    a. surgical treatment and repair of a fractured skull;
    b. placement of a halo brace upon her head and shoulders for stabilization and healing of vertebra fractures as C3 and 4;
    c. physical therapy to rehabilitate and restore the normal use of her head and neck;
    d. medical expenses related to the treatment and rehabilitation for the injuries sustained;
    e. time lost from school while hospitalized and unable to attend school;
    f. arranging and paying for private tutors to come to her home for missed school instruction;
    g. inability to participate in soccer, Daisy Scouts and other of life's pleasures, and;
    h. such other damages as will be established at the trial of this matter.

Wherefore plaintiff requests this Honorable court enter judgment in her favor and against the Defendants in an amount exceeding $25,000 plus interest, costs, attorneys fees and such other relief as deemed equitable.

Count IV - Plaintiff v. Defendant Smith

30. Plaintiff incorporates by reference the allegations contained in paragraphs 1 through 21 as though fully set forth at length herein.

31. Defendant Smith was negligent in the operation and control of a dump truck driving too fast for conditions while approaching an intersection with flashing yellow lights.

32. As a direct result of Defendant Smith's negligence the dump truck he was operating struck the school bus in which Plaintiff was a passenger.

33. Plaintiff was injured when upon impact of the dump truck with the school bus she was thrown about the interior of the school bus striking her head and shoulders on the side and roof of the bus resulting in a fractured skull and vertebra at C3 and 4.

34. As a result of the injuries sustained by Plaintiff she has suffered damages as follows:
    a. surgical treatment and repair of a fractured skull;
    b. placement of a halo brace upon her head and shoulders for stabilization and healing of vertebra fractures as C3 and 4;
    c. physical therapy to rehabilitate and restore the normal use of her head and neck;
    d. medical expenses related to the treatment and rehabilitation for the injuries sustained;

(continued)

Exhibit 7.2 Sample state trial court fact pleading complaint *(continued)*

e. time lost from school while hospitalized and unable to attend school;
f. arranging and paying for private tutors to come to her home for missed school instruction
g. inability to participate in soccer, Daisy Scouts and other of life's pleasures, and;
h. such other damages as will be established in the trial of this matter.

Wherefore plaintiff requests this Honorable court enter judgment in her favor and against the Defendants in an amount exceeding $25,000 plus interest, costs, attorneys fees and such other relief as deemed equitable.

Count V - Plaintiff v. Defendant Ace

35. Plaintiff incorporates by reference the allegations contained in paragraphs 1 through 21 as though fully set forth at length herein.

36. Defendant Ace was negligent in failing to inspect and correct mechanical deficiencies to the brake system, the air hose linking the truck and the trailer, and permitting use of a dump truck to pull a trailer.

37. Defendant Ace was negligent in allowing its driver to operate a vehicle not designed to pull a trailer and failed to properly supervise and train employee Smith concerning the rules of the road.

38. As a result of Defendant Ace's negligence the dump truck struck the school bus in which Plaintiff was a passenger.

39. Plaintiff was injured when upon impact of the dump truck with the school bus she was thrown about the interior of the school bus striking her head and shoulders on the side and roof of the bus resulting in a fractured skull and vertebra at C3 and 4.

40. As a result of the injuries sustained by Plaintiff she has suffered damages as follows:
a. surgical treatment and repair of a fractured skull;
b. placement of a halo brace upon her head and shoulders for stabilization and healing of vertebra fractures as C3 and 4;
c. physical therapy to rehabilitate and restore the normal use of her head and neck;
d. medical expenses related to the treatment and rehabilitation for the injuries sustained;
e. time lost from school while hospitalized and unable to attend school;
f. arranging and paying for private tutors to come to her home for missed school instruction;
g. inability to participate in soccer, Daisy Scouts and other of life's pleasures, and;
h. such other damages as will be established at the trial of this matter.

Wherefore plaintiff requests this Honorable court enter judgment in her favor and against the Defendants in an amount exceeding $25,000 plus interest, costs, attorneys fees and such other relief as deemed equitable

Respectfully submitted,
Mason, Marshall and Benjamin
ATTORNEYS FOR PLAINTIFF

____

Ethan Benjamin, Esquire
Attorney ID #
Mason, Marshall and Benjamin
Address
Albany, New York
Phone
Fax
Email

Exhibit 7.3 Bilingual notice to plead to a complaint

IN THE COURT OF COMMON PLEAS
OF PHILADELPHIA COUNTY, PENNSYLVANIA
CIVIL ACTION LAW

KATHRYN KELSEY	: NO.
vs.	: ATTORNEY I.D. NO.
KATHRYN CARROLL	: COMPLAINT IN EQUITY

COMPLAINT - CIVIL ACTION

NOTICE

You have been sued in court. If you wish to defend against the claims set forth in the following pages, you must take action within twenty (20) days after this complaint and notice are served, by entering a written appearance personally or by attorney and filing in writing with the court your defenses or objections to the claims set forth against you. You are warned that if you fail to do so the case may proceed without you and a judgment may be entered against you by the court without further notice for any money claimed in the complaint or for any other claims or relief requested by the plaintiff. You may lose money or property or other rights important to you.

You should take this paper to your lawyer at once. If you do not have a lawyer or cannot afford one, go to or telephone the office set forth below to find out where you can get legal help.

Philadelphia Bar Association
Lawyer Referral and
Information Service
One Reading Center
Philadelphia, Pennsylvania 19107
215-238-1701

AVISO

Le han demandado a usted en la corte. Si usted quiere defenderse de estas demandas expuestas en las paginas siguientes, usted tiene veinte (20) dias de plazo al partir de la fecha de la demanda y la notificacion. Hace falta asentar una compancia escrita o en persona o con un abogado y entregar a la corte en forma escrita sus defensas o sus objeciones a las demandas en contra de su persona. Sea avisado que si usted no se defiende, la corta tomara medidas y puede continuar la demanda en contra suya sin previo aviso o notificacion. Ademas, la corte puede decidir a favor del demandante y requiere que usted cumpla con todas las provisiones de esta demanda. Usted puede perer dinero o sus propiedades u oetros derechos importantes para usted.

Lieva esta demanda a un abogado immediatamente. Si no tiene abogado o si no tiene el dinero suficiente de pagartal servicio, vaya en persona o llame por telefono a la oficina cuya direccion se encuentra escrita abajo para averiguar donde se puede conseguir asistencia legal.

Asociacion de Licenciados de Filadelfia
Servicio de Referencia e
Informacion Legal
One Reading Center
Filadelfia, Pennsylvania 19107
215-238-1701

Court rules require an attorney to sign all documents filed. State court rules in most jurisdictions follow Federal Rules of Civil Procedure Rule 11. If a person is filing on his or her own behalf, called a ***pro se*** filing, an attorney's signature is not required. In federal court, Rule 11 governs the attorney's obligations and the potential penalties, as discussed in the following cases.

Web Exploration

Go to. www.eff.org/IP/digitalradio/XM_complaint.pdf to view a copy of a complaint filed in U.S. district court.

IN THE WORDS OF THE COURT . . .

NOTICE PLEADING

CONLEY V. GIBSON, 355 U.S. 41, 47–48 (1957) 78 S.CT. 99

. . . The respondents also argue that the complaint failed to set forth specific facts to support its general allegations of discrimination and that its dismissal is therefore proper. The decisive answer to this is that the Federal Rules of Civil Procedure do not require a claimant to set out in detail the facts upon which he bases his claim. To the contrary, all the Rules require is "a short and plain statement of the claim" that will give the defendant fair notice of what the plaintiff's claim is and the grounds upon which it rests. The illustrative forms appended to the Rules plainly demonstrate this. Such simplified "notice pleading" is made possible by the liberal opportunity for discovery and the other pretrial procedures established by the Rules to disclose more precisely the basis of both claim and defense and to define more narrowly the disputed facts and issues. Following the simple guide of Rule 8(f) that "all pleadings shall be so construed as to do substantial justice," we have no doubt that petitioners' complaint adequately set forth a claim and gave the respondents fair notice of its basis. The Federal Rules reject the approach that pleading is a game of skill in which one misstep by counsel may be decisive to the outcome and accept the principle that the purpose of pleading is to facilitate a proper decision on the merits. Cf. *Maty v. Grasselli Chemical Co.*, 303 U.S. 197. . . .

IN THE WORDS OF THE COURT . . .

FEDERAL RULE 11

LEAHY V. EDMONDS SCHOOL DISTRICT,
NO. C07-1979 RSM (W.D. WASH., MARCH 2, 2009)

. . . C. Rule 11 Sanctions

Defendants also argue that Plaintiff's counsel should personally be liable for attorney's fees under Rule 11. Rule 11 generally provides guidelines for attorneys to follow when submitting a pleading to the court. The rule "imposes a duty on attorneys to certify that they have conducted a reasonable inquiry and have determined that any papers filed with the court are well grounded in fact, legally tenable, and not interposed for any improper purpose." *Cooter & Gell v. Hartmarx Corp.*, 496 U.S. 384, 393 (1990). "The central purpose of Rule 11 is to deter baseless filing in district court[.]" *Id.* (internal quotations omitted). Additionally, "[s]anctions must be imposed on the signer of a paper if the paper is 'frivolous.'" *In re Keegan Mgmt. Co.*, 78 F.3d 431, 434 (9th Cir. 1996). Although the word "frivolous" does not appear in the text of the rule, it is well-established that it denotes "a filing that is *both* baseless *and* made without a reasonable and competent inquiry." *Id.* (citation omitted) (emphasis in original). The Ninth Circuit has explained that "there are basically three types of submitted papers which warrant sanctions: factually frivolous (not 'well grounded in fact'); legally frivolous (not 'warranted by existing law or a good faith argument for the extension, modification, or reversal of existing law'); and papers 'interposed for an improper purpose.'" *Business Guides, Inc. v. Chromatic Commc'ns Enterprises, Inc.*, 892 F.2d 802, 808 (9th Cir. 1989) (quoting FRCP *11*). . . .

CHECKLIST Preparing a Complaint

- ☐ Caption
- ☐ Body of the complaint
- ☐ Identification of parties
- ☐ Jurisdictional averments
- ☐ Background facts or those facts that apply to all causes of action
- ☐ Element of causes of action
- ☐ Negligence
- ☐ Breach of contract
- ☐ Professional malpractice
- ☐ Class actions
- ☐ Allegation of damages
- ☐ Prayer for relief (wherefore clause)
- ☐ Signature of attorney
- ☐ Affidavit or verification

Filing Fee

Filing fees must be paid at the time of filing of the complaint or summons to start the lawsuit, unless waived by the court. Most rules provide that the action is not considered commenced until the applicable fees have been paid to the court. In most cases, this is not an issue. However, it may be an issue if the person filing the pleading does not have the required fees and the applicable statute of limitations is going to expire unless the action is properly commenced by the deadline. Most court offices are open during specific business hours and expect that normal business, including the filing of pleadings, will occur during those hours. However, there is usually a procedure that provides an after-business-hours method for filing time-critical documents. It may involve a clerk or deputy who is on call, or a judge who is available to accept documents. It is not that unusual for a potential client to appear with a claim on the day the statute of limitations is to expire. The person who first learns of this deadline is the person conducting the initial interview, usually a paralegal conducting a screening interview. Therefore, paralegals must be alert to the issue and ask questions to determine the possible claims and dates of the alleged wrong. If a statute of limitations issue appears to be imminent, the paralegal must immediately contact his or her supervising attorney.

Electronic Filing

Increasingly, jurisdictions require electronic filing of pleadings and documents. Some courts permit but do not require electronic filing of all pleadings; others allow filings that do not add or change named parties. In either event, the requirements for electronic filing are not uniform or standardized. Each court has its own set of rules and requirements. The specific state or federal rules and local court rules for each court must be checked. The rules are constantly being changed as technology allows and experience requires. Typically, the complaint accompanied by the civil cover sheet will be the document that causes the creation of a file in the court's computer system. Some courts require that a request for permission to use electronic filing be submitted with the complaint. Other forms, such as that from a California court shown in Exhibit 7.4, seek permission of the litigants for consent to electronic filing. Exhibit 7.5 shows a form for the U.S. district court Waiver of the Service of Summons. Always consult the current local rules for the requirements for electronic filing, including the necessary format of the submitted files (Microsoft Word, Corel WordPerfect, PDF, PDF/A, or other file format). The importance of following the local rules cannot be underestimated with regard to electronic filing requirements.

Service of the Complaint

Summons A court order directing the defendant to appear in court and answer the complaint.

Defendant The party who files the answer.

In some jurisdictions, after a complaint has been filed, the court issues a **summons**—a court order directing the **defendant** to appear in court and answer the complaint. A fundamental requirement is that notice be given to the defendant. A sheriff, another government official, or a private process server may serve the complaint on the defendant and, where required, the summons. In some cases, as when the defendant cannot be found to be served personally, the defendant may be served by other means, such as by publication.

After filing the complaint and having the summons issued, the plaintiff must serve the defendant. In federal court, service must be made within 120 days. In state courts, the time period varies, but typically service must be made within 30 to 60 days

Exhibit 7.4 California consent to electronic service

(New, 12-01-02)

Form 13.
Consent to Electronic Service
Pursuant to Ninth Circuit Rule 25-3.3

I agree that ____________________________________,
(law firm or name of unrepresented litigant)

who represents ____________________ may electronically serve me
(name of party)

with copies of all documents filed with the court.

Electronic service shall be accomplished by (*check all that apply*):

______________ facsimile transmission to ______________ (facsimile number)

______________ electronic mail at ______________ (electronic mail address) limited to documents created in the following word proceeding formats: ____________________

______________ both facsimile transmission to ______________ (facsimile number) and electronic mail at ___________ (electronic mail address) limited to documents created in the following word processing formats______________

______________ Electronic service must be accompanied by simultaneous service by mail or commercial carrier of a paper copy of the electronically served document.

DATED: ______________ ____________________________

Attorney for ______________________
(name of party)
Or Pro Se Litigant

Exhibit 7.5 U.S. district court Waiver of the Service of Summons

AO 399 (01/09) Waiver of the Service of Summons

UNITED STATES DISTRICT COURT

for the

____

______________________ *Plaintiff*	)	
v.	)	Civil Action No. ______
______________________ *Defendant*	)	

WAIVER OF THE SERVICE OF SUMMONS

To: ______________________
(Name of the plaintiff's attorney or unrepresented plaintiff)

I have received your request to waive service of a summons in this action along with a copy of the complaint, two copies of this waiver form, and a prepaid means of returning one signed copy of the form to you.

I, or the entity I represent, agree to save the expense of serving a summons and complaint in this case.

I understand that I, or the entity I represent, will keep all defenses or objections to the lawsuit, the court's jurisdiction, and the venue of the action, but that I waive any objections to the absence of a summons or of service.

I also understand that I, or the entity I represent, must file and serve an answer or a motion under Rule 12 within 60 days from ______________, the date when this request was sent (or 90 days if it was sent outside the United States). If I fail to do so, a default judgment will be entered against me or the entity I represent.

Date: ______________

____
Signature of the attorney or unrepresented party

____
Printed name of party waiving service of summons

____
Printed name

____
Address

____
E-mail address

____
Telephone number

Duty to Avoid Unnecessary Expenses of Serving a Summons

Rule 4 of the Federal Rules of Civil Procedure requires certain defendants to cooperate in saving unnecessary expenses of serving a summons and complaint. A defendant who is located in the United States and who fails to return a signed waiver of service requested by a plaintiff located in the United States will be required to pay the expenses of service, unless the defendant shows good cause for the failure.

"Good cause" does *not* include a belief that the lawsuit is groundless, or that it has been brought in an improper venue, or that the court has no jurisdiction over this matter or over the defendant or the defendant's property.

If the waiver is signed and returned, you can still make these and all other defenses and objections, but you cannot object to the absence of a summons or of service.

If you waive service, then you must, within the time specified on the waiver form, serve an answer or a motion under Rule 12 on the plaintiff and file a copy with the court. By signing and returning the waiver form, you are allowed more time to respond than if a summons had been served.

after the initial filing. Failure to serve the complaint within the time limit can result in the complaint being dismissed. If it is dismissed on this basis, the plaintiff may file a motion seeking the court's permission to reinstate the complaint and reissue the summons.

The defendant also has a time limit within which to respond to the complaint by filing a responsive pleading. This time period begins to run when the complaint is actually served (not on the last day the complaint could have been served). In federal court, if served by a U.S. marshal, private process server, or other authorized person, the period is 20 days. If served by notice and waiver, it is 60 days. Calculating the due date is as important for the defendant as it is for the plaintiff. Failure to respond in a timely fashion allows the plaintiff to obtain a default judgment against the defendant. Default is not automatic, but it is a right the plaintiff may enforce. The defendant must know the rule and properly calculate the due date to avoid a **default judgment** for nonaction.

All pleadings after the initial complaint and answer also have a response time. This includes the plaintiff's response to counterclaims or affirmative defenses asserted by the defendant, and the responses to any motions.

SIDEBAR

RECOGNIZING A FRIVOLOUS LAWSUIT

Although paralegals are not lawyers, they should still have some concept of whether a lawsuit has merit or not. Consider the following case: The Chungs are Korean residents who came to the United States to open a dry cleaning business. They eventually owned three dry cleaning shops in the Washington, D.C., area. Roy L. Pearson was a District of Columbia administrative judge who was a customer at one of the Chungs' dry cleaning stores. Pearson walked to the Chungs' store because he did not have a car.

The Chungs had signs in the window of their store that stated "Satisfaction Guaranteed" and "Same Day Service." Pearson claimed that the Chungs lost a pair of his pants. He sued the Chungs for $67 million in damages, alleging that they had violated the D.C. consumer protection act. Pearson later reduced his demand to $54 million. He demanded $3 million for violation of the "Satisfaction Guaranteed" sign, $2 million for mental suffering and inconvenience, $500,000 in legal fees for representing himself, $6 million for ten years of rental car fees to drive to another cleaners, and $51 million to help similarly dissatisfied D.C. customers. Pearson stated that he had no choice but to take on "the awesome responsibility" of suing the Chungs on behalf of every D.C. resident. A website was set up to accept donations for the Chungs' legal fees of $83,000, which was eventually paid by donations.

Roy L. Pearson v. Soo Chung, et al., Superior Court of the District of Columbia (2009)

Do you think Pearson had a legitimate legal case, or was this a frivolous lawsuit?

Responsive Pleadings

Upon receipt of the complaint, petition, or summons, the defendant and counsel have some critical decisions to make. In many instances, defendants may already have anticipated that a lawsuit would be filed against them. Being served with a complaint may not be a surprise, but the quickly approaching deadlines can be intimidating for the legal defense team, especially if the client did not promptly advise them of having been served. If served personally, the defendant has a limited time in which to file a responsive pleading. In federal court, that time period is 20 days, which is probably insufficient time to thoroughly investigate and respond. Just as plaintiffs frequently wait until the last day before the statute of limitations has run, defendants frequently wait to meet with an attorney until the date the response is due. The first step may be to request from opposing counsel an **extension of time to respond**. In federal court and some state courts, the team must prepare and file a stipulation with the court if opposing counsel agrees to an extension. If the request is refused, the defense team must file a motion asking the court to grant an extension of time to respond.

Answer

The defendant is required to respond to the allegations contained in the plaintiff's complaint. This is done by preparing, filing, and serving an **answer**. Like a complaint, an answer is made up of the same sections, whether in federal or state court: a caption, numbered paragraphs, a prayer for relief, and alternative defenses.

When responding to the averments of the complaint, there are two basic choices:

1. **Admitted**—the facts of the averment in the complaint are true, or
2. **Denied**—the facts of the averment in the complaint are not true.

In some jurisdictions, simply denying averments of the complaint is not sufficient. The word "denied" with nothing more is considered a **general denial**, and the averment of the complaint is treated as if it were "admitted." In these jurisdictions, the reasons for the denial must be listed. These reasons may include the following types of responses:

1. Denied, as the facts are not as stated (and set forth specifically the alternate facts).

2. Denied, as after reasonable investigation the defendant lacks adequate knowledge to determine whether the information is true.
3. Denied, as the averment represents a conclusion of law to which no response is required.

In some instances, when the complaint is directed at multiple defendants, there may be paragraphs in the complaint that apply only to another defendant. In that event, the appropriate response would be: "No answer is required as the averments are addressed to another defendant."

Cross-Complaint and Reply

A defendant who believes that he or she has been injured by the plaintiff can file, in addition to an answer, a **cross-complaint**, or counterpetition as it is called in some jurisdictions, against the plaintiff in addition to an answer. In the cross-complaint, the defendant (now the **cross-complainant**) sues the plaintiff (now the **cross-defendant**) for damages or some other remedy. The original plaintiff must file a **reply**, or answer to the cross-complaint. Exhibit 7.6 is a sample answer. The reply—which can include affirmative defenses—must be filed with the court and served on the original defendant. Exhibit 7.7 illustrates the pleadings process.

Cross-complaint A pleading filed by a defendant against a plaintiff to seek damages or some other remedy.

Reply A pleading filed by the original plaintiff to answer the defendant's cross-complaint.

Web Exploration

Go to http://www.statutes-of-limitations.com/state/. On the left-hand side of the page is a list of states. Click on your state to find out what the statute of limitations is for filing a negligence action in your state.

Intervention and Consolidation

If other persons have an interest in the outcome of the dispute, they may step in and become parties to the lawsuit—called an **intervention**. For instance, in a lawsuit over ownership of a piece of real estate, a bank that has made a secured loan on the property can intervene because it has a stake in the outcome.

If several plaintiffs have filed separate lawsuits stemming from the same fact situation against the same defendant, the court can initiate a **consolidation** of the cases into one case if it would not cause undue prejudice to the parties. For example, if a commercial airplane crashes, killing and injuring many people, the court may consolidate all of the lawsuits against the defendant airplane company.

Web Exploration

Locate the U.S. district court that serves the county or parish in which you live. Go to that court's website and find and review the "Court Forms" for that court. http://uscourts.gov/.

Discovery

LEARNING OBJECTIVE 3

Explain the purpose of discovery in the litigation process.

The fundamental purpose of discovery is to obtain evidence that may be used at trial, as well as information that may lead to evidence that may be used at trial. This purpose remains the same whether the legal team is dealing with paper or electronic documents. In the past, most documents produced in discovery were on paper. But today, the documents are increasingly in an electronic form. Changes in discovery practice are the result of the switch from paper to electronically stored information. Discovery procedures had to be updated as governments, businesses, and individuals saved more of their records in electronic form. In the early days of personal computers, there were no standards for the creation and storage of electronic information. For example, for word processing some offices used WordPerfect while others used Microsoft Word, each with its own electronic file format. In addition to these word processing programs, there were many lesser-known programs used in some major corporations. Added to these word processor variations were the many specialized database formats used for the creation and storage of financial and other numerical data. Even today, there is still no universally accepted standard or common set of programs. Among the continuing issues is the inability of some programs to read the formats of other programs, or even different versions of the same program. In addition, there is no standard among the leading computer operating systems like Apple,

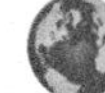

Web Exploration

Visit http://www.americanbar.org/groups/departments_offices/legal_technology_resources.htmlfand and search e-filing for a discussion of e-filings and the use of electronic documents.

Exhibit 7.6 Sample state answer to fact-pleading complaint

IN THE SUPREME COURT OF NEW YORK FOR ALBANY COUNTY

B.K., a minor by her Parents and guardians, Janice Knowles and Steven Knowles, Plaintiff	: : :	No.: 2007 - 19743 - N- 11 Civil Action - Negligence
v.	:	
Ronald Clemmons, Lower Council School District, Bud Smith, and Ace Trucking Company, Defendants	: : :	Jury Trial Demanded Attorney ID No. 097531

ANSWER OF DEFENDANT CLEMMONS TO PLAINTIFFS COMPLAINT
WITH AFFIRMATIVE DEFENSES

NOW comes Defendant Clemmons, by his attorneys, Li and Salva, and answers the complaint alleging as follows:

1. Admitted.
2. Admitted.
3. Admitted.
4. Admitted upon information and belief.
5. Admitted upon information and belief.
6. Admitted.
7. Admitted upon information and belief.
8. Admitted.
9. Admitted.
10. Admitted upon information and belief.
11. Admitted.
12. Admitted.
13. Denied that defendant Clemmons asked a chaperone o[r] anyone else for directions to the Pumpkin Patch. Although Clemmons had never been to the Pumpkin Patch he was familiar with the location and knew where it was and how to get there. A chaperone did provide a map and directions but it is specifically denied that this was at the request of defendant Clemmons.
14. Admitted in part and denied in part. It is admitted that each bus seat was equipped with three color coded lap belts, one for each passenger in a seat. It is specifically denied that each student on the bus was belted. After reason investigation, answering defendant lacks adequate knowledge, information or belief as the truth of the allegations concerning each child being belted or the reasons therefore. Strict proof thereof is demanded at trial.
15. Admitted.
16. Admitted in part and denied in part. It is admitted that Clemmons exited at the wrong exit, exit #24, reentered the Highway and continued to the correct exit, #23. The remaining allegations of the paragraph are denied. It is specifically denied that Clemmons was confused about the directions or the exit number. To the contrary, Clemmons was not confused when he exited at Exit 24. There was a traffic accident on the highway with police diverting thru-traffic around the

(continued)

Exhibit 7.6 Sample state answer to fact-pleading complaint *(continued)*

accident by use of the exit and entrance ramps of Exit 24. It is specifically denied that Clemmons turned the bus around on the exit ramp for Exit 24. To the contrary, Clemmons was following the directions of state police diverting traffic from the highway to the ramp and back onto the highway to go around an accident blocking the lanes.

17. Admitted.
18. Admitted.
19. Admitted based upon information and belief.
20. Denied as stated. The yelling and screaming of the children was not limited to the approach of the intersection. The children were uncontrolled, jumping about and switching seats, and loudly singing, yelling, and screaming throughout the ride from Public School No. 18. After reasonable investigation, answering defendant is unable to determine whether this behavior was attributable to seeing signs for the Pumpkin Patch or simply the uncontrolled behavior of the children.
21. Denied as stated. It is true that answering defendant slowed as he approached the intersection, which was accomplished by removing his foot from the accelerator of the vehicle. Upon attempting to apply the brakes to further slow and stop the vehicle, the defendant discovered the brakes were not operating properly, thus causing the vehicle to enter the intersection without stopping. It is admitted that the vehicle was then struck by a dump truck.

Count I
Plaintiff v. Defendant Clemmons

22. No answer is required to the averments set forth in this paragraph. To the extent [an] answer is required Defendant Clemmons incorporates paragraphs 1 through 21 hereof as though fully set forth at length.
23. Denied as a conclusion of law. Further denied that Defendant Clemmons was negligent or failed to observe the rules of the road. To the contrary, Clemmons complied with all rules of the road including following the instructions of the police officers controlling traffic patterns around an accident scene. Failure to bring the vehicle to a stop was a result of mechanical failure of the brakes not the action or inaction of Clemmons.
24. Denied as a conclusion of law and for the reasons set forth in paragraph 23 which are incorporated herein by reference.
25. Denied as a conclusion of law and for reasons set forth in paragraph 23 which are incorporated herein by reference. Further denied, as after reasonable investigation, answering defendant lacks adequate knowledge as to any of the injuries suffered by the plaintiff. Strict proof thereof is demanded at the trial of this matter.
26. Denied as a conclusion of law. Further denied, as after reasonable investigation, answering defendant lacks adequate knowledge as to any of the injuries suffered by the plaintiff. Strict proof thereof is demanded at the trial of this matter.

WHEREFORE, Defendant respectfully requests that plaintiff's complaint be dismissed with prejudice.

Paragraphs 27 - 40. No answer is required as they are addressed to defendants other than Clemmons.

Affirmative Defenses

27. Defendant Clemmons incorporates by reference his answers to paragraphs 1 through 40.
28. Plaintiff's claims are barred by the statute of limitations.
29. Plaintiff's claims are barred by the doctrine of sovereign immunity.
30. Plaintiff's claims are barred by the doctrine of contributory negligence.
31. Plaintiff's claims against the answering defendant are barred by the doctrine of respondeat superior.

WHEREFORE, Defendant respectfully requests plaintiff's complaint be dismissed.

Exhibit 7.7 Pleadings process

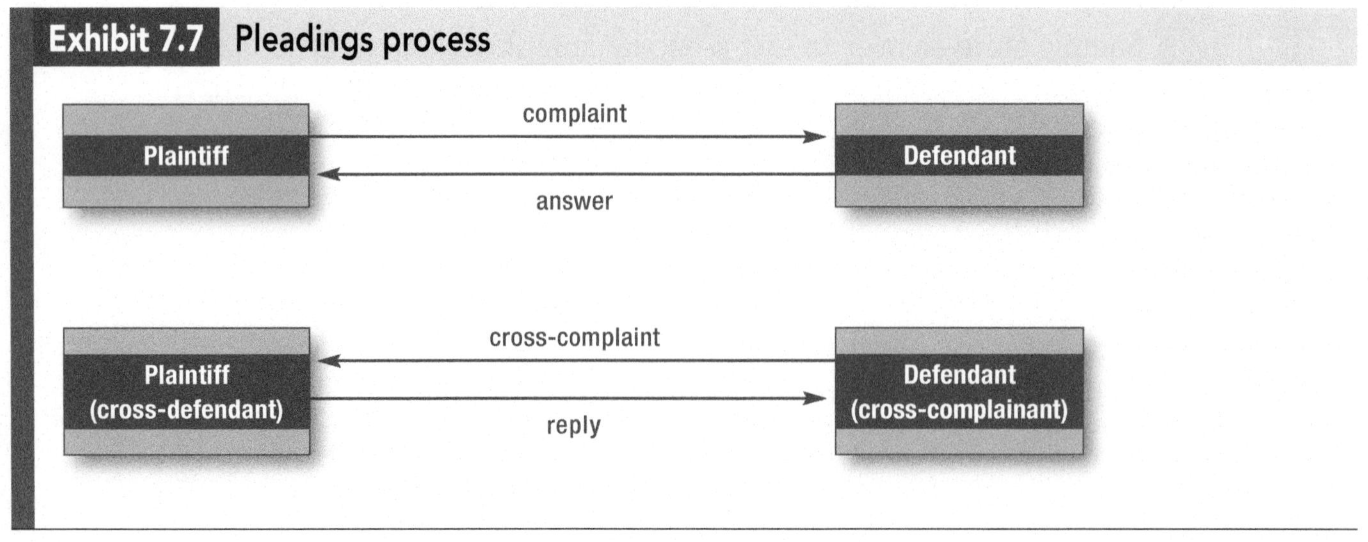

Exhibit 7.8 Sample time deadlines using Lawyers Toolbox

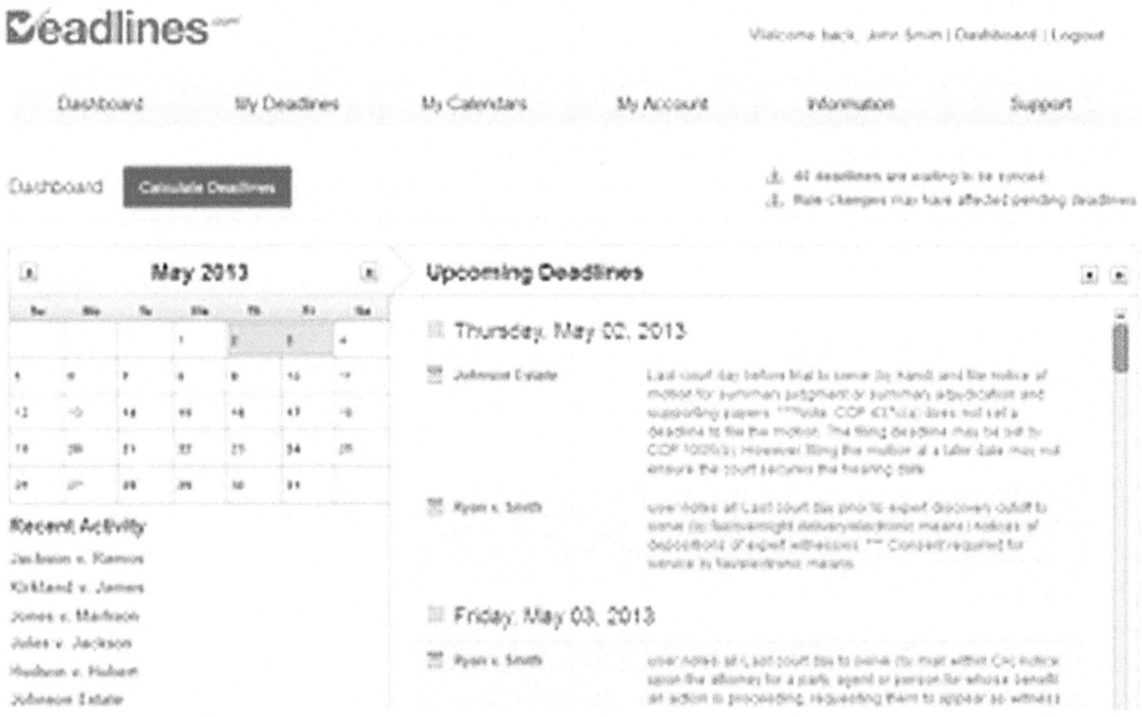

Reprinted with permission of Aderant

Microsoft, and Linux, which continue to compete for the computer market, or for smartphones like Android or Apple.

Advances in communication technology have created new sources of potential trial evidence in the form of video and audio files, emails, text messages, and social media data. Each type of media presents its own technical issues in locating, retrieving, and reviewing sources for evidence. As technology's playing field changes, the courts must establish rules for the discovery of electronically stored information.

The methods used to locate, preserve, and produce these cyber documents require a new set of skills. In large or complex cases, it is often necessary for a paralegal to work with information technology experts. Successful discovery also requires a familiarity with the rules of the court, and the rules relating to electronic files are becoming increasingly important.

Litigation Hold

A client who is concerned about a potential lawsuit can easily destroy evidence contained in electronic files. It is sometimes as easy as hitting the delete key. Paper documents can also be "deleted," usually with the help of a good paper shredder. If a client knows a lawsuit is imminent, is it appropriate to destroy files?

The common law and amendments to the Federal Rules of Civil Procedure suggest that once a client has a reasonable belief that litigation may arise from a dispute, a duty arises to preserve all documents related to that dispute, both paper and electronic. A lawsuit need not have been filed or a complaint served for the duty to apply, only a reasonable belief that litigation may arise. But it has been left to the courts to determine what constitutes a "reasonable belief."

An emerging line of cases suggests that the duty to preserve information arises if the party knows or should have known of the possibility of litigation. Preservation may require placing a matter and all documents related to it on **litigation hold**. A litigation hold is a notice to the company and its employees not to destroy or alter any documents related to the dispute, and to save them in their present forms. When litigation is filed, or when there is a reasonable expectation of litigation, the individual or company must cease any activity that will result in the destruction or loss of records.

When litigation is actually commenced, counsel must issue a litigation hold letter to the client. A sample letter is shown in Exhibit 7.9. Court opinions have held that lawyers have an affirmative duty to follow up with the client to ensure that the litigation hold procedures are implemented and maintained. This burden applies to both inside and outside counsel.

The Duty to Preserve Evidence

In addition to the obligations imposed by the rules of procedure, there is also a well-recognized common law duty to preserve evidence:

> Case law has developed the rule that when it is reasonably foreseeable that a claim may be asserted, a party must preserve relevant information.
> *Shamis v. Ambassador Factors Corp., 34 F. Supp. 2d 879, 888-889 (S.D.N.Y. 1999)*

It is clear that when actual notice of litigation is received, the duty to preserve potential evidence exists. But it is less clear at what point before litigation the duty arises. The case law is not consistent, with some cases taking the position that any preliminary activity that may lead to litigation creates the duty.

Case Evaluation

By answering each other's questions, the parties share information about the facts, documents, statements, and expert witnesses related to the dispute. By openly sharing information that may be used at trial, each side is forced to evaluate its case and its opponent's case. Seeing all the available evidence allows each side to determine the ability to meet its respective burdens of proof. Drawing on prior experience or similar reported cases, each side can put a potential value on a trial outcome. In many instances, the decision to try or settle a case is a business decision. Thus the sides must

Exhibit 7.9 Sample litigation hold letter

Sample Preservation Letter—To Client

[Date]

RE: [Case Name]—Data Preservation

Dear:

Please be advised that the Office of General Counsel assistance believes electronically stored information to be an important and irreplaceable source of discovery and/or evidence in [description of event, transaction, business unit, product, etc.]. The lawsuit requires preservation of all information from [Corporation's] computer systems, removable electronic media, and other locations relating to [description of event, transaction, business unit, product, etc.]. This includes, but is not limited to, e-mail and other electronic communication, word processing documents, spreadsheets, databases, calendars, telephone logs, contact manager information, Internet usage files, and network access information.

[Corporation] should also preserve the following platforms in the possession of the [Corporation] or a third party under the control of the [Corporation] (such as an employee or outside vendor under contract): databases, networks, computer systems, including legacy systems (hardware and software), servers, archives, backup or disaster recovery systems, tapes, discs, drives, cartridges and other storage media, laptops, personal computers, Internet data, personal digital assistants, handheld wireless devices, mobile telephones, paging devices, and audio systems (including voicemail).

Employees must take every reasonable step to preserve this information until further notice from the Office of General Counsel. Failure to do so could result in extreme penalties against [Corporation].

All of the information contained in the letter should be preserved for the following dates and time periods: [List dates and times].

Preservation Obligations

The laws and rules prohibiting destruction of evidence apply to electronically stored information in the same manner that they apply to other evidence. Due to its format, electronic information is easily deleted, modified, or corrupted. Accordingly, [Corporation] must take every reasonable step to preserve this information until the final resolution of this matter.

This includes, but is not limited to, an obligation to:

- Discontinue all data destruction and backup tape recycling policies;
- Preserve and not dispose of relevant hardware unless an exact replica of the file (a mirror image) is made

Kroll Ontrack.

ask whether the cost of a trial is outweighed by the potential recovery. If both sides are well prepared, their evaluations may be surprisingly close, and settlement may be within reach.

Preparing for Trial

If properly conducted, discovery can eliminate the potential for surprises in evidence presented at trial. Many of the "surprise" witnesses and evidence seen in television courtroom dramas would not be possible under actual court rules. Among these rules is the ethical obligation of fairness to opposing counsel and parties, which has been adopted in most states. Rule 3.4 of the Illinois Rules of Professional Conduct is set forth below.

Facilitating Settlement

Properly conducted discovery facilitates settlements. Careful analysis of the evidence revealed through discovery enables the legal team to evaluate the client's case and

ETHICAL PERSPECTIVES

Illinois Rules of Professional Conduct of 2010

RULE 3.4: FAIRNESS TO OPPOSING PARTY AND COUNSEL

A lawyer shall not:

(a) unlawfully obstruct another party's access to evidence or unlawfully alter, destroy or conceal a document or other material having potential evidentiary value. A lawyer shall not counsel or assist another person to do any such act;

(b) falsify evidence, counsel or assist a witness to testify falsely, or offer an inducement to a witness that is prohibited by law;

(c) knowingly disobey an obligation under the rules of a tribunal, except for an open refusal based on an assertion that no valid obligation exists;

(d) in pretrial procedure, make a frivolous discovery request or fail to make reasonably diligent effort to comply with a legally proper discovery request by an opposing party;

(e) in trial, allude to any matter that the lawyer does not reasonably believe is relevant or that will not be supported by admissible evidence, assert personal knowledge of facts in issue except when testifying as a witness, or state a personal opinion as to the justness of a cause, the credibility of a witness, the culpability of a civil litigant or the guilt or innocence of an accused; or

(f) request a person other than a client to refrain from voluntarily giving relevant information to another party unless:
   (1) the person is a relative or an employee or other agent of a client; and
   (2) the lawyer reasonably believes that the person's interests will not be adversely affected by refraining from giving such information.

Adopted July 1, 2009, effective January 1, 2010.
Source: http://www.state.il.us/court/supremecourt/rules/art_viii/ArtVIII_NEW.htm#3.4

that of the opposing side. Both sides are in a better position to evaluate their chances of success at trial based on the weight of evidence and the perceived credibility of witnesses.

Preserving Oral Testimony

Discovery can also be used for preserving oral testimony. There are times when witnesses may not be available to attend trial to testify. Examples include witnesses who are gravely ill and not expected to live until trial, those who are elderly or incapacitated and physically unable to come to the courthouse, and those who are outside the geographical jurisdiction of the court. Under limited circumstances, the deposition testimony of these unavailable witnesses may be presented at trial. The deposition of witnesses is given the same treatment as if the witness were in court testifying in person.

Federal Rules of Civil Procedure—Rule 26(a) Disclosure Requirements

For many years, much of the key information in a case was disclosed only after a formal written discovery request had been issued. In many cases, no action was taken on a file until one side moved the case forward with a formal discovery request. Now,

Advice from the Field

THE ELECTRONIC PARALEGAL

William Mulkeen, Past President, American Association for Paralegal Education

Paralegals must start thinking about the training and skills necessary to work on the electronic civil litigation team emerging in the present; for many the future is here now. The process of electronic discovery; the gathering and acquisition of electronic records; the filing and preparation of this discovery; and the presentation of it in electronic courtrooms is already upon us. Demand for advanced litigation skills including an understanding of the role of electronic databases and the management of electronic documents is becoming commonplace. Paralegals must understand the technology and the ethical considerations and implications of these technological advances.

under Rule 26(a), everything the legal team intends to rely upon to prove its claims must be disclosed early in the litigation. Insufficient time to investigate the claim is not a valid excuse for failure to comply.

Rule 26. Duty to Disclose; General Provisions Governing Discovery
(a) Required Disclosures.
  (1) *Initial Disclosure.*
    (A) *In General.* Except as exempted by Rule 26(a)(1)(B) or as otherwise stipulated or ordered by the court, a party must, without awaiting a discovery request, provide to the other parties:
      (i) the name and, if known, the address and telephone number of each individual likely to have discoverable information—along with the subjects of that information—that the disclosing party may use to support its claims or defenses, unless the use would be solely for impeachment;
      (ii) a copy—or a description by category and location—of all documents, electronically stored information, and tangible things that the disclosing party has in its possession, custody, or control and may use to support its claims or defenses, unless the use would be solely for impeachment;

The benefits of mandatory disclosure are twofold: (1) it provides for the early evaluation and settlement of claims; and (2) it reduces the amount, nature, and time necessary to conduct formal discovery. From a practical standpoint, the plaintiff's legal team must be prepared for disclosure at or shortly after filing the complaint.

While the new rules contemplate a specific time frame for disclosure, they do permit the attorneys to agree to some other time frame. Although the attorneys may agree to extend that time, the judge at the scheduling conference may encourage them to conclude the disclosure at a faster pace. The investigation that might have occurred under prior rules must now be completed before filing suit. For the defense team, the time to investigate and comply is very short. There is no time for procrastination in investigating and establishing the grounds to defend the claims.

IN THE WORDS OF THE COURT . . .

United States District Court, S.D. New York

SECURITIES AND EXCHANGE COMMISSION V. COLLINS & AIKMAN CORP.,
NO. 07-2419 (S.D.N.Y., JANUARY 13, 2009)

II. The Discovery Disputes

This opinion addresses four distinct but related discovery disputes. Stockman served a document request pursuant to Rule 34, asking the SEC to "produce for inspection and copying the documents and things identified" in fifty-four separate categories.[FN4] In response, the SEC produced 1.7 million documents (10.6 million pages) maintained in thirty-six separate Concordance databases—many of which use different metadata protocols.[FN5] Stockman raises the following objections. *First*, the SEC failed to identify documents responsive to requests for documents supporting particular factual allegations in the Complaint, preferring instead to "dump" 1.7 million potentially responsive documents on Stockman and then suggesting that he is capable of searching them to locate those that are relevant. *Second*, the SEC failed to perform a reasonable search for documents relating to accounting principles governing supplier rebates—both in general and with respect to the automobile industry. Instead, the SEC unilaterally limited its search to three of its divisions—and only if those divisions possessed "centralized compilations of non-privileged documents dealing specifically with rebates or accounting for rebates in the automobile industry."[FN6] *Third*, the SEC improperly asserted the deliberative process privilege with regard to certain documents. *Fourth*, the SEC failed to search its own e-mails, attachments thereto, and other records created and maintained solely in an electronic format that related to either "(i) the investigation and litigation of this matter or (ii) the handling of several large cases unrelated to C & A and the Commission's regulatory role in matters relating to rebates and rebate accounting."[FN7] The objections were raised in a series of letters rather than by formal motion.[FN8]

1. Attorney Work Product Protection Applied to Selection and Compilation

The Second Circuit has recognized that the selection and compilation of documents may fall within the protection accorded to attorney work product, despite the general availability of documents from both parties and non-parties during discovery.[FN18] However, it has labeled this protection a "narrow exception"[FN19] aimed at preventing requests with "the precise goal of learning what the opposing attorney's thinking or strategy may be."[FN20] Moreover, equity favors rejection of work product protection to a compilation of documents that are otherwise unavailable or "beyond reasonable access."[FN21] The Circuit has suggested that a court may permit *ex parte* communication of the strategy the withholding party wishes to conceal and *in camera* review of documents, so that the court may make an educated assessment whether production of the compilation will reveal a party's litigation strategy.[FN22]

C. Discussion

1. Work Product Protection

It is first necessary to determine the level of protection afforded to the *selection* of documents by an attorney to support factual allegations in a complaint. Such documents are not "core" work product. Core work product constitutes

(continued)

legal documents drafted by an attorney—her mental impressions, conclusions, opinions, and legal theories. This highest level of protection applies to a compilation only if it is organized by legal theory or strategy. The SEC's theory—that every document or word reviewed by an attorney is "core" attorney work product—leaves nothing to surround the core.[FN35] The first step in responding to any document request is an attorney's assessment of relevance with regard to potentially responsive documents. It would make no sense to then claim that an attorney's determination of relevance shields the selection of responsive documents from production.

With few exceptions, *Rule 26(f)* requires the parties to hold a conference and prepare a discovery plan. The Rule specifically requires that the discovery plan state the parties' views and proposals with respect to "the subject on which discovery may be needed . . . and whether discovery should be conducted in phases or be limited to or focused on particular issues"[FN66] and "any issues about disclosure or discovery of electronically stored information. . . ."[FN67] Had this been accomplished, the Court might not now be required to intervene in this particular dispute. I also draw the parties' attention to the recently issued Sedona Conference Cooperation Proclamation, which urges parties to work in a cooperative rather than an adversarial manner to resolve discovery issues in order to stem the "rising monetary costs" of discovery disputes.[FN68] The Proclamation notes that courts see the discovery rules "as a mandate for counsel to act cooperatively."[FN69] Accordingly, counsel are directly to meet and confer forthwith and develop a workable search protocol that would reveal *at least some* of the information defendant seeks. If the parties cannot craft an agreement, the Court will consider the appointment of a Special Master to assist in this effort. . . . The logic of *Rule 34* supports this limitation. When records do not result from "routine and repetitive" activity, there is no incentive to organize them in a predictable system. The purpose of the Rule is to facilitate production of records in a useful manner and to minimize discovery costs; thus it is reasonable to require litigants who do not create and/or maintain records in a "routine and repetitive" manner to organize the records in a usable[FN55] fashion prior to producing them.

. . . By rough analogy to *Rule 803(6)*, the option of producing documents "as they are kept in the usual course of business" under *Rule 34* requires the producing party to meet either of two tests. *First*, this option is available to commercial enterprises or entities that function in the manner of commercial enterprises. *Second*, this option may also apply to records resulting from "regularly conducted activity."[FN53] Where a producing party's activities are not "routine and repetitive" such as to require a well-organized record-keeping system—in other words when the records do not result from an "ordinary course of business"—the party must produce documents according to the sole remaining option under *Rule 34*: "organize[d] and label[ed] . . . to correspond to the categories in the request."[FN54]

B. Applicable Law

"A district court has wide latitude to determine the scope of discovery."[FN62] The general scope of discovery in civil litigation is defined by *Rule 26(b)(1)*.

FN62. *In re Agent Orange Product Liab. Litig.*, 517 F.3d 76, 103 (2d Cir. 2008).

Parties may obtain discovery regarding any nonprivileged matter that is relevant to any party's claim or defense. . . . For good cause, the court may order discovery of any matter relevant to the subject matter involved in the action. Relevant information need not be admissible at the trial if the discovery appears reasonably calculated to lead to the discovery of admissible evidence.

. . . A court must limit the "frequency or extent of discovery" if one of three conditions in *Rule 26(b)(2)(C)* is present. The third limits production when "the burden or expense of the proposed discovery outweighs its likely benefit, considering the needs of the case, the amount in controversy, the parties' resources, the importance of the issues at stake in the action, and the importance of the discovery in resolving the issues."[FN63] The burden or expense may be defined in terms of time, expense, or even the "adverse consequences of the disclosure of sensitive, albeit unprivileged material."[FN64] . . .

VII. Conclusion

When a government agency initiates litigation, it must be prepared to follow the same discovery rules that govern private parties (albeit with the benefit of additional privileges such as deliberative process and state secrets). For the reasons set forth above, the SEC is ordered to produce or identify documents organized in response to Stockman's requests; to negotiate an appropriate search protocol to locate documents responsive to requests described above in Part IV; to submit materials allegedly covered by the deliberative process privilege to the Court for *in camera* review, together with a supporting memorandum within twenty days of the date of this Order; and to negotiate an appropriately limited search protocol with respect to agency e-mail. While the SEC has raised legitimate concerns about the burdens imposed by particular requests, it cannot unilaterally determine that those burdens outweigh defendants' need for discovery. At the very least, the SEC must engage in a good faith effort to negotiate with its adversaries and craft a search protocol designed to retrieve responsive information without incurring an unduly burdensome expense disproportionate to the size and needs of the case. The parties are therefore directed to engage in a cooperative effort to resolve the scope and design of a search with respect to the rebate issues and a search of e-mail created and maintained by the SEC. A conference is scheduled for February 13, at 5:00 pm, by which date the parties should have completed the meet and confer process in the hope of establishing an acceptable discovery program. If the parties remain at an impasse, the Court will be prepared to resolve further disputes and will consider the appointment of a Special Master to supervise the remaining discovery in this case.

SO ORDERED.

Information Subject to Mandatory Disclosure

Almost anything relied upon in developing the claim must be disclosed, regardless of whether it is admissible at trial. This disclosure includes the identity of witnesses, copies of documents, a computation of damages, and a copy of any insurance policy that may be used to satisfy a judgment obtained in the litigation.

FRCP 26

(b) Discovery Scope and Limits.

(1) *Scope in General.* Unless otherwise limited by court order, the scope of discovery is as follows: Parties may obtain discovery regarding any nonprivileged matter that is relevant to any party's claim or defense—and proportional to the needs of the case, considering the importance of the issues at stake in the action, the amount in controversy, the parties' relative access to relevant information, the parties' resources, the importance of the discovery in resolving the issues, and whether the burden or expense of the proposed discovery outweighs its likely benefit.

> Information within this scope of discovery need not be admissible in evidence to be discoverable.

In the past, information used to compute damages represented the plaintiff attorney's thought process and was typically not released as part of discovery under the work product privilege. Under the current rule, however, the attorney's value on the case is made known within months of the complaint being filed.

From the defense standpoint, the disclosure of insurance coverage, which is not admissible at trial, is a significant change from previous discovery rules. A key element in settling most cases is the existence and limitations of insurance coverage. With both the plaintiff's calculation of damages and the defendant's insurance coverage known within months of filing the lawsuit, the chances for settlement are increased.

Experts and Witnesses

Expert witnesses expected to be called at trial must also be identified, accompanied by a copy of the expert's qualifications, a list of publications the witness has written over the preceding 10 years, a statement of compensation, and a list of other cases in which the expert has testified. The most critical element to be shared is the written report of the expert's opinion. The report states what the expert is expected to say at trial, and must include the opinion of the expert, the basis of that opinion, the information relied upon, and any assumptions made. The disclosure of the expert and his or her report must be made at least 90 days prior to trial. Some courts require the disclosure of the expert at the time of the initial disclosure, or within 30 days of receipt of the expert's report. Many lawsuits become a battle of the experts. The early disclosure of the expert and his or her opinion often leads to early resolution of the case.

Depositions

Deposition Oral testimony given by a party or witness prior to trial. The testimony is given under oath and is transcribed.

A **deposition** is oral testimony given, under oath, by a party or witness prior to trial. The person giving the deposition is called the **deponent**. The parties to the lawsuit must give their depositions if the other party requests them to do so. The deposition of a **witness** can be given voluntarily on request, or pursuant to a **subpoena** (court order). The deponent can be required to bring documents to the deposition.

Depositions are used to preserve evidence (such as when the deponent is terminally ill or otherwise not available at trial), to find out information that may lead to evidence, or to impeach testimony given by witnesses at trial. Most depositions are taken at the office of one of the attorneys. The deponent is placed under oath and then asked oral questions by the attorneys for one or more parties to the lawsuit. The questions and answers are recorded in written form by a court reporter. Depositions can also be videotaped. The deponent is given an opportunity to correct his or her answers prior to signing the deposition, depending on local practice or rules.

Interrogatories

Interrogatories Written questions submitted by one party to another. The questions must be answered in writing within a stipulated time.

Interrogatories are written questions submitted by one party to a lawsuit to another party. The questions can be highly detailed, as illustrated by the sample interrogatory in Exhibit 7.10. In some jurisdictions, certain documents must be attached to the answers. A party is required to answer the interrogatories in writing within a specified time period (typically 60 to 90 days). An attorney usually helps with the preparation of the answers, which are signed under oath.

Exhibit 7.10 Sample interrogatory

THOMAS F. GOLDMAN & ASSOCIATES
138 N. State Street
Newtown, PA 18940
(123) 555-1234

KATHRYN KELSEY	:	COURT OF COMMON PLEAS
	:	PHILADELPHIA COUNTY
	:	
vs.	:	APRIL TERM, 2011
KATHRYN CARROLL	:	NO. 1234

INTERROGATORIES ADDRESSED TO KATHRYN KELSEY

You are to answer the following interrogatories under oath or verification pursuant to the Pa. R.C.P. 4005 and 4006 within thirty days from the service hereof. The answering party is under a duty to supplement responses to any questions with information discovered after these answers were given.

Also, a party or expert witness must amend prior responses if he/she obtains information upon the basis of which:

(a) he/she knows the response was incorrect when made; or

(b) he/she knows that the response, though correct when made, is no longer true.

The words "your vehicle" as used in the following interrogatories are defined as the motor vehicle you were operating at the time of the accident.

When a Standard Interrogatory uses the word: "identify", the party served with the Interrogatory must identify all documents, things and persons known to that party or to that party's attorney, and the address of all persons identified MUST be set forth.

Where a Standard Interrogatory is marked with an asterisk (*), a Request for Production may accompany the Interrogatory.

STANDARD INTERROGATORIES PURSUANT TO PHILADELPHIA RULE OF CIVIL PROCEDURE *4005

INJURIES AND DISEASES ALLEGED

1. State in detail the injuries or diseases that you allege that you suffered as a result of the accident referred to in the Complaint.

MEDICAL TREATMENT & REPORTS*

2. If you received medical treatment or examinations (including x-rays) because of injuries or diseases you suffered as a result of the accident, identify:
   (a) Each hospital at which you were treated or examined;
   (b) The dates on which each such treatment or examination at a hospital was rendered and the charges by the hospital for each;
   (c) Each doctor or practitioner by whom you were treated or examined;
   (d) The dates on which each such treatment or examination by a doctor or practitioner was rendered and the charges for each;
   (e) All reports regarding any medical treatment or examinations, setting forth the author and date of such reports.

Production of Documents

Production of documents
Request by one party to another to produce all documents relevant to the case prior to the trial.

Very often, particularly in complex business cases, a substantial portion of the lawsuit is based on information contained in documents (such as memoranda, correspondence, and company records). One party to a lawsuit may request that the other party produce all documents that are relevant to the case prior to trial. This is called **production of documents.** If the documents sought are too voluminous to be moved, are in permanent storage, or if moving the documents would disrupt ongoing business, the requesting party may be required to examine the documents at the other party's premises. Exhibit 7.11 is an example of a request for production of documents.

Exhibit 7.11 Sample request for production of documents

THOMAS F. GOLDMAN & ASSOCIATES
138 N. State Street
Newtown, PA 18940
(123) 555-1234

KATHRYN KELSEY	: COURT OF COMMON PLEAS : PHILADELPHIA COUNTY
vs.	: APRIL TERM, 2011
KATHRYN CARROLL	: NO. 1259

REQUEST TO PRODUCE UNDER PA R.C.P. 4033 and 4009
DIRECTED TO PLAINTIFFS

Within thirty (30) days of service, please produce for inspection and copying at the office of THOMAS F. GOLDMAN & ASSOCIATES, 138 North State Street, Newtown, Pennsylvania 18940, the following:

1. All photographs and/or diagrams of the area involved in this accident or occurrence, the locale or surrounding area of the site of this accident or occurrence, or any other matter or things involved in this accident or occurrence.
2. All property damage estimates rendered for any object belonging to the Plaintiffs which was involved in this accident or occurrence.
3. All property damage estimates rendered for any object belonging to the Defendant which was involved in this accident or occurrence.
4. All statements concerning this action or its subject matter previously made by any party or witness. The statements referred to here are defined by Pa. R.C.P. 4003.4.
5. All transcriptions and summaries of all interviews conducted by anyone acting on behalf of the Plaintiff or Plaintiff's insurance carrier of any potential witness and/or person(s) who has any knowledge of the accident or its surrounding circumstances
6. All inter-office memorandum between representative of Plaintiffs' insurance carrier or memorandum to Plaintiffs' insurance carrier's file concerning the manner in which the accident occurred.
7. All inter-office memorandum between representative of Plaintiffs' insurance carrier or memorandum to Plaintiffs' insurance carrier's file concerning the injuries sustained by the Plaintiffs.
8. A copy of any written accident report concerning this accident or occurrence signed by or prepared by Plaintiff for Plaintiffs' insurance carrier or Plaintiff's employers.
9. A copy of the face sheet of any policy of insurance providing coverage to Plaintiffs for the claim being asserted by Plaintiff in this action.
10. All bills, reports, and records from any and all physicians, hospitals, or other health-care providers concerning the injuries sustained by the Defendant from this accident or occurrence.
11. All photographs and/or motion pictures of any and all surveillance of Defendant performed by anyone acting on behalf of Plaintiff, Plaintiffs' insurer and/or Plaintiffs' attorney.
12. All photographs taken of Plaintiffs' motor vehicle which depict any damage to said vehicle which was sustained as a result of this accident.
13. All photographs taken of Defendant's motor vehicle which depict any damage to said vehicle which was sustained as a result of this accident.
14. Any and all reports, writings, memorandum, Xeroxed cards and/or other writings, lists or compilations of the Defendant and others with similar names as indexed by the Metropolitan Index Bureau, Central Index Bureau or other Index Bureau in possession of the Plaintiffs or the Plaintiffs' insurance carrier.

Physical and Mental Examination

A **physical and mental examination** (in some jurisdictions called an **independent medical examination**, or **IME**) is permitted where the physical or mental condition of one of the parties is at issue. In a personal injury action, the physical injuries suffered, and the damages that result from those injuries, are elements of a cause of action for negligence. Thus, the defense team may obtain a physical examination of the plaintiff from a doctor of the defense team's choosing. In a guardianship proceeding, the plaintiff seeks to be appointed guardian over someone who lacks the mental capacity to handle financial and other matters. Because the cause of action is dependent on the mental state of the individual, a psychiatric examination would be appropriate.

Requests for Admission

Requests for admission are written requests issued by one party to the lawsuit to the other asking that certain facts or legal issues be admitted as true. Properly used, requests for admission can narrow the focus of trial and streamline the testimony to those issues that are actually contested. Some facts are usually not in controversy, such as names, addresses, and other personal information.

Locations of accidents, time of day, and related facts may also be admitted without calling witnesses. Facts such as whether someone was speeding, not observant, or otherwise negligent are facts rarely admitted because they represent an admission of liability. However, if liability is admitted, the only issue left is damages. Where the damages are minimal, parties may admit to the facts of liability to avoid the time and cost of trial to obtain a finding of fact of something obvious. The remaining issue of how much monetary value is assigned to the wrong may be agreed upon between the parties or determined by the trier of fact in very short order with less time and expense.

> Example If the defendant admits as true his liability for the automobile accident, then that issue is no longer in dispute. No evidence as to the cause of the accident will be required at trial. The trial will be limited to determining damages only, resulting in a more focused and streamlined case.

E-Discovery

The use in business of email, electronic records, websites, online transactions, and other digital technologies has exploded. This technology is also used extensively in conducting personal affairs. Therefore, in many lawsuits, much of the evidence is in digital form. Winning a lawsuit may depend on the ability of a party to conduct **electronic discovery**, or **e-discovery**.

Electronic discovery (e-discovery) The discovery of emails, electronically stored data, e-contracts, and other electronic records.

Modern discovery practices permit the electronic discovery of evidence. Most federal and state courts have adopted rules that permit the e-discovery of emails, electronically stored data, e-contracts, and other electronic records. E-discovery is fast becoming a burgeoning part of the preparation of a case for trial or settlement.

The lawyer and the paralegal must have a sound understanding of permissible e-discovery. Courts have consistently permitted the discovery of emails and electronic databases where relevant to a court case. A party seeking e-discovery must prepare the proper requests for such discovery as required by court rules.

In addition to discovery of emails and electronic information, courts permit the use of electronic interrogatories. Some courts also permit the taking of depositions electronically. This requires that the questions by the lawyers and the answers of the deponent be communicated electronically.

Federal and state courts have established rules of evidence that require the parties not to destroy or delete documents or other evidence that is relevant to a pending

Paralegals *in* Practice

PARALEGAL PROFILE
Emily A. Ewald

Emily A. Ewald is a graduate of Xavier University with a Bachelor of Science degree. She also has a Paralegal Certificate from Davenport University. Emily currently works in the area of civil/commercial and appellate litigation at the large law firm of Dickinson Wright in Grand Rapids, Michigan.

Although I have been a paralegal for six years, the first three were spent focused on one enormous case. During that period, I reviewed, organized, and managed over 450,000 documents, 1,650 deposition exhibits, a 98-page trial exhibit list, deposition designations from over 70 depositions, and numerous other assignments to assist attorneys preparing for discovery and trial. In this case, our client, the defendant, was being sued for $74 million. However, three weeks before the scheduled trial date, the case was settled for a much lower amount.

My current work duties include drafting interrogatories, interrogatory responses, motions and briefs, witness lists, juror questionnaires, and verdict forms. I also help prepare for and attend depositions, hearings, mediations, arbitrations, and trials. Additionally, I go to client meetings, expert witness meetings, and deposition preparation sessions.

More and more legal documents are being digitally produced and exchanged. For instance, we are required by all federal courts to file everything electronically through an online program called PACER (Public Access to Court Electronic Records). For e-discovery purposes, we use Summation®, a software program used to summarize case documents and search them for specific data. TrialDirector® software is used to load case exhibits, videos, and other documents onto a laptop computer, which can later be projected onto a courtroom screen for judge and jurors to see.

My main advice to new paralegals is to be flexible. You should expect to be asked to go back and forth between different case assignments, at a moment's notice. You are also likely to get some assignments in which you have little or no interest. However, always do them to the best of your ability because you will gain from the experience.

lawsuit. This prohibition is particularly important when the documents and evidence are in digital form. The destruction or deletion of e-evidence may subject the violating party to civil and criminal penalties.

In cases where digital evidence has been destroyed or deleted from electronic files, it may be possible to reconstruct the evidence. The use of computer experts will be necessary to find the missing evidence and digitally reconstruct it.

E-discovery will continue to increase as an important aspect of many lawsuits. The recovery of emails, mining of electronic databases, and reconstruction of electronic evidence will play an ever more important part of discovery in current and future lawsuits.

LEARNING OBJECTIVE 4
Explain the use of pretrial motions and settlement conferences.

Pretrial Motions

Paralegals employed in the civil litigation field are often called upon to prepare **pretrial motions** to try to dispose of all or part of a lawsuit prior to trial. The three major pretrial motions are the motion to dismiss, the motion for judgment on the pleadings, and the motion for summary judgment.

Pretrial motion A motion to try to dispose of all or part of a lawsuit prior to trial.

Motion to dismiss A motion that alleges that the plaintiff's complaint fails to state a claim for which relief can be granted. Also called a *demurrer.*

Motion to Dismiss

A defendant can file a **motion to dismiss** that may request that a plaintiff's complaint be dismissed for failure to state a claim for which relief can be granted. A motion to dismiss is sometimes called a **demurrer.** It alleges that even if the facts as presented in the plaintiff's complaint are true, there is no reason to continue the lawsuit. For example, a motion to dismiss would be granted if the plaintiff alleges that the defendant was negligent, but the facts as alleged in the complaint do not support a claim of negligence.

A motion to dismiss can be filed with the court prior to the defendant's having filed an answer in the case. If the motion to dismiss is denied, the defendant is given further time to answer. If the court grants the motion to dismiss, the defendant does not have to file an answer. The plaintiff usually is given time to file an amended complaint. If the plaintiff fails to file an amended complaint, judgment will be entered against the plaintiff. If the plaintiff files an amended complaint, the defendant must answer the complaint or file a new motion to dismiss.

Motion for Judgment on the Pleadings

Once the pleadings are complete, either party can make a **motion for judgment on the pleadings**. This motion alleges that if all of the facts presented in the pleadings are true, the party making the motion would win the lawsuit when the law is applied to these facts. In deciding this motion, the judge cannot consider any facts outside the pleadings.

Motion for judgment on the pleadings A motion that alleges that if all the facts presented in the pleadings are taken as true, the party making the motion would win the lawsuit when the law is applied to the asserted facts.

Motion for Summary Judgment

The trier of fact (the jury, or if no jury, the judge) determines *factual issues*. A **motion for summary judgment** asserts that there are no factual disputes to be decided by the trier of fact, and that the judge should apply the law to the undisputed facts and rule in the moving party's favor. Motions for summary judgment, which can be made by either party, are supported by evidence outside the pleadings. Affidavits from the parties and witnesses, documents (such as a written contract between the parties), and depositions are common forms of evidence used to support such a motion.

If, after examining the evidence, the court finds no factual dispute, it can decide the issues raised in the summary judgment motion. This may dispense with the entire case or with part of the case. If the judge finds that a factual dispute exists, the motion will be denied and the case will go to trial.

Motion for summary judgment A motion that asserts that there are no factual disputes to be decided by a jury and that the judge can apply the law to the undisputed facts and decide the case without a jury. These motions are supported by affidavits, documents, and deposition testimony.

Settlement Conference

Federal court rules and most state court rules permit the court to direct the attorneys or parties to appear before the court for a **pretrial hearing**, or **settlement conference**. One of the major purposes of these hearings is to facilitate settlement of the case. Pretrial conferences often are held informally in the judge's chambers. If no settlement is reached, the pretrial hearing is used to identify the major trial issues and other relevant factors.

More than 90 percent of all cases are settled before they go to trial. In cases that do proceed to trial, the trial judge may advise the attorneys of his or her own rules and timetable. The judge will also advise the attorneys of any deadlines for discovery and the deadline for submitting any final motions with regard to what may be offered at the trial, called *motions in limine*.

In a number of jurisdictions, cases are referred to arbitration or other forms of alternative dispute resolution. Depending on the amount of money in controversy, some cases are required to be submitted before court-approved panels of attorneys sitting as arbitrators. In other courts, arbitration is not required, but the litigants may elect to have the case heard before an arbitration panel. Appeal rights from arbitration panel decisions vary, but cases typically may be appealed *de novo* to the trial court as if no arbitration had occurred, except possibly with the payment of an appeal fee to cover part of the cost of the arbitration.

Exhibit 7.12 shows the timeline sequence of key events before trial.

Web Exploration

Go to http://www.legalzoom?.com/lawsuits-settlements/?personal-injury/top-?ten-frivolous-lawsuits and read the article "Top Ten Frivolous Lawsuits."

Trial

LEARNING OBJECTIVE 5
Describe the steps in a civil trial.

Pursuant to the Seventh Amendment to the U.S. Constitution, a party to an action at law is guaranteed the right to a **jury trial** in cases in federal court. Most state constitutions contain a similar guarantee for state court actions. The trial will be by jury only if either party demands it. The right to a jury is waived if neither party files a jury demand. In non-jury trials, the judge sits as the **trier of fact**. These trials also are

Exhibit 7.12 Timeline sequence of key events before trial

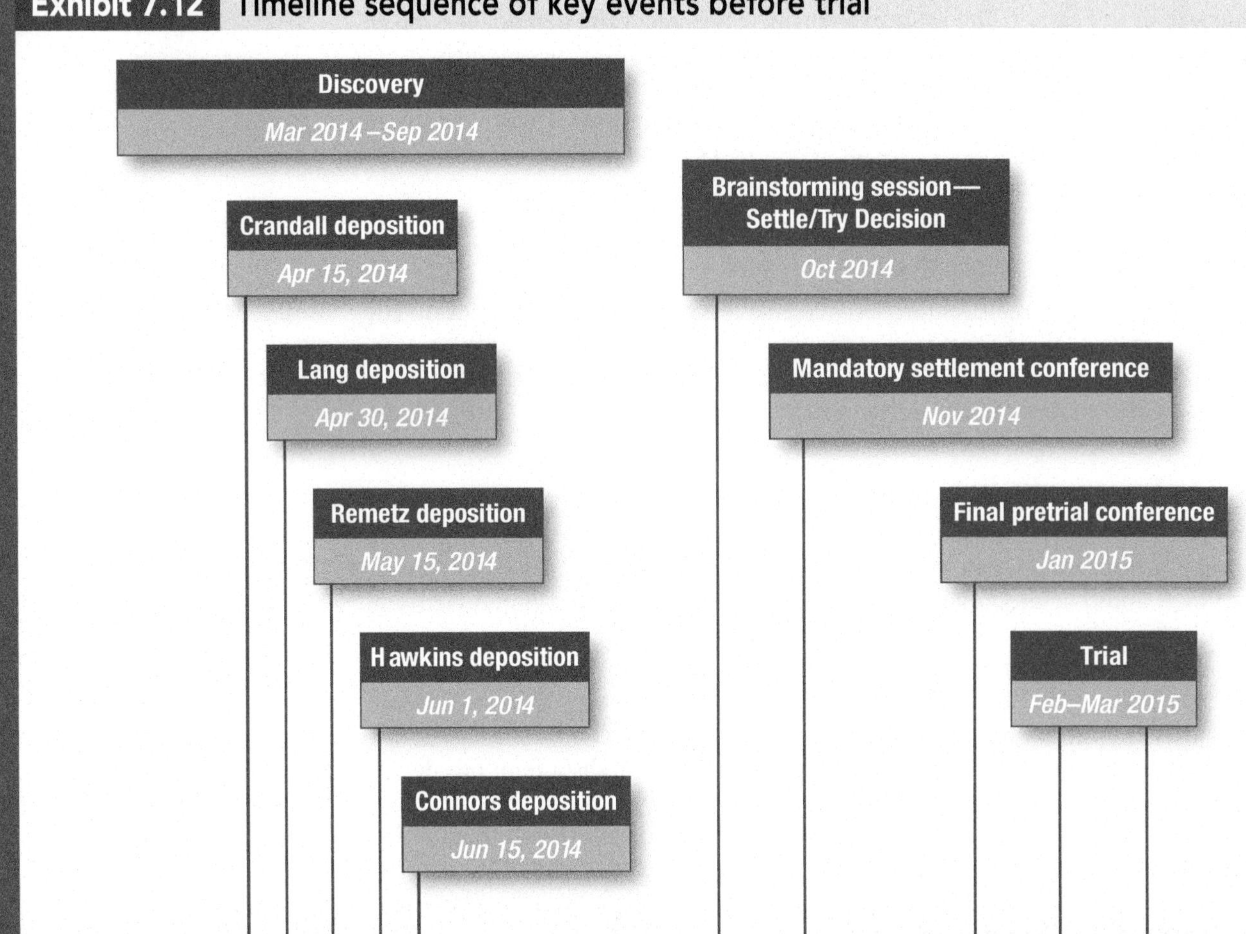

Source: Copyright 2015 LexisNexis, a division of Reed Elsevier Inc. All Rights Reserved. LexisNexis and the Knowledge Burst logo are registered trademarks of Reed Elsevier Properties Inc., and are used with permission of LexisNexis.

Trier of fact In a trial, the person or entity who decides questions of fact, as opposed to questions of law. In a jury trial, it is the jury; in a bench trial with no jury, the trier of fact is the judge.

Trial briefs Documents submitted to the judge by the parties' attorneys that contain legal support for their side of the case.

called *waiver trials* or **bench trials**. At the time of trial, the parties usually submit to the judge **trial briefs** containing legal support for their side of the case.

Trials usually are divided into the following phases:

- Jury selection
- Opening statements
- Plaintiff's case
- Defendant's case
- Rebuttal and rejoinder
- Closing arguments
- Jury instructions
- Jury deliberation
- Entry of judgment

Voir dire The process whereby prospective jurors are asked questions by the judge and attorneys to determine whether they would be biased in their decisions.

Jury Selection

In **jury selection**, the pool of the potential jurors is usually selected from voter or automobile registration lists. Potential jurors are asked to fill out a questionnaire such as that shown in Exhibit 7.13. Individuals are then selected through a process called ***voir dire***, which means "to speak the truth." Lawyers for each party and the judge can ask

Exhibit 7.13 Sample jury questionnaire

JURY QUESTIONNAIRE

(Please Print)

NAME JUROR NO.

(Last) *(First)* *(Middle initial)*

SECTION OF CITY

(Currently) *(Other sections of city lived in within past ten years)*

Marital Status ☐ Married ☐ Single ☐ Divorced ☐ Separated ☐ Widowed

Occupation

(Currently) *(Other occupations within past ten years)*

Occupation of ☐ Spouse *(or deceased spouse)* ☐ Other

(Currently) *(Other occupations within past ten years)*

No. of Male Children Ages

No. of Female Children Ages

Your Level of Schooling Completed

Race ☐ White ☐ Hispanic ☐ Black ☐ Other

STOP HERE
Writing below this line is prohibited until the juror video is shown

QUESTIONS TO BE ANSWERED IN THE JURY ASSEMBLY ROOM

1. Do you have any physical or psychological disability or are you presently taking any medication? ❑ YES ❑ NO
2. (a) Have you ever been a juror before? ❑ YES ❑ NO
   (b) If so, were you ever on a hung jury? ❑ YES ❑ NO

Questions 3 through 15 apply to criminal cases only

3. Do you have any religious, moral or ethical beliefs that would prevent you from sitting in judgment in a criminal case and rendering a fair verdict? ❑ YES ❑ NO
4. Have you or anyone close to you ever been a victim of a crime? ❑ YES ❑ NO
5. Have you or anyone close to you ever been charged with or arrested for a crime, other than a traffic violation? ❑ YES ❑ NO
6. Have you or anyone close to you ever been an eyewitness to a crime, whether or not it ever came to Court? ❑ YES ❑ NO

(continued)

Exhibit 7.13 Sample jury questionnaire *(continued)*

7. Have you, or has anyone close to you, ever worked as a police officer or in other law enforcement jobs? This includes prosecutors, public defenders, private criminal defense lawyers, detectives, and security or prison guards. ❑ YES ❑ NO
8. Would you be more likely to believe the testimony of a police officer or any other law enforcement officer just because of his job? ❑ YES ❑ NO
9. Would you be less likely to believe the testimony of a police officer or any other law enforcement officer just because of his job? ❑ YES ❑ NO
10. Would you have any problem following the Court's instruction that the defendant in a criminal case is presumed to be innocent until proven guilty beyond a reasonable doubt? ❑ YES ❑ NO
11. Would you have any problem following the Court's instruction that the defendant in a criminal case does not have to take the stand or present evidence, and it cannot be held against the defendant if he or she elects to remain silent? ❑ YES ❑ NO
12. Would you have any problem following the Court's instruction in a criminal case that just because someone is arrested, it does not mean that the person is guilty of anything? ❑ YES ❑ NO
13. In general, would you have any problem following and applying the judge's instructions on the law? ❑ YES ❑ NO
14. Would you have any problem during jury deliberations in a criminal case discussing the case fully but still making up your own mind? ❑ YES ❑ NO
15. Is there any other reason you could not be a fair juror in a criminal case? ❑ YES ❑ NO

Questions 16 through 24 apply to civil cases only

16. Have you or anyone close to you ever sued someone, been sued, or been a witness? ❑ YES ❑ NO
17. Have you or anyone close to you been employed as a lawyer or in a law-related job? ❑ YES ❑ NO
18. Have you or anyone close to you been employed as a doctor or nurse or in a medical-related job? ❑ YES ❑ NO
19. In a civil case, would you have any problem following the Court's instruction that the plaintiff has the burden or proof, but unlike in a criminal case, the test is not beyond a reasonable doubt but "more likely than not"? ❑ YES ❑ NO
20. In a civil case, would you have any problem putting aside sympathy for the plaintiff and deciding the case solely on the evidence? ❑ YES ❑ NO
21. In a civil case, would you have any problem following the Court's instruction to award money for damages for things like pain and suffering, loss of life's pleasures, etc., although it is difficult to put a dollar figure on them? ❑ YES ❑ NO
22. Would you have any problem during jury deliberations in a civil case discussing the case fully but still making up your own mind? ❑ YES ❑ NO
23. Is there any reason in a civil case that you cannot follow the Court's instructions on the law? ❑ YES ❑ NO
24. Is there any reason in a civil case that you cannot otherwise be a fair juror? ❑ YES ❑ NO

questions of prospective jurors to determine whether they would be biased in their decision. Jurors can be "stricken for cause" if the court believes that the potential juror is too biased to render a fair verdict. Lawyers may also use preemptory challenges to exclude a juror from sitting on a particular case without giving any reason for the dismissal.

Once the jurors are selected (usually six to twelve jurors), they are impaneled to hear the case and are sworn in. Then the trial is ready to begin. In cases in which the court is concerned for the safety of the jury, such as in a high-profile murder case, it can **sequester**, or separate, the jury from the outside world. Jurors are paid minimum fees for their service. Courts can hold people in contempt and fine or jail them for willful refusal to serve as jurors.

Opening Statements

Each party's attorney is allowed to make an **opening statement** to the jury. In opening statements, attorneys usually summarize the main factual and legal issues of the case and describe why they believe their client's position is valid. The information given in this statement is not considered evidence. It is the attorney's opportunity to tell the trier of fact what he or she intends to tell the jury through witnesses and evidence.

Plaintiff's Case

Plaintiffs bear the **burden of proof** to persuade the trier of fact of the merits of their case. This is called the **plaintiff's case**. The plaintiff's attorney calls witnesses to give testimony. After a witness has been sworn in, the plaintiff's attorney examines (questions) the witness. This is called **direct examination**. Documents and other evidence can be introduced through each witness.

After the plaintiff's attorney has completed his or her questions, the defendant's attorney can question the witness in **cross-examination**. The defendant's attorney can ask questions only about the subjects that were brought up during the direct examination. After the defendant's attorney completes his or her questions, the plaintiff's attorney can ask questions of the witness in **redirect examination**. The defendant's attorney then can ask questions of the witness again. This is called **recross examination**. Exhibit 7.14 illustrates this sequence for examining witnesses.

Defendant's Case

After the plaintiff has concluded his or her case, the **defendant's case** proceeds. The defendant's case must:

1. rebut the plaintiff's evidence;
2. prove any affirmative defenses asserted by the defendant; and
3. prove any allegations contained in the defendant's cross-complaint.

CONDUCTING A COST-BENEFIT ANALYSIS OF A LAWSUIT

SIDEBAR

A paralegal should have knowledge of how expensive and time-consuming a lawsuit is for both the client and the lawyer or law office. The choice of whether to bring or defend a lawsuit should be analyzed like any other business decision. This includes performing a **cost-benefit analysis** of the lawsuit.

The following factors should be considered in deciding whether to bring or settle a lawsuit:

- The probability of winning or losing
- The amount of money that could be won or lost
- Lawyers' fees and other costs of litigation
- Loss of time of managers and other personnel in the client's business
- The long-term effects on the relationship and reputation of the parties
- The amount of prejudgment interest provided by law
- The aggravation and psychological costs associated with a lawsuit
- The unpredictability of the legal system, and the possibility of error
- Other factors particular to the parties and claims being asserted

Exhibit 7.14 Sequence for examining witnesses

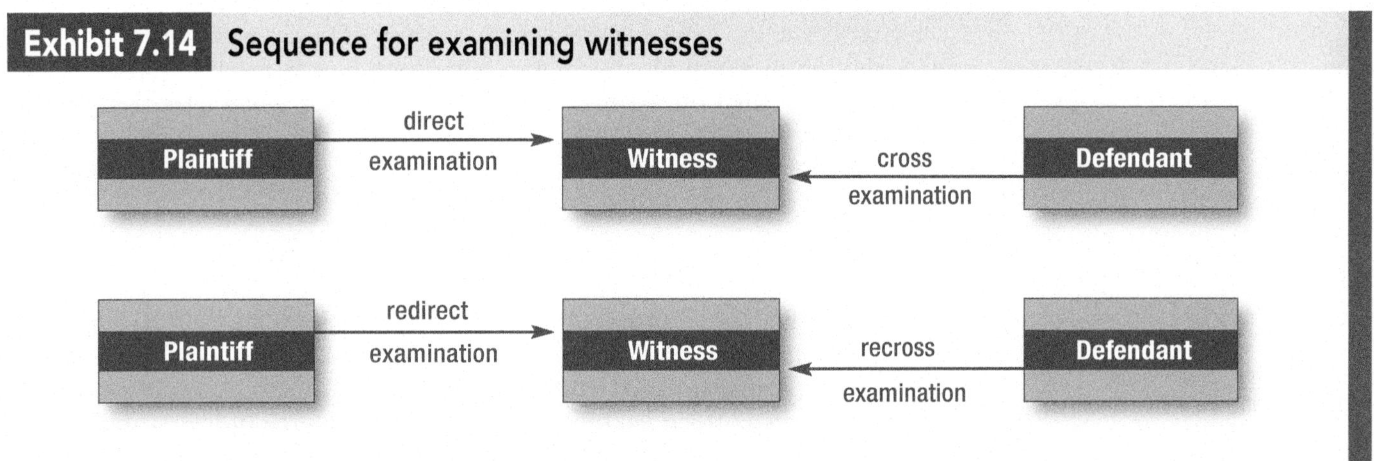

Plaintiff's case The portion of the trial in which the plaintiff calls witnesses and introduces evidence to prove the allegations contained in his or her complaint.

Defendant's case The portion of the case in which the defendant calls witnesses and introduces evidence to (1) rebut the plaintiff's evidence, (2) prove affirmative defenses, and (3) prove allegations made in a cross-complaint.

The defendant's witnesses are examined by the defendant's attorney. The plaintiff's attorney can cross-examine each witness. This is followed by redirect examination by the defendant, and recross examination by the plaintiff.

Rebuttal and Rejoinder

After the defendant's attorney has completed calling witnesses, the plaintiff's attorney can call witnesses and put forth evidence to rebut the defendant's case. This is called a **rebuttal**. The defendant's attorney can call additional witnesses and introduce other evidence to counter the rebuttal. This is called the **rejoinder**.

Closing Arguments

At the conclusion of the evidence, each party's attorney is allowed to make a **closing argument** to the jury. Each attorney tries to convince the jury to render a verdict for his or her client by pointing out the strengths in the client's case and the weaknesses in the other side's case.

Information given by the attorneys in their closing statements is not evidence. It is a chance for the attorneys to remind the jury what their opening statements said they would tell the jury through witnesses and evidence and how they had accomplished this during the trial.

Jury Instructions

Jury instructions (charges) Instructions given by the judge to the jury that inform them of the law to be applied in the case.

Once the closing arguments are completed, the judge reads the **jury instructions**, or **charges**, to the jury. These instructions inform the jury about the law they must apply in deciding the case (see Exhibit 7.15). For example, in a criminal trial the judge will read the jury the statutory definition of the crime the defendant is charged with. In an accident case, the judge will read the jury the legal definition of *negligence*.

Jury Deliberation and Verdict

Verdict Decision reached by the jury.

The jury then goes into the jury room to deliberate its findings. **Jury deliberation** can take from a few minutes to many weeks. After deliberation, the jury announces its **verdict**. In civil cases, the jury also assesses damages. In criminal cases, the judge imposes penalties.

Entry of Judgment

Judgment The official decision of the court.

In most cases, after the jury has returned its verdict, the judge enters **judgment** for the successful party, based on the verdict. This is the official decision of the court. But the court may overturn the verdict if it finds bias or jury misconduct. This is called a **judgment notwithstanding the verdict**, **judgment n.o.v.**, or **j.n.o.v.** (n.o.v. stands for the Latin *non obstante veredicto*.)

In a civil case, the judge may reduce the amount of monetary damages awarded by the jury if he or she finds the jury to have been biased, overly emotional, or inflamed. This is called **remittitur**. The trial court usually issues a **written memorandum** setting forth the reasons for the judgment. This memorandum, together with the trial transcript and evidence introduced at trial, constitutes the permanent *record* of the trial court proceeding.

LEARNING OBJECTIVE 6

Describe how a case is appealed and what decisions can be rendered by an appellate court.

Appeal

In a civil case, either party can **appeal** the trial court's decision once a final judgment is entered. However, in a criminal case, only the defendant can appeal. The appeal is made to the appropriate **appellate court** (see Exhibit 7.16). A notice of appeal must be filed within a prescribed time after judgment is entered (usually within 60 or 90 days). The appealing party is called the **appellant**, or **petitioner**. The responding

Exhibit 7.15 Sample jury instructions

6.01J (Civ) PROPERTY DAMAGE

The plaintiff is entitled to be compensated for the harm done to his (her) property. If you find that the property was a total loss, damages are to be measured by either its market value or its special value to plaintiff, whichever is greater. If the property was not a total loss, damages are measured by (the difference in value before and after the harm) (the reasonable cost of repairs) and you may consider such evidence produced by defendant by way of defense to plaintiff's claim. In addition, plaintiff is entitled to be reimbursed for incidental costs or losses reasonably incurred because of the damage to the property, such as (rental of a replacement vehicle during repairs), (towing charges), (loss of use of the property), (etc.).

SUBCOMMITTEE NOTE

Damage to property is covered generally by Restatement of Torts, §§ 927 and 928. Section 927 provides for damages to be measured by the "market value" or "damages based upon its special value to [plaintiff] if that is greater than its market value." Restatement of Torts, § 927, Comment c (1934). Section 928 provides, in the case of damages not amounting to total destruction, damages measured by "the difference between the value of the chattel before the harm and the value after the harm or, at plaintiff's election, the reasonable cost of repair or restoration." This accounts for the parenthesized phrases (the difference in value before and after the harm) and (the reasonable cost of repairs).

Incidental costs will depend on the nature of the property damage. Rental of a substitute vehicle has long been recognized as one such compensable item. *Bauer v. Armour & Co.*, 84 Pa.Super. 174 (1924). Compensation for loss of use is specifically authorized by Restatement of Torts, § 928(b), in the case of less than total loss. The Subcommittee can see no logical reason why such damages should not be awarded under Section 927 in the case of total loss. *Nelson v. Johnson*, 55 D. & C. 2d 21 (Somerset C.P. 1970). Any further expense, proximately resulting from the loss or damage is recoverable under general provisions of tort law. *Nelson v. Johnson*, *supra*, at 33-34.

In the case of damage to automobiles, however, the appellate courts have adhered to the ancient rule requiring testimony of the one who supervised or made the repairs, prior to admission of damage estimates. *Mackiw v. Pennsylvania Threshermen & Farmers Mut. Cas. Ins. Co.*, 201 Pa.Super. 626, 193 A.2d 745 (1963). This rule has been criticized as time-consuming and "technical" by the very courts adhering to it. *Mackiw*, *supra*, 193 A.2d at 745. It further creates an intolerable burden on the courts, in a period when backlog has led to "compulsory" arbitration in many counties of cases valued below $10,000. E.g., *Loughery v. Barnes*, 181 Pa.Super. 352, 124 A.2d 120 (1956) (appeal after verdict of $341.30 for property damage); *Wilk v. Borough of Mt. Oliver*, 152 Pa.Super. 539, 33 A.2d 73 (1943) (new trial ordered after verdict of $175). The Subcommittee therefore adopts a rule requiring only the submission of a repair bill or estimate in proof of damages to automobiles (such bill being submitted prior to trial to defense counsel); should defendant wish to challenge such an estimate, he may do so through cross-examination and through the introduction of evidence in his own case. See *Watsontown Brick Co. v. Hercules Powder Co.*, 265 F.Supp. 268, 275 (M.D.Pa.), *aff'd*, 387 F.2d 99 (3rd Cir. 1967) (after introduction of damage evidence, burden shifts to defendant to show reduction).

Absent stipulation, the issue of reasonable compensation remains a jury issue.

6.01F (Civ) FUTURE PAIN AND SUFFERING

The plaintiff is entitled to be fairly and adequately compensated for such physical pain, mental anguish, discomfort, inconvenience and distress as you believe he (she) will endure in the future as a result of his (her) injuries. [. . .]

party is called the **appellee**, or **respondent**. The appellant often is required to post an **appeal bond** (typically one-and-a-half times the judgment) on appeal.

Appeal The process of asking an appellate court to overturn a decision after the trial court's final judgment has been entered.

Appellant The appealing party in an appeal. Also known as the *petitioner*.

Appellee The responding party in an appeal. Also known as the *respondent*.

Briefs and Oral Argument

The parties may submit all or relevant portions of the trial record to the appellate court for review. The appellant's attorney may file an **opening brief** with the court, citing legal authority and other information to support his or her contentions on appeal. The appellee can file a **responding brief** answering the appellant's contentions.

The attorneys may make oral arguments to support their positions and clarify what they believe to be the appropriate law. But not every appellate court permits or allows oral argument in every case. In some appeals, a decision is based only upon

Exhibit 7.16 Form 1 of appellate rules

United States District Court for the *Eastern*

District of *Pennsylvania*

File Number *US3CA 01234*

Ethan Marshall

v.) Notice of Appeal

Sara Elliott

Notice is hereby given that *Ethan Marshall* (plaintiffs) in the above named case,* hereby appeal to the United States Court of Appeals for the *Third* Circuit *from the final judgment* entered in this action on the 06 day of February, 2011.

(s) Thomas F. Goldman

(Address)

Attorney for *Plaintiff*

Address: *138 North State Street*
Newtown, Pa, 18940

* See Rule 3(c) for permissible ways of identifying appellants.

the attorneys' written briefs. In some courts, the attorneys must, at the time of filing, make a request for oral argument or indicate a willingness to have the matter decided on the briefs alone. In some cases, oral argument is allowed automatically, and in other cases a reason for oral argument must be stated.

In the federal courts of appeals, oral argument is allowed unless a panel of three judges unanimously agrees, after reviewing the briefs, that the oral argument is unnecessary because the appeal is frivolous, the main issues have been correctly decided, or the facts and argument are presented adequately in the briefs and the record and their decision would not be aided by oral argument (F.R.A.P. 344).

Typically, oral arguments are made before the court without the presence of clients or witnesses. Because no additional fact-finding is permitted, it is a matter of making effective legal arguments to persuade the court to rule in favor of a legal position. Many appellate courts establish a time limit for each side. In some courts, the time limit is enforced by a warning light indicating when the time has nearly run out, and when the time has expired. The judges may waive the time limits, particularly when they have used up the attorneys' allotted time by asking questions. However, the court's treatment of the time limit is determined by local practice.

Web Exploration

Review Rule 29 of the Court Rules of the U.S. Supreme Court at http://www.supremecourt.gov/.

Actions by the Appellate Courts

After review of the briefs, the record in the form of the trial court transcript, and oral arguments by the attorneys, an appellate court may affirm, reverse, or remand the case to the lower court. If the appellate court believes there were no errors in application of the law, it will **affirm** the decision of the lower court, and the decision will stand.

An appellate court may **reverse** a lower court decision if it finds an **error of law** in the record. Such an error may be in either the procedural law or the substantive law of the case. Examples of such errors of law include: the jury has been improperly instructed by the trial court judge, prejudicial evidence was admitted at trial that should have been excluded, or prejudicial evidence was obtained through an unconstitutional search and seizure. An appellate court will not reverse a finding of fact unless such finding is unsupported by the evidence or is contradicted by the evidence.

The court also may find that the lower court has made an error that can be corrected, and **remand** the case to the lower court to take additional action or conduct further proceedings. For example, the lower court may be directed to hold further proceedings in which a jury hears testimony related only to the issue of damages and makes a new award. In other cases when the court finds a reversible error, the court may **reverse and remand** the case. This means that the appellate court feels their decision cannot correct the error and the case needs to be retried. The retrial will take place in front of a new judge and a new jury.

Concept Review *and* Reinforcement

LEGAL TERMINOLOGY

Admitted 264
Affirm 288
Answer 264
Appeal 286
Appeal bond 287
Appellant (petitioner) 286
Appellate court 286
Appellee (respondent) 287
Bench trials 282
Burden of proof 285
Civil litigation 242
Closing argument 286
Complaint 249
Consolidation 265
Cost-benefit analysis 285
Cross-complainant 265
Cross-complaint 265
Cross-defendant 265
Cross-examination 285
Default judgment 264
Defendant 262
Defendant's case 285
Demurrer 280
Denied 264
Deponent 276
Deposition 276
Direct examination 285
Discovery 245
Electronic discovery (e-discovery) 279
Electronic filing (e-filing) 265
Error of law 289
Expert witnesses 276
Extension of time to respond 264
Fact pleading 250
General denial 264
Independent medical examination (IME) 279
Interrogatories 276
Intervention 265
Judgment 286
Judgment notwithstanding the verdict (j.n.o.v.) 286
Jury deliberation 286
Jury instructions (charges) 286
Jury selection 282
Jury trial 281
Litigation 269
Motion for judgment on the pleadings 281
Motion for summary judgment 281
Motion to dismiss 280
Notice pleading 250
Opening brief 287
Opening statement 285
Petitioner 286
Physical and mental examination 279
Plaintiff 249
Plaintiff's case 285
Pleadings 247
Pretrial hearing 281
Pretrial motion 280
Pro se 261
Production of documents 278
Rebuttal 286
Recross examination 285
Redirect examination 285
Rejoinder 286
Remand 289
Remittitur 286
Reply 265
Requests for admission 279
Respondent 287
Responding brief 287
Reverse 289
Reverse and remand 289
Sequester 267
Settlement conference 281
Statute of limitations 247
Subpoena 276
Summons 262
Trial briefs 282
Trier of fact 281
Verdict 286
Voir dire 282
Witness 276
Written memorandum 286

SUMMARY OF KEY CONCEPTS

Civil Litigation

What Is Civil Litigation?	Civil litigation is the legal process for resolving disputes between parties. In civil litigation, the plaintiff sues a defendant to recover monetary damages or other remedy for the alleged harm the defendant caused the plaintiff.
Civil Litigation Paralegal Skills	The civil litigation paralegal may perform any number of different tasks, including conducting legal research, typing a pleading or a court brief, making copies, interviewing witnesses, and operating audiovisual equipment.
Managing Client Relationships	Maintaining positive client relationships is a critical area of the practice of law. Clients want to be kept informed and have their inquiries answered promptly. It is important that the legal team, and particularly the paralegal, understand the client's views and values.
Tasks of the Civil Litigation Paralegal	Interviewing clients and witnesses, investigating facts, organizing and managing case files, conducting factual and legal research, drafting pleadings and memos of law, scheduling and assisting in depositions, and even operating the trial presentation software in court.
Corporate Paralegals in Litigation	In-house paralegals may have a supervisory role in the litigation process, making sure deadlines are met, reviewing documents prepared by outside counsel, and monitoring the budgets for the litigation. When outside counsel is retained, the paralegal's primary role is the maintenance of the relationship among outside counsel, in-house counsel, and corporate officers and employees whose testimony may be required.
Litigation Support Manager	In large law firms, the litigation support manager may serve to coordinate the technology for the entire firm.

Pleadings

What Are Pleadings?	Pleadings consist of documents that initiate or respond to a lawsuit.
Complaint	A complaint (or petition) is filed by the plaintiff with the court and served, in some states, with a summons on the defendant. It sets forth the basis of the lawsuit.
Fact and Notice Pleading	Depending on the jurisdiction, the complaint must either provide a general description of the wrongful conduct alleged, which is called notice pleading, or plead specific facts alleged, which is called fact pleading.
Pleading Deadlines	Individual court rules provide a time within which the initial complaint or petition must be served, or the action will be dismissed. A responsive pleading must be filed within a certain time frame to avoid a default judgment.
Responsive Pleadings	The responding party (the defendant) must file a responsive pleading within the time allowed or request an extension of time to respond from the opposing attorney or from the court.
Answer	An answer is filed by the defendant with the court and served on the plaintiff. It usually denies most allegations of the complaint.
Cross-Complaint	A cross-complaint is filed and served by the defendant if he or she countersues the plaintiff. The defendant is the cross-complainant and the plaintiff is the cross-defendant. The cross-defendant must file and serve a reply (answer).

Intervention	In an intervention, a person who has an interest in a lawsuit becomes a party to the lawsuit.
Consolidation	Consolidation means that the court combines into one case the separate cases against the same defendant arising from the same incident, as long as doing so will not cause prejudice to the parties.
Statute of Limitations	A statute of limitations establishes the period during which a plaintiff must bring a lawsuit against a defendant. If a lawsuit is not filed within this time period, the plaintiff loses his or her right to sue.
Discovery	
What Is Discovery?	Discovery is the pretrial litigation process for eliciting facts of the case from the other parties and witnesses for purposes of understanding and evaluating the strengths and weaknesses of the client's case and those of opposing parties, preserving testimony, investigating information that may lead to evidence, finding information that may be used to impeach a witness, and potentially facilitating settlement.
Information Subject to Mandatory Disclosure	Almost anything relied upon in developing the claim must be disclosed, regardless of whether it is admissible at trial. This disclosure includes the identity of witnesses, copies of documents, a computation of damages, and a copy of any insurance policy.
Litigation Hold	Once a client has a reasonable belief that litigation may arise from a dispute, a duty arises to preserve all documents related to that dispute, both paper and electronic. A lawsuit need not have been filed or a complaint served for the duty to attach, only a reasonable belief that litigation may arise.
Depositions	Depositions are oral testimony given by *deponents*, either a party or a witness, and transcribed.
Interrogatories	Interrogatories are written questions submitted by one party to another party. These questions must be answered within a specified period of time.
Production of Documents	A party to a lawsuit may obtain copies of all relevant documents from the other party.
Physical and Mental Examination	Physical and mental examinations of a party are permitted upon order of the court where injuries are alleged that could be verified or disputed by such examination.
Requests for Admission	Written requests may be issued by one party in a lawsuit to another asking that certain facts or legal issues be admitted as true.
E-Discovery	In many lawsuits, much of the evidence is in digital form. Winning a lawsuit may depend on the ability of a party to conduct electronic discovery. The lawyer and the paralegal must have a sound understanding of permissible e-discovery.
Pretrial Motions	
Motion to Dismiss	A motion to dismiss alleges that even if the facts as presented in the plaintiff's complaint are true, there is no reason to continue the lawsuit. Also called a *demurrer*.
Motion for Judgment on the Pleadings	A motion for judgment on the pleadings alleges that if all facts as pleaded are true, the moving party would win the lawsuit. No facts outside the pleadings may be considered.
Motion for Summary Judgment	A motion for summary judgment alleges that there are no factual disputes, so the judge may apply the law and decide the case without a jury. Evidence outside the pleadings, however, may be considered (such as affidavits, documents, and depositions).

Settlement Conference	
Description	A settlement conference is held prior to trial between the parties in front of the judge to facilitate settlement of the case. Also called a *pretrial hearing*. If a settlement is not reached, the case proceeds to trial.
Trial	
Jury Selection	Jury selection is done through a process called *voir dire.* Biased jurors are dismissed and replaced.
Opening Statements	The parties' lawyers make opening statements to tell the jury what they intend to present at trial. These statements do not constitute evidence.
Plaintiff's Case	The plaintiff bears the burden of proof. The plaintiff calls witnesses and introduces evidence to try to prove his or her case.
Defendant's Case	The defendant calls witnesses and introduces evidence to rebut the plaintiff's case and to prove affirmative defenses and cross-complaints.
Rebuttal and Rejoinder	In rebuttal and rejoinder, the plaintiff and defendant may call additional witnesses and introduce additional evidence.
Closing Arguments	Closing arguments are made by the parties' lawyers. Their statements are not evidence.
Jury Instructions	The judge reads instructions to the jury as to what law the jurors are to apply to the case.
Jury Deliberation	The jury retires to the jury room and deliberates until it reaches a *verdict*.
Entry of Judgment	The judge may: 1. enter judgment on the verdict reached by the jury. 2. grant a motion of judgment n.o.v. if the judge finds that the jury was biased. This means that the jury's verdict does not stand. 3. order *remittitur* (reduction) of any damages awarded if the judge finds the jury to have been biased or overly emotional.
Appeal	
Appellate Court	1. Unlike the trial court, whose main function is to make findings of facts, the appellate court's main function is to make findings of law. 2. In a civil case, unlike a criminal case, either party can appeal the trial court's decision once a final judgment is entered. In a criminal case, only the defendant can appeal. The appeal is made to the appropriate appellate court.
Briefs	In some appeals, the attorneys submit their case on "brief" only, and ask the court to make a decision based upon the written submission.
Oral Arguments	In other cases, the attorneys may, on their own request or at the request of the court, make an oral argument to support their position and clarify what they believe to be the appropriate law. Not every appellate court permits or allows oral argument in every case.
Actions by the Appellate Courts	
Affirm	The appellate court believes there have been no errors in the application of the procedural law or the substantive law and allows the prior decision to stand.

Reverse	The appellate court rules that the lower court has made a substantial error in either the procedural or substantive law of the case.
Remand	The court finds that the lower court has made an error that can be corrected by sending the case back to the lower court for further proceedings.

WORKING THE WEB

1. Find the website for your local state trial court. Locate the local rules for filing complaints, answers, and other documents with the court.
2. Visit the website http://uscourts.gov/. Locate the U.S. district court that serves the county or parish in which you live. Go to that court's website. Does the court require electronic filing of documents? If so, review the "user manual" on how to make electronic filings with the court.
3. Visit the U.S. Supreme Court's website: http://www.supremecourt.gov/. Click on "Case Handling Guides" and then "Guide to Filing Paid Cases" and review the requirements for filing a petition. How much detail does a paralegal need to know when assisting an attorney to file documents with the U.S. Supreme Court? Explain.
4. Visit http://www.lawtoolbox.com/. Read about the deadline calculator services available. Are these useful services?
5. Find a state form for the state court that serves the county or parish where you live. Find a federal form for the U.S. district court that serves the county or parish where you live.

CRITICAL THINKING & WRITING QUESTIONS

1. Define "plaintiff." Define "defendant." In what procedural situations can a party be both a plaintiff and a defendant?
2. What is civil litigation? What remedy or remedies are sought by the plaintiff in civil litigation?
3. What are pleadings? Describe the following pleadings: (a) complaint, (b) answer, (c) cross-complaint, and (d) reply.
4. What is a summons? Describe service of process.
5. What is intervention? What is consolidation? Describe the purposes of these two procedures.
6. Explain statutes of limitations.
7. What is the process of discovery? What purposes does discovery serve? Explain.
8. Describe the following types of discovery: (a) deposition, (b) interrogatories, (c) production of documents, and (d) physical and mental examination.
9. Describe the differences between the following pretrial motions: (a) motion to dismiss, (b) motion for judgment on the pleadings, and (c) motion for summary judgment.
10. What is a settlement conference? What is its purpose?
11. How is a jury selected for a case? What is *voir dire*? What does *trier of fact* mean?
12. Describe the following phases of a trial: (a) opening statements, (b) plaintiff's case, (c) defendant's case, (d) rebuttal and rejoinder, and (e) closing arguments.
13. What are jury instructions? Explain. What is a verdict? What is a judgment?
14. What is an appeal? Define appellant (petitioner) and appellee (respondent).
15. Describe the following possible decisions by an appellate court: (a) affirm, (b) reverse, and (c) reverse and remand.

Building Paralegal Skills

VIDEO CASE STUDIES

Preparing for Trial: Preparing a Fact Witness

A paralegal is preparing a witness for deposition and trial and attempts to put the witness at ease by answering the witness's questions and explaining the procedures.

After viewing the video case study at the book website at www.pearsonhighered.com/careersresources, answer the following:

1. Why is it necessary to prepare a person for deposition or for trial?
2. What is the most important advice the paralegal gives the witness?
3. Is preparing a witness the unauthorized practice of law?

Trial: Direct and Cross-Examination of a Witness

The attorneys in a trial ask questions of a fact witness in direct and then in cross-examination to develop the facts of a case.

After viewing the video case study at the book website at www.pearsonhighered.com/careersresources, answer the following:

1. What is the purpose of direct examination?
2. What is the purpose of cross-examination?
3. Why would the attorney ask the judge whether it is acceptable to approach the witness?

ETHICS ANALYSIS & DISCUSSION QUESTIONS

1. Is there an ethical obligation not to file certain lawsuits?
2. What is meant by a "frivolous lawsuit"? Are there sanctions for filing frivolous lawsuits? Explain.
3. Should emails between lawyers and paralegals be treated as confidential and not subject to use as evidence in a case? Why or why not?
4. A former client of your firm sees you on the street at a local lunch stand and shows you a copy of a judgment rendered against him in a small claims court. He tells you he is out of work and cannot afford to hire a lawyer. Can you help the client proceed *pro se* (on his own, acting as his own lawyer)? Can you help him prepare the paperwork to appeal the judgment? Would any of this constitute the unauthorized practice of law? (See Pennsylvania comments to Ethics Rule 5.5.)
5. An ethical rule prohibits communication with an opponent who is represented by counsel. While surfing the Web, you decide to see if the opposing party has a website. You locate it and check it carefully for any information that might help the investigation of the case assigned to you. You send a request to the site and receive information related to the lawsuit. Have you violated the ethical prohibition barring communications with a represented party? (See Oregon State Bar Op 2001-164.)

DEVELOPING YOUR COLLABORATION SKILLS

With a group of other students, review the Paralegals at Work at the beginning of the chapter. As a group, discuss the following questions.

1. Identify what document or documents your law firm should prepare on behalf of Rowan, Isis, and their parents to start the lawsuit. Identify what document the trucking company will file with the court to begin to defend the lawsuit.
2. What are the time limits in your jurisdiction for filing and responding to a complaint? Are there any other local requirements to commence and respond to the lawsuit?
3. Why would the state court or the federal court be more preferable in this case?

PARALEGAL & PORTFOLIO EXERCISE

Refer to the Paralegals at Work opening scenario. Find online (if possible), from a law library or a U.S. district court, the proper form for filing a complaint for personal injuries in a U.S. district court that serves your area. Prepare as best as possible, from the facts of the case, the complaint and answer. If insufficient facts are provided to complete the complaint or answer, make up the missing information and complete these documents.

LEGAL ANALYSIS & WRITING CASES

Swierkiewicz v. Sorema N.A *534 U.S. 506, 122 S.Ct. 992, 152 L.Ed. 1, 2002 U.S. Lexis 1374 (U.S.)*

In April 1989, Akos Swierkiewicz, a native of Hungary, began working for Sorema N.A., a reinsurance company headquartered in New York. Swierkiewicz initially was employed as senior vice president and chief underwriting officer. Nearly six years later, the chief executive officer of the company demoted Swierkiewicz to a marketing position, and he was removed from his underwriting responsibilities. Swierkiewicz's underwriting responsibilities were transferred to a 32-year-old employee with less than 1 year of underwriting experience. Swierkiewicz, who was 53 years old at the time and had 26 years of experience in the insurance industry, was dismissed by Sorema.

Swierkiewicz sued Sorema to recover monetary damages for alleged age and national-origin discrimination in violation of federal antidiscrimination laws. Sorema moved to have Swierkiewicz's complaint dismissed. The District Court dismissed Swierkiewicz's complaint for not being specific enough, and the Court of Appeals affirmed. Swierkiewicz appealed to the U.S. Supreme Court.

Question

1. Under the notice pleading system, was plaintiff Swierkiewicz's complaint sufficiently stated to permit the case to go to trial? Explain why or why not.

Norgart v. The Upjohn Company *21 Cal.4th 383, 87 Cal.Rptr.2nd 453, 1999 Cal. Lexis 5308 (Cal.)*

Kristi Norgart McBride lived with her husband in Santa Rosa, California. Kristi suffered from manic-depressive mental illness (now called bipolar disorder). In this disease, the person cycles between manic (very happy, expansive, extroverted) episodes and depressive episodes. The disease is often treated with prescription drugs. In April 1984, Kristi attempted suicide. A psychiatrist prescribed an antianxiety drug. In May 1985, Kristi attempted suicide again by overdosing on drugs. The doctor prescribed Halcion, a hypnotic drug, and added Darvocet-N, a mild narcotic analgesic. On October 16, 1985, after descending into a severe depression, Kristi committed suicide by overdosing on Halcion and Darvocet-N.

On October 16, 1991, exactly six years after Kristi's death, Leo and Phyllis Norgart, Kristi's parents, filed a lawsuit against the Upjohn Company, the maker of Halcion, for wrongful death based on Upjohn's alleged failure to warn of the unreasonable dangers of taking the drug. The trial court granted Upjohn's motion for summary judgment based on the fact that the one-year statute of limitations for wrongful death actions had run. The Court of Appeals reversed, and Upjohn appealed to the Supreme Court of California.

Question

1. Is the plaintiff's action for wrongful death barred by the one-year statute of limitations? Explain.

Ferlito v. Johnson & Johnson Products, Inc. *771 F.Supp. 196, 1991 U.S. Dist. Lexis 11747 (E.D.Mich.)*

Susan and Frank Ferlito were invited to a Halloween party. They decided to attend as Mary (Mrs. Ferlito) and her little lamb (Mr. Ferlito). Mrs. Ferlito constructed a lamb costume for her husband by gluing cotton batting manufactured by Johnson & Johnson Products, Inc. (JJP), to a suit of long underwear. She used the same cotton batting to fashion a headpiece, complete with ears. The costume covered Mr. Ferlito from his head to his ankles, except for his face and hands, which were blackened with paint. At the party, Mr. Ferlito attempted to light a cigarette with a butane lighter. The flame passed close to his left arm, and the cotton batting ignited. He suffered burns over one-third of his body. The Ferlitos sued JJP to recover damages, alleging that the company failed to warn them of the flammability of the cotton batting. The jury returned a verdict for Mr. Ferlito in the amount of $555,000, and for Mrs. Ferlito in the amount of $70,000. JJP filed a motion for judgment notwithstanding the verdict (j.n.o.v.).

Question

1. Should defendant JJP's motion for j.n.o.v. be granted? Explain.

Pizza Hut, Inc. v. Papa John's International, Inc. 227 F.3d 489 2000 U.S. App. Lexis 23444 (5th Cir.)

Pizza Hut, Inc., the largest pizza chain in the United States, operates more than 7,000 restaurants. Papa John's International, Inc., is the third-largest pizza chain in the United States, with more than 2,050 locations. In May 1995, Papa John's adopted a new slogan, "Better Ingredients. Better Pizza," and applied for and received a federal trademark for this slogan. Papa John's spent more than $300 million building customer recognition and goodwill for this slogan. The slogan appeared on millions of signs, shirts, menus, pizza boxes, napkins, and other items and has regularly appeared as the tag line at the end of Papa John's radio and television advertisements.

On May 1, 1997, Pizza Hut launched a new advertising campaign in which it declared "war" on poor-quality pizza. The advertisements touted the "better taste" of Pizza Hut's pizza and "dared" anyone to find a better pizza. A few weeks later, Papa John's launched a comparative advertising campaign that touted the superiority of Papa John's pizza over Pizza Hut's pizza. Papa John's claimed it had sauce and dough superior to Pizza Hut's. Many of these advertisements were accompanied by Papa John's slogan, "Better Ingredients. Better Pizza."

In 1998, Pizza Hut filed a civil action in federal District Court, charging Papa John's with false advertising in violation of Section 43(a) of the federal Lanham Act. The District Court found that Papa John's slogan "Better Ingredients. Better Pizza," standing alone, was mere puffery and did not constitute false advertising. The District Court also found, however, that Papa John's claims of superior sauce and dough were misleading and that Papa John's slogan "Better Ingredients. Better Pizza" became tainted because it was associated with these misleading statements. The District Court enjoined Papa John's from using the slogan "Better Ingredients. Better Pizza." Papa John's appealed.

Question

1. Should the U.S. district court's opinion in favor of Pizza Hut, Inc. be reversed? Explain.

Haviland & Co. v. Montgomery Ward & Co. 31 F.R.D. 578, 1962 U.S. Dist. Lexis 5964 (S.D.N.Y.)

Haviland & Company filed suit against Montgomery Ward & Company in U.S. District Court, claiming that Ward used the trademark "Haviland" on millions of dollars' worth of merchandise. As the owner of the mark, Haviland & Company sought compensation from Ward. Ward served notice to take the deposition of Haviland & Company's president, William D. Haviland. The attorneys for Haviland told the court that Haviland was 80 years old, lived in Limoges, France, and was too ill to travel to the United States for the deposition. Haviland's physician submitted an affidavit confirming these facts.

Questions

1. Must Haviland give his deposition? Explain.
2. What alternative way to take the testimony may be used? Describe these methods and their purpose.

In Re M.C., 09-08-00465-CV (Tex.App.-Beaumont [9th Dist.] 3-5-2009)

On January 9, 2009, the court notified the parties that the appeal would be dismissed for want of prosecution unless arrangements were made for filing the record or the appellant explained why additional time was needed to file the record. It also notified the parties that the appeal would be dismissed unless the appellant remitted the filing fee for the appeal. The appellant, Blanca Carrillo, did not respond to the court's notices. The appellant did not file an affidavit of indigence and is not entitled to proceed without payment of costs. There was no satisfactory explanation for the failure to file the record, and no reasonable explanation for the failure to pay the filing fee for the appeal. The court dismissed the appeal for want of prosecution.

Questions

1. Why would a court dismiss a case for failure to meet a time deadline?
2. Why would a court dismiss a case for not paying the filing fees?
3. Is justice served by a court enforcing these time limits and filing requirements?

Goodman v. Praxair Services, Inc. Marc B. Goodman, Plaintiff, v. Praxair Services, Inc., Defendant. Case (D. Md. 2009) 632 F. Supp.2d 494 No. MJG-04-391.

United States District Court, D. Maryland. July 7, 2009.

MEMORANDUM OPINION

PAUL W. GRIMM, United States Magistrate Judge.

. . . The lesson to be learned from the cases that have sought to define when a spoliation motion should be filed in order to be timely is that there is a particular need for these motions to be filed as soon as reasonably possible after discovery of the facts that underlie the motion. This is because resolution of spoliation motions are fact intensive, requiring the court to assess when the duty to preserve commenced, whether the party accused of spoliation properly complied with its preservation duty, the degree of culpability involved, the relevance of the lost evidence to the case, and the concomitant prejudice to the party that was deprived of access to the evidence because it was not preserved. *See, e.g.*, Silvestri, 273 F.3d at 594-95. Before ruling on a spoliation motion, a court may have to hold a hearing, and if spoliation is found, consideration of an appropriate remedy can involve determinations that may end the litigation or severely alter its course by striking leadings, precluding proof of facts, foreclosing claims or defenses, or even granting a default judgment. And, in deciding a spoliation motion, the court may order that additional discovery take place either to develop facts needed to rule on the motion or to afford the party deprived of relevant evidence an additional opportunity to develop it from other sources. The least disruptive time to undertake this is *during* the discovery phase, not after it has closed. Reopening discovery, even if for a limited purpose, months after it has closed or after dispositive motions have been filed, or worse still, on the eve of trial, can completely disrupt the pretrial schedule, involve significant cost, and burden the court and parties. Courts are justifiably unsympathetic to litigants who, because of inattention, neglect, or purposeful delay aimed at achieving an unwarranted tactical advantage, attempt to reargue a substantive issue already ruled on by the court through the guise of a spoliation motion, or use such a motion to try to reopen or prolong discovery beyond the time allotted in the pretrial order. . . .

Questions

1. What action should be taken when it is suspected that evidence has been destroyed?
2. When should action be taken?

WORKING WITH THE LANGUAGE OF THE COURT CASE

Gnazzo v. G.D. Searle & Co.,

973 F.2d 136 1992 U.S. App. Lexis 19453
United States Court of Appeals, Second Circuit

Read the following case, excerpted from the court of appeals opinion. Review and brief the case. In your brief, answer the following questions:

1. What is a statute of limitations? What purposes does such a statute serve?
2. What was the Connecticut statute of limitations for the injury alleged by the plaintiff?
3. What is summary judgment? Under what circumstances will it be granted?
4. What was the decision of the trial court? Of the court of appeals? What was the basis for each of these decisions?

Pierce, Circuit Judge

On November 11, 1974, Gnazzo had a CU-7 intrauterine device (IUD) inserted in her uterus for contraceptive purposes. The IUD was developed, marketed, and sold by G.D. Searle & Co. (Searle). When Gnazzo's deposition was taken, she stated that her doctor had informed her that "the insertion would hurt, but not for long," and that she "would have uncomfortable and probably painful periods for the first three to four months." On October 11, 1975, Gnazzo found it necessary to return to her physician due to excessive

(continued)

pain and cramping. During this visit she was informed by her doctor that he thought she had pelvic inflammatory disease (PID). She recalled that he stated that the infection was possibly caused by venereal disease or the use of the IUD. The PID was treated with antibiotics and cleared up shortly thereafter. Less than one year later, Gnazzo was again treated for an IUD-associated infection. This infection was also treated with antibiotics. Gnazzo continued using the IUD until it was finally removed in December of 1977.

Following a laparoscopy in March of 1989, Gnazzo was informed by a fertility specialist that she was infertile because of PID-induced adhesions resulting from her prior IUD use. Subsequent to this determination, and at the request of her then-attorneys, Gnazzo completed a questionnaire dated May 11, 1989. In response to the following question, "When and why did you first suspect that your IUD had caused you any harm?" Gnazzo responded "sometime in 1981" and explained: "I was married in April 1981, so I stopped using birth control so I could get pregnant—nothing ever happened (of course), then I started hearing and reading about how damaging IUDs could be. I figured that was the problem; however, my marriage started to crumble, so I never pursued the issue."

On May 4, 1990, Gnazzo initiated the underlying action against Searle. In an amended complaint, she alleged that she had suffered injuries as a result of her use of the IUD developed by Searle. Searle moved for summary judgment on the ground that Gnazzo's claim was time-barred by Connecticut's three-year statute of limitations for product liability actions. Searle argued, inter alia, that Gnazzo knew in 1981 that she had suffered harm caused by her IUD. Gnazzo contended that her cause of action against Searle accrued only when she learned from the fertility specialist that the IUD had caused her PID and subsequent infertility.

In a ruling dated September 18, 1991, the district court granted Searle's motion for summary judgment on the ground that Gnazzo's claim was time-barred by the applicable statute of limitations. In reaching this result, the court determined that Connecticut law provided no support for Gnazzo's contention that she should not have been expected to file her action until she was told of her infertility and the IUD's causal connection. This appeal followed.

On appeal, Gnazzo contends that the district court improperly granted Searle's motion for summary judgment because a genuine issue of material fact exists as to when she discovered, or reasonably should have discovered, her injuries and their causal connection to the defendant's alleged wrongful conduct. Summary judgment is appropriate when there is no genuine issue as to any material fact and the moving party is entitled to judgment as a matter of law. We consider the record in the light most favorable to the non-movant. However, the non-movant "may not rest upon the mere allegations of denials of her pleading, but must set forth specific facts showing that there is a genuine issue for trial."

Under Connecticut law, a product liability claim must be brought within "three years from the date when the injury is first sustained or discovered or in the exercise of reasonable care should have been discovered." In Connecticut, a cause of action accrues when a plaintiff suffers actionable harm. Actionable harm occurs when the plaintiff discovers or should discover, through the exercise of reasonable care, that he or she has been injured and that the defendant's conduct caused such injury.

Gnazzo contends that "the mere occurrence of a pelvic infection or difficulty in becoming pregnant does not necessarily result in notice to the plaintiff of a cause of action." Thus, she maintains that her cause of action did not accrue until 1989 when the fertility specialist informed her both that she was infertile and that this condition resulted from her previous use of the IUD.

Under Connecticut law, however, "the statute of limitations begins to run when the plaintiff discovers some form of actionable harm, not the fullest manifestation thereof." Therefore, as Gnazzo's responses to the questionnaire indicate[,] she suspected "sometime in 1981" that the IUD had caused her harm because she had been experiencing trouble becoming pregnant and had "started hearing and reading about how damaging IUDs could be and had figured that was the problem."

Thus, by her own admission, Gnazzo had recognized, or should have recognized, the critical link between her injury and the defendant's causal connection to it. In other words, she had "discovered, or should have discovered through the exercise of reasonable care, that she had been injured and that Searle's conduct caused such injury." However, as Gnazzo acknowledged in the questionnaire, she did not pursue the "issue" at the time because of her marital problems. Thus, even when viewed in the light most favorable to Gnazzo, the non-moving party, we are constrained to find that she knew by 1981 that she had "some form of actionable harm." Consequently, by the time she commenced her action in 1990, Gnazzo was time-barred by the Connecticut statute of limitations.

Since we have determined that Gnazzo's cause of action commenced in 1981, we need not address Searle's additional contention that Gnazzo's awareness in 1975 of her PID and her purported knowledge of its causal connection to the IUD commenced the running of the Connecticut statute of limitations at that time.

We are sympathetic to Gnazzo's situation and mindful that the unavoidable result we reach in this case is harsh. Nevertheless, we are equally aware that "it is within the Connecticut General Assembly's constitutional authority to decide when claims for injury are to be brought. Where a plaintiff has failed to comply with this requirement, a court may not entertain the suit." The judgment of the district court is affirmed.

VIRTUAL LAW OFFICE EXPERIENCE MODULES

If your instructor has instructed you to complete assignments in the Virtual Law Office program, complete the Virtual Law Office assignments as assigned by your instructor. These assignments are designed to develop your workplace skills. Completing the assignments for this chapter will result in producing the following documents for inclusion in your portfolio:

VLOE 7.1

1. Completed Client Interview Form, including a short summary of the accident
2. Client summary from AbacusLaw
3. Calendar of the statute of limitations in AbacusLaw
4. A client engagement and fee letter

CHAPTER

8

Criminal Law and Procedure

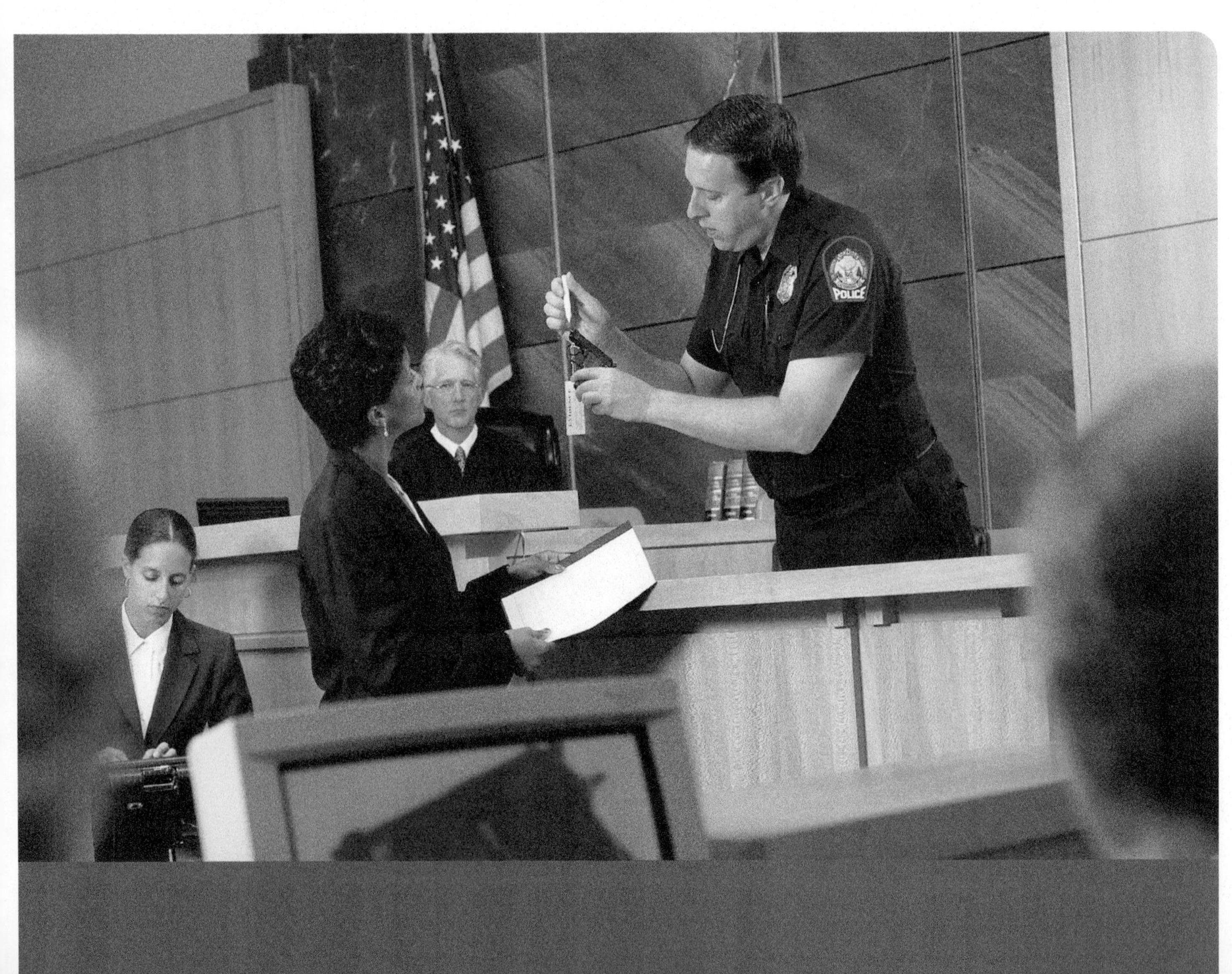

LEARNING OBJECTIVES

After studying this chapter, you should be able to:

1. Recognize the professional opportunities for paralegals in criminal law.
2. Identify and describe the parties and attorneys to a criminal action.
3. Describe pretrial criminal procedure.
4. Describe a criminal trial.
5. List and define the essential elements of a crime.
6. Describe the most important common crimes.
7. Explain the Fourth Amendment's protection from unreasonable search and seizure.
8. Describe the Fifth Amendment's privilege against self-incrimination, and describe *Miranda* rights.
9. Describe the Sixth Amendment's right to a public jury trial.
10. Explain a paralegal's duty to report criminal activity.

Paralegals at Work

You are a paralegal at a law firm that does criminal defense work. The law firm specializes in defending executives in white-collar criminal law matters. You work for Ms. Heather Josephson, a renowned attorney in the area of white-collar criminal defense. She informs you that the law firm has been retained to represent Mr. Keith Day, an executive now facing charges for alleged white-collar crimes. You will assist Ms. Josephson in preparing the defense of Mr. Day.

Ms. Josephson explains that Mr. Day was the founder and Chief Executive Officer (CEO) of the E-Run Corporation, one of the largest companies in the United States. Mr. Day has been served a complaint, *United States v. Day*, in which Mr. Day has been charged by the federal government with various crimes, including financial fraud.

The complaint alleges that Mr. Day, Mr. Don Scott, E-Run Corporation's Chief Financial Officer (CFO), and other corporate officers agreed to "cook the books" of the corporation to make the corporation appear to be making huge profits when it was not. The complaint further alleges that the executives failed to report large debts on the company's financial statements, causing it to show a large financial profit, when in fact the corporation was losing money. When the alleged misdeeds were discovered, E-Run Corporation failed and had to declare bankruptcy. Shareholders lost their entire investments, and the creditors of the corporation were not paid.

In addition, the complaint alleges that Mr. Day, Mr. Scott, and other officers stole money directly from the corporation and diverted corporate cash to their own personal bank accounts. Mr. Day is alleged to have used the mail, telephones, and computers to carry out the entire scheme. The complaint also alleges that Mr. Day purchased

> "It is better that ten guilty persons escape, than that one innocent suffer."
>
> Sir William Blackstone, *Commentaries on the Laws of England* (1809)

a restaurant and moved the stolen money through it to make it seem that the restaurant generated the cash.

Ms. Josephson explains that immediately after he was served with the complaint, federal government agents asked Mr. Day many questions concerning his employment at E-Run Corporation and his involvement in the financial affairs of the company. Mr. Day explained to the agents how the fraud worked and his involvement in this situation. Ms. Josephson asked Mr. Day whether the federal agents had read him any rights before they questioned him, and Mr. Day answered that they had not. Mr. Day is now concerned that the information he gave the federal agents "may come back to haunt him."

Ms. Josephson says that the federal government kept a wiretap on Mr. Day's telephones for 12 months, but the government failed to obtain a warrant to conduct this surveillance. Further, Mr. Day said that his spouse "knows everything," and she is willing to be a witness against him at trial. Also, the federal government has reached a plea bargain with Mr. Scott that grants Mr. Scott immunity from prosecution in return for his testimony against Mr. Day at trial.

LEARNING OBJECTIVE 1
Recognize the professional opportunities for paralegals in criminal law.

INTRODUCTION FOR THE PARALEGAL

Paralegals who work for criminal lawyers must have knowledge of the criminal legal process. Some private lawyers specialize in representing clients accused of criminal wrongdoing. Other lawyers work for the government, either as prosecutors representing the government in criminal cases or as government-appointed defense counsel representing defendants who cannot afford a private attorney.

For members of society to coexist peacefully and for commerce to flourish, people and their property must be protected from injury by other members of society. **Criminal laws** provide an incentive for persons to act reasonably in society and impose penalties on persons who injure others.

There can be no equal justice where the kind of trial a man gets depends on the amount of money he has.
Justice Black
Griffin v. Illinois, 351 U.S. 12 (1956)

Many common crimes involve taking or destroying property, such as arson, robbery, burglary, larceny, and other forms of theft. Other common crimes involve injury or death to other persons, such as the crimes of murder, rape, assault, and battery.

Another category of crimes is often referred to as "white-collar crimes." They are given this name because they are often committed by persons who are executives or employees of businesses. These crimes include bribery, civil fraud, and securities fraud. A business is liable for the crimes committed by its employees on behalf of the business.

A person charged with a crime in the United States is presumed innocent until proven guilty. The **burden of proof** is on the government to prove that the accused is guilty of the crime charged. The accused must be found guilty "**beyond a reasonable doubt**." Conviction requires a unanimous jury vote.

The following feature discusses the career opportunities for paralegal professionals in criminal law.

CAREER OPPORTUNITIES FOR PARALEGALS IN CRIMINAL LAW

Criminal law provides abundant job opportunities for paralegals. The criminal justice system is extremely large and requires the services of thousands of lawyers and, by extension, thousands of paralegals. The job opportunities for paralegals are quite varied in this area.

Most of the crimes prosecuted in the United States involve violations of state laws. These include many violent crimes against persons and property, such as assault, battery, robbery, and rape, as well as nonviolent crimes, such as illegal drug sales, fraud, and other violations.

In each case when a defendant is charged with a violation of state law, the state files a complaint against the alleged criminal. These actions are brought by prosecutors in the local jurisdiction where the crime is alleged to have been committed. The prosecutors are lawyers who are state government employees. The prosecutor is responsible for investigating the alleged crime and for assembling the government's case against the defendant. Paralegals have many opportunities to work for these prosecuting attorneys.

Paralegals also have opportunities to work for the attorneys who defend persons charged with criminal offenses. Many defendants in criminal cases cannot afford their own attorneys, so the government provides attorneys to represent them. These defense attorneys frequently are government employees and are referred to as public defenders. The paralegals who work for them are also state government employees. Sometimes the court will appoint an attorney in private practice to represent a defendant, and the government pays this attorney's fees.

Prosecutors and defense attorneys typically rely heavily on paralegals to conduct investigations, perform legal research, prepare documents to be filed with the court, and assist at trials. Thus, many job opportunities are available for paralegals in this area.

Many opportunities also exist in the area of prosecuting and defending matters involving white-collar crimes. These crimes involve allegations of fraud, securities violations, money laundering, racketeering, and other nonviolent activities by individuals, businesses, and other organizations. White-collar defendants may be charged with violating either state or federal criminal laws, depending on the crimes they are alleged to have committed. White-collar criminal cases are often complex. Substantial effort is required to investigate and prepare them for trial, and paralegals are indispensable in these efforts.

In a white-collar criminal case, whether in state or federal court, the government employs lawyers to prosecute the case against the accused. In state cases, the lawyers are state employees, and in federal cases, the lawyers are federal employees. There are excellent opportunities at both the state and federal levels for paralegals to assist these prosecuting attorneys.

On the other side, white-collar defendants, who are often wealthy individuals or corporations, often have the economic ability to employ private attorneys to represent them. Many paralegals work for the law firms that represent these white-collar persons and businesses or for the legal departments of the defendant corporations.

There will always be criminals and criminal defendants—and therefore, there will always be a need for attorneys to represent the government on one side and the defendants on the other. Consequently, there will always be a need for paralegals on both sides, and the area of criminal law will remain an important source of employment for paralegals.

Paralegals who work in the criminal law field must have a thorough understanding of the provisions in the U.S. Constitution that protect a person charged with a crime in the United States. These include protections against unreasonable search and seizure, against self-incrimination, against double jeopardy, and against cruel and unusual punishment; they also include the right to a public jury trial.

In this important and exciting area of the law, paralegals will be called on to conduct research and assist lawyers in preparing for trial. This chapter provides the knowledge that paralegals will be expected to have regarding crimes, criminal procedure, and constitutional safeguards relating to criminal charges.

Parties and Attorneys of a Criminal Action

LEARNING OBJECTIVE 2
Identify and describe the parties and attorneys of a criminal action.

In a criminal lawsuit, the government, rather than a private party, is the **plaintiff**. The government prosecuting a case can either be the federal government or a state or territorial government. The government is represented by a **prosecuting attorney** (or **prosecutor**). The lawyer who prosecutes criminal cases on behalf of a state is often called the state's attorney or **district attorney (DA)**. The lawyer who prosecutes federal criminal cases is called the **United States Attorney**.

The accused, usually either an individual or a business, is the **defendant**, who is represented by a **defense attorney**. Sometimes the accused will hire a private attorney to represent him or her if he or she can afford to do so. If the accused cannot afford a lawyer, the government will provide one free of charge. This defense attorney employed by the government is often called a **public defender**.

LEARNING OBJECTIVE 3

Describe pretrial criminal procedure.

Criminal Procedure

The court procedure for initiating and maintaining a criminal action is quite detailed, encompassing both pretrial procedures and the actual trial. Pretrial criminal procedure consists of several distinct stages: *arrest*, *indictment* or *information*, *arraignment*, and in some cases, *plea bargaining*.

The **Federal Rules of Criminal Procedure** (FRCP) govern all criminal proceedings in the courts of the United States, as stated in FRCP Rule 1. Each state has its own rules of criminal procedure that govern criminal proceedings in its courts.

Criminal Complaint

In criminal cases, the government must file a **criminal complaint** charging the defendant with the alleged crimes. FRCP Rule 3 defines a complaint as follows:

> The complaint is a written statement of the essential facts constituting the offense charged. It must be made under oath before a magistrate judge or, if none is reasonably available, before a state or local judicial officer.

States also have their own requirements for the information to be contained in a criminal complaint.

A complaint is usually filed after the government has obtained sufficient evidence to charge the accused with a crime. This government investigation may consist of observing the activities of the accused, monitoring wiretaps, obtaining information from informants or witnesses, and obtaining evidence through other means.

A copy of a criminal complaint filed by the United States government appears as Exhibit 8.1.

Arrest

Arrest warrant A document authorizing a person to be detained based upon a showing of probable cause that the person committed the crime.

Probable cause Evidence of the substantial likelihood that a person either committed or is about to commit a crime.

Before the police can arrest a person for committing a crime, they often must obtain an **arrest warrant** based upon a showing of **probable cause**—meaning there is a substantial likelihood that the person either committed or is about to commit a crime.

> Example The police are tipped off by a source that a person has been involved in selling illegal drugs. If the judge finds that the information is reliable and that it constitutes probable cause, the judge will issue an arrest warrant.

If the police do not have time to obtain a warrant, they may still arrest a suspect. **Warrantless arrests** are also judged by the standard of probable cause. A warrantless arrest can be made by the police if they arrive during the commission of a crime, when a person is fleeing from the scene of a crime, or when it is likely that evidence will be destroyed.

After a person is arrested, he or she is taken to the police station for *booking*—the administrative procedure for fingerprinting and recording information about the person.

Web Exploration

Go to www.fbi.gov and click on "Most Wanted" and then "Ten Most Wanted Fugitives." Who is the number-one fugitive listed, and what crime is he or she wanted for?

Bail

When a person is arrested, a **bail** amount is usually set. If the arrested person "posts" the amount of the bail, he or she can be released from prison until the date of the trial.

Exhibit 8.1 **Complaint filed by the U.S. government in *United States of America v. Bernard L. Madoff***

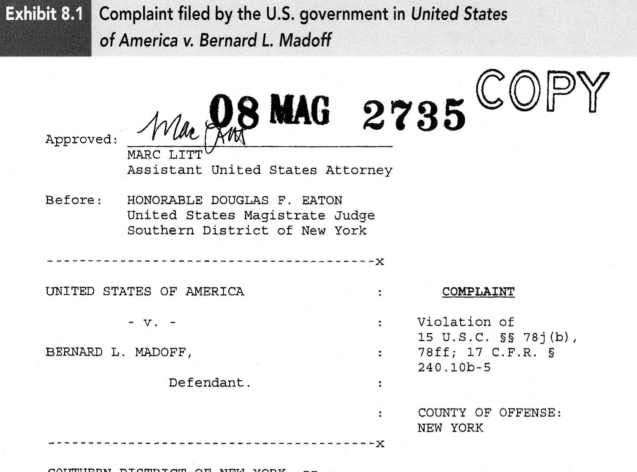

08 MAG 2735 COPY

Approved: [signature]
MARC LITT
Assistant United States Attorney

Before: HONORABLE DOUGLAS F. EATON
United States Magistrate Judge
Southern District of New York

---------------------------------------x

UNITED STATES OF AMERICA	:	**COMPLAINT**
- v. -	:	Violation of 15 U.S.C. §§ 78j(b), 78ff; 17 C.F.R. § 240.10b-5
BERNARD L. MADOFF,	:	
Defendant.	:	
	:	COUNTY OF OFFENSE: NEW YORK

---------------------------------------x

SOUTHERN DISTRICT OF NEW YORK, ss.:

THEODORE CACIOPPI, being duly sworn, deposes and says that he is a Special Agent with the Federal Bureau of Investigation, and charges as follows:

COUNT ONE
(Securities Fraud)

1. From at least in or about December 2008 through the present, in the Southern District of New York and elsewhere, BERNARD L. MADOFF, the defendant, unlawfully, wilfully and knowingly, by the use of the means and instrumentalities of interstate commerce and of the mails, directly and indirectly, in connection with the purchase and sale of securities, would and did use and employ manipulative and deceptive devices and contrivances in violation of Title 17, Code of Federal Regulations, Section 240.10b-5, by (a) employing devices, schemes, and artifices to defraud; (b) making untrue statements of material facts and omitting to state material facts necessary in order to make the statements made, in the light of the circumstances under which they were made, not misleading, and (c) engaging in acts, practices, and courses of business which operated and would operate as a fraud and deceit upon persons, to wit, MADOFF deceived investors by operating a securities business in which he traded and lost investor money, and then paid certain

(continued)

Exhibit 8.1 Complaint filed by the U.S. government in *United States of America v. Bernard L. Madoff* (*continued*)

WHEREFORE, deponent prays that BERNARD L. MADOFF, the defendant, be imprisoned, or bailed, as the case may be.

DEC 1 1 2008

THEODORE CACIOPPI
Special Agent
Federal Bureau of Investigation

Sworn to before me this
_____ day of December, 2008

HONORABLE DOUGLAS F. EATON
UNITED STATES MAGISTRATE JUDGE
SOUTHERN DISTRICT OF NEW YORK

Bail will not be set if the crime is especially severe (such as murder) or if the arrestee is a flight risk who might not later show up for trial.

Most arrestees (or a relative or friend) pay a professional bail bondsperson who operates a business to post the **bail bond**. Bail bondspersons usually require payment of 10 percent of the bail in order to post bond. If the bail is set at $100,000, then the amount for payment of the bail bond is $10,000. The bail bondsperson keeps this $10,000 payment and guarantees the court that he or she will pay the court $100,000 if the arrestee does not show up for trial. If this happens, the bail bondsperson will attempt to recover the amount of the bond from the arrestee. Bail bondspersons often require collateral (such as the title to an automobile or a second mortgage on a house) before they issue a bail bond.

Example Susan is arrested for possession of an illegal narcotic. The court sets a bail of $100,000. Susan can pay $100,000 to the court and get out of jail until the time of her trial. At the time of her trial, she will be paid back the $100,000. If Susan cannot post bail herself, she can pay a bail bondsperson $10,000 to post bail.

Indictment or Information

Accused persons must be formally charged with a crime before they can be brought to trial. This usually is done by the issuance of a **grand jury indictment** or a **magistrate's (judge's) information**. Evidence of serious crimes, such as murder, is usually presented to a **grand jury**.

FRCP Rule 6 states that a federal grand jury shall consist of between 6 and 23 citizens who are charged with evaluating the evidence presented by the government. State grand juries provide for a varying number of grand jurors. Grand jurors sit for a fixed time, such as one year.

If the grand jury determines that there is sufficient evidence to hold the accused for trial, it issues an **indictment**. Excerpts of a federal grand jury indictment appear as Exhibit 8.2. Note that the grand jury does not determine guilt. If an indictment is issued, the accused will be held until trial.

Indictment The charge of having committed a crime (usually a felony), based on the judgment of a grand jury.

Exhibit 8.2 Grand jury indictment in the Court of Common Pleas, County of Summit, Ohio

COPY

DANIEL M. HORRIGAN
2008 APR -9 PM 1:28
SUMMIT COUNTY
CLERK OF COURTS

IN THE COURT OF COMMON PLEAS
COUNTY OF SUMMIT, OHIO

INDICTMENT TYPE: BINDOVER CASE NO. 2008-03-0968

INDICTMENT FOR: MURDER (1) 2903.02(B) SF; FELONIOUS ASSAULT (1) 2903.11(A)(1) F-2; ENDANGERING CHILDREN (1) 2919.22(B)(1) F-2; ENDANGERING CHILDREN (1) 2919.22(A) F-3

In the Common Pleas Court of Summit County, Ohio, of the term of MARCH in the year of our Lord, Two Thousand and Eight.

The Jurors of the Grand Jury of the State of Ohio, within and for the body of the County aforesaid, being duly impaneled and sworn and charged to inquire of and present all offenses whatever committed within the limits of said County, on their oaths, IN THE NAME AND BY THE AUTHORITY OF THE STATE OF OHIO,

COUNT ONE

DO FIND AND PRESENT That **CRAIG R. WILSON** on or about the 12th day of March, 2008, in the County of Summit and State of Ohio, aforesaid, did commit the crime of **MURDER** in that he did cause the death of C.W. (DOB: 1/1/2008) as a proximate result of **CRAIG R. WILSON** committing or attempting to commit Endangering Children and/or Felonious Assault, an offense of violence that is a felony of the first or second degree, in violation of Section 2903.02(B) of the Ohio Revised Code, A SPECIAL FELONY, contrary to the form of the statute in such case made and provided and against the peace and dignity of the State of Ohio.

COUNT TWO

And the Grand Jurors of the State of Ohio, within and for the body of the County of Summit aforesaid, on their oaths in the name and by the authority of the State of Ohio, DO FURTHER FIND AND PRESENT, that **CRAIG R. WILSON** on or about the 12th day of March, 2008, in the County of Summit aforesaid, did commit the crime of **FELONIOUS ASSAULT** in that he did knowingly cause serious physical harm to C.W. (DOB: 1/1/2008), in violation of Section 2903.11(A)(1) of the Ohio Revised Code, A FELONY OF THE SECOND DEGREE, contrary to the form of the statute in such case made and provided and against the peace and dignity of the State of Ohio.

(continued)

Exhibit 8.2 **Grand jury indictment in the Court of Common Pleas, County of Summit, Ohio** *(continued)*

COPY

Criminal Indictment
Case No. 2008-03-0968
Page Two of Three

COUNT THREE

And the Grand Jurors of the State of Ohio, within and for the body of the County of Summit aforesaid, on their oaths in the name and by the authority of the State of Ohio, DO FURTHER FIND AND PRESENT, that **CRAIG R. WILSON** on or about the 12th day of March, 2008, in the County of Summit aforesaid, did commit the crime of **ENDANGERING CHILDREN** in that he did recklessly abuse C.W., 2 months, a child under eighteen years of age (DOB: 1/1/2008), resulting in serious physical harm to said child, in violation of Section 2919.22(B)(1) of the Ohio Revised Code, A FELONY OF THE SECOND DEGREE, contrary to the form of the statute in such case made and provided and against the peace and dignity of the State of Ohio.

COUNT FOUR

And the Grand Jurors of the State of Ohio, within and for the body of the County of Summit aforesaid, on their oaths in the name and by the authority of the State of Ohio, DO FURTHER FIND AND PRESENT, that **CRAIG R. WILSON** on or about the 1st day of January, 2008 to the 12th day of March, 2008, in the County of Summit aforesaid, did commit the crime of **ENDANGERING CHILDREN** in that he did being a parent, guardian, custody, person having custody or control, or person in loco parentis of C.W., 2 months, a child under eighteen years of age (DOB: 1/1/2008), did recklessly create a substantial risk to the health or safety of the child by violating a duty of care, protection or support resulting in serious physical harm to said child, in violation of Section 2919.22(A) of the Ohio Revised Code, A FELONY OF THE THIRD DEGREE, contrary to the form of the statute in such case made and provided and against the peace and dignity of the State of Ohio.

Sherri Bevan Walsh /mk
SHERRI BEVAN WALSH, Prosecutor/pw

Prosecutor, County of Summit, by

Margaret Kanelli

Date: 4-8-08

Grand Jury foreperson/Deputy Foreperson

A TRUE BILL

(continued)

Exhibit 8.2 Grand jury indictment in the Court of Common Pleas, County of Summit, Ohio *(continued)*

COPY

Case No. 2008-03-0968
Page Three of Three

ORDER

TO: DREW ALEXANDER, Sheriff
County of Summit, Ohio

CRAIG R. WILSON

THAT he has been indicted by the Grand Jury of the County of Summit and that the person named in the indictment is hereby ordered to personally appear for the purpose of arraignment at 8 a.m. on the **11th** day of **April, 2008** before the Honorable Magistrate John H. Shoemaker, Judge of the Court of Common Pleas in the County of Summit Courthouse at 209 South High Street, Akron, Ohio, and THAT FAILURE TO APPEAR WILL RESULT IN A WARRANT FOR ARREST, FORFEITURE OF BOND, IF ANY, OR ADDITIONAL CRIMINAL CHARGES FOR FAILURE TO APPEAR UNDER O.R.C. SECTION 2937.99.

I certify that this is a true copy of the original indictment on file in this office.

DANIEL HORRIGAN, Clerk
Court of Common Pleas

By______________________________
Deputy

Example Dominick is arrested for first-degree murder. Usually, with this type of crime, a defendant will not be granted bail and will remain in prison. Several months later, the government prosecutors will present evidence to the grand jury concerning Dominick's alleged crime. Dominick's lawyer will also introduce evidence claiming that Dominick did not commit the crime. After hearing this evidence, the grand jury issues an indictment. The grand jury has not made a decision that Dominick is guilty but only decided there is enough evidence to hold him for a future trial for first-degree murder. In this case, Dominick probably will be denied bail and will remain in prison until the trial.

For lesser crimes (such as burglary or shoplifting), the accused will be brought before a **magistrate (judge)**, who will decide whether there is enough evidence to hold the accused for trial. If the magistrate decides that there is enough evidence, he or she will issue an **information**. The case against the accused is dismissed if neither an indictment nor an information is issued.

Information The charge of having committed a crime (usually a misdemeanor), based on the judgment of a judge or magistrate.

Arraignment

Arraignment A hearing during which the accused is brought before a court and is (1) informed of the charges against him or her and (2) asked to enter a plea.

If an indictment or information is issued, the accused is brought before a court for an **arraignment** proceeding during which the accused is (1) informed of the charges against him or her, and (2) asked to enter a *plea*. The accused may plead **guilty**, **not guilty**, or *nolo contendere*.

A plea of ***nolo contendere*** means that the accused agrees to the imposition of a penalty but does not admit guilt. A *nolo contendere* plea cannot be used as evidence of liability against the accused at a subsequent civil trial. Corporate defendants often enter this plea. The government has the option of accepting a *nolo contendere* plea or requiring the defendant to plead guilty or not guilty. Depending on the nature of the crime, the accused may be released upon posting bail.

> Example The U.S. government sues a company for criminally violating federal pollution control laws. The company pleads *nolo contendere* and the government accepts the plea. The government and the company agree that the company must pay $100,000 in criminal fines, but the company does not admit guilt.

Plea Bargaining

Plea bargain agreement An agreement in which the accused admits to a lesser crime than charged. In return, the government agrees to impose a lesser sentence than might have been obtained had the case gone to trial.

Sometimes the accused and the government enter into a **plea bargain agreement**. The government engages in plea bargaining to save costs, avoid the risks of a trial, and prevent further overcrowding of the prisons. This arrangement allows the accused to admit to a lesser crime than charged. In return, the government agrees to impose a lesser penalty or sentence than might have been obtained had the case gone to trial. In the federal system, more than 90 percent of defendants plead guilty rather than go to trial.

> Example Harold is arrested for the crime of felony burglary, which typically carries a penalty of three years in jail if he is found guilty. The government and Harold reach a plea bargain under which he will plead guilty to misdemeanor burglary and agree to a sentence of six months in jail and three years' probation.

Criminal Trial

LEARNING OBJECTIVE 4
Describe a criminal trial.

Trier of fact The jury is the trier of fact.

A **criminal trial** and a civil trial have many similarities. The functions of the judge and jury are the same. The jury acts as the **trier of fact**. In cases in which the defendant exercises the right to proceed without a jury, also known as a **bench trial** or **waiver trial**, the judge acts as the trier of fact. The judge also determines questions of law. He or she acts as the arbiter of procedural rules covering the conduct of the trial, applies the law to findings of fact, and determines the sentence, fine, or other penalty if the defendant is found guilty. In some severe cases, such as murder trials, the jury may also play a role in deciding the sentence.

The order and presentation of evidence also are similar to those in civil cases. The prosecution goes first and puts on its case, followed by the defense's presentation of its evidence. In addition, motions for dismissal at the close of the prosecution's case are similar to those in a civil action.

A significant difference from civil litigation in many criminal cases is the concern for protecting the record (the trial transcript). Defense counsel tends to be especially concerned with making appropriate objections on the record that can be used as the basis for an appeal. Prosecutors are also very careful not to say anything on the record that the defendant can use as a basis for appeal in the event of a conviction.

Pretrial Discovery

A limited amount of **pretrial discovery** is permitted, with substantial restrictions to protect the identity of government informants and to prevent intimidation of witnesses. Defense attorneys often file motions to suppress evidence, which ask the court to exclude evidence from trial that the defendant believes the government obtained illegally. The government is also under an obligation to provide **exculpatory evidence** to the defense attorney.

Under the Federal Rules of Criminal Procedure Rule 16, upon the defendant's request, the government must disclose and make available for inspection, copying, or photographing any relevant written or recorded statements made by the defendant that are within the possession, custody, or control of the government; the existence of which is known; or that by the exercise of due diligence may become known to the attorney for the government.

Determination of Guilt

At a criminal trial, unlike a civil trial, all jurors must agree *unanimously* before the accused is found guilty of the crime charged. If even one juror disagrees (if he or she has reasonable doubt) about the guilt of the accused, the accused cannot be found guilty of the crime charged. If all of the jurors agree that the accused did not commit the crime, the accused is **innocent** of the crime charged.

After trial, the following rules apply:

- If the defendant is found guilty, he or she may appeal.
- If the defendant is found innocent, the government cannot appeal.
- If the jury cannot come to a unanimous decision about the defendant's guilt, the jury is considered a **hung jury**. The government may choose to retry the case before a new judge and jury.

Hung jury A jury that does not come to a unanimous decision about the defendant's guilt. The government may choose to retry the case.

Crimes

LEARNING OBJECTIVE 5
List and define the essential elements of a crime.

A **crime** is defined as any act by an individual in violation of those duties that he or she owes to society. It is the breach of a law that requires the wrongdoer to make amends to the public. Many activities have been considered crimes throughout the ages, whereas other crimes are of recent origin.

Crime A violation of a statute for which the government imposes a punishment.

Penal Codes and Regulatory Statutes

Statutes are the primary source of criminal law. Most states have adopted comprehensive **penal codes** that define in detail the activities that are crimes within their jurisdiction and the penalties that will be imposed for committing these crimes. Federal crimes are defined by a comprehensive federal criminal code (Title 18 of the U.S. Code). In addition, state and federal **regulatory statutes** often provide for criminal violations and penalties. The state and federal legislatures are continually adding to the list of crimes.

Penal codes Statutes that define crimes.

Regulatory statutes Statutes, such as environmental laws, securities laws, and antitrust laws, that provide for criminal violations and penalties.

The penalty for committing a crime may consist of a fine, imprisonment, or some other form of punishment (such as probation). Generally, imprisonment is imposed to (1) incapacitate the criminal so he or she will not harm others in society, (2) provide a means to rehabilitate the criminal, (3) deter others from similar conduct, and (4) inhibit personal retribution by the victim.

Classification of Crimes

Crimes are classified as *felonies*, *misdemeanors*, or *violations*.

- **Felonies** are the most serious crimes. They include crimes that are ***mala in se***—inherently evil. Most crimes against a person (such as murder or rape) and certain business-related crimes (such as embezzlement or bribery) are felonies in most jurisdictions.

  Felonies are usually punishable by imprisonment. In some jurisdictions, first-degree murder is punishable by death. Federal law and some state laws have mandatory sentencing for specified crimes. Many statutes define different degrees of crimes (such as first-, second-, and third-degree murder), with each degree earning different penalties.

- **Misdemeanors** are less serious than felonies and include many crimes against property, such as vandalism or trespassing, and violations of regulatory statutes. Many of these offenses are treated as crimes that are ***mala prohibita***—not inherently evil, but prohibited by society. Misdemeanors carry lesser penalties than felonies—they are usually punishable by fine or imprisonment for one year or less.
- **Violations** are infractions such as traffic offenses and jaywalking, which are neither felonies nor misdemeanors. These offenses are usually punishable by a fine. Occasionally, a few days of imprisonment are imposed.

Intent Crimes

Actus reus ("guilty act") The actual performance of the criminal act.

For a person to be found guilty of most crimes, a *criminal act* and *criminal intent* must be proven. To commit a **criminal act**, the defendant must have actually performed the prohibited act. Under common law, actual performance of the criminal act is called the ***actus reus* (guilty act)**. Under the Model Penal Code, the prohibited act may be analyzed in terms of conduct, circumstances, and results.

Example Killing someone without legal justification is an example of *actus reus*. Sometimes the omission of an act constitutes the requisite *actus reus*.

Example A crime has been committed if a taxpayer who is under a legal duty to file a tax return fails to do so. Merely thinking about committing a crime is not a crime, because no action has been taken.

Mens rea ("evil intent") The possession of the requisite state of mind to commit a prohibited act.

To be found guilty of a crime, the accused must also be found to have possessed the requisite subjective state of mind, or **criminal intent** (also called specific or general intent) when the act was performed. This is called the ***mens rea* (evil intent)** under traditional common law analysis, and *culpable mental state* under the Model Penal Code. The Model Penal Code has four levels of culpable mental state:

Web Exploration

Go to www.google.com and find the penal code of the state in which your college or university is located. Find and read your state's definition of murder.

1. Purposefully (or intentionally)
2. Knowingly
3. Recklessly
4. Negligently (in the criminal sense)

Specific intent is found where the accused purposefully, intentionally, or with knowledge commits a prohibited act. **General intent** is found where there is a showing of recklessness or a lesser degree of mental culpability. The individual criminal statutes state whether the crime requires a showing of specific or general intent. Juries may infer a defendant's intent from the facts and circumstances of the case. There is no crime if the requisite *mens rea* cannot be proven. Thus, no crime is committed if one person accidentally injures another person.

Non-Intent Crimes

Non-intent crime A crime that imposes criminal liability without a finding of *mens rea* (intent).

Most states provide for certain **non-intent crimes**. The crime of **involuntary manslaughter** is often imposed for reckless conduct.

Example If a person drives an automobile at a very high rate of speed (such as 20 miles over the speed limit) on a city street and hits and kills a pedestrian, the driver most likely will be found guilty of the crime of involuntary manslaughter and be sentenced to jail.

Criminal Acts as a Basis for Tort Actions

An injured party may bring a **civil tort action** against a wrongdoer who has caused the party injury during the commission of a criminal act. Civil lawsuits are separate from the government's criminal action against the wrongdoer. In many cases, a person injured by a criminal act will not sue the criminal to recover civil damages because the criminal is often **judgment-proof**—that is, the criminal does not have the money to pay a civil judgment.

LEARNING OBJECTIVE 6
Describe the most important common crimes.

Common Crimes

Crimes are often categorized as crimes against persons or crimes against property. The most important types of crimes against persons or property are discussed below.

Crimes Against the Person

Crimes against the person are considered by society to be the most heinous of crimes. The most common forms of crimes against the person are:

- **Assault:** A threat of immediate harm or offensive conduct toward another person coupled with apparent present ability to carry out the attempt. Actual physical contact is not necessary.
- **Battery:** Harmful or offensive physical contact with another person without his or her consent (such as punching someone in the face without just cause).
- **Mayhem:** Depriving another person of a member of his or her body (such as cutting off a person's finger).
- **Rape:** Sexual relations with a person forcibly and against the person's will.
- **Kidnapping:** Abduction and detention of a person against his or her will.
- **False imprisonment:** Confinement or restraint of another person without authority or justification and without his or her consent.

Murder

Murder is the unlawful killing of a human being by another with intent. Murder is often categorized by degrees—such as *first degree*, *second degree*, and *third degree*—depending on the circumstances of the case. Those convicted of murder receive the harshest jail sentences.

Murder The unlawful killing of a human being by another with intent.

Sometimes a murder is committed during the commission of another crime even though the criminal did not originally intend to commit murder. Most state laws hold the perpetrator liable for the crime of murder in addition to the other crime. This is called the **felony murder rule**. The intent to commit the murder is inferred from the intent to commit the other crime. Many states also hold accomplices liable under this doctrine.

In the feature on page 314, a paralegal professional shares her experiences as a criminal prosecution paralegal.

Robbery

At common law, **robbery** is defined as the taking of personal property from another person or business by the use of fear or force. Robbery with a deadly weapon is generally considered aggravated robbery (or armed robbery) and carries a harsher penalty.

Robbery The taking of personal property from another person by the use of fear or force.

> Examples If a robber demands that the victim surrender her purse and threatens the victim with a gun, this is the crime of robbery. If a person pickpockets somebody's wallet, it is not robbery because there has been no use of force or fear. It is instead a crime of theft.

Burglary

At common law, **burglary** is defined as "breaking and entering a dwelling at night" with the intent to commit a felony. Modern penal codes have broadened this definition to include daytime thefts from homes, offices, and other commercial

Burglary The taking of personal property from another's home, office, or other commercial building.

buildings. In addition, the "breaking in" element has been abandoned by most modern definitions of burglary. Thus, unauthorized entering of a building through an unlocked door is sufficient. Aggravated burglary (or armed burglary) carries stiffer penalties.

> Example Harold breaks into Sharon's home and steals jewelry and other items. Harold is guilty of the crime of burglary because he entered a dwelling and committed theft.

Larceny

Larceny The taking of another's personal property other than from his or her person or building.

At common law, **larceny** is defined as the wrongful and fraudulent taking of another person's personal property that is not robbery or burglary. The taking of most kinds of personal property—including tangible property, trade secrets, computer programs, and other business property—is larceny. Neither the use of force nor the entry of a building is required. Stealing of automobiles and car stereos and pickpocketing are examples of larceny. Some states distinguish between grand larceny and petit larceny. This distinction depends on the value of the property taken.

Theft

Some states have dropped the distinction among the crimes of robbery, burglary, and larceny. Instead, these states group these crimes under the more general term "**theft.**" Most of these states distinguish between grand theft and petit theft, depending on the value of the property taken.

Paralegals *in* Practice

PARALEGAL PROFILE

Debra K. Jennings

Debra K. Jennings is an Advanced Certified Paralegal in Trial Practice who works for the Campbell County Attorney's Office in Gillette, Wyoming. Of her 18 years as a paralegal, the first 11 were spent in civil practice and the last seven in criminal prosecution. Debra is a member of the National Association of Legal Assistants and currently serves on its Advanced Paralegal Certification board.

I'd like to share the following case description to help illustrate the various skills and knowledge needed by a criminal prosecution paralegal: A man slammed head-on into another vehicle while driving intoxicated at three times the legal limit. At impact, he was driving over 90 mph in a 65-mph zone, on a hill in a no-passing zone, while going around a double tractor-trailer. In the other car, the female driver and her young son were severely injured, and her mother died instantly. The drunk driver also sustained serious injuries. All three survivors eventually recovered.

The man was charged with one count of Aggravated Vehicular Homicide and two counts of Driving Under the Influence with Serious Bodily Injury. As the prosecuting attorney's paralegal, I first coordinated the gathering of information, materials, documents, reports, and evidence. This included researching the defendant's criminal history and identifying applicable laws and judicial decisions as they pertained to the case facts. All relevant information was analyzed and organized.

Next, my writing and communication skills were called into play. I prepared written explanatory material on laws and recommended courses of action. I then helped the prosecutor prepare legal arguments and write pleadings, traverses, motions, and briefs. I also assisted with hearing and pretrial groundwork. This included communicating with other agencies and law enforcement, interviewing and preparing witnesses, performing background checks of the potential jury pool, preparing exhibits and trial notebooks, as well as discussing legal issues with the prosecutor.

In the end, the evidence and arguments presented were overwhelming. The driver responsible for the crash eventually pleaded guilty. He was sentenced to 18 to 20 years on Count I and 9 to 10 years each on Counts II and III, all to run consecutively with one another. As you can see from this case, the key to any paralegal's success is being organized and able to multitask. Educationally, the social sciences provide a great background. The bottom line: Remember your real client is the attorney for whom you work.

Arson

At common law, **arson** is defined as the malicious or willful burning of the dwelling of another person. Modern penal codes have expanded this definition to include the burning of all types of private, commercial, and public buildings.

Arson The willful or malicious burning of a building.

Example An owner of a motel that is not doing well financially burns down the motel to collect insurance proceeds. The owner is guilty of the crime of arson. If arson is found, the insurance company does not have to pay the proceeds of any insurance policy on the burned property.

Forgery

The crime of **forgery** occurs if a written document is fraudulently made or altered and that change affects the legal liability of another person.

Forgery The fraudulent making or alteration of a written document that affects the legal liability of another person.

Examples Counterfeiting, falsifying public records, and materially altering legal documents are acts of forgery. One of the most common forms of forgery is the signing of another person's name to a check or changing the amount of a check. Note that signing another person's name without intent to defraud is not forgery. For instance, forgery is not committed if one spouse signs the other spouse's payroll check for deposit in a joint checking or savings account at the bank.

Extortion

The crime of **extortion** means obtaining property from another, with his or her consent, but induced by wrongful use of actual or threatened force, violence, or fear. Extortion occurs when a person threatens to expose something about another person unless that other person gives money or property. Extortion of private persons is commonly called **blackmail**. The truth or falsity of the information is immaterial. Extortion of public officials is called extortion "*under color of official right.*"

Extortion Threat to expose something about another person unless that other person gives money or property. Often referred to as "blackmail."

White-Collar Crimes

Businesspersons are sometimes prone to commit certain types of crimes. These crimes are often referred to as **white-collar crimes** and usually involve cunning and deceit rather than physical force. Many business and white-collar crimes are discussed in the paragraphs that follow.

White-collar crimes Crimes usually involving cunning and deceit rather than physical force.

Embezzlement

Unknown at common law, the crime of **embezzlement** is now a statutory offense. Embezzlement is the fraudulent conversion of property by a person to whom that property was entrusted. Typically, embezzlement is committed by an employer's employees, agents, or representatives (such as accountants, lawyers, trust officers, or treasurers). Embezzlers often try to cover their tracks by preparing false books, records, or entries.

Embezzlement The fraudulent conversion of property by a person to whom that property was entrusted.

The key element in embezzlement is that the stolen property was *entrusted* to the embezzler. This differs from robbery, burglary, and larceny, in which property is taken by someone not entrusted with the property.

There are some frauds so well conducted that it would be stupidity not to be deceived by them.

C. C. Colton
Lacon, Volume 1 (1820)

Example A bank teller absconds with money that was deposited by customers. The employer (the bank) entrusted the teller to take deposits from its customers, and therefore the teller is guilty of embezzlement.

Criminal Fraud

Criminal fraud A crime that involves obtaining the title to property through deception or trickery. Also known as "*false pretenses* or *deceit*."

Obtaining title to property through deception or trickery constitutes the crime of **criminal fraud**, also known as *false pretenses* or *deceit*. To prove fraud, the following elements must be shown:

1. ***The wrongdoer made a false representation of material fact.*** To be actionable as fraud, the misrepresentation must be of a past or existing material fact. Statements of opinion or predictions about the future generally do not form the basis for fraud.
2. ***The wrongdoer intended to deceive the innocent party.*** Thus, the person making the misrepresentation must either have had knowledge that the representation was false or must have made it without sufficient knowledge of the truth. This is called **scienter** (a "guilty mind").
3. ***The innocent party justifiably relied on the misrepresentation.*** A misrepresentation is not actionable unless the innocent party to whom the misrepresentation was directed acted upon it.
4. ***The innocent party was injured.*** To recover damages, the innocent party must prove that the fraud caused economic injury. The measure of damages is the difference between the value of the property as represented and the actual value of the property.

Example Robert Anderson, a stockbroker, promises Mary Greenberg, a prospective investor, that he will use any money she invests to purchase interests in oil wells. Based on this promise, Ms. Greenberg decides to make the investment. Mr. Anderson never intended to invest the money. Instead, he used the money for his personal needs. This is criminal fraud.

Bribery

Bribery A crime in which one person gives another person money, property, favors, or anything else of value for a favor in return. Often referred to as a "*payoff*" or "*kickback*."

Bribery is one of the most prevalent forms of white-collar crime. A bribe can be in the form of money, property, favors, or anything else of value. The crime of commercial bribery is the payment of bribes to private persons and businesses. This type of bribe is often called a **kickback** or a **payoff**. Intent is a necessary element of this crime. The offeror of a bribe commits the crime of bribery when the bribe is tendered. The offeree is guilty of the crime of bribery when he or she accepts the bribe. The offeror can be found liable for the crime of bribery even if the person to whom the bribe is offered rejects the bribe.

Example Harriet Landers, as the purchasing agent for the ABCD Corporation, is in charge of purchasing equipment to be used by the corporation. Neal Brown, sales representative of a company that makes a type of equipment that is used by the ABCD Corporation, offers to pay her a 10 percent kickback if she buys equipment from him. She accepts the bribe and orders the equipment. Both parties are guilty of bribery.

At common law, the crime of bribery was defined as the giving or receiving of anything of value in payment for an "official act" by a public official. Public officials include legislators, judges, jurors, witnesses at trial, administrative agency personnel, and other government officials. Modern penal codes also make it a crime to bribe public officials.

Example A real estate developer who is constructing an apartment building cannot pay the building inspector to overlook a building code violation.

New York Police Department, Times Square, New York City

Criminal Conspiracy

When two or more persons enter into an *agreement* to commit a crime, it is called **criminal conspiracy**. To be liable for a criminal conspiracy, the conspirators must commit an **overt act** to further the crime. The crime itself does not have to be committed, however. The government usually brings criminal conspiracy charges if (1) the defendants have been thwarted in their efforts to commit the underlying crime, or (2) insufficient evidence is available to prove the underlying crime.

Criminal conspiracy A crime in which two or more persons enter into an agreement to commit a crime, and an overt act is taken to further the crime.

Example Two securities brokers agree by telephone to commit a securities fraud. They also obtain a list of potential victims and prepare false financial statements necessary for the fraud. Because they entered into an agreement to commit a crime and took overt action, the brokers are guilty of the crime of criminal conspiracy even if they didn't carry out the securities fraud.

Constitutional Safeguards

Suspected criminals are provided many rights and protections by both the U.S. Constitution and state constitutions. People in this country are guaranteed the right to be free from unreasonable searches and seizures, and any evidence obtained illegally is considered "tainted" evidence and cannot be used in court. People who are suspected of a criminal act may assert their right of privilege against self-incrimination and may choose not to testify at any pretrial proceedings or at trial. Parties have a right to a public trial by a jury of their peers. In addition, if convicted of a crime, the criminal cannot be subjected to cruel and unusual punishment.

When the framers drafted the U.S. Constitution, they included provisions that protect persons from unreasonable government intrusion and provide safeguards for those accused of crimes. Although these safeguards originally applied only to federal cases, the Fourteenth Amendment's Due Process Clause makes them applicable to state criminal law cases as well. The most important constitutional safeguards and privileges are discussed in the following paragraphs.

LEARNING OBJECTIVE 7
Explain the Fourth Amendment's protection from unreasonable search and seizure.

Fourth Amendment Protection Against Unreasonable Searches and Seizures

The **Fourth Amendment** to the U.S. Constitution protects persons and corporations from overzealous investigative activities by the government. It protects the right of the people to be free from **unreasonable search and seizure** by the government and allows people to be secure in their persons, houses, papers, and effects.

Unreasonable search and seizure Any search and seizure by the government that violates the Fourth Amendment.

Search warrant A warrant issued by a court that authorizes the police to search a designated place for specified contraband, articles, items, or documents. A search warrant must be based on probable cause.

Search Warrants

Search and seizure by the government is lawful if it is "reasonable." **Search warrants** based on probable cause are necessary in most cases. If the police receive a tip from a reasonable source that someone is engaged in criminal activity, the police can present this information to a judge, who will issue a search warrant if he or she finds probable cause. These warrants specifically state the place and scope of the authorized search. General searches beyond the specified area are forbidden. A copy of a search warrant appears as Exhibit 8.3.

Warrantless Searches

Warrantless searches generally are permitted only (1) incident to arrest, (2) where evidence is in "plain view," or (3) when evidence will likely be destroyed. Warrantless searches are also judged by the probable cause standard.

Example The police are notified that a person of a certain description has committed a crime in a specific location. The police arrive on the scene and find a suspect nearby who meets the description. The police may conduct a warrantless search of the individual in order to protect themselves from danger while making the arrest.

Search of Business Premises

Generally, the government does not have the right to search business premises without a search warrant on probable cause or pursuant to a warrantless search based on probable cause. However, businesses in certain hazardous and regulated industries are subject to warrantless searches if proper statutory procedures are met.

Examples Sellers of firearms and liquor, coal mines, and automobile junkyards may be subject to warrantless searches.

A business may also give consent to search the premises, including employee desks and computers, because of the lack of an expectation of privacy in those items.

Exclusionary Rule

Exclusionary rule A rule that says evidence obtained in an unreasonable search and seizure can generally be prohibited from introduction at a trial or administrative proceeding against the person searched.

Evidence obtained in an unreasonable search and seizure is considered tainted evidence ("fruit of a poisonous tree"). Under the **exclusionary rule**, such evidence can be prohibited from introduction at a trial or administrative proceeding against the person searched. This evidence, however, is freely admissible against other persons.

The U.S. Supreme Court has created a *good-faith exception* to the exclusionary rule. This exception allows evidence otherwise obtained illegally to be introduced as evidence against the accused if the police officers who conducted the search reasonably believed they were acting pursuant to a lawful search warrant.

Exhibit 8.3 Search warrant of a federal U.S. district court

AO 93 (Rev. 01/09) Search and Seizure Warrant

UNITED STATES DISTRICT COURT

for the

In the Matter of the Search of)
(Briefly describe the property to be searched)
or identify the person by name and address)) Case No.
)
)
)

SEARCH AND SEIZURE WARRANT

To: Any authorized law enforcement officer

An application by a federal law enforcement officer or an attorney for the government requests the search of the following person or property located in the ______________ District of ______________
(identify the person or describe the property to be searched and give its location):

The person or property to be searched, described above, is believed to conceal *(identify the person or describe the property to be seized)*:

I find that the affidavit(s), or any recorded testimony, establish probable cause to search and seize the person or property.

YOU ARE COMMANDED to execute this warrant on or before ______________
(not to exceed 10 days)

❒ in the daytime 6:00 a.m. to 10 p.m. ❒ at any time in the day or night as I find reasonable cause has been established.

Unless delayed notice is authorized below, you must give a copy of the warrant and a receipt for the property taken to the person from whom, or from whose premises, the property was taken, or leave the copy and receipt at the place where the property was taken.

The officer executing this warrant, or an officer present during the execution of the warrant, must prepare an inventory as required by law and promptly return this warrant and inventory to United States Magistrate Judge

______________ .
(name)

❒ I find that immediate notification may have an adverse result listed in 18 U.S.C. § 2705 (except for delay of trial), and authorize the officer executing this warrant to delay notice to the person who, or whose property, will be searched or seized *(check the appropriate box)* ❒for ______ days *(not to exceed 30)*.
❒until, the facts justifying, the later specific date of ______________ .

Date and time issued: ______________ ______________
Judge's signature

City and state: ______________ ______________
Printed name and title

(continued)

Exhibit 8.3 Search warrant of a federal U.S. district court *(continued)*

AO 93 (Rev. 01/09) Search and Seizure Warrant (Page 2)

Return

Case No.:	Date and time warrant executed:	Copy of warrant and inventory left with:

Inventory made in the presence of :

Inventory of the property taken and name of any person(s) seized:

Certification

I declare under penalty of perjury that this inventory is correct and was returned along with the original warrant to the designated judge.

Date: ____________

____
Executing officer's signature

____
Printed name and title

Fifth Amendment Privilege Against Self-Incrimination

LEARNING OBJECTIVE 8

Describe the Fifth Amendment's privilege against self-incrimination, and describe *Miranda* rights.

The **Fifth Amendment** to the U.S. Constitution provides that no person "shall be compelled in any criminal case to be a witness against himself." Thus, a person cannot be compelled to give testimony against him- or herself. It is also improper for a jury to infer guilt from the defendant's exercise of his or her constitutional right to remain silent. A person who asserts this right is described as having "taken the Fifth." This protection applies to federal cases and is extended to state and local criminal cases through the Due Process Clause of the Fourteenth Amendment.

The privilege against **self-incrimination** applies only to natural persons who are accused of crimes. Therefore, "artificial" persons (such as corporations and partnerships) cannot raise this protection against self-incriminating testimony. Thus, business records of corporations and partnerships are not protected from disclosure, even if they incriminate individuals who work for the business. But certain "private papers" of businesspersons (such as personal diaries) are protected from disclosure.

Self-incrimination The Fifth Amendment states that no person shall be compelled in any criminal case to be a witness against him- or herself.

The Fifth Amendment protects only an individual from being forced to testify. It does not apply to nontestimonial evidence such as fingerprints, body fluids, and the like, which may be compelled without violating the Fifth Amendment.

Miranda Rights

Most people have not read and memorized the provisions of the U.S. Constitution. The U.S. Supreme Court recognized this fact when it decided the landmark case *Miranda v. Arizona*, 384 U.S. 436, 86 S.Ct. 1602, 1966 U.S. Lexis 2817 (U.S., 1966). The Court held that the Fifth Amendment right against self-incrimination is not meaningful unless a criminal suspect has knowledge of this right. Therefore, the Supreme Court required that the following warning—colloquially referred to as the ***Miranda* rights**—be read to a criminal suspect before he or she is interrogated by the police or other government officials:

***Miranda* rights** Rights that a suspect must be informed of before being interrogated so that the suspect will not unwittingly give up his or her Fifth Amendment right.

- You have the right to remain silent.
- Anything you say can and will be used against you.
- You have the right to consult a lawyer and to have a lawyer present with you during interrogation.
- If you cannot afford a lawyer, a lawyer will be appointed to represent you free of charge.

Many police departments read a more detailed version of the *Miranda* rights that is designed to cover all issues that a detainee might encounter while in police custody. A detainee may also be asked to sign a statement acknowledging that the *Miranda* rights have been read to him or her. A copy of the *Miranda* rights appears as Exhibit 8.4. Although the holding in *Miranda* has been questioned, the U.S. Supreme Court upheld it in *Dickerson v. United States*, 530 U.S. 428, 120 S.Ct. 2326, 2000 U.S. Lexis 4305 (U.S., 2000), stating, "[w]e do not think there is justification for overruling *Miranda*. *Miranda* has become embedded in routine police practice to the point where the warnings have become part of our national culture."

The criminal is to go free because the constable has blundered.

Chief Judge Cardozo
People v. Defore (1926)

Any statements or confessions obtained from a suspect prior to being read his or her *Miranda* rights can be excluded from evidence at trial.

Example Margaret is arrested by the police on suspicion of using and distributing illegal narcotics. The police start asking her questions about these issues before reading Margaret her *Miranda* rights. During this questioning, Margaret admits to the offenses. Margaret's statements are inadmissible at court because she had not been read her *Miranda* rights.

Exhibit 8.4 ***Miranda* rights form**

***Miranda* Rights**

- You have the right to remain silent and refuse to answer questions. Do you understand?
- Anything you do say may be used against you in a court of law. Do you understand?
- You have the right to consult an attorney before speaking to the police and to have an attorney present during questioning now or in the future. Do you understand?
- If you cannot afford an attorney, one will be appointed for you before any questioning if you wish. Do you understand?
- If you decide to answer questions now without an attorney present you will still have the right to stop answering at any time until you talk to an attorney. Do you understand?
- Knowing and understanding your rights as I have explained them to you, are you willing to answer my questions without an attorney present?

Immunity from Prosecution

Immunity from prosecution The government's agreement not to use against a person any evidence given by that person.

On occasion, the government wants to obtain information from a suspect who has asserted his or her Fifth Amendment privilege against self-incrimination. The government can try to achieve this by offering the suspect **immunity from prosecution**, meaning that the government agrees not to use any evidence given by a person who has been granted immunity. Once immunity is granted, the suspect loses the right to assert his or her Fifth Amendment privilege.

Grants of immunity often are given when the government wants the suspect to give information that will lead to the prosecution of other, more important criminal suspects. Partial grants of immunity are also available. For example, a suspect may be granted immunity from prosecution for a serious crime but not for a lesser crime in exchange for information. Some persons who are granted immunity are placed in witness protection programs in which they are given a new identity, are relocated, and are found new employment.

Attorney–Client Privilege

Attorney–client privilege A rule that says a client can tell his or her lawyer anything about the case without fear that the attorney will be called as a witness against the client.

To obtain a proper defense, an accused person must be able to tell his or her attorney facts about the case without fear that the attorney will be called as a witness against the accused. The **attorney–client privilege** is protected by the Fifth Amendment. Either the client or the attorney can raise this privilege. For the privilege to apply, the information must be told to the attorney in his or her capacity as an attorney, and not as a friend, neighbor, or similar relationship.

> Example Cedric is accused of murder. He employs Hillary, a renowned criminal attorney, to represent him. During the course of their discussions, Cedric confesses to the murder. Hillary cannot be a witness against Cedric at his criminal trial. Cedric is permitted to tell his lawyer the truth so that she can prepare the best defense she can for him.

Other Privileges

The following privileges have also been recognized under the Fifth Amendment, whereby the accused may keep the following individuals from being a witness against him or her. The reasons are stated in parentheses.

- **Psychiatrist/psychologist–patient privilege** (the accused may tell the truth in order to seek help for his or her condition)

- **Priest/rabbi/minister/imam–penitent privilege** (the accused may tell the truth in order to repent, to obtain help, and to seek forgiveness for his or her deed)
- **Spouse–spouse privilege** (the couple can be open with one another so that they will remain together)
- **Parent–child privilege** (the family can be open with one another so that they will remain together)

However, a spouse or child who is injured by a spouse or parent (as in cases of domestic abuse) may testify against the accused. In addition, if the accused discloses that he or she is planning to commit a crime in the future (such as murder), then the accused's lawyer, psychiatrist, psychologist, priest, rabbi, minister, or imam is required to report this to the police or other relevant authorities.

The U.S. Supreme Court has held that there is no accountant–client privilege under federal law. Thus, an accountant could be called as a witness in cases involving federal securities laws, federal mail or wire fraud, or other federal crimes he or she learns of while working for a client. Nevertheless, approximately 20 states have enacted special statutes that create an **accountant–client privilege**. An accountant cannot be called as a witness against a client in a court action in a state where these statutes are in effect. Federal courts do not recognize these laws, however.

Fifth Amendment Protection Against Double Jeopardy

The **Double Jeopardy Clause** of the Fifth Amendment protects persons from being tried twice for the same crime. For example, if the state tries a suspect for the crime of murder and the suspect is found innocent, the state cannot bring another trial against the accused for the same crime. But if the same criminal act involves several different crimes, the accused may be tried for each of the crimes without violating the Double Jeopardy Clause. For example, if the accused is alleged to have killed two people during a robbery, the accused may be tried for each of the two murders and for the robbery.

Double Jeopardy Clause A clause of the Fifth Amendment that protects persons from being tried twice for the same crime.

If the same act violates the laws of two or more jurisdictions, each jurisdiction may try the accused. For instance, if an accused person kidnaps a person in one state and takes the victim across a state border into another state, the act violates the laws of two states and the federal government. Thus, three jurisdictions can prosecute the accused without violating the Double Jeopardy Clause.

If an accused is tried once and the result is a hung jury—that is, the verdict is not unanimous—then the government can retry the case against the accused without violating the Double Jeopardy Clause.

> Example The government tries a defendant for the crime of murder, and the jury reaches a 10 to 2 verdict—that is, 10 jurors vote guilty and two jurors vote not guilty. This is a hung jury. Since no decision was reached, the government may, if it wants, retry the case against the accused. This does not violate the Double Jeopardy Clause.

LEARNING OBJECTIVE 9
Describe the Sixth Amendment's right to a public jury trial.

Sixth Amendment Right to a Public Trial

The **Sixth Amendment** guarantees that criminal defendants have these rights:

1. The right to be tried by an impartial jury of the state or district in which the alleged crime was committed.
2. The right to confront (cross-examine) witnesses against the accused.
3. The right to have the assistance of a lawyer.
4. The right to have a speedy trial.

The federal **Speedy Trial Act** requires that a criminal defendant be brought to trial within 70 days after indictment [18 U.S.C. Section 3161(c)(1)]. States have similar acts that require speedy trials for criminal defendants. However, courts may grant continuances to serve the "ends of justice."

LEARNING OBJECTIVE 10
Explain a paralegal's duty to report criminal activity.

Eighth Amendment Protection Against Cruel and Unusual Punishment

The **Eighth Amendment** protects criminal defendants from **cruel and unusual punishment**.

This means the government cannot use torture. The Eighth Amendment does not prohibit capital punishment, but it does limit the form of capital punishment that is imposed. For example, the U.S. Supreme Court has held that injection by lethal dosage of drugs generally is not cruel and unusual punishment and is permitted as a means of capital punishment.

ETHICAL PERSPECTIVE

Paralegal's Duty to Report Criminal Activity

Ms. Gutierrez is a paralegal who works at a white-collar criminal defense law firm. Ms. Gutierrez works directly for Mr. Darrow, a partner at the law firm.

One day, Mr. Darrow requests that Ms. Gutierrez sit in on a meeting with him and a client of the firm. The client, Mr. Elliot, owns Beta Corporation. Mr. Elliot explains that he and Beta Corporation are under investigation by the federal government for engaging in criminal fraud, insider trading, wire fraud, and mail fraud. Mr. Elliot has hired Mr. Darrow and his law firm to represent him and the company during the federal investigation and possible criminal lawsuit. At the meeting, Mr. Elliot discloses that he wants to get cash out of Beta Corporation before the federal government goes any further with its investigation.

Mr. Darrow, who is an expert in white-collar criminal matters, tells Mr. Elliot he can accomplish this if Mr. Elliot starts another business that is secretly owned by Mr. Elliot through a front, transfers the cash from Beta Corporation to this new business, and then transfers the cash to a bank located in the Bahamas and into a bank account in Mr. Elliot's name. Mr. Darrow explains that the Bahamas has bank secrecy laws that prevent any party, including the United States government, from discovering the owner of and the amount of money in bank accounts that are located in the Bahamas.

Mr. Elliot asks Mr. Darrow if he will help him do this, and Mr. Darrow agrees. The actions that Mr. Elliot proposes, and that Mr. Darrow has agreed to help accomplish, would constitute criminal conspiracy, criminal fraud, money laundering, and other federal crimes. Ms. Gutierrez has been a witness to this conversation and agreement.

What should Ms. Gutierrez do?

PARALEGAL'S ETHICAL DECISION

State paralegal codes of ethics and professional responsibility provide that a paralegal who possesses knowledge of future criminal activity must report this knowledge to the appropriate authorities. This is true even if the paralegal has become aware of the information in a situation where the attorney–client privilege or the work product rule would normally protect such information from being disclosed.

Ms. Gutierrez owes an ethical duty to report the criminal conspiracy between Mr. Elliot and attorney Mr. Darrow to the appropriate authorities. This decision is difficult for a paralegal professional to make because it would implicate her supervising attorney. Even so, Ms. Gutierrez owes an ethical duty to report the criminal conspiracy, regardless of the potential consequences to her employment.

Concept Review *and* Reinforcement

LEGAL TERMINOLOGY

Accountant–client privilege 323
Actus reus (guilty act) 312
Arraignment 310
Arrest warrant 304
Arson 315
Assault 313
Attorney–client privilege 322
Bail 304
Bail bond 306
Battery 313
Bench trial (waiver trial) 310
Beyond a reasonable doubt 302
Blackmail 315
Bribery 316
Burden of proof 302
Burglary 313
Crime 311
Criminal act 312
Criminal complaint 304
Criminal conspiracy 317
Criminal fraud 316
Criminal intent 312
Criminal laws 302
Criminal trial 310
Cruel and unusual punishment 323
Civil tort action 312
Defendant 304
Defense attorney 304
District attorney (DA) 304
Double Jeopardy Clause 323
Eighth Amendment protection against cruel and unusual punishment 323
Embezzlement 315
Exclusionary rule 318
Exculpatory evidence 311
Extortion 315
False imprisonment 313
Federal Rules of Criminal Procedure 304
Felonies 311
Felony murder rule 313
Fifth Amendment privilege against self-incrimination 321
Fifth Amendment protection against double jeopardy 323
Forgery 315
Fourth Amendment protection against unreasonable searches and seizures 318
General intent 312
Grand jury 306
Grand jury indictment 306
Guilty 310
Hung jury 311
Immunity from prosecution 322
Indictment 306
Information 309
Innocent 311
Involuntary manslaughter 312
Judgment-proof 313
Kickback 316
Kidnapping 313
Larceny 314
Magistrate (judge) 309
Magistrate's (judge's) information 306
Mala in se 311
Mala prohibita 312
Mayhem 313
Mens rea (evil intent) 312
Miranda rights 321
Misdemeanors 312
Murder 313
Nolo contendere 310
Non-intent crimes 312
Not guilty 310
Overt act 317
Parent–child privilege 323
Payoff 316
Penal codes 311
Plaintiff 303
Plea bargain agreement 310
Pretrial discovery 310
Priest/rabbi/minister/imam–penitent privilege warrants 323
Probable cause 304
Prosecuting attorney (prosecutor) 303
Psychiatrist/psychologist–patient privilege 322
Public defender 304
Rape 313
Regulatory statutes 311
Robbery 313
Scienter 316
Search warrants 318
Self-incrimination 321
Sixth Amendment right to a public jury trial 323
Specific intent 312
Speedy Trial Act 323
Spouse–spouse privilege 323
Theft 314
Trier of fact 310
United States Attorney 304
Unreasonable search and seizure 318
Violations 312
Waiver trial (bench trial) 310
Warrantless arrests 304
Warrantless searches 318
White-collar crimes 315

SUMMARY OF KEY CONCEPTS

Parties and Attorneys of a Criminal Action

Parties to a Criminal Lawsuit	*Plaintiff:* the government. *Defendant:* the person or business accused of the crime.
Attorneys in a Criminal Lawsuit	*Prosecuting attorney:* the attorney who represents the government. These can be: • District attorney (DA), who prosecutes criminal cases on behalf of the state. • United States Attorney, who prosecutes criminal cases on behalf of the federal government. *Defense attorney:* the attorney who represents the person or party accused of the crime. These can be: • Public defender: a government attorney who represents the accused. • Private attorney: a nongovernment attorney whom the accused hires to represent him or her.

Criminal Procedure

Pretrial Criminal Procedure	*Arrest:* The person is arrested pursuant to an arrest warrant based upon a showing of probable cause, or, where permitted, by a warrantless arrest. *Indictment or information:* Grand juries issue indictments; magistrates (judges) issue informations. These formally charge the accused with specific crimes. *Arraignment:* The accused is informed of the charges against him or her and enters a plea in court. The plea may be *not guilty, guilty,* or *nolo contendere.* *Plea bargaining:* The government and the accused may negotiate a settlement agreement wherein the accused agrees to admit to a lesser crime than charged.

Criminal Trial

Outcomes	*Conviction:* requires unanimous vote of jury. *Innocent:* requires unanimous vote of jury. *Hung jury:* nonunanimous vote of the jury; the government may prosecute the case again.
Crimes	A crime is an act done by a person in violation of certain duties that he or she owes to society, the breach of which the law provides a penalty for.
Penal Codes and Regulatory Statutes	Penal codes are state and federal statutes that define many crimes. Criminal conduct also is defined in many regulatory statutes.
Parties to a Criminal Lawsuit	*Plaintiff:* the government, which is represented by the prosecuting attorney or prosecutor or district attorney in the state court systems. In the federal system, this attorney is called the United States Attorney. *Defendant:* the person or business accused of the crime, who is represented by a defense attorney. If the defense attorney is a government attorney, that attorney is called a public defender.
Classification of Crimes	*Felonies:* the most serious kinds of crimes; *mala in se* (inherently evil); usually punishable by imprisonment. *Misdemeanors:* less serious crimes; usually punishable by fine or imprisonment for less than one year. Many are considered *mala prohibita* (not inherently evil, but prohibited by society). *Violations:* not a felony or a misdemeanor; generally punishable by a fine.

Elements of a Crime	Intent crimes require the following elements: *Actus reus:* guilty act. *Mens rea:* evil intent.
Non-Intent Crimes	Non-intent crimes do not require intent. An example is the crime of involuntary manslaughter, which can be based on reckless conduct, although death of the victim was not intended.
Common Crimes	
Crimes Against the Person	Crimes against the person include: • Assault • Battery • Mayhem • Rape • Kidnapping • False imprisonment
Murder	Murder is the unlawful killing of another human being with intent.
Robbery	Robbery is the taking of personal property from another by fear or force.
Burglary	Burglary is the unauthorized entering of a building to commit a felony.
Larceny	Larceny is the wrongful taking of another's property other than from his or her person or a building.
Theft	Theft is the wrongful taking of another's property, whether by robbery, burglary, or larceny.
Arson	Arson is the malicious and willful burning of a building.
Forgery	Forgery is the fraudulent making or altering of a written document that affects the legal liability of another person.
Extortion	Extortion is the threat to expose something about another person unless that person gives up money or property. Also called *blackmail.*
White-Collar Crimes	
	White-collar crimes are those that tend to be committed by businesspersons and involve cunning and trickery rather than physical force.
Embezzlement	Embezzlement is the fraudulent conversion of property by a person to whom the property was entrusted.
Criminal Fraud	Criminal fraud involves obtaining the title to another's property through deception or trickery. Also called *false pretenses* or *deceit.*
Bribery	Bribery is the offer of a payment of money or property or something else of value in return for an unwarranted favor. The payer of a bribe also is guilty of the crime of bribery. *Commercial bribery* is the offer of a payment of a bribe to a private person or a business. This often is referred to as a *kickback* or *payoff.* Bribery of a public official for an "official act" is a crime.

Constitutional Safeguards

The U.S. Constitution includes provisions that protect persons from unreasonable government intrusion and provide safeguards for those accused of crimes.

Fourth Amendment Protection Against Unreasonable Searches and Seizures

The Fourth Amendment protects persons and corporations from unreasonable searches and seizures.
Reasonable searches and seizures: those based on probable cause are lawful.
Search warrant: stipulates the place and scope of the search.
Warrantless search: permitted only:

1. incident to an arrest;
2. where evidence is in plain view;
3. where it is likely that evidence will be destroyed.

Exclusionary rule: evidence obtained from an unreasonable search and seizure is tainted evidence that may not be introduced at a government proceeding against the person searched.
Business premises: protected by the Fourth Amendment, except that certain regulated industries may be subject to warrantless searches authorized by statute.

Fifth Amendment Privilege Against Self-Incrimination

The Fifth Amendment provides that no person "shall be compelled in any criminal case to be a witness against himself." A person asserting this privilege is said to have "taken the Fifth."
Nontestimonial evidence: evidence (such as fingerprints or body fluids) that is not protected.
Businesses: the privilege applies only to natural persons; businesses cannot assert the privilege.
Miranda *rights:* a right of a criminal suspect to be informed of his or her Fifth Amendment rights before the suspect can be interrogated by the police or government officials.
Immunity from prosecution: granted by the government to obtain otherwise privileged evidence; the government agrees not to use the evidence given against the person who gave it.
Attorney–client privilege: An accused's lawyer cannot be called as a witness against the accused.
Other privileges: The following privileges have been recognized, with some limitations:

- psychiatrist/psychologist–patient
- priest/rabbi/minister/imam–penitent
- spouse–spouse
- parent–child

Accountant–client privilege: None recognized at the federal level. Some states recognize this privilege in state law actions.

Fifth Amendment Protection Against Double Jeopardy

The Fifth Amendment protects persons from being tried twice by the same jurisdiction for the same crime. If the act violates the laws of two or more jurisdictions, each jurisdiction may try the accused.

Sixth Amendment Right to a Public Trial

The Sixth Amendment guarantees criminal defendants the following rights:

1. to be tried by an impartial jury
2. to confront the witness
3. to have the assistance of a lawyer
4. to have a speedy trial (Speedy Trial Law)

Eighth Amendment Protection Against Cruel and Unusual Punishment

The Eighth Amendment protects criminal defendants from cruel and unusual punishment. Capital punishment is permitted.

WORKING THE WEB

1. Go to the website of Crime Stoppers USA at http://www.crimestopusa.com. Read about what the organization does.
2. Go to the website of the Federal Bureau of Investigation (FBI) at http://www.fbi.gov/. Read one of the articles under the section "Breaking News." What is the subject matter of this article?
3. Go to www.google.com or another Internet search engine and find the website for the prosecuting attorney's office for the county in which you are located. Read the information that describes the functions of the county prosecutor.
4. Go to the website of the U.S. Attorney at http://www.justice.gov/usao/. What is the mission of the United States Attorneys? Find the address and telephone number of the U.S. Attorney's office closest to you.

CRITICAL THINKING & WRITING QUESTIONS

1. Who are the parties to a criminal action? What lawyers are involved in a criminal action?
2. Describe the function of a criminal complaint.
3. Describe a grand jury. What is the function of a grand jury? What is an indictment?
4. What is a plea? Describe the process of plea bargaining.
5. What is a trier of fact? What is its function in a criminal trial?
6. What is a penal code? Give an example of a crime defined by the penal code. What types of crimes are prohibited by regulatory statutes? Give an example of this type of crime.
7. Define *actus reus*. Define *mens rea*. What is a non-intent crime? Give an example.
8. Define the following common crimes: (a) robbery, (b) burglary, (c) larceny, (d) murder, and (e) involuntary manslaughter.
9. Describe each of the following crimes: (a) forgery, (b) extortion, (c) bribery, (d) embezzlement, and (e) criminal fraud
10. What does the Fourth Amendment's protection against unreasonable search and seizure protect persons against? What is a search warrant? What is *probable cause*? Explain the exclusionary rule.
11. What does the Fifth Amendment privilege against self-incrimination protect against? Describe *Miranda* rights. Describe the attorney–client privilege.
12. Explain the Fifth Amendment's protection against double jeopardy. What is a hung jury?
13. Explain the Sixth Amendment's right to a public jury trial.

Building Paralegal Skills

VIDEO CASE STUDIES

Attorney–Client Privilege: Confidentiality Issue

In a meeting between a paralegal and a client, the client reveals to the paralegal conduct that may be criminal in nature.

After viewing the video case study at the book website at www.pearsonhighered.com/careersresources, answer the following:

1. Does the paralegal have a duty to disclose fraudulent activity?
2. Is the paralegal protected under the attorney–client privilege?
3. Is information about the commission of a crime covered under the duty of confidentiality?

ETHICS ANALYSIS & DISCUSSION QUESTIONS

1. Is the information given to a paralegal by a criminal client covered under the Fifth Amendment when he or she interviews the person?
2. What obligation does a paralegal have to make available exculpatory evidence discovered during the investigation of a case?
3. You are a paralegal who works for the state government assisting a public defender in the defense of common criminals. One defendant is accused of the attempted murder of his spouse. It is obvious the defendant is guilty of this charge. Can you report this fact to the judge overseeing the case? Explain.
4. In the prior example, you are at a meeting with the public defender and the defendant says, "I may have missed killing her before, but if I get off she's dead!" Do you have a duty to report this statement to the judge overseeing the case or other government official? Explain.

DEVELOPING YOUR COLLABORATION SKILLS

With a group of students, review the facts of the following case. Then, as a group, discuss the following questions.

1. What are the elements necessary to prove first-degree murder?
2. Did Wilson have the intent to commit murder?
3. What is the felony-murder rule? Would it apply in this case?
4. If Wilson is found guilty, what sentence should be imposed?

State of Ohio v. Wilson

Gregory O. Wilson, who had been arguing earlier in the day with his girlfriend, Melissa Spear, approached a parked car within which Ms. Spear was seated and poured gasoline from a beer bottle over her head. When Ms. Spear exited the car, Wilson ignited her with his cigarette lighter, setting her body on fire. As Ms. Spear became engulfed in flames, Wilson walked away.

Ms. Spear was transported to a hospital. When she arrived, she had third-degree burns over most of her body. She remained in a coma for 45 days, during which time she underwent 10 surgeries. She was subsequently transferred to a rehabilitation facility, and then home. Nine months after the incident, and five days before her thirtieth birthday, Ms. Spear's seven-year old son found her lying dead in her bed.

The state of Ohio brought murder charges against Wilson. Wilson argued that he was not liable for murder because there was not sufficient causation between Wilson's act of setting Ms. Spear on fire and Ms. Spear's death nine months later to warrant a conviction for murder. The jury disagreed and convicted Wilson of aggravated murder and he was sentenced to prison for 30 years to life. Wilson appealed to the Ohio court of appeals.

Source: State of Ohio v. Wilson, 2004 Ohio App. Lexis 2503 (Court of Appeals of Ohio, 2004)

PARALEGAL PORTFOLIO EXERCISE

Using a general Web search site, Westlaw or LexisNexis legal services, or a law library, find a copy of the jury instructions for first-degree murder in your state. Write a legal memorandum discussing the elements necessary to prove first-degree murder in your state.

LEGAL ANALYSIS & WRITING CASES

Kentucky v. King

Kentucky undercover police officers set up a controlled buy of cocaine outside an apartment complex. After the deal took place, uniformed police moved in on the suspect. The suspect ran to a breezeway of an apartment building. As the officers arrived in the area, they heard a door shut. At the end of the breezeway were two apartments, one on the left and one on the right. The officers smelled marijuana smoke emanating from the apartment on the left.

The officers banged on the door as loudly as they could, while yelling "Police!" As soon as the officers started banging on the door, they heard people moving inside and things being moved inside the apartment. These noises led the officers to believe that drug-related evidence was about to be destroyed. At that point, the officers kicked in the door and entered the apartment, where they found three people, including Hollis King, his girlfriend, and a guest. The officers saw marijuana and powder cocaine in plain view. A further search turned up crack cocaine, cash, and drug paraphernalia. Police eventually entered the apartment on the right side of the breezeway and found the suspect who was the initial target of their investigation.

King was indicted for criminal violations, including trafficking in marijuana, trafficking in controlled substances, and persistent felony offender status. King filed a motion to have the evidence suppressed as the fruits of an illegal warrantless search in violation of the Fourth Amendment. The government argued that the search was a valid warrantless search that was justified by exigent circumstances.

Question

1. Is the warrantless search constitutional?

Source: Kentucky v. King, 563 U.S. 452, 131 S.Ct. 1849, 2011 U.S. Lexis 3541 (Supreme Court of the United States, 2011)

Florida v. Jardines

Detective William Pedraja of the Miami-Dade Police Department received a "crime stoppers" unverified tip that one of the tipper's neighbors, Joelis Jardines, was growing marijuana in his house. Detective Pedraja, and Detective Bartelt and his drug detection dog Franky, went to Jardines' home. There were no cars in the driveway and the window blinds were closed. The two detectives and Franky went onto Jardines' porch. Franky sniffed the base of the front door and sat, alerting the detectives of the smell of drugs.

Based upon this investigation, the detectives obtained a search warrant to search Jardines' home. The search revealed marijuana plants. Jardines was arrested for the crime of trafficking in marijuana. At trial, Jardines made a motion to suppress the marijuana plants as evidence on the ground that the detectives and Franky's investigation was an unreasonable search in violation of the Fourth Amendment to the U.S. Constitution. The Florida trial court and the Florida Supreme Court held that there was an unreasonable search and suppressed the evidence. Jardines appealed to the U.S. Supreme Court.

Question

1. Was the canine investigation an unreasonable search?

Source: Florida v. Jardines, 133 S.Ct. 1409, 2013 U.S. Lexis 2542 (Supreme Court of the United States, 2013)

WORKING WITH THE LANGUAGE OF THE COURT CASE

United States of America v. $2,164,341 in U.S. Currency

2013 U.S. Dist. Lexis 79696 (2013)
United States District Court for the District of Arizona

Read the following excerpt from the opinion of the U.S. district court and brief the case. In your brief, answer the following questions.

1. Can the United States government sue for the forfeiture of money?
2. Does a defendant have to be proven guilty of a crime before the government can obtain the forfeiture of his or her money or property?
3. What elements must be shown for the government to obtain forfeiture of cash or other property?
4. Were these elements found in this case?
5. What remedy was ordered by the court in this case?

Campbell, District Judge

The government has filed a motion for summary judgment on its forfeiture claim regarding $2,164,341 seized from Claimant Leonardo Cornejo Reynoso ("Claimant"). During the course of this litigation, the government repeatedly arranged for Claimant to enter the United States from Mexico in order to be deposed. Claimant repeatedly refused to appear, asserting that he was not willing to enter the United States.

In April of 2011, Claimant drove a Budget rental truck on a one-way trip from Atlanta, Georgia, to Los Angeles, California. At approximately 5:00 a.m. on April 21, 2011, near Flagstaff, Arizona, a city about 700 miles from Los Angeles, Officer Gerard stopped Claimant for an unsafe lane change. Claimant produced a Georgia driver's license bearing the name Leonardo Cornejo-Reynoso and a copy of a Budget rental agreement which reflected a one-way rental from Atlanta to Los Angeles.

Officer Gerard explained the reason for the stop and asked Claimant to step out of the truck while he went back to his patrol car to prepare a warning citation. Claimant did not want to leave the truck. Officer Gerard asked Claimant where he was going, and Claimant stated that he was going to Los Angeles to donate used clothing and to purchase new clothing for his Atlanta-area clothing store. Claimant stated that the rental truck contained used clothing. Officer Gerard asked Claimant why he did not donate the clothing in Georgia, and Claimant explained that he would receive a discount on the new clothing in exchange for his donation. DPS Sergeant J. Hutton, who was assisting Officer Gerard, asked Claimant about the one-way rental, and Claimant explained that he planned to fly back to Atlanta and have the new clothing shipped there. Officer Gerard asked Claimant if the rental truck contained drugs, weapons, or large amounts of currency. Claimant said it did not.

At the officer's request, Claimant signed a form consenting to a search of the truck and confirmed that he was responsible for the truck's contents. After accessing the rear of the truck, Officer Gerard immediately smelled a strong odor of dirty clothing and body odor, and found garbage bags containing clothing inside. Officer Gerard inspected a small bag near the truck's cab and found that it contained a large bundle of money wrapped in plastic. Officer Gerard told Claimant about the money, and Claimant replied that he did not think the money was illegal and that it was his. When Officer Gerard asked how much money was in the truck, Claimant said that there was about two million dollars. Claimant told Officer Gerard that he had the money with him because he planned to purchase property in California.

After closing and securing the rear door of the rental truck, Officer Gerard advised Claimant that he was not under arrest, that he was under investigative detention, and that DPS would transport the truck to one of its facilities for a more extensive search. At the DPS facility, Officer Gerard used certified narcotic detention canine Crowe to examine the rental truck. Crowe positively alerted to the rear of the rental truck and to boxes containing the money discovered in the truck. Officers inventoried the rental truck's contents and found more money concealed inside the bags of used clothing, bound by rubber bands and wrapped in plastic containing axle grease. A total of $2,164,431.00 in cash was found inside the truck.

A laptop computer was found in the passenger compartment of the truck. When searched pursuant to a warrant, the laptop was found to contain a ledger that reflects receipts of more than $2 million during the month of March 2011.

Sometime after the seizure of the money found in the truck, Claimant returned to Guadalajara. Claimant remains in Mexico.

The government submits that Claimant's rental truck contained $2,164,341 in cash and that possession of a large amount of cash is strong evidence of a connection to illegal activity. Although not alone sufficient to show a connection to illegal drug transactions, this factor is significant given the large sum of money discovered in this case.

The government argues that the packaging of the money is also relevant. Cellophane is not a normal repository for carrying large amounts of money. Rather cellophane, which is largely impermeable to gas, is commonly used to conceal the smell of drugs and avoid detection by drug dogs. Packaging the $2,164,341 in bundles, banded with rubber bands, wrapped in plastic containing axle grease, is certainly consistent with efforts to block the odor of drugs and to conceal the money with an odor-masking grease.

The government contends that the method of concealing the bundled currency is another factor establishing a connection between the currency and drug crimes. The Court agrees. The method of concealment strongly suggests that the Claimant was attempting to hide the scent of drug-related money from law enforcement.

The government argues that the positive dog alert connects the money to illegal drug activity. The government has presented evidence establishing that Crowe is certified as a patrol and narcotics detection canine.

The Court concludes that the government has met its burden of providing sufficient evidence to conclude, by a preponderance standard, that the money was used or intended to be used to facilitate a violation of federal drug laws.

The Court concludes that no reasonable trier of fact—jury or judge—could find that Claimant was carrying the $2,164,341 in currency for legitimate, non-drug related reasons. The government has carried its burden of showing by a preponderance of the evidence that there is a substantial connection between the money seized and illegal drug activity. Claimant has failed to present evidence that raises a genuine issue of material fact for trial. The government is therefore entitled to summary judgment.

IT IS ORDERED: The government's motion for summary judgment is granted. Claimant's interest in $2,164,341 in U.S. Currency is forfeited to the United States. The Clerk is directed to terminate this action.

VIRTUAL LAW OFFICE EXPERIENCE MODULES

If your instructor has instructed you to complete assignments in the Virtual Law Office program, complete the Virtual Law Office assignments as assigned by your instructor. These assignments are designed to develop your workplace skills. Completing the assignments for this chapter will result in producing the following documents for inclusion in your portfolio:

VLOE 8.1	Memo listing the criminal code sections, elements of the crimes, and conduct observed on the video indicating violation of these criminal statutes
VLOE 8.2	Office memo on ethical rules concerning disclosure of a client's admission that they have committed a crime

CHAPTER

9

Administrative Law

LEARNING OBJECTIVES

After studying this chapter, you should be able to:

1. Recognize the professional opportunities for paralegals in the administrative law area.
2. Define *administrative law.*
3. Describe the types of government regulation of business.
4. List and explain the functions of administrative agencies.
5. Explain the scope of the Administrative Procedure Act.
6. Describe the powers of administrative agencies.
7. Describe administrative searches.
8. Explain the judicial review of administrative agency decisions.
9. List and describe important federal administrative agencies.
10. Describe public disclosure of administrative agency actions.

Paralegals at Work

You are a paralegal at a law firm that specializes in representing persons who allege that they have been discriminated against at work. Your supervisor is Ms. Emilia Ortiz, a renowned attorney in the area of equal opportunity in employment. Ms. Ortiz has informed you that the law firm has been retained to represent Ms. Ester Soto, an employee of the Sof-Tech Corporation, a midsize high-tech company that produces software for financial institutions. Ms. Ortiz said that you will assist her in preparing the case for Ms. Soto.

Ms. Ortiz explained that Ms. Soto would be coming to the law office for a consultation and that you would be attending the meeting, which would be held in the law firm's conference room. At the meeting, Ms. Soto explained that she is currently employed as the controller of Sof-Tech. The company has a niche market and has been very successful.

When Ms. Ortiz asked Ms. Soto her background, she explained that her parents immigrated to the United States from Paraguay when she was 15 years old. Ms. Soto attended high school in New York City, graduated from New York University with an undergraduate degree in economics, and obtained a master's of business administration (MBA) degree from the University of Chicago with a major in finance. Before being hired by Sof-Tech Corporation, Ms. Soto worked at two companies for a period of seven years. At the second of these two companies, she was promoted to controller. Ms. Soto was hired as controller of Sof-Tech Corporation five years ago, and has worked at that position ever since.

Ms. Soto explained that when the position of chief financial officer (CFO) became available at Sof-Tech Corporation, she had applied for the job. Although she met the work and educational requirements of the CFO position, she was rejected for the job. Instead, another applicant, a Caucasian male with less experience than she

> "Good government is an empire of laws."
>
> John Adams, *Thoughts on Government* (1776)

had, was hired for the position. Ms. Soto believes that she was not promoted because of her gender and her ethnicity. Ms. Soto explained more details of her case before the meeting ended.

After Ms. Soto left the meeting, Ms. Ortiz asked you to have the answers to the following questions ready when a follow-up meeting is held in a few days: What federal act has been violated, according to the facts alleged by Ms. Soto? What administrative agency has authority to hear the case? Can you go online and find a rule or regulation of the administrative agency that defines the type of discrimination being alleged by Ms. Soto? Can a complaint be filed on behalf of Ms. Soto at the administrative agency? Does the agency have the power to hear the case, and if so, who will hear the case? Are there any rules that the administrative agency must follow in hearing the case? Is the decision of the administrative agency subject to judicial review?

LEARNING OBJECTIVE 1
Recognize the professional opportunities for paralegals in the administrative law area.

INTRODUCTION FOR THE PARALEGAL

Justice is the end of government. It is the end of civil society. It ever has been, and ever will be pursued, until it be obtained, or until liberty be lost in the pursuit.

James Madison
The Federalist No. 51 (1788)

Many paralegal professionals work in the area of administrative law. Some work for federal administrative agencies such as the Securities and Exchange Commission (SEC), the Federal Trade Commission (FTC), and other federal agencies. Paralegals also often work for state administrative agencies, including state corporations departments, environmental protection agencies, and other regulatory agencies.

In the administrative law field, paralegals may also work for attorneys who represent clients who are subject to regulation by administrative agencies. For example, if a client is prosecuted by the SEC for violation of federal securities laws, an attorney will represent the client at the proceedings. Those who seek licenses from administrative agencies to conduct business are also often represented by attorneys. For example, someone who wishes to form a national bank must obtain permission from the Office of the Comptroller of the Currency. An attorney may assist the person in dealing with that agency. Paralegals often assist attorneys in preparing for such administrative agency matters.

The following feature discusses the career opportunities for paralegal professionals in administrative law.

CAREER OPPORTUNITIES FOR PARALEGAL PROFESSIONALS IN ADMINISTRATIVE LAW

Lawyers increasingly employ paralegals in areas of law that involve practice before administrative agencies. Administrative law has become extremely important for businesses and individuals alike. Administrative agencies govern many aspects of business, and our personal lives as well.

The number of administrative agencies in this country is staggering. The federal government alone has dozens of agencies. These range from agencies that regulate specific industries to agencies whose powers apply to large segments of society and the economy. The following are only a few of the major federal administrative agencies:

- Environmental Protection Agency (EPA): regulates air, water, hazardous waste, and other types of pollution.
- Equal Employment Opportunity Commission (EEOC): enforces many antidiscrimination laws that affect businesses and their employees.
- Federal Trade Commission (FTC): enforces many consumer protection laws.
- Food and Drug Administration (FDA): regulates the safety of foods, drugs, cosmetics, and medical devices.
- Federal Communications Commission (FCC): regulates radio, television, cable, and other broadcast media.

- National Labor Relations Board (NLRB): regulates labor union formation, elections, bargaining with employers, and other labor issues.
- Securities and Exchange Commission (SEC): regulates the issuance, sale, and purchase of securities, including stocks and bonds.
- Department of Homeland Security (DHS): coordinates certain federal agencies in protecting the country against terrorism and other threats.

In addition to federal administrative agencies, there are thousands of state and local administrative agencies. These include agencies that license and regulate corporations and financial institutions, protect the environment, and perform many other functions. At the local level, cities and municipalities have administrative agencies that regulate construction, set building codes, establish zoning regulations, issue water permits, and perform other duties.

Paralegals often work for lawyers who specialize in making appearances before specific federal, state, and local administrative agencies. For example, lawyers prepare applications for submission to the Federal Communications Commission (FCC) to obtain licenses to operate radio, television, or cable companies. Lawyers are also asked to prepare applications to the federal Food and Drug Administration (FDA) to obtain approval to market a new drug.

The federal government has enacted the Administrative Procedure Act (APA), which establishes rules for legal practice before federal administrative agencies. There are similar statutes that set administrative procedures at the state level. In addition, each administrative agency has its own rules and regulations for submitting applications and appearing at hearings before it.

Paralegals who work for lawyers specializing in certain areas of administrative law must become familiar with a particular agency's rules and procedures. Paralegals often are called upon to assist in drafting documents that will be submitted to administrative agencies and preparing cases that will be decided by these agencies. Thus, paralegals often become experts in certain areas of administrative law, and therefore can be indispensable to lawyers who practice before those administrative agencies.

Administrative Law

LEARNING OBJECTIVE 2
Define *administrative law.*

Businesses are generally free to produce goods or services, enter into contracts, and otherwise conduct business as they see fit. However, businesses are also subject to substantial federal, state, and local government regulations. Government regulation is designed to protect employees and the public from unsafe and abusive practices by businesses. Many times when a regulatory statute is enacted, an **administrative agency** (or **regulatory agency**) is created to enforce the law. Because of their importance, administrative agencies are informally referred to as the "fourth branch of government."

Administrative agency (regulatory agency) An agency that the government creates to enforce a statute.

Regulatory agencies, and the industries, businesses, and professionals they regulate, are governed by a body of **administrative law**. These laws are often referred to as **regulatory statutes**. Sometimes when the legislative branch enacts a new statute, it authorizes an existing administrative agency to administer and enforce the law (see Exhibit 9.1).

Administrative law (regulatory statute) Law that governments enact to regulate industries, businesses, and professionals.

Example When Congress enacted the **Securities Act of 1933** and the Securities Exchange Act of 1934, it created the Securities and Exchange Commission (SEC), a federal administrative agency, to administer and enforce those statutes.

General Government Regulation

LEARNING OBJECTIVE 3
Describe the types of government regulation of business.

Many administrative agencies regulate businesses and industries collectively. This is called **general government regulation**. Most of the industries and businesses in the United States are subject to these laws. These laws do not regulate a specific industry but apply to all industries and businesses except those that are specifically exempt from certain regulations.

General government regulation Laws that regulate businesses and industries collectively.

Examples The federal National Labor Relations Board (NLRB) is empowered to regulate the formation and operation of labor unions in most industries and businesses in the United States. The federal Occupational Safety and Health Administration (OSHA) is authorized to regulate workplace safety for most industries and businesses in the country. The U.S. Equal Employment Opportunity Commission (EEOC) enforces equal opportunity in employment laws that cover most workers in the United States.

Exhibit 9.1 Administrative agency

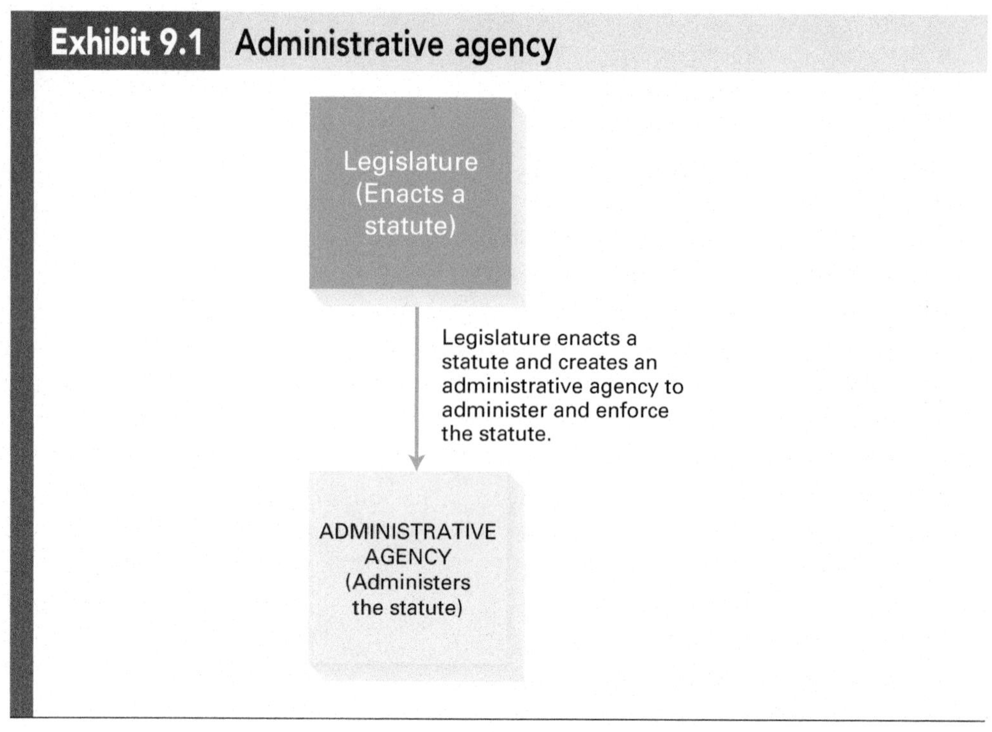
Legislature
(Enacts a
statute)
Legislature enacts a statute and creates an administrative agency to administer and enforce the statute.
ADMINISTRATIVE
AGENCY
(Administers
the statute)

Specific Government Regulation

Some administrative agencies, and the laws they enforce, are created to regulate specific industries or areas of commerce only. That is, an industry is subject to administrative laws that are specifically adopted to regulate that industry. This is called **specific government regulation** of business. Administrative agencies that are industry specific are created to administer those specific laws.

Specific government regulation Laws that regulate a specific industry or type of business.

Examples The Federal Communications Commission (FCC) regulates the operation of television and radio stations. The Federal Aviation Administration (FAA) regulates the operation of commercial airlines. The Office of the Comptroller of the Currency regulates the licensing and operation of national banks.

Federal and state governments have enacted many statutes to protect air, water, and the environment from pollution.

Administrative Agencies

LEARNING OBJECTIVE 4

List and explain the functions of administrative agencies.

Administrative agencies are created by federal, state, and local governments to enforce regulatory statutes. Government agencies range from large, complex federal agencies, such as the Department of Homeland Security, to local zoning boards. There are more than one hundred federal administrative agencies. Thousands of other administrative agencies have been created by state and local governments.

Cabinet-Level Federal Departments

At the federal level, the president can create **cabinet-level federal departments** that answer directly to the president. The president appoints cabinet members subject to confirmation by a majority vote of the U.S. Senate. Cabinet-level departments advise the president and are responsible for enforcing specific laws enacted by Congress. The fifteen departments of the executive branch are:

Cabinet-level federal agencies Federal agencies that advise the president and are responsible for enforcing specific administrative statutes enacted by Congress.

Department of Agriculture
Department of Commerce
Department of Defense
Department of Education
Department of Energy
Department of Health and Human Services
Department of Homeland Security
Department of Housing and Urban Development
Department of Interior
Department of Justice
Department of Labor
Department of State
Department of Transportation
Department of the Treasury
Department of Veterans Affairs

The organizational structure of the Department of Labor is set forth in Exhibit 9.2.

Department of Homeland Security

After the terrorist attacks of September 11, 2001, President George W. Bush issued an executive order creating the Office of Homeland Security. The president called for the office to be made into a cabinet-level department. Congress responded by enacting the **Homeland Security Act (HSA)** of 2002,[1] which created the cabinet-level **U.S. Department of Homeland Security (DHS)**. The creation of the DHS was the largest government reorganization in more than 50 years.

U.S. Department of Homeland Security (DHS) A cabinet-level federal administrative agency whose mission is to enforce laws to prevent terrorist attacks and related criminal activities.

The act placed 22 federal agencies, with approximately 200,000 employees, under the umbrella of the DHS. The DHS is the second-largest government agency, after the Department of Defense, and the agencies it oversees include:

- the Bureau of Customs and Border Protection,
- the Bureau of Citizenship and Immigration Services,
- the U.S. Secret Service,
- the Federal Emergency Management Agency,
- the Federal Computer Incident Response Center,
- the National Domestic Preparedness Office,
- the U.S. Coast Guard, and
- portions of the Federal Bureau of Investigation, Treasury Department, Commerce Department, and Justice Department.

---

[1] Public Law 107–295 (2002).

Exhibit 9.2 Organizational chart of the U.S. Department of Labor

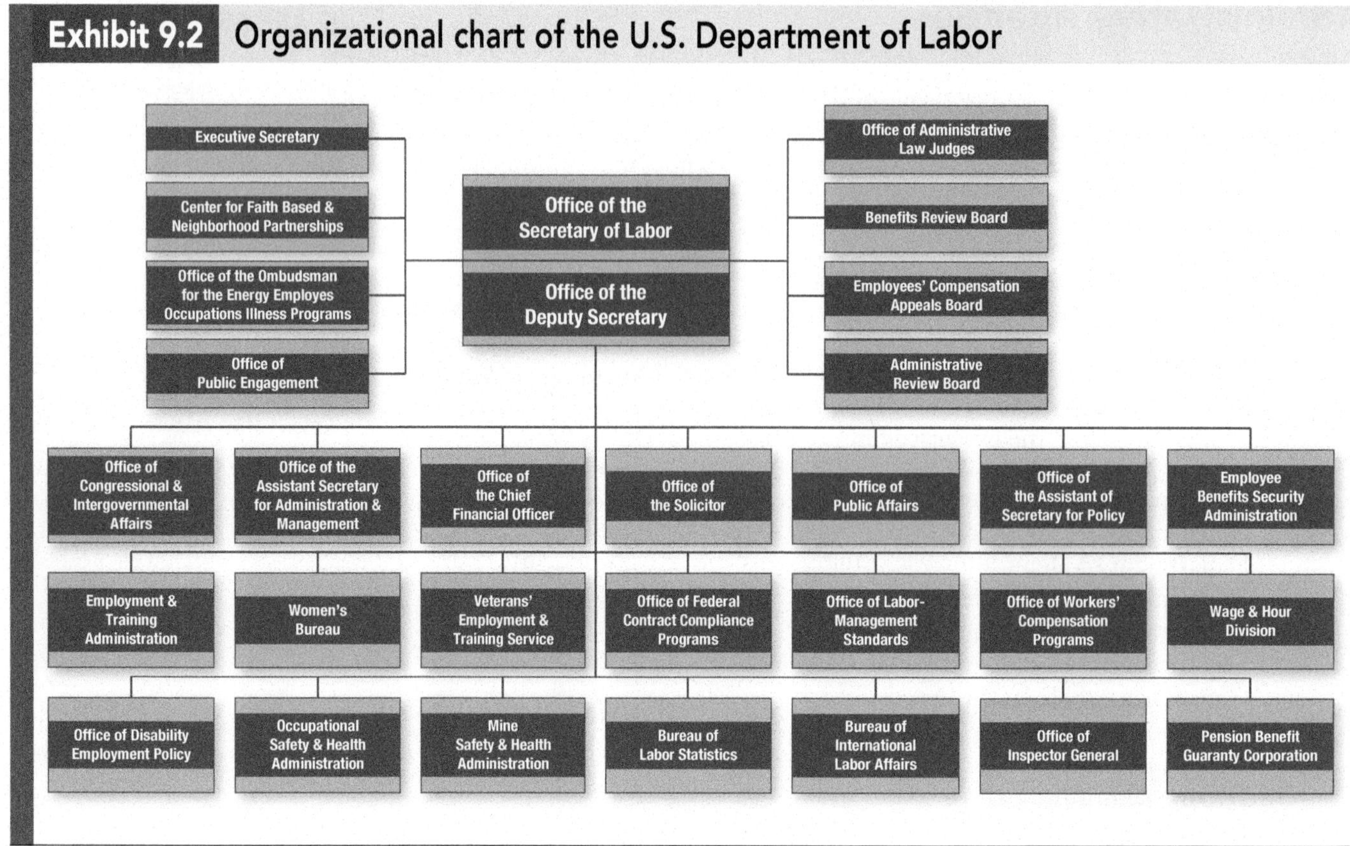

The mission of DHS is to enforce laws to prevent domestic terrorist attacks, reduce vulnerability to terrorist attacks, minimize the harm caused by such attacks, and assist in recovery in the event of a terrorist attack. The DHS provides services in the following critical areas:

(1) border and transportation security, including protecting airports, seaports, and borders, and providing immigration and visa processing;
(2) chemical, biological, radiological, and nuclear countermeasures, including metering the air for biological agents and developing vaccines and treatments for biological agents;
(3) information analysis and infrastructure protection, including protecting communications systems, power grids, transportation networks, telecommunications, and cyber systems; and
(4) emergency preparedness and response to terrorist incidents, including training first responders and coordinating government disaster relief.

Independent Federal Administrative Agencies

Independent federal administrative agencies
Federal agencies that have broad regulatory powers over key areas of the national economy.

At the federal level, Congress has created more than 100 administrative agencies called **independent federal administrative agencies**. These agencies have broad regulatory powers over key areas of the national economy and society.

Examples The Securities and Exchange Commission (SEC) regulates the issuance and trading of securities. The Federal Trade Commission (FTC) enforces federal antitrust and consumer protection laws. The Federal Communications Commission (FCC) regulates radio and television broadcasting and telecommunications.

State and Local Administrative Agencies

All states have created administrative agencies to enforce and interpret state regulatory law. **State administrative agencies** are empowered to enforce state statutes and have a profound effect on business. They have the power to adopt rules and regulations to interpret the statutes they are authorized to administer.

State administrative agencies Agencies created by legislative branches of states to administer state regulatory laws.

Examples Most states have a corporation department to enforce state corporation law and regulate the issuance of securities, a banking department to license and regulate the operation of banks, fish and game departments to regulate fishing and hunting within the state's boundaries, workers' compensation boards to decide workers' compensation claims for injuries that occur on the job, and environmental protection departments to regulate land, waterways, and other environmental matters.

Local governments such as cities, municipalities, and counties create **local administrative agencies** to administer local regulatory law.

Local administrative agencies Agencies created by cities, municipalities, and counties to administer local regulatory law.

Examples Counties have numerous administrative boards to regulate county activities. Cities and towns have school boards, zoning commissions, and other administrative bodies to regulate city and town matters.

In the following feature, a paralegal professional and owner of his own business discusses his position as a non-attorney Social Security Disability Appeals Representative. Exhibit 9.3 is an application form for an administrative hearing regarding a Social Security matter.

Paralegals *in* Practice

PARALEGAL PROFILE

Melvin E. Irvin

Since 1996, Melvin E. Irvin has worked as a non-attorney Social Security Disability Appeals Representative in the San Jose, California, area. He legally represents clients before the Social Security Administration (SSA) in appeals regarding Social Security disability benefits. In addition to being a Marine Corps veteran, Mel is a graduate of Santa Clara University Law School Institute for Paralegal Studies. He also earned the Certified Paralegal (CP) designation from the National Association of Legal Assistants.

As president of my own corporation, Melvin E. Irvin Disability Representative, Inc., I represent about 55–60 clients at any given time. The most important skills needed in my position are above-average communication skills and a good working knowledge of Social Security law. There are no specific educational requirements to become a non-attorney disability representative except that you cannot be a disbarred attorney, or disallowed by another government administration from practicing. Naturally, a college degree and a paralegal certificate are very helpful.

Over the past 20 years, successful representation has become more difficult as the SSA has significantly reduced its claim allowance rates. SSA representation fees are paid only on a contingency basis, whether you are an attorney or non-attorney. Since the SSA is backlogged on disability cases, currently more than 700,000 nationally, it may take two or more years before a new representative sees the first paycheck. This is due to the length of time it takes for a case to be resolved. Even so, my work is very rewarding because it allows me to help people who really need assistance.

I find that many people in the U.S. today still believe that paralegals can perform work directly for the public. According to Section 6450 of the California Business and Professions Code, those who call themselves paralegals must be attorney supervised, with few exceptions. One exception is legally representing the public in administrative law settings such as the SSA. As the current president of the California Alliance of Paralegal Associations, I help educate others about the paralegal profession. Part of my role is to encourage local paralegal associations to appoint public information officers who can respond to questions from the legal community, the public, and the media.

Exhibit 9.3 Application for Social Security administrative hearing

SOCIAL SECURITY ADMINISTRATION
OFFICE OF HEARINGS AND APPEALS

Form Approved
OMB No. 0960-0269

REQUEST FOR HEARING BY ADMINISTRATIVE LAW JUDGE
[Take or mail original and all copies to your local Social Security Office]

PRIVACY ACT NOTICE ON REVERSE SIDE OF FORM.

1. CLAIMANT	2. WAGE EARNER, IF DIFFERENT	3. SOC. SEC. CLAIM NUMBER	4. SPOUSE's CLAIM NUMBER

5. I REQUEST A HEARING BEFORE AN ADMINISTRATIVE LAW JUDGE. I disagree with the determination made on my claim because:

An Administrative Law Judge of the Office of Hearings and Appeals will be appointed to conduct the hearing or other proceedings in your case. You will receive notice of the time and place of a hearing at least 20 days before the date set for a hearing.

6. If you have additional evidence to submit check the following block and complete the statement: ☐

I have additional evidence to submit from (name and address of source): ______

(Please submit it to the Social Security Office within 10 days. Attach an additional sheet if you need more space.)

7. Check one of the blocks:

☐ I wish to appear at a hearing.

☐ I do not wish to appear and I request that a decision be made based on the evidence in my case. (Complete Waiver Form HA-4608)

You have a right to be represented at the hearing. If you are not represented but would like to be, your Social Security Office will give you a list of legal referral and service organizations. (If you are represented and have not done so previously, complete and submit form SSA-1696 (Appointment of Representative).)

[You should complete No. 8 and your representative (if any) should complete No. 9. If you are represented and your representative is not available to complete this form, you should also print his or her name, address, etc. in No. 9.]

8. (CLAIMANT'S SIGNATURE)	9. (REPRESENTATIVE'S SIGNATURE/NAME)
ADDRESS	(ADDRESS) ☐ ATTORNEY; ☐ NON ATTORNEY;
CITY STATE ZIP CODE	CITY STATE ZIP CODE
DATE AREA CODE AND TELEPHONE NUMBER	DATE AREA CODE AND TELEPHONE NUMBER

TO BE COMPLETED BY SOCIAL SECURITY ADMINISTRATION-ACKNOWLEDGMENT OF REQUEST FOR HEARING

10. **Request for Hearing RECEIVED for the Social Security Administration on** ______ by: ______

(TITLE) ADDRESS

11. Was the request for hearing received within 65 days of the reconsidered determination?
☐ YES ☐ NO

If no is checked, attach claimant's explanation for delay; and attach copy of appointment notice, letter, or other pertinent material or information in the Social Security Office.

12. Claimant not represented -
☐ list of legal referral and service organizations provided

13. Interpreter needed -
☐ enter language (including sign language): ______

14. Check one: ☐ Initial Entitlement Case
☐ Disability Cessation Case
☐ Other Postentitlement Case

15. Check claim type(s):
☐ RSI only ---(RSI)
☐ Title II Disability-worker or child---(DIWC)
☐ Title II Disability-widow(er) only---(DIWW)
☐ SSI Aged only---(SSIA)
☐ SSI Blind only---(SSIB)
☐ SSI Disability only ---(SSID)
☐ SSI Aged/Title II ---(SSAC)
☐ SSI Blind/Title II ---(SSBC)
☐ SSI Disability/Title II ---(SSDC)
☐ HI Entitlement ---(HIE)
☐ Other-Specify: (______)

16. **HO COPY SENT TO:** ______ HO on ______
☐ CF Attached: ☐ Title II; ☐ Title XVI; or
☐ Title II CF held in FO to establish CAPS ORBIT; or
☐ CF requested ☐ Title II; ☐ Title XVI
(Copy of teletype or phone report attached)

17. **CF COPY SENT TO:** ______ HO on ______
☐ CF Attached: ☐ Title II; ☐ Title XVI
☐ Other Attached: ______

FORM HA-501-U5 (5-1996) EF (7-2000)
Issue old stock

CLAIMS FOLDER

LEARNING OBJECTIVE 5
Explain the scope of the Administrative Procedure Act.

Administrative Procedure

Administrative law is a combination of *substantive* and *procedural law*. **Substantive administrative law** is law enacted by Congress or a state legislature that an administrative agency enforces. **Procedural administrative law** establishes the procedures that must be followed by an administrative agency while enforcing substantive laws.

Examples Congress created the federal Environmental Protection Agency (EPA) to enforce federal environmental laws to protect the environment. This is an example of substantive law—laws to protect the environment. In enforcing these laws, the EPA must follow certain established procedural rules (such as requirements to provide notice and a hearing). These are examples of procedural law.

Administrative Procedure Act

In 1946, Congress enacted the **Administrative Procedure Act (APA).**[2] This act is very important because it establishes procedures that federal administrative agencies must follow in conducting their affairs. The APA requires federal agencies to give notice of actions they plan on taking. It also requires hearings to be held in most cases, and it requires certain procedural safeguards and protocols to be followed at these proceedings.

Administrative Procedure Act (APA) A federal statute that establishes procedures to be followed by federal administrative agencies while conducting their affairs.

The APA also establishes how **rules and regulations** can be adopted by federal administrative agencies. This includes providing notice of proposed **rule making**, granting a time period for receiving comments from the public regarding proposed rule making, and holding hearings to take evidence. The APA provides a procedure for receiving evidence and hearing requests for the granting of federal licenses (such as a license to operate a national bank). The APA also establishes notice and hearing requirements, and rules for conducting agency adjudicative actions, such as actions to take away licenses from certain persons (for example, securities brokers' licenses). Most states have also enacted administrative procedural statutes that govern state administrative procedures.

Administrative Law Judges

Administrative law judges (ALJs) preside over administrative proceedings and decide questions of law and fact concerning each case. Each ALJ is an employee of the administrative agency that he or she serves. Both the administrative agency and the respondent may be represented by counsel. Witnesses may be examined and cross-examined, evidence may be introduced, and objections may be made. There is no jury, since the ALJ determines all questions of fact.

Administrative law judge (ALJ) An employee of an administrative agency who presides over an administrative proceeding and decides questions of law and fact concerning cases.

An ALJ's decision is issued in the form of an **administrative order**. The order must state the reasons for the ALJ's decision, and becomes final if it is not appealed. If appealed, the decision is reviewed by the administrative agency. Further appeal can be made to the appropriate federal court (in federal agency actions) or state court (in state agency actions).

Administrative order A decision issued by an administrative law judge.

Powers of Administrative Agencies

LEARNING OBJECTIVE 6
Describe the powers of administrative agencies.

When an administrative agency is created, it is delegated certain powers. The agency has only the legislative, judicial, and executive powers that are delegated to it. This is called the **delegation doctrine**. Thus, an agency can adopt a rule or regulation (a legislative function), prosecute a violation of the statute or rule (an executive function), and adjudicate the dispute (a judicial function). The courts have upheld as constitutional this combined power of administrative agencies. If an administrative agency acts outside the scope of its delegated powers, it is an unconstitutional act.

Delegation doctrine A doctrine that provides that when an administrative agency is created, it is delegated certain powers, and that the agency can use only the legislative, judicial, and executive powers that are delegated to it.

The legislative powers delegated to administrative agencies consist of substantive rule making, interpretative rule making, issuing statements of policy, and granting licenses.

[2] 5 U.S.C. Sections 551–706.

Rule Making

Substantive rule A rule issued by an administrative agency that has the force of law and to which covered persons and businesses must adhere.

Many federal statutes expressly authorize an administrative agency to issue **substantive rules**. A substantive rule is much like a statute: It has the force of law, and certain persons and businesses must adhere to it. Violators may be held civilly or criminally liable, depending on the rule. All substantive rules are subject to judicial review.

Example The Securities and Exchange Commission (SEC) is authorized to prohibit fraud in the purchase and sale of securities. The SEC therefore has the power to adopt rules that define what fraudulent conduct is prohibited by the federal securities laws.

A federal administrative agency that proposes to adopt a substantive rule must follow procedures set forth in the APA.[3] This means the agency must do the following:

1. It must publish a general notice of the proposed rule making in the ***Federal Register***. The notice must include:
   a. the time, place, and nature of the rule-making proceeding;
   b. the legal authority pursuant to which the rule is proposed; and
   c. the terms or substance of the proposed rule or a description of the subject and issues involved.
2. The agency must give interested persons an opportunity to participate in the rule-making process. This may involve oral hearings.
3. It must review all written and oral comments. Then the agency announces its *final rule making* in the matter. This procedure is often referred to as *notice-and-comment rule making*, or **informal rule making**.
4. The APA may require, in some instances, **formal rule making**. Here, the agency must conduct a trial-like hearing at which the parties may present evidence, engage in cross-examination, present rebuttal evidence, and similar procedures.

Interpretive rule A rule issued by an administrative agency that interprets existing statutory language.

Statement of policy A statement issued by an administrative agency that announces a proposed course of action that the agency intends to follow in the future.

Administrative agencies can issue an **interpretive rule** that interprets existing statutory language. Such rules do not establish new laws. Administrative agencies may issue a **statement of policy**. Such a statement announces a proposed course of action that an agency intends to follow in the future. Interpretive rules and statements of policy do not have the force of law and public notice and participation are not required.

A proposed rule published in the *Federal Register* is set forth in Exhibit 9.4.

Code of Federal Regulations

Code of Federal Regulations (CFR) A codification of the regulations that have been adopted by executive departments and administrative agencies of the federal government.

Rules and regulations adopted by federal administrative agencies are published in the *Federal Register*. The **Code of Federal Regulations (CFR)** is the codification of the regulations that have been adopted by executive departments and administrative agencies of the federal government. Each rule and regulation is assigned a CFR citation, such as 29 CFR 1604.11(a). This citation would be read as "title 29, part 1604, section 11, paragraph (a)."

The CFR is divided up into 50 titles that represent general areas subject to federal regulation. These titles are listed in Exhibit 9.5.

Each title is divided into chapters that state the name of the issuing department or agency. Each chapter is subdivided into parts that cover specific regulatory areas. Most parts are further subdivided into subparts. Each title of the CFR is updated once each calendar year and is available in printed form. Federal rules and regulations are also available in the **Electronic Code of Federal Regulations (e-CFR)** at www.ecfr.gov.

An example of an administrative rule adopted by the federal Equal Employment Opportunity Commission (EEOC) is shown in Exhibit 9.6.

Web Exploration

Go to the Electronic Code of Federal Regulations (e-CFR) website at www.ecfr.gov. Where the word "Browse" appears, select the title "Labor" and click on "Go." What regulatory entities are responsible for administering labor law?

[3] 5 U.S.C. Sections 553.

Exhibit 9.4 Proposed rule published in the *Federal Register*

12506

Proposed Rules

Federal Register

Vol. 77, No. 41

Thursday, March 1, 2012

This section of the FEDERAL REGISTER contains notices to the public of the proposed issuance of rules and regulations. The purpose of these notices is to give interested persons an opportunity to participate in the rule making prior to the adoption of the final rules.

DEPARTMENT OF TRANSPORTATION

Federal Aviation Administration

14 CFR Part 39

[Docket No. FAA–2012–0187; Directorate Identifier 2011–NM–094–AD]

RIN 2120–AA64

Airworthiness Directives; The Boeing Company Airplanes

AGENCY: Federal Aviation Administration (FAA), DOT.

ACTION: Notice of proposed rulemaking (NPRM).

SUMMARY: We propose to adopt a new airworthiness directive (AD) for certain The Boeing Company Model 757 airplanes. This proposed AD was prompted by fuel system reviews conducted by the manufacturer. This proposed AD would require modifying the fuel quantity indication system (FQIS) wiring or fuel tank systems to prevent development of an ignition source inside the center fuel tank. We are proposing this AD to prevent ignition sources inside the center fuel tank, which, in combination with flammable fuel vapors, could result in fuel tank explosions and consequent loss of the airplane.

DATES: We must receive comments on this proposed AD by April 30, 2012.

ADDRESSES: You may send comments, using the procedures found in 14 CFR 11.43 and 11.45, by any of the following methods:

- *Federal eRulemaking Portal:* Go to *http://www.regulations.gov.* Follow the instructions for submitting comments.
- *Fax:* 202–493–2251.
- *Mail:* U.S. Department of Transportation, Docket Operations, M–30, West Building Ground Floor, Room W12–140, 1200 New Jersey Avenue SE., Washington, DC 20590.
- *Hand Delivery:* Deliver to Mail address above between 9 a.m. and 5 p.m., Monday through Friday, except Federal holidays.

Examining the AD Docket

You may examine the AD docket on the Internet at *http://www.regulations.gov;* or in person at the Docket Management Facility between 9 a.m. and 5 p.m., Monday through Friday, except Federal holidays. The AD docket contains this proposed AD, the regulatory evaluation, any comments received, and other information. The street address for the Docket Office (phone: 800–647–5527) is in the **ADDRESSES** section. Comments will be available in the AD docket shortly after receipt.

FOR FURTHER INFORMATION CONTACT: Tak Kobayashi, Aerospace Engineer, Propulsion Branch, ANM–140S, FAA, Seattle Aircraft Certification Office (ACO), 1601 Lind Avenue SW., Renton, Washington 98057–3356; phone: 425–917–6499; fax: 425–917–6590; email: *takahisa.kobayashi@faa.gov.*

SUPPLEMENTARY INFORMATION:

Comments Invited

We invite you to send any written relevant data, views, or arguments about this proposal. Send your comments to an address listed under the **ADDRESSES** section. Include "Docket No. FAA–2012–0187; Directorate Identifier 2011–NM–094–AD" at the beginning of your comments. We specifically invite comments on the overall regulatory, economic, environmental, and energy aspects of this proposed AD. We will consider all comments received by the closing date and may amend this proposed AD because of those comments.

We will post all comments we receive, without change, to *http://www.regulations.gov,* including any personal information you provide. We will also post a report summarizing each substantive verbal contact we receive about this proposed AD.

Discussion

The FAA has examined the underlying safety issues involved in fuel tank explosions on several large transport airplanes, including the adequacy of existing regulations, the service history of airplanes subject to those regulations, and existing maintenance practices for fuel tank systems. As a result of those findings, we issued a regulation titled "Transport Airplane Fuel Tank System Design Review, Flammability Reduction and Maintenance and Inspection Requirements" (66 FR 23086, May 7, 2001). In addition to new airworthiness standards for transport airplanes and new maintenance requirements, this rule included Special Federal Aviation Regulation No. 88 ("SFAR 88," Amendment 21–78, and subsequent Amendments 21–82 and 21–83).

Among other actions, SFAR 88 requires certain type design (i.e., type certificate (TC) and supplemental type certificate (STC)) holders to substantiate that their fuel tank systems can prevent ignition sources in the fuel tanks. This requirement applies to type design holders for large turbine-powered transport airplanes and for subsequent modifications to those airplanes. It requires them to perform design reviews and to develop design changes and maintenance procedures if their designs do not meet the new fuel tank safety standards. As explained in the preamble to the rule, we intended to adopt airworthiness directives to mandate any changes found necessary to address unsafe conditions identified as a result of these reviews.

In evaluating these design reviews, we have established four criteria intended to define the unsafe conditions associated with fuel tank systems that require corrective actions. The percentage of operating time during which fuel tanks are exposed to flammable conditions is one of these criteria. The other three criteria address the failure types under evaluation: single failures, a combination of failures, and unacceptable service (failure) experience. For all four criteria, the evaluations included consideration of previous actions taken that may mitigate the need for further action.

We have determined that the actions identified in this proposed AD are necessary to reduce the potential of ignition sources inside the center fuel tank, which has been identified to have a high flammability exposure. Ignition sources inside the center fuel tank, in combination with flammable fuel vapors, could result in fuel tank explosions and consequent loss of the airplane.

The combination of a latent failure within the center fuel tank and a subsequent single failure of the fuel quantity indicating system (FQIS) wiring or components outside the fuel tank can cause development of an

(continued)

Exhibit 9.4 Proposed rule published in the *Federal Register* (continued)

Federal Register / Vol. 77, No. 41 / Thursday, March 1, 2012 / Proposed Rules 12507

ignition source inside the center fuel tank. Latent in-tank failures, including corrosion/deposits at wire terminals, conductive debris on fuel system probes, wires or probes contacting the tank structure, and wire faults, could create a conductive path inside the center fuel tank. Out-tank single failures including hot shorts in airplane wiring and/or the FQIS processor could result in electrical energy being transmitted into the center fuel tank via the FQIS wiring. The electrical energy, if combined with a latent in-tank failure, could be sufficient to create an ignition source inside the center fuel tank, which, combined with flammable fuel vapors could result in a catastrophic fuel tank explosion.

SFAR 88 and Fuel Tank Flammability Reduction Rule

The National Transportation Safety Board (NTSB) determined that the combination of a latent failure inside the center fuel tank and a subsequent single failure of the FQIS wiring or components outside the fuel tank was the most likely ignition source inside the center fuel tank that resulted in the TWA Flight 800 explosion. After the TWA 800 accident, we issued AD 99–03–04, Amendment 39–11018 (64 FR 4959, February 2, 1999), and AD 98–20–40, Amendment 39–10808 (63 FR 52147, September 30, 1998), mandating separation of the FQIS wiring that penetrates the fuel tank from high power wires and circuits on the classic Boeing 737 and 747 airplanes. Those ADs resulted in installation of Transient Suppression Units (TSUs), Transient Suppression Devices (TSDs), or Isolated Fuel Quantity Transmitter (IFQT) as a method of compliance with the AD requirements.

After we issued those ADs, the findings from the SFAR 88 review showed that most transport category airplanes with high flammability fuel tanks needed TSUs, TSDs, or IFQTs to prevent electrical energy from entering the fuel tanks via the FQIS wiring in the event of a latent failure in combination with a single failure.

Installation of those FQIS protection devices, however, was determined unnecessary on those airplanes that are required to comply with the "Reduction of Fuel Tank Flammability in Transport Category Airplanes" rule (73 FR 42444, July 21, 2008), referred to as the Fuel Tank Flammability Reduction (FTFR) rule. The FTFR rule requires incorporation of a flammability reduction means (FRM) that converts high flammability fuel tanks into low flammability fuel tanks for certain airplane models. Therefore, the unsafe condition identified by SFAR 88 is mitigated by incorporation of an FRM, as discussed in the FTFR rule.

This proposed AD is intended to address the unsafe condition associated with the FQIS wiring that penetrates the center fuel tank for all Boeing Model 757 airplanes that are not subject to the requirements of the FTFR rule. This proposed AD would apply to airplanes operated in all-cargo service and airplanes operated under Title 14 Code of Federal Regulations (CFR) part 91, since those airplanes are not subject to the requirements of the FTFR rule. Also, this proposed AD would apply to airplanes for which the State of Manufacture issued the original certificate of airworthiness or export airworthiness approval prior to January 1, 1992, since those airplanes are also not subject to the requirements of the FTFR rule. However, as explained in paragraph 2–5.a. of Advisory Circular 120–98, "Operator Requirements for Incorporation of Fuel Tank Flammability Reduction Requirements," dated May 7, 2009, to operate a pre-1992 airplane in passenger service after December 26, 2017, operators must incorporate an FRM that meets the requirements of § 26.33(c) before that date. For such airplanes on which an FRM is incorporated, further compliance with this proposed AD is not required.

The nitrogen generating system (NGS) being developed by Boeing to meet the FTFR rule addresses the unsafe condition of this AD, as well as providing other safety improvements. Paragraph (h) of this proposed AD provides that, for operators not required to comply with the FTFR rule, electing to comply with the FTFR rule would be an acceptable method of addressing the unsafe condition.

As discussed in the FTFR rule, the FAA recognized that separate airworthiness actions would be initiated to address the remaining fuel system safety issues for airplanes for which an FRM is not required. We have notified design approval holders that service instructions to support introduction of FQIS protection are now necessary for fuel tanks that are not required to be modified with an FRM by the FTFR rule. To date we have not received any service information from Boeing addressing this specific threat; therefore, we are proceeding with this proposal, which would require modifications using methods approved by the Manager of the Seattle Aircraft Certification Office.

We plan similar actions for those Boeing and Airbus airplanes with similar FQIS vulnerabilities that are not affected by the FTFR rule.

FAA's Determination

We are proposing this AD because we evaluated all the relevant information and determined the unsafe condition described previously is likely to exist or develop in other products of the same type design.

Proposed AD Requirements

This proposed AD would require modifying the FQIS wiring or fuel tank systems to prevent development of an ignition source inside the center fuel tank.

Costs of Compliance

We estimate that this proposed AD affects 352 airplanes of U.S. registry. We have been advised that some of those airplanes are subject to the requirements of the FTFR rule and therefore are excluded from the requirements of this AD.

Because the manufacturer has not yet developed a modification commensurate with the actions specified by this proposed AD, we cannot provide specific information regarding the required number of work hours or the cost of parts to do the proposed modification. In addition, modification costs will likely vary depending on the operator and the airplane configuration. The proposed compliance time of 60 months should provide ample time for the development, approval, and installation of an appropriate modification.

Based on similar modifications, however, we can provide some estimated costs for the proposed modification in this NPRM. The modifications mandated by AD 99–03–04, Amendment 39–11018 (64 FR 4959, February 2, 1999), and AD 98–20–40, Amendment 39–10808 (63 FR 52147, September 30, 1998), for the classic Boeing Model 737 and 747 airplanes (i.e., TSD, TSU, IFQT) are not available for Boeing Model 757 airplanes. But, based on the costs associated with those modifications, we estimate the cost of this new proposed modification to be no more than $100,000 per airplane. The Honeywell FQIS may need additional modifications, which may cost as much as $100,000 per airplane. The cost impact of the proposed AD therefore is estimated to be between $100,000 and $200,000 per airplane.

As indicated earlier in this preamble, we specifically invite the submission of comments and other data regarding the costs of this proposed AD.

(continued)

Exhibit 9.4 Proposed rule published in the *Federal Register* (continued)

12508 Federal Register / Vol. 77, No. 41 / Thursday, March 1, 2012 / Proposed Rules

Authority for This Rulemaking

Title 49 of the United States Code specifies the FAA's authority to issue rules on aviation safety. Subtitle I, section 106, describes the authority of the FAA Administrator. Subtitle VII: Aviation Programs, describes in more detail the scope of the Agency's authority.

We are issuing this rulemaking under the authority described in subtitle VII, part A, subpart III, section 44701: "General requirements." Under that section, Congress charges the FAA with promoting safe flight of civil aircraft in air commerce by prescribing regulations for practices, methods, and procedures the Administrator finds necessary for safety in air commerce. This regulation is within the scope of that authority because it addresses an unsafe condition that is likely to exist or develop on products identified in this rulemaking action.

Regulatory Findings

We determined that this proposed AD would not have federalism implications under Executive Order 13132. This proposed AD would not have a substantial direct effect on the States, on the relationship between the national Government and the States, or on the distribution of power and responsibilities among the various levels of government.

For the reasons discussed above, I certify this proposed regulation:

(1) Is not a "significant regulatory action" under Executive Order 12866,

(2) Is not a "significant rule" under the DOT Regulatory Policies and Procedures (44 FR 11034, February 26, 1979),

(3) Will not affect intrastate aviation in Alaska, and

(4) Will not have a significant economic impact, positive or negative, on a substantial number of small entities under the criteria of the Regulatory Flexibility Act.

List of Subjects in 14 CFR Part 39

Air transportation, Aircraft, Aviation safety, Incorporation by reference, Safety.

The Proposed Amendment

Accordingly, under the authority delegated to me by the Administrator, the FAA proposes to amend 14 CFR part 39 as follows:

PART 39—AIRWORTHINESS DIRECTIVES

1. The authority citation for part 39 continues to read as follows:

Authority: 49 U.S.C. 106(g), 40113, 44701.

§ 39.13 [Amended]

2. The FAA amends § 39.13 by adding the following new airworthiness directive (AD):

The Boeing Company: Docket No. FAA–2012–0187; Directorate Identifier 2011–NM–094–AD.

(a) Comments Due Date

We must receive comments by April 30, 2012.

(b) Affected ADs

None.

(c) Applicability

This AD applies to The Boeing Company Model 757–200, –200PF, –200CB, and –300 series airplanes; certificated in any category; for which compliance with 14 CFR 121.1117(d), 125.509(d), or 129.117(d) is not required; regardless of the date of issuance of the original certificate of airworthiness or export airworthiness approval.

(d) Subject

Joint Aircraft System Component (JASC)/Air Transport Association (ATA) of America Code 7397: Engine fuel system wiring.

(e) Unsafe Condition

This AD was prompted by fuel system reviews conducted by the manufacturer. We are issuing this AD to prevent development of an ignition source inside the center fuel tank caused by a latent in-tank failure combined with electrical energy transmitted into the center fuel tank via the fuel quantity indicating system (FQIS) wiring due to a single out-tank failure.

(f) Compliance

Comply with this AD within the compliance times specified, unless already done.

(g) Modification

Within 60 months after the effective date of this AD, modify the FQIS wiring or fuel tank systems to prevent development of an ignition source inside the center fuel tank, in accordance with a method approved by the Manager, Seattle Aircraft Certification Office (ACO), FAA.

Note 1 to paragraph (g) of this AD: After accomplishment of the actions required by paragraph (g) of this AD, maintenance and/or preventive maintenance under 14 CFR part 43 is permitted provided the maintenance does not result in changing the AD-mandated configuration (reference 14 CFR 39.7).

(h) Optional Installation of Flammability Reduction Means

As an alternative to the requirements of paragraph (g) of this AD, operators may elect to comply with the requirements of 14 CFR 121.1117 or 14 CFR 125.509 or 14 CFR 129.117 (not including the exclusion of cargo airplanes in Sections 121.1117(j), 129.117(j), and 125.509(j)). Following this election, failure to comply with Sections 121.1117, 129.117, and 125.509 is a violation of this AD.

(i) Alternative Methods of Compliance (AMOCs)

(1) The Manager, Seattle ACO, FAA, has the authority to approve AMOCs for this AD, if requested using the procedures found in 14 CFR 39.19. In accordance with 14 CFR 39.19, send your request to your principal inspector or local Flight Standards District Office, as appropriate. If sending information directly to the manager of the ACO, send it to the attention of the person identified in the Related Information section of this AD. Information may be emailed to: *9-ANM-Seattle-ACO-AMOC-Requests@faa.gov.*

(2) Before using any approved AMOC, notify your appropriate principal inspector, or lacking a principal inspector, the manager of the local flight standards district office/certificate holding district office.

(j) Related Information

For more information about this AD, contact Tak Kobayashi, Aerospace Engineer, Propulsion Branch, ANM–140S, FAA, Seattle Aircraft Certification Office (ACO), 1601 Lind Avenue SW., Renton, Washington 98057–3356; phone: 425–917–6499; fax: 425–917–6590; email: *takahisa.kobayashi@faa.gov.*

Issued in Renton, Washington, on February 21, 2012.

Ali Bahrami,

Manager, Transport Airplane Directorate, Aircraft Certification Service.

[FR Doc. 2012–4931 Filed 2–29–12; 8:45 am]

BILLING CODE 4910–13–P

DEPARTMENT OF JUSTICE

Drug Enforcement Administration

21 CFR Part 1308

[Docket No. DEA–345]

Schedules of Controlled Substances: Placement of Five Synthetic Cannabinoids Into Schedule I

AGENCY: Drug Enforcement Administration, Department of Justice.

ACTION: Notice of proposed rulemaking.

SUMMARY: The Drug Enforcement Administration (DEA) proposes placing five synthetic cannabinoids 1-pentyl-3-(1-naphthoyl)indole (JWH–018), 1-butyl-3-(1-naphthoyl)indole (JWH–073), 1-[2-(4-morpholinyl)ethyl]-3-(1-naphthoyl)indole (JWH–200), 5-(1,1-dimethylheptyl)-2-(3-hydroxycyclohexyl)-phenol (CP–47,497), and 5-(1,1-dimethyloctyl)-2-(3-hydroxycyclohexyl)-phenol (cannabicyclohexanol, CP–47,497 C8 homologue) including their salts, isomers, and salts of isomers whenever the existence of such salts, isomers, and salts of isomers is possible, into Schedule I of the Controlled Substances Act (CSA). This proposed action is pursuant to the CSA which requires that

Exhibit 9.5 Titles of the Code of Federal Regulations

Title 1	General Provisions	Title 26	Internal Review
Title 2	Grants and Agreements	Title 27	Alcohol, Tobacco Products, and Firearms
Title 3	The President	Title 28	Judicial Administration
Title 4	Accounts	Title 29	Labor
Title 5	Administrative Personnel	Title 30	Mineral Resources
Title 6	Homeland Security	Title 31	Money and Finance: Treasury
Title 7	Agriculture	Title 32	National Defense
Title 8	Aliens and Nationality	Title 33	Navigation and Navigable Waters
Title 9	Animals and Animal Products	Title 34	Education
Title 10	Energy	Title 35	Reserved (formerly Panama Canal)
Title 11	Federal Elections	Title 36	Parks, Forests, and Public Property
Title 12	Banks and Banking	Title 37	Patents, Trademarks, and Copyrights
Title 13	Business Credit and Assistance	Title 38	Pensions, Bonuses, and Veterans' Relief
Title 14	Aeronautics and Space	Title 39	Postal Service
Title 15	Commerce and Foreign Trade	Title 40	Protection of Environment
Title 16	Commercial Practices	Title 41	Public Contracts and Property Management
Title 17	Commodity and Securities Exchanges	Title 42	Public Health
Title 18	Conservation of Power and Water Resources	Title 43	Public Lands: Interior
Title 19	Custom Duties	Title 44	Emergency Management and Assistance
Title 20	Employees' Benefits	Title 45	Public Welfare
Title 21	Food and Drugs	Title 46	Shipping
Title 22	Foreign Relations	Title 47	Telecommunication
Title 23	Highways	Title 48	Federal Acquisition Regulations System
Title 24	Housing and Urban Development	Title 49	Transportation
Title 25	Indians	Title 50	Wildlife and Fisheries

Licensing Power

License Permission that an administrative agency grants to persons or businesses to conduct certain types of commerce or professions.

Statutes often require the issuance of a government **license** before a person or business can enter certain types of industries (such as banks, television and radio stations, and commercial airlines) or professions (such as doctors, lawyers, dentists, certified public accountants, and contractors). The administrative agency that regulates the specific area is given **licensing power** to determine whether to grant a license to an applicant.

Applicants must usually submit detailed applications to the appropriate administrative agency. In addition, the agency usually accepts written comments from interested parties and holds hearings on the matter. Courts generally defer to the expertise of administrative agencies in licensing matters.

> **Example** A group of persons wants to start a new national bank. To do this, the applicants must obtain approval from the Office of the Comptroller of Currency (OCC), a federal administrative agency that charters, supervises, and regulates national banks. The group will hire lawyers, economists, accountants, and other professionals to prepare the application. After considering the application, the OCC will either approve or reject it.

Judicial Authority

Judicial authority Authority of an administrative agency to adjudicate cases in an administrative proceeding.

Many administrative agencies have the **judicial authority** to decide cases through administrative proceedings. Such a proceeding is initiated when an agency serves a complaint on a party the agency believes has violated a statute or an administrative rule or order.

Exhibit 9.6 Administrative rule adopted by the Equal Employment Opportunity Commission

United States Code of Federal Regulations
Title 29-Labor

Subtitle B-Regulations Relating to Labor

Chapter XIV–Equal Employment Opportunity Commission
Part 1604–Guidelines on Discrimination Because of Sex

Section 1604.11–Sexual harassment

(a) Harassment on the basis of sex is a violation of section 703 of title VII. Unwelcome sexual advances, requests for sexual favors, and other verbal or physical conduct of a sexual nature constitute sexual harassment when (1) submission to such conduct is made either explicitly or implicitly a term or condition of an individual's employment, (2) submission to or rejection of such conduct by an individual is used as the basis for employment decisions affecting such individual, or (3) such conduct has the purpose or effect of unreasonably interfering with an individual's work performance or creating an intimidating, hostile, or offensive working environment.

(b) In determining whether alleged conduct constitutes sexual harassment, the Commission will look at the record as a whole and at the totality of the circumstances, such as the nature of the sexual advances and the context in which the alleged incidents occurred. The determination of the legality of a particular action will be made from the facts, on a case by case basis.

(c) [Reserved]

(d) With respect to conduct between fellow employees, an employer is responsible for acts of sexual harassment in the workplace where the employer (or its agents or supervisory employees) knows or should have known of the conduct, unless it can show that it took immediate and appropriate corrective action.

(e) An employer may also be responsible for the acts of non-employees, with respect to sexual harassment of employees in the workplace, where the employer (or its agents or supervisory employees) knows or should have known of the conduct and fails to take immediate and appropriate corrective action. In reviewing these cases the Commission will consider the extent of the employer's control and any other legal responsibility which the employer may have with respect to the conduct of such non-employees.

(f) Prevention is the best tool for the elimination of sexual harassment. An employer should take all steps necessary to prevent sexual harassment from occurring, such as affirmatively raising the subject, expressing strong disapproval, developing appropriate sanctions, informing employees of their right to raise and how to raise the issue of harassment under title VII, and developing methods to sensitize all concerned.

(g) Other related practices: Where employment opportunities or benefits are granted because of an individual's submission to the employer's sexual advances or requests for sexual favors, the employer may be held liable for unlawful sex discrimination against other persons who were qualified for but denied that employment opportunity or benefit.

The principles involved here continue to apply to race, color, religion or national origin.

Example The Occupational Safety and Health Administration (OSHA) is a federal administrative agency empowered to enforce worker safety rules. OSHA can bring an administrative proceeding against an employer for violating a federal worker safety rule. The agency can make a decision that the employer violated the rule and order the violator to pay a fine.

Procedural due process Due process that requires the respondent to be given proper and timely notice of the allegations or charges against him or her and an opportunity to present evidence on the matter.

In adjudicating cases, an administrative agency must comply with the Due Process Clause of the U.S. Constitution (or state constitution, if applicable). **Procedural due process** requires the respondent to be given proper and timely notice of the allegations or charges against him or her and an opportunity to present evidence on the matter.

A decision of an administrative law judge (ALJ) is set forth in Exhibit 9.7.

Exhibit 9.7 Decision of an administrative law judge

INITIAL DECISION RELEASE NO. 432

ADMINISTRATIVE PROCEEDING

FILE NO. 3-14161

UNITED STATES OF AMERICA

Before the

SECURITIES AND EXCHANGE COMMISSION

In the Matter of :

GORDON A. DRIVER : INITIAL DECISION

: September 22, 2011

APPEARANCES: Spencer E. Bendell and Susan F. Hannan for the Division of Enforcement, Securities and Exchange Commission. Gordon A. Driver, pro se.

BEFORE: Robert G. Mahony, Administrative Law Judge.

INTRODUCTION

The Securities and Exchange Commission (Commission) issued its Order Instituting Proceedings (OIP) on December 10, 2010, pursuant to Section 15(b) of the Securities Exchange Act of 1934 (Exchange Act). The OIP alleges that on December 14, 2009, a final judgment was entered by consent against Respondent Gordon A. Driver (Driver or Respondent) permanently enjoining him from future violations of the federal securities laws. The Commission instituted this proceeding to determine whether these allegations are true and, if so, to decide whether remedial action is appropriate in the public interest. The Division of Enforcement (Division) seeks to bar Driver from association with any broker or dealer. Additionally, the Division seeks to collaterally bar Driver under the Dodd-Frank Wall Street Reform and Consumer Protection Act of 2010 (Dodd-Frank Act) from association

(continued)

Exhibit 9.7 Decision of an administrative law judge *(continued)*

with any investment adviser, municipal securities dealer, municipal advisor, transfer agent, or nationally recognized statistical rating organization (NRSRO).

FINDINGS OF FACT

Driver, age fifty-one as of May 14, 2009, was a resident of Las Vegas, Nevada, and Hamilton, Ontario, Canada. From 1998 to 2007, during which Driver engaged in part of the conduct underlying the Judgment against him, Driver resided in Southern California.

From February 2006 to May 2009, Driver, acting as an unregistered broker, engaged in the misconduct underlying the Judgment against him. During this time, Driver was associated with Axcess Automation, LLC (Axcess), an entity registered as a Nevada limited liability company since October 17, 2007. Driver acted as Axcess' manager, was a signatory on the bank accounts into which investors wired funds, and had sole discretionary authority over the accounts through which he traded investor funds.

Driver raised at least $14.1 million from over 100 investors in the United States and Canada from approximately February 2006 to May 2009. Driver fraudulently misrepresented to investors that he would use their funds to trade "e-Mini S&P 500 futures" using proprietary software, and that he would provide investors with between one percent and five percent weekly return. Driver solicited friends, neighbors, and business acquaintances, and hired "finders" personally to recruit additional investors. Driver directed investors to wire transfer their funds into his personal bank account or into an account held in Axcess' name.

Driver used $3.7 million of the $14.1 million deposited into these accounts to engage in futures trading, ultimately resulting in a cumulative loss of $3.55 million. Additionally, Driver operated a "ponzi scheme" and misappropriated approximately $10.7 million of the $14.1 million by using funds received from new investors to pay existing investors. Further, over $1.1 million of the $14.1 million collected from investors was misappropriated by Driver and used by him to pay his personal expenses.

In February 2009, Driver prepared and provided a false annual statement, on Axcess letterhead, to forty-eight investors falsely showing an account balance of $9.6 million as of December 31, 2008, when, in fact, Driver only held a total of approximately $276,000 in all its bank accounts. Further, Driver fabricated and provided a trading account statement to at least one "finder" in October 2008, falsely stating an account balance of approximately $34.7 million when, in fact, the account balance was approximately $11,000.

On December 3, 2009, Driver consented to the entry of the Judgment permanently restraining and enjoining him from violating Sections 5 and 17(a) of the Securities Act of 1933, Sections 10(b) and 15(a) of the Exchange Act, and Rule 10b-5 promulgated thereunder. Additionally, Driver was ordered to pay disgorgement. On December 14, 2009, the Judgment was filed.

CONCLUSIONS OF LAW

Based on the foregoing, Driver is subject to Section 15(b)(6) of the Exchange Act, and the Administrative Law Judge has grounds to impose remedial sanctions, including a collateral bar under the Dodd-Frank Act, if such sanctions are in the public interest.

To determine whether sanctions under Section 15(b) of the Exchange Act are in the public interest, the Commission considers six factors: (1) the egregiousness of the respondent's actions; (2) whether the violations were isolated or recurrent; (3) the degree of scienter; (4) the sincerity of the respondent's assurances against future violations; (5) the respondent's recognition of the wrongful nature of his or her conduct; and (6) the likelihood that the respondent's occupation will present opportunities for future violations. No one factor is controlling. Remedial sanctions are not intended to punish a respondent, but to protect the public from future harm.

Driver's actions were egregious and recurrent. Driver engaged in a "ponzi scheme" spanning more than three years causing substantial harm to over 100 investors. He provided false and misleading information to certain of those investors and "finders." Additionally, Driver used significant investor funds for his own benefit.

Driver acted with scienter. Driver had sole discretion and authority over the bank accounts into which he directed investors to wire transfer their funds. He had actual knowledge of the trading losses he was incurring, while at the same time continuing to provide false and misleading information to investors regarding the account balances.

(continued)

Exhibit 9.7 Decision of an administrative law judge *(continued)*

Driver has not admitted the wrongful nature of his conduct. Likewise, he has made no assurances against future violations. Throughout his Deposition, Driver asserted his privilege against self-incrimination under the Fifth Amendment. Without an associational bar, the potential for Driver's future violations remains. Further, the Commission has often emphasized, the public interest determination extends to the public-at-large, the welfare of investors as a class, and standards of conduct in the securities business generally.

In view of the factors in their entirety, a collateral bar is necessary and appropriate in the public interest.

ORDER

IT IS ORDERED that, pursuant to Section 15(b)(6)(A) of the Securities Exchange Act of 1934, Gordon A. Driver is barred from association with any broker, dealer, investment adviser, municipal securities dealer, municipal advisor, transfer agent, and NRSRO, and from participating in an offering of penny stock.

The Commission will enter an order of finality unless a party files a petition for review or a motion to correct a manifest error of fact, or the Commission determines on its own initiative to review the Initial Decision as to a party. If any of these events occur, the Initial Decision shall not become final as to that party.

Robert G. Mahony
Administrative Law Judge

UNITED STATES OF AMERICA

Before the

SECURITIES AND EXCHANGE COMMISSION

SECURITIES EXCHANGE ACT OF 1934

Rel. No. 65707/November 8, 2011

Admin. Proc. File No. 3-14161

In the Matter of :
:
GORDON A. DRIVER :
:
:

NOTICE THAT INITIAL DECISION HAS BECOME FINAL

The time for filing a petition for review of the initial decision in this proceeding has expired. No such petition has been filed by Gordon A. Driver, and the Commission has not chosen to review the decision on its own initiative.

Accordingly, notice is hereby given, pursuant to Rule 360(d) of the Commission's Rules of Practice, that the initial decision of the administrative law judge has become the final decision of the Commission with respect to Gordon A. Driver. The order contained in that decision is hereby declared effective. That order barred Gordon A. Driver from association with any broker, dealer, investment adviser, municipal securities dealer, municipal advisor, transfer agent, and NRSRO, and from participating in an offering of penny stock.

For the Commission by the Office of the General Counsel, pursuant to delegated authority.

Elizabeth M. Murphy, Secretary

Executive Power

Administrative agencies are usually granted **executive powers**, such as the power to investigate and prosecute possible violations of statutes, administrative rules, and administrative orders.

Executive power Power that administrative agencies are granted, such as to investigate and prosecute possible violations of statutes, administrative rules, and administrative orders.

> Example The Antitrust Division of the United States Department of Justice suspects that three companies in the same line of commerce are engaged in illegal price fixing. The Department of Justice has the authority to investigate whether a criminal violation of the Sherman Antitrust Act has occurred. The Department of Justice can prosecute suspected criminal violators of criminal antitrust laws.

The legislative, judicial, and executive powers of administrative agencies are described in Exhibit 9.8.

Administrative Searches

LEARNING OBJECTIVE 7

Describe administrative searches.

To perform its functions, an agency must often obtain information from the persons and businesses under investigation, as well as from other sources. If the required information is not supplied voluntarily, or if those being investigated do not voluntarily give permission for the inspection of their premises, the agency may issue an administrative subpoena to search the premises and obtain the necessary evidence. This is called an **administrative search**.

Exhibit 9.8 Powers of administrative agencies

Power	Description of Power
1. Legislative Power	
A. Substantive rule making	To adopt rules that advance the purpose of the statutes that the agency is empowered to enforce. These rules have the force of law. Public notice and participation are required.
B. Interpretive rule making	To adopt rules that interpret statutes. These rules do not establish new laws. Neither public notice nor participation is required.
C. Statements of policy	To announce a proposed course of action the agency plans to take in the future. These statements do not have the force of law. Public participation and notice are not required.
D. Licensing	To grant licenses to applicants (e.g., television station licenses, bank charters) and to suspend or revoke licenses.
2. Judicial Power	The power to adjudicate cases through an administrative proceeding. This includes the power to issue a complaint, hold a hearing by an administrative law judge (ALJ), and issue an order deciding the case and assessing remedies.
3. Executive Power	The power to prosecute violations of statutes and administrative rules and orders. This includes the power to investigate suspected violations, issue administrative subpoenas, and conduct administrative searches.

Administrative subpoena An order that directs the subject of the subpoena to disclose requested information.

An administrative agency can issue an **administrative subpoena** to a business or person subject to its jurisdiction. The subpoena directs the party to disclose the requested information to the administrative agency. The administrative agency can seek judicial enforcement of the subpoena if the party does not comply.

Most inspections by administrative agencies are considered "searches" that are subject to the **Fourth Amendment to the U.S. Constitution**. This amendment protects persons (including businesses) from **unreasonable search and seizure**. Searches by administrative agencies are generally considered to be "reasonable," within the meaning of the Fourth Amendment, if

Unreasonable search and seizure Any search and seizure by the government that violates the Fourth Amendment to the U.S. Constitution.

- the party voluntarily agrees to the search;
- the search is conducted pursuant to a validly issued **search warrant**;
- a warrantless search is conducted in an emergency situation;
- the business is part of a special industry where warrantless searches are automatically considered valid (such as the sale of liquor or firearms); or
- the business is part of a hazardous industry and a statute expressly provides for non-arbitrary warrantless searches (such as coal mines).

Evidence from a search and seizure not meeting any of these requirements is considered "tainted evidence" and is inadmissible in court.

LEARNING OBJECTIVE 8
Explain the judicial review of administrative agency decisions.

Judicial Review of Administrative Agency Actions

Many federal statutes expressly provide for **judicial review of administrative agency actions**. Where an enabling statute does not provide for review by the agency, the APA authorizes judicial review of agency actions. The party appealing the decision of an administrative agency is called the **petitioner**.

Decisions of federal administrative agencies are appealed to the appropriate federal court. Decisions of state administrative agencies may be appealed to the proper state court. The federal appeal process is illustrated in Exhibit 9.9.

LEARNING OBJECTIVE 9
List and describe important federal administrative agencies.

Federal Administrative Agencies

The federal government has created numerous administrative agencies that have the authority to enforce federal statutes enacted by Congress. Several major **federal administrative agencies** and the areas of the law that they are empowered to regulate are discussed below.

Federal administrative agencies Federal administrative agencies that are created by Congress.

Equal Employment Opportunity Commission (EEOC)

Equal Employment Opportunity Commission (EEOC) The federal administrative agency that is responsible for enforcing most federal antidiscrimination laws.

The **Equal Employment Opportunity Commission (EEOC)** is the federal administrative agency responsible for enforcing certain federal antidiscrimination laws. Some of the federal statutes that the EEOC is empowered to enforce are:

- **Title VII of the Civil Rights Act of 1964**,[4] which prohibits job discrimination based on race, color, national origin, sex, and religion.
- **Pregnancy Discrimination Act of 1978**,[5] which forbids employment discrimination because of "pregnancy, childbirth, or related medical conditions."
- **Title I of the Americans with Disabilities Act of 1990**,[6] as amended by the **Americans with Disabilities Act Amendments Act of 2008 (ADAAA)**,[7] which prohibits employment discrimination against

We hold these truths to be self-evident, that all men and women are created equal.
Elizabeth Cady Stanton (1848)

[4]42 U.S.C. Sections 2000(d) et seq.
[5]42 U.S.C. Section 2000(e)(K).
[6]42 U.S.C. Sections 12111–12117.
[7]Public Law 110–325, 122 Stat. 3553

Exhibit 9.9 Appeal of a federal administrative agency rule, order, or decision

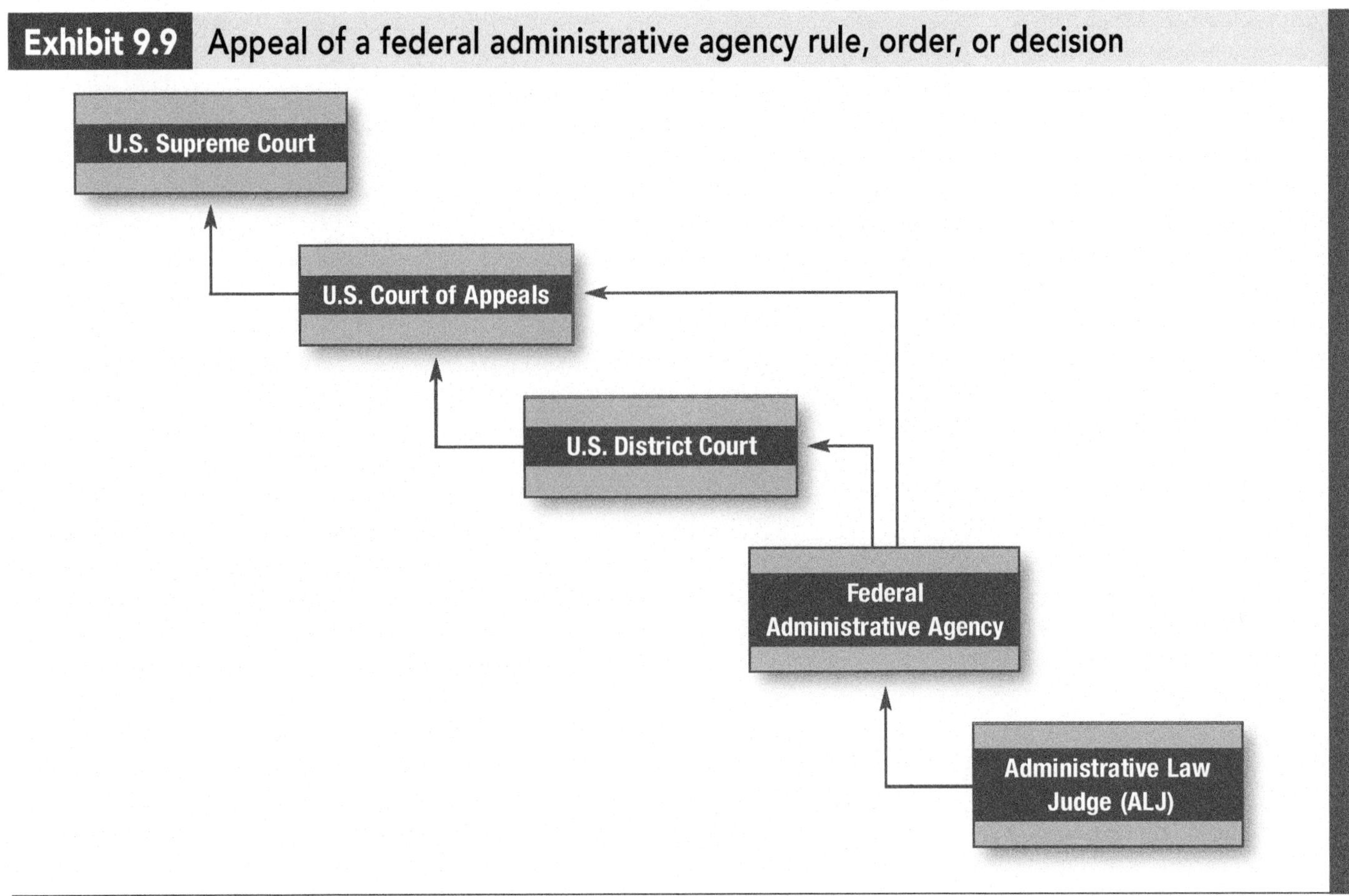

qualified individuals with disabilities with regard to job application procedures, hiring, compensation, training, promotion, and termination.

- **Equal Pay Act of 1963,**[8] which protects both sexes from pay discrimination based on sex.
- **Age Discrimination in Employment Act of 1967 (ADEA),**[9] which protects people who are 40 or older from discrimination because of their age.
- **Genetic Information Nondiscrimination Act of 2008 (GINA),**[10] which makes it illegal for an employer to discriminate against job applicants and employees based on genetic information.

The EEOC is empowered to interpret these statutes, conduct investigations, encourage conciliation between parties, and bring suits to enforce the law. The EEOC can also seek injunctive relief.

We won't have a society if we destroy the environment.
Margaret Mead

Environmental Protection Agency (EPA)

The **Environmental Protection Agency (EPA)** is a federal administrative agency that is empowered to enforce federal environmental protection laws. The EPA has broad rule-making powers to advance the environmental laws it is empowered to administer. The agency also has adjudicative powers to hold hearings, make decisions, and order remedies for violations of federal environmental laws. In addition, the EPA can initiate judicial proceedings in court against alleged violators.

Environmental Protection Agency (EPA) A federal administrative agency created by Congress to coordinate the implementation and enforcement of the federal environmental protection laws.

[8]29 U.S.C. Section 206(d).
[9]29 U.S.C. Sections 621–634.
[10]Public Law 110–233, 122 Stat. 881.

Civil Rights Act of 1964 This is a photograph of President Lyndon Baines Johnson signing the Civil Rights Act of 1964 on July 2, 1964. Dr. Martin Luther King, Jr. is standing directly behind the President. Dr. King was an influential civil rights leader who worked to end racial segregation and racial discrimination.

The EPA is charged with enforcing the Clean Air Act,[11] Clean Water Act,[12] Safe Drinking Water Act,[13] Endangered Species Act,[14] Comprehensive Environmental Response, Compensation, and Liability Act (CERCLA, or "the Superfund"),[15] Insecticide, Fungicide, and Rodenticide Act,[16] and numerous other federal laws designed to protect the environment.

Food and Drug Administration (FDA)

Food and Drug Administration (FDA) The federal administrative agency that administers and enforces the federal Food, Drug, and Cosmetic Act.

The **Food, Drug, and Cosmetic Act (FDCA or FDC Act)**[17] was enacted in 1938. This federal statute regulates the testing, manufacture, distribution, and sale of foods, drugs, cosmetics, and medicinal devices in the United States. The **Food and Drug Administration (FDA)** is the federal administrative agency empowered to enforce the FDCA.

Before certain food additives, drugs, cosmetics, and medicinal devices can be sold to the public, they must receive FDA approval. A manufacturer must submit an application to the FDA that contains relevant information about the safety and uses of the product. The FDA, after considering the evidence, will either approve or deny the application.

The FDA can seek search warrants and conduct inspections; obtain orders for the seizure, recall, and condemnation of products; seek injunctions; and turn over suspected criminal violations to the U.S. Department of Justice for prosecution.

Securities and Exchange Commission (SEC)

Securities and Exchange Commission (SEC) The federal administrative agency that is empowered to administer federal securities laws. The SEC can adopt rules and regulations to interpret and implement federal securities laws.

The **Securities and Exchange Commission (SEC)** is a federal administrative agency that is empowered to administer federal securities laws. Two of the primary statutes enforced by the SEC are the Securities Act of 1933 and the Securities

[11]Public Law 88-206.
[12]33 U.S.C. Sections 1251–1367.
[13]21 U.S.C. Section 349 and 300f–300j-25.
[14]16 U.S.C. Sections 1531–1544.
[15]42 U.S.C. Sections 9601–9675.
[16]7 U.S.C. Sections 135 et seq.
[17]21 U.S.C. Section 301.

Exchange Act of 1934. The Securities Act is a federal statute that primarily regulates the issue of securities by companies and other businesses. The **Securities Exchange Act of 1934**[18] is a federal statute primarily designed to prevent fraud in the trading of securities.

The major responsibilities of the SEC are as follows:

- The SEC can adopt rules (also called regulations) that further the purpose of the federal securities statutes. These rules have the force of law.
- It can investigate alleged securities violations and bring enforcement actions against suspected violators. This may include recommendations for criminal prosecution. Criminal prosecutions of violations of federal securities laws are brought by the U.S. Department of Justice.
- The SEC may bring a civil action to recover monetary damages from violators of securities laws.
- The SEC regulates the activities of securities brokers and advisors. This includes registering brokers and advisors and taking enforcement action against those who violate securities laws.

Occupational Safety and Health Administration (OSHA)

In 1970, Congress enacted the **Occupational Safety and Health Act**[19] to promote safety in the workplace. The **Occupational Safety and Health Administration (OSHA)** is the agency empowered to adopt rules and regulations to interpret and enforce the Occupational Safety and Health Act. OSHA has established thousands of specific workplace safety standards that employers must meet. The act also imposes record-keeping and reporting requirements on employers and requires them to post notices in the workplace informing employees of their rights under the act.

Occupational Safety and Health Administration (OSHA) A federal administrative agency that is empowered to enforce the Occupational Safety and Health Act.

OSHA is also empowered to inspect places of employment for health hazards and safety violations. If a violation is found, OSHA can issue a written citation that requires the employer to abate or correct the situation. Employers who violate the act, OSHA rules and regulations, or OSHA citations are subject to both civil and criminal penalties.

National Labor Relations Board (NLRB)

The **National Labor Relations Board (NLRB)** is a federal administrative body that oversees union elections, prevents employers and unions from engaging in illegal and unfair labor practices, and enforces and interprets certain federal labor laws. The decisions of the NLRB are enforceable in court.

National Labor Relations Board (NLRB) A federal administrative agency that oversees union elections, prevents employers and unions from engaging in illegal and unfair labor practices, and enforces and interprets certain federal labor laws.

Some of the federal statutes that the NLRB is empowered to enforce are:

- The **Norris-LaGuardia Act**. Enacted in 1932, this statute stipulates that it is legal for employees to organize.[20]
- The **National Labor Relations Act (NLRA)**. Also known as the **Wagner Act**, this statute was enacted in 1935.[21] The NLRA establishes the right of employees to form and join labor organizations, to bargain collectively with employers, and to engage in concerted activity to promote these rights.
- The **Labor Management Relations Act**. Also known as the **Taft-Hartley Act**, Congress enacted this statute in 1947 to (1) expand the activities that labor unions can engage in, (2) give employers the

---

[18] 15 U.S.C. Sections 78a–78mm.
[19] 29 U.S.C. Sections 553, 651–678.
[20] 29 U.S.C. Sections 101–110, 113–115.
[21] 29 U.S.C. Sections 151–169.

right to engage in free speech efforts against unions prior to a union election, and (3) give the president of the United States the right to seek an injunction (for up to 80 days) against a strike that would create a national emergency.[22]

- The **Labor Management Reporting and Disclosure Act**. In 1959, Congress enacted this statute, also known as the **Landrum-Griffin Act**, to regulate internal union affairs and establish the rights of union members.[23]

Consumer Product Safety Commission (CPSC)

Consumer Product Safety Commission (CPSC) A federal administrative agency empowered to adopt rules and regulations to interpret and enforce the Consumer Product Safety Act.

In 1972, Congress enacted the **Consumer Product Safety Act (CPSA)**[24] and created the **Consumer Product Safety Commission (CPSC)**. This agency is empowered to conduct research on the safety of consumer products, collect data regarding injuries caused by consumer products, and adopt rules and regulations to interpret and enforce the CPSA.

The CPSC issues product safety standards for consumer products that pose an unreasonable risk of injury. If a consumer product is found to be imminently hazardous—that is, if its use causes an unreasonable risk of death or serious injury or illness—the manufacturer can be required to recall, repair, or replace the product or take other corrective action. Alternatively, the CPSC can seek injunctions, bring actions to seize hazardous consumer products, seek civil penalties for knowing violations of the act, or seek criminal penalties for knowing and willful violations of the act or of CPSC rules. A notice of the recall of a hazardous toy by the Consumer Safety Product Commission appears as Exhibit 9.10.

Exhibit 9.10 Notice of recall of a hazardous toy by the Consumer Safety Product Commission

U.S. Consumer Product Safety Commission
www.cpsc.gov

Health Canada
www.hc-sc.gc.ca

FOR IMMEDIATE RELEASE
September 8, 2011
Release #11-321

Firm's Recall Hotline: (855) 880-4504
CPSC Recall Hotline: (800) 638-2772
CPSC Media Contact: (301) 504-7908
HC Media Contact: (613) 957-2983

Dolls Recalled by Pottery Barn Kids Due To Strangulation Hazard

WASHINGTON, D.C.-The U.S. Consumer Product Safety Commission and Health Canada, in cooperation with the firm named below, today announced a voluntary recall of the following consumer product. Consumers should stop using recalled products immediately unless otherwise instructed. It is illegal to resell or attempt to resell a recalled consumer product.

Name of Product: Chloe, Sophie and Audrey soft dolls

Units: About 81,000 in the United States and 1,300 in Canada

Importer: Pottery Barn Kids, a division of Williams-Sonoma Inc., of San Francisco, Calif.

(continued)

[22] 29 U.S.C. Section 141 et seq.
[23] 29 U.S.C. Section 401 et seq.
[24] 15 U.S.C. Section 2051.

Exhibit 9.10 Notice of recall of a hazardous toy by the Consumer Safety Product Commission *(continued)*

Hazard: The hair on the Chloe and Sophie dolls may contain loops that are large enough to fit around a child's head and neck, and the headband on the Audrey doll, if loosened, can form a loop that fits around a child's head and neck. These loops can pose a strangulation hazard.

Incidents/Injuries: The firm has received five reports of dolls with looped hair, including one report in which a loop of the Chloe doll's hair was found around the neck of a 21-month old child. The child was not injured.

Description: This recall involves soft dolls sold under the names Audrey, Chloe and Sophie. The dolls measure about 17 inches high and have hair made of yarn. Audrey's hair is black, Chloe's hair is dark brown and Sophie's hair is blonde. The dolls are part of Pottery Barn Kids' Girl Doll Collection. The doll's name can be found on a tag sewn onto her bottom.

Sold exclusively at: Pottery Barn Kids stores nationwide, online at www.potterybarnkids.com and through Pottery Barn Kids catalogs from July 2006 to April 2011 for about $40.

Manufactured in: China

Remedy: Consumers should take the dolls away from children immediately and cut the looped hair of the Chloe and Sophie dolls and remove the headband of the Audrey doll to eliminate the hazard. Consumers may also call Pottery Barn Kids for instructions on how to return the affected dolls for a merchandise credit.

Consumer Contact: For additional information, contact Pottery Barn Kids toll-free at (855) 880-4504 between 4 a.m. and 9 p.m. PT seven days a week or visit the firm's website at www.potterybarnkids.com

Note: Health Canada's press release is available at http://cpsr-rspc.hc-sc.gc.ca/PR-RP/recall-retrait-eng.jsp?re_id=1389

Federal Trade Commission (FTC)

The **Federal Trade Commission Act (FTC Act)** was enacted in 1914.[25] The **Federal Trade Commission (FTC)** is empowered to enforce the FTC Act as well as other federal consumer protection statutes. Section 5 of the FTC Act prohibits "unfair and deceptive practices." It has been used extensively to regulate unscrupulous business conduct. This section gives the FTC the authority to bring an administrative proceeding to end a deceptive or unfair practice, such as false and deceptive advertising.

Federal Trade Commission (FTC) A federal administrative agency empowered to enforce the Federal Trade Commission Act and other federal consumer protection statutes.

The FTC can also issue interpretive rules, general statements of policy, trade regulation rules, and guidelines that define unfair or deceptive practices, and it can conduct investigations of suspected antitrust violations. The FTC may issue cease-and-desist orders, require affirmative disclosures to consumers, order corrective advertising, or other actions. The FTC may also sue to obtain compensation on behalf of consumers.

Consumer Financial Protection Bureau (CFPB)

The **Consumer Financial Protection Bureau (CFPB)**, a new federal administrative agency, began operations in 2011. This agency has the authority to prohibit unfair, deceptive, or abusive acts or practices regarding consumer financial products and services. It also acts as a watchdog over credit cards, debit cards, mortgages, payday loans, and other consumer financial products and services. The CFPB has authority

Consumer Financial Protection Bureau (CFPB) A federal administrative agency that is responsible for enforcing federal consumer financial protection statutes.

[25] 15 U.S.C. Sections 41–51.

to supervise all participants in the consumer finance and mortgage area, including depository institutions such as commercial and savings banks and non-depository businesses such as insurance companies, mortgage brokers, credit counseling firms, and debt collectors. The CFPB has authority to enforce the following statutes:

- Consumer Financial Protection Act of 2010
- Mortgage Reform and Anti-Predatory Lending Act of 2010
- Truth in Lending Act (TILA)
- Equal Credit Opportunity Act
- Fair Credit Reporting Act
- Fair Debt Collection Practices Act
- Home Mortgage Disclosure Act
- Electronic Funds Transfer Act
- Truth in Savings Act

The CFPB is authorized to adopt rules to interpret and enforce the provisions of the acts it administers. The CFPB has investigative and subpoena powers, and may refer matters to the U.S. Attorney General for criminal prosecution.

LEARNING OBJECTIVE 10
Describe public disclosure of administrative agency actions.

Individual Rights and Disclosure of Administrative Agency Actions

Public concern over the possible secrecy of federal administrative agency actions led Congress to enact several statutes that promote public disclosure of agency activities and that protect parties from overly obtrusive agency actions. These statutes are discussed in the paragraphs that follow.

Freedom of Information Act

Freedom of Information Act (FOIA) A federal act that gives the public access to documents in the possession of federal administrative agencies. There are many exceptions to disclosure.

The **Freedom of Information Act (FOIA)**[26] was enacted to give the public access to most documents in the possession of federal administrative agencies. The act requires federal administrative agencies to publish agency procedures, rules, regulations, interpretations, and other such information in the *Federal Register*. The act also requires agencies to publish quarterly indexes of certain documents. In addition, the act specifies time limits for agencies to respond to requests for information, sets limits on copying charges, and provides for disciplinary action against agency employees who refuse to honor proper requests for information.

Example If a person suspects that he or she, or someone else, was subject to the Federal Bureau of Investigation (FBI) inquiry during the anti-communist McCarthy hearings, that person may submit a Freedom of Information Act request to obtain copies of any information on this subject from the FBI.

For purposes of privacy, the following documents are exempt from disclosure: (1) documents classified by the president to be in the interest of national security; (2) documents that are statutorily prohibited from disclosure; (3) records whose disclosure would interfere with law enforcement proceedings; (4) medical, personnel, and similar files; and (5) documents containing trade secrets or other confidential or privileged information. Decisions by federal administrative agencies to not publicly disclose documents requested under the act are subject to judicial review in a U.S. district court.

A sample letter to request information from the Federal Bureau of Investigation under the Freedom of Information Act appears as Exhibit 9.11. An actual FOIA request made to multiple government entities is shown in Exhibit 9.12.

[26] 5 U.S.C. Section 552.

Exhibit 9.11 Sample letter requesting information pursuant to the Freedom of Information Act

Date: ______________________
Federal Bureau of Investigation

Record/Information Dissemination Section
Attn: FOIA Request
170 Marcel Drive
Winchester, VA 22602-4843

Dear FOIA Officer,

This is a request under the Freedom of Information Act.

Date range of request: ______________________

Description of Request:

____

____

____

Please search the FBI's indices to the Central Records System for the information responsive to this request related to:

____

____

____

I am willing to pay up to [$ __] for the processing of this request. Please inform me if the estimated fees will exceed this limit before processing my request.
I am seeking information for personal use and not for commercial use.

Thank you for your consideration,

Name: ______________________________________

Title (optional): ______________________________

Business (if applicable): _________________________

Street Address: _______________________________

City/State/ZIP Code: ___________________________

Country (if applicable): _________________________

Telephone (optional): ___________________________

Email (optional): ______________________________

Government in the Sunshine Act

The **Government in the Sunshine Act**[27] was enacted to open most federal administrative agency meetings to the public. There are some exceptions to this rule. These include meetings (1) where a person is accused of a crime, (2) concerning an agency's issuance of a subpoena, (3) where attendance of the public would significantly frustrate the implementation of a proposed agency action, and (4) concerning day-to-day operations. Decisions by federal administrative agencies to close meetings to the public are subject to judicial review in U.S. district courts.

Government in the Sunshine Act A federal act that opens most federal administrative agency meetings to the public.

[27] 5 U.S.C. Section 552(b).

Exhibit 9.12 Request for information pursuant to the Freedom of Information Act

January 13, 2009

Director, Freedom of Information and Security Review
Department of Defense
1155 Defense Pentagon, Room 2C757
Washington, D.C. 20301-1155

FOIA/PA Mail Referral Unit
Department of Justice
Room 115
LOC Building
Washington, D.C. 20530-0001

Information and Privacy Coordinator
Central Intelligence Agency
Washington, D.C. 20505

Office of Information Programs and Services
A/GIS/IPS/RL
U.S. Department of State
Washington, D.C. 20522-8100

Re: REQUEST UNDER FREEDOM OF INFORMATION ACT
Expedited Processing Requested

To Whom It May Concern:

This letter constitutes a request ("Request") pursuant to the Freedom of Information Act ("FOIA") Section 552 *et seq*., the Department of Defense implementing regulations, 32 C.F.R. Section 286.1 *et seq*., the Department of Justice implementing regulations, 22 C.F.R. Section 171.1 *et seq*., the Central Intelligence Agency implementing regulations, 32 C.F.R. Section 1900.01 *et seq*., and the President's Memorandum of January 21, 2009, 74 Fed. Reg. 4683 (Jan. 26, 2009) and the Attorney General's Memorandum of March 19, 2009, 74 Fed. Reg. 49,892 (Sep. 29, 2009). The Request is submitted by the American Civil Liberties Union Foundation and the American Civil Liberties Union (collectively, the "ACLU").

This Request seeks records pertaining to the use of unmanned aerial vehicles ("UAVs")—commonly referred to as "drones" and including the MQ-1 Predator and MQ-9 Reaper—by the CIA and the armed forces for the purpose of killing targeted individuals. In particular, we seek information about the legal basis in domestic, foreign, and international law for the use of drones to conduct targeted killings. We request information regarding the rules and standards that the Armed Forces and the CIA use to determine when and where these weapons may be used, the targets that they may be used against, and the processes in place to decide whether their use is legally permissible in particular circumstances, especially in the face of anticipated civilian casualties. We also seek information about how these rules and standards are implemented and enforced. We request information about how the consequences of drone strikes are assessed, including methods for determining the number of civilian and non-civilian casualties. Finally, we request information about the frequency of drone strikes and the number of individuals—Al Qaeda, Afghan Taliban, other targeted individuals, innocent civilians, or otherwise—who have been killed or injured in these operations. . . .

I. Requested Records

1. All records created after September 11, 2001 pertaining to the legal basis in domestic, foreign and international law upon which unmanned aerial vehicles ("UAVs" or "drones") can be used to execute targeted killings ("drone strikes"). . . .

2. All records created after September 11, 2001 pertaining to agreements, understandings, cooperation or coordination between the U.S. and the governments of Afghanistan, Pakistan, or any other country regarding the use of drones to effect targeted killings in the territory of those countries. . . .

(continued)

Exhibit 9.12 Request for information pursuant to the Freedom of Information Act *(continued)*

3. All records created after September 11, 2001 pertaining to the selection of human targets for drone strikes and any limits on who may be targeted by a drone strike.

4. All records created after September 11, 2001 pertaining to civilian casualties in drone strikes, including but not limited to measures regarding the determination of the likelihood of civilian casualties, measures to limit civilian casualties, and guidelines about when drone strikes may be carried out despite a likelihood of civilian casualties. . . .

****

If the Request is denied in whole or in part, we ask that you justify all deletions by reference to specific exemptions to FOIA. We expect the release of all segregable portions of otherwise exempt material. We reserve the right to appeal a decision to withhold any information. . . .

Thank you for your prompt attention to this matter. Please furnish applicable records to:

Jonathan Manes
National Security Project
American Civil Liberties Union
125 Broad Street, 18th Floor
New York, NY 10004

Example The Federal Communications Commission (FCC) is debating whether to grant an applicant permission to purchase a television station license. This meeting is not protected by any of the exceptions in the Sunshine Act. The FCC must publish a public notice of place, date, and time of the meeting so that persons may appear at the meeting.

Equal Access to Justice Act

Congress enacted the **Equal Access to Justice Act**[28] to protect persons from harassment by federal administrative agencies. Under this act, a private party who is the subject of an unjustified federal administrative agency action can sue to recover attorneys' fees and other costs. The courts have generally held that the agency's conduct must be extremely outrageous before an award will be made under the act. A number of states have similar statutes.

Equal Access to Justice Act A federal act that protects persons from harassment by federal administrative agencies.

Privacy Act

The federal **Privacy Act**[29] concerns individual privacy. It stipulates that federal administrative agencies can maintain only such information about an individual as is relevant and necessary to accomplish a legitimate agency purpose. The act affords individuals the right to access agency records concerning themselves and to correct those records. Many states have enacted similar privacy acts.

Privacy Act A federal act that states that federal administrative agencies can maintain only information about an individual that is relevant and necessary to accomplish a legitimate agency purpose.

28 5 U.S.C. Section 504.
29 5 U.S.C. Section 552(a).

Concept Review *and* Reinforcement

LEGAL TERMINOLOGY

Administrative agency (regulatory agency) 337
Administrative law 337
Administrative law judge (ALJ) 343
Administrative order 343
Administrative Procedure Act (APA) 343
Administrative search 353
Administrative subpoena 354
Age Discrimination in Employment Act of 1967 (ADEA) 355
Americans with Disabilities Act Amendments Act of 2008 (ADAAA) 354
Cabinet-level federal departments 339
Code of Federal Regulations (CFR) 344
Consumer Financial Protection Bureau (CFPB) 359
Consumer Product Safety Act (CPSA) 358
Consumer Product Safety Commission (CPSC) 358
Delegation doctrine 343
Electronic Code of Federal Regulations (e-CFR) 344
Environmental Protection Agency (EPA) 355
Equal Access to Justice Act 363
Equal Employment Opportunity Commission (EEOC) 354
Equal Pay Act of 1963 355
Executive power 353
Federal administrative agencies 354
Federal Register 344
Federal Trade Commission (FTC) 359
Federal Trade Commission Act (FTC Act) 359
Food and Drug Administration (FDA) 356
Food, Drug, and Cosmetic Act (FDCA or FDC Act) 356
Formal rule making 344
Fourth Amendment to the U.S. Constitution 354
Freedom of Information Act (FOIA) 360
General government regulation 337
Genetic Information Nondiscrimination Act of 2008 (GINA) 355
Government in the Sunshine Act 361
Homeland Security Act (HSA) 339
Independent federal administrative agencies 340
Informal rule making 344
Interpretive rule 344
Judicial review of administrative agency actions 354
Judicial authority 348
Labor Management Relations Act (Taft-Hartley Act) 357
Labor Management Reporting and Disclosure Act (Landrum-Griffin Act) 358
License 348
Local administrative agencies 341
Licensing power 348
National Labor Relations Act (NLRA) (Wagner Act) 357
National Labor Relations Board (NLRB) 357
Norris-LaGuardia Act 357
Occupational Safety and Health Act 357
Occupational Safety and Health Administration (OSHA) 357
Petitioner 354
Pregnancy Discrimination Act of 1978 354
Privacy Act 363
Procedural administrative law 342
Procedural due process 350
Regulatory statutes 337
Rule making 343
Rules and regulations 343
Search warrant 354
Securities Act of 1933 337
Securities and Exchange Commission (SEC) 356
Securities Exchange Act of 1934 357
Specific government regulation 338
State administrative agencies 341
Statement of policy 344
Substantive administrative law 342
Substantive rule 344
Title I of the Americans with Disabilities Act of 1990 354
Title VII of the Civil Rights Act of 1964 354
Unreasonable search and seizure 354
U.S. Department of Homeland Security (DHS) 339

SUMMARY OF KEY CONCEPTS

Administrative Law

Administrative Law	Administrative law is enacted by governments to regulate industries, businesses, and professionals, and to protect consumers and other members of society.
General Government Regulation	General regulations are enacted by governments to regulate businesses and industries collectively.
Specific Government Regulation	Specific regulations are enacted by governments to regulate certain industries or areas of commerce only.

Administrative Agencies

Administrative Agencies	Agencies are created by federal and state legislative and executive branches. They are staffed by professionals who have expertise in a certain area of commerce and who interpret and apply designated statutes.
Cabinet-Level Federal Departments	Cabinet-level departments are created by the president to regulate certain activities and advise the president. The president appoints cabinet members subject to confirmation by a majority vote of the U.S. Senate.
Independent Federal Administrative Agencies	Independent administrative agencies are created by Congress to regulate areas of the national economy and society.
State and Local Administrative Agencies	State administrative agencies are created by states and local cities and municipalities to regulate areas of commerce and society.

Administrative Procedure

Administrative Procedure Act (APA)	The APA establishes procedures (e.g., notice, hearing) for federal agencies to follow in conducting their affairs. States have enacted their own procedural acts to govern state agencies.
Administrative Law Judge (ALJ)	The ALJ is an employee of the administrative agency who presides over the administrative proceeding, decides questions of law and fact, and issues a decision in the form of an order.

Powers of Administrative Agencies

Delegation Doctrine	When an administrative agency is created, it is delegated certain powers. The agency has rule-making power, licensing power, judicial authority, and executive power.
Rule Making	Rule making is the power to adopt substantive rules that have the force of law and must be adhered to by covered persons and businesses.
Licensing Power	Licensing power is the authority to issue licenses before a person or business can enter certain types of industries.
Judicial Authority	Judicial authority is the authority to decide cases in an administrative proceeding.
Executive Power	Executive power is the power to prosecute violations of statutes and administrative rules and regulations.

Administrative Searches	Administrative agencies have the power to conduct administrative searches and to issue administrative subpoenas to conduct searches and to obtain information and evidence.
Judicial Review of Administrative Agency Actions	The Administrative Procedure Act (APA), many federal statutes, and many state administrative statutes and local ordinances expressly provide for judicial review by courts of administrative agency actions.
Federal Administrative Agencies	
Equal Employment Opportunity Commission (EEOC)	The EEOC enforces federal antidiscrimination laws.
Environmental Protection Agency (EPA)	The EPA enforces federal environmental protection laws.
Food and Drug Administration (FDA)	The FDA regulates the testing, manufacture, distribution, and sale of foods, drugs, cosmetics, and medical devices.
Securities and Exchange Commission (SEC)	The SEC enforces federal securities laws.
Occupational Safety and Health Administration (OSHA)	OSHA enforces workplace safety standards.
National Labor Relations Board (NLRB)	The NLRB enforces federal labor laws.
Federal Trade Commission (FTC)	The FTC regulates business conduct and practices.
Consumer Product Safety Commission (CPSC)	The CPSC regulates the safety of consumer products.
Consumer Financial Protection Bureau (CFPB)	The CFPB regulates consumer financial products and services.
Individual Rights and Disclosure of Administrative Agency Actions	
Freedom of Information Act	The FOIA is a federal law that gives the public access to most documents in the possession of federal administrative agencies. It also requires federal administrative agencies to publish agency procedures, rules, regulations, interpretations, and other information in the *Federal Register.*
Government in the Sunshine Act	This federal law opens certain federal administrative agency meetings to the public.
Equal Access to Justice Act	This federal law protects persons from harassment by federal administrative agencies and provides certain penalties for its violation.
Privacy Act	The Privacy Act (a) restricts information a federal administrative agency can maintain about an individual, and (b) gives individuals the right to access agency records concerning themselves.

WORKING THE WEB

1. Go to the website www.fda.gov. This is the website for the federal Food and Drug Administration (FDA). Click on "Recalls" and select a subject matter that interests you and write a one-page report on that information.
2. Go to the website www.cpsc.gov. This is the website for the federal Consumer Product Safety Commission (CPSC). Go to the headings "Recalls" and "News." Find a recall of a product that interests you and write a half-page report describing the product and its recall.
3. Go to the website of the U.S. Environmental Protection Agency at www.epa.gov. Click on "News." Select your state and click on "Go." Read a current news release and summarize it.
4. Go to the website of the Federal Trade Commission at www.ftc.gov. Go to "Latest News."

CRITICAL THINKING & WRITING QUESTIONS

1. What is an administrative law?
2. What is the difference between general government regulation and specific government regulation?
3. How do cabinet-level federal departments differ from independent federal administrative agencies?
4. Explain the difference between substantive administrative law and procedural administrative law.
5. What is the Administrative Procedure Act (APA)? What is its main purpose?
6. What is an administrative law judge (ALJ)? What does an ALJ do?
7. Describe the following: (1) substantive rule, (2) interpretive rule, and (3) statement of policy.
8. Describe each of the following powers of an administrative agency: (1) licensing power, (2) judicial authority, and (3) executive power.
9. What is the Freedom of Information Act (FOIA)?
10. Describe each of the following: (1) Government in the Sunshine Act, (2) Equal Access to Justice Act, and (3) Privacy Act.

Building Paralegal Skills

VIDEO CASE STUDIES

Administrative Agency Hearing: The Role of the Paralegal

A school bus driver has been injured in what he claims to be a work-related injury. His employer—the school district—has raised objections, requiring a Workers' Compensation hearing. A paralegal appears before the Workers' Compensation hearing officer representing the school bus driver.

After viewing the video case study at the book website at www.pearsonhighered.com/careersresources, answer the following:

1. Why are matters of this type heard before administrative hearing officers instead of going directly to court?
2. Is the paralegal committing the unauthorized practice of law in representing the school bus driver in this matter?
3. Are paralegals in your jurisdiction permitted to represent clients before administrative agencies?

ETHICS ANALYSIS & DISCUSSION QUESTIONS

1. What ethical guidelines apply to the representation of parties before administrative agencies by a paralegal?
2. May paralegals advertise their availability to appear before administrative agencies? Explain.
3. As a recent graduate of a four-year degree program, you wish to get started in your career. At your local computer store, you purchase a copy of software that can be used to create various commonly used legal forms. You invite a group of friends and relatives to your home and offer to use the program to prepare powers of attorney and living wills (advance medical directives) for them. See *Unauthorized Practice of Law v. Parsons Tech.*, 179 F.3d 956 (5th Cir. 1999). Are there any UPL issues? Explain.

DEVELOPING YOUR COLLABORATION SKILLS

With a group of other students, review the facts of the following case. As a group, discuss the following questions.

1. What government agency was involved in this case?
2. Did the agency conduct a proper search of the business premises?
3. Did LaGrou knowingly engage in the improper storage of meat, poultry, and other food products, in violation of federal food safety laws?

United States of America v. LaGrou Distribution Systems, Incorporated

LaGrou Distribution Systems, Incorporated, operated a cold storage warehouse and distribution center in Chicago, Illinois. The warehouse stored raw, fresh, and frozen meat, poultry, and other food products that were owned by customers who paid LaGrou to do so. More than 2 million pounds of food went into and out of the warehouse each day. The warehouse had a rat problem for a considerable period of time. LaGrou workers consistently found rodent droppings and rodent-gnawed products, and they caught rats in traps throughout the warehouse on a daily basis. The manager of the warehouse and the president of LaGrou were aware of this problem and discussed it weekly. The problem became so bad that workers were assigned to "rat patrols" to search for rats and to put out traps to catch rats. At one point, the rat patrols were trapping as many as 50 rats per day. LaGrou did not inform its customers of the rodent infestation. LaGrou would throw out product that had been gnawed by rats.

One day, a food inspector for the United States Department of Agriculture (USDA), a federal administrative agency, went to the LaGrou warehouse and discovered the rat problem. The following morning, 14 USDA inspectors and representatives of the federal Food and Drug Administration (FDA) arrived at the warehouse to begin an extensive investigation. The inspectors found the extensive rat infestation and the contaminated meat. The contaminated meat could transmit bacterial, viral, parasitic, and fungal pathogens, including *E. coli* and *Salmonella*, which could cause severe illness in human beings.

The USDA ordered the warehouse shut down. Of the 22 million pounds of meat, poultry, and other food products stored at the warehouse, 8 million pounds were found to be adulterated and were destroyed. The remaining product had to be treated with strict decontamination procedures. The U.S. government brought charges against LaGrou for violating federal food safety laws. The U.S. District Court ordered LaGrou to pay restitution of $8.2 million to customers who lost product and to pay a $2 million fine, and it sentenced LaGrou to a 5-year term of probation. LaGrou appealed to the U.S. Court of Appeals.

Source: United States of America v. LaGrou Distribution Systems, Incorporated, 466 F.3d 585, 2006 U.S. App. Lexis 25986 (United States Court of Appeals for the Seventh Circuit, 2006)

PARALEGAL PORTFOLIO EXERCISE

Prepare a memorandum, no longer than three pages, that discusses the general powers of a federal administrative agency, and the specific powers of the Federal Food and Drug Administration (FDA).

LEGAL ANALYSIS & WRITING CASES

Entergy Corporation v. Riverkeeper, Inc.

Entergy Corporation operates large power plants that generate electrical power. In the course of generating power, these plants also generate large amounts of heat. To cool its facilities, Entergy uses cooling water intake structures that extract water from nearby water sources. These structures pose various risks to the environment, particularly to aquatic organisms that live in the affected water, by squashing them against intake screens (called "impingement") or suctioning them into the cooling system (called "entrainment"). The Clean Water Act, a federal statute, mandates that a point source of pollution, such as a power plant, install the "best technology" available for minimizing adverse environmental impact.

The Environmental Protection Agency (EPA), a federal administrative agency, adopted a rule that requires new power plants to install the "most effective technology" that would reduce impingement and entrainment mortality by up to 98 percent. The EPA conducted a cost-benefit analysis and adopted a different rule for existing power plants. This EPA rule allows existing plants to deploy a mix of less expensive technology that is "commercially available and practicable." This technology would reduce impingement and entrainment by more than 80 percent. Thus, the EPA chose not to require existing plants to deploy the more expensive[,] most effective technology that it requires for new power plants.

Riverkeeper, Inc. and other environmental groups (Riverkeeper) challenged the EPA rule for existing power plants, alleging that the EPA was not empowered to use cost-benefit analysis when setting performance standards for power plants. Riverkeeper asserts that the Clean Water Act's "best technology" language required existing power plants to deploy the most effective technology equal to that required of new power plants.

Question

1. Is the EPA permitted to use cost-benefit analysis in promulgating rules for technology to be deployed by existing point sources of water pollution under the Clean Water Act?

Source: Entergy Corporation v. Riverkeeper, Inc., 556 U.S. 208, 129 S.Ct. 1498, 2009 U.S. Lexis 2498 (Supreme Court of the United States, 2009)

People v. Paulson

Lee Stuart Paulson owned a liquor license for My House, a bar in San Francisco. The California Department of Alcoholic Beverage Control (Department) is the state administrative agency that regulates bars in that state. The California Business and Professions Code, which is administered by the Department, prohibit[s] "any kind of illegal activity on licensed premises." An anonymous informer tipped the Department that narcotics were being sold on the premises of My House, an establishment that sold liquor, and that the narcotics were kept in a safe behind the bar on the premises. A special department investigator entered the bar during its hours of operation, identified himself, and informed Paulson that he was conducting an inspection. The investigator, who did not have a search warrant, opened the safe without seeking Paulson's consent. Twenty-two bundles of cocaine, totaling 5.5 grams, were found in the safe. Paulson was arrested. At his criminal trial, Paulson challenged the lawfulness of the Department's search.

Question

1. Is the Department's search constitutional?

Source: People v. Paulson, 216 Cal. App. 3d 1480, 265 Cal. Rptr. 579, 1990 Cal. App. Lexis 10 (Court of Appeal of California, 1990)

WORKING WITH THE LANGUAGE OF THE COURT CASE

R. Williams Construction Company v. Occupational Safety & Health Review Commission

464 F.3d 1060, 2006 U.S. App. Lexis 24646 (2006)
United States Court of Appeals for the Ninth Circuit

Read the following case, excerpted from the court of appeals' opinion. Review and brief the case. In your brief, answer the following questions:

1. What administrative agency was involved in this case?
2. What administrative agency rules were alleged to have been violated in this case?

(continued)

3. What were the violations found by the administrative law judge (ALJ)?
4. Was the penalty assessed sufficient based on the facts of the case?

Fletcher, Circuit Judge

Petitioner R. Williams Construction Co. ("Williams" or "the Company") petitions for review of a final order of the Federal Occupational Safety and Health Review Commission (the "Commission"), affirming violations of the Occupational Safety and Health Act ("OSHA") in the wake of a trench collapse and death of an employee at a construction site in Santa Ynez, California.

On September 19, 2002, a trench collapse at a sewer-construction project at the Chumash Casino Project in Santa Ynez, California, killed Jose Aguiniga, a Williams employee, and seriously injured Adam Palomar, another Williams employee. On the day of the collapse, the trench was ten to twelve feet deep and between three and four feet wide at the bottom. The trench was about thirteen feet wide at the top and more than forty feet long. The sides of the trench rose vertically from the bottom for approximately five feet, after which they sloped backwards at about a forty-five degree angle. An earthen slope at the west end of the trench provided the workers' only access to and egress from the bottom. Ground water seeped into the soil continuously.

Williams used a number of submersible pumps to remove the ground water that seeped into the trench. Although the pumps could be pulled up and cleaned from the top of the trench, it was the practice to do so from inside the trench. Adam Palomar and Jose Aguiniga, two Williams employees, were generally responsible for cleaning the pumps and did so as needed throughout any given workday without receiving specific instructions.

On the day before the accident, a hydraulic jack shoring system, which supported the trench wall, had been removed. On the day of the accident, Palomar and Aguiniga entered the unshored trench to clean the pumps, remaining there for about fifteen minutes. As the two were exiting the trench, the north wall collapsed, burying Aguiniga completely and Palomar almost completely. Aguiniga died, and Palomar was severely injured.

OSHA conducted an investigation and cited the Company for safety violations. The first citation charged the Company with failing to instruct its employees in the recognition and avoidance of unsafe conditions and in the regulations applicable to their work environment, as required by 29 C.F.R. § 1926.21(b)(2). The second citation charged the Company with failing to ensure that no worker would have to travel more than 25 feet to reach a safe point of egress, as required by 29 C.F.R. § 1926.651(c)(2). The third citation charged the Company with failing to ensure that a "competent person"—i.e., one with specific training in soil analysis and protective systems and capable of identifying dangerous conditions—performed daily inspections of excavations for evidence of hazardous conditions, as required by 29 C.F.R. §§ 1926.651(k)(1). The fourth violation charged the Company with failing to ensure that the walls of the excavation be either sloped or supported, as required by 29 C.F.R. § 1926.652(a)(1).

The Administrative Law Judge (ALJ) conducted a two-day hearing, during which several Williams employees provided testimony. Palomar testified that he worked for Williams for approximately nine months prior to the accident and had never received any training in trench safety. He testified that there was no safety meeting at the beginning of the workday on September 19, 2002. He was never told not to enter the trench and did not know who his supervisor was. He received all of his work instructions from Sergio Lopez, who acted as translator because Palomar speaks only Spanish.

John (J.P.) Williams testified that he was the supervisor at the Santa Ynez worksite and was responsible for employee safety at the site. He admitted that he never looked at the company safety manual, which was located behind the seat of his truck; he also had not been trained as an OSHA "competent person" or received any other safety training other than on the job. He was unfamiliar with OSHA sloping and trenching requirements and did not conduct any physical tests on the soil in the trench.

Based on the testimony at the hearing, the ALJ affirmed the [OSHA] citations. This resulted in a total penalty of $22,000. The ALJ's findings, based upon the witnesses' testimony regarding Williams' lack of attention to safety standards, is supported by substantial evidence.

Williams violated 29 C.F.R. § 1926.21(b)(2) by failing to instruct each employee in the recognition and avoidance of unsafe conditions and for failing to eliminate other hazards: Williams provided no training in trenching hazards to at least the two employees working in the trench; moreover, no Williams supervisor was familiar with OSHA regulations.

Williams also violated 29 C.F.R. § 1926.651(c)(2) by providing only one safe means of egress at the east end of the 45-foot trench. A violation is established so long as employees have *access* to a dangerous area more than 25 feet from a means of egress. In addition, Williams violated 29 C.F.R. § 1926.651(k)(1) for failing to designate a "competent person" with sufficient training and knowledge to identify and correct existing and predictable hazards.

The ALJ findings, and the reasonable inferences drawn from them, easily satisfy the substantial-evidence standard. Consequently, the ALJ's decision affirming the citations is affirmed.

VIRTUAL LAW OFFICE EXPERIENCE MODULES

If your instructor has instructed you to complete assignments in the Virtual Law Office program, complete the Virtual Law Office assignments as assigned by your instructor. These assignments are designed to develop your workplace skills. Completing the assignments for this chapter will result in producing the following documents for inclusion in your portfolio:

VLOE 9.1	Office memo on when a paralegal may represent a client under our local state and federal rules, laws, and regulations

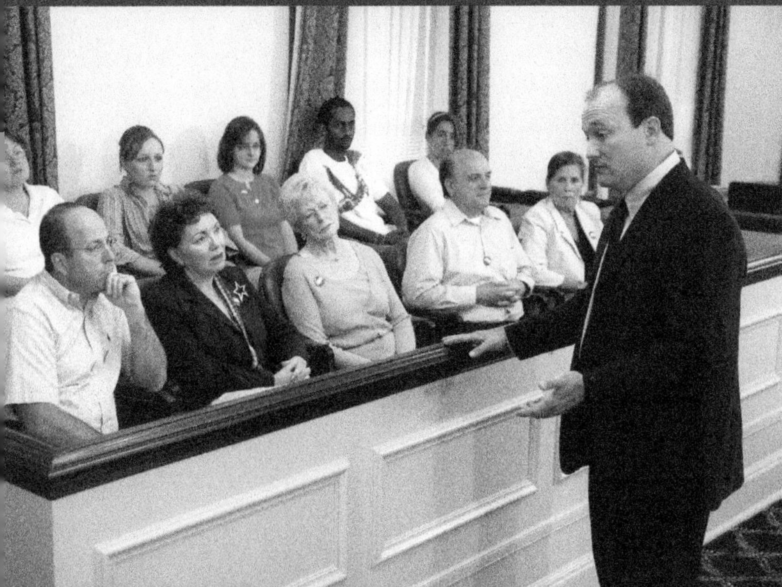

PART

III

Paralegal Skills

The aspiring paralegal professional must develop a certain set of basic skills to work as part of a legal team in the law office, the courts, administrative agencies, and in the alternative dispute resolution process. Excellent verbal and written skills are crucial for paralegals who will be interviewing clients and witnesses. Paralegals must also develop an ability to think critically and analytically when performing legal research and writing briefs, memoranda of the law, and general correspondence. Today's paralegal must be familiar with the technology used to conduct legal and factual research, such as digital libraries and Internet research services, as well as conventional sources of print information. Part III covers the basic skills needed for a paralegal professional to be successful in the job.

Chapter 10
Interviewing and Investigation Skills

Chapter 11
Legal Writing and Critical Legal Thinking

Chapter 12
Legal Research

CHAPTER

10

Interviewing and Investigation Skills

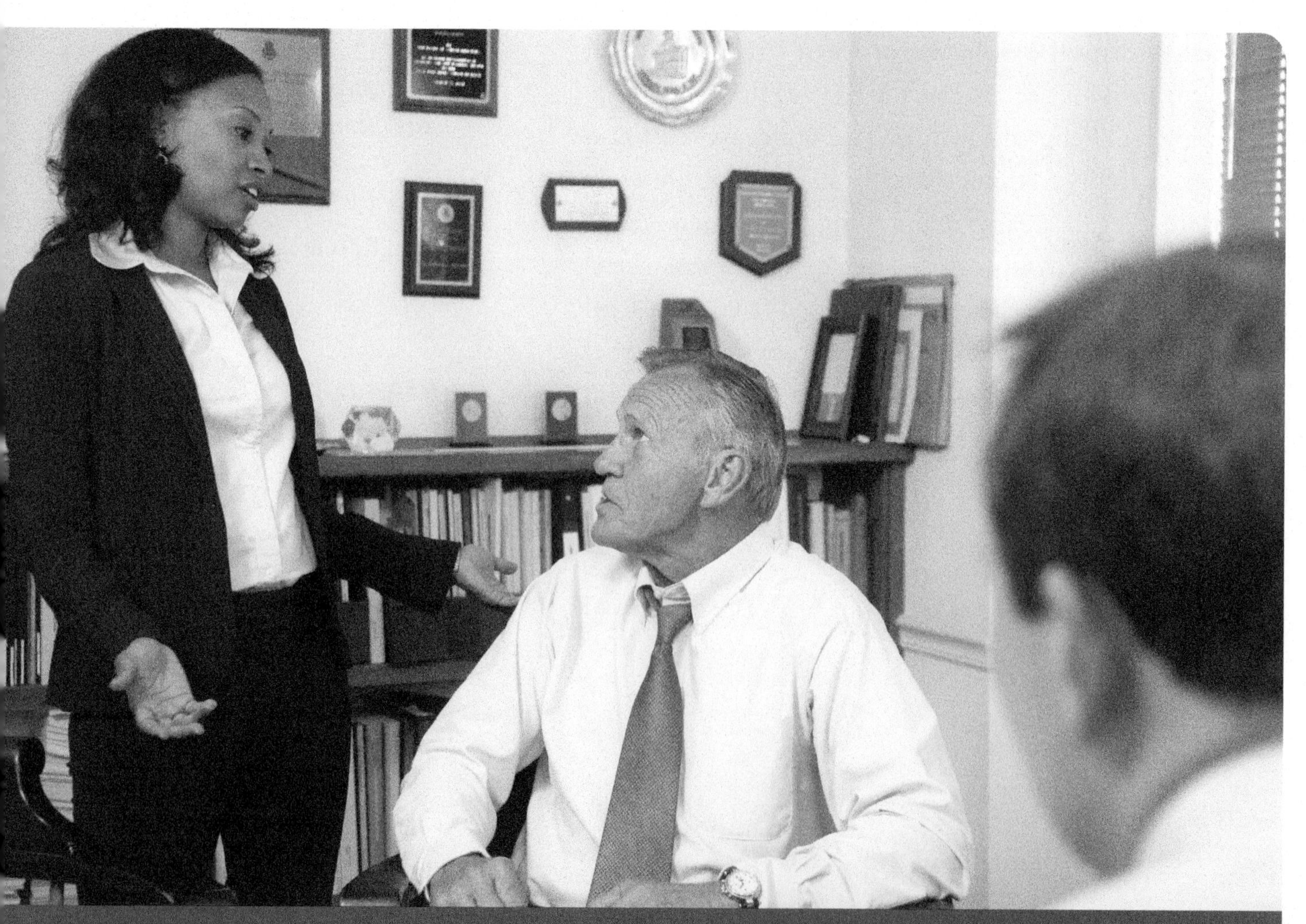

LEARNING OBJECTIVES

After studying this chapter, you should be able to:

1. Explain the importance of the initial contact with clients and witnesses.
2. Describe the issues in preparing for and conducting an interview.
3. Explain how expert witnesses are used in litigation.
4. Explain the steps and process of conducting an investigation.
5. Explain the function of the trial notebook and its relationship to case management.

Paralegals at Work

Sara had been working for only a few weeks as a paralegal intern for a small, boutique litigation firm. Mrs. Weiser, one of the two paralegals supporting the two trial attorneys, told Sara about the long-planned Alaskan cruise that she would be taking with her husband for their 25th anniversary. The reality of the situation started to set in when Sara was advised that the cruise would begin in Anchorage the next day, and Mrs. Weiser was scheduled to leave within the hour to catch a plane. Sara's concerns intensified when she and Mrs. Weiser reviewed the office calendar and it became obvious that Sara would be alone in the office during the time Mrs. Weiser was gone. The attorneys and the other full-time paralegal were involved in a major medical malpractice case in another state for at least the next two weeks. Clearly, it was expected that Sara would be in charge of the office, answering the phone and taking care of anyone who came in. Somewhat troubling was the fact that Sara would have no contact with Mrs. Weiser for the duration of the cruise or with the other paralegal or attorneys during the trial. The instructions Mrs. Weiser gave her left no doubt that she would be very busy:

Now remember—we advertise on TV, and Mr. Elliott expects us to screen potential clients without bothering him with loser cases. I've left a couple of files for you to work on while I'm gone. The Morales case just came in. It's an accident case that happened a few years ago, and you need to get her in for an initial interview. Get all the necessary facts and see what else we have to do to move it along and whether we need to settle it or file suit. Oh, by the way, you do speak Spanish, don't you? Mrs. Morales is from Puerto Rico.

"It is the spirit and not the form of law that keeps justice alive."

Earl Warren

The LaCorte case is on the trial list for next month. We don't have an expert yet who can substantiate our theory of the case. See what you can find. Oh, and you'd better get that case organized so they can start trial immediately in case the current trial lasts longer than the expected three weeks. All the material is in piles or in boxes in Mr. Martin's office. Prepare a trial notebook, or you can try that new case management software we just got that is supposed to make life easier. I'm sure, with your computer skills, that you can get it up and running and use it to get the case ready for trial.

Consider the issues involved in this scenario as you read the chapter.

INTRODUCTION TO INTERVIEWING AND INVESTIGATIONS

Communication skills are at the heart of a paralegal's ability to conduct successful interviews and investigations. The paralegal is often the firm's first point of contact with a new client or witness. The impression the paralegal makes is also the impression the firm makes. As someone once said, we have only one opportunity to make a good first impression. In some practices, the paralegal is the first one to meet with the client and conduct the initial interview before referring the client to the supervising attorney. In other practices, clients are interviewed first by the supervising attorney and then referred to the paralegal for a detailed factual interview.

The paralegal must be able to interview clients, fact witnesses, expert witnesses, investigators, and others, including public records custodians who may have access to information necessary for the preparation of a case. The skill of the interviewer or investigator can determine the accuracy and completeness of the information obtained—and, ultimately, the outcome of the case.

The impressions created and the relationship developed with a new client may also be the deciding factors in whether the client stays with the firm or seeks other counsel. Professional relationships developed with public officials, public records custodians, hospital records librarians, police investigators, and similar independent investigators can make the paralegal's job much easier and ultimately benefit the client.

LEARNING OBJECTIVE 1

Explain the importance of the initial contact with clients and witnesses.

Interviews

Paralegals frequently conduct the initial investigation of a client's case and make the initial contact with potential witnesses. This initial contact may be a telephone call to set up a meeting or a telephone interview. The meeting may take place in the office or at the witness's home or place of business. The initial contact with a potential witness, just as with a potential client, may set the tone for the interview and can influence the willingness of the person to cooperate. Any contact that a paralegal has with a client, or a prospective client, should be treated as an interview. It may involve limited contact, such as a **screening interview**, or it may be an initial in-depth, fact-gathering interview. In each case, the paralegal usually is the firm's first point of contact with the client.

Screening interview Limited first contact with a prospective new client.

A screening interview is the initial contact with the client. This usually begins with an initial telephone call to the firm, although a person may appear unexpectedly at the reception desk, looking for an attorney to determine whether the firm is interested in taking the case, and what it will cost.

Screening Interview

Many clients come to a law firm or lawyer from a referral source, such as a current or former client. This source of clients sometimes serves as a type of screening. The referral source has probably told the potential client something about the firm's practice and the perceived reputation or ability of the lawyer or firm. Other potential clients may have found the firm's name and phone number in the telephone book, on a website listing of attorneys, or from a law firm advertisement. Some simply appear at the office door and ask for an appointment or basic information about the firm's areas of practice or interest in taking a case. In smaller offices, the paralegal is often the one who handles these drop-in visits or calls, doubling as receptionist or phone operator.

The screening interview is often filled with potential landmines. If the paralegal solicits too much information or the prospective client volunteers too much information, an implied attorney–client relationship may be created. An implied attorney–client relationship has been found to exist, even if no fee is paid, if the party believes he or she is divulging confidential information for the purpose of obtaining legal advice. If too little information is obtained, the attorney will not have enough information to decide whether he or she wants to talk to the potential client. Therefore, the paralegal or receptionist has to decide how much information to take and how much information to give.

First Meeting

At the very least, it is prudent for the paralegal to advise the potential client that paralegals are not lawyers, and that only a lawyer can give legal advice. Also, the potential client should be advised that any information given to the paralegal in this initial meeting may not be subject to **attorney–client privilege**.

Attorney–client privilege A client's right to have anything told to a lawyer while seeking legal advice kept confidential in most instances.

The prospective client may want a quick answer to the question, "Do I have a case?" The answer requires a legal analysis that only the attorney can make. The attorney/employer probably does not want to be bothered with most early contacts but also does not want to lose a good case. Should the paralegal give advice or have this person speak with a lawyer? Most of these potential problems can be avoided by having a policy or strategy in place in advance. Most offices have a policy regarding the fee for an initial interview. Many offer a no-cost initial interview to determine the validity of a case and check for any potential conflicts of interest that might require the office to decline the case. In some offices, a nominal fee is charged. This may be a flat rate or an hourly rate. In many jurisdictions, referrals from the local lawyer referral office or legal aid office are charged a token fee, sometimes as little as $5, or for indigent cases, no fee as part of a local pro bono program. The paralegal should ask the firm's policy before attempting to give and receive information from potential clients.

Implied Attorney–Client Relationship

If too much information is taken, the potential client may think he or she is now represented by a lawyer. The courts have ruled on the side of the prospective client, holding that an **implied attorney–client relationship** exists, even where the attorney did not expressly agree to take the case. In this "implied" relationship, the client is entitled to expect the same degree of confidentiality under the attorney–client privilege. In addition, a **conflict of interest** may result if the firm is already representing another party in the same matter, which would result in disqualification of the attorney or require the establishment of an **ethical wall** to prevent access to information by members of the legal team who have a conflict.

Implied attorney–client relationship An implied attorney–client relationship may result when a prospective client divulges confidential information during a consultation with an attorney for the purpose of retaining the attorney, even if actual employment does not result.

Conflict of interest Representation of another with conflicting rights.

Ethical wall An artificial barrier preventing anyone who may have a conflict of interest from accessing client information.

IN THE WORDS OF THE COURT . . .

Implied Attorney–Client Relationship

PRO HAND SERVICES TRUST V. MONTHEI, 49 P.3D 56, 59 (MONT. 2002)

An implied attorney–client relationship may result when a prospective client divulges confidential information during a consultation with an attorney for the purpose of retaining the attorney, even if actual employment does not result.

IN THE WORDS OF THE COURT . . .

HUSTLER CINCINNATI, INC., ET AL., PLAINTIFFS V. PAUL J. CAMBRIA, JR., ET AL., DEFENDANT

Civil Action No. 1:11cv0718 (WOB-KKL).

UNITED STATES DISTRICT COURT, S.D. OHIO, WESTERN DIVISION. OCTOBER 14, 2014.

. . . [T]he attorney–client relationship may also be implied. *Cuyahoga Cnty. Bar Assn. v. Hardiman*, 798 N.E.2d 369, 373 (Ohio 2003) ("While it is true that an attorney–client relationship may be formed by the express terms of a contract, it can also be formed by implication based on conduct of the lawyer and expectations of the client."). "To establish an implied attorney–client relationship, plaintiff Jimmy Flynt must show (1) he submitted confidential information to the defendant attorneys during the time that the defendants represented the Larry Flynt Companies, and (2) that he did so with the reasonable belief that the defendant attorneys were acting as his personal attorney." . . .

"The determination of whether an attorney–client relationship was created turns largely on the reasonable belief of the prospective client." *Hardiman*, 798 N.E.2d at 373. "[T]he test for determining the existence of an attorney–client relationship is both a subjective and objective test." *Stuffleben v. Cowden*, No. 82537, 2003 WL 22805065, at ¶ 22 (Ct. Ap. Ohio 2003).

An attorney–client relationship "exists when an attorney advises others as to their legal rights, a method to be pursued, the forum to be selected, and the practice to be followed for the enforcement of their rights." . . . Further "[a]n essential element as to whether an attorney–client relationship has been formed is the determination that the relationship invoked such trust and confidence in the attorney that the communication became privileged and, thus, the information exchanged was so confidential as to invoke an attorney–client privilege." However, "payment of a fee is not an essential element" to establish an attorney–client relationship.

Web Exploration

Contrast and compare the Missouri Rule 4-1.18, http://www.courts.mo.gov/courts/ClerkHandbooksP2RulesOnly.nsf/publicSupremeCourtRules?OpenView&Start=1&Count=30&Expand=4#4, with ABA Rule 1.18 at www.abanet.org/cpr and the rule in your jurisdiction.

IMPLIED ATTORNEY–CLIENT RELATIONSHIP

SIDEBAR

The attorney–client privilege applies to all confidential communications made to an attorney during preliminary discussions of the prospective professional employment, as well as those made during the course of any professional relationship resulting from such discussions.

Hooser v. Superior Court, 101 Cal. Rptr. 2d 341, 346 (Ct. App. 2000).

ETHICAL PERSPECTIVE

Missouri Bar—Rules of Professional Conduct

RULE 4-1.18: DUTIES TO PROSPECTIVE CLIENT

(a) A person who discusses with a lawyer the possibility of forming a client–lawyer relationship with respect to a matter is a prospective client.

(b) Even when no client–lawyer relationship ensues, a lawyer who has had discussions with a prospective client shall not use or reveal information learned in the consultation, except as Rule 4-1.9 would permit with respect to information of a former client.

(c) A lawyer subject to Rule 4-1.18(b) shall not represent a client with interests materially adverse to those of a prospective client in the same or a substantially related matter if the lawyer received information from the prospective client that could be significantly harmful to that person in the matter, except as provided in Rule 4-1.18(d). If a lawyer is disqualified from representation under Rule 4-1.18(c), no lawyer in a firm with which that lawyer is associated may knowingly undertake or continue representation in such a matter, except as provided in Rule 4-1.18(d).

(d) When the lawyer has received disqualifying information as defined in Rule 4-1.18(c), representation is permissible if:

(1) both the affected client and the prospective client have given informed consent, confirmed in writing, or

(2) the lawyer who received the information took reasonable measures to avoid exposure to more disqualifying information than was reasonably necessary to determine whether to represent the prospective client and the disqualified lawyer is timely screened from any participation in the matter.

Statute of Limitations

One of the biggest sources of potential malpractice is missing a **statute of limitations** on a client's case. The statute of limitations is a time period within which a case must be filed with the court. If not filed within the required time frame, the right to bring a cause of action is lost. The statute of limitations is set by legislation, and each state has the power to set its own statute of limitations for each type of case. For example, in many states the time limit for filing a tort action arising out of an automobile accident is two years, and a contract action six years, but in some states the suit must be filed in as little as 30 days. A client seeking a lawyer may not be aware of the time frame. But to the lawyer, the failure to act before the statute runs out may result in a claim for malpractice.

Statute of limitations A time limit within which a case must be brought; if a case is not filed within that time frame, the right to seek redress in court is lost.

The timing of the statute of limitations deadline must always be considered when taking the initial call or during the first contact with the potential client. If a court holds that an implied attorney–client relationship exists at the time the statute of limitations has expired, the failure of the attorney to take action may be held to be malpractice. The remedy in such a malpractice claim would be for the lawyer to pay what would have been recovered if the case had gone forward and a recovery obtained. During this first point of contact with the potential client, the paralegal must be prepared to take appropriate action and refer the matter to the supervising attorney.

Like the statutes of limitation, court rules set time deadlines for taking action to avoid being denied court action or relief, such as filing responsive pleadings and appeals. As discussed in the following case, it is the attorney's responsibility to monitor all deadlines and not rely on electronic notifications. Unanswered is the question of the responsibility, if any, of the legal assistants who downloaded the electronic documents to review them for deadlines and advise the supervising attorney, who has the ultimate responsibility.

IN THE WORDS OF THE COURT . . .

UNITED STATE DISTRICT COURT FOR THE WESTERN DISTRICT OF TEXAS, SAN ANTONIO DIVISION

Two-Way Media, LLC, v. AT&T Operations, Inc., et al.

CASE 5:09-CV-00476-OLG DOCUMENT 633 FILED 02/06/14

Defendants argue that the e-mail notice of electronic filings (NEF's) that defense counsel received on November 25, 2013 did not provide them with "notice" that Defendants' substantive post-trial motions had been resolved. . . . Defendants contend that based on the NEFs they received, counsel believed the motions for JMOL and new trial on damages and non-infringement had not been disposed of and remained pending before the Court. That is, Defendants claim the fact they "did not receive sufficient notice of the substance of the orders entered justifies reopening the time to file an appeal." The Court respectfully disagrees.

II. Analysis

The timely filing of a notice of appeal is a jurisdictional requirement. . . . An untimely notice of appeal must be dismissed for lack of jurisdiction; the requirement cannot be waived, and is not subject to equitable tolling. *Id.* In this case, Defendants failed to timely file its notice of appeal, and now seek an extension of time to file it pursuant to Federal Rule of Appellate Procedure 4(a)(5). In the alternative, Defendants seek to reopen the time to file an appeal pursuant to Rule 4(a)(6). Rule 4(a)(5) of the Federal Rules of Appellate Procedure provides that:

> The district court may extend the time to file a notice of appeal if: (i) a party so moves no later than 30 days after the time prescribed by this Rule 4(a) expires; and (ii) regardless of whether its motion is filed before or during the 30 days after the time prescribed by this Rule 4(a) expires, that party shows excusable neglect or good cause.

. . . "notification by the clerk [of entry of judgment or of an order] is merely for the convenience of the litigants." . . . The Court finds that Rule 77(d) imposes on attorneys the responsibility to check on the status of their case. The Court notes it is every attorney's responsibility to read the substance of each order issued by the Court, and to read the order in its entirety. If any of defense counsel would have read the orders issued by the Court on November 22, 2013, which they were notified of on November 25, 2013, counsel would have realized that each of the substantive post-trial motions had been denied. Defense counsel admits that the orders were "downloaded and stored" by litigation assistants in two different firms representing Defendants; yet, it appears that nobody actually read the orders.

. . .The Court finds it is not sufficient for attorneys to rely on the electronic and e-mail notifications received from the ECF system, as the docket entries and notifications do not always convey the Court's disposition in its entirety. The substance of the orders carry validity under the law, not the electronic NEFs. . . . (noting time to appeal from judgment begins to run from date of its entry, not from notice of its entry). The Court must agree with Plaintiffs' opposition to Defendants' motion and finds it is very troublesome that: for almost 52 days after the entry of the orders, none of the at least eighteen counsel that received the NEFs on behalf of Defendants, even after admittedly having their assistants download and file such orders, bothered to read the orders issued by the Court, check the docket for activity, or check on the status of the case. Such an omission is particularly alarming in this case where a $40 million judgment has been entered against Defendants.

. . . The Court is not convinced that Defendants failed to receive notification that their substantive post-trial motions had been disposed of. Instead, the Court finds Defendants received notification that all their substantive post-trial motions had been denied the moment the corresponding orders were downloaded by legal assistants in both of defense counsel's law firms. In other words, the Court finds that "lack of notice" is not equivalent or excusable by an attorney's failure to read the Court's orders.

Letters of Engagement and Termination of Engagement

Good practice requires that the client be appropriately notified in writing of the decision of the law firm to accept or decline the representation. If the representation is accepted, a fee agreement should accompany the cover letter. Exhibit 10.1a is a sample hourly fee engagement letter, and Exhibit 10.1b is a contingent fee engagement letter. If representation is declined, the paralegal may draft a letter summarizing the facts as related by the client and the facts as determined by the firm, and including the reason for declining the representation. A recommendation to clients concerning the next step in their cause of action should be made as soon as possible. Quick action is particularly necessary if the client is a defendant who is mandated by the court's rules to file a timely, responsive pleading to the complaint served on the client.

It is also not unusual for a law office to receive calls not only from potential clients, but also from those attempting to get information about the firm's existing clients. Particularly in family law cases, a party may call as if seeking representation, but in reality is trying to find out whether the other party has retained the firm.

Many causes of friction between lawyers and their clients are related to fees and costs. Thus many states require a written fee agreement that is signed by the lawyer and the client. This agreement, also called an "engagement letter," is addressed to a client and sets out the specific duties the law firm agrees to undertake for the client. In other words, the letter states what the firm will or will not do for the client. It may also spell out the specific obligations the firm will undertake, the basis of the fee (contingent fee, hourly fee, flat fee, or a combination of these), and the terms of payment. In litigation cases, the engagement letter may clarify who is responsible for the payment of costs and expenses related to the investigation, such as deposition costs.

Non-Engagement

A non-engagement letter may be more important than an engagement letter. It tells the person (the would-be client) that the firm will not represent him or her. This is important when a statute of limitations may be approaching and the engagement is declined. The potential client must be clearly advised that the firm is not representing him or her and that he or she should seek other counsel immediately. If a person believes that he or she is represented, and the lawyer does not clearly express that the firm is not accepting the representation, an implied attorney–client relationship may arise. A sample non-engagement letter is shown in Exhibit 10.2.

Web Exploration

Sample engagement, non-engagement, and termination letters are available at http://www.abanet.org/genpractice/magazine/2007/jan-feb/sampleengageletters.html#letter-1.

Preparing for the Interview

LEARNING OBJECTIVE 2

Describe the issues in preparing for and conducting an interview.

The first step in preparing for an interview is to understand the purpose of the interview and the outcome desired. Understanding the goals of the interview, the background or cultural issues, and the nature of the situation of the individual will help in structuring a successful interview. The fundamental purpose of any interview is to obtain all of the relevant facts in the case. Another purpose of an initial interview with a new client is to instill confidence in the client regarding the firm and its personnel. Occasionally an interview must be conducted without time for preparation, such as when the paralegal is asked to fill in for someone else at the last moment.

Investigation Checklists

The investigation checklist should not be viewed as a static document, but should be supplemented according to the purposes and circumstances of each interview. The checklist should start with a listing of all of the parties that should be interviewed, including initial fact witnesses (see Exhibit 10.3). As additional parties and witnesses are interviewed, more people may be identified who need to be added to the list. Exhibit 10.4 is a witness information form that may be used to organize information received from a witness.

CHECKLISTS — SIDEBAR

Many forms used in investigations and interviews are used in paperless systems. These may be available for use with smartphones, tablets, laptops, or desktop computers. Most forms may be converted from word processing forms to fillable PDF forms, saving time inputting the information later.

Exhibit 10.1a Hourly fee engagement letter

January 29, 2013

Mr. and Mrs. Thomas Daniels

12 Route 189

Your town, State

RE: ***Employment of Mason, Marshall and Benjamin by Mr. and Mrs. Thomas Daniels***

Dear Mr. and Mrs. Daniels:

Thank you for selecting Mason, Marshall and Benjamin to represent you with respect to the breach of contract action against Honey Bee Pollinators, Ltd. This letter will confirm our recent discussion regarding the scope and terms of this engagement.

Our firm has agreed to represent you in this lawsuit. I personally will supervise the case. However, it is anticipated that other lawyers and legal assistants in the firm also will work on the case.

We will attempt to obtain compliance with the provisions of the contract to have fruit trees on your property pollinated as agreed or, in the alternative, to seek damages for breach of the contract.

You have agreed to pay for our services based on the time we spend working on the case. My current hourly rate is $250 per hour. The rates of our associates currently range between $125 and $225 per hour. Paralegals, who will be utilized where appropriate to avoid unnecessary attorney fees, currently are charged at $75 per hour. These rates are subject to change once a year, usually in December. Generally, you will be billed for all time spent on your matter, including telephone calls.

As discussed, our current estimate for this engagement is $5,000, not including any out-of-pocket expenses for experts, court reporter fees, or court fees. This estimate is imprecise as my knowledge of the facts at this time is limited. We will advise you if fees will be significantly higher than this estimate. At such time, you may decide to restrict the scope of our efforts or we may make other adjustments. This estimate does not include cost items.

You have paid us the sum of $3,000 as an advance against fees and costs, which we have deposited to our trust account. After your receipt of monthly statements, we will pay the amount of the statement from the trust account. If any portion of the advance is unexpended at the conclusion of the case, it will be refunded to you. If the advance is expended, you have agreed to pay subsequent monthly statements on receipt. An interest charge of one and one-half percent per month is charged on statement balances not paid within 30 days of billing.

You will appreciate we can make no guarantee of a successful conclusion in any case. However, the attorneys of this firm will make their best efforts on your behalf.

My objectives are to provide you with excellent legal services and to protect your interests in the event of my unexpected death, disability, impairment, or incapacity. To accomplish this, I have arranged with another lawyer to assist with closing my practice in the event of my death, disability, impairment, or incapacity. In such event, my office staff or the assisting lawyer will contact you and provide you with information about how to proceed.

If this letter fairly states our agreement, please so indicate by signing and returning the enclosed copy in the enclosed business reply envelope. If you have any questions or concerns, please call me to discuss them. We greatly appreciate the opportunity to represent you on this case and look forward to working with you.

Sincerely,

Owen Mason, Esq.

Mason, Marshall and Benjamin

Exhibit 10.1b Contingent fee engagement letter

RE: ***Employment of Mason, Marshall and Benjamin by Jonathan Leonard***

Dear Mr. Leonard:

Thank you for selecting our firm to represent you with respect to the personal injury action against Acme Trucking Company. This letter will confirm our recent discussion regarding the scope and terms of this engagement.

Our firm has agreed to represent you in this lawsuit. I personally will supervise the case. However, it is anticipated that other lawyers and legal assistants in the firm also will work on the case.

We will represent you in the investigation, preparation, and civil trial of your claim against Acme Trucking in the U.S. District Court or Local Trial Court to the rendering of a verdict. Our engagement at this time does not cover any appellate activity or post-trial work on your behalf.

We will be compensated on a contingent fee basis. We will receive for our services 25% of any recovery plus all out-of-pocket costs for service and filing fees, expert witness fees, court reporter fees, and charges for investigation, travel and accommodation, telephone long distance, photocopies. These out-of-pocket costs will be billed to you on a monthly basis itemizing the monies we have advanced on your behalf.

As discussed, our current estimate cost for out-of-pocket expenses for this engagement is $5,000. This estimate is imprecise as my knowledge of the facts at this time is limited.

You have paid us the sum of $1,000.00 as an advance against costs, which we have deposited to our trust account. After your receipt of monthly statements, we will pay the amount of the statement from the trust account. If any portion of the advance is unexpended at the conclusion of the case, it will be refunded to you. If the advance is expended, you have agreed to pay subsequent monthly statements on receipt.

You will appreciate we can make no guarantee of a successful conclusion in any case. However, the attorneys of this firm will use their best efforts on your behalf.

You understand that we represent other plaintiffs involved in the same case and, where possible, will prorate costs. You have agreed that our firm representing the other plaintiffs is acceptable to you.

If this letter fairly states our agreement, will you please so indicate by signing and returning the enclosed copy in the enclosed business reply envelope. If you have any questions or concerns, please call me to discuss them. We greatly appreciate the opportunity to represent you on this case and look forward to working with you.

Sincerely,

Owen Mason

Mason, Marshall and Benjamin

Investigation of locations and physical evidence may reveal other locations and evidence that should be investigated. Initial interviews may also reveal the need for one or more expert witnesses to be added to the investigation checklist.

A checklist can be a valuable tool in ensuring that all the information required for a case is obtained during the initial interview. The same checklist also offers a good foundation for developing a more detailed interview plan when there is more time for preparation.

Physical Surroundings

The physical surroundings in the interview location can set the tone for the interview. Depending upon the purpose of the interview and the person being interviewed, the paralegal may wish to create either a formal or an informal environment.

Exhibit 10.2 Non-engagement letter

Dear Mr. Wilkins:

Thank you for consulting our firm about your case against the Acme Trucking Company. After reviewing the facts, we regret that we cannot represent you in this matter.

I strongly recommend that you contact another lawyer immediately. Failure to act immediately may result in the barring your ability to file suit. If you do not have another lawyer in mind, I suggest you call the Bar Association Referral service at 218-555-1000.

Thank you for contacting me. I hope to be of service to you in the future.

Very truly yours,

____

Ethan Benjamin

Mason, Marshall and Benjamin

IN THE WORDS OF THE COURT . . .

Identity of Clients

HOOSER V. SUPERIOR COURT OF SAN DIEGO COUNTY, 84 CAL.APP.4TH 997, 101 CAL.RPTR.2D 341. (CAL. APP. 2000)

. . . the identity of an attorney's clients is sensitive personal information that implicates the clients' rights of privacy. "[E]very person [has the right] to freely confer with and confide in his attorney in an atmosphere of trust and serenity. . . ." (*Willis v. Superior Court* (1980) 112 Cal.App.3d 277, 293.)

Clients routinely exercise their right to consult with counsel, seeking to obtain advice on a host of matters that they reasonably expect to remain private. A spouse who consults a divorce attorney may not want his or her spouse or other family members to know that he or she is considering divorce.

Similarly, an employee who is concerned about conduct in his workplace, an entrepreneur planning a new business endeavor, an individual with questions about the criminal or tax consequences of his or her acts, or a family member who desires to rewrite a will may consult an attorney with the expectation that the consultation itself, as well as the matters discussed therein, will remain confidential until such time as the consultation is disclosed to third parties, through the filing of a lawsuit, the open representation of the client in dealing with third parties or in some other manner.

Upon such public disclosure of the attorney–client relationship, the client's privacy concerns regarding the fact of the consultation evaporate and there is no longer a basis for preventing the attorney from identifying the client. (See *Satterlee v. Bliss* (1869) 36 Cal. 489, 501.) However, until such a public disclosure occurs, the client's identity is itself a matter of privacy, subject to the protection against involuntary disclosure through compelled discovery against the attorney.

PRACTICE TIP

Investigation checklists, such as the one shown in Exhibit 10.3, are only starting points in gathering information. Be alert to additional information that may be available based on the responses of clients and witnesses. Update and modify the checklist to adapt it to each case. Do not allow yourself to become so preoccupied with filling in the blanks that you miss important clues that could lead to additional information.

Exhibit 10.3 Investigation checklist for auto accident

CLIENT INTERVIEW CHECKLIST

CLIENT PERSONAL INFORMATION

Name ______

Address ______

City ______ State ______ Zip ______

Phone (hm) ______ (wk) ______ (cell) ______

How long at this address ______

Date of birth ______ Place of birth ______

Social Security No. ______

Prior address ______

City ______ State ______ Zip ______

Dates at this address ______

Employer: ______

Job description ______

Marital status ______ Maiden name ______

Spouse's name ______ Date of birth ______

Child's name ______ Date of birth ______

Child's name ______ Date of birth ______

Child's name ______ Date of birth ______

CASE INFORMATION

Case referred by ______

Case type: ☐ Appeal ☐ Business ☐ Corporate ☐ Estate ☐ Litigation
☐ Municipal ☐ Real Estate ☐ Tax ☐ Trust ☐ Other

Opposing party(ies) ______

Opposing party ______

Address ______

Opposing attorney ______

Address ______

Date of incident ______ Statute of limitation date ______

Summary of facts ______

______

______

______

You can probably remember a situation in which someone interviewed you from across a desk. Didn't you feel a certain formality? Dealing with opposing counsel might best be handled in this type of meeting. However, interviewing clients or witnesses in such an environment may instill a feeling of subservience to the interviewer. By contrast, an informal setting with a low coffee table and living room–style

Exhibit 10.4 Witness information form

Witness Information

CLIENT PERSONAL DATA

Client Name | Case No. | File No.

Address | City, State, Zip | Phone

CASE DATA

File Label | Case issue | Date

Responsible Attorney(s)

WITNESS DATA

Witness Name

Aliases, if any | US Citizen ☐ Yes ☐ No

Current Address | City, State, Zip | Phone

Past Address(es)

Date & Place of Birth | Sex | Race | Age | Current Marital Status ☐ Single ☐ Divorced ☐ Married ☐ Widowed ☐ Separated

Name of Spouse | Number/Former Marriages | Number/Children

Name of Children (natural & adopted)	Age	Name	Age

Current Employer

Address | City, State, Zip | Phone

Job Title | Supervisor | From | To

Previous Employer

Address | City, State, Zip | Phone

Job Title | Supervisor | From | To

Education/Name of School	City/State	From	To	Degree
High School				
College				
Technical/Other				

Witness for ☐ Plaintiff ☐ Defendant | Type of Witness ☐ Expert ☐ Character ☐ Eye Witness | Have you ever been a party or witness in a court suit? ☐ No ☐ Yes

If yes, where & when

OTHER PERTINENT DATA

Form 8567 · 9/86 SYCOM Madison, WI Printed in U.S.A.

chairs may give the meeting a more personal tone and help the interviewee feel more relaxed and on an equal footing with the interviewer. In most cases, the paralegal will want to create the impression of being a competent professional, but in some situations, creating a more relaxed atmosphere may be beneficial. Some witnesses are more cooperative and helpful when they feel as if they are the ones in charge and are in the position of helping the interviewer.

Dress and Appearance

During an interview, first impressions are very important. The impression a paralegal makes when walking into the room for the initial interview may set the stage for the entire relationship with the client or witness. Clothing, posture, and manner of greeting help create this first impression.

Clothing sends a nonverbal message about the person and the firm. The impression a person makes upon walking into the room can enhance or destroy credibility. In the practice of law or in a corporate law department, professionals must be prepared for the unexpected. Many attorneys, male and female alike, keep a "going-to-court suit" in the office just in case it is needed at a moment's notice. When the new client comes in, attorneys can change quickly into more polished and professional dress while the receptionist or secretary buys them time.

A client may be put off by a paralegal's "casual Friday" appearance, believing that the paralegal is not taking the matter seriously. The working paralegal, however, usually doesn't have time to change when the unexpected arises, often being the one to "buy time" for the attorney. Therefore, paralegals always must be prepared to make a good impression and should tailor their appearance appropriately as the situation warrants. In the case of field interviews, a casual appearance may be preferred to put the potential witness at ease. In the office, suits with jackets are appropriate for men and women. In the field, removing the jacket may give the impression of less formality.

Communication Skills in a Multicultural Society*

Clients, witnesses, and others with whom the paralegal comes in contact should never be stereotyped. At the same time, paralegals should be aware of the gender, religious, and ethnic sensitivities of people. A paralegal's skill as an interviewer depends on the ability to appreciate how and why individuals act and react differently. Paralegals must not assume that everyone in each category believes and acts the same; they must be sensitive to issues that may cause a person to communicate in an unexpected way. The following discussion will point out some general differences in the way men and women communicate, followed by some cultural background considerations.

Web Exploration

Check religious holiday dates at http://www.interfaithcalendar.org/.

Gender differences

A man, in comparison to a woman, is more likely to

- be more aggressive and boast of his successes;
- be motivated by competition;
- view conflict as impersonal;
- be impressed by power, ability, and achievement;
- hear only the literal words and miss the underlying emotion;
- have a more direct communication style.

---

*This section on communication skills is adapted from *Crosstalk: Communicating in a Multicultural Workplace* by Sherron Kenton and Deborah Valentine (1997). Reprinted with permission of the authors.

A woman is more likely to

- work cooperatively and to be modest about her success;
- compromise and collaborate and be motivated by affiliation;
- compete primarily with herself;
- take conflict personally;
- be impressed by personal disclosure;
- be proficient at decoding nonverbal meanings and likely to display her feelings through facial expression and body language;
- have an indirect style, except with other women of equal rank.

Considering the receiver's attitudes about the paralegal:

- Man-to-man: He may afford the paralegal instant credibility based on being the same gender.
- Woman-to-woman: She may expect the paralegal to be friendly, nurturing, and concerned and may afford the paralegal instant credibility based on same-gender assumptions.
- Paralegal man-to-woman: She may expect that the paralegal will not really listen to her.
- Paralegal woman-to-man: He may expect the paralegal to be friendly and nurturing, even passive-dependent. Any deviation from his expectation he may simply disregard the female paralegal.

Cultural Sensitivity

The culturally sensitive person is aware of how religious and ethnic backgrounds and belief systems influence behavior. As the cultural makeup of the United States has become more diverse, the need for **cultural sensitivity** in the legal and paralegal professions has grown. Just as men and women are said to be different in some ways, so are those of differing cultural backgrounds.

Interviewing a Latino male, for example, may require a different approach than interviewing an Asian female. Even subtleties of eye contact can affect an interview. Whereas Americans view eye contact as a sign of sincerity, some Asian cultures view it as aggressive. In developing communication skills, paralegals must become sensitive to how they are perceived and learn to fashion their approach to maximize accuracy of communication.

The effectiveness of paralegals is also influenced by how well they "read" the cultural backgrounds of those with whom they interact. This involves manners of speaking, dressing, and acting, and whether one is a man or a woman in that culture. What is heard may not be what was intended. What is intended to be perceived may not be what the other person actually perceives because of cultural differences that affect the interpretation of words and body language. We will briefly highlight some general characteristics of four cultural groups.

European background

Generally, the countries of Western Europe, including Scandinavia, are the sources of those of European background. This group is extraordinarily large and complex, which limits attempts to make cultural generalities. In terms of gender differences, men and women with roots in European culture may have different initial reactions to the paralegal and attitudes about the topic at hand. Male and female listeners alike tend to perceive men as having more credibility than women of equal rank, experience, and training. Men tend to be more credible to other men, and women may be more credible to other women.

Now consider the cultural implications of graphic pictures of physical injuries from car crashes. These photos are acceptable in the United States, but Germans tend to dislike the sight of blood, and the British are likely to be offended by violence.

Latino background

Collectively, Latin America encompasses 51 countries—generally considered to be those south of the U.S. border: Mexico and the countries of Central America, South America, and the Caribbean islands. With so vast an area, many differences can be expected from country to country and even from city to city. The languages, too, are not the same. Portuguese is spoken in Brazil, and the Spanish that is spoken in South America differs from the Spanish spoken in Puerto Rico. The Latino-American population has moved closer to becoming the largest minority group in the United States.

Asian background

More than 30 countries can be considered Asian—among them, China, Malaysia, Japan, the Philippines, India, and Korea. They, too, demonstrate vast differences from culture to culture. Some generalizations may be made, however. Asian cultures generally consider that being direct and to the point is rude, and relationships are considered the top priority. The Japanese, for example, tend to prefer an indirect style of communication. In communicating with people who have an Asian background, then, it might be best to begin with pleasantries about the weather, sports, or the well-being of the individual and his or her family.

Roots in African culture

African-Americans represent the largest ethnic group in the United States. A distinction should be made between African-Americans who are recent immigrants and who have stronger cultural ties to African culture and African-Americans with long family ties within the United States and whose cultural roots are American.

Conducting the Interview

In the first meeting, the paralegal must make clear that he or she is a paralegal and not an attorney. During the first few minutes of the interview, paralegals must build a relationship with the interviewee, explain the reason for the interview, and eliminate any barriers that would prevent the interviewee from sharing the necessary information. Sometimes the interviewee may seem to be fully cooperative, when in fact he or she is not cooperating. The subject matter may be embarrassing, he or she may have a fear of authority figures, or the interviewee might be uncomfortable using certain terms that are necessary to describe the situation.

Effective interviewers learn the verbal and nonverbal cues that help them understand the reasons for the interviewee's reluctance to answer questions. In some situations, the solution is first to ask easy questions, such as the person's name and address. Once the interviewee starts speaking, he or she often has less trouble answering well thought-out questions that build logically on the previous information.

This is not always the case, though. In times of great stress, clients have been known to read the name on a nameplate in the office and state it as their own name!

The interviewer must be careful to avoid embarrassing the interviewee and have questions prepared that can be answered easily, thereby helping the person gain composure, such as, "My records show that you live at 123 South Main Street. Is that correct?" or "How do you spell your name?"

Listening Skills

A good interviewer must master the skill of listening. Most of us hear the words being said but may not be listening to *what* is being said. Instead of concentrating on what is being said, the interviewer may be emotionally influenced by the speaker's message, distracted by the speaker's physical behavior, or thinking about the next question he or she wants to ask.

CHECKLIST Tips for Being a Good Listener

- ☐ Give your full attention to the person who is speaking. Don't look out the window or at what else is going on in the room.
- ☐ Make sure your mind is focused, too. It can be easy to let your mind wander if you think you know what the person is going to say next, but you might be wrong! If you feel your mind wandering, change the position of your body and try to concentrate on the speaker's words.
- ☐ Let the speaker finish before you begin to talk. Speakers appreciate having the chance to say everything they would like to say without being interrupted. When you interrupt, it looks like you aren't listening, even if you really are.
- ☐ Let yourself finish listening before you begin to speak! You can't really listen if you are busy thinking about what you want to say next.
- ☐ Listen for main ideas. The main ideas are the most important points the speaker wants to get across. They may be mentioned at the start or end of a talk, and repeated a number of times. Pay special attention to statements that begin with phrases such as "My point is . . ." or "The thing to remember is. . . ."
- ☐ Ask questions. If you are not sure you understand what the speaker has said, just ask. It is a good idea to repeat in your own words what the speaker said so that you can be sure your understanding is correct. For example, you might say, "When you said that no two zebras are alike, did you mean that the stripes are different on each one?"
- ☐ Give feedback. Sit up straight and look directly at the speaker. Now and then, nod to show that you understand. At appropriate points you may also smile, frown, laugh, or be silent. These are all ways to let the speaker know that you are really listening. Remember, you listen with your face.

Interviewing clients and witnesses requires understanding not only their background, but also what type of witness they are—friendly, hostile, or expert—and how that might result in a bias toward the client or the type of case for which they are being interviewed. Fact witnesses may not want to get involved in the case. A hostile witness might say either what he or she thinks you want to hear or only what will advance his or her own agenda. Some fact witnesses may be influenced by religious, ethnic, or racial prejudice, and may not be as concerned with the truth as they are with someone "paying" for committing a wrongful act.

When listening, the paralegal must focus on what is said, and not on how it is said. Some people are not articulate, and the facts may be lost if the interviewer doesn't listen carefully. Others may try to shock or put off the interviewer by using words intended to cause a reaction, similar to the "trash talk" used in sports to get the listener to react emotionally and lose concentration.

Good listeners avoid distractions. They do not allow themselves to lose focus because of noise or activity in the area of the interview or a speaker's annoying physical habits, such as tapping fingers or feet. Good listeners focus on the message and block out distractions.

More importantly, good interviewers do not make assumptions about the facts of the case. Professional interviewers must listen in a nonjudgmental, impartial manner to what is really being said. They listen with an open mind. Making assumptions about people or facts can lead to attempts to make the facts fit the interviewer's preconceived notions. Sometimes the facts are not what they first seem to be. Many people have been released from jail after DNA evidence proved they did not commit a crime that everyone assumed they had committed. Even though fact witnesses were interviewed and gave different versions of the incident, it was the DNA evidence that proved the person to be innocent.

Leading Questions

Leading questions are those that suggest the desired answer. In conducting a cross-examination, lawyers in trial frequently use leading questions to force a witness to answer in a desired manner. Leading questions do not lead to open-ended answers but are directed toward a desired answer, often yes or no, such as: "You ran the red light, didn't you?" or "Have you stopped kicking your dog?"

Leading question A question that suggests the answer.

Open-Ended Questions

Open-ended questions are designed to give interviewees an opportunity to tell their story instead of limiting their response to "yes" or "no." Open-ended questions create a **narrative opportunity** for the witness. For example, the interviewer may ask: "Tell me what you did today" or "Tell me about your life since the accident."

Open-ended question A question that usually does not have a yes or no answer.

Narrative opportunity A question that allows the witness to give a full explanation.

In fact interviews, the witness should receive the opportunity for open-ended narrative answers. Asking a leading question to obtain only an answer that you desire may prevent the witness from sharing information that is important to your case. For example, if an interviewer wants to know whether the client was observed at the scene, a leading question might be "Did you see my client at the scene of the accident?" The answer to this question may be "yes" or "no" and will not elicit very much additional information. A better question might be "Who was present at the scene of the accident?" This kind of question may lead to information about additional witnesses who could be interviewed. Similarly, the question "How fast were the cars going prior to the impact?" is much better than "Were the cars speeding before the impact?" In this context, the term "speeding" may be interpreted as "exceeding the speed limit" instead of "going too fast for the conditions."

With the witness's statements in hand at the time of trial, the trial attorney might then ask a leading question such as "My client wasn't present at the scene of the accident, was she?" or "Isn't it true that the defendant was speeding before the impact?" With knowledge of the earlier statement, there should be no surprise in the answer at trial. If there is, the earlier statement can be used to impeach the credibility of the witness as part of the trial strategy.

At times, the interviewer may want to focus clients or witnesses by asking questions that give them a perspective of time or place, such as "What did you observe at noon on Saturday?" or "Tell me what happened on September 11, 2001." The tragedy of that day will haunt the memories of Americans and most of the rest of the world, so little stimulus will be needed to elicit where they were and what they observed. In the case of traumatic events in people's lives—the loss of a loved one, the birth of a child, or a serious accident in which they were injured—little stimulus will be needed to elicit where they were and what they observed. Other, less important days and times tend to blur and have to be brought to the consciousness of the witness by questions such as "Let's think back to August 19, 2015" and "What happened to you that day?"

Discovery Limitations

Discovery is the pretrial process during which the parties try to learn everything relevant about the case. This includes the investigation phase, in which basic information is gathered without the formality of statements signed under oath, such as written interrogatories, or before a court reporter authorized to administer oaths such as in a formal deposition.

In discovery, the scope of the inquiry is only limited generally to that which is **relevant**. Evidence is relevant if the fact is logically connected and tends to prove or disprove a fact in issue. "Under the federal rules of evidence, effective December 1, 2015."

RULE 26(b)

> b) Discovery Scope and Limits.
> *(1)Scope in General.*
> Unless otherwise limited by court order, the scope of discovery is as follows: Parties may obtain discovery regarding any nonprivileged matter that is relevant to any party's claim or defense—and proportional to the needs of the case, considering the importance of the issues at stake in the action, the amount in controversy, the parties' relative access to relevant information, the parties' resources, the importance of the discovery in resolving the issues, and whether the burden or expense of the proposed discovery outweighs its likely benefit. Information within this scope of discovery need not be admissible in evidence to be discoverable.

For the investigator or interviewer, the general rule is that information may be sought, even if it is not admissible, as long as it is relevant and may lead to relevant information that will be admissible at trial. This includes information that may be used in trial to show bias, lack of credibility, and challenges to the qualifications of an expert.

Moral Versus Ethical Considerations

Moral obligation An obligation based on one's own conscience.

Ethical obligation A minimum standard of conduct, usually within one's profession.

In the investigation of a case, it is often necessary to understand the difference between moral and ethical obligations. A **moral obligation** is one based on one's own conscience or a person's personal rules of correct conduct, which may come from within the person's own community. Some communities, for instance, may consider it to be morally improper to ask someone to give information about another person. An **ethical obligation** is a responsibility of the legal profession under the ABA Model Rules of Professional Conduct, which includes thoroughness in representing a client. Ethical obligations apply to all members of the legal team, including those acting on behalf of a supervising attorney.

Is it ethically improper to ask someone to tell the truth surrounding the facts of a case that may lead to a neighbor, relative, or friend being held liable for his or her actions? For the paralegal and the legal team, the primary ethical obligation is the duty to the client. Some members of the legal team, for example, may be offended by asking a mother to testify against her child. This is a moral issue for the mother if testifying will result in financial hardship or ruin because of a verdict based on the child's negligent conduct. However, the ethical duty to the client may require the paralegal to take this course of action.

Privileged Communication

Certain forms of communication are considered privileged and not usable at trial unless the privilege is waived. Forms of **privileged communication** are:

Privileged communication A communication that a person has a right to be kept confidential based on the relationship with the other person, such as attorney and client.

1. Attorney–client communications
2. Doctor–patient communications
3. Priest–penitent communications
4. Spousal communications during marriage

Each of these privileges can be waived, but the waiver must come from the client, patient, penitent, or spouse making the statement with the belief that the information is privileged. Some rules of ethics now permit certain otherwise privileged communications to be revealed in order to prevent harm or injury to another. In some cases, such as when another person's life may be in danger, these people may be compelled by a court to testify even when they believe it is a violation of their moral duty to the person from whom they have received the information.

Information gathered from a client is privileged if it is part of the representation of the client and necessary for rendering competent legal advice. When the paralegal is acting on behalf of the attorney, communications between a client and the paralegal are protected by the same privilege as those between the client and the attorney. The paralegal, therefore, is in the same position as the attorney to whom the confidential information has been communicated. The paralegal must carefully guard the confidential information and not inadvertently or intentionally reveal it.

ETHICAL PERSPECTIVE

New Hampshire Rules of Professional Conduct

RULE 1.6. CONFIDENTIALITY OF INFORMATION

(a) A lawyer shall not reveal information relating to the representation of a client unless the client gives informed consent. The disclosure is impliedly authorized in order to carry out the representation or the disclosure is permitted by paragraph (B).

Web Exploration

Contrast and compare the New Hampshire Rule at http://www.courts.state.nh.us/rules/pcon/pcon-1_6.htm with the ABA Model Rules at http://www.americanbar.org/groups/professional_responsibility.html and the analogous rule in your jurisdiction.

Expert Witnesses

LEARNING OBJECTIVE 3

Explain how expert witnesses are used in litigation.

Expert witnesses are individuals whose background, education, and experience are such that courts recognize them as qualified to give opinions in a certain subject based on a set of facts. An expert witness may be a doctor certified by a board of medical experts or an engineer specializing in an area of science such as the flammability of fabrics. A report of an expert may advise, based on the facts of the potential case, whether there is sufficient evidence to support a cause of action. Without this report, the lawyers may be obligated to advise clients that they have no actionable cause of action.

Expert witness A person qualified by education or experience to render an opinion based on a set of facts.

There is no clear rule on whether what is revealed to an expert in the preparation of a case is protected by attorney–client privilege. The question is whether the information given to the testifying expert is protected to the same extent as that revealed to a member of the trial team, including other attorneys, paralegals, and secretarial staff working on the case. Certainly, anything revealed to an expert who is listed as an expert witness on the list of witnesses to be called at trial is discoverable.

Some law firms retain an expert to advise them but do not ask that expert to testify. The advice and information provided by these experts to help in the preparation for trial may be protected under the attorney–client privilege or the work product doctrine. Although the privilege is the client's, the paralegal and others on the legal team must be careful not to divulge privileged or confidential material without authorization.

The expert retained for background trial advice must have as much confidence in the legal team as the legal team has in the expert's advice and integrity. Some experts fear that the legal team will give them only selected information. With the limited information provided, they might give an expert opinion that is not what they would have given if they had received the complete set of facts.

Exhibit 10.5 indicates factors to be considered in arranging for an expert witness.

IN THE WORDS OF THE COURT . . .

FEDERAL RULES OF CIVIL PROCEDURE 26 F.R.C.P. 26(B)(4)

(4) Trial Preparation: Experts.

(A) *Deposition of an Expert Who May Testify.* A party may depose any person who has been identified as an expert whose opinions may be presented at trial. If Rule 26(a)(2)(B) requires a report from the expert, the deposition may be conducted only after the report is provided.

(B) *Trial-Preparation Protection for Draft Reports or Disclosures.* Rules 26(b)(3)(A) and (B) protect drafts of any report or disclosure required under Rule 26(a)(2), regardless of the form in which the draft is recorded.

(C) *Trial-Preparation Protection for Communications Between a Party's Attorney and Expert Witnesses.* Rules 26(b)(3)(A) and (B) protect communications between the party's attorney and any witness required to provide a report under Rule 26(a)(2)(B), regardless of the form of the communications, except to the extent that the communications:

(i) relate to compensation for the expert's study or testimony;

(ii) identify facts or data that the party's attorney provided and that the expert considered in forming the opinions to be expressed; or

(iii) identify assumptions that the party's attorney provided and that the expert relied on in forming the opinions to be expressed.

(D) *Expert Employed Only for Trial Preparation.* Ordinarily, a party may not, by interrogatories or deposition, discover facts known or opinions held by an expert who has been retained or specially employed by another party in anticipation of litigation or to prepare for trial and who is not expected to be called as a witness at trial. But a party may do so only:

(i) as provided in Rule 35(b); or

(ii) on showing exceptional circumstances under which it is impracticable for the party to obtain facts or opinions on the same subject by other means.

(E) *Payment.* Unless manifest injustice would result, the court must require that the party seeking discovery:

(i) pay the expert a reasonable fee for time spent in responding to discovery under Rule 26(b)(4)(A) or (D); and

(ii) for discovery under (D), also pay the other party a fair portion of the fees and expenses it reasonably incurred in obtaining the expert's facts and opinions.

Exhibit 10.5 Expert witness form

EXPERT WITNESS CHECKLIST

BACKGROUND

Full name	Date of birth
Business address	
Business telephone number	Business fax number
Business email address	Business website
Locations of prior offices	
Home address	
Home telephone number	

EDUCATION

Schools attended	Dates of attendance
Degrees or honors awarded	
Continuing education courses	

WORK HISTORY

Place of employment	Dates of employment
Job description	
Reasons for leaving	
Specific area of expertise	
Published articles and books	
Professional affiliations	
Professional magazines subscribed to	
Licenses and jurisdictions	
Litigations or disciplinary action	

PRIOR LEGAL EXPERIENCE

Ratio of plaintiff/defense cases

Prior clients including date (plaintiff or defendant)

Types of investigations with dates

Deposition testimony given with dates

Court testimony with dates

Legal references

AVAILABILITY

Vacation plans and dates	Potential meeting dates

In the deposition, verify the accuracy and currency of the expert's professional information, including all résumé and curriculum vitae items. Verify that the opinions are those of the expert and, if based on the work of others, who these others are and what other experts' writings were consulted. It is important to have on the record the assumptions upon which the expert has formed the opinion and the steps followed in reaching the opinion.

Investigating Claims

LEARNING OBJECTIVE 4
Explain the steps and process of conducting an investigation.

The legal team must gather all relevant information about a cause of action before making a recommendation to a client to file a lawsuit or respond to a claim of wrongdoing. In most cases, the paralegal has some indication of the area of law or the nature

Web Exploration

For more information on the changes in the revised Restatement of the Law Third, Torts, visit the American Law Institute website, http://www.ali.org/index.cfm?fuseaction=publications.ppage&node_id=54.

Strict liability Liability without requiring a finding of fault.

Restatement of the Law Third, Torts A legal treatise with suggested rules of laws relating to torts.

of the claim before the first interview with the client. This may be determined from a brief telephone interview when the client calls for an appointment, or by talking to the supervising attorney when the paralegal is assigned to the investigation. If paralegals specialize in certain areas of law, they are likely to already have some understanding of the elements of the claims or rights the client wishes to assert. Those in general practice and those entering a new area of law must try to understand the rules of law as they apply to the client's issue.

For example, in a product liability case, understanding the common law elements of negligence is not enough. One must also understand the law of **strict liability** for product defect cases, as found in the **Restatement of the Law Third, Torts: Product Liability**. Whereas in common law negligence, a breach of duty must be proven, strict liability does not require a finding of fault. An interview considering only negligence as the basis for a legal action could result in the client being advised that he or she does not have a claim when, under the concept of no-fault liability for defective products, a claim might exist.

The first step is to determine the legal basis of a client's claim. With an understanding of the legal basis of the claim and the applicable law, an investigative plan can be prepared to obtain the necessary witness statements, locate physical evidence, and obtain photographs, reports, and other evidence for use in preparation for trial. Knowing what elements of the action must be proven dictates what evidence must be located, such as witnesses, photographs, reports, and physical evidence. Knowing the elements of the claim will also ensure that the proper questions are asked in the interview, which will then dictate the necessary steps in the investigation.

For example, where a claim of negligence is to be made, photographic evidence may be essential in demonstrating the hazard that gave rise to the claim. If a client has been injured in a fall at a store, photographs showing the hazardous condition should be obtained as quickly as possible. In the case of strict liability involving a product, preservation of the defective product or photographic documentation of the defect becomes essential as a matter of proof.

One of the most useful tools for gathering information about a case is the digital camera. Digital photographs may be shared on computer networks or may be transmitted via the Internet to clients, possible witnesses, and other members of the legal team. It also is useful to take pictures of potential witnesses so that other members of the legal team may recognize them at the time of depositions and trial. If the photographs are going to be used as evidence at trial, it should be kept in mind that the photographer may need to be called as a witness to authenticate them.

A Defense Perspective

Most people quite naturally think of a lawsuit from the plaintiff's perspective, in terms of the violation of rights and the resulting injury. In a perfect world, only legitimate actions would be filed and the law would provide a perfect remedy for all wrongs committed. But not every plaintiff is in the right, and frivolous or even fraudulent lawsuits are sometimes filed.

The balance in the American legal system is achieved in part by allowing a vigorous defense on behalf of the defendant. A plaintiff may claim, for example, that she slipped and was injured as a result of the negligence of a storeowner. But the defendant storeowner might be innocent of any wrongdoing or breach of any duty to the plaintiff. It is good to remember that for every plaintiff there is a defendant, and for each party there is a law firm and an attorney willing to represent him or her.

Obtaining Official Reports

Most incidents giving rise to litigation have some type of official report associated with them. In a negligence action, it may be a police accident or incident report, emergency medical services report, fire department call report, or an incident report of safety violations from a federal, state, or local authority. These reports are filed in central depositories as public records. A useful starting point in an investigation is thus to obtain any official reports associated with the case. These reports frequently indicate the time and location of the incident and the names of fact witnesses. In some cases, detailed diagrams or photographs may accompany the reports. Exhibit 10.6 is an example of a police accident report form.

Fact Analysis

Analyzing the facts begins with interviewing the client and obtaining her or his account of the time, place, circumstances, and other participants or witnesses involved. Exhibit 10.7 is a sample client interview form. A complete analysis usually requires further field investigation of the location, the objects involved (such as an automobile), and interviews of the parties and witnesses. One person's perception may not reflect reality. A client's recollection and description of the physical surroundings may not be consistent with the investigator's observations at the location. For example, what one person describes as a narrow, congested walkway may actually be a standard-width, open sidewalk.

The ultimate trier of fact will be the jury, a panel of arbitrators, or a judge acting as the trier of fact. Therefore, analysis of the facts must support the presentation of a client's claim or defense in an **arbitration** proceeding or a trial.

Arbitration A form of ADR in which the parties choose an impartial third party to hear and decide the dispute.

Locations

Careful analysis of a claim includes verification of the physical aspects of the actual location where the incident occurred. Ask any group of people to describe a location, and you're likely to get a different description from each person. The direction from which the person viewed the location (from the south, north, east, or west) may affect the person's description, as will many other factors. The driver's view from behind the wheel of a large tractor-trailer might be different from the view from behind the wheel of a small sports car.

Web Exploration

Find your home on Google Earth at http://www.google.com/earth/.

Investigation of a case should include a trip to the location where the incident occurred. The trier of fact will be relying upon the presentations of the attorneys to describe the location. They will also be looking at the place from a neutral point of view, usually without any prior familiarity with the location. The diagrams presented at trial are usually sterile, two-dimensional aerial views, and photographs from the points of view of all the participants can make the difference in understanding the duties and responsibilities of the litigants. Unlike diagrams of the location, photographs typically will be from the point of view of the plaintiff, defendant, or witnesses who may have been at ground level, behind the wheel of a vehicle, or looking out of a building window.

Satellite photos are available of locations around the world. Google Earth™ offers Web access to images that may be modified to add descriptions such as street names and points of interest, such as lodgings, restaurants, schools, churches, and other places.

Tangible Evidence

Tangible evidence consists of the physical objects that may have caused an injury. Examples of such objects might include a giveaway toy from a fast-food restaurant that was swallowed by a two-year-old, a bottle that exploded, or an automobile with brakes that failed or seatbelts that snapped. In some cases, the tangible evidence is essential to proving negligence or an element of strict liability.

Much has been written about the effects of a plaintiff's or defendant's failure to preserve critical tangible evidence. In some cases, failure to preserve evidence has resulted in the plaintiff or defendant losing the case.

Exhibit 10.6 Sample police accident report form

COMMONWEALTH OF PENNSYLVANIA
POLICE ACCIDENT REPORT

(XX) REFER TO OVERLAY SHEETS

REPORTABLE ☐ NON - REPORTABLE ☐

PENNDOT USE ONLY

POLICE INFORMATION		ACCIDENT LOCATION	
1. INCIDENT NUMBER		20. COUNTY	CODE
2. AGENCY NAME		21. MUNICIPALITY	CODE
3. STATION/ PRECINCT	4. PATROL ZONE	PRINCIPAL ROADWAY INFORMATION	
5. INVESTIGATOR	BADGE NUMBER	22. ROUTE NO. OR STREET NAME	
6. APPROVED BY	BADGE NUMBER	23. SPEED LIMIT; (24) TYPE HIGHWAY	(25) ACCESS CONTROL
7. INVESTIGATION DATE	8. ARRIVAL TIME	INTERSECTING ROAD:	
ACCIDENT INFORMATION		26. ROUTE NO. OR STREET NAME	
9. ACCIDENT DATE	10. DAY OF WEEK	27. SPEED LIMIT; (28) TYPE HIGHWAY	(29) ACCESS CONTROL
11. TIME OF DAY	12. NUMBER OF UNITS	IF NOT AT INTERSECTION:	
13. # KILLED; 14. # INJURED	15. PRIV. PROP. ACCIDENT Y ☐ N ☐	30. CROSS STREET OR SEGMENT MARKER	
16. DID VEHICLE HAVE TO BE REMOVED FROM THE SCENE? UNIT 1 Y ☐ N ☐ UNIT 2 Y ☐ N ☐	17. VEHICLE DAMAGE 0 - NONE 1 - LIGHT 2 - MODERATE 3 - SEVERE; UNIT 1 ☐ UNIT 2 ☐	31. DIRECTION FROM SITE N S E W	32. DISTANCE FROM SITE FT. MI.
		33. DISTANCE WAS MEASURED ☐ ESTIMATED ☐	
		(34) CONSTRUCTION ZONE ☐	(35) TRAFFIC CONTROL DEVICE PRINCIPAL ☐ INTERSECTING ☐
18. HAZARDOUS MATERIALS Y ☐ N ☐	19. PENNDOT PROPERTY Y ☐ N ☐		

UNIT # 1			UNIT # 2		
36. LEGALLY PARKED ? Y ☐ N ☐	37. REG. PLATE	38. STATE	36. LEGALLY PARKED ? Y ☐ N ☐	37. REG. PLATE	38. STATE
39. PA TITLE OR OUT-OF-STATE VIN			39. PA TITLE OR OUT-OF-STATE VIN		
40. OWNER			40. OWNER		
41. OWNER ADDRESS			41. OWNER ADDRESS		
42. CITY, STATE & ZIPCODE			42. CITY, STATE & ZIPCODE		
43. YEAR	44. MAKE		43. YEAR	44. MAKE	
45. MODEL - (NOT BODY TYPE)		46. INS. Y ☐ N ☐ UNK ☐	45. MODEL - (NOT BODY TYPE)		46. INS. Y ☐ N ☐ UNK ☐
(47) BODY TYPE	(48) SPECIAL USAGE	(49) VEHICLE OWNERSHIP	(47) BODY TYPE	(48) SPECIAL USAGE	(49) VEHICLE OWNERSHIP
(50) INITIAL IMPACT POINT	(51) VEHICLE STATUS	(52) TRAVEL SPEED	(50) INITIAL IMPACT POINT	(51) VEHICLE STATUS	(52) TRAVEL SPEED
(53) VEHICLE GRADIENT	(54) DRIVER PRESENCE ☐	(55) DRIVER CONDITION	(53) VEHICLE GRADIENT	(54) DRIVER PRESENCE ☐	(55) DRIVER CONDITION
56. DRIVER NUMBER		57. STATE	56. DRIVER NUMBER		57. STATE
58. DRIVER NAME			58. DRIVER NAME		
59. DRIVER ADDRESS			59. DRIVER ADDRESS		
60. CITY, STATE & ZIPCODE			60. CITY, STATE & ZIPCODE		
61. SEX	62. DATE OF BIRTH	63. PHONE	61. SEX	62. DATE OF BIRTH	63. PHONE
64. COMM. VEH. Y ☐ N ☐	65. DRIVER CLASS	66. DRIVER SS #	64. COMM. VEH. Y ☐ N ☐	65. DRIVER CLASS	66. DRIVER SS #
67. CARRIER			67. CARRIER		
68. CARRIER ADDRESS			68. CARRIER ADDRESS		
69. CITY, STATE & ZIPCODE			69. CITY, STATE & ZIPCODE		
70. USDOT #	ICC #	PUC #	70. USDOT #	ICC #	PUC #
(72) VEH. CONFIG.	(73) CARGO BODY TYPE	74. GVWR	(72) VEH. CONFIG.	(73) CARGO BODY TYPE	74. GVWR
75. NO. OF AXLES	(76) HAZ ARDOUS MATERIALS	77. RELEASE OF HAZ MAT Y ☐ N ☐ UNK ☐	75. NO. OF AXLES	(76) HAZ ARDOUS MATERIALS	77. RELEASE OF HAZ MAT Y ☐ N ☐ UNK ☐

AA-45 (1/92) PAGE: CENTER FOR HIGHWAY SAFETY

(continued)

Exhibit 10.6 Sample police accident report form (*continued*)

78. RESPONDING EMS AGENCY | INCIDENT #:
79. MEDICAL FACILITY | ACCIDENT DATE:

80. PEOPLE INFORMATION

A	B	C	D	E	F	G	NAME	ADDRESS	H	I	J	K	L	M

81. ILLUMINATION ☐ 82. WEATHER ☐
83. ROAD SURFACE ☐

84. PENNSYLVANIA SCHOOL DISTRICT (IF APPLICABLE)

85. DESCRIPTION OF DAMAGED PROPERTY

OWNER

ADDRESS

PHONE

86. DIAGRAM

87. NARRATIVE - IDENTIFY PRECIPITATING EVENTS, CAUSATION FACTORS, SEQUENCE OF EVENTS, WITNESS STATEMENTS, AND PROVIDE ADDITIONAL DETAILS. LIKE INSURANCE INFORMATION AND LOCATION OF TOWED VEHILCES, IF KNOWN.

INSURANCE INFORMATION	COMPANY	INSURANCE INFORMATION	COMPANY
UNIT 1	POLICY NO	UNIT 2	POLICY NO

88. WINTESSES	NAME	ADDRESS	PHONE
	NAME	ADDRESS	PHONE

	89. VIOLATIONS INDICATED	90. SECTION NUMBERS (ONLY IF CHARGED)	TC NTC
UNIT 1			☐ ☐
UNIT 2			☐ ☐

	91. PROBABLE USE	92. TYPE TEST	93. RESULTS			91. PROBABLE USE	92. TYPE TEST	93. RESULTS		94. INVESTIGATION COMPLETE ?
UNIT 1			0.__%	☐ NO TEST ☐ REFUSE ☐ UNK	UNIT 2			0.__%	☐ NO TEST ☐ REFUSE ☐ UNK	YES ☐ NO ☐

AA-45 (1/92) PAGE: CENTER FOR HIGHWAY SAFETY

Source: Pennsylvania Department of Transportation, Bureau of Highway Safety and Traffic Engineering. Used with permission.

Exhibit 10.7 Initial client interview form

CLIENT INTERVIEW CHECKLIST

CLIENT PERSONAL INFORMATION

Name ____________________

Address ____________________

City ____________ State ____________ Zip ____________

Phone (hm) ____________ (wk) ____________ (cell) ____________

How long at this address ____________________

Date of birth ____________ Place of birth ____________

Social Security No. ____________________

Prior address ____________________

City ____________ State ____________ Zip ____________

Dates at this address ____________________

Employer ____________________

Job description ____________________

Marital status ____________ Maiden name ____________

Spouse's name ____________ Date of birth ____________

Child's name ____________ Date of birth ____________

Child's name ____________ Date of birth ____________

Child's name ____________ Date of birth ____________

CASE INFORMATION

Case referred by ____________________

Case type ☐ Appeal ☐ Business ☐ Corporate ☐ Estate ☐ Litigation
☐ Municipal ☐ Real Estate ☐ Tax ☐ Trust ☐ Other

Opposing party(ies) ____________________

Opposing party ____________________

Address ____________________

Opposing attorney ____________________

Address ____________________

Date of incident ____________ Statute of limitation date ____________

Summary of facts ____________________

____

____

____

Spoliation of evidence Destruction of evidence.

It is important to understand the local rules with regard to the loss or destruction of evidence, or **spoliation of evidence**, and its effect on a cause of action. In determining the appropriate penalty for spoliation of evidence, courts are most likely to consider:

1. the degree of fault of the party who altered or destroyed the evidence;
2. the degree of prejudice suffered by the opposing party; and
3. the availability of a lesser sanction that will protect the opposing party's rights and deter future similar conduct [see *Schroeder v. Department of Transportation*, 710 A2d 23 (1998)].

Exhibit 10.8 Sample timeline using LexisNexis TimeMap

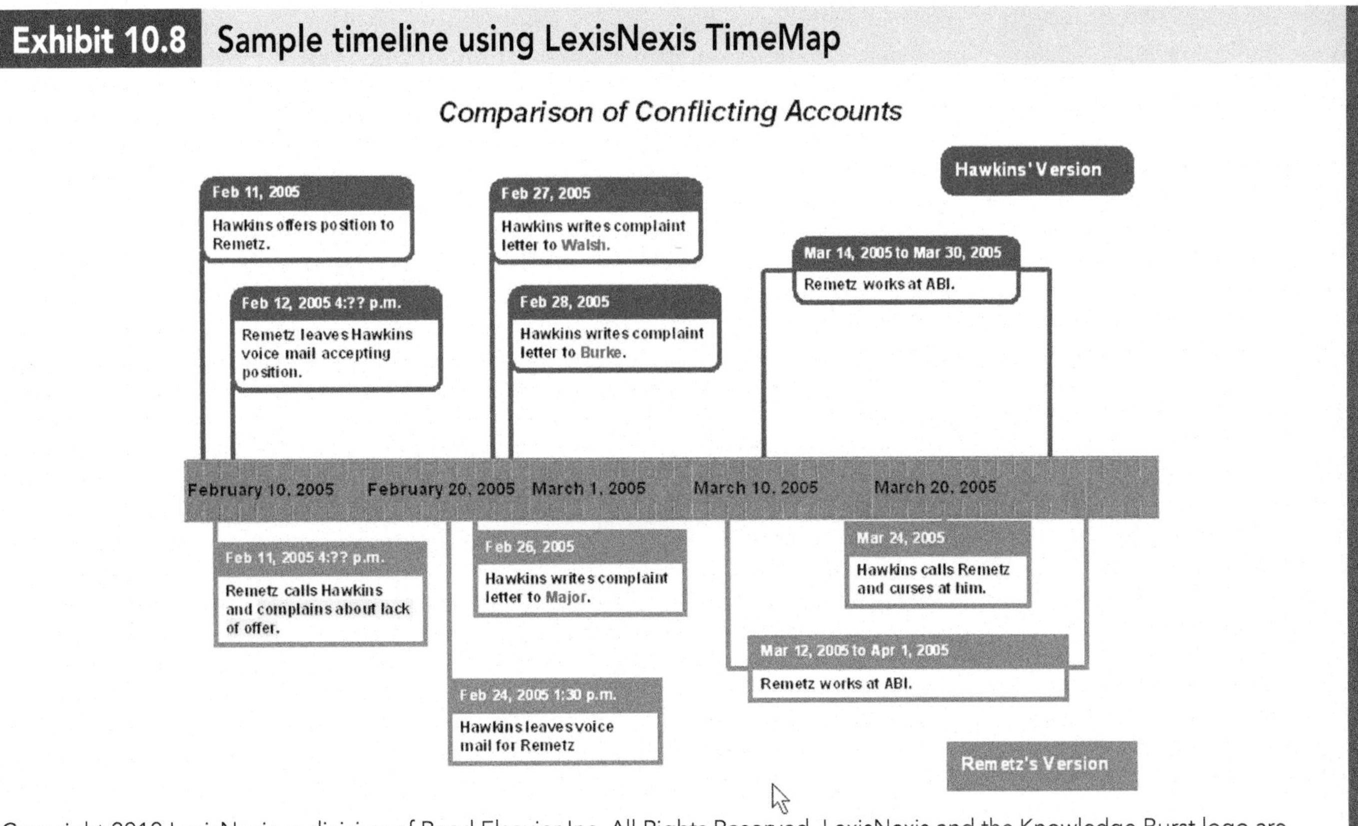

Following a Timeline

An investigation should explore not only the incident itself, but also events leading up to the incident, as well as the events and occurrences that followed it. (See Exhibit 10.8 for a comparison of conflicting accounts.) Some of the facts leading up to and following the incident may be critical. An essential question in some cases may be whether the incident could have occurred in the time period asserted by the parties. For example, could a party have taken only 20 minutes to drive 30 miles through crowded rush-hour traffic on city streets? In a food-poisoning case, could ingestion of the food at noon have caused the reaction claimed by 1:00 p.m.? Most food-poisoning cases take 6 to 12 hours from ingestion of the tainted food until the onset of symptoms. If the ingestion occurred only an hour prior, this may indicate that the claimant might have been negligent or the wrong source was identified as the cause of the illness.

The starting point for developing a timeline is the time of the alleged injury. Also important, from the standpoint of proving fault or the absence of fault, are the events that led up to the incident. From the damages standpoint, the events after the incident, including treatment and subsequent changes in the person's life or lifestyle, are important.

Freedom of Information Act (FOIA)

The **Freedom of Information Act (FOIA)** is a federal statute designed to make available to the public information possessed by the federal government and its agencies. The federal government can be a good source of information. Many documents filed by persons or businesses are available through the government and

Freedom of Information Act (FOIA) A federal statute permitting access to federal agency records.

are frequently provided online, such as corporate filings with the Securities and Exchange Commission. Other information may be available by request. However, some limitations apply to the information available. The general exceptions in FOIA, 5 U.S.C. § 552, are:

> **(b)** This section does not apply to matters that are—
>
> **(1)**
> **(A)** specifically authorized under criteria established by an Executive order to be kept secret in the interest of national defense or foreign policy and
> **(B)** are in fact properly classified pursuant to such Executive order;
> **(2)** related solely to the internal personnel rules and practices of an agency;
> **(3)** specifically exempted from disclosure by statute (other than section 552b of this title), if that statute—
> **(A)**
> **(i)** requires that the matters be withheld from the public in such a manner as to leave no discretion on the issue; or
> **(ii)** establishes particular criteria for withholding or refers to particular types of matters to be withheld; and
> **(B)** if enacted after the date of enactment of the OPEN FOIA Act of 2009, specifically cites to this paragraph.
> **(4)** trade secrets and commercial or financial information obtained from a person and privileged or confidential;
> **(5)** inter-agency or intra-agency memorandums or letters which would not be available by law to a party other than an agency in litigation with the agency;
> **(6)** personnel and medical files and similar files the disclosure of which would constitute a clearly unwarranted invasion of personal privacy;
> **(7)** records or information compiled for law enforcement purposes, but only to the extent that the production of such law enforcement records or information
> **(A)** could reasonably be expected to interfere with enforcement proceedings,
> **(B)** would deprive a person of a right to a fair trial or an impartial adjudication,
> **(C)** could reasonably be expected to constitute an unwarranted invasion of personal privacy,
> **(D)** could reasonably be expected to disclose the identity of a confidential source, including a State, local, or foreign agency or authority or any private institution which furnished information on a confidential basis, and, in the case of a record or information compiled by criminal law enforcement authority in the course of a criminal investigation or by an agency conducting a lawful national security intelligence investigation, information furnished by a confidential source,
> **(E)** would disclose techniques and procedures for law enforcement investigations or prosecutions, or would disclose guidelines for law enforcement investigations or prosecutions if such disclosure could reasonably be expected to risk circumvention of the law, or
> **(F)** could reasonably be expected to endanger the life or physical safety of any individual;
> **(8)** contained in or related to examination, operating, or condition reports prepared by, on behalf of, or for the use of an agency responsible for the regulation or supervision of financial institutions; or
> **(9)** geological and geophysical information and data, including maps, concerning wells.
>
> Any reasonably segregable portion of a record shall be provided to any person requesting such record after deletion of the portions which are exempt under this subsection. The amount of information deleted, and the exemption under which the deletion is made, shall be indicated on the released portion of the record, unless including that indication would harm an interest protected by the exemption in this subsection under which the deletion is made. If technically feasible, the amount of the information deleted, and the exemption under which the deletion is made, shall be indicated at the place in the record where such deletion is made.

Many federal agencies do not require a formal FOIA request. Some federal agencies, such as the National Transportation Safety Board (NTSB), make information available online. The Consumer Product Safety Commission (CPSC) site is

SIDEBAR

CPSC LIMITATIONS OF FOIA DISCLOSURE

15 U.S.C. § 2055. Public disclosure of information release date: 2005-08-01

(a) Disclosure requirements for manufacturers or private labelers; procedures applicable
  (1) Nothing contained in this Act shall be construed to require the release of any information described by subsection (b) of section 552 of title 5 or which is otherwise protected by law from disclosure to the public.
  (2) All information reported to or otherwise obtained by the Commission or its representative under this Act[,] which information contains or relates to a trade secret or other matter referred to in section 1905 of title 18 or subject to section 552 (b)(4) of title 5[,] shall be considered confidential and shall not be disclosed.
  (3) The Commission shall, prior to the disclosure of any information which will permit the public to ascertain readily the identity of a manufacturer or private labeler of a consumer product, offer such manufacturer or private labeler an opportunity to mark such information as confidential and therefore barred from disclosure under paragraph (2).
  (4) All information that a manufacturer or private labeler has marked to be confidential and barred from disclosure under paragraph (2), either at the time of submission or pursuant to paragraph (3), shall not be disclosed, except in accordance with the procedures established in paragraphs (5) and (6). . . .

helpful in finding information about defective products that may be a cause of a client's injuries, but limitations are placed on the information that an agency may disclose under federal law.

Under the provisions of the Electronic Freedom of Information Act (FOIA) Amendments of 1996, all federal agencies are required to use electronic information technology to foster public availability of FOIA records. The Act requires each agency to make electronically available the documents described in 5 U.S.C. Sec. 552(a)(2) that the agency created after November 1, 1996.

Web Exploration

For the Consumer Product Safety Commission Guide to Public Information, see: http://www.cpsc.gov/Newsroom/FOIA/Guide-to-Public-Information/.

Locating Witnesses

Most witnesses can be located by the use of directories. The Web has also become a valuable tool for locating witnesses.

Directories

Investigators traditionally keep a collection of telephone books and directories of the areas in which they work. But the availability and use of printed telephone directories has declined in favor of online, Internet-based directories, which may be searched by phone number, address, or last name. Directories are not limited to the United States but are available online for most parts of the world. Businesses may also be located using commercial or industrial directories, both domestically and internationally.

In addition to online telephone directories, online directories are published by trade organizations, professional groups, and educational institutions in both print and online versions. These directories may be limited to their memberships but can be useful in cases where the name and the association are known, but not the city, state, or country where the person can be found.

The Web

As paper is replaced by electronic media, more directories are being placed online. In addition, search engines can be used to locate individuals, businesses, and organizations on the Internet. Communications companies and other private firms offer a number of online directories. Many organizations and publishers of professional directories now offer their directories online. These services may change or cancel their Web address and others may be added, so the list of websites must be kept continually up to date.

The Web is also a good source of information about both expert and lay witnesses. Normal search engines such as Bing, Google, or Yahoo! frequently will provide some information using a person's name as a search term. Social networking sites, such as Facebook, offer information on millions of people who otherwise would not be in a directory. A search of Facebook, YouTube, blogs, and other similar websites may produce information that can be used for finding people and learning about them. The sites may also provide information about a witness's good or questionable behavior that might demonstrate a credibility issue. For example, the posting of a Web camera image of a high-profile athlete or celebrity at a party has resulted in a loss of endorsement contracts because of questions of improper conduct. Public postings by potential parties and witnesses may also indicate a potential bias, hostility, or, in the case of a potential juror, a predisposition or prejudice about a particular party. In some cases, jurors posting to their websites, Facebook, or other social networking sites may show a violation of jury deliberation secrecy that might result in a new trial.

Web Exploration

For information or making an FOIA request to the Department of Justice is available at http://www.justice.gov/oip/foia-resources.html.

Web Exploration

Check frequently requested information at the NTSB website: http://www.ntsb.gov.

Web Exploration

Experts can be located using the free LexisNexis/Martindale-Hubbell website at http://experts.martindale.com/.

CHECKLIST Investigation Information Sources

Information Source	Web Address	Physical Location	Comments
Police Records—Local	www.		
Police Records—State	www.		
Birth Records	www.		
Death Records	www.		
Driver's License	www.		
Vehicle Registration	www.		
Corporate Records	www.		
Real Estate—Recorder	www.		
Real Estate—Tax	www.		
Real Estate—Land Mapping	www.		
Register of Wills	www.		
Trial Court	www.		
Federal District Court—Clerk's Office	www.	Room________Federal Courthouse	
Federal Bankruptcy Court	www.		
Occupational License	www.		
Weather Reports	www.		

Personalize this list by adding the local or regional office web address, mailing addresses, and room numbers for personal visits. Add comments and note any applicable contact people, costs, or hours of operation.

LEARNING OBJECTIVE 5
Explain the function of the trial notebook and its relationship to case management.

Interviews, Investigations, and Trials

It is never too early to start preparing for trial. Trial preparation starts with the first client contact or with gathering the first document related to a case. Good preparation for trial also includes an assessment of how well clients and witnesses will react in depositions or in court under the pressure of cross-examination and how they will be perceived by opposing counsel, the judge, or the jury. An important practical consideration in deciding whether to try a case is how the parties will appear to the jury. Will they come across as being truthful and likeable? Or will they appear dishonest, unpleasant, or untrustworthy? These observational notes may be of great interest when the legal team must decide whether to settle or try the case.

Effectively managing a case may involve reviewing, sorting, and marking for identification hundreds or even thousands of documents, photographs, and other items. Careful tracking and organizing should start at the beginning of the case management process. Good case management requires a thoughtful process for storing, handling, examining, evaluating, and indexing every page. In the computer age, case management also includes making decisions on whether to use electronic display technologies in addition to conventional paper exhibits. **Demonstrative evidence**, such as the defective products in a strict liability action or an automobile in a motor vehicle accident, may need to be obtained and preserved for examination by expert witnesses or for use at trial.

Trial notebook A summary of the case, tabbed for each major activity, witness, or element of proof.

There are almost as many different approaches to setting up case files and managing cases as there are legal teams. One of the traditional approaches is the case or **trial notebook**. Summary information about the case is maintained in a notebook with tabs for each major activity, party, expert, or element of proof needed. A sample of the sections is shown in Exhibit 10.9. If a trial notebook system is used, the team must maintain and organize the case file, file boxes, or file cabinets where the hard copies of documents, exhibits, and other evidence are maintained. If only one trial or case notebook is kept for the team, someone working on the case must take responsibility for being certain that there is no duplication of effort and that the most current activities are entered. When multiple copies of the notebook are used, each trial notebook must be updated regularly so that all members of the legal team are using the same information.

Case and Practice Management Software

The legal team may be working on a number of cases at the same time, and each case may be in a different stage of preparation. With the team approach to handling cases, each member of the team must be able to access case information and know what the other members of the team have done, as well as what remains to be done. In the traditional paper file approach, the physical file is the repository for everything in the case, including interview notes, pleadings, and exhibits. To work on a specific part of a case, the physical file has to be located and the needed folder pulled.

In the **"paperless" office**, everything, in theory, is available on the computer screen. Documents are scanned into an electronic format and saved on the computer. Pleadings and notes are saved as word processor files. Transcripts of depositions and court hearings are also stored in electronic form. In a case with voluminous paperwork and days or weeks of deposition transcripts, case management software can allow relevant documents or appropriate deposition notes to be accessed quickly and efficiently.

Case management or practice management software can be used to manage both the law office itself and the cases within the office. This software has evolved from earlier programs that tracked time spent on cases, sometimes with a calendar component that could be used to track deadlines and statutes of limitation. Modern programs also include practice management functions such as time and cost tracking, conflict checking, scheduling, and contact management. Others allow for management of the individual cases, including the tracking of documents, parties, issues, and events.

Software

Case management software is constantly evolving as the various vendors try to meet the demands and needs of their customers. Some non-legal software has case or practice management-type functions. Microsoft Outlook provides a combination contact manager, calendar/scheduler, task "to do" list, and email function. More sophisticated programs, such as AbacusLaw from Abacus Data Systems and Practice Manager from Tabs3, provide the same functions, as well as outlining, billing, integrated research management, timelines, and other functions. LexisNexis CaseSoft offers individual programs that can share data, including CaseMap, TimeMap, TextMap,

SIDE BAR

It is important to check individual judges' policies and procedures before taking action; see, for example, the following from the Policies and Procedures of PETRESE B. TUCKER, Chief Judge of the United States District Court for the Eastern District of Pennsylvania.

1. General Policies

The parties **shall not** file any dispositive motions before attending a settlement conference with Magistrate Judge Caracappa. All motions to amend the complaint, join or add additional defendants or name John Doe defendants shall be filed on or before the date set by the Court. All motions in limine shall be filed and served at least five (5) business days before the trial date. All other motions shall be filed and served prior to the close of the discovery period.

All briefs must be on 8.5 by 11 inch sequentially numbered pages. The text must be double-spaced. Headings and footnotes may be single-spaced. The font must be twelve (12) point. The margins must be one (1) inch on all four sides. No brief filed in support of or in opposition to any motion shall exceed twenty-five (25) pages in length without prior leave of Court. Any brief filed in support of or in opposition to any motion that exceeds ten (10) pages in length must be accompanied by a table of contents.

Exhibit 10.9 Sample case file tabs

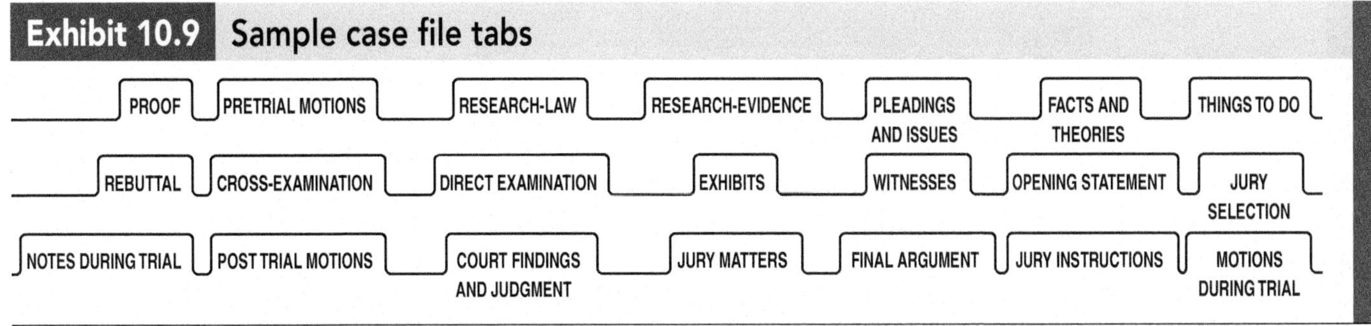

Paralegals *in* Practice

PARALEGAL PROFILE

Kevin D. Gasiewski

Kevin D. Gasiewski is a Certified Legal Assistant Specialist in Intellectual Property. After a career in law enforcement, he obtained his first paralegal job in the City Attorney's Office of Ann Arbor, Michigan. Later, he worked for Ford Global Technologies, LLC, and is now employed by Brooks Kushman P.C. Kevin is an active member of the Legal Assistants Section of the State Bar of Michigan, of which he is a past chairperson and a recipient of its 2003 Mentor Award.

My work focuses mainly on trademark prosecution, maintenance, and protection. During the initial interview with a client interested in registering a trademark, it is important to fully identify all team members, vendors, and third-party manufacturers connected to the proposed mark. I also ask questions regarding the mark itself and who designed it, as well as the goods, services, and countries for which it is intended. This data will be needed if the trademark is challenged, and for future maintenance or protection requirements.

My job also includes protecting trademarks from illegal use. When customs officials notify us that they are detaining suspected counterfeit goods, I initiate an investigation. I examine the subject trademark, determine the origin of the goods, and ascertain the final destination of the goods. The results of this investigation help me confirm whether or not the suspect goods are genuine.

Interview and investigation data are stored electronically, including contacts' information, specimen images showing use of the trademark, evidence showing the fame of the mark, and documents filed in support of the mark. The databases I use also contain a field for listing key phrases, words, and acronyms to make data searches easier and more efficient.

Although formal education is a definite plus in my field, it is equally important to stress your skills when applying for a paralegal position. Not only were my police investigation and interview skills attractive to employers; these abilities also provided me with the confidence to complete the wide variety of assignments typically encountered as a trademark paralegal.

"Paperless" office An office with electronic documents.

and NoteMap. One of the features of CaseMap is the ability to organize a case by facts, objects, or parties and create a chronology, as shown in Exhibit 10.10. CaseMap can then seamlessly create timelines from the chronological information by using the TimeMap program (see Exhibit 11.11).

Exhibit 10.10 **CaseMap features**

Back | Facts | 38 Records

Main | Facts | Objects | Issues

Date & Time	Fact Text	Source(s)	Key	Status +	Linked Issues	Eval by CA	Eval
06/??/1999	William Lang makes decision to reduce size of staff.	Deposition of William Lang, 43:19	☐	Undisputed	Age Discrim Against Hawkins	↘	
07/??/1999	Susan Sheridan is terminated.	Deposition of Philip Hawkins	☐	Undisputed	Pattern & Practice	↓	
Sun 07/04/1999	Philip Hawkins allegedly makes derogatory remarks about Linda Collins to Karen Thomas during Anstar Biotech Industries Fourth of	Interview Notes	☑	Disputed by:	Hawkins Deserved Termination	↗	
Mon 07/12/1999	Anstar Biotech Industries second quarter sales announced. Sales have dropped by 8%.		☐	Undisputed	Demotion, Hawkins Deserved Termination	→	
Fri 07/30/1999	Philip Hawkins *demoted* to sales manager.	Deposition of Philip Hawkins, p. 24, l15.	☐	Undisputed	Demotion	↘	
Thu 08/05/1999 #1	Philip Hawkins and William Lang meet.	????	☐	Undisputed	Age Discrim Against Hawkins	→	
Thu 08/05/1999 #2	Philip Hawkins alleges that William Lang tells him "The old wood must be trimmed back hard."	Complaint, p. 8; Deposition of Philip	☑	Disputed by: Us	Pattern & Practice, Demotion	↓	
Mon 08/09/1999	Philip Hawkins transferred to Anstar Biotech Industries office in Fresno.	Deposition of Philip Hawkins, p.43, l18.	☐	Undisputed	Transfer, Hawkins Deserved Termination	↘	
09/23/1999	Philip Hawkins writes letter to William Lang complaining about the way he's being treated and alleging plan to eliminate older staff	Hawkins Letter of 9/23/99	☐	Undisputed	Wrongful Termination, Age Discrim Against Hawkins	↘	
Fri 11/12/1999	Reduction in force takes place. 55 Anstar Biotech Industries employees are let go including Philip Hawkins.		☑	Undisputed	Wrongful Termination, Age Discrim Against Hawkins	↓	
Mon 11/22/1999	Philip Hawkins files suit.	Complaint	☐	Undisputed		→	
Tue 12/14/1999	Philip Hawkins turns down job offer from Converse Chemical Labs.	Rumor William Lang heard	☐	Prospective	Failure to Mitigate	↗	
01/??/2000	Philip Hawkins meets with Susan Sheridan	Rumor William Lang heard	☐	Prospective		?	
01/??/2000	Philip Hawkins is diagnosed as suffering Post Traumatic Stress Disorder.		☐		Mental Anguish	↗	

Exhibit 10.11 TimeMap features

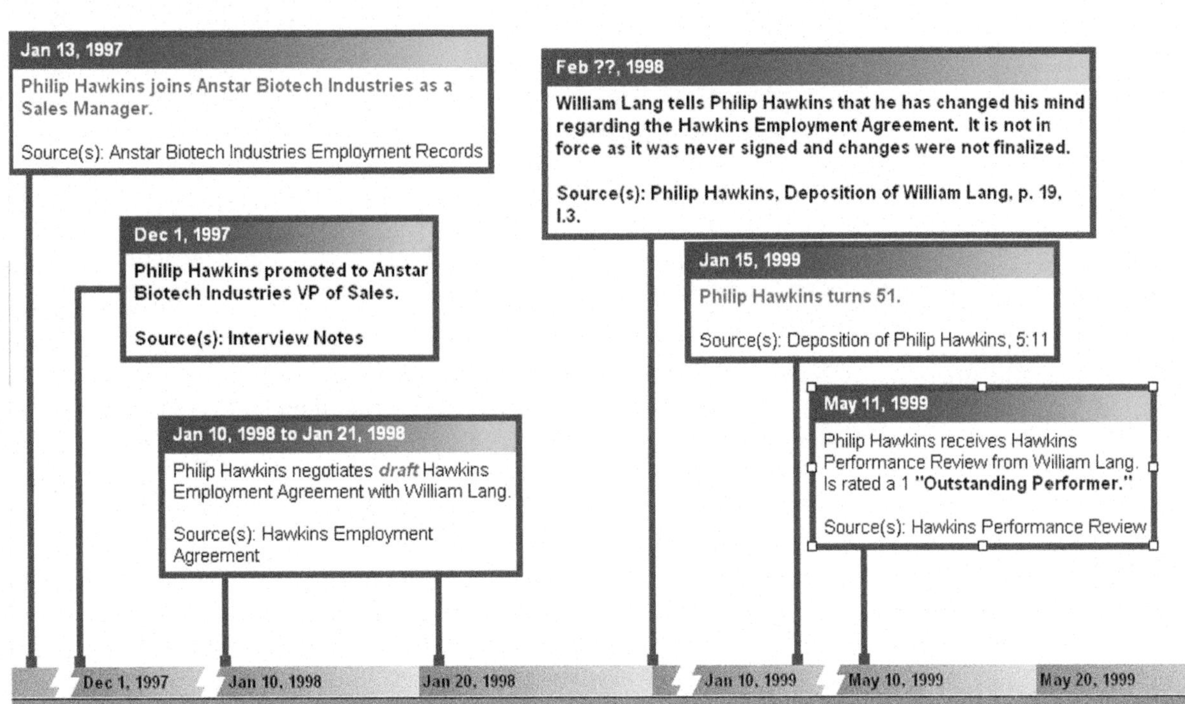

Concept Review *and* Reinforcement

LEGAL TERMINOLOGY

Arbitration, 397
Attorney–client privilege, 377
Conflict of interest, 377
Ethical obligation, 392
Ethical wall, 377
Expert witnesses, 393
Freedom of Information Act (FOIA), 401
Implied attorney–client relationship, 377
Leading questions, 391
Moral obligation, 392
Narrative opportunity, 391
Open-ended questions, 391
"Paperless" office, 406
Privileged communication, 393
Restatement of the Law Third, Torts, 396
Screening interview, 376
Spoliation of evidence, 400
Strict liability, 396
Statute of limitations, 379
Trial notebook, 404

SUMMARY OF KEY CONCEPTS

Interviews/Interviewing

Interview	Any contact you have with a client, or prospective client, is a type of interview.
Screening Interview	The typical first contact with a client usually is a telephone call, but some people just appear at the office door, asking for an appointment or basic information about the firm's ability or interest in taking a case.
First Meeting	1. The paralegal must be careful to make clear that he or she is a paralegal and not an attorney. 2. The paralegal must build a relationship with the individual, let him or her understand the purpose of the interview, and eliminate any barriers that would prevent obtaining the necessary information.
Implied Attorney–Client Relationship	If too much information is taken, the potential client will think he or she is now represented by a lawyer. The courts have ruled on the side of the potential client, holding that an implied attorney–client relationship exists.
Cultural Sensitivity	The culturally sensitive person is aware of the reasons for differences in the way people behave based on religious and ethnic backgrounds and belief systems.

Preparing for the Interview

Outcomes	1. The first step is to understand the outcomes desired, one of which is to instill confidence in the firm and its personnel. 2. The ideal outcome of any interview is to obtain all the necessary and relevant facts in the case.
Physical Surroundings	Depending upon the purpose of the interview and the person being interviewed, a formal or an informal environment may be desired.
Dress and Appearance	Clothing worn in an interview sends a nonverbal message about the paralegal and the firm or business, and the initial impression can enhance or destroy credibility.
Communication Skills in a Multicultural Society	Interviewers must appreciate how and why individuals act and react differently.
Listening Skills	An interviewer must learn to listen to what is actually being said and not just to the words themselves.
Leading Questions	Leading questions are questions that suggest the desired answer. Lawyers in conducting a cross-examination in trial frequently use leading questions to force the witness to answer in a desired manner.
Open-Ended Questions	Open-ended questions are designed to create a narrative opportunity for the witness.

Moral versus Ethical Considerations

Moral Obligations	Moral obligations are based on one's own conscience or perceived rules of correct conduct, generally held by the person's own community.
Ethical Obligations	Ethical obligations are obligations of the legal professional under the ABA Model Rules of Professional Conduct. An important ethical obligation is thoroughness in representing a client.

Privileged Communications

Forms of Privileged Communications	Attorney–client communications Doctor–patient communications Priest–penitent communications Spousal communications during marriage
Waivers	Privileges can be waived, but the waiver must come from the client, patient, penitent, or spouse making the statement with the belief that it is privileged.

Investigating Claims

Expert Witnesses	Expert witnesses are individuals whose background, education, and experience are such that courts will recognize them as qualified to give opinions based on a set of facts.

Freedom of Information Act (FOIA)

	FOIA is a federal statute designed to open to the public information in the possession of the federal government and its agencies.

Locating Witnesses

Directories	1. Phone books 2. Cross-reference directories 3. Membership directories
The Web	Search engines can help locate individuals, businesses, and organizations on the Internet. The Web is also a source of information about individuals from public sources and social networking sites.

Interviews, Investigations, and Trials

Trial Preparation	Trial preparation starts with the first client contact and the gathering of the first document. Good preparation for trial includes an assessment of how well clients and witnesses will react in depositions or in court under the pressure of cross-examination and how they will be perceived by opposing counsel, the judge, or the jury.
Case Management	Good case management requires a thoughtful process for storing, handling, examining, evaluating, and indexing every page. In the computer age, case management involves decisions on the appropriateness and potential use of electronic display technologies, as well as conventional paper exhibits.
Traditional Case Management	The case notebook or trial notebook was one of the common traditional approaches to case management.
Case and Practice Management Software	Case management or practice management programs can be used to manage the law office and the cases within the office.

WORKING THE WEB

1. Use the Internet to find and print out a map of the local area around your home.
2. Use the Internet to obtain driving directions from your home to your school's main entrance. Print out the directions and related maps.
3. Obtain a satellite image of your school from Google Earth: https://www.google.com/earth/. How might this be more helpful in investigating a case than other maps available on the Internet?
4. Use Findlaw to locate an accounting expert in your state: www.findlaw.com. Print out a list of experts listed.
5. Use the LexisNexis Martindale-Hubbell website to locate an expert witness for a patent intellectual property case involving an electronic device. Print out a copy of the contact information.
6. Using the search function of your computer browser, find and print out a copy of Rule 26 of the Federal Rules of Civil Procedure.
7. Download a trial copy of TimeMap from LexisNexis using the link on the Technology Resources website: http://media.pearsoncmg.com/ph/chet/chet_goldman_techresources_2/pages/index.html.
8. Prepare a timeline of the assignments and exams for the courses you are currently taking. Print a copy of the timeline.
9. Assume you have been asked to work on a case in which a pedestrian was struck by a car going north on the west side of the Flat Iron Building in Manhattan (New York City). Print out a satellite image of the location showing the building and the traffic flow using Google Earth: http://www.google.com/earth/index.html. Note that you will have to download the Google Earth viewer. Check with your instructor before downloading on a school computer. What is the proper direction of the vehicle traffic? Was the crosswalk visible? Were any other potential images available? Prepare a short memorandum about your findings.

CRITICAL THINKING & WRITING QUESTIONS

1. What are the legal and ethical issues involved for the paralegal when the potential client says he or she just wants a quick answer to a question such as, "Do I have a case?" Explain fully, including references to the applicable state statute.
2. What is a screening interview? What potential ethical and malpractice issues are involved?
3. How is the implied attorney–client relationship created? What are the critical issues for the law firm when this relationship is established?
4. Does the attorney have a duty to keep the names of clients confidential? Explain the ethical rules that apply.
5. What are the ethical or legal implications of not advising a party that you are a paralegal and not a lawyer?
6. What is the difference between "listening" and "hearing" during an interview? Explain.
7. How can stereotypes prevent hearing what is said in interviews?
8. What role do cultural issues play in the interview process? Explain.
9. What are the strategic reasons for using leading questions and for using open-ended questions? Give an example of when each would be better used than the other.
10. In representing a client, is it acceptable or required to ignore an ethical or moral consideration? Explain, giving an example and a reason for breaching each.
11. Explain fully the reasons for conducting a thorough investigation of a case. What ethical issues dictate how an investigation is to be conducted?
12. How can the Internet be used to effectively conduct an investigation of a case? Explain, comparing with examples of conventional methods that could also be used.
13. Using the facts in the *Palsgraf* case in Appendix A, prepare a list of witnesses who might be called in that case. Prepare an interview checklist for each of the witnesses.
14. Using the facts in the *Palsgraf* case in Appendix A, prepare an investigative checklist, including a list of the evidence that should be gathered in the case and a list and description of any photographs needed.
15. In conducting an interview, when would it be appropriate to dress in "casual Friday" attire?
16. Why is it important to visit the site of the accident in a motor vehicle case being prepared for trial?
17. Under what circumstances might it be advisable for someone in the firm other than you to handle an interview with a client or witness?
18. Why would someone feel a moral obligation to not answer questions in an interview?
19. Why would a law firm hire an expert witness, but then not call that person as a witness at trial?

20. How useful is the Freedom of Information Act in obtaining state or local government documents? Explain.
21. Can a client restrict the use of information obtained as part of the investigation in preparation for trial even if doing so will have adverse consequences, in the opinion of the attorney? Why or why not?
22. What are the issues and potential problems in using a trial notebook?
23. How does the use of case management software improve the effectiveness of the legal team? Who has the ultimate responsibility for managing the case file when using case management software?

Building Paralegal Skills

VIDEO CASE STUDIES

UPL Issue: Working with a Witness

A paralegal investigating an accident case creates the impression that he is acting in an official capacity when requesting a fact witness to appear to give a formal statement. When the fact witness appears for the statement, he is offered compensation for his time.

After viewing the video case study at the book website at www.pearsonhighered.com/careersresources, answer the following:

1. Does the paralegal have a duty to divulge his role as a paralegal when interviewing potential witnesses?
2. Is it appropriate to offer compensation to a fact witness?
3. Should the same rules of ethics apply to investigators as well as to paralegals?

Zealous Representation Issue: When You Are Asked to Lie

A paralegal has been instructed by his supervising attorney to do whatever is necessary to obtain information needed in a particular case.

After viewing the video case study at the book website at www.pearsonhighered.com/careersresources, answer the following:

1. What is pretexting?
2. Is it ethical to lie to obtain needed information?
3. Is a paralegal bound by ethical rules when acting as an investigator?

ETHICS ANALYSIS & DISCUSSION QUESTIONS

Review the opening scenario of this chapter. What are the ethical issues involved? Prepare a suggested policy, referencing the specific ethics code sections, to present to the supervising attorney of the firm. Address the issues of how to answer the phone and what should and should not be said. Your instructor may provide you with specifics, such as the fee for an initial consultation.

DEVELOPING YOUR COLLABORATION SKILLS

Working on your own or with a group of other students, review the scenario at the beginning of the chapter and the discussion that takes place between Sara and Mrs. Weiser.

1. a. Prepare a list of questions Sara should ask before starting work. Discuss who should be asked these questions, and what actions Sara should or should not take.
   b. What are the ethical issues facing Sara?
   c. What are the potential malpractice issues facing the firm?
2. Write a summary of the advice the group would give to Sara.
3. Form groups of three. Designate one person who will act as Sara, one as a potential client, and the third as a supervising paralegal.
   a. As the paralegal interviewer of a client who has just walked into the office after being injured in an

accident, use the facts of the *Palsgraf* case in Appendix A or another assigned by your instructor.

b. As the client, be sure you understand whether you have a case and that the fee is acceptable.

c. As the supervising paralegal, comment on the interview, what issues were raised, and what you would have done differently.

PARALEGAL PORTFOLIO EXERCISE

Using the current information for your area or jurisdiction, complete the Investigation Information Sources checklist. Print out a copy for your portfolio.

LEGAL ANALYSIS & WRITING CASES

Limitations on Obtaining Information in Criminal Cases Under the FOIA

Department of Justice v. Landano, 508 U.S. 165 (1993)

The FOIA can be a good source of information in criminal cases as well as civil litigation. As with discovery-limitation exemptions in civil cases, additional exemptions exist under the Act in criminal cases. Landano was convicted in New Jersey state court for murdering a police officer during what may have been a gang-related robbery. In an effort to support his claim in subsequent state court proceedings that his rights were violated by withholding material exculpatory evidence, he filed Freedom of Information Act requests with the Federal Bureau of Investigation (FBI) for information it had compiled in connection with the murder investigation.

When the FBI redacted some documents and withheld others, Landano filed an action, seeking disclosure of the contents of the requested files. The court held that the government is not entitled to a presumption that all sources supplying information to the FBI in the course of a criminal investigation are confidential sources within the meaning of Exemption 7(D). Further, a source should be deemed "confidential" if the source furnished information with the understanding that the FBI would not divulge the communication except to the extent it thought necessary for law-enforcement purposes.

Questions

1. Does this unfairly subject an informant to potential harassment?
2. Does limiting information unfairly prevent the defendant from receiving a fair trial?
3. Does the limitation effectively limit any usefulness in making a request under FOIA?

Spoliation of Evidence

In Re *Daimlerchrysler Ag Securities Litigation* No. 00-993-JJF (D. Del. Nov. 25, 2003)

Defendants requested relief in the form of sanctions against the plaintiff for the spoliation of evidence[,] contending that a personal assistant to one of the Plaintiffs, Jaclyn Thode, had destroyed documents that she used to prepare a list of meetings and/or conversations prepared at the request of general counsel, who had failed to instruct her to preserve the documents used in making the list. The court in ruling on the defendant's motion concluded that sanctions were not warranted as a result of the alleged spoliation of evidence. The unrebutted deposition testimony and affidavit of Ms. Thode establish that she discarded her handwritten notes after converting them into typewritten form, consistent with her practice in the past. Ms. Thode had no information or understanding about the substance of the litigation and no information as to the purpose of counsel's request, and thus she had no reason to alter or omit any information from the documents and that she acted unintentionally when she discarded the steno pads and pink message notes. The Court also found the Defendants did not suffer any prejudice, because they had a complete and accurate chronology of the contents of the documents that were discarded. The court cited *Son, Inc. v. Louis & Nashville R.R. Co.*, 695 F.2d 253, 259 (7th Cir.1982) (finding that destruction of evidence was not intentional where handwritten notes were discarded after being typed and [the] person handling evidence had no reason to omit or alter necessary information).

Questions

1. Should the investigation of a case where documents include transcription also include inquiry into the source of transcribed notes? Why or why not?
2. Why would not knowing the purpose of creating the notes matter in determining the potential spoliation of evidence?
3. What advice would you give to someone who has the responsibility of transcribing or keeping minutes of meetings?

WORKING WITH THE LANGUAGE OF THE COURT CASE

Carol M. Douglas v. Deidre Monroe, Esq., 743 N.E.2d 1181 (2001)

Read, and if assigned, brief this case. In your brief, answer the following questions.

1. What actions may constitute the creation of an attorney–client relationship?
2. What steps should an attorney take to avoid creating an attorney–client relationship?

CASE SUMMARY

Appellant-plaintiff Carol M. **Douglas** ("Carol"), individually and as administratrix of the estate of her deceased son, Curtis K. **Douglas** ("Curtis"), appeals from the entry of summary judgment on Carol's legal malpractice claim in favor of appellee-defendant Deidre **Monroe** ("**Monroe**"). We affirm.

ISSUE

Carol presents one issue, which we restate as whether a genuine issue of material fact regarding the existence of an attorney–client relationship between **Monroe** and Carol should have precluded summary judgment.

FACTS AND PROCEDURAL HISTORY

On April 20, 1997, Curtis, an eighteen-year-old freshman at Indiana University Purdue University at Indianapolis ("IUPUI"), drowned at the Natatorium swimming facility. In August of that year, Carol began considering the possibility of filing a lawsuit in connection with Curtis's death. Because Carol was still grieving, her brother, Lionel **Douglas** ("Lionel"), looked into the possibility of bringing suit.

Shortly thereafter, while working as a security guard at a bank in Gary, Indiana, Lionel saw **Monroe** in the bank's lobby. He had gone to high school with her and knew she was now an attorney, but he had never engaged her professional services. They had a short conversation during which Lionel told her about his nephew's passing,[1] indicated that counsel might be sought, and inquired as to whether there was a time limit in which to bring suit. **Monroe** responded that he had two years. **Monroe** mentioned neither the 180-day limit in which to file a tort claims notice nor that Lionel should not rely on her advice. They had another short conversation in the bank lobby thereafter. Lionel did not believe that **Monroe** was representing him or Carol when he was talking to her. Supp. Record at 66. Lionel conveyed to Carol the two-year statute of limitations.

In November 1997, Carol spoke with her current counsel and first learned about the tort claims notice requirement. By then, more than 180 days had lapsed since Curtis's death. On March 26, 1999, Carol filed a wrongful death/legal malpractice complaint against IUPUI, IUPUI Natatorium, Trustees of Indiana University, Edward Merkling, David Thibodeau, Chris Chin, Julie McKenney, Ryan J. Ellis, Danny A. Huffman, Jr., Adam Boatman, Jeff Ellis & Associates, Inc., and **Monroe**.[2] Carol alleged that **Monroe's** failure to inform Lionel of the 180-day tort claims notice requirement and Carol's subsequent failure to file a timely notice resulted in the barring of her wrongful death suit.

Monroe answered, denying the allegations. She then moved for summary judgment, asserting that no attorney–client relationship existed between her and Carol at any time, and that therefore, Carol's claim must fail. After Carol filed a response, the trial court held a hearing on the matter. On March 27, 2000, the trial court granted **Monroe's** motion for summary judgment.

DISCUSSION AND DECISION

Carol argues that summary judgment was improperly granted because "there is at the very least a question of fact about the existence of the attorney–client relationship." She boldly contends that in "no way is **Monroe** entitled as a matter of law to escape all accountability for willingly giving incorrect legal advice about a critically important legal issue to someone who consulted her in her capacity as an attorney." Encompassed in her argument are assertions of detrimental reliance and agency.

"The purpose of summary judgment is to terminate litigation about which there can be no factual dispute and which can be determined as a matter of law." *Bamberger & Feibleman v. Indianapolis Power & Light Co.*, 665 N.E.2d 933, 936 (Ind.Ct. App.1996); *see* Ind. Trial Rule 56(C). "The trial court's grant of summary judgment is clothed with a presumption of validity and the appellant bears the burden of proving that the trial court erred." *Bamberger*, 665 N.E.2d at 936. In reviewing a motion for summary judgment, we apply the same standard as the trial court, and we resolve any question of fact

(continued)

or an inference to be drawn therefrom in favor of the non-moving party. *Id.* "We will affirm a trial court's grant of summary judgment if it is sustainable on any theory found in the evidence designated to the trial court." *Id.*

"To prove a legal malpractice claim, 'a plaintiff-client must show (1) employment of an attorney (duty); (2) failure by the attorney to exercise ordinary skill and knowledge (breach); (3) proximate cause (causation); and (4) loss to the plaintiff (damages).'" *Bernstein v. Glavin*, 725 N.E.2d 455, 462 (Ind.Ct.App.2000) (quoting *Fricke v. Gray*, 705 N.E.2d 1027, 1033 (Ind.Ct.App.1999), *trans. denied*), *trans. denied.* A defendant is entitled to judgment as a matter of law "when undisputed material facts negate at least one element of a plaintiff's claim." *McDaniel v. Bus. Inv. Group, Ltd.*, 709 N.E.2d 17, 20 (Ind. Ct.App.1999), *trans. denied.*

"[A]n attorney–client relationship need not be express, but may be implied by the conduct of the parties." *Matter of Kinney*, 670 N.E.2d 1294, 1297-98 (Ind. 1996) (citing *In re Anonymous*, 655 N.E.2d 67, 70 (Ind.1995) and *Hacker v. Holland*, 570 N.E.2d 951, 955 (Ind.Ct.App. 1991)). "Attorney–client relationships have been implied where a person seeks advice or assistance from an attorney, where the advice sought pertains to matters within the attorney's professional competence, and where the attorney gives the desired advice or assistance." *Anonymous*, 655 N.E.2d at 71. "An important factor is the putative client's subjective belief that he is consulting a lawyer in his professional capacity and on his intent to seek professional advice." *Id.* at 70. However, "[t]he relationship is consensual, existing only after both attorney and client have consented to its formation." *Kinney*, 670 N.E.2d at 1297. Hence, a "would-be client's unilateral belief cannot create an attorney–client relationship." *Hacker*, 570 N.E.2d at 955.

In addressing Carol's argument, we briefly review cases concerning the question of an attorney–client relationship for legal malpractice purposes. In relation to a medical malpractice action, attorney Kinney helped a woman "answer some interrogatories, attended a deposition with her, and, at a court hearing which the woman apparently failed to attend, managed to secure a continuance of certain discovery deadlines." *Kinney*, 670 N.E.2d at 1297. Yet, our supreme court concluded:

. . . the opportunity to file a formal appearance on the client's behalf, but declined to do so. Each of these facts indicates that the respondent did not consent to the formation of an attorney–client relationship and that his actions should have put the woman on notice that he did not represent her.

. . . However, *the mere provision of nominal legal advice is not automatically dispositive where the existence of an attorney–client relationship is disputed.*

Id. at 1298 (emphasis added). Similarly, we have concluded that a buyer's attorney's preparation of closing documents and his act of presiding over a closing, standing alone, were insufficient to create a relationship or to render the attorney liable to the seller for any negligent acts associated with the transaction. *Hacker*, 570 N.E.2d at 956.

In contrast, our supreme court concluded that both an attorney and a putative client consented to the formation of an attorney–client relationship in *Anonymous*, 655 N.E.2d 67. In that case, however, (1) the attorney met with the putative client on several occasions and discussed a potential wrongful termination suit, a matter within the respondent's professional competence; (2) the attorney concluded that the putative client had a strong wrongful termination case; (3) the putative client thought the attorney was acting as his attorney; and (4) the attorney should have been aware that the putative client thought the attorney was representing him, but did nothing to dispel this belief. *Id.* at 70-71.

We find the present case more similar to *Kinney* and *Hacker* than to *Anonymous*. Here, Carol never met or spoke with **Monroe**. Moreover, she did not attempt to contact **Monroe**, schedule an appointment with her, or consent to the formation of an attorney–client relationship with her. Carol neither entered into a contract for legal services with **Monroe** nor paid for advice from her. Carol never thought **Monroe** was representing her in the matter of Curtis's death. Indeed, when later contacted by her current counsel and asked if she was being represented, Carol replied "no." Further, there is no evidence that **Monroe** believed she was in any way representing Carol or that **Monroe** consented to the formation of an attorney–client relationship. **Monroe's** brief statement regarding the statute of limitations appears to have been fostered by sympathy, not by any desire to provide professional services to a woman she did not know.

As for the detrimental reliance theory, we have stated:

In certain cases, an attorney–client relationship may also be created by a client's detrimental reliance on the attorney's statements or conduct. An attorney has in effect consented to the establishment of an attorney–client relationship if there is "proof of detrimental reliance, when the person seeking legal services reasonably relies on the attorney to provide them and the attorney, aware of such reliance, does nothing to negate it."

Hacker, 570 N.E.2d at 956 (quoting *Kurtenbach v. TeKippe*, 260 N.W.2d 53, 56 (Iowa 1977)). "The cases actually applying this rule to find attorney liability are few, and liability has been found only when the attorney undertook, gratuitously or otherwise, to complete an affirmative act for the party who later brought suit." *Id.* We stressed in *Hacker* that the appellant would not be able to obtain an instruction on her reliance theory upon retrial unless she could "demonstrate either that she had a prior, continuous attorney–client relationship with [the attorney] or that [the attorney] agreed to act in her behalf in the transaction." *Id.* at 957. Here, **Monroe** undertook no affirmative act; there was no prior, continuous attorney–client relationship; and **Monroe** did not agree to act on Carol's behalf in any transaction. Rather, Carol's brother had a brief conversation with an attorney passing through a bank lobby one day, and during that conversation the attorney responded that the relevant statute of limitation was two years. Under the circumstances, **Monroe** did not know Carol would rely on this isolated statement, and any reliance Carol placed on the statement was not reasonable. Thus, we find Carol's detrimental reliance theory unavailing.

Finally, we address Carol's assertions of agency. To establish an actual agency relationship, three elements must be shown: (1) a manifestation of consent by the principal to the agent; (2) an acceptance of the authority by the agent; and (3) control exerted by the principal over the agent. *Johnson v. Blankenship*, 679 N.E.2d 505, 507 (Ind.Ct.App.1997), *aff'd* 688 N.E.2d 1250 (Ind.1997). Apparent agency is also initiated by a manifestation of the principal. *Swanson v. Wabash College*, 504 N.E.2d 327, 331 (Ind.Ct.App. 1987).

However, the necessary manifestation is one made by the principal to a third party who in turn is instilled with a reasonable belief that another individual is an agent of the principal. It is essential that there be some form of communication, direct or indirect, by the principal, which instills a reasonable belief in the mind of the third party. Statements or manifestations made by the agent are not sufficient to create an apparent agency relationship.

Id. at 332 (citations omitted). "*Generally*, the question of whether an agency relationship exists is a question of fact." *Id.* (emphasis added). However, if the evidence is undisputed, there are times when summary judgment is appropriate in agency cases. *See, e.g., Drake v. Maid-Rite Co.*, 681 N.E.2d 734 (Ind.Ct.App.1997); *Jarvis Drilling, Inc. v. Midwest Oil Producing Co.*, 626 N.E.2d 821 (Ind.Ct.App.1993), *trans. denied*; Swanson, 504 N.E.2d 327.

Here, there is evidence, albeit conflicting, regarding the first two prongs of the agency test. Resolving this evidence in favor of Carol as we must, *see Bamberger*, 665 N.E.2d at 936, we presume that there was a manifestation of consent by Carol to Lionel and that he accepted the authority. As for the third prong, Lionel's affidavit provides the only potential support for the notion that Carol had control over Lionel. Lionel's affidavit, submitted after **Monroe** filed her motion for summary judgment, states, "[a]t all times that I sought Deidre **Monroe's** advice, I was doing so under the direction and control of my sister Carol, who had asked for my help."

. . . Specifically, there is no evidence that Carol instructed Lionel to seek a lawyer's advice, let alone **Monroe's** advice. There is no evidence that Carol told him when or where to speak with **Monroe**, gave him questions to ask her, outlined potential terms of employment, or gave him the power to bind her to an agreement, such as would support an attorney–client relationship. Further, there is no evidence that Carol was unaware of how to form such an attorney–client relationship, as she eventually did enter into such a relationship with her current counsel. Especially telling is Carol's previously mentioned deposition testimony that she never thought **Monroe** was representing her in the matter of Curtis's death. Under these circumstances, we conclude that Carol has failed to set forth sufficient specific facts to support an actual agency theory. *See id.* at 601.

Carol's apparent agency argument is likewise unpersuasive. Carol submitted no evidence regarding the necessary manifestation made by the principal to a third party who in turn is instilled with a reasonable belief that another individual is an agent of the principal. *See Swanson, 504 N.E.2d at 332.* That is, there was no form of communication, direct or indirect, by Carol, which instilled a reasonable belief in the mind of **Monroe** that Lionel was acting as her agent. Lionel's statements are simply insufficient to create an apparent agency relationship.

Although we sympathize with Carol's immense loss, we must conclude that the trial court properly granted summary judgment in **Monroe's** favor in this legal malpractice action.

Affirmed.

Department of the Interior v. Klamath Water Users Protective Association, 532 U.S. 1 (2001)

Supreme Court of the United States

Read, and if assigned, brief this case. In your brief, answer the following questions.

1. What are the two conditions under which a document qualifies for exemption under the Freedom of Information Act, Exemption 5?
2. How is "agency" defined under FOIA?
3. What is the "deliberative process" privilege? Does nongovernmental litigation have an equivalent privilege?

(continued)

4. What is the purpose of the deliberative process privilege?

5. What is the "general philosophy" behind FOIA?

Justice Souter delivered the opinion of the Court. Documents in issue here, passing between Indian Tribes and the Department of the Interior, addressed tribal interests subject to state and federal proceedings to determine water allocations. The question is whether the documents are exempt from the disclosure requirements of the Freedom of Information Act, as "intra-agency memorandums or letters" that would normally be privileged in civil discovery [5 U.S.C. § 552(b)(5)]. We hold they are not.

I

. . . [T]he Department's Bureau of Indian Affairs (Bureau) filed claims on behalf of the Klamath Tribe alone in an Oregon state-court adjudication intended to allocate water rights. Since the Bureau is responsible for administering land and water held in trust for Indian tribes . . . it consulted with the Klamath Tribe, and the two exchanged written memorandums on the appropriate scope of the claims ultimately submitted. . . . The Bureau does not, however, act as counsel for the Tribe, which has its own lawyers and has independently submitted claims on its own behalf.[1]

. . . [T]he Klamath Water Users Protective Association is a nonprofit association of water users in the Klamath River Basin, most of whom receive water from the Klamath Project, and whose interests are adverse to the tribal interests owing to scarcity of water. The Association filed a series of requests with the Bureau under the Freedom of Information Act (FOIA) [5 U.S.C. § 552] seeking access to communications between the Bureau and the Basin Tribes during the relevant time period. The Bureau turned over several documents but withheld others as exempt under the attorney work-product and deliberative process privileges. These privileges are said to be incorporated in FOIA Exemption 5, which exempts from disclosure "inter-agency or intra-agency memorandums or letters which would not be available by law to a party other than an agency in litigation with the agency" [§ 552(b)(5)]. The Association then sued the Bureau under FOIA to compel release of the documents. . . .

Upon request, FOIA mandates disclosure of records held by a federal agency, see 5 U.S.C. § 552, unless the documents fall within enumerated exemptions. . . .

A

Exemption 5 protects from disclosure "inter-agency or intra-agency memorandums or letters which would not be available by law to a party other than an agency in litigation with the agency" [5 U.S.C. § 552(b)(5)]. To qualify, a document must thus satisfy two conditions: Its source must be a Government agency, and it must fall within the ambit of a privilege against discovery under judicial standards that would govern litigation against the agency that holds it.

Our prior cases on Exemption 5 have addressed the second condition, incorporating civil discovery privileges. . . . So far as they might matter here, those privileges include the privilege for attorney work-product and what is sometimes called the "deliberative process" privilege. Work-product protects "mental processes of the attorney" while deliberative process covers "documents reflecting advisory opinions, recommendations and deliberations comprising part of a process by which governmental decisions and policies are formulated." The deliberative process privilege rests on the obvious realization that officials will not communicate candidly among themselves if each remark is a potential item of discovery and front-page news, and its object is to enhance "the quality of agency decisions," . . . by protecting open and frank discussion among those who make them within the Government. . . .

The point is not to protect Government secrecy pure and simple, however, and the first condition of Exemption 5 is no less important than the second; the communication must be "inter-agency or intra-agency" [5 U.S.C. § 552(b)(5)]. . . . With exceptions not relevant here, "agency" means "each authority of the Government of the United States," and "includes any executive department, military department, Government corporation, Government-controlled corporation, or other establishment in the executive branch of the Government . . . , or any independent regulatory agency." . . .

Although neither the terms of the exemption nor the statutory definitions say anything about communications with outsiders, some Courts of Appeals have held that in some circumstances a document prepared outside the Government may . . . qualify . . . under Exemption 5. . . .

[1] The Government is "not technically acting as [the Tribes'] attorney. That is, the Tribes have their own attorneys, but the United States acts as trustee" [Tr. of Oral Arg. 5]. "The United States has also filed claims on behalf of the Project and on behalf of other Federal interests" in the Oregon adjudication [Id. At 6]. The Hoopa Valley, Karuk, and Yurok Tribes are not parties to the adjudication. [Brief for Respondent 7]

It is . . . possible . . . to regard as an intra-agency memorandum one that has been received by an agency, to assist it in the performance of its own functions, from a person acting in a governmentally conferred capacity other than on behalf of another agency—e.g., in a capacity as . . . consultant to the agency.

Typically, courts taking the latter view have held that the exemption extends to communications between Government agencies and outside consultants hired by them. . . . In such cases, the records submitted by outside consultants played essentially the same part in an agency's process of deliberation as documents prepared by agency personnel might have done. . . . [T]he fact about the consultant that is constant . . . is that the consultant does not represent an interest of its own, or the interest of any other client, when it advises the agency that hires it. Its only obligations are to truth and its sense of what good judgment calls for, and in those respects the consultant functions just as an employee would be expected to do.

B

. . . The Tribes, on the contrary, necessarily communicate with the Bureau with their own, albeit entirely legitimate, interests in mind. While this fact alone distinguishes tribal communications from the consultants' examples recognized by several Courts of Appeals, the distinction is even sharper, in that the Tribes are self-advocates at the expense of others seeking benefits inadequate to satisfy everyone.

. . . All of this boils down to requesting that we read an "Indian trust" exemption into the statute, a reading that is out of the question for reasons already explored. There is simply no support for the exemption in the statutory text, which we have elsewhere insisted be read strictly in order to serve FOIA's mandate of broad disclosure, which was obviously expected and intended to affect Government operations. In FOIA, after all, a new conception of Government conduct was enacted into law, "a general philosophy of full agency disclosure." Congress had to realize that not every secret under the old law would be secret under the new.

The judgment of the Court of Appeals is affirmed. *It is so ordered.*

The differences among the various circuits on the use of unpublished opinions was clarified by the Amendment to the Federal Rules of Appellate Procedure approved by the United States Supreme Court on April 12, 2006, when it approved the citation of unpublished opinions.

The proposed new Rule 32.1 as submitted for comment to Congress provided:

> Proposed new Rule 32.1 permits the citation in briefs of opinions, orders, or other judicial dispositions that have been designated as "not for publication," "non-precedential," or the like and supersedes limitations imposed on such citation by circuit rules. New Rule 32.1 takes no position on whether unpublished opinions should have any precedential value, leaving that issue for the circuits to decide. The Judicial Conference amended the proposed rule so as to apply prospectively to unpublished opinions filed on or after January 1, 2007. A court may, by local rule, continue to permit or restrict citation to unpublished opinions filed before that date.

VIRTUAL LAW OFFICE EXPERIENCE MODULES

If your instructor has instructed you to complete assignments in the Virtual Law Office program, complete the Virtual Law Office assignments as assigned by your instructor. These assignments are designed to develop your workplace skills. Completing the assignments for this chapter will result in producing the following documents for inclusion in your portfolio:

VLOE 10.1	Summary of the information from the on-site investigation
VLOE 10.2	Summary of the interview with the witness
VLOE 10.3	Memo to Mr. Saunders with opinion on using a paid fact witness
VLOE 10.4	List of additional investigation that should be undertaken

CHAPTER

11

Legal Writing and Critical Legal Thinking

LEARNING OBJECTIVES

After studying this chapter, you should be able to:

1. Explain the process of critical legal thinking.
2. Explain the ethical duty of candor toward the tribunal.
3. Describe the similarities and differences between a memorandum of law and a court brief.
4. Explain the need for proper citation form, and describe how to use it.

Paralegals at Work

Sylvia White had worked for the law firm of Thomas and Daniels for only a few weeks when the senior partner, who specialized in mergers and acquisitions, asked her to sit in on a meeting with a long-term client, Bill Johnson, and his daughter, Tonya. One of the senior paralegals on the staff told Sylvia that her role was to take notes, since the partner never took notes in meetings. He conducted the interviews, asked the questions, and didn't want anyone else to interfere.

After escorting the client and his daughter from the reception area to the partner's office, Sylvia was asked to take a seat in the corner and record the meeting notes. Mr. Johnson made it clear that he expected his attorney to get the charges of driving under the influence against Tonya dropped. Tonya acknowledged that she had been drinking at a country-western bar and knew she was well over the legal drinking limit. She had tested her alcohol level on a breath analyzer that the bar made available to its patrons.

Upon leaving the bar, Tonya went out to her car, got in, started it, and then fell asleep at the wheel. A police officer found her in this condition, woke her, and took her to the hospital for a blood alcohol test. The officer cited her for operating a vehicle while under the influence of alcohol, based on her .09 percent blood alcohol level.

After the clients left, the partner told Amanda to prepare a memorandum of law that he could use to get the charges against the client's daughter dismissed.

After doing a little research, Amanda realized that the law was against getting the charges dismissed. Furthermore, in the meeting with her father and the partner, Tonya had admitted to being intoxicated. Based on advice from the other paralegals, Amanda was concerned about putting anything negative into the memo and decided to write a memo presenting a case for dismissal.

Consider the issues involved in this scenario as you read the chapter.

> "Justice is the end of government. It is the end of civil society. It ever has been, and ever will be pursued, until it be obtained, or until liberty be lost in the pursuit."
>
> *James Madison*

INTRODUCTION TO LEGAL WRITING AND CRITICAL LEGAL THINKING

Legal writing can take a number of forms: memos, letters, opinions, memoranda of law for internal purposes, and briefs for the court. The presentation formats of these documents are very different, depending on the intended audience. But all of these types of writing share the need for clarity and accuracy. Preparation of these documents starts with an understanding of the material facts of a case and identifying the legal issues.

LEARNING OBJECTIVE 1
Explain the process of critical legal thinking.

Critical legal thinking The process of identifying the issue, the material facts, and the applicable law and then applying the law to come to a conclusion.

Issue The legal matter in dispute.

Critical Legal Thinking

Critical legal thinking is the process by which the law is applied to the facts to answer a client's issue. The writer must identify the **issue** presented by a case (the legal matter in dispute), the material (key or relevant) facts in the case, and the applicable law, and then apply the law to the facts to come to a conclusion that answers the issue or issues presented. Critical legal thinking puts the pieces of the legal puzzle together. The critical thinking process starts with a clear understanding of the facts of the client's case and identifying the legal issues in that case.

Before starting the research, the researcher must have a clear picture of all the material facts. An important purpose of the interview with the client is to determine those facts. However, some of the facts that the client thinks are important may actually not be relevant in deciding the legal issue. And some of the facts that seem unimportant to the client may actually be relevant or even critical to the outcome of the case. For example, it may not seem important to the client that he was struck by a driver going north. But this may turn out to be a material fact when it is determined that the street was a one-way street going south.

Identifying relevant facts can also be important in all types of claims, whether in tort, contract, or some other area of the law. For example, if a client signed an employee noncompetition agreement, state law may say that the agreement is unenforceable unless it was signed before commencing employment, or unless full and adequate consideration was given for signing the agreement after commencing employment. It may be essential to ask the client exactly when the agreement was signed.

Understanding the relevant facts enables the researcher to review the case and statutory law to determine which cases or statutes are applicable to the client's case. A difference in one key fact may make all the difference in the outcome of the case. Consider the case of the client charged with killing King Kong. According to the facts of the case, King Kong is a giant ape, and not a human being. The murder statute of the jurisdiction defines murder as the taking of the life of a human being by another human being; therefore, if King Kong is not a human being, the statute has not been violated. The client may be guilty of hunting out of season, hunting without a license, or killing an endangered species, but not of murder.

However, if the killer were sued in court for a civil cause of action, additional facts that were immaterial in the murder prosecution may become material. King Kong's owner may file a suit for damages for loss of an irreplaceable item. In that case, other facts may indicate that the killer is liable for damages. Determining which facts are relevant depends on the type of case (civil or criminal), the wrong that was alleged, or the right that was alleged to have been violated.

The American justice system is based on both statutory and case law. Just as in the criminal law case discussed above, factual analysis requires determining the elements of the crime, looking at the statute, and applying the facts to those elements. It may also be necessary to look at case law for precedent on how those facts are applied. For example, all states have laws prohibiting driving under the influence of alcohol. Some of these statutes use the terms "vehicle" and "operating." The researcher may

IN THE WORDS OF THE COURT . . .

WHITING V. STATE, NO. A-8755 (ALASKA APP. OCTOBER 12, 2005)

MANNHEIMER, JUDGE.

Michael T. Whiting appeals his conviction for felony driving under the influence, . . . the facts . . . : Whiting and his girlfriend and his girlfriend's six-year-old son decided to go fishing in Gastineau Channel. Whiting piloted a skiff into the channel and then turned the motor off. The three occupants of the skiff fished while the skiff drifted in the channel; Whiting sat in the rear of the skiff near the motor. While Whiting was fishing, he was also drinking alcoholic beverages.

A Coast Guard vessel approached the skiff . . . , discovered that he was under the influence. Whiting claimed that he had been sober when he piloted the boat into the channel, and that he did not become intoxicated until after he stopped the motor and the fishing began.

. . . Whiting's argument hinges on his assertion that the statutory definition of driving under the influence, AS 28.35.030(a)[,] does not include the situation where an intoxicated person is in control of a watercraft whose engine is not running. Whiting's assertion is incorrect. . . . [T]his Court held that "operating" a watercraft includes being in control of the watercraft, even if its engine is not running.

We addressed essentially the same argument in *Kingsley v. State*, 11 p. 3d 1001 (Alaska App. 2000). The defendant in *Kingsley* drove his car into a snow berm, where it became stuck. Kingsley turned the engine off and decided to remain in the car. According to Kingsley, it was only then that he consumed a bottle of whiskey and became intoxicated.

Kingsley argued that, under these circumstances, he was not intoxicated when he was operating the vehicle, and he was never in "control" of the vehicle after he became intoxicated. We rejected this narrow definition of "control."

As Kingsley acknowledges in his brief to this court, a person who engages the engine of a vehicle and allows it to run is not merely exercising physical control over the vehicle but is also "operating" it. Thus, if the engine of Kingsley's vehicle had been running when the police arrived, the State might have proved that Kingsley was operating the vehicle while intoxicated. But the State had to prove only that Kingsley was in actual physical control of the vehicle while intoxicated.

. . . A person's attempt to operate a vehicle may furnish convincing proof that the person is in actual physical control of the vehicle, but a person may exercise actual physical control over a vehicle without making active attempts to operate it.

Whiting was the one who had piloted the skiff into the channel, and Whiting remained primarily in the rear of the skiff, nearest the motor, while his girlfriend and her son sat in the front of the skiff. Under these facts, as a matter of law, Whiting was in physical control of the skiff, and he was therefore operating the skiff for purposes of the DUI statute.

---

need to determine how courts have defined a "vehicle" and what conduct is considered "operating." Defense counsel must examine the case law carefully to try to differentiate the client's fact pattern from decided cases. Slight variations in facts can be important in making a compelling argument.

Facts Information or details that are not based on theory, opinion, or conjecture.

Facts are pieces of information or details that exist in reality, or have occurred, and are not based on theory, supposition, or conjecture. Facts, in the law, are circumstances, events, actions, occurrences, or states, rather than opinions or interpretations. A statement that a car was traveling south on State Street at 60 miles per hour, as shown on a police officer's radar unit, is a statement of fact. A statement by a witness standing on the sidewalk that the car appeared to be traveling faster than 55 miles per hour is an opinion or conjecture, not a fact.

Material facts Facts significant or essential to the issue.

Immaterial facts Facts that are not essential to the matter or issue at hand.

Facts may be divided into **material facts** and **immaterial facts.** A material fact is a fact that has some significant or essential connection with the issue or matter at hand. An immaterial fact is one that has no probative value in the matter at issue. Some facts, while not relevant because they do not prove or disprove a matter in issue, may lead to relevant material facts.

For example, the information revealed in an investigation may show that a defendant was coming from a doctor's office and driving within the speed limit when he struck another car in the rear at a red stoplight. Is the fact that he was coming from the doctor's office a relevant fact in the accident? It may be, if he was given medication at the doctor's office that caused blurred vision or drowsiness and if the doctor had told him not to drive or operate any machinery. The information that he was coming from the doctor's office was not in itself relevant to proving the allegations, but it led to the discovery of other relevant material facts.

Legal Writing

The purpose of writing is to communicate. If the writing does not communicate the subject to the reader, it has not served its purpose. But there are many types of written communication, and there are as many writing styles as there are writers. A writer of a novel may devote pages to setting the stage for the characters and many more pages to developing those characters. Readers probably come to expect this and look forward to long paragraphs that create the setting and describe the characters.

Skilled legal writers are more like the writers of short stories. They must quickly and accurately set the stage in only a few words and tell the story in a small space. Skilled legal writers are able to explain, persuade, and state facts for the record accurately, concisely, and clearly. Unlike the novelist or poet, the legal writer must follow a set of guidelines dictated by ethical and procedural rules, while at the same time clearly presenting an answer to a client, or persuading a court to adopt a certain position.

Paralegals *in* Practice

PARALEGAL PROFILE

Ann L. Atkinson

Ann L. Atkinson is a graduate of the University of Nebraska with a Bachelor of Science degree in Education. She is also an Advanced Certified Paralegal with over 27 years of legal experience. Her professional memberships include the Nebraska Paralegal Association, the National Association of Legal Assistants, and the National Association of Bond Lawyers. Ann is currently employed by the law firm of Kutak Rock LLP in their Omaha, Nebraska, office.

I specialize in public finance law, which generally is transactional in nature—preparing, reviewing, and revising contracts or negotiated "deals" between parties. Specifically, I assist the attorneys as they work with state housing agencies or municipalities when they issue bonds for public purposes. The bonds represent a "loan" of money from bondholders. The attorneys with whom I work often act as bond counsel (where we are counsel for the bond issue itself), or we may also serve as underwriter's counsel (in which we are counsel to the underwriter of the bonds).

Since our department focuses primarily on single-family housing, we prepare all the documents that enable an issuer to issue bonds. These bonds then provide proceeds from which the issuer can offer single-family homes to first-time homebuyers at a "below market" interest rate. Our department also handles transactions for multi-family housing such as apartment buildings being constructed, acquired, and/or rehabilitated.

In my position, I coordinate all the things that need to be done in order for a bond issue to close. In order to do so, I rely heavily on writing and critical thinking skills. Tasks include preparing initial drafts of bond documents, researching statutes, proofing and reviewing offering documents and third-party opinions, and assisting with bond closings, including the preparation of closing transcripts. Thus, a knowledge of correct grammar, spelling, and punctuation is essential. Critical thinking skills are very useful when preparing documents because they help you follow document processes—the flow of funds, the timing requirements for notices, and knowing when and how to obtain amendment approvals.

Legal writing is a process. It requires research, analysis, organization, writing, editing, and proofreading. Sometimes it requires starting over when the final document, viewed from the position of the ultimate reader, does not communicate the necessary information or tell the story.

In the legal working environment, time to rethink, re-research, and rewrite is a luxury the paralegal will not often have. The paralegal must develop strong research and writing skills to be able to work efficiently and minimize the time necessary to produce an acceptable document, whether it is a letter, an office memorandum, or a court brief.

Writing Styles

Two of the most common types of legal documents are the brief and the memorandum. Both address a legal issue and apply a set of facts to applicable law. However, each requires a totally different writing style. The **memorandum** is a working document that is used by the legal team in the preparation of a case. It must give an objective analysis of the case and describe any alternative interpretations of the facts and the law. The analysis should be similar to the objective analysis used by a court to decide a case. For example, the Ninth Circuit Court of Appeals used this type of analysis in determining whether consent to a search was "voluntary":

Memorandum A working document for the legal team to use in the preparation of a case.

> Fed.R.Crim.P. 12(e) states that "[w]here factual issues are involved in determining a [pretrial] motion, the court shall state its essential findings on the record." Such a record is necessary to our review. . . . Compliance with the rule 12(e) requirement is particularly important in a case such as this, where we examine "all the surrounding circumstances." . . . Factual subtleties may well affect a determination of voluntariness under this test . . . *U.S. v. Castrillon*, 716 F.2d 1279 (9th Cir. 1983).

A brief written by an advocate before a court will have a different style than an internal memorandum. The brief is designed to advocate the client's point of view and convince the court to adopt a position favorable to the client.

The **opinion letter** to a client requires a different style. The opinion letter must explain to a client, who is generally untrained in the law, what legal options the client has and what can and cannot be done based on the set of facts provided by the client. In some ways it is an educational document—it must be informative and provide options with sufficient detail to allow the client to make an appropriate decision.

Opinion letter A formal statement of advice to the client based on the lawyer's expert knowledge.

Duty of Candor

LEARNING OBJECTIVE 2
Explain the ethical duty of candor toward the tribunal.

The **duty of candor** is the ethical obligation to be honest with the court. In some jurisdictions, such as Indiana, the ethical rule is titled "Candor Toward the Tribunal." The duty of candor is set forth in Rule 3.3 in the Model Rules of Professional Conduct:

A WORD OF CAUTION

The speed, ease of use, and widespread availability of email have created a new writing style that is more casual and uses shorthand terminology to communicate. Those in the legal profession must remember that every email could potentially become a piece of evidence in an electronic discovery request. Emails are frequently forwarded to others without the knowledge of the original writer, and hundreds of copies may be unintentionally distributed to other recipients.

In the legal setting, shortcuts should not be taken in writing emails. The same formality and care that go into writing a letter on legal stationery should be used in writing an email. Even greater care should be used when the email may contain privileged or confidential information. Such information may accidentally end up in the hands of those not covered by the ethical obligation to maintain confidentiality. In some cases, an email may be accidentally sent to opposing counsel, resulting in a breach of the attorney–client or work product privileges.

Duty of candor The duty of honesty to the court.

The duty of candor means that although lawyers must be zealous advocates, they also have an ethical obligation to not mislead the court. A brief that intentionally distorts or hides the truth or intentionally misleads the court can potentially destroy a legal career. Even if it doesn't result in sanctions, suspension, or disbarment, judges talk with their colleagues, and a reputation for questionable integrity is hard to correct. At the least, the court will always remember the attorney's shoddy work and may question his or her credibility in the future, even if the attorney's later cases are accurate, honest, and well prepared.

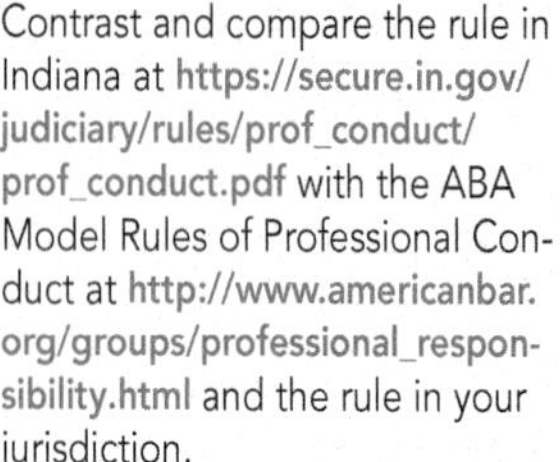

Contrast and compare the rule in Indiana at https://secure.in.gov/judiciary/rules/prof_conduct/prof_conduct.pdf with the ABA Model Rules of Professional Conduct at http://www.americanbar.org/groups/professional_responsibility.html and the rule in your jurisdiction.

RULE 3.3. CANDOR TOWARD THE TRIBUNAL

(a) A lawyer shall not knowingly:
  (1) make a false statement of fact or law to a tribunal or fail to correct a false statement of material fact or law previously made to the tribunal by the lawyer;
  (2) fail to disclose to the tribunal legal authority in the controlling jurisdiction known to the lawyer to be directly adverse to the position of the client and not disclosed by opposing counsel; or
  (3) offer evidence that the lawyer knows to be false. If a lawyer, the lawyer's client, or a witness called by the lawyer, has offered material evidence and the lawyer comes to know of its falsity, the lawyer shall take reasonable remedial measures, including, if necessary, disclosure to the tribunal. A lawyer may refuse to offer evidence, other than the testimony of a defendant in a criminal matter, that the lawyer reasonably believes is false.

(b) A lawyer who represents a client in an adjudicative proceeding and who knows that a person intends to engage, is engaging or has engaged in criminal or fraudulent conduct related to the proceeding shall take reasonable remedial measures, including, if necessary, disclosure to the tribunal.

(c) The duties stated in paragraphs (a) and (b) continue to the conclusion of the proceeding, and apply even if compliance requires disclosure of information otherwise protected by Rule 1.6.

(d) In an ex parte proceeding, a lawyer shall inform the tribunal of all material facts known to the lawyer which will enable the tribunal to make an informed decision, whether or not the facts are adverse.

Indiana Rules of Court, Rules of Professional Conduct, including Amendments made through January 1, 2012.

CHECKLIST Memorandum of Law Template

- ☐ To:
- ☐ From:
- ☐ Date:
- ☐ Subject:
- ☐ Facts
- ☐ Issue(s)
- ☐ Discussion
- ☐ Conclusion

LEARNING OBJECTIVE 3
Describe the similarities and differences between a memorandum of law and a court brief.

Preparing Office Memoranda

In researching and writing a memorandum of law, the paralegal must be careful to include all the relevant statutes and case law, even those that negatively impact the client's case. Some paralegals are intimidated by the gruff and even downright nasty attitude of certain lawyers, particularly trial counsel in the middle of a stressful case, and are fearful of including information that will upset them. In these situations, the paralegal is afraid the lawyer will "shoot the messenger" if the memorandum contains bad news. However, the reality is that the attorney *must* know the weaknesses in the case, along with the strengths. Nothing is more upsetting to an attorney, whether in court or in a meeting with a client or opposing counsel, than to be surprised by a case, facts, or law that has not been covered in the office memorandum of law.

Office memoranda are frequently filed in the office for future reference and are usually indexed by subject. If another case arises that has a similar fact pattern, a previous memorandum may provide a good starting point and can be a major time saver. The facts upon which the conclusion is based must be clearly stated so that the memorandum may be indexed properly and easily found for later use. All statutes, regulations, and cases must be cited properly so that anyone reading the memorandum in the future can look them up. Listing relevant websites that were used in preparing the memorandum is also helpful.

Starting Point

The starting point for the legal researcher is to make sure the assignment is understood. What has the researcher been asked to research? For the memorandum of law, the assignment is usually to answer a question:

- "What is the current law on . . . ?"
- "What is the current law on alcohol blood level for driving under the influence?"
- "What happens if . . . ?"
- "What happens if this is a second conviction for driving under the influence?"
- "What is the procedure for . . . ?"
- "What is the procedure for appealing a small claims judgment to a trial court?"

Before starting an assignment, the paralegal must be certain what is really being asked. Any uncertainties should be resolved by asking the person for whom the assignment is being prepared. It is often useful for the paralegal to restate, in the form of a question, what he believes he is being asked to research, such as "What are the rights of an individual who . . . ?" This will help clarify the issue in the mind of the researcher and confirm that he is researching the precise issue that the attorney is requesting.

At the outset, paralegals must also be sure to have all the relevant facts. Knowing certain facts may change the outcome—for example, the requirement in some states that a subscribing witness to a decedent's will cannot be a beneficiary. The paralegal should ascertain all the necessary facts about the case in order to prepare an accurate memorandum.

Memorandum of Law Format

The supervising attorney will usually prepare an assignment memo with a request to research and prepare an office memorandum on a specific subject or case. A sample of an assignment memo is shown in Exhibit 11.1. Frequently, the assignment is given to the paralegal in a face-to-face meeting. When the assignment is made orally, it is a good idea to confirm the specific assignment if there is any uncertainty about what is being requested.

The format or template for office memoranda is fairly standard, as shown in the memorandum of law template. Some offices may add, for identification purposes, headings such as office file numbers or client identifiers. The format in some offices includes subject matter with legal terms or areas of law so that memoranda can be filed and retrieved if future cases require research on the same subject. Copies of memoranda and other documents are now often stored electronically as word processor files or templates that can be retrieved and used as samples for new projects, as shown in Exhibit 11.2.

Exhibit 11.1 Assignment memo

MEMORANDUM

To: **Edith Hannah**
From: **Glenn Hains**
Date: **January 23, 2006**
File **Number: GH 06-1002**
Re: **Commonwealth of Pennsylvania vs. Kevin Dones**

Our client was stopped by a police officer at the bottom of the hill on route 332 in Northhampton Township, at 3:30 on Sunday afternoon, January 15, 2006. He was riding a bicycle south on route 332 and was given a citation for speeding. The police used a radar unit and claimed a speed of 35 mph in a 25 mph zone. He administered a field sobriety test, which gave a reading over the legal limit, and client was given a citation for driving under the influence. He tells me he was riding a bike because his license was suspended for a previous DUI.

Please prepare a brief memorandum of law, with citations and cases.

Exhibit 11.2 Word search function

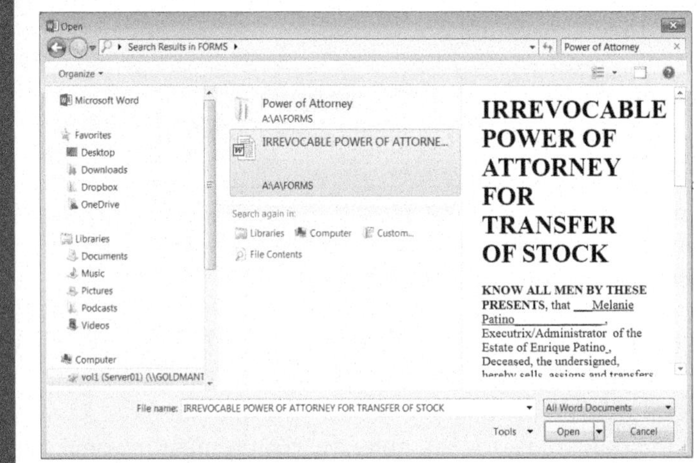

Source: Microsoft product box shots reprinted with permission from Microsoft Corporation.

When taking an assignment to research and write a memorandum, a few basics should be remembered. The attorney probably will not redo the research or add much content, and will refer to the material submitted with the memorandum. The memorandum must be an unbiased presentation of the law as it exists, and it must be clearly presented. If the content of the memorandum is not accurate and complete, the attorney relying on the analysis and discussion may be embarrassed before opposing counsel or the court, or caught off guard by information he or she was unaware of.

Points to remember in preparing a memorandum of law:

- **Never** rely on case law headnotes. Headnotes are not a primary source of the law.
- **Always** check the actual language of the court cases. It is the primary authority.
- **Check** the dates of the cases and statutes. Be sure they are current law.

- **Shepardize** (GlobalCite, KeyCite, V.Cite) the cases you cite to be certain they have not been overruled by a later case or statute.
- **Don't** be afraid to show the cases and statutes that are against the client's position.
- **Cite all** sources used. Never plagiarize.
- **Analyze** opposing case law for any differences that may give the attorney a chance to distinguish the negative cases in some way based on the facts or the law.
- **Ask** the attorney if you don't understand the issues or questions involved. It is better to admit that you are having a problem with the research than to give the attorney incorrect, incomplete, or unintelligible information.

The format of the memorandum of law is determined by the nature of the assignment, the number of issues, and the ultimate use of the memorandum, as well as personal preferences of the person giving the assignment.

The components of a memorandum of law and the components of a court opinion (case) are similar. Exhibit 11.3 presents a comparison. Some case opinions have a brief summary or syllabus of the case that is prepared by an editor, such as the editors of West Publishing Company, or Supreme Court editors. The syllabus is not an official part of the case but is provided for the reader's convenience. Some attorneys prefer to have a short "Answer" under the "Statement of the Assignment." The Answer is generally a shortened version of the main points of the conclusion.

Samples of a traditional memorandum of law and one prepared for internal government use are shown in Exhibits 11.4 and 11.5.

If you have ever "briefed" a case, you will notice the similarity to the list of items shown in the comparison above. A sample of a case and a case brief are provided in Appendix A: How to Brief a Case.

Facts

The writer of a legal memorandum must have a clear statement of the facts from which to work. All of the facts relied upon in writing the assignment memo must be included as part of the final memorandum. Other members of the firm may read the

Exhibit 11.3 Components of court opinions and memorandums of law

COURT OPINIONS	MEMORANDUMS OF LAW
Caption: Parties, citation, relevant dates	**Heading:** Assigning party, client, file number
Judicial history: Prior proceeding (how the case got to this court)	**Statement of the assignment:** History of what happened and why the client sought representation
Issue: Legal question before the court	**Issue:** Legal issues of clients raised in statement of assignment
Facts: Relevant facts used to decide case	**Statement of facts:** Relevant facts
Analysis and discussion: Discussion of the facts, rules of law, issues, judicial reasons for decision	**Analysis and discussion:** Discussion of each issue, how the applicable law applies, what relevant facts impact the decision
Conclusion: Holding of the Court	**Conclusion:** Restatement of the conclusion to each issue analyzed and discussed above, summarizing the main points

Exhibit 11.4 Sample memorandum of law prepared by leading legal research provider

MEMORANDUM OF LAW

TO: Ellen Holroyd, Esq.

FROM: [redacted]

DATE: January 29, 2004

RE: SEC Definitions of Terms Under the Sarbanes-Oxley Act of 2002

QUESTION PRESENTED

With regard to its regulations promulgated pursuant to the Sarbanes-Oxley Act of 2002, how does the Security and Exchange Commission define the concepts "material violation", "credible evidence", and "reasonable behavior" by an attorney?

DISCUSSION

Section 307 of the Sarbanes-Oxley Act of 2002 ("Sarbanes-Oxley") requires the Securities and Exchange Commission ("SEC") to "prescribe minimum standards of professional conduct for attorneys appearing and practicing before the Commission in any way in the representation of issuers." Implementation of Standards of Professional Conduct for Attorneys, Securities Act Release No. 33,8185, 68 Fed. Reg. 6,296 (Feb. 6, 2003.) According to the SEC, these standards "must include a rule requiring an attorney to report evidence of a material violation of securities laws or breach of fiduciary duty or similar violation by the issuer." Id., at 6,296. This memorandum discusses the definitions embraced by the SEC for "material violation," "credible evidence," and "reasonable behavior" by an attorney, three concepts found in the regulations adopted by the SEC pertaining to Sarbanes-Oxley.

Page 4 of 27

Exhibit 11.4 Sample memorandum of law prepared by leading legal research provider *(continued)*

III. Definition of "Reasonable Behavior" By An Attorney

Such a definition necessarily brings up next the question of what the SEC deems to be "reasonable behavior" for attorneys with regard to their duty to report actual or suspected Sarbanes-Oxley violations. In its formulation of what constitutes "reasonable behavior" on the part of an attorney under the Sarbanes-Oxley regulations, the SEC points out that it is not a "bright line" test, and that it is dependent on the circumstances surrounding not just the alleged violation, but also the attorney involved:

> This formulation, while intended to adopt an objective standard, also recognizes that there is a range of conduct in which an attorney may engage without being unreasonable. The "circumstances" are the circumstances at the time the attorney decides whether he or she is obligated to report the information. These circumstances may include, among others, the attorney's professional skills, background and experience, the time constraints under which the attorney is acting, the attorney's previous experience and familiarity with the client, and the availability of other lawyers with whom the lawyer may consult.

Implementation of Standards of Professional Conduct for Attorneys, Securities Act Release No. 33,8185, 68 Fed. Reg. 6,296, 6,302 (Feb. 6, 2003.) Thus, what is deemed reasonable behavior for one attorney could differ significantly from that for another attorney, depending on the various factors laid out by the SEC.

CONCLUSION

While the SEC provided guidance as to the meanings of all three concepts discussed in this memo, it is clear that it intended there to be no "bright line", "one size fits all" definitions for these phrases. That said, a "material violation" for purposes of the SEC's Sarbanes-Oxley rules would appear to be a violation of such consequence that a reasonable and prudent investor would consider it important to know about when determining whether to buy, sell, or hold a particular security. "Credible evidence" would appear to be evidence of a material violation substantial enough that a prudent

Page 9 of 27

memorandum, and they need to understand the specific facts upon which the analysis is based, particularly if the paralegal is not available to answer questions about the memorandum. It is often necessary to recite other facts that were not relied upon in the analysis and the reasons for not considering them. It may also be necessary to explain how a result would be different if a particular fact were different. For example, a memorandum may have a notation that the fact pattern was based upon all of the

Exhibit 11.5 Sample memorandum of law prepared by the U.S. Department of Justice

U.S. Department of Justice
Immigration and Naturalization Service

HQADN 70/23

Office of the Executive Associate Commissioner

425 1 Street NW
Washington, DC 20536

May 24, 2001

MEMORANDUM FOR Michael A. Pearson
Executive Associate Commissioner
Office of Field Operations

FROM: Michael D. Cronin /s/
Acting Executive Associate Commissioner
Office of Programs

SUBJECT: Public Law 106-378, adjustment of status of certain Syrian nationals.

This memorandum provides eligibility information and adjudication policy guidance for the implementation of Public Law 106-378, which pertains to the adjustment of certain Syrian nationals who were granted asylum after arriving in the United States after December 31, 1991.

ELIGIBILITY

Public Law 106-378 provides for the adjustment of status of a principal alien as well as an alien who is the spouse, child, or unmarried son or daughter of a principal alien.

Principal alien. In order to be eligible for adjustment under this law, the principal alien must:

1. Be a Jewish national of Syria;
2. Have arrived in the United States after December 31, 1991, after being permitted by the Syrian government to depart from Syria;
3. Be physically present in the United States at the time of filing the application to adjust status;
4. Apply for adjustment of status under Public Law 106-378 no later than October 26, 2001, or, have applied for adjustment of status under another provision of law prior to October 27, 2000, and request to have the basis of that application changed to Public Law 106-378;
5. Have been physically present in the United States for at least one year after being granted asylum;
6. Not be firmly resettled in any foreign country; and Memorandum: Public Law 106-378, adjustment of status of certain Syrian nationals.

REQUIRED FIELD OFFICE ACTION

Field offices are to identify all potentially eligible Syrian asylee adjustment applications and forward them and the related A-files to NSC within 30-days of this memorandum. The appropriate code, "SY6, 7 or 8" and reference to Public Law 106-378 must be noted. A-files are to be routed to the NSC in separate batches, with individual cover sheets attached to the outside face of each file reflecting "**SYRIAN ASYLEE P. L. 106-378**". If, for whatever reason, a field office cannot accomplish this goal, they are to provide a report to their respective region identifying each case, explaining the reason(s), and advising the anticipated date of completion of the A-file transfer. Regions are requested to review the report and take appropriate action.

SERVICE CENTER ACTION ON APPROVED ASYLEE APPLICATIONS

The NSC must review all asylum adjustment cases received via Direct Mail as well as all cases forwarded to them from the field to cull out those Syrian nationals whose applications contain evidence of Syrian nationality, arrival

Exhibit 11.5 Sample memorandum of law prepared by the U.S. Department of Justice *(continued)*

in the United States after December 31, 1991, and a grant of asylum or asylee dependent status. The NSC must also retrieve A-files belonging to qualifying Syrian applicants inappropriately coded as "AS" adjustments, and take corrective action. A list containing the names of Syrian asylees has already been provided to the NSC to help in this regard. The NSC will also track the total number of cases approved. After the NSC approves 2,000 principal beneficiaries under this law, the NSC will stop adjudicating applications, and will notify HQ ISD and HQ ADN that the numerical limitation has been reached.

SUPPLEMENTAL FILING INSTRUCTIONS

The Form I-485 supplemental filing instructions are being modified to instruct qualified applicants to identify themselves by writing "**SYRIAN ASYLEE P. L. 106-378**" in Part 2, Block 2. Since many qualified Syrian asylees may be unaware of their special classification or the correct way to claim it, the NSC should review all newly submitted asylee adjustment applications, and, when appropriate, endorse the Form I-485 as described above. When an applicant's eligibility to adjust under Public Law 106-378 has been verified, the adjudicator will check the "other" block in the "Section of Law" portion of the FOR INS USE ONLY Section of Form I-485 and will enter the notation, "**Public Law 106-378**."

CONCLUSION

Segregating the Syrian asylum adjustments for proper adjudication is essential to preserve the use of the 10,000 visa numbers authorized annually for other asylees who are eligible to adjust their status. If you have questions regarding the adjudication of Syrian-processed asylum adjustments, please contact your center or regional representative. If needed, service center. . . .

Source: United States Department of Justice.

participants being over the age of majority for contracting, or over the age to purchase and consume alcoholic beverages.

Analysis

Critical legal thinking is essential to the legal writing process. It involves analyzing the law to find the similarities and differences in cases that could be used to argue for or against the client's position. The memorandum the paralegal prepares may be the basis for the court brief that the attorney or someone else will prepare. To be able to meet the ethical obligation to the court, the person who presents a persuasive argument on behalf of the client must know all the relevant statutory and case law, and understand how it applies to the client's case.

A memorandum must present both sides of the issue and be a neutral, objective presentation of applicable laws as they apply to the facts of the case. Any issues that the opposing attorney or the judge may raise should be considered and presented. A good analysis will include a discussion of cases that may be used by opposing counsel, and how those cases can be distinguished from the client's case.

Editing and Rewriting

The written word is a reflection of the writer. Although the paralegal may have written the memorandum for a particular person, many others may eventually read it, and everyone who reads it will evaluate the writer's abilities. In other words, every memorandum could potentially impact the writer's reputation. Therefore, the memorandum should be carefully reread, revised, and proofread before sending the final draft to the recipient. Certain elements should be considered when editing and revising, such as:

- Is the writing clear?
- Are words used properly?
- Is the spelling correct?
- Is the grammar correct?

Language differences may also be an important consideration. If the memorandum is being written for an audience for whom English is a second language, the writer should indicate this in the memorandum. Where there are variations in the translation of certain foreign-language terms, those variations should be clarified. For example, if the facts were translated from Spanish, it may be important to note which Spanish dialect they were translated from.

Preparing Court Briefs

Amicus curiae Briefs submitted by interested parties, as a "friend of the court," who do not have standing in the action.

A brief is written for the court and is designed to persuade the court to accept the client's position. Each court has rules specifying the requirements for briefs submitted by the parties and by an ***amicus curiae***—"friend of the court" (plural: *amici curiae*) The rules determine the format and the sections that must be included in the brief. In some courts, the format is based on the personal preferences of the judge. Before undertaking the task of writing a brief, the writer should always obtain a current copy of the court rules and contact the judge's law clerk for any additional limitations or requirements.

Sometimes the court is unable to read the brief thoroughly before the oral argument. In these situations, the brief's preliminary statement becomes a critical part of the brief because it focuses the court on the issues presented and the arguments being made. Being able to state the client's side of the case briefly is not easy, but it is worth the effort. It requires a clear, concise, and careful choice of words. An effective preliminary statement will be remembered as the hearing progresses, and later when the court is making its analysis and decision.

A table of contents, partial table of authorities, summary of the argument, and conclusion of an *amicus curiae* brief submitted in a case to the U.S. Supreme Court is shown in Exhibit 11.6.

LEARNING OBJECTIVE 4

Explain the need for proper citation format, and describe how to use it.

Citations

Citation A reference to the source of the information.

A legal **citation** is a reference to the source of information that allows the reader to find that source. The citation must be sufficient for the reader to be able to find the material, and the format must be one that others in the legal community generally accept and use. If a person in California submits a brief to a court, a person in New York or in Florida must be able to use the citations to locate the items referred to in the document in a traditional legal library or electronic law source such as Loislaw, VersusLaw, LexisNexis, or WestlawNext.

Primary authority The actual law itself.

Secondary authority Writings that explain or comment on the law.

All legal authorities are either primary authorities or secondary authorities. A **primary authority** is the law itself, which includes constitutions, statutes, cases, and administrative regulations. A **secondary authority** explains and comments on the primary authority, or is used as a tool for locating primary authority (such as treatises, encyclopedias, digests, or dictionaries). With a consistent citation format, the reader can locate the primary or secondary authorities referenced in a document.

Judges and lawyers in some states are abandoning the long-standing tradition of putting citations in the body of a document and now are putting the citations at the bottom of each page of the document in footnotes. They claim it makes reading legal opinions easier by eliminating the citations' interference with the flow of words.

Traditional Print Sources

The traditional method for publishing primary and secondary authority is in paper form, in books or as a collection or series of books. Where a case, statute, or regulation is available in more than one series of books, citation to both locations—known as parallel citations—is required. For example, if a case is published in both the official reporter of the state and a private publication, such as those published by West Publishing, both citations must be given. The citation form is basically the same for each:

Volume	Reporter and Series	Page
232	Atlantic 2d	44

Exhibit 11.6 *Amicus curiae* brief filed with the U.S. Supreme Court

No. 08-479

In The
Supreme Court of the United States

SAFFORD UNIFIED SCHOOL DISTRICT #1, *et al.*,
Petitioners,

v.

APRIL REDDING,
LEGAL GUARDIAN OF MINOR CHILD,
Respondent.

On Writ of Certiorari to the
United States Court of Appeals
for the Ninth Circuit

BRIEF OF *AMICI CURIAE* THE RUTHERFORD INSTITUTE, GOLDWATER INSTITUTE AND CATO INSTITUTE IN SUPPORT OF RESPONDENT

John W. Whitehead
Counsel of Record
Douglas R. McKusick
THE RUTHERFORD INSTITUTE
1440 Sachem Place
Charlottesville, VA 22911
(434) 978-3888

Timothy Lynch
Ilya Shapiro
CATO INSTITUTE
1000 Massachusetts Ave., NW
Washington, DC 20001
(202) 218-4600

Clint Bolick
Nicholas C. Dranias
GOLDWATER INSTITUTE
SCHARF-NORTON CENTER FOR CONSTITUTIONAL LITIGATION
500 E. Coronado Road
Phoenix, AZ 85004
(602) 462-5000

LANTAGNE LEGAL PRINTING
801 East Main Street Suite 100 Richmond, Virginia 23219 (800) 847-0477

TABLE OF AUTHORITIES

Cases

Bell v. Wolfish, 441 U.S. 520 (1979)........................7, 9

C.B. by and through Breeding v. Driscoll, 82 F.3d 383 (11th Cir. 1996)..13

Calabretta v. Floyd, 189 F.3d 808 (9th Cir. 1991).......5

Camara v. Municipal Court, 387 U.S. 523 (1967)..6, 7

Cornfield by Lewis v. Consol. High Sch. Dist. No. 230, 991 F.2d 1316 (7th Cir. 1993) 8, 11, 17

Doe v. Renfrow, 631 F.2d 91 (7th Cir.), *reh'g denied*, 635 F.2d 582 (7th Cir. 1980), *cert. denied*, 451 U.S. 1022 (1981) 5

Edwards v. Aguillard, 482 U.S. 578 (1987)..............19

Illinois v. Gates, 462 U.S. 213 (1983)........................16

Leatherman v. Tarrant County Narcotics, Intelligence & Coordination Unit, 507 U.S. 163 (1993) 22

Lilly v. Virginia, 527 U.S. 116 (1999).......................12

Mary Beth G. v. City of Chicago, 723 F.2d 1263 (7th Cir. 1983)...5

Maryland v. Garrison, 480 U.S. 79 (1987) 15

New Jersey v. T.L.O., 469 U.S. 325 (1985) ....passim

O'Connor v. Ortega, 480 U.S. 709 (1987)....................6

Pearson v. Callahan, 129 S.Ct. 808 (2009).........21, 22

Phaneuf v.Fraikin, 448 F.3d 591 (2d Cir. 2006) 5, 8, 11

(continued)

Exhibit 11.6 *Amicus curiae* **brief filed with the U.S. Supreme Court** *(continued)*

SUMMARY OF THE ARGUMENT

In *New Jersey v. T.L.O.*, 469 U.S. 325 (1985), this Court accommodated the interests of public school educators and administrators in maintaining order and discipline in public schools by easing the restrictions on searches normally imposed upon state actors by the Fourth Amendment. In ruling that in-school searches of students in the school setting need not be supported by probable cause, however, the *T.L.O.* decision made clear that the "reasonableness" of a school search largely depends on whether the search is "excessively intrusive in light of the age and sex of the student and nature of the infraction." *Id.* at 342. This Court clearly signaled that the severity of the privacy invasion must be considered when deciding whether school officials have violated a student's Fourth Amendment rights.

In light of *T.L.O.*'s direction to consider the intrusiveness of a search, the *en banc* Ninth Circuit correctly understood here that a strip search of a student will be reasonable only when school officials have clear evidence to justify it. Strip searches are unquestionably privacy invasions of a different order and higher degree than "ordinary" searches and should be undertaken rarely. Only when school officials have highly credible evidence showing (1) the student is in possession of objects posing a significant danger to the school and (2) that the student has secreted the objects in a place only a strip search will uncover is such a search reasonable.

CONCLUSION

Throughout their merits brief, Petitioners decry a regrettable consequence of the decision below: educators must now "school themselves" in Fourth Amendment jurisprudence and allows courts to second-guess their judgment. But, given the seriousness of the intrusion effected by strip searches, this consequence is unavoidable.

School officials must realize that they may conduct strip searches only in extremely limited circumstances, and only on the basis of compelling evidence. The alternative implicit in the Petitioners' suggested resolution of this case is an unblinking deference to school officials that places students' privacy and security in grave jeopardy.

For the above reasons, the Ninth Circuit properly found that the strip search of Savana Redding was not reasonable and therefore violated the Fourth Amendment. That decision should be affirmed as guidance to school officials, and to ensure that the practice of strip-searching students remains appropriately rare.

In this example, in the citation "232 A.2d 44," "232" refers to the volume in the Atlantic 2d series of the reporter service of West Publishing Company, and "44" refers to the page on which the case may be found.

Bluebook

The most commonly used guide to citation form is the publication *The Bluebook: A Uniform System of Citation*. This is the generally accepted authority for proper citation form, unless the rules of a particular court dictate a different citation format. For example, the executive administrator of the Superior Court of Pennsylvania issued this notice:

> Pennsylvania Superior Court will be issuing opinions containing a Universal Citation. This citation will be as follows:
>
> Jones v. Smith, 1999 PA Super, 1.
>
> The second number is a Court-issued number on the opinion. Each opinion will also have numbered paragraphs, to be used for pinpoint citation, e.g., Jones v. Smith, 1999 PA Super, 1, 15. Citation to opinions that have not yet been issued an Atlantic 2d citation are to be in the Universal Citation number. After the official citation has been issued, citation is to be only the official citation, and not the Universal Citation.

Therefore, an attorney submitting a brief to the Superior Court of Pennsylvania must use that court's specified citation form.

ALWD Citation Format

The **Association of Legal Writing Directors (ALWD)** is a society for professors who coordinate legal writing instruction in legal education. They have compiled a system of citation that is specified in the *ALWD Citation Manual: A Professional System of Citation.*

The *ALWD Citation Manual,* as set out in its preface, is "a set of rules that reflects a consensus in the legal profession about how citations should function." The *ALWD Manual* includes, in addition to the general citation rules, an appendix containing court citation rules for the individual states. With the publication of the 19th edition of the *Bluebook* and the fifth edition of the AWLD guide, the two are almost the same, though with slight variations.

Association of Legal Writing Directors (ALWD) A society for professors who coordinate legal writing instruction.

Web Exploration

Check the ALWD website for the latest updates at www.alwd.org.

Universal Citation Format

The *Universal Citation Guide* represents an attempt by the American Association of Law Libraries' (AALL) Committee on Citation Formats to create a set of universal citation rules for American law that is vendor (publisher) neutral and medium (print and electronic) neutral.

The various forms of electronic distribution require a system of citation that can be applied consistently to allow researchers to find a referenced authority regardless of the research tool used. Whereas traditional, book-based citations reference the page numbers of the books, the **Universal Citation Format** relies upon the courts to use numbered paragraphs in their opinions. Any publisher of case law must then preserve the information provided by the court, including the citation references to the case and paragraph.

Universal Citation Format A system for citation relying on the courts to number the paragraphs in their opinions.

Anyone who has read and compared a case in a book with a case online is aware that the page size and the display are different. Unless the online computer display is in a photo-image format, such as PDF, locating a specific page or reference can be difficult. Librarians and courts are recognizing the need for the on-screen user to be able to pinpoint citations, and the Universal Citation Format represents an attempt to make such pinpointing possible. The difficulty with some courts is the requirement that the Universal Citation Format be used only until the hard copy is published, at which time the traditional citation must be used. As a result, you may see the following citation format within documents:

Jones v. Smith, 1999 Pennsylvania Superior 1, ___Pa Super___, ___A2d___ (1999)

The blank spaces are provided for eventual insertion of the volume and page numbers in the print version when they become available. Appendix D lists court name abbreviations.

Other Citation Formats

Many states, including Pennsylvania, have adopted as their official citation format one that originally was created by publishers such as West Publishing Company. These sometimes are referred to as **vendor-specific citation formats**. The West Publishing Company format is based on the West Regional Reporter system and its publications of federal material.

Vendor-specific citation format The citation format of a legal publisher adopted by a court.

New methods of electronic information technology, such as databases, CD-ROMs, and the Internet, have created a number of problems with the traditional citation formats. Some vendors have claimed copyright protection for their pagination systems. In 1985, West Publishing Company, in a case against Mead Data Central, argued successfully that the wholesale use of its pagination by a competing online publisher infringed upon West's copyright interest in the arrangement of cases in its court reports. But in a 1998 case involving Matthew Bender & Company and West Publishing Company, the Second Circuit held that West's pagination was not protected by copyright. Obviously, all claims to a pagination system or citation system that is vendor specific will result in some action to protect the corporate claim for copyright, trademark, or potential patent for some electronic methodology.

Exhibit 11.7 Comparison of selected ALWD fifth edition rules and *The Bluebook* 19th edition rules

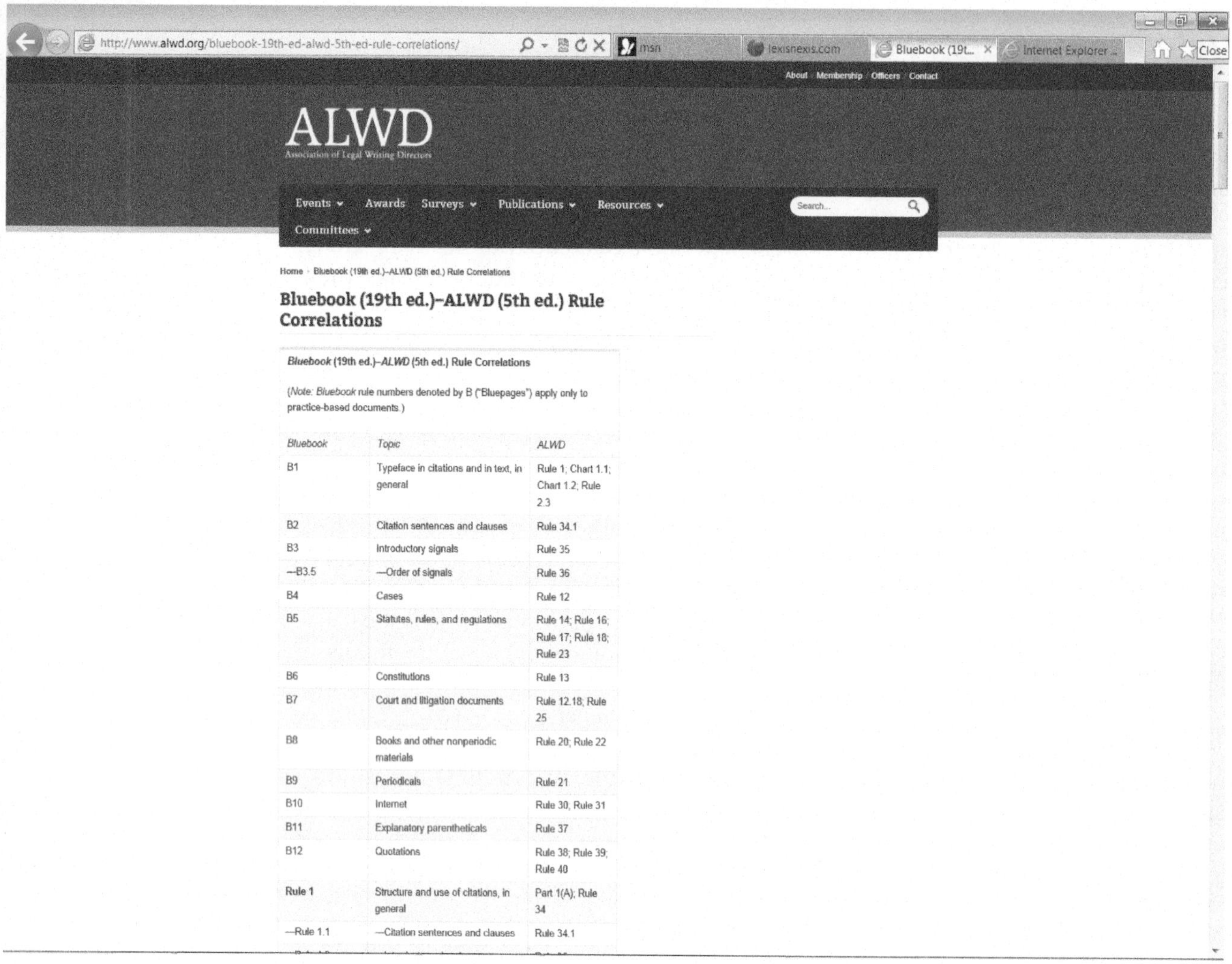

http://www.alwd.org/bluebook-19th-ed-alwd-5th-ed-rule-correlations/

About / Membership / Officers / Contact

ALWD

Association of Legal Writing Directors

Events · Awards · Surveys · Publications · Resources · Committees

Home › Bluebook (19th ed.)–ALWD (5th ed.) Rule Correlations

Bluebook (19th ed.)–ALWD (5th ed.) Rule Correlations

Bluebook (19th ed.)–*ALWD* (5th ed.) Rule Correlations

(*Note: Bluebook* rule numbers denoted by B ("Bluepages") apply only to practice-based documents.)

Bluebook	*Topic*	*ALWD*
B1	Typeface in citations and in text, in general	Rule 1; Chart 1.1; Chart 1.2; Rule 2.3
B2	Citation sentences and clauses	Rule 34.1
B3	Introductory signals	Rule 35
—B3.5	—Order of signals	Rule 36
B4	Cases	Rule 12
B5	Statutes, rules, and regulations	Rule 14; Rule 16; Rule 17; Rule 18; Rule 23
B6	Constitutions	Rule 13
B7	Court and litigation documents	Rule 12.18; Rule 25
B8	Books and other nonperiodic materials	Rule 20; Rule 22
B9	Periodicals	Rule 21
B10	Internet	Rule 30; Rule 31
B11	Explanatory parentheticals	Rule 37
B12	Quotations	Rule 38; Rule 39; Rule 40
Rule 1	Structure and use of citations, in general	Part 1(A); Rule 34
—Rule 1.1	—Citation sentences and clauses	Rule 34.1

Exhibit 11.7 Comparison of selected ALWD fifth edition rules and *The Bluebook* 19th edition rules (*continued*)

Rule 1	Structure and use of citations, in general	Part 1(A); Rule 34
—Rule 1.1	—Citation sentences and clauses	Rule 34.1
—Rule 1.2	—Introductory signals	Rule 35
—Rule 1.3	—Order of signals	Rule 36
—Rule 1.4	—Order of authorities within a signal	Rule 36
—Rule 1.5	—Parenthetical information	Rule 37; Sidebar 37.1
—Rule 1.6	—Related authority	Rule 37
Rule 2	Typeface in academic writing, in general	Rule 1; Rule 1.4
—Rule 2.1	—Typeface in footnotes	Rule 1.4
—Rule 2.2	—Typeface in text	Rule 1; Rule 1.3
Rule 3	Subdivisions, in general	Rule 6; Rule 7; Rule 8; Rule 9
—Rule 3.1	—Volumes, parts, and supplements	Rule 8; Rule 9
—Rule 3.2	—Pages, footnotes, endnotes, graphical materials	Rule 7; Rule 9
—Rule 3.3	—Sections and paragraphs	Rule 6
—Rule 3.4	—Appended material	Rule 9
—Rule 3.5	—Internal cross-references	Rule 10
Rule 4	Short citation forms, in general	Rule 11.2
—Rule 4.1	—*Id.*	Rule 11.3
—Rule 4.2	—*Supra* and "hereinafter"	Rule 11.4; Rule 11.5
Rule 5	Quotations, in general	Rule 38
—Rule 5.1	—Formatting quotations	Rule 38.3; Rule 38.4; Rule 38.5
—Rule 5.2	—Alterations and quotations within quotations	Rule 38.4(c); Rule 38.5(b); Rule 39
—Rule 5.3	—Omissions	Rule 40
Rule 6	Abbreviations, numerals, and symbols, in general	Rule 2; Rule 2.2 (e); Rule 4; Rule 6
—Rule 6.1	—Abbreviations, in general	Rule 2; Chart 2.1
—Rule 6.2	—Numerals and symbols, in general	Rule 4; Rule 6.2
Rule 7	Italicization for style and in unique circumstances	Rule 1.3

Rule 7	Italicization for style and in unique circumstances	Rule 1.3
Rule 8	Capitalization	Rule 3.2; Rule 3.3; Rule 3.4; Chart 3.1
Rule 9	Titles of judges, officials, and terms of court	Rule 3; Sidebar 3.1; Chart 3.1
Rule 10	Cases	Rule 12
—Rule 10.1	—Basic citation forms	Rule 12.1
—Rule 10.2	—Case names	Rule 12.2
—Rule 10.3	—Reporters and other sources	Rule 12.3; Rule 12.4; Chart 12.2; Sidebar 12.3
—Rule 10.3.1	—Parallel citations	Rule 12.4(c); Sidebar 12.4
—Rule 10.3.2	—Reporter volume number; nominative reporters	Rule 12.3; Rule 12.4(b)(4); Sidebar 12.3
—Rule 10.3.3	—Public domain formats	Rule 12.17; Appendix 2
—Rule 10.4	—Court and jurisdiction	Rule 12.6
—Rule 10.5	—Date or year	Rule 12.7
—Rule 10.6	—Parenthetical information regarding cases	Rule 12.8(g); Rule 12.10
—Rule 10.7	—Prior and subsequent history	Rule 12.8; Rule 12.9
—Rule 10.7.1	—Explanatory phrases and weight of authority	Rule 12.8(e); Rule 12.8(f); Chart 12.2; Chart 12.3
—Rule 10.7.2	—Different case name on appeal	Rule 12.8(d)
—Rule 10.8	—Special citation forms	Rules 12.11–12.15
—Rule 10.8.1	—Pending and unreported cases	Rule 12.12; Rule 12.13; Rule 12.15
—Rule 10.8.2	—Fifth Circuit split	Rule 12.6(c)(3)
—Rule 10.8.3	—Briefs, court filings, and transcripts	Rule 12.18
—Rule 10.9	—Short citation forms	Rule 12.19
Rule 11	Constitutions	Rule 13
Rule 12	Statutes	Rule 14
—Rule 12.1; Rule 12.2	—Basic citation forms	Rule 14.2; Rule 14.3; Rule 14.4

(continued)

Exhibit 11.7 Comparison of selected ALWD fifth edition rules and *The Bluebook* 19th edition rules (*continued*)

Rule 12	Statutes	Rule 14
—Rule 12.1; Rule 12.2	—Basic citation forms	Rule 14.2; Rule 14.3; Rule 14.4
—Rule 12.3	—Current official and unofficial codes	Rule 14.1; Sidebar 14.1
—Rule 12.4	—Session laws	Rule 14.6
—Rule 12.5	—Electronic media and other sources	Rule 14.2(f)
—Rule 12.6	—Other secondary sources	Rule 14.6(d)
—Rule 12.7	—Invalidation, repeal, amendment, and prior history	Rule 14.3(a), (b)
—Rule 12.8	—Explanatory parenthetical phrases	Rule 14.2(g)
—Rule 12.9.1	—Internal Revenue Code	Rule 14.2(b), (d); Appendix 6
—Rule 12.9.2	—Ordinances	Rule 17
—Rule 12.9.3	—Rules of evidence and procedure	Rule 16
—Rule 12.9.4	—Uniform acts	Rule 23.5
—Rule 12.9.5	—Model codes, restatements, sentencing guidelines	Rule 23
—Rule 12.9.6	—ABA code of professional responsibility, ethics opinions	Rule 23.3
—Rule 12.10	—Short citation forms	Rule 14.5
Rule 13	Legislative materials	Rule 15
—Rule 13.1	—Basic citation forms	Rule 15.1; Rule 15.13
— Rule 13.2	—Bills and resolutions	Rule 15.1; Rule 15.3; Rule 15.4; Rule 15.13; Rule 15.15
— Rule 13.3	—Hearings	Rule 15.5; Rule 15.16
— Rule 13.4	—Reports, documents, and committee prints	Rule 15.7; Rule 15.9; Rule 15.17
— Rule 13.5	—Debates	Rule 15.10; Rule 15.18
— Rule 13.6	—Separately bound legislative histories	Rule 15.11; Rule 15.20
— Rule 13.7	—Electronic media and online sources	Rule 15.1(g); Rule 15.13(f)
— Rule 13.8	—Short citation forms	Rule 15.2; Rule 15.6; Rule 15.8; Rule 15.10(b); Rule 15.10(d); Rule 15.11(c); Rule 15.14; Rule 15.15(b); Rule 15.16(b); Rule 15.19; Rule 15.20 (b), (c)
Rule 14	Administrative and executive materials	Rule 18
— Rule 14.1	—Basic citation forms	Rule 18.1; Rule 18.3; Rule 18.5; Rule 18.7; Rule 18.9; Rule 18.13; Rule 18.14; Rule 18.15
—Rule 14.2	—Rules, regulations, and other publications	Rule 18.1; Rule 18.3; Rule 18.13; Rule 18.14
— Rule 14.3	—Administrative adjudications and arbitrations	Rule 18.5; Rule 18.15
— Rule 14.4	—Short citation forms	Rule 18.2; Rule 18.4; Rule 18.6; Rule 18.8; Rule 18.10
Rule 15	Books, reports, and other nonperiodic materials	Rule 20
— Rule 15.1	—Author	Rule 20.1(b)
— Rule 15.2	—Editor or translator	Rule 20.1(e)
— Rule 15.3	—Title	Rule 20.1(c)
— Rule 15.4	—Edition, publisher, and date	Rule 20.1(e)
— Rule 15.5	—Shorter works in collection	Rule 20.3
— Rule 15.6	—Prefaces, forewords, introductions, and epilogues	Rule 20.3(b)
—Rule 15.7	—Serial number	Rule 20.1(e)(4)
—Rule 15.8	—Special citation forms	Rule 22
—Rule 15.8(b)	—Star edition	Rule 20.2
— Rule 15.9	—Electronic media and other sources	Rule 20.4
— Rule 15.10	—Short citation forms	Rule 20.6
Rule 16	Periodicals	Rule 21
— Rule 16.1	—Basic citation forms	Rule 21.2; Rule 21.3

Exhibit 11.7 Comparison of selected ALWD fifth edition rules and *The Bluebook* 19th edition rules (continued)

Rule 16	Periodicals	Rule 21
— Rule 16.1	—Basic citation forms	Rule 21.2; Rule 21.3
— Rule 16.2	—Author	Rule 21.2(a), (b); Rule 21.3(a); Sidebar 21.1
— Rule 16.3	—Title	Rule 21.2(c); Rule 21.3(b)
— Rule 16.4	—Consecutively paginated periodicals	Rule 21.1; Rule 21.2
— Rule 16.5	—Nonconsecutively paginated periodicals	Rule 21.1; Rule 21.3
— Rule 16.6	—Newspapers	Rule 21.3(f)
— Rule 16.7	—Special citation forms	Rule 21.2(b); Sidebar 21.1; Rule 21.2(h), (i); Rule 22.6
— Rule 16.8	—Electronic media and online sources	Rule 21.5
— Rule 16.9	—Short citation forms	Rule 21.7
Rule 17	Unpublished and forthcoming sources	Rule 29
—Rule 17.1	—Basic citation forms	Rule 29.1; Rule 29.2
—Rule 17.2	—Unpublished materials, in general	Rule 29.2
—Rule 17.2.1	—Manuscripts	Rule 29.2
—Rule 17.2.2	—Dissertations and theses	Rule 29.2(e)
—Rule 17.2.3	—Letters, memoranda, and press releases	Rule 27.3; Rule 27.4
—Rule 17.2.4	—Email correspondence and listserv postings	Rule 33.1; Rule 33.2
—Rule 17.2.5	—Interviews	Rule 27.1; Rule 27.2
—Rule 17.2.6	—Speeches and addresses	Rule 26
—Rule 17.3	—Forthcoming publications	Rule 29.1
—Rule 17.4	—Working papers	Rule 29.3
—Rule 17.5	—Electronic media and online sources	Rule 27.3(g); Rule 29.1(c); Rule 29.2(e); Rule 30.1(a)
—Rule 17.6	—Short citation forms	Rule 26.4; Rule 27.5; Rule 29.5

Rule 18	Internet, electronic media, and other nonprint resources	Rule 28; Rules 30–34; Chart 30.1
—Rule 18.1	—Basic citation forms	Rule 31; Chart 30.1
—Rule 18.2	—Internet	Rule 31; Sidebar 30.1; Sidebar 30.2
—Rule 18.3	—Commercial databases	Rule 32
—Rule 18.4	—CD-ROM and other electronic storage media	Rule 33
—Rule 18.5	—Microform	Rule 28.6
—Rule 18.6	—Films, broadcasts, and noncommercial video materials	Rule 28
—Rule 18.7	—Audio recordings	Rule 28.3; Rule 28.4; Rule 28.5
—Rule 18.8	—Short citation forms	Rule 28.7; Rule 31.5; Rule 32.4; Rule 33.7
Rule 19	Looseleaf services	Rule 24
—Rule 19.1	—Basic citation forms for services	Rule 24.1; Rule 24.3
—Rule 19.2	—Short citation forms	Rule 24.2; Rule 24.4
Rule 20	Foreign materials	Rule 19.4; *Guide to Foreign and International Legal Citations* (2d ed. 2009)
Rule 21	International materials	Rule 19.4; *Guide to Foreign and International Legal Citations* (2d ed. 2009)
Bluepages Table BT1	Court documents	Appendix 3(G)
Bluepages Table BT2	Local rules	Appendix 2
Table T1	United States jurisdictions	Appendix 1
—T1.1	—Federal judicial and legislative materials	Appendix 1(A)
—T1.2	—Federal administrative and executive materials	Appendix 1(A)
—T1.3	—States and the District of Columbia	Appendix 1(B)

(continued)

Exhibit 11.7 Comparison of selected ALWD fifth edition rules and *The Bluebook* 19th edition rules (*continued*)

Bluepages Table BT1	Court documents	Appendix 3(G)
Bluepages Table BT2	Local rules	Appendix 2
Table T1	United States jurisdictions	Appendix 1
—T1.1	—Federal judicial and legislative materials	Appendix 1(A)
—T1.2	—Federal administrative and executive materials	Appendix 1(A)
—T1.3	—States and the District of Columbia	Appendix 1(B)
—T1.4	—Other United States jurisdictions	Appendix 1(C)
Table T2	Foreign jurisdictions	*See Guide to Foreign and International Legal Citations* (2d ed. 2009).
Table T3	Intergovernmental organizations	*See Guide to Foreign and International Legal Citations* (2d ed. 2009).
Table T4	Treaty sources	Chart 19.1
Table T5	International arbitral reporters	*See Guide to Foreign and International Legal Citations* (2d ed. 2009).
Table T6	Case names and institutional authors (abbreviations)	Appendix 3(E)
Table T7	Court names (abbreviations)	Appendix 4
Table T8	Explanatory phrases (abbreviations)	Chart 12.3; Chart 12.4; Sidebar 37.1
Table T9	Legislative documents (abbreviations)	Appendix 3(F)
Table T10	Geographical terms (abbreviations)	Appendix 3(B)
Table T11	Judges and officials (abbreviations)	Chart 12.5
Table T12	Months (abbreviations)	Appendix 3(A)
Table T13	Periodicals (abbreviations)	Appendix 5
Table T14	Publishing terms (abbreviations)	Appendix 3(D)
Table T15	Services (abbreviations)	Chart 24.1; Appendix 5

Table T6	Case names and institutional authors (abbreviations)	Appendix 3(E)
Table T7	Court names (abbreviations)	Appendix 4
Table T8	Explanatory phrases (abbreviations)	Chart 12.3; Chart 12.4; Sidebar 37.1
Table T9	Legislative documents (abbreviations)	Appendix 3(F)
Table T10	Geographical terms (abbreviations)	Appendix 3(B)
Table T11	Judges and officials (abbreviations)	Chart 12.5
Table T12	Months (abbreviations)	Appendix 3(A)
Table T13	Periodicals (abbreviations)	Appendix 5
Table T14	Publishing terms (abbreviations)	Appendix 3(D)
Table T15	Services (abbreviations)	Chart 24.1; Appendix 5

Table T16	Subdivisions (abbreviations)	Appendix 3(C)

Source: ALWD Association of Legal Writing Directors *© Copyright 2007, 2013 ALWD*

Table of Authorities

A **table of authorities** is a listing of the citations or other references that are used in a document, along with the page numbers where they are mentioned. A tool for creating a table of authorities is included in the two most popular word processor programs used in the law office, WordPerfect and Microsoft Word. WordPerfect uses an add-in program, Perfect Authority, to automatically create tables of authorities by selecting the add-in from the tool bar, which automatically creates the table as shown in Exhibit 11.8.

In Word, each authority is first identified and marked by opening the Table of Authorities menu (pressing ALT+SHIFT+I). The authorities are then organized by category, as shown in Exhibit 11.9. Each authority is marked and an identifier

Table of authorities A listing of the citations or other references in a document and the page numbers where they are located.

Exhibit 11.8 Table of Authorities prepared with WordPerfect Perfect Authority

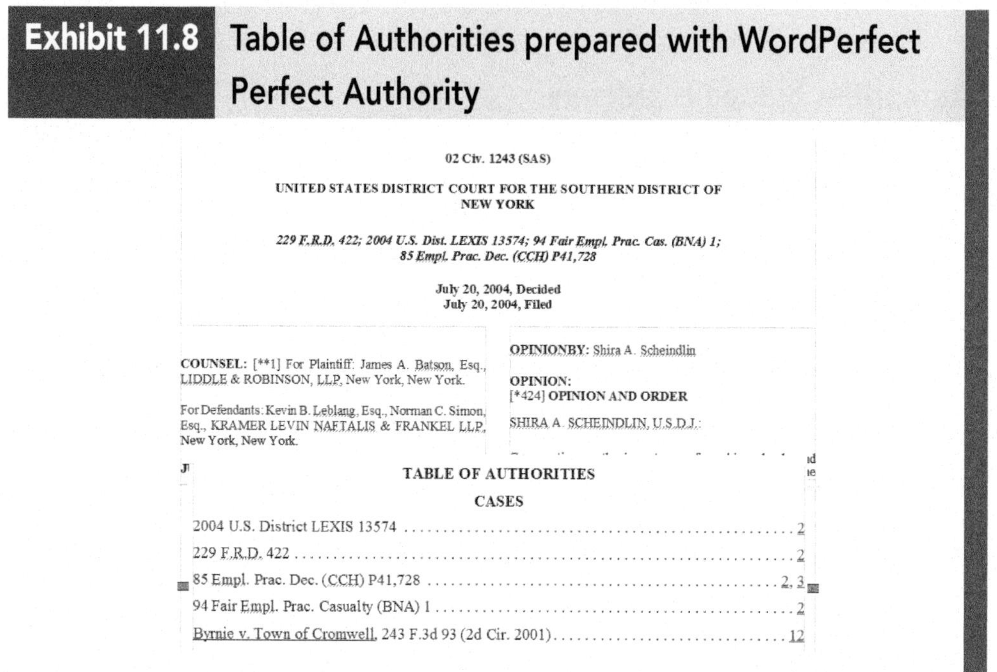

02 Civ. 1243 (SAS)

UNITED STATES DISTRICT COURT FOR THE SOUTHERN DISTRICT OF NEW YORK

229 F.R.D. 422; 2004 U.S. Dist. LEXIS 13574; 94 Fair Empl. Prac. Cas. (BNA) 1; 85 Empl. Prac. Dec. (CCH) P41,728

July 20, 2004, Decided
July 20, 2004, Filed

COUNSEL: [**1] For Plaintiff: James A. Batson, Esq., LIDDLE & ROBINSON, LLP, New York, New York.

For Defendants: Kevin B. Leblang, Esq., Norman C. Simon, Esq., KRAMER LEVIN NAFTALIS & FRANKEL LLP, New York, New York.

OPINIONBY: Shira A. Scheindlin

OPINION:
[*424] OPINION AND ORDER

SHIRA A. SCHEINDLIN, U.S.D.J.:

TABLE OF AUTHORITIES

CASES

2004 U.S. District LEXIS 13574 2
229 F.R.D. 422 2
85 Empl. Prac. Dec. (CCH) P41,728 .... 2, 3
94 Fair Empl. Prac. Casualty (BNA) 1 2
Byrnie v. Town of Cromwell, 243 F.3d 93 (2d Cir. 2001) 12

Exhibit 11.9 Table of Authorities selection menus

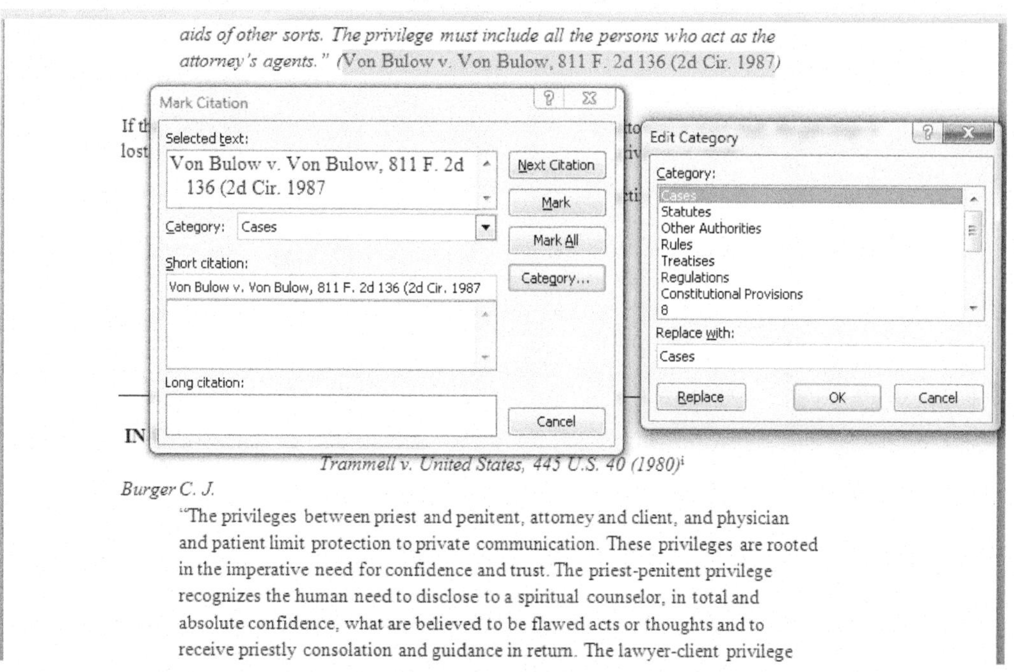

inserted into the document, called a TA or Table of Authority Entry in MS Word. These marks are visible when the Hidden Marks button is selected, as shown in Exhibit 11.10. The table of authorities may be inserted using the Insert Table of Authorities selection in the Reference tab, as shown in Exhibit 11.11.

Cite Checking

Cite checking The process of verifying proper citation format in a document.

Cite checking is the process of checking each referenced case or statute to determine that it is valid and that it has not been repealed or overturned. Cite checking also involves verifying that the proper citation format has been used for each citation. The format to be used—*Bluebook*, *ALWD Citation Manual*, or Universal Citation Format—as well as the rigor with which the citation rules must be applied, depend on

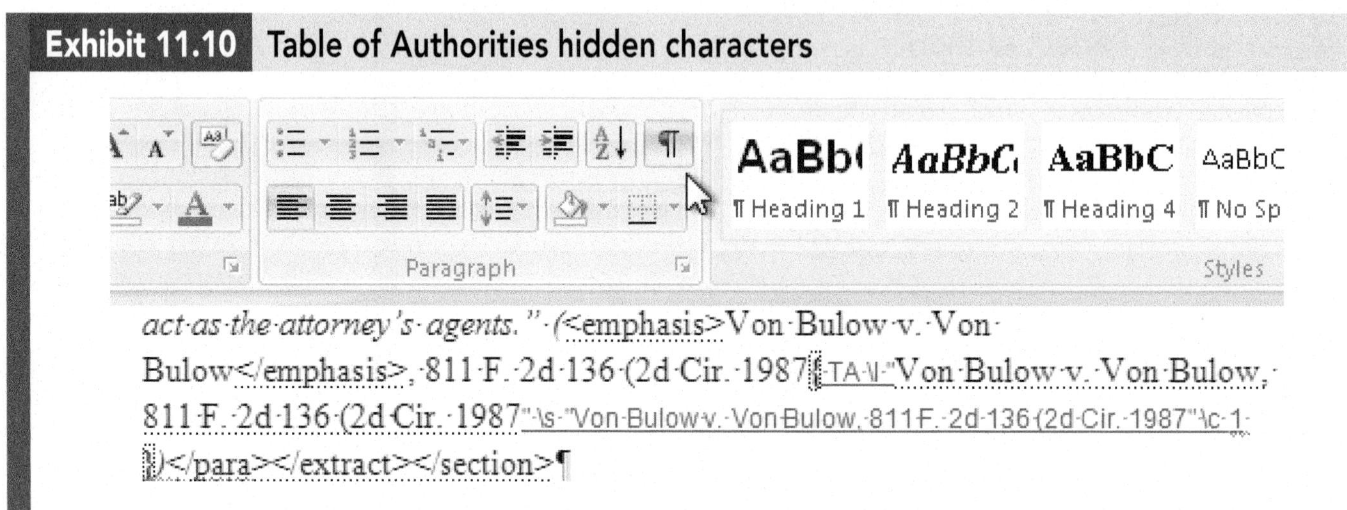

Exhibit 11.10 Table of Authorities hidden characters

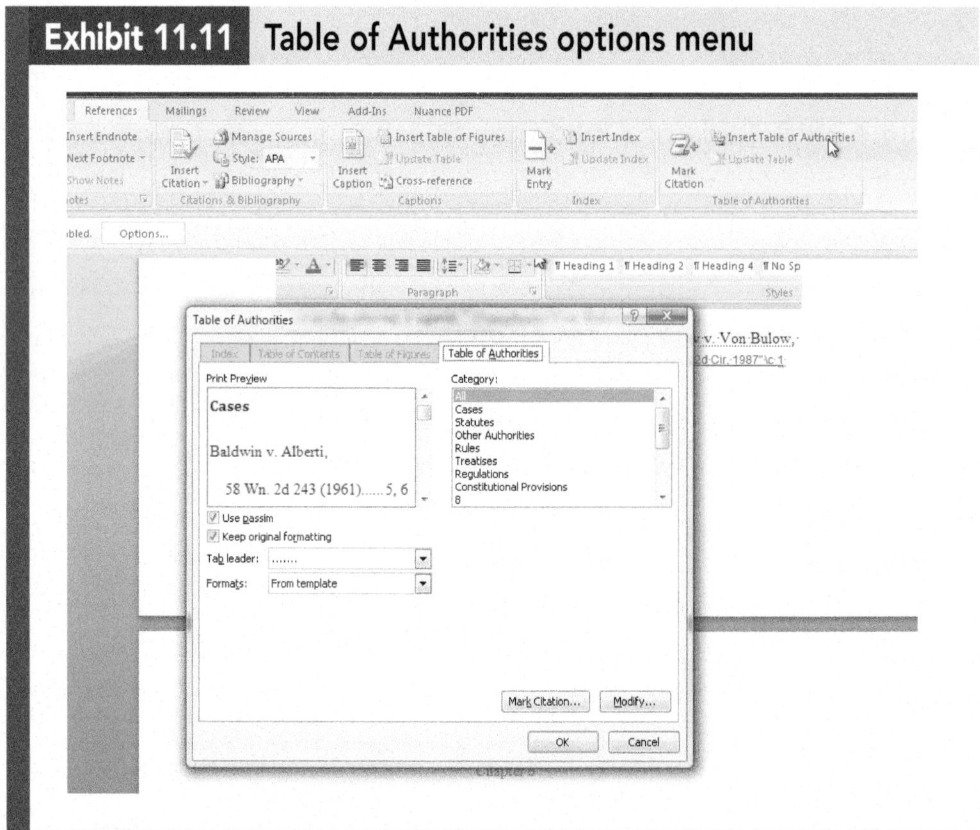

Exhibit 11.11 Table of Authorities options menu

the preferences of the attorney for whom the document is prepared, or those of the court or judge to whom it is submitted. Some courts view improper citation format with a jaundiced eye, the same way they view incorrect punctuation, spelling, and grammar. Others may be upset if the citations do not reference the paper or online legal research service available to them.

Bluebook and ALWD Compared

The citation format to be used depends on local custom and the courts in which the firm or supervising attorney practices. The two forms used most commonly used—the *Bluebook* and the *ALWD Citation Manual*—have a number of similarities.

Both of these manuals are divided into parts—the *Bluebook* into three parts and the ALWD manual into seven. The parts are further divided into rules. The *Bluebook* has 20 basic rules, and the ALWD has 50 rules. Most of the rules have a common pattern, and some rules are the same for each manual. For example, *Bluebook* Rule 12 and *ALWD* Rule 14, on the method of citing statutes, are the same. They both dictate the same format for citing the United States Code, such as 18 U.S.C. § 1965 (1994). Other rules have minor variations in presentation. For example, *Bluebook* Rule 10.2.2 states, "Do not abbreviate 'United States,'" whereas ALWD Rule 12.2(g) states, "United States as party: Cite as U.S. Omit 'America.'"

Sample *Bluebook* citation formats:

Rule 11 Constitutions:	U.S.Const.art.I, § 9, cl.2.
Rule 10 Cases:	United States v Shaffer Equip. Co., 11 F.3d 450 (4th Cir. 1993)
Rule 12 Statutes:	42 U.S.C. § 1983 (1994)

Sample ALWD citation formats:

Rule 13 Constitutions:	U.S. Const.art. IV, § 5(b)
Rule 12 Cases:	Brown v. Bd. Of Educ., 349 U.S. 294
	U.S. v. Chairse, 18 F.Supp. 2d 1021 (D. Minn. 1998)
Rule 14 Statutory Codes:	18 U.S.C. § 1965 (1994)

Advice *from the* Field

PROFESSIONAL COMMUNICATION

by Kathryn L. Myers, Associate Professor and Coordinator of Paralegal Studies at Saint Mary-of-the-Woods College in Saint Mary-of-the-Woods, IN

There are countless misunderstandings, conflicts, and disagreements in every organization in the United States. Effective listening skills are almost extinct in many firms, and gossip among colleagues has become commonplace. The result is lost productivity, hurt feelings, hidden agendas, loss of innovative ideas, and mistrust among coworkers.

The importance of professional communication skills in dealing with these problems cannot be overstressed. *The Wall Street Journal* recently reported a study involving more than one hundred Fortune 500 executives who ranked interpersonal communication first, across the board, as the most valuable skill they considered in hiring or promotion decisions. Lack of interpersonal communication skills impedes professional effectiveness in influencing[,] persuading, and negotiating, all of which are crucial to success.

Professional communication may take the form of written communication, active listening, or nonverbal communication, all of which require interpersonal communication skills. All three skills work together to define professional communication, but this article focuses specifically on written communication.

Writing intimidates many people, but there are times when writing is the best way to communicate and often is the only way to get a message across. Good writers must have access to at least one quality writing guide. Some good choices are: *The Elements of Style*, by William Strunk, Jr., and E.B. White for lawyers, paralegals, and others engaged in formal writing; *The Bedford*

(continued)

Handbook, by Diana T. Hacker; *How 10: A Handbook for Office Professionals*, by James L. and Lyn R. Clark; and *The Associated Press Stylebook* for traditional journalists is the professional bible.

The following tips are offered as examples of what careful writers must consider.

BE CAUTIOUS

Written communication is more concrete than verbal communication and is less forgiving of errors. Once something is written and sent, it cannot be taken back; and it cannot be nuanced or explained away as readily as can be done with the spoken word.

Communicators in writing must meet the challenges of spelling, grammar, punctuation, and style in addition to the actual wording (rhetoric). Modern technology superficially makes writing seem easier by providing grammar and spelling checks, but these tools are not failsafe. They may actually contribute to egregious errors if the writer is not carefully involved with the writing and proofreading the material for sense.

REMEMBER THE ABC'S OF WRITING

Accuracy—Proof and reproof

Brevity—Keep sentences short

Clarity—Use active voice for clear meaning

BEWARE OF COMMON ERRORS

Commas—Use commas after each part of full dates (*e.g.*, "Wednesday, July 13, 2005," or "July 13, 2005," unless the year falls at the end of the sentence. No comma is used with a calendar date expressed alone (*e.g.*, "February 14.") Do not use commas where the year stands by itself (*e.g.*, "the year 2005 was special.").

Restrictive words, phrases, or clauses modify the main idea and are essential to its meaning. These are not set off by commas. Nonrestrictive words, phrases, or clauses, however, do not significantly change the meaning of the sentence and are set off by commas. Place commas inside quotation marks and parentheses.

Semicolons—Use semicolons when there are two or more independent clauses that do not have coordinating conjunctions, or when the clauses are joined by a transitional expression such as "however." Also use them to separate clauses in a series which have internal commas. Place semicolons outside quotation marks and parentheses.

Colons—Use colons after independent clauses that introduce a formal list or enumeration of items, but not if a verb of being precedes the list. Use a colon after a business salutation and to introduce formal quotations (*e.g.*, the court held: "no offense was proven . . . ").

Dashes—Use dashes instead of commas to achieve greater pause and emphasis to what follows. Also use them in place of commas with parenthetical expressions or appositives that contain internal commas.

Ellipsis—An ellipsis is a series of three periods to indicate one or more words are missing from the middle of a sentence in the quoted text. If the missing text is at the end of a sentence, this fact is indicated with a fourth period—the sentence period—at the end of the series.

Quotation Marks—Quotation marks are used to show directly quoted speech or text as well as the titles of published articles. Quotations of 50 words or more do not use quotation marks but, rather, are written as separate paragraph(s), single spaced, and indented on the right and left margins greater than the normal text.

Apostrophe—The apostrophe is used to indicate a missing letter in a contraction (*e.g.*, "it's" for "it is" or "don't" for "do not") or to denote singular possession (*e.g.*, "Mary's"), or plural possession (*e.g.*, "the companies' policies.") "Its" is the correct (albeit counterintuitive) possessive form of "it." No apostrophe is used. All possessive case pronouns (my, your, yours, their, its, whose, theirs, ours) are written without apostrophes.

When there is joint ownership, the apostrophe attaches to the last noun (*e.g.*, "it was Dick and Jane's home"). With individual possession where there are two or more nouns, each noun shows ownership (*e.g.*, "it was either Dick's or Jane's").

WATCH YOUR GRAMMAR

Active Voice—Using action verbs and active voice provides clear and readable sentences.

Noun/Pronoun Agreement—A singular noun (legal assistant) must have a singular pronoun (his/her). Plural nouns (legal assistants) must have plural pronouns (their). Avoid confusion by writing in the plural form when possible.

Subjective Case—Use the subjective case of a pronoun (I, he, she, you, we, they, who, it, whoever) for the subject, for the complement of a "being" verb, and after the infinitive "to be" when this verb does not have a subject directly preceding it.

Objective Case—Use the objective case of a pronoun (me, him, her, you, us, them, whom, it, whomever) as the direct or indirect object of a verb, the object of a preposition, the subject of any infinitive, the object of the infinitive "to be" when it has a subject directly preceding it, and the object of any other infinitive.

Noun/Verb Agreement—Singular nouns take singular verbs. Know the difference among present, past, and future tenses. Do not switch verb tenses in documents unless the material requires the switch.

Identifiers (Modifiers)—Place identifiers (modifiers) (*e.g.*, adjectives and adverbs) as close as possible to the words they identify (modify).

Proper Pairs—Certain words (correlative conjunctions) must be used in pairs (*e.g.*, either/or, neither/nor, not only/but also).

Clichés, Slang, and Jargon—Avoid clichés: use them only when there is a sound reason to believe that a particular cliché will strengthen your rhetoric. Use slang and "legalese" only when it would be awkward for the reader not to do so, and only if you are sure the reader will understand the reference. A judge, for example, expects to read some amount of legalese. He or she likely would be disappointed to see none at all in a trial brief.

Spelling—Use your spelling checker, but proofread to make sure you do not have correct spelling of the wrong word (*e.g.*, "she was soaking in the tube."). Great care should be taken to spell the names of people and companies correctly.

Acronyms and Abbreviations—Except for acronyms and abbreviations in common usage and which are self-explanatory in context (*e.g.*, "the Hon. James Parker" or "she is an interpreter with NATO"), give full titles and names when the acronym or abbreviation first is mentioned. Err on the side of spelling it out if there is any doubt.

Numbers—In general, single-digit numbers should be written as words; double digit, as numerals in written materials unless the number is used to begin a sentence (*e.g.*, "I had only 10 reference books when I began five years ago.").

Source Acknowledgement—The source of borrowed material of any kind must be attributed with quotation marks if directly quoted, or by attribution if not directly quoted (*e.g.*, "I shall return," Gen. MacArthur promised, or, "General Douglas MacArthur promised he would be back"). In formal research and in legal writing, complete citations must be provided according to the legal convention or the style prescribed by the particular publication.

LETTERS

Correspondence is a primary form of communication between the law firm and the world. It is vital that correspondence be crafted well to properly reflect both the reputation of the law office and your own professionalism. Correspondence must be free of grammar and spelling errors, and the research and analysis must be absolutely correct.

There are different types of letters for different purposes: informational letters, opinion letters, and demand letters, to name a few. Although paralegals would not sign their names to opinion or demand letters, it is quite common for them to draft substantial portions of this correspondence.

There are certain parts to a letter that are necessary for successful correspondence.

Format—There are three primary formats: 1) full block, 2) modified block with blocked paragraphs, and 3) modified block with indented paragraphs.

Letterhead—Preprinted letterhead needs no additional information; but subsequent pages need to contain an identification of the letter, or a header including the name of the addressee, the date, and the page number.

Date—The full date appears below the letterhead at the left or right margin depending on the format used.

Method of Delivery—This appears at the left margin below the date if delivery other than U.S. Postal Service is used.

Recipient's Address Block—The inside address is placed at the left margin and should include:

The recipient

The recipient's title (if any)

The name of the business (if appropriate)

The address

Reference Line—Usually introduced with "Re:" the reference line identifies the subject of the letter. Depending upon office requirements, it may contain case identification.

Salutation—Legal correspondence generally is formal; and the salutation is followed with a colon, such as "Dear Ms. Myers:" You can use the first name if you know the person well, although it is a safer practice to remain formal. It is best to address the letter to a named individual. This may mean calling the recipient business and identifying a person to whom the letter should be addressed.

Body—The body of the letter should have three components:

1. Introduction: For normal business letters, your letter should start with an overall summary, showing in the first paragraph why the letter is relevant to the reader. Don't make [the] reader go past the first paragraph to find out why the letter was sent.
2. Main section: The body of the letter needs to explain the reason for the correspondence, including any relevant background and current information. Make sure the information flows logically to make your points effectively.
3. Requests/instructions: The closing of the letter is the final impression you leave with the reader. End with an action point such as, "I will call you later this week to discuss the matter."

Closing—Following the body of the letter, the closing consists of a standard statement and/or an action item.

Signature and Title—Clearly identify the writer by name and title.

Initials of Drafter—This is a reference to the author (KLM) and the typist (sbk).

Enclosure Notation—"Enc." or "Encs." notations are used to identify one or more enclosures.

Copies to Others—The traditional "cc" notation, formerly meaning "carbon copy," now means "courtesy copy" and is used universally. Some writers, however, will use only "c" or "copy to," along with the name(s), to identify others receiving copies of the document.

PROOFREADING

Even when you believe your draft is exactly what you want, read it one more time. This rule is for everything you write whether it is a memorandum, letter, proposal, or some other document. It is true no matter how many drafts you have written.

Use both the grammar and spelling checker on your computer, paying very close attention to every word highlighted. Do not place total faith in your computer. Instead, have both a printed dictionary and a thesaurus nearby to double-check everything your computer's editing tools highlight, because the computer tools are not always reliable.

Make sure your document is clear and concise. Is there anything that could be misinterpreted? Does it raise questions or fail to make the point you need to make? Can you reduce the number of words or unnecessarily long words? Do not use a long word when a short one works as well; do not use two words when one will do; and do not waste the reader's time with unnecessary words or phrases.

Is your written communication well organized? Does each idea proceed logically from one paragraph to the next? Make sure written communications are easy to read, contain the necessary information, use facts where needed, and avoid information that is not relevant. Be sure to specify the course of action you expect, such as a return call or an order.

Close appropriately, whether formally or informally, according to the nature of the communication. This may seem obvious, but it is sometimes overlooked and can make written communications look amateurish. This diminishes your chances of meeting your written communication's goals.

Communication is vital to the success of any workplace; and in the legal arena, professionals live or die by the communicated word. Well-crafted documents are a positive step toward being a successful professional.

Concept Review *and* Reinforcement

LEGAL TERMINOLOGY

Amicus curiae 432
Association of Legal Writing Directors (ALWD) 435
Citation 432
Cite checking 442
Critical legal thinking 440
Duty of candor 424
Facts 421
Immaterial facts 422
Issue 420
Material facts 422
Memorandum 423
Opinion letter 423
Primary authority 432
Secondary authority 432
Table of authorities 441
Universal Citation Format 435
Vendor-specific citation format 435

SUMMARY OF KEY CONCEPTS

Critical Legal Thinking: Definitions

Critical Legal Thinking	Critical legal thinking is the process of identifying legal issues, determining relevant facts, and applying the applicable law to those facts to reach a conclusion that answers the legal questions or issues presented. The paralegal must understand the audience for whom the document is being prepared: the client, the supervising attorney, other members of the legal team, or the court.
Facts	Facts are pieces of information or details that actually exist, or have occurred, as opposed to theories, suppositions, or conjectures. In the law, facts are circumstances of an event, actions, occurrences, or states of affairs, rather than interpretations of their significance.
Material Fact	A material fact is a fact that is significant or essential to the issue or matter at hand.

Immaterial Fact	An immaterial fact is one that is not essential to the matter at issue.

Legal Writing

Standards	1. The language used must be clear to the intended reader. 2. The writer must make an honest presentation of the facts and arguments. 3. Arguments advocating a new interpretation to the existing law, as well as the current law, must be clearly stated. 4. The ethical obligation to the court must be obeyed, including the presentation of any adverse authority in the jurisdiction. 5. Any factual variation must be presented and the sources used clearly identified by proper citation in a format acceptable to the reader.
Duty of Candor	There is an obligation to be honest with the court and not to mislead the court.

Preparing Office Memoranda

Purpose	1. The memorandum is a working document, written for the legal team, to be used in the preparation and presentation of a case. 2. The paralegal must understand the specific assignment. For the memorandum of law, the assignment is usually to answer a question. 3. Office memoranda are frequently indexed by subject and filed in the office for future reference. If a similar fact pattern requires research, a prior memorandum may be a good starting point and can be a major timesaver. 4. The facts relied upon in writing the assignment memorandum must be a part of the final memorandum; other people who read the memorandum need to understand the specific facts it is based on. 5. A memorandum must present both sides of the issue and in that respect be a neutral, unbiased, objective presentation of the law as it applies to the facts of the case. Issues that the opposing attorney or the judge may raise should be considered and presented. A good analysis includes a discussion of how the fact pattern may differ in cases that are not on point.

Preparing Court Briefs

	Written for the court, the brief provides written advocacy of the client's position and must be written to convince the court to adopt a position favorable to the client.

Citations

Purpose	A citation should allow someone else to find the case or other material mentioned in a document. The format must be generally accepted and used by others in the legal community.
Traditional Sources: Print Citation Format	The basic paper citation form is: Volume, Book or Series, Page Number Example: 232 Atlantic 2d 44 "232" refers to the volume in the Atlantic 2d series reporter service of West Publishing Company, and "44" refers to the page on which the case may be found.
Bluebook Citation Format	The *Bluebook* has been the generally accepted authority for proper citation form, unless the rules of a particular court dictate a different citation format.
ALWD Citation Format	This citation format authority was written by the Association of Legal Writing Directors.

Universal Citation Format	Traditionally, book-based citation used information based on internal page numbers. Universal Citation Format relies upon the courts to provide numbered paragraphs in their opinions.
Table of Authorities	A table of authorities is a listing of the citations or other references in a document and the page numbers where they are located.
Cite Checking	Documents must be checked to verify that the referenced cases and statutes are valid, that the cases and statutes have not been repealed or overturned, and that they are written in the proper citation format. The strictness with which the citation rules must be applied, as well as the method used—*Bluebook*, ALWD, or Universal Citation Format—depend on the wishes and demands of the attorney for whom the document is being prepared, or those of the court or judge to whom it will be submitted.

WORKING THE WEB

1. Summarize in a memo the requirements for briefs submitted to the U.S. Supreme Court, and the citation to the applicable rule. http://www.supremecourt.gov/ctrules/ctrules.aspx or http://www.law.cornell.edu/ rules/supct.
2. Use the Internet to find information on preparing an internal office memorandum or the requirements for filing briefs in your jurisdiction's highest court.
3. The Legal Law Institute at Cornell Law School offers a number of sources for the legal writer, including citation information. Use the LII website to download the section from *Introduction to Basic Legal Citation* by Peter W. Martin—"Who Sets Citation Norms"—at http://www.law.cornell.edu/citation/.
4. Use the homepage link from the Web page in question 3, and download your personal copy of the reference document.
5. If you are using the *ALWD Citation Manual* for citation rules, download a copy of the latest updates at www.alwd.org.

CRITICAL THINKING & WRITING QUESTIONS

1. What is critical legal thinking? Explain and give an example.
2. Why is it important to have all the material facts before beginning the research to prepare a memorandum of law?
3. What is meant by "material facts"? Give an example of a material fact.
4. What is meant by an "immaterial fact"? Give an example.
5. What is the goal of legal writing?
6. Why should headnotes not be used in legal writing?
7. How important is it to Shepardize the cases in a memorandum of law or brief? When should this be done? Why?
8. How are the memorandum of law and the court brief similar? How are they different? Explain.
9. Contrast and compare the fact situation in the opening scenario and the Alaskan case of *Whiting v. State* presented in this chapter. What are the similarities, and what are the points that could be used to argue that the law does not apply?
10. How does the general duty to inform the court preserve the integrity of the judicial process? See *Hazel-Atlas Glass Co. v. Hartford-Empire Co.*, 322 U.S. 238 (1944).
11. Are sanctions against attorneys for failing to observe a duty of candor to the court an appropriate remedy? See *Beam v. IPCO Corp.*, 838 F.2d 242 (7th Cir. 1998).
12. What are the relevant facts in the *Palsgraf v. LIRR* case found in Appendix A? What facts are interesting but not relevant? Create a computer search query using the facts in the *Palsgraf* case, and search the case law of your jurisdiction using these relevant facts. Prepare a short brief of the latest case you find, using proper *Bluebook* and ALWD citation formats.
13. What questions should a paralegal ask before preparing a memorandum of law or a brief?
14. Why should both sides of a case be presented in an office memorandum of law?

15. Why would an attorney request that all parallel citations be listed for each case listed in a memorandum of law?
16. How would knowing the intended audience influence the writing of a memorandum of law or a brief?
17. What level of confidentiality should be attached to the preparation and handling of a memorandum of law? Why?

Building Paralegal Skills

VIDEO CASE STUDIES

Zealous Representation Issue: Candor to the Court

The supervising attorney is due in another courtroom and asks the paralegal to appear for him and submit a brief, which the paralegal has prepared. The lawyer does not read the petition and accepts the paralegal's statement that it includes the current law on the subject.

After viewing the video case study at the book website at www.pearsonhighered.com/careersresources, answer the following:

1. What is the duty of the legal team to present up-to-date information to the court when seeking relief?
2. Can legal research from a prior case be used in an argument to the court?
3. Who is held responsible for misleading the court on the accuracy of legal authority, the paralegal or the attorney?

Zealous Representation Issue: Signing Documents

Court rules require that pleadings be signed by the attorney. With the court about to close and the statute of limitations running out that day, the paralegal signs the attorney's name and files the paperwork.

After viewing the video case study at the book website at www.pearsonhighered.com/careersresources, answer the following:

1. What is the purpose of having the attorney sign all pleadings?
2. Would electronic filing have avoided this problem?
3. What are the dangers in relying upon electronic filing of documents?

ETHICS ANALYSIS & DISCUSSION QUESTIONS

1. What are the ethical issues in failing to properly cite authorities used in a document?
2. What are the ethical obligations in arguing to the court for a change in the law and not following the current law?
3. What are the ethical obligations to the client when analysis of the law indicates there is no valid claim?
4. Assume you have been working for a legal specialist in estate law for a number of years and have taken a number of advanced courses in the field. You are highly regarded in the paralegal community and are seen as the person to call for help in the field. Your supervising attorney decides to take a three-week bicycle trip through the Swiss Alps and leaves you in charge of the office.

    During his absence, you give a talk to a local senior citizens group on the advantages of preparing a will. You meet with most of the people in the audience after the talk and tell them that a simple will can be prepared for $25 (your office's standard fee) and proceed to take the information from them for a will. You prepare the individual wills and send copies marked DRAFT to each person, along with an invoice for the $25 fee and a note to return the fee if they wish to have the will completed. Everyone accepts and sends in the fee.

    Upon his return, the attorney looks over the wills, tells you they are "letter perfect," and says, "It's just what I would have done." See *Cincinnati Bar v. Kathman*, 92 Ohio St. 92 (2001) quoting *People v. Cassidy*, 884 P.2d 309 (Colo. 1994).

    What are the legal and ethical issues?

5. It is the week between Christmas and New Year's Day. You are the only one covering the office while all of the lawyers and support personnel are on vacation. A client who is traveling in Asia calls and asks you to fax to his hotel a copy of an opinion letter prepared by your supervising attorney. You helped prepare the opinion letter and know that it contains a summary of the facts, including details about the opposing parties, case strategy, and potential violations of law. May you send it? What are the ethical issues, if any?
6. You are working for the local prosecutor as a paralegal. The district attorney asks you to prepare an office memorandum of law on the question: Is there any duty to advise the court of any changes in the law or facts after the case has been presented?
7. You prepared a memorandum of law for the firm's trial attorney, and a brief for the court that was used in the case that started today. Closing arguments will be made tomorrow. You now discover case law that is favorable to the other side and that effectively overturns the case law you used in the memorandum of law and brief. What do you do? Are there any ethical issues? Explain fully.

DEVELOPING YOUR COLLABORATION SKILLS

Working on your own or with a group of other students assigned by your instructor, review the scenario at the beginning of the chapter.

1. Divide the group into two teams.
   a. One team is to prepare a memorandum for the court in the form of a brief.
   b. One team is to prepare a memorandum of law for the partner.
   c. After the memorandums are finished, each group will compare the two documents and write a report on the differences between them.
2. As a group, prepare a memo that Amanda might prepare for the supervising paralegal or other attorney on the handling of the interview and any concerns or recommendations.
3. Discuss any ethical concerns that Amanda might have, based on the interview and the potential handling of the case.

PARALEGAL PORTFOLIO EXERCISE

Prepare a memorandum of law for the supervising attorney using the information in the memorandum assignment below. Use the statutory and case law of your local jurisdiction.

Memorandum Assignment

To:	Edith Hannah
From:	Richard Wasserbly
Date:	January 23, 2016
File	Number: GH 06-1002
Re:	State of [your state] v. Kevin Dones

Our client was stopped by a police officer at the bottom of a 1-mile-long 10% grade hill on State Route 332 in Northampton Township, at 3:30 p.m. on Sunday afternoon, January 15, 2016. He was riding a bicycle south on State Route 332. He was given a motor vehicle citation for speeding. They used a radar unit and claim a speed of 35 mph in a 25 mph zone. He also was administered a field sobriety test, which gave a reading over the legal limit, and was given a citation for driving under the influence. He tells me he was riding a bike because his license was suspended for having two previous DUIs.

Please prepare a brief memorandum of law, with citations and cases.

LEGAL ANALYSIS & WRITING CASES

The Continuing Duty to Inform the Court of Changes in the Law

United States v. Shaffer Equipt. Co., 11 F.3d 450 (4th Cir. 1993)

Government counsel learned that its expert witness had lied about his credentials and that the witness had lied in other litigation. The attorney did not immediately notify the court or opposing counsel. In finding against the government, the court extended the duty of candor to include a continuing duty to inform the court of any development that may conceivably affect the outcome of litigation.

Questions

1. Is preserving the integrity of the judicial process more important than the duty to vigorously pursue a client's case?
2. Is there a duty to inform the court when an attorney suspects that a client may have committed perjury?
3. What additional burden is placed on the paralegal in preparing material for a case in light of this decision?

WORKING WITH THE LANGUAGE OF THE COURT CASE

Golden Eagle Distributing Corp. v. Burroughs, 801 F.2d. 1531 (9th Cir. 1986)

United States Court of Appeals, Ninth Circuit

Read and brief this case. In your brief, answer the following questions.

1. What is the intent of Federal Rules of Civil Procedure Rule 11?
2. What test does the court use to determine whether sanctions should be imposed under FRCP Rule 11?
3. What is meant by the "ethical duty of candor"?
4. Is there a conflict between the attorney's ethical obligations under the ABA Model Rules of Professional Conduct and the requirements of FRCP 11?
5. Do attorneys have any duty to cite cases adverse to their client's case? Explain.

Schroeder, Circuit Judge

This is an appeal from the imposition of sanctions under Rule 11 of the Federal Rules of Civil Procedure as amended in 1983. The appellant, a major national law firm, raises significant questions of first impression.

The relevant portions of the amended Rule provide: Every pleading, motion, and other paper of a party represented by an attorney shall be signed by at least one attorney. . . . The signature of an attorney . . . constitutes a certificate by him that he has read the pleading, motion, or other paper; that to the best of his knowledge, information, and belief formed after reasonable inquiry, it is well grounded in fact and is warranted by existing law or a good faith argument for the extension, modification, or reversal of existing law. . . . If a pleading, motion, or other paper is signed in violation of this rule, the court, upon motion or upon its own initiative, shall impose upon the person who signed it, a represented party, or both, an appropriate sanction. . . .

In this appeal, we must decide whether the district court correctly interpreted Rule 11.

. . . Golden Eagle Distributing Corporation filed the underlying action in Minnesota state court for fraud, negligence, and breach of contract against Burroughs, because of an allegedly defective computer system. Burroughs removed the action to the federal district court in Minnesota. Burroughs then moved pursuant to 28 U.S.C. § 1404(a) to transfer the action to the Northern District of California. . . . Burroughs next filed the motion for summary judgment, which gave rise to the sanctions at issue here. It argued that the California, rather than the Minnesota, statute of limitations applied and that all of Golden Eagle's claims were time-barred under California law. It also contended that Golden Eagle's claim for economic loss arising from negligent manufacture lacked merit under California law. Golden Eagle filed a response, arguing that Minnesota law governed the statute of limitations question and that Burroughs had misinterpreted California law regarding economic loss. . . .

After a hearing, the district judge denied Burroughs' motion and directed the Kirkland & Ellis attorney who had been responsible for the summary judgment motion to submit a memorandum explaining why sanctions should not be imposed under Rule 11. . . . Proper understanding of this appeal requires some comprehension of the nature of Burroughs' arguments and the faults which the district court found with them. . . .

Kirkland & Ellis's opening memorandum argued that Golden Eagle's claims were barred by California's

(continued)

three-year statute of limitations. The question was whether the change of venue from Minnesota to California affected which law applied. . . . In imposing sanctions, the district court held that Kirkland & Ellis's argument was "misleading" because it suggested that there already exists a *forum non conveniens* exception to the general rule that the transferor's law applies. . . . [The case cited] raised the issue but did not decide it. . . . Kirkland & Ellis's corollary argument, that a Minnesota court would have dismissed the case on *forum non conveniens* grounds, was found to be "misleading" because it failed to note that one prerequisite to such a dismissal is that an alternative forum be available. . . .

Kirkland & Ellis also argued that Golden Eagle's claim for negligent manufacture lacked merit because Golden Eagle sought damages for economic loss, and such damages are not recoverable under California law [as demonstrated in the *Seely* case]. . . . The district court sanctioned Kirkland & Ellis for not citing three cases whose holdings it concluded were adverse to *Seely*. . . . The district court held that these omissions violated counsel's duty to disclose adverse authority, embodied in Model Rule 3.3, Model Rules of Professional Conduct Rule 3.3 (1983), which the court viewed as a "necessary corollary to Rule 11."

. . . The district court's application of Rule 11 in this case strikes a chord not otherwise heard in discussion of this Rule. The district court did not focus on whether a sound basis in law and in fact existed for the defendant's motion for summary judgment. Indeed it indicated that the motion itself was nonfrivolous. . . . Rather, the district court looked to the manner in which the motion was presented. The district court in this case held that Rule 11 imposes upon counsel an ethical "duty of candor." . . . It said:

The duty of candor is a necessary corollary of the certification required by Rule 11. A court has a right to expect that counsel will state the controlling law fairly and fully; indeed, unless that is done the court cannot perform its task properly. A lawyer must not misstate the law, fail to disclose adverse authority (not disclosed by his opponent), or omit facts critical to the application of the rule of law relied on. . . .

With the district court's salutary admonitions against misstatements of the law, failure to disclose directly adverse authority, or omission of critical facts, we have no quarrel. It is, however, with Rule 11 that we must deal. The district court's interpretation of Rule 11 requires district courts to judge the ethical propriety of lawyers' conduct with respect to every piece of paper filed in federal court. This gives us considerable pause. . . .

The district court's invocation of Rule 11 has two aspects. The first, which we term "argument identification," is the holding that counsel should differentiate between an argument "warranted by existing law" and an argument for the "extension, modification, or reversal of existing law." The second is the conclusion that Rule 11 is violated when counsel fails to cite what the district court views to be directly contrary authority.

. . . The text of the Rule . . . does not require that counsel differentiate between a position which is supported by existing law and one that would extend it. The Rule on its face requires that the motion be either one or the other. . . . The district court's ruling appears to go even beyond the principle of Rule 3.3 of the ABA Model Rules, which proscribes "knowing" false statements of material fact or law. The district court made no finding of a knowing misstatement, and, given the well-established objective nature of the Rule 11 standard, such a requirement would be inappropriate. Both the earnest advocate exaggerating the state of the current law without knowingly misrepresenting it, and the unscrupulous lawyer knowingly deceiving the court, are within the scope of the district court's interpretation.

This gives rise to serious concerns about the effect of such a rule on advocacy. It is not always easy to decide whether an argument is based on established law or is an argument for the extension of existing law. Whether the case being litigated is . . . materially the same as earlier precedent is frequently the very issue which prompted the litigation in the first place. Such questions can be close.

Sanctions under Rule 11 are mandatory. . . . In even a close case, we think it extremely unlikely that a judge, who has already decided that the law is not as a lawyer argued it, will also decide that the loser's position was warranted by existing law. Attorneys who adopt an aggressive posture risk more than the loss of the motion if the district court decides that their argument is for an extension of the law which it declines to make. What is at stake is often not merely the monetary sanction but the lawyer's reputation.

The "argument identification" requirement adopted by the district court therefore tends to create a conflict between the lawyer's duty zealously to represent his client, Model Code of Professional Responsibility Canon 7, and the lawyer's own interest in avoiding rebuke. The concern on the part of the bar that this type of requirement will chill advocacy is understandable. . . .

Were the scope of the rule to be expanded as the district court suggests, mandatory sanctions would ride on close decisions concerning whether or not one case is or is not the same as another. We think Rule 11 should not impose the risk of sanctions in the event that the court later decides that the lawyer was wrong. The burdens of research and briefing by a diligent lawyer anxious to avoid any possible rebuke would be great. And the burdens would not be merely on the lawyer. If the mandatory provisions of the Rule are to be interpreted literally, the court would have a duty to research authority beyond that provided by the parties to make sure that they have not omitted something.

The burden is illustrated in this case, where the district court based its imposition of sanctions in part upon Kirkland & Ellis's failure to cite authorities which the court concluded were directly adverse to a case it did cite. The district court charged the appellant with constructive notice of these authorities because they were identified in Shepard's as "distinguishing" the case Kirkland & Ellis relied on.

. . . Amended Rule 11 of the Federal Rules of Civil Procedure does not impose upon the district courts the burden of evaluating under ethical standards the accuracy of all lawyers' arguments. Rather, Rule 11 is intended to reduce the burden on district courts by sanctioning, and hence deterring, attorneys who submit motions or pleadings which cannot reasonably be supported in law or in fact. We therefore reverse the district court's imposition of sanctions for conduct which it felt fell short of the ethical responsibilities of the attorney. Reversed.

VIRTUAL LAW OFFICE EXPERIENCE MODULES

If your instructor has instructed you to complete assignments in the Virtual Law Office program, complete the Virtual Law Office assignments as assigned by your instructor. These assignments are designed to develop your workplace skills. Completing the assignments for this chapter will result in producing the following documents for inclusion in your portfolio:

VLOE 11.1 Printout of the weather on the day of the accident (one year ago today in your home town)

VLOE 11.2 Aerial view of the scene (at the intersection nearest your home)

CHAPTER

12

Legal Research

LEARNING OBJECTIVES

After studying this chapter, you should be able to:

1. Define "legal research" and create a legal research plan.
2. Explain the differences among primary resources, secondary resources, and finding tools.
3. Create a search query.
4. Explain the need for, and the methods of, updating legal research.

Paralegals at Work

Mr. Mulkeen, the managing partner of a large multinational law firm, was preparing for an executive committee meeting with the senior partners from the firm's offices around the world. The diverse group ranged from young partners on the fast track seeking direct experience to older senior partners concerned more with developing client contacts than working on cases directly. Some of the firm's newer offices specialized in specific areas of law, such as their five-person healthcare group in Chicago and their 20-person intellectual property office in San Francisco.

As with all law firms, reducing costs was high on the agenda. One of the major items on the firm's budget was the law library. Some partners wanted to expand the library, while others wanted to cut it. Mr. Mulkeen wanted to keep as many staff members as possible happy and reach a consensus among a cross-section of the firm's members. At the meeting, he indicated that the firm was at a crossroads in making a decision about the firm's law library. They needed to decide what to keep, what to get rid of, and what to commit resources to. The cost of the space for the library was a major issue for the firm, as was the increasing cost of law reporters and upkeep services.

Mr. Wasserbly, a senior partner who had been with the firm more than 25 years, reminded everyone that when he started with the firm, the library didn't have the same resources as it had currently, and that the law book collection was an object of pride that he frequently pointed out to new clients. He said the firm could research case law in most jurisdictions back to the first volume of the case reporters, and the firm had all of the volumes of the state and federal statutes and codes. Research could be done on weekends if necessary, and pages were copied out of the books. He didn't feel comfortable eliminating any of the hardbound volumes and said that there was value in being

> *"Books are the quietest and most constant of friends; they are the most accessible and wisest of counselors, and the most patient of teachers."*
>
> —Charles William Eliot

able to thumb through the pages to find something, even if you weren't sure what you were looking for.

Kathryn, one of the senior paralegals, said that she didn't use the library that much, and that it was mostly a place for her to spread things out. She and her supervising attorney did most of their research at their desks, using computers to access online research services. She felt limited, she said, in using the hourly fee research services for research because the cost could not always be billed to the client and the bookkeeping department was critical about the office having to absorb the fees. Kathryn also pointed out that the litigation team was always in court or trying cases out of town, so the in-house library didn't really do the litigation team much good anyway.

Kelsey, one of the firm's long-term secretaries, expressed concern about eliminating the current library. She explained that when working for one of the general-practice attorneys, it was often necessary to get up to speed on a new area of law, and she had to browse through some of the encyclopedias and treatises just to understand the basic issues and terminology. She said she couldn't do this using the computer—at least not until the terminology was understood.

Consider the issues involved in this scenario as you read the chapter.

INTRODUCTION TO RESEARCH FOR THE PARALEGAL

One of the most important skills a paralegal can develop is the ability to find current legal and factual information in a timely manner. Knowing where to look is just as important as knowing what to look for. Clients expect their legal counsel to use the most current law in advising them. The paralegal is expected to be able to analyze the relevant facts and find the current statutory and case law that applies to those facts.

The frequent changes in court decisions and statutes present a challenge to the legal profession. Traditional law libraries consisting of printed materials may not have the latest versions of cases, statutes, or regulations until days or weeks after they are issued because of the time required to assemble, print, and send out printed versions of the updates.

Internet and computer technology allows for more rapid access to the latest information. Many courts now issue the electronic version of a court opinion as soon as the opinion is handed down. Instant availability of these decisions is necessary because the ethical duty of candor requires the most current decision to be used in court filings, even before the printed version is available.

Although the ability to obtain current case law is important, in many cases an older common law case may still be precedent. The problem is that some electronic or online services, such as VersusLaw, may not have included the older cases in their database of available cases. For example, VersusLaw only includes state appellate court cases from Illinois and Pennsylvania from 1950 and the California Court of

Appeals from 1930. For that reason, being able to find the case the old-fashioned way by checking through the books is a valuable skill. When using an electronic case service, the dates of the available cases should be checked to be certain that they cover the time period needed for the search.

Legal Research

LEARNING OBJECTIVE 1
Define "legal research" and create a legal research plan.

Legal research is the process of finding the answer to a legal question. The legal question usually involves a specific set of facts, and the answer may include federal, state, and local statutory law, administrative agency regulation, and case law.

Legal research The process of finding the answer to a legal question.

Before starting, the researcher must have a clear picture of the relevant facts, the legal question, and what information the person who assigned the research needs. With this in mind, proceeding in a systematic way will save time and ensure that all research avenues have been considered. A systematic approach begins with planning the research and knowing what issues must be addressed and covered.

Creating a Research Plan

The first step in legal research is setting up a research plan. The research plan helps the researcher focus on the issues, the sources, and the methods for finding the answer and the controlling law. A few basic questions should be considered in setting up the research plan.

1. What is the issue or legal question?
   a. a statute or regulation
   b. a legal question involving a set of facts
2. What is the appropriate search terminology?
   a. words
   b. phrases
   c. legal terms
   d. popular names of statutes or cases
3. What type of research material is available?
   a. traditional
   b. computer
4. What jurisdiction or jurisdictions are involved?
   a. federal
   b. state
   c. local
5. What is the controlling law?
   a. statutory
   b. regulatory
   c. case law
6. What are the types of resources to be used?
   a. primary
   b. secondary
   c. finding tools
7. Where is the needed research material located?
   a. in-house traditional materials
   b. fee-based legal services
   c. free Web-based remote libraries

Using checklists for each search, such as the Research Plan: Words and Phrases and the Research Search Items checklists shown later in the chapter, is a good way to be sure all appropriate terms and sources have been used. When the checklist has been filled out, a record of the results is available for follow-up by the researcher or a colleague.

Paralegals *in* Practice

PARALEGAL PROFILE

Ann G. Hill

Returning to school after spending over 10 years as a legal secretary, Ann G. Hill earned a paralegal certificate at Illinois State University in 2000. She also earned the Insurance Institute of America Certificate in General Insurance in 2003, and obtained her paralegal certification through the National Association of Legal Assistants in 2004. Ann is currently a legal assistant for a major insurance company in Bloomington, Illinois. In her spare time, she serves as a pro bono paralegal providing legal assistance to Social Security clients of the local legal aid society.

I currently specialize in records/information management, legal research, and project management. Legal research is often similar to putting together a massive jigsaw puzzle. When researching a specific issue, I initially review applicable statutes and case law. Then I look for agency rules, since agencies often have statutory authority to enact rules that carry the force of law. When researching contracts issues, I examine project funding since funds are often tied to federal and state grant programs with many stipulations. I also look at professional organizations' websites for legal information relevant to their particular field.

A good research paralegal must be able to "step back," view the issue from different perspectives, and analyze the data. I try to identify factors that could impact the outcome of the legal opinion. I then ask the client more questions. Since clients are not always aware of relevant factors and potential issues, you must be able to "think outside the box" in order to know what questions will prove most helpful to the case.

During the research process, I take advantage of credible research already completed. I use a variety of online search services including Westlaw®, LexisNexis®, and PACER. Law journal and legal news articles posted on the Internet often contain information about specific laws, regulations, and cases relevant to a particular issue. No matter what research methods are used, I always "Shepardize" case law, use annotated statutes when possible, and strive to be thorough.

To be truly successful in the paralegal profession, continue to pursue a variety of learning opportunities. For example, consider helping to fill the need for legal services among low-income families and senior citizens who cannot afford private attorneys. By partnering with a legal aid society, you can gain valuable experience while serving your community.

What Is the Issue or Legal Question?

Legal research is like a puzzle to be solved. To solve it, understanding the assigned question is essential. Valuable time may be wasted if the paralegal takes the wrong research path because the question was not clear or the lawyer requesting the research was not clear about the information needed. At times the question is framed with some specificity:

> **Find the statute . . .**
> **Example: "What is the statute of limitations for filing a tort action for . . . ?"**
> **Get me the case of . . .**
> **Example: "What is the language of the *Miranda* decision on . . . ?"**

More often, however, the question is much more vague:

> **How does the law address this set of facts . . . ?**
> **Example: "How does the law address a case where our client suffered a broken leg three years ago when the car in which he was a passenger was hit . . . ?"**

In such cases, the paralegal should follow up by asking questions to determine exactly what legal issue he or she is being asked to research.

Researchers must first understand which facts are relevant and what areas of law apply to the case they are being asked to research. Unlike the cases in textbooks and court opinions, in real life, the **relevant facts** and the specific area of substantive or procedural law that applies are usually not so clear. The initial interview with the

Relevant facts Facts crucial to the case and having legal significance.

client may have focused on what the client or the interviewer *thought at that time* was the applicable law. Further research may indicate that other areas of law must also be considered.

For example, what may seem to be a simple rear-end automobile accident caused by negligent driving may in actuality be a case of product liability caused by a manufacturing defect on the part of the automobile manufacturer or the supplier of a defective part. To analyze a case properly, the researcher must know the factual elements of both a negligence case and a product liability case. The researcher must also understand the facts of the case at hand. Some facts are crucial to the case; others may not be important or have any legal significance.

What Is the Appropriate Search Terminology?

Knowing the legal terminology used in research materials is critical. The indexes of printed research materials use words selected by the editors of the publishing company. Different publishers do not always use the same words or legal terms to index the same rules of law. For example, one publisher may use the term "infant" to identify people under the age of majority, while another publisher uses the term "minor." If the researcher is presented with the question, "What are the contract rights of a person under the age of majority?" using "minor" to search an index in one source will not produce the desired results if that source's publisher listed the information under "infant."

Computer research is not dependent on using the terms selected by the publishers in its index. Most computer research allows for searches of words found in the documents themselves using a **search query**, in which the computer looks through the entire document for every instance of the selected words. For example, a computer search might include multiple terms: "enforceability of contracts of infants or minors."

Search query Specific words used in a computerized search.

It is also important to keep in mind the differences in terminology used in legal and factual research. Finding cases and statutes requires the use of the legal terminology used by the courts, legal professionals, and authors of legal treatises. However, these words and phrases may not be the most useful in locating factual information on the Internet or elsewhere where the authors of the articles are non-legally trained laypersons such as reporters and writers. For example, whereas the term "infant" is often used by legal texts to describe those under the age of majority, this term may not be useful for finding information on underage drinking in newspaper articles. Or statutes may use the expression "driving under the influence," while newspaper articles may use the terms "drunk driving" or "driving while intoxicated."

What Type of Research Material Is Available?

Traditionally, the law library consisted of books in paper form such as case reporters, legal encyclopedias, legal dictionaries, and a host of finding tools such as paper card indexes and digests. Increasingly, law libraries are replacing books with Internet access to free research sources such as the Cornell Law School Legal Information Institute and fee-based online computer services such as Westlaw, LexisNexis, VersusLaw, and Loislaw. Others combine traditional paper-based materials with electronic research tools.

"Are books obsolete?" is a question frequently asked in legal circles. Paralegal students who have grown up in the era of online research frequently ask why they need to learn how to use traditional paper-based research material. Depending on the Internet tools and paid service used, everything needed to properly conduct a research project may not be available electronically. For example, in some states, applicable precedent may be from a period before the material was digitized for electronic delivery. Before researching a legal issue, the date range of available material must be checked. Exhibit 12.1 shows a portion of the VersusLaw library directories coverage for the U.S. Supreme Court and federal circuit courts.

In some cases, researchers may find the use of print material more effective. For example, some find use of digests covering a broad range more efficient when

Exhibit 12.1 VersusLaw libraries directory

U.S. Supreme Court

U.S. Supreme Court	1886

back to top

Federal Circuit Courts

Court	Year
1st Circuit (MA,ME,NH,PR,RI)	1930
2nd Circuit (CT,NY,VT)	1930
3rd Circuit (DE,NJ,PA,VI)	1930
4th Circuit (MD,NC,SC,VA,WV)	1930
5th Circuit (LA,MS,TX)	1930
6th Circuit (KY,MI,OH,TN)	1920
7th Circuit (IL,IN,WI)	1930
8th Circuit (AR,IA,MN,MO,ND,NE,SD)	1930
9th Circuit (AK,AZ,CA,GU,HI,ID,MP,MT,NV,OR,WA)	1941
10th Circuit (CO,KS,NM,OK,UT,WY)	1930
11th Circuit (AL,FL,GA)	1981
D. C. Circuit (DC)	1945
Federal Circuit (null)	1982

learning about a new area or find the serendipity of discovery from flipping pages rapidly and making a discovery. Novice researchers may not appreciate the terminology used in indexing statutory law, making online research a hit-or-miss effort. Following the "paper trail" of the original enacted legislative statute through integration with the state or federal consolidated statutes makes computer searches easier because of knowledge of how the specific sections are disseminated across a consolidated code.

Occasionally, the legal team is faced with situations where they are trying a case out of town or in a different courthouse and need to check an unexpected case or statute, only to find that online resources are unavailable or their Internet access is blocked in that location. Frequently, paralegals accompany the lawyer to court. During the trial, they may be asked to slip out of the courtroom and conduct a quick bit of legal research. In some courthouses, a public computer terminal is not available in the law library, laptop computers cannot be connected to outgoing phone lines for security reasons, and cell phones are held at the security desk. In these situations, the paralegal must conduct the research quickly and accurately using traditional book methods. In short, the paralegal must be able to find the information needed when the familiar resources are not available.

What Jurisdictions Are Involved?

Research may involve federal, state, or local law. Some questions point to a certain jurisdiction—for example, "What is the age of majority in Florida?" At other times, the jurisdiction is not as clear: "What law controls the situation of an unruly passenger on a flight from Los Angeles to Philadelphia?" Here the paralegal must consider jurisdictional issues related to California, Pennsylvania, and federal statutes. Or consider the case of the driver from Georgia who is driving a truck belonging to a South Carolina company and has an accident in Alabama. The legal team working on that case might want to know the law in each jurisdiction before deciding where to file suit. Determining at the outset the appropriate jurisdictions to be searched reduces the number of books that must be searched and reduces the amount of online computer search time needed.

What Is the Controlling Law?

The controlling law is found in primary sources—statutes, regulations, and case law. Knowing which set of materials to use—the statutes of a jurisdiction, the regulations of a certain administrative agency, or the courts of a specific jurisdiction—will save time when doing the research. Irrelevant sources can be eliminated from consideration, and the source of the needed material can be located on-site or online. The controlling law may be narrowed to that of a local city, county, or parish, such as municipal zoning ordinances or local plumbing code.

What Types of Resources Should Be Used?

Law libraries usually have both primary and secondary sources of the law. A **primary source** is the actual law itself, which consists of the statutes and the case law that are reprinted in the text. **Secondary sources** are not the laws themselves but, instead, are writings about the law, such as legal encyclopedias and digests. A third set of resources is referred to as "finding tools"—publications, such as digests or the *Index to Legal Periodicals*, that are used to find primary and secondary sources. Frequently, sources contain both secondary sources and **finding tools** in one publication, such as the *American Law Reports*. Some services combine all three into one service or publication. Exhibit 12.2 delineates primary sources, secondary sources, and finding tools.

Primary source of law The actual law itself.

Secondary source of law Writings about the law.

Finding tools Publications used to find primary and secondary sources.

Ultimately, only primary sources of law are used in preparing a legal memorandum or brief. Secondary sources are useful, efficient ways to get an overview of an area of law or learn the terminology used in a certain field of law that the researcher is not familiar with. A torts specialist may suddenly be asked to research an issue related to a different area of law, such as negotiable instruments, and may be lost trying to remember the terminology and rules from courses taken long ago. Secondary sources such as legal encyclopedias can thus supply a quick review of that area and point the researcher to the appropriate primary sources, such as the commercial code of the relevant state. Legal dictionaries frequently list cases that have defined certain legal terms and thus can also be a starting point for case research.

Where Is the Needed Research Material Located?

It would be ideal to have a complete print and electronic library available on-site, such as the libraries at most law schools. However, law libraries are costly to acquire and maintain. The materials can run into hundreds of dollars per volume, and the annual upkeep for pocket parts, supplemental volumes, and new case reporters is nearly as expensive. The availability of space is another factor. Office space is expensive, and as a library grows, more floor space must be used for books instead of people. Finally,

Exhibit 12.2 Research materials

Primary Sources	Secondary Sources	Finding Tools
Constitutions	Legal dictionaries	Digests
Statutes	Legal encyclopedias	Citators
Court decisions	Treatises	Indexes
Common-law cases	Law reviews	
Administrative regulations	Textbooks	
Ordinances	Legal periodicals	
Court rules		

the cost of filing the updates and keeping the space orderly must be considered. If the collection is large enough, a full-time librarian may be needed. In smaller offices, these tasks take up the time of paralegals, time that could better be spent performing billable services for clients.

These issues have spurred the adoption of electronic libraries such as the fee-based online services provided by Loislaw, LexisNexis, Westlaw, and VersusLaw, as well as the free online services provided by some colleges and universities. Virtually all primary material is available online. Some proprietary secondary materials, such as encyclopedias, are not available from all sources. Depending on the resources needed to complete an assignment, the paralegal may have to locate the needed material at a remote library such as a bar association or a law school library.

Executing the Research Plan

After laying out a plan of action based on the preliminary questions in the assignment, the research plan can be executed. As with the execution of any plan, detours should be expected. The law is constantly evolving, as new statutes are enacted and new cases are handed down. During the research process, the researcher must look for changes or potential changes due to pending legislation and cases on appeal. Word lists and citations must be updated and new search paths followed.

The time spent initially in creating a list of search terms and phrases will save time when the research plan is executed. In looking for a statute, knowing the subject matter of the desired law, such as "blood alcohol level for driving," or the popular name of the law, such as "Sarbanes-Oxley," will save time by focusing the search on a specific statutory or popular name index.

The research plan should be executed in a systematic way using a checklist of terms and research materials. Not every search term will result in a successful search. However, some search terms may lead to other search terms. When a circular search brings the researcher back to a previous result, this indicates a dead end, and the researcher must proceed on a more fruitful path.

The researcher must also keep a list of citations, both successful and unsuccessful, which should be continually updated as the research progresses. When the time comes to finalize the research in a written document, the researcher will have the citation references available and will not have to go back and find the material again. In the event of additional, similar research assignments, the researcher will also have a ready reference to pick up the search and proceed quickly, using relevant terms and citations.

LEARNING OBJECTIVE 2

Explain the differences among primary resources, secondary resources, and finding tools.

Finding the Law

Finding "the law" seems like it should be an easy thing to accomplish. We go to the original source and read it. But what is the original source, and how is it located in a modern law library?

Statutory law is found in the statutes and regulations passed by the **legislative branch** of government. Case law is found in court decisions of the **judicial branch**. In the United States, laws are created at the federal, state, and local levels. At the federal legislative level, laws are passed by the U.S. Congress, which is a **bicameral** legislative body—meaning that there are two legislative houses, the House of Representatives and the Senate. At the state government level, all of the state legislatures are bicameral except Nebraska's, which has only one legislative body. Local governing bodies include cities, towns, and boroughs. At the judicial level, both federal and state courts create case law through their court decisions. The law is also found in the regulations enacted by administrative agencies as a result of the authority granted to them by the legislative branch of government, whether federal, state, or local.

Usually, the assignment is to find the current controlling law. However, occasionally the research assignment is to find the law that was in control at a point in the

Legislative branch The part of the government that makes law by enacting legislation. At the federal legal, the legislative branch is Congress (the Senate and the House of Representatives).

Judicial branch The court system.

Bicameral In the American system, a legislature consisting of two bodies—usually a House of Representatives and a Senate.

CHECKLIST Research

Primary Sources	Secondary Sources
Case ☐ Name ☐ Citation	Encyclopedia—National ☐ Name ☐ Key or descriptive word
Federal statute ☐ Federal citation ☐ Popular name	Encyclopedia—State ☐ Name ☐ Key or descriptive word
State (name) ☐ State citation ☐ Popular name	Treatises ☐ Name ☐ Citation
Local jurisdiction name ☐ Local citation ☐ Popular name	Restatement of law ☐ Name ☐ Citation
Administrative regulations ☐ Federal agency name ☐ Citation	Periodicals ☐ Citation
State agency name ☐ Citation	Practice books ☐ Name ☐ Citation
Local agency name ☐ Citation	Dictionary ☐ Name
Constitution ☐ Federal citation ☐ State citation	Digest ☐ Name ☐ Citation

past, such as what the blood alcohol limit was last year when the client was cited for driving under the influence.

When looking for the applicable law, we might start by asking:

- Is there a statute?
- Are there administrative regulations?
- Is there case law on the point?

If there is a statute in the applicable jurisdiction, that statute will be controlling. Regulations enacted to enforce the statute will also be controlling, subject to compliance with the statutory authority under which they are enacted. Case law may also exist to clarify and explain the law based on the facts of the cases before the courts.

Primary Sources and Authority

Primary sources are the law. This includes constitutions, both state and federal. Primary law includes statutes enacted by the legislative branch of government and the regulations of the administrative agencies established by the legislature to carry out the statutory enactments. Court rules and court decisions are sources of primary law from the judicial branch of government.

Mandatory and Persuasive Authority

Research should start with primary sources that are **mandatory authority**. Mandatory authority is the legal authority that the courts must follow when making decisions.

Mandatory authority Court decisions that are binding on all lower courts.

WHEN ARE COURT DECISIONS PRECEDENTS?

Courts issue published and unpublished opinions. A **published opinion** is a court's written explanation of its decision on a case, which is intended to be relied upon as a statement of the law based on the facts of the case. In some cases, the court will issue an informal statement of its ruling—an **unpublished opinion**—which is intended to apply only to the parties before the court and to the very narrow issue of the particular case based on the specific facts before the court. Unlike published opinions, the courts generally do not intend unpublished opinions to be used as precedent in other cases. However, it should be understood that unpublished opinions are not "secret" opinions. Many are available online, and others are available from the clerk's office.

There is some controversy with regard to the use of unpublished opinions in other court proceedings. The controversy has centered on the right of lawyers to use the unpublished opinions in arguments to the court. In reviewing the issue, the Eighth Circuit Court of Appeals made the following observations:

> Before concluding, we wish to indicate what this case is not about. It is not about whether opinions should be published, whether that means printed in a book or available in some other accessible form to the public in general. Courts may decide, for one reason or another, that some of their cases are not important enough to take up pages in a printed report. Such decisions may be eminently practical and defensible, but in our view they have nothing to do with the authoritative effect of any court decision.
>
> The question presented here is not whether opinions ought to be published, but whether they ought to have precedential effect, whether published or not. We point out, in addition, that "unpublished" in this context has never meant "secret." So far as we are aware, every opinion and every order of any court in this country, at least of any appellate court, is available to the public. You may have to walk into a clerk's office and pay a per-page fee, but you can get the opinion if you want it. Indeed, most appellate courts now make their opinions, whether labeled "published" or not, available to anyone online.

Anastasoff v. U.S., 223 F. 3d 898 (8th cir. 2000).

Following the publication of the initial opinion, the court declared the issues in the case, which concerned the recovery of tax payments, as moot, since the taxpayer received her refund, stating,

> . . . Here, the case having become moot, the appropriate and customary treatment is to vacate our previous opinion and judgment, remand to the District Court, and direct that Court to vacate its judgment as moot. We now take exactly that action. The constitutionality of that portion of Rule 28A(i) which says that unpublished opinions have no precedential effect remains an open question in this Circuit. . . .

Anastasoff v. U.S., No. 99-3917EM, (8th Cir. Dec. 18, 2000).

The issue of using unpublished opinions has been resolved among federal courts with the passage of federal Rule 32.1, Citing Judicial Dispositions, which permits the inclusion of those cases issued after January 1, 2007:

Rule 32.1. Citing Judicial Dispositions

(a) Citation Permitted. A court may not prohibit or restrict the citation of federal judicial opinions, orders, judgments, or other written dispositions that have been:

   (i) designated as "unpublished," "not for publication," "non-precedential," "not precedent," or the like; and

   (ii) issued on or after January 1, 2007.

(b) Copies Required. If a party cites a federal judicial opinion, order, judgment, or other written disposition that is not available in a publicly accessible electronic database, the party must file and serve a copy of that opinion, order, judgment, or disposition with the brief or other paper in which it is cited.

Published opinion A court's written explanation of its decision on a case intended to be relied upon as a statement of the law based on the facts of the case.

Unpublished opinions Cases that the court does not feel have precedential effect and are limited to a specific set of facts.

In addition to statutes and administrative regulations and ordinances, mandatory authority includes case law from higher courts. The highest court in the United States is the U.S. Supreme Court. The decisions of the Supreme Court are mandatory for all lesser federal and state courts. The decisions of the highest appellate court of a state are mandatory authority for all lesser courts of that state.

If mandatory authority cannot be found, the researcher should search for **persuasive authority**, which is authority the courts are not required to follow, but is from a respected source and is well reasoned. Decisions of some state courts traditionally have been looked at as being so well reasoned that courts in other states have been persuaded to follow that legal reasoning in deciding cases for their own state when they did not have any previously decided cases or statutes on the point at issue.

A good example of a persuasive opinion is that of Justice Cardozo in the New York Court of Appeals case of *Palsgraf v. Long Island Railroad Company*, 248 N.Y. 339, 192 N.E. 99 (N.Y. 1928) (see Appendix A, "How To Brief a Case"). Many courts, even today, find the logic and reasoning of Justice Cardozo in *Palsgraf* to be persuasive, and the case is frequently quoted by courts in other states.

Persuasive authority Court decisions the court is not required to follow but are well reasoned and from a respected court.

Constitutions

Web Exploration

View a high-resolution version of the original copy of the U.S. Constitution at www.archives.gov.

The United States Constitution is the ultimate primary law that sets the guidelines, limits, and authority of federal and state governments. The state constitutions are the ultimate law for the individual states, and they set the guidelines, limits, and authority of the government and the local governing bodies of that state. Constitutions are primary sources—the original or primary source of law.

Finding a section of the U.S. Constitution is probably the easiest task in legal research. This document is reproduced in many publications, including many textbooks, is available in virtually every public library, and is easily available on the Internet from many sources, including the National Archives. Finding the Constitution for individual states, however, is not as easy. Although some are posted on general-interest websites, most require access to specialty legal research websites, or to the paper version, generally found in the bound volumes of the state statutes.

Web Exploration

Read the latest U.S. Supreme Court opinion at http://www.supremecourt.gov/opinions/opinions.aspx.

Visit the homepage of the Legal Information Institute at Cornell University Law School to see the information provided, at http://www.law.cornell.edu/.

Statutes enacted by the legislative branch of government are primary sources of the law. The statutes of the United States—the *United States Code*—are available online from a number of free sources, including the U.S. Government Printing Office. Many states currently make their state statutes available online through an official state website. Until a few years ago, this free-access source was generally limited to state legislators. However, Web-based resources should be used with caution. Some unofficial sites appear to be "official" primary sources of the law, but in reality are not complete or up-to-date.

Court Decisions

Court decisions are also primary authority. The U.S. Supreme Court and some federal courts provide their current opinions and decisions online. Notably, the Legal Information Institute at Cornell University provides free access to the U.S. Supreme Court opinions, as well as those of many other courts. But many court decisions are not generally available from free Web sources and require the use of a paid subscription or fee-based services such as LexisNexis, Westlaw, Loislaw, and VersusLaw. Exhibit 12.3 shows the homepage of U.S. Courts with judiciary links.

Courts such as the U.S. Supreme Court issue opinions from the "bench," called **bench opinions**. A **slip opinion** is then sent for printing. This second version may contain corrections to the bench opinion. See the U.S. Supreme Court comments on the difference in Exhibit 12.4.

Bench opinion The initial version of a decision issued from the bench of the court.

Slip opinion A copy of the opinion sent to the printer.

Within cases, the court's actual language is the primary source of the law. However, the **case syllabus**, summaries, interpretations, or abstracts of the points of law presented by the editorial staff of the publishers of the case law, usually called **headnotes**, are *not* the primary source of law. Rather, they are explanations, interpretations, or comments that help the reader understand the legal concepts. As such, they are secondary sources. Note the cautionary comment in the syllabus of the Supreme Court case in Exhibit 12.5. Contrast the syllabus of the case with the opinion of the court in Exhibit 12.6.

Case syllabus In a court opinion, a headnote for the convenience of the reader.

Headnotes The syllabus or summary of the points of law prepared by the editorial staff of a publisher.

Legal dictionaries and encyclopedias also use headnotes—short, single-concept definitions and summaries—to provide basic information. When doing research, it should be kept in mind that these short "snippets" are taken out of the context of the case in which they were presented. None of the factual or procedural background is given in the headnote describing how the decision came about.

Exhibit 12.3 U.S. Courts website

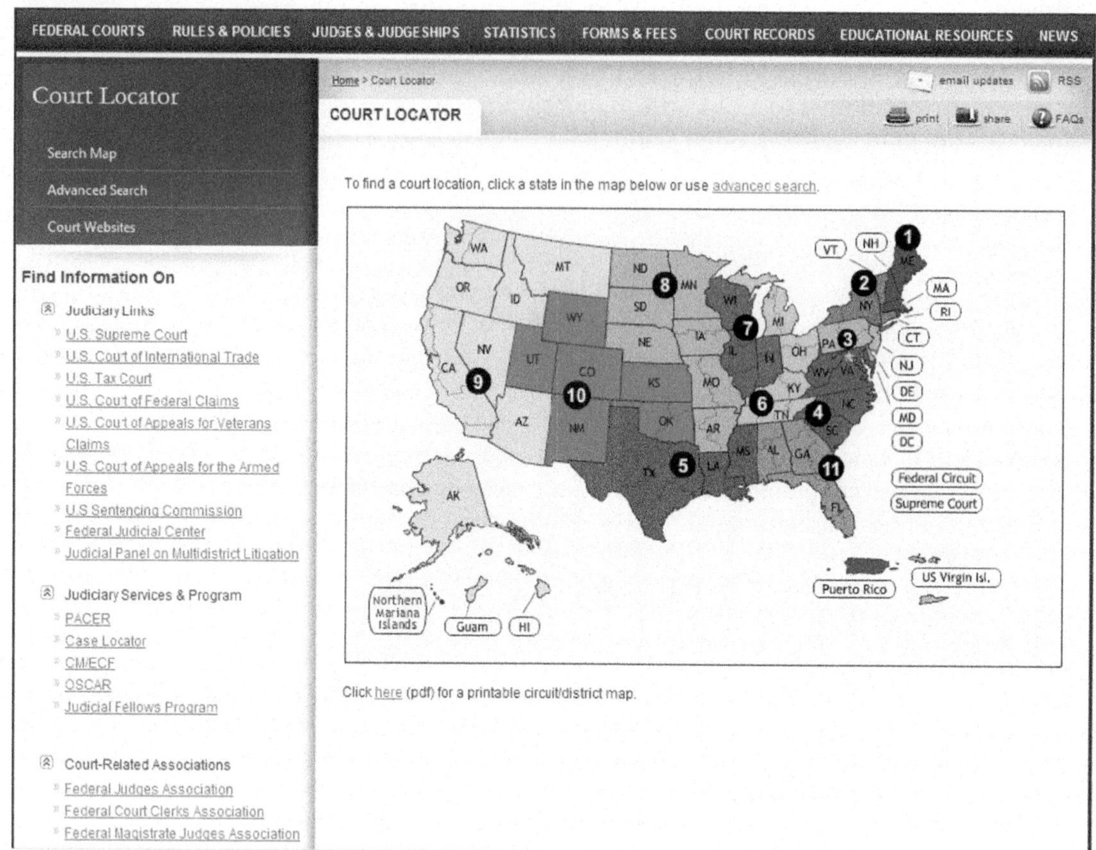

Source: http://www.uscourts.gov/Court_Locator.aspx, Administrative Office of the U.S. Courts, Washington, DC.

Holding The actual decision on the specific point of law the court was asked to decide.

Dicta Court comments on issues not directly related to the holding and therefore not having precedential effect.

Taking court statements out of the context of the case in which they appeared, and relying on case headnotes or summaries, can present many problems for the researcher—the most obvious of which is accuracy. Was the headnote or summary copied correctly from the final version of the opinion? Judges have been known to correct errors in the language of opinions. Did the editor writing the note use the final version of the opinion? More importantly—does the statement accurately reflect the majority view, or does it reflect a minority or dissenting view? Was it the actual decision on the point of law before the court, therefore having the precedential weight of a "**holding**" of the court? Or was it merely **dicta**—comments having no precedential authority because they were not related directly to the court decision? Contrast the headnote and the full court opinion in the case in Exhibit 12.7.

Doing legal research requires finding the most current and accurate statement of the legislative enactments and of the court. Presenting editorial headnotes, judges' dicta, or a dissenting opinion as current and accurate legal authority is a potentially career-ending act. The members of your legal team may rely on the potentially erroneous statements to prepare the case and their prosecution or defense strategy based on inaccurate information. Notwithstanding the potential effect on the outcome of the case, it may result in a severe reprimand or dismissal from employment.

Presenting erroneous information to the court is also an ethical violation of the duty of candor toward the tribunal under Rule 3.3 of the Model Rules of Professional Conduct. It does not matter to the court that it was prepared by someone other than the attorney presenting the case, the brief, or the oral argument; it is treated as a breach of the duty of candor to the court by the attorney.

Exhibit 12.4 Supreme Court explanation on differences between bench and slip opinions

2005 TERM OPINIONS OF THE COURT

Slip Opinions, *Per Curiams* (PC), and Original Case Decrees (D)

The "slip" opinion is the second version of an opinion. It is sent to the printer later in the day on which the "bench" opinion is released by the Court. Each slip opinion has the same elements as the bench opinion--majority or plurality opinion, concurrences or dissents, and a prefatory syllabus--but may contain corrections not appearing in the bench opinion. The slip opinions collected here are those issued during October Term 2005 (October 3, 2005, through October 1, 2006). These opinions are posted on this Website within hours after the bench opinions are issued and will remain posted until the opinions are published in a bound volume of the United States Reports. For further information, see Column Header Definitions and the file entitled Information About Opinions.

Caution: These electronic opinions may contain computer-generated errors or other deviations from the official printed slip opinion pamphlets. Moreover, a slip opinion is replaced within a few months by a paginated version of the case in the preliminary print, and--one year after the issuance of that print--by the final version of the case in a U. S. Reports bound volume. In case of discrepancies between the print and electronic versions of a slip opinion, the print version controls. In case of discrepancies between the slip opinion and any later official version of the opinion, the later version controls.

Source: Supreme Court of the United States.

Exhibit 12.5 Sample of a U.S. Supreme Court syllabus

Syllabus

NOTE: Where it is feasible, a syllabus (headnote) will be released, as is being done in connection with this case, at the time the opinion is issued.
The syllabus constitutes no part of the opinion of the Court but has been prepared by the Reporter of Decisions for the convenience of the reader.
See United States v. Detroit Timber & Lumber Co., 200 U.S. 321, 337.

SUPREME COURT OF THE UNITED STATES

ROPER, SUPERINTENDENT, POTOSI CORRECTIONAL CENTER v. SIMMONS

CERTIORARI TO THE SUPREME COURT OF MISSOURI

No. 03—633.Argued October 13, 2004-Decided March 1, 2005

At age 17, respondent Simmons planned and committed a capital murder. After he had turned 18, he was sentenced to death. His direct appeal and subsequent petitions for state and federal postconviction relief were rejected. This Court then held, in *Atkins* v. *Virginia*, 536 U.S. 304, that the Eighth Amendment, applicable to the States through the Fourteenth Amendment, prohibits the execution of a mentally retarded person. Simmons filed a new petition for state postconviction relief, arguing that *Atkins'* reasoning established that the Constitution prohibits the execution of a juvenile who was under 18 when he committed his crime. The Missouri Supreme Court agreed and set aside Simmons' death sentence in favor of life imprisonment without eligibility for release. It held that, although *Stanford* v. *Kentucky*, 492 U.S. 361, rejected the proposition that the Constitution bars capital punishment for juvenile offenders younger than 18, a national consensus has developed against the execution of those offenders since *Stanford*.

Held: The Eighth and Fourteenth Amendments forbid imposition of the death penalty on offenders who were under the age of 18 when their crimes were committed. Pp. 6–25.

(a) The Eighth Amendment's prohibition against "cruel and unusual punishments" must be interpreted according to its text, by considering history,

Source: Supreme Court of the United States.

Exhibit 12.6 Sample opinion of the U.S. Supreme Court

Opinion of the Court

NOTICE: This opinion is subject to formal revision before publication in the preliminary print of the United States Reports. Readers are requested to notify the Reporter of Decisions, Supreme Court of the United States, Washington, D. C. 20543, of any typographical or other formal errors, in order that corrections may be made before the preliminary print goes to press.

SUPREME COURT OF THE UNITED STATES

No. 03–633

DONALD P. ROPER, SUPERINTENDENT, POTOSI CORRECTIONAL CENTER, PETITIONER *v.* CHRISTOPHER SIMMONS

ON WRIT OF CERTIORARI TO THE SUPREME COURT OF MISSOURI

[March 1, 2005]

Justice Kennedy delivered the opinion of the Court.

This case requires us to address, for the second time in a decade and a half, whether it is permissible under the Eighth and Fourteenth Amendments to the Constitution of the United States to execute a juvenile offender who was older than 15 but younger than 18 when he committed a capital crime. In *Stanford* v. *Kentucky*, 492 U.S. 361 (1989), a divided Court rejected the proposition that the Constitution bars capital punishment for juvenile offenders in this age group. We reconsider the question.

I

At the age of 17, when he was still a junior in high school, Christopher Simmons, the respondent here, committed murder. About nine months later, after he had turned 18, he was tried and sentenced to death. There is little doubt that Simmons was the instigator of the crime. Before its commission Simmons said he wanted to murder someone. In chilling, callous terms he talked about his plan, discussing it for the most part with two friends, Charles Benjamin and John Tessmer, then aged 15 and 16 respectively. Simmons proposed to commit burglary and murder by breaking and entering, tying up a

Source: Supreme Court of the United States.

This is not to say that dissenting opinions and dicta may not be used when presenting an argument to the court. Although this material is not binding authority, it may have persuasive value in making an argument. Many of the finest jurists have issued dissenting views that eventually became the law in later cases. And dicta in another case may well be a valid argument in the present case being decided. The researcher's duty is to make clear whether the information is binding or persuasive authority. Sometimes it is not clear whether something is binding authority, as stated by one court:

> What exactly constitutes "dicta" is hotly contested and judges often disagree about what is or is not dicta in a particular case. See *United States v. Johnson*, 256 F.3d 895, 914–16 (9th Cir. 2001) (en banc) (Kozinski, J., concurring). In Johnson, Judge Kozinski explained that, "where a panel confronts an issue germane to the eventual resolution of the case, and resolves it after reasoned consideration in a published opinion, that ruling becomes the law of the circuit, regardless of whether doing so is necessary in some strict logical sense." Id. at 914; accord *Cetacean Cmty. v. Bush*, 386 F.3d 1169,1173 (9th Cir. 2004) (quoting Johnson); *Miranda B. v. Kitzhaber*, 328 F.3d 1181, 1186 (9th Cir. 2003) (per curiam) (same).
>
> Only "[w]here it is clear that a statement is made casually and without analysis, where the statement is uttered in passing without due consideration of the alternatives, or where it is merely a prelude to another legal issue that commands the panel's full attention, it may be appropriate to re-visit the issue in a later case." *Johnson*, 256 F.3d at 915. Nevertheless, "any such reconsideration should be done cautiously and rarely—only where the later panel is convinced that the earlier panel did not make a deliberate decision to adopt the rule of law it announced." Id. If, however, "it is clear

Exhibit 12.7 Regional reporter sample page

Reference to Volume and Name of Reporter

Case Name

COM. v. ZAENGLE Pa. 1335 ← Reporter Page Number

Cite as 497 A.2d 1335 (Pa.Super. 1985)

COMMONWEALTH of Pennsylvania
v.
John Stephen ZAENGLE, Appellant.
Superior Court of Pennsylvania.
Argued April 3, 1984.
Date of Opinion → Filed Aug. 16, 1985.

Beginning of West's Editor Summary → Defendant was convicted in the Court of Common Pleas, Criminal Division, Cumberland County, No. 886 Criminal 1982, Keller, J., of one count of driving while under the influence and three counts of homicide by vehicle, and he appealed his sentences. The Superior Court remanded for resentencing, 332 Pa.Super. 137, 480 A.2d 1224, and State appealed. The Supreme Court, 497 A.2d 1330, remanded for proceedings consistent with *Commonwealth v. Frisbie*. The Superior Court, No. 175 Harrisburg 1983, Olszewski, J., held that imposing multiple sentences upon defendant for the multiple deaths which resulted from his single violation of the homicide by vehicle statute was permissible.

End of Summary → Sentences reinstated.

West Digest Topic and Corresponding West Key Number → Criminal Law 984(7)

Legislature authorized multiple sentences for multiple deaths resulting from a single violation of homicide by vehicle statute, 75 Pa.C.S.A. § 3732.

Lawyers → Taylor P. Andrews, Public Defender, Carlisle, for appellant.

Kevin A. Hess, Asst. Dist. Atty., Carlisle, for Commonwealth, appellee. ← Lawyers

Before WICKERSHAM, OLSZEWSKI, AND HOFFMAN, JJ. ← Judges Who Heard Case

OLSZEWSKI, Judge:

By order of the Supreme Court, 497 A.2d 1330, this case has been remanded for proceedings consistent with *Commonwealth v. Frisbie*, 506 Pa. 461, 485 A.2d 1098 (1984). *Frisbie* holds that, where legislatively authorized, the imposition of multiple sentences upon a defendant whose single unlawful act injures multiple victims is legal. In the instant case, appellee driving drunk killed three people. The test of legislative authorization under *Frisbie* looks to the language of the statute defining the offense. *See id.* at 466, 485 A.2d at 1100 (comparing the language of 18 Pa.C.S. Sec 2705 with that of 18 Pa.C.S. Sec. 2707 and 2710). The operative language in 75 Pa.C.S. Sec. 3732 penalizes "(a)ny person who unintentionally causes *the death of another person.*" (Emphasis added.) Applying the *Frisbie* analysis to the facts of this case, we conclude that the legislature did authorize multiple sentences for multiple deaths resulting from a single violation of 75 Pa.C.S. Sec. 3732. Accord *Commonwealth v. Zaengle*, 332 Pa.Super. 137, 141, 480 A.2d 1224, 1228 (1984) (Olszewski J., dissenting). ← Beginning of Court's Opinion

The sentences imposed by the trial court are reinstated.

---

that a majority of the panel has focused on the legal issue presented by the case before it and made a deliberate decision to resolve the issue, that ruling becomes the law of the circuit and can only be overturned by an en banc court or by the Supreme Court." Id. at 916; see also *Cetacean Cmty.*, 386 F.3d at 1173; *Miranda B.*, 328 F.3d at 1186.

This understanding of binding circuit authority was further articulated in *Barapind v. Enomoto*, 400 F.3d 744 (9th Cir. 2005) (en banc) (per curiam), where we said that when a panel has "addressed [an] issue and decided it in an opinion joined in relevant part by a majority of the panel," the panel's decision becomes "law of the circuit." Id. at 750-51 (footnote omitted).

Padilla v. Lever, No. 03-56259 (9th Cir. November 23, 2005)

Secondary Sources

Secondary sources explain the law. Trying to understand a new area of law can be difficult, and secondary sources are useful sources on the history of an area of law, the issues involved, and in some situations the direction the law may be taking. A secondary source may also be the editorial headnotes of a case or an in-depth scholarly interpretation, such as a treatise, a law review article, or an article in a scholarly journal or other periodical.

Legal Dictionaries

Legal dictionaries, as opposed to general English or other specialized dictionaries, define words and phrases as used in the law. The "law," as with most professions, trades, and occupations, has developed its own specialized vocabulary. Each specialized area of law also develops its own specialized terminology. Lawyers in specialty fields, such as antitrust law, use terms that have developed specialized meaning through case decisions. For example, in antitrust law, the term "tying arrangement" is used to describe the situation in which one product can be purchased only with another product. This term comes from the 1947 antitrust case of *International Salt v. United States*, 332 U.S. 392 (1947), which held that a patent is presumed to give the patent holder "market power" (another legal term), making it illegal to "tie the sale of the patented product to the sale of another." Without an understanding of the basic terminology and legal concepts, it is hard to conduct proper legal research using either traditional books or computer-based services. Exhibit 12.8 is a sample page from *Black's Law Dictionary* illustrating the term "tying."

Secondary Sources—Legal Encyclopedias

Legal encyclopedias, like legal dictionaries, can provide basic background and understanding of an area in order to start research. They can provide an overview of the concepts and history of an area of law, the basic legal issues involved, and the terminology. The annotations (lists of case citations) can also provide a starting point for case law research. National encyclopedias such as *Corpus Juris Secundum* (CJS) and *American Jurisprudence* (Am Jur) provide selected cases from all jurisdictions for reference and research. Exhibit 12.9 is a sample page from *American Jurisprudence*.

State-specific encyclopedias generally limit case references or citations to that jurisdiction. Where the research is on a new area of law for the jurisdiction, the national coverage may be preferable in order to find information on persuasive authority from other jurisdictions. Exhibit 12.10 is a sample page from *Corpus Juris Secundum*.

Exhibit 12.8 ***Black's Law Dictionary*, sample page**

confesses in open court. U.S. Const. Art. IV, § 2, cl. 2.

tying, *adj. Antitrust.* Of or relating to an arrangement whereby a seller sells a product to a buyer only if the buyer purchases another product from the seller <tying agreement>.

tying arrangement. *Antitrust.* **1.** A seller's agreement to sell one product or service only if the buyer also buys a different product or service. The product or service that the buyer wants to buy is known as the *tying product* or *tying service*; the different product or service that the seller insists on selling is known as the *tied product* or *tied service*. Tying arrangements may be illegal under the Sherman or Clayton Act if their effect is too anticompetitive. **2.** A seller's refusal to sell one product or service unless the buyer also buys a different product or service. — Also termed *tying agreement; tie-in; tie-in arrangement*. Cf. RECIPROCAL DEALING.

tying product. See TYING ARRANGEMENT (1).

tyranny, *n.* Arbitrary or despotic government; the severe and autocratic exercise of sovereign power, whether vested constitutionally in one ruler or usurped by that ruler by breaking down the division and distribution of governmental powers. — **tyrannical, tyrannous**, *adj.*

tyrant, *n.* A sovereign or ruler, legitimate or not, who wields power unjustly and arbitrarily to oppress the citizenry; a despot.

Source: *Black's Law Dictionary*, 7/e, 1995. Reprinted with permission of Thomson/West Publishing.

Exhibit 12.9 *American Jurisprudence, sample page*

68 Am Jur 2d SCHOOLS § 317

is infected with a contagious disease[90] or has been dangerously exposed to such a disease.[91]

§ 317. —Children infected with the AIDS virus

Acquired Immune Deficiency Syndrome (AIDS) disables victims of the disease by collapsing their immune systems, making them unable to fight infection.[92] State education authorities, rather than local school authorities, are the appropriate parties to promulgate regulations concerning the right of AIDS-infected children to attend public school, since the state's power to regulate on the issue, inferable from its broad grant of authority to supervise the schools, pre-empts any rights of local authorities under their statutory discretion to exclude children from school to prevent the spread of contagious disease.[93]

◆ *Caution:* State statutes and local health regulations concerning contagious diseases in general, which make no specific reference to AIDS, do not apply to the decision whether AIDS-infected students should be allowed to attend public school.[94]

Procedures for determining whether AIDS-infected children should be excluded from a public school have withstood a due process challenge, one court having upheld the constitutionality of a plan which provided for an impartial decision by a medical panel, proper notice, and the opportunity to call and cross-examine witnesses.[95] However, distinguishing between students known to be infected with AIDS and students who were unidentified carriers of AIDS-related complex or asymptomatic carriers is constitutionally unacceptable since the proposed exclusion from public school of only the known AIDS-infected children constitutes an equal protection violation.[96]

◆ *Practice Guide:* Numerous organizations, both medical and educational, have formulated guidelines on when AIDS carriers should be segregated from the rest of the population. In cases concerning the right of a student with AIDS to attend school, courts have received evidence of the guidelines

90. Kenney v. Gurley, 208 Ala. 623, 95 So. 34, 26 A.L.R. 813 (1923); Nutt v. Board of Education of City of Goodland, Sherman County, 128 Kan. 507, 278 P. 1065 (1929).

As to the right to public education, generally, see §§ 242 et seq.

Forms: Answer—Defense—School district providing home teaching to student with contagious or infectious disease pending determination whether student's attendance at school would be danger to others. 22 Am Jur Pl & Pr Forms (Rev), Schools, Form 182.

91. Bright v. Beard, 132 Minn. 375, 157 N.W. 501 (1916).

92. Board of Educ. of City of Plainfield, Union County v. Cooperman, 105 N.J. 587, 523 A.2d 655, 38 Ed. Law Rep. 607, 60 A.L.R.4th 1 (1987).

Law Reviews: AIDS in public schools: Resolved issues and continuing controversy, 24 J Law and Educ 1:69 (1995).

Students with AIDS: Protecting an infected child's right to a classroom education and developing a school's AIDS policy, 40 S Dakota LR 1:72 (1995).

93. Board of Educ. of City of Plainfield, Union County v. Cooperman, 105 N.J. 587, 523 A.2d 655, 38 Ed. Law Rep. 607, 60 A.L.R.4th 1 (1987).

94. District 27 Community School Bd. by Granirer v. Board of Educ. of City of New York, 130 Misc. 2d 398, 502 N.Y.S.2d 325, 32 Ed. Law Rep. 740 (Sup. Ct. 1986).

95. Board of Educ. of City of Plainfield, Union County v. Cooperman, 105 N.J. 587, 523 A.2d 655, 38 Ed. Law Rep. 607, 60 A.L.R.4th 1 (1987).

Forms: Complaint, petition, or declaration—To enjoin expulsion of student who tested positive for AIDS virus—By guardian. 22 Am Jur Pl & Pr Forms (Rev), Schools, Form 177.

96. District 27 Community School Bd. by Granirer v. Board of Educ. of City of New York, 130 Misc. 2d 398, 502 N.Y.S.2d 325, 32 Ed. Law Rep. 740 (Sup. Ct. 1986).

537

Source: *American Jurisprudence, 2/e*, 2000. Reprinted with permission of Thomson/West Publishing.

Exhibit 12.10 Page from *Corpus Juris Secundum*, a legal encyclopedia

§§ 58–59 SOCIAL SECURITY 81 C.J.S.

individual who died fully insured,[65] and have physical or mental impairments which, under regulations promulgated for the purpose, are deemed to be of such severity as to preclude engaging in any gainful activity.[66] The requirements for obtaining disability benefits by such persons are more restrictive than requirements for the insured individual himself.[67] The physical impairment necessary to a finding of disability is placed on a level of severity to be determined administratively,[68] and the regulations adopted to carry out the statutory provisions have been upheld.[69]

A claim for disability is judged solely by medical criteria,[70] without regard to non-medical factors[71] such as age, education, and work experience,[72] in contrast to the considerations given to an insured individual's age, education, and work experience, in determining his ability to engage in substantial gainful activity, as discussed supra § 56. An individual cannot qualify for disability insurance benefits unless suffering from an impairment listed in the appendix to the regulations applicable to disabilities, or from one or more unlisted impairments that singly or in combination are the medical equivalent of a listed impairment.[73] The benefits are to be paid only for a disabling medical impairment,[74] and not simply for the inability to obtain employment.[75]

§ 59. Benefits of Disabled Child

A disabled child of an insured individual who is, or would have been, eligible for social security benefits, may be entitled to disability insurance benefits.

Research Note

Status as child eligible for benefits under statute generally is discussed supra § 41.

Library References

Social Security and Public Welfare ⚿123, 140.5.

Under the provisions of the Social Security Act,[76] disabled children of retired or disabled insured individuals, and of insured individuals who have died, may be paid benefits if they have been disabled since before they reached twenty-two years of age, and if they meet the other conditions of eligibility.[77] The purpose of the provision is to provide a measure of income and security to those who have lost a wage-earner on whom they depended,[78] or to provide support for the dependents of a disabled wage earner,[79] and not to replace only that support enjoyed by the child prior to the onset of disability.[80] The liberal perspective of the Act applies to the award of children's disability benefits.[81]

In order to be entitled to recover benefits under this provision, the child must have been disabled,[82] as defined elsewhere in the Act,[83] prior to attaining a specified age,[84] and must be un-

65. U.S.—Sullivan v. Weinberger, C.A. Ga., 493 F.2d 855, certiorari denied 95 S.Ct. 1958, 421 U.S. 967, 44 L.Ed.2d 455.

66. U.S.—Wokojance v. Weinberger, C. A.Ohio, 513 F.2d 210, certiorari denied 96 S.Ct. 106, 423 U.S. 856, 46 L.Ed.2d 82.

Hendrix v. Finch, D.C.S.C., 310 F. Supp. 513.

Baby sitting; domestic work
U.S.—Dixon v. Weinberger, C.A.Ga., 495 F.2d 202.

Time impairment manifest
U.S.—Sullivan v. Weinberger, C.A.Ga., 493 F.2d 855, certiorari denied 95 S.Ct. 1958, 421 U.S. 967, 44 L.Ed.2d 455.

67. U.S.—Wokojance v. Weinberger, C. A.Ohio, 513 F.2d 210, certiorari denied 96 S.Ct. 106, 423 U.S. 856, 46 L.Ed.2d 82.

Solis v. U. S. Secretary of Health, Ed. and Welfare, D.C.Puerto Rico, 372 F.Supp. 1223—Truss v. Richardson, D. C.Mich., 338 F.Supp. 741—Nickles v. Richardson, D.C.S.C., 326 F.Supp. 777.

68. U.S.—Gillock v. Richardson, D.C. Kan., 322 F.Supp. 354.

69. U.S.—Sullivan v. Weinberger, C.A. Ga., 493 F.2d 855, certiorari denied 95 S.Ct. 1958, 421 U.S. 967, 44 L.Ed.2d 455.

Gunter v. Richardson, D.C.Ark., 335 F.Supp. 907—Zanoviak v. Finch, D.C. Pa., 314 F.Supp. 1152—Frasier v. Finch, D.C.Ala., 313 F.Supp. 160, affirmed, C. A., 434 F.2d 597.

70. U.S.—Wokojance v. Weinberger, C. A.Ohio, 513 F.2d 210, certiorari denied 96 S.Ct. 106, 423 U.S. 856, 46 L.Ed.2d 82.

71. U.S.—Sullivan v. Weinberger, C.A. Ga., 493 F.2d 855, certiorari denied 95 S.Ct. 1958, 421 U.S. 967, 44 L.Ed.2d 455.

72. U.S.—Gillock v. Richardson, D.C. Kan., 322 F.Supp. 354.

73. U.S.—Wokojance v. Weinberger, C. A.Ohio, 513 F.2d 210, certiorari denied 96 S.Ct. 106, 423 U.S. 856, 46 L.Ed.2d 82.

Gillock v. Richardson, D.C.Kan., 322 F.Supp. 354—Hendrix v. Finch, D.C.S. C., 310 F.Supp. 513.

74. U.S.—Sullivan v. Weinberger, C.A. Ga., 493 F.2d 855, certiorari denied 95 S.Ct. 1958, 421 U.S. 967, 44 L.Ed.2d 455.

75. U.S.—Sullivan v. Weinberger, C.A. Ga., 493 F.2d 855, certiorari denied 95 S.Ct. 1958, 421 U.S. 967, 44 L.Ed.2d 455.

76. 42 U.S.C.A. § 402(d).

77. U.S.—Lowe v. Finch, D.C.Va., 297 F.Supp. 667—Blevins v. Fleming, D.C. Ark., 180 F.Supp. 287.

78. U.S.—Ziskin v. Weinberger, D.C. Ohio, 379 F.Supp. 124.

79. U.S.—Jimenez v. Weinberger, Ill., 94 S.Ct. 2496, 417 U.S. 628, 41 L.Ed.2d 363, appeal after remand, C.A., 523 F.2d 689, certiorari denied 96 S.Ct. 3200.

80. U.S.—Jimenez v. Weinberger, Ill., 94 S.Ct. 2496, 417 U.S. 628, 41 L.Ed.2d 363, appeal after remand, C.A., 523 F.2d 689, certiorari denied 96 S.Ct. 3200.

81. U.S.—Ziskin v. Weinberger, D.C. Ohio, 379 F.Supp. 124.

82. U.S.—Ziskin v. Weinberger, D.C. Ohio, 379 F.Supp. 124.

83. 42 U.S.C.A. § 423.

84. U.S.—Ziskin v. Weinberger, D.C. Ohio, 379 F.Supp. 124—Moon v. Richardson, D.C.Va., 345 F.Supp. 1182.

Source: From *Corpus Juris Secundum*, © The West Group, a Thomson Company. Reproduced with permission.

Treatises, Law Reviews, and Legal Periodicals

Some secondary sources are considered very authoritative, and may be of sufficient scholarly value to be persuasive to the court. For example, the treatise on Torts by Prosser is frequently used in arguments and is accepted as persuasive authority by most courts. In new areas of the law such as cyber law, or emerging and changing areas such as privacy rights, courts frequently welcome a well-reasoned scholarly article from a law review or other legal journal that makes a clear and convincing argument using thorough research and well-reasoned thought. In some instances, these articles are like the ***amicus curiae*** briefs submitted to the court by interested parties that have no actual standing as a party but have a clear interest in the outcome.

Amicus curiae Briefs submitted by interested parties, as "friends of the court," who do not have standing in the action.

Finding Tools

Finding tools are resources that help to "find" the law. Finding the right case, statute, or regulation can be difficult, particularly if it is a challenge to find the correct term or phrase to conduct the search. For example, West Publishing might use the phrase "Bills and Notes" and another publisher might use the term "holder" to refer to the same cases and material on negotiable instruments. In these instances, a finding tool may be a helpful resource.

Indexes are valuable finding tools. Among the more useful sets of indexes and **citators** are those that cross-reference material. Some indexes use the commonly used or popular name of a case or statute to provide the citation or reference to the original source. For example, the commonly used or popular name for the statement of rights read to criminal defendants when arrested is "Miranda Rights." Using a popular name index provides the citation to the case in which the U.S. Supreme Court established the reading of these rights to defendants: *Miranda v. Arizona*, 384 U.S 436 (1966).

Citator An index of cases.

Legal digests provide lists of cases in subject topic format, with cases generally in chronological order from the earliest to the latest. Digests do not, however, offer the detailed analysis found in encyclopedias. Exhibit 12.11 is a sample page from *West's Digest*.

Personal Research Strategy

Over time, each paralegal develops his or her own personal search strategy, which may be adapted based on the nature of the problem, the issue to be researched, and the resources available. When the legal issue in an assignment is well defined and focuses on a specific case or statute, it may be possible to start with the original primary source. More likely, however, the research assignment will be less well defined and may only recite a set of facts describing the client's situation. A possible area of law may be suggested, such as "driving too fast for conditions," or "personal injury from an automobile accident." But the precise legal issue may not be defined.

In this situation, the facts must be used to determine the area of law. If the paralegal is unfamiliar with the area of law, the connection may not be obvious. Secondary sources provide a good reference source to acquire a general understanding about an area of law. As the paralegal learns more about the specifics of the area of law and the essential elements of its causes of action, the applicable law should become clearer. One of the advantages of using the traditional book form of research is the ability to flip pages back and forth and scan many items that can lead to a specific point of law. This is sometimes referred to as "the serendipity of research."

Computer search engines can also lead to specific case law and statutes. The challenge is in how to construct the search query or question. If the researcher does not know what facts to include in the query, the resulting report may not be accurate. Computers, for the most part, are limited to finding only the things the search query specifically asks for. Learning the relevant facts to create the proper question may involve using the print resources first to determine the relevant facts or the proper terminology. For example, in a case of an alleged copyright violation under the fair-use doctrine, is the status of the alleged violator as a nonprofit organization relevant?

Exhibit 12.11 *West's Federal Digest*, sample page

CRIMINAL LAW

SUBJECTS INCLUDED

Acts and omissions in violation of law punishable as offenses against the public

Nature and elements of crime in general

Capacity to commit crime, nature and extent of responsibility therefore in general, and responsibility of principals, accessories, etc.

Jurisdiction over and place of prosecution of crimes

Limitation of time for prosecution

Preliminary complaints, warrants, examination and commitment

Arraignment and pleas

Evidence in criminal proceedings

Trial, and acquittal or conviction

Motions in arrest of judgment and for new trial

Judgment or sentence and final commitment

Review on appeal, writ of error or certiorari

Prosecution and punishment of successive offenses or of habitual criminals

Modes of punishment and prevention of crime in general

SUBJECTS EXCLUDED AND COVERED BY OTHER TOPICS

Arrest, see ARREST

Bail, see BAIL

Constitutional rights and privileges of accused not peculiar to matters within scope of this topic, see CONSTITUTIONAL LAW, INDICTMENT AND INFORMATION, JURY, SEARCHES AND SEIZURES, WITNESSES and other specific topics

Convicts, disabilities and regulation, see CONVICTS

Costs in criminal prosecutions, see COSTS

Extradition of fugitives, see EXTRADITION AND DETAINERS

Fines in general, see FINES

Grand juries and inquisitions by them, see GRAND JURY

Habeas corpus to obtain discharge from imprisonment, see HABEAS CORPUS

Included offenses, conviction under indictment for broader offense, see INDICTMENT AND INFORMATION

Indictments or other accusations, see INDICTMENT AND INFORMATION and specific topics relating to particular offenses

Injunction against commission of crime, see INJUNCTION

Judgment of acquittal, conviction or sentence, effect as adjudication, see JUDGMENT

Jury trial, right to and waiver, and qualifications and selection of jurors, see JURY

Juvenile offenders, special rules and proceedings, see INFANTS

Source: *West's Federal Digest*, 4/e. Reprinted with permission of Thomson/West Publishing.

Always verify that the law to be cited in the memorandum of law is current. Look for pending cases and legislation that might change the answer to the legal question. Look in legal journals, periodicals, and legal newspapers, as well as newspapers of general circulation, for cases that are on appeal and that involve the same legal issues. Check the legislative services for pending legislation that may have an impact on the case. Research that is concerned with giving clients advice on future actions may depend on knowing about changes that may alter the basic parameters of the law. For example, should a smoking section be installed in a new restaurant if there is not yet an ordinance that prohibits smoking? Are the tax rates for estate planning going to change next year?

A Final Word on Executing the Legal Research Plan

This final piece of advice must be emphasized: *know when to ask for help*. Everyone on the legal team who has done legal research has hit a dead end at one time or another. Sometimes taking a few minutes to ask a question will yield the "magic" word, term, or phrase that will lead to the answer.

Using Printed Legal Reference Works

Most legal references have a set of common features. They generally have a section, usually in the introduction, that explains its coverage and how to use the book or service. This section typically includes the abbreviations used throughout the work (see Exhibit 12.12), and describes the method of pagination—for example, standard page numbering or section numbers. The table of contents (see Exhibit 12.13) also provides a general list of major topics. The index at the end provides the details of the coverage. Multivolume sets might have a separate set of volumes containing this index. Each volume might also contain an index for that specific volume.

Most of these legal reference works also contain a table of the cases that are mentioned in the text. This is a useful feature when a case seems to be relevant or on point, and the paralegal wants to see other cases on the same issue. A table of statutes may also be included to help the researcher find cases or discussions of a statute.

Exhibit 12.12 Sample list of abbreviations

ABBREVIATIONS

A. *Atlantic Reporter*
A.2d *Atlantic Reporter, Second Series*
Abb. *Abbott's Circuit Court Reports, U.S.*
Abb.Adm. *Abbott's Admiralty Reports, U.S.*
Adams L.J. *Adams County Legal Journal*
Add. *Addison's Reports*
Am.Dec. *American Decisions*
Am.L.J., N.S. *American Law Journal, New Series*
Am.L.J.,O.S. *American Law Journal, Hall's*
Am.L.Reg., N.S. *American Law Register, New Series*
Am.L.Reg., O.S. *American Law Register, Old Series*
Am.Rep. *American Reports*
Am.St.Rep. *American State Reports*
Ann.Cas. *American & English Annotated Cases*
Ashm. *Ashmead's Reports*
Baldw. *Baldwin's Reports, U.S.*
Beaver *Beaver County Legal Journal*
Ben. *Benedict's Reports, U.S.*
Berks *Berks County Legal Journal*
Binn. *Binney's Reports*
Binns' Just. *Binns' Justice*
Biss. *Bissell's Reports, U.S.*
Black *Black's United States Supreme Court Reports*
Blair *Blair County Law Reports*
Blatchf.C.C. *Blatchford's Reports, U.S.*
Bond *Bond's Reports, U.S.*
B.R. *Bankruptcy reports*
Bright.E.C. *Brightly's Election Cases*
Bright.N.P. *Brightly's Nisi Prius Reports*
Browne *P.A. Browne's reports*
Brock. *Brockenbrough's Reports, U.S.*
Bucks *Bucks County Law Reporter*
C.A. *United States Court of Appeals*
C.C.A. *United States Circuit Court of Appeals*
Cambria *Cambria County Legal Journal*
Cambria C.R. *Cambria County Reports*
Camp. *Campbell's Legal Gazette Reports*
Cent. *Central Reporter*
C.C. *(see Pa.C.C.) County Court Reports*
Chest. *Chester County Reports*

Source: From *Purdon's Pennsylvania Statutes Annotated*, © 1994 by West Group, a Thomson Company. Reproduced with permission.

Exhibit 12.13 Sample table of contents

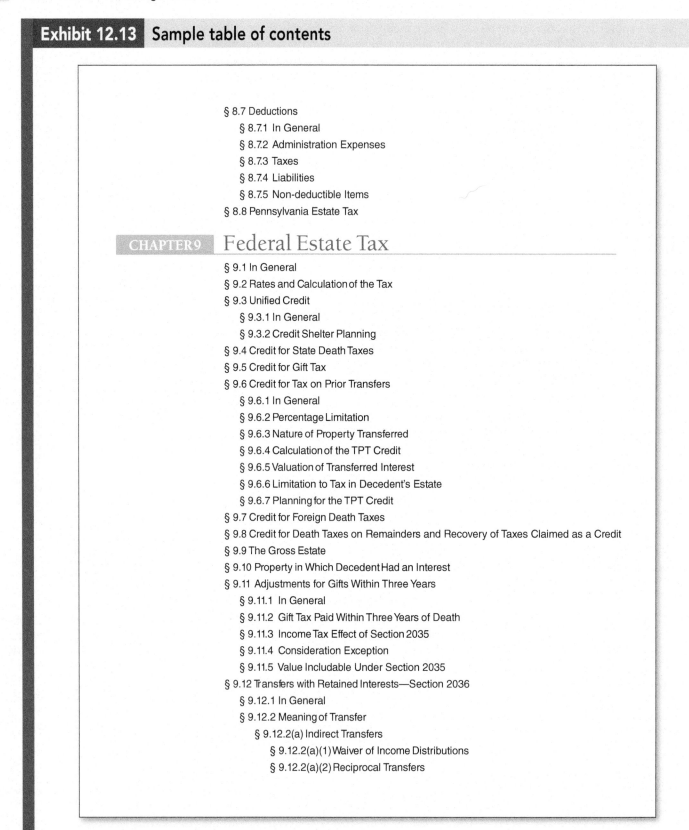

§ 8.7 Deductions
§ 8.7.1 In General
§ 8.7.2 Administration Expenses
§ 8.7.3 Taxes
§ 8.7.4 Liabilities
§ 8.7.5 Non-deductible Items
§ 8.8 Pennsylvania Estate Tax

CHAPTER 9 Federal Estate Tax

§ 9.1 In General
§ 9.2 Rates and Calculation of the Tax
§ 9.3 Unified Credit
§ 9.3.1 In General
§ 9.3.2 Credit Shelter Planning
§ 9.4 Credit for State Death Taxes
§ 9.5 Credit for Gift Tax
§ 9.6 Credit for Tax on Prior Transfers
§ 9.6.1 In General
§ 9.6.2 Percentage Limitation
§ 9.6.3 Nature of Property Transferred
§ 9.6.4 Calculation of the TPT Credit
§ 9.6.5 Valuation of Transferred Interest
§ 9.6.6 Limitation to Tax in Decedent's Estate
§ 9.6.7 Planning for the TPT Credit
§ 9.7 Credit for Foreign Death Taxes
§ 9.8 Credit for Death Taxes on Remainders and Recovery of Taxes Claimed as a Credit
§ 9.9 The Gross Estate
§ 9.10 Property in Which Decedent Had an Interest
§ 9.11 Adjustments for Gifts Within Three Years
§ 9.11.1 In General
§ 9.11.2 Gift Tax Paid Within Three Years of Death
§ 9.11.3 Income Tax Effect of Section 2035
§ 9.11.4 Consideration Exception
§ 9.11.5 Value Includable Under Section 2035
§ 9.12 Transfers with Retained Interests—Section 2036
§ 9.12.1 In General
§ 9.12.2 Meaning of Transfer
§ 9.12.2(a) Indirect Transfers
§ 9.12.2(a)(1) Waiver of Income Distributions
§ 9.12.2(a)(2) Reciprocal Transfers

Source: From *Pennsylvania Estate Planning and Drafting*, 2/e, by Robert J. Weinberg.

Updates

Print material is updated in a number of ways. One of the most frequent methods is the use of **pocket parts**, so called because they are slipped into a pocket in the back of the hardcover volume. Usually these are annual updates, but they may also be produced more or less frequently, depending on the publisher and the need for updates. Materials may also be updated by supplemental pamphlets, which are usually paperbacks. Updates may be issued monthly, quarterly, annually, or semi-annually.

It is essential that the pocket parts or supplements be consulted every time a primary source is used. In statutory research, for example, the main volumes may be many years old, and sections of the law may have been amended or repealed. The pocket parts or other supplements, not the main volume, contain the latest information. For this reason, some researchers look at the pocket parts before consulting the main volume. More and more frequently, additional updates are provided online. The paralegal must learn how each resource is updated and the frequency of the updates. Exhibit 12.14 is a sample pocket part supplement.

Web Explorations

VersusLaw Research Manual: https://server.iad.liveperson.net/hc/s-65442687/cmd/kbresource/kb-5427540797510340552/front_page!PAGETYPE?category=8
LexisNexis: www.lexisnexis.com/
WestlawNext: http://legal-solutions.thomsonreuters.com/law-products/west-law-legal-research/reviews/corporate-librarian
VersusLaw: www.versuslaw.com
Loislaw: www.loislaw.com

Pocket parts Updates to a book; they are separate documents that slip into a pocket in the back of the main volume.

Constructing a Computer Search Query

LEARNING OBJECTIVE 3
Create a search query.

Successful computer research requires the use of appropriate search words in a search query. In the English language, some words have different meanings in different contexts, or to different groups or professions. For example, the word "head" usually means the top of a person's body. But to a sailor, it means a bathroom. To a bartender, it means the foam at the top of a beverage.

As with any profession, the legal profession also has its own vocabulary. This includes words defined by the courts over the years to have specific meanings when used in a legal context. For example, in commercial law, the definition of the term "holder" is "a person to whom a negotiable instrument has been properly negotiated." To the layperson, the term may mean a person holding something in their hand—not necessarily a negotiable instrument—or holding something with any legal formality attached to it.

People in all areas of life develop words and phrases that help them understand their fields of interest. In creating laws, legislatures use language in special ways that may not be clear to laypersons, or even to legal researchers who are not accustomed to the terminology of the lawmakers. The editors who create indexes to legal reference tools also have their own vocabulary and methods of indexing material. For example, West Publishing Company editors originally created the index of 450 West Digest Topics for indexing cases published in case reporters (see Exhibit 12.15). These offer excellent starting points for creating search queries.

Finding print materials requires that the paralegal understand what items are included under each index classification. The word "holder," for example, is listed in the West Digest index under "Statutes," but the word "holder," as defined above, is also found under the West Digest Topic "Bills and Notes." *Black's Law Dictionary* defines the same word in the language of the negotiable instrument law. Using the West Topic heading "Bills and Notes" and "holder" in some computer searches of conventional Westlaw products will not return cases of negotiable instrument holders. But using the terms "negotiable instrument" and "holder" as the search words in a computer search will yield the desired result. Because paralegals cannot be sure whether the research will be done using a traditional paper library or a computer search or, if online, which particular online research service, they must understand how each resource organizes the information.

Knowing how to use both traditional and computer methods, and recognizing the strengths and weaknesses of each system, are important in conducting searches. Traditional research may be a better option when general background research is needed or when the paralegal isn't familiar with an area of law. Indexing systems are grouped by concept, and once paralegals get into the right area of law, they can browse easily. The ability to flip pages back and forth when they are in the right general area is particularly helpful in statutory research, as many of the computer-based

SIDEBAR

ELECTRONIC SEARCHING STRATEGY

Searching is a process, not an event. . . . Searching a library is not about spending time and mental energy formulating the "golden query" that retrieves your desired information in a single stroke. In practice, good online searching involves formulating a succession of queries until you are satisfied with the results. As you view results from one search, you'll come across additional leads that you did not identify in your original search. You can incorporate these new terms into your existing query or create a new one. After each query, evaluate its success by asking:

- Did I find what I was looking for?
- What better information could still be out there?
- How can I refine my query to find better information?

Issuing multiple queries can be frustrating or rewarding, depending on how long it takes you to identify the key material you need to answer your research problem.

Source: CASELAW.

Exhibit 12.14 Sample pocket part supplement

13 Pa.C.S.A. § 1105 COMMERCIAL CODE

DIVISION 1
GENERAL PROVISIONS

CHAPTER 11

SHORT TITLE, CONSTRUCTION, APPLICATION AND SUBJECT MATTER OF TITLE

§ 1105. Territorial application of title; power of parties to choose applicable law

Notes of Decisions

Bankruptcy 6

1. In general

In re Eagle Enterprises, Inc., Bkrtcy.E.D.Pa. 1998, 223 B.R. 290, [main volume] affirmed 237 B.R. 269.

2. Law governing

When parties agree to apply foreign law, pursuant to which their contract to "lease" goods kept in Pennsylvania will be deemed a true "lease," despite fact that contract does not permit lessor to terminate agreement but affords him an option to purchase goods for nominal consideration, Pennsylvania law will not give effect to that choice. In re Eagle Enterprises, Inc., E.D.Pa.1999, 237 B.R. 269.

4. Third parties

In re Eagle Enterprises, Inc., Bkrtcy.E.D.Pa. 1998, 223 B.R. 290, [main volume] affirmed 237 B.R. 269.

6. Bankruptcy

While Chapter 7 debtor and equipment lessor were generally free, under Pennsylvania statute, to agree what law would govern their rights and duties, debtor and equipment lessor could not impose their choice of law on Chapter 7 trustee, as party who never agreed to choice-of-law provision, in order to prevent trustee from challenging parties' characterization, as equipment "lease," of agreement which required debtor to pay alleged rent throughout full term of lease, and which then allowed debtor to acquire equipment at end of lease for nominal consideration of one dollar, merely because lease would allegedly have been recognized as true lease under law of foreign country that parties chose to govern their agreement. In re Eagle Enterprises, Inc., E.D.Pa.1999, 237 B.R. 269.

CHAPTER 12

GENERAL DEFINITIONS AND PRINCIPLES OF INTERPRETATION

§ 1201. General definitions

Notes of Decisions

11. Lease or lease intended as security

Under Pennsylvania law, "lease" transaction in which "lessee" cannot terminate "lease" during its term, but may thereafter become owner of "leased" goods for no additional or nominal additional consideration, does not create lease, but rather a security interest. In re Eagle Enterprises, Inc., E.D.Pa.1999, 237 B.R. 269.

When parties agree to apply foreign law, pursuant to which their contract to "lease" goods kept in Pennsylvania will be deemed a true "lease," despite fact that contract does not permit lessor to terminate agreement but affords him an option to purchase goods for nominal consideration, Pennsylvania law will not give effect to that choice. In re Eagle Enterprises, Inc., E.D.Pa.1999, 237 B.R. 269.

13. Security interest

Revised Pennsylvania statute defining term "security interest" seeks to correct shortcomings of its predecessor by focusing inquiry of lease/security interest analysis on economics of the transaction, rather than on intent of the parties. In re Kim, Bkrtcy.E.D.Pa.1999, 232 B.R. 324.

Whether, under Pennsylvania law, lease or security interest is created by a particular transaction is no longer within exclusive control of the parties and subject to possible manipulation through artful document drafting; rather, issue is to be determined by reference to uniform criteria set forth in revised statute defining term "security interest." In re Kim, Bkrtcy.E.D.Pa.1999, 232 B.R. 324.

In determining whether debtor's lease was a disguised security interest or a true lease under Pennsylvania law, bankruptcy court was required to consider entire "transaction" and was not constrained to look solely to documents signed by the parties which were designated "lease" or which made use of terms commonly found in leases, but could examine both parol and extrin-

4

Source: From *Purdon's Pennsylvania Consolidated Statutes Annotated, 2001 Cumulative Annual Pocket Part.*

Exhibit 12.15 West Digest Topics and their numerical designations

No.	Topic
1	Abandoned and Lost Property
2	Abatement and Revival
4	Abortion and Birth Control
5	Absentees
6	Abstracts of Title
7	Accession
8	Accord and Satisfaction
9	Account
10	Account, Action on
11	Account Stated
11a	Accountants
12	Acknowledgment
13	Action
14	Action on the Case
15	Adjoining Landowners
15a	Administrative Law and Procedure
16	Admiralty
17	Adoption
18	Adulteration
19	Adultery
20	Adverse Possession
21	Affidavits
23	Agriculture
24	Aliens
25	Alteration of Instruments
26	Ambassadors and Consuls
27	Amicus Curiae
28	Animals
29	Annuities
30	Appeal and Error
31	Appearance
33	Arbitration
34	Armed Services
35	Arrest
36	Arson
37	Assault and Battery
38	Assignments
40	Assistance, Writ of
41	Associations
42	Assumpsit, Action of
43	Asylums
44	Attachment
45	Attorney and Client
46	Attorney General
47	Auctions and Auctioneers
48	Audita Querela
48a	Automobiles
48b	Aviation
49	Bail
50	Bailment
51	Bankruptcy
52	Banks and Banking
54	Beneficial Associations
55	Bigamy
56	Bills and Notes
58	Bonds
59	Boundaries
60	Bounties
61	Breach of Marriage Promise
62	Breach of the Peace
63	Bribery
64	Bridges
65	Brokers
66	Building and Loan Associations
67	Burglary
68	Canals
69	Cancellation of Instruments
70	Carriers
71	Cemeteries
72	Census
73	Certiorari
74	Champerty and Maintenance
75	Charities
76	Chattel Mortgages
76a	Chemical Dependence
76h	Children Out-of-Wedlock
77	Citizens
78	Civil Rights
79	Clerks of Courts
80	Clubs
81	Colleges and Universities
82	Collision
83	Commerce
83h	Commodity Futures Trading Regulation
84	Common Lands
85	Common Law
88	Compounding Offenses
89	Compromise and Settlement
89a	Condominium
90	Confusion of Goods
91	Conspiracy
92	Constitutional Law
92b	Consumer Credit
92h	Consumer Protection
93	Contempt
95	Contracts
96	Contribution
97	Conversion
98	Convicts
99	Copyrights and Intellectual Property
100	Coroners
101	Corporations
102	Costs
103	Counterfeiting
104	Counties
105	Court Commissioners
106	Courts (see also Topic 170b Federal Courts)
107	Covenant, Action of
108	Covenants
108a	Credit Reporting Agencies
110	Criminal Law
111	Crops
113	Customs and Usages
114	Customs Duties
115	Damages
116	Dead Bodies
117	Death
117g	Debt, Action of
117t	Debtor and Creditor
118a	Declaratory Judgment
119	Dedication
120	Deeds
122a	Deposits and Escrows
123	Deposits in Court
124	Descent and Distribution
125	Detectives
126	Detinue
129	Disorderly Conduct
130	Disorderly House
131	District and Prosecuting Attorneys
132	District of Columbia
133	Disturbance of Public Assemblage
134	Divorce
135	Domicile
135h	Double Jeopardy
136	Dower and Curtesy
137	Drains
138	Drugs and Narcotics
141	Easements
142	Ejectment
143	Election of Remedies
144	Elections
145	Electricity
146	Embezzlement
148	Eminent Domain
148a	Employers' Liability
149	Entry, Writ of
150	Equity
151	Escape
152	Escheat
154	Estates in Property
156	Estoppel
157	Evidence
158	Exceptions, Bill of
159	Exchange of Property
160	Exchanges
161	Execution
162	Executors and Administrators
163	Exemptions
164	Explosives
165	Extortion and Threats
166	Extradition and Detainers
167	Factors
168	False Imprisonment
169	False Personation
170	False Pretenses
170a	Federal Civil Procedure
170b	Federal Courts
171	Fences
172	Ferries
174	Fines
175	Fires
176	Fish
177	Fixtures
178	Food
179	Forcible Entry and Detainer
180	Forfeitures
181	Forgery
183	Franchises
184	Fraud
185	Frauds, Statute of
186	Fraudulent Conveyances
187	Game
188	Gaming
189	Garnishment
190	Gas
191	Gifts
192	Good Will
193	Grand Jury
195	Guaranty
196	Guardian and Ward
197	Habeas Corpus
198	Hawkers and Peddlers
199	Health and Environment
200	Highways
201	Holidays
202	Homestead
203	Homicide
204	Hospitals
205	Husband and Wife
205h	Implied and Constructive Contracts
206	Improvements
207	Incest
208	Indemnity
209	Indians

(continued)

Exhibit 12.15 West Digest Topics and their numerical designations (*continued*)

No.	Topic
210	Indictment and Information
211	Infants
212	Injunction
213	Innkeepers
216	Inspection
217	Insurance
218	Insurrection and Sedition
219	Interest
220	Internal Revenue
221	International Law
222	Interpleader
223	Intoxicating Liquors
224	Joint Adventures
225	Joint-Stock Companies and Business Trusts
226	Joint Tenancy
227	Judges
228	Judgment
229	Judicial Sales
230	Jury
231	Justices of the Peace
232	Kidnapping
232a	Labor Relations
233	Landlord and Tenant
234	Larceny
235	Levees and Flood Control
236	Lewdness
237	Libel and Slander
238	Licenses
239	Liens
240	Life Estates
241	Limitation of Actions
242	Lis Pendens
245	Logs and Logging
246	Lost Instruments
247	Lotteries
248	Malicious Mischief
249	Malicious Prosecution
250	Mandamus
251	Manufactures
252	Maritime Liens
253	Marriage
255	Master and Servant
256	Mayhem
257	Mechanics' Liens
257a	Mental Health
258a	Military Justice
259	Militia
260	Mines and Minerals
265	Monopolies
266	Mortgages
267	Motions
268	Municipal Corporations
269	Names
270	Navigable Waters
271	Ne Exeat
272	Negligence
273	Neutrality Laws
274	Newspapers
275	New Trial
276	Notaries
277	Notice
278	Novation
279	Nuisance
280	Oath
281	Obscenity
282	Obstructing Justice
283	Officers and Public Employees
284	Pardon and Parole
285	Parent and Child
286	Parliamentary Law
287	Parties
288	Partition
289	Partnership
290	Party Walls
291	Patents
292	Paupers
294	Payment
295	Penalties
296	Pensions
297	Perjury
298	Perpetuities
299	Physicians and Surgeons
300	Pilots
302	Pleading
303	Pledges
304	Poisons
305	Possessory Warrant
306	Postal Service
307	Powers
307a	Pretrial Procedure
308	Principal and Agent
309	Principal and Surety
310	Prisons
311	Private Roads
313	Process
313a	Products Liability
314	Prohibition
315	Property
316	Prostitution
316a	Public Contracts
317	Public Lands
317a	Public Utilities
318	Quieting Title
319	Quo Warranto
319h	Racketeer Influenced and Corrupt Organizations
320	Railroads
321	Rape
322	Real Actions
323	Receivers
324	Receiving Stolen Goods
325	Recognizances
326	Records
327	Reference
328	Reformation of Instruments
330	Registers of Deeds
331	Release
332	Religious Societies
333	Remainders
334	Removal of Cases
335	Replevin
336	Reports
337	Rescue
338	Reversions
339	Review
340	Rewards
341	Riot
342	Robbery
343	Sales
344	Salvage
345	Schools
346	Scire Facias
347	Seals
348	Seamen
349	Searches and Seizures
349a	Secured Transactions
349b	Securities Regulation
350	Seduction
351	Sequestration
352	Set-Off and Counterclaim
353	Sheriffs and Constables
354	Shipping
355	Signatures
356	Slaves
356a	Social Security and Public Welfare
357	Sodomy
358	Specific Performance
359	Spendthrifts
360	States
361	Statutes
362	Steam
363	Stipulations
365	Submission of Controversy
366	Subrogation
367	Subscriptions
368	Suicide
369	Sunday
370	Supersedeas
371	Taxation
372	Telecommunications
373	Tenancy in Common
374	Tender
375	Territories
376	Theaters and Shows
378	Time
379	Torts
380	Towage
381	Towns
382	Trade Regulation
384	Treason
385	Treaties
386	Trespass
387	Trespass to Try Title
388	Trial
389	Trover and Conversion
390	Trusts
391	Turnpikes and Toll Roads
392	Undertakings
393	United States
394	United States Magistrates
395	United States Marshals
396	Unlawful Assembly
396a	Urban Railroads
398	Usury
399	Vagrancy
400	Vendor and Purchaser
401	Venue
402	War and National Emergency
403	Warehousemen
404	Waste
405	Waters and Water Courses
406	Weapons
407	Weights and Measures
408	Wharves
409	Wills
410	Witnesses
411	Woods and Forests
413	Workers' Compensation
414	Zoning and Planning
450	Merit Systems Protection (Merit Systems Protection Board Reporter)

Source: West Digest Topics. Reprinted with permission of Thomson/West Publishing.

systems perform that task slowly, if at all—and that is assuming the paralegal can figure out how the index has been developed to create the computer search term.

By contrast, for a narrow, fact-based question, or if the researcher already has a citation or case name to work from, computer-based research usually is the better approach. Success in research depends on recognizing the best tools for a specific problem and using them efficiently.

Knowing the legal terminology used in the indexes of the research materials is critical. As noted previously, publishers of legal materials do not always use the same words or legal terms to index the same rules of law. One publisher may use the term "infant" to identify people under the age of majority, whereas another publisher may index that group of people under "minor." Different online services may require the use of different sets of search terms when formulating a query.

Creating a List of Research Terms

The paralegal should create one list of words for online searches and a separate list for searches of traditional print sources. The list should be updated as the paralegal performs research, adding or deleting words and phrases and annotating the list with citations for future research. The word list should be developed from the facts of the question, the parties, the locations, the case-specific goods and services, their status, or the relationships among them.

Consider the case of the off-duty police officer who had just come from a doctor's visit where he had been given a medication to reduce his blood pressure. He was involved in a rear-end collision with a van of schoolchildren returning from selling candy at a fundraiser. The driver of the van was one of the children's mothers, and was also a teacher at the school. A skateboarder darted in front of one of the vehicles, resulting in the collision. The checklist Research Plan: Words and Phrases is a good way to put together a list of the words and phrases to be searched.

What are some of the words and terms with which to start researching the issue of liability? As with most cases, each person has multiple roles or statuses that must be considered: teacher, parent, driver, police officer, student, child, principal, agent of school, agent of other parents, or patient. Further, the situation may have been caused by any of a number of factors—road conditions, weather, time of day, speed, medical issues, carelessness, and/or distractions. Also to be considered are the vehicles' braking abilities, possible manufacturing defects, and airbag deployment issues.

Obviously, not every issue comes into play in every case. Before starting the research, the researcher must identify the relevant terms that apply to the case being researched. The time spent creating the list will save time chasing dead ends or irrelevant issues. In creating the word list, the researcher should think of words, legal terms, and phrases, and consider alternatives to those words—synonyms, antonyms, and related terms. Appropriate language may be found using secondary sources and finding tools such as legal dictionaries, encyclopedias, and treatises.

Computer Research Providers

The three primary full-service online providers of computer research services—LexisNexis, Loislaw, and WestlawNext—provide a broad range of legal materials, including cases, statutes, and regulations. In addition, there are limited-service search providers that specialize in providing cases and limited access to additional items, such as the Code of Federal Regulations.

In using a limited-service provider, it is important to check the coverage dates and content. In some cases, the same information is available from other sources, such as the United States Code and the Code of Federal Regulations, which are available online through the GPO Access website. In all cases, researchers must be certain that they have checked for all the latest update sources.

CHECKLIST Research Plan: Words and Phrases

Concepts and Issues	Generic Words and Phrases	Text-Based Research Terms	Computer-Based Research Terms
Persons Status Relationship Occupation Group Class			
Item(s) Involved			
Location(s)			
Subject Matter			
Jurisdiction Federal State City Locality			
Cause of Action Tort Contract Family Law Commercial			
Relief Sought Injunction Damages Compensatory Punitive Mandamus			
Defenses			

Search Method and Query

Each of the online providers uses words to find and retrieve documents. As part of the publication process, indexes are prepared of every word in the document, and the words are tabulated for frequency. The query the researcher creates will be used by the service to search this index. VersusLaw uses a full-text retrieval method that searches every word except "stop words"—words that are used too commonly in documents to be used in a search, such as "the," "not," "of," and "and."

Creating the Query

When you conduct a search, you are asking the search engine to find the indexed words you have chosen. These may be legal specialty words or common English words. Single words may be in any of the Internet or legal search engines. Frequently you will be looking for more detailed information. Using combinations of words in the search can narrow the search results. Usually, the most productive search contains a combination of words, which may consist of multiple-word terms and phrases, such as "strict liability," "legal malpractice," "automobile accident," or "reckless indifference."

Using Connectors

Connectors Instructions in a search query on how to treat the words in the query.

Connectors are words that tell the search engine to look for documents containing combinations of words. Connectors may be thought of as instructions to the search engine, such as "Find me documents in which the words 'strict' AND 'liability' appear." The word AND is a connector that instructs the search engine to return only the documents in which *both* of the words are found. Exhibit 12.16 shows a Loislaw search with the AND connector.

The connector OR instructs the search engine to retrieve those documents that have *either* term—the word "strict" OR the word "liability." Exhibit 12.17 depicts a LexisNexis search with the OR connector.

Exhibit 12.16 Loislaw search with AND connector

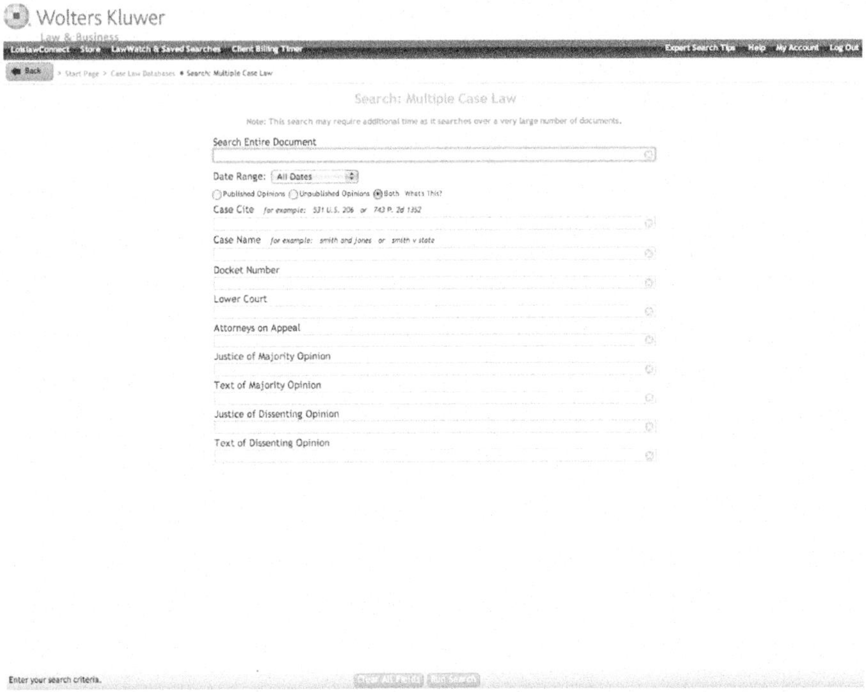

Wolters Kluwer
Law & Business

Search: Multiple Case Law

Search Entire Document

Date Range: All Dates

Case Cite

Case Name

Docket Number

Lower Court

Attorneys on Appeal

Justice of Majority Opinion

Text of Majority Opinion

Justice of Dissenting Opinion

Text of Dissenting Opinion

Enter your search criteria.

Source: Reproduced with permission of Aspen Publishers, Loislaw screen shot.

Exhibit 12.17 LexisNexis search with OR connector

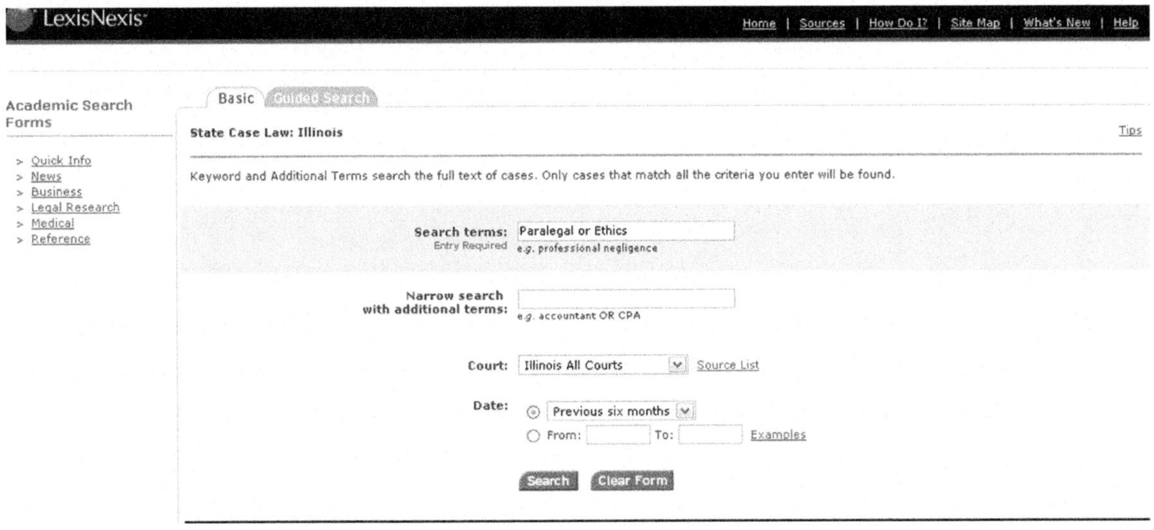

Source: Copyright 2009 LexisNexis, a division of Reed Elsevier Inc. All Rights Reserved. LexisNexis and the Knowledge Burst logo are registered trademarks of Reed Elsevier Properties Inc. and are used with the permission of LexisNexis.

The NOT connector instructs the search engine to eliminate certain words. For example, you may wish to review documents in which the word "malpractice" is found, but *not* documents with the word "medical."

In some cases, it might be assumed that there will be other words between the desired terms, such as in the phrase "Paralegals are bound by the ethics of their profession." The NEAR connector helps to locate documents where the terms are near each other—for example: "Find 'paralegal' NEAR 'ethics.'" The NEAR connector allows the paralegal to search for words near each other by specifying the maximum number of words apart.

Exhibit 12.18 gives a comparison of these concepts in VersusLaw, and Exhibit 12.19 provides a guide to connectors for Westlaw.

Exhibit 12.18 Comparison grid from VersusLaw

VersusLaw	LEXIS	Westlaw
Connectors		
and	and	and, &
or	or	or, *space*
not	and not	but not, %
Proximity operators		
w/n	w/n	w/n, /n
w/n	pre/n	pre/n, +n
Exact phrase match		
unlawful entry	unlawful entry	"unlawful entry"
Wild Cards - end of root words		
*	!	!
Wild Cards - single character		
?	*	*
Order of operators		
proximity operators, not, and, or	or, *proximity operators*, and, and not	or, *proximity operators*, and, but not

Source: © Copyright 2009 VersusLaw, Inc. Redmond, WA, USA. All rights reserved. www.versuslaw.com.

Exhibit 12.19 Westlaw guide to connectors

USING CONNECTORS

Connector	You type	Westlaw retrieves documents
AND	&	containing both search terms: **workplace & safety**
OR	a space	containing either search term or both search terms: **landlord lessor**
Grammatical Connectors	/p	containing search terms in the same paragraph: **warrant! /p habitat!**
	/s	containing search terms in the same sentence: **danger! /s defect!**
	+s	in which the first term precedes the second within the same sentence: **capital +s gain**
Numerical Connectors	/n (where *n* is a number)	containing search terms with *n* terms of each other: **issues /5 fact**
	+n (where *n* is a number)	in which the first term precedes the second by *n* terms: **20 + 5 1080**
BUT NOT	%	not containing the term or terms following the percent symbol (%): **tax taxation % tax taxation/3 income**

Source: Reproduced with permission from West Group.

Search Engines

Great advances have been made in computer search methods. It is no longer necessary to know the exact word or phrase to be able to find the desired information in a computer database. Boolean searches with words and connectors are being supplemented with advanced search engines that can conduct searches using phrases or sentences, sometimes referred to as "natural language" searches. For example, a query may ask, "What is the statute of limitations for a person injured as a result of a defective brake part in an automobile?"

Modern search engines can also automatically substitute words that are conceptually similar. When "automobile" is used in a search query, the search engine also searches using words such as "vehicle," "motor vehicle," "truck," "bus," and other similar terms. This is referred to as a "conceptual search." Still other search engines automatically search for the singular or plural and may even search for similar terms in other languages.

Updating Legal Research

LEARNING OBJECTIVE 4
Explain the need for, and the methods of, updating legal research.

The legal team must always use the most current statutory and case law in advising clients and arguing cases before the court. The ethical rules of the legal profession require candor to the court, which in turn demands that the latest information be provided to the court. One of the features of the American legal system is its constant change. Courts attempt to meet the needs of a changing society by reviewing prior case law and, when appropriate, overruling or modifying it as the contemporary American view of justice dictates. The American legal system's concept of ***stare decisis*** provides that we use prior case law as **precedent**, but the law may be adapted to new situations or changed as American society changes. Occasionally, existing case law may be held unconstitutional, as in the landmark case of *Roe v. Wade*, 410 U.S. 113 (1973).

Stare decisis The legal principle that prior case law should apply unless there is a substantial change in society necessitating a change in the case law.

Precedent Prior case law that is controlling.

Knowing whether the case law being used in a legal argument is current is a vital part of the lawyer's obligation to the client and to the court. Up to the moment before the arguments are made to the court or the brief is submitted, a case that the attorney or the opponent is using as a basis for a legal argument may be overturned. The ethical obligation of candor (see the Ethical Perspective on the following page) requires the use of most current case law.

For paralegals, an essential part of legal research is verifying that they have the latest case or statute. The process is complicated by the method by which changes in statutes or case law are released to the public. Ultimately, new statutes and new case law are reported in a published form, both in paper and online, but not all publications are able to disseminate the information daily. Paper versions take time to print and distribute. Not all electronic versions are posted immediately. Therefore, it becomes important to know how quickly the reporting services used by the law firm distribute new cases or changes in statutes. More and more courts have their own websites and release case opinions electronically, along with the print versions, to the public and publishing companies. For example, you can check decisions of the U.S. Supreme Court daily by accessing its website.

The greatest difficulty is in knowing whether the cases or statutes have affected the case being researched. When the court specifically mentions a case being cited in a memorandum of law or a court brief, the paralegal has to know if the new case follows, reverses, or in some way differs from the older case.

As soon as a case is entered into an electronic case law database, such as WestlawNext, LexisNexis, Loislaw, or VersusLaw, a general search can be made for references to the case name or citation. Before the case is entered, however, the same search will not show the newest reference. Even a reference to the case will not indicate whether the case law has changed. It will only indicate that another case has referred to it. Someone must actually read the case to see how the court has used it or referred to it in the opinion.

ETHICAL PERSPECTIVE

Idaho Rules of Professional Conduct

RULE 3.3 CANDOR TOWARD THE TRIBUNAL

(a) A lawyer shall not knowingly:

(1) make a false statement of fact or law to a tribunal or fail to correct a false statement of material fact or law previously made to the tribunal by the lawyer;

(2) fail to disclose to the tribunal legal authority in the controlling jurisdiction known to the lawyer to be directly adverse to the position of the client and not disclosed by opposing counsel; or

(3) offer evidence that the lawyer knows to be false. If a lawyer, the lawyer's client, or a witness called by the lawyer, has offered material evidence and the lawyer comes to know of its falsity, the lawyer shall take reasonable remedial measures, including, if necessary, disclosure to the tribunal. A lawyer may refuse to offer evidence, other than the testimony of a defendant in a criminal matter, that the lawyer reasonably believes is false.

(b) A lawyer who represents a client in an adjudicative proceeding and who knows that a person intends to engage, is engaging or has engaged in criminal or fraudulent conduct related to the proceeding shall take reasonable remedial measures, including, if necessary, disclosure to the tribunal.

(c) The duties stated in paragraphs (a) and (b) continue to the conclusion of the proceeding, and apply even if compliance requires disclosure of information otherwise protected by Rule 1.6.

(d) In an ex parte proceeding, a lawyer shall inform the tribunal of all material facts known to the lawyer that will enable the tribunal to make an informed decision, whether or not the facts are adverse.

Web Exploration

Contrast and compare the Idaho rule at http://isb.idaho.gov/pdf/rules/irpc.pdf with the ABA Model Rules of Professional Conduct at www.abanet.org/cpr and the rule in your jurisdiction.

Shepard's

Shepard's Citations is a multivolume set of books listing cases and statutes by their respective citations and giving the citation of every other case in which the listed case was mentioned. *Shepard's* has long been a standard tool of legal research in law libraries. The listings were originally compiled by editors who physically read through every reported case to find citations. These were then reported by case citation, with every other mention of the case reported by its citation in chronological fashion, and notations indicating whether the opinion was reversed, affirmed, followed, overruled, or distinguished. The process of using *Shepard's* to check legal citations came to be called "Shepardizing"—a term that many legal assistants still use, even when using other citation-checking services such as Westlaw's KeyCite. An advantage to using the *Shepard's Citator* is the editorial symbol system, which indicates how the new case affects the case being checked, as shown in Exhibit 12.20.

The problem with the traditional paper form of *Shepard's* was the lag in time for the print version to be prepared and sent out to subscribers. *Shepard's* now provides the same service online through the LexisNexis service. One of the difficulties in using the print version of *Shepard's* is the number of hardbound volumes and paperback updates needing to be consulted, and finding the latest update pamphlet if someone has misfiled it in the law library. Exhibit 12.21 is an example of the print version for cases in *Shepard's*.

Many educational institutions and public libraries subscribe to the Web-based LexisNexis Academic Universe. *Shepard's* citation service (shown in Exhibit 12.22) is usually available for the U.S. Supreme Court as part of the service, but other federal and state *Shepard's* citation services may not be included because of the additional license fees involved.

Exhibit 12.20 ***Shepard's* symbols showing effects of new cases**

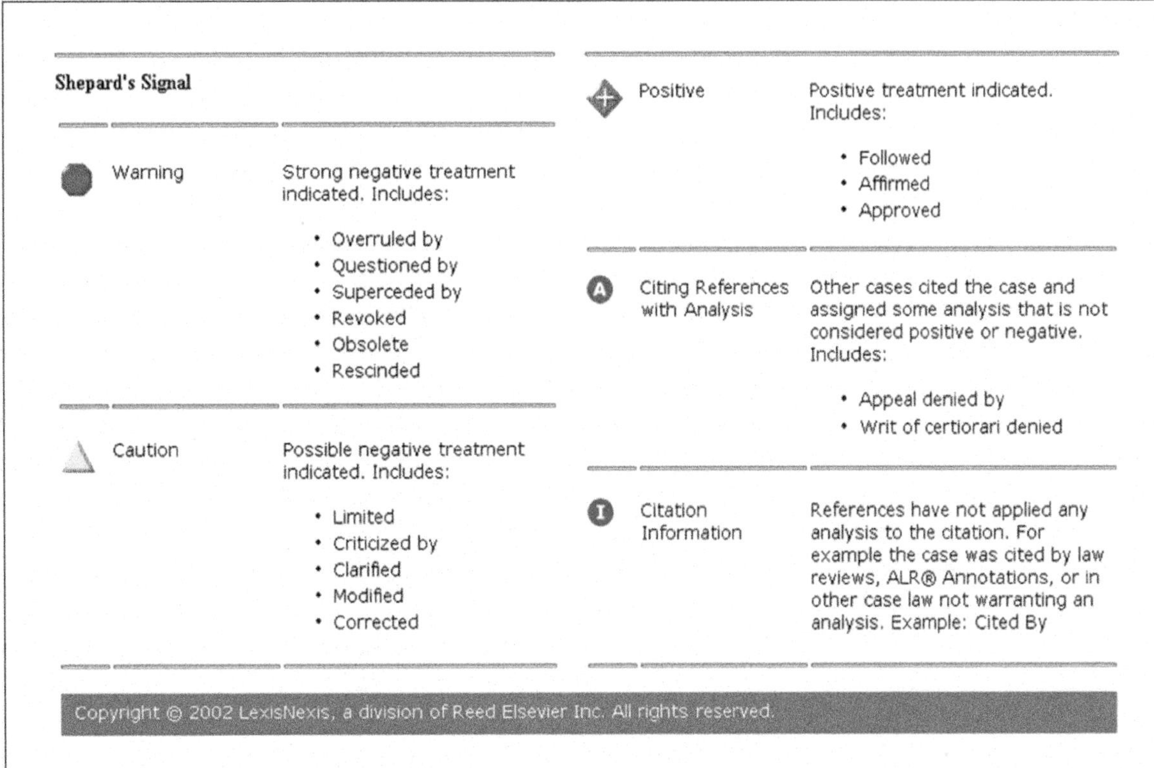

Shepard's Signal

Signal		Description
Warning		Strong negative treatment indicated. Includes: • Overruled by • Questioned by • Superceded by • Revoked • Obsolete • Rescinded
Caution		Possible negative treatment indicated. Includes: • Limited • Criticized by • Clarified • Modified • Corrected
Positive		Positive treatment indicated. Includes: • Followed • Affirmed • Approved
A	Citing References with Analysis	Other cases cited the case and assigned some analysis that is not considered positive or negative. Includes: • Appeal denied by • Writ of certiorari denied
I	Citation Information	References have not applied any analysis to the citation. For example the case was cited by law reviews, ALR® Annotations, or in other case law not warranting an analysis. Example: Cited By

Source: Copyright 2009 LexisNexis, a division of Reed Elsevier Inc. All Rights Reserved. LexisNexis and the Knowledge Burst logo are registered trademarks of Reed Elsevier Properties, Inc. and are used with the permission of LexisNexis.

GlobalCite™

Loislaw's **GlobalCite** provides a reverse chronological list of the case law, the statutes ordered by number of citation occurrences, the regulations listed in order of relevancy, and references to other databases in the Loislaw library. Exhibit 12.23 shows a GlobalCite screen.

Web Exploration

Read about *Shepard's Citations* in the How to Shepardize at http://www.lexisnexis.com/shepards-citations/printsupport/shepardize_print.pdf.

GlobalCite Loislaw's tool for searching cases containing references to another case.

KeyCite™

KeyCite is the Westlaw online citation update service. The Westlaw KeyCite is a combination citator and case finder. Unlike other similar services, KeyCite uses the West Key number system and West Headnotes.

KeyCite Westlaw's tool for searching cases containing references to another case.

V. Cite™

V. Cite, VersusLaw's citation tool, will produce a list of all cases within the selected jurisdictions that have cited the case being searched. The list that a V. Cite search produces will include cases that have cited the initial case, which most likely will discuss similar issues. An additional V. Cite feature allows one to append a specific term to the search request. For example, including the word "damages" in the "additional query information" section of the V. Cite form will restrict the search to cases that cite the searched case and also discuss "damages."

V. Cite VersusLaw's tool for searching cases containing references to another case.

Exhibit 12.21 Example of print version case presentation in *Shepard's*

—157—	**—558—**	**—558—**
Oregon v Plowman 1992	**Oregon v Plowman 1992**	**Oregon v Plowman 1992**
(838P2d558)	(314Ore157)	(314Ore157)
s 107OrA782	s 813P2d1114	s 813P2d1114
cc 314Ore170	cc 813P2d1115	cc 813P2d1115
e 315Ore375	cc 838P2d566	cc 838P2d566
315Ore380	840P2d1324	840P2d1324
317Ore⁴258	e 840P2d1325	e 840P2d1325
317Ore451	841P2d650	841P2d650
f 317Ore452	e 845P2d1285	e 845P2d1285
j 317Ore472	845P2d1289	845P2d1289
f 318Ore488	j 851P2d1147	j 851P2d1147
318Ore492	j 852P2d888	j 852P2d888
d 318Ore497	854P2d959	854P2d959
116OrA189	855P2d⁴625	855P2d⁴625
e 116OrA192	857P2d107	Calif
h 116OrA265	f 857P2d108	17CaR2d296
j 119OrA303	j 857P2d119	e 19CaR2d448
j 120OrA333	f 871P2d458	e 19CaR2d449
121OrA384	871P2d461	Iowa
j 128OrA14	d 871P2d463	500N W 42
71OLR689	j 874P2d1348	
22A5268n		
Shepard's Oregon Citations, *Oregon Reports division, shows citations from:* • *state reports* • Oregon Law Review • *annotations (ALR® 5th)*	Shepard's Oregon Citations, *Oregon Cases division, shows citations from Oregon as published in the* Pacific Reporter.	Shepard's Pacific Reporter Citations, *P.2d division, shows citations from all cases published in a West regional reporter.*

Parallel Citations

Parallel citation Citation to the same case in a different publication.

Most cases are reported in more than one service or set of books. A **parallel citation** is a cite to the same material, usually a case, in another source. Frequently a state will have an official publication, such as the court's own publication, and a private publication, such as the *West Reporter*. In some cases, *West* was, and is, the official reporter, and there may not be a parallel print source. One of the many uses of *Shepard's* is to find parallel citations to other locations for the same case.

Shepard's also provides updated information on statutory citations. Amendments to and repeals of statutory information are listed in *Shepard's*. Citations to any cases in which the statute has been cited are also listed, with information on how the case law considered the statute.

Exhibit 12.22 LexisNexis Total *Shepard's*® Table of Authorities

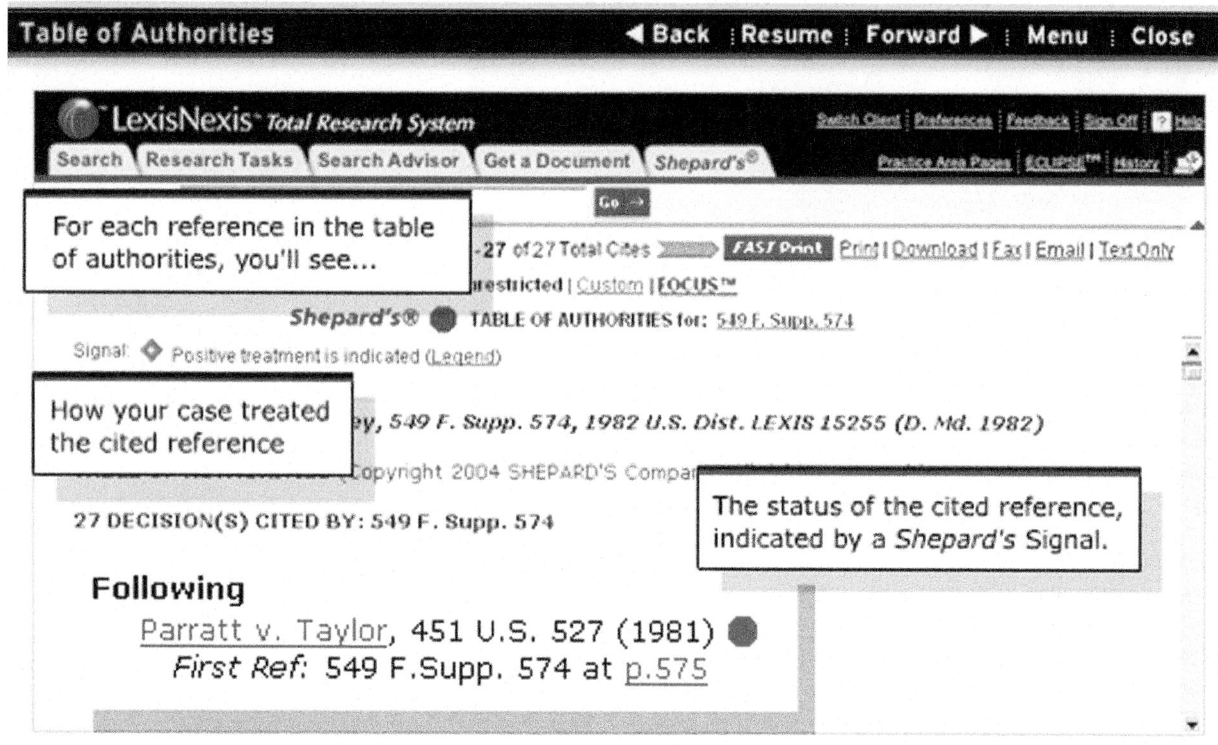

Source: Copyright 2009 LexisNexis, a division of Reed Elsevier Inc. All Rights Reserved. LexisNexis and the Knowledge Burst logo are registered trademarks of Reed Elsevier Properties, Inc. and are used with the permission of LexisNexis.

Exhibit 12.23 GlobalCite screen

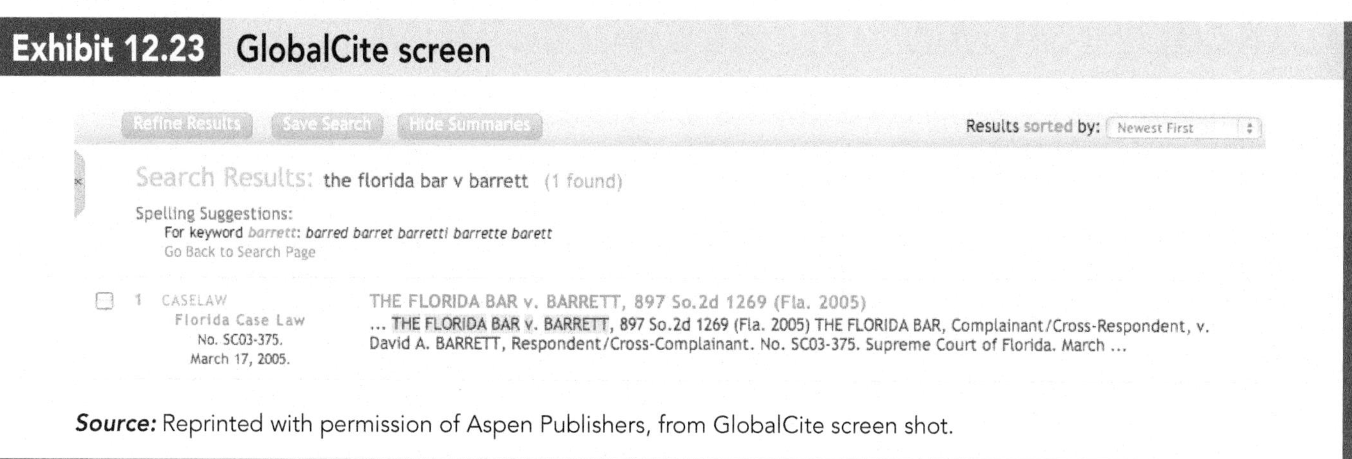

Source: Reprinted with permission of Aspen Publishers, from GlobalCite screen shot.

CHECKLIST Research Search Items

- ☐ Client:
- ☐ Issue:
- ☐ Search terms and phrases:
- ☐ Search combinations used:
- ☐ Date:

CHECKLIST Research Sources Checked

Checked Source	Citation	Update Service Checked	Web Location
Primary Sources			
	State statute		www.
	USC		www.
	USCA		www.
	CFR		www.
	Local ordinance		www.
			www.
Secondary Sources			
	State digest		www.
	Federal digest		www.
	ALR		www.
			www.
	Encyclopedia		www.
	State		www.
	C.J.S.		www.
	Periodicals		www.
	Treatises		www.

Concept Review *and* Reinforcement

LEGAL TERMINOLOGY

Amicus curiae 473
Bench opinion 465
Bicameral 462
Case syllabus 465
Citator 473
Connectors 482
Dicta 466
Finding tools 461
GlobalCite 487
Headnotes 465
Holding 466
Judicial branch 462
KeyCite 487
Legal research 457
Legislative branch 462
Mandatory authority 463
Parallel citation 488
Persuasive authority 465
Pocket parts 477
Precedent 485
Primary source of law 461
Published opinion 464
Relevant facts 458
Search query 459
Secondary source of law 461
Slip opinion 465
Stare decisis 485
Unpublished opinions 464
V. Cite 487

SUMMARY OF KEY CONCEPTS

Legal Research

Legal research is the process of finding the answer to a legal question.

Creating a Research Plan

The research plan helps to focus on the issues, sources, and methods for finding the answer to a legal question and the controlling law.

What Is the Issue or Legal Question?	After clarifying the question being asked, the next step is to determine the relevant facts based on the applicable law.
What Is the Appropriate Search Terminology?	Print research materials require finding material based on a printed index of individual words as selected by editors of the service. Computer research allows for searches of words found in the documents using a text search of requested words in the search query.
What Type of Research Material Is Available?	The paralegal must be able to find the information needed when the familiar resources are not available. Because paralegals cannot always be sure whether the research can be done using a traditional paper library or a computer search, they must understand how to use each system.
What Jurisdictions Are Involved?	Focusing on a single jurisdiction or a minimum number of jurisdictions reduces the number of books necessary and saves online computer search time.
What Is the Controlling Law?	Knowing which set of materials to use, the statutes of the jurisdiction, the regulation of a given administrative agency, or the courts of a given jurisdiction will save time in doing the research.
What Types of Resources Should Be Used?	1. Primary sources of law are used in preparing the legal memo or brief. 2. Secondary sources are useful, efficient ways to get an overview of an area of law or learn the terminology of a particular field that the paralegal is not familiar with. 3. Finding tools are publications for finding both primary and secondary sources.
Where Is the Needed Research Material Located?	The needed material may have to be located at a remote library such as a bar association library or a law school library.
Creating a List of Research Terms	Separate lists should be created for online searches and traditional print source searches.
Executing the Research Plan	As with the execution of any plan, detours should be expected, as the law is constantly evolving. New statutes are enacted, and new judicial opinions are handed down. During the research process, the researcher must look for changes and potential changes in pending legislation and cases on appeal.

Finding the Law

The Controlling Law	The controlling law may be found at federal, state, or local legislative or judicial levels.
Primary Sources and Authority	Primary sources include the law—constitutions, statutes, regulations, court rules, and case decisions.
Mandatory and Persuasive Authority	1. Mandatory authority is legal authority that the courts must follow. 2. Persuasive authority is legal authority the courts are not required to follow but is from a respected source and is well reasoned.
Constitutions	Constitutions are primary sources that set the guidelines, limits, and authority of the federal and state governments.
Statutes	Statutes are enacted by the legislative branch of government.
Court Decisions	The actual court language is a primary source of the law. The syllabus, summaries, interpretations, or abstracts of the points of law presented by the editorial staffs of the publishers—usually called headnotes—are *not* a primary source of law.

Secondary Sources	Secondary sources explain the law. 1. Legal dictionaries, as opposed to general English or other specialized dictionaries, define words and phrases as used in the law. 2. Legal encyclopedias provide the background to understand the area sufficiently to start the research. They provide an overview of the concepts and history of an area of law, the legal issues involved, and the terminology. 3. Treatises, law reviews, and legal periodicals are authoritative or of sufficient scholarly value to be persuasive to the court.
Finding Tools	Finding tools help to "find" the law. 1. Digests provide lists of cases in a subject topic format, with cases generally in chronological order. 2. Indexes and citators cross-reference material such as by the commonly used or popular name of a case or statute.
Personal Research Strategy	
	Over time, each paralegal develops a personal search strategy based on the nature of the problem or issue to be researched and the resources available.
	A personal research strategy includes methods of verifying that the law cited in the memorandum of law is current law, and methods for looking for pending cases and legislation that might change the answer to the legal question.
A Final Word on Executing the Legal Research Plan	
	Know when to ask for help.
Using Printed Legal Reference Works	
Common Features	• Table of abbreviations • Table of contents in the front • Index of terms in the back • Table of cases and citations
Updates	Print material is frequently updated with pocket parts, usually issued annually and slipped into the back of the volume in a pocket. Paperback supplements are issued annually, semi-annually, quarterly, or monthly. Online updates from the publishers are increasingly available for some materials.
Constructing a Computer Search Query	
Creating a List of Research Terms	A query is a combination of words, phrases, and connectors used to search for an answer.
Search Method and Query	Each online provider uses words to find and retrieve documents. As part of the publication process, indexes are prepared of every word in the document, the words are tabulated for frequency, and a word index is prepared. The query is used to search this index.
Creating the Query	The search engine is used to find the indexed words the paralegal has chosen; they may be legal specialty words or common English words. Using combinations of words in the search can narrow the search results.
Using Connectors	AND instructs the search to return documents in which two words are found.
	OR instructs the search engine to find documents that contain either of two terms.
	NEAR may be used to find the occurrence of desired words within a set number of words of each other.
Updating Legal Research	
	1. *Shepard's*: A multivolume set of books listing cases and statutes by their respective citations and giving the citation of every other case in which the listed case was mentioned; checking citations is often called "Shepardizing."

2. GlobalCite (Loislaw): Provides a reverse chronological list of the case law, a list of statutes in the order of the highest number of citation occurrences, regulations in relevancy order, and reference to other databases in the Loislaw library.
3. KeyCite (Westlaw): An online citation update service.
4. V. Cite (VersusLaw): An online citation tool.

Parallel Citation	
	A citation to the same material, usually a case, in another source.
Statutory Law Updates	*Shepard's* provides updated information on amendments and repeals of statutory information. Citations to any cases in which the statute has been cited are also listed, with information on how the case law considered the statute.

WORKING THE WEB

1. Use the Government Printing Office website (www.gpoaccess.gov) to find and print out the summary and purpose of 21 CFR 404, or any other section assigned by your instructor.
2. Make a list of the federal primary sources available on the Government Printing Office website.
3. From the sitemap of the VersusLaw website, http://www.versuslaw.com/features/sitemap.htm, print out for your future computer searches the printable version of the *VersusLaw Research Manual.*
4. Use the Legal Information Institute at the Cornell University website (http://www.law.cornell.edu) to find title 44 C.F.R. 201 and print out the list of key responsibilities of FEMA and state and local/tribal governments. Does this site provide direct access or a link to another source? Explain. What primary federal sources does this site offer?
5. Conduct a search for information on paralegal ethics using two different search engines, and print out a copy of the first page of each result. Are they the same? What is the difference in results and order of presentation? Possible search engines include: Google, www.google.com; Yahoo!, www.yahoo.com; Ask, www.ask.com; and Findlaw, www.findlaw.com.
6. If you have access to Loislaw, LexisNexis, Westlaw, or VersusLaw, conduct a search for paralegal ethics cases for your jurisdiction. Prepare a list of authorities cited in the search.
7. Print out the current list of opinions of the U.S. Supreme Court at http://www.supremecourt.gov.
8. Print out the complete version of Rule 3.3, Candor Toward the Tribunal, of the ABA Model Rules of Professional Conduct, at http://www.abanet.org/cpr/mrpc/mrpc_toc.html.
9. Under the theory of *stare decisis*, on which courts would the decisions of a court have a binding effect? Would a decision in a case be binding on future cases if the decision were available only in the clerk's office?
10. Would your answer be the same if the decision were available in the clerk's office at first but then available in printed form or online at a later date? When would the decision become effective as precedent?
11. Where is the "law" found?
12. Who makes the "law" under the United States legal system?
13. What is meant by a "bicameral" legislature?
14. In legal research, what is meant by "primary source"?
15. What is a "treatise"? Is it a primary source? Explain.
16. What is a headnote in legal research? Is it a primary source? Explain.
17. What are dicta? What are their effect on other courts? Explain.
18. What weight do courts give secondary sources? Explain fully.
19. Why are finding tools important to the legal researcher? Give an example of how a finding tool might be used.
20. Do unpublished opinions have precedential effect? Explain.

CRITICAL THINKING & WRITING QUESTIONS

1. Using the facts in the *Palsgraf* case in Appendix A, prepare a search query using connectors to locate the law or a similar case in your jurisdiction. Run the search using an online legal research service, if available.
2. Why does a paralegal have to be familiar with both traditional and electronic research tools and methods?

3. Why does the paralegal have to know how quickly changes in statutory and case law are updated by online and traditional primary and secondary sources?
4. Why is knowledge of the underlying law in an area important in constructing a question for online research?
5. How can a researcher be certain that a case that seems to be on point is still the current case law?
6. Why should secondary sources not be relied upon in citing binding authority?
7. Why would a researcher use a traditional paper resource before using an online research tool?
8. How does the use of connectors help in conducting online research? Give an example.
9. Why might an identical search query return different results?
10. Why must researchers clearly understand the question they are being asked to research? How can they be certain they do?

Building Paralegal Skills

VIDEO CASE STUDIES

Legal Research: Are Books Obsolete?

In the middle of a trial, a trial attorney sends his paralegal to the courthouse law library to find a case that has been cited as precedent by opposing counsel in oral argument. Without a valid password, the paralegal is advised to use traditional "paper" research methods.

After viewing the video case study at the book website at www.pearsonhighered.com/careersresources, answer the following:

1. What are the differences between using books and using electronic legal research?
2. Are traditional paper-based reference materials as current as electronic reference sources?
3. Are there any differences among the different legal research services such as LexisNexis, Westlaw, Loislaw, or VersusLaw?

Fees and Billing Issue: Using Time Effectively

A paralegal has responded to the request of her supervising attorney for information on a question of law. After spending considerable time, she is helped by another paralegal, who quickly provides the information she is looking for. However, she also finds out that her supervising attorney was merely "curious," and there was no client to bill for the research time.

After viewing the video case study at the book website at www.pearsonhighered.com/careersresources, answer the following:

1. What questions should a paralegal ask before commencing the research?
2. At what point should the paralegal ask for help, and from whom should the help be sought?
3. Is there any value in doing legal research when there is no specific client or case to which it will apply?

ETHICS ANALYSIS & DISCUSSION QUESTIONS

1. Is there an ethical obligation under the Model Rules to perform legal research competently? Explain.
2. What is the ethical obligation under the Model Rules to provide the court with legal authority that is not favorable to your client's legal position?
3. What is the ethical obligation to "Shepardize" cases and statutes before submitting a brief or memorandum of law to the court?

For answers, look at American Bar Association Rule 3.3, Candor Toward the Tribunal, and Rule 1.1, Competence (ABA Model Rules of Professional Conduct, 2002).

Confidentiality

There are few certainties in the area of ethics, for paralegals or in any profession. What qualifies as ethical conduct is in most cases based on state law and court interpretation applied to a set of facts. The citation listed below represents one legal opinion and is provided as a research starting point. Do not assume that the same rule applies in your jurisdiction. For the following:

- Prepare a written statement based on your state law.
- Use your state bar association website as a starting point.

You are waiting for a fax needed for a case on which you are working. While you are standing by the fax machine, a fax comes in from an attorney at an opposing firm containing a letter about settlement that was clearly intended for the attorney's client and not for opposing counsel. It was sent by your best friend, the paralegal who is working on that case at the opposing firm. She is stressed out by the case and made the mistake of dialing your fax number rather than the client's. From your reading of the letter, it appears the information would greatly help your law office win the case. See *State Compensation Insurance Fund v. The WPS, Inc.*, 70 Cal.App. 4th 644 (1999).

Do you quietly return the fax to your friend and say nothing to anyone? Do you read it carefully to be sure of the contents? Do you return it to opposing counsel? Do you tell your supervising attorney about the letter, and describe its contents?

DEVELOPING YOUR COLLABORATION SKILLS

Working on your own or with a group of other students assigned by your instructor, review the scenario at the beginning of the chapter and discuss the different views on law libraries, including traditional versus computer legal research.

1. Write a summary of the potential advantages and disadvantages of each point of view.
2. Prepare a report to the executive committee considering the different views of members of the firm with a solution that might satisfy most users of the firm's library.
3. The group should divide into two teams. One team will conduct a research assignment using traditional methods and the other will conduct the assignment using computer research tools.
    a. Each team is to complete the checklist Research Sources Checked, and prepare a copy for the members of the other team and your instructor.
    b. After you have completed the research, prepare a short memorandum of law to submit to your instructor.
4. Complete a second research project, with each team now using the other approach to research. The traditional methods team now will use computer tools, and the computer tools team will conduct the research using traditional tools. Prepare a short memorandum and complete the checklist Research Sources Checked.
5. Based on your experience doing traditional and computer research, what recommendations would you make to the managing partner in the opening scenario?

PARALEGAL PORTFOLIO EXERCISE

Complete the "Web Location" section of the checklist Research Sources Checked. When preparing the list, include alternative sources where available. Print a copy for your portfolio for future use and a copy for your instructor.

LEGAL ANALYSIS & WRITING CASES

Copying of Material for Future Research and Law Library Archives from Copyrighted Magazines and Journals

American Geophysical Union v. Texaco Inc., 37 F.3d 881 (2d Cir. 1994)

Most researchers understand that misuse of copyrighted material may subject them to liability under the copyright laws. The case of *American Geophysical Union v. Texaco* illustrates the potential liability in regularly copying copyrighted articles for personal archives. Researchers at Texaco regularly made copies of articles for future reference from the works of the plaintiff and 82 other publishers of scientific and technical journals. Texaco raised the defense of "fair use" as permitted under the copyright law.

Fair use as a defense depends on four tests: (1) the purpose and character of the use—including whether for nonprofit educational purposes or commercial use; (2) the nature of copyright work—the law generally recognizes a greater need to disseminate factual works than works of fiction or fantasy; (3) amount and substantiality of portion used—whether the quantity used was reasonable in relation to the purpose of the copying; and (4) the effect on potential market or value—will the copying have an impact on the sale of the works, and is there an efficient mechanism for the licensing of the works?

Questions

1. How does copyright law apply to a student copying copyrighted materials while doing research for a class project?
2. Would the answer be the same if the student were doing the research as part of an assignment while working in a law office?
3. Does it matter whether the work copied is a court case or an article by an expert in automobile airbags liability? Why?

WORKING WITH THE LANGUAGE OF THE COURT CASE

Hart v. Massanari, 266 F.3d 1155 (9th Cir. 2001)

United States Court of Appeals, Ninth Circuit

Read and brief this case. In your brief, answer the following questions:

1. Why are unpublished decisions of courts not valid as precedent in future cases?
2. What is the difference between controlling authority and persuasive authority?
3. How might an unpublished opinion be used in this case?
4. Has the adoption of Rule 32.1 changed the effect of this case?
5. Why does this court believe it is important, in writing an opinion of the court, to recite all the relevant facts?
6. What is the effect of binding precedent on other courts?

Kozinski, Circuit Judge

Appellant's . . . brief cites . . . an unpublished disposition, not reported in the *Federal Reporter*. . . . The full text . . . is marked with the following notice: "This disposition is not appropriate for publication and may not be cited to or by the courts of this circuit. . . . Unpublished dispositions and orders of this Court are not binding precedent . . . [and generally] may not be cited to or by the courts of this circuit." . . . [9th Cir.R.36-3.]

We ordered counsel to show cause as to why he should not be disciplined for violating Ninth Circuit Rule 36-3. Counsel responds by arguing that Rule 36-3 may be unconstitutional . . . [relying] . . . on the Eighth Circuit's opinion in *Anastasoff v. United States*, [which] while vacated, continues to have persuasive force. . . .

A. *Anastasoff* held that Eighth Circuit Rule 28A(i), ... that unpublished dispositions are not precedential[,]* . . . violates Article III of the Constitution. . . . We believe that *Anastasoff* overstates the case. . . . *Anastasoff* focused on one aspect of the way federal courts do business—the way they issue opinions—and held that they are subject to a constitutional limitation derived from the [constitutional] framers' conception of what it means to exercise the judicial power. . . . We question whether the "judicial power" clause contains any limitation at all, separate from the specific limitations of Article III and other parts of the Constitution . . . . The term "judicial power" in Article III is more likely descriptive than prescriptive. . . .

**Our rule operates . . . differently from . . . the Eighth Circuit. . . . Rule 28A(i) [that] says that "[u]npublished decisions are not precedent." [W]e say that unpublished dispositions are "not binding precedent." . . . Our rule . . . prohibits citation of an unpublished disposition to any of the courts of our circuit. The Eighth Circuit's rule allows citation . . . , but provides that the authority is persuasive rather than binding.*

B. Modern federal courts are the successors of the English courts that developed the common law. . . . Common law judges did not make law as we understand that concept; rather, they "found" the law with the help of earlier cases that had considered similar matters. An opinion was evidence of what the law is, but it was not an independent source of law. . . . The idea that judges declared rather than made the law remained firmly entrenched in English jurisprudence until the early nineteenth century. . . . For centuries, the most important sources of law were not judicial opinions themselves, but treatises that restated the law. . . .

The modern concept of binding precedent . . . came about only gradually over the nineteenth and early twentieth centuries. Lawyers began to believe that judges made, not found, the law. This coincided with monumental improvements in the collection and reporting of case authorities . . . and [as] a more comprehensive reporting system began to take hold, it became possible for judicial decisions to serve as binding authority. . . .

II

Federal courts today do follow some common law traditions. When ruling on a novel issue of law, they will generally consider how other courts have ruled on the same issue. . . . Law on point is the law. If a court must decide an issue governed by a prior opinion that constitutes binding authority, the later court is bound to reach the same result, even if it considers the rule unwise or incorrect. Binding authority must be followed unless and until overruled by a body competent to do so.

In determining whether it is bound by an earlier decision, a court considers not merely the "reason and spirit of cases" but also "the letter of particular precedents." . . . This includes not only the rule announced, but also the facts giving rise to the dispute, other rules considered and rejected, and the views expressed in response to any dissent or concurrence. Thus, when crafting binding authority, the precise language employed is often crucial to the contours and scope of the rule announced.

. . . A decision of the Supreme Court will control that corner of the law unless and until the Supreme Court itself overrules or modifies it. . . . Thus, the first panel to consider an issue sets the law not only for all the inferior courts in the circuit, but also future panels of the court of appeals. Once a panel resolves an issue in a precedential opinion, the matter is deemed resolved, unless overruled by the court itself sitting en banc, or by the Supreme Court. . . .

Controlling authority has much in common with persuasive authority. Using the techniques developed at common law, a court confronted with apparently controlling authority must parse the precedent in light of the facts presented and the rule announced. Insofar as there may be factual differences between the current case and the earlier one, the court must determine whether those differences are material to the application of the rule or allow the precedent to be distinguished on a principled basis. . . . But there are also very important differences between controlling and persuasive authority. . . . [I]f a controlling precedent is determined to be on point, it must be followed. . . . Thus, an opinion of our court is binding within our circuit, not elsewhere. . . .

III

While we agree with *Anastasoff* that the principle of precedent was well established in the common law courts by the time Article III of the Constitution was written, we do not agree that it was known and applied in the strict sense in which we apply binding authority today. . . .

In writing an opinion, the court must be careful to recite all facts that are relevant to its ruling, while omitting facts that it considers irrelevant. Omitting relevant facts will make the ruling unintelligible to those not already familiar with the case; including inconsequential facts can provide a spurious basis for distinguishing the case in the future. . . .

While federal courts of appeals generally lack discretionary review authority, they use their authority to decide cases by unpublished—and nonprecedential—dispositions to achieve the same end. . . . That a case is decided without a precedential opinion does not mean it is not fully considered. . . . The disposition is not written in a way that makes it suitable for governing future cases. . . . An unpublished disposition is, more or less, a letter from the court to parties familiar with the facts, announcing the result and the essential rationale of the court's decision. . . .

IV

We conclude that Rule 36-3 is constitutional. We also find that counsel violated the rule. Nevertheless, we are aware that *Anastasoff* may have cast doubt on our rule's constitutional validity. Our rules are obviously not meant to punish attorneys who, in good faith, seek to test a rule's constitutionality. We therefore conclude that the violation was not willful and exercise our discretion not to impose sanctions.

The order to show cause is DISCHARGED.

In a footnote in the case of *Cogan v. Barnhart*, USDC Mass, 03-12421-WGY, the court commented:

"Citation to unpublished opinions has been an issue of considerable debate, which continues until today. The Eighth and Ninth Circuits are on extreme ends of the debate. *Anastasoff v. US*, 223 F. 3d 898 . . . (holding that unpublished opinions have precedential effect); *Hart v. Massanari*, . . . (upholding its local rule prohibiting the citation of unpublished decisions as constitutional). . . .

VIRTUAL LAW OFFICE EXPERIENCE MODULES

If your instructor has instructed you to complete assignments in the Virtual Law Office program, complete the Virtual Law Office assignments as assigned by your instructor. These assignments are designed to develop your workplace skills. Completing the assignments for this chapter will result in producing the following documents for inclusion in your portfolio:

VLOE 12.1	Electronic copies of documents to proceed with the case using the American Arbitration Association procedures
VLOE 12.2	Office memo summary of the law on product liability and strict liability in your state

APPENDIX A

How to Brief a Case

CRITICAL LEGAL THINKING

Judges apply legal reasoning in reaching a decision in a case. In doing so, the judge must specify the issue presented by the case, identify the key facts in the case and the applicable law, and then apply the law to the facts to come to a conclusion that answers the issue presented. This process is called **critical legal thinking**. Skills of analysis and interpretation are important in deciding legal cases.

Key Terms

Before embarking upon the study of law, the student should be familiar with the following key legal terms:

Plaintiff The party who originally brought the lawsuit.

Defendant The party against whom the lawsuit has been brought.

Petitioner or Appellant The party who has appealed the decision of the trial court or lower court. The petitioner may be either the plaintiff or the defendant, depending on who lost the case at the trial court or lower court level.

Respondent or Appellee The party who must answer the petitioner's appeal. The respondent may be either the plaintiff or the defendant, depending upon which party is the petitioner. In some cases, both the plaintiff *and* the defendant may disagree with the trial court's or lower court's decision and both parties may appeal the decision.

Briefing a Case

"Briefing" a case is important to clarify the legal issues involved and to gain a better understanding of the case.

The student must summarize (brief) the court's decision in no more than 400 words (some professors may shorten or lengthen this limit). The format is highly structured, consisting of five parts, each of which is numbered and labeled:

Part	Maximum Words
1. Case name and citation	25
2. Summary of key facts in the case	125
3. Issue presented by the case, stated as a one-sentence question answerable only by yes or no	25
4. Holding—the court's resolution of the issue	25
5. A summary of the court's reasoning justifying the holding	200
Total words	400

1. Case Name and Citation

The name of the case is placed at the beginning of each briefed case. The case name usually contains the names of the parties to the lawsuit. If there are multiple plaintiffs or defendants, however, some of the names of the parties may be omitted from the case name. Abbreviations often are used in case names.

The case citation—which consists of a number plus the year in which the case was decided, such as "126 L.Ed.2d 295 (1993)"—is set forth below the case name. The case citation identifies the book in the law library in which the case may be found. For example, the case in the above citation may be found in volume 126 of the *Supreme Court Reporter Lawyer's Edition (Second)*, page 295. The name of the court that decided the case appears below the case name.

2. Summary of Key Facts in the Case

The important facts of a case are stated briefly. Extraneous facts and facts of minor importance are omitted from the brief. The facts of the case usually can be found at the beginning of the case, but not necessarily. Important facts may be found throughout the case.

3. Issue Presented by the Case

It is crucial in briefing a case to identify the issue presented to the court to decide. The issue on appeal is most often a legal question, although questions of fact sometimes are the subject of an appeal. The issue presented in each case usually is quite specific and should be asked in a one-sentence question that is answerable only by a *yes* or *no*. For example, the issue statement, "Is Mary liable?" is too broad. A more proper statement of the issue would be, "Is Mary liable to Joe for breach of the contract made between them based on her refusal to make the payment due on September 30?"

4. Holding

The holding is the decision reached by the present court. It should be *yes* or *no*. The holding also states which party won.

5. Summary of the Court's Reasoning

When an appellate court or supreme court issues a decision—which often is called an *opinion*—the court normally states the reasoning it used in reaching its decision. The rationale for the decision may be based on the specific facts of the case, public policy, prior law, or other matters. In stating the reasoning of the court, the student should reword the court's language into the student's own language. This summary of the court's reasoning should pick out the meat of the opinions and weed out the nonessentials.

Following are two U.S. Supreme Court opinions for briefing. The case is presented in the language of the U.S. Supreme Court. A "Brief of the Case" follows each of the two cases. A third case, from the New York State Court of Appeals, also is included for briefing.

CASE 1

For Briefing

Harris v. Forklift Systems, Inc.	CASE NAME	
510 U.S. 17, 114 S.CT. 367, 126 L.ED.2D 295	CITATION	**1993 U.S. LEXIS 7155 (1993)**
	COURT	**Supreme Court of the United States**

OPINION OF THE COURT. O'CONNOR, JUSTICE

FACTS. Teresa Harris worked as a manager at Forklift Systems, Inc., an equipment rental company, from April 1985 until October 1987. Charles Hardy was Forklift's president. Throughout Harris's time at Forklift, Hardy often insulted her because of her gender and often made her the target of unwanted sexual innuendos. Hardy told Harris on several occasions, in the presence of other employees, "You're a woman, what do you know" and "We need a man as the rental manager"; at least once, he told her she was "a dumb-ass woman." Again in front of others, he suggested that the two of them "go to the Holiday Inn to negotiate Harris' raise." Hardy occasionally asked Harris and other female employees to get coins from his front pants pocket. He threw objects on the ground in front of Harris and other women, and asked them to pick the objects up. He made sexual innuendos about Harris' and other women's clothing.

In mid-August 1987, Harris complained to Hardy about his conduct. Hardy said he was surprised that Harris was offended, claimed he was only joking, and apologized. He also promised he would stop and based on his assurance Harris stayed on the job. But in early September, Hardy began anew: While Harris was arranging a deal with one of Forklift's customers, he asked her, again in front of other employees, "What did you do, promise the guy some sex Saturday night?" On October 1, Harris collected her paycheck and quit.

LOWER COURTS' OPINIONS. Harris then sued Forklift, claiming that Hardy's conduct had created an abusive work environment for her because of her gender. The United States District Court for the Middle District of Tennessee found this to be "a close case," but held that Hardy's conduct did not create an abusive environment. The court found that some of Hardy's comments offended Harris, and would offend the "reasonable woman," but that they were not "so severe as to be expected to seriously affect Harris' psychological well-being." A reasonable woman manager under like circumstances would have been offended by Hardy, but his conduct would not have risen to the level of interfering with that person's work performance. The United States Court of Appeals for the Sixth Circuit affirmed in a brief unpublished decision.

ISSUE. We granted certiorari to resolve a conflict among the Circuits on whether conduct, to be actionable as "abusive work environment" harassment, must "seriously affect an employee's psychological well-being" or lead the plaintiff to "suffer injury."

STATUTE BEING INTERPRETED. Title VII of the Civil Rights Act of 1964 makes it "an unlawful employment practice for an employer . . . to discriminate against any individual with respect to his compensation, terms, conditions, or privileges of employment, because of such individual's race, color, religion, sex, or national origin." 42 U.S.C. §2000e-2(a)(1).

U.S. SUPREME COURT'S REASONING. When the workplace is permeated with discriminatory intimidation, ridicule, and insult that is sufficiently severe or pervasive to alter the conditions of the victim's employment and create an abusive working environment, Title VII is violated. This standard takes a middle path between making actionable any conduct that is merely offensive and requiring the conduct to cause a tangible psychological injury. Mere utterance of an epithet which engenders offensive feelings in an employee does not sufficiently affect the conditions of employment to implicate Title VII. Conduct that is not severe or pervasive enough to create an objectively hostile or abusive work environment—an environment that a reasonable person would find hostile or abusive—is beyond Title VII's purview. Likewise, if the victim does not subjectively perceive the environment to be abusive, the conduct has not actually altered the conditions of the victim's employment, and there is no Title VII violation.

But Title VII comes into play before the harassing conduct leads to a nervous breakdown. A discriminatorily abusive work environment, even one that does not seriously affect employees' psychological well-being, can and often will detract from employees' job performance, discourage employees from remaining on the job, or keep them from advancing in their careers. Moreover, even without regard to these tangible effects, the very fact that the discriminatory conduct was so severe or pervasive that it created a work environment abusive to employees because of their race, gender, religion, or national origin offends Title VII's broad rule of workplace equality.

HOLDING. We therefore believe the district court erred in relying on whether the conduct "seriously affected plaintiff's psychological well-being" or led her to "suffer injury." Such an inquiry may needlessly focus the factfinder's attention on concrete psychological harm, an element Title VII does not require. So long as the environment would reasonably be perceived, and is perceived, as hostile or abusive, there is no need for it also to be psychologically injurious. This is not, and by its nature cannot be, a mathematically precise test. But we can say that whether an environment is "hostile" or "abusive" can be determined only by looking at all the circumstances.

We therefore reverse the judgment of the Court of Appeals, and remand the case for further proceedings consistent with this opinion.

CONCURRING OPINION. GINSBURG, JUSTICE
The critical issue, Title VII's text indicates, is whether members of one sex are exposed to disadvantageous terms or conditions of employment to which members of the other sex are not exposed. The adjudicator's inquiry should center, dominantly, on whether the discriminatory conduct has reasonably interfered with the plaintiff's work performance. To show such interference, the plaintiff need not prove that his or her tangible productivity has declined as a result of the harassment.

Brief of the Case: *Harris v. Forklift Systems, Inc.*

1. Case Name, Citation, and Court

Harris v. Forklift Systems, Inc.
126 L.Ed.2d. 295 (1993)
United States Supreme Court

2. Summary of the Key Facts

A. While Harris worked at Forklift, Hardy continually insulted her because of her gender and made her the target of unwanted sexual innuendos.
B. This conduct created an abusive and hostile work environment, causing Harris to terminate her employment.
C. Harris sued Forklift, alleging sexual harassment in violation of Title VII of the Civil Rights Act of 1964, which makes it an unlawful employment practice for an employer to discriminate in employment because of an individual's sex.

3. The Issue

Must an employee prove that she suffered psychological injury before she can prove a Title VII claim for sexual harassment against her employer?

4. The Holding

No. The Supreme Court remanded the case for further proceedings consistent with its opinion.

5. Summary of the Court's Reasoning

The Supreme Court held that a workplace that is permeated with discriminatory intimidation, ridicule, and insult so severe that it alters the conditions of the victim's employment creates an abusive and hostile work environment that violates Title VII. The Court held that the victim is not required to prove that she suffered tangible psychological injury to prove her Title VII claim. The Court noted that Title VII comes into play before the harassing conduct leads the victim to have a nervous breakdown.

CASE 2

For Briefing

PGA Tour, Inc. v. Martin	**CASE NAME**	
121 S.CT. 1879, 149 L.ED.2D 904 (2001)	**CITATION**	***2001 U.S. LEXIS 4115***
	COURT	***Supreme Court of the United States***

OPINION OF THE COURT. STEVEN, JUSTICE

ISSUE. This case raises two questions concerning the application of the Americans with Disabilities Act of 1990 [42 U.S.C. § 12101 *et seq.*] to a gifted athlete: first, whether the Act protects access to professional golf tournaments by a qualified entrant with a disability; and second, whether a disabled contestant may be denied the use of a golf cart because it would "fundamentally alter the nature" of the tournaments to allow him to ride when all other contestants must walk.

FACTS. Petitioner PGA TOUR, Inc., a nonprofit entity formed in 1968, sponsors and cosponsors professional golf tournaments conducted on three annual tours. About 200 golfers participate in the PGA TOUR; about 170 in the NIKE TOUR; and about 100 in the SENIOR PGA TOUR. PGA TOUR and NIKE TOUR tournaments typically are 4-day events, played on courses leased and operated by petitioner. The revenues generated by television, admissions, concessions, and contributions from cosponsors amount to about $300 million a year, much of which is distributed in prize money. The "Conditions of Competition and Local Rules," often described as the "hard card," apply specifically to petitioner's professional tours. The hard cards for the PGA TOUR and NIKE TOUR require players to walk the golf course during tournaments, but not during open qualifying rounds. On the SENIOR PGA TOUR, which is limited to golfers age 50 and older, the contestants may use golf carts. Most seniors, however, prefer to walk.

RESPONDENT. Casey Martin is a talented golfer. As an amateur, he won 17 Oregon Golf Association junior events before he was 15, and won the state championship as a high school senior. He played on the Stanford University golf team that won the 1994 National Collegiate Athletic Association (NCAA) championship. As a professional, Martin qualified for the NIKE TOUR in 1998 and 1999, and based on his 1999 performance, qualified for the PGA TOUR in 2000. In the 1999 season, he entered 24 events, made the cut 13 times, and had 6 top-10 finishes, coming in second twice and third once.

Martin is also an individual with a disability as defined in the Americans with Disabilities Act of 1990 (ADA or Act). Since birth he has been afflicted with Klippel-Trenaunay-Weber Syndrome, a degenerative circulatory disorder that obstructs the flow of blood from his right leg back to his heart. The disease is progressive; it causes severe pain and has atrophied his right leg. During the latter part of his college career, because of the progress of the disease, Martin could no longer walk an 18-hole golf course. Walking not only caused him pain, fatigue, and anxiety, but also created a significant risk of hemorrhaging, developing blood clots, and fracturing his tibia so badly that an amputation might be required.

When Martin turned pro and entered the petitioner's Qualifying-School, the hard card permitted him to use a cart during his successful progress through the first two stages. He made a request, supported by detailed medical records, for permission to use a golf cart during the third stage. Petitioner refused to review those records, or to waive its walking rule for the third stage. Martin therefore filed this action.

DISTRICT COURT'S DECISION 994 F.SUPP. 1242 [DISTRICT: OREGON (1998)]. At trial, petitioner PGA TOUR did not contest the conclusion that Martin has a disability covered by the ADA, or the fact that his disability prevents him from walking the course during a round of golf. Rather, petitioner asserted that the condition of walking is a substantive rule of competition, and that waiving it as to any individual for any reason would fundamentally alter the nature of the competition. Petitioner's evidence included the testimony of a number of experts, among them some of the greatest golfers in history. Arnold Palmer, Jack Nicklaus, and Ken Venturi explained that fatigue can be a critical factor in a tournament, particularly on the last day when psychological pressure is at a maximum. Their testimony makes it clear that, in their view, permission to use a cart might well give some players a competitive advantage over other players who must walk.

The judge found that the purpose of the rule was to inject fatigue into the skill of shot-making, but that the fatigue injected "by walking the course cannot be deemed significant under normal circumstances." Furthermore, Martin presented evidence, and the judge found, that even with the use of a cart, Martin must walk over a mile during an 18-hole round, and that the fatigue he suffers from coping with his disability is "undeniably greater" than the fatigue his able-bodied competitors endure from walking the course. As a result, the judge concluded that it would "not fundamentally alter the nature of the PGA Tour's game to accommodate him with a cart." The judge accordingly entered a permanent injunction requiring petitioner to permit Martin to use a cart in tour and qualifying events.

COURT OF APPEALS DECISION 204 F.3D 994 [9TH CIRCUIT (2000)]. The Court of Appeals concluded that golf courses remain places of public accommodation during PGA tournaments. On the merits, because there was no serious dispute about the fact that permitting Martin to use a golf cart was both a reasonable and a necessary solution to the problem of providing him access to the tournaments, the Court of Appeals regarded the central dispute as whether such permission would "fundamentally alter" the nature of the PGA TOUR or

NIKE TOUR. Like the District Court, the Court of Appeals viewed the issue not as "whether use of carts generally would fundamentally alter the competition, but whether the use of a cart by Martin would do so." That issue turned on "an intensively fact-based inquiry," and, the court concluded, had been correctly resolved by the trial judge. In its words, "all that the cart does is permit Martin access to a type of competition in which he otherwise could not engage because of his disability."

FEDERAL STATUTE BEING INTERPRETED. Congress enacted the ADA in 1990 to remedy widespread discrimination against disabled individuals. To effectuate its sweeping purpose, the ADA forbids discrimination against disabled individuals in major areas of public life, among them employment (Title I of the Act), public services (Title II), and public accommodations (Title III). At issue now is the applicability of Title III to petitioner's golf tours and qualifying rounds, in particular to petitioner's treatment of a qualified disabled golfer wishing to compete in those events.

U.S. SUPREME COURT'S REASONING. It seems apparent, from both the general rule and the comprehensive definition of "public accommodation," that petitioner's golf tours and their qualifying rounds fit comfortably within the coverage of Title III, and Martin within its protection. The events occur on "golf courses," a type of place specifically identified by the Act as a public accommodation. Section 12181(7)(L). In this case, the narrow dispute is whether allowing Martin to use a golf cart, despite the walking requirement that applies to the PGA TOUR, the NIKE TOUR, and the third stage of the Qualifying-School, is a modification that would "fundamentally alter the nature" of those events.

As an initial matter, we observe that the use of carts is not itself inconsistent with the fundamental character of the game of golf. From early on, the essence of the game has been shot-making—using clubs to cause a ball to progress from the teeing ground to a hole some distance away with as few strokes as possible. Golf carts started appearing with increasing regularity on American golf courses in the 1950s. Today they are everywhere. And they are encouraged. For one thing, they often speed up play, and for another, they are great revenue producers. There is nothing in the Rules of Golf that either forbids the use of carts, or penalizes a player for using a cart.

Petitioner, however, distinguishes the game of golf as it is generally played from the game that it sponsors in the PGA TOUR, NIKE TOUR, and the last stage of the Qualifying-School—golf at the "highest level." According to petitioner, "the goal of the highest-level competitive athletics is to assess and compare the performance of different competitors, a task that is meaningful only if the competitors are subject to identical substantive rules." The waiver of any possibly "outcome-affecting" rule for a contestant would violate this principle and therefore, in petitioner's view, fundamentally alter the nature of the highest level athletic event. The walking rule is one such rule, petitioner submits, because its purpose is "to inject the element of fatigue into the skill of shot-making," and thus its effect may be the critical loss of a stroke. As a consequence, the reasonable modification Martin seeks would fundamentally alter the nature of petitioner's highest level tournaments.

The force of petitioner's argument is, first of all, mitigated by the fact that golf is a game in which it is impossible to guarantee that all competitors will play under exactly the same conditions or that an individual's ability will be the sole determinant of the outcome. For example, changes in the weather may produce harder greens and more head winds for the tournament leader than for his closest pursuers. A lucky bounce may save a shot or two. Whether such happenstance events are more or less probable than the likelihood that a golfer afflicted with Klippel-Trenaunay-Weber Syndrome would one day qualify for the NIKE TOUR and PGA TOUR, they at least demonstrate that pure chance may have a greater impact on the outcome of elite golf tournaments than the fatigue resulting from the enforcement of the walking rule.

Further, the factual basis of petitioner's argument is undermined by the District Court's finding that the fatigue from walking during one of petitioner's 4-day tournaments cannot be deemed significant. The District Court credited the testimony of a professor in physiology and expert on fatigue, who calculated the calories expended in walking a golf course (about five miles) to be approximately 500 calories—"nutritionally less than a Big Mac." What is more, that energy is expended over a 5-hour period, during which golfers have numerous intervals for rest and refreshment. In fact, the expert concluded, because golf is a low intensity activity, fatigue from the game is primarily a psychological phenomenon in which stress and motivation are the key ingredients. And even under conditions of severe heat and humidity, the critical factor in fatigue is fluid loss rather than exercise from walking. Moreover, when given the option of using a cart, the majority of golfers in petitioner's tournaments have chosen to walk, often to relieve stress or for other strategic reasons. As NIKE TOUR member Eric Johnson testified, walking allows him to keep in rhythm, stay warmer when it is chilly, and develop a better sense of the elements and the course than riding in a cart. As we have demonstrated, the walking rule is at best peripheral to the nature of petitioner's athletic events, and thus it might be waived in individual cases without working a fundamental alteration.

HOLDING AND REMEDY. Under the ADA's basic requirement that the need of a disabled person be evaluated on an individual basis, we have no doubt that allowing Martin to use a golf cart would not fundamentally alter the nature of petitioner's tournaments. As we have discussed, the purpose of the walking rule is to subject players to fatigue, which in turn may influence the outcome of tournaments. Even if the rule does serve that purpose, it is an uncontested finding of the District Court that Martin "easily endures greater fatigue even with a cart than his able-bodied competitors do by walking." The purpose of the walking rule is therefore not compromised in the slightest by allowing Martin to use a cart. A modification that provides an exception to a peripheral tournament rule without impairing its purpose cannot be said to "fundamentally alter" the tournament. What it can be said to do, on the other hand, is to allow Martin the chance to qualify for and compete in the athletic events petitioner offers to those members of the public who have the skill and desire to enter. That is exactly what the ADA requires. As a result, Martin's request for a waiver of the walking rule should have been granted.

The judgment of the Court of Appeals is affirmed. It is so ordered.

DISSENTING OPINION. SCALIA, JUSTICE

In my view, today's opinion exercises a benevolent compassion that the law does not place it within our power to impose. The judgment distorts the text of Title III, the structure of the ADA, and common sense. I respectfully dissent.

The Court, for its part, assumes that conclusion for the sake of argument, but pronounces respondent to be a "customer" of the PGA TOUR or of the golf courses on which it is played. That seems to me quite incredible. The PGA TOUR is a professional sporting event, staged for the entertainment of a live and TV audience. The professional golfers on the tour are no more "enjoying" (the statutory term) the entertainment that the tour provides, or the facilities of the golf courses on which it is held, than professional baseball players "enjoy" the baseball games in which they play or the facilities of Yankee Stadium. To be sure, professional baseball players *participate* in the games, and *use* the ballfields, but no one in his right mind would think that they are *customers* of the American League or of Yankee Stadium. They are themselves the entertainment that the customers pay to watch. And professional golfers are no different. A professional golfer's practicing his profession is not comparable to John Q. Public's frequenting "a 232-acre amusement area with swimming, boating, sun bathing, picnicking, miniature golf, dancing facilities, and a snack bar."

Having erroneously held that Title III applies to the "customers" of professional golf who consist of its practitioners, the Court then erroneously answers—or to be accurate simply ignores—a second question. The ADA requires covered businesses to make such reasonable modifications of "policies, practices, or procedures" as are necessary to "afford" goods, services, and privileges to individuals with disabilities; but it explicitly does not require "modifications that would fundamentally alter the nature" of the goods, services, and privileges. Section 12182(b)(2)(A)(ii). In other words, disabled individuals must be given *access* to the same goods, services, and privileges that others enjoy.

A camera store may not refuse to sell cameras to a disabled person, but it is not required to stock cameras specially designed for such persons. It is hardly a feasible judicial function to decide whether shoe stores should sell single shoes to one-legged persons and if so at what price, or how many Braille books the Borders or Barnes and Noble bookstore chains should stock in each of their stores. Eighteen-hole golf courses, 10-foot-high basketball hoops, 90-foot baselines, 100-yard football fields—all are arbitrary and none is essential. The only support for any of them is tradition and (in more modern times) insistence by what has come to be regarded as the ruling body of the sport—both of which factors support the PGA TOUR's position in the present case. One can envision the parents of a Little League player with attention deficit disorder trying to convince a judge that their son's disability makes it at least 25% more difficult to hit a pitched ball. (If they are successful, the only thing that could prevent a court order giving a kid four strikes would be a judicial determination that, in baseball, three strikes are metaphysically necessary, which is quite absurd.)

Agility, strength, speed, balance, quickness of mind, steadiness of nerves, intensity of concentration—these talents are not evenly distributed. No wild-eyed dreamer has ever suggested that the managing bodies of the competitive sports that test precisely these qualities should try to take account of the uneven distribution of God-given gifts when writing and enforcing the rules of competition. And I have no doubt Congress did not authorize misty-eyed judicial supervision of such revolution. The year was 2001, and "everybody was finally equal." K. Vonnegut, Harrison Bergeron, in *Animal Farm and Related Readings* 129 (1997).

Brief of the Case: *PGA TOUR, Inc. v. Martin*

1. Case Name, Citation, and Court

PGA TOUR, Inc. v. Martin

121 S.Ct. 1879, 2001 LEXIS 415 (2001)

Supreme Court of the United States

2. Summary of the Key Facts

A. PGA TOUR, Inc. is a nonprofit organization that sponsors professional golf tournaments.

B. The PGA establishes rules for its golf tournaments. A PGA rule requires golfers to walk the golf course, and not use golf carts.

C. Casey Martin is a professional golfer who suffers from Klippel-Trenaunay-Weber Syndrome, a degenerative circulatory disorder that atrophied Martin's right leg and causes him pain, fatigue, and anxiety when walking.

D. When Martin petitioned the PGA to use a golf cart during golf tournaments, the PGA refused.

E. Martin sued the PGA, alleging discrimination against a disabled individual in violation of the American with Disabilities Act of 1990, a federal statute.

3. Issue

Does the Americans with Disabilities Act require the PGA to accommodate Martin by permitting him to use a golf cart while playing in PGA golf tournaments?

4. Holding

Yes. The Supreme Court held that the PGA must allow Martin to use a golf cart when competing in PGA golf tournaments. Affirmed.

5. Court's Reasoning

The Supreme Court held that:

A. Martin was disabled and covered by the Act.
B. Golf courses are "public accommodations" covered by the Act.
C. The use of golf carts is not a fundamental characteristic of the game of golf.
D. Other than the PGA rule, no Rule of Golf forbids the use of golf carts.
E. It is impossible to guarantee all players in golf will play under the exact same conditions, so allowing Martin to use a golf cart gives him no advantage over other golfers.
F. Martin, because of his disease, will probably suffer more fatigue playing golf using a golf cart than other golfers will suffer without using a cart.
G. The PGA's "walking rule" is only peripheral to the game of golf and not a fundamental part of golf.
H. Allowing Martin to use a golf cart will not fundamentally alter the PGA's highest-level professional golf tournaments.

CASE 3

For Briefing

Palsgraf v. Long Island R.R. Co.	CASE NAME	
248 N.Y. 339 (1928)	CITATION	***162 N.E. 99***
	COURT	***Court of Appeals of the State of New York***

OPINION OF THE COURT. CARDOZO, CH. J.

FACTS. Plaintiff was standing on a platform of defendant's railroad after buying a ticket to go to Rockaway Beach. A train stopped at the station, bound for another place. Two men ran forward to catch it. One of the men reached the platform of the car without mishap, though the train was already moving. The other man, carrying a package, jumped aboard the car, but seemed unsteady as if about to fall. A guard on the car, who had held the door open, reached forward to help him in, and another guard on the platform pushed him from behind. In this act, the package was dislodged, and fell upon the rails. It was a package of small size, about fifteen inches long, and was covered by a newspaper. In fact it contained fireworks, but there was nothing in its appearance to give notice of its contents. The fireworks when they fell exploded. The shock of the explosion threw down some scales at the other end of the platform, many feet away. The scales struck the plaintiff, causing injuries for which she sues.

The conduct of the defendant's guard, if a wrong in its relation to the holder of the package, was not a wrong in its relation to the plaintiff, standing far away. Relatively to her it was not negligence at all. Nothing in the situation gave notice that the falling package had in it the potency of peril to persons thus removed. Negligence is not actionable unless it involves the invasion of a legally protected interest, the violation of a right. "Proof of negligence in the air, so to speak, will not do" (Pollock, *Torts* [11th ed.], p. 455; *Martin v. Herzog*, 228 N.Y. 164, 170; cf. Salmond, Torts [6th ed.], p. 24). "Negligence is the absence of care, according to the circumstances" (WILLES, J., in *Vaughan v. Taff Vale Ry. Co.*, 5 H. & N. 679, 688; 1 Beven, Negligence [4th ed.], 7; *Paul v. Consol. Fireworks Co.*, 212 N.Y. 117; *Adams v. Bullock*, 227 N.Y. 208, 211; *Parrott v. Wells-Fargo* Co., 15 Wall. [U.S.] 524). The plaintiff as she stood upon the platform of the station might claim to be protected against intentional invasion of her bodily security. Such invasion is not charged. She might claim to be protected against unintentional invasion by conduct involving in the thought of reasonable men an unreasonable hazard that such invasion would ensue. These, from the point of view of the law, were the bounds of her immunity, with perhaps some rare exceptions, survivals for the most part of ancient forms of liability, where conduct is held to be at the peril of the actor (*Sullivan v. Dunham*, 161 N.Y. 290 Page 342). If no hazard was apparent to the eye of ordinary vigilance, an act innocent and harmless, at least to outward seeming, with reference to her, did not take to itself the quality of a tort because it happened to be a wrong, though apparently not one involving the risk of bodily insecurity, with reference to some one else. "In every instance, before negligence can be predicated of a given act, back of the act must be sought and found a duty to the individual complaining, the observance of which would have averted or avoided the injury" (McSHERRY, C.J., in *W. Va. Central R. Co. v. State*, 96 Md. 652, 666; cf. *Norfolk & Western Ry. Co. v. Wood*, 99 Va. 156, 158, 159; *Hughes v. Boston & Maine R.R. Co.*, 71 N.H. 279, 284; *U.S. Express Co. v. Everest*, 72 Kan. 517; *Emry v. Roanoke Nav. Co.*, 111 N.C. 94, 95; *Vaughan v. Transit Dev. Co.*, 222 N.Y. 79; *Losee v. Clute*, 51 N.Y. 494; *DiCaprio v. N.Y.C.R.R. Co.*, 231 N.Y. 94; 1 Shearman & Redfield on Negligence, § 8, and cases cited; Cooley on Torts [3d ed.], p. 1411; Jaggard on Torts, vol. 2, p. 826; Wharton, *Negligence*, § 24; Bohlen, *Studies in the Law of Torts*, p. 601). "The ideas of negligence and duty are strictly correlative" (BOWEN, L.J., in *Thomas v. Quartermaine*, 18 Q.B.D. 685, 694). The plaintiff sues in her own right for a wrong personal to her, and not as the vicarious beneficiary of a breach of duty to another.

A different conclusion will involve us, and swiftly too, in a maze of contradictions. A guard stumbles over a package which has been left upon a platform. It seems to be a bundle of newspapers. It turns out to be a can of dynamite. To the eye of ordinary vigilance, the bundle is abandoned waste, which may be kicked or trod on with impunity. Is a passenger at the other end of the platform protected by the law against the unsuspected hazard concealed beneath the waste? If not, is the result to be any different, so far as the distant passenger is concerned, when the guard stumbles over a valise which a truckman or a porter has left upon the walk? The passenger far away, if the victim of a wrong at all, has a cause of action, not derivative, but original and primary. His claim to be protected against invasion of his bodily security is neither greater nor less because the act resulting in the invasion is a wrong to another far removed. In this case, the rights that are said to have been violated, the interests said to have been invaded, are not even of the same order. The man was not injured in his person nor even put in danger. The purpose of the act, as well as its effect, was to make his person safe. If there was a wrong to him at all, which may very well be doubted, it was a wrong to a property interest only, the safety of his package. Out of this wrong to property, which threatened injury to nothing else, there has passed, we are told, to the plaintiff by derivation or succession a right of action for the invasion of an interest of another order, the right to bodily security. The diversity of interests emphasizes the futility of the effort to build the plaintiff's right upon the basis of a wrong to some one else. The gain is one of emphasis, for a like result would follow if the interests were the same. Even then, the orbit of the danger as disclosed to the eye of reasonable vigilance would be the orbit of the duty. One who jostles one's neighbor in a crowd does not invade the rights of others standing at the outer fringe when the unintended contact casts a bomb upon the ground. The wrongdoer as to them is the man who carries the bomb, not the one who explodes it without suspicion of the danger. Life will have to be made over, and human nature transformed, before prevision so extravagant can be accepted as the norm of conduct, the customary standard to which behavior must conform. The argument for the plaintiff is built upon the shifting meanings of such words as "wrong" and "wrongful," and shares their instability. What the plaintiff must show is "a wrong" to herself, i.e., a violation of her own right, and not merely a wrong to some one else, nor conduct "wrongful" because unsocial, but not "a wrong" to any one. We are told that one who drives at reckless speed through a crowded city street is guilty of a negligent act and, therefore, of a wrongful one irrespective of the consequences. Negligent the act is, and wrongful in the sense that it is unsocial, but wrongful and unsocial in relation to other travelers, only because the eye of vigilance perceives the risk of damage. If the same act were to be committed on a speedway or a race course, it would lose its wrongful quality. The risk reasonably to be perceived defines the duty to be obeyed, and risk imports relation; it is risk to another or to others within the range of apprehension (Seavey, Negligence, Subjective or Objective, 41 H.L. Rv. 6; *Boronkay v. Robinson & Carpenter*, 247 N.Y. 365). This does not mean, of course, that one who launches a destructive force is always relieved of liability if the force, though known to be destructive, pursues an unexpected path. "It was not necessary that the defendant should have had notice of the particular method in which an accident would occur, if the possibility of an accident was clear to the ordinarily prudent eye" (*Munsey v. Webb*, 231 U.S. 150, 156; *Condran v. Park & Tilford*, 213 N.Y. 341, 345; *Robert v. U.S.E.F. Corp.*, 240 N.Y. 474, 477). Some acts, such as shooting, are so imminently dangerous to any one who may come within reach of the missile, however unexpectedly, as to impose a duty of prevision not far from that of an insurer. Even today, and much oftener in earlier stages of the law, one acts sometimes at one's peril (Jeremiah Smith, Tort and Absolute Liability, 30 H.L. Rv. 328; Street, *Foundations of Legal Liability*, vol. 1, pp. 77, 78). Under this head, it may be, fall certain cases of what is known as transferred intent, an act willfully dangerous to A resulting by misadventure in injury to B (*Talmage v. Smith*, 101 Mich. 370, 374). These cases aside, wrong is defined in terms of the natural or probable, at least when unintentional (*Parrot v. Wells-Fargo Co.* [The Nitro-Glycerine Case], 15 Wall. [U.S.] 524). The range of reasonable apprehension is at times a question for the court, and at times, if varying inferences are possible, a question for the jury. Here, by concession, there was nothing in the situation to suggest to the most cautious mind that the parcel wrapped in newspaper would spread wreckage through the station. If the guard had thrown it down knowingly and willfully, he would not have threatened the plaintiff's safety, so far as appearances could warn him. His conduct would not have involved, even then, an unreasonable probability of invasion of her bodily security. Liability can be no greater where the act is inadvertent.

Negligence, like risk, is thus a term of relation. Negligence in the abstract, apart from things related, is surely not a tort, if indeed it is understandable at all (BOWEN, L.J., in *Thomas v. Quartermaine*, 18 Q.B.D. 685, 694). Negligence is not a tort unless it results in the commission of a wrong, and the commission of a wrong imports the violation of a right, in this case, we are told, the right to be protected against interference with one's bodily security. But bodily security is protected, not against all forms of interference or aggression, but only against some. One who seeks redress at law does not make out a cause of action by showing without more that there has been damage to his person. If the harm was not willful, he must show that the act as to him had possibilities of danger so many and apparent as to entitle him to be protected against the doing of it though the harm was unintended. Affront to personality is still the keynote of the wrong. Confirmation of this view will be found in the history and development of the action on the case. Negligence as a basis of civil liability was unknown to mediaeval law (8 Holdsworth, *History of English Law*, p. 449; *Street, Foundations of Legal Liability*, vol. 1, pp. 189, 190). For damage to the person, the sole remedy was trespass, and trespass did not lie in the absence of aggression, and that direct and personal (Holdsworth, op. cit. p. 453; Street, op. cit. vol. 3, pp. 258, 260, vol. 1, pp. 71, 74.) Liability for other damage, as where a servant without orders from the master does or omits something to the damage of another, is a plant of later growth (Holdsworth, op. cit. 450, 457; Wigmore, *Responsibility or Tortious Acts*, vol. 3, *Essays in Anglo- American Legal History*, 520, 523, 526, 533). When it emerged out of the legal soil, it was thought of as a variant of trespass, an offshoot of the parent stock. This appears in the form of action, which was known as trespass on the case (Holdsworth, op. cit. p. 449; cf. *Scott v. Shepard*, 2 Wm. Black. 892; Green, *Rationale of Proximate Cause*, p. 19). The victim does not sue derivatively, or by right of subrogation, to vindicate an interest invaded in the person of another. Thus to view his cause of action is to ignore the fundamental difference between tort and crime (Holland, *Jurisprudence* [12th ed.], p. 328). He sues for breach of a duty owing to himself.

The law of causation, remote or proximate, is thus foreign to the case before us. The question of liability is always anterior to the question of the measure of the consequences that go with liability. If there is no tort to be redressed, there is no occasion to consider what damage might be recovered if there were a finding of a tort. We may assume, without deciding, that negligence, not at large or in the abstract, but in relation to the plaintiff, would entail liability for any and all consequences, however novel or extraordinary (*Bird v. St. Paul F. & M. Ins. Co.*, 224 N.Y. 47, 54; *Ehrgott v. Mayor*, etc., *of NY*, 96 N.Y. 264; *Smith v. London & S.W. Ry. Co.*, L.R. 6 C.P. 14; 1 Beven, Negligence, 106; Street, op. cit. vol. 1, p. 90; Green, *Rationale of Proximate Cause*, pp. 88, 118; cf. *Matter of Polemis*, L.R. 1921, 3 K.B. 560; 44 *Law Quarterly Review*, 142). There is room for argument that a distinction is to be drawn according to the diversity of interests invaded by the act, as where conduct negligent in that it threatens an insignificant invasion of an interest in property results in an unforeseeable invasion of an interest of another order, as, e.g., one of bodily security. Perhaps other distinctions may be necessary. We do not go into the question now. The consequences to be followed must first be rooted in a wrong.

HOLDING. The judgment of the Appellate Division and that of the Trial Term should be reversed, and the complaint dismissed, with costs in all courts.

DISSENTING OPINION. ANDREWS, J.

Assisting a passenger to board a train, the defendant's servant negligently knocked a package from his arms. It fell between the platform and the cars. Of its contents the servant knew and could know nothing. A violent explosion followed. The concussion broke some scales standing a considerable distance away. In falling they injured the plaintiff, an intending passenger.

Upon these facts may she recover the damages she has suffered in an action brought against the master? The result we shall reach depends upon our theory as to the nature of negligence. Is it a relative concept—the breach of some duty owing to a particular person or to particular persons? Or where there is an act which unreasonably threatens the safety of others, is the doer liable for all its proximate consequences, even where they result in injury to one who would generally be thought to be outside the radius of danger? This is not a mere dispute as to words. We might not believe that to the average mind the dropping of the bundle would seem to involve the probability of harm to the plaintiff standing many feet away whatever might be the case as to the owner or to one so near as to be likely to be struck by its fall. If, however, we adopt the second hypothesis we have to inquire only as to the relation between cause and effect. We deal in terms of proximate cause, not of negligence.

Negligence may be defined roughly as an act or omission which unreasonably does or may affect the rights of others, or which unreasonably fails to protect oneself from the dangers resulting from such acts. Here I confine myself to the first branch of the definition. Nor do I comment on the word "unreasonable." For present purposes it sufficiently describes that average of conduct that society requires of its members.

There must be both the act or the omission, and the right. It is the act itself, not the intent of the actor, that is important. (*Hover v. Barkhoof*, 44 N.Y. 113; *Mertz v. Connecticut Co.*, 217 N.Y. 475.) In criminal law both the intent and the result are to be considered. Intent again is material in tort actions, where punitive damages are sought, dependent on actual malice—not on merely reckless conduct. But here neither insanity nor infancy lessens responsibility. (*Williams v. Hays*, 143 N.Y. 442.)

As has been said, except in cases of contributory negligence, there must be rights which are or may be affected. Often though injury has occurred, no rights of him who suffers have been touched. A licensee or trespasser upon my land has no claim to affirmative care on my part that the land be made safe. (*Meiers v. Koch Brewery*, 229 N.Y. 10.) Where a railroad is required to fence its tracks against cattle, no man's rights are injured should he wander upon the road because such fence is absent. (*DiCaprio v. N.Y.C.R.R.*, 231 N.Y. 94.) An unborn child may not demand immunity from personal harm. (Drobner v. Peters, 232 N.Y. 220.)

But we are told that "there is no negligence unless there is in the particular case a legal duty to take care, and this duty must be one which is owed to the plaintiff himself and not merely to others." (Salmond Torts [6th ed.], 24.) This, I think too narrow a conception. Where there is the unreasonable act, and some right that may be affected there is negligence whether damage does or does not result. That is immaterial. Should we drive down Broadway at a reckless speed, we are negligent whether we strike an approaching car or miss it by an inch. The act itself is wrongful. It is a wrong not only to those who happen to be within the radius of danger but to all who might have been there—a wrong to the public at large. Such is the language of the street. Such the language of the courts when speaking of contributory negligence. Such again and again their language in speaking of the duty of some defendant and discussing proximate cause in cases where such a discussion is wholly irrelevant on any other theory. (*Perry v. Rochester Line Co.*, 219 N.Y. 60.) As was said by Mr. Justice HOLMES many years ago, "the measure of the defendant's duty in determining whether a wrong has been committed is one thing, the measure of liability when a wrong has been committed is another." (*Spade v. Lynn & Boston R.R. Co.*, 172 Mass. 488.) Due care is a duty imposed on each one of us to protect society from unnecessary danger, not to protect A, B or C alone.

It may well be that there is no such thing as negligence in the abstract. "Proof of negligence in the air, so to speak, will not do." In an empty world negligence would not exist. It does involve a relationship between man and his fellows. But not merely a relationship between man and those whom he might reasonably expect his act would injure. Rather, a relationship between him and those whom he does in fact injure. If his act has a tendency to harm some one, it harms him a mile away as surely as it does those on the scene. We now permit children to recover for the negligent killing of the father. It was never prevented on the theory that no duty was owing to them. A husband may be compensated for the loss of his wife's services. To say that the wrongdoer was negligent as to the husband as well as to the wife is merely an attempt to fit facts to theory. An insurance company paying a fire loss recovers its payment of the negligent incendiary. We speak of subrogation—of suing in the right of the insured. Behind the cloud of words is the fact they hide, that the act, wrongful as to the insured, has also injured the company. Even if it be true that the fault of father, wife or insured will prevent recovery, it is because we consider the original negligence not the proximate cause of the injury. (Pollock, *Torts* [12th ed.], 463.)

In the well-known *Polemis* case (1921, 3 K.B. 560), SCRUTTON, L.J., said that the dropping of a plank was negligent for it might injure "workman or cargo or ship." Because of either possibility the owner of the vessel was to be made good for his loss. The act being wrongful the doer was liable for its proximate results. Criticized and explained as this statement may have been, I think it states the law as it should be and as it is. (*Smith v. London & Southwestern Ry. Co.*, [1870-71] 6 C.P. 14; *Anthony v. Slaid, 52 Mass. 290; Wood v. Penn. R.R.Co.*, 177 Penn. St. 306; *Trashansky v. Hershkovitz*, 239 N.Y. 452.)

The proposition is this. Every one owes to the world at large the duty of refraining from those acts that may unreasonably threaten the safety of others. Such an act occurs. Not only is he wronged to whom harm might reasonably be expected to result, but he also who is in fact injured, even if he be outside what would generally be thought the danger zone. There needs be duty due the one complaining but this is not a duty to a particular individual because as to him harm might be expected. Harm to some one being the natural result of the act, not only that one alone, but all those in fact injured may complain. We have never, I think, held otherwise. Indeed in the Di Caprio case we said that a breach of a general ordinance defining the degree of care to be exercised in one's calling is evidence of negligence as to every one. We did not limit this statement to those who might be expected to be exposed to danger. Unreasonable risk being taken, its consequences are not confined to those who might probably be hurt.

If this be so, we do not have a plaintiff suing by "derivation or succession." Her action is original and primary. Her claim is for a breach of duty to herself—not that she is subrogated to any right of action of the owner of the parcel or of a passenger standing at the scene of the explosion.

The right to recover damages rests on additional considerations. The plaintiff's rights must be injured, and this injury must be caused by the negligence. We build a dam, but are negligent as to its foundations. Breaking, it injures property down stream. We are not liable if all this happened because of some reason other than the insecure foundation. But when injuries do result from our unlawful act we are liable for the consequences. It does not matter that they are unusual, unexpected, unforeseen and unforeseeable. But there is one limitation. The damages must be so connected with the negligence that the latter may be said to be the proximate cause of the former.

These two words have never been given an inclusive definition. What is a cause in a legal sense, still more what is a proximate cause, depend in each case upon many considerations, as does the existence of negligence itself. Any philosophical doctrine of causation does not help us. A boy throws a stone into a pond. The ripples spread. The water level rises. The history of that pond is altered to all eternity. It will be altered by other causes also. Yet it will be forever the resultant of all causes combined. Each one will have an influence. How great only omniscience can say. You may speak of a chain, or if you please, a net. An analogy is of little aid. Each cause brings about future events. Without each the future would not be the same. Each is proximate in the sense it is essential. But that is not what we mean by the word. Nor on the other hand do we mean sole cause. There is no such thing.

Should analogy be thought helpful, however, I prefer that of a stream. The spring, starting on its journey, is joined by tributary after tributary. The river, reaching the ocean, comes from a hundred sources. No man may say whence any drop of water is derived. Yet for a time distinction may be possible. Into the clear creek, brown swamp water flows from the left. Later, from the right comes water stained by its clay bed. The three may remain for a space, sharply divided. But at last, inevitably no trace of separation remains. They are so commingled that all distinction is lost.

As we have said, we cannot trace the effect of an act to the end, if end there is. Again, however, we may trace it part of the way. A murder at Sarajevo may be the necessary antecedent to an assassination in London twenty years hence. An overturned lantern may burn all Chicago. We may follow the fire from the shed to the last building. We rightly say the fire started by the lantern caused its destruction.

A cause, but not the proximate cause. What we do mean by the word "proximate" is, that because of convenience, of public policy, of a rough sense of justice, the law arbitrarily declines to trace a series of events beyond a certain point. This is not logic. It is practical politics. Take our rule as to fires. Sparks from my burning haystack set on fire my house and my neighbor's. I may recover from a negligent railroad. He may not. Yet the wrongful act as directly harmed the one as the other. We may regret that the line was drawn just where it was, but drawn somewhere it had to be. We said the act of the railroad was not the proximate cause of our neighbor's fire. Cause it surely was. The words we used were simply indicative of our notions of public policy. Other courts think differently. But somewhere they reach the point where they cannot say the stream comes from any one source.

Take the illustration given in an unpublished manuscript by a distinguished and helpful writer on the law of torts. A chauffeur negligently collides with another car which is filled with dynamite, although he could not know it. An explosion follows. A, walking on the sidewalk nearby, is killed. B, sitting in a window of a building opposite, is cut by flying glass. C, likewise sitting in a window a block away, is similarly injured. And a further illustration. A nursemaid, ten blocks away, startled by the noise, involuntarily drops a baby from her arms to the walk. We are told that C may not recover while A may. As to B it is a question for court or jury. We will all agree that the baby might not. Because, we are again told, the chauffeur had no reason to believe his conduct involved any risk of injuring either C or the baby. As to them he was not negligent.

But the chauffeur, being negligent in risking the collision, his belief that the scope of the harm he might do would be limited is immaterial. His act unreasonably jeopardized the safety of any one who might be affected by it. C's injury and that of the baby were directly traceable to the collision. Without that, the injury would not have happened. C had the right to sit in his office, secure from such dangers. The baby was entitled to use the sidewalk with reasonable safety.

The true theory is, it seems to me, that the injury to C, if in truth he is to be denied recovery, and the injury to the baby is that their several injuries were not the proximate result of the negligence. And here not what the chauffeur had reason to believe would be the result of his conduct, but what the prudent would foresee, may have a bearing. May have some bearing, for the problem of proximate cause is not to be solved by any one consideration.

It is all a question of expediency. There are no fixed rules to govern our judgment. There are simply matters of which we may take account. We have in a somewhat different connection spoken of "the stream of events." We have asked whether that stream was deflected—whether it was forced into new and unexpected channels. (*Donnelly v. Piercy Contracting Co.*, 222 N.Y. 210.) This is rather rhetoric than law. There is in truth little to guide us other than common sense.

There are some hints that may help us. The proximate cause, involved as it may be with many other causes, must be, at the least, something without which the event would not happen. The court must ask itself whether there was a natural and continuous sequence between cause and effect. Was the one a substantial factor in producing the other? Was there a direct connection between them, without too many intervening causes? Is the effect of cause on result not too attenuated? Is the cause likely, in the usual judgment of mankind, to produce the result? Or by the exercise of prudent foresight could the result be foreseen? Is the result too remote from the cause, and here we consider remoteness in time and space. (*Bird v. St. Paul F. & M. Ins. Co.*, 224 N.Y. 47, where we passed upon the construction of a contract—but something was also said on this subject.) Clearly we must so consider, for the greater the distance either in time or space, the more surely do other causes intervene to affect the result. When a lantern is overturned the firing of a shed is a fairly direct consequence. Many things contribute to the spread of the conflagration—the force of the wind, the direction and width of streets, the character of intervening structures, other factors. We draw an uncertain and wavering line, but draw it we must as best we can.

Once again, it is all a question of fair judgment, always keeping in mind the fact that we endeavor to make a rule in each case that will be practical and in keeping with the general understanding of mankind.

Here another question must be answered. In the case supposed it is said, and said correctly, that the chauffeur is liable for the direct effect of the explosion although he had no reason to suppose it would follow a collision. "The fact that the injury occurred in a different manner than that which might have been expected does not prevent the chauffeur's negligence from being in law the cause of the injury." But the natural results of a negligent act—the results which a prudent man would or should foresee—do have a bearing upon the decision as to proximate cause. We have said so repeatedly. What should be foreseen? No human foresight would suggest that a collision itself might injure one a block away. On the contrary, given an explosion, such a possibility might be reasonably expected. I think the direct connection, the foresight of which the courts peak, assumes prevision of the explosion, for the immediate results of which, at least, the chauffeur is responsible.

It may be said this is unjust. Why? In fairness he should make good every injury flowing from his negligence. Not because of tenderness toward him we say he need not answer for all that follows his wrong. We look back to the catastrophe, the fire kindled by the spark, or the explosion. We trace the consequences—not indefinitely, but to a certain point. And to aid us in fixing that point we ask what might ordinarily be expected to follow the fire or the explosion.

This last suggestion is the factor which must determine the case before us. The act upon which defendant's liability rests is knocking an apparently harmless package onto the platform. The act was negligent. For its proximate consequences the defendant is liable. If its contents were broken, to the owner; if it fell upon and crushed a passenger's foot, then to him. If it exploded and injured one in the immediate vicinity, to him also as to A in the illustration. Mrs. Palsgraf was standing some distance away. How far cannot be told from the record—apparently twenty-five or thirty feet. Perhaps less. Except for the explosion, she would not have been injured. We are told by the appellant in his brief "it cannot be denied that the explosion was the direct cause of the plaintiff's injuries." So it was a substantial factor in producing the result—there was here a natural and continuous sequence—direct connection. The only intervening cause was that instead of blowing her to the ground the concussion smashed the weighing machine which in turn fell upon her. There was no remoteness in time, little in space. And surely, given such an explosion as here it needed no great foresight to predict that the natural result would be to injure one on the platform at no greater distance from its scene than was the plaintiff. Just how no one might be able to predict. Whether by flying fragments, by broken glass, by wreckage of machines or structures no one could say. But injury in some form was most probable.

Under these circumstances I cannot say as a matter of law that the plaintiff's injuries were not the proximate result of the negligence. That is all we have before us. The court refused to so charge. No request was made to submit the matter to the jury as a question of fact, even would that have been proper upon the record before us.

The judgment appealed from should be affirmed, with costs.

National Federation of Paralegal Associations, Inc.

Model Code of Ethics and Professional Responsibility and Guidelines for Enforcement

PREAMBLE

The National Federation of Paralegal Associations, Inc. ("NFPA") is a professional organization comprised of paralegal associations and individual paralegals throughout the United States and Canada. Members of NFPA have varying backgrounds, experiences, education, and job responsibilities that reflect the diversity of the paralegal profession. NFPA promotes the growth, development, and recognition of the paralegal profession as an integral partner in the delivery of legal services.

In May 1993 NFPA adopted its Model Code of Ethics and Professional Responsibility ("Model Code") to delineate the principles for ethics and conduct to which every paralegal should aspire.

Many paralegal associations throughout the United States have endorsed the concept and content of NFPA's Model Code through the adoption of their own ethical codes. In doing so, paralegals have confirmed the profession's commitment to increase the quality and efficiency of legal services, as well as recognized its responsibilities to the public, the legal community, and colleagues.

Paralegals have recognized, and will continue to recognize, that the profession must continue to evolve to enhance their roles in the delivery of legal services. With increased levels of responsibility comes the need to define and enforce mandatory rules of professional conduct. Enforcement of codes of paralegal conduct is a logical and necessary step to enhance and ensure the confidence of the legal community and the public in the integrity and professional responsibility of paralegals.

In April 1997 NFPA adopted the Model Disciplinary Rules ("Model Rules") to make possible the enforcement of the Canons and Ethical Considerations contained in the NFPA Model Code. A concurrent determination was made that the Model Code of Ethics and Professional Responsibility, formerly aspirational in nature, should be recognized as setting forth the enforceable obligations of all paralegals.

The Model Code and Model Rules offer a framework for professional discipline, either voluntarily or through formal regulatory programs.

§1 NFPA Model Disciplinary Rules and Ethical Considerations

1.1. A Paralegal Shall Achieve and Maintain a High Level of Competence.

Ethical Considerations

EC-1.1 (a) A paralegal shall achieve competency through education, training, and work experience.

EC-1.1 (b) A paralegal shall aspire to participate in a minimum of twelve (12) hours of continuing legal education, to include at least one (1) hour of ethics education, every two (2) years in order to remain current on developments in the law.

EC-1.1 (c) A paralegal shall perform all assignments promptly and efficiently.

1.2. A Paralegal Shall Maintain a High Level of Personal and Professional Integrity.

Ethical Considerations

EC-1.2 (a) A paralegal shall not engage in any ex parte communications involving the courts or any other adjudicatory body in an attempt to exert undue influence or to obtain advantage or the benefit of only one party.

EC-1.2 (b) A paralegal shall not communicate, or cause another to communicate, with a party the paralegal knows to be represented by a lawyer in a pending matter without the prior consent of the lawyer representing such other party.

EC-1.2 (c) A paralegal shall ensure that all timekeeping and billing records prepared by the paralegal are thorough, accurate, honest, and complete.

EC-1.2 (d) A paralegal shall not knowingly engage in fraudulent billing practices. Such practices may include, but are not limited to: inflation of hours billed to a client or employer; misrepresentation of the nature of tasks performed; and/or submission of fraudulent expense and disbursement documentation.

EC-1.2 (e) A paralegal shall be scrupulous, thorough, and honest in the identification and maintenance of all funds, securities, and other assets of a client and shall provide accurate accounting as appropriate.

EC-1.2 (f) A paralegal shall advise the proper authority of non-confidential knowledge of any dishonest or fraudulent acts by any person pertaining to the handling of the funds, securities or other assets of a client. The authority to whom the report is made shall depend on the nature and circumstances of the possible misconduct (e.g., ethics committees of law firms, corporations and/or paralegal associations, local or state bar associations, local prosecutors, administrative agencies, etc.). Failure to report such knowledge is in itself misconduct and shall be treated as such under these rules.

1.3. A Paralegal Shall Maintain a High Standard of Professional Conduct.

Ethical Considerations

EC-1.3 (a) A paralegal shall refrain from engaging in any conduct that offends the dignity and decorum of proceedings before a court or other adjudicatory body and shall be respectful of all rules and procedures.

EC-1.3 (b) A paralegal shall avoid impropriety and the appearance of impropriety and shall not engage in any conduct that would adversely affect his/her fitness to practice. Such conduct may include, but is not limited to: violence, dishonesty, interference with the administration of justice, and/or abuse of a professional position or public office.

EC-1.3 (c) Should a paralegal's fitness to practice be compromised by physical or mental illness, causing that paralegal to commit an act that is in direct violation of the Model Code/Model Rules and/or the rules and/or laws governing the jurisdiction in which the paralegal practices, that paralegal may be protected from sanction upon review of the nature and circumstances of that illness.

EC-1.3 (d) A paralegal shall advise the proper authority of non-confidential knowledge of any action of another legal professional that clearly demonstrates fraud, deceit, dishonesty, or misrepresentation. The authority to whom the report is made shall depend on the nature and circumstances of the possible misconduct (e.g., ethics committees of law firms, corporations and/or paralegal associations, local or state bar associations, local prosecutors, administrative agencies, etc.). Failure to report such knowledge is in itself misconduct and shall be treated as such under these rules.

EC-1.3 (e) A paralegal shall not knowingly assist any individual with the commission of an act that is in direct violation of the Model Code/Model Rules and/or the rules and/or laws governing the jurisdiction in which the paralegal practices.

EC-1.3 (f) If a paralegal possesses knowledge of future criminal activity, that knowledge must be reported to the appropriate authority immediately.

1.4. A Paralegal Shall Serve the Public Interest by Contributing to the Improvement of the Legal System and Delivery of Quality Legal Services, Including Pro Bono Publico Services.

Ethical Considerations

EC-1.4 (a) A paralegal shall be sensitive to the legal needs of the public and shall promote the development and implementation of programs that address those needs.

EC-1.4 (b) A paralegal shall support efforts to improve the legal system and access thereto and shall assist in making changes.

EC-1.4 (c) A paralegal shall support and participate in the delivery of Pro Bono Publico services directed toward implementing and improving access to justice, the law, the legal system or the paralegal and legal professions.

EC-1.4 (d) A paralegal should aspire annually to contribute twenty-four (24) hours of Pro Bono Publico services under the supervision of an attorney or as authorized by administrative, statutory or court authority to:

1. persons of limited means; or
2. charitable, religious, civic, community, governmental and educational organizations in matters that are designed primarily to address the legal needs of persons with limited means; or
3. individuals, groups or organizations seeking to secure or protect civil rights, civil liberties or public rights.

The twenty-four (24) hours of Pro Bono Publico services contributed annually by a paralegal may consist of such services as detailed in this EC-1.4(d), and/or administrative matters designed to develop and implement the attainment of this aspiration as detailed above in EC-1.4(a) or (c), or any combination of the two.

1.5. A Paralegal Shall Preserve All Confidential Information Provided by the Client or Acquired from Other Sources Before, During, and After the Course of the Professional Relationship.

Ethical Considerations

EC-1.5 (a) A paralegal shall be aware of and abide by all legal authority governing confidential information in the jurisdiction in which the paralegal practices.

EC-1.5 (b) A paralegal shall not use confidential information to the disadvantage of the client.

EC-1.5 (c) A paralegal shall not use confidential information to the advantage of the paralegal or of a third person.

EC-1.5 (d) A paralegal may reveal confidential information only after full disclosure and with the client's written consent; or, when required by law or court order; or, when necessary to prevent the client from committing an act that could result in death or serious bodily harm.

EC-1.5 (e) A paralegal shall keep those individuals responsible for the legal representation of a client fully informed of any confidential information the paralegal may have pertaining to that client.

EC-1.5 (f) A paralegal shall not engage in any indiscreet communications concerning clients.

1.6. A Paralegal Shall Avoid Conflicts of Interest and Shall Disclose Any Possible Conflict to the Employer or Client, as Well as to the Prospective Employers or Clients.

Ethical Considerations

EC-1.6 (a) A paralegal shall act within the bounds of the law, solely for the benefit of the client, and shall be free of compromising influences and loyalties. Neither the paralegal's personal or business interest, nor those of other clients or third persons, should compromise the paralegal's professional judgment and loyalty to the client.

EC-1.6 (b) A paralegal shall avoid conflicts of interest that may arise from previous assignments, whether for a present or past employer or client.

EC-1.6 (c) A paralegal shall avoid conflicts of interest that may arise from family relationships and from personal and business interests.

EC-1.6 (d) In order to be able to determine whether an actual or potential conflict of interest exists, a paralegal shall create and maintain an effective recordkeeping system that identifies clients, matters, and parties with which the paralegal has worked.

EC-1.6 (e) A paralegal shall reveal sufficient non-confidential information about a client or former client to reasonably ascertain if an actual or potential conflict of interest exists.

EC-1.6 (f) A paralegal shall not participate in or conduct work on any matter where a conflict of interest has been identified.

EC-1.6 (g) In matters where a conflict of interest has been identified and the client consents to continued representation, a paralegal shall comply fully with the implementation and maintenance of an Ethical Wall.

1.7. A Paralegal's Title Shall Be Fully Disclosed.

Ethical Considerations

EC-1.7 (a) A paralegal's title shall clearly indicate the individual's status and shall be disclosed in all business and professional communications to avoid misunderstandings and misconceptions about the paralegal's role and responsibilities.

EC-1.7 (b) A paralegal's title shall be included if the paralegal's name appears on business cards, letterhead, brochures, directories, and advertisements.

EC-1.7 (c) A paralegal shall not use letterhead, business cards or other promotional materials to create a fraudulent impression of his/her status or ability to practice in the jurisdiction in which the paralegal practices.

EC-1.7 (d) A paralegal shall not practice under color of any record, diploma, or certificate that has been illegally or fraudulently obtained or issued or which is misrepresentative in any way.

EC1.7 (e) A paralegal shall not participate in the creation, issuance, or dissemination of fraudulent records, diplomas, or certificates.

1.8. A Paralegal Shall Not Engage in the Unauthorized Practice of Law.

Ethical Considerations

EC-1.8 (a) A paralegal shall comply with the applicable legal authority governing the unauthorized practice of law in the jurisdiction in which the paralegal practices.

§2 NFPA Guidelines for the Enforcement of the Model Code of Ethics and Professional Responsibility

2.1. Basis for Discipline

2.1(a) Disciplinary investigations and proceedings brought under authority of the Rules shall be conducted in accord with obligations imposed on the paralegal professional by the Model Code of Ethics and Professional Responsibility.

2.2. Structure of Disciplinary Committee

2.2(a) The Disciplinary Committee ("Committee") shall be made up of nine (9) members including the Chair.

2.2(b) Each member of the Committee, including any temporary replacement members, shall have demonstrated working knowledge of ethics/professional responsibility-related issues and activities.

2.2(c) The Committee shall represent a cross-section of practice areas and work experience. The following recommendations are made regarding the members of the Committee.

1. At least one paralegal with one to three years of law-related work experience.
2. At least one paralegal with five to seven years of law related work experience.
3. At least one paralegal with over ten years of law related work experience.
4. One paralegal educator with five to seven years of work experience; preferably in the area of ethics/professional responsibility.
5. One paralegal manager.
6. One lawyer with five to seven years of law-related work experience.
7. One lay member.

2.2(d) The Chair of the Committee shall be appointed within thirty (30) days of its members' induction. The Chair shall have no fewer than ten (10) years of law-related work experience.

2.2(e) The terms of all members of the Committee shall be staggered. Of those members initially appointed, a simple majority plus one shall be appointed to a term of one year, and the remaining members shall be appointed to a term of two years. Thereafter, all members of the Committee shall be appointed to terms of two years.

2.2(f) If for any reason the terms of a majority of the Committee will expire at the same time, members may be appointed to terms of one year to maintain continuity of the Committee.

2.2(g) The Committee shall organize from its members a three-tiered structure to investigate, prosecute, and/or adjudicate charges of misconduct. The members shall be rotated among the tiers.

2.3. Operation of Committee

2.3(a) The Committee shall meet on an as-needed basis to discuss, investigate, and/or adjudicate alleged violations of the Model Code/Model Rules.

2.3(b) A majority of the members of the Committee present at a meeting shall constitute a quorum.

2.3(c) A Recording Secretary shall be designated to maintain complete and accurate minutes of all Committee meetings. All such minutes shall be kept confidential until a decision has been made that the matter will be set for hearing as set forth in Section 6.1 below.

2.3(d) If any member of the Committee has a conflict of interest with the Charging Party, the Responding Party, or the allegations of misconduct, that member shall not take part in any hearing or deliberations concerning those allegations. If the absence of that member creates a lack of a quorum for the Committee, then a temporary replacement for the member shall be appointed.

2.3(e) Either the Charging Party or the Responding Party may request that, for good cause shown, any member of the Committee not participate in a hearing or deliberation. All such requests shall be honored. If the absence of a Committee member under those circumstances creates a lack of a quorum for the Committee, then a temporary replacement for that member shall be appointed.

2.3(f) All discussions and correspondence of the Committee shall be kept confidential until a decision has been made that the matter will be set for hearing as set forth in Section 6.1 below.

2.3(g) All correspondence from the Committee to the Responding Party regarding any charge of misconduct and any decisions made regarding the charge shall be mailed certified mail, return receipt requested, to the Responding Party's last known address and shall be clearly marked with a "Confidential" designation.

2.4. Procedure for the Reporting of Alleged Violations of the Model Code/Disciplinary Rules

2.4(a) An individual or entity in possession of non-confidential knowledge or information concerning possible instances of misconduct shall make a confidential written report to the Committee within thirty (30) days of obtaining same. This report shall include all details of the alleged misconduct.

2.4(b) The Committee so notified shall inform the Responding Party of the allegation(s) of misconduct no later than ten (10) business days after receiving the confidential written report from the Charging Party.

2.4(c) Notification to the Responding Party shall include the identity of the Charging Party, unless, for good cause shown, the Charging Party requests anonymity.

2.4(d) The Responding Party shall reply to the allegations within ten (10) business days of notification.

2.5. Procedure for the Investigation of a Charge of Misconduct

2.5(a) Upon receipt of a Charge of Misconduct ("Charge"), or on its own initiative, the Committee shall initiate an investigation.

2.5(b) If, upon initial or preliminary review, the Committee makes a determination that the charges are either without basis in fact or, if proven, would not constitute professional misconduct, the Committee shall dismiss the allegations of misconduct. If such determination of dismissal cannot be made, a formal investigation shall be initiated.

2.5(c) Upon the decision to conduct a formal investigation, the Committee shall:

1. mail to the Charging and Responding Parties within three (3) business days of that decision notice of the commencement of a formal investigation. That notification shall be in writing and shall contain a complete explanation of all Charge(s), as well as the reasons for a formal investigation and shall cite the applicable codes and rules;
2. allow the Responding Party thirty (30) days to prepare and submit a confidential response to the Committee, which response shall address each charge specifically and shall be in writing; and
3. upon receipt of the response to the notification, have thirty (30) days to investigate the Charge(s). If an extension of time is deemed necessary, that extension shall not exceed ninety (90) days.

2.5(d) Upon conclusion of the investigation, the Committee may:

1. dismiss the Charge upon the finding that it has no basis in fact;
2. dismiss the Charge upon the finding that, if proven, the Charge would not constitute Misconduct;
3. refer the matter for hearing by the Tribunal; or
4. in the case of criminal activity, refer the Charge(s) and all investigation results to the appropriate authority.

2.6. Procedure for a Misconduct Hearing Before a Tribunal

2.6(a) Upon the decision by the Committee that a matter should be heard, all parties shall be notified and a hearing date shall be set. The hearing shall take place no more than thirty (30) days from the conclusion of the formal investigation.

2.6(b) The Responding Party shall have the right to counsel. The parties and the Tribunal shall have the right to call any witnesses and introduce any documentation that they believe will lead to the fair and reasonable resolution of the matter.

2.6(c) Upon completion of the hearing, the Tribunal shall deliberate and present a written decision to the parties in accordance with procedures as set forth by the Tribunal.

2.6(d) Notice of the decision of the Tribunal shall be appropriately published.

2.7. Sanctions

2.7(a) Upon a finding of the Tribunal that misconduct has occurred, any of the following sanctions, or others as may be deemed appropriate, may be imposed upon the Responding Party, either singularly or in combination:

1. letter of reprimand to the Responding Party; counseling;
2. attendance at an ethics course approved by the Tribunal; probation;
3. suspension of license/authority to practice; revocation of license/authority to practice;
4. imposition of a fine; assessment of costs; or
5. in the instance of criminal activity, referral to the appropriate authority.

2.7(b) Upon the expiration of any period of probation, suspension, or revocation, the Responding Party may make application for reinstatement. With the application for reinstatement, the Responding Party must show proof of having complied with all aspects of the sanctions imposed by the Tribunal.

2.8. Appellate Procedures

2.8(a) The parties shall have the right to appeal the decision of the Tribunal in accordance with the procedure as set forth by the Tribunal.

DEFINITIONS

"Appellate Body" means a body established to adjudicate an appeal to any decision made by a Tribunal or other decision-making body with respect to formally heard Charges of Misconduct.

"Charge of Misconduct" means a written submission by any individual or entity to an ethics committee, paralegal association, bar association, law enforcement agency, judicial body, government agency, or other appropriate body or entity, that sets forth non-confidential information regarding any instance of alleged misconduct by an individual paralegal or paralegal entity.

"Charging Party" means any individual or entity who submits a Charge of Misconduct against an individual paralegal or paralegal entity.

"Competency" means the demonstration of: diligence, education, skill, and mental, emotional, and physical fitness reasonably necessary for the performance of paralegal services.

"Confidential Information" means information relating to a client, whatever its source, that is not public knowledge nor available to the public. ("Non-Confidential Information" would generally include the name of the client and the identity of the matter for which the paralegal provided services.)

"Disciplinary Hearing" means the confidential proceeding conducted by a committee or other designated body or entity concerning any instance of alleged misconduct by an individual paralegal or paralegal entity.

"Disciplinary Committee" means any committee that has been established by an entity such as a paralegal association, bar association, judicial body, or government agency to: (a) identify, define, and investigate general ethical considerations and concerns with respect to paralegal practice; (b) administer and enforce the Model Code and Model Rules and; (c) discipline any individual paralegal or paralegal entity found to be in violation of same.

"Disclose" means communication of information reasonably sufficient to permit identification of the significance of the matter in question.

"Ethical Wall" means the screening method implemented in order to protect a client from a conflict of interest. An Ethical Wall generally includes, but is not limited to, the following elements: (1) prohibit the paralegal from having any connection with the matter; (2) ban discussions with or the transfer of documents to or from the paralegal; (3) restrict access to files; and (4) educate all members of the firm, corporation, or entity as to the separation of the paralegal (both organizationally and physically) from the pending matter. For more information regarding the Ethical Wall, see the NFPA publication entitled "The Ethical Wall—Its Application to Paralegals."

"Ex parte" means actions or communications conducted at the instance and for the benefit of one party only, and without notice to, or contestation by, any person adversely interested.

"Investigation" means the investigation of any charge(s) of misconduct filed against an individual paralegal or paralegal entity by a Committee.

"Letter of Reprimand" means a written notice of formal censure or severe reproof administered to an individual paralegal or paralegal entity for unethical or improper conduct.

"Misconduct" means the knowing or unknowing commission of an act that is in direct violation of those Canons and Ethical Considerations of any and all applicable codes and/or rules of conduct.

"Paralegal" is synonymous with "Legal Assistant" and is defined as a person qualified through education, training, or work experience to perform substantive legal work that requires knowledge of legal concepts and is customarily, but not exclusively, performed by a lawyer. This person may be retained or employed by a lawyer, law office, governmental agency, or other entity or may be authorized by administrative, statutory, or court authority to perform this work.

"Pro Bono Publico" means providing or assisting to provide quality legal services in order to enhance access to justice for persons of limited means; charitable, religious, civic, community, governmental, and educational organizations in matters that are designed primarily to address the legal needs of persons with limited means; or individuals, groups or organizations seeking to secure or protect civil rights, civil liberties or public rights.

"Proper Authority" means the local paralegal association, the local or state bar association, Committee(s) of the local paralegal or bar association(s), local prosecutor, administrative agency, or other tribunal empowered to investigate or act upon an instance of alleged misconduct.

"Responding Party" means an individual paralegal or paralegal entity against whom a Charge of Misconduct has been submitted.

"Revocation" means the recision of the license, certificate, or other authority to practice of an individual paralegal or paralegal entity found in violation of those Canons and Ethical Considerations of any and all applicable codes and/or rules of conduct.

"Suspension" means the suspension of the license, certificate, or other authority to practice of an individual paralegal or paralegal entity found in violation of those Canons and Ethical Considerations of any and all applicable codes and/or rules of conduct.

"Tribunal" means the body designated to adjudicate allegations of misconduct.

APPENDIX C

Model Standards and Guidelines for Utilization of Legal Assistants—Paralegals

Table of Contents:

INTRODUCTION
PREAMBLE
DEFINITION
STANDARDS
GUIDELINES
Addendum (include case law references and summary of state activity)

INTRODUCTION

The purpose of this annotated version of the National Association of Legal Assistants, Inc. Model Standards and Guidelines for the Utilization of Legal Assistants (the "Model," "Standards" and/or the "Guidelines") is to provide references to the existing case law and other authorities where the underlying issues have been considered. The authorities cited will serve as a basis upon which conduct of a legal assistant may be analyzed as proper or improper.

The Guidelines represent a statement of how the legal assistant may function. The Guidelines are not intended to be a comprehensive or exhaustive list of the proper duties of a legal assistant. Rather, they are designed as guides to what may or may not be proper conduct for the legal assistant. In formulating the Guidelines, the reasoning and rules of law in many reported decisions of disciplinary cases and unauthorized practice of law cases have been analyzed and considered. In addition, the provisions of the American Bar Association's Model Rules of Professional Conduct, as well as the ethical promulgations of various state courts and bar associations, have been considered in the development of the Guidelines.

These Guidelines form a sound basis for the legal assistant and the supervising attorney to follow. This Model will serve as a comprehensive resource document and as a definitive, well-reasoned guide to those considering voluntary standards and guidelines for legal assistants.

I
PREAMBLE

Proper utilization of the services of legal assistants contributes to the delivery of cost-effective, high-quality legal services. Legal assistants and the legal profession should be assured that measures exist for identifying legal assistants and their role in assisting attorneys in the delivery of legal services. Therefore, the National Association of Legal Assistants, Inc., hereby adopts these Standards and Guidelines as an educational document for the benefit of legal assistants and the legal profession.

Comment

The three most frequently raised questions concerning legal assistants are (1) How do you define a legal assistant; (2) Who is qualified to be identified as a legal assistant; and (3) What duties may a legal assistant perform? The definition adopted in 1984 by the National Association of Legal Assistants answers the first question. The Model sets forth minimum education, training, and experience through standards which will assure that an individual utilizing the title "legal assistant" or "paralegal" has the qualifications to be held out to the legal community and the public in that capacity. The Guidelines identify those acts which the reported cases hold to be proscribed and give examples of services which the legal assistant may perform under the supervision of a licensed attorney.

These Guidelines constitute a statement relating to services performed by legal assistants, as defined herein, as approved by court decisions and other sources of authority. The purpose of the Guidelines is not to place limitations or restrictions on the legal assistant profession. Rather, the Guidelines are intended to outline for the legal profession an acceptable course of conduct. Voluntary recognition and utilization of the Standards and Guidelines will benefit the entire legal profession and the public it serves.

II
DEFINITION

The National Association of Legal Assistants adopted the following definition in 1984:

> Legal assistants, also known as paralegals, are a distinguishable group of persons who assist attorneys in the delivery of legal services. Through formal education, training, and experience, legal assistants have knowledge and expertise regarding the legal system and substantive and procedural law which qualify them to do work of a legal nature under the supervision of an attorney.

In recognition of the similarity of the definitions and the need for one clear definition, in July 2001, the NALA membership approved a resolution to adopt the definition of the American Bar Association as well. The ABA definition reads as follows:

> A legal assistant or paralegal is a person qualified by education, training or work experience who is employed or retained by a lawyer, law office, corporation, governmental agency or other entity who performs specifically delegated substantive legal work for which a lawyer is responsible. (Adopted by the ABA in 1997)

Comment

These definitions emphasize the knowledge and expertise of legal assistants in substantive and procedural law obtained through education and work experience. They further define the legal assistant or paralegal as a professional working under the supervision of an attorney as distinguished from a non-lawyer who delivers services directly to the public without any intervention or review of work product by an attorney. Such unsupervised services, unless authorized by court or agency rules, constitute the unauthorized practice of law.

Statutes, court rules, case law, and bar association documents are additional sources for legal assistant or paralegal definitions. In applying the Standards and Guidelines, it is important to remember that they were developed to apply to the legal assistant as defined herein. Lawyers should refrain from labeling those as paralegals or legal assistants who do not meet the criteria set forth in these definitions and/or the definitions set forth by state rules, guidelines or bar associations. Labeling secretaries and other administrative staff as legal assistants/paralegals is inaccurate.

For billing purposes, the services of a legal secretary are considered part of overhead costs and are not recoverable in fee awards. However, the courts have held that fees for paralegal services are recoverable as long as they are not clerical functions, such as organizing files, copying documents, checking docket, updating files, checking court dates, and delivering papers. As established in Missouri v. Jenkins, 491 U.S. 274, 109 S.Ct. 2463, 2471, n.10 (1989) tasks performed by legal assistants must be substantive in nature which, absent the legal assistant, the attorney would perform.

There are also case law and Supreme Court Rules addressing the issue of a disbarred attorney serving in the capacity of a legal assistant.

III
STANDARDS

A legal assistant should meet certain minimum qualifications. The following standards may be used to determine an individual's qualifications as a legal assistant:

1. Successful completion of the Certified Legal Assistant (CLA)/Certified Paralegal (CP) certifying examination of the National Association of Legal Assistants, Inc.;
2. Graduation from an ABA approved program of study for legal assistants;
3. Graduation from a course of study for legal assistants which is institutionally accredited but not ABA approved, and which requires not less than the equivalent of 60 semester hours of classroom study;
4. Graduation from a course of study for legal assistants, other than those set forth in (2) and (3) above, plus not less than six months of in-house training as a legal assistant;
5. A baccalaureate degree in any field, plus not less than six months in-house training as a legal assistant;
6. A minimum of three years of law-related experience under the supervision of an attorney, including at least six months of in-house training as a legal assistant; or
7. Two years of in-house training as a legal assistant.

For purposes of these Standards, "in-house training as a legal assistant" means attorney education of the employee concerning legal assistant duties and these Guidelines. In addition to review and analysis of assignments, the legal assistant should receive a reasonable amount of instruction directly related to the duties and obligations of the legal assistant.

Comment

The Standards set forth suggest minimum qualifications for a legal assistant. These minimum qualifications, as adopted, recognize legal related work backgrounds and formal education backgrounds, both of which provide the legal assistant with a broad base in exposure to and knowledge of the legal profession. This background is necessary to assure the public and the legal profession that the employee identified as a legal assistant is qualified.

The Certified Legal Assistant (CLA)/Certified Paralegal (CP) examination established by NALA in 1976 is a voluntary nationwide certification program for legal assistants. *(CLA and CP are federally registered certification marks owned by NALA.)* The CLA/CP designation is a statement to the legal profession and the public that the legal assistant has met the high levels of knowledge and professionalism required by NALA's certification program. Continuing education requirements, which all certified legal assistants must meet, assure that high standards are maintained. The CLA/CP designation has been recognized as a means of establishing the qualifications of a legal assistant in supreme court rules, state court and bar association standards, and utilization guidelines.

Certification through NALA is available to all legal assistants meeting the educational and experience requirements. Certified Legal Assistants may also pursue advanced certification in specialty practice areas through the APC, Advanced Paralegal Certification, credentialing program. Legal assistants/paralegals may also pursue certification based on state laws and procedures in California, Florida, Louisiana, and Texas.

IV GUIDELINES

These Guidelines relating to standards of performance and professional responsibility are intended to aid legal assistants and attorneys. The ultimate responsibility rests with an attorney who employs legal assistants to educate them with respect to the duties they are assigned and to supervise the manner in which such duties are accomplished.

Comment

In general, a legal assistant is allowed to perform any task which is properly delegated and supervised by an attorney, as long as the attorney is ultimately responsible to the client and assumes complete professional responsibility for the work product.

ABA Model Rules of Professional Conduct, Rule 5.3 provides:

With respect to a non-lawyer employed or retained by or associated with a lawyer:

a. a partner in a law firm shall make reasonable efforts to ensure that the firm has in effect measures giving reasonable assurance that the person's conduct is compatible with the professional obligations of the lawyer;
b. a lawyer having direct supervisory authority over the non-lawyer shall make reasonable efforts to ensure that the person's conduct is compatible with the professional obligations of the lawyer; and
c. a lawyer shall be responsible for conduct of such a person that would be a violation of the rules of professional conduct if engaged in by a lawyer if:
    1. the lawyer orders or, with the knowledge of the specific conduct ratifies the conduct involved; or
    2. the lawyer is a partner in the law firm in which the person is employed, or has direct supervisory authority over the person, and knows of the conduct at a time when its consequences can be avoided or mitigated but fails to take remedial action.

There are many interesting and complex issues involving the use of legal assistants. In any discussion of the proper role of a legal assistant, attention must be directed to what constitutes the practice of law. Proper delegation to legal assistants is further complicated and confused by the lack of an adequate definition of the practice of law.

Kentucky became the first state to adopt a Paralegal Code by Supreme Court Rule. This Code sets forth certain exclusions to the unauthorized practice of law:

> For purposes of this rule, the unauthorized practice of law shall not include any service rendered involving legal knowledge or advice, whether representation, counsel or advocacy, in or out of court, rendered in respect to the acts, duties, obligations, liabilities or business relations of the one requiring services where:
> a. The client understands that the paralegal is not a lawyer;
> b. The lawyer supervises the paralegal in the performance of his or her duties; and
> c. The lawyer remains fully responsible for such representation including all actions taken or not taken in connection therewith by the paralegal to the same extent as if such representation had been furnished entirely by the lawyer and all such actions had been taken or not taken directly by the attorney. Paralegal Code, Ky.S.Ct. R3.700, Sub-Rule 2.

South Dakota Supreme Court Rule 97-25 Utilization Rule a(4) states:

> The attorney remains responsible for the services performed by the legal assistant to the same extent as though such services had been furnished entirely by the attorney and such actions were those of the attorney.

GUIDELINE 1

Legal assistants should:

1. Disclose their status as legal assistants at the outset of any professional relationship with a client, other attorneys, a court or administrative agency or personnel thereof, or members of the general public;
2. Preserve the confidences and secrets of all clients; and
3. Understand the attorney's Rules of Professional Responsibility and these Guidelines in order to avoid any action which would involve the attorney in a violation of the Rules, or give the appearance of professional impropriety.

Comment

Routine early disclosure of the paralegal's status when dealing with persons outside the attorney's office is necessary to assure that there will be no misunderstanding as to the responsibilities and role of the legal assistant. Disclosure may be made in any way that avoids confusion. If the person dealing with the legal assistant already knows of his/her status, further disclosure is unnecessary. If at any time in written or oral communication the legal assistant becomes aware that the other person may believe the legal assistant is an attorney, immediate disclosure should be made as to the legal assistant's status.

The attorney should exercise care that the legal assistant preserves and refrains from using any confidence or secrets of a client, and should instruct the legal assistant not to disclose or use any such confidences or secrets.

The legal assistant must take any and all steps necessary to prevent conflicts of interest and fully disclose such conflicts to the supervising attorney. Failure to do so may jeopardize both the attorney's representation of the client and the case itself.

Guidelines for the Utilization of Legal Assistant Services adopted December 3, 1994, by the Washington State Bar Association Board of Governors states:

> Guideline 7: A lawyer shall take reasonable measures to prevent conflicts of interest resulting from a legal assistant's other employment or interest insofar as such other employment or interests would present a conflict of interest if it were that of the lawyer.

In Re Complex Asbestos Litigation, 232 Cal. App. 3d 572 (Cal. 1991), addresses the issue wherein a law firm was disqualified due to possession of attorney-client confidences by a legal assistant employee resulting from previous employment by opposing counsel.

In Oklahoma, in an order issued July 12, 2001, in the matter of *Mark A. Hayes, M.D. v. Central States Orthopedic Specialists, Inc.*, a Tulsa County District Court Judge disqualified a law firm from representation of a client on the basis that an ethical screen was an impermissible device to protect from disclosure confidences gained by a nonlawyer employee while employed by another law firm. In applying the same rules that govern attorneys, the court found that the Rules of Professional Conduct pertaining to confidentiality apply to nonlawyers who leave firms with actual knowledge of material, confidential information, and a screening device is not an appropriate alternative to the imputed disqualification of an incoming legal assistant who has moved from one firm to another during ongoing litigation and has actual knowledge of material, confidential information. The decision was appealed and the Oklahoma Supreme Court determined that, under certain circumstances, screening is an appropriate management tool for non-lawyer staff.

In 2004, the Nevada Supreme Court also addressed this issue at the urging of the state's paralegals. The Nevada Supreme Court granted a petition to rescind the Court's 1997 ruling in *Ciaffone v. District Court*. In this case, the court clarified the original ruling, stating "mere opportunity to access confidential information does not merit disqualification." The opinion stated instances in which screening may be appropriate, and listed minimum screening requirements. The opinion also set forth guidelines that a district court may use to determine if screening has been or may be effective. These considerations are:

1. substantiality of the relationship between the former and current matters
2. the time elapsed between the matters
3. size of the firm
4. number of individuals presumed to have confidential information
5. nature of their involvement in the former matter
6. timing and features of any measures taken to reduce the danger of disclosure
7. whether the old firm and the new firm represent adverse parties in the same proceeding rather than in different proceedings.

The ultimate responsibility for compliance with approved standards of professional conduct rests with the supervising attorney. The burden rests upon the attorney who employs a legal assistant to educate the latter with respect to the duties which may be assigned and then to supervise the manner in which the legal assistant carries out such duties. However, this does not relieve the legal assistant from an independent obligation to refrain from illegal conduct. Additionally, and notwithstanding that the Rules are not binding upon non-lawyers, the very nature of a legal assistant's employment imposes an obligation not to engage in conduct which would involve the supervising attorney in a violation of the Rules.

The attorney must make sufficient background investigation of the prior activities and character and integrity of his or her legal assistants.

Further, the attorney must take all measures necessary to avoid and fully disclose conflicts of interest due to other employment or interests. Failure to do so may jeopardize both the attorney's representation of the client and the case itself.

Legal assistant associations strive to maintain the high level of integrity and competence expected of the legal profession and, further, strive to uphold the high standards of ethics.

NALA's Code of Ethics and Professional Responsibility states "A legal assistant's conduct is guided by bar associations' codes of professional responsibility and rules of professional conduct."

GUIDELINE 2

Legal assistants should not:

1. Establish attorney-client relationships; set legal fees; give legal opinions or advice; or represent a client before a court, unless authorized to do so by said court; nor
2. Engage in, encourage, or contribute to any act which could constitute the unauthorized practice of law.

Comment

Case law, court rules, codes of ethics and professional responsibilities, as well as bar ethics opinions now hold which acts can and cannot be performed by a legal assistant. Generally, the determination of what acts constitute the unauthorized practice of law is made by state supreme courts.

Numerous cases exist relating to the unauthorized practice of law. Courts have gone so far as to prohibit the legal assistant from preparation of divorce kits and assisting in preparation of bankruptcy forms and, more specifically, from providing basic information about procedures and requirements, deciding where information should be placed on forms, and responding to questions from debtors regarding the interpretation or definition of terms.

Cases have identified certain areas in which an attorney has a duty to act, but it is interesting to note that none of these cases state that it is improper for an attorney to have the initial work performed by the legal assistant. This again points out the importance of adequate supervision by the employing attorney.

An attorney can be found to have aided in the unauthorized practice of law when delegating acts which cannot be performed by a legal assistant.

GUIDELINE 3

Legal assistants may perform services for an attorney in the representation of a client, provided:

1. The services performed by the legal assistant do not require the exercise of independent professional legal judgment;
2. The attorney maintains a direct relationship with the client and maintains control of all client matters;
3. The attorney supervises the legal assistant;
4. The attorney remains professionally responsible for all work on behalf of the client, including any actions taken or not taken by the legal assistant in connection therewith; and
5. The services performed supplement, merge with, and become the attorney's work product.

Comment

Paralegals, whether employees or independent contractors, perform services for the attorney in the representation of a client. Attorneys should delegate work to legal assistants commensurate with their knowledge and experience and provide appropriate instruction and supervision concerning the delegated work, as well as ethical acts of their employment. Ultimate responsibility for the work product of a legal assistant rests with the attorney. However, a legal assistant must use discretion and professional judgment and must not render independent legal judgment in place of an attorney.

The work product of a legal assistant is subject to civil rules governing discovery of materials prepared in anticipation of litigation, whether the legal assistant is viewed as an extension of the attorney or as another representative of the party itself. Fed.R.Civ.P. 26 (b) (3) and (5).

GUIDELINE 4

In the supervision of a legal assistant, consideration should be given to

1. Designating work assignments that correspond to the legal assistant's abilities, knowledge, training, and experience;
2. Educating and training the legal assistant with respect to professional responsibility, local rules and practices, and firm policies;
3. Monitoring the work and professional conduct of the legal assistant to ensure that the work is substantively correct and timely performed;
4. Providing continuing education for the legal assistant in substantive matters through courses, institutes, workshops, seminars, and in-house training; and
5. Encouraging and supporting membership and active participation in professional organizations.

Comment

Attorneys are responsible for the actions of their employees in both malpractice and disciplinary proceedings. In the vast majority of cases, the courts have not censured attorneys for a particular act delegated to the legal assistant, but rather, have been critical of and imposed sanctions against attorneys for failure to adequately supervise the legal assistant. The attorney's responsibility for supervision of his or her legal assistant must be more than a willingness to accept responsibility and liability for the legal assistant's work. Supervision of a legal assistant must be offered in both the procedural and substantive legal areas. The attorney must delegate work based upon the education, knowledge, and abilities of the legal assistant and must monitor the work product and conduct of the legal assistant to insure that the work performed is substantively correct and competently performed in a professional manner.

Michigan State Board of Commissioners has adopted Guidelines for the Utilization of Legal Assistants (April 23, 1993). These guidelines, in part, encourage employers to support legal assistant participation in continuing education programs to ensure that the legal assistant remains competent in the fields of practice in which the legal assistant is assigned.

The working relationship between the lawyer and the legal assistant should extend to cooperative efforts on public service activities wherever possible. Participation in pro bono activities is encouraged in ABA Guideline 10.

GUIDELINE 5

Except as otherwise provided by statute, court rule or decision, administrative rule or regulation, or the attorney's rules of professional responsibility, and within the preceding parameters and proscriptions, a legal assistant may perform any function delegated by an attorney, including, but not limited to the following:

1. Conduct client interviews and maintain general contact with the client after the establishment of the attorney-client relationship, so long as the client is aware of

the status and function of the legal assistant, and the client contact is under the supervision of the attorney.
2. Locate and interview witnesses, so long as the witnesses are aware of the status and function of the legal assistant.
3. Conduct investigations and statistical and documentary research for review by the attorney.
4. Conduct legal research for review by the attorney.
5. Draft legal documents for review by the attorney.
6. Draft correspondence and pleadings for review by and signature of the attorney.
7. Summarize depositions, interrogatories, and testimony for review by the attorney.
8. Attend executions of wills, real estate closings, depositions, court or administrative hearings, and trials with the attorney.
9. Author and sign letters providing the legal assistant's status is clearly indicated and the correspondence does not contain independent legal opinions or legal advice.

Comment

The United States Supreme Court has recognized the variety of tasks being performed by legal assistants and has noted that use of legal assistants encourages cost-effective delivery of legal services, *Missouri v. Jenkins*, 491 U.S. 274, 109 S.Ct. 2463, 2471, n.10 (1989). In Jenkins, the court further held that legal assistant time should be included in compensation for attorney fee awards at the market rate of the relevant community to bill legal assistant time.

Courts have held that legal assistant fees are not a part of the overall overhead of a law firm. Legal assistant services are billed separately by attorneys, and decrease litigation expenses. Tasks performed by legal assistants must contain substantive legal work under the direction or supervision of an attorney, such that if the legal assistant were not present, the work would be performed by the attorney.

In *Taylor v. Chubb*, 874 P.2d 806 (Okla. 1994), the Court ruled that attorney fees awarded should include fees for services performed by legal assistants and, further, defined tasks which may be performed by the legal assistant under the supervision of an attorney including, among others: interview clients; draft pleadings and other documents; carry on legal research, both conventional and computer aided; research public records; prepare discovery requests and responses; schedule depositions and prepare notices and subpoenas; summarize depositions and other discovery responses; coordinate and manage document production; locate and interview witnesses; organize pleadings, trial exhibits, and other documents; prepare witness and exhibit lists; prepare trial notebooks; prepare for the attendance of witnesses at trial; and assist lawyers at trials.

Except for the specific proscription contained in Guideline 1, the reported cases do not limit the duties which may be performed by a legal assistant under the supervision of the attorney.

An attorney may not split legal fees with a legal assistant, nor pay a legal assistant for the referral of legal business. An attorney may compensate a legal assistant based on the quantity and quality of the legal assistant's work and value of that work to a law practice.

CONCLUSION

These Standards and Guidelines were developed from generally accepted practices. Each supervising attorney must be aware of the specific rules, decisions, and statutes applicable to legal assistants within his/her jurisdiction.

ADDENDUM

For further information, the following cases may be helpful to you:

Duties

Taylor v. Chubb, 874 P.2d 806 (Okla. 1994)

McMackin v. McMackin, 651 A.2d 778 (Del.Fam Ct 1993)

Work Product

Fine v. Facet Aerospace Products Co., 133 F.R.D. 439 (S.D.N.Y. 1990)

Unauthorized Practice of Law

Akron Bar Assn. v. Green, 673 N.E.2d 1307 (Ohio 1997)

In Re Hessinger & Associates, 192 B.R. 211 (N.D. Calif. 1996)

In the Matter of Bright, 171 B.R. 799 (Bkrtcy. E.D. Mich)

Louisiana State Bar Assn v. Edwins, 540 So.2d 294 (La. 1989)

Attorney/Client Privilege

In Re Complex Asbestos Litigation, 232 Cal. App. 3d 572 (Calif. 1991)

Makita Corp. v. U.S., 819 F.Supp. 1099 (CIT 1993)

Conflicts

In Re Complex Asbestos Litigation, 232 Cal. App. 3d 572 (Calif. 1991)

Makita Corp. v. U.S., 819 F.Supp. 1099 (CIT 1993)

Phoenix Founders, Inc., v. Marshall, 887 S.W.2d 831 (Tex. 1994)

Smart Industries v. Superior Court, 876 P.2d 1176 (Ariz. App. Div.1 1994)

Supervision

Matter of Martinez, 754 P.2d 842 (N.M. 1988)

State v. Barrett, 483 P.2d 1106 (Kan. 1971)

Hayes v. Central States Orthopedic Specialists, Inc., 2002 OK 30, 51 P.3d 562

Liebowitz v. Eighth Judicial District Court of Nevada, Nev Sup Ct., No 39683, November 3, 2003 clarified in part and overrules in part *Ciaffone v. District Court*, 113 Nev 1165, 945. P2d 950 (1997)

Fee Awards

In Re Bicoastal Corp., 121 B.R. 653 (Bktrcy.M.D.Fla. 1990)

In Re Carter, 101 B.R. 170 (Bkrtcy.D.S.D. 1989)

Taylor v. Chubb, 874 P.2d 806 (Okla.1994)

Missouri v. Jenkins, 491 U.S. 274, 109 S.Ct. 2463, 105 L.Ed.2d 229 (1989) 11 U.S.C.A.§ 330

McMackin v. McMackin, Del.Fam.Ct. 651 A.2d 778 (1993)

Miller v. Alamo, 983 F.2d 856 (8th Cir. 1993)

Stewart v. Sullivan, 810 F.Supp. 1102 (D.Hawaii 1993)

In Re Yankton College, 101 B.R. 151 (Bkrtcy. D.S.D. 1989)

Stacey v. Stroud, 845 F.Supp. 1135 (S.D.W.Va. 1993)

Court Appearances

Louisiana State Bar Assn v. Edwins, 540 So.2d 294 (La. 1989)

In addition to the above referenced cases, you may contact your state bar association for information regarding guidelines for the utilization of legal assistants that may have been adopted by the bar, or ethical opinions concerning the utilization of legal assistants. The following states have adopted a definition of "legal assistant" or "paralegal" either through bar association guidelines, ethical opinions, legislation or case law:

Legislation

California
Florida
Illinois
Indiana
Maine
Pennsylvania

Supreme Court Cases or Rules

Kentucky
New Hampshire
New Mexico
North Dakota
Rhode Island
South Dakota
Virginia

Cases

Arizona
New Jersey
Oklahoma

Cases (Cont.)

South Carolina
Washington

Guidelines

Colorado
Connecticut
Georgia
Idaho
New York
Oregon
Utah
Wisconsin

Bar Association Activity

Alaska
Arizona
Colorado
Connecticut
Florida
Illinois

Bar Association Activity (Cont.)

Iowa
Kansas
Kentucky
Massachusetts
Michigan
Minnesota
Missouri
Nevada
New Mexico
New Hampshire
North Carolina
North Dakota
Ohio
Oregon
Rhode Island
South Carolina
South Dakota
Tennessee
Texas
Virginia
Wisconsin

Federal Court Name Abbreviations

Court	Abbrev.
United States Supreme Court	U.S.
UNITED STATES COURTS OF APPEALS	
First Circuit	1st Cir.
Second Circuit	2d Cir.
Third Circuit	3d Cir.
Fourth Circuit	4th Cir.
Fifth Circuit	5th Cir.
Sixth Circuit	6th Cir.
Seventh Circuit	7th Cir.
Eighth Circuit	8th Cir.
Ninth Circuit	9th Cir.
Tenth Circuit	10th Cir.
Eleventh Circuit	11th Cir.
D.C. Circuit	D.C. Cir.
Federal Circuit	Fed. Cir.
UNITED STATES DISTRICT COURTS	
Middle District of Alabama	M.D. Ala.
Northern District of Alabama	N.D. Ala.
Southern District of Alabama	S.D. Ala.
District of Alaska	D. Alaska
District of Arizona	D. Ariz.
Eastern District of Arkansas	E.D. Ark.
Western District of Arkansas	W.D. Ark.
Central District of California	C.D. Cal.
Eastern District of California	E.D. Cal.

(Note: The D.C.Z. ceased to exist on March 31, 1982.)

Court	Abbrev.
Northern District of California	N.D. Cal.
Southern District of California	S.D. Cal.
District of the Canal Zone	D.C.Z.
District of Colorado	D. Colo.
District of Connecticut	D. Conn.
District of Delaware	D. Del.
District of D.C.	D.D.C.
Middle District of Florida	M.D. Fla.
Northern District of Florida	N.D. Fla.
Southern District of Florida	S.D. Fla.
Middle District of Georgia	M.D. Ga.
Northern District of Georgia	N.D. Ga.
Southern District of Georgia	S.D. Ga.
District of Guam	D. Guam
District of Hawaii	D. Haw.
District of Idaho	D. Idaho
Central District of Illinois	C.D. Ill.
Northern District of Illinois	N.D. Ill.
Southern District of Illinois	S.D. Ill.
Northern District of Indiana	N.D. Ind.
Southern District of Indiana	S.D. Ind.
Northern District of Iowa	N.D. Iowa
Southern District of Iowa	S.D. Iowa
District of Kansas	D. Kan.
Eastern District of Kentucky	E.D. Ky.
Western District of Kentucky	W.D. Ky.
Eastern District of Louisiana	E.D. La.
Middle District of Louisiana	M.D. La.
Western District of Louisiana	W.D. La.
District of Maine	D. Me.
District of Maryland	D. Md.
District of Massachusetts	D. Mass.
Eastern District of Michigan	E.D. Mich.
Western District of Michigan	W.D. Mich.
District of Minnesota	D. Minn.
Northern District of Mississippi	N.D. Miss.
Southern District of Mississippi	S.D. Miss.
Eastern District of Missouri	E.D. Mo.
Western District of Missouri	W.D. Mo.
District of Montana	D. Mont.
District of Nebraska	D. Neb.

Court	Abbrev.
District of Nevada	D. Nev.
District of New Hampshire	D. N.H.
District of New Jersey	D. N.J.
District of New Mexico	D. N.M.
Eastern District of New York	E.D. N.Y.
Northern District of New York	N.D. N.Y.
Southern District of New York	S.D. N.Y.
Western District of New York	W.D. N.Y.
Eastern District of North Carolina	E.D. N.C.
Middle District of North Carolina	M.D. N.C.
Western District of North Carolina	W.D. N.C.
District of North Dakota	D. N.D.
District of the Northern Mariana Islands	D.N. Mar. I.
Northern District of Ohio	N.D. Ohio
Southern District of Ohio	S.D. Ohio
Eastern District of Oklahoma	E.D. Okla.
Northern District of Oklahoma	N.D. Okla.
Western District of Oklahoma	W.D. Okla.
District of Oregon	D. Or.
Eastern District of Pennsylvania	E.D. Pa.
Middle District of Pennsylvania	M.D. Pa.
Western District of Pennsylvania	W.D. Pa.
District of Puerto Rico	D. P.R.
District of Rhode Island	D. R.I.
District of South Carolina	D. S.C.
District of South Dakota	D. S.D.
Eastern District of Tennessee	E.D. Tenn.
Middle District of Tennessee	M.D. Tenn.
Western District of Tennessee	W.D. Tenn.
Eastern District of Texas	E.D. Tex.
Northern District of Texas	N.D. Tex.
Southern District of Texas	S.D. Tex.
Western District of Texas	W.D. Tex.
District of Utah	D. Utah
District of Vermont	D. Vt.
Eastern District of Virginia	E.D. Va.
Western District of Virginia	W.D. Va.
District of the Virgin Islands	D. V.I.
Eastern District of Washington	E.D. Wash.
Western District of Washington	W.D. Wash.

Court	Abbrev.
Northern District of West Virginia	N.D. W.Va.
Southern District of West Virginia	S.D. W.Va.
Eastern District of Wisconsin	E.D. Wis.
Western District of Wisconsin	W.D. Wis.
District of Wyoming	D. Wyo.
MILITARY COURTS	
United States Court of Appeals for the Armed Forces	Armed Forces App.
United States Court of Veterans Appeals	Vet. App.
United States Air Force Court of Criminal Appeals	A.F. Crim. App.
United States Army Court of Criminal Appeals	Army Crim. App.
United States Coast Guard Court of Criminal Appeals	Coast Guard Crim. App.
United States Navy-Marine Corps Court of Criminal Appeals	Navy-Marine Crim. App.

BANKRUPTCY COURTS

Each United States District Court has a corresponding bankruptcy court. To cite a bankruptcy court, add Bankr. to the district court abbreviation.

Examples:

Bankr. N.D. Ala.

Bankr. D. Mass.

OTHER FEDERAL COURTS

Court	Abbrev.
Court of Federal Claims	Fed. Cl.
Court of Customs and Patent Appeals	Cust. & Pat. App.
Court of Claims	Ct. Cl.
Claims Court	Cl. Ct.
Court of International Trade	Ct. Intl. Trade
Tax Court	Tax

APPENDIX E

Effective Learning

How to Study

Everyone learns differently. Some people seem to absorb information like a sponge, while others must work hard to soak up any information. Although some people truly do have photographic memories, they are few and far between. Most likely, the people who seem to absorb information "like a sponge" have learned how to maximize their learning experiences. Most of us do not take the time to figure out how we learn best and, as a result, probably spend more time than necessary to achieve the same results as more proficient learners.

Have you ever wondered how some people who are just average students seem to always get As? If you were to ask them, they probably would tell you that they spend more time than most people studying and preparing, or that they have learned how to study more effectively and efficiently in the time they have available. A good starting point is to determine how you learn best and work out methods to maximize the time and effort you have available.

LEARNING STYLES

A learning style is the way you learn most effectively. Everyone has his or her own learning style, and there are no "better" or "correct" ways to learn. Somewhere in your school career you may have been given tests—such as the Hogan/Champagne Personal Style Indicator or the Kolb Learning Style Inventory—to determine your personal learning styles. These and similar assessments are available through most school advisors and guidance counselors. If you want help in determining your learning styles, take the initiative for your own success and make an appointment with someone who can administer an assessment.

Learning styles fall into these categories:

- independent (competitive) versus collaborative
- structured versus unstructured
- auditory versus visual
- spatial versus verbal
- practical versus creative
- applied versus conceptual
- factual versus analytical
- emotional versus logical

This sounds like a lot to consider, but taking a few minutes to determine which learning style best suits you can save you countless hours of frustration—hours that could be better devoted to studying or other activities.

Independent Versus Collaborative

Do you prefer to work with a group or independently? Some people like to avoid all distractions by working alone. Others prefer to work in a study group and share information.

If you prefer to work independently, you may want to obtain additional course information from study guides and computer-assisted instruction. You may prefer lecture-format classes to small discussion courses. If you prefer to work collaboratively, you may wish to form study groups early in the semester or find a tutor to work with, and you should choose courses that include small discussion groups or group projects.

Structured Versus Unstructured

Structured learners feel more comfortable when they formalize their study habits—for example, by selecting a definite time and place in which to study every day. If you are a structured learner, you may find it useful to create "to-do" lists and keep a written schedule of classes, study times, and activities.

Unstructured learners tend to resist formalizing their study plan and try to avoid feeling "locked in." They tend to procrastinate. Procrastinators need to find ways to give more structure to their learning activities. One method is to join a study group of students who are more organized.

Auditory Versus Visual

Auditory learners learn best by listening. Visual learners learn best from what they see. Visual learners cannot always learn everything by listening to lectures or by reading and watching video presentations. Auditory learners may find it more efficient to listen to lectures and then read related material. Visual learners may do better reading the book first, and then attending lectures. Auditory learners may also find group discussion and study group activities beneficial.

Spatial Versus Verbal

Spatial learners are better then verbal learners at reading and interpreting maps, charts, and other graphics. Verbal learners prefer to read words rather than to interpret graphics. Spatial learners need to create and incorporate their own diagrams, maps, timelines, and other graphics into their notes.

Verbal learners need to translate or obtain translations of graphics into words. A useful technique for verbal learners is to take notes that describe the material, including the graphics, in such a way that a visually impaired student could understand the graphic representation from the verbal description. Teaming up with a visually impaired student may be mutually beneficial.

Practical Versus Creative

Practical learners tend to be methodical and systematic. They prefer specific instruction that is directed and focused. Creative learners prefer experimentation and creative activities. Practical learners may benefit from creating an organized study plan for each course, including detailed "to-do" lists and a calendar. For creative learners, courses that allow writing and other creative approaches may be more satisfying.

Applied Versus Conceptual

Applied learners want to know how information can be transferred to given situations. Conceptual learners are not so much concerned with the application as with the underlying concepts. Applied learners need to focus on ways in which the ideas presented in courses and lectures can be applied. Taking notes that include examples for applying the concepts helps them recall the concepts later. Conceptual learners may find it useful to consider the concepts in a broader context than that of the narrow lecture presentation.

Factual Versus Analytical

Factual learners are good with details and enjoy learning interesting and unusual facts. They prefer objective tests. Analytical learners like to break down a topic into its component parts to understand how the parts relate to each other. Analytical learners prefer essay exams that allow them to demonstrate how their knowledge relates to the question. Factual learners may want to make lists of facts, which they can associate with prior knowledge. Analytical learners may want to analyze the organization as they read a textbook, looking for trends and patterns.

Emotional Versus Logical

Emotional learners tend to prefer human-interest stories to material that presents just facts and logic. Logical learners want to understand the factual basis, including statistics, of an argument. Emotional learners may find that reading biographical sketches helps them understand factual subjects.

PUTTING IT ALL TOGETHER

1. ***Understand yourself.*** From the previous list of types of learners, select the descriptions in each category that best fit your style of learning. Look back at courses and classes you have taken in which you have done well or that you enjoyed the most. You may see a pattern that will help you understand your learning style.

2. ***Set goals.*** Determine your personal and occupational goals. Do you want a career working with people or with things? Do you want a professional career working directly with people or behind the scenes supporting others? What courses will help you acquire the skills and knowledge you need to achieve these goals?

3. ***Make a plan.*** Your educational path should lead to a goal. It may be a personal goal to be an outstanding parent or partner, or it may be a goal to be a generalist or a specialist in an occupation or profession. To achieve these goals, you will have to focus on courses that give you the necessary skills and knowledge. Within the courses may be options that accommodate your learning style, such as large lecture classes versus small-group discussion classes, face-to-face courses versus distance-learning courses, and so on.

   Create a personal plan that allows for flexibility as your goals or interests change. A good foundation will allow you more flexibility in courses and curriculum. Don't be afraid to admit that you did not enjoy some courses you expected to enjoy or that you enjoyed some classes you didn't think would give you pleasure. These insights may help you fine-tune your personal and professional goals.

4. ***Check your progress.*** Periodically assess how well you are doing in individual classes, as well as in your overall program of study. Use the opportunity to assess why you are doing better than you expected in some classes and not as well in others. You may have to adjust your overall plan or merely your learning methods. Or outside influences such as work, family, or personal issues may be interfering with your learning. Periodic self-assessment is the first step in modifying your goals.

5. ***Make adjustments.*** As your goals change, so will your plan. Don't be afraid to make the adjustments necessary to achieve your goals or to change your goals as your interests change. Life rarely follows a straight path. Be adaptable and make adjustments when necessary.

SCHEDULING TIME

Most people use a calendar to keep track of information such as birthdays, appointments, or upcoming events. Calendars may include vacations, concerts, and other special events or activities. Depending on your personal style, you might include "to-do" lists or an hour-by-hour schedule of classes and other activities. Scheduling school and study time is helpful to most students.

Whichever method works best for you, use it to track the amount of time you spend in all of your activities so you can budget your time more accurately. When scheduling, keep in mind that the power of concentration has a limitation for everyone. Don't schedule so many activities that they exceed your mental or physical abilities.

SUPPLEMENTAL LEARNING AIDS

1. ***Study guides.*** Many textbooks have a study guide that will give you additional information, including sample tests and quizzes. Your instructor may or may not require the use of a study guide. If you need additional reinforcement, you may want to purchase a study guide even if it is not a required part of the course.

2. ***Flash cards.*** Flash cards are available in college bookstores for many courses. But you will learn more by preparing your own and customizing them to the course you are taking. On the front side of an index card, write a word, phrase, or concept, and write the definition or explanation on the reverse side. With a properly prepared set of flash cards, you may not have to refer to the text or your notes when studying for a test.

3. ***Companion websites.*** Many publishers offer companion websites for their textbooks. These websites frequently are available on the publisher's website without cost or for a nominal fee. Often these websites are the equivalent of an online study guide. Others offer self-tests. The publisher may post information that has become available since the publication of the textbook.

4. ***Outlining.*** Few people have a photographic memory or the ability to absorb material on one reading. The following approach can help you use your textbook effectively.

   a. ***How long is the chapter?*** Before you start, check the length of the chapter and your reading assignment. Most textbooks are filled with graphics and illustrations that reduce the amount of actual reading time to a manageable level.
   b. ***Scan the chapter.*** Look over the material quickly to get a sense of what will be covered.
   c. ***Chapter objectives.*** At the beginning of each chapter, most textbooks list what you should learn from reading the chapter. These chapter objectives help you focus on important topics, information, and themes.
   d. ***Read the chapter.*** Quickly read through the chapter to get an overall sense of the material and how the sections relate to each other.
   e. ***Underline the important items.*** After you have done this, go back over the material and underline in pencil the items you believe are important.
   f. ***Go to class.*** From the instructor's lecture and class discussion, you may find that what you think is important changes.
   g. ***Highlight the important material.*** After class, use a highlighter to highlight what you now believe to be the important information in the text. You probably will find that it is substantially less than what you underlined in pencil.
   h. ***Make your flash cards.*** From the highlighted information, create a set of flash cards for each chapter.

5. *Tutors.* Not everyone can afford the luxury of a personal tutor, but most colleges and universities have a tutoring center or offer some form of tutoring assistance. If you are having difficulty, don't be afraid to ask for help before it is too late. At the beginning of the semester, determine what personalized help is available for each course. You may not need to use this information, but having it available will reduce your anxiety and panic if you realize that you need some help.

Don't be afraid to ask your instructor for help. Your instructor wants you to succeed. If you are doing everything you can to be successful in a class, the instructor should be more than happy to help you or direct you for help.

6. *Study groups.* If you are the type of learner who benefits from working with others, form a study group at the beginning of each semester in each course. After the first class, ask if others wish to form a study group, or post a notice on the course bulletin board website.

One advantage of study groups is the opportunity to share class notes as well as ideas. Verbal learners can benefit from having visual learners in the study group to interpret and explain charts, graphs, and maps. Study groups can motivate procrastinators to complete tasks on time.

7. *Tests.* Most students suffer from some form of test anxiety. At the beginning of each course, ask the instructor for the exam schedule and the type of tests he or she will be giving. Some schools maintain copies of all tests that students can use for practice. If your school does not maintain these, ask your instructors if they will make available sample tests and quizzes. Practice tests may be available in the study guide for the text or on a companion website. If you are in a study group, members can prepare practice tests as part of test preparation.

For more detailed information about study skills, see *Effective Study Skills: Maximizing Your Academic Potential*, by Judy M. Roberts (Prentice Hall, 1998).

The Constitution of the United States of America

PREAMBLE

We the People of the United States, in Order to form a more perfect Union, establish Justice, insure domestic Tranquility, provide for the common defense, promote the general Welfare, and secure the Blessings of Liberty to ourselves and our Posterity, do ordain and establish this Constitution for the United States of America.

ARTICLE I

Section 1. All legislative Powers herein granted shall be vested in a Congress of the United States, which shall consist of a Senate and House of Representatives.

Section 2. The House of Representatives shall be composed of Members chosen every second Year by the People of the several States, and the Electors in each State shall have the Qualifications requisite for Electors of the most numerous Branch of the State Legislature.

No Person shall be a Representative who shall not have attained to the Age of twenty five Years, and been seven Years a Citizen of the United States, and who shall not, when elected, be an Inhabitant of that State in which he shall be chosen.

Representatives and direct Taxes shall be apportioned among the several States which may be included within this Union, according to their respective Numbers, which shall be determined by adding to the whole Number of free Persons, including those bound to Service for a Term of Years, and excluding Indians not taxed, three fifths of all other Persons. The actual Enumeration shall be made within three Years after the first Meeting of the Congress of the United States, and within every subsequent Term of ten Years, in such Manner as they shall by Law direct. The Number of Representatives shall not exceed one for every thirty Thousand, but each State shall have at Least one Representative; and until such enumeration shall be made, the State of New Hampshire shall be entitled to chuse three, Massachusetts eight, Rhode Island and Providence Plantations one, Connecticut five, New York six, New Jersey four, Pennsylvania eight, Delaware one, Maryland six, Virginia ten, North Carolina five, South Carolina five, and Georgia three.

When vacancies happen in the Representation from any State, the Executive Authority thereof shall issue Writs of Election to fill such Vacancies.

The House of Representatives shall chuse their Speaker and other Officers; and shall have the sole Power of Impeachment.

Section 3. The Senate of the United States shall be composed of two Senators from each State, chosen by the Legislature thereof for six Years; and each Senator shall have one Vote.

Immediately after they shall be assembled in Consequence of the first Election, they shall be divided as equally as may be into three Classes. The Seats of the Senators of the first Class shall be vacated at the Expiration of the second Year, of the second Class at the Expiration of the fourth Year, and of the third Class at the Expiration of the sixth Year, so that one third may be chosen every second Year; and if Vacancies happen by Resignation, or otherwise, during the Recess of the Legislature of any State, the Executive thereof may make temporary Appointments until the next Meeting of the Legislature, which shall then fill such Vacancies.

No Person shall be a Senator who shall not have attained to the Age of thirty Years, and been nine Years a Citizen of the United States, and who shall not, when elected, be an Inhabitant of that State for which he shall be chosen.

The Vice President of the United States shall be President of the Senate, but shall have no Vote, unless they be equally divided.

The Senate shall chuse their other Officers, and also a President pro tempore, in the Absence of the Vice President, or when he shall exercise the Office of President of the United States.

The Senate shall have the sole Power to try all Impeachments. When sitting for that Purpose, they shall be on Oath or Affirmation. When the President of the United States is tried, the Chief Justice shall preside: And no Person shall be convicted without the Concurrence of two thirds of the Members present.

Judgment in Cases of Impeachment shall not extend further than to removal from Office, and disqualification to hold and enjoy any Office of honor, Trust or Profit under the United States: but the Party convicted shall nevertheless be liable and subject to Indictment, Trial, Judgment and Punishment, according to Law.

Section 4. The Times, Places and Manner of holding Elections for Senators and Representatives, shall be prescribed in each State by the Legislature thereof; but the Congress may at any time by Law make or alter such Regulations, except as to the Places of chusing Senators.

The Congress shall assemble at least once in every Year, and such Meeting shall be on the first Monday in December, unless they shall by Law appoint a different Day.

Section 5. Each House shall be the Judge of the Elections, Returns and Qualifications of its own Members, and a Majority of each shall constitute a Quorum to do Business; but a smaller Number may adjourn from day to day, and may be authorized to compel the Attendance of absent Members, in such Manner, and under such Penalties as each House may provide.

Each House may determine the Rules of its Proceedings, punish its Members for disorderly Behaviour, and, with the Concurrence of two thirds, expel a Member.

Each House shall keep a Journal of its Proceedings, and from time to time publish the same, excepting such Parts as may in their Judgment require Secrecy; and the Yeas and Nays of the Members of either House on any question shall, at the Desire of one fifth of those Present, be entered on the Journal.

Neither House, during the Session of Congress, shall, without the Consent of the other, adjourn for more than three days, nor to any other Place than that in which the two Houses shall be sitting.

Section 6. The Senators and Representatives shall receive a Compensation for their Services, to be ascertained by Law, and paid out of the Treasury of the United States. They shall in all Cases, except Treason, Felony and Breach of the Peace, be privileged from Arrest during their Attendance at the Session of their respective Houses, and in going to and returning from the same; and for any Speech or Debate in either House, they shall not be questioned in any other Place.

No Senator or Representative shall, during the Time for which he was elected, be appointed to any civil Office under the Authority of the United States, which shall have been created, or the Emoluments whereof shall have been encreased during such time; and no Person holding any Office under the United States, shall be a Member of either House during his Continuance in Office.

Section 7. All Bills for raising Revenue shall originate in the House of Representatives; but the Senate may propose or concur with Amendments as on other Bills.

Every Bill which shall have passed the House of Representatives and the Senate, shall, before it become a Law, be presented to the President of the United States: If he approve he shall sign it, but if not he shall return it, with his Objections to that House in which it shall have originated, who shall enter the Objections at large on their Journal, and proceed to reconsider it. If after such Reconsideration two thirds of that House shall agree to pass the Bill, it shall be sent, together with the Objections, to the other House, by which it shall likewise be reconsidered, and if approved by two thirds of that House, it shall become a Law. But in all such Cases the Votes of both Houses shall be determined by yeas and Nays, and the Names of the Persons voting for and against the Bill shall be entered on the Journal of each House respectively. If any Bill shall not be returned by the President within ten Days (Sundays excepted) after it shall have been presented to him, the Same shall be a Law, in like Manner as if he had signed it, unless the Congress by their Adjournment prevent its Return, in which Case it shall not be a Law.

Every Order, Resolution, or Vote to which the Concurrence of the Senate and House of Representatives may be necessary (except on a question of Adjournment) shall be presented to the President of the United States; and before the Same shall take Effect, shall be approved by him, or being disapproved by him, shall be repassed by two thirds of the Senate and House of Representatives, according to the Rules and Limitations prescribed in the Case of a Bill.

Section 8. The Congress shall have Power To lay and collect Taxes, Duties, Imposts and Excises, to pay the Debts and provide for the common Defence and general Welfare of the United States; but all Duties, Imposts and Excises shall be uniform throughout the United States;

To borrow Money on the credit of the United States;

To regulate Commerce with foreign Nations, and among the several States, and with the Indian Tribes;

To establish an uniform Rule of Naturalization, and uniform Laws on the subject of Bankruptcies throughout the United States;

To coin Money, regulate the Value thereof, and of foreign Coin, and fix the Standard of Weights and Measures;

To provide for the Punishment of counterfeiting the Securities and current Coin of the United States;

To establish Post Offices and post Roads;

To promote the Progress of Science and useful Arts, by securing for limited Times to Authors and Inventors the exclusive Right to their respective Writings and Discoveries;

To constitute Tribunals inferior to the supreme Court;

To define and punish Piracies and Felonies committed on the high Seas, and Offences against the Law of Nations;

To declare War, grant Letters of Marque and Reprisal, and make Rules concerning Captures on Land and Water;

To raise and support Armies, but no Appropriation of Money to that Use shall be for a longer Term than two Years; To provide and maintain a Navy;

To make Rules for the Government and Regulation of the land and naval Forces;

To provide for calling forth the Militia to execute the Laws of the Union, suppress Insurrections and repel Invasions;

To provide for organizing, arming, and disciplining, the Militia, and for governing such Part of them as may be employed in the Service of the United States, reserving to the States respectively, the Appointment of the Officers, and the Authority of training the Militia according to the discipline prescribed by Congress;

To exercise exclusive Legislation in all Cases whatsoever, over such District (not exceeding ten Miles square) as may, by Cession of particular States, and the Acceptance of Congress, become the Seat of the Government of the United States, and to exercise like Authority over all Places purchased by the Consent of the Legislature of the State in which the Same shall be, for the Erection of Forts, Magazines, Arsenals, dock-Yards, and other needful Buildings;—And

To make all Laws which shall be necessary and proper for carrying into Execution the foregoing Powers, and all other Powers vested by this Constitution in the Government of the United States, or in any Department or Officer thereof.

Section 9. The Migration or Importation of such Persons as any of the States now existing shall think proper to admit, shall not be prohibited by the Congress prior to the Year one thousand eight hundred and eight, but a Tax or duty may be imposed on such Importation, not exceeding ten dollars for each Person.

The Privilege of the Writ of Habeas Corpus shall not be suspended, unless when in Cases of Rebellion or Invasion the public Safety may require it.

No Bill of Attainder or ex post facto Law shall be passed.

No Capitation, or other direct, Tax shall be laid, unless in Proportion to the Census or enumeration herein before directed to be taken.

No Tax or Duty shall be laid on Articles exported from any State.

No Preference shall be given by any Regulation of Commerce or Revenue to the Ports of one State over those of another; nor shall Vessels bound to, or from, one State, be obliged to enter, clear, or pay Duties in another.

No Money shall be drawn from the Treasury, but in Consequence of Appropriations made by Law; and a regular Statement and Account of the Receipts and Expenditures of all public Money shall be published from time to time.

No Title of Nobility shall be granted by the United States: And no Person holding any Office of Profit or Trust under them, shall, without the Consent of the Congress, accept of any present, Emolument, Office, or Title, of any kind whatever, from any King, Prince, or foreign State.

Section 10. No State shall enter into any Treaty, Alliance, or Confederation; grant Letters of Marque and Reprisal; coin Money; emit Bills of Credit; make any Thing but gold and silver Coin a Tender in Payment of Debts; pass any Bill of Attainder, ex post facto Law, or Law impairing the Obligation of Contracts, or grant any Title of Nobility.

No State shall, without the Consent of the Congress, lay any Imposts or Duties on Imports or Exports, except what may be absolutely necessary for executing it's inspection Laws: and the net Produce of all Duties and Imposts, laid by any State on Imports or Exports, shall be for the Use of the Treasury of the United States; and all such Laws shall be subject to the Revision and Controul of the Congress.

No State shall, without the Consent of Congress, lay any Duty of Tonnage, keep Troops, or Ships of War in time of Peace, enter into any Agreement or Compact with another State, or with a foreign Power, or engage in War, unless actually invaded, or in such imminent Danger as will not admit of delay.

ARTICLE II

Section 1. The executive Power shall be vested in a President of the United States of America. He shall hold his Office during the Term of four Years, and, together with the Vice President, chosen for the same Term, be elected, as follows:

Each State shall appoint, in such Manner as the Legislature thereof may direct, a Number of Electors, equal to the whole Number of Senators and Representatives to which the State may be entitled in the Congress: but no Senator or Representative, or Person holding an Office of Trust or Profit under the United States, shall be appointed an Elector.

The Electors shall meet in their respective States, and vote by Ballot for two Persons, of whom one at least shall not be an Inhabitant of the same State with themselves. And they shall make a List of all the Persons voted for, and of the Number of Votes for each; which List they shall sign and certify, and transmit sealed to the Seat of the Government of the United States, directed to the President of the Senate. The President of the Senate shall, in the Presence of the Senate and House of Representatives, open all the Certificates, and the Votes shall then be counted. The Person having the greatest Number of Votes shall be the President, if such Number be a Majority of the whole Number of Electors appointed; and if there be more than one who have such Majority, and have an equal Number of Votes, then the House of Representatives shall immediately chuse by Ballot one of them for President; and if no Person have a Majority, then from the five highest on the List the said House shall in like Manner chuse the President. But in chusing the President, the Votes shall be taken by States, the Representation from each State having one Vote; A quorum for this purpose shall consist of a Member or Members from two thirds of the States, and a Majority of all the States shall be necessary to a Choice. In every Case, after the Choice of the President, the Person having the greatest Number of Votes of the Electors shall be the Vice President. But if there should remain two or more who have equal Votes, the Senate shall chuse from them by Ballot the Vice President.

The Congress may determine the Time of chusing the Electors, and the Day on which they shall give their Votes; which Day shall be the same throughout the United States.

No Person except a natural born Citizen, or a Citizen of the United States, at the time of the Adoption of this Constitution, shall be eligible to the Office of President; neither shall any Person be eligible to that Office who shall not have attained to the Age of thirty five Years, and been fourteen Years a Resident within the United States.

In Case of the Removal of the President from Office, or of his Death, Resignation, or Inability to discharge the Powers and Duties of the said Office, the Same shall devolve on the Vice President, and the Congress may by Law provide for the Case of Removal, Death, Resignation or Inability, both of the President and Vice President, declaring what Officer shall then act as President, and such Officer shall act accordingly, until the Disability be removed, or a President shall be elected.

The President shall, at stated Times, receive for his Services, a Compensation, which shall neither be increased nor diminished during the Period for which he shall have been elected, and he shall not receive within that Period any other Emolument from the United States, or any of them.

Before he enter on the Execution of his Office, he shall take the following Oath or Affirmation:—"I do solemnly swear (or affirm) that I will faithfully execute the Office of President of the United States, and will to the best of my Ability, preserve, protect and defend the Constitution of the United States."

Section 2. The President shall be Commander in Chief of the Army and Navy of the United States, and of the Militia of the several States, when called into the actual Service of the United States; he may require the Opinion, in writing, of the principal Officer in each of the executive Departments, upon any Subject relating to the Duties of their respective Offices, and he shall have Power to grant Reprieves and Pardons for Offences against the United States, except in Cases of Impeachment.

He shall have Power, by and with the Advice and Consent of the Senate, to make Treaties, provided two thirds of the Senators present concur; and he shall nominate, and by and with the Advice and Consent of the Senate, shall appoint Ambassadors, other public Ministers and Consuls, Judges of the supreme Court, and all other Officers of the United States, whose Appointments are not herein otherwise provided for, and which shall be established by Law: but the Congress may by Law vest the Appointment of such inferior Officers, as they think proper, in the President alone, in the Courts of Law, or in the Heads of Departments.

The President shall have Power to fill up all Vacancies that may happen during the Recess of the Senate, by granting Commissions which shall expire at the End of their next Session.

Section 3. He shall from time to time give to the Congress Information of the State of the Union, and recommend to their Consideration such Measures as he shall judge necessary and expedient; he may, on extraordinary Occasions, convene both Houses, or either of them, and in Case of Disagreement between them, with Respect to the Time of Adjournment, he may adjourn them to such Time as he shall think proper; he shall receive Ambassadors and other public Ministers; he shall take Care that the Laws be faithfully executed, and shall Commission all the Officers of the United States.

Section 4. The President, Vice President and all civil Officers of the United States, shall be removed from Office on Impeachment for, and Conviction of, Treason, Bribery, or other high Crimes and Misdemeanors.

ARTICLE III

Section 1. The judicial Power of the United States shall be vested in one supreme Court, and in such inferior Courts as the Congress may from time to time ordain and establish. The Judges, both of the supreme and inferior Courts, shall hold their Offices during good Behaviour, and shall, at stated Times, receive for their Services a Compensation, which shall not be diminished during their Continuance in Office.

Section 2. The judicial Power shall extend to all Cases, in Law and Equity, arising under this Constitution, the Laws of the United States, and Treaties made, or which shall be made, under their Authority;—to all Cases affecting Ambassadors, other public Ministers and Consuls;—to all Cases of admiralty and maritime Jurisdiction;—to Controversies to which the United States shall be a Party;—to Controversies between two or more States;—between a State and Citizens of another State;—between Citizens of different States;—between Citizens of the same State claiming Lands under Grants of different States, and between a State, or the Citizens thereof, and foreign States, Citizens or Subjects.

In all Cases affecting Ambassadors, other public Ministers and Consuls, and those in which a State shall be Party, the supreme Court shall have original Jurisdiction. In all the other Cases before mentioned, the supreme Court shall have appellate Jurisdiction, both as to Law and Fact, with such Exceptions, and under such Regulations as the Congress shall make.

The Trial of all Crimes, except in Cases of Impeachment, shall be by Jury; and such Trial shall be held in the State where the said Crimes shall have been committed; but when not committed within any State, the Trial shall be at such Place or Places as the Congress may by Law have directed.

Section 3. Treason against the United States, shall consist only in levying War against them, or in adhering to their Enemies, giving them Aid and Comfort. No Person shall be convicted of Treason unless on the Testimony of two Witnesses to the same overt Act, or on Confession in open Court.

The Congress shall have Power to declare the Punishment of Treason, but no Attainder of Treason shall work Corruption of Blood, or Forfeiture except during the Life of the Person attainted.

ARTICLE IV

Section 1. Full Faith and Credit shall be given in each State to the public Acts, Records, and judicial Proceedings of every other State. And the Congress may by general Laws prescribe the Manner in which such Acts, Records and Proceedings shall be proved, and the Effect thereof.

Section 2. The Citizens of each State shall be entitled to all Privileges and Immunities of Citizens in the several States.

A Person charged in any State with Treason, Felony, or other Crime, who shall flee from Justice, and be found in another State, shall on Demand of the executive Authority of the State from which he fled, be delivered up, to be removed to the State having Jurisdiction of the Crime.

No Person held to Service or Labour in one State, under the Laws thereof, escaping into another, shall, in Consequence of any Law or Regulation therein, be discharged from such Service or Labour, but shall be delivered up on Claim of the Party to whom such Service or Labour may be due.

Section 3. New States may be admitted by the Congress into this Union; but no new State shall be formed or erected within the Jurisdiction of any other State; nor any State be formed by the Junction of two or more States, or Parts of States, without the Consent of the Legislatures of the States concerned as well as of the Congress.

The Congress shall have Power to dispose of and make all needful Rules and Regulations respecting the Territory or other Property belonging to the United States; and nothing in this Constitution shall be so construed as to Prejudice any Claims of the United States, or of any particular State.

Section 4. The United States shall guarantee to every State in this Union a Republican Form of Government, and shall protect each of them against Invasion; and on Application of the Legislature, or of the Executive (when the Legislature cannot be convened), against domestic Violence.

ARTICLE V

The Congress, whenever two thirds of both Houses shall deem it necessary, shall propose Amendments to this Constitution, or, on the Application of the Legislatures of two thirds of the several States, shall call a Convention for proposing Amendments, which, in either Case, shall be valid to all Intents and Purposes, as Part of this Constitution, when ratified by the Legislatures of three fourths of the several States, or by Conventions in three fourths thereof, as the one or the other Mode of Ratification may be proposed by the Congress; Provided that no Amendment which may be made prior to the Year One thousand eight hundred and eight shall in any Manner affect the first and fourth Clauses in the Ninth Section of the first Article; and that no State, without its Consent, shall be deprived of its equal Suffrage in the Senate.

ARTICLE VI

All Debts contracted and Engagements entered into, before the Adoption of this Constitution, shall be as valid against the United States under this Constitution, as under the Confederation.

This Constitution, and the Laws of the United States which shall be made in Pursuance thereof; and all Treaties made, or which shall be made, under the Authority of the United States, shall be the supreme Law of the Land; and the Judges in every State shall be bound thereby, any Thing in the Constitution or Laws of any State to the Contrary notwithstanding.

The Senators and Representatives before mentioned, and the Members of the several State Legislatures, and all executive and judicial Officers, both of the United States and of the several States, shall be bound by Oath or Affirmation, to support this Constitution; but no religious Test shall ever be required as a Qualification to any Office or public Trust under the United States.

ARTICLE VII

The Ratification of the Conventions of nine States, shall be sufficient for the Establishment of this Constitution between the States so ratifying the Same.

AMENDMENTS TO THE CONSTITUTION OF THE UNITED STATES

[Amendments I–X make up the Bill of Rights]

AMENDMENT I

Congress shall make no law respecting an establishment of religion, or prohibiting the free exercise thereof; or abridging the freedom of speech, or of the press; or the right of the people peaceably to assemble, and to petition the Government for a redress of grievances.

AMENDMENT II

A well regulated Militia, being necessary to the security of a free State, the right of the people to keep and bear Arms, shall not be infringed.

AMENDMENT III

No Soldier shall, in time of peace be quartered in any house, without the consent of the Owner, nor in time of war, but in a manner to be prescribed by law.

AMENDMENT IV

The right of the people to be secure in their persons, houses, papers, and effects, against unreasonable searches and seizures, shall not be violated, and no Warrants shall issue, but upon probable cause, supported by Oath or affirmation, and particularly describing the place to be searched, and the persons or things to be seized.

AMENDMENT V

No person shall be held to answer for a capital, or otherwise infamous crime, unless on a presentment or indictment of a Grand Jury, except in cases arising in the land or naval forces, or in the Militia, when in actual service in time of War or public danger; nor shall any person be subject for the same offence to be twice put in jeopardy of life or limb; nor shall be compelled in any criminal case to be a witness against himself, nor be deprived of life, liberty, or property, without due process of law; nor shall private property be taken for public use, without just compensation.

AMENDMENT VI

In all criminal prosecutions, the accused shall enjoy the right to a speedy and public trial, by an impartial jury of the State and district wherein the crime shall have been committed, which district shall have been previously ascertained by law, and to be informed of the nature and cause of the accusation; to be confronted with the witnesses against him; to have compulsory process for obtaining witnesses in his favor, and to have the Assistance of Counsel for his defence.

AMENDMENT VII

In suits at common law, where the value in controversy shall exceed twenty dollars, the right of trial by jury shall be preserved, and no fact tried by a jury, shall be otherwise reexamined in any Court of the United States, than according to the rules of the common law.

AMENDMENT VIII

Excessive bail shall not be required, nor excessive fines imposed, nor cruel and unusual punishments inflicted.

AMENDMENT IX

The enumeration in the Constitution, of certain rights, shall not be construed to deny or disparage others retained by the people.

AMENDMENT X

The powers not delegated to the United States by the Constitution, nor prohibited by it to the States, are reserved to the States respectively, or to the people.

AMENDMENT XI

The Judicial power of the United States shall not be construed to extend to any suit in law or equity, commenced or prosecuted against one of the United States by Citizens of another State, or by Citizens or Subjects of any Foreign State.

AMENDMENT XII

The Electors shall meet in their respective states and vote by ballot for President and Vice-President, one of whom, at least, shall not be an inhabitant of the same state with themselves; they shall name in their ballots the person voted for as President, and in distinct ballots the person voted for as Vice-President, and they shall make distinct lists of all persons voted for as President, and of all persons voted for as Vice-President, and of the number of votes for each, which lists they shall sign and certify, and transmit sealed to the seat of the government of the United States, directed to the President of the Senate;—the President of the Senate shall, in the presence of the Senate and House of Representatives, open all the certificates and the votes shall then be counted;—The person having the greatest number of votes for President, shall be the President, if such number be a majority of the whole number of Electors appointed; and if no person have such majority, then from the persons having the highest numbers not exceeding three on the list of those voted for as President, the House of Representatives shall choose immediately, by ballot, the President. But in choosing the President, the votes shall be taken by states, the representation from each state having one vote; a quorum for this purpose shall consist of a member or members from two-thirds of the states, and a majority of all the states shall be necessary to a choice. [And if the House of Representatives shall not choose a President whenever the right of choice shall devolve upon them, before the fourth day of March next following, then the Vice-President shall act as President, as in case of the death or other constitutional disability of the President.—]* The person having the greatest number of votes as Vice-President, shall be the Vice-President, if such number be a majority of the whole number of Electors appointed, and if no person have a majority, then from the two highest numbers on the list, the Senate shall choose the Vice-President; a quorum for the purpose shall consist of two-thirds of the whole number of Senators, and a majority of the whole number shall be necessary to a choice. But no person constitutionally ineligible to the office of President shall be eligible to that of Vice-President of the United States.

AMENDMENT XIII

Section 1. Neither slavery nor involuntary servitude, except as a punishment for crime whereof the party shall have been duly convicted, shall exist within the United States, or any place subject to their jurisdiction.

Section 2. Congress shall have power to enforce this article by appropriate legislation.

AMENDMENT XIV

Section 1. All persons born or naturalized in the United States, and subject to the jurisdiction thereof, are citizens of the United States and of the State wherein they reside. No State shall make or enforce any law which shall abridge the privileges or immunities of citizens of the United States; nor shall any State deprive any person of life, liberty, or property, without due process of law; nor deny to any person within its jurisdiction the equal protection of the laws.

Section 2. Representatives shall be apportioned among the several States according to their respective numbers, counting the whole number of persons in each State, excluding Indians not taxed. But when the right to vote at any election for the choice of electors for President and Vice-President of the United States, Representatives in Congress, the Executive and Judicial officers of a State, or the members of the Legislature thereof, is denied to any of the male inhabitants of such State, being twenty-one years of age,* and citizens of the United States, or in any way abridged, except for participation in rebellion, or other crime, the basis of representation therein shall be reduced in the proportion which the number of such male citizens shall bear to the whole number of male citizens twenty-one years of age in such State.

Section 3. No person shall be a Senator or Representative in Congress, or elector of President and Vice-President, or hold any office, civil or military, under the United States, or under any State, who, having previously taken an oath, as a member of Congress, or as an officer of the United States, or as a member of any State legislature, or as an executive or judicial officer of any State, to support the Constitution of the United States, shall have engaged in insurrection or rebellion against the same, or given aid or comfort to the enemies thereof. But Congress may by a vote of two-thirds of each House, remove such disability.

Section 4. The validity of the public debt of the United States, authorized by law, including debts incurred for payment of pensions and bounties for services in suppressing insurrection or rebellion, shall not be questioned. But neither the United States nor any State shall assume or pay any debt or obligation incurred in aid of insurrection or rebellion against the United States, or any claim for the loss or emancipation of any slave; but all such debts, obligations and claims shall be held illegal and void.

Section 5. The Congress shall have the power to enforce, by appropriate legislation, the provisions of this article.

AMENDMENT XV

Section 1. The right of citizens of the United States to vote shall not be denied or abridged by the United States or by any State on account of race, color, or previous condition of servitude.

Section 2. The Congress shall have the power to enforce this article by appropriate legislation.

AMENDMENT XVI

The Congress shall have power to lay and collect taxes on incomes, from whatever source derived, without apportionment among the several States, and without regard to any census or enumeration.

AMENDMENT XVII

The Senate of the United States shall be composed of two Senators from each State, elected by the people thereof, for six years; and each Senator shall have one vote. The electors in each State shall have the qualifications requisite for electors of the most numerous branch of the State legislatures.

When vacancies happen in the representation of any State in the Senate, the executive authority of such State shall issue writs of election to fill such vacancies: Provided, That the legislature of any State may empower the executive thereof to make temporary appointments until the people fill the vacancies by election as the legislature may direct.

This amendment shall not be so construed as to affect the election or term of any Senator chosen before it becomes valid as part of the Constitution.

AMENDMENT XVIII

Section 1. After one year from the ratification of this article the manufacture, sale, or transportation of intoxicating liquors within, the importation thereof into, or the exportation thereof from the United States and all territory subject to the jurisdiction thereof for beverage purposes is hereby prohibited.

Section 2. The Congress and the several States shall have concurrent power to enforce this article by appropriate legislation.

Section 3. This article shall be inoperative unless it shall have been ratified as an amendment to the Constitution by the legislatures of the several States, as provided in the Constitution, within seven years from the date of the submission hereof to the States by the Congress.

AMENDMENT XIX

The right of citizens of the United States to vote shall not be denied or abridged by the United States or by any State on account of sex.

Congress shall have power to enforce this article by appropriate legislation.

AMENDMENT XX

Section 1. The terms of the President and the Vice President shall end at noon on the 20th day of January, and the terms of Senators and Representatives at noon on the 3d day of January, of the years in which such terms would have ended if this article had not been ratified; and the terms of their successors shall then begin.

Section 2. The Congress shall assemble at least once in every year, and such meeting shall begin at noon on the 3d day of January, unless they shall by law appoint a different day.

Section 3. If, at the time fixed for the beginning of the term of the President, the President elect shall have died, the Vice President elect shall become President. If a President shall not have been chosen before the time fixed for the beginning of his term, or if the President elect shall have failed to qualify, then the Vice President elect shall act as President until a President shall have qualified; and the Congress may by law provide for the case wherein neither a President elect nor a Vice President shall have qualified, declaring who shall then act as President, or the manner in which one who is to act shall be selected, and such person shall act accordingly until a President or Vice President shall have qualified.

Section 4. The Congress may by law provide for the case of the death of any of the persons from whom the House of Representatives may choose a President whenever the right of choice shall have devolved upon them, and for the case of the death of any of the persons from whom the Senate may choose a Vice President whenever the right of choice shall have devolved upon them.

Section 5. Sections 1 and 2 shall take effect on the 15th day of October following the ratification of this article.

Section 6. This article shall be inoperative unless it shall have been ratified as an amendment to the Constitution by the legislatures of three-fourths of the several States within seven years from the date of its submission.

AMENDMENT XXI

Section 1. The eighteenth article of amendment to the Constitution of the United States is hereby repealed.

Section 2. The transportation or importation into any State, Territory, or Possession of the United States for delivery or use therein of intoxicating liquors, in violation of the laws thereof, is hereby prohibited.

Section 3. This article shall be inoperative unless it shall have been ratified as an amendment to the Constitution by conventions in the several States, as provided in the Constitution, within seven years from the date of the submission hereof to the States by the Congress.

AMENDMENT XXII

Section 1. No person shall be elected to the office of the President more than twice, and no person who has held the office of President, or acted as President, for more than two years of a term to which some other person was elected President shall be elected to the office of President more than once. But this Article shall not apply to any person holding the office of President when this Article was proposed by Congress, and shall not prevent any person who may be holding the office of President, or acting as President, during the term within which this Article becomes operative from holding the office of President or acting as President during the remainder of such term.

Section 2. This article shall be inoperative unless it shall have been ratified as an amendment to the Constitution by the legislatures of three-fourths of the several States within seven years from the date of its submission to the States by the Congress.

AMENDMENT XXIII

Section 1. The District constituting the seat of Government of the United States shall appoint in such manner as Congress may direct:

A number of electors of President and Vice President equal to the whole number of Senators and Representatives in Congress to which the District would be entitled if it were a State, but in no event more than the least populous State; they shall be in addition to those appointed by the States, but they shall be considered, for the purposes of the election of President and Vice President, to be electors appointed by a State; and they shall meet in the District and perform such duties as provided by the twelfth article of amendment.

Section 2. The Congress shall have power to enforce this article by appropriate legislation.

AMENDMENT XXIV

Section 1. The right of citizens of the United States to vote in any primary or other election for President or Vice President, for electors for President or Vice President, or for Senator or Representative in Congress, shall not be denied or abridged by the United States or any State by reason of failure to pay poll tax or other tax.

Section 2. The Congress shall have power to enforce this article by appropriate legislation.

AMENDMENT XXV

Section 1. In case of the removal of the President from office or of his death or resignation, the Vice President shall become President.

Section 2. Whenever there is a vacancy in the office of the Vice President, the President shall nominate a Vice President who shall take office upon confirmation by a majority vote of both Houses of Congress.

Section 3. Whenever the President transmits to the President pro tempore of the Senate and the Speaker of the House of Representatives his written declaration that he is unable to discharge the powers and duties of his office, and until he transmits to them a written declaration to the contrary, such powers and duties shall be discharged by the Vice President as Acting President.

Section 4. Whenever the Vice President and a majority of either the principal officers of the executive departments or of such other body as Congress may by law provide, transmit to the President pro tempore of the Senate and the Speaker of the House of Representatives their written declaration that the President is unable to discharge the powers and duties of his office, the Vice President shall immediately assume the powers and duties of the office as Acting President.

Thereafter, when the President transmits to the President pro tempore of the Senate and the Speaker of the House of Representatives his written declaration that no inability exists, he shall resume the powers and duties of his office unless the Vice President and a majority of either the principal officers of the executive department or of such other body as Congress may by law provide, transmit within four days to the President pro tempore of the Senate and the Speaker of the House of Representatives their written declaration that the President is unable to discharge the powers and duties of his office. Thereupon Congress shall decide the issue, assembling within forty-eight hours for that purpose if not in session. If the Congress, within twenty-one days after receipt of the latter written declaration, or, if Congress is not in session, within twenty-one days after Congress is required to assemble, determines by two-thirds vote of both Houses that the President is unable to discharge the powers and duties of his office, the Vice President shall continue to discharge the same as Acting President; otherwise, the President shall resume the powers and duties of his office.

AMENDMENT XXVI

Section 1. The right of citizens of the United States, who are eighteen years of age or older, to vote shall not be denied or abridged by the United States or by any State on account of age.

Section 2. The Congress shall have power to enforce this article by appropriate legislation.

AMENDMENT XXVII

No law, varying the compensation for the services of the Senators and Representatives, shall take effect, until an election of representatives shall have intervened.

Internet Resources

Courts—Alternative Dispute Resolution—Government

U.S. Courts	www.uscourts.gov
U.S. Tax Court	www.ustaxcourt.gov
U.S. Court of Federal Claims	www.uscfc.uscourts.gov/
U.S. Court of International Trade	www.cit.uscourts.gov/
U.S Court of Appeals for the Federal Circuit	www.cafc.uscourts.gov/
U.S. Supreme Court	www.supremecourt.gov
National Mediation Board	www.nmb.gov
American Arbitration Association	www.adr.org
Pacer System	http://pacer.psc.uscourts.gov/
U.S. Court of Appeals	www.uscourts.gov/courtsofappeals.html
Internal Revenue Service	www.irs.gov
Government Printing Office	www.gpo.gov/
Code of Federal Regulations	http://www.ecfr.gov/cgi-bin/ECFR?page=browse

Legal Research

VersusLaw	www.versuslaw.com/
Lexis	www.lexisnexis.com/
Westlaw	www.westlaw.com/
Library of Congress	www.loc.gov
Loislaw	www.loislaw.com
Cornell University LII	www.law.cornell.edu/citation
ALWD Manual	www.alwd.org

Legal Organizations

American Bar Association	www.abanet.org
National Federation of Paralegal Associations, Inc.	www.paralegals.org
National Association of Legal Assistants	www.nala.org
American Association of Legal Administrators	www.alanet.org/home.html
American Association for Paralegal Education	www.aafpe.org
ABA Standing Committee on Legal Assistants	www.abanet.org/legalassts
Legal Nurse Consultants	www.aalnc.org

State Bar Associations

Alabama	www.alabar.org
Alaska	www.alaskabar.org
Arizona	www.azbar.org
Arkansas	www.arkbar.org
California	www.calbar.org
Colorado	www.cobar.org
Connecticut	www.ctbar.org
Delaware	www.dsba.org
District of Columbia	www.dcbar.org
Florida	www.flabar.org
Georgia	www.gabar.org
Hawaii	www.hsba.org
Idaho	https://isb.idaho.gov/
Illinois	www.isba.org
Indiana	www.inbar.org
Iowa	www.iowabar.org
Kansas	www.ksbar.org
Kentucky	www.kybar.org
Louisiana	www.lsba.org
Maine	www.maine.org
Maryland	www.msba.org
Massachusetts	www.massbar.org
Michigan	www.michbar.org
Minnesota	www.mnbar.org
Mississippi	www.msbar.org
Missouri	www.mobar.org
Montana	www.montanabar.org
Nebraska	www.nebar.org
Nevada	www.nvbar.org
New Hampshire	www.nhbar.org
New Jersey	www.njsba.com
New Mexico	www.nmbar.org
New York	www.nysba.org
North Carolina	www.ncbar.com
North Dakota	www.sband.org
Ohio	www.ohiobar.org
Oklahoma	www.okbar.org
Oregon	www.osbar.org
Pennsylvania	www.pabar.org
Rhode Island	www.ribar.com
South Carolina	www.scbar.org
South Dakota	www.sdbar.org
Tennessee	www.tba.org

Texas	www.texasbar.com
Utah	www.utahbar.org
Vermont	www.vtbar.org
Virginia	www.vsb.org
Washington	www.wsba.org
West Virginia	www.wvbar.org
Wisconsin	www.wisbar.org
Wyoming	www.wyomingbar.org

Other

Religious calendar	www.interfaithcalendar.org/
AOL	www.aol.com
Compuserve	www.compuserve.com
The Affiliate	www.futurelawoffice.com/practice.html
Adobe Systems	www.adobe.com
Mapquest	www.mapquest.com

Internet Search Engines

Bing	www.bing.com
Ask Jeeves	www.askjeeves.com
Dogpile	www.dogpile.com
Excite	www.excite.com
Google	www.google.com
Netscape	www.netscape.com
Yahoo!	www.yahoo.com
Findlaw	www.findlaw.com

APPENDIX H

Glossary of Spanish Equivalents for Important Legal Terms

A

a priori Desde antes, del pasado.

AAA Siglas para **American Arbitration Association** Asociación de Arbitraje.

ABA Siglas para **American Bar Association** Colegio de Abogados Estadounidenses.

accept Aceptar, admitir, aprobar, recibir reconocer.

accession Accesión, admisión, aumento, incremento.

accord Acuerdo, convenio, arreglo, acordar, conceder.

acquittal Absolución, descargo, veredicto de no culpable.

act Acto, estatuto, decreto, actuar, funcionar.

actionable Justiciable, punible, procesable.

adjourn Levantar, posponer, suspender la sesión.

adjudicate Adjudicar, decidir, dar fallo a favor de, sentenciar, declarar.

administrative Administrativo, ejecutivo.

administrative agency Agencia administrativa.

administrative hearing Juicio administrativo.

administrative law Derecho administrativo.

administrative law judge Juez de derecho, administrativo.

administrator Administrador.

admit Admitir, conceder, reconocer, permitir entrada, confesar, asentir.

adverse Adverso, contrario, opuesto.

adverse possession Posesión adversa.

advice Consejo, asesoramiento, notificación.

affected class Clase afectada, grupo iscriminado.

affidavit Declaración voluntaria, escrita y bajo uramento, afidávit, atestiguación, testificata.

affirmative action Acción positiva.

affirmative defense Defensa justificativa.

after acquired property Propiedad adquirida con garantía adicional.

against En contra.

agency Agencia, oficina, intervención.

agent Agente, representante autorizado.

aggrieved party Parte dañada, agraviada, perjudicada.

agreement Acuerdo, arreglo, contrato, convenio, pacto.

alibi Coartada.

alien Extranjero, extraño, foráneo.

annul Anular, cancelar, invalidar, revocar, dejar sin efecto.

answer Contestación, réplica, respuesta, alegato.

antecedent Antecedente, previo, preexistente.

appeal Apelar, apelación.

appear Aparecer, comparecer.

appellate court Tribunal de apelaciones.

appellate jurisdiction Competencia de apelación.

applicable Aplicable, apropiado, pertinente a, lo que puede ser aplicado.

arraign Denunciar, acusar, procesar, instruir de cargos hechos.

arrears Retrasos, pagos atrasados, decursas.

arrest Arresto, arrestar, aprehensión, aprehender, detener.

arson Incendio intencional.

articles of incorporation Carta de organización corporativa.

assault Agresión, asalto, ataque, violencia carnal, agredir, atacar, acometer.

assault and battery Amenazas y agresión, asalto.

assign Asignar, ceder, designar, hacer cesión, traspasar, persona asignada un derecho.

attachment Secuestro judicial.

attorney Abogado, consejero, apoderado.

award Fallo, juicio, laudo, premio.

B

bail Caución, fianza.

bail bondsman Fiador, fiador judicial.

bailee Depositario de bienes.

bailment Depósito, encargo, depósito mercantil, depósito comercial.

bailment For hire, depósito oneroso.

bailor Fiador.

bankruptcy Bancarrota, quiebra, insolvencia.

battery Agravio, agresión.

bearer bond Título mobiliario.

bearer instrument Título al portador.

bench Tribunal, los jueces, la magistratura.

beneficiary Beneficiario, legatario.

bequeath Legar.

bilateral contract Contrato bilateral.

bill of lading Póliza de embarque, boleto de carga, documento de tránsito.

bill of rights Las primeras diez enmiendas a la Constitución de los Estados Unidos de América.

binder Resguardo provisional, recibo para garantizar el precio de un bien inmueble.

birth certificate Acta de nacimiento, partida de nacimiento, certificado de nacimiento.

blue sky laws Estatutos para prevenir el fraude en la compraventa de valores.

bond Bono, título, obligación, deuda inversionista, fianza.

booking Término dado en el cuartel de policía al registro de arresto y los cargos hechos al arrestado.

breach of contract Violación, rotura, incumplimiento de contrato.

brief Alegato, escrito memorial.

burglary Escalamiento, allanamiento de morada.

buyer Comprador.

bylaws Estatutos sociales, reglamentos internos.

C

capacity to contract Capacidad contractual.

case Causa, caso, acción legal, proceso, proceso civil, asunto, expediente.

case law Jurisprudencia.

cashier's check Cheque bancario.

cease and desist order Orden judicial de cese.

censure Censura.

certificate of deposit Certificado de depósito.

certified check Cheque certificado.

certify Certificar, atestiguar.

charge Cobrar, acusar, imputar.

charitable trust Fideicomiso caritativo.

chattel Bienes muebles, bártulos.

cheat Fraude, engaño, defraudador, trampa, tramposo, estafar.

check Cheque, talón, comprobación.

cite Citación, citar, referir, emplazar.

citizenship Ciudadanía.

civil action Acción, enjuiciamiento civil, demanda.

civil law Derecho civil.

Claims Court Tribunal federal de reclamaciones.

client Cliente.

closing arguments Alegatos de clausura.

closing costs Gastos ocasionados en la venta de bienes raíces.

clue Pista, indicio.

codicil Codicilo.

coercion Coerción, coacción.

collateral Colateral, auxiliar, subsidiario, seguridad colateral, garantía prendaria.

collect Cobrar, recobrar, recaudar.

collision Choque, colisión.

common law Derecho consuetudinario.

comparative negligence Negligencia comparativa.

compensatory damages Indemnización compensatoria por daños y perjuicios, daños compensatorios.

competency Competencia, capacidad legal.

concurrent conditions Condiciones concurrentes.

concurrent jurisdiction Jurisdicción simultanea, conocimiento acumulativo.

concurrent sentences Sentencias que se cumplen simultáneamente.

concurring opinion Opinión coincidente.

condemn Condenar, confiscar, expropiar.

condition precedent Condición precedente.

condition subsequent Condición subsecuente.

confession Confesión, admisión.

confidential Confidencial, íntimo, secreto.

confiscation Confiscación, comiso, decomiso.

consent decree Decreto por acuerdo mutuo.

consequential damages Daños especiales.

consideration Contraprestación.

consolidation Consolidación, unión, concentración.

constructive delivery Presunta entrega.

contempt of court Desacato, contumacia o menosprecio a la corte.

contract Contrato, convenio, acuerdo, pacto.

contributory negligence Negligencia contribuyente.

conversion Conversión, canje.

conviction Convicción, fallo de culpabilidad, convencimiento, sentencia condenatoria, condena.

copyright Derecho de autor, propiedad literaria, propiedad intelectual, derecho de impresión.

corroborate Corroborar, confirmar.

counterclaim Contrademanda, excepción de compensación.

counteroffer Contra oferta.

courts Cortes o tribunales establecidas por la constitución.

covenant for quiet enjoyment Convenio de disfrute y posesión pacífica.

creditor Acreedor.

crime Crimen, delito.

criminal act Acto criminal.

criminal law Derecho penal.

cross examination Contrainterrogatorio, repregunta.

cure Curar, corregir.

D

damages Daños y perjuicios, indemnización pecuniaria.

d.b.a. Sigla para doing business as En negociación comercial.

deadly force Fuerza mortífera.

debt Deuda, débito.

debtor Deudor.

decision Decisión judicial, fallo, determinación auto, sentencia.

deed Escritura, título de propiedad, escritura de traspaso.

defamation Difamación, infamación.

default Incumplir, faltar, no comparecer, incumplimiento.

defendant Demandado, reo, procesado, acusado.

delinquent Delincuente, atrasado en pagos, delictuoso.

denial Denegación, negación, denegatoria.

deponent Deponente, declarante.

deportation Deportación, destierro.

deposition Deposición, declaración bajo juramento.

detain Detener, retardar, retrasar.

devise Legado de bienes raíces.

direct examination Interrogatorio directo, interrogatorio a testigo propio.

directed verdict Veredicto expedido por el juez, veredicto por falta de pruebas.

disaffirm Negar, rechazar, repudiar, anular.

discharge Descargo, cumplimiento, liberación.

disclose Revelar.

discovery Revelación de prueba, exposición reveladora.

discriminate Discriminar.

dismiss Despedir, desechar, desestimar.

dissenting opinion Opinión en desacuerdo.

dissolution Disolución, liquidación.

diversity of citizenship Diversidad de ciudadanías, ciudadanías diferentes.

dividend Acción librada, dividendo.

divorce Divorcio, divorciar.

docket Orden del día, lista de casos en la corte.

double jeopardy Non bis in idem.

driving under the influence Manejar bajo los efectos de bebidas alcohólicas o drogas.

duress Coacción.

E

earnest money Arras, señal.

easement Servidumbre.

edict Edicto, decreto, auto.

embezzlement Malversación de fondos.

eminent domain Dominio eminente.

encroachment Intrusión, usurpación, invasión, uso indebido.

encumbrance Gravamen, afectación, cargo.

enforce Hacer cumplir, dar valor, poner en efecto.

entitlement Derecho, título.

equal protection clause Cláusula de protección de igualdad ante la ley.

equal protection of the law Igualdad ante la ley.

equity Equidad, derecho equitativo.

escheat Reversión al estado al no haber herederos.

estate Bienes, propiedad, caudal hereditario, cuerpo de la herencia, caudal, derecho, título, interés sobre propiedad.

estop Impedir, detener, prevenir.

ethics Sistema ético.

eviction Evicción, desalojo, desalojamiento, desahucio, lanzamiento.

evidence Testimonio, prueba, pruebas documentales, pieza de prueba.

examination Examen, reconocimiento, interrogatorio.

executed contract Contrato firmado, contrato ejecutado.

execution Ejecución, desempeño, cumplimiento.

executory contract Contrato por cumplirse.

executory interests Intereses futuros.

exempt Franquear, exentar, exencionar, eximir, libre, franco, exento, inmune.

exoneration Exoneración, descargo, liberación.

expert witness Testigo perito.

express contract Contrato explícito.

expropriation Expropiación, confiscación.

eyewitness Testigo ocular o presencial.

F

fact Hecho falsificado.

failure to appear Incomparecencia.

fault Falta, defecto, culpa, negligencia.

fee Honorarios, retribución, cuota, cargo, derecho, dominio, asesoría, propiedad, bienes raíces.

fee simple estate Propiedad en dominio pleno.

felon Felón, autor de un delito.

felony Delito mayor o grave.

fiduciary Fiduciario.

find against Fallar o decidir en contra.

find for Fallar o decidir a favor.

finding Determinación de los hechos.

fine Multa, castigo.

fixture Accesorio fijo.

foreclose Entablar juicio hipotecario, embargar bienes hipotecados.

forgery Falsificación.

franchise Franquicia, privilegio, patente, concesión social, derecho de votar.

fraud Fraude, engaño, estafa, trampa, embuste, defraudación.

full disclosure Revelación completa.

G

garnishment Embargo de bienes.

gift Regalo, dádiva, donación.

gift causa mortis Donación de propiedad en expectativa de muerte.

gift inter vivos Donación entre vivos.

gift tax Impuesto sobre donaciones.

good and valid consideration Causa contractual válida.

good faith Buena fe.

goods Mercaderías, bienes, productos.

grace period Período de espera.

grantee Concesionario, cesionario.

grantor Otorgante, cesionista.

grievance Agravio, injuria, ofensa, queja formal.

gross negligence Negligencia temeraria, negligencia grave.

H

habitation Habitación, lugar donde se vive.

harassment Hostigamiento.

hearing Audiencia, vista, juicio.

hearsay Testimonio de oídas.

holder Tenedor, poseedor.

holding Decisión, opinión, tenencia posesión, asociación, grupo industrial.

holographic will Testamento hológrafo.

homeowner Propietario, dueño de casa.

homestead Casa, solariega, hogar, heredad, excepción de embargo, bien de familia.

hung jury Jurado sin veredicto.

I

identify Identificar, verificar, autenticar.

illegal Ilegal, ilícito, ilegítimo.

illegal entry Entrada ilegal.

illegal search Registro domiciliario, allanamiento ilegal, cacheo ilegal.

immunity Inmunidad, exención.

implied warranty Garantía implícita.

impossibility of performance Imposibilidad de cumplimiento.

impound Embargar, incautar, confiscar, secuestrar.

inadmissible Inadmisible, inaceptable.

income Ingreso, ganancia, entrada, renta, rédito.

incriminate Incriminar, acriminar.

indictment Procesamiento, acusación por jurado acusatorio, inculpatoria.

indorsement Endose, endoso, respaldo, garantía.

informant Informador, denunciante, delator.

information Información, informe, acusación por el fiscal, denuncia.

informed consent Conformidad por información.

inherit Heredar, recibir por herencia.

injunction Mandato judicial, amparo, prohibición judicial, interdicto.

innocent Inocente, no culpable.

inquiry Indagatoria judicial, pesquisa.

insufficient evidence Prueba insuficiente.

interrogation Interrogación.

interstate commerce Comercio interestatal.

intestate Intestado, intestar, sin testamento.

intestate succession Sucesión hereditaria.

investigation Investigación, indagación, encuesta.

issue Emisión, cuestión, punto, edición, número, tirada, sucesión, descendencia, resultado, decisión.

J

jail Cárcel, calabozo, encarcelar.

joint tenancy Condominio.

judge Magistrado, juez, juzgar, adjudicar, enjuiciar, fallar.

judgment Sentencia, fallo, juicio, decisión, dictamen, criterio.

judicial proceeding Proceso o diligencia judicial.

judicial review Revisión judicial.

jump bail Fugarse bajo fianza.

jurisdiction Jurisdicción, fuero competencia.

jury Jurado

L

landlord Arrendatario, propietario.

larceny Hurto, latrocinio, ladronicio.

law Ley, derecho.

lease Contrato de arrendamiento, arrendamiento, arriendo, contrato de locación, arrendar, alquilar.

leasehold estate Bienes forales.

legatee Legatario, asignatario.

lender Prestamista.

lessee Arrendatario, locatario, inquilino.

lessor Arrendatario, arrendador, arrendante, locador.

letter of credit Letra de crédito.

liability Responsiva, responsabilidad.

libel Libelo por difamación por escrito.

license Licencia, permiso, privilegio, matrícula, patente, título, licenciar, permitir.

lien Gravamen, derecho prendario o de retención, embargo preventivo.

life estate Hipoteca legal, dominio vitalicio.

limited liability company Sociedad de responsabilidad limitada.

limited partnership Sociedad en comandita, sociedad comanditaria.

litigated Pleiteado, litigado, sujeto a litigación.

M

majority opinion Opinión que refleja la mayoría de los miembros de la corte de apelaciones.

maker Otorgante, girador.

malice Malicia, malignidad, maldad.

malpractice Incompetencia profesional.

manslaughter Homicidio sin premeditación.

material witness Testigo esencial.

mechanics lien Gravamen de construcción.

mediation Mediación, tercería, intervención, interposición.

medical examiner Médico examinador.

merger Fusión, incorporación, unión, consolidación.

minor Menor, insignificante, pequeño, trivial.

misdemeanor Delito menor, fechoría.

mitigation of damages Mitigación de daños, minoración, atenuación.

monetary damages Daños pecuniarios.

mortgage Hipoteca, gravamen, hipotecar, gravar.

motion to dismiss Petición para declaración sin lugar.

motion to suppress Moción para suprimir, reprimir o suspender.

motive Motivo.

murder Asesinato, asesinar, homicidio culposo.

N

naturalization Naturalización.

negligence Negligencia, descuido, imprudencia.

negotiable Negociable.

negotiate Negociar, agenciar, hacer efectivo, traspasar, tratar.

net assets Haberes netos.

notice Aviso, notificación, advertencia, conocimiento.

novation Novación, delegación de crédito.

nuisance Daño, molestia, perjuicio.

nuncupative will Testamento abierto.

O

oath Juramento.

objection Objeción, oposición, disconformidad, recusación, impugnación, excepción, réplica, reclamación.

obstruction of justice Encubrimiento activo.

offer Oferta, ofrecimiento, propuesta, ofrecer, proponer.

omission Omisión, falla, falta.

opinion Opinión, dictamen, decisión de la corte.

oral argument Alegato oral.

order instrument Instrumento de pago a la orden.

owe Deber, estar en deuda, adeudo.

owner Dueño, propietario, poseedor.

P

pain and suffering Angustia mental y dolor físico.

pardon Perdón, indulto, absolución, indultar, perdonar.

parol evidence rule Principio que prohíbe la modificación de un contrato por prueba verbal.

parole Libertad vigilada.

partnership Sociedad, compañía colectiva, aparcería, consorcio, sociedad personal.

patent Patente, obvio, evidente, aparente, privilegio de invención, patentar.

penalty Pena, multa, castigo, penalidad, condena.

pending Pendiente, en trámite, pendiente de, hasta que.

per capita Por cabeza.

performance Cumplimiento, desempeño, ejecución, rendimiento.

perjury Perjurio, testimonio falso, juramento falso.

personal property Bienes personales, bienes mobiliarios.

plea bargain Declaración de culpabilidad concertada.

plea of guilty Alegación de culpabilidad.

pleadings Alegatos, alegaciones, escritos.

pledge Prenda, caución, empeño, empeñar, dar en prenda, pignorar.

police power Poder policial.

policy Póliza, escritura, práctica política.

possession Posesión, tenencia, goce, disfrute.

possibility of reverter Posibilidad de reversión.

power of attorney Poder de representación, poder notarial, procura.

precedent Precedente, decisión previa por el mismo tribunal.

preemptive right Derecho de prioridad.

prejudicial Dañoso, perjudicial.

preliminary hearing Audiencia preliminar.

premeditation Premeditación.

presume Presumir, asumir como hecho basado en la experiencia, suponer.

prevail Prevalecer, persuadir, predominar, ganar, triunfar.

price discrimination Discriminación en el precio.

principal Principal, jefe, de mayor importancia, valor actual.

privileged communication Comunicación privilegiada.

privity Coparticipación, intereses comunes.

procedural Procesal.

proceeds Ganancias.

profit Ganancia, utilidad, lucro, beneficio.

prohibited Prohibido.

promise Promesa.

promissory estoppel Impedimento promisorio.

promissory note Pagaré, vale, nota de pago.

proof Prueba, comprobación, demostración.

prosecutor Fiscal, abogado público acusador.

proximate cause Causa relacionada.

proxy Poder, delegación, apoderado, mandatario.

punishment Pena, castigo.

punitive damages Indemnización punitiva por daños y perjuicios, daños ejemplares.

Q

qualification Capacidad, calidad, preparación.

qualified indorsement Endoso limitado endoso con reservas.

quasi contract Cuasicontrato.

query Pregunta, interrogación.

question of fact Cuestión de hecho.

question of law Cuestión de derecho.

quiet enjoyment Uso y disfrute.

quitclaim deed Escritura de traspaso de finiquito.

R

race discrimination Discriminación racial.

rape Estupro, violación, ultraje, rapto, violar.

ratification Ratificación, aprobación, confirmación.

ratify Aprobar, confirmar, ratificar, convalidar, adoptar.

real property Bienes raíces, bienes inmuebles, arraigo.

reasonable doubt Duda razonable.

rebut Rebatir, refutar, negar, contradecir.

recognizance Obligación impuesta judicialmente.

recordation Inscripción oficial, grabación.

recover Recobrar, recuperar, obtener como resultado de decreto.

redress Reparación, compensación, desagravio, compensar, reparar, satisfacer, remediar.

regulatory agency Agencia reguladora.

reimburse Reembolsar, repagar, compensar, reintegrar.

rejoinder Respuesta, réplica, contrarréplica.

release Descargo, liberación, librar, relevar, descargar, libertar.

relevance Relevancia.

remainder Resto, restante, residuo, derecho expectativo a un bien raíz.

remedy Remedio, recurso.

remuneration Remuneración, compensación.

reply Réplica, contestación, contestar, responder.

reprieve Suspensión de la sentencia, suspensión, indulto, indultar, suspender.

reprimand Reprender, regañar, reprimenda, reprensión.

repudiate Repudiar, renunciar, rechazar.

rescission Rescisión, abrogación, cancelación de un contrato.

respondeat superior Responsabilidad civil al supervisor.

respondent Apelado, demandado.

restitution Restitución, devolución.

restraining order Inhibitoria, interdicto, orden de amparo.

retain Retener, emplear, guardar.

reversion Reversión, derecho de sucesión.

revocation Revocación, derogación, anulación.

reward Premio.

right of first refusal Retracto arrendaticio.

right of subrogation Derecho de sustituir.

right of survivorship Derecho de supervivencia entre dueños de propiedad mancomunada.

right to work laws Leyes que prohíben la filiación sindical como requisito para poder desempeñar un puesto, derecho de trabajo.

rights Derechos.

robbery Robo, atraco.

ruling Determinación oficial, auto judicial.

S

sale Venta.

sale on approval Venta por aprobación.

satisfaction Satisfacción, liquidación, cumplimiento, pago, finiquito.

scope of authority Autoridad explícitamente otorgada o implícitamente concedida.

search and seizure Allanamiento, registro e incautación.

search warrant Orden de registro o de allanamiento.

secured party Persona con interés asegurado.

secured transaction Transacción con un interés asegurado.

securities Valores, títulos, obligaciones.

security agreement Acuerdo que crea la garantía de un interés.

security deposit Deposito de seguridad.

seize Arrestar, confiscar, secuestrar, incautar.

settlement Arreglo, composición, ajuste, liquidación, componenda, acomodo.

sex discrimination Discriminación sexual.

sexual harassment Acoso sexual.

shoplifting Ratería en tiendas.

signature Firma.

slander Calumnia, difamación oral, calumniar.

source of income Fuente de ingresos.

specific performance Prestación específica contractual.

split decision Decisión con opiniones mixtas.

spousal abuse Abuso conyugal.

stare decisis Vinculación con decisiones judiciales anteriores.

state of mind Estado de ánimo, estado mental.

statement Alegación, declaración, relato, estado de cuentas.

statutory foreclosure Ejecución hipotecaria estatutaria.

statutory law Derecho estatutario.

statutory rape Estupro, violación de un menor de edad.

steal Robar, hurtar, robo, hurto.

stock Acciones, capital, existencias, semental.

stock option Opción de comprar o vender acciones.

stop payment order Suspensión de pago.

strict liability Responsabilidad rigurosa.

sublease Subarriendo, sublocación, subarrendar.

subpoena Citación, citatorio, comparendo, cédula de citación, citación judicial, subpoena.

sue Demandar, procesar.

summary judgment Sentencia sumaria.

summon Convocar, llamar, citar.

suppress Suprimir, excluir pruebas ilegalmente obtenidas, reprimir, suspender.

surrender Rendir, entregar, entrega, rendirse, entregarse.

surviving spouse Cónyuge sobreviviente.

suspect Sospecha, sospechar, sospechoso.

T

tangible evidence Prueba real.

tangible property Propiedad tangible, bienes tangibles.

tenancy at sufferance Tenencia o posesión por tolerancia.

tenancy at will Tenencia o inquilinato sin plazo fijo.

tenancy by the entirety Tenencia conyugal.

tenancy for life Tenencia vitalicia.

tenancy for years Inquilinato por tiempo fijo.

tender Propuesta, oferta, presentar.

testator Testador.

testify Atestar, atestiguar, dar testimonio.

theft Hurto.

title Título, derecho de posesión, rango, denominación.

tort Agravio, torticero, entuerto, daño legal, perjuicio, acto ilícito civil.

Totten trust Fideicomiso bancario Totten.

trade name Nombre comercial, marca de fábrica, marca comercial.

trademark Marca registrada, marca industrial.

transgression Ofensa, delito, transgresión.

trespass Transgresión, violación de propiedad ajena, translimitación, traspasar, violar, infringir, transgredir.

trial court Tribunal de primera instancia.

trust Fideicomiso, confianza, confidencia, confianza, crédito, combinación, consorcio, grupo industrial.

truth Verdad, verdadero, veracidad.

try Probar, juzgar.

U

ultra vires Mas allá de la facultad de actuar.

unanimous verdict Veredicto unánime.

unbiased Imparcial, neutral.

unconditional pardon Perdón, amnistía, indulto incondicional.

unconscionable Reprochable, repugnante, desmedido.

under arrest Arrestado, bajo arresto.

underwrite Subscribir, asegurar, firmar.

undisclosed Escondido, no revelado.

undue influence Influencia indebida, coacción, abuso de poder.

unenforceable Inejecutable.

unilateral contract Contrato unilateral.

unlawful Ilegal, ilícito, ilegítimo.

unsound mind Privado de razón, de mente inestable.

usury Usura, agiotaje, logrería.

V

vagrancy Vagancia, vagabundeo.

validity Validez, vigencia.

valuable consideration Causa contractual con cierto valor, causa contractual onerosa.

venue Partido judicial.

verbal contract Contrato verbal.

verbatim Al pié de la letra.

verdict Veredicto, fallo, sentencia, decisión.

victim Víctima.

voidable Anulable, cancelable.

W

wage Salario, jornal, sueldo.

waive Renunciar, ceder, suspender, abdicar.

waiver Renunciar, desistir, ceder, suspender, abdicar, renuncia.

warrant Autorización, resguardo, comprobante, certificado, justificación, decisión judicial.

warranty Garantía, seguridad.

warranty of habitability Garantía de habitabilidad.

welfare Asistencia pública.

will Testamento, voluntad.

willful misconduct Mala conducta intencional.

withhold Retener, detener.

witness Testigo, declarante, atestar, testificar, atestiguar.

writ of attachment Mandamiento de embargo.

writ of certiorari Pedimento de avocación.

writ of execution Auto de ejecución, ejecutoria.

Glossary

ABA Model Rules of Professional Conduct A recommended set of ethics and professional conduct guidelines for lawyers, prepared by American Bar Association, originally released in 1983; prior release was Model Code of Professional Conduct.

Abandoned property Property that an owner has discarded with the intent to relinquish his or her rights in it; mislaid or lost property that the owner has given up any further attempts to locate.

Abatement If the property the testator leaves is not sufficient to satisfy all the beneficiaries named in a will and there are both general and residuary bequests, the residuary bequest is abated first (i.e., paid last).

Acceptance A manifestation of assent by the offeree to the terms of the offer in a manner invited or required by the offer as measured by the objective theory of contracts.

Actus reus "Guilty act"—the actual performance of the criminal act.

Ademption A principle that says if a testator leaves a specific devise of property to a beneficiary, but the property is no longer in the estate when the testator dies, the beneficiary receives nothing.

Administrative agencies Agencies that the legislative and executive branches of federal and state governments establish.

Administrative law Substantive and procedural law that governs the operation of administrative agencies.

Administrative law judge (ALJ) A judge who presides over an administrative proceeding and who decides the questions of law and fact that arise in the proceeding.

Administrative Procedure Act (APA) An act that establishes certain administrative procedures that federal administrative agencies must follow in conducting their affairs.

Admitted A possible response of the defendant to the complaint which accepts the facts of the averment are true.

Adoption A situation in which a person becomes the legal parent of a child who is not his or her biological child.

Adverse possession A situation in which a person who wrongfully possesses someone else's real property obtains title to that property if certain statutory requirements are met.

Affirm The appellate court agrees with the outcome of trial and can find no reversible error and the decision of the trial court stands.

Age Discrimination in Employment Act (ADEA) A federal statute that prohibits age discrimination practices against employees who are age 40 and older.

Agency A principal–agent relationship; the fiduciary relationship "which results from the manifestation of consent by one person to another that the other shall act in his behalf and subject to his control, and consent by the other so to act."

Agency adoption An adoption that occurs when a person adopts a child from a social service organization of a state.

Agency by ratification An agency that occurs when (1) a person misrepresents himself or herself as another's agent when in fact he or she is not and (2) the purported principal ratifies the unauthorized act.

Agent A party who agrees to act on behalf of another.

Agreement The manifestation by two or more persons of the substance of a contract.

Aiding and abetting the commission of a crime Rendering support, assistance, or encouragement to the commission of a crime; harboring a criminal after he or she has committed a crime.

Alien corporation A corporation that is incorporated in another country.

ALS (Acredited Legal Secretary) The basic certification for legal professionals from NALS.

Alternative dispute resolution (ADR) Methods of resolving disputes other than litigation.

American Arbitration Association (AAA) A private nonprofit organization providing lists of potential arbitrators for the parties to select from and a set of rules for conducting the private arbitration.

American Association for Paralegal Education (AAfPE) National organization of paralegal educators and institutions offering paralegal education programs.

American Bar Association (ABA) Largest professional legal organization in the United States.

American Inventors Protection Act A federal statute that permits an inventor to file a *provisional application* with the U.S. Patent and Trademark Office (PTO) three months before the filing of a final patent application, among other provisions.

Americans with Disabilities Act (ADA) A federal statute that imposes obligations on employers and providers of public transportation, telecommunications, and public accommodations to accommodate individuals with disabilities.

Amicus curiae Briefs submitted by interested parties who do not have standing in the action as a "friend of the court."

Annulment An order of the court declaring that a marriage did not exist.

Answer Document by which the defendant responds to the allegations contained in the plaintiff's complaint.

Antenuptial agreement A contract entered into after marriage to specify how property will be distributed upon termination of the marriage.

Apparent agency Agency that arises when a principal creates the appearance of an agency that in actuality does not exist.

Appeal The act of asking an appellate court to overturn a decision after the trial court's final judgment has been entered.

Appellant The appealing party in an appeal. Also known as *petitioner*.

Appellate courts Courts which review the record from the trial court to determine if the trial judge made an error in applying the procedural or substantive law.

Appellee The responding party in an appeal. Also known as *respondent*.

Applications software Applications programs are software that perform generic tasks such as word processing.

Arbitration A form of ADR in which the parties choose an impartial third party to hear and decide the dispute.

Arbitration clause A clause in contracts that requires disputes arising out of the contract to be submitted to arbitration. A clause contained in many international contracts that stipulates that any dispute between the parties concerning the performance of the contract will be submitted to an arbitrator or arbitration panel for resolution.

Arraignment A hearing during which the accused is brought before a court and is (1) informed of the charges against him or her and (2) asked to enter a plea.

Arrest warrant A document for a person's detainment based upon a showing of probable cause that the person committed the crime.

Arson Willfully or maliciously burning another's building.

Article 2 (Sales) of the Uniform Commercial Code (UCC) An article of the UCC that governs the sale of goods.

Article 2A (Leases) of the Uniform Commercial Code (UCC) An article of the UCC that governs the lease of goods.

Articles of incorporation The basic governing document of the corporation. This document must be filed with the secretary of state of the state of incorporation.

Articles of limited liability partnership A public document that must be filed with the secretary of state to form a limited liability partnership.

Articles of organization The formal document that must be filed with the secretary of state to form an LLC.

Assault The threat of immediate harm or offensive contact or (2) any action that arouses reasonable apprehension of imminent harm. Actual physical contact is unnecessary.

Associate's degree A college degree in science (AS), arts (AA), or applied arts (AAS) generally requiring two years of full-time study.

Association of Legal Writing Directors (ALWD) A society for professors who coordinate legal writing instruction.

Assumption of the risk A defense a defendant can use against a plaintiff who knowingly and voluntarily enters into or participates in a risky activity that results in injury.

Attachment A popular method of transmitting text files and graphic images by attaching the file to an email.

Attempt to commit a crime When a crime is attempted but not completed.

Attestation The action of a will being witnessed by the required number of competent people.

Attestation clause Section of a will where witnesses sign to acknowledge testation of the will.

Attorney–client privilege A client's right to have anything told to a lawyer while seeking legal advice, kept confidential in most instances.

Automatic stay The result of the filing of a voluntary or involuntary petition; the suspension of certain actions by creditors against the debtor or the debtor's property.

Bachelor's degree A college degree generally requiring four years of full-time study.

Backup of data Making a copy of critical files and programs in case of a loss of the original computer files.

Bailee A holder of goods who is not a seller or a buyer (e.g., a warehouse or common carrier).

Bailment A transaction in which an owner transfers his or her personal property to another to be held, stored, delivered, or for some other purpose. Title to the property does not transfer.

Bailor The owner of property in a bailment.

Bankruptcy Abuse Prevention and Consumer Protection Act of 2005 A federal act that substantially amended federal bankruptcy law. It makes it more difficult for debtors to file for bankruptcy and have their unpaid debts discharged.

Bankruptcy courts Special federal courts that hear and decide bankruptcy cases.

Bankruptcy estate A debtor's property and earnings that comprise the estate of a bankruptcy proceeding.

Battery Unauthorized and harmful or offensive physical contact with another person. Direct physical contact is not necessary.

Bench opinions The initial version of a decision issued from the bench of the court.

Beneficiary A person or organization designated in the will that receives all or a portion of the testator's property at the time of the testator's death.

Bequest A gift of personal property by will. Also known as a legacy.

Best interests of the child A legal doctrine used by the court to decide what is best for the child.

Bicameral In the American system, a legislature of a house of representatives and a senate.

Bill of Rights The first 10 amendments to the Constitution. They were added to the U.S. Constitution in 1791.

Board of directors A panel of decision makers, the members of which are elected by a corporation's shareholders.

Bona fide occupational qualification (BFOQ) Lawful employment discrimination that is based on a protected class (other than race or color) and is *job-related* and a *business necessity*. This exception is narrowly interpreted by the courts.

Breach of contract A contracting party's failure to perform an absolute duty owed under a contract.

Breach of duty of care Failure to exercise care or to act as a reasonable person would act.

Bribery A crime in which one person gives another person money, property, favors, or anything else of value for a favor in return. Often referred to as a payoff or *kickback*.

Briefs Documents submitted by the parties' attorneys to the judge that contain legal support for their side of the case.

Building A structure constructed on land.

Burden of proof The level of proof required to establish an entitlement to recovery.

Burglary The taking of personal property from another's home, office, or commercial or other type of building.

Business judgment rule A rule stating that directors and officers are not liable to the corporation or its shareholders for honest mistakes of judgment.

Bylaws A detailed set of rules adopted by the board of directors after the corporation is incorporated that contains provisions for managing the business and the affairs of the corporation.

Candor A duty of honesty to the court.

Case and litigation management software Case and litigation management programs are used to manage documents and the facts and issues of cases.

Case syllabus In a court opinion, a headnote for the convenience of the reader.

Causation The two types of causation that must be proven are (1) causation in fact (actual cause) and (2) proximate cause (legal cause).

Causation in fact or **actual cause** The actual cause of negligence. A person who commits a negligent act is not liable unless causation in fact can be proven.

Central processing unit (CPU) The computer chip and memory module that perform the basic computer functions.

Certificate A recognition of the completion of a program of study that requires less than that needed for a degree.

Certificate of limited partnership A document that two or more persons must execute and sign that makes the limited partnership legal and binding.

Certified Legal Assistant (CLA) Designation by National Association of Legal Assistants for those who take and pass the NALA certification program two-day comprehensive examination.

Chain of distribution All manufacturers, distributors, wholesalers, retailers, lessors, and subcomponent manufacturers involved in a transaction.

Chapter 7 discharge The termination of the legal duty of a debtor to pay unsecured debts that remain unpaid upon the completion of a Chapter 7 proceeding.

Chapter 7 liquidation A form of bankruptcy in which the debtor's nonexempt property is sold for cash, the cash is distributed to the creditors, and any unpaid debts are discharged.

Chapter 11 reorganization A bankruptcy method that allows the reorganization of the debtor's financial affairs under the supervision of the bankruptcy court.

Chapter 12 adjustment of debts of a family farmer or family fisherman with regular income A form of bankruptcy reorganization permitted to be used by family farmers and family fishermen.

Chapter 12 discharge A discharge in a Chapter 12 case that is granted to a family farmer or family fisherman debtor after the debtor's plan of payment is completed (which is usually three years but could be up to five years).

Chapter 13 adjustment of debts of an individual with regular income A rehabilitation form of bankruptcy that permits bankruptcy courts to supervise the debtor's plan for the payment of unpaid debts in installments over the plan period.

Chapter 13 discharge A discharge in a Chapter 13 case that is granted to the debtor after the debtor's plan of payment is completed (which could be up to three or up to five years).

Charitable trust A trust for the benefit of a charity.

Child custody The awarding of legal custody of a child to a parent based on the best interests of the child. The parent awarded custody is called the *custodial parent*.

Child neglect Failure to provide necessities to a child for whom one is legally responsible.

Child support Payments made by the noncustodial parent to help pay for the financial support of his or her children.

Choice-of-law clause Clause in an international contract that designates which nation's laws will be applied in deciding a dispute.

Chronological résumé format Presents education and job history in chronological order with the most recent experience listed first.

Citation A reference to the source of the information.

Citator An index of cases.

Cite checking The process of verifying proper citation format in a document.

Civil litigation Resolution of legal disputes between parties seeking a remedy for a civil wrong or to enforce a contract.

Civil Rights Act A federal statute that prohibits racial discrimination in the transfer of real property.

Civil Rights Act of 1866 A federal statute enacted after the Civil War that says all persons "have the same right . . . to make and enforce contracts . . . as is enjoyed by white persons." It prohibits racial and national origin employment discrimination.

Closing arguments The last opportunity for the attorneys to address the jury, summing up the client's case and persuading the jury to decide in his client's favor.

Codicil A separate document that must be executed to amend a will. It must be executed with the same formalities as a will.

Collective bargaining The act of negotiating contract terms between an employer and the members of a union.

Collective bargaining agreement The resulting contract from a collective bargaining procedure.

"Coming and going" rule A rule that says a principal is generally not liable for injuries caused by its agents and employees while they are on their way to and from work.

Commerce Clause A clause of the U.S. Constitution that grants Congress the power "to regulate commerce with foreign nations, and among the several states, and with Indian tribes."

Commercial speech Speech used by businesses, such as advertising. It is subject to time, place, and manner restrictions.

Common carrier A firm that offers transportation services to the general public. The bailee. Owes a duty of strict liability to the bailor.

Common interest privilege To permit a client to share confidential information with the attorney for another who shares a common legal interest.

Common law Developed by judges who issue their opinions when deciding cases. The principles announced in these cases became precedent for later judges deciding similar cases.

Common law of contracts Contract law developed primarily by state courts.

Common stock A type of equity security that represents the residual value of the corporation.

Common stockholder (common shareholders) A person who owns common stock.

Common-law marriage A type of marriage recognized in some states where a marriage license has not been issued but certain requirements are met.

Community property A form of ownership in which each spouse owns an equal one-half share of the income of both spouses and the assets acquired during the marriage.

Comparative negligence A doctrine under which damages are apportioned according to fault.

Compensatory damages An award of money intended to compensate a nonbreaching party for loss of the bargain. Compensatory damages place the nonbreaching party in the same position as if the contract had been fully performed by restoring the "benefit of the bargain."

Competence/competent The minimum level of knowledge and skill required of a professional.

Complaint The document the plaintiff files with the court and serves on the defendant to initiate a lawsuit.

Complete performance A situation in which a party to a contract renders performance exactly as required by the contract. Complete performance discharges that party's obligations under the contract.

Complex litigation Cases involving many parties as in a class action or multiple or complex legal issues.

Computer addresses and locations The modern equivalent of a person's telephone number is the email address. Pages on the Internet also have addresses known as the Uniform Resource Locator (URL), made up of three parts: protocol, computer, and path.

Computer hardware Hardware is the term that encompasses all of the tangible or physical items, including computers, monitors, printers, fax machines, duplicators, and similar items that usually have either an electrical connection or use batteries as a power source.

Computer network A set of workstations connected together.

Computer system A combination of an input device, a processor, and an output device.

Computer viruses Viruses are programs that attack and destroy computer programs, internal computer operating systems, and occasionally the hard disk drives of computers.

Conciliation A form of dispute resolution in which a conciliator transmits offers and counteroffers between the disputing parties in helping to reach a settlement of their dispute.

Conciliator A third party in a conciliation proceeding who assists the disputing parties in reaching a settlement of their dispute. The conciliator cannot make a decision or an award.

Concurrent jurisdiction Jurisdiction shared by two or more courts.

Concurrent ownership (co-ownership) When two or more persons own a piece of real property.

Condition precedent A condition that requires the occurrence of an event before a party is obligated to perform a duty under a contract.

Condominium A common form of ownership in a multiple-dwelling building in which the purchaser has title to the individual unit and owns the common areas as a tenant in common with the other condominium owners.

Confidentiality A duty imposed on the attorney to enable clients to obtain legal advice by allowing the client to freely and openly give the attorney all the relevant facts.

Confirmation The bankruptcy court's approval of a plan of reorganization.

Conflict checking Verifying that the attorneys in the firm do not have a personal conflict and have not previously represented and are not currently representing any party with an adverse interest or conflict with the potential client.

Conflict of interest The representation of one client being directly adverse to the interest of another client.

Connectors Instructions in a search query on how to treat the words in the query.

Consequential damages Foreseeable damages that arise from circumstances outside the contract. To be liable for these damages, the breaching party must know or have reason to know that the breach will cause special damages to the other party.

Consideration Something of legal value given in exchange for a promise.

Consolidation The act of a court to combine two or more separate lawsuits into one lawsuit. Occurs when two or more corporations combine to form an entirely new corporation.

Constitution of the United States of America The supreme law of the United States. The Constitution of the United States of America establishes the structure of the federal government, delegates powers to the federal government, and guarantees certain fundamental rights.

Constructive trust An equitable trust that is implied by law to avoid fraud, unjust enrichment, and injustice.

Contract An agreement entered by two parties for valid consideration.

Contracts contrary to public policy Contracts that have a negative impact on society or that interfere with the public's safety and welfare.

Contributory negligence An affirmative defense which states there is no recovery where the plaintiff's negligence contributed to his injuries.

Controlling the Assault of Non-Solicited Pornography and Marketing Act (CAN-SPAM Act) A federal statute that prohibits certain deceptive and misleading email. The act is administered by the Federal Trade Commission (FTC).

Conversion of personal property A tort that deprives a true owner of the use and enjoyment of his or her personal property by taking over such property and exercising ownership rights over it.

Cooling-off period Requires a union to give an employer at least 60 days' notice before a strike can commence.

Cooperative A form of coownership of a multiple-dwelling building in which a corporation owns the building and the residents own shares in the corporation.

Co-ownership (concurrent ownership) A situation in which two or more persons own a piece of real property. Also called *concurrent ownership*.

Copyright infringement An act in which a party copies a substantial and material part of the plaintiff's copyrighted work without permission. A copyright holder may recover damages and other remedies against the infringer.

Copyright Revision Act A federal statute that (1) establishes the requirements for obtaining a copyright and (2) protects copyrighted works from infringement.

Corporate bylaws A detailed set of rules that are adopted by the board of directors after the corporation is incorporated, containing provisions for managing the business and the affairs of the corporation.

Corporation A fictitious legal entity that is created according to statutory requirements.

Cost-benefit analysis Process by which a litigant determines the costs of pursuing litigation and compares that to what is likely to be gained.

Counterfeit Access Device and Computer Fraud and Abuse Act (CFAA) A federal statute that makes it a federal crime to access a computer knowingly to obtain (1) restricted federal government information, (2) financial records of financial institutions, and (3) consumer reports of consumer reporting agencies.

Counteroffer A response by an offeree that contains terms and conditions different from or in addition to those of the offer. A counteroffer terminates an offer.

Court accounting An accounting with the local court that administers or supervises trust and estate matters. These reports are designed to show that the fiduciary has properly administered the estate or trust.

Court of Appeals for the Federal Circuit A court of appeals in Washington, DC, that has special appellate jurisdiction to review the decisions of the Claims Court, the Patent and Trademark Office, and the Court of International Trade.

Court of Chancery Court that granted relief based on fairness. Also called *equity court*.

Courts of record Those courts in which the testimony and evidence presented are recorded and preserved.

Covenant An unconditional promise to perform.

Cover letter A brief letter sent with a document identifying the intended recipient and the purpose of the attachment.

Creditors' committee The creditors holding the seven largest unsecured claims are usually appointed to the creditors' committee. Representatives of the committee appear at Bankruptcy Court hearings, participate in the negotiation of a plan of reorganization, assert objections to proposed plans, and so on.

Crime An act done by an individual in violation of those duties that he or she owes to society and for the breach of which the law provides that the wrongdoer shall make amends to the public.

Criminal conspiracy A crime in which two or more persons enter into an agreement to commit a crime and an overt act is taken to further the crime.

Criminal fraud (false pretenses or deceit) Obtaining title to property through deception or trickery. Also known as false pretenses or deceit.

Criminal laws A violation of a statute for which the government imposes a punishment.

Criminal trial A trial to determine if a person has violated a statue for which the government imposes a penalty.

Critical legal thinking The process of identifying the issue, the material facts, and the applicable law and applying the law to come to a conclusion.

Cross-complaint Filed by the defendant against the plaintiff to seek damages or some other remedy.

Cross-examination Opportunity of defense (opposing) counsel to question a witness after the direct examination of the witness.

Crossover worker A person who does not honor a strike who either (1) chooses not to strike or (2) returns to work after joining the strikers for a time.

Cruel and unusual punishment A clause of the Eighth Amendment that protects criminal defendants from torture or other abusive punishment.

Custodial parent The parent to whom physical custody of the child is legally given.

Damages Compensation for loss suffered.

Database program A database program is an electronic repository of information of all types that can be sorted and presented in a meaningful manner.

Deathbed will Oral will that is made as a dying declaration before a witness during the testator's last illness.

Decree of divorce A court order that terminates a marriage.

Deed A writing that describes a person's ownership interest in a piece of real property.

Defamation of character False statement(s) made by one person about another. In court, the plaintiff must prove that (1) the defendant made an untrue statement of fact about the plaintiff and (2) the statement was intentionally or accidentally published to a third party.

Default judgment Judgment obtained by the plaintiff against the defendant where the defendant has failed to respond in a timely fashion to the complaint.

Defect Something wrong, inadequate, or improper in manufacture, design, packaging, warning, or safety measures of a product.

Defect in design A flaw that occurs when a product is improperly designed.

Defect in manufacture A defect that occurs when the manufacturer fails to (1) properly assemble a product, (2) properly test a product, or (3) adequately check the quality of the product.

Defect in packaging A defect that occurs when a product has been placed in packaging that is insufficiently tamperproof.

Defendant The party who files the answer.

Defendant's case Process by which the defendant calls witnesses and introduces evidence to (1) rebut the plaintiff's evidence, (2) prove affirmative defenses, and (3) prove allegations made in a cross-complaint.

Defense of Marriage Act (DOMA) A federal statute banning same-sex couples from federal benefits given heterosexual couples.

Delegation doctrine A doctrine that says when an administrative agency is created, it is delegated certain powers; the agency can only use those legislative, judicial, and executive powers that are delegated to it.

Denied A possible response of the defendant to the complaint which asserts the facts of the averment are not true.

Deponent Party who gives his or her deposition.

Deposition Oral testimony given by a party or witness prior to trial. The testimony is given under oath and is transcribed.

Devise A gift of real estate by will.

Dicta Court comments on issues not directly related to the holding and therefore not having precedential effect.

Digital format A computerized format utilizing a series of 0's and 1's.

Digital Millennium Copyright Act (DMCA) A federal statute that prohibits unauthorized access to copyrighted digital works by circumventing encryption technology or the manufacture and distribution of technologies designed for the purpose of circumventing encryption protection of digital works.

Digital (or electronic) signature Some electronic method that identifies an individual.

Direct examination Questions addressed to a witness by the attorney who has called that witness to testify on behalf of his client.

Disaffirm The act of a minor to rescind a contract under the infancy doctrine. Disaffirmance may be done orally, in writing, or by the minor's conduct.

Discharge Actions or events that relieve certain parties from liability on negotiable instruments. There are three methods of discharge: (1) payment of the instrument; (2) cancellation; and (3) impairment of the right of recourse. The termination of the legal duty of a debtor to pay debts that remain unpaid upon the completion of a bankruptcy proceeding. Creditors' claims that are not included in a Chapter 11 reorganization are discharged. A discharge is granted to a debtor in a Chapter 13 consumer debt adjustment bankruptcy only after all the payments under the plan are completed by the debtor.

Discovery A legal process during which both parties engage in various activities to elicit facts of the case from the other party and witnesses prior to trial.

Diversity of citizenship A case between (1) citizens of different states, (2) a citizen of a state and a citizen or subject of a foreign country, and (3) a citizen of a state and a foreign country where a foreign country is the plaintiff.

Divorce An order of the court that terminates a marriage.

Doctrine of Equity A doctrine that permits judges to make decisions based on fairness, equality, moral rights, and natural law.

Doctrine of strict liability A tort doctrine that makes manufacturers, distributors, wholesalers, retailers, and others in the chain of distribution of a defective product liable for the damages caused by the defect irrespective of fault.

Doctrine of transferred intent An offender may be held responsible for an intent crime or intentional tort when someone other than the intended victim is injured.

Domain name A unique name that identifies an individual's or a company's website.

Domestic corporation A corporation in the state in which it was formed.

Dominant easement The land that benefits from the easement.

Donee A person who receives a gift.

Donor A person who gives a gift.

Double Jeopardy Clause A clause of the Fifth Amendment that protects persons from being tried twice for the same crime.

Dram Shop Act Statute that makes taverns and bartenders liable for injuries caused to or by patrons who are served too much alcohol.

Dual-purpose mission An errand or another act that a principal requests of an agent while the agent is on his or her own personal business.

Due Process Clause A clause that provides that no person shall be deprived of "life, liberty, or property" without due process of the law.

Duty not to willfully or wantonly injure The duty an owner or renter of real property owes a trespasser to prevent intentional injury or harm to the trespasser when the trespasser is on his or her premises.

Duty of candor Honesty to the court.

Duty of care The obligation we all owe each other not to cause any unreasonable harm or risk of harm. A responsibility of corporate directors and officers to use care and diligence when acting on behalf of the corporation.

Duty of loyalty A responsibility of directors and officers not to act adversely to the interests of the corporation and to subordinate their personal interests to those of the corporation and its shareholders.

Duty of ordinary care The duty an owner or renter of real property owes an invitee or a licensee to prevent injury or harm when the invitee or licensee steps on the owner's premises.

Duty of reasonable care The duty that a reasonable bailee in like circumstances would owe to protect the bailed property.

Duty of utmost care A duty of care that goes beyond ordinary care.

Easement A given or required right to make limited use of someone else's land without owning or leasing it.

Easement by grant One party gives another party an easement across his or her property.

Easement by implication A right erected on division of land to allow each owner use.

Easement by necessity Right to access another's property in order to reach one's landlocked property.

Easement by reservation A retained right to use land after a transfer.

E-commerce The sale of goods and services by computer over the Internet.

Economic Espionage Act A federal statute that makes it a crime for any person to convert a trade secret for his or another's benefit, knowing or intending to cause injury to the owners of the trade secret.

E-contract A contract that is entered into by email and over the World Wide Web.

E-discovery The discovery of emails, electronically stored data, e-contracts, and other electronically stored records.

E-filing The electronic filing of pleadings, briefs, and other documents related to a lawsuit with the court.

Elder law Advocacy for the elderly.

Electronic Communications Privacy Act (ECPA) A federal statute that makes it a crime to intercept an electronic communication at the point of transmission, while in transit, when stored by a router or server, or after receipt by the intended recipient.

Electronic mail (email) Electronic written communication between individuals using computers connected to the Internet.

Electronic repository A secure protected file server to which everyone authorized has access over the internet.

Electronic Signature in Global and National Commerce Act (E-SIGN Act) A federal statute that recognizes that electronic contracts, or e-contracts, meet the writing requirement of the Statute of Frauds and gives electronic signatures, or e-signatures, the same force and effect as peninscribed signatures on paper.

E-license A contract that transfers limited rights in intellectual property and informational rights.

Emancipation When a minor voluntarily leaves home and lives apart from his or her parents.

Embezzlement The fraudulent conversion of property by a person to whom that property was entrusted.

Eminent domain The government's power to take private property for public use, provided that just compensation is paid to the private property holder.

Employer–employee relationship A relationship that results when an employer hires an employee to perform some form of physical service.

Encryption Encryption is technology that allows computer users to put a "lock" around information to prevent discovery by others.

Engagement (1) A formal entrance into a contract between a client and an accountant; (2) the period between acceptance of an offer to marry and the marriage.

Entity theory A theory that holds that partnerships are separate legal entities that can hold title to personal and real property, transact business in the partnership name, sue in the partnership name, and the like.

Enumerated powers Certain powers delegated to the federal government by the states.

Environmental law An area of the law dealing with the protection of the environment.

Equal Access to Justice Act An act that was enacted to protect persons from harassment by federal administrative agencies.

Equal Employment Opportunity Commission (EEOC) A federal administrative agency responsible for enforcing most federal antidiscrimination laws.

Equal Pay Act of 1963 A federal statute that protects both sexes from pay discrimination based on sex. It extends to jobs that require equal skill, equal effort, equal responsibility, and similar working conditions.

Equal Protection Clause A clause that provides that state, local, and federal governments cannot deny to any person the "equal protection of the laws."

Equitable distribution A law used by many states where the court orders a *fair distribution* of marital property to the divorcing spouses.

Equitable remedies Used where no amount of monetary damages can make the injured party whole.

Escheat When property goes to the state in the absence of claim by heir.

Establishment Clause A clause to the First Amendment that prohibits the government from either establishing a state religion or promoting one religion over another.

Estate (estate in land) Ownership rights in real property; the bundle of legal rights of the owner to possess, use, and enjoy the property.

Ethical wall An environment in which an attorney or a paralegal is isolated from a particular case or client to avoid a conflict of interest or to protect a client's confidences and secrets.

Exclusionary rule A rule that says evidence obtained from an unreasonable search and seizure can generally be prohibited from introduction at a trial or administrative proceeding against the person searched.

Exclusive agency contract A contract a principal and agent enter into that says the principal cannot employ any agent other than the exclusive agent.

Exculpatory evidence Evidence which tends to prove the innocence of the accused or prove the facts of the defendant's case.

Executed contract A contract that has been fully performed on both sides; a completed contract.

Executive branch One of the three co-equal branches of government represented by the president and administrative agencies.

Executor/executrix (male/female) A person representative named in a will.

Executory contract or unexpired lease A contract or lease that has not been fully performed. With the bankruptcy court's approval, executor contracts and unexpired leases may be rejected by a debtor in bankruptcy.

Exempt property Property that may be retained by a debtor pursuant to federal or state law that does not become part of the bankruptcy estate.

Expert witness A person qualified by education or experience to render an opinion based on a set of facts.

Express agency An agency that occurs when a principal and an agent expressly agree to enter into an agency agreement with each other.

Express contract An agreement that is expressed in written or oral words.

Express trust A trust created voluntarily by the settlor.

Extension of time to respond Request by the defendant to enlarge the time to respond to the complaint beyond that which is permitted under the rules.

Extortion Threat to expose something about another person unless that other person gives money or property. Often referred to as "blackmail."

Fact pleading Pleadings required to include all relevant facts in support of all claims asserted.

Facts Information or details.

Failure to provide adequate instructions A defect that occurs when a manufacturer does not provide detailed directions for safe assembly and use of a product.

Failure to warn A defect that occurs when a manufacturer does not place a warning on the packaging of products that could cause injury if the danger is unknown.

Fair Housing Act A federal statute that makes it unlawful for a party to refuse to rent or sell a dwelling to any person because of his or her race, color, national origin, sex, or religion.

Fair Labor Standards Act (FLSA) A federal act enacted in 1938 to protect workers that prohibits child labor and establishes minimum wage and overtime pay requirements.

Fair-use doctrine A doctrine that permits certain limited use of a copyright by someone other than the copyright holder without the permission of the copyright holder.

False imprisonment The intentional confinement or restraint of another person without authority or justification and without that person's consent.

Father's registry Where a male may register as the father of a child.

Federal administrative agencies Agencies established by legislative and executive branches of federal and state governments.

Federal Arbitration Act (FAA) A federal statute that provides that arbitration agreements in commercial contracts are valid, irrevocable, and enforceable unless some legal or equitable (fraud, duress) grounds exist to invalidate them.

Federal Patent Statute A federal statute that establishes the requirements for obtaining a patent and protects patented inventions from infringement.

Federal question A case arising under the U.S. Constitution, treaties, or federal statutes and regulations.

Federal Trade Commission (FTC) Federal government agency empowered to enforce federal franchising rules. Federal administrative agency empowered to enforce the Federal Trade Commission Act and other federal consumer protection statutes.

Federalism The U.S. form of government; the federal government and the 50 state governments share powers.

Fee simple absolute (fee simple) A type of ownership of real property that grants the owner the fullest bundle of legal rights that a person can hold in real property.

Fee simple defeasible (qualified fee) A type of ownership of real property that grants the owner all the incidents of a fee simple absolute except that it may be taken away if a specified condition occurs or does not occur.

Felony The most serious type of crime; inherently evil crime. Most crimes against the person and some business-related crimes are felonies.

Fiduciary relationship A relationship under which one party has a duty to act for the interest and benefit of another while acting within the scope of the relationship.

File attachment The attachment is a popular method for transmitting text files, and occasionally graphic images, by attaching the file to an email.

File extension When a file is saved, a file extension (a period followed by three characters) is added to the end of the filename to identify the program or format in which the file has been saved.

Finding tools Publications used to find primary and secondary sources.

Firewalls Programs designed to limit access to authorized users and applications.

Fixtures Goods that are affixed to real estate so as to become part thereof.

Foreign corporation A corporation in any state or jurisdiction other than the one in which it was formed.

Foreign Corrupt Practices Act (FCPA) A federal statute that makes it illegal for U.S. companies, or their officers, directors, agents, or employees, to bribe a foreign official or foreign political party official to influence the awarding of new business or the retention of continuous business activity.

Forgery The fraudulent making or alteration of a written document that affects the legal liability of another person.

Form I-9 "Employment Eligibility Verification" A form that must be completed by prospective employees.

Formal will A will that meets all the requirements of the state will statute.

Forum-selection clause Contract provision that designates a certain court to hear any dispute concerning nonperformance of the contract.

Foster care Parent care, sponsored by the state, by those not the adoptive or biological parents.

Fraud A knowing misrepresentation or concealment of a material fact to induce another to act to their detriment.

Fraudulent transfer Occurs when (1) a debtor transfers property to a third person within one year before the filing of a petition in bankruptcy and (2) the transfer was made by the debtor with an intent to hinder, delay, or defraud creditors.

Free Exercise Clause A clause to the First Amendment that prohibits the government from interfering with the free exercise of religion in the United States.

Freedom of Information Act A law that was enacted to give the public access to most documents in the possession of federal administrative agencies.

Freedom of speech The right to engage in oral, written, and symbolic speech protected by the First Amendment.

Freehold estate An estate in which the owner has a present possessory interest in the real property.

Frolic and detour A situation in which an agent does something during the course of his or her employment to further his or her own interests rather than the principal's interests.

Functional résumé format Lists a summary of the individual's qualifications with current experience and education without any emphasis on dates of employment.

Future interest The interest that the grantor retains for him- or herself or a third party.

General denial In some jurisdictions, the word "Denied" alone is insufficient and the averment of the complaint is treated as if it were "Admitted."

General gift A gift that does not identify the specific property from which the gift is to be made.

General government regulation Government regulation that applies to many industries collectively.

General law practice A general law practice is one that handles all types of cases.

General partner A partner of a general partnership who is liable for the debts and obligations of the general partnership. Also, partners in a limited partnership who invest capital, manage the business, and are personally liable for partnership debts.

General partnership A voluntary association of two or more persons for carrying on a business as co-owners for profit. Also called a *partnership*.

General-jurisdiction trial court (courts of record) A court that hears cases of a general nature that are not within the jurisdiction of limited-jurisdiction trial courts.

Generally known dangers A defense that acknowledges that certain products are inherently dangerous and are known to the general population to be so.

Generic name A term for a mark that has become a common term for a product line or type of service and therefore has lost its trademark protection.

Gift A voluntary transfer of title to property without payment of consideration by the donee. To be a valid gift, three elements must be shown: (1) *donative intent*, (2) *delivery*, and (3) *acceptance*.

Gift *causa mortis* A gift that is made in contemplation of death.

Gift *inter vivos* A gift made during a person's lifetime that is an irrevocable present transfer of ownership.

Gift promise A promise that is unenforceable because it lacks consideration.

GlobalCite Loislaw's tool for searching cases containing references to another case.

Good Samaritan law A state statute that relieves medical professionals from liability for ordinary negligence when they stop and render aid to victims in emergency situations.

Goods Tangible things that are movable at the time of their identification to the contract.

Government employment Working for federal, state, and local government agencies and authorities.

Government in the Sunshine Act An act that was enacted to open certain federal administrative agency meetings to the public.

Grantee The party to whom an interest in real property is transferred.

Grantor The party who transfers an ownership interest in real property.

Grantor (trustor) The person who creates a living trust. Also called the *trustor*.

Graphic user interface (GUI) A set of screen presentations and metaphors that utilize graphic elements such as icons in an attempt to make an operating system easier to operate.

H-1B visa A nonimmigrant visa that allows U.S. employers to employ foreign nationals in the United States that are skilled in specialty occupations.

Hacking Unauthorized access to a computer or computer network.

Hardcopy Paper copies of documents.

Headnotes The syllabus or summary of the points of law prepared by the editorial staff of a publisher.

Healthcare agent One designated by a person in a healthcare directive to act for a person in making healthcare decisions.

Healthcare directive (healthcare proxy) A document in which the maker should name someone to be his or her healthcare agent to make all healthcare decisions in accordance with his or her wishes in the living will.

Heir One who receives property from a deceased relative under intestacy statute.

Highest state court The top court in a state court system; it hears appeals from intermediate state courts and certain trial courts.

Holding The actual decision on the specific point of law the court was asked to decide.

Holographic will Will that is entirely handwritten and signed by the testator.

Homestead exemption Equity in a debtor's home that the debtor is permitted to retain.

Hot spot A wireless access point, generally in a public area.

Hung jury A jury that does not come to a unanimous decision about the defendant's guilt. The government may choose to retry the case.

Identity theft (ID theft) A crime where one person steals information about another person and poses as that person and takes the innocent person's money or property or purchases goods and services using the victim's credit information.

Identity Theft and Assumption Deterrence Act A federal statute that makes identity theft a felony that is punishable by a prison sentence.

Illegal contract A contract to perform an illegal act. Cannot be enforced by either party to the contract.

Immaterial facts A fact not essential to the matter or issue at hand.

Immigration Reform and Control Act of 1986 (IRCA) A federal statute that makes it unlawful for employers to hire illegal immigrants.

Immunity from prosecution The government agrees not to use any evidence given by a person granted immunity against that person.

Implied agency An agency that occurs when a principal and an agent do not expressly create an agency, but it is inferred from the conduct of the parties.

Implied attorney–client relationship Implied attorney–client relationship may result when a prospective client divulges confdential information during a consultation with an attorney for the purpose of retaining the attorney, even if actual employment does not result.

Implied warranty of habitability A warranty that provides that leased premises must be fit, safe, and suitable for ordinary residential use.

Implied-in-fact contract A contract in which agreement between parties has been inferred from their conduct.

***In personam* (personal) jurisdiction** Jurisdiction over the parties to a lawsuit.

***In rem* jurisdiction** Jurisdiction to hear a case because of jurisdiction over the property of the lawsuit.

Income beneficiary Person or entity to be paid income from the trust.

Indemnification Right of a partner to be reimbursed for expenditures incurred on behalf of the partnership.

Independent adoption An adoption in which there is a private arrangement between the biological parents and adoptive parents.

Independent contractor A person or business that is not an employee and is employed by a principal to perform a certain task on his or her behalf.

Independent Medical Examination (IME) Term formerly used to describe a defense medical evaluation.

Indictment The charge of having committed a crime (usually a felony), based on the judgment of a grand jury.

Infancy doctrine A doctrine that allows minors to disaffirm (cancel) most contracts they have entered into with adults.

Inferior performance A situation in which a party fails to perform express or implied contractual obligations and impairs or destroys the essence of the contract.

Information The charge of having committed a crime (usually a misdemeanor), based on the judgment of a judge (magistrate).

Information Infrastructure Protection Act (IIP Act) A federal statute that makes it a federal crime for anyone to intentionally access and acquire information from a protected computer without authorization.

Injunction A court order that prohibits a person from doing a certain act.

Injury The plaintiff must suffer personal injury or damage to his or her property to recover monetary damages for the defendant's negligence.

Innkeeper The owner of a facility that provides lodging to the public for compensation.

Inside director A member of the board of directors who is also an officer of the corporation.

Intangible property Rights that cannot be reduced to physical form such as stock certificates, certificates of deposit, bonds, and copyrights.

Intellectual property and information rights Patents, copyrights, trademarks, trade secrets, trade names, domain names, and other valuable business assets. Federal and state laws protect intellectual property rights from misappropriation and infringement.

Intentional infliction of emotional distress A tort that occurs when a person's extreme and outrageous conduct intentionally or recklessly causes severe emotional distress to another person. Also known as the *tort of outrage*.

Intentional torts A category of torts that requires that the defendant possessed the intent to do the act that caused the plaintiff's injuries.

***Inter vivos* trust** A trust that is created while the settlor is alive.

Intermediate appellate court An intermediate court that hears appeals from trial courts.

Intermediate scrutiny test Test that is applied to classifications based on protected classes other than race (e.g., sex or age).

International Paralegal Management Association (IPMA) A North American association for legal assistant managers.

Internet A collection of millions of computers that provide a network of electronic connections between the computers.

Internet (Web) browsers An Internet or Web browser is a software program that allows a person to use a computer to access the Internet. The two most popular Web browsers are Microsoft Internet Explorer and Google Chrome.

Internet search engine An Internet search engine is a program designed to take a word or set of words and locate websites on the Internet.

Internet service provider (ISP) The company providing the connection between the user and the Internet.

Interpretive rules Rules issued by administrative agencies that interpret existing statutory language.

Interrogatories Written questions submitted by one party to another party. The questions must be answered in writing within a stipulated time.

Interstate commerce Commerce that moves between states or that affects commerce between states.

Intervention The act of others to join as parties to an existing lawsuit.

Intestacy statute A state statute that specifies how a deceased's property will be distributed if he or she dies without a will or if the last will is declared void and there is no prior valid will.

Intestate The state of having died without leaving a will.

Intoxicated person A person who is under contractual incapacity because of ingestion of alcohol or drugs to the point of incompetence.

Invasion of the right to privacy A tort that constitutes the violation of a person's right to live his or her life without being subjected to unwarranted and undesired publicity.

Invitee One expressly or by implication invited onto the premises of the owner for mutual benefit.

Involuntary petition A petition filed by creditors of the debtor; alleges that the debtor is not paying his or her debts as they become due.

IOLTA account Where the amount is too small to earn interest, court rules require the funds be deposited into a special interest-bearing account, and the interest generally paid to support legal aid projects (Interest on Lawyers Trust Accounts).

Irreconcilable differences The legal matter in dispute.

Joint and several liability Tort liability where general partners are liable as a group or separately. This means that the plaintiff can sue one or more of the partners separately. If successful, the plaintiff can recover the entire amount of the judgment from any or all of the defendant–partners.

Joint custody Custody given to both parents with each having a period of physical custody and shared decision-making power.

Joint liability Partners are jointly liable for contracts and debts of the partnership. This means that a plaintiff must name the partnership and all of the partners as defendants in a lawsuit.

Joint tenancy A form of co-ownership that includes the right of survivorship.

Joint will A will that is executed by two or more testators.

Judgment The official decision of the court.

Judicial branch The court system.

Judicial decision A ruling about an individual lawsuit issued by federal and state courts.

Jurisdiction The authority of the court to hear disputes and impose resolution of the dispute upon the litigants.

Jurisprudence The philosophy or science of law.

Jury deliberation The process where the jury meets to discuss and resolve the dispute.

Jury instructions (charges) Instructions given by the judge to the jury that informs them of the law to be applied in the case.

Jury selection Process by which a group of six or more people is chosen to serve on the jury.

Just Compensation Clause A clause of the U.S. Constitution that requires the government to compensate the property owner, and possibly others, when the government takes property under its power of eminent domain.

KeyCite Westlaw's tool for searching cases containing references to another case.

Land The most common form of real property; includes the land and buildings and other structures permanently attached to the land.

Landlord/lessor An owner who transfers a leasehold.

Landlord–tenant relationship A relationship created when the owner of a freehold estate (landlord) transfers a right to exclusively and temporarily possess the owner's property to another (tenant).

Land-use control or land-use regulation The collective term for the laws that regulate the possession, ownership, and use of real property.

Lanham Trademark Act A federal statute that (1) establishes the requirements for obtaining a federal mark, and (2) protects marks from infringement.

Larceny The taking of another's personal property other than from his or her person or building.

Large law offices Large law offices are an outgrowth of traditional law offices that have expanded over the years, adding partners and associates along the way.

Law That which must be obeyed and followed by citizens subject to sanctions or legal consequences; a body of rules of action or conduct prescribed by controlling authority, and having binding legal force.

Law court A court that developed and administered a uniform set of laws decreed by the kings and queens after William the Conqueror; legal procedure was emphasized over merits at this time.

Leading question A question which suggests the answer.

Lease A transfer of the right to the possession and use of real property for a set term in return for certain consideration; the rental agreement between a landlord and a tenant.

Leasehold estate/leasehold A tenant's interest in property.

Legal assistant See *Paralegal*.

Legal research The process for finding the answer to a legal question.

Legally enforceable A contract in which if one party fails to perform as promised, the other party can use the court system to enforce the contract and recover damages or other remedy.

Legislative branch The part of the government that consists of Congress (the Senate and the House of Representatives).

Lessee The person who acquires the right to possession and use of goods under the lease.

Lessor The person who transfers the right of possession and use of goods under the lease.

Libel A false statement that appears in a letter, newspaper, magazine, book, photograph, movie, video, or other media.

License A contract that transfers limited rights in intellectual property and information rights. Grants a person the right to enter upon another person's property for a specified and usually short period of time.

Licensee A party who is granted limited rights in or access to intellectual property or informational rights owned by a licensor.

Licensing agreement A detailed and comprehensive written agreement between a licensor and a licensee that sets forth the express terms of their agreement.

Licensor An owner of intellectual property or informational rights who transfers rights in the property or information to the licensee.

Life estate An interest in land for a person's lifetime; upon that person's death, the interest will be transferred to another party.

Limited liability Members are liable for the LLC's debts, obligations, and liabilities only to the extent of their capital contributions. Liability that shareholders have only to the extent of their capital contribution. Shareholders are generally not personally liable for debts and obligations of the corporation.

Limited liability company (LLC) An unincorporated business entity that combines the most favorable attributes of general partnerships, limited partnerships, and corporations.

Limited liability partnership (LLP) A form of partnership in which all partners are limited partners and there are no general partners.

Limited partners Partners in a limited partnership who invest capital but do not participate in management and are not personally liable for partnership debts beyond their capital contribution.

Limited partnership A special form of partnership that is formed only if certain formalities are followed. A limited partnership has both general and limited partners.

Limited partnership agreement A document that sets forth the rights and duties of the general and limited partners, the terms and conditions regarding the operation, termination, and dissolution of the partnership, and so on.

Limited-jurisdiction trial courts Courts authorized to hear certain types of disputes such as divorce or bankruptcy.

Lineal descendants The testator's children, grandchildren, great-grandchildren, and so on.

Liquidated damages Damages to which parties to a contract agree in advance should be paid if the contract is breached.

Litigation The process of bringing, maintaining, and defending a lawsuit.

Living trust A method for holding property during a person's lifetime and distributing the property upon that person's death. Also called a *grantor's trust* and a *revocable trust*.

Living will A document that states which life-saving measures the signor does and does not want, and can specify that he or she wants such treatments withdrawn if doctors determine that there is no hope of a meaningful recovery.

Local area network (LAN) A network of computers at one location.

Long-arm statute A statute that extends a state's jurisdiction to nonresidents who were not served a summons within the state.

Lost property Property that the owner leaves somewhere because of negligence, carelessness, or inadvertence.

Mainframe A large computer system used primarily for bulk processing of data and financial information.

Malicious prosecution A lawsuit in which the original defendant sues the original plaintiff for bringing a lawsuit without probable cause and with malice.

Mandatory authority Court decisions that are binding on all lower courts.

Marital property Property acquired during the course of marriage using income earned during the marriage, and separate property that has been converted to marital property.

Mark The collective name for trademarks, service marks, certification marks, and collective marks.

Marketable title Title to real property that is free from any encumbrances or other defects that are not disclosed but would affect the value of the property. Also called *good title*.

Marriage A legal union between two people that confers certain legal rights and duties upon the parties and upon the children born of the marriage.

Marriage ceremony A mutual exchange of intent to be married.

Marriage license A legal document issued by a state certifying that two people are married.

Marriage requirements Minimum standards for marriage under state law.

Material breach A breach that occurs when a party renders inferior performance of his or her contractual duties.

Material facts A fact significant or essential to the issue.

Mediation A form of negotiation in which a neutral third party assists the disputing parties in reaching a settlement of their dispute.

Mediator A neutral third party who assists the disputing parties in reaching a settlement of their dispute. The mediator cannot make a decision or an award.

Member An owner of an LLC.

Memorandum A working legal document for the legal team for use in preparation and presentation of a case.

Mens rea "Evil intent"—the possession of the requisite state of mind to commit a prohibited act.

Merchant protection statute A state statute that allows merchants to stop, detain, and investigate suspected shoplifters without being held liable for false imprisonment if (1) there are reasonable grounds for the suspicion, (2) suspects are detained for only a reasonable time, and (3) investigations are conducted in a reasonable manner.

Mineral rights (subsurface rights) Rights to the earth located beneath the surface of the land.

Minitrial A voluntary private proceeding in which the lawyers for each side present a shortened version of their case to representatives of the other side, and usually to a neutral third party, in an attempt to reach a settlement of the dispute.

Minor A person who has not reached the age of majority.

Minor breach A breach that occurs when a party renders substantial performance of his or her contractual duties.

***Miranda* rights** Rights that a suspect must be informed of before being interrogated, so that the suspect will not unwittingly give up his or her Fifth Amendment right.

Mirror image rule A rule that states that for an acceptance to exist, the offeree must accept the terms as stated in the offer.

Misappropriation of the right to publicity A tort in which one party appropriates a person's name or identity for commercial purposes.

Misdemeanor A less serious crime; not inherently evil but prohibited by society. Many crimes against property are misdemeanors.

Mislaid property Property that an owner voluntarily places somewhere and then inadvertently forgets.

Mitigation of damages A nonbreaching party's legal duty to avoid or reduce damages caused by a breach of contract.

Model Guidelines for the Utilization of Legal Assistant Services A set of guidelines by ABA policymaking body, the House of Delegates, intended to govern conduct of lawyers when utilizing paralegals or legal assistants.

Modem A device to translate electrical signals to allow computers to communicate with each other.

Monetary damages An award of money.

Money Laundering Control Act A federal statute that makes it a crime to (1) knowingly engage in a *money transaction* through a financial institution involving property worth more than $10,000 and (2) knowingly engage in a *financial transaction* involving the proceeds of an illegal activity.

Moral obligation An obligation based on one's own conscience.

Motion for judgment on the pleadings A motion that alleges that if all the facts presented in the pleadings are taken as true, the party making the motion would win the lawsuit when the proper law is applied to these asserted facts.

Motion for summary judgment A motion that asserts that there are no factual disputes to be decided by the jury and that the judge can apply the proper law to the undisputed facts and decide the case without a jury. These motions are supported by affidavits, documents, and deposition testimony.

Motion to dismiss A motion that alleges that the plaintiff's complaint fails to state a claim for which relief can be granted. Also called a *demurrer*.

Motivation test A test to determine the liability of the principal; if the agent's motivation in committing the intentional tort is to promote the principal's business, then the principal is liable for any injury caused by the tort.

Murder The unlawful killing of a human being by another with intent.

Mutual benefit bailment A bailment for the mutual benefit of the bailor and bailee. The bailee owes a duty of ordinary care to protect the bailed property.

Mutual (reciprocal) will Occurs where two or more testators execute separate wills that leave their property to each other on the condition that the survivor leave the remaining property on his or her death as agreed by the testators.

Narrative opportunity A question that allows the giving of a full explanation.

National Association of Legal Assistants (NALA) Professional organization for legal assistants that provides continuing education and professional certification for paralegals, incorporated in 1975.

National Association of Legal Secretaries (NALS) Since 1999, an association for legal professionals, originally formed in 1949 as an association for legal secretaries.

National Federation of Paralegal Associations (NFPA) Professional organization of state and local paralegal associations founded in 1974.

National Labor Relations Board (NLRB) A federal administrative agency that oversees union elections, prevents employers and unions from engaging in illegal and unfair labor practices, and enforces and interprets certain federal labor laws.

Necessaries of life A minor must pay the reasonable value of food, clothing, shelter, medical care, and other items considered necessary to the maintenance of life.

Negligence Failure of a corporate director or officer to exercise the duty of care while conducting the corporation's business.

Negligence *per se* Tort where the violation of a statute or ordinance constitutes the breach of the duty of care.

Negligent infliction of emotional distress A tort that permits a person to recover for emotional distress caused by the defendant's negligent conduct.

Negotiation A procedure in which the parties to a dispute engage in negotiations to try to reach a voluntary settlement of their dispute.

Network administrator The network administrator usually is the person with the highest-level access to the network file server.

Network file server A separate computer in a network that acts as the traffic cop of the system controlling the flow of data.

Network rights and privileges Rights or privileges determine who has access to the server, the data stored on the server, and the flow of information between connections.

Networking The establishment of contact with others with whom questions and information are shared.

No Electronic Theft Act (NET Act) A federal statute that makes it a crime for a person to willfully infringe on a copyright work that exceeds $1,000 in retail value.

No-fault divorce A divorce recognized by the law of a state whereby neither party is blamed for the divorce.

Noncupative will Oral will that is made before a witness during the testator's last illness.

Nonfreehold estate An estate in which the tenant has a right to possession of the property but not title to the property.

Non-intent crime A crime that imposes criminal liability without a finding of *mens rea* (intent).

Notice pleading Pleadings required to include sufficient facts to put the parties on notice of the claims asserted against them.

Nurse paralegals Nurses who have gained medical work experience and combine it with paralegal skills. Also referred to as *legal nurse consultants*.

Objective rule A rule stating that if an engagement is broken off, the prospective bride must return the engagement ring, regardless of which party broke off the engagement.

Obscene speech Speech that (1) appeals to the prurient interest, (2) depicts sexual conduct in a patently offensive way, and (3) lacks serious literary, artistic, political, or scientific value.

Occupational Safety and Health Act A federal act enacted in 1970 that promotes safety in the workplace.

Offensive speech Speech that is offensive to many members of society. It is subject to time, place, and manner restrictions.

Offer The manifestation of willingness to enter into a bargain, so made as to justify another person in understanding that his assent to that bargain is invited and will conclude it.

Offeree The party to whom an offer to enter into a contract is made.

Offeror The party who makes an offer to enter into a contract.

Office software suites This software consists of commonly used office software programs that manage data and database programs; manipulate financial or numeric information, spreadsheet programs; or display images and presentation graphics programs.

Officers of the corporation Employees of a corporation who are appointed by the board of directors to manage the day-to-day operations of the corporation.

One-year rule An executory contract that cannot be performed by its own terms within one year of its formation must be in writing.

Online collaboration Using the Internet to conduct meetings and share documents.

Open adoption Where biological and adoptive parents are known to each other.

Open-ended question A question that usually does not have a yes or no answer.

Opening brief The first opportunity for the attorneys to address the jury and describe the nature of the lawsuit.

Operating agreement An agreement entered into by members that governs the affairs and business of the LLC and the relations among members, managers, and the LLC.

Operating system The operating system is a basic set of instructions to the computer on how to handle basic functions—how to process input from "input devices" such as the keyboard and mouse, the order in which to process information, and what to show on the computer monitor.

Opinion letter A formal statement of advice based on the lawyer's expert knowledge.

Order Decision issued by an administrative law judge.

Ordinances Laws enacted by local government bodies such as cities and municipalities, counties, school districts, and water districts.

Organizational meeting A meeting that must be held by the initial directors of the corporation after the articles of incorporation are filed.

Outside director A member of the board of directors who is not an officer of the corporation.

Outsourcing Use of persons or services outside of the immediate office staff.

Paperless office The paperless office is one in which documents are created and stored electronically.

Paralegal A person qualified by education, training, or work experience who is employed or retained by a lawyer, law office, corporation, governmental agency, or other entity who performs specifically delegated substantive legal work for which a lawyer is responsible. Also referred to as *legal assistant*.

Paralegal Advanced Competency Exam (PACE) National Association of Paralegal Association's certification program that requires the paralegal to have two years of experience and a bachelor's degree and have completed a paralegal course at an accredited school.

Paralegal manager Someone who hires, supervises, trains, and evaluates paralegals.

Parallel citation The citation to the same case in a different publication.

Parent A person who by adoption or as the biological parent is legally responsible for a child.

Partnership Two or more natural (human) or artificial (corporation) persons who have joined together to share ownership and profit or loss.

Partnership agreement A written partnership agreement that the partners sign. Also called articles of partnership.

Partnership at will A partnership with no fixed duration.

Partnership for a term A partnership with a fixed duration.

Patent infringement Unauthorized use of another's patent. A patent holder may recover damages and other remedies against a patent infringer.

Paternity action A legal proceeding that determines the identity of the father of a child.

Penal codes Statutes that define crimes.

***Per capita* distribution** A distribution of the estate that makes each grandchild and greatgrandchild of the deceased inherit equally with the children of the deceased.

***Per stirpes* distribution** A distribution of the estate that makes grandchildren and greatgrandchildren of the deceased inherit by representation of their parent.

Periodic tenancy A tenancy created when a lease specifies intervals at which payments are due but does not specify the length of the lease.

Permanent (lifetime) alimony Payments of spousal support paid until remarriage or death of recipient.

Personal jurisdiction Requires the court to have authority over the persons as well as the subject matter of the lawsuit.

Personal property Tangible property such as automobiles, furniture, and equipment, and intangible property such as securities, patents, and copyrights.

Personal representative The person(s) appointed by the court to administer an estate.

Persuasive authority Court decisions the court is not required to follow but are well reasoned and from a respected court.

Petition for bankruptcy A document filed with the bankruptcy court that starts a bankruptcy proceeding.

Petition for *certiorari* A petition asking the Supreme Court to hear one's case.

Petition for divorce A document filed with the proper state court that commences a divorce proceeding.

Petitioner The party appealing the decision of an administrative agency.

Physical and mental examination A form of discovery that permits the physical or mental examination of a party by a qualified expert of the opposing party's choosing where the physical or mental condition of the party is at issue in the lawsuit.

Picketing The action of strikers walking in front of the employer's premises carrying signs announcing their strike.

Piercing the corporate veil A doctrine that says that if a shareholder dominates a corporation and misuses it for improper purposes, a court of equity can disregard the corporate entity and hold the shareholder personally liable for the corporation's debts and obligations.

Plaintiff The party who files the complaint.

Plaintiff's case Process by which the plaintiff calls witnesses and introduces evidence to prove the allegations contained in his or her complaint.

Plan of reorganization A plan that sets forth a proposed new capital structure for the debtor to have when it emerges from Chapter 11 reorganization bankruptcy.

Plant life and vegetation Real property that is growing in or on the surface of the land.

Plea bargain agreement An agreement in which the accused admits to a lesser crime than charged. In return, the government agrees to impose a lesser sentence than might have been obtained had the case gone to trial.

Pleadings The paperwork that is filed with the court to initiate and respond to a lawsuit.

Pocket parts An update to a book that is a separate document that slips into a pocket in the back of the main volume.

Police power The power of states to regulate private and business activity within their borders.

Pour-over will A will that, upon the grantor's death, distributes the grantor's property that is not in the living will.

Power of attorney An express agency agreement that is often used to give an agent the power to sign legal documents on behalf of the principal.

Precedent Prior case law that is controlling.

Preemption doctrine The concept that federal law takes precedence over state or local law.

Pregnancy Discrimination Act Amendment to Title VII that forbids employment discrimination because of "pregnancy, childbirth, or related medical conditions."

Prenuptial agreement A contract entered into prior to marriage that specifies how property will be distributed upon the termination of the marriage or death of a spouse. Also referred to as a *premarital agreement*.

Pretrial hearing A hearing before the trial in order to facilitate the settlement of a case. Also called a settlement conference.

Pretrial motion A motion a party can make to try to dispose of all or part of a lawsuit prior to trial.

Primary authority The actual law itself.

Primary source of law The actual law itself.

Principal A party who employs another person to act on his or her behalf.

Principal–agent relationship A relationship in which an employer hires an employee and gives that employee authority to act and enter into contracts on his or her behalf.

Privacy Act An act stipulating that federal administrative agencies can maintain only information about an individual that is relevant and necessary to accomplish a legitimate agency purpose.

Privilege A special legal right.

Privileged communication A communication that the person has a right to be kept confidential based on the relationship with the other part such as attorney and client.

Pro bono Working without compensation on behalf of individuals and organizations that otherwise could not afford legal assistance.

Pro se Parties represent themselves.

Probate (settlement of estate) The process of a deceased's property being collected, debts and taxes being paid, and the remainder of the estate being distributed.

Procedural due process Due process that requires the respondent to be given (1) proper and timely notice of the allegations or charges against him or her and (2) an opportunity to present evidence on the matter.

Procedural law Law which realtes to how the trial is conducted and is usually based upon Rules of Court and Rules of Evidence.

Production of documents Request by one party to another party to produce all documents relevant to the case prior to the trial.

Products liability The liability of manufacturers, sellers, and others for the injuries caused by defective products.

Professional Legal Secretary (PLS) The advanced certification for legal professionals from NALS.

Professional malpractice The liability of a professional who breaches his or her duty of ordinary care.

Professional Paralegal (PP) Certification from NALS for those performing paralegal duties.

Promise to marry An offer to marry that is accepted.

Proof of claim A document required to be filed by unsecured creditors that states the amount of their claim against the debtor.

Proprietary school Private, as opposed to public, institution, generally for profit, offering training and education.

Protocol In a URL, the required format of the Web address.

Proximate cause A point along a chain of events caused by a negligent party after which this party is no longer legally responsible for the consequences of his or her actions. Also referred to as *legal cause*.

Published opinion A court's written explanation of its decision on a case intended to be relied upon as a statement of the law based on the facts of the case.

Punitive damages Damages that are awarded to punish the defendant, to deter the defendant from similar conduct in the future, and to set an example for others.

***Quasi in rem* (attachment) jurisdiction** Jurisdiction allowed a plaintiff who obtains a judgment in one state to try to collect the judgment by attaching property of the defendant located in another state.

Quasi-contract (implied-in-law contract) An equitable doctrine whereby a court may award monetary damages to a plaintiff for providing work or services to a defendant even though no actual contract existed.

Quiet title An action brought by a party seeking an order of the court declaring who has title to disputed property. By its decision, the court "quiets title."

Racketeer Influenced Corrupt Organizations Act (RICO) A federal statute that defines the crime of racketeering and provides for both criminal and civil penalties for racketeering.

Random access memory (RAM) Temporary computer memory that stores work in processs.

Rational basis test Test that is applied to classifications not involving a suspect or protected class.

Real property The land itself as well as buildings, trees, soil, minerals, timber, plants, and other things permanently affixed to the land.

Reasonable person standard Acting as a responsible, prudent person would act under the same or similar circumstances.

Reasonable professional standard Acting as a responsible, prudent professional would act as measured by other similar professionals.

Rebuttal Phase of the trial that gives the plaintiff the chance to address or respond to information contained in the defendant's case-in-chief.

Receiving stolen property A person (1) knowingly receives stolen property and (2) intends to deprive the rightful owner of that property.

Recording statute A state statute that requires a mortgage or deed of trust to be recorded in the county recorder's office of the county in which the real property is located.

Recross examination Permits opposing counsel to again challenge the credibility of the witness but only as to matters questioned on redirect examination.

Redirect examination After cross-examination, counsel who originally called the witness on direct examination may ask the witness additional questions.

Reformation An equitable doctrine that permits the court to rewrite a contract to express the parties' true intentions.

Registrar of Deeds A public official with whom property deeds are filed and maintained.

Regulatory statutes Statutes, such as environmental laws, securities laws, and antitrust laws that provide for criminal violations and penalties.

Rejection Express words or conduct by the offeree that rejects an offer. Rejection terminates the offer.

Relevant facts Facts crucial to the case and having legal significance.

Religious discrimination Discrimination against a person solely because of his or her religion or religious practices.

Remainder (remainderman) A right of possession that returns to a third party upon the expiration of a limited or contingent estate.

Remainder beneficiary Person or entity to receive the trust *corpus* upon termination of the trust.

Remand When the basis of federal jurisdiction is resolved and only state claims remain to be litigated, the federal court must send the matter back to the state trial court. Also, when the appellate court disagrees with the outcome of the trial court but sends the matter back to the trial court for further proceeding in accordance with its opinion, which may include additional proceedings or a new trial to correct the error, in accordance with the appellate court's decision.

Remote collaboration Working on a common document utilizing remote access by two or more parties.

Renounce an inheritance A beneficiary rejection of a bequest or right to take property.

Replacement workers Workers who are hired to take the place of striking workers. They can be hired on either a temporary or permanent basis.

Reply Filed by the original plaintiff to answer the defendant's cross-complaint.

Request for admission A form of discovery in which written requests are made to the opposing party asking him to admit the truth of certain facts or liability.

Res ipsa loquitur Tort where the presumption of negligence arises because (1) the defendant was in exclusive control of the situation, and (2) the plaintiff would not have suffered injury but for someone's negligence. The burden switches to the defendant(s) to prove they were not negligent.

Residuary gift A gift of the estate left after the debts, taxes, and specific and general gifts have been paid.

Respondeat superior A rule that says an employer is liable for the tortious conduct of its employees or agents while they are acting within the scope of its authority.

Respondent The party who must respond to the appeal, usually the verdict winner at trial.

Restatement of the Law Third, Torts A legal treatise with suggested rules of laws relating to torts.

Restraining order A court order directing one party to avoid contact with another.

Resulting trust A trust that is implied from the conduct of the parties.

Résumé A short description of a person's education, a summary of work experience, and other related and supporting information that potential employers use in evaluating a person's qualifications for a position in a firm or an organization.

Retainer A payment at the beginning of the handling of a new matter for a client. This amount may be used to offset the fees for services rendered or costs advanced on behalf of the client.

Reverse The appellate court disagrees with the outcome of the trial and finds reversible error was made and judgment should be overturned and entered in favor of the appellant.

Reversion A right of possession that returns to the grantor after the expiration of a limited or contingent estate.

Revised Model Business Corporation Act (RMBCA) A 1984 revision of the MBCA that arranged the provisions of the original act more logically, revised the language to be more consistent, and made substantial changes in the provisions.

Revised Uniform Limited Partnership Act (RULPA) A 1976 revision of the ULPA that provides a more modern, comprehensive law for the formation, operation, and dissolution of limited partnerships.

Revocation Withdrawal of an offer by the offeror which terminates the offer.

Robbery The taking of personal property from another person by the use of fear or force.

Rules of court A court's rules for the processing and presentation of cases.

S corporation A corporation that has elected S corporation status. An S corporation pays no federal income tax at the corporate level. The gains or losses of an S corporation flow-through to the shareholders.

Sale The passing of title from a seller to a buyer for a price. Also called a *conveyance*.

Sales contract under UCC A passage of the title to goods for a price.

Scienter Means international conduct. Scienter is required for there to be a violation of Section 10(b) and Rule 10b-5.

Screening interview Limited first contact with a prospective new client.

Search query Specific words used in a computerized search.

Search warrant A warrant issued by a court that authorizes the police to search a designated place for specified contraband, articles, items, or documents. The search warrant must be based on probable cause.

Secondary authority Writings that explain the law.

Secondary meaning When an ordinary term has become a brand name.

Secondary source of law Writings about the law.

Section 7 of the NLRA A law that gives employees the right to join together and form a union.

Section 8(a) of the NLRA A law that makes it an unfair labor practice for an employer to interfere with, coerce, or restrain employees from exercising their statutory right to form and join unions.

Self-employment Working independently either as a freelance paralegal for different lawyers or, when authorized by state or federal law, performing services for the public.

Self-incrimination The Fifth Amendment states that no person shall be compelled in any criminal case to be a witness against him or herself.

Separate property Property owned by a spouse prior to marriage, as well as inheritances and gifts received by a spouse during the marriage.

Service mark A mark that distinguishes the services of the holder from those of its competitors.

Service of process settlement agreement A summons is served on the defendant to obtain personal jurisdiction over him or her.

Servient easement The land that is used by dominant easement.

Settlement agreement An agreement voluntarily entered into by the parties to a dispute that settles the dispute. In a divorce, a written document signed by divorcing parties that evidences their agreement settling property rights and other issues of their divorce.

Settlor, trustor, or transferor Person who creates a trust. Also referred to as *trustor* or *transferor*.

Sex discrimination Discrimination against a person solely because of his or her sex.

Sexual harassment Lewd remarks, touching, intimidation, posting of pinups, and other verbal or physical conduct of a sexual nature that occur on the job.

Shareholders The owners of corporations, whose ownership interests are evidenced by stock certificates.

Slander Oral defamation of character.

Slip opinion A copy of the opinion sent to the printer.

Small offices Small-office arrangements range from individual practitioners sharing space to partnerships.

Small-claims court A court that hears civil cases involving small dollar amounts.

Software Refers to programs containing sets of instructions that tell the computer and the other computer-based electronic devices what to do and how to do it.

Sole proprietorship A form of business in which the owner is actually the business; the business is not a separate legal entity.

Solo practice One lawyer practicing alone without the assistance of other attorneys.

Special federal courts Federal courts that hear matters of specialized or limited jurisdiction.

Specialty application programs Specialty programs combine many of the basic functions found in software suites, word processing, database management, spreadsheets, and graphic presentations to perform law office, case, and litigation management.

Specialty practice A specialty practice is involved in practice in one area of law.

Specific duty An OSHA standard that addresses a safety problem of a specific duty nature (e.g., requirement for a safety guard on a particular type of equipment).

Specific gift A gift of a specifically named piece of property.

Specific government regulation Government regulation that applies to individual industries.

Specific performance A remedy that orders the breaching party to perform the acts promised in the contract. Specific performance usually is awarded in cases where the subject matter is unique, such as in contracts involving land, heirlooms, and paintings.

Spendthrift trust A trust for a beneficiary with limits on the use of the funds to prevent claims of the beneficiary's creditors.

Spoliation of evidence Destruction of evidence.

Spousal support Payments made by one divorced spouse to the other divorced spouse. Also called *alimony*.

Spreadsheet programs Programs that permit the calculation and presentation of financial information in a grid format of rows and columns.

Standing to sue The plaintiff must have some stake in the outcome of the lawsuit.

Stare decisis Latin: "to stand by the decision." Adherence to precedent. The legal principle that prior case law should apply unless there is a substantial change in society necessitating a change in the case law.

State administrative agencies Administrative agencies that states create to enforce and interpret state law.

Statement of policy A statement issued by administrative agencies announcing a proposed course of action that an agency intends to follow in the future.

Statute Written law enacted by the legislative branch of the federal and state governments that establishes certain courses of conduct that the covered parties must adhere to.

Statute of Frauds A state statute that requires certain types of contracts to be in writing.

Statute of limitations A time limit within which a case must be brought or lose the right to seek redress in court.

Statute of repose A statute that limits the seller's liability to a certain number of years from the date when the product was first sold.

Statute of Wills A state statute that establishes the requirements for making a valid will.

Strict liability A tort doctrine that makes manufacturers, distributors, wholesalers, retailers, and others in the chain of distribution of a defective product liable for the damages caused by the defect *irrespective of fault*. Also, liability without fault.

Strict scrutiny test Test that is applied to classifications based on race.

Strike Cessation of work by union members to obtain economic benefits or correct an unfair labor practice.

Subject-matter jurisdiction Jurisdiction over the subject matter of a lawsuit.

Subpoena A court order compelling a witness to attend and testify, must accompany a notice of deposition served on a non-party witness.

Substantial performance Performance by a contracting party that deviates only slightly from complete performance.

Substantive due process Due process that requires that the statute or rule that the respondent is charged with violating be clearly stated.

Substantive law Law which relates to the law of the case, such as the law of negligence or contract.

Substantive rule A rule issued by an administrative agency that has much the same power as a statute: It has the force of law and must be adhered to by covered persons and businesses.

Subsurface rights (mineral rights) Rights to the earth located beneath the surface of the land.

Summons A court order directing the defendant to appear in court and answer the complaint.

Superseding (or intervening) event A defendant is not liable for injuries caused by a superseding or intervening event for which he or she is not responsible.

Supervising attorney The member of the legal team to whom all others on the team report and who has the ultimate responsibility for the actions of the legal team.

Supremacy Clause A clause of the U.S. Constitution that establishes that the federal Constitution, treaties, federal laws, and federal regulations are the supreme law of the land.

Tangible property All real property and physically defined personal property such as buildings, goods, animals, and minerals.

Teleworker People who work from remote locations, typically home.

Temporary (rehabilitation) alimony Spousal support paid for a limited period of time.

Tenancy at sufferance A tenancy created when a tenant retains possession of property after the expiration of another tenancy or a life estate without the owner's consent.

Tenancy at will A tenancy created by a lease that may be terminated at any time by either party.

Tenancy by the entirety A form of co-ownership of real property that can be used only by married couples.

Tenancy for years A tenancy created when the landlord and the tenant agree on a specific duration for a lease.

Tenancy in common A form of co-ownership in which the interest of a surviving tenant in common passes to the deceased tenant's estate and not to the co-tenants.

Tenant The party to whom a leasehold is transferred.

Tender of performance Tender is an unconditional and absolute offer by a contracting party to perform his or her obligations under the contract. Occurs when a party who has the ability and willingness to perform offers to complete the performance of his or her duties under the contract.

Testamentary trust A trust created by will: the trust comes into existence when the settlor dies.

Testator or **testatrix** The person who makes a will.

Thin client A computer system where programs and files are maintained on a centralized server.

Third-party documents Documents prepared by a third party in the ordinary course of business that would have been prepared in similar form if there was no litigation.

Title III of the Americans with Disabilities Act A federal statute that prohibits discrimination on the basis of disability in places of public accommodation by private entities.

Title VII of the Civil Rights Act of 1964 A title of a federal statute enacted to eliminate job discrimination based on five protected classes: *race*, *color*, *religion*, *sex*, and *national origin*.

Title insurance Insurance that owners of real property purchase to insure that they have clear title to the property.

Tort A wrong. There are three categories of torts: (1) intentional torts, (2) unintentional torts (negligence), and (3) strict liability.

Totten trust Typically a bank account payable to a benefactor only on death of the person opening the account.

Track Changes Track Changes, as found in MS Word, shows the original text, the deleted text, and the new text as well as a strike through for deleted text, underlining or highlighting of new text, as well as margin notes on the document.

Trade secret A product formula, pattern, design, compilation of data, customer list, or other business secret.

Trademark A distinctive mark, symbol, name, word, motto, or device that identifies the goods of a particular business.

Trademark infringement Unauthorized use of another's mark. The holder may recover damages and other remedies from the infringer.

Treaty A compact made between two or more nations.

Trespass to land A tort that interferes with an owner's right to exclusive possession of land.

Trespass to personal property A tort that occurs whenever one person injures another person's personal property or interferes with that person's enjoyment of his or her personal property.

Trial brief Document presented to the court setting forth a legal argument to persuade the court to rule in a particular way on a procedural or substantive legal issue.

Trial notebook A summary of the case tabbed for each major activity, witness, or element of proof.

Trier of facts The trier of facts decides what facts are to be accepted and used in making the decision. It is usually a jury, but may be a judge who hears a case without a jury and decides the facts and applies the law.

Trust A legal arrangement established when one person transfers title to property to another person to be held and used for the benefit of a third person.

Trust account The funds of the client.

Trust *corpus* or trust *res* The property and assets held in trust.

Trustee Person or entity that holds legal title to the trust *corpus* and manages the trust for the benefit of the beneficiary or beneficiaries.

Trustee in bankruptcy A legal representative of a debtor's estate.

UCC Statute of Frauds A rule that requires all contracts for the sale of goods costing $500 or more and lease contracts involving payments of $1,000 or more to be in writing.

U.S. Courts of Appeals The federal court system's intermediate appellate courts.

U.S. District Courts The federal court system's trial courts of general jurisdiction.

U.S. Immigration and Customs Enforcement (ICE) The federal administrative agency that enforces federal immigration laws.

U.S. Supreme Court The Supreme Court was created by Article III of the U.S. Constitution. The Supreme Court is the highest court in the land. It is located in Washington, DC.

Unauthorized Practice of Law (UPL) Giving legal advice, if legal rights may be affected, by anyone not licensed to practice law.

Undue influence Occurs where one person takes advantage of another person's mental, emotional, or physical weakness and unduly persuades that person to make a will; the persuasion by the wrongdoer must overcome the free will of the testator.

Uniform Arbitration Act A uniform act adopted by more than half of the states; similar to the Federal Arbitration Act, it describes procedures that must be followed for arbitration to be initiated, how the panel of arbitrators is to be selected, and the procedures for conducting arbitration hearings.

Uniform Commercial Code (UCC) A comprehensive statutory scheme that includes laws covering aspects of commercial transactions.

Uniform Computer Information Transactions Act (UCITA) A model state law that creates contract law for the licensing of information technology rights.

Uniform Gift to Minors Act or Revised Uniform Gift to Minors Act Acts that establish procedures for adults to make gifts of money and securities to minors.

Uniform Limited Liability Company Act (ULLCA) A model act that provides comprehensive and uniform laws for the formation, operation, and dissolution of LLCs.

Uniform Partnership Act (UPA) A model act that codifies partnership law. Most states have adopted the UPA in whole or in part.

Uniform Probate Code (UPC) A model law promulgated to establish uniform rules for the creation of wills, the administration of estates, and the resolution of conflicts in settling estates.

Uniform resource locator (URL) The address of a site on the Internet.

Uniform Simultaneous Death Act An act that provides that if people who would inherit property from each other die simultaneously, each person's property is distributed as though he or she survived.

Unintentional tort/negligence The omission to do something which a reasonable person would do or doing something a reasonable person would refrain from doing.

Uninterruptable power supply (UPS) A battery system that can supply power to a computer or computer peripheral for a short period of time.

Universal Citation Format A system for citation relying on the courts to number the paragraphs in their opinions.

Unprotected speech Speech that is not protected by the First Amendment and may be forbidden by the government.

Unpublished opinions Cases which the court does not feel have precedential effect and are limited to a specific set of facts.

Unreasonable search and seizure Any search and seizure by the government that violates the Fourth Amendment.

V. Cite VersusLaw's tool for searching cases containing references to another case.

Variance An exception that permits a type of building or use in an area that would not otherwise be allowed by a zoning ordinance.

Vendor-specific citation format Citation format of a legal publisher adopted by a court.

Venue A concept that requires lawsuits to be heard by the court with jurisdiction that is nearest the location in which the incident occurred or where the parties reside.

Verdict Decision reached by the jury.

Videoconferencing Conferencing from multiple locations using high-speed Internet connections to transmit sound and images.

Violation A crime that is neither a felony nor a misdemeanor that is usually punishable by a fine.

Visitation rights A time period for visitation by noncustodial parent with the child.

Voice recognition Computer programs for converting speech into text or commands without the use of other input devices such as keyboards.

VoIP Voice over Internet protocol is a computer Internet replacement for traditional telephone connections.

Voir dire Process whereby prospective jurors are asked questions by the judge and attorneys to determine if they would be biased in their decision.

Voluntary petition A petition filed by the debtor; states that the debtor has debts.

White-collar crimes Crimes usually involving cunning and deceit rather than physical force.

Wide area network A wide area network is a network of networks. Each network is treated as if it were a connection on the network.

Will A declaration of how a person wants his or her property to be distributed upon death.

Wire fraud The use of telephone or telegraph to defraud another person.

Wireless computer networks A wireless network uses wireless technology in place of wires for connecting to the network.

Wireless network A wireless network uses wireless technology instead of wires for connecting to the network.

Workers' compensation acts Laws that compensate workers and their families if workers are injured in connection with their jobs.

Work–product doctrine A qualified immunity from discovery for "work product of the lawyer" except on a substantial showing of "necessity or justification" of certain written statements and memoranda prepared by counsel in representation of a client, generally in preparation for trial.

Work-related test A test that says if an agent commits an intentional tort within a work-related time or space, the principal is liable for any injury caused by the agent's intentional tort.

Workstation A computer connected to a network that is used for access consisting of a monitor, input device, and computer.

World Wide Web An electronic connection of millions of computers that support a standard set of rules for the exchange of information.

Writ of *certiorari* An official notice that the Supreme Court will review one's case.

Wrongful death action Lawsuit seeking compensation for damage caused by death of a relative.

Wrongful dissolution When a partner withdraws from a partnership without have the right to do so at that time.

Wrongful termination of an agency The termination of an agency contract in violation of the terms of the agency contract. In this situation, the nonbreaching party may recover damages from the breaching party.

Zoning commission A local administrative body that formulates zoning ordinances, conducts public hearings, and makes recommendations to the city council.

Zoning ordinances Local laws that are adopted by municipalities and local governments to regulate land use within their boundaries.

Case Index

A

Agent Orange Product Liab. Litig., In re (2008), 274
Akron Bar Assn. v. Green (1997), 531
Allen v. United States Steel Corp. (1982), 105
American Geophysical Union v. Texaco Inc. (1994), 495
Anastasoff v. U.S. (2000), 464, 496–497
Anonymous, In re (1995), 414
Aretakis, In re (2005), 78

B

Bamberger & Feibleman v. Indianapolis Power & Light Co. (1996), 413–414, 415
Barapind v. Enomoto (2005), 469
Barrett, State v, (1971), 531
Bell Atlantic Corp. v. Twombly (2005), 250
Bernstein v. Glavin (2000), 414
Bertram v. Norden, et al. (2004), 238
Bicoastal Corp., In re (1990), 531
Blake v. Greyhound Lines, Inc. (2006), 132–133
Bright, In the Matter of, 531
Broadcast Music, Inc. v. McDade & Sons, Inc. (2013), 797
Browne of New York City, Inc. v. Ambase Corp. (1993), 56
Brown v. Board of Education (1954), 178, 219–220
Business Guides, Inc. v. Chromatic Commc'ns Enterprises, Inc., (1989), 260
Busy Beaver Bldg. Centers, Inc. In re (1994), 127–128

C

Carmona v. Sheffield (1971, *aff'd* 1973), 132
Carter, In re (1989), 531
Castrillon, United States v. (1983), 423
Cetacean Cmty. v. Bush (2004), 468, 469
Ciaffone v. District Court (1997), 103–104, 527, 531
Cincinnati Bar Assn. v. Kathman (2001), 77
Complex Asbestos Litigation, In re (1991), 527, 531
Conley v. Gibson (1957), 260
Cooter & Gell v. Hartmarx Corp. (1990), 260
Cuyahoga Cnty. Bar Assn. v. Hardiman (2003), 378

D

Daimlerchrysler Ag Securities Litigation, In re (2003), 412
Department of Justice v. Landano (1993), 412
Department of the Interior v. Klamath Water Users Protective Association (2001), 415–417
Devine v. Beinfield (1997), 103
Dickerson v. United States (2000), 321
Doe v. Condon (2000), 38
Carol M. Douglas v. Deidre Monroe, Esq. (2001), 413–415
Drake v. Maid-Rite Co. (1997), 415
Duell v. Kawasaki Motors Corporation, U.S.A. and East Coast Cycles, Inc. (2013), 238–239

E

Electronic Data Systems Corporation v. Steingraber (2003), 59
Entergy Corporation v. Riverkeeper, Inc. (2009), 369

F

Facobellis v. Ohio (1964), 189
Ferlito v. Johnson & Johnson Products, Inc. (1991), 295–296
Fine v. Facet Aerospace Products Co. (1990), 531
First Fed. Sav. & Loan Ass'n v. Oppenheim, Appel, Dixon & Co. (1986), 58
Fisher v. The University of Texas at Austin (2011), 215–218
Flagiello v. Pennsylvania (1965), 182
Florida Bar v. Brumbaugh (1978), 83–84
Florida v. Jardines (2013), 331
Fricke v. Gray (1999), 414
Fteja v. Facebook, Inc. (2012), 237

G

Gnazzo v. G.D. Searle & Co. (1992), 297–299
Golden Eagle Distributing Corp. v. Burroughs (1986), 451–453
Goodman v. Praxair Services, Inc. (2009), 297
Grand Jury Subpoenas, In re (2002), 59
Grand Jury Subpoenas dated March 24, 2003 directed to (A) Grand Jury Witness Firm and (B) Grand Jury Witness, In re (2003), 57
Griffin v. Illinois (1956), 302

H

Hacker v. Holland (1991), 414–415
Harris v. Forklift Systems, Inc. (1993), 502–503
Hart v. Massanari (2001), 496–497
Haviland & Co. v. Montgomery Ward & Co. (1962), 296
Hawkins v. District Court of Fourth Judicial Dist. (1982), 60–61
Mark A. Hayes, M.D. v. Central States Orthopedic Specialists, Inc. (2001), 527
Hayes v. Central States Orthopedic Specialists, Inc. (2002), 531
Hearn v. Rhay (1975), 58
Hessinger & Associates, In re (1996), 531
Hickman v. Taylor (1947), 59–60
Hooser v. Superior Court of San Diego County (2000), 378, 384
Hulse v. Criger (1952), 83, 84
Hustler Cincinnati, Inc. et al. v. Paul J. Cambria, Jr., et al. (2014), 378

I

In re/In the Matter of. *See name of party*
International Salt v. United States (1947), 470
International Shoe Co. v. Washington (1945), 223, 239

J

Janson v. Legalzoom.com, Inc. (2011), 82–85
Jarvis Drilling, Inc. v. Midwest Oil Producing Co. (1993), 415
Jean v. Nelson (1988), 105, 127
Johnson, United States v. (2001), 468–469
Johnson v. Blankenship (1997), 415

K

Kaitangian, In re (1998), 77
Keegan Mgmt. Co., In re (1996), 260
Kentucky v. King (2011), 331
Kingsley v. State (2000), 421
Kinney, Matter of (1996), 414
Kovel, United States v. (1961), 57
Kurtenbach v. TeKippe (1977), 414

L

LaGrou Distribution Systems, Incorporated, United States v. (2006), 368
Leahy v. Edmonds School District (2009), 260
Leibowitz v. Eighth Judicial District Court (2003), 103–104, 531
Louisiana State Bar Assn v. Edwins (1989), 531

M

Madoff, United States v. (2009), 305–306
Makita Corp. v. U.S. (1993), 531
Martinez, Matter of (1988), 531
Martinez v. Triad Controls, Inc. (2009), 132–133
Mason v. Balcom (1976), 53
M.C., In re (2009), 296
McCreary County, Kentucky v. American Civil Liberties Union of KY (2005), 190n4, 200
McDaniel v. Bus. Inv. Group, Ltd. (1999), 414
McMackin v. McMackin (1993), 531
Meyerhofer v. Empire Fire & Marine Ins. Co. (1974), 58
Mid-America Living Trust Assocs., In re (1996), 63, 64–65
Miller v. Alamo (1993), 531
Miller v. California (1973), 189
Miranda B. v. Kitzhaber (2003), 468, 469
Miranda v. Arizona (1966), 321, 473
Miranda v. So. Pac. Transp. Co. (1983), 58
Missouri v. Jenkins (1989), 38–40, 524, 530, 531
Mutual Pharmaceutical Company, Inc. v. Bartlett (2013), 199

N

Norgart v. The Upjohn Company (1999), 295

O

Obergefell v. Hodges (2015), 200–202
O'Boyle v. Borough of Longport (2014), 56

P

Padilla v. Lever (2005), 468–469
Palsgraf v. Long Island Railroad Company (1928), 465, 507–511
Paulson, People v. (1990), 369
Pavlik v. Lane Ltd./Tobacco Exps. Int'l (1998), 133
Roy L. Pearson v. Soo Chung, et al. (2009), 264
Penny v. Little (1841), 179–180
People v. Paulson (1990), 369
PGA Tour, Inc. v. Martin (2001), 504–506
Phoenix Founders, Inc. v. Marshall (1994), 80, 128–130, 531
Pizza Hut, Inc. v. Papa John's International, Inc. (2000), 296
Pro Hand Services Trust v. Monthei (2002), 57, 378

R

Ramirez v. Plough, Inc. (1992), 130–131
Ramirez v. Plough, Inc. (1993), 132, 133
Ray v. Atlantic Richfield Co. (1978), 185
Reno, Attorney General of the United States v. Condon, Attorney General of South Carolina (2000), 200
Reno v. American Civil Liberties Union (1997), 189n2
Richtone Design Group v. Live Siri Art (2013), 237
Rico v. Mitsubishi Motors Corp. (2007), 61–62
Roe v. Wade (1973), 485
Rubin v. Enns (2000), 80–81
R. Williams Construction Company v. Occupational Safety & Health Review Commission (2006), 369–371

S

Satterlee v. Bliss (1869), 384
Schroeder v. Department of Transportation (1998), 400
Securities and Exchange Commission v. Collins & Aikman Corp. (2009), 273–275
Shaffer Equipt. Co., United States v. (1993), 450–451
Shamis v. Ambassador Factors Corp. (1999), 269
Smart Industries v. Superior Court (1994), 531
Son, Inc. v. Louis & Nashville R.R. Co. (1982), 412
Sperry v. Florida ex rel. Florida Bar (1963), 30, 38
SR Int'l Bus. Ins. Co. v. World Trade Ctr. Prop. (2002), 56
Stacey v. Stroud (1993), 531
Standefer v. United States (1980), 177
Stanley Indus., Inc. v. W.M. Barr & Co. (1992), 133
State Comp. Ins. Fund v. WPS, Inc. (1999), 62
State of Ohio v. Wilson (2004), 330
State v. Barrett (1971), 531
Stewart v. Sullivan (1993), 531
Stuffleben v. Cowden (2003), 378
Swanson v. Wabash College (1987), 415
Swierkiewicz v. Sorema N.A. (2002), 295

T

Taylor v. Chubb (1994), 530, 531
Tegman v. Accident & Medical Investigations (2001), 52, 78–80
Thompson, In re (1978), 83–84
Trammell v. United States (1980), 57
$2,164,341 in US Currency, United States v. (2013), 332–333
Two-Way Media, LLC v. AT&T Operations, Inc., et al. (2014), 380

U

Unauthorized Practice of Law v. Parsons Tech. (1999), 368
United States v. $2,164,341 in US Currency (2013), 332–333
United States v. Castrillon (1983), 423
United States v. Johnson (2001), 468–469
United States v. Kovel (1961), 57
United States v. LaGrou Distribution Systems, Incorporated (2006), 368
United States v. Madoff (2009), 305–306
United States v. Shaffer Equipt. Co. (1993), 450–451

V

Von Bulow v. Von Bulow (1987), 55, 56

W

Wallace v. Jaffree (1985), 190n3
Whiting v. State (2005), 421
Wickard, Secretary of Agriculture v. Filburn (1942), 186

Y

Yankton College, In re (1989), 531

Z

Ziegler v. Nickel (1998), 236
Zippo Manufacturing Company v. Zippo Dot Com, Inc. (1997), 223–224

Subject Index

A

AbacusLaw, 106, 405
Accountant-client privilege, 323
Accounting
  client retainers and costs in, 110–111
  costs advanced tracked in, 111
  court accounting in, 113, 114–115
  escrow accounts in, 111, 112–113
  family law-specific, 106, 107–108
  fiduciary accounting standards for, 112
  IOLTA accounts in, 112
  in law offices and firms, 106–113, 124
  litigation-related, 106, 111
  maintaining financial information in, 106–107, 109
  money laundering avoidance via, 112–113
  safekeeping clients' property in, 109
  timely disbursements in, 111
  trust accounts in, 109, 111–112
Accredited Legal Secretary (ALS), 18
Actus reus (guilty act), 312
Adams, John, 335
Administrative agencies. *See also specific agencies*
  administrative law by, 181–182, 335–371
  administrative procedures for, 342–343, 365
  administrative searches by, 353–354
  administrative subpoenas by, 353–354
  appeals of decisions of, 354, 355
  cabinet-level federal departments as, 339
  Code of Federal Regulations of, 344, 348, 349
  definition of, 337
  delegation doctrine empowering, 343
  electronic filing with, 153
  Equal Access to Justice Act impacting, 363
  executive power of, 353
  federal administrative agencies as, 336–337, 354–360, 366
  Freedom of Information Act impacting, 360–361, 362–363
  government employment with, 94
  Government in the Sunshine Act impacting, 361, 363
  independent federal agencies as, 340
  individual rights and disclosure of actions of, 360–363, 366
  judicial authority of, 348, 350–352
  judicial review of actions of, 354, 361
  licensing power, 348
  paralegal practice before, 30–31, 70–71, 95
  powers of, 343–354, 365–366
  Privacy Act impacting, 363
  rule making by, 343, 344, 345–347
  state and local administrative agencies as, 341
  statements of policy by, 344
  types of, 339–343, 365
Administrative law
  Administrative Procedure Act on, 337, 343, 344
  administrative procedure under, 342–343, 365
  federal administrative agencies under, 336–337, 354–360, 366
  individual rights and disclosure of agency actions under, 360–363, 366
  overview of, 181–182, 336–338, 365–366
  paralegal career opportunities in, 336–337
  powers of administrative agencies under, 343–354, 365–366
  procedural, 342–343
  substantive, 342–343
  types of administrative agencies administering, 339–343, 365
Administrative law judges (ALJs), 343, 350–352
Administrative orders, 343
Administrative Procedure Act (APA), 337, 343, 344
Administrative procedures
  in administrative agencies, 342–343, 365
  conflict checking as, 102–104
  in law offices and firms, 102–106, 124
  time keeping and billing as, 104–106, 111 (*see also* Fees)
Adobe Acrobat, 151, 161
Adolescents. *See* Minors
Affirmation of judicial decisions, 288
Age Discrimination in Employment Act of 1967 (ADEA), 355
Agency
  ethics and professional responsibility based on, 50, 51
  extension of privilege based on, 57
Agreements
  fee, 110, 381, 382–383
  plea bargain, 310
  settlement, 225, 231
  submission, 225
Alabama
  freedom of religion in, 190
  state court system in, 209
Alaska, state court system in, 209
Alternative dispute resolution (ADR)
  ADR procedure, 227
  ADR providers, 227
  arbitration as, 225–228, 231, 281, 397
  for civil litigation, 281
  conciliation as, 229
  counteroffers in, 231
  decision and award in, 227–228
  fact-finding for, 229–230
  judicial referees in, 230
  mediation as, 228–229, 230, 231
  minitrials as, 229
  negotiation as, 224–225
  online, 231
  overview of, 206, 224, 234–235
  paralegal career opportunities in, 225
  settlement agreements from, 225, 231

ALWD Citation Manual: A Professional System of Citation, 435, 436–440, 443
American Arbitration Association (AAA), 225, 227
American Association for Paralegal Education (AAfPE), 13, 18
American Association of Legal Nurse Consultants (AALNC), 92
American Bar Association (ABA)
  Center for Professional Responsibility, 44, 65
  Ethics Opinion 92-368 (inadvertent disclosure), 61
  House of Delegates, 4, 50
  Model Guidelines for the Utilization of Paralegal Services, 50
  Model Rules of Professional Conduct, 21, 44, 45, 48, 49, 51, 53, 54, 63, 68, 105, 109, 393, 423–424, 466
  paralegal definition by, 4, 523
  paralegal educational program approval by, 13, 14
  on paralegal profession regulation, 22
  Standing Committee on Paralegals, 4, 14, 18, 92
  on state ethics resources, 45
American Jurisprudence, 470, 471
American Law Reports, 461
Americans with Disabilities Act of 1990/2008 (ADA), 354–355
Amicus curiae briefs, 432, 433–434, 473
Analytical school, 178
Analytical skills, 9
Answer to pleadings, 264–265, 266–267
Appeals
  actions of court in response to, 288–289
  administrative agency, 354, 355
  appeal bonds in, 287
  appellants or petitioners in, 286, 500
  appellate courts hearing, 208, 211–212, 213, 286–289
  appellees or respondents in, 287, 500
  civil litigation, 286–289, 292–293
  criminal litigation, 310, 311
  opening and responding briefs in, 287
  oral arguments in, 287–288
  timely filing of, 380
Apple
  FaceTime, 163
  operating system, 155, 268
Applications software, 142, 155–158
Arbitration, 225–228, 231, 281, 397
Aristotle, 229
Arizona
  domain names in, 152
  ethics rules in, 62, 152
  practice of law regulations in, 46, 47
  state court system in, 209
  Supreme Court of, 47
Arkansas
  Rules of Professional Conduct, 63
  state court system in, 209
Arraignments, 310
Arrest warrants, 304
Arson, 315
Ask.com, 148, 150
Assault, 313
Associate degrees, 14, 15
Association of Legal Administrators
  ethics guidelines of, 50
  website of, 13
Association of Legal Writing Directors *ALWD Citation Manual: A Professional System of Citation*, 435, 436–440, 443
Atkinson, Ann L., 422
Attachment jurisdiction, 223
Attachments, electronic, 136, 137, 151–152
Attorney-client privilege
  claim of, 56
  common interest exception to, 56
  constitutional safeguards for, 322
  definition of, 55
  discovery under, 273
  ethical duty of confidentiality and, 49, 55–58, 61–62, 73–74, 393
  expert witnesses and, 393–394
  extension of, to others, 56–57
  implied attorney-client relationship and, 57, 377–379
  inadvertent disclosure and, 61–62
  interview issues of, 377–379, 393–394, 409
  self-defense exception to, 57–58
  waiver of, 55, 61–62, 393
Attorneys. *See* Lawyers
Automatic waiver, 61

B

Bachelor degrees, 14, 15–16
Backup of data, 144
Bail/bail bond, 304, 306
Balancing test, 61
Bankruptcy law
  bankruptcy courts adjudicating, 536
  paralegals' tasks or functions in, 97
  U.S. Bankruptcy Court for, 210
Bar exams, 46
Beecher, Henry Ward, 177
Bench opinions, 465, 467
Bench trials, 282, 310
Beyond a reasonable doubt, 302
Bicameral legislative body, 180, 462
Bilingual pleadings, 259
Billing, 104–106, 111. *See also* Accounting; Fees
Bill of Rights, 187–192
Binding arbitration, 227–228
Bing, 137, 403
Black, Hugo, 302
Blackmail, 315
Black's Law Dictionary, 470, 477
Blackstone, William, 301
The Bluebook: A Uniform System of Citation, 434–435, 436–440, 443
Bribery, 316
Briefs
  amicus curiae, 432, 433–434, 473
  in appeals, 287
  briefing a case, 427, 500–511
  legal writing in, 432, 433–434, 447
  opening, 287
  responding, 287
  submitted for trials, 282
Burden of proof, 285, 302
Burger, Warren, 177
Burglary, 313–314

Bush, George W., 182, 339
Business law and organization
  commercial litigation in, 106
  corporations in, 94, 98, 244–245, 246–247
  paralegals' tasks and functions in, 97
Business premises searches, 318

C

Cabinet-level federal agencies, 339. *See also* Administrative agencies
California
  Business and Professional Code, 22, 47, 69
  civil litigation in, 262
  document specialists in, 95
  inadvertent disclosure rulings in, 61–62
  paralegal profession regulation in, 22, 23, 46–48, 525
  practice of law regulations in, 22, 23, 46, 48
  state court system in, 209
  unauthorized practice of law in, 46, 48, 69
Call, Kathleen, 6–7
Candor
  ethical duty of, 48, 65, 66–67, 74, 423–424, 466, 485, 486
  in legal research, 466, 485, 486
  in legal writing, 423–424
Capital punishment, 324
Cardozo, Benjamin, 465
Careers, paralegal
  in administrative law, 336–337
  in alternative dispute resolution, 225
  career planning, 13–17, 34–35
  in constitutional law, 176
  in courts and litigation, 206
  in criminal law, 206, 303
  getting started in, 31–33
Case and practice management software, 401, 405–407
Case law, 462, 464, 465–469, 485. *See also separate Index of Cases*
Case syllabus, 465, 467
Central processing units (CPUs), 142
Certificate programs, 15, 16, 18, 19–21, 22, 23, 30, 525
Certified Paralegal/Certified Legal Assistant (CP/CLA), 18, 19–21, 525
Certiorari, petition for/writ of, 214, 215–218
Chancery (equity) courts, 179
Change of venue, 223
Checks and balances, 184
Chicago School, 178
Children. *See* Minors
Choice-of-law clauses, 224
Chronological résumé format, 117
Citations
  ALWD Citation Manual: A Professional System of Citation for, 435, 436–440, 443
  The Bluebook: A Uniform System of Citation for, 434–435, 436–440, 443
  briefing a case including, 501
  cite checking of, 442–443, 486–489
  legal writing including, 432–443, 445, 447–448, 501
  parallel, 433, 488
  primary authorities for, 432
  secondary authorities for, 432
  Shepard's Citations of, 486–489
  tables of authorities including, 441–442
  technology impacts on, 435–436
  traditional print sources for, 433–434
  Universal Citation Format for, 435
  vendor-specific formats for, 435–436
Citators, 473
Citizenship
  diversity of, 221–222
Civil law system, 180
Civil litigation
  alternative dispute resolution for, 281
  appeal of decisions in, 286–289, 292–293
  case analysis for, 248–249, 269–270
  civil tort action based on criminal acts, 312–313 (*see also* Torts)
  client and witness interviews in, 245
  client relationship management in, 244–245
  complaints in, 249–261
  conducting discovery for, 245
  contract cases in, 249
  corporations in, 244–245, 246–247
  court system for (*see* Courts)
  damages in, 276, 286, 313
  default judgments in, 264
  defendants in, 262, 264, 268, 285–286
  depositions in, 276
  discovery in, 245, 265, 268–280, 291
  drafting documents for, 246
  duty to preserve evidence in, 269, 270
  electronic filing in, 261, 262, 265
  fact investigations for, 245
  Federal Rules of Civil Procedure on, 60–61, 141–142, 250, 259–260, 271–276, 394
  fee and cost billing in, 111
  filing fees in, 261
  frivolous suits in, 260, 264, 288
  interrogatories in, 276–277
  intervention into, 265
  legal team in, 244
  litigation holds for, 269, 270
  litigation support managers for, 247
  medical malpractice claims in, 249
  obtaining documents and records for, 246
  overview of, 242–244, 290–293
  paralegal career opportunities in, 206
  paralegal skills and tasks for, 242, 244–247
  physical and mental examinations in, 279
  plaintiffs in, 249–250, 268, 285, 286
  pleadings in, 246, 247–268, 290–291
  preparing for trial in, 270
  pretrial motions in, 280–281, 291
  records reviews for, 246
  requests for admission in, 279
  retrials in, 289
  sanctions for filing frivolous, 260
  service of complaint in, 262–264
  settlement conference in, 281, 292
  statutes of limitations for, 247, 249, 265
  technology in, 141–142, 261, 262, 265, 268, 279–280
  timeline of key pretrial events in, 282
  torts as, 312–313
  trials in, 246, 270, 281–286, 292
  witnesses in, 245, 272, 276, 285–286, 394

Civil Rights Acts, 354, 356
Clean Air Act, 356
Clean Water Act, 356
Clients
  client data sheets for, 96
  client interview forms, 400
  engagement letters with, 381, 382–383
  fees charged to (*see* Fees)
  filling out forms for, 70, 96
  identity of, 381, 384
  implied attorney-client relationship, 57, 377–379
  interviews with, 95–96, 245, 376–395, 397, 400
  investigating claims of (*see* Investigations)
  legal advice to, 69–70, 95–96
  relationship management with, 244–245
  representation of, 70–71
  retainers and costs of, 110–111
  safekeeping property of, 109
  thin, 166–167
Closing arguments, 286
Cloud computing, 166–167
Cobo, Michael E., 145
Code of Federal Regulations (CFR), 344, 348, 349, 481
Codified law, 181
Colorado
  Rules of Professional Conduct, 68
  state court system in, 209
  Supreme Court of, 68
Command school, 178
Commerce
  Commerce Clause on, 181, 185–187
  contracts in (*see* Contracts)
  Uniform Commercial Code on, 249
Commercial litigation, 106
Commercial speech, 188
Commitment, 9
Common interest exception, 56
Common law, 179–180
Communication
  communication skills in multicultural society, 387–388
  electronic (*see* Internet; Technology)
  freedom of speech, 187–190
  gender differences in, 387–388
  interviews involving (*see* Interviews)
  listening skills in, 390–391, 443
  paralegals' skill in, 7, 10–11
  writing as means of (*see* Legal writing; Writing)
Communications Decency Act, 189
Competence
  ethical duty of, 48, 53–54, 513
  in technological language/lexicon, 53, 138, 139, 140
Complaints, 249–261, 304, 305–306
Complex litigation, 93, 100–102
Comprehensive Environmental Response, Compensation, and Liability Act, 356
Computers. *See also* Internet; Technology
  addresses and locations, 148, 149–150
  backup of, 144
  central processing units in, 142
  computer systems, 142
  file servers, 144, 145–146
  firewalls in, 153
  hacking into, 153
  hardware, 142–145
  mainframe, 142
  miniaturization and portability of, 164
  networks, 138, 143–146, 166
  notetaking via, 167
  operating systems, 142, 143, 154–155, 265, 268
  skills needed with, 136–139
  software, 138, 142, 155–160, 164, 265, 405–406
  storage of data from, 138, 141, 144, 166–167
  training to use, 159–160
  viruses and antivirus programs in, 154
  workstations, 143, 144, 146
Conciliation/conciliators, 229
Concurrent jurisdiction, 222
Confidentiality. *See also* Privacy issues; Privilege
  attorney-client privilege and, 49, 55–58, 61–62, 73–74, 393
  client identity and, 381, 384
  definition of, 54
  ethical duty of, 48, 49, 54–62, 68, 73–74, 137, 144, 154, 381, 384, 393, 515, 527
  inadvertent disclosure of confidential information, 61–62
  technology impacting, 54–55, 137, 144, 154
  work product doctrine and, 49, 58–61, 73–74
Conflicts of interest
  conflict checking for, 102–104
  ethical duty related to, 48, 63–65, 102–104, 193, 377, 515, 526
  for in-house counsel, 63–65
  paralegals' duty to avoid, 193, 526
  paralegals' duty to disclose, 515
Connecticut
  conflicts of interest in, 103
  state court system in, 209
Connectors, 482–484
Consolidation of civil litigation, 265
Conspiracy, criminal, 317
Constitution, U.S.
  amendments to, 187–193, 317–324, 328–329, 354, 548, 549–556
  Bill of Rights, 187–192
  checks and balances in, 184
  Commerce Clause in, 181, 185–187
  criminal law and procedure under, 303, 317–324, 328–329
  cruel and unusual punishment protection in, 324
  Double Jeopardy Clause in, 323
  drafting and ratification of, 183
  Due Process Clause in, 191–192, 317–318, 350
  Eighth Amendment, 324, 550
  Equal Protection Clause in, 192–193
  executive branch in, 184, 546–547
  federalism and delegated/enumerated powers under, 184
  Fifth Amendment, 191–192, 321–323, 550
  First Amendment, 187–191, 549
  Fourteenth Amendment, 191–193, 317–318, 551–552
  Fourth Amendment, 318–320, 354, 549
  freedom of religion under, 190–191
  freedom of speech under, 187–190
  functions of, 183
  judicial branch in, 184, 210, 218, 221, 547–548 (*see also* Federal courts)

Just Compensation Clause in, 192
law based on, 181, 183–193, 195–197, 328–329, 350 (*see also* Constitutional law)
legislative branch in, 184, 542–545 (*see also* U.S. Congress)
Preamble to, 175, 542
as primary sources of law, 465
privilege against self-incrimination in, 321–323
right to a public trial in, 323–324
separation of powers based on, 184
Sixth Amendment, 323–324, 550
Supremacy Clause in, 184–185
text of, 542–556
unreasonable searches and seizures under, 318–320, 354
visual image of, 183

Constitutional law
Bill of Rights in, 187–192
checks and balances in, 184
Commerce Clause in, 185–187
constitutional amendments in, 187–193, 317–324, 328–329, 354, 548, 549–556
Constitution as foundation of, 181, 183–193, 195–197, 317–324, 328–329, 350, 354, 542–556
criminal law and procedure under, 303, 317–324, 328–329
Due Process Clause in, 191–192, 317–318, 350
Equal Protection Clause in, 192–193
federalism and delegated/enumerated powers in, 184
freedom of religion under, 190–191
freedom of speech under, 187–190
overview of, 195–197
paralegal career opportunities in, 176
separation of powers doctrine in, 184
Supremacy Clause in, 184–185

Constitutions, state, 181, 317, 465
Consumer Financial Protection Act, 360
Consumer Financial Protection Bureau (CFPB), 359–360
Consumer Product Safety Act, 358
Consumer Product Safety Commission (CPSC), 358–359, 402–403
Contracts. *See also* Agreements
arbitration clauses in, 225
choice-of-law clauses in, 224
civil litigation related to, 249
forum selection clauses in, 224
Uniform Commercial Code on, 249

Controlling law, 461, 462–463
Copyrights
for citation formats/pagination systems, 436
copyright form for, 101

Corel
DB, 158
Quattro Pro, 157
WordPerfect™, 151, 155–156, 162, 265, 441
WordPerfect Office, 159
WordPerfect Presentation, 158

Cornell University
Cornell Law School, 150
Legal Information Institute, 459, 465

Corporations
civil litigation involving, 244–245, 246–247
client relationship management with, 244–245
corporate legal departments of, 94
paralegals' tasks or functions in, 98, 246–247

Corpus Juris Secundum (CJS), 470, 472
Courts
alternative dispute resolution *vs.* (*see* Alternative dispute resolution)
appellate, 208, 211–212, 213, 286–289
bankruptcy, 536
case law from, 462, 464, 485 (*see also separate Index of Cases*)
chancery (equity), 179
court accounting, 113, 114–115
court briefs to, 432, 433–434, 447, 473
court decisions by, 465–469 (*see also* Case law; *court opinions* and *judicial decisions subentries*)
court opinions, 427, 464, 465–469, 501
courts of record, 207
dicta by, 466, 468–469
electronic filing in, 137, 153, 224
electronic or e-courts, 160, 161, 224
federal (*see* Federal courts)
holding of, 466, 501
judicial decisions by, 182, 214, 218, 219–220
jurisdiction of, 206, 207, 210–211, 221–224, 233–234
law, 179
litigation in (*see* Litigation)
merchant, 179
military, 536
overview of court system, 206, 232–234
paralegal career opportunities in, 206
rules of court, 53, 288
service of process by, 222, 262–264
standing to sue in, 222
stare decisis doctrine in, 182, 485
state (*see* State courts)
Supreme Courts (*see under specific states;* U.S. Supreme Court)

Cover letters, 118
Criminal law and procedure
appeals under, 310, 311
arraignments under, 310
arrests under, 304
arson under, 315
bail in, 304, 306
beyond a reasonable doubt standard in, 302
bribery under, 316
burden of proof in, 302
burglary under, 313–314
capital punishment under, 324
civil tort action based on criminal acts, 312–313
classification of crimes under, 311–312
constitutional safeguards for, 303, 317–324, 328–329
court system for (*see* Courts)
crimes against the person under, 313
crimes under, 311–317, 326–327
criminal acts under, 312
criminal complaint under, 304, 305–306
criminal conspiracy under, 317
criminal fraud under, 316
criminal intent under, 312
criminal procedure, 304–310, 326
criminal trials under, 310–311, 323–324, 326
cruel and unusual punishment protection under, 324

Criminal law and procedure (*Continued*)
determination of guilt under, 311
double jeopardy under, 323
due process in, 192
embezzlement under, 315
ethical duty to report criminal activity, 324
exculpatory evidence in, 65
extortion under, 315
Federal Rules of Criminal Procedure on, 304, 306, 311
felonies under, 311, 313
forgery under, 315
guilty, not guilty, or *nolo contendere* pleas in, 310
immunity from prosecution under, 322
indictment or information under, 306–309, 310
intent crimes *vs.* non-intent crimes under, 312, 316 (*see also* Intentional torts; Unintentional torts)
involuntary manslaughter under, 312
larceny under, 314
Miranda rights under, 321–322
misdemeanors under, 312
murder under, 313
overview of, 302–303, 326–329
paralegal career opportunities in, 206, 303
parties and attorneys in criminal actions, 303–304, 326
penal codes and regulatory statutes in, 311
penalties for violation of, 311–312
plea bargain agreements in, 310
pretrial discovery under, 310–311
privilege against self-incrimination under, 321–323
probable cause in, 304
right to a public trial under, 323–324
robbery under, 313
theft under, 314
unauthorized practice of law under, 46
unreasonable searches and seizures under, 318–320
violations under, 312
white-collar crimes in, 303, 315–317, 327
Critical legal studies school, 178
Critical legal thinking, 420–422, 431, 446–447, 500–511
Cross-complaints, 265
Cross-examination, 285
Cruel and unusual punishment protection, 324
Culture
African roots, 389
Asian background, 389
communication skills in multicultural society, 387–388
cultural sensitivity, in interviews, 388–389
European background, 388–389
Latino background, 389

D

Damages
award of, 286
discovery related to, 276
judgment-proof, 313
Database programs, 158
Death
capital punishment, 324
estate planning before (*see* Estates; Wills)
Debtor or creditor rights, 97. *See also* Bankruptcy law
DecisionQuest, 248–249
Default judgments, 264
Defendants
in civil litigation, 262, 264, 268, 285–286
in criminal actions, 304, 310
definition of, 500
investigating from perspective of, 396
Defense attorney, 304
Delaware
state court system in, 209
Delegated powers, 184
Delegation doctrine, 343
Demonstrative evidence, 404
Demurrers, 280–281
Departments, U.S. *See U.S. Department entries*
Depositions, 160, 276
Dicta, 466, 468–469
Digital photographs, 396
Direct examination, 285
Disabilities, persons with
Americans with Disabilities Act for, 354–355
Disbarment, 46, 66
Discovery
case evaluation using, 269–270
civil litigation, 245, 265, 268–280, 291
criminal litigation, 310–311
depositions in, 276
disclosure requirements for, 271–275
duty to preserve evidence for, 269, 270
electronic, 137, 141–142, 245, 265, 268–269, 279–280
expert witness testimony in, 276
facilitating settlement with, 271–272
Federal Rules of Civil Procedure on, 271–276
Federal Rules of Criminal Procedure on, 311
Federal Rules of Evidence on, 392
information subject to mandatory, 275–276
interrogatories in, 276–277
limitations for, 392
litigation holds for, 269, 270
physical and mental examinations in, 279
preparing for trial with, 270
preserving oral testimony with, 272
privilege impacting, 273–274
production of documents for, 278
requests for admission in, 279
Discrimination
age, 355
Civil Rights Acts on, 354, 356
EEOC role in combating, 336, 337, 344, 349, 354–355
Equal Protection Clause on, 192–193
District attorney (DA), 304
District of Columbia, state court system in, 209
Diversity of citizenship, 221–222
Doctor-patient privilege, 322, 393
Document specialists, 95
Dogpile, 148
Domain names, 150, 152
Dormant Commerce Clause, 186–187
Double jeopardy clause, 323
Douglas, William, 179–180

Douglas, William O., 178
Dragon Naturally Speaking, 164
Driver's Privacy Protection Act (1994), 200
DropBox, 54–55, 166
Due process, 57, 191–192, 317–318, 350
DuPont Legal Model, 94
Duty
  of candor, 48, 65, 66–67, 74, 423–424, 466, 485, 486
  of confidentiality, 48, 49, 54–62, 68, 73–74, 137, 144, 154, 381, 384, 393, 515, 527
  to disclose conflicts of interest, 515
  to disclose paralegal status, 516, 526
  ethical, 48–51, 72, 378–379, 392, 423–424, 466, 485, 486, 513–516 (*see also* Ethics and professional responsibility)
  to preserve evidence, 269, 270
  to prospective client, 378–379
  to report criminal activity, 324

E

Education
  associate degrees in, 14, 15
  bachelor degrees in, 14, 15–16
  certificate programs in, 15, 16, 18, 19–21, 22, 23, 30, 525
  continuing, 244
  effective learning and, 537–541
  electives selection in, 17
  graduate programs in, 16
  for paralegals, 13–21, 22–23, 27, 30, 31–33, 34–35, 92, 244, 272, 524–525, 537–541
  student portfolios from, 31–33, 121–122
  study techniques in, 537–541
  technology training as, 159–160, 272
Eighth Amendment, 324, 550
Elder law
  specialty practice in, 93
Electronic Communications Privacy Act (1986/1994), 154
Electronic data. *See* Computers; Internet; Technology
Electronic Freedom of Information Act, 403
Electronic Funds Transfer Act, 360
Eliot, Charles William, 455
Emails
  attachments to, 136, 137, 151–152
  electronic discovery of, 141–142
  interpersonal skills applied in, 10
  legal writing in, 423
  receiving and downloading, 151–152
  sample display of, 148
  sending, 152
Embezzlement, 315
Employment law. *See also* Workplace
  Age Discrimination in Employment Act of 1967 as, 355
  Americans with Disabilities Act of 1990/2008 as, 354–355
  Equal Opportunity Employment Commission in, 336, 337, 344, 349, 354–355
  Equal Pay Act of 1963 as, 355
  labor union law as, 337, 357–358
  Occupational Safety and Health Act as, 357
Encryption technology, 153–154
Endangered Species Act, 356
Engagement letters, 381, 382–383
English common law, 179–180
Enumerated powers, 184
Environmental law
  enactment of statutes in, 338
  EPA role in, 336, 343, 355–356
  paralegals' tasks or functions in, 98
  as specialty practice, 93
Environmental Protection Agency (EPA), 336, 343, 355–356
Equal Access to Justice Act, 363
Equal Credit Opportunity Act, 360
Equal Opportunity Employment Commission (EEOC), 336, 337, 344, 349, 354–355
Equal Pay Act of 1963, 355
Equal Protection Clause, 192–193
Errors of law, 289
Escrow accounts, 111, 112–113
Establishment Clause, 190
Ethics and professional responsibility
  billing and fees as, 105–106
  candor in, 48, 65, 66–67, 74, 423–424, 466, 485, 486
  competence in, 48, 53–54, 513
  confidentiality in, 48, 49, 54–62, 68, 73–74, 137, 144, 154, 381, 384, 393, 515, 527 (*see also* Privacy issues; Privilege)
  conflicts of interest in, 48, 63–65, 102–104, 193, 377, 515, 526
  definition and description of, 44, 48
  disclosure of paralegal status as, 516, 526
  duty to report criminal activity as, 324
  enforcement of, 516–521
  ethical duties and obligations, 48–51, 72, 378–379, 392, 423–424, 466, 485, 486, 513–516
  ethical guidelines and rules, 49, 72–73
  ethical walls/Chinese walls for, 89, 90, 103–104, 144, 377
  fairness in, 48, 65–68, 74, 270, 271
  interview consideration of, 377, 378–379, 392, 393, 408
  Model Guidelines for the Utilization of Paralegal Services on, 50
  Model Rules of Professional Conduct on, 21, 44, 45, 48, 49, 51, 53, 54, 63, 68, 105, 109, 393, 423–424, 466
  NALA Model Standards and Guidelines for Utilization of Legal Assistants-Paralegals on, 5, 12, 71, 522–532
  NFPA Model Code of Ethics and Professional Responsibility on, 44, 45, 49, 50, 512–521
  overview of, 44, 72–75
  pro bono work in, 94, 231, 514
  regulating practice of law as, 21, 45–48, 72
  safekeeping clients' property as, 109
  sanctions for violation of, 66
  state codes of ethics on, 21, 44, 46, 49, 50, 51, 52, 53, 54, 58, 62, 63, 66–68, 105
  supervision in, 48, 51–52, 63–65, 73, 89, 529
  unauthorized practice of law as violation of, 21, 30, 46–48, 63–65, 67, 69–71, 74–75, 91–92, 95–96, 504, 528
  workplace creating issues of, 89, 90, 95–96, 102–104, 109
Evidence
  demonstrative, 404
  discovery of (*see* Discovery)
  duty to preserve, 269, 270
  exclusionary rule on, 318
  exculpatory, 65, 311
  Federal Rules of Evidence on, 49, 54

Evidence (*Continued*)
litigation holds for potential, 269, 270
spoliation of, 400
tainted, 354
tangible, 397, 400
Ewald, Emily A., 280
Excite, 148
Exclusionary rule, 318
Exclusive jurisdiction, 222
Exculpatory evidence, 65, 311
Executive branch, 184, 546–547
Executive orders, 182
Executive power, 353
Expert witnesses
attorney-client privilege and, 393–394
civil litigation, 276, 394
Federal Rules of Civil Procedure on, 394
interviews with, 393–395
locating, 403
Extortion, 315

F

Facebook, 403
Fact pleadings, 250, 255–258, 266–267
Facts
ADR fact-finding, 229–230
briefing a case including, 501
civil litigation fact investigations, 245
civil litigation fact pleadings, 250, 255–258, 266–267
critical legal thinking relevant fact analysis, 420–422, 501
definition of, 421
immaterial, 422
investigation fact analysis, 397
legal research relevant fact analysis, 458–459
material, 422
relevant, 420–422, 458–459
statements of facts for legal writing, 427, 429, 431
triers of fact, 65, 281, 282, 310, 397
Fair Credit Reporting Act, 360
Fair Debt Collection Practices Act, 360
Fairness
ethical duty of, 48, 65–68, 74, 270, 271
of the law, 177
False imprisonment, 313
Family law
accounting related to, 106, 107–108
child custody and child support in, 99
paralegals' tasks or functions in, 98, 99
Federal administrative agencies, 336–337, 354–360, 366. *See also* Administrative agencies; *specific agencies*
Federal Arbitration Act (FAA), 227
Federal Aviation Administration (FAA), 338, 345–347
Federal Bureau of Investigation (FBI), 360, 361
Federal Communications Commission (FCC), 188, 336, 338, 340, 363
Federal courts. *See also* U.S. Supreme Court
appellate process in, 211–212, 213, 288, 354, 355
bankruptcy courts as, 536
civil litigation deadlines in, 262, 263, 264
court forms for, 265
criminal procedures and actions in, 304, 305–306
judges in, 210
jurisdiction of, 221–222
military courts as, 536
name abbreviations of, 533–536
overview of court system, 210–212, 213, 233
right to practice before, 46
special, 210
U.S. Courts of Appeals as, 211–212, 288, 355, 533
U.S. District Courts as, 210–211, 263, 265, 533–536
Federal government. *See* Administrative agencies; Constitution, U.S.; *federal and U.S. entries*
Federalism, 184
Federal question cases, 221
Federal Register, 344, 345–347, 360
Federal Rules of Civil Procedure
discovery under, 271–276
expert witnesses under, 394
pleadings under, 250, 259–260
technology impacts of, 141–142
work product doctrine under, 60–61
Federal Rules of Criminal Procedure
criminal complaint under, 304
grand juries under, 306
pretrial discovery under, 311
Federal Rules of Evidence
discovery under, 392
privilege under, 49, 54
Federal Trade Commission (FTC), 181, 336, 340, 359
Federal Trade Commission Act, 359
Fees
accounting to calculate, 106–113
contingent, 110, 381, 383
fee agreements on, 110, 381, 382–383
fee and cost billing, 111
filing, 261
hourly, 381, 382
for initial interviews, 377
for paralegal services, 12, 105, 524
time keeping and billing for, 104–106, 111
Felonies, 311, 313
Fiduciary accounting standards, 112
Fiduciary relationships, 51
Fifth Amendment, 191–192, 321–323, 550
File extensions, 155–156
Finding tools, legal research using, 461, 473, 474
Firefox, 147
Firewalls, 153
First Amendment, 187–191, 549
Flexibility of the law, 177
Florida
paralegal profession regulation in, 23, 525
penalties for unauthorized practice of law in, 47
practice of law regulations in, 23, 46
State Bar Association, 23
state court system in, 209
unauthorized practice of law in, 69, 70
Food, Drug, and Cosmetic Act, 356
Food and Drug Administration (FDA), 336, 356
Foreign commerce, 186
Forgery, 315
Formal rule making, 344

Forum selection clauses, 224
Fourteenth Amendment, 191–193, 317–318, 551–552
Fourth Amendment, 318–320, 354, 549
Frank, Jerome, 177
Franklin, Benjamin, 135
Fraud
  criminal, 316
Freedom of Information Act (FOIA), 360–361, 362–363, 401–403, 409
Freedom of religion, 190–191
Freedom of speech, 187–190
Free Exercise Clause, 190–191
Fully protected speech, 188
Functional résumé format, 116, 117

G

Gasiewski, Kevin D., 406
Gender issues
  gender differences in communication, 387–388
General government regulation, 337
General intent, 312
General jurisdiction trial courts, 207
General law practice, 90–91
Genetic Information Nondiscrimination Act of 2008, 355
Georgia, state court system in, 209
Gladstone, W. E., 189
GlobalCite™, 487, 489
Glossary
  English, 567–585
  Spanish, 560–566
Google
  browser, 147
  Earth™, 397
  search engine, 137, 147, 148, 150, 403
Government employment
  criminal law positions as, 303
  specialty practice in, 94
Government in the Sunshine Act, 361, 363
Graduate programs, 16
Grand juries, 306
Guam, state court system in, 209
Guilt
  actus reus (guilty act), 312
  determination of, 311
  guilty, not guilty pleas, 310

H

Hacking, 153
Hawaii
  paralegal profession regulation in, 22
  State Bar Association, 22
  state court system in, 209
  Supreme Court of, 22
Headnotes, 465–466, 469
Hill, Ann G., 458
Historical school, 178
Holding, 466, 501
Homeland Security Act (HSA), 339
Home Mortgage Disclosure Act, 360
Hotspots, 166
Human resources law, 100
Hung juries, 311, 323

I

Idaho
  duty of candor in, 486
  Rules of Professional Conduct in, 486
  state court system in, 209
Illinois
  Rules of Professional Conduct in, 45, 51, 271
  state court system in, 209
  Supreme Court of, 45
Immaterial facts, 422
Immigration law
  paralegals' tasks or functions in, 98, 100
  sample Citizenship and Immigration Services form in, 100
Immunity from prosecution, 322
Implied attorney-client relationship, 57, 377–379
Inadvertent disclosure of confidential information, 61–62
Independent federal administrative agencies, 340. *See also* Administrative agencies
Independent medical examinations, 279
Index to Legal Periodicals, 461
Indiana
  duty of candor in, 423–424
  Rules of Professional Conduct in, 423–424
  state court system in, 209
Indian Gaming Regulatory Act, 185
Indictments, 306–309, 310
Informal rule making, 344
Information, magistrate's, 306, 309
Information Technology, 139–141. *See also* Technology
In-house counsel
  civil litigation role of, 245, 246–247
  conflicts of interest for, 63–65
Innocent, ruling of, 311
in personam jurisdiction, 222
in rem jurisdiction, 222–223
Insecticide, Fungicide, and Rodenticide Act, 356
Insurance coverage
  discovery related to, 276
Intel Corporation, 154–155
Intellectual property law
  copyrights in, 101, 436
  paralegals' tasks or functions in, 98, 101
  specialty practice in, 93
Intent crimes, 312, 316. *See also* Intentional torts
Intentional torts
  assault as, 313
  battery as, 313
  false imprisonment as, 313
Interest
  interest-bearing escrow accounts, 112–113
  IOLTA (Interest on Lawyers Trust Account) accounts, 112
Intermediate appellate courts, 208
Intermediate scrutiny test, 192–193
Internal Revenue Service (IRS), 149, 150, 153
International Paralegal Management Association (IPMA), 13, 15, 18, 93

International Practice Management Association, 136
Internet. *See also* Technology
attachments via, 136, 137, 151–152
communication structure via, 145–147
computer addresses and locations on, 148, 149–150
definition of, 145
digital photograph transmission via, 396
domain names on, 150, 152
emails via, 10, 136, 137, 141–142, 148, 151–152, 245, 423
freedom of speech via, 189
hacking via, 153
Internet browsers, 147–148, 149, 151
Internet resources, 147–150, 557–559
Internet search engines, 137, 147, 148–149, 150, 403, 485
Internet service providers, 146, 151, 152
jurisdiction of cyberspace, 223–224
legal research via, 150
locating witnesses via, 403–404
online alternative dispute resolution via, 231
online computer resources via, 147–150, 557–559
receiving and downloading files via, 151–152
remote access via, 140, 153, 162, 164, 165
search queries via, 459, 477, 479–485, 492
sending files via, 152
social networking sites via, 403
transmission speed via, 146–147
videoconferencing via, 163, 165
VoiP (Voice over Internet Protocol), 163–164
websites, 137, 148–149, 152, 557–559
wireless technology to access, 164–165, 166
Interpersonal skills, 9–10
Interpretive rules, 344
Interrogatories, 276–277
Interstate commerce, 186–187
Intervention, into civil litigation, 265
Interviews
attorney-client privilege issues in, 377–379, 393–394, 409
checklists for, 381, 383, 384, 385, 386
client, 95–96, 245, 376–395, 397, 400
conducting, 389–392
cultural consideration and sensitivity in, 387–389
discovery limitations and, 392
dress and appearance for, 387
ethical and moral considerations with, 377, 378–379, 392, 393, 408
expert witness, 393–395
fee issues considered in, 377, 381, 382–383
first or initial, 377
goals and purpose of, 381
implied attorney-client relationship from, 377–379
job, 120, 121–122, 125
leading questions in, 391
letters of engagement or termination of engagement after, 381, 382–383
letters of non-engagement after, 381, 384
listening skills in, 390–391
narrative opportunity in, 391–392
open-ended questions in, 391–392
overview of skills for, 376, 408–409
physical surroundings for, 383, 385–387
preparing for, 381, 383, 385–389, 408
privileged communication in, 393, 409
screening, 376, 377
statutes of limitations considered in, 379–380
trial preparation with, 404–407, 409
witness, 245, 376, 381, 383, 386–387, 390–392, 393–395
Intrastate commerce, 186
Investigations
defense perspective in, 396
digital photographs in, 396
fact analysis in, 397
Freedom of Information Act use in, 401–403, 409
information sources for, 403–404
investigating claims via, 395–401, 409
locating witnesses in, 403–404, 409
location analysis in, 397
obtaining official reports in, 396–397, 398–399
paralegals' role in, 96–97, 395–407
tangible evidence in, 397, 400
timelines for, 401
trial preparation with, 404–407, 409
Involuntary manslaughter, 312
IOLTA accounts, 112
Iowa, state court system in, 209
Irvin, Melvin E., 341
Issues
critical legal thinking about, 420, 501
legal research of specific, 458–459

J

Jackson, Andrew, 3
Jennings, Debra K., 314
Johnson, Lyndon B., 356
Judgment, entry of, 286
Judgment notwithstanding the verdict (j.n.o.v.), 286
Judgment-proof damages, 313
Judicial authority of administrative agencies, 348, 350–352
Judicial branch, 184, 462, 547–548. *See also* Federal courts
Judicial referees, 230
Judicial review of administrative agency actions, 354, 361
Juries
grand, 306
hung, 311, 323
jury deliberation and verdict, 286, 311
jury instructions (charges), 286, 287
jury selection, 282–285
jury trials, 281, 282–287, 310–311
Jurisdiction
choice-of-law clauses on, 224
concurrent, 222
courts', 206, 207, 210–211, 221–224, 233–234
in cyberspace, 223–224
diversity of citizenship and, 221–222
exclusive, 222
forum selection clauses and, 224
general jurisdiction trial courts, 207
in personam or personal, 222
in rem, 222–223
legal research consideration of, 460–461
limited jurisdiction trial courts, 207
long-arm statutes and, 223
quasi in rem or attachment, 223

standing to sue in, 222
subject matter, 221
venue and, 223
Jurisprudence, 177–178, 195
Just Compensation Clause, 192

K

Kagan, Elena, 221
Kansas, state court system in, 209
Kant, Immanuel, 43
Karayan, Vicki L., 5
Kentucky
freedom of religion in, 190
paralegal profession regulation in, 526
state court system in, 209
KeyCite™, 486, 487
Kickbacks, 316
Kidnapping, 313
King, Martin Luther, Jr., 356
Kurzweil, Raymond, 162–163

L

Labor Management Relations Act, 357–358
Labor Management Reporting and Disclosure Act, 358
Labor union law
Labor Management Relations Act, 357–358
Labor Management Reporting and Disclosure Act as, 358
National Labor Relations Act as, 357
National Labor Relations Board role in, 337, 357–358
Norris-LaGuardia Act as, 357
Landrum-Griffin Act, 358
Larceny, 314
Large law offices, 89–90
Law. *See also* Regulations; Statutes
administrative, 181–182, 335–371
analytical school on, 178
business, 97, 106, (*see also* Corporations)
case, 462, 464, 465–469, 485 (*see also separate Index of Cases*)
civil law system, 180 (*see also* Civil litigation; Torts)
codified, 181
command school on, 178
common, 179–180
constitutional (*see* Constitution, U.S.; Constitutional law; Constitutions, state)
contract (*see* Contracts)
controlling, 461, 462–463
criminal (*see* Criminal law and procedure)
critical legal studies school on, 178
definition and description of, 176–178, 194–195
elder, 93
employment (*see* Employment law)
environmental, 93, 98, 336, 338, 343, 355–356
errors of law, 289
executive orders as, 182
fairness of the, 177
family (*see* Family law)
finding, in legal research, 462–473, 491–492
flexibility of the, 177
functions of the, 178
historical school on, 178
history of American, 179–180, 195
human resources, 100
immigration, 98, 100
intellectual property (*see* Intellectual property law)
judicial decisions in, 182
law and economics school on, 178
natural law school on, 177
overview of, 176, 194–197
practice of law, defined, 47
property or real estate (*see* Property law)
regulating practice of, 21–31, 35, 45–48, 72
schools of jurisprudential thought on, 177–178, 195
securities, 181, 336, 337, 340, 344, 350–352, 356–357
sociological school on, 178
sources of, in U.S., 180–182, 195
stare decisis doctrine in, 182, 195, 485
state (*see* State laws and regulations)
treaties in, 181
unauthorized practice of, 21, 30, 46–48, 63–65, 67, 69–71, 74–75, 91–92, 95–96, 516, 528
Law courts, 179
Law offices and firms
accounting in, 106–113, 124
administrative procedures in, 102–106, 124
conflict checking in, 102–104
ethical issues impacted by structure of, 89, 90
general law practice in, 90–91
large law offices as, 89–90
paperless offices as, 160–167, 405, 406
partnerships as, 89
small offices as, 89
solo practice as, 88
specialty practice in, 90 (*see also* Specialty practice)
technology in, 136–142, 152, 160–167
time keeping and billing in, 104–106, 111 (*see also* Fees)
websites of, 137, 152
as workplace for paralegals, 88–91, 102–113, 123, 124
Law reviews, 473
Lawsuits. *See* Litigation
Lawyers
bar exams for, 46
compensation for, 90
defense attorneys as, 304
disbarment of, 46, 66
ethical codes for (*see* Ethics and professional responsibility)
in-house counsel as, 63–65, 245, 246–247
licensing of, 21, 45–46
offices and firms of (*see* Law offices and firms)
privilege obligations of (*see* Privilege)
prosecutors as, 303–304
public defenders as, 304
sanctions against, 66, 260
supervision by, 48, 51–52, 63–65, 73, 89, 529
suspension of, 66
Lawyers Toolbox, 268
Leading questions, 391
Learning, effective, 537–541. *See also* Education
Legal advice, 69–70, 95–96
Legal assistants, 4. *See also* Paralegals
Legal dictionaries, 470, 477

Legal encyclopedias, 470–472
Legal nurse consultants, 92
Legal periodicals, 473
Legal research
checklists for, 457, 463, 481, 482, 489–490
citation-checking services for, 486–489
computer research providers for, 481 (*see also specific companies by name*)
connectors in searches for, 482–484
controlling law identified in, 461, 462–463
creating a research plan for, 457–462, 491
definition of, 457
ethical duty of candor in, 466, 485, 486
executing research plan for, 462, 475
finding the law in, 462–473, 491–492
finding tools for, 461, 473, 474
issue or legal question to be answered via, 458–459
jurisdictions involved considered in, 460–461
location of research materials for, 461–462
overview of, 456–457, 491–493
personal research strategy for, 473, 475, 492
pocket parts/updates for, 477, 478
primary sources for, 461, 463–469
printed legal references works for, 475–477, 492
research material available for, 459–460
research term list for, 481
resource types used for, 461
search engines for, 485
search queries for, 459, 477, 479–485, 492
search terminology for, 459, 477, 481–484
secondary sources for, 461, 463, 465–466, 469, 470–473
technology use for, 150, 456–457, 459–460, 462, 465, 473, 477, 479–485, 486–487, 489
updating, 485–488, 492–493
workplace functions including, 97
Legal writing
ABCs (accuracy, brevity, clarity) of, 444
advice from the field on, 443–446
analysis in, 431
Association of Legal Writing Directors, 435, 436–440, 443
briefing a case using, 427, 500–511
citations in, 432–443, 445, 447–448, 501
cite checking for, 442–443
common errors in, 444
in court briefs, 432, 433–434, 447
critical legal thinking for, 420–422, 431, 446–447
duty of candor in, 423–424
editing and rewriting, 431–432
in emails, 423
foreign-language terms in, 432
grammar use in, 444–445
in letters, 445
in memoranda, 423, 424–431, 447
in opinion letters, 423
overview of, 422–423, 446–448
proofreading of, 446
punctuation in, 444
samples of, 428–429, 430–431
statements of facts for, 427, 429, 431
tables of authorities in, 441–442
technology impacts on, 435–436, 444
workplace functions including, 97
writing styles for, 423
Legislative branch, 184, 462, 542–545. *See also* U.S. Congress
Letters
cover, 118
engagement/termination of engagement, 381, 382–383
legal writing in, 445
non-engagement, 381, 384
opinion, 423
LexisNexis
Academic Universe, 486
CaseMap, 405–406
CaseSoft, 405–406
citations to, 432
e-filing systems, 224
legal research using, 97, 150, 459, 462, 465, 481, 483, 486, 489
locating expert witnesses via, 403
NoteMap, 406
Shepard's Citations, 486, 489
TextMap, 405
TimeMap, 401, 405, 406, 407
Liability
product, 396, 404
strict liability, 396
tort, 312–313
Licenses
lawyers' requirements for, 21, 45–46
licensing power of administrative agencies, 348
paralegal requirements for, 21, 22–30, 46–47
Limited jurisdiction trial courts, 207
Limited protected speech, 188
Lincoln, Abraham, 87, 106, 241
Linux, 268
Listening skills, 390–391, 443
Litigation
accounting related to, 106, 111
civil (*see* Civil litigation)
commercial, 106
complex, 93, 100–102
court system for (*see* Courts)
criminal (*see* Criminal law and procedure)
definition of, 206, 242
litigation holds for, 269, 270
paralegal career opportunities in, 206
paralegals' tasks and functions in, 100–102, 242, 244–247
subpoenas in, 102, 276, 353–354
technology used for, 138, 139–140, 141–142, 145, 160, 162, 163, 261, 262, 265, 268, 279–280
Local administrative agencies, 341
Local area network (LAN), 146
Loislaw
citations to, 432
GlobalCite™, 487, 489
legal research using, 97, 150, 459, 462, 465, 481, 483, 487, 489
Long-arm statutes, 223
Louisiana
law in, 179, 180, 192
paralegal profession regulation in, 525
state court system in, 209

M

Madison, James, 336, 419
Maine
  document specialists in, 95
  paralegal profession regulation in, 46
  state court system in, 209
Mainframe computers, 142
Mala in se crimes, 311
Mala prohibita crimes, 312
Malpractice
  medical, in civil litigation, 249
  missing statutes of limitations as cause for, 379
Mandatory authority, 463–464
Marriage
  spouse-spouse privilege in, 323, 393
Maryland, state court system in, 209
Massachusetts, state court system in, 209
Material facts, 422
Matthew Bender & Company, 436
Mayhem, 313
McAfee, 154
Mead, Margaret, 355
Mead Data Central, 436
Medical practice
  doctor-patient privilege in, 322, 393
  malpractice in, 249
  physical and mental examinations in, 279
Memoranda
  court opinions *vs.* memorandums of law, 427
  legal writing in, 423, 424–431, 447
  samples of, 428–429, 430–431
Mens rea (evil intent), 312
Mentors, 7
Merchant courts, 179
Michigan
  Guidelines for the Utilization of Legal Assistants in, 529
  Standards for Imposing Lawyer Sanctions, 66
  state court system in, 209
Microsoft
  Access, 158
Edge, 147
  e-filing systems, 224
  Excel, 157
  Internet Explorer, 147, 151
  Office 365, 167
  Office Suite, 143, 159
  OneDrive, 54, 166
  OneNote, 167
  operating system, 155, 268
  Outlook, 405
  PowerPoint, 158
  Windows™, 155
  Windows Explorer, 146, 151
  Word™, 151, 155–156, 162, 265, 441–442
Military courts, 536
Minitrials, 229
Minnesota, state court system in, 209
Minors
  child support for, 99
  civil litigation brought after age of majority of, 249
  court accounting for, 113, 114–115
  custody of, 99
  family law on, 99
Miranda rights, 321–322, 473
Misdemeanors, 312
Mississippi, state court system in, 209
Missouri
  Rules of Professional Conduct in, 52, 378–379
  state court system in, 207, 209
Modems, 146
Money laundering, 112–113
Montana, state court system in, 209
Moral obligations, 392. *See also* Ethics and professional responsibility
Mortgage Reform and Anti-Predatory Lending Act of 2010, 360
"Most Wanted" fugitives, 304
Motions
  motions for judgment on the pleadings, 281
  motions for summary judgment, 281
  motions in limine, 281
  motions to dismiss, 280–281
Motorola, 155
Mulkeen, William, 272
Murder, 313
Musmanno, Michael, 182
Myers, Kathryn, 31–33, 121–122, 443–446

N

Narrative opportunity, 391–392
National Archives, 465
National Association of Legal Assistants (NALA)
  Certified Paralegal/Certified Legal Assistant designation by, 18, 19–21, 525
  Code of Ethics and Professional Responsibility of, 44, 45, 49, 50–51
  Model Standards and Guidelines for Utilization of Legal Assistants-Paralegals of, 5, 12, 71, 522–532
  paralegal definition by, 4, 523–524
  website of, 13
National Association of Legal Secretaries (NALS)
  description of, 12
  ethics guidelines of, 50
  Professional Paralegal designation by, 18, 19–21
  website of, 13
National Federation of Paralegal Associations (NFPA)
  definition of paralegal by, 4
  Model Code of Ethics and Professional Responsibility and Guidelines for Enforcement, 44, 45, 49, 50, 512–521
  Paralegal Advance Competency Exam by, 18, 19–21
  Paralegal CORE Competency Exam by, 19–21
  website of, 13
National Labor Relations Act (NLRA), 357
National Labor Relations Board (NLRB), 337, 357–358
National Museum of the American Indian, 185
National Transportation Safety Board (NTSB), 402, 403
Native Americans, commerce with, 185
Natural law school, 177
Nebraska, state court system in, 209
Negligence
  investigating claims of, 396
Negotiation, 224–225

Network administrators, 144
Networking, 95
Networking, social media, 403
Network rights and privileges, 144
Networks, computer, 138, 143–146, 166
Neutrals, 227
Nevada
- conflicts of interest in, 103–104
- federal courts in, 211
- Rules of Professional Conduct in, 527
- state court system in, 209
- Supreme Court of, 103–104

New Hampshire
- fiduciary accounting standards in, 112
- Rules of Professional Conduct, 393
- state court system in, 209

New Jersey
- family law in, 107–108
- paralegal profession regulation in, 22
- state court system in, 209
- Supreme Court of, 22, 56

New Mexico, state court system in, 209
New York
- civil litigation in, 251–258, 266–267
- paralegal profession regulation in, 23, 28–30
- professional and judicial ethics in, 53
- state court system in, 209

Nolo contendere pleas, 310
Non-binding arbitration, 227
Non-engagement letters, 381, 384
Non-intent crimes, 312. *See also* Unintentional torts
Norris-LaGuardia Act, 357
North Carolina
- paralegal profession regulation in, 30, 46
- State Bar Association, 30
- state court system in, 209
- Supreme Court of, 30

North Dakota, state court system in, 209
Norton, 154
Notice pleadings, 250–254, 259, 260
No waiver, 61
Nuance
- OmniPage, 162
- PaperPort, 162
- PDF Creator, 161

Nurse paralegals/legal nurse consultants, 92

O

Obama, Barack, 221
Obscene speech, 188–189
Occupational Safety and Health Act, 357
Occupational Safety and Health Administration (OSHA), 337, 350, 357
Offensive speech, 188
Offers
- counteroffers, 231
- offerees and offerors in, 316

Office of the Comptroller of the Currency, 336, 338, 348
Office of the Solicitor General, 94
Office software suites, 159
Ohio
- commercial law-related websites in, 152
- criminal law and procedure in, 307–309
- paralegal profession regulation in, 23
- State Bar Association, 23
- state court system in, 209
- Supreme Court of, 23

Oklahoma
- Rules of Professional Conduct in, 527
- state court system in, 209

Online data. *See* Computers; Internet; Technology
Open-ended questions, 391–392
Opening briefs, 287
Opening statements, 285
Operating systems, 142, 143, 154–155, 265, 268
Opinion letters, 423
Optical character recognition (OCR), 162
Ordinances, 181
Oregon
- Rules of Professional Conduct, 67
- state court system in, 209

P

Paperless office, 160–167, 405, 406
Paralegal Advance Competency Exam (PACE), 18, 19–21
Paralegal CORE Competency Exam (PCCE), 19–21
Paralegals
- advice from the field for, 6–7, 13, 31–33, 121–122, 145, 248–249, 272, 443–446
- analytical skills of, 9
- background and skills assessment by, 17
- career planning for (*see* Careers, paralegal)
- certificates/certifications for, 15, 16, 18, 19–21, 22, 23, 30, 525
- civil litigation work of (*see* Civil litigation)
- commitment of, 9
- communication skills of, 7, 10–11
- compensation for, 11
- court system for (*see* Courts)
- criminal law work of (*see* Criminal law and procedure)
- critical legal thinking by, 420–422, 431, 446–447, 500–511
- definition and description of, 4, 33, 523–524
- document specialists *vs.*, 95
- education for, 13–21, 22–23, 27, 30, 31–33, 34–35, 92, 244, 272, 524–525, 537–541
- ethical codes for (*see* Ethics and professional responsibility)
- federal practice by, 30–31, 70–71, 95
- fees charged for services of, 12, 105, 530
- future of profession for, 12, 35
- getting started in career as, 31–33
- goal setting by, 16–17
- interpersonal skills of, 9–10
- interview skills of (*see* Interviews)
- investigation skills of (*see* Investigations)
- law applied by (*see* Law)
- legal research by (*see* Legal research)
- legal writing skills of (*see* Legal writing; Writing)
- licensing requirements for, 21, 22–30, 46–47
- opportunities or, 11, 13, 35
- overview of paralegal profession, 4, 33–35
- paralegal managers, 92

people skills critical to, 6–7
portfolios of, 31–33, 121–122
pro bono, 93–94, 231, 514
professional skills of, 7–11, 14, 34
profiles of, 5, 49, 91, 191, 228, 280, 314, 341, 406, 422, 458
qualifications of, 12, 18–21, 22–30, 524–525
regulating profession of, 21–31, 35 (*see also* Law; Regulations)
resourcefulness of, 8
role or function of, 5, 7, 34, 88, 95–102, 124
specialty fields for, 16–17
technology and (*see* Technology)
unauthorized practice of law by, 21, 30, 46–48, 63–65, 67, 69–71, 74–75, 91–92, 95–96, 516, 528
workplace of (*see* Workplace)
at work scenarios for, 3, 43, 87–88, 135–136, 175, 205, 241, 301–302, 335–336, 375–376, 419, 455–456
Parallel citations, 433, 488
Parents
child support by, 99
parent-child privilege, 323
Partnerships
law offices and firms as, 89
Payoffs, 316
Penal codes, 311, 312
Pennsylvania
civil litigation in, 259
court accounting in, 114–115
penalties for unauthorized practice of law in, 47
Rules of Professional Conduct, 58, 67, 68
State Bar Association, 67
state court system in, 210
Superior Court of, 434–435
Perfect Authority, 441
Personal jurisdiction, 222
Persuasive authority, 464–465
Petitions
petitioners, 286, 354, 500
petition for *certiorari*, 214, 215–218
Physical and mental examinations, 279
Plaintiffs
in civil litigation, 249–250, 268, 285, 286
in criminal actions, 303, 310
definition of, 500
Plato, 176
Plea bargain agreements, 310
Pleadings
answer, 264–265, 266–267
bilingual, 259
civil litigation, 246, 247–268, 290–291
complaint, 249–261
cross-complaint, 265
definition of, 247
electronic filing of, 261, 262, 265
fact, 250, 255–258, 266–267
filing fees for, 261
motions for judgment on, 281
notice, 250–254, 259, 260
pro se filing of, 259
reply to cross-complaint, 265
responsive, 264
service of complaint, 262–264
time limits and deadlines for, 247–249, 262–264, 268
Pocket parts, 477, 478
Police power, 186
Political speech, 188, 190
Portable document format (PDF), 161
Portfolios, 31–33, 121–122
Practice Manager, 405
Precedents, 485
Preemption doctrine, 185
Pregnancy Discrimination Act of 1978, 354
Presentation graphics programs, 158–159
Pretrial hearings, 281
Pretrial motions
in civil litigation, 280–281, 291
motion for judgment on the pleadings as, 281
motion for summary judgment as, 281
motions in limine as, 281
motion to dismiss as, 280–281
Price, Ann W., 91
Primary authorities/sources
citations of, 432
constitutions as, 465
court decisions/opinions as, 465–469
legal research using, 461, 463–469
mandatory authority, 463–464
persuasive authority, 464–465
Privacy issues. *See also* Confidentiality
client identity as, 381, 384
Electronic Communications Privacy Act on, 154
Privacy Act on, 363
Privilege
accountant-client, 323
attorney-client (*see* Attorney-client privilege)
claim of, 56
confidentiality distinction from, 54
constitutional safeguards for, 322–323
definition of, 54
discovery impacted by, 273–274
doctor-patient, 322, 393
parent-child, 323
privileged communication in interviews, 393, 409
religious leader-penitent, 323, 393
against self-incrimination, 321–323
spouse-spouse, 323, 393
waiver of, 55, 61–62, 393
work product (*see* Work product doctrine)
Probable cause, 304
Pro bono paralegals, 93–94, 231, 514
Procedural administrative law, 342–343
Procedural due process, 192, 350
Production of documents, 278
Product liability
demonstrative evidence for, 404
investigating claims of, 396
strict liability with, 396
Professional Legal Secretary (PLS), 18
Professional Paralegal (PP), 18, 19–21
Professional responsibility. *See* Ethics and professional responsibility
Proofreading, of legal writing, 446
Property law
specialty practice in, 92
Proprietary schools, 14

Prosecuting attorney/prosecutors, 303–304
Pro se filing, 259
Protocol, 138, 149
Public defenders, 304
Published opinions, 464
Puerto Rico, state court system in, 210

Q

Quasi in rem jurisdiction, 223
Questions
  federal question cases, 221
  leading, 391
  legal research on issue or legal question, 458–459
  open-ended, 391–392

R

Random access memory (RAM), 142
Rape, 313
Rational basis test, 193
Real estate law. *See* Property law
Rebuttals, 286
Records and reports
  civil litigation obtainment of, 246
  civil litigation records reviews, 246
  courts of record, 207
  investigation obtainment of official, 396–397, 398–399
  time keeping, 104–106, 111
  trial records, 286, 310
Recross examination, 285
Redirect examination, 285
References, 118
Registered Paralegal (RP), 18, 23
Regulations. *See also* Law; Statutes
  administrative (*see* Administrative law)
  federal regulatory statutes, 311
  general government regulation, 337
  legal research of, 462
  practice of law, 21–31, 35, 45–48, 72
  specific government regulation, 338
  state (*see* State laws and regulations)
  unauthorized practice of law, 21, 30, 46–48
Regulatory agencies. *See* Administrative agencies
Rejoinders, 286
Relevant facts, 420–422, 458–459. *See also* Facts
Religious issues
  cultural sensitivity to, 387, 388
  freedom of religion, 190–191
  religious leader-penitent privilege, 323, 393
Remand of case, 289
Remittitur, 286
Remote access, 140, 153, 162, 164, 165
Remote collaboration, 165
Rentals. *See* Leases; Tenants
Reply to cross-complaints, 265
Reports. *See* Records and reports
Representation, unauthorized practice of law related to, 70–71
Requests for admission, 279
Research, legal. *See* Legal research
Resourcefulness, 8
Respondents, 287, 500
Responding briefs, 287
Responsive pleadings, 264
Restatement of the Law Third, Torts, 396
Résumé
  checklist for, 120
  common elements of, 118
  cover letters with, 118
  electronic, 118–120
  formats for, 116–118
  preparing, for workplace, 113, 116–120, 124–125
  references with, 118
  sample, 116, 117
Retainers, 110
Reversal of judicial decisions, 289
Rhode Island
  Rules of Professional Conduct, 66–67
  state court system in, 210
Robbery, 313
Robert Half Legal, 6
Rule making, 343, 344, 345–347
Rules of court, 53

S

Safe Drinking Water Act, 356
Sanctions, 66, 260
Scanning, 162
Screening interviews, 376, 377
Searches
  administrative searches, 353–354
  business premises searches, 318
  connectors in, 482–484
  legal research involving, 459
  search engines, 137, 147, 148–149, 150, 403, 485
  search queries, 459, 477, 479–485, 492
  search terminology, 459, 477, 481–484
  search warrants, 318, 319–320, 354
  unreasonable searches and seizures, 318–320, 354
  warrantless searches, 318
Secondary authorities/sources
  citations of, 432
  headnotes as, 465–466, 469
  law reviews as, 473
  legal dictionaries as, 470
  legal encyclopedias as, 470–472
  legal periodicals as, 473
  legal research using, 461, 463, 465–466, 469, 470–473
  treatises as, 473
Securities and Exchange Commission (SEC), 181, 336, 337, 340, 344, 350–352, 356–357, 402
Securities laws
  ethical considerations under, 50
  SEC role in administering, 181, 336, 337, 340, 344, 350–352, 356–357, 402
  Securities Act of 1933, 337, 356

Securities Exchange Act of 1934, 337, 356–357
Self-defense exception, 57–58
Self-employment, 94–95
Self-incrimination, privilege against, 321–323
Separation of powers doctrine, 184
Sequestering juries, 285
Service of process, 222, 262–264
Settlement
  discovery facilitating, 271–272
  settlement agreements, 225, 231
  settlement conferences, 281, 292
Shepard's Citations, 486–489
Sheraden-Baker, Charlotte A., 191
Sixth Amendment, 323–324, 550
Skype, 163, 164
Slip opinions, 465, 467
Small claims courts, 207
Small offices, 89
Smoking gun, 141
Social networking sites, 403
Social Security Administration, 30–31, 71, 94, 95, 110, 341–342
Sociological school, 178
Software
  applications, 142, 155–158
  case and practice management, 401, 405–407
  database, 158
  document comparison, 156
  litigation support, 160
  office suites, 159
  online collaboration, 138
  presentation graphics, 158–159
  Software as a Service (SaaS), 167
  specialty application, 159
  spreadsheet, 157–158
  training to use, 159–160
  voice recognition, 164
  wordprocessing, 142, 151, 155–157, 265
Solo practice, 88
Sotomayor, Sonia, 221
South Carolina, state court system in, 210
South Dakota
  paralegal profession regulation in, 526
  Rules of Professional Conduct in, 109
  safekeeping property in, 109
  state court system in, 210
Special federal courts, 210
Specialty application programs, 159
Specialty practice
  business law as, 97 (*see also* Corporations)
  complex litigation in, 93, 100–102
  corporate legal departments/practice in, 94, 98
  debtor or creditor rights in, 97 (*see also* Bankruptcy law)
  elder law in, 93
  environmental law in, 93, 98
  family law in, 98, 99, 106
  government employment in, 94
  human resources law in, 100
  immigration law in, 98, 100
  intellectual property in, 93, 98, 101
  networking in, 95
  nurse paralegals/legal nurse consultants in, 92
  paralegal managers in, 92
  paralegals' tasks or functions in, 97–102
  pro bono paralegals in, 93–94
  real estate law in, 92
  self-employment in, 94–95
  specialty certificates for, 16, 18
  workplace as, 90, 91–95, 97–102, 106, 123
Specific government regulation, 338
Specific intent, 312
Speech
  commercial, 188
  freedom of, 187–190
  fully protected, 188
  limited protected, 188
  obscene, 188–189
  offensive, 188
  political, 188, 190
  unprotected, 188–189
Speedy Trial Act, 323
Spoliation of evidence, 400
Spouse-spouse privilege, 323, 393
Spreadsheet programs, 157–158
Standing to sue, 222
Stare decisis doctrine, 182, 195, 485
State administrative agencies, 341
State bar associations, 558–559
State constitutions, 181, 317, 465
State courts
  civil litigation deadlines in, 262, 264, 265
  criminal procedures and actions in, 304
  general jurisdiction trial courts as, 207
  highest or supreme courts as, 208 (*see also Supreme Courts in specific states*)
  intermediate appellate courts as, 208
  jurisdiction of, 221–222, 223
  limited jurisdiction trial courts as, 207
  overview of court system, 206–210, 232
  right to practice before, 46
  small claims courts as, 207
  websites for, 209–210
State laws and regulations. *See also specific states*
  codes of ethics under, 21, 44, 46, 49, 50, 51, 52, 53, 54, 58, 62, 63, 66–68, 105
  crimes violating, 303, 304, 311 (*see also* Criminal law and procedure)
  licensing requirements under, 21, 22–30, 46–47
  long-arm statutes as, 223
  paralegal profession regulation under, 21–30
  penal codes and regulatory statutes as, 311, 312
  police power of, 186
  practice of law regulation under, 21–30, 46–48
  state statutes as (*see* Statutes)
  supremacy/preemption of federal laws over, 184–185, 186–187
  technology constraints and allowances under, 152, 153
  Uniform laws as (*see Uniform entries*)
Statements of policy, 344
Statutes. *See also* Law; Regulations
  codified law via, 181
  definition of, 181

Statutes (*Continued*)
finding, in legal research, 462, 465
regulatory statutes, 311
statutes of limitations, 247, 249, 265, 379–380
Stewart, Potter, 189
Stradley, Kathleen A., 228
Strict liability, 396
Strict scrutiny test, 192
Study techniques, 537–541
Subject matter jurisdiction, 221
Submission agreements, 225
Subpoenas, 102, 276, 353–354
Substantive administrative law, 342–343
Substantive due process, 191–192
Substantive rules, 344
Summons, 222, 262
Supervision
conflicts of interest impacting, 63–65
document specialists *vs.* paralegals without, 95
ethical duty of, 48, 51–52, 63–65, 73, 89, 527
workplace structure for, 89
Supremacy Clause, 184–185
Supreme Courts. *See under specific states;* U.S. Supreme Court
Suspension, 66

T

Tables of authorities, 441–442
Tabs 3 Practice Manager, 405
Taft-Hartley Act, 357–358
Taxes
accounting related to, 107
electronic filing of returns, 153
Technology. *See also* Internet
attachments in, 136, 137, 151–152
backup of data using, 144
central processing units as, 142
citation formats impacted by, 435–436
competence in language/lexicon of, 53, 138, 139, 140
computer addresses and locations via, 148, 149–150
computer hardware as, 142–145
computer skills needed for, 136–139
computer software as, 138, 142, 155–160, 164, 265, 405–406
computer systems as, 142
computer viruses and antivirus programs in, 154
confidentiality issues with, 54–55, 137, 144, 154
digital format in, 136, 137
digital photographs using, 396
domain names in, 150, 152
effectiveness and cost-efficiency of, 142, 145, 162
electronic Code of Federal Regulations using, 344
electronic courtroom using, 160, 161, 224
electronic discovery using, 137, 141–142, 245, 265, 268–269, 279–280
electronic documents using, 137, 141–142, 245–246
electronic filing using, 137, 153, 224, 261, 262, 265
Electronic Freedom of Information Act on, 403
electronic repository/storage using, 138, 141, 144, 166–167
electronic résumé using, 118–120
emails via, 10, 136, 137, 141–142, 148, 151–152, 245, 423
encryption, 153–154
Federal Rules of Civil Procedure impacting, 141–142
file servers as, 144, 145–146
firewalls in, 153
formats for available information, 151–152
future trends in, 162–167
hacking into, 153
hard copy *vs.*, 136, 137
Information Technology staff and consultants for, 139–141
knowledge needed to use, 138–193
law offices and firms using, 136–142, 152, 160–167
law-specific uses of, 139
legal research via, 150, 456–457, 459–460, 462, 465, 473, 477, 479–485, 486–487, 489
legal writing impacted by, 435–436, 444
local area network as, 146
locating witnesses using, 403–404
mainframe computers as, 142
metadata in, 157
miniaturization and portability of, 164
modems as, 146
network administrators managing, 144
network systems in, 138, 143–146, 166
notetaking via, 167
online alternative dispute resolution using, 231
online collaboration software as, 138
online computer resources via, 147–150, 557–559
operating systems as, 142, 143, 154–155, 265, 268
outsourcing, 140–141
overview of, 136, 168–169
paperless offices using, 160–167, 405, 406
power sources for, 143
protocol in, 138, 149
random access memory as, 142
receiving and downloading files via, 151–152
remote access via, 140, 153, 162, 164, 165
remote collaboration using, 165
search engines using, 137, 147, 148–149, 150, 403, 485
search queries via, 459, 477, 479–485, 492
security issues with, 54–55, 153–154
sending files via, 152
social networking sites using, 403
training in, 159–160, 272
transmission speed via, 146–147
videoconferencing, 163, 165
VoiP (Voice over Internet Protocol), 163–164
websites via, 137, 148–149, 152, 557–559
wide area networks as, 145
wireless, 164–165, 166
workstations as, 143, 144, 146
Teleworkers, 162
Tennessee
state court system in, 210
unauthorized practice of law in, 70
Termination
of engagement, 381
Texas
paralegal profession regulation in, 525
state court system in, 210

Theft, 314
Thin client, 166–167
Time
  chronological résumé format, 117
  pleading time limits and deadlines, 247–249, 262–264, 268
  statutes of limitations, 247, 249, 265, 379–380
  time keeping, 104–106, 111
  timeline of key pretrial events in civil litigation, 282
  timelines/chronologies in case management software, 401, 406, 407
  timelines for investigations, 401
  timely accounting disbursements, 111
  timely appeals filing, 380
Torts
  assault as, 313
  battery as, 313
  criminal acts as basis for, 312–313
Track Changes tool, 155, 156, 157
Treaties, 181
Treatises, 473
Trials
  bench or waiver, 282, 310
  burden of proof in, 285
  case and practice management software for, 401, 405–407
  civil litigation, 246, 270, 281–286, 292
  closing arguments in, 286
  criminal litigation, 310–311, 323–324, 326
  defendant's case in, 285–286, 310
  entry of judgment in, 286
  interviews, investigations and, 404–407, 409
  jury, 281, 282–287, 310–311
  jury deliberation and verdict in, 286
  jury instructions (charges) in, 286, 287
  jury selection in, 282–285
  minitrials, 229
  opening statements in, 285
  paralegals assisting at, 246
  plaintiff's case in, 285, 286, 310
  preparing for, 270, 404–407
  rebuttal and rejoinder in, 286
  record of, 286, 310
  retrials, 289, 311, 323
  right to public, 323–324
  trial briefs submitted for, 282
  trial notebooks for, 404–405
Triers of fact, 65, 281, 282, 310, 397
Trust accounts, 109, 111–112
Truth in Lending Act, 360
Truth in Savings Act, 360

U

Unauthorized practice of law (UPL)
  avoiding, 67, 69–71, 74–75
  client interviews leading to, 95–96
  conflicts of interest impacting, 63–65
  as ethical violation, 21, 30, 46–48, 63–65, 67, 69–71, 74–75, 91–92, 95–96, 516, 528
  filling out forms as, 70, 96
  giving advice as, 69–70, 95–96
  guidelines for avoiding, 71
  holding oneself out as, 69
  penalties for, 47–48
  regulations on, 21, 30, 46–48
  representing clients as, 70–71
  specialty practice expertise and, 91–92
Uniform Arbitration Act, 227
Uniform Commercial Code (UCC), 249
Uniform system of accounts, 113
Uninterruptible power supply (UPS), 143
Universal Citation Format, 435
Unprotected speech, 188–189
Unpublished opinions, 464
Unreasonable searches and seizures, 318–320, 354
URLs (uniform resource locators), 148, 149–150
U.S. Attorney, 304
U.S. Attorney's Office, 94
U.S. Bankruptcy Court, 210
U.S. Code, 311, 465, 481
U.S. Congress
  as bicameral system, 180, 462
  laws enacted by, 181, 189, 227, 339, 462
  legislative branch as, 184, 542–545
  Supreme Court justice approval by, 218, 221
U.S. Court of Appeals, 211–212, 288, 355, 533
U.S. Court of Federal Claims, 210
U.S. Court of International Trade, 210
U.S. Department of Agriculture, 339
U.S. Department of Commerce, 339
U.S. Department of Defense, 339
U.S. Department of Education, 339
U.S. Department of Energy, 339
U.S. Department of Health and Human Services, 339
U.S. Department of Homeland Security (DHS), 337, 339–340
U.S. Department of Housing and Urban Development, 339
U.S. Department of Interior, 339
U.S. Department of Justice, 339, 353, 403
U.S. Department of Labor
  Bureau of Labor Statistics of, 11, 13
  as cabinet-level department, 339, 340
  Occupational Outlook Handbook of, 11, 13
U.S. Department of State, 339
U.S. Department of the Treasury, 339
U.S. Department of Transportation, 339, 345–347
U.S. Department of Veterans Affairs, 339
U.S. District Courts, 210–211, 263, 265, 355, 533–536
U.S. Government Printing Office, 465, 481
U.S. Patent and Trademark Office (UPTO), 30, 71, 95
U.S. Supreme Court
  administrative agency appeals to, 355
  arbitration upheld by, 225, 226
  on bench *vs.* slip opinions, 467
  briefing opinions of, 501–507
  case syllabus of, 467
  concurring *vs.* dissenting opinions in, 218, 219–220
  constitutional interpretation by, 176, 185, 186, 187–190, 192–193, 321, 324
  Court Rules of, 288
  decisions of as primary authority, 464, 465, 468

U.S. Supreme Court (*Continued*)
fairness of law under, 177
justices of, 212–213, 214, 218, 221
mandatory authority of decision of, 464
name abbreviation of, 533
notice pleading requirements, 250
overview of, 212–221, 233
petition for *certiorari* to, 214, 215–218
votes/decisions of, 214, 218, 219–220
writ of *certiorari* by, 214
U.S. Tax Court, 210
Utah
Rules of Professional Conduct in, 105
state court system in, 210

V

V. Cite™, 487
Venue, 223
Verdicts, 286
Vermont, state court system in, 210
VersusLaw
citations of, 432
legal research using, 97, 150, 456–457, 459, 460, 462, 465, 482, 484, 487
V. Cite™, 487
Videoconferencing, 163, 165
Violations, criminal, 312
Virginia, state court system in, 210
Virgin Islands, state court system in, 210
Virtual courthouses, 224
Voice recognition software, 164
VoiP (Voice over Internet Protocol), 163–164
Voir dire, 282–285
Voisin, Vicki, 49
Voltaire, 205
Volunteerism, 7

W

Waiver trials, 282, 310
Warrants
arrest, 304
search, 318, 319–320, 354
warrantless arrests, 304
warrantless searches, 318
Warren, Earl, 178, 375
Washington
federal preemption of laws of, 185
Limited Practice Rules of Legal Technicians in, 23–27
paralegal profession regulation in, 23–27, 526
state court system in, 210
Supreme Court of, 23
Web-based data. *See* Computers; Internet; Technology; Websites; World Wide Web
Websites, 137, 148–149, 152, 557–559
Westlaw
citations of, 432
KeyCite™, 486, 487
legal research using, 97, 150, 459, 462, 465, 481, 484, 486, 487
West Publishing Company, 435–436, 473, 477, 479–480
West Reporter, 488
West's Digest, 473, 474, 477, 479–480
West Virginia, state court system in, 210
White-collar crimes, 303, 315–317, 327
Wide area networks, 145
Wilbraham, Thomas, 206
Wilson, Woodrow, 183
Wireless computer networks, 166
Wireless devices, 166
Wireless technology, 164–165, 166
Wisconsin
Rules of Professional Conduct in, 53, 54
state court system in, 210
Supreme Court of, 163
videoconferencing rules in, 163
Witnesses
civil litigation, 245, 272, 276, 285–286, 394
expert, 276, 393–395, 403
interviews with, 245, 376, 381, 383, 386–387, 390–392, 393–395
locating, 403–404, 409
oral testimony of, 272
Word™, Microsoft, 151, 155–156, 162, 265, 441–442
WordPerfect™, 151, 155–156, 162, 265, 441
WordPerfect Office, 159
WordPerfect Presentation, 158
Wordprocessing software, 142, 151, 155–157, 265
Workplace. *See also* Employment law
accounting in, 106–113, 124
administrative procedures in, 102–106, 124
client interviews in, 95–96
conflict checking in, 102–104
ethical issues considered in, 89, 90, 95–96, 102–104, 109
general law practice in, 90–91
investigations in, 96–97
job interviews in, 120, 121–122, 125
law offices and firms as, 88–91, 102–113, 123, 124
legal research in, 97
legal writing in, 97
networking in, 95
OSHA safety standards in, 337, 350, 357
overview of, 88, 123–125
paralegal tasks and functions in, 95–102, 124
preparing résumé for, 113, 116–120, 124–125
self-employment in, 94–95
specialty practice in, 90, 91–95, 97–102, 106, 123
teleworkers in, 162
time keeping and billing in, 104–106, 111
Work product doctrine
definition of, 58
discovery under, 273–274, 276
ethical duty of confidentiality and, 49, 58–61, 73–74

exceptions and limitations to, 59–61
Federal Rules of Civil Procedure on, 60–61
Workstations, computer, 143, 144, 146
World Wide Web, 147. *See also* Internet
Writing
civil litigation document drafting, 246
legal, 97, 422–453, 500–511
paralegals' skill in, 7
styles, 423
written memorandum regarding judgments, 286
Writ of *certiorari*, 214
Wyoming, state court system in, 210

Y

Yahoo!, 137, 147, 148, 150, 403
Yahoo Messenger, 164
Youth. *See* Minors
YouTube, 403

Z

Zoo, 148